United States Supreme Court Decisions, 1778–1996

An Index to Excerpts, Reprints, and Discussions, 1980–1995

Kelly S. Janousek

The Scarecrow Press, Inc.
Lanham, Maryland, and London
2001

SCARECROW PRESS, INC.

Published in the United States of America
by Scarecrow Press, Inc.
4720 Boston Way, Lanham, Maryland 20706
www.scarecrowpress.com

4 Pleydell Gardens, Folkestone
Kent CT20 2DN, England

First edition © 1976 by Nancy Anderman: *United States Supreme Court Decisions:
An Index to Their Locations*. Metuchen, N.J.: Scarecrow Press. ISBN 0-8108-0932-X.
Second edition © 1983 by Nancy Anderman Guenther: *United States Supreme Court Decisions: An
Index to Excerpts, Reprints, and Discussions*. Metuchen, N.J.: Scarecrow Press. ISBN 0-8108-1578-8.

British Library Cataloguing in Publication Information Available

Library of Congress Cataloging-in-Publication Data

Janousek, Kelly S., 1960–
    United States Supreme Court decisions, 1778–1996 : an index to excerpts, reprints, and
  discussions, 1980–1995 / Kelly S. Janousek.
        p. cm.
    Rev. ed. of: United States Supreme Court decisions / by Nancy Anderman Guenther.
  2nd ed. 1983.
    Includes bibliographical references and index.
    ISBN 0-8108-3998-9 (cloth : alk. paper)
      1. Law reports, digests, etc.—United States—Indexes. 2. Constitutional law—United
  States—Bibliography. 3. Constitutional law—United States—Indexes. I. Guenther, Nancy
  Anderman, 1949– United States Supreme Court decisions. II. Title.
  KF101.6 .G83 2001
  342.73'084'02648—dc21   00-066188

CONTENTS

Introduction   v

Acknowledgments   vi

Instructions for Use   vii

Books Cited   viii

Journals Cited   xiii

United States Supreme Court Decisions   1

Words and Phrases Index   717

Popular Law Name Index   721

Case Subject Index   733

Case Names and Popular Case Names Index   769

About the Author   877

INTRODUCTION

The objective of this publication is to continue the work of Nancy A. Guenther's first two editions of *United States Court Decisions: An Index to Excerpts, Reprints, and Discussions*. Ms. Guenther's work ended with 1980 cases and that is where this title starts. The index covers the literature published from 1980 to 1995 and indexes any case heard by the Supreme Court. There are articles appearing for cases of 1995-1995 United States Supreme Court, hence the cases go beyond the 1995 year. The focus has changed slightly with the same basic presumption: to provide for undergraduate and high school students discussions and reprints of United States Supreme Court decisions from nonlaw-oriented and easily accessible publications.

The journals and book titles chosen were found by searching indexes and book reviews. These included *ABI/Inform*; *America: History and Life*; *Business Periodical Index*; *Education Index*; *ERIC*; *Essay and General Literature Index*; *General Science Abstracts*; *PsycInfo*; *PAIS: Public Affairs Information Service*; *Readers' Guide to Periodical Literature*; and *Social Science Abstracts*. There are 114 journal titles indexed and included because they contained more than five articles about decisions in the years 1980 to 1995 and were on *OCLC Top Serials List* of 1995. This means they are readily available at most public and academic libraries. There are 108 books indexed. These books were included because more than 50 California public and academic libraries owned the title, allowing hopefully easy access. Some books have more than one edition during 1980-1995; the edition included was owned by more libraries according to *OCLC's WorldCat*.

The index is larger than planned because of the workload of the Supreme Court during the early 1980s. They heard more cases per year during this time than any other time in their history. Normal years have 90 to 110 decisions; during the early 1980s they made more than 140 decisions per year.

ACKNOWLEDGMENTS

Every attempt was made to minimize errors but some have probably slipped through. The author would appreciate information on these errors. I must also thank my family, colleagues and friends for putting up with me during this project.

INSTRUCTIONS FOR USE

The bibliography is arranged by date of each decision. Most entries contain:

1436.[a] Gillette v. United States[b]   March 8, 1971[c]
            Coupled with Negre v. Larsen[d]
401 US 437   28 LEd2d 168   91 SCt 828[e]
Documents (v. 2):753-756R[f]
En Am Con 352-353, 1538-1545
Godless 60
Regan, Richard J. Supreme Court roundup: 1980 term. *Thought* 56(223):491-502 (December 1981).[g]
————. Supreme Court roundup: 1984 term. *Thought* 61(241):290-302 (June 1986).
Vile, John R. Bob Jones before the bench. *Christian Century* 100(23):707-711 (August 3-10, 1983).

a.   This is the entry number used in the index for locating this case.
b.   These are the parties involved and part of the citation. Included are names that the case may also go by, e.g. Collector v. Day is also known as Buffington, Collector of Internal Revenue v. Day.
c.   Date of the case. Arranged chronologically by date allows finding decision during the 1970s by following the date of the case.
d.   Links cases decided together so one can see the connections. Not all cases are coupled with other decisions.
e.   These are all reporter citations to the case. The official one is first; not everyone has the official *United States Reports* (US), hence citations for *United States Supreme Court Reports, Lawyers' Edition* (LEd and LEd2d) and West's *Supreme Court Reporter* (SCt) are listed.
f.   First list usually is the books. Abbreviations are used; see the next page for the full book title. Some are multiset encyclopedias hence volume then pages are given. Use of the capital R means that is a reprint of the case decision. Use of + sign after a page means there are more pages later in the book, usually highlighting another case but mentioning this case and the relationship. Not all of the decisions are mentioned in books, especially the more current cases.
g.   Second are the journals. Full and actual titles are used; see the following pages for journal titles indexed. Use of [Editorial] means that is an editorial about the case and not necessarily information. Not all of the decisions are mentioned in journals, especially the older cases.

There are several indexes at the back of the book. The first index is the **Words and Phrases Index**, starting on page 717. This index gives an entry number to cases that have argued words or phrases in court. The next index is the **Popular Law Name Index**, starting on page 721. This index gives an entry number to the case that argued a particular law like Federal Employers' Liability Act (FELA). It is arranged by full act name and acronym name, e.g. FELA (Federal Employers' Liability Act). The third index is the **Case Subject Index**, starting on page 733. The index gives an entry number to link cases to the topic or the subject of that case. Finally the biggest index is the **Case Names and Popular Case Names Index**, starting on page 769. Each entry leads to the case by any parties involved, including coupled cases. Note that government agencies are not under their abbreviation but the full agency name is given, e.g. INS is filed under Immigration and Naturalization Service (INS). Use of city names is a problem so look both under the official city name and under City of, e.g. Los Angeles and City of Los Angeles. Any popular case names are given in quotation marks like "Alabama and Mississippi Boundary Case," 2790.

BOOKS CITED

The following are the abbreviations used to identify books. They include the full citation information for locating the book.

Abortion (Frohock)	*Abortion, A Case Study in Law and Morals*. Fred M. Frohock. Westport, Conn.: Greenwood Press, 1983.
Abortion Am	*Abortion and American Politics*. Barbara Hickson Craig. Chatham, N.J.: Chatham House, 1993.
Abortion Con	*The Abortion Controversy: A Documentary History*. Westport, Conn.: Greenwood Press, 1994.
Abortion Dec	*Abortion Decisions of the Supreme Court, 1973 through 1989: A Comprehensive Review with Historical Commentary*. Dan Drucker. Jefferson, N.C.: McFarland & Co., 1990.
Abortion Dec 70s	*Abortion Decisions of the United States Supreme Court: The 1970's*. Beverly Hills, Calif.: Excellent Books, 1993.
Abortion Dec 80s	*Abortion Decisions of the United States Supreme Court: The 1980's*. Beverly Hills, Calif.: Excellent Books, 1993.
Abortion Dec 90s	*Abortion Decisions of the United States Supreme Court: The 1990's*. Maureen Harrison and Steve Gilbert (eds.). Beverly Hills, Calif.: Excellent Books, 1993.
Abortion Moral	*Abortion, Moral and Legal Perspectives*. Jay L. Garfield. Amherst: University of Massachusetts Press, 1984.
Abortion Pol (Jaffe)	*Abortion Politics: Private Morality and Public Policy*. Frederick S. Jaffe. New York: McGraw-Hill, 1981.
Abortion Pol (Rubin)	*Abortion, Politics, and the Courts: Roe v. Wade and Its Aftermath*. Eva R. Rubin. Westport, Conn.: Greenwood Press, 1982.
Abortion Quest	*The Abortion Question*. Hyman Rodman. New York: Columbia University Press, 1987.
Affirmative (Greene)	*Affirmative Action and Principles of Justice*. Kathanne W. Greene. Westport, Conn.: Greenwood Press, 1989.
Affirmative (Woods)	*Affirmative Action*. Geraldine Woods. New York: Watts, 1989.
Almanac (year)	*Congressional Quarterly Almanac*. Washington, D.C.: Congressional Quarterly, annuals for years 1980-1995.
Am Educators	*American Educators' Encyclopedia*. Edward L. Dejnozka. Westport, Conn.: Greenwood Press, 1991.
Am Indian (Deloria)	*American Indian Policy in the Twentieth Century*. Vine Deloria, Jr. (ed.). Norman, Okla.: University of Oklahoma Press, 1985.
Am Indians (Wilkinson)	*American Indians, Time, and the Law: Native Societies in a Modern Constitutional Democracy*. Charles F. Wilkinson. New Haven: Yale University Press, 1987.
Amending	*Amending America: If We Love the Constitution So Much, Why Do We Keep Trying to Change It?* Richard B. Bernstein. New York: Times Books, 1993.
Antagonists	*The Antagonists: Hugo Black, Felix Frankfurter, and Civil Liberties in Modern America*. James F. Simon. New York: Simon & Schuster, 1989.
Ascent	*The Ascent of Pragmatism: The Burger Court in Action*. Bernard Schwartz. Reading, Mass.: Addison-Wesley Publishing Co., 1990.

Bakke	*Bakke and the Politics of Equality: Friends and Foes in the Classroom of Litigation.* Timothy J. O'Neill. Middletown, Conn.: Wesleyan University Press, 1985.
Behind Bakke	*Behind Bakke: Affirmative Action and the Supreme Court.* Bernard Schwartz. New York: New York University Press, 1988.
Black	*Black Mondays: Worst Decisions of the Supreme Court.* Joel D. Joseph. Bethesda, Md.: National Press, 1987.
Brennan	*Brennan vs. Rehnquist: The Battle for the Constitution.* Peter H. Irons. New York: Knopf, 1994.
Burden	*The Burden of Brown: Thirty Years of School Desegregation.* Raymond Wolters. Knoxville: University of Tennessee Press, 1984.
Burger Court	*The Burger Court: The Counter-revolution That Wasn't.* Vincent Blasi (ed.). New Haven: Yale University Press, 1983.
Burger Years	*The Burger Years: Rights and Wrongs in the Supreme Court, 1969-1986.* Herman Schwartz (ed.). New York: Viking, 1987.
Capital Punish	*Capital Punishment: Criminal Law and Social Evolution.* Jan Gorecki. New York: Columbia University Press, 1983.
Center	*The Center Holds: The Power Struggle inside the Rehnquist Court.* James F. Simon. New York: Simon & Schuster, 1995.
Chadha	*Chadha: The Story of an Epic Constitutional Struggle.* Barbara Hinkson Craig. New York: Oxford University Press, 1988.
Civil 19th	*Civil Rights Decisions of the United States Supreme Court: The 19th Century.* Maureen Harrison and Steve Gilbert (eds.). San Diego, Calif.: Excellent Books, 1994.
Civil 20th	*Civil Rights Decisions of the United States Supreme Court: The 20th Century.* Maureen Harrison and Steve Gilbert (eds.). San Diego, Calif.: Excellent Books, 1994.
Conflict	*A Conflict of Rights: The Supreme Court and Affirmative Action.* Melvin I. Urofsky. New York: Scribner's Sons, 1991.
Congress	*Congress Reconsidered.* 2nd Edition. Lawrence C. Dodd (ed.). Washington, D.C.: CQ Press, 1981.
Const (Currie)	*The Constitution in the Supreme Court: The Second Century, 1888-1986.* David P. Currie. Chicago: University of Chicago Press, 1990.
Const (Friendly)	*The Constitution—That Delicate Balance.* Fred W. Friendly. New York: Random House, 1984.
Const Law	*Constitutional Law for a Changing America: Rights, Liberties, and Justice.* Lee Epstein and Thomas G. Walker. Washington, D.C.: CQ Press, 1992.
Courage	*The Courage of Their Convictions.* Peter H. Irons. New York: Free Press, 1988.
Court Const	*The Court and the Constitution.* Archibald Cox. Boston: Houghton Mifflin, 1987.
Court Public	*The Court and Public Policy.* Robert H. Birkby. Washington, D.C.: CQ Press, 1983.
Culture	*Culture in an Age of Money: The Legacy of the 1980s in America.* Nicolaus Mills (ed.). Chicago: Ivan R. Dee, 1990.
Death Penalty (Bedau)	*The Death Penalty in America.* 3rd Edition. Hugo A. Bedau. New York: Oxford University Press, 1982.
Death Penalty (Streib)	*Death Penalty for Juveniles.* Victor L. Streib. Bloomington: Indiana University Press, 1987.
Death Penalty (Tushnet)	*The Death Penalty.* Mark V. Tushnet. New York: Facts on File, 1994.
Death Penalty 80s	*The Death Penalty in the Eighties: An Examination of the Modern System of Capital Punishment.* Welsh S. White. Ann Arbor: University of Michigan Press, 1987.

Death Penalty 90s   *The Death Penalty in the Nineties: An Examination of the Modern System of Capital Punishment*. Welsh S. White. Ann Arbor: University of Michigan Press, 1991.

Documents (v. 1-2)   *Documents of American History*. 10th Edition. Henry S. Commager and Milton Cantor. Englewood Cliffs, N.J.: Prentice Hall, 1988. 2 volumes.

Economics   *The Economics of Justice*. Richard A. Posner. Cambridge: Harvard University Press, 1981.

Editorials (year)   *Editorials on File*. New York: Facts on File, annuals for years 1980-1995.

En Am Con   *Encyclopedia of the American Constitution*. Leonard W. Levy (ed.). New York: Macmillan, 1986. Volumes 1-4.

Equal (Baldus)   *Equal Justice and the Death Penalty: A Legal and Empirical Analysis*. David C. Baldus. Boston: Northeastern University Press, 1990.

Equal (Harrell)   *Equal Justice under Law: The Supreme Court in American Life*. 4th Edition. Mary Ann Harrell and Burnett Anderson. Washington, D.C.: Supreme Court Historical Society, 1982.

Equal Pay   *Equal Pay for Comparable Worth: The Working Women's Issue of the Eighties*. Frances C. Hutner. New York: Praeger, 1986.

Equal Rights   *Equal Rights, The Male Stake*. Leo Kanowitz. Albuquerque: University of New Mexico Press, 1981.

Establishment   *The Establishment Clause: Religion and the First Amendment*. Leonard W. Levy. New York: Macmillan, 1986.

Ethics   *The Ethics of Abortion: Pro-life! vs. Pro-choice!* Buffalo, N.Y.: Prometheus Books, 1989.

Eyes   *The Eyes on the Prize Civil Rights Reader: Documents, Speeches, and Firsthand Accounts from the Black Freedom Struggle, 1954-1990*. Revised Edition. New York: Penguin Books, 1991.

Fighting   *Fighting Faiths: The Abrams Case, the Supreme Court, and Free Speech*. Richard Polenberg. New York: Viking, 1987.

Financing   *Financing Politics: Money, Elections, and Political Reform*. 3rd Edition. Herbert E. Alexander. Washington, D.C.: CQ Press, 1984.

First   *The First Freedom: The Tumultuous History of Free Speech in America*. Nat Hentoff. New York: Delacorte Press, 1980.

Founders (v. 1-5)   *The Founders' Constitution*. Philip B. Kurland and Ralph Lerner (eds.). Chicago: University of Chicago Press, 1987. 5 volumes.

Fourth   *The Fourth Estate and the Constitution: Freedom of the Press in America*. Lucas A. Powe, Jr. Berkeley: University of California Press, 1991.

Freedom (Cox)   *Freedom of Expression*. Archibald Cox. Cambridge: Harvard University Press, 1981.

Godless   *That Godless Court?: Supreme Court Decisions on Church-State Relationships*. Ronald B. Flowers. Louisville, Ky.: Westminster John Knox Press, 1994.

Guide (CQ)   *Congressional Quarterly's Guide to the U.S. Supreme Court*. 2nd Edition. Elder Witt. Washington, D.C.: Congressional Quarterly, 1990.

Guide (West)   *The Guide to American Law: Everyone's Legal Encyclopedia*. St. Paul: West Pub. Co., 1983. Volumes 1-10, including 1987 yearbook and 1990-1995 supplements.

Hard Choices   *Hard Choices, Lost Voices: How the Abortion Conflict Has Divided America, Distorted Constitutional Rights, and Damaged the Courts*. Donald P. Judges. Chicago: Ivan R. Dee, 1993.

Japanese   *Japanese American History: An A-to-Z Reference from 1868 to Present*. Brian Niijay (ed.). New York: Facts on File, 1993.

Jerry   *Jerry Falwell v. Larry Flynt: The First Amendment on Trial*. Rodney A. Smolla. New York: St. Martin's Press, 1988.

Just War   *Justice at War*. Peter H. Irons. New York: Oxford University Press, 1983.

Landmark (v. 1-5) — *Landmark Decisions of the United States Supreme Court.* Maureen Harrison and Steve Gilbert (eds.). Beverly Hills, Calif.: Excellent Books, 1991-1995. Volumes 1-5.

Law Governing — *The Law Governing Abortion, Contraception, and Sterilization.* Irving J. Sloan. London: Oceana Publications, 1988.

Law (Rembar) — *The Law of the Land: The Evolution of Our Legal System.* Charles Rembar. New York: Simon & Schuster, 1980.

Let Us — *Let Us Pray: A Plea for Prayer in Our Schools.* William J. Murray. New York: W. Morrow, 1995.

Letting Go — *Letting Go: Death, Dying, and the Law.* Melvin I. Urofsky. New York: Charles Scribner's Sons, 1993.

Liberty — *Liberty and Sexuality: The Right to Privacy and the Making of Roe v. Wade.* David J. Garrow. New York: Macmillan Publishing Co., 1994.

Loud — *Loud Hawk: The United States versus the American Indian Movement.* Kenneth S. Stern. Norman: University of Oklahoma Press, 1994.

Magic — *The Magic Mirror: Law in American History.* Kermit Hall. New York: Oxford University Press, 1989.

Make — *Make No Law: The Sullivan Case and the First Amendment.* Anthony Lewis. New York: Random House, 1991.

Making — *Making Civil Rights Law: Thurgood Marshall and the Supreme Court, 1936-1961.* New York: Oxford University Press, 1994.

Marbury — *Marbury v. Madison and Judicial Review.* Robert L. Clinton. Lawrence: University Press of Kansas, 1989.

May It — *May It Please the Court: The Most Significant Oral Arguments Made before the Supreme Court since 1955.* Peter Irons (ed.). New York: The New Press, 1993.

Minnesota — *Minnesota Rag: The Dramatic Story of the Landmark Supreme Court Case That Gave New Meaning to Freedom of the Press.* Fred W. Friendly. New York: Random House, 1981.

Mutiny — *Mutiny on the Amistad: The Saga of a Slave Revolt and Its Impact on American Abolition, Law, and Diplomacy.* Howard Jones. New York: Oxford University Press, 1987.

New Right (Schwartz) — *The New Right and the Constitution: Turning Back the Legal Clock.* Bernard Schwartz. Boston: Northeastern University Press, 1990.

New Right (Whitaker) — *The New Right Papers.* Robert W. Whitaker (ed.). New York: St. Martin's Press, 1982.

Nobody's — *Nobody's Business: Paradoxes of Privacy.* Alida Brill. Reading, Mass.: Addison-Wesley Publishing Co., 1990.

One — *100 Key Documents in American Democracy.* Peter B. Levy (ed.). Westport, Conn.: Greenwood Press, 1994.

Original (Davis) — *Original Intent: Chief Justice Rehnquist and the Course of American Church/State Relations.* Derek Davis. Buffalo, N.Y.: Prometheus Books, 1991.

Owners — *Owners versus Players: Baseball and Collective Bargaining.* James B. Dworkin. Boston: Auburn House Publishing Co., 1981.

Plessy — *The Plessy Case: A Legal-Historical Interpretation.* Charles A. Lofgren. New York: Oxford University Press, 1987.

Price — *The Price We Pay: The Case against Racist Speech, Hate Propaganda, and Pornography.* Laura J. Lederer and Richard Delgado (eds.). New York: Hill & Wang, 1995.

Powers — *Powers of Congress.* 2nd Edition. Washington, D.C.: Congressional Quarterly, 1982.

Quarrels — *Quarrels That Have Shaped the Constitution.* Revised Edition. New York: Harper & Row, 1987.

Reader's   *The Reader's Companion to American History*. Eric Foner and John H.
                      Garraty (eds.). Boston: Houghton-Mifflin, 1991.

Religion   *Religion, State, and the Burger Court*. Leo Pfeffer. Buffalo, N.Y.:
                      Prometheus Books, 1984.

Sup Ct Church   *The Supreme Court on Church and State*. Robert S. Alley (ed.). New York:
                      Oxford University Press, 1988.

Sup Ct Ind   *The Supreme Court and Individual Rights*. 2nd Edition. Elder Witt.
                      Washington, D.C.: Congressional Quarterly, 1988.

Sup Ct Review (year) *The Supreme Court Review*. Philip B. Kurland (ed.). Chicago: University
                      of Chicago Press, annual from 1980 to 1995.

Sup Ct Yearbook (year) *Supreme Court Yearbook*. Joan Biskopic and Kenneth Jost (eds.).
                      Washington, D.C.: Congressional Quarterly, annual from 1989 to
                      1995.

Super   *Super Chief, Earl Warren and His Supreme Court: A Judicial Biography*.
                      Unabridged Edition. Bernard Schwartz. New York: New York
                      University Press, 1983.

Tenth   *The Tenth Justice: The Solicitor General and the Rule of Law*. Lincoln
                      Caplan. New York: Knopf, 1987.

Thurgood   *Thurgood Marshall: Justice for All*. Roger L. Goldman. New York: Carroll
                      & Graf, 1992.

Tolerant   *The Tolerant Society: Freedom of Speech and Extremist Speech in
                      America*. Lee C. Bollinger. New York: Oxford University Press, 1986.

Trial   *Trial and Error: The American Controversy over Creation and Evolution*.
                      Edward J. Larson. New York: Oxford University Press, 1985.

Turning   *Turning Right: The Making of the Rehnquist Supreme Court*. Expanded
                      and Updated Edition. David G. Savage. New York: Wiley 1993.

Wars   *The Wars of Watergate: The Last Crisis of Richard Nixon*. Stanley I.
                      Kutler. New York: Knopf, 1990.

Without   *Without Fear or Favor: The "New York Times" and Its Times*. Harrison E.
                      Salisbury. New York: Times Books, 1980.

JOURNALS CITED

Listed below are the magazines and journals in this index. Included are title variations used between 1980 and 1995.

ABA Banking Journal
Academe
Across the Board
Advertising Age
America
American City and County
American Heritage
American Journal of International Law
American Political Science Review
American Politics Quarterly
American Psychologist
American School Board Journal
Annals of the American Academy of Political and Social Science
Aviation Week and Space Technology
Barron's
Best's Review
Best's Review (Property/Casualty Insurance Edition)
Best's Review (Life/Health Insurance Edition)
Black Enterprise
Boston College Environmental Affairs Law Review
Business Credit
Business History Review
Business Horizons
Business Insurance
Business Week
Business Week (Industrial Edition)
Business Week (Industrial/Technology Edition)
Center Magazine
Chemical and Engineering News
Chemical Marketing Reporter
Chemical Week
Christian Century
Christianity Today
Chronicle of Higher Education
Clearing House
Columbia Journalism Review
Commentary
Commonweal
Congressional Digest
CPA Journal
Credit and Financial Management
Crisis
Ebony
Economist

Editor and Publisher
Education Digest
Electrical World
Electronic News
Engineering News
Engineering News Record
ENR
Environment
Forbes
Fortnightly
Fortune
Governing
HR Focus
Humanist
Industry Week
JAMA: The Journal of the American Medical Association
Jet
Journal of Accountancy
Journal of American History
Journal of Criminal Law and Criminology
Journal of Marketing
Journal of Negro Education
Journal of Politics
Journal of State Government
Journal of Taxation
Journalism and Mass Communications Quarterly
Journalism Quarterly
Law and Contemporary Problems
Life
Monthly Labor Review
Ms.
NASSP Bulletin
Nation
National Civic Review
National Review
Nation's Business
New England Journal of Medicine
New Republic
New Statesman
New Statesman and Society
New York Review of Books
New York Times Magazine
New Yorker
Newsweek

Oil and Gas Journal
People Weekly
Personnel
Personnel Journal
Phi Delta Kappan
Planning
Political Research Quarterly
Practical Accountant
Progressive
Public Administration Review
Public Interest
Public Personnel Management
Public Utilities Fortnightly
Publishers' Weekly
Reader's Digest
Review of Politics
Scholastic Update
Scholastic Update (Teachers' Edition)
Science
Science News

Scientific American
Senior Scholastic
Social Education
Society
Sports Illustrated
State Government
Supervision
Taxes
Teachers College Record
Thought
Time
Trial
Trusts and Estates
USA Today
U.S. News and World Report
Vital Speeches
Washington Monthly
Western Political Quarterly
Wilson Quarterly

UNITED STATES SUPREME COURT DECISIONS

1. United States v. Carlisle   September Sessions 1778
   Respublica v. Carlisle
   1 US (1 Dallas) 35   1 LEd 26
   Founders (v. 4):431R

2. United States v. Chapman   April Term 1781
   Respublica v. Chapman
   1 US (1 Dallas) 53   1 LEd 33
   Founders (v. 4):431-433R

3. United States v. De Longchamps   October Session 1784
   Respublica v. De Longchamps
   1 US (1 Dallas) 111   1 LEd 59
   Founders (v. 3):67-68R

4. Wharton v. Morris   April Term 1785
   1 US (1 Dallas) 125   1 LEd 65
   Founders (v. 3):7R

5. Pirate alias Belt v. Dalby   April Term 1786
   1 US (1 Dallas) 167   1 LEd 84
   Founders (v. 3):279R

6. James v. Allen   September Term 1786
   1 US (1 Dallas) 188   1 LEd 93
   Founders (v. 4):470-471R

7. United States v. Shaffer   February Sessions 1788
   Respublica v. Shaffer
   1 US (1 Dallas) 236   1 LEd 116
   Founders (v. 5):261-262R

8. Bolton v. Martin   September 6, 1788
   1 US (1 Dallas) 296   1 LEd 144
   Founders (v. 2):329-330R

9. United States v. Oswald   July Term 1788
   Respublica v. Oswald
   1 US (1 Dallas) 319   1 LEd 155
   Founders (v. 5):124-128R

10. Holmes v. Comegys   June Term 1789
    1 US (1 Dallas) 439   1 LEd 213
    Founders (v. 5):263R

11. United States, Respublica v. Weidle   November Session 1781
    Respublica v. Weidle

2 US (2 Dallas) 88   1 LEd 301
  Founders (v. 4):433-434R

12. Collet v. Collet   April Term 1792
    2 US (2 Dallas) 294   1 LEd 387
      Founders (v. 2):568-569R

13. Van Horne's Lessee v. Dorrance   April Term 1795
    2 US (2 Dallas) 304   1 LEd 391
      En Am Con 1960-1961, 1962-1964
      Founders (v. 1):599-600R; (v. 5):317-321R

14. United States v. Worrall   April Term 1798
    2 US (2 Dallas) 384   1 LEd 426
      Founders (v. 4):261-262

15. Georgia v. Brailsford   April Term 1794
    2 US (2 Dallas) 402, 415   1 LEd 433, 438
    Founders (v. 5):364R
    Guide (CQ) 6-7

16. Hayburn's Case   June 8, 1792
    2 US (2 Dallas) 409   1 LEd 436
      Const (Currie) 89-92
      En Am Con 908-909, 1659-1664
      Founders (v. 4):255-257

17. Chisholm v. Georgia   February 18, 1793
    2 US (2 Dallas) 419   1 LEd 440
      Amending 48-59, 271-272+
      Const (Currie) 568-569
      Documents (v. 1):160-162R
      En Am Con 251, 622-624, 1046-1054
      Equal (Harrell) 15-16
      Founders (v. 5):408-429R
      Guide (CQ) 6
      Magic 76-77
      Marbury 154-159
      Reader's 167-168
    Mathias, Charles McC., Jr. The federal courts under siege. *Annals of the American Academy of Political and Social Science* 462:26-33 (July 1982).
    McDowell, Gary L. Modest remedy for judicial activism. *Public Interest* (67):3-20 (Spring 1982).
    O'Brien, David M. Federalism as a metaphor in the constitutional politics of public administration. *Public Administration Review* 49(5):411-419 (September/October 1989).

18. Glass v. the Sloop Betsey   February Term 1794
    3 US (3 Dallas) 6   1 LEd 485
      Equal (Harrell) 16, 21
      Founders (v. 4):260-261R

19. Hylton v. United States   February Term 1796
    3 US (3 Dallas) 171   1 LEd 556
      En Am Con 564-565, 944-945
      Founders (v. 3):357-362R
      Guide (CQ) 7, 69, 111, 288

20. Ware v. Hylton February Term 1796
 3 US (3 Dallas) 199 1 LEd 568
  En Am Con 2007
  Equal (Harrell) 20
  Founders (v. 4):607-610R
  Guide (CQ) 7, 13
 Orren, Karen. The primacy of labor in American constitutional development. *American Political Science Review* 89(2):377-388 (June 1995).
 Raymond, John M., and Barbara J. Frischholz. Lawyers who established international law in the United States, 1776-1914. *American Journal of International Law* 76(4):802-829 (October 1982).

21. Arcambel v. Wiseman August Term 1796
 3 US (3 Dallas) 306 1 LEd 613
 O'Connor, Karen, and Lee Epstein. Bridging the gap between Congress and the Supreme Court: interest groups and the erosion of the American rule governing awards of attorneys' fees. *Western Political Quarterly* 38(2):238-249 (June 1985).

22. Wiscart v. D'Auchy August 12, 1796
 3 US (3 Dallas) 321 1 LEd 619
  Founders (v. 4):379-382R

23. Hollingsworth v. Virginia February Term 1798
 3 US (3 Dallas) 378 1 LEd 644
  Amending 48-59
  Founders (v. 5):429
  Guide (CQ) 151-152

24. Calder v. Bull August Term 1798
 3 US (3 Dallas) 386 1 LEd 648
  En Am Con 194-195, 676-677, 827-828, 914-917, 1558-1560, 1796-1803, 1962-1964
  Founders (v. 3):349-353; (v. 3):402-408R
  Guide (CQ) 7, 77
  Hard Choices 118-119
 Orren, Karen. The primacy of labor in American constitutional development. *American Political Science Review* 89(2):377-388 (June 1995).

25. Fowler v. Lindsey February Term 1799
 3 US (3 Dallas) 411 1 LEd 658
  Founders (v. 4):262-264R

26. Coxe v. McClenachan December Term 1798
 Coxe v. M'Clenachan
 3 US (3 Dallas) 478 1 LEd 687
  Founders (v. 2):37R

27. Turner v. President, Directors and Company of the Bank of North America August Term 1799
 4 US (4 Dallas) 8 1 LEd 718
  Founders (v. 4):264R

28. Mossman v. Higginson February Term 1800
 4 US (4 Dallas) 12 1 LEd 720
  Founders (v. 4):264R

29. Cooper v. Telfair February 13, 1800
 4 US (4 Dallas) 14 1 LEd 721

Founders (v. 4):265-266R

Orren, Karen. The primacy of labor in American constitutional development. *American Political Science Review* 89(2):377-388 (June 1995).

30. Bas v. Tingy   August Term 1800
     4 US (4 Dallas) 37   1 LEd 731
     Founders (v. 3):97-100R

31. Gyer's Lessee v. Irwin   April Term 1790
     4 US (4 Dallas) 107   1 LEd 762
     Founders (v. 2):330-331R

32. Commonwealth of Pennsylvania v. Dillon   January Term 1792
     4 US (4 Dallas) 116   1 LEd 765
     Founders (v. 5):263-264R

33. Hurst v. Hurst   November 4, 1804
     In re Hurst
     4 US (4 Dallas) 387   1 LEd 878
     Founders (v. 2):341-342R

34. United States v. Schooner Peggy   August Term 1801
     5 US (1 Cranch) 103   2 LEd 49
     Founders (v. 4):616-617R

35. Marbury v. Madison   February 24, 1803
     5 US (1 Cranch) 137   2 LEd 60
     Burger Years 3-20
     Const (Friendly) 7-10
     Court Const 45-53, 57-61+
     Court Public 14, 27-34R
     Documents (v. 1):191-195R
     En Am Con 357-358, 391-399, 464-471, 1031-1038, 1046-1054, 1054-1061, 1136-1143, 1199-1202, 1420-1422, 1659-1664
     Equal (Harrell) 24-27+
     Founders (v. 4):269-277
     Guide (CQ) 8-9, 63-64, 69-71
     Guide (West) (v. 7):262-263, 267-269, 278-286
     Hard Choices 115-117, 305-306
     Landmark (v. 3):155-175R
     Magic 80, 82-84
     Make 46-55
     Marbury 1-30, 81-127, 161-175, 211-233+
     New Right (Whitaker) 142-168
     One 77-81R
     Powers 234-235, 285
     Quarrels 7-19
     Sup Ct Review (1993):329-446

Baker, banker, clergyman, thief. *Life* 10(10):84-88 (Fall 1987).

Barrett, Edward L. The Supreme Court: why the Constitution survives: long-term view of the Court. *Trial* 25(12):30-35 (December 1989).

Berns, Walter. Government by lawyers and judges. *Commentary* 83(6):17-24 (June 1987).

Funk, William. The exception that approves the rule: FDF variances under the Clean Water Act. *Boston College Environmental Affairs Law Review* 13(1):1-60 (Fall 1985).

Flaherty, Francis J. Abortion, the Constitution, and the Human Life Statute. *Commonweal* 108(19):586-593 (October 23, 1981).

Garraty, John Arthur. 101 things every college graduate should know about American history. *American Heritage* 38(1):24-32 (December 1986).

Gest, Ted. Courts: a major battleground of social upheaval. *U.S. News & World Report* 98(3):48-50 (January 28, 1985).

Goldstein, Leslie Friedman. Judicial review and democratic theory: guardian democracy vs. representative democracy. *Western Political Quarterly* 40(3):391-412 (September 1987).

Graglia, Lino A. How the Constitution disappeared. *Commentary* 81(2):19-27 (February 1986).

Gunther, Gerald. Judicial Review. *Society* 24(1):18-23 (November/December 1986).

———. The power of the courts—any practicable limits? *Center Magazine* 18(5):52-64 (September/October 1985).

Heffner, Judith C. The Constitution in court. *Scholastic Update* (Teachers' Edition) 116(5):16-18 (October 28, 1983).

Howard, A. E. Dick. Making it work. *Wilson Quarterly* 11(2):122-133 (Spring 1987).

Meese, Edwin, 3d. Interpreting the Constitution. *USA Today* 115(2496):36-39 (September 1986).

———. Saving the Constitution: The law of the Constitution. *National Review* 39(13):30-33 (July 17, 1987).

Murphy, Walter F. The Constitution and the 14th Amendment. *Center Magazine* 20(4):9-30 (July/August 1987).

Orren, Karen. The primacy of labor in American constitutional development. *American Political Science Review* 89(2):377-388 (June 1995).

Pawelek, Dick. Call five cases that shaped Congress. *Scholastic Update* (Teachers' Edition) 119(9):12-14 (January 12, 1987).

Polin, Raymond. The Supreme Court's dilemma and defense. *USA Today* 115(2496):43-45 (September 1986).

Rabinove, Samuel, William E. Johnston, Jr., Lawrence E. Mitchell, Christopher C. Faille, Wallace M. Rudolph, David A. Frolick, Ronald K. L. Collins, Herb Greer, H. Elliot Wales, Thomas A. Bustin, and Lino A. Graglia. The Constitution and the Court. [Editorial] *Commentary* 81(6):2-11 (June 1986).

Rees, Grover, 3d. Constitution, the court, and the President-elect. *National Review* 32(26):1595-1602 (December 31, 1980).

Relin, David Oliver. Five landmark decisions. *Scholastic Update* 120(15):20 (April 8, 1988).

Stephenson, D. Grier, Jr. John Marshall and the evolution of judicial review. *USA Today* 116(2506):37-39 (July 1987).

Winkler, Karen J. Who says what the Constitution means? Supreme Court's authority to decide is debated. *Chronicle of Higher Education* 34(27):A4-A7 (March 16, 1988).

Wise, Charles, and Rosemary O'Leary. Is federalism dead or alive in the Supreme Court?: implications for public administrators. *Public Administration Review* 52(6):559-572 (November/December 1992).

36. Stuart v. Laird — February Term 1803
   5 US (1 Cranch) 299 — 2 LEd 115
   En Am Con 1793
   Founders (v. 4):187-188R

37. Murry v. Schooner The Charming Betsy — February Term 1804
   6 US (2 Cranch) 64 — 2 LEd 208
   Sup Ct Review (1994):295-343

Glennon, Michael J. State-Sponsored Abduction: A Comment on United States v. Alvarez-Machain. *American Journal of International Law* 86(4):746-756 (October 1992).

Trimble, Phillip R. The Supreme Court and international law: the demise of Restatement section 403. [Editorial] *American Journal of International Law* 89(1):53-57 (January 1995).

38. Little v. Barreme — February 27, 1804
   6 US (2 Cranch) 170 — 2 LEd 243
   En Am Con 316-317
   Founders (v. 3):102-104R

Deering, Christopher J. Congress, the President, and Military Policy. *Annals of the American Academy of Political and Social Science* 499:136-147 (September 1988).

39. United States v. Fisher, Assignees of Blight   February Term 1804
    6 US (2 Cranch) 358   2 LEd 304
       Founders (v. 2):622R
    Orren, Karen. The primacy of labor in American Constitutional development. *American Political Science Review* 89(2):377-388 (June 1995).
    Van Alstyne, William W. Implied powers. *Society* 24(1):56-60 (November/December 1986).

40. Hepburn and Dundas v. Ellzey   February Term 1804
    6 US (2 Cranch) 445   2 LEd 332
       Founders (v. 3):230R

41. Huidekoper's Lessee v. Douglass   February Term 1805
    7 US (3 Cranch) 1   2 LEd 347
    Orren, Karen. The primacy of labor in American constitutional development. *American Political Science Review* 89(2):377-388 (June 1995).

42. United States v. More   March 2, 1805
    7 US (3 Cranch) 159   2 LEd 397
       Founders (v. 4):382-383R

43. Strawbridge v. Curtiss   February Term 1806
    7 US (3 Cranch) 267   2 LEd 435
       Founders (v. 4):285R

44. Ex Parte Burford   February Term 1806
    7 US (3 Cranch) 448   2 LEd 495
       Founders (v. 5):239

45. Ex Parte Bollman   February Term 1807
    8 US (4 Cranch) 75   2 LEd 554
       Const (Currie) 294-299
       En Am Con 133, 1903-1909
       Founders (v. 3):336-341R; (v. 4):439-443R

46. Bank of the United States v. Deveaux   February Term 1809
    9 US (5 Cranch) 61   3 LEd 38
       Founders (v. 4):285-287R

47. United States v. Judge Peters   February Term 1809
    9 US (5 Cranch) 115   3 LEd 53
       En Am Con 1030-1031, 1211-1218
       Founders (v. 4):287-289R
       Sup Ct Review (1984):149-168

48. Harrison v. Sterry   February Term 1809
    9 US (5 Cranch) 289   3 LEd 104
       Founders (v. 2):622-623R

49. Hodgson and Thompson v. Bowerbank   February Term 1809
    9 US (5 Cranch) 303   3 LEd 108
       Am En Con 41-43, 919-920
       Founders (v. 4):289-290

50. Owings v. Norwood's Lessee February Term 1809
   9 US (5 Cranch) 344 3 LEd 120
      Founders (v. 4):290R

51. Fletcher v. Peck March 16, 1810
   10 US (6 Cranch) 87 3 LEd 162
      Documents (v. 1):205-207R
      En Am Con 493-499, 537-539, 744-745, 914-917
      Founders (v. 3):408-413R
      Guide (CQ) 10-11
      Guide (West) (v. 5):266-267
      Let Us 113
      Magic 82-84, 122-123
      Marbury 143-160
      Reader's 403-404, 1050-1052
   Duesenberg, Richard W. Washington is stifling economic liberties. *USA Today* 123(2596):14-16 (January 1995).
   Kens, Paul. Liberty and the public ingredient of private property. *Review of Politics* 55(1):85-116 (Winter 1993).
   Melone, Albert P. Mendelson v. Wright: understanding the contract clause. *Western Political Quarterly* 41(4):791-799 (December 1988).
   Mendelson, Wallace. B. F. Wright on the contract clause: a progressive misreading of the Marshall-Taney era. *Western Political Quarterly* 38(2):262-275 (June 1985).
   Orren, Karen. The primacy of labor in American constitutional development. *American Political Science Review* 89(2):377-388 (June 1995).

52. Durousseau v. United States March 15, 1810
   10 US (6 Cranch) 307 3 LEd 232
      Founders (v. 4):383-385R

53. Sere and Laralde v. Pitot March 17, 1810
   10 US (6 Cranch) 332 3 LEd 240
      Founders (v. 4):556R

54. United States v. Hudson and Goodwin March 14, 1812
   11 US (7 Cranch) 32 3 LEd 259
      Founders (v. 4):294, 318
      Guide (CQ) 11
      Magic 84-86, 168
      Sup Ct Review (1994):209-245, 345-428

55. Schooner Exchange v. M'Faddon March 3, 1812
   11 US (7 Cranch) 116 3 LEd 287
      Founders (v. 3):78-82R
      Sup Ct Review (1991):179-224
   Raymond, John M., and Barbara J. Frischholz. Lawyers who established international law in the United States, 1776-1914. *American Journal of International Law* 76(4):802-829 (October 1982).

56. New Jersey v. Wilson March 3, 1812
   11 US (7 Cranch) 164 3 LEd 303
      En Am Con 1308-1309
      Marbury 143-160
   Orren, Karen. The primacy of labor in American constitutional development. *American Political Science Review* 89(2):377-388 (June 1995).

57. M'Kim v. Voorhies   March 14, 1812
     McKim v. Voorhies
     11 US (7 Cranch) 279   3 LEd 342
        Founders (v. 4):617R

58. Mima Queen v. Hepburn   February 13, 1813
     Queen v. Hepburn
     11 US (7 Cranch) 290   3 LEd 348
        Founders (v. 5):364-365R

59. Mills v. Duryee   March 11, 1813
     11 US (7 Cranch) 481   3 LEd 411
        Founders (v. 4):477-478R

60. McIntire v. Wood   March 15, 1813
     11 US (7 Cranch) 504   3 LEd 420
        Founders (v. 4):294-295R

61. Fairfax's Devisee v. Hunter's Lessee   March 15, 1813
     11 US (7 Cranch) 603   3 LEd 453
        Founders (v. 4):617-622R

62. Brown v. United States   March 2, 1814
     12 US (8 Cranch) 110   3 LEd 504
        Founders (v. 3):104-115R

63. Terrett v. Taylor   February 17, 1815
     13 US (9 Cranch) 043   3 LEd 650
        En Am Con 914-917, 1796-1803, 1877
     Orren, Karen. The primacy of labor in American constitutional development. *American Political Science Review* 89(2):377-388 (June 1995).

64. Town of Pawlet v. Clark   March 10, 1815
     Pawlet v. Clark
     13 US (9 Cranch) 292   3 LEd 735
        Founders (v. 4):301R

65. Corporation of New Orleans v. Winter   February Term 1816
     New Orleans v. Winter
     14 US (1 Wheaton) 91   4 LEd 44
        Founders (v. 4):304R

66.   Martin v. Hunter's Lessee   March 20, 1816
     14 US (1 Wheaton) 304   4 LEd 97
        Court Const 63-67+
        En Am Con 305-308, 1046-1054, 1211-1218, 1219-1222
        Founders (v. 4):304-318R
        Guide (CQ) 11-12
     Barrett, Edward L. The Supreme Court: why the Constitution survives: long-term view of the Court. *Trial* 25(12):30-35 (December 1989).
     Gunther, Gerald. The power of the courts—any practicable limits? *Center Magazine* 18(5):52-64 (September/October 1985).

67. United States v. Coolidge   March 21, 1816
     14 US (1 Wheaton) 415   4 LEd 124

Founders (v. 4):318R

68. Laidlaw v. Organ   February Term 1817
    15 US (2 Wheaton) 178   4 LEd 214
    Magic 121-122

69. Morgan's Heirs v. Morgan   February Term 1817
    15 US (2 Wheaton) 290   4 LEd 242
    Founders (v. 4):321R

70. United States v. Bevans   February Term 1818
    16 US (3 Wheaton) 336   4 LEd 404
    Founders (v. 4):323-325R

71. United States v. Palmer   February Term 1818
    16 US (3 Wheaton) 610   4 LEd 471
    Mutiny 81-84
    White, G. Edward. The Marshall Court and international law: the piracy cases. *American Journal of International Law* 83(4):727-735 (October 1989).

72. Sturges v. Crowninshield   February Term 1819
    17 US (4 Wheaton) 122   4 LEd 529
    En Am Con 464-471, 493-499, 1794
    Founders (v. 2):632-636R
    Guide (CQ) 11,13
    Marbury 143-160
    Mendelson, Wallace. B. F. Wright on the contract clause: a progressive misreading of the Marshall-Taney era. *Western Political Quarterly* 38(2):262-275 (June 1985).
    Orren, Karen. The primacy of labor in American constitutional development. *American Political Science Review* 89(2):377-388 (June 1995).

73. Bank of Columbia v. Okely   February Term 1819
    17 US (4 Wheaton) 235   4 LEd 559
    Founders (v. 5):365-366R

74. McCulloch v. Maryland   March 7, 1819
    17 US (4 Wheaton) 316   4 LEd 579
    Const (Currie) 563-568
    Const (Friendly) 255-262
    Court Const 75-83+
    Documents (v. 1):213-220R
    En Am Con 305-308, 343-344, 346-348, 464-471, 962-966, 1043-1046, 1234-1237, 1270-1273+
    Equal (Harrell) 29-34
    Founders (v. 1):238; (v. 2):15-16R; (v. 3):252-259R; (v. 4):626-627R
    Guide (CQ) 11-12, 73-74, 121, 127
    Guide (West) (v. 7):314-315
    Hard Choices 115-117, 119-120+
    Landmark (v. 4):1-22R
    Magic 89-93
    Marbury 102-115, 194-199+
    Quarrels 37-53
    Reader's 712, 1050-1052
    Sup Ct Review (1995):125-215
    Baker, banker, clergyman, thief. *Life* 10(10):84-88 (Fall 1987).

Blasi, Ronald W., and C. James Judson. Supreme Court provides guideline for taxing of federal securities by states. *Journal of Taxation* 64(1):42-45 (January 1986).

Clinton, Robert Lowry. Judicial review, nationalism, and the commerce clause: contrasting antebellum and postbellum Supreme Court decision making. *Political Research Quarterly* 47(4):857-876 (December 1994).

Garraty, John Arthur. 101 things every college graduate should know about American history. *American Heritage* 38(1):24-32 (December 1986).

Gunther, Gerald. Judicial review. *Society* 24(1):18-23 (November/December 1986).

Heffner, Judith C. The Constitution in court. *Scholastic Update* (Teachers' Edition) 116(5):16-18 (October 28, 1983).

Howard, A. E. Dick. Making it work. *Wilson Quarterly* 11(2):122-133 (Spring 1987).

Johnston, Richard E., and John T. Thompson. Burger court and federalism: a revolution in 1976? *Western Political Quarterly* 33(2):197-216 (June 1980).

Kens, Paul. Liberty and the public ingredient of private property. *Review of Politics* 55(1):85-116 (Winter 1993).

Moss, David A. Kindling a flame under federalism: progressive reformers, corporate elites, and the phosphorous match campaign of 1909-1912. *Business History Review* 68(2):244-275 (Summer 1994).

O'Brien, David M. The framers' muse on republicanism, the Supreme Court, and pragmatic constitutional interpretivism. *Review of Politics* 53(2):251-288 (Spring 1991).

Orren, Karen. The primacy of labor in American constitutional development. *American Political Science Review* 89(2):377-388 (June 1995).

Plater, Zygmunt J.B., and William Lund Norine. Through the looking glass of eminent domain: exploring the "arbitrary and capricious" test and substantive rationality review of governmental decisions. *Boston College Environmental Affairs Law Review* 16(4):661-752 (Summer 1989).

Polin, Raymond. The Supreme Court's dilemma and defense. *USA Today* 115(2496):43-45 (September 1986).

Relin, David Oliver. Five landmark decisions. *Scholastic Update* 120(15):20 (April 8, 1988).

Van Alstyne, William W. Implied powers. *Society* 24(1):56-60 (November/December 1986).

75. Trustees of Dartmouth College v. Woodward   February 2, 1819
    17 US (4 Wheaton) 518   4 LEd 629
    Am Educators 156
    Const (Friendly) 252-255
    Documents (v. 1):220-223R
    En Am Con 255-257, 493-499, 537-539, 1560
    Founders (v. 3):415-435R
    Guide (CQ) 11
    Guide (West) (v. 4):30-32
    Magic 109-111, 122-123+
    Marbury 143-160
    Quarrels 21-35
    Reader's 266, 333-334

Kens, Paul. Liberty and the public ingredient of private property. *Review of Politics* 55(1):85-116 (Winter 1993).

Melone, Albert P. Mendelson v. Wright: understanding the contract clause. *Western Political Quarterly* 41(4):791-799 (December 1988).

Mendelson, Wallace. B. F. Wright on the contract clause: a progressive misreading of the Marshall-Taney era. *Western Political Quarterly* 38(2):262-275 (June 1985).

Orren, Karen. The primacy of labor in American constitutional development. *American Political Science Review* 89(2):377-388 (June 1995).

76. Houston v. Moore   February 16, 1820
    18 US (5 Wheaton) 1   5 LEd 19
    Founders (v. 3):188-197R

77. United States v. Wiltberger   February Term 1820
    18 US (5 Wheaton) 76   5 LEd 37

Sup Ct Review (1994):345-428

78. United States v. Klintock   February Term 1820
    18 US (5 Wheaton) 144   5 LEd 55
    White, G. Edward. The Marshall Court and international law: the piracy cases. *American Journal of International Law* 83(4):727-735 (October 1989).

79. United States v. Smith   February Term 1820
    18 US (5 Wheaton) 153   5 LEd 57
        Founders (v. 3):82-85R
    White, G. Edward. The Marshall Court and international law: the piracy cases. *American Journal of International Law* 83(4):727-735 (October 1989).

80. Loughborough v. Blake   February Term 1820
    18 US (5 Wheaton) 317   5 LEd 98
        Founders (v. 3):363-365R

81. Owings v. Speed   February Term 1820
    18 US (5 Wheaton) 420   5 LEd 124
        Founders (v. 4):670-671R

82. Cohens v. Virginia   February Term 1821
    19 US (6 Wheaton) 264   5 LEd 257
        Documents (v. 1):228-232R
        En Am Con 305-308
        Equal (Harrell) 35-37
        Founders (v. 4):326-339R; (v. 5):429-442R
        Guide (CQ) 12, 14-15
        Marbury 143-160, 194-199+
    Gunther, Gerald. Judicial review. *Society* 24(1):18-23 (November/December 1986).

83. M'Clung v. Silliman   February Term 1821
    19 US (6 Wheaton) 598   5 LEd 340
        Founders (v. 4):339-340R

84. In re The Santissima Trinidad   February Term 1822
    20 US (7 Wheaton) 283   5 LEd 454
        Founders (v. 2):596R

85. Green v. Biddle   February Term 1823
    21 US (8 Wheaton) 1   5 LEd 547
        En Am Con 866-867
        Founders (v. 3):482R

86. In re Sarah   February Term 1823
    21 US (8 Wheaton) 391   5 LEd 644
        Founders (v. 4):340-341R

87. Johnson & Graham's Lessee v. William M'Intosh   February Term 1823
    21 US (8 Wheaton) 543   5 LEd 681
        Am Indian (Deloria) 22-29, 63-82, 239-256
        Am Indians (Wilkinson) 24, 39-41, 50, 153
        Founders (v. 2):533-540R
    Orlando, Caroline L. Aboriginal title claims in the Indian Claims Commission: U.S. v. Dann and its due process limitations. *Boston College Environmental Affairs Law Review* 13(2):241-280 (Winter 1986).

88. Gibbons v. Ogden   March 3, 1824
     22 US (9 Wheaton) 1   6 LEd 23
       Court Const 84-91+
       Documents (v. 1):238-242R
       En Am Con 596-600, 602-606, 613-614, 841-843, 993-994, 1744-1751, 1751-1755
       Equal (Harrell) 36-40
       Founders (v. 2):496-509R
       Guide (CQ) 12-13, 64-65, 83, 85-86, 87, 95
       Guide (West) (v. 5):374
       Marbury 194-199+
       Powers 129-131, 133-137+
       Quarrels 57-69
       Reader's 449
       Sup Ct Review (1995):125-215
     Baker, banker, clergyman, thief. *Life* 10(10):84-88 (Fall 1987).
     Clinton, Robert Lowry. Judicial review, nationalism, and the commerce clause: contrasting antebellum and
       postbellum Supreme Court decision making. *Political Research Quarterly* 47(4):857-876 (December 1994).
     Deering, Christopher J. Congress, the President, and military policy. *Annals of the American Academy of
       Political and Social Science* 499:136-147 (September 1988).
     Garraty, John Arthur. 101 things every college graduate should know about American history. *American
       Heritage* 38(1):24-32 (December 1986).
     Johnston, Richard E., and John T. Thompson. Burger court and federalism: a revolution in 1976? *Western
       Political Quarterly* 33(2):197-216 (June 1980).
     Mendelson, Wallace. B. F. Wright on the contract clause: a progressive misreading of the Marshall-Taney era.
       Western Political Quarterly 38(2):262-275 (June 1985).
     O'Brien, David M. Federalism as a metaphor in the constitutional politics of public administration. *Public
       Administration Review* 49(5):411-419 (September/October 1989).
     Orren, Karen. The primacy of labor in American constitutional development. *American Political Science
       Review* 89(2):377-388 (June 1995).
     Pawelek, Dick. Call five cases that shaped Congress. *Scholastic Update* (Teacher' Edition) 119(9):12-14
       (January 12, 1987).
     ———. Put yourself on the U.S. Supreme Court. *Senior Scholastic* 113(8):12-13, 27 (December 12, 1980).
     Powers, Carol L. State taxation of energy resources: affirmation of Commonwealth Edison Co. v. Montana.
       Boston College Environmental Affairs Law Review 10(2):503-564 (September 1982).
     Schwartz, Edward B. Water as an article of commerce: state embargoes spring a leak under Sporhase v.
       Nebraska. *Boston College Environmental Affairs Law Review* 12(1):103-169 (Fall 1985).

89. Appollon   February Term 1824
     22 US (9 Wheaton) 362   6 LEd 111
     White, G. Edward. The Marshall Court and international law: the piracy cases. *American Journal of
       International Law* 83(4):727-735 (October 1989).

90. United States v. Perez   March 17, 1824
     22 US (9 Wheaton) 579   6 LEd 165
       Founders (v. 5):285R

91. Osborn v. President, Directors and Co. of the Bank of the United States   February Term 1824
     22 US (9 Wheaton) 738   6 LEd 204
       En Am Con 391-399, 622-624, 1046-1054, 1350-1351
       Founders (v. 4):342-350R; (v. 5):442-445R
       Guide (CQ) 145
       Quarrels 37-53
       Sup Ct Review (1984):149-168
     Meese, Edwin, III. Interpreting the Constitution. *USA Today* 115(2496):36-39 (September 1986).

92. Bank of the United States v. Planters' Bank of Georgia   February Term 1824
    22 US (9 Wheaton) 904   6 LEd 244
    Founders (v. 5):445-446R

93. Wayman v. Southard   February Term 1825
    23 US (10 Wheaton) 1   6 LEd 253
    Founders (v. 2):37-38R

94. Bank of the United States v. Halstead   February Term 1825
    23 US (10 Wheaton) 51   6 LEd 264
    Founders (v. 2):38-39R

95. The Antelope   March 18, 1825
    23 US (10 Wheaton) 66   6 LEd 268
    Founders (v. 3):302-304R; (v. 5):242-244R
    Landmark (v. 5):1-11R
    Mutiny 74-79+
    White, G. Edward. The Marshall Court and international law: the piracy cases. *American Journal of
        International Law* 83(4):727-735 (October 1989).

96. Elmendorf v. Taylor   February Term 1825
    23 US (10 Wheaton) 152   6 LEd 289
    Founders (v. 4):478-479

97. McCormick v. Sullivant   March 16, 1825
    M'Cormick v. Sullivant
    23 US (10 Wheaton) 192   6 LEd 300
    Founders (v. 4):479R

98. Marianna Flora   February Term 1826
    24 US (11 Wheaton) 1   6 LEd 405
    White, G. Edward. The Marshall Court and international law: the piracy cases. *American Journal of
        International Law* 83(4):727-735 (October 1989).

99. United States v. Ortega   February Term 1826
    24 US (11 Wheaton) 467   6 LEd 521
    Founders (v. 4):356R

100. Martin v. Mott   February 2, 1827
    25 US (12 Wheaton) 19   6 LEd 537
    Documents (v. 1):246-247R
    En Am Con 413-419, 1222
    Founders (v. 3):198-202R

101. Ogden v. Saunders   January Term 1827
    25 US (12 Wheaton) 213   6 LEd 606
    En Am Con 493-499, 600-602, 1340-1341
    Founders (v. 3):435-457R
    Guide (CQ) 13
    Marbury 143-160
    Kens, Paul. Liberty and the public ingredient of private property. *Review of Politics* 55(1):85-116 (Winter
        1993).
    Mendelson, Wallace. B. F. Wright on the contract clause: a progressive misreading of the Marshall-Taney era.
        Western Political Quarterly 38(2):262-275 (June 1985).

Orren, Karen. The primacy of labor in American constitutional development. *American Political Science Review* 89(2):377-388 (June 1995).

102. Mason v. Haile   January Term 1827
      25 US (12 Wheaton) 370   6 LEd 660
         Founders (v. 3):457-459R
         Guide (CQ) 13, 308, 888

103. Brown v. Maryland   January Term 1827
      25 US (12 Wheaton) 419   6 LEd 678
         Ascent 120-122
         En Am Con 164, 1349-1350, 1757-1760
         Founders (v. 2):509-517R
         Guide (CQ) 13
      Clinton, Robert Lowry. Judicial review, nationalism, and the commerce clause: contrasting antebellum and postbellum Supreme Court decision making. *Political Research Quarterly* 47(4):857-876 (December 1994).

104. United States v. Gooding   January Term 1827
      25 US (12 Wheaton) 460   6 LEd 693
         Founders (v. 5):287R

105. United States v. Marchant & Colson   March 12, 1827
      25 US (12 Wheaton) 480   6 LEd 700
         Founders (v. 5):287-289R

106. United States v. Saline Bank of Virginia   January Term 1828
      26 US (1 Peters) 100   7 LEd 69
         Founders (v. 5):289R

107. Sundry African Slaves v. Madrazo   January Term 1828
      Governor of Georgia v. Sundry African Slaves
      26 US (1 Peters) 110   7 LEd 73
         Sup Ct Review (1984):149-168

108. American Insurance Co. and the Ocean Insurance Co.   January Term 1828
         v. 356 Bales of Cotton, Canter, Claimant
      26 US (1 Peters) 511   7 LEd 242
         Documents (v. 1):248-249R
         En Am Con 52-53, 407-413, 1144-1145, 1877-1878, 1878-1879
         Founders (v. 3):63-65R
      White, G. Edward. The Marshall Court and international law: the piracy cases. *American Journal of International Law* 83(4):727-735 (October 1989).

109. Boyce v. Anderson   January Term 1829
      27 US (2 Peters) 150   7 LEd 379
         Guide (CQ) 13, 377

110. Wilson v. Black Bird Creek Marsh Co.   January Term 1829
      27 US (2 Peters) 245   7 LEd 412
         En Am Con 2066-2067
         Founders (v. 2):509-517R
         Guide (CQ) 13, 86-87, 312, 318, 887
         Marbury 147-150+
         Sup Ct Review (1995):125-215

Clinton, Robert Lowry. Judicial review, nationalism, and the commerce clause: contrasting antebellum and postbellum Supreme Court decision making. *Political Research Quarterly* 47(4):857-876 (December 1994).

111. Foster and Elam v. Neilson   January Term 1829
    27 US (2 Peters) 253   7 LEd 415
       En Am Con 1910-1911
       Guide (CQ) 17, 66, 133
    Raymond, John M., and Barbara J. Frischholz. Lawyers who established international law in the United States, 1776-1914. *American Journal of International Law* 76(4):802-829 (October 1982).

112. Satterlee v. Mathewson   January Term 1829
    27 US (2 Peters) 380   7 LEd 458
       Founders (v. 3):349-353

113. Weston v. City of Charleston   January Term 1829
    27 US (2 Peters) 449   7 LEd 481
       En Am Con 2046
       Guide (CQ) 13, 118, 120b, 351, 888
    Blasi, Ronald W., and C. James Judson. Supreme Court provides guideline for taxing of federal securities by states. *Journal of Taxation* 64(1):42-45 (January 1986).

114. Beatty v. Kurtz   January Term 1829
    27 US (2 Peters) 566   7 LEd 521
       Sup Ct Review (1983):459-507

115. Shanks v. DuPont   January Term 1830
    28 US (3 Peters) 242   7 LEd 666
       Founders (v. 2):611-618R

116. Craig v. Missouri   January Term 1830
    29 US (4 Peters) 410   7 LEd 903
       Documents (v. 1):252-253R
       En Am Con 112, 513
       Founders (v. 3):459-463R
       Guide (CQ) 13, 15, 663, 888

117. Providence Bank v. Billings and Pittman   January Term 1830
    29 US (4 Peters) 514   7 LEd 939
       En Am Con 493-499, 1483
       Guide (CQ) 13
       Marbury 147-150
    Kens, Paul. Liberty and the public ingredient of private property. *Review of Politics* 55(1):85-116 (Winter 1993).
    Mendelson, Wallace. B. F. Wright on the contract clause: a progressive misreading of the Marshall-Taney era. *Western Political Quarterly* 38(2):262-275 (June 1985).
    Orren, Karen. The primacy of labor in American constitutional development. *American Political Science Review* 89(2):377-388 (June 1995).

118. Cherokee Nation v. Georgia   March 18, 1831
    30 US (5 Peters) 1   8 LEd 25
       Am Indian (Deloria) 22-29, 63-82, 105-133
       Am Indians (Wilkinson) 24, 55, 153
       Civil 19th 4, 9, 13-22R+
       Documents (v. 1):255-258R
       En Am Con 240-242

Founders (v. 2):540-550R
Landmark (v. 4):23-32R
Magic 147-148
Reader's 160

Allen, Mark. Native American control of tribal natural resource development in the context of the federal trust and tribal self-determination. *Boston College Environmental Affairs Law Review* 16(4):857-895 (Summer 1989).

Baer, Susan D. The public trust doctrine—a tool to make federal administrative agencies increase protection of public land and its resources. *Boston College Environmental Affairs Law Review* 15(2):385-436 (Winter 1988).

Cohn, Bob. Supreme but not final. *Newsweek* 120(15):78-79 (October 12, 1992).

McDowell, Gary L. Modest remedy for judicial activism. *Public Interest* (67):3-20 (Spring 1982).

Williams, Walter L. United States Indian policy and the debate over Philippine annexation: implications for the origins of American imperialism. *Journal of American History* 66(4):810-831 (March 1980).

119. Ex Parte Crane   January Term 1831
          Coupled with Jackson v. Kelly
      30 US (5 Peters) 190   8 LEd 92
          Founders (v. 4):362-366R

120. Hawkins v. Barney's Lessee   January Term 1831
      30 US (5 Peters) 457   8 LEd 190
          Founders (v. 3):482-484R

121. Worcester v. Georgia   March 2, 1832
      31 US (6 Peters) 515   8 LEd 483
          Am Indian (Deloria) 22-29, 63-82, 197-220
          Am Indians (Wilkinson) 24, 30-37, 55-56, 59-62, 95-96+
          Civil 19th 4, 9, 23-46R
          Const (Friendly) 11
          Documents (v. 1):258-259R
          En Am Con 240-242
          Guide (CQ) 13-14
          Landmark (v. 4):32-56R

Allen, Mark. Native American control of tribal natural resource development in the context of the federal trust and tribal self-determination. *Boston College Environmental Affairs Law Review* 16(4):857-895 (Summer 1989).

Jones, Peter M. Three great decisions: what would you have done? Indian land. *Scholastic Update* 120(12):18 (February 26, 1988).

Ott, Brian R. Indian fishing rights in the Pacific Northwest: The need for federal intervention. *Boston College Environmental Affairs Law Review* 14(2):313-343 (Winter 1987).

Peck, Ira. Worcester v. Georgia: the campaign to move the Cherokee Nation. *Senior Scholastic* 115(6):17-18, 21, 24 (November 12, 1982).

Williams, Walter L. United States Indian policy and the debate over Philippine annexation: Implications for the origins of American imperialism. *Journal of American History* 66(4):810-831 (March 1980).

122. United States v. Percheman   January Term 1833
      32 US (7 Peters) 51   8 LEd 604
Raymond, John M., and Barbara J. Frischholz. Lawyers who established international law in the United States, 1776-1914. *American Journal of International Law* 76(4):802-829 (October 1982).

123. United States v. Wilson   January Term 1833
      32 US (7 Peters) 150   8 LEd 640
          Founders (v. 4):24-25R

124. Barron v. Mayor and City Council of Baltimore   January Term 1833
      32 US (7 Peters) 243   8 LEd 672
         Amending 201, 203-213
         Const (Friendly) 3-6, 10-15, 22-28
         Const Law 14-17, 38-39
         En Am Con 102, 630-632, 757-761, 970-973, 1744-1751, 1796-1803
         Founders (v. 5):339-340R
         Guide (CQ) 14, 25-26, 143b
         Let Us 113-114
         Magic 117-118
      Meese, Edwin III. The attorney general's view of the Supreme Court: toward a jurisprudence of original
         intention. *Public Administration Review* 45(Special Issue):701-704 (November 1985).
      Rabinove, Samuel, William E. Johnston, Jr., Lawrence E. Mitchell, Christopher C. Faille, Wallace M. Rudolph,
         David A. Frolick, Ronald K. L. Collins, Herb Greer, H. Elliot Wales, Thomas A. Bustin, and Lino A. Graglia.
         The Constitution and the Court. [Editorial] *Commentary* 81(6):2-11 (June 1986).
      Rutland, Robert Allen. The dark century. *Life* 14 (13 Special Issue):48 (Fall 1991).

125. Lessee of Livingston v. Moore   January Term 1833
      32 US (7 Peters) 469   8 LEd 751
         Founders (v. 4):198-200R

126. Wheaton v. Peters   January Term 1834
      33 US (8 Peters) 591   8 LEd 1055
         En Am Con 504-505
         Founders (v. 3):44-60R
         Guide (West) (v. 10):365-367

127. Mayor, Aldermen and Commonalty of the City of New York v. Miln   January Term 1837
      New York v. Miln
      36 US (11 Peters) 102   9 LEd 648, 961
         En Am Con 1231, 1954-1955
         Guide (CQ) 15
         Sup Ct Review (1995):125-215
      Clinton, Robert Lowry. Judicial review, nationalism, and the commerce clause: contrasting antebellum and
         postbellum Supreme Court decision making. *Political Research Quarterly* 47(4):857-876 (December 1994).
      Orren, Karen. The primacy of labor in American constitutional development. *American Political Science
         Review* 89(2):377-388 (June 1995).

128. Briscoe v. President and Directors of the Bank   January Term 1837
         of Commonwealth of Kentucky
      36 US (11 Peters) 257   9 LEd 709, 928
         En Am Con 155
         Guide (CQ) 14-15, 888

129. Charles River Bridge v. Warren Bridge   January Term 1837
      36 US (11 Peters) 420   9 LEd 773, 938
         Documents (v. 1):285-287R
         En Am Con 227-229, 493-499, 1962-1964
         Equal (Harrell) 38-44
         Guide (CQ) 15
         Guide (West) (v. 2):286-289
         Magic 96-99, 117-118
         Marbury 147-150
         Quarrels 71-85
         Reader's 158

Heffner, Judith C. The Constitution in court. *Scholastic Update* (Teachers' Edition) 116(5):16-18 (October 28, 1983).

Kens, Paul. Liberty and the public ingredient of private property. *Review of Politics* 55(1):85-116 (Winter 1993).

Melone, Albert P. Mendelson v. Wright: understanding the contract clause. *Western Political Quarterly* 41(4):791-799 (December 1988).

Mendelson, Wallace. B. F. Wright on the contract clause: a progressive misreading of the Marshall-Taney era. *Western Political Quarterly* 38(2):262-275 (June 1985).

Orren, Karen. The primacy of labor in American constitutional development. *American Political Science Review* 89(2):377-388 (June 1995).

130. Williams v. Suffolk Insurance Co.   January Term 1839
    38 US (13 Peters) 415   10 LEd 226

Halberstam, Malvina. Sabbatino resurrected: the act of state doctrine in the revised restatement of U.S. foreign relations law. *American Journal of International Law* 79(1):68-91 (January 1985).

131. Bank of Augusta v. Earle   January Term 1839
    38 US (13 Peters) 519   10 LEd 274
     En Am Con 98

Merkel, Philip L. Going national: the life insurance industry's campaign for federal regulation after the Civil War. *Business History Review* 65(3):528-553 (Autumn 1991).

132. Groves v. Slaughter   January Term 1841
    40 US (15 Peters) 449   10 LEd 800
     En Am Con 874
     Guide (CQ) 16, 312, 319, 377

133. United States v. Schooner Amistad   January Term 1841
    40 US (15 Peters) 518   10 LEd 826
     Landmark (v. 5):13-25R
     Mutiny 136-154, 170-219+
     Reader's 35-36

Levy, Todd. The Amistad incident: a classroom reenactment. *Social Education* 59(5):303-308 (September1995).

134. Swift v. Tyson   January Term 1842
    41 US (16 Peters) 1   10 LEd 865
     En Am Con 689-691, 1841-1842
     Guide (West) (v.10):8-10
     Magic 122-123, 229-230+
     Sup Ct Review (1994):209-245

Lipartito, Kenneth. What have lawyers done for American business? the case of Baker and Botts of Houston. *Business History Review* 64(3):489-580 (September 22, 1990).

Merkel, Philip L. Going national: the life insurance industry's campaign for federal regulation after the Civil War. *Business History Review* 65(3):528-553 (Autumn 1991).

135. Martin v. Lessee of Waddell   January Term 1842
    41 US (16 Peters) 367   10 LEd 997

Bader, Harry R. Antaeus and the Public Trust Doctrine: a new approach to substantive environmental protection in the common law. *Boston College Environmental Affairs Law Review* 19(4):749-763 (Summer 1992).

Brady, Timothy Patrick. "But most of it belongs to those yet to be born:" The public trust doctrine, NEPA,and the stewardship ethic. *Boston College Environmental Affairs Law Review* 17(3):621-646 (Spring 1990).

136. Prigg v. Pennsylvania   March 1, 1842
    41 US (16 Peters) 593   10 LEd 1060

Civil 19th 4, 10, 59-83R
Documents (v. 1):292-295R
En Am Con 287-289, 400-406, 811-812, 1382, 1452, 1688-1695
Guide (CQ) 16
Guide (West) (v. 8):269-271
Law 138-139
Sup Ct Review (1992):155-194; (1994):247-294
McCurdy, Charles W. Waite Court. *Society* 24(1):40-45 (November/December 1986).

137. Bronson v. Kinzie   January Term 1843
    42 US (1 Howard) 311   11 LEd 143
     En Am Con 159-160

138. Vidal v. Girard's Executors   January Term 1844
    Vidal v. Mayor, Aldermen and Citizens of Philadelphia, Executors of Girard
    43 US (2 Howard) 127   11 LEd 205
     Guide (West) (v.10):240-242
Pfeffer, Leo. Religious exemptions. *Society* 21(4):17-22 (May/June 1984).

139. Pollard, Lessee v. Hagan   January Term 1845
    44 US (3 Howard) 212   11 LEd 565
     Guide (CQ) 135-136
Baer, Susan D. The Public Trust Doctrine—a tool to make federal administrative agencies increase protection of public land and its resources. *Boston College Environmental Affairs Law Review* 15(2):385-436 (Winter 1988).
McCurdy, Charles W. Waite Court. *Society* 24(1):40-45 (November/December 1986).

140. Permoli v. Municipality No. 1 of the City of New Orleans   January Term 1851
    44 US (3 Howard) 589   11 LEd 739
     Let Us 113

141. Thurlow v. Massachusetts   January Term 1847
    46 US (5 Howard) 504   12 LEd 256
     En Am Con 588-589, 1159-1160, 1744-1751
     Guide (CQ) 17-18, 86, 312, 889

142. West River Bridge Co. v. Dix   January Term 1848
    47 US (6 Howard) 507   12 LEd 535
     En Am Con 630-632, 1489-1492, 1962-1964, 2046-2047
     Magic 117-118
     Marbury 147-150

143. Luther v. Borden   January Term 1849
    48 US (7 Howard) 1   12 LEd 581
     En Am Con 419-425, 874-875, 1185-1186, 1558-1560
     Guide (CQ) 17, 217-218, 291, 350, 485-486, 889

144. Smith v. Turner   January Term 1849
    48 US (7 Howard) 283   12 LEd 702
     En Am Con 1366
     Guide (CQ) 17-18, 86, 105, 313, 319, 889

145. Strader v. Graham   December Term 1850
    51 US (10 Howard) 82   13 LEd 337
     En Am Con 1688-1695, 1786

Guide (CQ) 17-18, 138-140, 377

146. Cooley v. Board of Wardens of Port of Philadelphia   December Term 1851
      53 US (12 Howard) 299   13 LEd 996
          Ascent 110-114
          Court Const 90-92+
          En Am Con 322-329, 500-501, 575-576, 1648, 1751-1755, 1794-1795
          Guide (CQ) 17-18, 83, 95
          Sup Ct Review (1995):125-215
      Clinton, Robert Lowry. Judicial review, nationalism, and the commerce clause: contrasting antebellum and
          postbellum Supreme Court decision making. *Political Research Quarterly* 47(4):857-876 (December 1994).
      Schwartz, Edward B. Water as an article of commerce: state embargoes spring a leak under Sporhase v.
          Nebraska. *Boston College Environmental Affairs Law Review* 12(1):103-169 (Fall 1985).

147. Propeller Genessee Chief v. Fitzhugh   December Term 1851
      53 US (12 Howard) 443   13 LEd 1058
          En Am Con 1483

148. United States v. Ferreira   December Term 1851
      54 US (13 Howard) 40   14 LEd 42
          Founders (v. 4):259-260

149. Pennsylvania v. Wheeling and Belmont Bridge Co.   December Term 1851
      54 US (13 Howard) 518   14 LEd 249
          Guide (CQ) 18
      Briggett, Marlissa S. State supremacy in the federal realm: the interstate compact. *Boston College
          Environmental Affairs Law Review* 18(4):751-772 (Summer 1991).

150. Smith v. Swormstedt   December Term 1853
      57 US (16 Howard) 288   14 LEd 942
          Sup Ct Review (1983):459-507

151. Piqua Branch of the State Bank of Ohio v. Knoop   December Term 1853
      57 US (16 Howard) 369   14 LEd 977
          En Am Con 573-574, 1391

152. Den, Murray's Lessee v. Hoboken Land and Improvement Co.   February 19, 1856
      59 US (18 Howard) 272   15 LEd 372
          Const (Currie) 245-246
          En Am Con 589-590, 1288, 1472-1479
          Guide (CQ) 18
          Sup Ct Review (1982):85-125
      Fisher, Louis. The administrative world of Chadha and Bowsher. *Public Administration Review* 47(3):213-219
          (May/June 1987).

153. Dodge v. Woolsey   April 8, 1856
      59 US (18 Howard) 331   15 LEd 401
          En Am Con 573-574

154. Scott v. Sandford   March 6, 1857
      60 US (19 Howard) 393   15 LEd 691
          Amending 79-80+
          Black 135-145
          Burger Years 95-108
          Civil 19th 4, 10, 93-114R

Const (Currie) 377-381
Const (Friendly) 17-22
Const Law 470-474+
Court Const 105-109
Documents (v. 1):339-345R
En Am Con 273-280, 281, 407-413, 584-587, 640-647, 914-917, 1688-1695, 1878-1879
Equal (Harrell) 43-48+
Guide (CQ) 18-19, 71-73, 122b, 137-138, 141b
Guide (West) (v. 4):188-199
Landmark (v. 2):13-34R
Magic 141-142, 232-233+
Make 15-22
Marbury 116-127+
Quarrels 87-99
Reader's 295-296, 1050-1053
Sup Ct Ind 4-5, 229

Baker, banker, clergyman, thief. *Life* 10(10):84-88 (Fall 1987).

Berns, Walter. Government by lawyers and judges. *Commentary* 83(6):17-24 (June 1987).

Cecil, Andrew R. Moral values in a free society: individualism and social conscience. *Vital Speeches of the Day* 60(7):204-209 (January 15, 1994).

A curb on state powers. *U.S. News & World Report* 111(25):50 (December 16, 1991).

Garraty, John Arthur. 101 things every college graduate should know about American history. *American Heritage* 38(1):24-32 (December 1986).

Gest, Ted. Courts: a major battleground of social upheaval. *U.S. News & World Report* 98(3):48-50 (January 28, 1985).

Heffner, Judith C. The Constitution in court. *Scholastic Update* (Teachers' Edition) 116(5):16-18 (October 28, 1983).

Karst, Kenneth L. Equal protection of the laws. *Society* 24(1):24-30 (November/December 1986).

Katz, Stanley N. The strange birth and unlikely history of constitutional equality. *Journal of American History* 75(3):747-762 (December 1988).

LaFeber, Walter. The Constitution and United States foreign policy: an interpretation. *Journal of American History* 74(3):695-717 (December 1987).

Lasser, William. The Supreme Court in periods of critical realignment. *Journal of Politics* 47(4):1174-1187 (November 1985).

Lehrman, Lewis E. The right to life and the restoration of the American republic. *National Review* 38(16):25-28 (August 29, 1986).

Marshall, Thomas R. Public opinion, representation, and the modern Supreme Court. *American Politics Quarterly* 16(3):296-316 (July 1988).

Marshall, Thurgood. The real meaning of the Constitution bicentennial. *Ebony* 42(11):62-68 (September 1987).

McDowell, Gary L. Rights without roots. *Wilson Quarterly* 15(1):71-79 (Winter 1991).

Meese, Edwin, 3d. Interpreting the Constitution. *USA Today* 115(2496):36-39 (September 1986).

————. Saving the Constitution: The law of the Constitution. *National Review* 39(13):30-33 (July 17, 1987).

Orren, Karen. The primacy of labor in American constitutional development. *American Political Science Review* 89(2):377-388 (June 1995).

Quirk, William J. Judicial dictatorship. *Society* 31(2):34-38 (January/February 1994).

Sudo, Phil. Five "little" people who changed U.S. history. *Scholastic Update* 122(10):8-10 (January 16, 1990).

155. Ableman v. Booth   March 7, 1859
      62 US (21 Howard) 506   16 LEd 169
      Civil 19th 4, 10, 85-91R
      Court Const 109-111
      Documents (v. 1):358-361R
      En Am Con 1-2, 287-289, 811-812, 1688-1695
      Guide (CQ):19
      Reader's 1

Pawelek, Dick. Put yourself on the U.S. Supreme Court. *Senior Scholastic* 113(8):12-13, 27 (December 12, 1980).

156. Kentucky v. Dennison   March 14, 1861
     65 US (24 Howard) 66   16 LEd 717
        Almanac (1987):18A
        En Am Con 810-811
     McCurdy, Charles W. Waite Court. *Society* 24(1):40-45 (November/December 1986).

157. Preciat v. United States   March 10, 1863
            Coupled with Currie v. United States
            Coupled with Miller v. United States
     67 US (2 Black) 635   17 LEd 459
        En Am Con 1462
        Guide (CQ):20-21, 127-128
     Deering, Christopher J. Congress, the President, and military policy. *Annals of the American Academy of Political and Social Science* 499:136-147 (September 1988).
     Orren, Karen. The primacy of labor in American constitutional development. *American Political Science Review* 89(2):377-388 (June 1995).
     Raymond, John M., and Barbara J. Frischholz. Lawyers who established international law in the United States, 1776-1914. *American Journal of International Law* 76(4):802-829 (October 1982).

158. Gelpcke v. City of Dubuque   January 11, 1864
     68 US (1 Wallace) 175   17 LEd 520
        En Am Con 836-837

159. Ex Parte Vallandigham   February 15, 1864
     68 US (1 Wallace) 243   17 LEd 589
        En Am Con 1957

160. The Plymouth   February 5, 1866
     Hough v. The Western Transportation Co.
     70 US (3 Wallace) 20   18 LEd 125
     Arsenault, Richard J., and Richard W. Beard. Bringing pleasure boat accidents under the admiralty forum. *Trial* 18(10):66-71, 88 (October 1982).
     George, James A. The "triple crown" of admiralty cases: from definitions to damages. *Trial* 27(10):46-53 (October 1991).

161. The Bermuda   March 12, 1866
            Coupled with Haigh v. United States
            Coupled with Blakely v. United States
            Coupled with Fraser, Trenholm and Co. v. United States
     70 US (3 Wallace) 514   18 LEd 200
     Raymond, John M., and Barbara J. Frischholz. Lawyers who established international law in the United States, 1776-1914. *American Journal of International Law* 76(4):802-829 (October 1982).

162. Ex Parte Milligan   December 17, 1866
     71 US (4 Wallace) 2   18 LEd 281
        Const (Currie) 280-281, 285-289, 400-403
        Documents (v. 1):472-476R
        En Am Con 628-629, 879-886, 1260
        Equal (Harrell) 48-52
        First 93-97
        Guide (CQ) 20-21, 76-77
        Guide (West) (v. 7):344

Just War 146-149, 177-178, 221-222, 249-250

Landmark (v. 4):55-74R

Quarrels 101-118

Sup Ct Review (1981):367-412; (1986):259-316

Barrett, Edward L. The Supreme Court: why the Constitution survives: long-term view of the Court. *Trial* 25(12):30-35 (December 1989).

Murphy, Walter F. The Constitution and the 14th Amendment. *Center Magazine* 20(4):9-30 (July/August 1987).

Pfeffer, Leo. Religious exemptions. *Society* 21(4):17-22 (May/June 1984).

163. Cummings v. Missouri   January 14, 1867
    71 US (4 Wallace) 277   18 LEd 356
    En Am Con 111-112, 676-677, 1883-1884
    Guide (CQ) 21, 76-77, 332, 502, 890

164. Ex Parte Garland   January 14, 1867
    71 US (4 Wallace) 333   18 LEd 366
    Documents (v. 1):477-478R
    En Am Con 111-112, 1883-1884
    Guide (CQ) 21, 76-77, 122b, 222-224, 279, 332, 502, 890, 1001
    Pawelek, Dick. Call five cases that shaped Congress. *Scholastic Update* (Teachers' Edition) 119(9):12-14 (January 12, 1987).

165. Mississippi v. Johnson   April 15, 1867
    71 US (4 Wallace) 475   18 LEd 437
    Const (Currie) 585-588
    Documents (v. 1):478-479R
    En Am Con 1267
    Guide (CQ) 21, 227-228, 273, 664, 891

166. The Bark Springbok   January 3, 1867
    The Springbok
    72 US (5 Wallace) 1   18 LEd 480
    Raymond, John M., and Barbara J. Frischholz. Lawyers who established international law in the United States, 1776-1914. *American Journal of International Law* 76(4):802-829 (October 1982).

167. The Peterhoff   April 15, 1867
    The Steamer Peterhoff
    72 US (5 Wallace) 28   18 LEd 564
    Raymond, John M., and Barbara J. Frischholz. Lawyers who established international law in the United States, 1776-1914. *American Journal of International Law* 76(4):802-829 (October 1982).

168. Pervear v. Commonwealth of Massachusetts   April 29, 1867
    72 US (5 Wallace) 475   18 LEd 608
    Schwartz, Charles Walter. Eighth Amendment proportionality analysis and the compelling case of William Rummel. *Journal of Criminal Law and Criminology* 71(4):378-420 (Winter 1980).

169. Georgia v. Stanton   February 10, 1868
        Coupled with Mississippi v. Stanton
    73 US (6 Wallace) 50   18 LEd 721
    En Am Con 1267

170. Twitchell v. Commonwealth of Pennsylvania   April 5, 1869
    74 US (7 Wallace) 321   19 LEd 223
    Marbury 199-207

171. Ex Parte McCardle   April 12, 1869
      74 US (7 Wallace) 506   19 LEd 264
        En Am Con 346-348, 1232
        Guide (CQ) 21-22
      American Survey: How supreme is the Supreme Court? *Economist* 279(7188):23-24 (June 6-12, 1981).
      Gunther, Gerald. The power of the courts—any practicable limits? *Center Magazine* 18(5):52-64
        (September/October 1985).
      Mathias, Charles McC., Jr. The federal courts under siege. *Annals of the American Academy of Political and
        Social Science* 462: 26-33 (July 1982).
      Regan, Richard J. Supreme Court roundup: 1981 term. *Thought* 57(227):514-527 (December 1982).
      Tortora, Anthony. Ex Parte McCardle. *National Review* 32(19):1140-1141,1157 (September 19, 1980).

172. Randall v. Brigham   April 15, 1869
      74 US (7 Wallace) 523   19 LEd 285
      Plotkin, Steven R., and Carol D. Mazorol. Judicial malpractice: Pulliam is not the answer. *Trial* 20(12):24-26
        (December 1984).

173. Texas v. White   April 12, 1869
      74 US (7 Wallace) 700   19 LEd 227
        Documents (v. 1):509-513R
        En Am Con 1884
        Guide (West) (v.10):76-77

174. Woodruff v. Parham   November 8, 1869
      75 US (8 Wallace) 123   19 LEd 382
        En Am Con 2075

175. Paul v. Virginia   November 1, 1869
      75 US (8 Wallace) 168   19 LEd 357
        En Am Con 1370, 1751-1755
        Guide (CQ) 106
        Powers 150
      McNamara, Daniel J. Toward a new environment. *Best's Review* (Property/Casualty Insurance Edition)
        91(2):53-58 (June 1990).
      Merkel, Philip L. Going national: the life insurance industry's campaign for federal regulation after the Civil
        War. *Business History Review* 65(3):528-553 (Autumn 1991).
      Vinyard, Walter D., Jr. Retaliatory taxation—a crack in the foundation? *Best's Review* (Property/Casualty
        Insurance Edition) 81(12):14, 94-100 (April 1981).

176. Veazie Bank v. Fenno   December 13, 1869
      75 US (8 Wallace) 533   19 LEd 482
        Documents (v. 1):508-509R
        En Am Con 1270-1273, 1869-1871, 1961
        Guide (CQ) 114-115
        Sup Ct Review (1981):367-412
      Moss, David A. Kindling a flame under federalism: progressive reformers, corporate elites, and the
        phosphorous match campaign of 1909-1912. *Business History Review* 68(2):244-275 (Summer 1994).

177. Hepburn v. Griswold   February 7, 1870
      75 US (8 Wallace) 603   19 LEd 513
        Documents (v. 1):514-517R
        En Am Con 1135-1136, 1270-1273
        Equal (Harrell) 55-56
        Guide (CQ) 22, 65-66, 71, 122b, 123-124
        Marbury 159-160+

New Right (Schwartz) 10-14
Sup Ct Review (1981):367-412

178. Steamer Daniel Ball v. United States January 23, 1871
77 US (10 Wallace) 557 19 LEd 999
Guide (CQ) 95
Proctor, Michael G. Section 10 of the Rivers and Harbors Act and Western Water Allocations—are the western states up a creek without a permit? *Boston College Environmental Affairs Law Review* 10(1):111-182 (1982-83).

179. Collector v. Day April 3, 1871
Buffington, Collector of Internal Revenue v. Day
78 US (11 Wallace) 113 20 LEd 122
Documents (v. 1):518-520R
En Am Con 311, 989-991
Guide (CQ) 118
Johnston, Richard E., and John T. Thompson. Burger court and federalism: a revolution in 1976? *Western Political Quarterly* 33(2):197-216 (June 1980).

180. Miller v. United States April 3, 1871
Page, Excecutor of Miller v. United States
78 US (11 Wallace) 268 20 LEd 135
En Am Con 346

181. New York v. Central Railroad Co. January 22, 1872
79 US (12 Wallace) 455 20 LEd 458
Briggett, Marlissa S. State supremacy in the federal realm: the interstate compact. *Boston College Environmental Affairs Law Review* 18(4):751-772 (Summer 1991).

182. Knox v. Lee May 1, 1871
Coupled with Parker v. Davis
79 US (12 Wallace) 457 20 LEd 287
Documents (v. 1):514-517R
En Am Con 1135-1136, 1270-1273
Guide (CQ) 22, 122b, 123-124, 130
Sup Ct Review (1981):367-412
Taylor, John B. The Supreme Court and political eras: a perspective on judicial power in a democratic polity. *Review of Politics* 54(3):345-68 (Summer 1992).

183. Low v. Austin January 29, 1872
80 US (13 Wallace) 29 20 LEd 517
Ascent 121-123
En Am Con 1349-1350

184. United States v. Klein January 29, 1872
80 US (13 Wallace) 128 20 LEd 519
Mathias, Charles McC., Jr. The federal courts under siege. *Annals of the American Academy of Political and Social Science* 462: 26-33 (July 1982).

185. Pumpelly v. Green Bay Co. February 19, 1872
Pumpelly v. Green Bay and Mississippi Canal Co.
80 US (13 Wallace) 166 20 LEd 557
Marbury 199-207

Hippler, Thomas A. Reexamining 100 years of the Supreme Court regulatory taking doctrine: the principles of "noxious use," "average reciprocity of advantage," and "bundle of rights" from Mugler to Keystone Bituminous Coal. *Boston College Environmental Affairs Law Review* 14(4):653-727 (Summer 1987).

Randle, Ellen M. The national reserve system and transferable development rights: is the New Jersey pinelands plan in unconstitutional "taking"? *Boston College Environmental Affairs Law Review* 10(1):183-241 (1982-83).

186. Bradley v. Fisher   April 8, 1872
      80 US (13 Wallace) 335   20 LEd 646
      Plotkin, Steven R., and Carol D. Mazorol. Judicial malpractice: Pulliam is not the answer. *Trial* 20(12):24-26 (December 1984).

187. Watson v. Jones   April 15, 1872
      80 US (13 Wallace) 679   20 LEd 666
        Ascent 212-214
        En Am Con 1538-1545
        Godless 45-47+
        Religion 260-264+
      Taylor, Barry W. Diversion of church funds to personal use: state, federal, and private sanctions. *Journal of Criminal Law and Criminology* 73(3):1204-1237 (Fall 1982).

188. Philadelphia and Reading Railroad Co. v. Pennsylvania   March 3, 1873
      82 US (15 Wallace) 232   21 LEd 146
        En Am Con 1384, 1757-1760

189. Butchers' Benevolent Association v. Crescent City   April 14, 1873
          Live-stock Landing and Slaughter-House Co.
              Coupled with Esteben v. Louisiana ex rel. Belden
      83 US (16 Wallace) 36   21 LEd 394
        Civil 19th 4, 11, 115-138R
        Const (Currie) 249
        Const Law 17-20R+
        Court Public 95-96
        Documents (v. 1):520-525R
        En Am Con 1031-1038, 1458-1461, 1640-1641, 1687-1688, 1979-1987
        First 131-135
        Guide (CQ) 22-25
        Guide (West) (v. 9):261-262
        Magic 233-236
        Marbury 199-211
        Reader's 990
      Gillman, Howard. Preferred freedoms: the progressive expansion of state power and the rise of modern civil liberties jurisprudence. *Political Research Quarterly* 47(3):623-653 (September 1994).
      Katz, Stanley N. The strange birth and unlikely history of constitutional equality. *Journal of American History* 75(3):747-762 (December 1988).
      McCurdy, Charles W. Waite Court. *Society* 24(1):40-45 (November/December 1986).
      Murphy, Walter F. The Constitution and the 14th Amendment. *Center Magazine* 20(4):9-30 (July/August 1987).
      Orren, Karen. The primacy of labor in American constitutional development. *American Political Science Review* 89(2):377-388 (June 1995).
      Rabinove, Samuel, William E. Johnston, Jr., Lawrence E. Mitchell, Christopher C. Faille, Wallace M. Rudolph, David A. Frolick, Ronald K. L. Collins, Herb Greer, H. Elliot Wales, Thomas A. Bustin, and Lino A. Graglia. The Constitution and the Court. [Editorial] *Commentary* 81(6):2-11 (June 1986).
      Smith, Rogers M. The "American Creed" and American identity: the limits of liberal citizenship in the United States. *Western Political Quarterly* 41(2):225-251 (June 1988).

Tollett, Kenneth S., Jeanette J. Leonard, and Portia P. James. A color-conscious constitution: the one pervading purpose redux. *Journal of Negro Education* 52(3):189-212 (Summer 1983).

Welsh, Robert, and Ronald K. L. Collins. Taking state constitutions seriously: the protection of civil liberties has been shifting away from the U.S. Supreme Court. *Center Magazine* 14(5):6-35, 38-43 (September/October 1981).

190. Bradwell v. Illinois
       83 US (16 Wallace) 130   21 LEd 442
       Abortion Pol (Rubin) 3, 31
       Brennan 294-302
       En Am Con 140, 1666-1673
       Magic 327-329

April 15, 1873

Binion, Gayle. The case for an Equal Rights Act. *Center Magazine* 16(6):2-7 (November/December 1983).

Cortes, Carlos E., and Van L. Perkins. U.S. Supreme Court decisions on diversity. *Education Digest* 46(6):21-24 (February 1981).

Press, Aric, Ann McDaniel, Alexander Stille, and Nadine Joseph. With justice for some. *Newsweek* 103(23):85-86 (June 4, 1984).

Segal, Jeffrey A., and Cheryl D. Reedy. The Supreme Court and sex discrimination: the role of the Solicitor General. *Western Political Quarterly* 41(3):553-568 (September 1988).

Smith, Rogers M. The "American Creed" and American identity: the limits of liberal citizenship in the United States. *Western Political Quarterly* 41(2):225-251 (June 1988).

191. American Steamboat Co. v. Chase
       Steamboat Co. v. Chase
       83 US (16 Wallace) 522   21 LEd 369

March 31, 1873

Edelman, Paul S. Wrongful death on the high seas: Tallentire says federal law governs. *Trial* 23(4):58-61 (April 1987).

192. Citizens' Savings and Loan Association of Cleveland v. Topeka
       Loan Association v. Topeka
       87 US (20 Wallace) 655   22 LEd 455
       Documents (v. 1):526-528R
       En Am Con 1174, 1489-1492, 1796-1803

February 1, 1875

193. Minor v. Happersett
       88 US (21 Wallace) 162   22 LEd 627
       Amending 129-134
       Black 186-192
       Documents (v. 1):534-536R
       En Am Con 1262, 1315-1316, 1558-1560, 1979-1987
       Landmark (v. 2):35-41R
       Magic 327-329
       Reader's 734-735

March 29, 1875

194. Welton v. Missouri
       91 US (1 Otto) 275   23 LEd 347
       En Am Con 1757-1760
       Magic 236-238

January 17, 1876

Merkel, Philip L. Going national: the life insurance industry's campaign for federal regulation after the Civil War. *Business History Review* 65(3):528-553 (Autumn 1991).

195. Kohl v. United States
       91 US (1 Otto) 367   23 LEd 449
       McCurdy, Charles W. Waite Court. *Society* 24(1):40-45 (November/December 1986).

March 27, 1876

Plater, Zygmunt J. B., and William Lund Norine. Through the looking glass of eminent domain: exploring the "arbitrary and capricious" test and substantive rationality review of governmental decisions. *Boston College Environmental Affairs Law Review* 16(4):661-752 (Summer 1989).

196. Walker v. Sauvinet   April 24, 1876
     92 US (2 Otto) 90   23 LEd 678
     En Am Con 2005-2006

197. United States v. Reese   March 27, 1876
     92 US (2 Otto) 214   23 LEd 563
     En Am Con 727-728, 746-747, 1528
     Guide (CQ) 153-154, 471
     McCurdy, Charles W. Waite Court. *Society* 24(1):40-45 (November/December 1986).

198. United States v. Cruikshank   March 27, 1876
     92 US (2 Otto) 542   23 LEd 588
     En Am Con 527, 727-728, 746-747, 770-773
     Eyes 83-89
     McCurdy, Charles W. Waite Court. *Society* 24(1):40-45 (November/December 1986).
     Orren, Karen. The primacy of labor in American constitutional development. *American Political Science Review* 89(2):377-388 (June 1995).
     Spitzer, Robert J., Shooting down gun myths. *America* 152(22):468-469 (June 8, 1985).

199. Sherlock v. Alling   November 6, 1876
     93 US (3 Otto) 99   23 LEd 819
     Edelman, Paul S. Wrongful death on the high seas: Tallentire says federal law governs. *Trial* 23(4):58-61 (April 1987).

200. Munn v. Illinois   March 1, 1877
     94 US (4 Otto) 113   24 LEd 77
     Const (Currie) 41-44
     Court Const 121-131+
     Documents (v. 1):541-544R
     En Am Con 32-33, 602-606, 862-863, 1744-1751
     Equal (Harrell) 56-59
     Guide (CQ) 25, 40
     Guide (West) (v. 5):394-395
     Magic 233-236
     Marbury 199-207
     New Right (Schwartz) 191-193
     Quarrels 119-138
     Reader's 759
     Cleaves, Robert E., IV. Constitutional protection for the utility investor: the confiscation doctrine after Cleveland Electric Illuminating Co. v. Public Utilities Commission of Ohio. *Boston College Environmental Affairs Law Review* 12(3):527-558 (Spring 1985).
     Garraty, John Arthur. 101 things every college graduate should know about American history. *American Heritage* 38(1):24-32 (December 1986).
     Kens, Paul. Liberty and the public ingredient of private property. *Review of Politics* 55(1):85-116 (Winter 1993).
     McCurdy, Charles W. Waite Court. *Society* 24(1):40-45 (November/December 1986).
     Orren, Karen. The primacy of labor in American constitutional development. *American Political Science Review* 89(2):377-388 (June 1995).

201. Chicago, Burlington and Quincy Railroad Co. v. Cutts   March 1, 1877
     Chicago, Burlington and Quincy Railroad Co. v. Iowa

C.B. & Q. R. R. Co. v. Iowa
94 US (4 Otto) 155, 183   24 LEd 94
  En Am Con 862-863, 1494

202. Peik v. Chicago and Northwestern Railway Co.   March 1, 1877
         Coupled with Lawrence v. Paul
      94 US (4 Otto) 164   24 LEd 97
         En Am Con 862-863

203. Chicago, Milwaukee and St. Paul Railroad Co. v. Ackley   March 1, 1877
      94 US (4 Otto) 179   24 LEd 99
         En Am Con 862-863

204. Winona and St. Peter Railroad Co. v. Blake   March 1, 1877
      94 US (4 Otto) 180   24 LEd 99
         En Am Con 862-863

205. Stone v. Wisconsin   March 1, 1877
      94 US (4 Otto) 181   24 LEd 102
         En Am Con 862-863

206. Hall v. De Cuir   January 14, 1878
      95 US (5 Otto) 485   24 LEd 547
         En Am Con 888-889
         Guide (CQ) 25-26, 105-107, 316, 598, 891

207. Pensacola Telegraph Co. v. Western Union Telegraph Co.   March 25, 1878
      96 US (6 Otto) 1   24 LEd 708
         En Am Con 1377

208. Davidson v. City of New Orleans   January 7, 1878
      96 US (6 Otto) 97   24 LEd 616
         Guide (CQ) 143b
         Marbury 199-207

209. Ex Parte Jackson   May 13, 1878
      96 US (6 Otto) 727   24 LEd 877
         Magic 160-162
      Murchison, Kenneth M. Prohibition and the Fourth Amendment: a new look at some old cases. *Journal of
      Criminal Law and Criminology* 73(2):471-532 (Summer 1982).

210. Boston Beer Co. v. Massachusetts   May 13, 1878
      97 US (7 Otto) 25   24 LEd 989
         En Am Con 135, 967-968, 1744-1751

211. Northwestern Fertilizer Co. v. Hyde Park   November 11, 1878
      97 US (7 Otto) 659   24 LEd 1036
         En Am Con 1328

212. Reynolds v. United States   May 5, 1879
      98 US (8 Otto) 145   25 LEd 244
         Brennan 116-119
         En Am Con 541-542, 686-688, 730-738, 1425-1426, 1538-1545, 1567-1568
         Godless 20-21+
         Magic 155-158

Original (Davis) xiv, 64-66+

Sup Ct Church 349-356R

Cox, Archibald. First Amendment. *Society* 24(1):8-15 (November/December 1986).

Ignagni, Joseph A. U.S. Supreme Court decision-making and the free exercise clause. *Review of Politics* 55(3):511-529 (Summer 1993).

Lawton, Kim A. Uncle Sam v. First Church. *Christianity Today* 35(11):38-41 (October 7, 1991).

Lesly, Elizabeth, and Elliott Beard. Pennies from Heaven. *Washington Monthly* 23(4):40-45 (April 1991).

Minow, Martha. We, the family: constitutional rights and American families. *Journal of American History* 74(3):959-983 (December 1987).

Regan, Richard J. Regulating cult activities: the limits of religious freedom. *Thought* 61(241):185-196 (June1986).

Roelofs, H. Mark. Church and state in America: toward a biblically derived reformulation of their relationship. *Review of Politics* 50(4):561-581 (Fall 1988).

213. Wilkerson v. Utah   March 17, 1879

    99 US (9 Otto) 130   25 LEd 345

    Court Public 238-239

    Death Penalty (Tushnet) 150

Schwartz, Charles Walter. Eighth Amendment proportionality analysis and the compelling case of William Rummel. *Journal of Criminal Law and Criminology* 71(4):378-420 (Winter 1980).

214. Union Pacific Railroad Co. v. United States   May 5, 1879

    99 US (9 Otto) 700   25 LEd 496

    En Am Con 1684

McCurdy, Charles W. Waite Court. *Society* 24(1):40-45 (November/December 1986).

215. United States v. Steffens   November 17, 1879

    100 US (10 Otto) 82   25 LEd 550

McCurdy, Charles W. Waite Court. *Society* 24(1):40-45 (November/December 1986).

216. Strauder v. West Virginia   March 1, 1880

    100 US (10 Otto) 303   25 LEd 664

    Const (Currie) 482-488

    En Am Con 273-280, 1082-1085, 1786-1787

    Make 15-22

    Sup Ct Review (1987):97-156

Katz, Stanley N. The strange birth and unlikely history of constitutional equality. *Journal of American History* 75(3):747-762 (December 1988).

McCurdy, Charles W. Waite Court. *Society* 24(1):40-45 (November/December 1986).

Rabinove, Samuel, William E. Johnston, Jr., Lawrence E. Mitchell, Christopher C. Faille, Wallace M. Rudolph, David A. Frolick, Ronald K. L. Collins, Herb Greer, H. Elliot Wales, Thomas A. Bustin, and Lino A. Graglia. The Constitution and the Court. [Editorial] *Commentary* 81(6):2-11 (June 1986).

Serr, Brian J., and Mark Maney. Racism, peremptory challenges, and the democratic jury: the jurisprudence of a delicate balance. *Journal of Criminal Law and Criminology* 79(1):1-65 (Spring 1988).

Tollett, Kenneth S., Jeanette J. Leonard, and Portia P. James. A color-conscious constitution: the one pervading purpose redux. *Journal of Negro Education* 52(3):189-212 (Summer 1983).

217. Ex Parte Virginia   March 1, 1880

    Virginia v. Rives

    100 US (10 Otto) 313   25 LEd 667

    En Am Con 1786-1787

218. Ex Parte Virginia and Coles   May 1, 1880

    100 US (10 Otto) 339   25 LEd 676

    En Am Con 1786-1787

219. Ex Parte Siebold   March 8, 1880
     100 US (10 Otto) 371,404   25 LEd 717
     McCurdy, Charles W. Waite Court. *Society* 24(1):40-45 (November/December 1986).
     Put yourself on the U.S. Supreme Court. *Senior Scholastic* 114(8):22-23,27 (December 11, 1981).

220. Stone v. Mississippi   May 10, 1880
     101 US (11 Otto) 814   25 LEd 1079
     En Am Con 1776
     Melone, Albert P. Mendelson v. Wright: understanding the contract clause. *Western Political Quarterly* 41(4):791-799 (December 1988).

221. Springer v. United States   January 24, 1881
     102 US (12 Otto) 586   26 LEd 253
     En Am Con 1719

222. Kilbourn v. Thompson   January 24, 1881
     103 US (13 Otto) 168   26 LEd 377
     En Am Con 1103, 1148-1151, 1659-1664
     Powers 205-206, 208

223. Neal v. Delaware   May 2, 1881
     103 US (13 Otto) 370   26 LEd 567
     En Am Con 1303
     Serr, Brian J., and Mark Maney. Racism, peremptory challenges, and the democratic jury: the jurisprudence of a delicate balance. *Journal of Criminal Law and Criminology* 79(1):1-65 (Spring 1988).

224. Barton v. Barbour   November 14, 1881
     104 US (14 Otto) 126   26 LEd 672
     Sup Ct Review (1989):261-282

225. United States v. McBratney   March 6, 1882
     104 US (14 Otto) 621   26 LEd 869
     Am Indian (Deloria) 63-82
     Am Indians (Wilkinson) 24-25, 34-35, 88, 154, 196-197

226. Trustees v. Greenough   May 8, 1882
     105 US (15 Otto) 527   26 LEd 1157
     Jordan, Scott J. Awarding attorney's fees to environmental plaintiffs under a private attorney general theory. *Boston College Environmental Affairs Law Review* 14(2):287-311 (Winter 1987).
     O'Connor, Karen, and Lee Epstein. Bridging the gap between Congress and the Supreme Court: interest groups and the erosion of the American rule governing awards of attorneys' fees. *Western Political Quarterly* 38(2):238-249 (June 1985).

227. United States v. Lee   December 4, 1882
     Coupled with Kaufman v. Lee
     106 US (16 Otto) 196   27 LEd 171   1 SCt 240
     Sup Ct Review (1984):149-168
     Rosenbloom, David H. Public administrators' official immunity and the Supreme Court: developments during the 1970s. *Public Administration Review* 40(2):166-173 (March/April 1980).

228. Pace v. Alabama   January 29, 1883
     106 US (16 Otto) 583   27 LEd 207   1 SCt 637
     En Am Con 1265-1266, 1359
     McCurdy, Charles W. Waite Court. *Society* 24(1):40-45 (November/December 1986).

229. United States v. Harris   January 22, 1883
          106 US (16 Otto) 629   27 LEd 290   1 SCt 601
             En Am Con 746-747, 868, 904
             Sup Ct Review (1993):199-243
          McCurdy, Charles W. Waite Court. *Society* 24(1):40-45 (November/December 1986).

230. Louisiana v. Jumel   March 5, 1883
             Coupled with Elliott v. Wiltz
          107 US (17 Otto) 711   27 LEd 448   2 SCt 128
             Sup Ct Review (1984):149-168

231. United States v. Stanley   October 15, 1883
             Coupled with United States v. Ryan
             Coupled with United States v. Nichols
             Coupled with United States v. Singleton
             Coupled with Robinson v. Memphis and Charleston Railroad Co.
          109 US 3   27 LEd 835   3 SCt 18
             Amending 203-213
             Black 147-154
             Civil 19th 4, 11, 139-162R
             Const Law 446-447, 471+
             Court Const 252-254+
             Court Public 95
             Documents (v. 1):536-538R
             En Am Con 287-289, 640-647, 1729-1736
             Guide (CQ) 25-26, 105-106, 153
             Guide (West) (v. 2):354-355, 356-361
             Magic 145-146
             Powers 149-150
             Quarrels 139-156, 165-174
             Sup Ct Ind 247+
             Sup Ct Review (1989):1-51
          Chemerinsky, Erwin. Supreme Court review: state action. *Trial* 31(9):82-84 (September 1995).
          Karst, Kenneth L. Equal protection of the laws. *Society* 24(1):24-30 (November/December 1986).
          Orren, Karen. The primacy of labor in American constitutional development. *American Political Science
             Review* 89(2):377-388 (June 1995).
          Wilson, Margaret Bush. American judiciary in historical perspective. *Crisis* 89(2):37-40 (February 1982).

232. Ex Parte Kan-gi-Shun-ca (Otherwise known as Crow Dog)   December 17, 1883
          109 US 556   27 LEd 1030   3 SCt 396
             Am Indians (Wilkinson) 24-25, 56, 153

233. Juilliard v. Greenman   March 3, 1884
          110 US 421   28 LEd 204   4 SCt 122
             Documents (v. 1):563-566R
             En Am Con 1135-1136, 1270-1273
             Marbury 166-175+
             Sup Ct Review (1981):367-412
          McCurdy, Charles W. Waite Court. *Society* 24(1):40-45 (November/December 1986).

234. Hurtado v. California   March 3, 1884
          110 US 516   28 LEd 232   4 SCt 111, 292
             Const (Currie) 245-249
             Const Law 20-25R+
             En Am Con 942-943, 970-973, 1472-1479, 1796-1803

Guide (CQ) 25-26
Guide (West) (v. 6):103
Magic 262-264
Sup Ct Ind 160-161+
Sup Ct Review (1982):85-125; (1991):303-390
McCurdy, Charles W. Waite Court. *Society* 24(1):40-45 (November/December 1986).

235. Ex Parte Yarbrough   March 3, 1884
    110 US 651   28 LEd 274   4 SCt 152
    Documents (v. 1):538-541R
    En Am Con 2082
    McCurdy, Charles W. Waite Court. *Society* 24(1):40-45 (November/December 1986).

236. Burrow-Giles Lithographic Co. v. Sarony   March 17, 1884
    111 US 53   28 LEd 349   4 SCt 279
    Sup Ct Review (1991):143-177

237. Butchers' Union Slaughterhouse and Live stock Landing Co. v.   May 5, 1884
    Crescent City Live stock Landing and Slaughter-house Co.
    Butchers' Union Slaughterhouse v. Crescent City Slaughterhouse
    111 US 746   28 LEd 585   4 SCt 652
    En Am Con 186
    Gillman, Howard. Preferred freedoms: the progressive expansion of state power and the rise of modern civil liberties jurisprudence. *Political Research Quarterly* 47(3):623-653 (September 1994).

238. Elk v. Wilkins   November 3, 1884
    112 US 94   28 LEd 643   5 SCt 41
    Am Indian (Deloria) 105-133
    Civil 19th 4, 9, 47-58R

239. Barbier v. Connolly   January 5, 1885
    113 US 27   28 LEd 923   5 SCt 357
    Gillman, Howard. Preferred freedoms: the progressive expansion of state power and the rise of modern civil liberties jurisprudence. *Political Research Quarterly* 47(3):623-653 (September 1994).

240. Pleasants v. Greenhow   April 20, 1885
    114 US 323   29 LEd 204   5 SCt 931, 962
    Sup Ct Review (1984):149-168

241. Wurts v. Hoagland   May 4, 1885
    114 US 606   29 LEd 229   5 SCt 1086
    Hippler, Thomas A. Reexamining 100 years of the Supreme Court regulatory taking doctrine: the principles of "noxious use," "average reciprocity of advantage," and "bundle of rights" from Mugler to Keystone Bituminous Coal. *Boston College Environmental Affairs Law Review* 14(4):653-727 (Summer 1987).

242. Missouri Pacific Railroad v. Humes   November 23, 1885
    115 US 512   29 LEd 463   6 SCt 110
    En Am Con 1269

243. Presser v. Illinois   January 4, 1886
    116 US 252   29 LEd 615   6 SCt 580
    Spitzer, Robert J. Shooting down gun myths. *America* 152(22):468-469 (June 8, 1985).

244. Stone v. Farmers' Loan and Trust Co.   January 4, 1886
    116 US 307   29 LEd 636   6 SCt 334, 388, 1191

En Am Con 1775

Cleaves, Robert E., IV. Constitutional protection for the utility investor: the confiscation doctrine after Cleveland Electric Illuminating Co. v. Public Utilities Commission of Ohio. *Boston College Environmental Affairs Law Review* 12(3):527-558 (Spring 1985).

McCurdy, Charles W. Waite Court. *Society* 24(1):40-45 (November/December 1986).

245. Boyd v. United States		February 1, 1886
116 US 616	29 LEd 746	6 SCt 524

Almanac (1994):51

Const (Friendly) 135

Economics 316-317+

En Am Con 137-138, 1569-1577, 1628-1635, 1947-1949

Guide (CQ) 25-26

Alter, Robert J. Shareholder's Fifth Amendment privilege bars summons of corporate records. *Journal of Taxation* 63(4):208-210 (October 1985).

Bayh, Birch. Search and seizure: aftermath of Stanford daily. *Trial* 16(8):30-33, 70 (August 1980).

Caginalp, O. A. Fifth Amendment privilege against self-incrimination and compulsory self-disclosure under the Clean Air and Clean Water Acts. *Boston College Environmental Affairs Law Review* 9(2):359-395 (1980-1981).

Comisky, Ian M., and Matthew J. Comisky. Supreme Court in Doe limits Fifth Amendment protection, but uncertainty remains. *Journal of Taxation* 61(2):66-70 (August 1984).

Fifth Amendment: compulsory production of incriminating business records. *Journal of Criminal Law and Criminology* 71(1):51-55 (Spring 1980).

Staas, John August. Supreme Court review: Fifth Amendment—statutory dilution of the privilege against self-incrimination. *Journal of Criminal Law and Criminology* 71(4):610-621 (Winter 1980).

Taylor, Stuart, Jr. Meese v. Brennan. *New Republic* 194(1):17-21 (January 6-13, 1986).

Use of the exclusionary rule. *Congressional Digest* 71(4):104-105 (April 1992).

Yeager, Daniel B. Search, seizure, and the positive law: expectations of privacy outside the Fourth Amendment. *Journal of Criminal Law and Criminology* 84(2):249-309 (Summer 1993).

246. Northern Pacific Railroad Co. v. Herbert		February 1, 1886
116 US 642	29 LEd 755	6 SCt 590

Garcia, Diana. Remittitur in environmental cases: developing a standard of review for federal courts. *Boston College Environmental Affairs Law Review* 16(1):119-147 (Fall 1988).

247. Eastern Band of Cherokee Indians v. United States March 1, 1886		
117 US 288	29 LEd 880	6 SCt 718

Orlando, Caroline L. Aboriginal title claims in the Indian Claims Commission U.S. v. Dann and its due process limitations. *Boston College Environmental Affairs Law Review* 13(2):241-280 (Winter 1986).

248. Yick Wo v. Hopkins		May 10, 1886
Coupled with Wo Lee v. Hopkins		
118 US 356	30 LEd 220	6 SCt 1064

Brennan 244-246

Civil 19th 12, 179-185R

Const Law 462, 464-465+

Court Public 95-96

En Am Con 273-280, 640-647, 2084

Just War 125-126

Magic 148-149+

Making 82-83, 113-115, 253-256+

Gillman, Howard. Preferred freedoms: the progressive expansion of state power and the rise of modern civil liberties jurisprudence. *Political Research Quarterly* 47(3):623-653 (September 1994).

Karst, Kenneth L. Equal protection of the laws. *Society* 24(1):24-30 (November/December 1986).

Katz, Stanley N. The strange birth and unlikely history of constitutional equality. *Journal of American History* 75(3):747-762 (December 1988).

Pawelek, Dick. Two high court cases that test the U.S. Constitution on human rights. *Scholastic Update* (Teachers' Edition) 119(3):39, 36 (October 6, 1986).

Tish, Martin H. Duplicative statutes, prosecutorial discretion, and the Illinois Armed Violence Statute. *Journal of Criminal Law and Criminology* 71(3):226-243 (Fall 1980).

249. United States v. Kagama alias Pactah Billy   May 10, 1886
      118 US 375   30 LEd 228   6 SCt 1109
        Am Indian (Deloria)   105-133
        Am Indians (Wilkinson) 24-25, 57+

250. Santa Clara County v. Southern Railway Co.   May 10, 1886
        Coupled with California v. Southern Pacific Railroad Co.
        Coupled with California v. Central Pacific Railroad Co.
      118 US 394   30 LEd 118   6 SCt 1132
        Guide (CQ) 26-27
        Guide (West) (v. 9):101-102
        Magic 233-236
        Wilson, Margaret Bush. American judiciary in historical perspective. *Crisis* 89(2):37-40 (February 1982).

251. Wabash, St. Louis and Pacific Railway v. Illinois   October 25, 1886
      118 US 557   30 LEd 244   7 SCt 4
        Documents (v. 1):572-574R
        En Am Con 602-606, 1989
        Guide (CQ) 26-27, 89
        Magic 204-206, 233-236
        Powers 138-139
        Pisani, Donald J. Promotion and regulation: Constitutionalism and the American economy. *Journal of American History* 74(3):740-768 (December 1987).

252. The Harrisburg   November 15, 1886
      Steamer Harrisburg v. Rickards
      119 US 199   30 LEd 358   7 SCt 140
      Edelman, Paul S. Wrongful death on the high seas: Tallentire says federal law governs. *Trial* 23(4):58-61 (April 1987).
      George, James A. The "triple crown" of admiralty cases: from definitions to damages. *Trial* 27(10):46-53 (October 1991).

253. United States v. Rauscher   December 6, 1886
      119 US 407   30 LEd 425   7 SCt 234
      Dripps, Donald A. Supreme Court review: making right of two wrongs. *Trial* 28(9):81-83 (September 1992).
      Lonner, Jonathan A. Supreme Court review: official government abductions in the presence of extradition treaties. *Journal of Criminal Law and Criminology* 83(4):998-1023 (Winter 1993).

254. Ker v. Illinois   December 6, 1886
      119 US 436   30 LEd 421   7 SCt 225
      Dripps, Donald A. Supreme Court review: making right of two wrongs. *Trial* 28(9):81-83 (September 1992).
      Fagan, Terence P. Supreme Court review: Fourth Amendment—in-court identifications. *Journal of Criminal and Criminology* 71(4):488-498 (Winter 1980).
      Halberstam, Malvina. Agora: international kidnaping—in defense of the Supreme Court decision in Alvarez-Machain. *American Journal of International Law* 86(4):736-746 (October 1992).
      Lonner, Jonathan A. Supreme Court review: official government abductions in the presence of extradition treaties. *Journal of Criminal Law and Criminology* 83(4):998-1023 (Winter 1993).

255. Mali and Wildenhus v. Keeper of the Common Jail   January 10, 1887
     In re Wildenhus
     120 US 1   30 LEd 565   7 SCt 385
     Raymond, John M., and Barbara J. Frischholz. Lawyers who established international law in the United States,
        1776-1914. *American Journal of International Law* 76(4):802-829 (October 1982).

256. Ex Parte Ayers   December 5, 1887
        Coupled with Ex Parte Scott
        Coupled with Ex Parte McCabe
     123 US 443   31 LEd 216   8 SCt 164
        En Am Con 622-624
        Sup Ct Review (1984):149-168

257. Mugler v. Kansas   December 5, 1887
        Coupled with Kansas ex rel. Tufts v. Ziebold
     123 US 623   31 LEd 205   8 SCt 273
        En Am Con 630-632, 1283, 1482, 1744-1751
        Marbury 116-127, 161-175+
     Cohen, Jonathan E. A constitutional safety valve: the variance in zoning and land-use based environmental
        controls. *Boston College Environmental Affairs Law Review* 22(2):307-364 (Winter 1995).
     Folsom, Robin E. Executive Order 12,630: a president's manipulation of the Fifth Amendment's just
        compensation clause to achieve control over executive agency regulatory decisionmaking. *Boston College
        Environmental Affairs Law Review* 20(4):639-697 (Summer 1993).
     Gillman, Howard. Preferred freedoms: the progressive expansion of state power and the rise of modern civil
        liberties jurisprudence. *Political Research Quarterly* 47(3):623-653 (September 1994).
     Hanley, Thomas. A developer's dream: the United States Claims Court's new analysis of Section 404 takings
        challenges. *Boston College Environmental Affairs Law Review* 19(2):317-353 (Fall/Winter 1991).
     Hippler, Thomas A. Reexamining 100 years of the Supreme Court regulatory taking doctrine: the principles of
        "noxious use," "average reciprocity of advantage," and "bundle of rights" from Mugler to Keystone
        Bituminous Coal. *Boston College Environmental Affairs Law Review* 14(4):653-727 (Summer 1987).
     Note: the public use test: would a ban on the possession of firearms require just compensation? *Law and
        Contemporary Problems* 49(1):223-249 (Winter 1986).
     Randle, Ellen M. The national reserve system and transferable development rights: is the New Jersey pinelands
        plan in unconstitutional "taking"? *Boston College Environmental Affairs Law Review* 10(1):183-241 (1982-
        83).
     Sharp, Andrew H. An ounce of prevention: rehabilitating the Anticipatory Nuisance Doctrine. *Boston College
        Environmental Affairs Law Review* 15(3-4):627-653 (Spring 1988).
     Skelton, Harold N. Houses on the sand: taking issues surrounding statutory restrictions on the use of oceanfront
        property. *Boston College Environmental Affairs Law Review* 18(1):125-158 (Fall 1990).

258. Bowman v. Chicago and Northwestern Railway Co.   March 19, 1888
     125 US 465   31 LEd 700   8 SCt 689, 1062
        En Am Con 136

259. Powell v. Pennsylvania   April 9, 1888
     127 US 678   32 LEd 253   8 SCt 992, 1257
        En Am Con 774-780
     Hippler, Thomas A. Reexamining 100 years of the Supreme Court regulatory taking doctrine: the principles of
        "noxious use," "average reciprocity of advantage," and "bundle of rights" from Mugler to Keystone
        Bituminous Coal. *Boston College Environmental Affairs Law Review* 14(4):653-727 (Summer 1987).
     Katz, Stanley N. The strange birth and unlikely history of constitutional equality. *Journal of American History*
        75(3):747-762 (December 1988).
     McCurdy, Charles W. Waite Court. *Society* 24(1):40-45 (November/December 1986).

260. Kidd v. Pearson   October 22, 1888
     128 US 1   32 LEd 346   9 SCt 6
     En Am Con 1103, 1751-1755
     Guide (CQ) 92, 95
     Sup Ct Review (1995):125-215

261. Dent v. West Virginia   January 14, 1889
     129 US 114   32 LEd 623   9 SCt 231
     McCurdy, Charles W. Waite Court. *Society* 24(1):40-45 (November/December 1986).

262. Arkansas Valley Land and Cattle Co. v. Mann   March 5, 1889
     130 US 69   32 LEd 854   9 SCt 458
     Garcia, Diana. Remittitur in environmental cases: developing a standard of review for federal courts. *Boston
        College Environmental Affairs Law Review* 16(1):119-147 (Fall 1988).

263. Chae Chan Ping v. United States   May 13, 1889
     130 US 581   32 LEd 1068   9 SCt 623
     Civil 19th 4, 12, 187-198R
     Const (Currie) 14-16
     Const (Friendly) 237
     En Am Con 224, 747-755, 949-951
     Guide (CQ) 147b
     Sup Ct Review (1984):255-307
     Halberstam, Malvina. Agora: international kidnaping—in defense of the Supreme Court decision in Alvarez-
        Machain. *American Journal of International Law* 86(4):736-746 (October 1992).
     Orren, Karen. The primacy of labor in American constitutional development. *American Political Science
        Review* 89(2):377-388 (June 1995).
     Smith, Rogers M. The "American Creed" and American identity: the limits of liberal citizenship in the United
        States. *Western Political Quarterly* 41(2):225-251 (June 1988).

264. DeGeofroy v. Riggs   February 3, 1890
     133 US 258   33 LEd 642   10 SCt 295
     En Am Con 1910-1911
     Moss, David A. Kindling a flame under federalism: progressive reformers, corporate elites, and the
        phosphorous match campaign of 1909-1912. *Business History Review* 68(2):244-275 (Summer 1994).

265. Davis v. Beason   February 3, 1890
     133 US 333   33 LEd 637   10 SCt 299
     En Am Con 541-542, 1425-1426
     Original (Davis) 64-66
     McKown, Delos Banning. Deism and the Supreme Court. *Humanist* 52(2):25-28, 48 (March/April 1992).
     Regan, Richard J. Regulating cult activities: the limits of religious freedom. *Thought* 61(241):185-196 (June
        1986).

266. Louisville, New Orleans and Texas Railway Co. v. Mississippi   March 3, 1890
     133 US 587   33 LEd 784   10 SCt 348
     En Am Con 1180
     Guide (CQ) 29, 47, 106, 316, 598, 894

267. Hans v. Louisiana   March 3, 1890
     134 US 1   33 LEd 842   10 SCt 504
     Const (Currie) 7-9, 572-574
     Sup Ct Review (1988):43-60

268. Chicago, Milwaukee and St. Paul Railroad Co. v. Minnesota   March 24, 1890
      134 US 418   33 LEd 970   10 SCt 462, 702
            Const (Currie) 41-44
            Documents (v. 1):582-583R
            En Am Con 242, 682-683
            Guide (CQ) 29, 89-90
            Magic 233-236
      Cleaves, Robert E., IV. Constitutional protection for the utility investor: the confiscation doctrine after
        Cleveland Electric Illuminating Co. v. Public Utilities Commission of Ohio. *Boston College Environmental
        Affairs Law Review* 12(3):527-558 (Spring 1985).

269. Cunningham v. Neagle   April 14, 1890
      In re Neagle
      135 US 1   34 LEd 55   10 SCt 658
            Guide (CQ) 30
      LaFeber, Walter. The Constitution and United States foreign policy: an interpretation. *Journal of American
        History* 74(3):695-717 (December 1987).
      Orren, Karen. The primacy of labor in American constitutional development. *American Political Science
        Review* 89(2):377-388 (June 1995).
      Rodriguez, Leon. Constitutional and statutory limits for cost-benefit analysis pursuant to Executive Orders
        12,291 and 12,498. *Boston College Environmental Affairs Law Review* 15(3-4):505-546 (Spring 1988).

270. Gus. Leisy and Co. v. Hardin   April 28, 1890
      135 US 100   34 LEd 128   10 SCt 681
            Const (Currie) 32-33
            En Am Con 1155, 1349-1350, 1751-1755, 2042

271. Late Corporations of the Church of Jesus Christ of Latter-Day Saints v. United States   May 19, 1890
            Coupled with Romney v. United States
      136 US 1   34 LEd 478   10 SCt 792
            En Am Con 252-253, 1425-1426

272. Minnesota v. Barber   May 19, 1890
      136 US 313   34 LEd 455   10 SCt 862
            En Am Con 1261

273. Ex Parte Kemmler   May 23, 1890
      136 US 436   34 LEd 519   10 SCt 930
            Court Public 235, 239
            Death Penalty (Tushnet) 14, 22, 150
            En Am Con 1099
      Schwartz, Charles Walter. Eighth Amendment proportionality analysis and the compelling case of William
        Rummel. *Journal of Criminal Law and Criminology* 71(4):378-420 (Winter 1980).

274. Handley v. Stutz   December 8, 1890
      137 US 366   34 LEd 706   11 SCt 117
            Sup Ct Review (1983):459-507

275. Joy v. St. Louis   January 19, 1891
      138 US 1   34 LEd 843   11 SCt 243
            Sup Ct Review (1986):259-316

276. Wilkerson v. Rahrer   May 25, 1891
      In re Rahrer
      140 US 545   35 LEd 572   11 SCt 865

Const (Currie) 34-36

277. McElvaine v. Brush   December 21, 1891
     142 US 155   35 LEd 971   12 SCt 156
     En Am Con 1099

278. Knight v. United States Land Association   December 21, 1891
     142 US 161   35 LEd 974   12 SCt 258
     Baer, Susan D. The Public Trust Doctrine—a tool to make federal administrative agencies increase protection
       of public land and its resources. *Boston College Environmental Affairs Law Review* 15(2):385-436 (Winter
       1988).

279. Counselman v. Hitchcock   January 11, 1892
     142 US 547   35 LEd 1110   125 SCt 195
     En Am Con 165-166, 509-510, 952-953, 1569-1577
     Staas, John August. Supreme Court review: Fifth Amendment—statutory dilution of the privilege against self-
       incrimination. *Journal of Criminal Law and Criminology* 71(4):610-621 (Winter 1980).

280. Ekiu v. United States   January 18, 1892
     142 US 651   35 LEd 1146   12 SCt 336
     Japanese 31, 267-268

281. Boyd v. Nebraska ex. rel. Thayer   February 1, 1892
     143 US 135   36 LEd 103   12 SCt 375
     En Am Con 1300-1301

282. Field and Co. v. Clark   February 29, 1892
         Coupled with Boyd v. United States
         Coupled with Sternbach v. United States
     143 US 649   36 LEd 294   12 SCt 495
     Const (Currie) 16-22
     En Am Con 725

283. United States v. Ballin   February 29, 1892
     144 US 1   36 LEd 321   12 SCt 507
     Franck, Thomas M., and Clifford A. Bob. The return of Humpty-Dumpty: foreign relations law after the
       Chadha case. *American Journal of International Law* 79(4):912-960 (October 1985).
     Vanderziel, Kathleen M. The Hatfield Riders and environmental preservation: what process is due? *Boston
       College Environmental Affairs Law Review* 19(2):431-479 (Fall/Winter 1991).

284. O'Neil v. Vermont   April 4, 1892
     144 US 323   36 LEd 450   12 SCt 693
     Death Penalty (Tushnet) 151
     En Am Con 1099
     Schwartz, Charles Walter. Eighth Amendment proportionality analysis and the compelling case of William
       Rummel. *Journal of Criminal Law and Criminology* 71(4):378-420 (Winter 1980).

285. Coosaw Mining Co. v. South Carolina   April 4, 1892
     144 US 550   36 LEd 537   12 SCt 689
     Sharp, Andrew H. An ounce of prevention: rehabilitating the Anticipatory Nuisance Doctrine. *Boston College
       Environmental Affairs Law Review* 15(3-4):627-653 (Spring 1988).

286. McPherson v. Blacker   October 17, 1892
     146 US 1   36 LEd 869   13 SCt 3
     Founders (v. 3):552-553

287. Illinois Central Railroad Co. v. Illinois   December 5, 1892
     146 US 387   36 LEd 1018   13 SCt 110
          Const (Currie) 10-13
     Bader, Harry R. Antaeus and the Public Trust Doctrine: a new approach to substantive environmental protection
         in the common law. *Boston College Environmental Affairs Law Review* 19(4):749-763 (Summer 1992).
     Baer, Susan D. The Public Trust Doctrine—a tool to make federal administrative agencies increase protection
         of public land and its resources. *Boston College Environmental Affairs Law Review* 15(2):385-436 (Winter
         1988).
     Brady, Timothy Patrick. "But most of it belongs to those yet to be born:" the Public Trust Doctrine, NEPA, and
         the stewardship ethic. *Boston College Environmental Affairs Law Review* 17(3):621-646 (Spring 1990).
     Grady, Kevin T. Commonwealth of Puerto Rico v. SS Zoe Colocotroni: state actions for damage to non-
         commercial living natural resources. *Boston College Environmental Affairs Law Review* 9(2):397-429 (1980-
         1981).

288. Huntington v. Attrill   December 12, 1892
     146 US 657   36 LEd 1123   13 SCt 224
          Const (Currie) 66-67

289. American Construction Co. v. Jacksonville, Tampa and Key West Railway Co.   March 27, 1893
          Coupled with American Construction Co. v. Pennsylvania Company for Insurance on Lives and
          Granting Annuities
     148 US 372   37 LEd 486   13 SCt 758
          Sup Ct Review (1986):259-316

290. Virginia v. Tennessee   April 3, 1893
     148 US 503   37 LEd 537   13 SCt 728
          En Am Con 747-755
     Briggett, Marlissa S. State supremacy in the federal realm: the Interstate Compact. *Boston College
         Environmental Affairs Law Review* 18(4):751-772 (Summer 1991).

291. Wilson v. United States   April 17, 1893
     149 US 60   37 LEd 650   13 SCt 765
     Gromer, Sharon K. Supreme Court review: Fifth Amendment—the right to a no "adverse inference" jury
         instruction. *Journal of Criminal Law and Criminology* 72(4):1307-1325 (Winter 1981).

292. Nix v. Hedden   May 10, 1893
     149 US 304   37 LEd 745   13 SCt 881
     Put yourself on the U.S. Supreme Court. *Senior Scholastic* 114(8):22-23, 27 (December 11, 1981).
     Scott, Jack Denton. The tangy, tantalizing tomato. *Reader's Digest* 126(753):27-31 (January 1985).

293. Lees v. United States   December 4, 1893
     150 US 476   37 LEd 1150   14 SCt 163
     Caginalp, O. A. Fifth Amendment privilege against self-incrimination and compulsory self-disclosure under the
         Clean Air and Clean Water Acts. *Boston College Environmental Affairs Law Review* 9(2):359-395 (1980-
         1981).

294. Lawton v. Steele   March 5, 1894
     152 US 133   38 LEd 385   14 SCt 499
     Gillman, Howard. Preferred freedoms: the progressive expansion of state power and the rise of modern civil
         liberties jurisprudence. *Political Research Quarterly* 47(3):623-653 (September 1994).
     Hippler, Thomas A. Reexamining 100 years of the Supreme Court regulatory taking doctrine: the principles of
         "noxious use," "average reciprocity of advantage," and "bundle of rights" from Mugler to Keystone
         Bituminous Coal. *Boston College Environmental Affairs Law Review* 14(4):653-727 (Summer 1987).

Plater, Zygmunt J. B., and William Lund Norine. Through the looking glass of eminent domain: exploring the"arbitrary and capricious" test and substantive rationality review of governmental decisions. *Boston College Environmental Affairs Law Review* 16(4):661-752 (Summer 1989).

295. Miller v. Texas   May 4, 1894
    153 US 535   38 LEd 812   14 SCt 874
    Spitzer, Robert J. Shooting down gun myths. *America* 152(22):468-469 (June 8, 1985).

296. Ex Parte Lockwood   March 26, 1894
    154 US 116   38 LEd 929   14 SCt 1082
       Magic 115, 216-218, 327-329

297. Reagan v. Farmers' Loan and Trust Co.   May 26, 1894
    154 US 362   38 LEd 1014   14 SCt 1047
       Documents (v. 1):582, 585-586R
       En Am Con 682-683, 1518
    Lipartito, Kenneth. What have lawyers done for American business? The case of Baker and Botts of Houston. *Business History Review* 64(3):489-584 (September 22, 1990).
    Lodge, Arthur. The Supreme Court as center ring. *Journal of Accountancy* 161(6):95 (June 1986).

298. Plumley v. Massachusetts   December 10, 1894
    155 US 461   39 LEd 223   15 SCt 154
       Const (Currie) 34-36

299. United States v. E.C. Knight Co.   January 21, 1895
    156 US 1   39 LEd 325   15 SCt 249
       Const (Currie) 22-24, 26-30
       Documents (v. 1):618-620R
       En Am Con 602-606, 613-614, 1106-1107, 1678-1679, 1787-1788
       Guide (CQ) 30-31, 92, 95
       Magic 236-238, 279-281
       Marbury 116-127+
       Reader's 1097
       Sup Ct Review (1995):125-215
    Clinton, Robert Lowry. Judicial review, nationalism, and the commerce clause: contrasting antebellum and postbellum Supreme Court decision making. *Political Research Quarterly* 47(4):857-876 (December 1994).
    Johnston, Richard E., and John T. Thompson. Burger Court and federalism: a revolution in 1976? *Western Political Quarterly* 33(2):197-216 (June 1980).
    Lipartito, Kenneth. What have lawyers done for American business? The case of Baker and Botts of Houston. *Business History Review* 64(3):489-584 (September 22, 1990).
    Pisani, Donald J. Promotion and regulation: Constitutionalism and the American economy. *Journal of American History* 74(3):740-768 (December 1987).
    Supreme Court: attack and retreat. *Economist* 335(7913):29 (May 6-12, 1995).

300. Coffin v. United States   March 4, 1895
    156 US 432   39 LEd 481   15 SCt 394
       Law 407-410

301. Pollock v. Farmers' Loan and Trust Co.   April 8, 1895
             Coupled with Hyde v. Continental Trust Co.
    157 US 429   39 LEd 759, 821   15 SCt 673
       Const (Currie) 24-26
       Documents (v. 1):605-609R
       En Am Con 1423-1424, 1685-1686, 1770-1771

Guide (CQ) 112, 122b

Lodge, Arthur. The Supreme Court as center ring. *Journal of Accountancy* 161(6):95 (June 1986).

Wise, Charles, and Rosemary O'Leary. Is federalism dead or alive in the Supreme Court?: implications for public administrators. *Public Administration Review* 52(6):559-572 (November/December 1992).

302. In re Debs   May 27, 1895
      158 US 564   39 LEd 1092   15 SCt 900
         Const (Currie) 20-22
         Documents (v. 1):613-616R
         En Am Con 544
         Guide (CQ) 30-31, 94
         Jerry 216-219
         Magic 244-245
      Orren, Karen. The primacy of labor in American constitutional development. *American Political Science Review* 89(2):377-388 (June 1995).

303. Pollock v. Farmers' Loan and Trust Co.   May 20, 1895
            Coupled with Hyde v. Continental Trust Co.
      158 US 601   39 LEd 1108   15 SCt 912
         Amending 118-122
         En Am Con 564-565, 596-600, 1423-1424
         Guide (CQ) 30-31, 57, 71-73, 76-77, 112-113, 122
         Guide (West) (v. 8):231
         Magic 236-238
         Marbury 116-127, 176-181+
      Flaherty, Francis J. Abortion, the Constitution and the Human Life Statute. *Commonweal* 108(19):586-593 (October 23, 1981).

304. Hilton v. Guyot   June 3, 1895
      159 US 113   40 LEd 95   16 SCt 139
      Lowenfeld, Andreas F. Conflict, balancing of interests, and the exercise of jurisdiction to prescribe: reflections on the Insurance Antitrust Case. [Editorial] *American Journal of International Law* 89(1):42-53 (January 1995).
      Raymond, John M., and Barbara J. Frischholz. Lawyers who established international law in the United States, 1776-1914. *American Journal of International Law* 76(4):802-829 (October 1982).
      Salter, Leonard M. A growth industry? International insolvencies and law: a case sampling. *Credit and Financial Management* 87(8):30-32 (October 1985).

305. Missouri v. Moore   November 25, 1895
      159 US 673   40 LEd 301   16 SCt 179
      Schwartz, Charles Walter. Eighth Amendment proportionality analysis and the compelling case of William Rummel. *Journal of Criminal Law and Criminology* 71(4):378-420 (Winter 1980).

306. United States v. Gettysburg Electric Railway Co.   January 27, 1896
      160 US 668   40 LEd 576   16 SCt 427
         En Am Con 630-632
      Cavarello, Daniel T. From Penn Central to United Artists' I and II: the rise to immunity of historic preservation designation from successful takings challenges. *Boston College Environmental Affairs Law Review* 22(3):593-622 (Spring 1995).
      Kourtis, Jane Papademetriou. The constructive trust: equity's answer to the need for a strong deterrent to the destruction of historic landmarks. *Boston College Environmental Affairs Law Review* 16(4):793-820 (Summer 1989).

307. Spalding v. Vilas   March 2, 1896
      161 US 483   40 LEd 780   16 SCt 631

Rosenbloom, David H. Public administrators' official immunity and the Supreme Court: developments during the 1970s. *Public Administration Review* 40(2):166-173 (March/April 1980).

308. Geer v. Connecticut — March 2, 1896
161 US 519 — 40 LEd 793 — 16 SCt 600
Grady, Kevin T. Commonwealth of Puerto Rico v. SS Zoe Colocotroni: state actions for damage to noncommercial living natural resources. *Boston College Environmental Affairs Law Review* 9(2):397-429 (1980-1981).
Schwartz, Edward B. Water as an article of commerce: state embargoes spring a leak under Sporhase v. Nebraska. *Boston College Environmental Affairs Law Review* 12(1):103-169 (Fall 1985).

309. Brown v. Walker — March 23, 1896
161 US 591 — 40 LEd 819 — 16 SCt 644
En Am Con 165-166, 952-953, 1569-1577

310. Talton v. Mayes — May 18, 1896
163 US 376 — 41 LEd 196 — 16 SCt 986
Am Indians (Wilkinson) 24-28, 56, 153-154

311. Ward v. Race Horse — May 25, 1896
163 US 504 — 41 LEd 244 — 16 SCt 1076
Ott, Brian R. Indian fishing rights in the Pacific Northwest: the need for federal intervention. *Boston College Environmental Affairs Law Review* 14(2):313-343 (Winter 1987).

312. Plessy v. Ferguson — May 18, 1896
163 US 537 — 41 LEd 256 — 16 SCt 1138
Abortion Pol (Rubin) 1, 3, 31
Am Educators 439
Amending 203-213
Black 155-162
Brennan 241-244
Burger Years 95-108
Civil 19th 11, 163-177R
Civil 20th 61
Const Law 471-475R, 482-484, 578-580+
Court Public 98, 101
Documents (v. 1):628-630R
En Am Con 273-280, 557-561, 640-647, 1396-1397, 1649-1650, 1729-1736
Equal (Harrell) 59-62, 97, 100, 102+
Guide (CQ) 31-32, 105-106
Guide (West) (v. 6):341; (v. 8):216-217
Landmark (v. 4):74-104R
Magic 146-147, 218-219, 322-324, 330-331
Make 15-22
Making 70-71, 135-147, 169-176, 189-190+
Marbury 207-211
Plessy 148-173+
Price 169-175
Quarrels 157-174, 307-309, 322-323+
Reader's 15-17, 131-132, 844-845, 1050-1052
Sup Ct Ind 232-233, 247-249+
Sup Ct Review (1988):245-267
Super 74-75+
Baker, banker, clergyman, thief. *Life* 10(10):84-88 (Fall 1987).
Basic court ruling: the Brown decision. *Congressional Digest* 59(2):34-35, 64 (February 1981).

Belz, Herman. Equality before the law: the Civil War Amendments. *Center Magazine* 20(6):4-19 (November/December 1987).

Bennett, Lerone., Jr. The day race relations changed forever. *Ebony* 40(7):108-116 (May 1985).

———. The second time around. *Ebony* 50(11):86-90, 144 (September 1995).

Bersoff, Donald N., and Donald B. Verrilli, Jr. In the Supreme Court of the United States Price Waterhouse v.Ann B. Hopkins: Amicus Curiae Brief for the American Psychological Association. *American Psychologist* 46(10):1061-1070 (October 1991).

Carlin, David R. As American as freeways: abortion's roots in our culture. *Commonweal* 116(13):392-393 (July 14, 1989).

Cecil, Andrew R. Moral values in a free society: individualism and social conscience. *Vital Speeches of the Day* 60(7):204-209 (January 15, 1994).

Cohen, Carl. Naked racial preference. *Commentary* 81(3):24-31 (March 1986).

Delon, Floyd G. The legacy of Thurgood Marshall. *Journal of Negro Education* 63(3):278-288 (Summer 1994).

Erler, Edward J. Brown v. Board of Education at 30. *National Review* 36(17):26-28, 30-31, 53 (September 7, 1984).

Garraty, John Arthur. 101 things every college graduate should know about American history. *American Heritage* 38(1):24-32 (December 1986).

Heffner, Judith C. The Constitution in court. *Scholastic Update* (Teacher' Edition) 116(5):16-18 (October 28, 1983).

Hobbs, Gardner J. Public school finance and the courts. *Clearing House* 53(9):405-409 (May 1980) .

Karst, Kenneth L. Equal protection of the laws. *Society* 24(1):24-30 (November/December 1986).

Katz, Stanley N. The strange birth and unlikely history of constitutional equality. *Journal of American History* 75(3):747-762 (December 1988).

Lamb, Charles M. Legal foundations of civil rights and pluralism America. *Annals of the American Academy of Political and Social Science* 454:13-25 (March 1981).

Levinson, Sanford. Looking at the Constitution: could Meese be right this time? *Nation* 243(21):689, 704-707 (December 20, 1986).

Meese, Edwin, III. Interpreting the Constitution. *USA Today* 115(2496):36-39 (September 1986).

Motley, Constance Baker. The legacy of Brown v. Board of Education. *Teachers College Record* 96(4):637-643 (Summer 1995).

Mueller, Jean West, and Wynell Burroughs Schamel. Teaching with documents: Plessy v. Ferguson mandate. *Social Education* 53(2):120-122 (February 1989).

O'Neill, Charles E. Separate but never equal. *America* 172(11):13-14 (April 1, 1995).

Parker, Franklin. A 30-year perspective on school desegregation. *Education Digest* 51(7):26-28 (March 1986).

Polin, Raymond. The Supreme Court's dilemma and defense. *USA Today* 115(2496):43-45 (September 1986).

Reid, Herbert O., and Frankie M. Foster-Davis. Three decades of "all deliberate speed". *Crisis* 91(5):12-15 (May 1984).

Relin, David Oliver. Five landmark decisions. *Scholastic Update* 120(15):20 (April 8, 1988).

Reynolds, William Bradford. Affirmative action and its negative repercussions. *Annals of the American Academy of Political and Social Science* 523:38-49 (September 1992).

Rutland, Robert Allen. The dark century. *Life* 14 (13 Special Issue):48 (Fall 1991).

Stefkovich, Jacqueline A., and Terrence Leas. A legal history of desegregation in higher education. *Journal of Negro Education* 63(3):406-420 (Summer 1994).

The talk of the town: notes and comment. [Editorial] *New Yorker* 68(7):23-24 (April 6, 1992).

Timberlake, Constance H. A historical perspective of school desegregation. *Crisis* 91(5):26-29 (1984).

Tollett, Kenneth S., Jeanette J. Leonard, and Portia P. James. A color-conscious constitution: the one pervading purpose redux. *Journal of Negro Education* 52(3):189-212 (Summer 1983).

Wilson, Margaret Bush. American judiciary in historical perspective. *Crisis* 89(2):37-40 (February 1982).

313. Wiborg v. United States   May 25, 1896
      163 US 632   41 LEd 289   16 SCt 1127, 1197

Lowry, Jeffrey L. Supreme Court review: plain error rule—clarifying plain error analysis under Rule 52(b) of the Federal Rules of Criminal Procedure. *Journal of Criminal Law and Criminology* 84(4):1065-1085 (Winter/Spring 1994).

314. Fallbrook Irrigation District v. Bradley — November 16, 1896
   164 US 112   41 LEd 369   17 SCt 56
   En Am Con 1489-1492
   Hippler, Thomas A. Reexamining 100 years of the Supreme Court regulatory taking doctrine: the principles of "noxious use," "average reciprocity of advantage," and "bundle of rights" from Mugler to Keystone Bituminous Coal. *Boston College Environmental Affairs Law Review* 14(4):653-727 (Summer 1987).

315. Allen v. United States — December 7, 1896
   164 US 492   41 LEd 528   17 SCt 154
   Guide (West) (v. 1):191

316. Covington and Lexington Turnpike Road Co. v. Sandford — December 14, 1896
   164 US 578   41 LEd 560   17 SCt 198
   Cleaves, Robert E., IV. Constitutional protection for the utility investor: the confiscation doctrine after Cleveland Electric Illuminating Co. v. Public Utilities Commission of Ohio. *Boston College Environmental Affairs Law Review* 12(3):527-558 (Spring 1985).

317. Allgeyer v. Louisiana — March 1, 1897
   165 US 578   41 LEd 832   17 SCt 427
   Const (Currie) 45-47
   En Am Con 45, 602-606, 774-780, 1577-1581, 1796-1803
   Guide (CQ) 32
   Magic 233-236
   Marbury 199-207
   Sup Ct Review (1992):235-293
   Galie, Peter J. State courts and economic rights. *Annals of the American Academy of Political and Social Science* 496:76-87 (March 1988).

318. United States v. The Three Friends — March 1, 1897
   In re The Three Friends
   166 US 1   41 LEd 897   17 SCt 495
   Sup Ct Review (1986):259-316

319. Chicago, Burlington and Quincy Railroad Co. v. Chicago — March 1, 1897
   166 US 226   41 LEd 979   17 SCt 581
   En Am Con 242
   Guide (CQ) 32, 143b
   Marbury 199-211

320. United States v. Trans-Missouri Freight Association — March 22, 1897
   166 US 290   41 LEd 1007   17 SCt 540
   Documents (v. 2):55-56R
   En Am Con 1615, 1903
   Guide (CQ) 94
   Sup Ct Review (1984):69-184
   Graglia, Lino A. One hundred years of antitrust. *Public Interest* (104):50-66 (Summer 1991).

321. Davis v. Massachusetts — May 10, 1897
   167 US 43   42 LEd 71   17 SCt 731
   Const (Currie) 263-266
   Sup Ct Review (1992):79-122

322. Interstate Commerce Commission (ICC) v. — May 24, 1897
   Cincinnati, New Orleans and Texas Pacific Railway Co.
   167 US 479   42 LEd 243   17 SCt 896

En Am Con 994-995

323. Camfield v. United States   March 24, 1897
     167 US 518   42 LEd 260   17 SCt 864
     Shepard, Blake. The scope of Congress's constitutional power under the property clause: regulating non-federal
       property to further the purposes of national parks and wilderness areas. *Boston College Environmental Affairs
       Law Review* 11(3): 479-538 (April 1984).

324. Interstate Commerce Commission (ICC) v. Alabama Midland Railway Co.   November 8, 1897
     168 US 144   42 LEd 414   18 SCt 45
     En Am Con 995, 1178

325. Underhill v. Hernandez   November 29, 1897
     168 US 250   42 LEd 456   18 SCt 83
     Raymond, John M., and Barbara J. Frischholz. Lawyers who established international law in the United States,
       1776-1914. *American Journal of International Law* 76(4):802-829 (October 1982).

326. Nobles v. Georgia   November 29, 1897
     168 US 398   42 LEd 515   18 SCt 87
     Pastroff, Sanford M. Supreme Court review: Eighth Amendment—the constitutional rights of the insane on
       death row. *Journal of Criminal Law and Criminology* 77(3):844-866 (Fall 1986).

327. Bram v. United States   December 13, 1897
     168 US 532   42 LEd 568   18 SCt 183
     En Am Con 1400-1408, 1569-1577
     Sup Ct Review (1991):103-142

328. Holden v. Hardy   February 28, 1898
     169 US 366   42 LEd 780   18 SCt 383
     Documents (v. 1):630-631R
     En Am Con 602-606, 774-780, 920, 1229-1230, 1796-1803
     Guide (CQ) 32
     Magic 240-242+
     Gillman, Howard. Preferred freedoms: the progressive expansion of state power and the rise of modern civil
       liberties jurisprudence. *Political Research Quarterly* 47(3):623-653 (September 1994).
     Orren, Karen. The primacy of labor in American constitutional development. *American Political Science
       Review* 89(2):377-388 (June 1995).

329. Smyth v. Ames   March 7, 1898
         Coupled with Smyth v. Smith
         Coupled with Smyth v. Higginson
     169 US 466   42 LEd 819   18 SCt 418
     Const (Currie) 41-44, 50-54
     Documents (v. 1):582, 583-585R
     En Am Con 682-683, 1699
     Guide (CQ) 32
     Cleaves, Robert E., IV. Constitutional protection for the utility investor: the confiscation doctrine after
       Cleveland Electric Illuminating Co. v. Public Utilities Commission of Ohio. *Boston College Environmental
       Affairs Law Review* 12(3):527-558 (Spring 1985).
     Miranti, Paul J., Jr. The mind's eye of reform: the ICC's Bureau of Statistics and Accounts and a vision of
       regulation, 1887-1940. *Business History Review* 63(3):469-509 (September 22, 1989).

330. United States v. Wong Kim Ark   March 28, 1898
     169 US 649   42 LEd 890   18 SCt 456
     En Am Con 2073-2074

Guide (CQ) 144
Japanese 33, 342
Just War 176

331. Williams v. Mississippi   April 25, 1898
      170 US 213   42 LEd 1012   18 SCt 583
      En Am Con 1169, 2065-2066
      Guide (CQ) 32
      Making 112

332. United States v. Rio Grande Dam and Irrigation Co.   May 22, 1899
      174 US 690   43 LEd 1136   19 SCt 770
      Proctor, Michael G. Section 10 of the Rivers and Harbors Act and Western Water Allocations—are the western
      states up a creek without a permit? *Boston College Environmental Affairs Law Review* 10(1):111-182(1982-83).

333. Addyston Pipe and Steel Co. v. United States   December 4, 1899
      175 US 211   44 LEd 136   20 SCt 96
      Sup Ct Review (1984):69-148

334. Bradfield v. Roberts, Treasurer of the United States   December 4, 1899
      175 US 291   44 LEd 168   20 SCt 121
      En Am Con 1650-1658
      Rayer, Thomas A. The bicentennial and church-related schools. *America* 157(17):427-429, 438 (December 5,
      1987).

335. Cumming v. County Board of Education Richmond, Georgia   December 18, 1899
      175 US 528   44 LEd 262   20 SCt 197
      Basic court ruling: the Brown decision. *Congressional Digest* 59(2):34-35, 64 (February 1981).
      Hobbs, Gardner J. Public school finance and the courts. *Clearing House* 53(9):405-409 (May 1980) .
      Tollett, Kenneth S., Jeanette J. Leonard, and Portia P. James. A color-conscious constitution: the one pervading
      purpose redux. *Journal of Negro Education* 52(3):189-212 (Summer 1983).

336. The Paquete Habana   January 8, 1900
      175 US 677   44 LEd 320   20 SCt 290
      Sup Ct Review (1994):295-343
      Glennon, Michael J. State-sponsored abduction: a comment on United States v. Alvarez-Machain. *American
      Journal of International Law* 86(4):746-756 (October 1992).
      Raymond, John M., and Barbara J. Frischholz. Lawyers who established international law in the United States,
      1776-1914. *American Journal of International Law* 76(4):802-829 (October 1982).

337. Maxwell v. Dow   February 26, 1900
      176 US 581   44 LEd 597   20 SCt 448, 494
      En Am Con 1231, 1472-1479
      Guide (CQ) 32, 33
      Sup Ct Ind 161+

338. Clarke v. Clarke   May 21, 1900
      178 US 186   44 LEd 1028   20 SCt 873
      Const (Currie) 70-72

339. Missouri v. Illinois   January 28, 1901
      180 US 208   45 LEd 497   21 SCt 331
      Collins, Michael. The dilemma of the downstream state: the untimely demise of federal common law nuisance.
      Boston College Environmental Affairs Law Review 11(2):295-412 (January 1984).

Sharp, Andrew H. An ounce of prevention: rehabilitating the Anticipatory Nuisance Doctrine. *Boston College Environmental Affairs Law Review* 15(3-4):627-653 (Spring 1988).

340. McDonald v. Massachusetts   February 25, 1901
    180 US 311   45 LEd 542   21 SCt 389
    Schwartz, Charles Walter. Eighth Amendment proportionality analysis and the compelling case of William Rummel. *Journal of Criminal Law and Criminology* 71(4):378-420 (Winter 1980).

341. Atherton v. Atherton   April 15, 1901
    181 US 155   45 LEd 794   21 SCt 544
    Const (Currie) 73-75

342. De Lima v. Bidwell   May 27, 1901
    182 US 1   45 LEd 1041   21 SCt 743
    Const (Currie) 59-65
    Guide (CQ) 66, 140

343. Dooley v. United States   May 27, 1901
    182 US 222   45 LEd 1074   21 SCt 762
    Const (Currie) 59-62

344. Downes v. Bidwell   May 27, 1901
    182 US 244   45 LEd 1088   21 SCt 770
    Const (Currie) 59-62
    Documents (v. 2):12-17R
    Guide (CQ) 66, 140-142

345. Knoxville Iron Co. v. Harbison   October 21, 1901
    183 US 13   46 LEd 55   22 SCt 1
    Magic 242-243

346. Lone Wolf v. Hitchcock   January 5, 1903
    187 US 553   47 LEd 299   23 SCt 216
    Am Indians (Wilkinson) 24-25, 78, 80-82, 154
    Norgren, Jill, and Petra T. Shattuck. Black Hills whitewash. *Nation* 230(18):557-560 (May 10, 1980).

347. Andrews v. Andrews   January 19, 1903
    188 US 14   47 LEd 366   23 SCt 237
    Const (Currie) 75-76

348. Champion v. Ames   February 23, 1903
    188 US 321   47 LEd 492   23 SCt 321
    Documents (v. 2):26-28R
    En Am Con 226-227, 893-894, 1295-1299
    Guide (CQ) 32-33, 95, 96-97

349. Yamataya v. Fisher   April 6, 1903
    189 US 86   47 LEd 721   23 SCt 611
    Japanese 35, 356

350. The Osceola   March 2, 1903
    189 US 158   47 LEd 760   23 SCt 483
    George, James A. The "triple crown" of admiralty cases: from definitions to damages. *Trial* 27(10):46-53 (October 1991).

351. Giles v. Harris   April 27, 1903
     189 US 475   47 LEd 909   23 SCt 639
     Making 112-113

352. James v. Bowman   May 4, 1903
     190 US 127   47 LEd 979   23 SCt 678
     En Am Con 1009-1010

353. Howard v. Fleming   November 16, 1903
     191 US 126   48 LEd 121   24 SCt 49
     Schwartz, Charles Walter. Eighth Amendment proportionality analysis and the compelling case of William
        Rummel. *Journal of Criminal Law and Criminology* 71(4):378-420 (Winter 1980).

354. Buttfield v. Stranahan   February 23, 1904
     192 US 470   48 LEd 525   24 SCt 349
     Const (Currie) 16-19
     Guide (CQ) 75

355. Northern Securities Co. v. United States   March 14, 1904
     193 US 197   48 LEd 679   24 SCt 436
     Documents (v. 2):35-39R
     En Am Con 1327-1328
     Equal (Harrell) 60-61, 67
     Guide (CQ) 32-33, 34, 93
     Quarrels 175-192

356. Houghton v. Payne   April 11, 1904
     194 US 88   48 LEd 888   24 SCt 590
     Kielbowicz, Richard B. Postal subsidies for the press and the business of mass culture, 1880-1920. *Business
        History Review* 64(3):451-488 (September 22, 1990).

357. McCray v. United States   May 31, 1904
     195 US 27   49 LEd 78   24 SCt 769
     En Am Con 1234, 1869-1871
     Guide (CQ) 36, 95, 115-116
     Moss, David A. Kindling a flame under federalism: progressive reformers, corporate elites, and the
        phosphorous match campaign of 1909-1912. *Business History Review* 68(2):244-275 (Summer 1994).

358. Schick v. United States   May 31, 1904
              Coupled with Broadwell v. United States
     195 US 65   49 LEd 99   24 SCt 826
     Law 391-395

359. Dorr v. United States   May 31, 1904
     195 US 138   49 LEd 128   24 SCt 808
     Const (Currie) 59-65
     Guide (CQ) 142

360. Dobbins v. Los Angeles   November 14, 1904
     195 US 223   49 LEd 169   25 SCt 18
     Hippler, Thomas A. Reexamining 100 years of the Supreme Court regulatory taking doctrine: the principles of
        "noxious use," "average reciprocity of advantage," and "bundle of rights" from Mugler to Keystone
        Bituminous Coal. *Boston College Environmental Affairs Law Review* 14(4):653-727 (Summer 1987).

361. Swift and Co. v. United States   January 30, 1905
      196 US 375   49 LEd 518   25 SCt 276
         En Am Con 613-614, 1787-1788, 1842
         Guide (CQ) 32-33, 93, 95
         Sup Ct Review (1995):125-215
      Pawelek, Dick. Call five cases that shaped Congress. *Scholastic Update* (Teachers' Edition) 119(9):12-14
         (January 12, 1987).
      ———. Put yourself on the U.S. Supreme Court. *Senior Scholastic* 114(8):22-23, 27 (December 11, 1981).

362. Jacobson v. Massachusetts   February 20, 1905
      197 US 11   49 LEd 643   25 SCt 358
         En Am Con 1009, 1538-1545, 1953
      Bodine, Margot R. Opening the schoolhouse door for children with AIDS: the Education for All Handicapped
         Children Act. *Boston College Environmental Affairs Law Review* 13(4):583-641 (Summer 1986).
      Pawelek, Dick. Put yourself on the U.S. Supreme Court. *Senior Scholastic* 113(8):12-13, 27 (December 12,
         1980).

363. Lochner v. New York   April 17, 1905
      198 US 45   49 LEd 937   25 SCt 539
         Abortion (Frohock) 61, 66
         Abortion Am 340-344+
         Amending 203-213
         Brennan 65-77
         Const (Currie) 47-50, 252-253
         Court Const 131-137, 150-151+
         Documents (v. 2):39-42R
         En Am Con 169-170, 506-508, 602-606, 774-780, 1112-1119, 1175, 1229-1230, 1796-1803
         Equal (Harrell) 62-64, 70-72, 77-79
         Guide (CQ) 33, 35, 37, 42
         Guide (West) (v. 7):176-178, 179-181, 212
         Hard Choices 126-127+
         Magic 240-242+
         New Right (Schwartz) 73-97+
         Reader's 677
         Sup Ct Review (1989):333-372; (1995):217-276
      Baker, banker, clergyman, thief. *Life* 10(10):84-88 (Fall 1987).
      Duesenberg, Richard W. Washington is stifling economic liberties. *USA Today* 123(2596):14-16 (January
         1995).
      Farber, Daniel A. 'Taking' liberties. *New Republic* 198(26):19-20 (June 27, 1988).
      Feitshans, Ilise L. Job security for pregnant employees: the model employment termination act. *Annals of the
         American Academy of Political and Social Science* 536:119-134 (November 1994).
      Galie, Peter J. State courts and economic rights. *Annals of the American Academy of Political and Social
         Science* 496:76-87 (March 1988).
      Gillman, Howard. Preferred freedoms: the progressive expansion of state power and the rise of modern civil
         liberties jurisprudence. *Political Research Quarterly* 47(3):623-653 (September 1994).
      Howard, A. E. Dick. Making it work. *Wilson Quarterly* 11(2):122-133 (Spring 1987).
      Minow, Martha. We, the family: constitutional rights and American families. *Journal of American History*
         74(3):959-983 (December 1987).
      Orren, Karen. The primacy of labor in American constitutional development. *American Political Science
         Review* 89(2):377-388 (June 1995).
      Plater, Zygmunt J. B., and William Lund Norine. Through the looking glass of eminent domain: exploring the
         "arbitrary and capricious" test and substantive rationality review of governmental decisions. *Boston College
         Environmental Affairs Law Review* 16(4):661-752 (Summer 1989).
      Quirk, William J. Judicial dictatorship. *Society* 31(2):34-38 (January/February 1994).

Van Alstyne, William W. Academic freedom and the First Amendment in the Supreme Court of the United States: an unhurried historical review. *Law and Contemporary Problems* 53(3):79-154 (Summer 1990).

Zimmerman, Joan G. The jurisprudence of equality: the women's minimum wage, the first equal rights amendment, and Adkins v. Children's Hospital, 1905-1923. *Journal of American History* 78(1):188-225 (June 1991).

364. United States v. Winans   May 15, 1905
     198 US 371   49 LEd 1089   25 SCt 662
     Ott, Brian R. Indian fishing rights in the Pacific Northwest: the need for federal intervention. *Boston College Environmental Affairs Law Review* 14(2):313-343 (Winter 1987).

365. Manigualt v. Springs   December 4, 1905
     199 US 473   50 LEd 274   26 SCt 127
     Const (Currie) 10-13

366. Hale and Henkel   March 12, 1906
     201 US 43   50 LEd 652   26 SCt 370
     Causey, Denzil, and Frances McNair. Protecting taxpayers privacy from the IRS. *Journal of Accountancy* 168(4):44-48 (October 1989).

367. Haddock v. Haddock   April 12, 1906
     201 US 562   50 LEd 867   26 SCt 525
     Const (Currie) 76-78

368. Hodges v. United States   May 28, 1906
     203 US 1   51 LEd 65   27 SCt 6
     En Am Con 919, 1892-1894

369. Patterson v. Colorado ex rel. Attorney General of Colorado   April 15, 1907
     205 US 454   51 LEd 879   27 SCt 556
     Fourth 1-16
     Magic 262-264
     Make 67-79, 90-102
     Minnesota 109, 131-132
     Gillman, Howard. Preferred freedoms: the progressive expansion of state power and the rise of modern civil liberties jurisprudence. *Political Research Quarterly* 47(3):623-653 (September 1994).

370. Georgia v. Tennessee Copper Co.   May 13, 1907
     206 US 230   51 LEd 1038   27 SCt 618
     Collins, Michael. The dilemma of the downstream state: the untimely demise of federal common law nuisance. *Boston College Environmental Affairs Law Review* 11(2):295-412 (January 1984).
     Feldman, Stuart P. Curbing the recalcitrant polluter: post-decree judicial agents in environmental litigation. *Boston College Environmental Affairs Law Review* 18(4):809-840 (Summer 1991).
     Giesser, John L. The National Park Service and external development: addressing park boundary-area threats through public nuisance. *Boston College Environmental Affairs Law Review* 20(4):761-809 (Summer 1993).

371. Hunter v. Pittsburgh   November 18, 1907
     207 US 161   52 LEd 151   28 SCt 40
     En Am Con 255-257

372. Old Dominion Steamship Co. v. Gilmore   December 23, 1907
     207 US 398   52 LEd 264   28 SCt 133
     Edelman, Paul S. Wrongful death on the high seas: Tallentire says federal law governs. *Trial* 23(4):58-61 (April 1987).

373. Howard v. Illinois Central Railroad Co.   January 6, 1908
          Coupled with Brooks v. Southern Pacific Co.
      207 US 463   52 LEd 297   28 SCt 141
          En Am Con 632-633

374. Winters v. United States   January 6, 1908
      207 US 564   52 LEd 340   28 SCt 207
          Am Indian (Deloria)   197-220
          Am Indians (Wilkinson) 67-71+

375. Adair v. United States   January 27, 1908
      208 US 161   52 LEd 436   28 SCt 277
          Documents (v. 2):45-48R
          En Am Con 15-16, 2083
          Guide (CQ) 33, 90, 95, 123b
          Magic 244-245
          Sup Ct Review (1992):235-293
      Coulson, Robert. The way it is—rules of the game—how to fire. *Across the Board* 19(2):20-48 (February
          1982).
      Gillman, Howard. Preferred freedoms: the progressive expansion of state power and the rise of modern civil
          liberties jurisprudence. *Political Research Quarterly* 47(3):623-653 (September 1994).

376. Loewe v. Lawlor   February 3, 1908
      208 US 274   52 LEd 488   28 SCt 301
          En Am Con 1177-1178
          Guide (CQ) 33, 90, 95

377. Muller v. Oregon   February 24, 1908
      208 US 412   52 LEd 551   28 SCt 324
          Documents (v. 2):43-45R
          En Am Con 144-145, 169-170, 602-606, 774-780, 1229-1230, 1283-1284, 1666-1673, 1796-1803
          Equal (Harrell) 73+
          Equal Rights (Kanowitz) 17-42, 65+
          Magic 239-240+
          Quarrels 193-208
          Reader's 759
      Baer, Judith A. Women's rights and the limits of constitutional doctrine. *Western Political Quarterly* 44(4):821-
          852 (December 1991).
      Feitshans, Ilise L. Job security for pregnant employees: the model employment termination act. *Annals of the
          American Academy of Political and Social Science* 536:119-134 (November 1994).
      Gillman, Howard. Preferred freedoms: the progressive expansion of state power and the rise of modern civil
          liberties jurisprudence. *Political Research Quarterly* 47(3):623-653 (September 1994).
      Hogan, Joyce, and Ann M. Quigley. Physical standards for employment and the courts. *American Psychologist*
          41(11):1193-1217 (November 1986).
      Orren, Karen. The primacy of labor in American constitutional development. *American Political Science
          Review* 89(2):377-388 (June 1995).
      Segal, Jeffrey A., and Cheryl D. Reedy. The Supreme Court and sex discrimination: the role of the Solicitor
          General. *Western Political Quarterly* 41(3):553-568 (September 1988).
      Zimmerman, Joan G. The jurisprudence of equality: the women's minimum wage, the first equal rights
          amendment, and Adkins v. Children's Hospital, 1905-1923. *Journal of American History* 78(1):188-225
          (June 1991).

378. Ex Parte Young   March 23, 1908
      209 US 123   52 LEd 714   28 SCt 441
          Const (Currie) 574-580

En Am Con 622-624, 961, 1898, 2084

Sup Ct Review (1984):149-168

Colton, Roger D., Kathleen Uehling, and Michael F. Sheehan. Seven-cum-eleven: rolling the toxic dice in the U.S. Supreme Court. *Boston College Environmental Affairs Law Review* 14(3):345-379 (Spring 1987).

379. Hudson County Water Co. v. McCarter   April 6, 1908
    209 US 349   52 LEd 828   28 SCt 529
    Schwartz, Edward B. Water as an article of commerce: state embargoes spring a leak under Sporhase v. Nebraska. *Boston College Environmental Affairs Law Review* 12(1):103-169 (Fall 1985).

380. Quick Bear v. Leupp   May 18, 1908
    210 US 50   52 LEd 954   28 SCt 690
    En Am Con 1650-1658
    Rayer, Thomas A. The bicentennial and church-related schools. *America* 157(17):427-429, 438 (December 5, 1987).

381. Deslions v. LaCompagnie General Transatlantique   May 18, 1908
    210 US 95   52 LEd 973   28 SCt 664
    Edelman, Paul S. Wrongful death on the high seas: Tallentire says federal law governs. *Trial* 23(4):58-61 (April 1987).

382. Fauntleroy v. Lum   May 18, 1908
    210 US 230   52 LEd 1039   28 SCt 641
    Const (Currie) 68-70

383. Londoner v. Denver   June 1, 1908
    210 US 373   52 LEd 1103   28 SCt 708
    Sup Ct Review (1988):1-41
    Vanderziel, Kathleen M. The Hatfield Riders and environmental preservation: what process is due? *Boston College Environmental Affairs Law Review* 19(2):431-479 (Fall/Winter 1991).

384. Berea College v. Kentucky   November 9, 1908
    211 US 45   53 LEd 81   29 SCt 33
    En Am Con 108
    Stefkovich, Jacqueline A., and Terrence Leas. A legal history of desegregation in higher education. *Journal of Negro Education* 63(3):406-420 (Summer 1994).
    Van Alstyne, William W. Academic freedom and the First Amendment in the Supreme Court of the United States: an unhurried historical review. *Law and Contemporary Problems* 53(3):79-154 (Summer 1990).

385. Twining v. New Jersey   November 9, 1908
    211 US 78   53 LEd 97   29 SCt 14
    Amending 203-213
    Antagonists 177-178
    Const (Currie) 362-364
    Const Law 25-28R
    En Am Con 164-165, 1569-1577, 1929-1930
    Guide (CQ) 33
    Sup Ct Ind 161-162+
    Sup Ct Review (1982):85-125

386. Hepner v. United States   April 5, 1909
    213 US 103   53 LEd 720   29 SCt 474
    Caginalp, O. A. Fifth Amendment privilege against self-incrimination and compulsory self-disclosure under the Clean Air and Clean Water Acts. *Boston College Environmental Affairs Law Review* 9(2):359-395 (1980-1981).

387. American Banana Co. v. United Fruit Co.   April 26, 1909
      213 US 347   53 LEd 826   29 SCt 511
      En Am Con 677-678
      Sup Ct Review (1991):179-224
      Goldfarb, Joan R. Extraterritorial compliance with NEPA amid the current wave of environmental alarm. *Boston College Environmental Affairs Law Review* 18(3):543-603 (Spring 1991).
      Kramer, Larry. Extraterritorial application of American law after the insurance antitrust case: a reply to professors Lowenfeld and Trimble. *American Journal of International Law* 89(4):750-758 (October 1995).

388. Interstate Commerce Commission (ICC) v. Illinois Central Railroad Co.   January 10, 1910
      215 US 452   54 LEd 280   30 SCt 155
      En Am Con 995-996

389. St. Louis, Kansas City and Colorado Railroad Co. v. Wabash Railroad Co.   April 11, 1910
      217 US 247   54 LEd 752   30 SCt 510
      Sup Ct Review (1986):259-316

390. Weems v. United States   May 2, 1910
      217 US 349   54 LEd 793   30 SCt 544
      Death Penalty (Tushnet) 14-16, 48, 142-148R, 149-154, 158-159
      En Am Con 524-526, 2044
      Bernstein, Sidney. Supreme Court review. *Trial* 19(11):20, 22 (November 1983).
      Dripps, Donald A. Supreme Court review: cruel, unusual, and constitutional. *Trial* 28(5):87-89 (May 1992).
      Nevares-Muniz, Dora. The Eighth Amendment revisited: a model of weighted punishments. *Journal of Criminal Law and Criminology* 75(1):272-289 (Spring 1984).
      Schwartz, Charles Walter. Eighth Amendment proportionality analysis and the compelling case of William Rummel. *Journal of Criminal Law and Criminology* 71(4):378-420 (Winter 1980).

391. Shevlin-Carpenter Co. v. Minnesota   May 31, 1910
      218 US 57   54 LEd 930   30 SCt 663
      Goldberg, Andrew M. Corporate officer liability for federal environmental statute violations. *Boston College Environmental Affairs Law Review* 18(2):357-379 (Winter 1991).

392. Mobile, Jackson and Kansas City Railroad Co. v. Turnipseed   December 19, 1910
      219 US 35   55 LEd 78   31 SCt 136
      Harris, Leslie J. Constitutional limits on criminal presumptions as an expression of changing concepts of fundamental fairness. *Journal of Criminal Law and Criminology* 77(2):308-357 (Summer 1986).

393. Noble State Bank v. Haskell   January 3, 1911
      219 US 104   55 LEd 112   31 SCt 186
      En Am Con 1744-1751
      Hippler, Thomas A. Reexamining 100 years of the Supreme Court regulatory taking doctrine: the principles of "noxious use," "average reciprocity of advantage," and "bundle of rights" from Mugler to Keystone Bituminous Coal. *Boston College Environmental Affairs Law Review* 14(4):653-727 (Summer 1987).

394. Bailey v. Alabama   January 3, 1911
      219 US 219   55 LEd 191   31 SCt 145
      Const (Currie) 105-109
      En Am Con 91-92, 1378-1379

395. Muskrat v. United States   January 23, 1911
      219 US 346   55 LEd 246   31 SCt 250
      Const (Currie) 89-92, 182
      En Am Con 1288
      McDowell, Gary L. Modest remedy for judicial activism. *Public Interest* (67):3-20 (Spring 1982).

396. Hipolite Egg Co. v. United States   March 13, 1911
      220 US 45   55 LEd 364   31 SCt 364
          En Am Con 918, 1496

397. Lindsley v. Natural Carbonic Gas Co.   March 13, 1917
      220 US 61   55 LEd 369   31 SCt 337
      Katz, Stanley N. The strange birth and unlikely history of constitutional equality. *Journal of American History*
          75(3):747-762 (December 1988).

398. Dr. Miles Medical Co. v. John D. Park and Sons Co.   April 3, 1911
      220 US 373   55 LEd 502   31 SCt 376
          Almanac (1990):539-540
          Sup Ct Review (1984):69-148
      Dolan, Michael W. Congress, the executive, and the court: the great resale price maintenance affair of 1983.
          Public Administration Review 45(Special Issue):718-722 (November 1985).
      Graglia, Lino A. One hundred years of antitrust. *Public Interest* (104):50-66 (Summer 1991).
      Sheffet, Mary Jane, and Debra L. Scammon. Resale price maintenance: is it safe to suggest retail prices?
          Journal of Marketing 49(4):82-92 (Fall 1985).
      Werner, Ray O. Marketing and the Supreme Court in transition, 1982-1984. *Journal of Marketing* 49(3):97-105
          (Summer 1985).

399. United States v. Grimaud   May 1, 1911
      220 US 506   55 LEd 563   31 SCt 480
          En Am Con 870

400. Light v. United States   May 1, 1911
      220 US 523   55 LEd 570   31 SCt 485
      Baer, Susan D. The Public Trust Doctrine—a tool to make federal administrative agencies increase protection
          of public land and its resources. *Boston College Environmental Affairs Law Review* 15(2):385-436 (Winter 1988).

401. Standard Oil Co. of New Jersey v. United States   May 15, 1911
      221 US 1   55 LEd 619   31 SCt 502
          Documents (v. 2):55, 57-58R
          En Am Con 719, 1721-1722
          Guide (CQ) 95
          Landmark (v. 4):105-113R
          Sup Ct Review (1984):69-148
      Dolan, Michael W. Congress, the executive, and the court: the great resale price maintenance affair of 1983.
          Public Administration Review 45(Special Issue):718-722 (November 1985).
      Pisani, Donald J. Promotion and regulation: Constitutionalism and the American economy. *Journal of American
          History* 74(3):740-768 (December 1987).

402. West v. Kansas Natural Gas Co.   May 15, 1911
      221 US 229   55 LEd 716   31 SCt 564
      Schwartz, Edward B. Water as an article of commerce: state embargoes spring a leak under Sporhase v.
          Nebraska. *Boston College Environmental Affairs Law Review* 12(1):103-169 (Fall 1985).

403. Gompers v. Buck's Stove and Range Co.   May 15, 1911
      221 US 418   55 LEd 797   31 SCt 492
          En Am Con 852

404. Coyle v. Smith   May 29, 1911
      221 US 559   55 LEd 853   31 SCt 688
          En Am Con 512
          Guide (CQ) 135-136

O'Brien, David M. Federalism as a metaphor in the constitutional politics of public administration. *Public Administration Review* 49(5):411-419 (September/October 1989).

405. Southern Railway Co. v. United States   October 30, 1911
     222 US 20   56 LEd 72   32 SCt 2
        Guide (CQ) 90-91
        Sup Ct Review (1995):125-215

406. Curtin v. Benson   November 20, 1911
     222 US 78   56 LEd 102   32 SCt 31
     Hippler, Thomas A. Reexamining 100 years of the Supreme Court regulatory taking doctrine: the principles of "noxious use," "average reciprocity of advantage," and "bundle of rights" from Mugler to Keystone Bituminous Coal. *Boston College Environmental Affairs Law Review* 14(4):653-727 (Summer 1987).

407. Southern Railway Co. v. Reid   January 9, 1912
     222 US 424   56 LEd 257   32 SCt 140
        Sup Ct Review (1995):125-215

408. Henry v. A.B. Dick Co.   March 11, 1912
     224 US 1   56 LEd 645   32 SCt 364
        En Am Con 632-633

409. Interstate Commerce Commission (ICC) v. Goodrich Transit Co.   April 1, 1912
        Coupled with United States v. White Star Line
     224 US 194   56 LEd 729   32 SCt 436
        Sup Ct Review (1995):125-215

410. Graham v. West Virginia   May 13, 1912
     224 US 616   56 LEd 917   32 SCt 583
     Schwartz, Charles Walter. Eighth Amendment proportionality analysis and the compelling case of William Rummel. *Journal of Criminal Law and Criminology* 71(4):378-420 (Winter 1980).

411. Yazoo and Mississippi Valley Railroad Co. v. Jackson Vinegar Co.   December 2, 1912
     226 US 217   57 LEd 193   33 SCt 40
        Sup Ct Review (1981):1-39

412. Hoke v. United States   February 24, 1913
     227 US 308   57 LEd 523   33 SCt 281
        En Am Con 920, 1198
        Guide (CQ) 97

413. United States v. Pacific and Arctic Railway and Navigation Co.   April 7, 1913
     228 US 87   57 LEd 742   33 SCt 443
     Kramer, Larry. Extraterritorial application of American law after the insurance antitrust case: a reply to professors Lowenfeld and Trimble. *American Journal of International Law* 89(4):750-758 (October   1995).

414. Lewis Publishing Co. v. Morgan   June 10, 1913
        Coupled with Journal of Commerce and Commercial Bulletin v. Burleson
     229 US 288   57 LEd 1190   33 SCt 867
     Kielbowicz, Richard B. Postal subsidies for the press and the business of mass culture, 1880-1920. *Business History Review* 64(3):451-488 (September 22, 1990).

415. Sturges and Burn Manufacturing Co. v. Beauchamp   December 1, 1913
     231 US 320   58 LEd 245   34 SCt 60
        Magic 239

416. Weeks v. United States   February 24, 1914
     232 US 383   58 LEd 652   34 SCt 341
         Const Law 364-368+
         En Am Con 662-665, 1636-1637, 1947-1949, 2044
         Guide (CQ) 35
         Magic 320-322
         Sup Ct Review (1983):283-304

     Bloom, Robert M. Judicial integrity: a call for its reemergence in the adjudication of criminal cases. *Journal of Criminal Law and Criminology* 84(3):462-501 (Fall 1993).

     Couleur, Terri M. The use of illegally obtained evidence to rebut the insanity defense: a new exception to the exclusionary rule? *Journal of Criminal Law and Criminology* 74(2):391-427 (Summer 1983).

     Gest, Ted. Courts: a major battleground of social upheaval. *U.S. News & World Report* 98(3):48-50 (January 28, 1985).

     Halberstam, Malvina. Agora: international kidnaping—in defense of the Supreme Court decision in Alvarez-Machain. *American Journal of International Law* 86(4):736-746 (October 1992).

     Jensen, D. Lowell, and Rosemary Hart. The good faith restatement of the exclusionary rule. *Journal of Criminal Law and Criminology* 73(3):916-938 (Fall 1982).

     Murchison, Kenneth M. Prohibition and the Fourth Amendment: a new look at some old cases. *Journal of Criminal Law and Criminology* 73(2):471-532 (Summer 1982).

     Repa, Barbara Kate, and Joseph L. Daly. A Supreme Court case preview: does the Fourth Amendment belong in school? *Social Education* 49(1):76-78 (January 1985).

     Schlag, Pierre J. Assaults on the exclusionary rule: good faith limitations and damage remedies. *Journal of Criminal Law and Criminology* 73(3):875-915 (Fall 1982).

     Scully, Leon. Civil wrongs. *National Review* 44(10):22-24, 26-28 (May 25, 1992).

     Use of the exclusionary rule. *Congressional Digest* 71(4):104-105 (April 1992).

     Yeager, Daniel B. Search, seizure, and the positive law: expectations of privacy outside the Fourth Amendment. *Journal of Criminal Law and Criminology* 84(2):249-309 (Summer 1993).

417. Plymouth Coal Co. v. Pennsylvania   February 24, 1914
     232 US 531   58 LEd 713   34 SCt 359
     Hippler, Thomas A. Reexamining 100 years of the Supreme Court regulatory taking doctrine: the principles of "noxious use," "average reciprocity of advantage," and "bundle of rights" from Mugler to Keystone Bituminous Coal. *Boston College Environmental Affairs Law Review* 14(4):653-727 (Summer 1987).

418. German Alliance Insurance Co. v. Lewis   April 20, 1914
     233 US 389   58 LEd 1011   34 SCt 612
     Stamp, Zack. A Modest Proposal. *Best's Review* (Property/Casualty Insurance Edition) 91(9):45-50 (January 1991).

419. Richards v. Washington Terminal Co.   May 4, 1914
     233 US 546   58 LEd 1088   34 SCt 654
     Brown, Todd D. The power line plaintiff and the inverse condemnation alternative. *Boston College Environmental Affairs Law Review* 19(3):655-694 (Spring 1992).

     Hippler, Thomas A. Reexamining 100 years of the Supreme Court regulatory taking doctrine: the principles of "noxious use," "average reciprocity of advantage," and "bundle of rights" from Mugler to Keystone Bituminous Coal. *Boston College Environmental Affairs Law Review* 14(4):653-727 (Summer 1987).

     Kahn, Richard. Inverse condemnation and the highway cases: compensation for abutting landowners. *Boston College Environmental Affairs Law Review* 22(3):563- 591 (Spring 1995).

420. Atlantic Transport Co. of West Virginia v. Imbrovek   May 25, 1914
     234 US 52   58 LEd 1208   34 SCt 733
     Arsenault, Richard J., and Richard W. Beard. Bringing pleasure boat accidents under the admiralty forum. *Trial* 18(10):66-71, 88 (October 1982).

421. Houston, East and West Texas Railway Co. v. United States   June 8, 1914
         Coupled with Texas and Pacific Railway Co. v. United States
      234 US 342   58 LEd 1341   34 SCt 833
         Const (Currie) 93-96
         Documents (v. 2):95-96R
         En Am Con 613-614, 928-929, 993-994, 1681-1682
         Guide (CQ) 89-90, 95

422. Coppage v. Kansas   January 25, 1915
      236 US 1   59 LEd 441   35 SCt 240
         En Am Con 504, 2083
         Hard Choices 308
         Magic 244-245
         Sup Ct Review (1992):235-293

423. Miller v. Wilson   February 23, 1915
      236 US 373   59 LEd 628   35 SCt 342
      Zimmerman, Joan G. The jurisprudence of equality: the women's minimum wage, the first equal rights
         amendment, and Adkins v. Children's Hospital, 1905-1923. *Journal of American History* 78(1):188-225
         (June 1991).

424. United States v. Midwest Oil Co.   February 23, 1915
      236 US 459   59 LEd 673   35 SCt 309
      Lee, William P. FLPMA's legislative veto provisions and INS v. Chadha: who controls the federal lands?
         Boston College Environmental Affairs Law Review 12(4):791-821 (Summer 1985).

425. Reinman v. Little Rock   April 5, 1915
      237 US 171   59 LEd 900   35 SCt 511
      Hippler, Thomas A. Reexamining 100 years of the Supreme Court regulatory taking doctrine: the principles of
         "noxious use," "average reciprocity of advantage," and "bundle of rights" from Mugler to Keystone
         Bituminous Coal. *Boston College Environmental Affairs Law Review* 14(4):653-727 (Summer 1987).

426. Georgia v. Tennessee Copper Co.   May 10, 1915
      237 US 474   59 LEd 1054   35 SCt 631
      Feldman, Stuart P. Curbing the recalcitrant polluter: post-decree judicial agents in environmental litigation.
         Boston College Environmental Affairs Law Review 18(4):809-840 (Summer 1991).

427. Guinn and Beal v. United States   June 21, 1915
      Guinn v. United States
      238 US 347   59 LEd 1340   35 SCt 926
         En Am Con 727-728, 859, 877, 1169, 1979-1987
         Guide (CQ) 35
         Magic 146-147, 264-265
      Cassimere Jr., Ralph. Flashback: 80 years ago the NAACP goes to court. *Crisis* 102(4):34-36 (May/June 1995).
      Karst, Kenneth L. Equal protection of the laws. *Society* 24(1):24-30 (November/December 1986).

428. Hadacheck v. Sebastian   December 20, 1915
      239 US 394   60 LEd 348   36 SCt 143
      Hippler, Thomas A. Reexamining 100 years of the Supreme Court regulatory taking doctrine: the principles of
         "noxious use," "average reciprocity of advantage," and "bundle of rights" from Mugler to Keystone
         Bituminous Coal. *Boston College Environmental Affairs Law Review* 14(4):653-727 (Summer 1987).
      Skelton, Harold N. Houses on the sand: taking issues surrounding statutory restrictions on the use of oceanfront
         property. *Boston College Environmental Affairs Law Review* 18(1):125-158 (Fall 1990).

429. Bi-Metallic Investment Co. v. State Board of Equalization of Colorado   December 20, 1915
     239 US 441   60 LEd 372   36 SCt 141
     Sup Ct Review (1988):1-41
     Vanderziel, Kathleen M. The Hatfield Riders and environmental preservation: what process is due? *Boston College Environmental Affairs Law Review* 19(2):431-479 (Fall/Winter 1991).

430. Brushaber v. Union Pacific Railroad Co.   January 24, 1916
     240 US 1   60 LEd 493   36 SCt 236
     Guide (CQ) 35

431. Badders v. United States   March 6, 1916
     240 US 391   60 LEd 706   36 SCt 367
     Schwartz, Charles Walter. Eighth Amendment proportionality analysis and the compelling case of William Rummel. *Journal of Criminal Law and Criminology* 71(4):378-420 (Winter 1980).

432. New York State on Relation of Kennedy v. Becker   June 12, 1916
     New York State ex rel. Kennedy v. Becker
     241 US 556   60 LEd 1166   36 SCt 705
     Ott, Brian R. Indian fishing rights in the Pacific Northwest: the need for federal intervention. *Boston College Environmental Affairs Law Review* 14(2):313- 343 (Winter 1987).

433. Clark Distilling Co. v. Western Maryland Railway Co.   January 8, 1917
     James Clark Distilling Co. v. Western Maryland Railway Co.
           Coupled with James Clark Distilling Co. v. American Express Co.
     242 US 311   61 LEd 326   37 SCt 180
     En Am Con 293, 2042

434. Caminetti v. United States   January 15, 1917
           Coupled with Diggs v. United States
           Coupled with Hays v. United States
     242 US 470   61 LEd 442   37 SCt 192
     En Am Con 920
     Guide (CQ) 97

435. New York Central Railroad Co. v. White   March 6, 1917
     243 US 188   61 LEd 667   37 SCt 247
     En Am Con 1311, 2076-2077

436. Swift and Co. v. Hocking Valley Railway Co.   March 6, 1917
     243 US 281   61 LEd 722   37 SCt 287
     Spillenger, Clyde. Reading the judicial canon: Alexander Bickel and the book of Brandeis. *Journal of American History* 79(1):125-151 (June 1992).

437. Wilson v. New   March 19, 1917
     243 US 332   61 LEd 755   37 SCt 298
     Documents (v. 2):123-125R
     En Am Con 1229-1230, 2071
     Guide (CQ) 35, 91, 95
     Orren, Karen. The primacy of labor in American Constitutional development. *American Political Science Review* 89(2):377-388 (June 1995).

438. Utah Power and Light Co. v. United States   March 19, 1917
           Coupled with Beaver River Power Co. v. United States
           Coupled with Nunn v. United States
     243 US 389   61 LEd 791   37 SCt 387

Baer, Susan D. The Public Trust Doctrine—a tool to make federal administrative agencies increase protection of public land and its resources. *Boston College Environmental Affairs Law Review* 15(2):385-436 (Winter 1988).

439. Bunting v. Oregon   April 9, 1917
     243 US 426   61 LEd 830   37 SCt 435
          Const (Currie) 102-104
          Documents (v. 2):134-135R
          En Am Con 169-170, 602-606, 1229-1230, 1796-1803
          Guide (CQ) 35
          Magic 240-242
     Gillman, Howard. Preferred freedoms: the progressive expansion of state power and the rise of modern civil liberties jurisprudence. *Political Research Quarterly* 47(3):623-653 (September 1994).

440. Adams v. Tanner   June 11, 1917
     244 US 590   61 LEd 1336   37 SCt 662
          En Am Con 23
     Gillman, Howard. Preferred freedoms: the progressive expansion of state power and the rise of modern civil liberties jurisprudence. *Political Research Quarterly* 47(3):623-653 (September 1994).

441. Buchanan v. Warley   November 5, 1917
     245 US 60   62 LEd 149   38 SCt 16
          Const (Currie) 105-109
          En Am Con 167, 1561-1562, 1645-1646, 1729-1736
          Magic 264-265
          Making 83-85
     Karst, Kenneth L. Equal protection of the laws. *Society* 24(1):24-30 (November/December 1986).
     Spillenger, Clyde. Reading the judicial canon: Alexander Bickel and the book of Brandeis. *Journal of American History* 79(1):125-151 (June 1992).

442. Hitchman Coal and Coke Co. v. Mitchell   December 10, 1917
     245 US 229   62 LEd 260   38 SCt 65
          En Am Con 918-919, 1326, 2083
          Sup Ct Review (1992):235-293

443. Arver v. United States   January 7, 1918
          Coupled with Grahl v. United States
          Coupled with Wangerin v. United States
          Coupled with Kramer v. United States
          Coupled with Graubard v. United States
     245 US 366   62 LEd 349   38 SCt 159
          En Am Con 1647-1648
          Guide (CQ) 130
     Pfeffer, Leo. Religious exemptions. *Society* 21(4):17-22 (May/June 1984).

444. Hammer v. Dagenhart   June 3, 1918
     247 US 251   62 LEd 1101   38 SCt 529
          Const (Currie) 96-98, 173-176
          Documents (v. 2):119-122R
          En Am Con 536-537, 602-606, 893-894, 1098, 1295-1299
          Equal (Harrell) 64-65
          Guide (CQ) 35, 44, 71-73, 83-84, 95, 97-99, 103-104, 116-117, 123b
          Guide (West) (v. 6):1-2
          Landmark (v. 4):115-124R
          Magic 239

Powers 141-143+

Sup Ct Review (1995):125-215

Clinton, Robert Lowry. Judicial review, nationalism, and the commerce clause: contrasting antebellum and postbellum Supreme Court decision making. *Political Research Quarterly* 47(4):857-876 (December 1994).

O'Brien, David M. Federalism as a metaphor in the constitutional politics of public administration. *Public Administration Review* 49(5):411-419 (September/October 1989).

Orren, Karen. The primacy of labor in American constitutional development. *American Political Science Review* 89(2):377-388 (June 1995).

Pawelek, Dick. Call five cases that shaped Congress. *Scholastic Update* (Teachers' Edition) 119(9):12-14 (January 12, 1987).

Spillenger, Clyde. Reading the judicial canon: Alexander Bickel and the book of Brandeis. *Journal of American History* 79(1):125-151 (June 1992).

445. International News Service v. Associated Press   December 23, 1918
     248 US 215   63 LEd 211   39 SCt 68
        Sup Ct Review (1983):509-581

446. Schenck v. United States   March 3, 1919
        Coupled with Baer v. United States
     249 US 47   63 LEd 470   39 SCt 247
        Brennan 143-150
        Const (Currie) 115-120
        Const Law 110-111R+
        Documents (v. 2):146-147R
        En Am Con 298-301, 514-516, 652-653, 730-738, 968-970, 1623-1624, 1804-1807
        Equal (Harrell) 67-69
        Fighting 212-224, 233-235+
        First 123-130
        Fourth 70-72+
        Guide (CQ) 35-36
        Guide (West) (v.9):106
        Landmark (v. 3):39-45R
        Magic 262-264
        Make 67-79+
        Sup Ct Ind 24-25+
        Sup Ct Review (1991):303-390; (1994):209-245
        Tolerant 166-168, 176-179+

Cox, Archibald. First Amendment. *Society* 24(1):8-15 (November/December 1986).

Gillman, Howard. Preferred freedoms: the progressive expansion of state power and the rise of modern civil liberties jurisprudence. *Political Research Quarterly* 47(3):623-653 (September 1994).

Greenawalt, Kent. Free speech in the United States and Canada. *Law and Contemporary Problems* 55(1):5-33 (Winter 1992).

Novick, Sheldon M. Holmes, Brennan, and the flag-burning cases. *Trial* 26(11):24-29 (November 1990).

Orren, Karen. The primacy of labor in American constitutional development. *American Political Science Review* 89(2):377-388 (June 1995).

447. United States v. Doremus   March 3, 1919
     249 US 86   63 LEd 493   39 SCt 214
        Const (Currie) 98-101
        En Am Con 575, 906, 1869-1871
        Guide (CQ) 115-116

Moss, David A. Kindling a flame under federalism: progressive reformers, corporate elites, and the phosphorous match campaign of 1909-1912. *Business History Review* 68(2):244-275 (Summer 1994).

448. Frohwerk v. United States   March 10, 1919
      249 US 204   63 LEd 561   39 SCt 249
          En Am Con 808-809, 1804-1807
          Fourth 70-78+
          Magic 262-264
          Sup Ct Ind 25-26+
          Sup Ct Review (1991):303-390

449. Debs v. United States   March 10, 1919
      249 US 211   63 LEd 566   39 SCt 252
          Const Law 111-112+
          Court Const 214-219
          En Am Con 544-545, 1804-1807
          Fighting 212, 216-217, 219-235+
          Fourth 70-72+
          Magic 262-264
          Make 67-89
          Sup Ct Ind 25+
          Sup Ct Review (1991):303-390
      Gillman, Howard. Preferred freedoms: the progressive expansion of state power and the rise of modern civil
          liberties jurisprudence. *Political Research Quarterly* 47(3):623-653 (September 1994).
      Lewis, Anthony. Staving off the silencers. *New York Times Magazine* (section 6, part 1):72-77 (December 1,
          1991).

450. United States v. Colgate and Co.   June 2, 1919
      250 US 300   63 LEd 992   39 SCt 465
          Sup Ct Review (1984):69-148
      Sheffet, Mary Jane, and Debra L. Scammon. Resale price maintenance: is it safe to suggest retail prices?
          Journal of Marketing 49(4):82-92 (Fall 1985).

451. Abrams v. United States   November 10, 1919
      250 US 616   63 LEd 1173   40 SCt 17
          Brennan 150-153
          Const (Currie) 120-125
          Const Law 112-114R+
          Documents (v. 2):148-149R
          En Am Con 7-8, 730-738, 790-797, 1203-1204, 1804-1807
          Fighting 1-242+
          First 123-130
          Guide (West) (v. 1):22-23
          Jerry 219-220+
          Magic 262-264
          Make 67-89+
          One 299-302R
          Sup Ct Ind 25-26+
          Sup Ct Review (1991):303-390; (1994):209-245
          Tolerant 15-23+
      Bork, Robert H. What to do about the First Amendment. *Commentary* 99(2):23-29 (February 1995).
      Cox, Archibald. First Amendment. *Society* 24(1):8-15 (November/December 1986).
      Gillman, Howard. Preferred freedoms: the progressive expansion of state power and the rise of modern civil
          liberties jurisprudence. *Political Research Quarterly* 47(3):623-653 (September 1994).
      Novick, Sheldon M. Holmes, Brennan, and the flag-burning cases. *Trial* 26(11):24-29 (November 1990).
      Orren, Karen. The primacy of labor in American constitutional development. *American Political Science
          Review* 89(2):377-388 (June 1995).

Rabinove, Samuel, Josef Joffe, Sheldon F. Gottlieb, Adam Simms, Stephen F. Rohde, Jeffrey Valle, and Robert H. Bork. The First Amendment. [Editorial] *Commentary* 99(5):7-15 (May 1995).

452. Stroud v. United States   November 24, 1919
     251 US 15   64 LEd 103   40 SCt 50
     Lane, James R. Supreme Court review: Fifth Amendment—the covert narrowing of double jeopardy precedent: the Supreme Court's real reason for hearing Schiro v. Farley. *Journal of Criminal Law and Criminology* 85(4):909-935 (Spring 1995).

453. Los Angeles v. Los Angeles Gas and Electric Corp. December 8, 1919
     City of Los Angeles v. Los Angeles Gas and Electric Corp.
     251 US 32   64 LEd 121   40 SCt 76
     Hippler, Thomas A. Reexamining 100 years of the Supreme Court regulatory taking doctrine: the principles of "noxious use," "average reciprocity of advantage," and "bundle of rights" from Mugler to Keystone Bituminous Coal. *Boston College Environmental Affairs Law Review* 14(4):653-727 (Summer 1987).

454. Hamilton v. Kentucky Distilleries and Warehouse Co.   December 15, 1919
          Coupled with Dryfoos v. Edwards
     251 US 146   64 LEd 194   40 SCt 106
     Const (Currie) 98-101

455. Silverthorne Lumber Co. v. United States   January 26, 1920
     251 US 385   64 LEd 319   40 SCt 182
     En Am Con 1628-1635, 1683
     Cohn, William M. Supreme Court review: Sixth Amendment—inevitable discovery: a valuable but easily abused exception to the exclusionary rule. *Journal of Criminal Law and Criminology* 75(3):729-754 (Fall 1984).
     Yeager, Daniel B. Search, seizure, and the positive law: expectations of privacy outside the Fourth Amendment. *Journal of Criminal Law and Criminology* 84(2):249-309 (Summer 1993).

456. Schaeffer v. United States   March 1, 1920
          Coupled with Vogel v. United States
          Coupled with Werner v. United States
          Coupled with Darkow v. United States
          Coupled with Lemke v. United States
     251 US 466   64 LEd 360   40 SCt 259
     Fighting 263-271
     Sup Ct Review (1991):303-390

457. Eisner v. Macomber   March 8, 1920
     252 US 189   64 LEd 521   40 SCt 189
     En Am Con 616, 1685-1686
     Guide (CQ) 114

458. Pierce v. United States   March 8, 1920
     252 US 239   64 LEd 542   40 SCt 205
     Fighting 203-204, 263-271
     Sup Ct Ind 27, 30+
     Sup Ct Review (1991):303-390

459. Missouri v. Holland   April 19, 1920
     252 US 416   64 LEd 641   40 SCt 382
     Const (Currie) 98-101
     Documents (v. 2):163-164R
     En Am Con 637-639, 1031-1038, 1267-1268, 1910-1911

Guide (CQ) 133

Sup Ct Review (1994):295-343

Ott, Brian R. Indian fishing rights in the Pacific Northwest: the need for federal intervention. *Boston College Environmental Affairs Law Review* 14(2):313- 343 (Winter 1987).

460. Hawke v. Smith   June 1, 1920
     253 US 221   64 LEd 871   40 SCt 495
     Guide (CQ) 152-153
     Gaugush, Bill. Principles governing the interpretation and exercise of Article 5 powers. *Western Political Quarterly* 35(2):212-221 (June 1982).

461. Hawke v. Smith   June 1, 1920
     253 US 231, 232   64 LEd 877   40 SCt 498
     Gaugush, Bill. Principles governing the interpretation and exercise of Article 5 powers. *Western Political Quarterly* 35(2):212-221 (June 1982).

462. Green v. Frazier   June 1, 1920
     253 US 233   64 LEd 878   40 SCt 499
     Documents (v. 2):170-172R

463. Rhode Island v. Palmer   June 7, 1920
     National Prohibition Cases
            Coupled with New Jersey v. Palmer
            Coupled with Dempsey v. Boynton
            Coupled with Kentucky Distilleries and Warehouse Co. v. Gregory
            Coupled with Christian Feigenspan, Corp. v. Bodine
            Coupled with Sawyer v. Manitowoc Products Co.
            Coupled with St. Louis Brewing Association v. Moore
     253 US 350   64 LEd 946   40 SCt 486
     Const (Currie) 176-181
     Documents (v. 2):156-157R
     En Am Con 614-615
     Guide (CQ) 151-152
     Magic 250-251
     Gaugush, Bill. Principles governing the interpretation and exercise of Article 5 powers. *Western Political Quarterly* 35(2):212-221 (June 1982).

464. F.S. Royster Guano Co. v. Virginia   June 7, 1920
     253 US 412   64 LEd 989   40 SCt 560
     Lamb, Charles M. Legal foundations of civil rights and pluralism in America. *Annals of the American Academy of Political and Social Science* 454:13-25 (March 1981).

465. Federal Trade Commission (FTC) v. Gratz   June 7, 1920
     253 US 421   64 LEd 993   40 SCt 572
     En Am Con 718-719
     Tedlow, Richard S. From competitor to consumer: the changing focus of federal regulation of advertising, 1914-1938. *Business History Review* 55(1): 35-58 (Spring 1981).

466. Gilbert v. Minnesota   December 13, 1920
     254 US 325   65 LEd 287   41 SCt 125
     Fighting 263-271
     First 126-130
     Sup Ct Review (1991):303-390
     Gillman, Howard. Preferred freedoms: the progressive expansion of state power and the rise of modern civil liberties jurisprudence. *Political Research Quarterly* 47(3):623-653 (September 1994).

467. Duplex Printing Press v. Deering   January 3, 1921
      254 US 443   65 LEd 349   41 SCt 172
         Documents (v. 2):177-178R
         En Am Con 593, 1326
         Guide (CQ) 95-96
      Orren, Karen. The primacy of labor in American constitutional development. *American Political Science Review* 89(2):377-388 (June 1995).

468. Gouled v. United States   February 28, 1921
      255 US 298   65 LEd 647   41 SCt 261
      Murchison, Kenneth M. Prohibition and the Fourth Amendment: a new look at some old cases. *Journal of Criminal Law and Criminology* 73(2):471-532 (Summer 1982).
      Yeager, Daniel B. Search, seizure, and the positive law: expectations of privacy outside the Fourth Amendment. *Journal of Criminal Law and Criminology* 84(2):249-309 (Summer 1993).

469. Supreme Tribe of Ben-Hur v. Cauble   March 7, 1921
      255 US 356   65 LEd 673   41 SCt 338
         Sup Ct Review (1983):459-507

470. Economy Light and Power Co. v. United States   April 11, 1921
      256 US 113   65 LEd 847   41 SCt 409
      Proctor, Michael G. Section 10 of the Rivers and Harbors Act and Western Water Allocations—are the western states up a creek without a permit? *Boston College Environmental Affairs Law Review* 10(1):111-182 (1982-83).

471. Block v. Hirsh   April 18, 1921
      256 US 135   65 LEd 865   41 SCt 458
      Hippler, Thomas A. Reexamining 100 years of the Supreme Court regulatory taking doctrine: the principles of "noxious use," "average reciprocity of advantage," and "bundle of rights" from Mugler to Keystone Bituminous Coal. *Boston College Environmental Affairs Law Review* 14(4):653-727 (Summer 1987).

472. Marcus Brown Holding Co., Inc. v. Feldman   April 18, 1921
      256 US 170   65 LEd 877   41 SCt 465
      Hippler, Thomas A. Reexamining 100 years of the Supreme Court regulatory taking doctrine: the principles of "noxious use," "average reciprocity of advantage," and "bundle of rights" from Mugler to Keystone Bituminous Coal. *Boston College Environmental Affairs Law Review* 14(4):653-727 (Summer 1987).

473. New York v. New Jersey   May 2, 1921
      256 US 296   65 LEd 937   41 SCt 492
      Briggett, Marlissa S. State supremacy in the federal realm: the Interstate Compact. *Boston College Environmental Affairs Law Review* 18(4):751-772 (Summer 1991).

474. Dillon v. Gloss   May 16, 1921
      256 US 368   65 LEd 994   41 SCt 510
         Almanac (1992):58
         Amending 250-256
         Guide (CQ) 152, 152b
      Gaugush, Bill. Principles governing the interpretation and exercise of Article 5 powers. *Western Political Quarterly* 35(2):212-221 (June 1982).

475. Burdeau v. McDowell   June 1, 1921
      256 US 465   65 LEd 1048   41 SCt 574
      Murchison, Kenneth M. Prohibition and the Fourth Amendment: a new look at some old cases. *Journal of Criminal Law and Criminology* 73(2):471-532 (Summer 1982).

476. Western Fuel Co. v. Garcia   December 5, 1921
      257 US 233   66 LEd 210   42 SCt 89
      Edelman, Paul S. Wrongful death on the high seas: Tallentire says federal law governs. *Trial* 23(4):58-61
         (April 1987).

477. Truax v. Corrigan   December 19, 1921
      257 US 312   66 LEd 254   42 SCt 124
         Const (Currie) 139-143, 263-266
         Documents (v. 2):174-177R
         En Am Con 1921-1922

478. Railroad Commission of Wisconsin v. Chicago, Burlington and Quincy Railroad Co.   February 27, 1922
      257 US 563   66 LEd 371   42 SCt 232
         Documents (v. 2):167-168R

479. Fairchild v. Hughes   February 27, 1922
      258 US 126   66 LEd 499   42 SCt 274
      Gaugush, Bill. Principles governing the interpretation   and exercise of Article 5 powers. *Western Political
         Quarterly* 35(2):212-221 (June 1982).

480. Leser v. Garnett   February 27, 1922
      258 US 130   66 LEd 505   42 SCt 217
         Guide (CQ) 152-153
      Gaugush, Bill. Principles governing the interpretation and exercise of Article 5 powers. *Western Political
         Quarterly* 35(2):212-221 (June 1982).

481. United States v. Balint   March 27, 1922
      258 US 250   66 LEd 604   42 SCt 301
      Webber, Rebecca S. Element analysis applied to environmental crimes: what did they know and when did they
         know it? *Boston College Environmental Affairs Law Review* 16(1):53-93 (Fall 1988).

482. Balzac v. Porto Rico   April 10, 1922
      258 US 298   66 LEd 627   42 SCt 343
         Documents (v. 2):178-181R

483. Stafford v. Wallace   May 1, 1922
      258 US 495   66 LEd 735   42 SCt 397
         En Am Con 1719-1720, 1787-1788
         Guide (CQ) 95
      Orren, Karen. The primacy of labor in American constitutional development. *American Political Science
         Review* 89(2):377-388 (June 1995).

484. Atherton Mills v. Johnston   May 15, 1922
      259 US 13   66 LEd 814   42 SCt 422
      Spillenger, Clyde. Reading the judicial canon: Alexander Bickel and the book of Brandeis. *Journal of American
         History* 79(1):125-151 (June 1992).

485. Bailey v. Drexel Furniture Co.   May 15, 1922
      259 US 20   66 LEd 817   42 SCt 449
         Documents (v. 2):153-154R
         En Am Con 92
         Guide (CQ) 36, 71-73, 95, 116-117, 123b
         Magic 239
      Spillenger, Clyde. Reading the judicial canon: Alexander Bickel and the book of Brandeis. *Journal of American
         History* 79(1):125-151 (June 1992).

486. Hill v. Wallace   May 15, 1922
     259 US 44   66 LEd 822   42 SCt 453

     Orren, Karen. The primacy of labor in American constitutional development. *American Political Science Review* 89(2):377-388 (June 1995).

     Spillenger, Clyde. Reading the judicial canon: Alexander Bickel and the book of Brandeis. *Journal of American History* 79(1):125-151 (June 1992).

487. Federal Baseball Club of Baltimore, Inc. v. National League   May 29, 1922
     of Professional Baseball Clubs
     259 US 200   66 LEd 898   42 SCt 465
     Almanac (1995):3-45-46
     Law 63-64
     Owners 55-56+

     Kaplan, David A. Congress takes a school. *Newsweek* 120(24):67 (December 14, 1992).

488. United Mine Workers v. Coronado Coal Co.   June 5, 1922
     259 US 344   66 LEd 975   42 SCt 570
     En Am Con 1937-1938

489. Prudential Insurance Co. v. Cheek   June 5, 1922
     259 US 530   66 LEd 1044   42 SCt 516

     Cox, Archibald. First Amendment. *Society* 24(1):8-15 (November/December 1986).

490. Jackson v. Rosenbaum Co.   October 23, 1922
     260 US 22   67 LEd 107   43 SCt 9

     Hippler, Thomas A. Reexamining 100 years of the Supreme Court regulatory taking doctrine: the principles of "noxious use," "average reciprocity of advantage," and "bundle of rights" from Mugler to Keystone Bituminous Coal. *Boston College Environmental Affairs Law Review* 14(4):653-727 (Summer 1987).

491. United States v. Bowman   November 13, 1922
     260 US 94   67 LEd 149   43 SCt 39

     Goldfarb, Joan R. Extraterritorial compliance with NEPA amid the current wave of environmental alarm. *Boston College Environmental Affairs Law Review* 18(3):543-603 (Spring 1991).

492. Keogh v. Chicago and Northwestern Railway   November 13, 1922
     260 US 156   67 LEd 183   43 SCt 47
     Almanac (1986):12A

     Moskowitz, Daniel B. Breaking down immunity to antitrust. *Business Week* (Industrial/Technology Edition) (2936):34-36 (March 10, 1986).

493. Ozawa v. United States   November 13, 1922
     260 US 178   67 LEd 199   43 SCt 65
     Brennan 267-270
     Japanese 46, 280-281
     Just War 11-13

494. Yamashita v. Hinkle   November 13, 1922
     260 US 199   67 LEd 209   43 SCt 69
     Japanese 46, 355

495. Heisler v. Thomas Colliery Co.   November 27, 1922
     260 US 245   67 LEd 237   43 SCt 83

     Powers, Carol L. State taxation of energy resources: affirmation of Commonwealth Edison Co. v. Montana. *Boston College Environmental Affairs Law Review* 10(2):503-564 (September 1982).

496. Portsmouth Harbor Land and Hotel Co. v. United States   December 4, 1922
     260 US 327   67 LEd 287   43 SCt 135
     Brown, Todd D. The power line plaintiff and the inverse condemnation alternative. *Boston College Environmental Affairs Law Review* 19(3):655-694 (Spring 1992).

497. United States v. Lanza   December 11, 1922
     260 US 377   67 LEd 314   43 SCt 141
     En Am Con 1124

498. Pennsylvania Coal Co. v. Mahon   December 11, 1922
     260 US 393   67 LEd 322   43 SCt 158
     En Am Con 630-632, 998-999, 1744-1751, 1855-1857, 2088-2089
     New Right (Schwartz) 116-120+
     Sup Ct Review (1987):1-46
     Cleaves, Robert E., IV. Constitutional protection for the utility investor: the confiscation doctrine after Cleveland Electric Illuminating Co. v. Public Utilities Commission of Ohio. *Boston College Environmental Affairs Law Review* 12(3):527-558 (Spring 1985).
     Cohen, Jonathan E. A constitutional safety valve: the variance in zoning and land-use based environmental controls. *Boston College Environmental Affairs Law Review* 22(2):307-364 (Winter 1995).
     Folsom, Robin E. Executive Order 12,630: a president's manipulation of the Fifth Amendment's just compensation clause to achieve control over executive agency regulatory decisionmaking. *Boston College Environmental Affairs Law Review* 20(4):639-697 (Summer 1993).
     Halper, Louise A. Law: A new view of regulatory takings? *Environment* 36(1):2-5, 39-40 (January/February 1994).
     Hippler, Thomas A. Reexamining 100 years of the Supreme Court regulatory taking doctrine: the principles of "noxious use," "average reciprocity of advantage," and "bundle of rights" from Mugler to Keystone Bituminous Coal. *Boston College Environmental Affairs Law Review* 14(4):653-727 (Summer 1987).
     LaRusso, Joseph. "Paying for the change": First English Evangelical Lutheran Church of Glendale v. County of Los Angeles and the calculation of interim damages for regulatory takings. *Boston College Environmental Affairs Law Review* 17(3):551-583 (Spring 1990).
     Note: the public use test: would a ban on the possession of firearms require just compensation? *Law and Contemporary Problems* 49(1):223-249 (Winter 1986).
     Singer, Saul Jay. Flooding the Fifth Amendment: the National Flood Insurance Program and the "takings" clause. *Boston College Environmental Affairs Law Review* 17(2):323-379 (Winter 1990).
     Skelton, Harold N. Houses on the sand: taking issues surrounding statutory restrictions on the use of oceanfront property. *Boston College Environmental Affairs Law Review* 18(1):125-158 (Fall 1990).

499. Moore v. Dempsey   February 19, 1923
     261 US 86   67 LEd 543   43 SCt 265
     Civil 20th 3, 7, 37-44R
     En Am Con 516-522, 1277-1278
     Equal (Harrell) 71-72, 81
     Guide (CQ) 37

500. Cramer v. United States   February 19, 1923
     261 US 219   67 LEd 622   43 SCt 342
     Const (Currie) 294-299
     En Am Con 910, 1903-1909
     Orlando, Caroline L. Aboriginal title claims in the Indian Claims Commission: U.S. v. Dann and its due process limitations. *Boston College Environmental Affairs Law Review* 13(2):241-280 (Winter 1986).

501. Adkins v. Children's Hospital of the District of Columbia   April 9, 1923
          Coupled with Adkins v. Lyons
     261 US 525   67 LEd 785   43 SCt 394
     Documents (v. 2):187-191R

En Am Con 25-27, 602-606, 774-780, 1229-1230, 1796-1803
Equal (Harrell) 77-79
Guide (CQ) 37, 42
Magic 242-243, 277-279
Minnesota 114-118+
Quarrels 268-280

Brown, Martin, Jens Christiansen, and Peter Philips. The decline of child labor in the U.S. fruit and vegetable canning industry: law or economics? *Business History Review* 66(4):723-771 (December 22, 1992).

Caldeira, Gregory A. Public opinion and the U.S. Supreme Court: FDR's court-packing plan. *American Political Science Review* 81(4):1139-1153 (December 1987).

Leuchtenburg, William Edward. The case of the chambermaid and the nine old men. *American Heritage* 38(1):34-41 (December 1986).

Zimmerman, Joan G. The jurisprudence of equality: the women's minimum wage, the first equal rights amendment, and Adkins v. Children's Hospital, 1905-1923. *Journal of American History* 78(1):188-225 (June 1991).

502. Oliver Iron Mining Co. v. Lord   May 7, 1923
        Coupled with Cleveland-Cliffs Iron Co. v. Lord
        Coupled with Mesaba-Cliffs Iron Mining Co. v. Lord
        Coupled with Bennett Mining Co. v. Lord
        Coupled with Republic Iron and Steel Co. v. Lord
        Coupled with Biwabic Mining Co. v. Lord
        Coupled with Interstate Iron Co. v. Lord
    262 US 172   67 LEd 929   43 SCt 526
    Powers, Carol L. State taxation of energy resources: affirmation of Commonwealth Edison Co. v. Montana. *Boston College Environmental Affairs Law Review* 10(2):503-564 (September 1982).

503. Hart v. B.F. Keith Vaudeville Exchange   May 21, 1923
    262 US 271   67 LEd 977   43 SCt 540
        Law 63-64

504. Missouri ex rel. Southwestern Bell Telephone Co. v. Public Service   May 21, 1923
        Commission of Missouri
    262 US 276   67 LEd 981   43 SCt 544
    Cleaves, Robert E., IV. Constitutional protection for the utility investor: the confiscation doctrine after Cleveland Electric Illuminating Co. v. Public Utilities Commission of Ohio. *Boston College Environmental Affairs Law Review* 12(3):527-558 (Spring 1985).

505. Meyer v. Nebraska   June 4, 1923
    262 US 390   67 LEd 1042   43 SCt 625
        Const (Currie) 153-154, 252-253
        En Am Con 686-688, 782, 1090-1093, 1252, 1538-1545, 1796-1803
        Hard Choices 131-133+
        Liberty 242-245+
    Bernstein, Sidney. Supreme Court review. *Trial* 21(4):14-15 (April 1985).

    Gillman, Howard. Preferred freedoms: the progressive expansion of state power and the rise of modern civil liberties jurisprudence. *Political Research Quarterly* 47(3):623-653 (September 1994).

    McKown, Delos Banning. Deism and the Supreme Court. *Humanist* 52(2):25-28,48 (March/April 1992).

    Minow, Martha. We, the family: constitutional rights and American families. *Journal of American History* 74(3):959-983 (December 1987).

    Van Alstyne, William W. Academic freedom and the First Amendment in the Supreme Court of the United States: an unhurried historical review. *Law and Contemporary Problems* 53(3):79-154 (Summer 1990).

    Wulf, Melvin L. On the origins of privacy. *Nation* 252(20):700, 702-704 (May 27, 1991).

506. Bartels v. Iowa   June 4, 1923
      Coupled with Bohning v. Iowa
      Coupled with Pohl v. Ohio
      Coupled with Nebraska District of Evangelical Lutheran Synod v. McKelvie
      262 US 404   67 LEd 1047   43 SCt 628
      Van Alstyne, William W. Academic freedom and the First Amendment in the Supreme Court of the United
      States: an unhurried historical review. *Law and Contemporary Problems* 53(3):79-154 (Summer 1990).

507. Massachusetts v. Mellon   June 4, 1923
      Coupled with Frothingham v. Mellon
      262 US 447   67 LEd 1078   43 SCt 597
      Const (Currie) 442-446
      En Am Con 503-504, 809, 1871-1872
      Godless 67-69
      Guide (CQ) 37, 118-119
      Alpert, Peter A. Citizen suits under the Clean Air Act: universal standing for the uninjured private attorney
      general? *Boston College Environmental Affairs Law Review* 16(2):283-328 (Winter 1988).
      Quirk, William J. Judicial dictatorship. *Society* 31(2):34-38 (January/February 1994).

508. Charles Wolff Packing Co. v. Court of Industrial Relations   June 11, 1923
      Wolff Packing Co. v. Court of Industrial Relations
      262 US 522   67 LEd 1103   43 SCt 630
      Documents (v. 2):186-187R
      En Am Con 2073

509. Terance v. Thompson   November 12, 1923
      263 US 197   68 LEd 255   44 SCt 15
      Japanese 47, 327-328

510. Porterfield v. Webb   November 12, 1923
      263 US 225   68 LEd 278   44 SCt 21
      Japanese 45, 47, 284-285

511. Webb v. O'Brien   November 19, 1923
      263 US 313   68 LEd 318   44 SCt 112
      Japanese 45, 47, 349

512. Frick v. Webb   November 19, 1923
      263 US 326   68 LEd 323   44 SCt 115
      Japanese 45, 47, 139

513. Dayton-Goose Creek Railway Co. v. United States   January 7, 1924
      263 US 456   68 LEd 388   44 SCt 169
      Documents (v. 2):169-170R
      En Am Con 543, 652

514. LaCoste v. Department of Conservation of Louisiana   January 7, 1924
      263 US 545   68 LEd 437   44 SCt 186
      Grady, Kevin T. Commonwealth of Puerto Rico v. SS Zoe Colocotroni: state actions for damage to non-
      commercial living natural resources. *Boston College Environmental Affairs Law Review* 9(2):397-429 (1980-
      1981).

515. Jay Burns Baking Co. v. Bryan   April 14, 1924
      264 US 504   68 LEd 813   44 SCt 412
      En Am Con 183

Guide (CQ) 38
Quarrels 204-206

516. Hester v. United States   May 5, 1924
 265 US 57   68 LEd 898   44 SCt 445
 Const (Currie) 163-164, 167-169

Andersen, Robert M. Technology, pollution control, and EPA access to commercial property: a constitutional and policy framework. *Boston College Environmental Affairs Law Review* 17(1):1-74 (Fall 1989).

Bazarian, Stephen C. Dow Chemical Company v. United States and aerial surveillance by the EPA: an argument for post-surveillance notice to the observed. *Boston College Environmental Affairs Law Review* 15(3-4):593-626 (Spring 1988).

Murchison, Kenneth M. Prohibition and the Fourth Amendment: a new look at some old cases. *Journal of Criminal Law and Criminology* 73(2):471-532 (Summer 1982).

517. Asakura v. City of Seattle   May 26, 1924
 265 US 332   68 LEd 1041   44 SCt 515
 Japanese 47, 106-107

518. Sanitary District of Chicago v. United States   January 5, 1925
 266 US 405   69 LEd 352   45 SCt 176

Proctor, Michael G. Section 10 of the Rivers and Harbors Act and Western Water Allocations—are the western states up a creek without a permit? *Boston College Environmental Affairs Law Review* 10(1):111-182 (1982-83).

519. Hygrade Provision Co., Inc. v. Sherman   January 5, 1925
      Coupled with Lewis and Fox Co. v. Sherman
      Coupled with Satz v. Sherman
 266 US 497   69 LEd 402   45 SCt 141

Sullivan, Catherine Beth. Are kosher food laws constitutionally kosher? *Boston College Environmental Affairs Law Review* 21(1):201-245 (Fall 1993).

520. Ex Parte Grossman   March 2, 1925
 267 US 87   69 LEd 527   45 SCt 332
 En Am Con 872

521. Carroll v. United States   March 2, 1925
 267 US 132   69 LEd 543   45 SCt 280
 Burger Court 75-79+, 279
 Const (Currie) 165-167
 Const Law 358-361+
 En Am Con 155, 216, 1628-1635, 1947-1949

Bernstein, Sidney, and Michael Eisenstein. 1982 Supreme Court update: the criminal law. *Trial* 18(9):45-50, 81 (September 1982).

Katz, Lewis R. United States v. Ross: evolving standards for warrantless searches. *Journal of Criminal Law and Criminology* 74(1):172-208 (Spring 1983).

Murchison, Kenneth M. Prohibition and the Fourth Amendment: a new look at some old cases. *Journal of Criminal Law and Criminology* 73(2):471-532 (Summer 1982).

Nugent, Shane V. Supreme Court review: Fourth Amendment—function over form: the automobile exception applied to motor homes. *Journal of Criminal Law and Criminology* 76(4):955-971 (Winter 1985).

Ray, Kent S. Supreme Court review: Fourth Amendment—overextending the automobile exception to justify the warrantless search of closed containers in cars. *Journal of Criminal Law and Criminology* 73(4):1430-1451 (Winter 1982).

Searching Cars: court gives police more power. *Time* 119(24):70 (June 14, 1982).

522. Brooks v. United States   March 9, 1925
      267 US 432   69 LEd 699   45 SCt 345
          Const (Currie) 175-176

523. Steele v. United States, No. 1   April 13, 1925
      267 US 498   69 LEd 757   45 SCt 414
      Murchison, Kenneth M. Prohibition and the Fourth Amendment: a new look at some old cases. *Journal of
          Criminal Law and Criminology* 73(2):471-532 (Summer 1982).

524. Steele v. United States, No. 2   April 13, 1925
      267 US 505   69 LEd 761   45 SCt 417
      Murchison, Kenneth M. Prohibition and the Fourth Amendment: a new look at some old cases. *Journal of
          Criminal Law and Criminology* 73(2):471-532 (Summer 1982).

525. Cockrill v. California   May 11, 1925
      268 US 258   69 LEd 944   45 SCt 490
          Japanese 47

526. Coronado Coal Co. v. United Mine Workers of America   May 25, 1925
      268 US 295   69 LEd 963   45 SCt 551
          En Am Con 1937-1938

527. Dumbra v. United States   May 25, 1925
      268 US 435   69 LEd 1032   455 SCt 546
      Murchison, Kenneth M. Prohibition and the Fourth Amendment: a new look at some old cases. *Journal of
          Criminal Law and Criminology* 73(2):471-532 (Summer 1982).

528. Pierce v. Society of Sisters of Holy Names of Jesus and Mary   June 1, 1925
          Coupled with Pierce v. Hill Military Academy
      268 US 510   69 LEd 1070   45 SCt 571
          Abortion (Frohock) 62
          Abortion Am 8+
          Am Educators 408
          Documents (v. 2):197-198R
          En Am Con 608-612, 1389, 1538-1545, 1650-1658, 1796-1803
          Godless 63-64
          Guide (CQ) 38
          Hard Choices 131-133+
          Liberty 241-245+
          Sup Ct Church 31-35R
      Abram, Morris B. Is "strict separation" too strict? *Public Interest* (82):81-90 (Winter 1986).
      Gillman, Howard. Preferred freedoms: the progressive expansion of state power and the rise of modern civil
          liberties jurisprudence. *Political Research Quarterly* 47(3):623-653 (September 1994).
      Glazer, Nathan. The Constitution and American diversity. *Public Interest* (86):10-21 (Winter 1987).
      Hammond, Phillip E. The courts and secular humanism. *Society* 21(4):11-16 (May/June 1984).
      Lines, Patricia M. The new private schools and their historic purpose. *Phi Delta Kappan* 67(5):373-379
          (January 1986).
      Minow, Martha. We, the family: constitutional rights and American families. *Journal of American History*
          74(3):959-983 (December 1987).
      Pfeffer, Leo. Religious exemptions. *Society* 21(4):17-22 (May/June 1984).
      Rabinove, Samuel, William E. Johnston, Jr., Lawrence E. Mitchell, Christopher C. Faille, Wallace M. Rudolph,
          David A. Frolick, Ronald K. L. Collins, Herb Greer, H. Elliot Wales, Thomas A. Bustin, and Lino A. Graglia.
          The Constitution and the Court. [Editorial] *Commentary* 81(6):2-11 (June 1986).
      Rayer, Thomas A. The bicentennial and church-related schools. *America* 157(17):427-429, 438 (December 5,
          1987).

Wulf, Melvin L. On the origins of privacy. *Nation* 252(20):700, 702-704 (May 27, 1991).

529. Gitlow v. New York   June 8, 1925
    268 US 652   69 LEd 1138   45 SCt 625
       Amending 203-213
       Const (Currie) 154-160, 252-253, 255-257
       Const (Friendly) 78-79
       Const Law 116-121R+
       Documents (v. 2):198-201R
       En Am Con 88-89, 730-738, 782-789, 847, 968-970, 1804-1807
       Equal (Harrell) 68-69
       Establishment 166-167+
       First 126-135, 315-316
       Guide (CQ) 38
       Guide (West) (v. 5):383-384
       Let Us 114
       Magic 262-264
       Make 79-89+
       Minnesota 96-97+
       Original (Davis) 66-69, 91+
       Sup Ct Ind 30-31+
       Sup Ct Review (1994):209-245

Bork, Robert H. What to do about the First Amendment. *Commentary* 99(2):23-29 (February 1995).

Cox, Archibald. First Amendment. *Society* 24(1):8-15 (November/December 1986).

Freidman, Robert. Freedom of the press: how far can they go? *American Heritage* 33(6):16-26 (October/ November 1982).

The other amendment. *Life* 14 (13 Special Issue):32 (Fall 1991).

Rabinove, Samuel, William E. Johnston, Jr., Lawrence E. Mitchell, Christopher C. Faille, Wallace M. Rudolph, David A. Frolick, Ronald K. L. Collins, Herb Greer, H. Elliot Wales, Thomas A. Bustin, and Lino A. Graglia. The Constitution and the Court. [Editorial] *Commentary* 81(6):2-11 (June 1986).

530. Agnello v. United States   October 12, 1925
    269 US 20   70 LEd 145   46 SCt 4
       En Am Con 37, 1636-1637

Murchison, Kenneth M. Prohibition and the Fourth Amendment: a new look at some old cases. *Journal of Criminal Law and Criminology* 73(2):471-532 (Summer 1982).

531. White v. Mechanics Securities Corp.   December 14, 1925
       Coupled with United States v. Securities Corporation General
       Coupled with White v. Securities Corporation General
       Coupled with United States v. Equitable Trust Co. of New York
       Coupled with Hicks v. Merchantile Trust Co.
       Coupled with United States v. Mercantile Trust Co.
    269 US 283   70 LEd 275   46 SCt 116
       Sup Ct Review (1986):259-316

532. Tutun v. United States   April 12, 1926
    270 US 568   70 LEd 738   46 SCt 425
       Const (Currie) 182-186

533. Corrigan v. Buckley   May 24, 1926
    271 US 323   70 LEd 969   46 SCt 521
       En Am Con 508, 1561-1562, 1676-1677
       Guide (CQ) 38
       Making 85-86

534. Frost dba Frost and Frost Trucking Co. v. Railroad Commission of California   June 7, 1926
     271 US 583   70 LEd 1101   46 SCt 605
     Van Alstyne, William W. Academic freedom and the First Amendment in the Supreme Court of the United
        States: an unhurried historical review. *Law and Contemporary Problems* 53(3):79-154 (Summer 1990).

535. International Stevedoring Co. v. Haverty   October 18, 1926
     272 US 50   71 LEd 157   47 SCt 19
     George, James A. The 'triple crown' of admiralty cases: from definitions to damages. *Trial* 27(10):46-53
        (October 1991).

536. Myers v. United States   October 25, 1926
     272 US 52   71 LEd 160   47 SCt 21
         Almanac (1988):124-125
         Ascent 65-68, 70-73+
         Const (Currie) 193-195, 588-593
         Documents (v. 2):206-208R
         En Am Con 940-941, 1289, 1659-1664
         Guide (CQ) 38
         Powers 244-245
         Sup Ct Review (1986):41-97; (1991):225-260
     Franck, Thomas M., and Clifford A. Bob. The return of Humpty-Dumpty: foreign relations law after the
        Chadha case. *American Journal of International Law* 79(4):912-960 (October 1985).
     Mathias, Charles McC., Jr. The federal courts under siege. *Annals of the American Academy of Political and
        Social Science* 462: 26-33 (July 1982).
     Orren, Karen. The primacy of labor in American constitutional development. *American Political Science
        Review* 89(2):377-388 (June 1995).
     Rodriguez, Leon. Constitutional and statutory limits for cost-benefit analysis pursuant to Executive Orders
        12,291 and 12,498. *Boston College Environmental Affairs Law Review* 15(3-4):505-546 (Spring 1988).
     Rohr, John A., and Rosemary O'Leary. Public administration, executive power, and constitutional confusion;
        response to John Rohr. *Public Administration Review* 49(2):108-115 (March/April 1989).

537. Village of Euclid v. Ambler Realty Co.   November 22, 1926
     272 US 365   71 LEd 303   47 SCt 114
         En Am Con 630-632, 656, 1744-1751, 2088-2089
         Guide (CQ) 38
         Magic 292-293
         New Right (Schwartz) 111-116
     Blackwell, Robert J. Overlay zoning, performance standards, and environmental protection after Nollan. *Boston
        College Environmental Affairs Law Review* 16(3):615-659 (Spring 1989).
     Cavarello, Daniel T. From Penn Central to United Artists' I and II: the rise to immunity of historic preservation
        designation from successful takings challenges. *Boston College Environmental Affairs Law Review*
        22(3):593-622 (Spring 1995).
     Cohen, Jonathan E. A constitutional safety valve: the variance in zoning and land-use based environmental
        controls. *Boston College Environmental Affairs Law Review* 22(2):307-364 (Winter 1995).
     Gallogly, Richard J. Opening the door for Boston's poor: will "linkage" survive judicial review? *Boston
        College Environmental Affairs Law Review* 14(3):447-480 (Spring 1987).
     Hippler, Thomas A. Reexamining 100 years of the Supreme Court regulatory taking doctrine: the principles of
        "noxious use," "average reciprocity of advantage," and "bundle of rights" from Mugler to Keystone
        Bituminous Coal. *Boston College Environmental Affairs Law Review* 14(4):653-727 (Summer 1987).
     Randle, Ellen M. The national reserve system and transferable development rights: Is the New Jersey pinelands
        plan in unconstitutional "taking"? *Boston College Environmental Affairs Law Review* 10(1):183-241 (1982-
        83).
     Singer, Saul Jay. Flooding the Fifth Amendment: the National Flood Insurance Program and the "takings"
        clause. *Boston College Environmental Affairs Law Review* 17(2):323-379 (Winter 1990).

538. United States v. General Electric Co.   November 23, 1926
     272 US 476   71 LEd 362   47 SCt 192
     Reich, Leonard S. Lighting the path to profit: GE's control of the electric lamp industry, 1892-1941. *Business History Review* 66(2):305-334 (Summer 1992).

539. Florida v. Mellon   January 3, 1926
     273 US 12   71 LEd 511   47 SCt 265
     Moss, David A. Kindling a flame under federalism: progressive reformers, corporate elites, and the phosphorous match campaign of 1909-1912. *Business History Review* 68(2):244-275 (Summer 1994).

540. Byars v. United States   January 3, 1927
     273 US 28   71 LEd 520   47 SCt 248
     Murchison, Kenneth M. Prohibition and the Fourth Amendment: a new look at some old cases. *Journal of Criminal Law and Criminology* 73(2):471-532 (Summer 1982).

541. DiSanto v. Pennsylvania   January 3, 1927
     273 US 34   71 LEd 524   47 SCt 267
     En Am Con 565
     Schwartz, Edward B. Water as an article of commerce: state embargoes spring a leak under Sporhase v. Nebraska. *Boston College Environmental Affairs Law Review* 12(1):103-169 (Fall 1985).

542. Public Utilities Commission of Rhode Island v. Attleboro Steam and Electric Co.   January 3, 1927
     273 US 83   71 LEd 549   47 SCt 294
     Martin, Stanley A. Problems with PURPA: the need for state legislation to encourage cogeneration and small power production. *Boston College Environmental Affairs Law Review* 11(1):149-202 (October 1983).
     O'Neill Andrew J. Retail electric rates: drawing the line between federal and state authority under the commerce clause. *Public Utilities Fortnightly* 112(9):52-55 (October 27, 1983).

543. McGrain v. Daugherty   January 17, 1927
     273 US 135   71 LEd 580   47 SCt 319
     En Am Con 1237-1238
     Guide (West) (v. 7):315-316
     Powers 206-208

544. Farrington v. Tokushige   February 21, 1927
     273 US 284   71 LEd 646   47 SCt 406
     Japanese 48, 136-137

545. Tyson and Brother-United Theatre Ticket Officers, Inc. v. Banton   February 28, 1927
     273 US 418   71 LEd 718   47 SCt 426
     Documents (v. 2):204-206R
     En Am Con 1932

546. Tumey v. Ohio   March 7, 1927
     273 US 510   71 LEd 749   47 SCt 437
     En Am Con 683-686
     Guide (CQ) 38
     Sup Ct Review (1982):85-125

547. Nixon v. Herndon   March 7, 1927
     273 US 536   71 LEd 759   47 SCt 446
     Civil 20th 3, 9, 123-127R
     Documents (v. 2):217-218R
     En Am Con 727-728, 1325, 1413-1417, 1736-1738, 1979-1987
     Guide (CQ) 38, 40

Magic 264-265
Sup Ct Ind 112+

548. Ford v. United States　　　　　　　　　　　　　　　　　　　　　　　April 11, 1927
　　　273 US 593　　　　　　　　　　　71 LEd 793　　　　　　　　　　　　47 SCt 531
　　　Riesenfeld, Stefan A. Doctrine of self-executing treaties and U.S. v. Postal: win any price? [Editorial] *American Journal International Law* 74(4):892-904 October 1980.

549. Bedford Cut Stone Co. v. Journeymen Stone Cutters' Association of North America　　April 11, 1927
　　　274 US 37　　　　　　　　　　　　71 LEd 916　　　　　　　　　　　　47 SCt 522
　　　En Am Con 106, 593

550. Buck v. Bell　　　　　　　　　　　　　　　　　　　　　　　　　　　　May 2, 1927
　　　274 US 200　　　　　　　　　　　71 LEd 1000　　　　　　　　　　　47 SCt 584
　　　Abortion Am 8
　　　Documents (v. 2):216-217R
　　　En Am Con 167-168, 686-688, 1249-1251, 1763
　　　Guide (CQ) 38
　　　Hard Choices 309
　　　Landmark (v. 3):47-52R
　　　Magic 155-158
　　　Baer, Judith A. Burger Court and the rights of the handicapped: the case for starting all over again. *Western Political Quarterly* 35(3):339-358 (September 1982).
　　　Katz, Stanley N. The strange birth and unlikely history of constitutional equality. *Journal of American History* 75(3):747-762 (December 1988).
　　　Kevles, Daniel J. Annals of Eugenics (III). *New Yorker* 60(36):92-151 (October 22, 1984).

551. United States v. Alford　　　　　　　　　　　　　　　　　　　　　　　May 16, 1927
　　　274 US 264　　　　　　　　　　　71 LEd 1040　　　　　　　　　　　47 SCt 597
　　　Shepard, Blake. The scope of Congress's constitutional power under the property clause: regulating non-federal property to further the purposes of national parks and wilderness areas. *Boston College Environmental Affairs Law Review* 11(3): 479-538 (April 1984).

552. United States v. Sisal Sales Corp.　　　　　　　　　　　　　　　　　　May 16, 1927
　　　274 US 268　　　　　　　　　　　71 LEd 1042　　　　　　　　　　　47 SCt 592
　　　Kramer, Larry. Extraterritorial application of American law after the insurance antitrust case: a reply to professors Lowenfeld and Trimble. *American Journal of International Law* 89(4):750-758 (October 1995).

553. Hope Natural Gas Co. v. Hall　　　　　　　　　　　　　　　　　　　　May 16, 1927
　　　274 US 284　　　　　　　　　　　71 LEd 1049　　　　　　　　　　　47 SCt 639
　　　Powers, Carol L. State taxation of energy resources: affirmation of Commonwealth Edison Co. v. Montana. *Boston College Environmental Affairs Law Review* 10(2):503-564 (September 1982).

554. Whitney v. California　　　　　　　　　　　　　　　　　　　　　　　May 16, 1927
　　　274 US 357　　　　　　　　　　　71 LEd 1095　　　　　　　　　　　47 SCt 641
　　　Const (Currie) 160-162, 252-255
　　　En Am Con 298-301, 522-523, 730-738, 770-773, 1804-1807, 2060
　　　Fourth 93-97, 237-241
　　　Make 79-89+
　　　Sup Ct Ind 31-32+
　　　Bork, Robert H. What to do about the First Amendment. *Commentary* 99(2):23-29 (February 1995).
　　　Cox, Archibald. First Amendment. *Society* 24(1):8-15 (November/December 1986).
　　　Gillman, Howard. Preferred freedoms: the progressive expansion of state power and the rise of modern civil liberties jurisprudence. *Political Research Quarterly* 47(3):623-653 (September 1994).

Spillenger, Clyde. Reading the judicial canon: Alexander Bickel and the book of Brandeis. *Journal of American History* 79(1):125-151 (June 1992).

555. Fiske v. Kansas May 16, 1927
274 US 380 71 LEd 1108 47 SCt 655
Const (Currie) 160-162, 252-255
Sup Ct Ind 32

556. United States v. Lee May 31, 1927
274 US 559 71 LEd 1202 47 SCt 746
Const (Currie) 167-169, 531-533
Junker, John M. The structure of the Fourth Amendment: the scope of the protection. *Journal of Criminal Law and Criminology* 79(4):1105-1183 (Winter 1989).
Murchison, Kenneth M. Prohibition and the Fourth Amendment: a new look at some old cases. *Journal of Criminal Law and Criminology* 73(2):471-532 (Summer 1982).

557. Gong Lum v. Rice November 21, 1927
275 US 78 72 LEd 172 48 SCt 91
En Am Com 273-280, 852
Eyes 89-94+
Quarrels 309-310
Basic court ruling: the Brown decision. *Congressional Digest* 59(2):34-35,64 (February 1981).
Hobbs, Gardner J. Public school finance and the courts. *Clearing House* 53(9):405-409 (May 1980) .
Katz, Stanley N. The strange birth and unlikely history of constitutional equality. *Journal of American History* 75(3):747-762 (December 1988).

558. Marron v. United States November 21, 1927
275 US 192 72 LEd 231 48 SCt 74
Murchison, Kenneth M. Prohibition and the Fourth Amendment: a new look at some old cases. *Journal of Criminal Law and Criminology* 73(2):471-532 (Summer 1982).

559. Robins Dry Dock and Repair Co. v. Flint December 12, 1927
275 US 303 72 LEd 290 48 SCt 134
Mulhern, Pegeen. Marine pollution, fishes, and the pillars of the land: a tort recovery standard for pure economic losses. *Boston College Environmental Affairs Law Review* 18(1):85-123 (Fall 1990).

560. Gambino v. United States December 12, 1927
275 US 310 72 LEd 293 48 SCt 137
Murchison, Kenneth M. Prohibition and the Fourth Amendment: a new look at some old cases. *Journal of Criminal Law and Criminology* 73(2):471-532 (Summer 1982).

561. Miller v. Schoene February 20, 1928
276 US 272 72 LEd 568 48 SCt 246
New Right (Schwartz) 107-111
Andersen, Robert M. Technology, pollution control, and EPA access to commercial property: a constitutional and policy framework. *Boston College Environmental Affairs Law Review* 17(1):1-74 (Fall 1989).
Hippler, Thomas A. Reexamining 100 years of the Supreme Court regulatory taking doctrine: the principles of "noxious use," "average reciprocity of advantage," and "bundle of rights" from Mugler to Keystone Bituminous Coal. *Boston College Environmental Affairs Law Review* 14(4):653-727 (Summer 1987).

562. J. W. Hampton, Jr. and Co. v. United States April 9, 1928
276 US 394 72 LEd 624 48 SCt 348
Const (Currie) 195-198
En Am Con 894
Guide (CQ) 38, 75

563. Ferry v. Ramsey   May 14, 1928
        Coupled with Harris v. Ramsey
        Coupled with Ferry v. James
        Coupled with Harris v. James
        Coupled with Ferry v. Ramsey Petroleum Co.
        Coupled with Harris v. Ramsey Petroleum Co.
        Coupled with Ferry v. Chastain
        Coupled with Ferry v. Lloyd
        Coupled with Harris v. Lloyd
      277 US 88   72 LEd 796   48 SCt 443
      Harris, Leslie J. Constitutional limits on criminal presumptions as an expression of changing concepts of
        fundamental fairness. *Journal of Criminal Law and Criminology* 77(2):308-357 (Summer 1986).

564. Nectow v. City of Cambridge   May 14, 1928
      277 US 183   72 LEd 842   48 SCt 447
      Randle, Ellen M. The national reserve system and transferable development rights: is the New Jersey pinelands
        plan in unconstitutional "taking"? *Boston College Environmental Affairs Law Review* 10(1):183-241 (1982-
        83).
      Singer, Saul Jay. Flooding the Fifth Amendment: the National Flood Insurance Program and the "takings"
        clause. *Boston College Environmental Affairs Law Review* 17(2):323-379 (Winter 1990).

565. Willing v. Chicago Auditorium Association   May 21, 1928
      277 US 274   72 LEd 880   48 SCt 507
      Spillenger, Clyde. Reading the judicial canon: Alexander Bickel and the book of Brandeis. *Journal of
        American History* 79(1):125-151 (June 1992).

566. Ribnik v. McBride   May 28, 1928
      277 US 350   72 LEd 913   48 SCt 545
        En Am Con 1568-1569

567. Olmstead v. United States   June 4, 1928
        Coupled with Green v. United States
        Coupled with McInnis v. United States
      277 US 438   72 LEd 944   48 SCt 564
        Amending 170-177
        Burger Court 63-64
        Economics 311-322
        En Am Con 516-522, 618-621, 1341-1342, 1577-1581, 1796-1803, 1947-1949, 2071-2072
        Guide (West) (v. 8):79-81,293-294
        Hard Choices 130-131
        Liberty 261-264+
        Magic 317-320
        Sup Ct Review (1981):111-155; (1995):125-215
        Super 386-387, 462-463+
      Bloom, Robert M. Judicial integrity: a call for its reemergence in the adjudication of criminal cases. *Journal of
        Criminal Law and Criminology* 84(3):462-501 (Fall 1993).
      Christopher, Maura. How the Constitution protects your "right to be let alone". *Scholastic Update* 119(1):12-13
        (September 8, 1986).
      Gillman, Howard. Preferred freedoms: the progressive expansion of state power and the rise of modern civil
        liberties jurisprudence. *Political Research Quarterly* 47(3):623-653 (September 1994).
      Goldsmith, Michael. The Supreme Court and Title III: rewriting the law of electronic surveillance. *Journal of
        Criminal Law and Criminology* 74(1):1-171 (Spring 1983).
      Murchison, Kenneth M. Prohibition and the Fourth Amendment: a new look at some old cases. *Journal of
        Criminal Law and Criminology* 73(2):471-532 (Summer 1982).
      Rosenblatt, Roger. The Bill of Rights. *Life* 14(13 Special Issue):9-30 (Fall 1991).

Schlesinger, Arthur M. Roosevelt and the courts. *Society* 24(1):53-56 (November/December 1986).

Webber, Dawn. Supreme Court review: Fourth Amendment—of warrants, electronic surveillance, expectations of privacy, and tainted fruits. *Journal of Criminal Law and Criminology* 75(3):630-652 (Fall 1984).

Wulf, Melvin L. On the origins of privacy. *Nation* 252(20):700, 702-704 (May 27, 1991).

568. Foster-Fountain Packing Co. v. Haydel — October 15, 1928
  278 US 1   73 LEd 147   49 SCt 1
  En Am Con 1751-1755
  Winn, John. Alaska v. F/V Baranof: state regulation beyond the territorial sea after the Magnuson Act. *Boston College Environmental Affairs Law Review* 13(2):281-327 (Winter 1986).

569. New York ex rel. Bryant v. Zimmerman — November 19, 1928
  Bryant v. Zimmerman
  278 US 63   73 LEd 184   49 SCt 61
  Padgett, Gregory L. Racially-motivated violence and intimidation: inadequate state enforcement and federal civil rights remedies. *Journal of Criminal Law and Criminology* 75(1):103-138 (Spring 1984).

570. Sinclair v. United States — April 8, 1929
  279 US 263   73 LEd 692   49 SCt 268
  Powers 207-208
  Sup Ct Yearbook (1994-95):87-88

571. Ex Parte Bakelite Corp. — May 20, 1929
  279 US 438   73 LEd 789   49 SCt 411
  Const (Currie) 593-596

572. United States v. Schwimmer — May 27, 1929
  279 US 644   73 LEd 889   49 SCt 448
  En Am Con 1627
  Godless 53-55+
  Guide (CQ) 144-145
  Make 79-89

573. Okanogan Indians v. United States — May 27, 1929
  279 US 655   73 LEd 894   49 SCt 463
  En Am Con 1399, 1964-1965

574. United Railways and Electric Co. of Baltimore v. West — January 6, 1930
  280 US 234   74 LEd 390   50 SCt 123
  En Am Con 1939

575. Clarke v. Haberle Crystal Springs Brewing Co. — January 27, 1930
  280 US 384   74 LEd 498   50 SCt 155
  Sup Ct Review (1983):32-82

576. Lucas v. Earl — March 17, 1930
  281 US 111   74 LEd 731   50 SCt 241
  Anspach, William N., Paul L. Marlin, and Charles J. Muller III. Deferred compensation: a case study of purposeful negation of Supreme Court jurisdiction over income tax laws. *Taxes* 59(10):691-711 (October 1981).
  Karjala, Dennis S. Deferred compensation and the Supreme Court. *Taxes* 60(9):684-694 (September 1982).

577. Patton v. United States — April 14, 1930
  281 US 276   74 LEd 854   50 SCt 253
  En Am Con 1085-1086, 1369

578. Cochran v. Louisiana Board of Education   April 28, 1930
      281 US 370   74 LEd 913   50 SCt 335
          Am Educators 103-104, 111
          En Am Con 304
          Godless 64-66, 70-71+
          Sup Ct Church 35-37R
      Hammond, Phillip E. The courts and secular humanism. *Society* 21(4):11-16 (May/June 1984).
      Rayer, Thomas A. The bicentennial and church-related schools. *America* 157(17):427-429, 438 (December 5,
          1987).

579. Corliss v. Bowers, Collector of Internal Revenue   April 28, 1930
      281 US 376   74 LEd 916   50 SCt 336
      Anspach, William N., Paul L. Marlin, and Charles J. Muller III. Deferred compensation: a case study of
          purposeful negation of Supreme Court jurisdiction over income tax laws. *Taxes* 59(10):691-711 (October
          1981).

580. Cincinnati v. Vester   May 19, 1930
          Coupled with Cincinnati v. Richards
          Coupled with Cincinnati v. Reakirt
      281 US 439   74 LEd 950   50 SCt 360
      Plater, Zygmunt J. B., and William Lund Norine. Through the looking glass of eminent domain: exploring the
          "arbitrary and capricious" test and substantive rationality review of governmental decisions. *Boston College
          Environmental Affairs Law Review* 16(4):661-752 (Summer 1989).

581. Texas and New Orleans Railroad Co. v. Brotherhood of Railway and Steamship Clerks   May 26, 1930
      281 US 548   74 LEd 1034   50 SCt 427
          Sup Ct Review (1992):235-293

582. Baldwin v. Missouri   May 26, 1930
      281 US 586   74 LEd 1056   50 SCt 436
      Rotunda, Ronald D. The Supreme Court: eschewing bright lines. *Trial* 25(12):52-56 (December 1989).

583. Poe, Collector of Internal Revenue v. Seaborn   November 24, 1930
      282 US 101   75 LEd 239   51 SCt 58
      Anspach, William N., Paul L. Marlin, and Charles J. Muller III. Deferred compensation: a case study of
          purposeful negation of Supreme Court jurisdiction over income tax laws. *Taxes* 59(10):691-711 (October
          1981).

584. Go-Bart Importing Co. v. United States   January 5, 1931
      282 US 344   75 LEd 374   51 SCt 153
      Murchison, Kenneth M. Prohibition and the Fourth Amendment: a new look at some old cases. *Journal of
          Criminal Law and Criminology* 73(2):471-532 (Summer 1982).

585. Husty v. United States   February 24, 1931
      282 US 694   75 LEd 629   51 SCt 240
      Murchison, Kenneth M. Prohibition and the Fourth Amendment: a new look at some old cases. *Journal of
          Criminal Law and Criminology* 73(2):471-532 (Summer 1982).

586. American Fruit Growers, Inc. v. Brogdex Co.   March 2, 1931
      283 US 1   75 LEd 801   51 SCt 328
      Rosenblatt, David P. The regulation of recombinant DNA research: the alternative of local control. *Boston
          College Environmental Affairs Law Review* 10(1):37-78 (1982-83).
      Smith, Donna H., and Jonathan King. Proprietary rights and public interest: the legal and legislative
          background. *Environment* 24(6):24-26, 33-37 (July/August 1982).

587. McBoyle v. United States March 9, 1931
283 US 25 75 LEd 816 51 SCt 340
Sup Ct Review (1994):345-428

588. Aldridge v. United States April 20, 1931
283 US 308 75 LEd 1054 51 SCt 470
Mar, Linda. Supreme Court review: probing racial prejudice on voir dire: the Supreme Court provides illusory
justice for minority defendants. *Journal of Criminal Law and Criminology* 72(4):1444-1461 (Winter 1981).
Schultz, Marjorie S. Jury defined: a review of Burger court decisions. *Law and Contemporary Problems*
43(4):8-23 (Autumn 1980).
Wyckoff, Maria. Supreme Court review: Sixth Amendment—right to inquire into juror's racial prejudices.
Journal of Criminal Law and Criminology 77(3):713-742 (Fall 1986).

589. Stromberg v. California May 18, 1931
283 US 359 75 LEd 1117 51 SCt 532
Const (Currie) 252-253, 255-257, 348-350
Const Law 121-123R+
En Am Con 1791, 1843-1844
Guide (CQ) 39
Magic 262-264
Minnesota 144-146+
Gillman, Howard. Preferred freedoms: the progressive expansion of state power and the rise of modern civil
liberties jurisprudence. *Political Research Quarterly* 47(3):623-653 (September 1994).

590. Burnet, Commissioner of Internal Revenue v. Logan May 18, 1931
283 US 404 75 LEd 1143 51 SCt 550
Wootton, Robert R. Mrs. Logan's ghost: the open transaction doctrine today. *Taxes* 71(12):725-745 (December
1993).

591. United States v. Macintosh May 25, 1931
283 US 605 75 LEd 1302 51 SCt 570
Godless 54-55
Religion 150-152
Demerath, N. J., III, and Rhys H. Williams. A mythical past and uncertain future. *Society* 21(4):3-10 (May/June
1984).
McKown, Delos Banning. Deism and the Supreme Court. *Humanist* 52(2):25-28, 48 (March/April 1992).

592. United States v. Bland May 25, 1931
283 US 636 75 LEd 1319 51 SCt 569
Godless 54

593. Fetters v. United States ex rel. Cunningham May 25, 1931
283 US 638 75 LEd 1321 51 SCt 596
Sup Ct Review (1986):259-316

594. Federal Trade Commission (FTC) v. Raladam Co. May 25, 1931
283 US 643 75 LEd 1324 51 SCt 587
Tedlow, Richard S. From competitor to consumer: the changing focus of federal regulation of advertising,
1914-1938. *Business History Review* 55(1): 35-58 (Spring 1981).

595. Near v. Minnesota ex rel. Olsen June 1, 1931
283 US 697 75 LEd 1357 51 SCt 625
Amending 203-213
Const (Currie) 252-253, 257-259
Const (Friendly) 31-49

Const Law 190-195R+
Court Public 315
En Am Con 797-804, 1303-1304, 1453-1456
Equal (Harrell) 69-71, 111
First 187-199
Fourth 140-147+
Magic 262-264+
Make 90-102+
Minnesota 82-155, 207-233R+
Quarrels 209-232
Sup Ct Review (1980):1-25

Boylan, James. Pleading the First. *Columbia Journalism Review* 30(4):41-43 (November/December 1991).

Freidman, Robert. Freedom of the press: how far can they go? *American Heritage* 33(6):16-26 (October/November 1982).

Gersh, Debra. Supreme Court and the media. *Editor and Publisher* 120(50):18-19 (December 12, 1987).

Lewin, Nathan. High court hexes free speech. *New Republic* 182(12):18-21 (March 22, 1980).

Near v. Minnesota: a landmark decision. *Editor and Publisher* 114(23):82 (June 6, 1981).

Rose, Jonathan. Decide 10 landmark cases that define your rights. *Scholastic Update* 119(1):7-9, 21 (September 8, 1986).

Welsh, Robert, and Ronald K. L. Collins. Taking state constitutions seriously: the protection of civil liberties has been shifting away from the U.S. Supreme Court. *Center Magazine* 14(5):6-35, 38-43 (September/October 1981).

596. Hoeper v. Tax Commission of Wisconsin   November 30, 1931
      284 US 206   76 LEd 248   52 SCt 120
      Blase, James G. Is the kiddie tax unconstitutional? *Trusts and Estates* 127(6):46-48, 67 (June 1988).

597. Blockburger v. United States   January 4, 1932
      284 US 299   76 LEd 306   52 SCt 180
      Bernstein, Sidney. Supreme Court review. *Trial* 19(11):20, 22 (November 1983).

      Donofrio, Anthony J. Supreme Court review: the double jeopardy clause of the Fifth Amendment—the Supreme Court's cursory treatment of underlying conduct in successive prosecutions. *Journal of Criminal Law and Criminology* 83(4):773-803 (Winter 1993).

      Dripps, Donald A. Supreme Court review: double jeopardy: what is the 'same offense'? *Trial* 28(11):90-91 (November 1992).

      Pace, Kirstin. Supreme Court review: Fifth Amendment—the adoption of the "same elements" test: the Supreme Court's failure to adequately protect defendants from double jeopardy. *Journal of Criminal Law and Criminology* 84(4):769-804 (Winter/Spring 1994).

598. Crowell v. Benson   February 23, 1932
      285 US 22   76 LEd 598   52 SCt 285
      Const (Currie) 593-596
      Sup Ct Review (1989):261-282

599. Burnet v. Leininger   March 14, 1932
      285 US 136   76 LEd 665   52 SCt 345
      Anspach, William N., Paul L. Marlin, and Charles J. Muller III. Deferred compensation: a case study of purposeful negation of Supreme Court jurisdiction over income tax laws. *Taxes* 59(10):691-711 (October 1981).

600. New State Ice Co. v. Liebmann   March 21, 1932
      285 US 262   76 LEd 747   52 SCt 371
      Const (Currie) 210-211
      Documents (v. 2):229-232R
      En Am Con 1310

Magic 277-279

New Right (Schwartz) 80-83

Spillenger, Clyde. Reading the judicial canon: Alexander Bickel and the book of Brandeis. *Journal of American History* 79(1):125-151 (June 1992).

601. United States v. Lefkowitz April 11, 1932
285 US 452 76 LEd 877 52 SCt 466
Murchison, Kenneth M. Prohibition and the Fourth Amendment: a new look at some old cases. *Journal of Criminal Law and Criminology* 73(2):471-532 (Summer 1982).

602. Taylor v. United States May 2, 1932
286 US 1 76 LEd 951 52 SCt 466
Murchison, Kenneth M. Prohibition and the Fourth Amendment: a new look at some old cases. *Journal of Criminal Law and Criminology* 73(2):471-532 (Summer 1982).

603. Nixon v. Condon May 2, 1932
286 US 73 76 LEd 984 52 SCt 484
Civil 20th 3, 9, 123, 128-137R
Const (Currie) 250-251
En Am Con 727-728, 1324, 1413-1417, 1979-1987
Making 100-102
Sup Ct Ind 112

604. United States v. Swift and Co. May 2, 1932
Coupled with American Wholesale Grocers Association v. Swift and Co.
Coupled with National Wholesale Grocers Association v. Swift and Co.
286 US 106 76 LEd 999 52 SCt 460
Fieweger, Michael J. Supreme Court review: consent decrees in prison and jail reform—relaxed standard of review for government motions to modify consent decrees. *Journal of Criminal Law and Criminology* 83(4):1024-1054 (Winter 1993).

605. North American Oil Consolidated v. Burnet, Commissioner of Internal Revenue May 23, 1932
286 US 417 76 LEd 1197 52 SCt 613
Anspach, William N., Paul L. Marlin, and Charles J. Muller III. Deferred compensation: a case study of purposeful negation of Supreme Court jurisdiction over income tax laws. *Taxes* 59(10):691-711 (October 1981).
Lynch, James M. Indianapolis Power and Light Company: issues and planning opportunities where the government seeks the acceleration of income. *Taxes* 68(12):931-944 (December 1990).

606. Powell v. Alabama November 7, 1932
Coupled with Patterson v. Alabama
Coupled with Weems v. Alabama
287 US 45 77 LEd 158 53 SCt 55
Civil 20th 3, 7, 45-60R
Const (Currie) 246-249, 252-253
Const Law 400-403R+
Death Penalty (Tushnet) 22-23
En Am Con 1433-1434, 1472-1479, 1585-1592
Fourth 197-199+
Guide (CQ) 39-40
Guide (West) (v. 8):246-247; (v. 9):124-126
Landmark (v. 3):53-68R
Law 376-385
Magic 264-265, 320-322
Reader's 971-972

Sup Ct Review (1982):85-125

Baer, Harold, Jr. Sequestering witnesses: does the practice interfere with the defendants' constitutional rights? *Trial* 22(7):99-102 (July 1986).

Bahl, Martin. The Sixth Amendment as constitutional theory: does originalism require that Massiah be abandoned? *Journal of Criminal Law and Criminology* 82(2):423-463 (Summer 1991).

Goldberg, Steven H. Harmless error: constitutional sneak thief. *Journal of Criminal Law and Criminology* 71(4):421-442 (Winter 1980).

Rosenblatt, Roger. The Bill of Rights. *Life* 14(13 Special Issue):9-30 (Fall 1991).

607. United States v. Shreveport Grain and Elevator Co.   November 7, 1932
      287 US 77   77 LEd 175   53 SCt 42
      Thomas, Charlotte E. The Cape Cod national seashore: a case study of federal administrative control over traditionally local land use decisions. *Boston College Environmental Affairs Law Review* 12(2):225-272 (Winter 1985).

608. Schoenthal v. Irving Trust Co.   November 7, 1932
      287 US 92   77 LEd 185   53 SCt 50
      Sup Ct Review (1989):261-282

609. Grau v. United States   November 7, 1932
      287 US 124   77 LEd 212   53 SCt 38
      Murchison, Kenneth M. Prohibition and the Fourth Amendment: a new look at some old cases. *Journal of Criminal Law and Criminology* 73(2):471-532 (Summer 1982).

610. Sgro v. United States   December 5, 1932
      287 US 206   77 LEd 260   53 SCt 138
      Murchison, Kenneth M. Prohibition and the Fourth Amendment: a new look at some old cases. *Journal of Criminal Law and Criminology* 73(2):471-532 (Summer 1982).

611. Sterling v. Constantin   December 12, 1932
      287 US 378   77 LEd 375   53 SCt 190
      Just War 177-178, 223

612. Sorrells v. United States   December 19, 1932
      287 US 435   77 LEd 413   53 SCt 210
      En Am Con 635-636
      Sup Ct Review (1981):111-155
      Dripps, Donald A. Supreme Court review: The riddle of entrapment. *Trial* 28(7):97-100 (July 1992).

613. Cook v. United States   January 23, 1933
      288 US 102   77 LEd 641   53 SCt 305
      En Am Con 1910-1911
      Riesenfeld, Stefan A. Doctrine of self-executing treaties and U.S. v. Postal: win any price? [Editorial] *American Journal International Law* 74(4):892-904 (October 1980).

614. United States v. Flores   April 10, 1933
      289 US 137   77 LEd 1086   53 SCt 580
      Raymond, John M., and Barbara J. Frischholz. Lawyers who established international law in the United States, 1776-1914. *American Journal of International Law* 76(4):802-829 (October 1982).

615. Reinecke, formerly Collector of Internal Revenue v. Smith   April 10, 1933
      289 US 172   77 LEd 1109   53 SCt 570
      Anspach, William N., Paul L. Marlin, and Charles J. Muller III. Deferred compensation: a case study of purposeful negation of Supreme Court jurisdiction over income tax laws. *Taxes* 59(10):691-711 (October 1981).

616. City of Harrisonville v. W. S. Dickey Clay Manufacturing Co.   May 8, 1933
      289 US 334   77 LEd 1208   53 SCt 602
      Giesser, John L. The national park service and external development: addressing park boundary-area threats
      through public nuisance. *Boston College Environmental Affairs Law Review* 20(4):761-809 (Summer 1993).

617. United States ex rel. Greathouse v. Dern   May 8, 1933
      289 US 352   77 LEd 1250   53 SCt 614
      Proctor, Michael G. Section 10 of the Rivers and Harbors Act and Western Water Allocations—are the western
      states up a creek without a permit? *Boston College Environmental Affairs Law Review* 10(1):111-182 (1982-
      83).

618. Burnet, Commissioner of Internal Revenue v. Wells   May 29, 1933
      289 US 670   77 LEd 1439   53 SCt 761
      Anspach, William N., Paul L. Marlin, and Charles J. Muller III. Deferred compensation: a case study of
      purposeful negation of Supreme Court jurisdiction over income tax laws. *Taxes* 59(10):691-711 (October
      1981).

619. Welch v. Helvering, Commissioner of Internal Revenue   November 6, 1933
      290 US 111   78 LEd 212   54 SCt 8
      Hume, Evelyn C., and Ernest R. Larkins. Takeover expenses: National Starch and the IRS add new wrinkles.
      Journal of Accountancy 174(2):87-93 (August 1992).

620. United States v. Murdock   December 11, 1933
      290 US 389   78 LEd 381   54 SCt 223
      Silverman, Elliot. Turning the other cheek: tax fraud, tax protest, and the willfulness requirement. *Taxes*
      69(5):302-307 (May 1991).

621. Home Building and Loan Association v. Blaisdell   January 8, 1934
      290 US 398   78 LEd 413   54 SCt 231
          Const (Currie) 211-213
          Documents (v. 2):296-298R
          En Am Con 159-160, 464-471, 925, 1560, 1962-1964
          Magic 277-279

622. Morrison v. California   January 8, 1934
      291 US 82   78 LEd 664   54 SCt 281
      Harris, Leslie J. Constitutional limits on criminal presumptions as an expression of changing concepts of
      fundamental fairness. *Journal of Criminal Law and Criminology* 77(2):308-357 (Summer 1986).

623. United States v. Chambers   February 5, 1934
      291 US 217   78 LEd 763   54 SCt 434
      Gaugush, Bill. Principles governing the interpretation and exercise of Article 5 powers. *Western Political
      Quarterly* 35(2):212-221 (June 1982).

624. Nebbia v. New York   March 5, 1934
      291 US 502   78 LEd 940   54 SCt 505
          Documents (v. 2):298-301R
          En Am Con 1304-1305, 1796-1803
          Equal (Harrell) 80, 89
          Guide (CQ) 40
          Hard Choices 308
          Magic 277-279
          Sup Ct Review (1992):235-293
      Duesenberg, Richard W. Washington is stifling economic liberties. *USA Today* 123(2596):14-16 (January
      1995).

Goldberg, Andrew M. Corporate officer liability for federal environmental statute violations. *Boston College Environmental Affairs Law Review* 18(2):357-379 (Winter 1991).

625. Local Loan Co. v. Hunt   April 30, 1934
     292 US 234   78 LEd 1230   54 SCt 695
     Cerne, Kathleen M. Honor thy creditors? the religious debtor's constitutional conflict with Section 1325(b). *Business Credit* 96(3):37-40 (March 1994).

626. Hamilton v. Regents of the University of California   December 3, 1934
     293 US 245   79 LE 343   55 SCt 197
        En Am Con 892
        Guide (CQ) 338, 378, 454

627. Panama Refining Co. v. Ryan   January 7, 1935
     293 US 388   79 LEd 446   55 SCt 241
        Const (Currie) 216-218
        En Am Con 530-531, 1363
        Guide (CQ) 40, 78, 123b
        Magic 279-281
        Sup Ct Review (1986):19-40

628. Gregory v. Helvering, Commissioner of Internal Revenue   January 7, 1935
     293 US 465   79 LEd 596   55 SCt 266
     Flesher, Tonya K. A turning point in tax history. *Journal of Accountancy* 163(5):193-194 (May 1987).

629. Dimick v. Schiedt   January 7, 1935
     293 US 474   79 LEd 603   55 SCt 296
     Garcia, Diana. Remittitur in environmental cases: developing a standard of review for federal courts. *Boston College Environmental Affairs Law Review* 16(1):119-147 (Fall 1988).

630. Mooney v. Holohan, Warden   January 21, 1935
     294 US 103   79 LEd 791   55 SCt 340
        Const (Currie) 247-248
        Equal (Harrell) 74-77, 86-87

631. Norman v. Baltimore and Ohio Railroad Co.   February 18, 1935
        Coupled with United States v. Bankers Trust Co.
     294 US 240   79 LEd 885   55 SCt 407
        Documents (v. 2):263-266
        En Am Con 850-851, 1270-1273
        Guide (CQ) 40, 124-125

632. Nortz v. United States   February 18, 1935
     294 US 317   79 LEd 907   55 SCt 428
        Documents (v. 2):263
        En Am Con 850-851, 1270-1273
        Guide (CQ) 40, 124-125

633. Perry v. United States   February 18, 1935
     294 US 330   79 LEd 912   55 SCt 432
        Documents (v. 2):263, 266-269R
        En Am Con 850-851, 1270-1273
        Guide (CQ) 40, 120, 124-125
     Schlesinger, Arthur M. Roosevelt and the courts. *Society* 24(1):53-56 (November/December 1986).

634. Norris v. Alabama   April 1, 1935
      294 US 587   79 LEd 1074   55 SCt 579
        En Am Con 1326
        Equal (Harrell) 73-77
        Guide (CQ) 39-40
        Guide (West) (v. 9):124-126
      Serr, Brian J., and Mark Maney. Racism, peremptory challenges, and the democratic jury: the jurisprudence of a
        delicate balance. *Journal of Criminal Law and Criminology* 79(1):1-65 (Spring 1988).

635. Grovey v. Townsend   April 1, 1935
      295 US 45   79 LEd 1292   55 SCt 622
        Const (Currie) 250-251
        Const Law 586-589, 1979-1987
        En Am Con 874
        Guide (CQ) 40, 46
        Making 102, 104-107
        Sup Ct Ind 112

636. Railroad Retirement Board (RRB) v. Alton Railroad Co.   May 6, 1935
      295 US 330   79 LEd 1468   55 SCt 758
        Const (Currie) 225-226
        Documents (v. 2):305-308R
        En Am Con 1509
        Guide (CQ) 40, 91, 95
        Sup Ct Review (1986):259-316

637. ALA Schechter Poultry Corp. v. United States   May 27, 1935
      295 US 495   79 LEd 1570   55 SCt 837
        Const (Currie) 218-220, 222-223, 300-301
        Documents (v. 2):278-283R
        En Am Con 322-329, 530-531, 1622-1623
        Guide (CQ) 40, 78, 95, 99-102
        Guide (West) (v.9):107-109
        Magic 279-281
        Powers 143-144
        Quarrels 233-252
        Sup Ct Review (1986):19-40
      Orren, Karen. The primacy of labor in American constitutional development. *American Political Science
        Review* 89(2):377-388 (June 1995).
      Rodriguez, Leon. Constitutional and statutory limits for cost-benefit analysis pursuant to Executive Orders
        12,291 and 12,498. *Boston College Environmental Affairs Law Review* 15(3-4):505-546 (Spring 1988).
      Schlesinger, Arthur M. Roosevelt and the courts. *Society* 24(1):53-56 (November/December 1986).
      Tish, Martin H. Duplicative statutes, prosecutorial discretion, and the Illinois armed violence statute. *Journal of
        Criminal Law and Criminology* 71(3):226-243 (Fall 1980).

638. Louisville Joint Stock Land Bank v. Radford   May 27, 1935
      295 US 555   79 LEd 1593   55 SCt 854
        En Am Con 769, 1180

639. Humphrey's Executor (Rathbun) v. United States   May 27, 1935
      295 US 602   79 LEd 1611   55 SCt 869
        Ascent 65-68, 70-73+
        Const (Currie) 220-222
        Documents (v. 2):308-311R
        En Am Con 940-941, 1659-1664

New Right (Schwartz) 196-221+

Powers 244-245

Sup Ct Review (1986):19-40, 41-97

Daugherty, Donald A. Supreme Court review: the separation of powers and abuses in prosecutorial discretion. *Journal of Criminal Law and Criminology* 79(3):953-996 (Fall 1988).

Orren, Karen. The primacy of labor in American constitutional development. *American Political Science Review* 89(2):377-388 (June 1995).

Rodriguez, Leon. Constitutional and statutory limits for cost-benefit analysis pursuant to Executive Orders 12,291 and 12,498. *Boston College Environmental Affairs Law Review* 15(3-4):505-546 (Spring 1988).

Rohr, John A., and Rosemary O'Leary. Public administration, executive power, and constitutional confusion; response to John Rohr. *Public Administration Review* 49(2):108-115 (March/April 1989).

640. General Utilities and Operating Co. v. Helvering,   December 9, 1935
Commissioner of Internal Revenue

296 US 200   80 LEd 154   56 SCt 185

Gans, Mitchell M. The repeal of General Utilities: estate tax implications. *Trusts and Estates* 126(7):43-48 (July 1987).

Deats, Richard G., D. Reed Maughan, and Danni S. Dunn. Wringing the division bell. *Taxes* 72(8):427-443 (August 1994).

641. United States v. Constantine   December 9, 1935

296 US 287   80 LEd 233   56 SCt 223

Caginalp, O. A. Fifth Amendment privilege against self-incrimination and compulsory self-disclosure under the Clean Air and Clean Water Acts. *Boston College Environmental Affairs Law Review* 9(2):359-395 (1980-1981).

642. Colgate v. Harvey, Tax Commissioner of Vermont   December 16, 1935

296 US 404   80 LEd 299   56 SCt 252

En Am Con 310

643. United States v. Butler   January 6, 1936

297 US 1   80 LEd 477   56 SCt 312

Documents (v. 2):246-255R

En Am Con 187-188, 322-329, 837-838, 1869-1871

Magic 279-281

Sup Ct Review (1986):259-316; (1988):85-127

Hickok, Eugene W., Jr. Federalism's future before the U.S. Supreme Court. *Annals of the American Academy of Political and Social Science* 509:73-82 (May 1990).

Jensen, Laura S. Subsidies, strings, and the courts: judicial action and conditional federal spending. *Review of Politics* 55(3):491-509 (Summer 1993).

Schlesinger, Arthur M. Roosevelt and the courts. *Society* 24(1):53-56 (November/December 1986).

644. Rickert Rice Mills v. Fontenot   January 13, 1936

297 US 110   80 LEd 513   56 SCt 374

Sup Ct Review (1986):259-316

645. United States v. Atkinson   February 3, 1936

297 US 157   80 LEd 555   56 SCt 391

Lowry, Jeffrey L. Supreme Court review: plain error rule—clarifying plain error analysis under Rule 52(b) of the Federal Rules of Criminal Procedure. *Journal of Criminal Law and Criminology* 84(4):1065-1085 (Winter/Spring 1994).

646. Grosjean v. American Press Co.   February 10, 1936

297 US 233   80 LEd 660   56 SCt 444

Const (Currie) 252-253, 260-261, 315-317

Documents (v. 2):311-313R
En Am Con 797-804, 871-872
Fourth 221-226

647. Brown v. Mississippi   February 17, 1936
    297 US 278   80 LEd 682   56 SCt 461
      Const (Currie) 247-248
      Death Penalty (Tushnet) 23-24
      En Am Con 164-165, 225-226, 1400-1408
      Guide (CQ) 41
      Magic 320-322
      Sup Ct Review (1982):85-125
    Methvin, Eugene H. The case of common sense vs. Miranda. *Reader's Digest* 131(784):96-100 (August 1987).
    Pace, Michael R. Supreme Court review: Fifth and Fourteenth Amendments—defining the protections of the Fifth and Fourteenth Amendments against self-incrimination for the mentally impaired. *Journal of Criminal Law and Criminology* 78(4):877-914 (Winter 1988).

648. Ashwander v. Tennessee Valley Authority (TVA)   February 17, 1936
    297 US 288   80 LEd 688   56 SCt 466
      Documents (v. 2):257-262R
      En Am Con 78-79, 1031-1038, 1770-1771
      Guide (CQ) 87-88
      Sup Ct Review (1995):71-90
    McGuire, Kevin T., and Barbara Palmer. Issue fluidity on the U.S. Supreme Court. *American Political Science Review* 89(3):691-702 (September 1995).

649. Bayside Fish Flour Co. v. Gentry   March 2, 1936
    297 US 422   80 LEd 772   56 SCt 513
    Winn, John. Alaska v. F/V Baranof: state regulation beyond the territorial sea after the Magnuson Act. *Boston College Environmental Affairs law Review* 13(2):281-327 (Winter 1986).

650. Jones v. Securities and Exchange Commission (SEC)   April 6, 1936
    298 US 1   80 LEd 1015   56 SCt 654
      En Am Con 1030

651. Carter v. Carter Coal Co.   May 18, 1936
          Coupled with Helvering v. Carter
          Coupled with R. C. Tway Coal Co. v. Glenn
          Coupled with R. C. Tway Coal Co. v. Clark
    298 US 238   80 LEd 1160   56 SCt 855
      Const (Currie) 223-225
      Documents (v. 2):344-353R
      En Am Con 119, 217-218, 322-329, 530-531, 1665-1666, 1770-1771
      Guide (CQ) 41, 71-73, 78, 95, 100-102, 114-115
      Powers 144-145
      Sup Ct Review (1986):259-316; (1995):125-215

652. Ashton v. Cameron County Water Improvement District, No. One   May 25, 1936
    298 US 513   80 LEd 1309   56 SCt 892
      En Am Con 78,1285

653. Morehead v. New York ex rel. Tipaldo   June 1, 1936
    298 US 587   80 LEd 1347   56 SCt 918
      Brennan 65-77
      Const (Currie) 231-232

En Am Con 1229-1230, 1279-1280

Guide (CQ) 41, 42

Magic 277-279

Quarrels 269-275

Caldeira, Gregory A. Public opinion and the U.S. Supreme Court: FDR's court-packing plan. *American Political Science Review* 81(4):1139-1153 (December 1987).

Leuchtenburg, William Edward. The case of the chambermaid and the nine old men. *American Heritage* 38(1):34-41 (December 1986).

Schlesinger, Arthur M. Roosevelt and the courts. *Society* 24(1):53-56 (November/December 1986).

654. Gully v. First National Bank in Meridian   November 9, 1936
      299 US 109   81 LEd 70   57 SCt 96
      En Am Con 715-716

Winn, John. Alaska v. F/V Baranof: state regulation beyond the territorial sea after the Magnuson Act. *Boston College Environmental Affairs Law Review* 13(2):281-327 (Winter 1986).

655. Old Dearborn Distributing Co. v. Seagram Distillers Corp.   December 7, 1936
            Coupled with McNeil v. Joseph Triner Corp.
      299 US 183   81 LEd 109   57 SCt 139

Sheffet, Mary Jane, and Debra L. Scammon. Resale price maintenance: is it safe to suggest retail prices? *Journal of Marketing* 49(4):82-92 (Fall 1985).

656. United States v. Curtiss-Wright Export Corp. et al.   December 21, 1936
      299 US 304   81 LEd 255   57 SCt 216
      Almanac (1988):125
      Documents (v. 2):362-365R
      En Am Con 530-531, 677-678, 747-755, 962-966
      Guide (CQ) 41, 78-79, 127, 132-133, 201
      Quarrels 253-265

Driesen, David M. The congressional role in international environmental law and its implications for statutory interpretation. *Boston College Environmental Affairs Law Review* 19(2):287-315 (Fall/Winter 1991).

Fisher, Louis. Foreign policy powers of the President and Congress. *Annals of the American Academy of Political and Social Science* 499:149-159 (September 1988).

Franck, Thomas M., and Clifford A. Bob. The return of Humpty-Dumpty: foreign relations law after the Chadha case. *American Journal of International Law* 79(4):912-960 (October 1985).

Halberstam, Malvina. Agora: international kidnaping—in defense of the Supreme Court decision in Alvarez-Machain. *American Journal of International Law* 86(4):736-746 (October 1992).

LaFeber, Walter. The Constitution and United States foreign policy: an interpretation. *Journal of American History* 74(3):695-717 (December 1987).

Pawelek, Dick. Your Constitution: can the president ban private arms sales? *Scholastic Update* (Teachers' Edition) 119(13):20, 25 (March 9, 1987).

Schlesinger, Arthur M. Roosevelt and the courts. *Society* 24(1):53-56 (November/December 1986).

Van Alstyne, William W. Implied powers. *Society* 24(1):56-60 (November/December 1986).

657. DeJonge v. Oregon   January 4, 1937
      299 US 353   81 LEd 278   57 SCt 255
      Amending 203-213
      Const (Currie) 252-253, 255-257
      Const (Friendly) 69-80+
      Const Law 122-123+
      Documents (v. 2):365-368R
      En Am Con 522-523, 551-552, 770-773
      Sup Ct Ind 32-33+

Gillman, Howard. Preferred freedoms: the progressive expansion of state power and the rise of modern civil liberties jurisprudence. *Political Research Quarterly* 47(3):623-653 (September 1994).

658. West Coast Hotel Co. v. Parrish   March 29, 1937
     300 US 379   81 LEd 703   57 SCt 578
        Abortion Am 340-341+
        Brennan 65-77
        Documents (v. 2):368-373R
        En Am Con 774-780, 1229-1230, 1796-1803, 2045-2046
        Guide (CQ) 42
        Guide (West) (v. 10):357-358
        Magic 282-284
        Quarrels 266-284
        Sup Ct Review (1994):57-128
     Caldeira, Gregory A. Public opinion and the U.S. Supreme Court: FDR's court-packing plan. *American Political Science Review* 81(4):1139-1153 (December 1987).
     Leuchtenburg, William Edward. The case of the chambermaid and the nine old men. *American Heritage* 38(1):34-41 (December 1986).
     Marshall, Thomas R. Public opinion, representation, and the modern Supreme Court. *American Politics Quarterly* 16(3):296-316 (July 1988).
     Minow, Martha. We, the family: constitutional rights and American families. *Journal of American History* 74(3):959-983 (December 1987).
     Mishler, William, and Reginald S. Sheehan. The Supreme Court as a countermajoritarian institution? The impact of public opinion on Supreme Court decisions. *American Political Science Review* 87(1):87-101 (March 1993).
     Orren, Karen. The primacy of labor in American constitutional development. *American Political Science Review* 89(2):377-388 (June 1995).
     Quirk, William J. Judicial dictatorship. *Society* 31(2):34-38 (January/February 1994).
     Schlesinger, Arthur M. Roosevelt and the courts. *Society* 24(1):53-56 (November/December 1986).
     Taylor, John B. The Supreme Court and political eras: a perspective on judicial power in a democratic polity. *Review of Politics* 54(3):345-68 (Summer 1992).

659. Wright v. Vinton Branch of the Mountain Trust Bank of Roanoke, Virginia   March 29, 1937
     300 US 440   81 LEd 736   57 SCt 556
        En Am Con 2077

660. Sonzinsky v. United States   March 29, 1937
     300 US 506   81 LEd 772   57 SCt 554
        En Am Con 1710
        Guide (CQ) 117-118

661. Virginian Railway Co. v. System Federation, No. 40, March 29, 1937
     Railway Employees Department of the American Federation of Labor
     300 US 515   81 LEd 789   57 SCt 592
        Sup Ct Review (1992):235-293

662. National Labor Relations Board (NLRB) v. Jones and Laughlin Steel Co.   April 12, 1937
     301 US 1   81 LEd 893   57 SCt 615
        Court Const 156-168+
        Documents (v. 2):318-324R
        En Am Con 602-606, 613-614, 1112-1119, 1913-1920, 1990-1992
        Equal (Harrell) 82-83, 94
        Guide (CQ) 42, 95, 101-102
        Guide (West) (v. 8):46-48
        Magic 282-284
        Powers 145-146
        Sup Ct Review (1995):125-215

Caldeira, Gregory A. Public opinion and the U.S. Supreme Court: FDR's court-packing plan. *American Political Science Review* 81(4):1139-1153 (December 1987).

Goddy, David. The Court's broad impact on our economic life. *Scholastic Update* (Teachers' Edition) 117(7):17-18 (November 30, 1984).

Heffner, Judith C. The Constitution in court. *Scholastic Update* (Teachers' Edition) 116(5):16-18 (October 28, 1983).

Mishler, William, and Reginald S. Sheehan. The Supreme Court as a countermajoritarian institution? The impact of public opinion on Supreme Court decisions. *American Political Science Review* 87(1):87-101 (March 1993).

O'Brien, David M. Federalism as a metaphor in the constitutional politics of public administration. *Public Administration Review* 49(5):411-419 (September/October 1989).

Orren, Karen. The primacy of labor in American constitutional development. *American Political Science Review* 89(2):377-388 (June 1995).

Schlesinger, Arthur M. Roosevelt and the courts. *Society* 24(1):53-56 (November/December 1986).

663. National Labor Relations Board (NLRB) v. Fruehauf Trailer Co.   April 12, 1937
      301 US 49   81 LEd 893   57 SCt 642
         En Am Con 1990-1992

664. National Labor Relations Board (NLRB) v. Friedman-Harry Marks Clothing Co., Inc.   April 12, 1937
      301 US 58   81 LEd 893, 921   57 SCt 645
         En Am Con 1900-1992
         Guide (CQ) 102-103

665. Associated Press v. National Labor Relation Board (NLRB)   April 12, 1937
      301 US 103   81 LEd 953   57 SCt 650
         Documents (v. 2):324-325R
         En Am Con 1990-1992
         Guide (CQ) 102-103
      Pfeffer, Leo. Religious exemptions. *Society* 21(4):17-22 (May/June 1984).

666. Washington, Virginia and Maryland Coach Co. v.   April 12, 1937
         National Labor Relations Board (NLRB)
      301 US 142   81 LEd 965   57 SCt 648
         Guide (CQ) 102-103
         Sup Ct Review (1992):235-293

667. Herndon v. Lowry   April 26, 1937
      301 US 242   81 LEd 1066   57 SCt 732
         Const (Currie) 254-255, 257-259
         Documents (v. 2):373-378R
         En Am Con 914, 968-970
         Sup Ct Ind 33+

668. United States v. Belmont   May 3, 1937
      301 US 324   81 LEd 1134   57 SCt 758
         En Am Con 106-107, 747-755, 1390-1391
      Halberstam, Malvina. Agora: international kidnaping—in defense of the Supreme Court decision in Alvarez-Machain. *American Journal of International Law* 86(4):736-746 (October 1992).
      LaFeber, Walter. The Constitution and United States foreign policy: an interpretation. *Journal of American History* 74(3):695-717 (December 1987).

669. Carmichael v. Southern Coal and Coke Co.   May 24, 1937
      301 US 495   81 LEd 1245   57 SCt 868
         New Right (Schwartz) 124-128

670. Steward Machine Co. v. Davis   May 24, 1937
      301 US 548   81 LEd 1279   57 SCt 883
        Documents (v. 2):334-339R
        En Am Con 695-697, 837-838, 1704-1705, 1768
        Guide (CQ) 42, 95, 119-121, 123b
        Magic 282-284
        New Right (Schwartz) 124-128
        Sup Ct Review (1988):85-127
     Hickok, Eugene W., Jr. Federalism's future before the U.S. Supreme Court. *Annals of the American Academy of Political and Social Science* 509:73-82 (May 1990).
     Jensen, Laura S. Subsidies, strings, and the courts: judicial action and conditional federal spending. *Review of Politics* 55(3):491-509 (Summer 1993).
     Stephens, Pamela J. Implementing federal energy policy at the state and local levels: "every power requisite". *Boston College Environmental Affairs Law Review* 10(4):875-904 (May 1983).

671. Helvering, Commissioner of Internal Revenue v. Davis   May 24, 1937
      301 US 619   81 LEd 1307   57 SCt 904
        Documents (v. 2):339-341R
        En Am Con 912, 1704-1705, 1869-1871
        Guide (CQ) 42, 95, 119-121, 123b
        New Right (Schwartz) 124-128

672. Breedlove v. Suttles, as Tax Collector   December 6, 1937
      302 US 277   82 LEd 252   58 SCt 205
        En Am Con 148, 1979-1987
        Sup Ct Review (1986):317-393

673. Palko v. Connecticut   December 6, 1937
      302 US 319   82 LEd 288   58 SCt 149
        Const (Currie) 247-248
        Const (Friendly) 28-29
        Const Law 29-31R+
        Court Const 240-243
        En Am Con 592, 829-830, 970-973, 1360-1361, 1472-1479, 1569-1577
        Hard Choices 129-130, 309
        Magic 313
     Gillman, Howard. Preferred freedoms: the progressive expansion of state power and the rise of modern civil liberties jurisprudence. *Political Research Quarterly* 47(3):623-653 (September 1994).

674. Nardone v. United States   December 20, 1937
      302 US 379   82 LEd 314   58 SCt 275
        En Am Con 1292

675. Ex Parte Levitt   October 11, 1937
      302 US 633   82 LEd 493   58 SCt 1
     Alpert, Peter A. Citizen suits under the Clean Air Act: universal standing for the uninjured private attorney general? *Boston College Environmental Affairs Law Review* 16(2):283-328 (Winter 1988).

676. Connecticut General Life Insurance Co. v. Johnson   January 31, 1938
      303 US 77   82 LEd 673   58 SCt 436
        Documents (v. 2):400-402R

677. South Carolina State Highway Department v. Barnwell Brothers, Inc.   February 14, 1938
      303 US 177   82 LEd 734   58 SCt 510
        Ascent 111-114

Const (Currie) 325-328
Court Const. 94-99
En Am Con 1751-1755

678. Lauf v. E.G. Shinner and Co.   February 28, 1938
      303 US 323   82 LEd 872   58 SCt 578
      Guide (CQ) 96
      Mathias, Charles McC., Jr. The federal courts under siege. *Annals of the American Academy of Political and Social Science* 462: 26-33 (July 1982).

679. Helvering, Commissioner of Internal Revenue v. Mitchell   March 7, 1938
      303 US 391   82 LEd 917   58 SCt 630
      Caginalp, O. A. Fifth Amendment privilege against self-incrimination and compulsory self-disclosure under the Clean Air and Clean Water Acts. *Boston College Environmental Affairs Law Review* 9(2):359-395 (1980-1981).
      Staas, John August. Supreme Court review: Fifth Amendment—statutory dilution of the privilege against self-incrimination. *Journal of Criminal Law and Criminology* 71(4):610-621 (Winter 1980).

680. Lovell v. City of Griffin   March 28, 1938
      303 US 444   82 LEd 949   58 SCt 666
      Const (Currie) 261-263
      En Am Con 1180-1181
      Guide (CQ) 44-45
      Sup Ct Ind 56-57+
      Boedecker, Karl A., and Fred W. Morgan. The evolution of First Amendment protection for commercial speech. *Journal of Marketing* 59(1):38-47 (January 1995).
      Mehra, Achal. Iskcon court decisions: setback for proselytizing rights. *Journalism Quarterly* 61(1):109-116 (Spring 1984).

681. Erie Railroad Co. v. Tompkins   April 25, 1938
      304 US 64   82 LEd 1188   58 SCt 817
      Const (Currie) 239-244
      En Am Con 357-358, 570-571, 650, 689-691
      Guide (West) (v. 4):371-375
      Law 84-86
      Magic 282-284
      Sup Ct Review (1983):509-581; (1994):295-343
      Arsenault, Richard J., and Richard W. Beard. Maritime personal injury on foreign waters. *Trial* 20(6):72-76 (June 1984).
      Collins, Michael. The dilemma of the downstream state: the untimely demise of federal common law nuisance. *Boston College Environmental Affairs Law Review* 11(2):295-412 (January 1984).
      Giesser, John L. The National Park Service and external development: addressing park boundary-area threats through public nuisance. *Boston College Environmental Affairs Law Review* 20(4):761-809 (Summer 1993).
      Spillenger, Clyde. Reading the judicial canon: Alexander Bickel and the book of Brandeis. *Journal of American History* 79(1):125-151 (June 1992).

682. Hinderlider v. La Plata River and Cherry Creek Ditch Co.   April 25, 1938
      304 US 92   82 LEd 1202   58 SCt 803
      Briggett, Marlissa S. State supremacy in the federal realm: the interstate compact. *Boston College Environmental Affairs Law Review* 18(4):751-772 (Summer 1991).
      Collins, Michael. The dilemma of the downstream state: the untimely demise of federal common law nuisance. *Boston College Environmental Affairs Law Review* 11(2):295-412 (January 1984).

683. United States v. Carolene Products Co.   April 25, 1938
      304 US 144   82 LEd 1234   58 SCt 778

Behind Bakke 73-74, 82
Brennan 65-77
Const (Currie) 308-334
Const (Friendly) 28-29
Documents (v. 2):410
En Am Con 213-215, 566-568, 730-738, 829-830, 914-917, 1031-1038, 1796-1803
Guide (CQ) 43
Guide (West) (v. 2):235-236
Magic 313
Sup Ct Review (1987):397-428

Cox, Archibald. First Amendment. *Society* 24(1):8-15 (November/December 1986).

Erler, Edward J. Brown v. Board of Education at 30. *National Review* 36(17):26-28, 30-31, 53 (September 7, 1984).

Gillman, Howard. Preferred freedoms: the progressive expansion of state power and the rise of modern civil liberties jurisprudence. *Political Research Quarterly* 47(3):623-653 (September 1994).

Howard, A. E. Dick. Making it work. *Wilson Quarterly* 11(2):122-133 (Spring 1987).

Kens, Paul. Liberty and the public ingredient of private property. *Review of Politics* 55(1):85-116 (Winter 1993).

Lamb, Charles M. Legal foundations of civil rights and pluralism America. *Annals of the American Academy of Political and Social Science* 454:13-25 (March 1981).

Marshall, Thomas R. Public opinion, representation, and the modern Supreme Court. *American Politics Quarterly* 16(3):296-316 (July 1988).

Rievman, Joshua D. Judicial scrutiny of Native American free exercise rights: Lyng and the decline of the Yoder doctrine. *Boston College Environmental Affairs Law Review* 17(1):169-199 (Fall 1989).

Wilkinson, J. Harvie, III. The dimensions of American constitutional equality. *Law and Contemporary Problems* 55(1):236-251 (Winter 1992).

684. National Labor Relations Board (NLRB) v. Mackay Radio and Telegraph Co.   May 16, 1938
304 US 333   82 LEd 1381   58 SCt 904
Almanac (1994):402

Donahue, Thomas R. AFL-CIO, should the Senate approve S.55, the Workplace Fairness Act? *Congressional Digest* 72(6-7):184, 186, 188, 190 (June 1993).

Finkin, Matthew W. Regulation by agreement: the case of private higher education. *Academe* 67(2):67-80 (April 1981).

Ford, William D., Marge Roukema, Harris W. Fawell, and Howard L. Berman. Should the House approve H.R. 5, the Workplace Fairness Act? *Congressional Digest* 70(11):270-273, 275, 277-280 (November 1991).

GAO report. *Congressional Digest* 70(11):267-268 (November 1991).

Higgins, George. Strike one, you're out. *Commonweal* 117(14):448-450 (August 10, 1990).

Miller, William H. Next year's big labor issue. *Industry Week* 239(13):56-57 (July 2, 1990).

Replacement of striking workers. *Congressional Digest* 72(6-7):162 (June 1993).

The right to strike. *Congressional Digest* 70(11):264-265 (November 1991).

685. Helvering, Commissioner of Internal Revenue v. Gerhardt   May 23, 1938
      Coupled with Helvering, Commissioner of Internal Revenue v. Wilson
      Coupled with Same v. Mulcahy
304 US 405   82 LEd 1427   58 SCt 969
Documents (v. 2):402-405R

686. Johnson v. Zerbst   May 23, 1938
304 US 458   82 LEd 1461   58 SCt 1019
En Am Con 1028, 1585-1592, 2003-2005
Guide (CQ) 44-45

687. Consolidated Edison Co. of New York v. National Labor Relations Board (NLRB)   December 5, 1938
      Coupled with International Brotherhood of Electrical Workers v. National Labor Relations Board

(NLRB)
305 US 197   83 LEd 126   59 SCt 206
  Guide (CQ) 102-103
Bangser, Paul M. An inherent role for cost-benefit analysis in judicial review of agency decisions: a new
  perspective on OSHA rulemaking. *Boston College Environmental Affairs Law Review* 10(2):365-444
  (September 1982).

688. Missouri ex rel. Gaines v. Canada   December 12, 1938
      305 US 337   83 LEd 208   59 SCt 232
        Const (Currie) 249-250
        En Am Con 1269
        Guide (CQ) 44-45
        Making 70, 121-123, 129-130, 181-182
      Basic court ruling: the Brown decision. *Congressional Digest* 59(2):34-35, 64 (February 1981).
      Delon, Floyd G. The legacy of Thurgood Marshall. *Journal of Negro Education* 63(3):278-288 (Summer 1994).
      Gregory, David L. The continuing vitality of affirmative action diversity principles in professional and graduate
        school student admissions and faculty hiring. *Journal of Negro Education* 63(3):421-429 (Summer 1994).
      Hobbs, Gardner J. Public school finance and the courts. *Clearing House* 53(9):405-409 (May 1980).
      Lamb, Charles M. Legal foundations of civil rights and pluralism America. *Annals of the American Academy of
        Political and Social Science* 454:13-25 (March 1981).
      Stefkovich, Jacqueline A., and Terrence Leas. A legal history of desegregation in higher education. *Journal of
        Negro Education* 63(3):406-420 (Summer 1994).
      White, Forrest R. Brown revisited. *Phi Delta Kappan* 76(1):12-19 (September 1994).

689. Currin v. Wallace, Secretary of Agriculture   January 30, 1939
      306 US 1   83 LEd 441   59 SCt 379
      Franck, Thomas M., and Clifford A. Bob. The return of Humpty-Dumpty: foreign relations law after the
        Chadha case. *American Journal of International Law* 79(4):912-960 (October 1985).

690. Graves v. New York ex rel. O'Keefe   March 27, 1939
      306 US 466   83 LEd 927   59 SCt 595
        Documents (v. 2):404-410R
        En Am Con 864

691. United States v. Miller   May 15, 1939
      307 US 174   83 LEd 1206   59 SCt 816
      Buckley, William F., Jr. Ban the guns? *National Review* 41(7):54-55 (April 21, 1989).
      Rosenblatt, Roger. The Bill of Rights. *Life* 14(13 Special Issue):9-30 (Fall 1991).
      Spitzer, Robert J. Shooting down gun myths. *America* 152(22):468-469 (June 8, 1985).
      Welsh, Robert, and Ronald K. L. Collins. Taking state constitutions seriously: the protection of civil liberties
        has been shifting away from the U.S. Supreme Court. *Center Magazine* 14(5):6-35, 38-43 (September/
        October 1981).

692. Lane v. Wilson   May 22, 1939
      307 US 268   83 LEd 1281   59 SCt 872
        Const (Currie) 249-250

693. Coleman v. Miller   June 5, 1939
      307 US 433   83 LEd 1385   59 SCt 972
        Almanac (1992):58
        Amending 248-256
        En Am Con 47-49, 310
        Equal Rights (Kanowitz) 125-127+
        Guide (CQ) 152, 152b, 153
      Lewin, Nathan. Judgment time for ERA. *New Republic* 186(6):8,10-13 (February 10, 1982).

Orren, Karen. The primacy of labor in American constitutional development. *American Political Science Review* 89(2):377-388 (June 1995).

694. Hague v. Committee for Industrial Organization (CIO) June 5, 1939
307 US 496 83 LEd 1423 59 SCt 954
Const (Currie) 263-266
En Am Con 770-773, 888, 1112-1119, 1488-1489
Guide (CQ) 44-45
Sup Ct Review (1992):79-122

695. United States v. Rock Royal Co-operative Inc. June 5, 1939
    Coupled with Noyes v. Rock Royal Co-operative, Inc.
    Coupled with Dairymen's League Cooperative Association v. Rock Royal Co-operative, Inc.
    Coupled with Metropolitan Cooperative Milk Products Bargaining Agency v. Rock Royal Co-operative, Inc.
307 US 533 83 LEd 1446 59 SCt 993
En Am Con 2077-2078

696. Case v. Los Angeles Lumber Products Co. November 6, 1939
308 US 106 84 LEd 110 60 SCt 1
Weintraub, Benjamin. Cramming down a plan: help or hindrance for creditors? *Credit and Financial Management* 84(3):27-28 (March 1982).

697. Schneider v. State of New Jersey (Town of Irvington) November 22, 1939
    Coupled with Young v. California
    Coupled with Snyder v. Milwaukee
    Coupled with Nichols v. Massachusetts
308 US 147 84 LEd 155 60 SCt 146
Const (Currie) 261-266, 268-270
Boedecker, Karl A., and Fred W. Morgan. The evolution of First Amendment protection for commercial speech. *Journal of Marketing* 59(1):38-47 (January 1995).
Gillman, Howard. Preferred freedoms: the progressive expansion of state power and the rise of modern civil liberties jurisprudence. *Political Research Quarterly* 47(3):623-653 (September 1994).

698. Bruno v. United States December 4, 1939
308 US 287 84 LEd 257 60 SCt 198
Gromer, Sharon K. Supreme Court review: Fifth Amendment—the right to a no "adverse inference" jury instruction. *Journal of Criminal Law and Criminology* 72(4):1307-1325 (Winter 1981).

699. Pepper v. Litton December 4, 1939
308 US 295 84 LEd 281 60 SCt 238
Weintraub, Benjamin. Legally speaking: equity—a court of conscience. *Credit and Financial Management* 82(8):11 (September 1980).

700. Nardone v. United States December 11, 1939
308 US 338 84 LEd 307 60 SCt 266
Stratton, Brent D. The attenuation exception to the exclusionary rule: a study in attenuated principle and dissipated logic. *Journal of Criminal Law and Criminology* 75(1):139-165 (Spring 1984).

701. Kalb v. Feuerstein January 2, 1940
    Coupled with Kalb v. Luce
308 US 433 84 LEd 370 60 SCt 343
Sup Ct Review (1986):135-155

702. Deputy v. du Pont   January 8, 1940
      308 US 488   84 LEd 416   60 SCt 363
      Bond, James G., and Royce E. Chaffin. Can securities trading be a trade or business? *Taxes* 65(11):727-732
          (November 1987).
      Gulledge, Dexter E., and Zoel W. Daughtrey. Gambling—a trade or business? *CPA Journal* 58(3):12-20
          (March 1988).

703. Yearsley v. W.A. Ross Construction Co.   January 29, 1940
      309 US 18   84 LEd 554   60 SCt 413
      Schwarz, Stephen G. The government contractor defense after Boyle: it can still be overcome. *Trial* 24(9):88-92
          (September 1988).

704. Madden v. Kentucky   January 29, 1940
      309 US 83   84 LEd 590   60 SCt 406
          En Am Con 1189

705. Chambers v. Florida   February 12, 1940
      309 US 227   84 LEd 716   60 SCt 472
          Documents (v. 2):424-427R
          En Am Con 225-226
          Making 50-51, 57, 68

706. South Chicago Coal and Dock Co. v. Bassett   February 26, 1940
      309 US 251   84 LEd 732   60 SCt 544
      Arsenault, Richard J. Seaman status: has the traditional mariner been forgotten? *Trial* 28(9):66-71 (September
          1992).
      George, James A. The 'triple crown' of admiralty cases: from definitions to damages. *Trial* 27(10):46-53
          (October 1991).

707. Helvering, Commissioner of Internal Revenue v. Clifford   February 26, 1940
      309 US 331   84 LEd 788   60 SCt 554
      Pratt, James W., and Sandra Leigh Bell. Trust-leaseback arrangements: where do they stand? *Trusts and
          Estates* 120(1):45-51 (January 1981).

708. National Licorice Co. v. National Labor Relations Board   March 4, 1940
      309 US 350   84 LEd 799   60 SCt 569
      Finkin, Matthew W. Regulation by agreement: the case of private higher education. *Academe* 67(2):67-80
          (April 1981).

709. United States v. City and County of San Francisco   April 22, 1940
      310 US 16   84 LEd 1050   60 SCt 749
      Fregeau, Jason David. Statutes and judicial discretion: against the law . . . sort of. *Boston College
          Environmental Affairs Law Review* 18(3):501-542 (Spring 1991).
      Shepard, Blake. The scope of Congress's constitutional power under the property clause: regulating non-federal
          property to further the purposes of national parks and wilderness areas. *Boston College Environmental Affairs
          Law Review* 11(3): 479-538 (April 1984).

710. Thornhill v. Alabama   April 22, 1940
      310 US 88   84 LEd 1093   60 SCt 736
          Const (Currie) 268-270, 311-313
          En Am Con 997-998, 1112-1119, 1352-1354, 1387-1388, 1896
          Guide (CQ) 44-45
          Sup Ct Review (1981):1-39

711. United States v. Socony-Vacuum Oil Co.
    310 US 150   84 LEd 1129
    Documents (v. 2):427-430R
    May 6, 1940   60 SCt 811

712. Cantwell v. Connecticut   May 20, 1940
    310 US 296   84 LEd 1213   60 SCt 900
    Amending 203-213
    Const (Currie) 252-253, 266-268, 348-350
    Const (Friendly) 113
    Const Law 49-52R+
    En Am Con 200-201, 770-773, 1538-1545, 1546-1547
    Godless 22-24+
    Landmark (v. 5):27-40R
    Let Us 114-115, 118-119
    Original (Davis) 66-69+
    Sup Ct Church 356-364R
    Boedecker, Karl A., and Fred W. Morgan. The evolution of First Amendment protection for commercial speech. *Journal of Marketing* 59(1):38-47 (January 1995).
    Greenlaw, Paul S., and John P. Kohl. Religious freedom and unemployment compensation benefits. *Public Personnel Management* 24(3):315-330 (Fall 1995).
    Ignagni, Joseph A. U.S. Supreme Court decision-making and the free exercise clause. *Review of Politics* 55(3):511-529 (Summer 1993).
    Lawton, Kim A. Uncle Sam v. First Church. *Christianity Today* 35(11):38-41 (October 7, 1991).
    Regan, Richard J. Regulating cult activities: the limits of religious freedom. *Thought* 61(241):185-196 (June 1986).
    Sullivan, Catherine Beth. Are kosher food laws constitutionally kosher? *Boston College Environmental Affairs Law Review* 21(1):201-245 (Fall 1993).
    Tushnet, Mark. The Constitution of religion. *Review of Politics* 50(4):628-658 (Fall 1988).

713. Nashville, Chattanooga and St. Louis Railway v. Browning   May 20, 1940
    310 US 362   84 LEd 1254   60 SCt 968
    Sup Ct Review (1989):223-259

714. Delaware River Joint Toll Bridge Commission v. Colburn   May 27, 1940
    310 US 419   84 LEd 1287   60 SCt 1039
    Briggett, Marlissa S. State supremacy in the federal realm: the Interstate Compact. *Boston College Environmental Affairs Law Review* 18(4):751-772 (Summer 1991).

715. Securities and Exchange Commission (SEC) v. United States Realty   May 27, 1940
    and Improvement Co.
    310 US 434   84 LEd 1293   60 SCt 1044
    Weintraub, Benjamin. Legally speaking: equity—a court of conscience. *Credit and Financial Management* 82(8):11 (September 1980).

716. Apex Hosiery Co. v. Leader   May 27, 1940
    310 US 469   84 LEd 1311   60 SCt 982
    En Am Con 63-64

717. United States v. American Trucking Association, Inc.   May 27, 1940
    310 US 534   84 LEd 1345   60 SCt 1059
    Sup Ct Review (1994):429-540

718. Minersville School District v. Gobitis   June 3, 1940
    310 US 586   84 LEd 1375   60 SCt 1010
    Abortion (Frohock) 10-12

> *Am Educators* 221
> *Antagonists* 106-119+
> *Black* 39-47
> *Brennan* 77-83
> *Const* (Friendly) 113-116
> *Courage* 13-36, 424-435
> *Court Const* 192-195
> *Documents* (v. 2):433-437R
> *En Am Con* 741-743, 1538-1545
> *Equal* (Harrell) 83-86, 97
> *First* 175-180
> *Godless* 7-8+
> *Guide (CQ)* 45
> *Just War* 230
> *Landmark* (v. 3):69-80R
> *Quarrels* 285-306
> *Sup Ct Church* 365-376R
> *Sup Ct Review* (1990):69-103

Brewster, Todd, and Temma Ehrenfeld. First and foremost. *Life* 14 (13 Special Issue):60-66 (Fall 1991).

Gillman, Howard. Preferred freedoms: the progressive expansion of state power and the rise of modern civil liberties jurisprudence. *Political Research Quarterly* 47(3):623-653 (September 1994).

Knowles, Trudy. Continued legal developments on the school flag movement. *Social Education* 56(1):52-54 (January 1992).

Simon, James F. Conflict and leadership: the U.S. Supreme Court from Marshall to Rehnquist. *Vital Speeches of the Day* 53(2):44-48 (November 1, 1986).

719. Hansberry v. Lee   November 12, 1940
      311 US 32   85 LEd 22   61 SCt 115
      En Am Con 294-295
      Making 86-87

Orlando, Caroline L. Aboriginal title claims in the Indian Claims Commission: U.S. v. Dann and its due process limitations. *Boston College Environmental Affairs Law Review* 13(2):241-280 (Winter 1986).

720. Helvering v. Horst   November 25, 1940
      311 US 112   85 LEd 75   61 SCt 144

Anspach, William N., Paul L. Marlin, and Charles J. Muller III. Deferred compensation: a case study of purposeful negation of Supreme Court jurisdiction over income tax laws. *Taxes* 59(10):691-711 (October 1981).

721. Helvering, Commissioner of Internal Revenue v. Eubank   November 25, 1940
      311 US 122   85 LEd 81   61 SCt 149

Anspach, William N., Paul L. Marlin, and Charles J. Muller III. Deferred compensation: a case study of purposeful negation of Supreme Court jurisdiction over income tax laws. *Taxes* 59(10):691-711 (October 1981).

722. United States v. Appalachian Electric Power Co.   December 16, 1940
      311 US 377   85 LEd 243   61 SCt 291
      En Am Con 64
      Guide (CQ) 88

Proctor, Michael G. Section 10 of the Rivers and Harbors Act and Western Water Allocations—are the western states up a creek without a permit? *Boston College Environmental Affairs Law Review* 10(1):111-182 (1982-83).

723. Sibbach v. Wilson and Co.   January 13, 1941
      312 US 1   85 LEd 479   61 SCt 422

Franck, Thomas M., and Clifford A. Bob. The return of Humpty-Dumpty: foreign relations law after the Chadha case. *American Journal of International Law* 79(4):912-960 (October 1985).

Schroeter, Leonard W. Privacy Rights can limit discovery. *Trial* 26(11):49-54 (November 1990).

724. Hines v. Davidowitz   January 20, 1941
     312 US 52   85 LEd 581   61 SCt 399
     En Am Con 918, 1146-1148

     Adams, Nancy D. Title VI of the 1990 Clean Air Act Amendments and state and local initiatives to reverse the stratospheric ozone crisis: an analysis of preemption. *Boston College Environmental Affairs Law Review* 19(1):173-216 (Fall 1991).

     Sherman, RuthAnn. Chemical warfare agent research regulation: the conflict between federal and local control. *Boston College Environmental Affairs Law Review* 14(1):131-163 (Fall 1986).

725. United States v. Darby   February 3, 1941
     312 US 100   85 LEd 609   61 SCt 451
     Documents (v. 2):453-456R
     En Am Con 536-537, 602-606, 680-682, 1229-1230, 1295-1299
     Equal (Harrell) 83
     Guide (CQ) 43-44, 95, 103-104, 123b
     Magic 282-284
     Powers 147

     Murphy, Walter F. The Constitution and the 14th Amendment. *Center Magazine* 20(4):9-30 (July/August 1987).

     Orren, Karen. The primacy of labor in American constitutional development. *American Political Science Review* 89(2):377-388 (June 1995).

726. Opp Cotton Mills v. Administrator of Wage and Hour   February 3, 1941
        Division of Department of Labor
     312 US 126   85 LEd 624   61 SCt 524

     Orren, Karen. The primacy of labor in American constitutional development. *American Political Science Review* 89(2):377-388 (June 1995).

727. Higgins v. Commissioner of Internal Revenue   February 3, 1941
     312 US 212   85 LEd 783   61 SCt 475

     Bond, James G., and Royce E. Chaffin. Can securities trading be a trade or business? *Taxes* 65(11):727-732 (November 1987).

728. United States v. Hutcheson   February 3, 1941
     312 US 219   85 LEd 788   61 SCt 463

     Orren, Karen. The primacy of labor in American constitutional development. *American Political Science Review* 89(2):377-388 (June 1995).

729. Milk Wagon Drivers Union of Chicago, Local 753 v. Meadowmoor Dairies, Inc.   February 10, 1941
     312 US 287   85 LEd 836   61 SCt 552
     Const (Currie) 269, 311-313

730. Railroad Commission of Texas v. Pullman Co.   March 3, 1941
     312 US 496   85 LEd 971   61 SCt 643
     En Am Con 9-11
     Guide (CQ) 273

731. Helvering v. Le Gierse   March 3, 1941
     312 US 531   85 LEd 996   61 SCt 646

     Adler, Stacy. Captive premiums deductible: court. *Business Insurance* 23(32):1, 49 (August 7, 1989).

Curley, Stephen C., and David Wawro. To what extent does deductibility of insurance premiums depend on risk shifting? *Journal of Taxation* 53(2):116-119 (August 1980).

Knight, Lee G., and Ray A. Knight. New possibility for captive insurance subsidiaries. *CPA Journal* 58(5):48-55 (May 1988).

Lenrow, Gerald I., and Philip K. Marblestone. The tax court affirms itself: bail bond arrangements do not constitute insurance. *Best's Review* (Property/Casualty Insurance Edition) 81(4):74-80 (August 1980).

732. Cox v. New Hampshire   March 31, 1941
312 US 569   85 LEd 1049   61 SCt 762
   Const (Currie) 261-263
   En Am Con 511-512, 1538-1545

Regan, Richard J. Regulating cult activities: the limits of religious freedom. *Thought* 61(241):185-196 (June 1986).

733. Skiriotes v. Florida   April 28, 1941
313 US 69   85 LEd 1193   61 SCt 924
   Sup Ct Review (1994):295-343

Winn, John. Alaska v. F/V Baranof: state regulation beyond the territorial sea after the Magnuson Act. *Boston College Environmental Affairs Law Review* 13(2):281-327 (Winter 1986).

734. Mitchell v. United States   April 28, 1941
313 US 80   85 LEd 1201   61 SCt 873
   Documents (v. 2):457-459R
   Making 71-72

735. Olsen v. Nebraska ex rel. Western Reference and Bond Association, Inc.   April 28, 1941
313 US 236   85 LEd 1305   61 SCt 862
   En Am Con 1343, 1744-1751

736. United States v. Classic   May 26, 1941
313 US 299   85 LEd 1368   61 SCt 1031
   Const Law 586-587+
   Documents (v. 2):459-463R
   En Am Con 295, 727-728, 1413-1417
   Guide (CQ) 43-44, 45
   Make 103-112
   Making 103-109
   Sup Ct Ind 112

Bernstein, Sidney, and Michael Eisenstein. 1982 Supreme Court update: the criminal law, part two. *Trial* 18(10):58-65 (October 1982).

737. Edwards v. California   November 24, 1941
314 US 160   86 LEd 119   62 SCt 164
   Documents (v. 2):463-464R
   En Am Con 613, 640-647, 975, 1458-1461, 1593-1596, 1954-1955
   Guide (CQ) 105

Karst, Kenneth L. Equal protection of the laws. *Society* 24(1):24-30 (November/December 1986).

738. Bridges v. California   December 8, 1941
     Coupled with Times-Mirror Co. v. Superior Court of California
314 US 252   86 LEd 192   62 SCt 190
   Antagonists 121-129+
   Const (Currie) 309-311
   Court Public 316
   En Am Con 154, 805-808, 1492-1494

Guide (West) (v. 2):161-163, 378-379
Make 90-102+

Simon, James F. Conflict and leadership: the U.S. Supreme Court from Marshall to Rehnquist. *Vital Speeches of the Day* 53(2):44-48 (November 1, 1986).

739. Textile Mills Securities Corp. v. Commissioner of Internal Revenue   December 8, 1941
      314 US 326   86 LEd 249   62 SCt 272
      Sup Ct Review (1983):32-82

740. United States v. Santa Fe Pacific Railroad   December 8, 1941
      United States ex rel. Hualpai Indians v. Santa Fe Pacific Railroad
      314 US 339   86 LEd 260   62 SCt 248

Orlando, Caroline L. Aboriginal title claims in the Indian Claims Commission: U.S. v. Dann and its due process limitations. *Boston College Environmental Affairs Law Review* 13(2):241-280 (Winter 1986).

741. Glasser v. United States   January 19, 1942
          Coupled with Kretske v. United States
          Coupled with Roth v. United States
      315 US 60   86 LEd 680   62 SCt 457

Baer, Harold, Jr. Sequestering witnesses: does the practice interfere with the defendants' constitutional rights? *Trial* 22(7):99-102 (July 1986).

Bleiweiss, Shell J. Supreme court review: Sixth Amendment—conflicts of interest in multiple representation of codefendants. *Journal of Criminal Law and Criminology* 71(4):529-537 (Winter 1980).

Hanusa, Julie. Supreme Court review: Sixth Amendment—the co-conspirator exemption to the hearsay rule: the confrontation clause and preliminary factual determinations relevant to Federal Rule of Evidence 801(d)(2)(E). *Journal of Criminal Law and Criminology* 78(4):915- 936 (Winter 1988).

742. United States v. Wrightwood Dairy Co.   February 2, 1942
      315 US 110   86 LEd 726   62 SCt 523
      En Am Con 2077
      Guide (CQ) 104

743. United States v. Pink   February 2, 1942
      315 US 203   86 LEd 796   62 SCt 552
      En Am Con 1390-1391

Halberstam, Malvina. Agora: international kidnaping—in defense of the Supreme Court decision in Alvarez-Machain. *American Journal of International Law* 86(4):736-746 (October 1992).

744. Chaplinsky v. New Hampshire   March 9, 1942
      315 US 568   86 LEd 1031   62 SCt 766
      Black 77-82
      Brennan 153-155+
      Const (Currie) 314-315, 396-398
      Const Law 154-156R+
      En Am Con 227, 728-729, 790-797, 797-804, 1335-1337, 1930
      First 300-310+
      Freedom (Cox) 49-52
      Jerry 184-194, 224-226+
      Price 8-13, 194-198
      Sup Ct Review (1992):29-77
      Tolerant 179-182+

Ennis, Bruce J. Protecting individual rights: hate speech and the heckler's veto. *Trial* 27(12):27-30 (December 1991).

Greenawalt, Kent. Free speech in the United States and Canada. *Law and Contemporary Problems* 55(1):5-33 (Winter 1992).

McGuire, Kevin T. Obscenity, libertarian values, and decision making in the Supreme Court. *American Politics Quarterly* 18(1):47-67 (January 1990).

Pawelek, Dick. Put yourself on the U.S. Supreme Court. *Senior Scholastic* 113(8):12-13, 27 (December 12, 1980).

Regan, Richard J. Regulating cult activities: the limits of religious freedom. *Thought* 61(241):185-196 (June 1986).

Rehnquist, William H. The United States Supreme Court: dissent. *Congressional Digest* 68(8-9):197, 199, 201 (August/September 1989).

Smolla, Rodney A. Academic freedom, hate speech, and the idea of a university. *Law and Contemporary Problems* 53(3):195-225 (Summer 1990).

745. Federal Power Commission (FPC) v. Natural Gas Pipeline Co.   March 16, 1942
     315 US 575   86 LEd 1037   62 SCt 736
     Documents (v. 2):471-474R

746. Tulee v. Washington   March 30, 1942
     315 US 681   86 LEd 1115   62 SCt 862
     Ott, Brian R. Indian fishing rights in the Pacific Northwest: the need for federal intervention. *Boston College Environmental Affairs Law Review* 14(2):313- 343 (Winter 1987).

747. Carpenters and Joiners Union of America, Local No. 213 v. Ritter's Cafe   March 30, 1942
     315 US 722   86 LEd 1143   62 SCt 807
     Const (Currie) 311-313

748. Bakery and Pastry Drivers & Helpers Local 802   March 30, 1942
     of the International Brotherhood of Teamsters v. Wohl
     315 US 769   86 LEd 1178   62 SCt 816
     Const (Currie) 311-313

749. Valentine v. Chrestensen   April 13, 1942
     316 US 52   86 LEd 1262   62 SCt 920
     Ascent 131-133
     Const (Currie) 513-518
     En Am Con 330-331
     Boedecker, Karl A., and Fred W. Morgan. The evolution of First Amendment protection for commercial speech. *Journal of Marketing* 59(1):38-47 (January 1995).

750. Goldman v. United States   April 27, 1942
     316 US 129   86 LEd 1322   62 SCt 993
     Webber, Dawn. Supreme Court review: Fourth Amendment—of warrants, electronic surveillance, expectations of privacy, and tainted fruits. *Journal of Criminal Law and Criminology* 75(3):630-652 (Fall 1984).

751. Seminole Nation v. United States   May 11, 1942
     316 US 286   86 LEd 1480   62 SCt 1049
     Baer, Susan D. The Public Trust Doctrine—a tool to make federal administrative agencies increase protection of public land and its resources. *Boston College Environmental Affairs Law Review* 15(2):385-436 (Winter 1988).

752. Hill v. Texas   June 1, 1942
     316 US 400   86 LEd 1559   62 SCt 1159
     Making 59-61
     Serr, Brian J., and Mark Maney. Racism, peremptory challenges, and the democratic jury: the jurisprudence of a delicate balance. *Journal of Criminal Law and Criminology* 79(1):1-65 (Spring 1988).

753. Betts v. Brady, Warden   June 1, 1942
      316 US 455   86 LEd 1595   62 SCt 1252
        Black 195-201
        Const (Currie) 320-322, 446-450
        Const Law 403-407+
        En Am Con 108, 844-845, 1472-1479, 1585-1592
        Guide (CQ) 45, 50
        Quarrels 340-347
        Super 407-409, 458-460+
      Wohleber, Curt. 1963 twenty-five years ago. *American Heritage* 39(2):36 (March 1988).

754. Kirschbaum v. Walling   June 1, 1942
          Coupled with Arsenal Building Corp. v. Walling
      316 US 517   86 LEd 1638   62 SCt 1116
        En Am Con 1105-1106

755. Skinner v. Oklahoma ex rel. Williamson   June 1, 1942
      316 US 535   86 LEd 1655   62 SCt 1110
        Abortion (Frohock) 62
        Abortion Am 8+
        Abortion Moral 37
        Court Public 97
        En Am Con 782-789, 1552-1558, 1577-1581, 1686, 1763, 1796-1803
        Hard Choices 131-132
      Gillman, Howard. Preferred freedoms: the progressive expansion of state power and the rise of modern civil
          liberties jurisprudence. *Political Research Quarterly* 47(3):623-653 (September 1994).
      Kaplan, David A. Is Roe good law? *Newsweek* 119(17):49-51 (April 27, 1992).

756. Jones v. Opelika   June 8, 1942
          Coupled with Bowden v. Fort Smith
          Coupled with Jobin v. Arizona
      316 US 584   86 LEd 1691   62 SCt 1231
        Antagonists 115-117+
        Const (Currie) 315-317
        Guide (CQ) 45
        Quarrels 300-302
      Gillman, Howard. Preferred freedoms: the progressive expansion of state power and the rise of modern civil
          liberties jurisprudence. *Political Research Quarterly* 47(3):623-653 (September 1994).

757. Ex Parte Quirin   October 29, 1942
      Quirin v. Cox
          Coupled with Ex Parte Haupt
          Coupled with Ex Parte Kerling
          Coupled with Ex Parte Burger
          Coupled with Ex Parte Heinek
          Coupled with Ex Parte Thiel
          Coupled with Ex Parte Neubauer
      317 US 1   87 LEd 3   63 SCt 1, 2
        Const (Currie) 280-281
        En Am Con 1497, 1903-1909
        Equal (Harrell) 88-89, 92
        Guide (CQ) 45
        Sup Ct Review (1986):259-316

758. Wickard, Secretary of Agriculture v. Filburn   November 9, 1942
     317 US 111   87 LEd 122   63 SCt 82
       Const (Currie) 299
       En Am Con 596-600, 602-606, 613-614, 962-966, 2061-2062
       Guide (CQ) 95, 104
       Magic 282-284
       Powers 147-148
     Orren, Karen. The primacy of labor in American constitutional development. *American Political Science Review* 89(2):377-388 (June 1995).
     Quirk, William J. Judicial dictatorship. *Society* 31(2):34-38 (January/February 1994).
     Solimine, Michael E. Constitutionality of congressional legislation to overrule Zurcher v. Stanford Daily. *Journal of Criminal Law and Criminology* 71(2):147-162 (Summer 1980).
     Van Alstyne, William W. Implied powers. *Society* 24(1):56-60 (November/December 1986).

759. Parker, Director of Agriculture v. Brown   January 4, 1943
     317 US 341   87 LEd 315   63 SCt 307
       Almanac (1980):10A
       En Am Con 1365, 1714-1716, 1744-1751
       Sup Ct Review (1984):69-148; (1986):157-173
     Hamlin, Ross J. Application of the Sherman Act state action exemption to municipal environmental regulation: a case for broader local discretion. *Boston College Environmental Affairs Law Review* 11(3):609-664 (April 1984).
     Roberts, Robert N. Municipal antitrust immunity and the state-action exemption: developments in the law. *State Government* 58(4):164-171 (Winter 1986).
     Ross, Douglas. Safeguarding our federalism: lessons for the states from the Supreme Court. *Public Administration Review* 45(Special Issue):723-731 (November 1985).
     Werner, Ray O. Marketing and the Supreme Court in transition. 1982-1984. *Journal of Marketing* 49(3):97-105 (Summer 1985).
     ———. Marketing and the United States Supreme Court, 1975-1981. *Journal of Marketing* 46(2):73-81 (Spring 1982).

760. Spies v. United States   January 11, 1943
     317 US 492   87 LEd 418   63 SCt 364
     Silverman, Elliot. Is affirmative misconduct necessary for tax evasion? *Journal of Taxation* 66(2):112-113 (February 1987).
     Silverman, Elliot. Turning the other cheek: tax fraud, tax protest, and the willfulness requirement. *Taxes* 69(5):302-307 (May 1991).

761. United States ex rel. Marcus v. Hess   January 18, 1943
     317 US 537   87 LEd 443   63 SCt 379
     Caginalp, O. A. Fifth Amendment privilege against self-incrimination and compulsory self-disclosure under the Clean Air and Clean Water Acts. *Boston College Environmental Affairs Law Review* 9(2):359-395 (1980-1981).
     Morenberg, Paul W. Environmental fraud by government contractors: a new application of the False Claims Act. *Boston College Environmental Affairs Law Review* 22(3):623-669 (Spring 1995).

762. Tileston v. Ullman   February 1, 1943
     318 US 44   87 LEd 603   63 SCt 493
       Abortion Am 6-7
       Liberty 94-106, 123-128+

763. Securities Exchange Commission (SEC) v. Chenery Corp.   February 1, 1943
     318 US 80   87 LEd 626   63 SCt 454
       Sup Ct Review (1991):261-301

764. McNabb v. United States March 1, 1943
318 US 332 87 LEd 819 63 SCt 608
En Am Con 1242-1243
Guide (West) (v. 7):319-320

Bloom, Robert M. Judicial integrity: a call for its reemergence in the adjudication of criminal cases. *Journal of Criminal Law and Criminology* 84(3):462-501 (Fall 1993).

Mitchells, Rebecca Ann. Supreme Court review: supervisory power meets the harmless error rule in Federal Grand Jury proceedings. *Journal of Criminal Law and Criminology* 79(3):1037-1063 (Fall 1988).

765. Jamison v. Texas March 8, 1943
318 US 413 87 LEd 869 63 SCt 669

Boedecker, Karl A., and Fred W. Morgan. The evolution of First Amendment protection for commercial speech. *Journal of Marketing* 59(1):38-47 (January 1995).

Regan, Richard J. Regulating cult activities: the limits of religious freedom. *Thought* 61(241):185-196 (June 1986).

766. Ex Parte Republic of Peru April 5, 1943
The Ucayali
318 US 578 87 LEd 1014 63 SCt 793
Sup Ct Review (1986):259-316

Halberstam, Malvina. Agora: international kidnaping—in defense of the Supreme Court decision in Alvarez-Machain. *American Journal of International Law* 86(4):736-746 (October 1992).

767. Murdock v. Pennsylvania May 3, 1943
     Coupled with Perisich v. Pennsylvania
     Coupled with Mowder v. Pennsylvania
     Coupled with Seders v. Pennsylvania
     Coupled with Lamborn v. Pennsylvania
     Coupled with Maltezos v. Pennsylvania
     Coupled with Tzanes v. Pennsylvania
319 US 105 87 LEd 1292 63 SCt 890
Const (Currie) 315-317
En Am Con 330-331, 1286
Godless 115-116+
Guide (CQ) 45

Boedecker, Karl A., and Fred W. Morgan. The evolution of First Amendment protection for commercial speech. *Journal of Marketing* 59(1):38-47 (January 1995).

Regan, Richard J. Regulating cult activities: the limits of religious freedom. *Thought* 61(241):185-196 (June 1986).

768. Martin v. City of Struthers, Ohio May 3, 1943
319 US 141 87 LEd 1313 63 SCt 862
Const (Currie) 317-320

Boedecker, Karl A., and Fred W. Morgan. The evolution of First Amendment protection for commercial speech. *Journal of Marketing* 59(1):38-47 (January 1995).

Regan, Richard J. Regulating cult activities: the limits of religious freedom. *Thought* 61(241):185-196 (June 1986).

769. Adams v. United States May 24, 1943
319 US 312 87 LEd 1421 63 SCt 1122
Making 64-66

770. Galloway v. United States May 24, 1943
319 US 372 87 LEd 1458 63 SCt 1077

Hogan, R. Ben, III. The Seventh Amendment: the Founders' views. *Trial* 23(9):76, 78, 80, 82 (September 1987).

771. Moline Properties, Inc. v. Commissioner of Internal Revenue   June 1, 1943
     319 US 436   87 LEd 1499   63 SCt 1132

Adler, Stacy. Captive premiums deductible: Court. *Business Insurance* 23(32):1, 49 (August 7, 1989).

Seto, Theodore P., and Susan D. Glimcher. When will a related corporate nominee be a partnership''s agent? *Journal of Taxation* 68(6):380-385 (June 1988).

Turner, Mark A. Agent vs. nominee: a suspended decision for dummy corporations. *Taxes* 67(4):263-268 (April 1989).

772. Tot v. United States   June 7, 1943
     319 US 463   87 LEd 1519   63 SCt 1241

     Sup Ct Review (1982):85-125
     Super 575-576

Harris, Leslie J. Constitutional limits on criminal presumptions as an expression of changing concepts of fundamental fairness. *Journal of Criminal Law and Criminology* 77(2):308-357 (Summer 1986).

773. West Virginia State Board of Education v. Barnette   June 14, 1943
     319 US 624   87 LEd 1628   63 SCt 1178

     Abortion (Frohock) 10
     Amending 188-193
     Antagonists 117-119+
     Brennan 77-83
     Center 26-269, 272+
     Const (Currie) 317-320, 353-354+
     Const (Friendly) 115-116
     Const Law 57-61R+
     Court Const 195-198+
     Documents (v. 2):437-442R
     En Am Con 608-612, 741-743, 1538-1545
     First 177-180, 183-184
     Godless 7-8+, 26-27
     Guide (CQ) 45
     Just War 230, 245-246
     Landmark (v. 3):81-96R
     Quarrels 285-306
     Sup Ct Church 376-400R
     Sup Ct Review (1990):69-103; (1994):57-128

Baird, Peter D., Oyez, oyez, oyez. *American Heritage* 45(7):32-37 (November 1994).

Bernstein, Sidney. Supreme Court review. *Trial* 21(4):14-15 (April 1985).

Brennan, William. The United States Supreme Court: decision. *Congressional Digest* 68(8-9)196, 198, 200 (August/September 1989).

Buckley, William F., Jr. Do you pledge allegiance? *National Review* 40(19):64-65 (September 30, 1988).

Eskin, Leah. Do you know your rights? *Scholastic Update* 120(15):9 (April 8, 1988).

Gillman, Howard. Preferred freedoms: the progressive expansion of state power and the rise of modern civil liberties jurisprudence. *Political Research Quarterly* 47(3):623-653 (September 1994).

Glasser, Ira. Preserving our liberty. *American School Board Journal* 178[179](11):22-26 (November 1992).

Gluckman, Ivan B. Separating myth from reality. *NASSP Bulletin* 69(485):60-66 (December 1985).

Kaplan, David A., and Bob Cohn. The hands-off Court. *Newsweek* 120(1):32-36 (July 6, 1992).

Knowles, Trudy. Continued legal developments on the school flag movement. *Social Education* 56(1):52-54 (January 1992).

Norpoth, Helmut, Jeffrey A. Segal, William Mishler, and Reginald S. Sheehan. Popular influence on Supreme Court decisions. *American Political Science Review* 88(3):711-724 (September 1994).

Olson, Tod. Marie and Cathie Barnett. *Scholastic Update* 126(2):21 (September 17, 1993).

Prayer in public schools. *Congressional Digest* 74(1):3-32 (January 1995).

Rabinove, Samuel. Religious liberty and church-state separation. *Vital Speeches of the Day* 52(17):526-530 (June 15, 1986).

Rehnquist, William H. The United States Supreme Court: dissent. *Congressional Digest* 68(8-9):197, 199, 201 (August/September 1989).

774. Hirabayashi v. United States   June 21, 1943
      320 US 81   87 LEd 1774   63 SCt 1375
      Antagonists 150-154+
      Brennan 83-86
      Civil 20th 2, 6, 13-26R
      Const (Currie) 285-289
      Courage 37-62, 425
      Documents (v. 2):465-470R
      En Am Con 877, 1010-1012
      Equal (Harrell) 86-87, 98
      Japanese 61, 83, 85, 86, 163-165
      Just War 87-93, 220-228, 231-250+
      Magic 264-265

775. Yasui v. United States   June 21, 1943
      320 US 115   87 LEd 1793   63 SCt 1392
      Japanese 360-361
      Just War 81-87, 222-227+

776. Schneiderman v. United States   June 21, 1943
      320 US 118   87 LEd 1796   63 SCt 1333
      Guide (CQ) 145
      Just War 243
      Murphy, Walter F. The Constitution and the 14th Amendment. *Center Magazine* 20(4):9-30 (July/August 1987).

777. United States v. Dotterweich   November 22, 1943
      320 US 277   88 LEd 48   64 SCt 134
      Goldberg, Andrew M. Corporate officer liability for federal environmental statute violations. *Boston College Environmental Affairs Law Review* 18(2):357-379 (Winter 1991).
      Webber, Rebecca S. Element analysis applied to environmental crimes: what did they know and when did they know it? *Boston College Environmental Affairs Law Review* 16(1):53-93 (Fall 1988).

778. Commissioner of Internal Revenue v. Heininger   December 20, 1943
      320 US 467   88 LEd 171   64 SCt 249
      Sup Ct Review (1983):32-82

779. Falbo v. United States   January 3, 1944
      320 US 549   88 LEd 305   64 SCt 346
      Const (Currie) 304-307

780. Federal Power Commission v. Hope Natural Gas Co.   January 3, 1944
            Coupled with Cleveland v. Hope Natural Gas Co.
      320 US 591   88 LEd 333   64 SCt 281
      En Am Con 682-683, 711
      Cleaves, Robert E., IV. Constitutional protection for the utility investor: the confiscation doctrine after Cleveland Electric Illuminating Co. v. Public Utilities Commission of Ohio. *Boston College Environmental Affairs Law Review* 12(3):527-558 (Spring 1985).

Marshall, Thomas R. Public opinion, representation, and the modern Supreme Court. *American Politics Quarterly* 16(3):296-316 (July 1988).

781. Prince v. Massachusetts   January 31, 1944
     321 US 158   88 LEd 645   64 SCt 438
       En Am Con 1453, 1538-1545
       Godless 24-25
     Minow, Martha. We, the family: constitutional rights and American families. *Journal of American History* 74(3):959-983 (December 1987).
     Regan, Richard J. Regulating cult activities: the limits of religious freedom. *Thought* 61(241):185-196 (June 1986).

782. Hecht Co. v. Bowles   February 28, 1944
     321 US 321   88 LEd 754   64 SCt 587
     Fregeau, Jason David. Statutes and judicial discretion: against the law . . . sort of. *Boston College Environmental Affairs Law Review* 18(3):501-542 (Spring 1991).

783. J.I. Case Co. v. National Labor Relations Board (NLRB)   February 28, 1944
     321 US 332   88 LEd 762   64 SCt 576
     Finkin, Matthew W. Regulation by agreement: the case of private higher education. *Academe* 67(2):67-80 (April 1981).

784. Yakus v. United States   March 27, 1944
     321 US 414   88 LEd 834   64 SCt 660
       Const (Currie) 300-303
       En Am Con 628, 2081
       Guide (CQ) 131
     Franck, Thomas M., and Clifford A. Bob. The return of Humpty-Dumpty: foreign relations law after the Chadha case. *American Journal of International Law* 79(4):912-960 (October 1985).
     Vanderziel, Kathleen M. The Hatfield Riders and environmental preservation: what process is due? *Boston College Environmental Affairs Law Review* 19(2):431-479 (Fall/Winter 1991).

785. Norton v. Warner, Co.   March 27, 1944
     321 US 565   88 LEd 931   64 SCt 747
     George, James A. The 'triple crown' of admiralty cases: from definitions to damages. *Trial* 27(10):46-53 (October 1991).

786. Follett v. Town of McCormick, South Carolina   March 27, 1944
     321 US 573   88 LEd 938   64 SCt 717
     Regan, Richard J. Regulating cult activities: the limits of religious freedom. *Thought* 61(241):185-196 (June 1986).

787. Smith v. Allwright   April 3, 1944
     321 US 649   88 LEd 987   64 SCt 757
       Const (Currie) 322-325
       Const Law 587-590R
       Documents (v. 2):485-487R
       En Am Con 727-728, 1698, 1979-1987
       Guide (CQ) 45
       Magic 322-324
       Making 105-109+
       Sup Ct Ind 112-113+
     Cutler, Lloyd N. Can the parties regulate campaign financing? *Annals of the American Academy of Political and Social Science* 486:115-120 (July 1986).
     Higginbotham, A. Leon, Jr. 50 years of civil rights. *Ebony* 51(1):148-154 (November 1995).

Klarman, Michael J. How Brown changed race relations: the backlash thesis. *Journal of American History* 81(1):81-118 (June 1994).

788. Pollock v. Williams, Sheriff   April 10, **1944**
    322 US 4   88 LEd 1095   64 SCt **792**
    En Am Con 1425

789. United States v. Ballard   April 24, **1944**
    322 US 78   88 LEd 1148   64 SCt **882**
    En Am Con 730-738, 1537, 1538-1545
    Godless 27-29+
    Religion 205-207, 226+
Cox, Archibald. First Amendment. *Society* 24(1):8-15 (November/December 1986).
Demerath, N. J., III, and Rhys H. Williams. A mythical past and uncertain future. *Society* 21(4):3-10 (May/June 1984).
McKown, Delos Banning. Deism and the Supreme Court. *Humanist* 52(2):25-28, 48 (March/April 1992).
Regan, Richard J. Regulating cult activities: the limits of religious freedom. *Thought* 61(241):185-196 (June 1986).
Taylor, Barry W. Diversion of church funds to personal use: state, federal, and private sanctions. *Journal of Criminal Law and Criminology* 73(3):1204-1237 (Fall 1982).

790. National Labor Relations Board v. Hearst Publications, Inc.   April 24, **1944**
        Coupled with National Labor Relations Board v. Stockholders Publishing Co.
        Coupled with National Labor Relations Board v. Times-Mirror Co.
    322 US 111   88 LEd 1170   64 SCt 851
Sheehan, Reginald S. Federal agencies and the Supreme Court: an analysis of litigation outcomes, 1953-1988. *American Politics Quarterly* 20(4):478-500 (October 1992).

791. Ashcraft v. Tennessee   May 1, **1944**
    322 US 143   88 LEd 1192   64 SCt 921
    En Am Con 1400-1408

792. United States v. South-Eastern Underwriters Association   June 5, **1944**
    322 US 533   88 LEd 1440   64 SCt 1162
    En Am Con 1713
    Guide (CQ) 106
McNamara, Daniel J. Toward a new environment. *Best's Review* (Property/Casualty Insurance Edition) 91(2):53-58 (June 1990).
Morrill, Thomas C. Nine dramatic decades. *Best's Review* (Property/Casualty Insurance Edition) 91(2):44-48, 126-128 (June 1990).
Stamp, Zack. A modest proposal. *Best's Review* (Property/Casualty Insurance Edition) 91(9):45-50 (January 1991).
Vinyard, Walter D., Jr. Retaliatory taxation—a crack in the foundation? *Best's Review* (Property/Casualty Insurance Edition) 81(12):14, 94-100 (April 1981).

793. Lyons v. Oklahoma   June 5, **1944**
    322 US 596   88 LEd 1481   64 SCt 1208
    Making 61-64

794. United States v. White   June 12, **1944**
    322 US 694   88 LEd 1542   65 SCt 1248
    En Am Con 1569-1577

795. Commissioner of Internal Revenue v. Harmon   November 20, **1944**
    323 US 44   89 LEd 60   65 SCt 103

Aspach, William N., Paul L. Marlin, and Charles J. Muller III. Deferred compensation: a case study of purposeful negation of Supreme Court jurisdiction over income tax laws. *Taxes* 59(10):691-711 (October 1981).

796. Kann v. United States   December 4, 1944
     323 US 88   89 LEd 88   65 SCt 148
     Maurer, Virginia G. The continuing expansion of RICO in business litigation. *Business Horizons* 33(5):80-87 (September/October 1990).

797. Smith v. Davis   December 4, 1944
     323 US 111   89 LEd 107   65 SCt 157
     Grillo, Alfred T. Ginnie Maes are not exempt from state taxation. *CPA Journal* 58(1):75-76 (January 1988).

798. Skidmore v. Swift and Co.   December 4, 1944
     323 US 134   89 LEd 124   65 SCt 161
     Sheehan, Reginald S. Federal agencies and the Supreme Court: an analysis of litigation outcomes, 1953-1988. *American Politics Quarterly* 20(4):478-500 (October 1992).

799. Steele v. Louisville and Nashville Railroad   December 18, 1944
     323 US 192   89 LEd 173   65 SCt 226
         Burger Court 161-162
     Higginbotham, A. Leon, Jr. 45 years in law and civil rights. *Ebony* 46(1):80-86 (November 1990).

800. Korematsu v. United States   December 18, 1944
     323 US 214   89 LEd 194   65 SCt 193
         Antagonists 147-155
         Black 163-182
         Brennan 83-86
         Civil 20th 2, 6, 27-36R
         Const (Currie) 289-292
         En Am Con 877, 1010-1012
         Equal (Harrell) 86-87
         Guide (CQ) 45
         Guide (West) (v. 7):26-27
         Japanese 61, 65, 209-211
         Just War 93-99, 226-307, 311-341+
         Landmark (v. 2):49-65R
         Magic 264-265
         One 361-367R
         Sup Ct Review (1995):1-43
         Sup Ct Yearbook (1993-94):30-31
     Bad landmark: righting a racial wrong. *Time* 122(22):51 (November 21, 1983).
     Higginbotham, A. Leon, Jr. 45 years in law and civil rights. *Ebony* 46(1):80-86 (November 1990).
     Karst, Kenneth L. Equal protection of the laws. *Society* 24(1):24-30 (November/December 1986).
     Katz, Stanley N. The strange birth and unlikely history of Constitutional equality. *Journal of American History* 75(3):747-762 (December 1988).
     Lamb, Charles M. Legal foundations of civil rights and pluralism America. *Annals of the American Academy of Political and Social Science* 454:13-25 (March 1981).
     Mishler, William, and Reginald S. Sheehan. The Supreme Court as a countermajoritarian institution? The impact of public opinion on Supreme Court decisions. *American Political Science Review* 87(1):87-101 (March 1993).
     Quirk, William J. Judicial dictatorship. *Society* 31(2):34-38 (January/February 1994).
     Raskin, Jamin B. A precedent for Arab-Americans? *Nation* 252(4):117, 119 (February 4, 1991).

801. Ex Parte Mitsuye Endo   December 18, 1944
     323 US 283   89 LEd 243   65 SCt 208
         Const (Currie) 292-293
         En Am Con 1010-1012
         Japanese 65, 134-135
         Just War 99-103, 143-151, 307-310, 317-319, 323-325, 341-345+

802. United States v. General Motors Co.   January 8, 1945
     323 US 373   89 LEd 311   65 SCt 357
     LaRusso, Joseph. "Paying for the change": First English Evangelical Lutheran Church of Glendale v. County of Los Angeles and the calculation of interim damages for regulatory takings. *Boston College Environmental Affairs Law Review* 17(3):551-583 (Spring 1990).

803. Thomas v. Collins   January 8, 1945
     323 US 516   89 LEd 430   65 SCt 315
         En Am Con 1112-1119
     Boedecker, Karl A., and Fred W. Morgan. The evolution of First Amendment protection for commercial speech. *Journal of Marketing* 59(1):38-47 (January 1995).

804. Republic of Mexico v. Hoffman   February 5, 1945
     324 US 30   89 LEd 729   65 SCt 530
     Halberstam, Malvina. Agora: international kidnaping—in defense of the Supreme Court decision in Alvarez-Machain. *American Journal of International Law* 86(4):736-746 (October 1992).

805. Commissioner of Internal Revenue v. Wemyss   March 5, 1945
     324 US 303   89 LEd 958   65 SCt 652
     Loutos, William A. Interest-free loans: an endangered species. *Taxes* 62(7):445-450 (July 1984).

806. Georgia v. Pennsylvania Railroad Co.   March 26, 1945
     324 US 439   89 LEd 1051   65 SCt 716
     Grady, Kevin T. Commonwealth of Puerto Rico v. SS Zoe Colocotroni: state actions for damage to non-commercial living natural resources. *Boston College Environmental Affairs Law Review* 9(2):397-429 (1980-1981).

807. Corn Products Refining Co. v. Federal Trade Commission (FTC)   April 23, 1945
     324 US 726   89 LEd 1320   65 SCt 961
     Boyles, Jesse V. The Supreme Court kills the Corn Products Doctrine—but will it rest in peace? *Taxes* 66(10):723-735 (October 1988).
     Briggs, Virginia L., and H. Ward Classen. Corn Products and its progeny: where do we go from here? *Taxes* 6(1):74-88 (January 1988).
     Marino, Francis A. Corn Products: evolution of tax doctrine. *CPA Journal* 50(11):21-27 (November 1980).
     Maydew, Gary L. Capital assets—the Arkansas Best and Circle K Cases. *CPA Journal* 61(11):56-61 (November 1991).
     Millman, Gregory J. The tale of Arkansas Best; when markets move faster than laws. [Editorial] *Barron's* 72(45):10 (November 9, 1992).
     Tatz, Reuben. Foreign currency hedges after Arkansas Best decision. *CPA Journal* 58(11):131-132 (November 1988).

808. Cramer v. United States   April 23, 1945
     325 US 1   89 LEd 1441   65 SCt 918
         En Am Con 513
         Equal (Harrell) 88-89
         Landmark (v. 5):41-66R
     Pawelek, Dick. Put yourself on the U.S. Supreme Court. *Senior Scholastic* 113(8):12-13, 27 (December 12, 1980).

809. Screws v. United States   May 7, 1945
      325 US 91   89 LEd 1495   65 SCt 1031
          En Am Con 1628, 1955-1957
          Making 49-50

810. Jewel Ridge Coal Corp. v. Local No. 6167, United Mine Workers   May 7, 1945
      325 US 161   89 LEd 1534   65 SCt 1063
          Sup Ct Review (1988):203-243

811. In re Summers   June 11, 1945
      325 US 561   89 LEd 1795   65 SCt 1307
          Black 47-55

812. Southern Pacific Co. v. Arizona ex rel. Sullivan   June 18, 1945
      325 US 761   89 LEd 1915   65 SCt 1515
          Const (Currie) 325-328
          En Am Con 596-600, 1145-1146, 1713-1714, 1751-1755
      Schwartz, Edward B. Water as an article of commerce: state embargoes spring a leak under Sporhase v.
          Nebraska. *Boston College Environmental Affairs Law Review* 12(1):103-169 (Fall 1985).

813. Allen Bradley Co. v. Local Union No. 3,   June 18, 1945
          International Brotherhood of Electrical Workers
      325 US 797   89 LEd 1939   65 SCt 1533
          En Am Con 45

814. Associated Press (AP) v. United States   June 18, 1945
          Coupled with Tribune Co. v. United States
      326 US 1   89 LEd 2013   65 SCt 1416
          Documents (v. 2):507-510R
          Fourth 207-221
          Freedom (Cox) 62-67
          Sup Ct Review (1994):57-128
      Blanchard, Margaret A. The Associated Press antitrust suit: a philosophical clash over ownership of First
          Amendment rights. *Business History Review* 61(1): 43-85 (Autumn 1984).

815. Guaranty Trust Co. of New York v. York   June 18, 1945
      326 US 99   89 LEd 2079   65 SCt 1464
          Law 85-89

816. Bridges v. Wixon, District Director, Immigration and Naturalization Service   June 18, 1945
      326 US 135   89 LEd 2103   65 SCt 1443
          Documents (v. 2):496-498R
      Cole, David. Non-alien speech. [Editorial] *Nation* 248(7):220-221 (February 20, 1989).

817. International Shoe Co. v. Washington   December 3, 1945
      326 US 310   90 LEd 95   66 SCt 154
      Arsenault, Richard J., and Richard W. Beard. Maritime personal injury on foreign waters. *Trial* 20(6):72-76
          (June 1984).
      Jurinski, James John. A primer on the unitary business concept. *CPA Journal* 56(9):52-64 (September 1986).

818. New York ex rel Ray v. Martin   January 7, 1946
      326 US 496   90 LEd 261   66 SCt 307
          Am Indian (Deloria)   63-82

819. Marsh v. Alabama   January 7, 1946
     326 US 501   90 LEd 265   66 SCt 276
     Burger Court 34-37
     En Am Con 273-280, 1205, 1729-1736, 1736-1738
     Sup Ct Review (1982):195-241; (1988):129-161
     Sullivan, Harold J. Privatization of public services: a growing threat to constitutional rights. *Public Administration Review* 47(6):461-467 (November/December 1987).

820. New York v. United States   January 14, 1946
     326 US 572   90 LEd 326   66 SCt 310
     Johnston, Richard E., and John T. Thompson. Burger court and federalism: a revolution in 1976? *Western Political Quarterly* 33(2):197-216 (June 1980).

821. In Re Yamashita   February 4, 1946
     Yamashita v. Styer
     327 US 1   90 LEd 499   66 SCt 340
     Const (Currie) 282-283
     Documents (v. 2):522-525R
     En Am Con 2081-2082

822. Estep v. United States   February 4, 1946
     327 US 114   90 LEd 567   66 SCt 423
     Const (Currie) 304-307

823. Duncan v. Kahanamoku   February 25, 1946
     Coupled with White v. Steer
     327 US 304   90 LEd 688   66 SCt 606
     Const (Currie) 283-285
     En Am Con 592, 628-629

824. United States v. Petty Motors Co.   February 25, 1946
     Coupled with United States v. Brockbank dba Brockbank Apparel Co.
     Coupled with United States v. Grimsdell dba Grocer Printing Co.
     Coupled with United States v. Wiggs dba Chicago Flexible Shaft Co.
     Coupled with United States v. Galigher Co.
     Coupled with United States v. Gray-Cannon Lumber Co.
     327 US 372   90 LEd 729   66 SCt 596
     LaRusso, Joseph. "Paying for the change": First English Evangelical Lutheran Church of Glendale v. County of Los Angeles and the calculation of interim damages for regulatory takings. *Boston College Environmental Affairs Law Review* 17(3):551-583 (Spring 1990).

825. Girouard v. United States   April 22, 1946
     328 US 61   90 LEd 1084   66 SCt 826
     En Am Con 846-847
     Godless 55-56
     Guide (CQ) 46-47, 144-145

826. Seas Shipping Co. v. Sieracki   April 22, 1946
     328 US 85   90 LEd 1099   66 SCt 872
     Due, Paul H. Proof of Negligence under the LHWCA. *Trial* 20(2):60-65 (February 1984).

827. United States v. Causby   May 27, 1946
     328 US 256   90 LEd 1206   66 SCt 1062
     En Am Con 1855-1857

Brown, Todd D. The power line plaintiff and the inverse condemnation alternative. *Boston College Environmental Affairs Law Review* 19(3):655-694 (Spring 1992).

Kahn, Richard. Inverse condemnation and the highway cases: compensation for abutting landowners. *Boston College Environmental Affairs Law Review* 22(3):563- 591 (Spring 1995).

828. United States v. Lovett   June 3, 1946
      Coupled with United States v. Watson
      Coupled with United States v. Dodd
   328 US 303   90 LEd 1252   66 SCt 1073
    Documents (v. 2):510-512R
    En Am Con 111-112, 1181, 1485-1487
    Guide (CQ) 76-77

829. Pennekamp v. Florida   June 3, 1946
   328 US 331   90 LEd 1295   66 SCt 1029
    Court Public 316

830. Morgan v. Virginia   June 3, 1946
   328 US 373   90 LEd 1317   66 SCt 1050
    Civil 20th 3, 9, 139-147R
    En Am Con 1280
    Guide (CQ) 46-47, 106
    Making 73-76+

831. Porter v. Warner Holding Co.   June 3, 1946
   328 US 395   90 LEd 1332   66 SCt 1086
Jordan, Scott J. Awarding attorney's fees to environmental plaintiffs under a private attorney general theory. *Boston College Environmental Affairs Law Review* 14(2):287-311 (Winter 1987).

McDowell, Gary L. Modest remedy for judicial activism. *Public Interest* (67):3-20 (Spring 1982).

832. Prudential Insurance Co. v. Benjamin   June 3, 1946
   328 US 408   90 LEd 1342   66 SCt 1142
    En Am Con 1383-1384
    Guide (CQ) 106
Vinyard, Walter D., Jr. Retaliatory taxation—a crack in the foundation? *Best's Review* (Property/Casualty Insurance Edition) 81(12):14, 94-100 (April 1981).

833. Colegrove v. Green   June 10, 1946
   328 US 549   90 LEd 1432   66 SCt 1198
    Const (Currie) 330-332
    Const Law 608+
    Court Public 48-49
    En Am Con 309-310, 1344, 1420-1422, 1518-1524
    Guide (CQ) 46-47, 50
    Super 410-412+
Rush, Mark E. In search of a coherent theory of voting rights: challenges to the Supreme Court's vision of fair and effective representation. *Review of Politics* 56(3):503-523 (Summer 1994).

834. Davis v. United States   June 10, 1946
   328 US 582   90 LEd 1453   66 SCt 1256
Goldberger, Peter. Consent, expectations of privacy, and the meaning of "searches" in the Fourth Amendment. *Journal of Criminal Law and Criminology* 75(2):319-362 (Summer 1984).

835. Kotteakos v. United States   June 10, 1946
   328 US 750   90 LEd 1557   66 SCt 1239

Liebman, James S., and Randy Hertz. Brecht v. Abrahamson: harmful error in habeas corpus law. *Journal of Criminal Law and Criminology* 84(4):1109-1056 (Winter/Spring 1994).

836. United States v. Carmack   December 9, 1946
    329 US 230   91 LEd 209   67 SCt 252
    Plater, Zygmunt J. B., and William Lund Norine. Through the looking glass of eminent domain: exploring the "arbitrary and capricious" test and substantive rationality review of governmental decisions. *Boston College Environmental Affairs Law Review* 16(4):661-752 (Summer 1989).

837. Freeman v. Hewit   December 16, 1946
    329 US 249   91 LEd 265   67 SCt 274
    En Am Con 804-805, 1757-1760

838. Louisiana ex rel. Francis v. Resweber   January 13, 1947
    329 US 459   91 LEd 422   67 SCt 374
    Const (Friendly) 161-172
    Death Penalty (Tushnet) 24-26, 154-155, 157
    Pawelek, Dick. Two high court cases that test the U.S. Constitution on human rights. *Scholastic Update* (Teachers' Edition) 119(3):39, 36 (October 6, 1986).
    Schwartz, Charles Walter. Eighth Amendment proportionality analysis and the compelling case of William Rummel. *Journal of Criminal Law and Criminology* 71(4):378-420 (Winter 1980).

839. Everson v. Board of Education of Ewing Township   February 10, 1947
    330 US 1   91 LEd 711   67 SCt 504
    Am Educators 209+
    Amending 203-213
    Antagonists 180-183+
    Burger Years 56-91
    Const (Currie) 339-342+
    Const (Friendly) 116-118
    Const Law 67-72R+
    Documents (v. 2):534-537R
    En Am Con 653-655, 657-658, 854-856, 1650-1658
    Establishment 123-128, 167, 172
    Godless 69-71+, 147-152
    Let Us 116-117
    Original (Davis) 66-71, 94-95, 102-104+
    Religion 22-26, 74
    Sup Ct Church 37-71R
    Sup Ct Review (1985):1-59
    Trial 93-94, 156-157
    Abram, Morris B. Is "strict separation" too strict? *Public Interest* (82):81-90 (Winter 1986).
    Buzzard, Lynn Robert and Samuel Ericsson. Public aid to private schools: Caesar rendering to God? *Christianity Today* 27(10):20-23 (June 17, 1983).
    Byrne, Harry J. Thanksgiving Day and the Supreme Court. *America* 162(5):121-123 (February 10, 1990).
    Card, Robert L. Church-state relations: where is the Supreme Court going? *Vital Speeches of the Day* 51(24):752-755 (October 1, 1985).
    Cord, Robert L. Church, state, and the Rehnquist Court. *National Review* 44(16):35-37 (August 17, 1992).
    ———. Understanding the First Amendment. *National Review* 34(1):26-32 (January 22, 1982).
    Coughlin, John J. Religion, education and the First Amendment. *America* 168(17):12-15 (May 15, 1993).
    Devins, Neal E., and Benjamin Feder. Reading the establishment clause. *Commonweal* 112(16):492-494 (September 20, 1985).
    Hammond, Phillip E. The courts and secular humanism. *Society* 21(4):11-16 (May/June 1984).
    Kobylka, Joseph F. Leadership on the Supreme Court of the United States: Chief Justice Burger and the establishment clause. *Western Political Quarterly* 42(4):545-568 (December 1989).

Lawton, Kim A. Uncle Sam v. First Church. *Christianity Today* 35(11):38-41 (October 7, 1991).

Lesly, Elizabeth, and Elliott Beard. Pennies from Heaven. *Washington Monthly* 23(4):40-45 (April 1991).

Manion, Maureen. The impact of state aid on sectarian higher education: the case of New York State. *Review of Politics* 1986 48(2): 264-288.

McBride, James. Tillich in an Alice-in-Wonderland world. [Editorial] *Christian Century* 104(18):519-520 (June 3-10, 1987).

Morrison, Richard Brandon. The wall of separation. *American Heritage* 35(5):77-79 (August/September 1984).

Mosk, Stanley. The emerging agenda in state constitutional rights law. *Annals of the American Academy of Political and Social Science* 496:54-64 (March 1988).

Ostling, Richard, Anne Constable, and Michael P. Harris. Threatening the wall: church-state separation has powerful new critics. *Time* 130(1):70-71 (July 6, 1987).

Pfeffer, Leo. Religious exemptions. *Society* 21(4):17-22 (May/June 1984).

Rabinove, Samuel, Josef Joffe, Sheldon F. Gottlieb, Adam Simms, Stephen F. Rohde, Jeffrey Valle, and Robert H. Bork. The First Amendment. [Editorial] *Commentary* 99(5):7-15 (May 1995).

Rabinove, Samuel. Religious liberty and church-state separation. *Vital Speeches of the Day* 52(17):526-530 (June 15, 1986).

Rayer, Thomas A. The bicentennial and church-related schools. *America* 157(17):427-429, 438 (December 5, 1987).

Regan, Richard J. Supreme Court roundup: 1979 term. *Thought* 55(219):487-455 (December 1980).

———. Supreme Court roundup: 1980 term. *Thought* 56(223):491-502 (December 1981).

———. Supreme Court roundup: 1986 term. *Thought* 63(251):429-441 (December 1988).

Roelofs, H. Mark. Church and state in America: toward a biblically derived reformulation of their relationship. *Review of Politics* 50(4):561-581 (Fall 1988).

Schamel, Wynell Burroughs, and Jean West Mueller. Teaching with documents: Abington v. Schempp: a study in the establishment clause. *Social Education* 53(1):61-66R (January 1989).

Stephenson, D. Grier, Jr. Religion and the Constitution: the Supreme Court speaks, again. *USA Today* 118(2538):21-23 (March 1990).

Sullivan, Catherine Beth. Are kosher food laws constitutionally kosher? *Boston College Environmental Affairs Law Review* 21(1):201-245 (Fall 1993).

Tushnet, Mark. The Constitution of religion. *Review of Politics* 50(4):628-658 (Fall 1988).

Weber, Paul J. Excessive entanglement: a wavering First Amendment standard. *Review of Politics* 46(4):483-501 (October 1984).

840. United Public Workers of America v. Mitchell   February 10, 1947
      330 US 75   91 LEd 754   67 SCt 556
          Const (Currie) 355-358
          En Am Con 907, 1597
          New Right (Schwartz) 62-67
      Supreme Court rulings. *Congressional Digest* 72(8-9):201, 224 (August/September 1993).

841. Oklahoma v. United States Civil Service Commission   February 10, 1947
      330 US 127   91 LEd 794   67 SCt 544
          Sup Ct Review (1988):85-113
      Jensen, Laura S. Subsidies, strings, and the courts: judicial action and conditional federal spending. *Review of Politics* 55(3):491-509 (Summer 1993).

      Johnston, Richard E., and John T. Thompson. Burger court and federalism: a revolution in 1976? *Western Political Quarterly* 33(2):197-216 (June 1980).

842. United States v. United Mine Workers of America   March 6, 1947
              Coupled with United States v. Lewis
      330 US 258   91 LEd 884   67 SCt 677
          En Am Con 1938

843. Testa v. Katt   March 10, 1947
      330 US 386   91 LEd 967   67 SCt 810

Martin, Stanley A. Problems with PURPA: the need for state legislation to encourage cogeneration and small power production. *Boston College Environmental Affairs Law Review* 11(1):149-202 (October 1983).

844. Gulf Oil Corp. v. Gilbert   March 10, 1947
330 US 501   91 LEd 1055   67 SCt 839
Arsenault, Richard J., and Richard W. Beard. Maritime personal injury on foreign waters. *Trial* 20(6):72-76 (June 1984).

845. Haupt v. United States   March 31, 1947
330 US 631   91 LEd 1145   67 SCt 874
En Am Con 908, 1903-1909
Equal (Harrell) 88-89, 92
Pawelek, Dick. Put yourself on the U.S. Supreme Court. *Senior Scholastic* 113(8):12-13, 27 (December 12, 1980).

846. Crane v. Commissioner of Internal Revenue   April 14, 1947
331 US 1   91 LEd 1301   67 SCt 1047
Bolling, Rodger A., and Philip P. Storrer. The Supreme Court's second look at Crane: what should it do? *Taxes* 61(2):138-144 (February 1983).
Bromberg, Barbara Schwartz. Trust taxes. *Trusts and Estates* 121(8):56 (August 1982).
Dorr, Patrick B., and Melvin E. Lacy. Crane after Tufts: still some unanswered questions. *Taxes* 62(3):162-169 (March 1984).
Duhl, Stuart and Jeffrey L. Kwall. Supreme Court holds that net gift triggers income to donor: an analysis of Diedrich. *Journal of Taxation* 57(3):130-134 (September 1982).
Hicks, Zoe M., and Rebecca F. Bracewell. Charitable contributions of partnership interests can produce unexpected results. *Journal of Taxation* 59(6):394-397 (December 1983).
Protass, Steven, and Gary Albert. Supreme Court decides Crane controversy. *CPA Journal* 53(11):64-65 (November 1983).
Sanders, Michael I. Supreme Court ending Crane controversy, says nonrecourse debt is always part of sales price. *Journal of Taxation* 59(1):2-5 (July 1983).
Yang, Wesley. Tufts: footnote to Crane. *Taxes* 62(2):118-124 (February 1984).

847. Rice v. Santa Fe Elevator Corp.   May 5, 1947
           Coupled with Illinois Commerce Commission v. Santa Fe Elevator Corp.
331 US 218   91 LEd 1447   67 SCt 1146
Sherman, RuthAnn. Chemical warfare agent research regulation: the conflict between federal and local control. *Boston College Environmental Affairs Law Review* 14(1):131-163 (Fall 1986).

848. Craig v. Harney, Sheriff   May 19, 1947
331 US 367   91 LEd 1546   67 SCt 1249
Court Public 316
En Am Con 805-808

849. United States v. California   June 23, 1947
332 US 19   91 LEd 1889   67 SCt 1658
Guide (CQ) 136b
Raymond, John M., and Barbara J. Frischholz. Lawyers who established international law in the United States, 1776-1914. *American Journal of International Law* 76(4):802-829 (October 1982).

850. Adamson v. California   June 23, 1947
332 US 46   91 LEd 1903   67 SCt 1672
Amending 203-213
Antagonists 176-179+
Const (Currie) 320-322, 362-364
En Am Con 23-24, 592, 757-761, 970-973, 1472-1479

Hard Choices 129, 309
Magic 313,317-320

851. Securities and Exchange Commission (SEC) v. Chenery Corp.   June 23, 1947
          Coupled with Securities and Exchange Commission v. Federal Water and Gas Corp.
      332 US 194   91 LEd 1995   67 SCt 1575, 1760
      Sup Ct Review (1991):261-301
      Funk, William. The exception that approves the rule: FDF variances under the Clean Water Act. *Boston College Environmental Affairs Law Review* 13(1):1-60(Fall 1985).

852. United States v. Yellow Cab Co.   June 23, 1947
      332 US 218   91 LEd 2010   67 SCt 1560
      Sup Ct Review (1984):69-148

853. Fay v. New York   June 23, 1947
          Coupled with Bove v. New York
      332 US 261   91 LEd 2043   67 SCt 1613
      En Am Con 130, 1082-1085, 1666-1673
      Magic 327-329

854. Federal Crop Insurance Corp. v. Merrill   November 10, 1947
      332 US 380   92 LEd 10   68 SCt 1
      Fisher, Bruce D. Positive law as the ethic of our time. *Business Horizons* 33(5):28-39 (September/October 1990).

855. International Salt Co., Inc. v. United States   November 10, 1947
      332 US 392   92 LEd 20   68 SCt 12
      Sup Ct Review (1984):69-148

856. Sipuel v. Board of Regents of the University of Oklahoma   January 12, 1948
      332 US 631   92 LEd 247   68 SCt 299
      Amending 203-213
      En Am Con 1684
      Making 129-131, 133-134
      Basic court ruling: the Brown decision. *Congressional Digest* 59(2):34-35, 64 (February 1981).
      Delon, Floyd G. The legacy of Thurgood Marshall. *Journal of Negro Education* 63(3):278-288 (Summer 1994).
      Lamb, Charles M. Legal foundations of civil rights and pluralism America. *Annals of the American Academy of Political and Social Science* 454:13-25 (March 1981).
      Stefkovich, Jacqueline A., and Terrence Leas. A legal history of desegregation in higher education. *Journal of Negro Education* 63(3):406-420 (Summer 1994).

857. Oyama v. California   January 19, 1948
      332 US 633   92 LEd 249   68 SCt 269
      En Am Con 1357-1358
      Japanese 67-68, 280

858. United States v. Sullivan   January 19, 1948
      332 US 689   92 LEd 297   68 SCt 331
      En Am Con 1808

859. Lee v. Mississippi   January 19, 1948
      332 US 742   92 LEd 330   68 SCt 300
      Making 68-69

860. Johnson v. United States   February 2, 1948
      333 US 10   92 LEd 436   68 SCt 367
      Misner, Robert L. Justifying searches on the basis of equality of treatment. *Journal of Criminal Law and Criminology* 82(3):547-578 (Fall 1991).

861. Bob-Lo Excursion Co. v. Michigan   February 2, 1948
      333 US 28   92 LEd 455   68 SCt 358
      En Am Con 132

862. C. & S. Airlines v. Waterman Corp.   February 9, 1948
      Chicago and Southern Airlines v. Waterman Steamship Corp.
            Coupled with Civil Aeronautics Board v. Waterman Steamship Corp.
      333 US 103   92 LEd 568   68 SCt 431
      Fisher, Louis. Foreign policy powers of the President and Congress. *Annals of the American Academy of Political and Social Science* 499:149-159 (September 1988).

863. Funk Brothers Seed Co. v. Kalo Inoculant Co.   February 16, 1948
      333 US 127   92 LEd 588   68 SCt 440
      Rosenblatt, David P. The regulation of recombinant DNA research: the alternative of local control. *Boston College Environmental Affairs Law Review* 10(1):37-78 (1982-83).
      Smith, Donna H., and Jonathan King. Proprietary rights and public interest: the legal and legislative background. *Environment* 24(6):24-26,33-37 (July/August 1982).

864. Woods v. Cloyd W. Miller Co.   February 16, 1948
      333 US 138   92 LEd 596   68 SCt 421
      En Am Con 2076
      Guide (CQ) 132

865. Illinois ex rel McCollum v. Board of Education of School District   March 8, 1948
            No. 71, Champaign County
      McCollum v. Board of Education
      333 US 203   92 LEd 649   68 SCt 461
            Am Educators 341-342
            Burger Years 56-91
            Const (Currie) 342-343+
            Const (Friendly) 116-118
            Documents (v. 2): 544-546
            En Am Con 34, 1535-1537, 1537-1538, 1650-1658
            First 165-168
            Godless 82-84+
            Let Us 118-119+
            Original (Davis) 69-72, 103-104+
            Religion 63-67, 79-82
            Sup Ct Church 173-183R, 183-194
      The court decisions. *Congressional Digest* 63(5):132-134,160 (May 1984).
      Gow, Haven Bradford. U.S. Supreme Court curbs student press rights. [Editorial] *Clearing House* 63(6)244 (February 1990).
      Hammond, Phillip E. The courts and secular humanism. *Society* 21(4):11-16 (May/June 1984).
      Prayer in public schools. *Congressional Digest* 74(1):3-32 (January 1995).
      Redlich, Norman. Some cracks in the wall. *Nation* 239(9):277-280 (September 29, 1984).
      Regan, Richard J. Supreme Court roundup: 1981 term. *Thought* 57(227):514-527 (December 1982).
      ———. Supreme Court roundup: 1986 term. *Thought* 63(251):429-441 (December 1988).
      Schamel, Wynell Burroughs, and Jean West Mueller. Teaching with documents: Abington v. Schempp: a study in the establishment clause. *Social Education* 53(1):61-66R (January 1989).

Sendor, Benjamin. When it comes to coercion, context is all. *American School Board Journal* 181(6):14-15 (June 1994).

866. In re Oliver   March 8, 1948
      333 US 257   92 LEd 682   68 SCt 499
          En Am Con 1341
          Law 388-389

867. Andres v. United States   April 26, 1948
      333 US 740   92 LEd 1055   68 SCt 880
          Death Penalty (Tushnet) 160, 163

868. Shelley v. Kraemer   May 3, 1948
      J. D. Shelley v. Kraemer
          Coupled with McGhee v. Sipes
      334 US 1   92 LEd 1161   68 SCt 836
          Brennan 255-257
          Civil 20th 3, 10, 149-166R
          Const (Currie) 358-360, 421-425
          Const Law 492-495R+
          Courage 63-79, 425
          Court Public 95
          En Am Con 273-280, 656-657, 727-728, 1500-1506, 1561-1562, 1676-1677, 1729-1736
          Guide (CQ) 46-47
          Making 96-98
          Sup Ct Review (1988):129-161
Halberstam, Malvina. Sabbatino resurrected: the act of state doctrine in the revised restatement of U.S. foreign relations law. *American Journal of International Law* 79(1):68-91 (January 1985).
Karst, Kenneth L. Equal protection of the laws. *Society* 24(1):24-30 (November/December 1986).

869. Hurd v. Hodge   May 3, 1948
          Coupled with Urciolo v. Hodge
      334 US 24   92 LEd 1187   68 SCt 847
          En Am Con 1676-1677

870. United States v. Paramount Pictures, Inc.   May 3, 1948
          Coupled with Loew's Inc. v. United States
          Coupled with Columbia Pictures Corp. v. United States
          Coupled with United Artists Corp. v. United States
          Coupled with Universal Pictures Corp. v. United States
          Coupled with American Theatres Association v. United States
          Coupled with Allred v. United States
      334 US 131   92 LEd 1260   68 SCt 915
Conant, Michael. Paramount decrees reconsidered. *Law and Contemporary Problems* 44(4):79-107 (Autumn 1981).

871. Toomer v. Witsell   June 7, 1948
      334 US 385   92 LEd 1460   68 SCt 1156
Grady, Kevin T. Commonwealth of Puerto Rico v. SS Zoe Colocotroni: state actions for damage to non-commercial living natural resources. *Boston College Environmental Affairs Law Review* 9(2):397-429 (1980-1981).
Winn, John. Alaska v. F/V Baranof: state regulation beyond the territorial sea after the Magnuson Act. *Boston College Environmental Affairs Law Review* 13(2):281-327 (Winter 1986).

872. Takahashi v. Fish and Game Commission   June 7, 1948
      334 US 410   92 LEd 1478   68 SCt 1138
         En Am Con 1855
         Japanese 68, 323

873. Phyle v. Duffy, Warden   June 7, 1948
      334 US 431   92 LEd 1494   68 SCt 1131
      Pastroff, Sanford M. Supreme Court review: Eighth Amendment—the constitutional rights of the insane on
         death row. *Journal of Criminal Law and Criminology* 77(3):844-866 (Fall 1986).

874. Saia v. New York   June 7, 1948
      334 US 558   92 LEd 1574   68 SCt 1148
         Const (Currie) 343-345

875. Central Greyhound Lines v. Mealey   June 14, 1948
      334 US 653   92 LEd 1633   68 SCt 1260
      Dell'Isola, Mark, and Sara Ann Hull. State sales tax on interstate transportation service valid. *CPA Journal*
         65(7):62-64 (August 1995).

876. Shapiro v. United States   June 21, 1948
      335 US 1   92 LEd 1787   68 SCt 1375
      Caginalp, O. A. Fifth Amendment privilege against self-incrimination and compulsory self-disclosure under the
         Clean Air and Clean Water Acts. *Boston College Environmental Affairs Law Review* 9(2):359-395 (1980-
         1981).
      Rosenblatt, Leonard R. The Fifth Amendment and the production of business records: and Braswell Begat
         Bouknight. *Taxes* 68(6):418-424 (June 1990).

877. Vermilya-Brown Co., Inc. v. Connell   December 6, 1948
      335 US 377   93 LEd 76   69 SCt 140
         Sup Ct Review (1991):179-224

878. Goesaert v. Cleary   December 20, 1948
      335 US 464   93 LEd 163   69 SCt 198
         Const (Currie) 360-362
         En Am Con 848, 1666-1673

879. Kovacs v. Cooper   January 31, 1949
      336 US 77   93 LEd 513   69 SCt 448
         Const (Currie) 343-345, 350-352
         En Am Con 330-331, 1109, 1711
      Marcy, William R. To protect or not to protect—that is the question. *Social Education* 54(6):364-365 (October
         1990).
      Winter, Ralph K. Political financing and the Constitution. *Annals of the Academy of Political and Social
         Science* 486:34-48 (July 1986).

880. Railway Express Agency v. New York   January 31, 1949
      336 US 106   93 LEd 533   69 SCt 463
         Const (Currie) 360-362
         En Am Con 1136-1143, 1509
      Lamb, Charles M. Legal foundations of civil rights and pluralism America. *Annals of the American Academy of
         Political and Social Science* 454:13-25 (March 1981).

881. Daniel v. Family Security Life Insurance Co.   February 28, 1949
      336 US 220   93 LEd 632   69 SCt 550
         Sup Ct Review (1982):127-166

882. Foley Bros., Inc. v. Filardo   March 7, 1949
     336 US 281   93 LEd 680   69 SCt 575
     Goldfarb, Joan R. Extraterritorial compliance with NEPA amid the current wave of environmental alarm.
        Boston College Environmental Affairs Law Review 18(3):543-603 (Spring 1991).

883. National Carbide Corp. v. Commissioner of Internal Revenue   March 28, 1949
           Coupled with Air Reduction Sales Co. v. Commissioner of Internal Revenue
           Coupled with Pure Carbonic, Inc. v. Commissioner of Internal Revenue
     336 US 422   93 LEd 779   69 SCt 726
     Seto, Theodore P., and Susan D. Glimcher. When will a related corporate nominee be a partnership's agent?
        Journal of Taxation 68(6):380-385 (June 1988).
     Turner, Mark A. Agent vs. nominee: a suspended decision for dummy corporations. *Taxes* 67(4):263-268 (April
        1989).

884. Giboney v. Empire Storage and Ice Co.   April 4, 1949
     336 US 490   93 LEd 834   69 SCt 684
        En Am Con 843, 1387-1388

885. Terminiello v. Chicago   May 16, 1949
     337 US 1   93 LEd 1131   69 SCt 894
        Const (Currie) 348-350
        Const Law 155-157+
        En Am Con 1877
        First 302-310
        Jerry 226-228
        Sup Ct Review (1990):257-299
     Melton, Gary B. Public policy and private prejudice: psychology and law on gay rights. *American Psychologist*
        44(6):933-940 (June 1989).

886. Brooks v. United States   May 16, 1949
     James M. Brooks v. United States
     337 US 49   93 LEd 1200   69 SCt 918
     Ball, Howard. The U.S. Supreme Court's glossing of the Federal Tort Claims Act: statutory construction and
        veterans' tort actions. *Western Political Quarterly* 41(3):529-552 (September 1988).

887. Williams v. New York   June 6, 1949
     337 US 241   93 LEd 1337   69 SCt 1079
        Death Penalty (Tushnet) 159
     Silets, Harvey M., and Susan W. Brenner. Commentary on the preliminary draft of the sentencing guidelines
        issued by the United States Sentencing Commission in September, 1986. *Journal of Criminal Law and
        Criminology* 77(4):1069-1111 (Winter 1986).

888. Larson v. Domestic and Foreign Commerce Corp.   June 27, 1949
     337 US 682   93 LEd 1628   69 SCt 1457
        Const (Currie) 577-580
        En Am Con 1125
        Sup Ct Review (1984):149-168

889. Kimball Laundry Co. v. United States   June 27, 1949
     338 US 1   93 LEd 1765   69 SCt 1434
     LaRusso, Joseph. "Paying for the change": First English Evangelical Lutheran Church of Glendale v. County of
        Los Angeles and the calculation of interim damages for regulatory takings. *Boston College Environmental
        Affairs Law Review* 17(3):551-583 (Spring 1990).

890. Wolf v. Colorado
   June 27, 1949
   338 US 25   93 LEd 1782   69 SCt 1359
      Const (Currie) 362-364, 407-410
      Const Law 365-368+
      En Am Con 662-665, 1199, 1472-1479, 1562-1564, 1628-1635, 1683, 2073
      Guide (CQ) 46-47
      Liberty 171-172
      Magic 320-322
      Sup Ct Ind 178+
      Super 391-398+
   Jensen, D. Lowell, and Rosemary Hart. The good faith restatement of the exclusionary rule. *Journal of Criminal Law and Criminology* 73(3):916-938 (Fall 1982).
   Schlag, Pierre J. Assaults on the exclusionary rule: good faith limitations and damage remedies. *Journal of Criminal Law and Criminology* 73(3):875-915 (Fall 1982).
   Use of the exclusionary rule. *Congressional Digest* 71(4):104-105 (April 1992).
   Wulf, Melvin L. On the origins of privacy. *Nation* 252(20):700, 702-704 (May 27, 1991).

891. Christoffel v. United States
   June 27, 1949
   338 US 84   93 LEd 1826   69 SCt 1447
   Vanderziel, Kathleen M. The Hatfield Riders and environmental preservation: what process is due? *Boston College Environmental Affairs Law Review* 19(2):431-479 (Fall/Winter 1991).

892. Brinegar v. United States
   June 27, 1949
   338 US 160   93 LEd 1879   69 SCt 1302
      En Am Con 155, 516-522, 1628-1635
   Wieber, Michael C. The theory and practice of Illinois v. Rodriguez: why an officer's reasonable belief about a third party's authority to consent does not protect a criminal suspect's rights. *Journal of Criminal Law and Criminology* 84(3):604-641 (Fall 1993).

893. Solesbee v. Balkcom
   February 20, 1950
   339 US 9   94 LEd 604   70 SCt 457
   Pastroff, Sanford M. Supreme Court review: Eighth Amendment—the constitutional rights of the insane on death row. *Journal of Criminal Law and Criminology* 77(3):844-866 (Fall 1986).

894. Mullane v. Central Hanover Bank and Trust Co.
   April 24, 1950
   339 US 306   94 LEd 865   70 SCt 652
   Weintraub, Benjamin. Is your claim scheduled? The problem lies with flawed rules. *Credit and Financial Management* 87(1):24 (January/February 1985).

895. American Communications Association v. Douds   May 8, 1950
            Coupled with United Steelworkers of America v. National Labor Relations Board (NLRB)
   339 US 382   94 LEd 925   70 SCt 674
      Const (Currie) 355-358
      En Am Con 50-51, 770-773, 877
      Guide (CQ) 47-48, 77

896. Sweatt v. Painter
   June 5, 1950
   339 US 629   94 LEd 1114   70 SCt 848
      Amending 203-213
      Antagonists 216-219
      Burden 71-73
      Const Law 478-480R+
      En Am Con 273-280, 1841
      Guide (CQ) 48
      Magic 322-324

Making 128-129, 131-138, 140-147+

Basic court ruling: the Brown decision. *Congressional Digest* 59(2):34-35, 64 (February 1981).

Delon, Floyd G. The legacy of Thurgood Marshall. *Journal of Negro Education* 63(3):278-288 (Summer 1994).

Gregory, David L. The continuing vitality of affirmative action diversity principles in professional and graduate school student admissions and faculty hiring. *Journal of Negro Education* 63(3):421-429 (Summer 1994).

Hobbs, Gardner J. Public school finance and the courts. *Clearing House* 53(9):405-409 (May 1980) .

Hooks, Benjamin L. Thirty years after Brown v. Board of Education. *Crisis* 91(5):24 (May 1984).

Hyde, Alison A. School desegregation: the role of the courts and means of achievement. *NASSP Bulletin* 78(565):28-37 (November 1994).

Lamb, Charles M. Legal foundations of civil rights and pluralism America. *Annals of the American Academy of Political and Social Science* 454:13-25 (March 1981).

Orren, Karen. The primacy of labor in American constitutional development. *American Political Science Review* 89(2):377-388 (June 1995).

Reid, Herbert O., and Frankie M. Foster-Davis. Three decades of "all deliberate speed". *Crisis* 91(5):12-15 (May 1984).

Russo, Charles J., J. John Harris III, and Rosetta F. Sandidge. Brown v. Board of Education at 40: a legal history of equal educational opportunity in American public education. *Journal of Negro Education* 63(3):297-309 (Summer 1994).

Simmons, Althea T. L. From Brown to Grove City: blueprint for education. *Crisis* 91(5):6-10 (May 1984).

Stefkovich, Jacqueline A., and Terrence Leas. A legal history of desegregation in higher education. *Journal of Negro Education* 63(3):406-420 (Summer 1994).

White, Forrest R. Brown revisited. *Phi Delta Kappan* 76(1):12-19 (September 1994).

897. McLaurin v. Oklahoma State Regents for Higher Education   June 5, 1950
      339 US 637   94 LEd 1149   70 SCt 851
         Amending 203-213
         Antagonists 215-219
         En Am Con 273-280, 1841
         Guide (CQ) 48
         Magic 322-324
         Making 134-136+

Basic court ruling: the Brown decision. *Congressional Digest* 59(2):34-35,64 (February 1981).

Delon, Floyd G. The legacy of Thurgood Marshall. *Journal of Negro Education* 63(3):278-288 (Summer 1994).

Hobbs, Gardner J. Public school finance and the courts. *Clearing House* 53(9):405-409 (May 1980) .

Hyde, Alison A. School desegregation: the role of the courts and means of achievement. *NASSP Bulletin* 78(565):28-37 (November 1994).

Lamb, Charles M. Legal foundations of civil rights and pluralism America. *Annals of the American Academy of Political and Social Science* 454:13-25 (March 1981).

Orren, Karen. The primacy of labor in American constitutional development. *American Political Science Review* 89(2):377-388 (June 1995).

Reid, Herbert O., and Frankie M. Foster-Davis. Three decades of "all deliberate speed". *Crisis* 91(5):12-15 (May 1984).

Russo, Charles J., J. John Harris III, and Rosetta F. Sandidge. Brown v. Board of Education at 40: a legal history of equal educational opportunity in American public education. *Journal of Negro Education* 63(3):297-309 (Summer 1994).

Simmons, Althea T. L. From Brown to Grove City: blueprint for education. *Crisis* 91(5):6-10 (May 1984).

Stefkovich, Jacqueline A., and Terrence Leas. A legal history of desegregation in higher education. *Journal of Negro Education* 63(3):406-420 (Summer 1994).

Timberlake, Constance H. A historical perspective of school desegregation. *Crisis* 91(5):26-29 (1984).

White, Forrest R. Brown revisited. *Phi Delta Kappan* 76(1):12-19 (September 1994).

898. Henderson v. United States   June 5, 1950
      339 US 816   94 LEd 1302   70 SCt 843
         Guide (CQ) 106
         Making 135-136, 139-141, 172-173+

899. Feres v. United States   December 4, 1950
            Coupled with Jefferson v. United States
            Coupled with United States v. Griggs
      340 US 135   95 LEd 152   71 SCt 153
         Almanac (1987):15A; (1988):81-82; (1989):291
         Guide (West) (1987):162-163, 543-544
      Ball, Howard. The U.S. Supreme Court's glossing of the Federal Tort Claims Act: statutory construction and
         'veterans' tort actions. *Western Political Quarterly* 41(3):529-552 (September 1988).
      Justice for all. [Editorial] *Aviation Week and Space Technology* 129(1):7 (July 4, 1988).
      Mangan, Joseph F. Government contractors: their defense rests. *Best's Review* (Property/Casualty Insurance
         Edition) 91(2):82, 84 (June 1990).
      Mecham, Michael. Supreme Court weighs liability in military contractor suit. *Aviation Week and Space
         Technology* 127(17):81-82 (October 26, 1987).
      Schwarz, Stephen G. The government contractor defense after Boyle: it can still be overcome. *Trial* 24(9):88-92
         (September 1988).

900. Kiefer-Stewart Co. v. Joseph E. Seagrams and Sons, Inc.   January 2, 1951
      340 US 211   95 LEd 219   71 SCt 259
         Sup Ct Review (1984):69-148

901. Niemotko v. Maryland   January 15, 1951
            Coupled with Kelley v. Maryland
      340 US 268   95 LEd 267   71 SCt 325, 328
         Const (Currie) 360-362
         En Am Con 1315
      Regan, Richard J. Regulating cult activities: the limits of religious freedom. *Thought* 61(241):185-196 (June
         1986).

902. Kunz v. New York   January 15, 1951
      340 US 290   95 LEd 280   71 SCt 312
         En Am Con 1109, 1538-1545
      McKown, Delos Banning. Deism and the Supreme Court. *Humanist* 52(2):25-28, 48 (March/April 1992).
      Regan, Richard J. Regulating cult activities: the limits of religious freedom. *Thought* 61(241):185-196 (June
         1986).

903. Feiner v. New York   January 15, 1951
      340 US 315   95 LEd 295   71 SCt 303
         Black 93-101
         Const (Currie) 348-350
         Const Law 155-156, 159+
         En Am Con 719, 927
      Marcy, William R. To protect or not to protect—that is the question. *Social Education* 54(6):364-365 (October
         1990).
      Regan, Richard J. Regulating cult activities: the limits of religious freedom. *Thought* 61(241):185-196 (June
         1986).

904. Blau v. United States   January 15, 1951
      340 US 332   95 LEd 306   71 SCt 301
         Powers 208-209

905. Dean Milk Co. v. City of Madison, Wisconsin   January 15, 1951
      340 US 349   95 LEd 329   71 SCt 295
         Const (Currie) 580-585
         En Am Con 544, 1132, 1751-1755

906. Rogers v. United States   February 26, 1951
      340 US 367   95 LEd 344   71 SCt 438
        Powers 208-209

907. Universal Camera Corp. v. National Labor Relations Board (NLRB)   February 26, 1951
      340 US 474   95 LEd 456   71 SCt 456
      Bangser, Paul M. An inherent role for cost-benefit analysis in judicial review of agency decisions: a new
        perspective on OSHA rulemaking. *Boston College Environmental Affairs Law Review* 10(2):365-444
        (September 1982).
      Plater, Zygmunt J. B., and William Lund Norine. Through the looking glass of eminent domain: exploring the
        "arbitrary and capricious" test and substantive rationality review of governmental decisions. *Boston College
        Environmental Affairs Law Review* 16(4):661-752 (Summer 1989).

908. Norton Co. v. Department of Revenue of Illinois   February 26, 1951
      340 US 534   95 LEd 517   71 SCt 377
      Quirk, William J. Minimizing state taxation of interstate business. *Journal of Taxation* 65(3):180-186
        (September 1986).

909. West Virginia ex re. Dyer v. Sims   April 9, 1951
      Dryer v. Sims
      341 US 22   95 LEd 713   71 SCt 557
        En Am Con 637-639
      Briggett, Marlissa S. State supremacy in the federal realm: the Interstate Compact. *Boston College
        Environmental Affairs Law Review* 18(4):751-772 (Summer 1991).

910. Gerende v. Board of Supervisors of Elections of Baltimore City   April 12, 1951
      341 US 56   95 LEd 745   71 SCt 565
        En Am Con 838
        Sup Ct Ind 146-148+

911. Joint Anti-Fascist Refugee Committee v. McGrath   April 30, 1951
            Coupled with National Council of American-Soviet Friendships, Inc. v. McGrath
            Coupled with International Workers Order, Inc. v. McGrath
      341 US 123   95 LEd 817   71 SCt 624
        En Am Con 1028, 1465-1472

912. Tenney v. Brandhove   May 21, 1951
      341 US 367   95 LEd 1019   71 SCt 783
        En Am Con 1146, 1716-1717, 1874-1875
      Ball, Howard. The U.S. Supreme Court's glossing of the Federal Tort Claims Act: statutory construction and
        'veterans' tort actions. *Western Political Quarterly* 41(3):529-552 (September 1988).

913. Schwegmann Brothers v. Calvert Distillers Corp.   May 21, 1951
            Coupled with Schwegmann Brothers v. Seagram Distillers Corp.
      341 US 384   95 LEd 1035   71 SCt 745
      Sheffet, Mary Jane, and Debra L. Scammon. Resale price maintenance: is it safe to suggest retail prices?
        Journal of Marketing 49(4):82-92 (Fall 1985).

914. Dennis v. United States   June 4, 1951
      341 US 494   95 LEd 1137   71 SCt 857
        Antagonists 198-201
        Brennan 86-90
        Const (Currie) 353-354
        Const Law 127-132R+
        Documents (v. 2):561-567R

En Am Con 145-146, 289-301, 555-556, 968-970, 1804-1807, 1930
First 136-150
Fourth 160-167
Guide (CQ) 47-48, 49-50
Guide (West) (v. 4):91-92
Magic 314-315
Sup Ct Ind 134,136-138+
Sup Ct Review (1991):303-390; (1994):209-245

Marshall, Thomas R. Public opinion, representation, and the modern Supreme Court. *American Politics Quarterly* 16(3):296-316 (July 1988).

Spillenger, Clyde. Reading the judicial canon: Alexander Bickel and the book of Brandeis. *Journal of American History* 79(1):125-151 (June 1992).

915. Breard v. Alexandria, Louisiana   June 4, 1951
     341 US 622   95 LEd 1233   71 SCt 920
       Black 108-114

     Boedecker, Karl A., and Fred W. Morgan. The evolution of First Amendment protection for commercial speech. *Journal of Marketing* 59(1):38-47 (January 1995).

916. Collins v. Hardyman   June 4, 1951
     341 US 651   95 LEd 1253   71 SCt 937
       Sup Ct Review (1993):199-243

917. Rochin v. California   January 2, 1952
     342 US 165   96 LEd 183   72 SCt 205
       Const (Currie) 362-364
       En Am Con 148, 1472-1479, 1602
       Super 135-136, 206-207+

     Mandell, Leonard Bruce, and L. Anita Richardson. Surgical search: removing a scar on the Fourth Amendment. *Journal of Criminal Law and Criminology* 75(3):525-552 (Fall 1984).

     Wulf, Melvin L. On the origins of privacy. *Nation* 252(20):700, 702-704 (May 27, 1991).

918. Morissette v. United States   January 7, 1952
     342 US 246   96 LEd 288   72 SCt 240

     Goldberg, Andrew M. Corporate officer liability for federal environmental statute violations. *Boston College Environmental Affairs Law Review* 18(2):357-379 (Winter 1991).

919. Doremus v. Board of Education of Borough of Hawthorne   March 3, 1952
     342 US 429   96 LEd 475   72 SCt 394
       En Am Con 575, 1871-1872

920. Adler v. Board of Education of the City of New York   March 3, 1952
     342 US 485   96 LEd 517   72 SCt 380

     Van Alstyne, William W. Academic freedom and the First Amendment in the Supreme Court of the United States: an unhurried historical review. *Law and Contemporary Problems* 53(3):79-154 (Summer 1990).

921. Frisbie v. Collins   March 10, 1952
     342 US 519   96 LEd 541   72 SCt 509

     Fagan, Terence P. Supreme court review: Fourth Amendment—in-court identifications. *Journal of Criminal Law and Criminology* 71(4):488-498 (Winter 1980).

     Glennon, Michael J. State-sponsored abduction: a comment on United States v. Alvarez-Machain. *American Journal of International Law* 86(4):746-756 (October 1992).

     Halberstam, Malvina. Agora: international kidnaping—in defense of the Supreme Court decision in Alvarez-Machain. *American Journal of International Law* 86(4):736-746 (October 1992).

Riesenfeld, Stefan A. Doctrine of self-executing treaties and U.S. v. Postal: win any price? [Editorial] *American Journal International Law* 74(4):892-904 (October 1980).

922. Harisiades v. Shaughnessy   March 10, 1952
         Coupled with Mascitti v. McGrath
         Coupled with Coleman v. McGrath
     342 US 580   96 LEd 586   72 SCt 512
       En Am Con 556-557
       Sup Ct Review (1984):255-307

923. Sacher, et al. v. United States   March 10, 1952
     343 US 1   96 LEd 717   72 SCt 451
       Antagonists 197-198, 201-202

924. Lilly v. Commissioner of Internal Revenue Service   March 10, 1952
     343 US 90   96 LEd 769   72 SCt 497
       Sup Ct Review (1983):32-82

925. Ray v. Blair   April 15, 1952
     343 US 214   96 LEd 894   72 SCt 654
       Const (Currie) 370-371

926. Beauharnais v. Illinois   April 28, 1952
     343 US 250   96 LEd 919   72 SCt 725
       Const (Currie) 350-352
       En Am Con 105, 873-874
       Jerry 187-190+
       Price 8-13, 169-175
       Sup Ct Review (1982):285-317
     Garvey, John H. Black and white images. *Law and Contemporary Problems* 56(4):189-216 (Autumn 1993).
     Greenawalt, Kent. Free speech in the United States and Canada. *Law and Contemporary Problems* 55(1):5-33 (Winter 1992).
     Smolla, Rodney A. Academic freedom, hate speech, and the idea of a university. *Law and Contemporary Problems* 53(3):195-225 (Summer 1990).

927. Zorach v. Clauson   April 28, 1952
     343 US 306   96 LEd 954   72 SCt 679
       Burger Years 56-91
       Const (Friendly) 116-118
       En Am Con 1535-1537, 1650-1658, 2090
       Establishment 145-146, 214+
       First 165-168
       Godless 83-84+
       Let Us 119, 124
       Original (Davis) 71-72+
       Religion 65-67, 103-107+
       Sup Ct Church 183-194R
       Sup Ct Review (1985):1-59
     Abram, Morris B. Is "strict separation" too strict? *Public Interest* (82):81-90 (Winter 1986).
     The court decisions. *Congressional Digest* 63(5):132-134, 160 (May 1984).
     Demerath, N. J., III and Rhys H. Williams. A mythical past and uncertain future. *Society* 21(4):3-10 (May/June 1984).
     Gaffney, Edward McGlynn, Jr. O'Connor fumbles 'Christian nation' case. [Editorial] *Christian Century* 106(12):373-375 (April 12, 1989).
     Hammond, Phillip E. The courts and secular humanism. *Society* 21(4):11-16 (May/June 1984).

Kilpatrick, James J. What in God's name is going on? *National Review* 37(2):36, 38-39 (February 8, 1985).

McKown, Delos Banning. Deism and the Supreme Court. *Humanist* 52(2):25-28, 48 (March/April 1992).

Prayer in public schools. *Congressional Digest* 74(1):3-32 (January 1995).

Regan, Richard J. Supreme Court roundup: 1981 term. *Thought* 57(227):514-527 (December 1982).

———. Supreme Court roundup: 1983 term. *Thought* 60(236):99-111 (March 1985).

———. Supreme Court roundup: 1986 term. *Thought* 63(251):429-441 (December 1988).

Schamel, Wynell Burroughs, and Jean West Mueller. Teaching with documents: Abington v. Schempp: a study in the establishment clause. *Social Education* 53(1):61-66R (January 1989).

Sullivan, Catherine Beth. Are kosher food laws constitutionally kosher? *Boston College Environmental Affairs Law Review* 21(1):201-245 (Fall 1993).

928. Public Utilities Commission of District of Columbia v. Pollak   May 26, 1952
343 US 451   96 LEd 1068   72 SCt 813
    Const (Currie) 345-348

929. Joseph Burstyn, Inc. v. Wilson   May 26, 1952
343 US 495   96 LEd 1098   72 SCt 777
    En Am Con 128-129, 183-184

O'Neil, Robert M. Artistic freedom and academic freedom. *Law and Contemporary Problems* 53(3):177-193 (Summer 1990).

930. Youngstown Sheet and Tube Co. v. Sawyer   June 2, 1952
343 US 579   96 LEd 1153   72 SCt 863
    Almanac (1988):124
    Const (Currie) 337-338, 365-369
    Documents (v. 2):574-578R
    En Am Con 491-492, 1441-1446, 1659-1664, 1761-1762, 2085-2086
    Guide (CQ) 48
    Guide (West) (v.10):443-444
    Sup Ct Review (1986):19-40

Commager, Henry Steele. The Constitution and original intent. *Center Magazine* 19(6):4-17 (November/December 1986).

Driesen, David M. The congressional role in international environmental law and its implications for statutory interpretation. *Boston College Environmental Affairs Law Review* 19(2):287-315 (Fall/Winter 1991).

Fisher, Louis. Foreign policy powers of the President and Congress. *Annals of the American Academy of Political and Social Science* 499:149-159 (September 1988).

Franck, Thomas M., and Clifford A. Bob. The return of Humpty-Dumpty: foreign relations law after the Chadha case. *American Journal of International Law* 79(4):912-960 (October 1985).

Heffner, Judith C. The Constitution in court. *Scholastic Update* (Teachers' Edition) 116(5):16-18 (October 28, 1983).

Mishler, William, and Reginald S. Sheehan. The Supreme Court as a countermajoritarian institution? The impact of public opinion on Supreme Court decisions. *American Political Science Review* 87(1):87-101 (March 1993).

Murphy, Walter F. The Constitution and the 14th Amendment. *Center Magazine* 20(4):9-30 (July/August 1987).

Orren, Karen. The primacy of labor in American constitutional development. *American Political Science Review* 89(2):377-388 (June 1995).

Rodriguez, Leon. Constitutional and statutory limits for cost-benefit analysis pursuant to Executive Orders 2,291 and 12,498. *Boston College Environmental Affairs Law Review* 15(3-4):505-546 (Spring 1988).

Van Alstyne, William W. Implied powers. *Society* 24(1):56-60 (November/December 1986).

931. Kawakita v. United States   June 2, 1952
343 US 717   96 LEd 1249   725 SCt 950
    Japanese 69, 198

932. On Lee v. United States   June 2, 1952
     343 US 747   96 LEd 1270   72 SCt 967
          En Am Con 618-621, 1344-1345
          Super 462-463+
     Goldberger, Peter. Consent, expectations of privacy, and the meaning of "searches" in the Fourth Amendment.
          Journal of Criminal Law and Criminology 75(2):319-362 (Summer 1984).
     Turley, Jonathan. The not-so-noble lie: the nonincorporation of state consensual surveillance standards in
          federal court. *Journal of Criminal Law and Criminology* 79(1):66-134 (Spring 1988).
     Webber, Dawn. Supreme Court review: Fourth Amendment—of warrants, electronic surveillance, expectations
          of privacy, and tainted fruits. *Journal of Criminal Law and Criminology* 75(3):630-652 (Fall 1984).

933. United States v. Beacon Brass Co.   November 10, 1952
     344 US 43   97 LEd 61   73 SCt 77
     Tish, Martin H. Duplicative statutes, prosecutorial discretion, and the Illinois armed violence statute. *Journal of*
          Criminal Law and Criminology 71(3):226-243 (Fall 1980).

934. Kedroff v. Saint Nicholas Cathedral of Russian Orthodox Church in North America   November 24, 1952
     344 US 94   97 LEd 120   73 SCt 143
          Godless 47

935. Wieman v. Updegraff   December 15, 1952
     344 US 183   97 LEd 216   73 SCt 215
          Const (Currie) 355-358, 385-386
          En Am Con 2063
          First 38-54
     Van Alstyne, William W. Academic freedom and the First Amendment in the Supreme Court of the United
          States: an unhurried historical review. *Law and Contemporary Problems* 53(3):79-154 (Summer 1990).

936. Steele v. Bulova Watch Co.   December 22, 1952
     344 US 280   97 LEd 319   73 SCt 252
          Sup Ct Review (1991):179-224
     Kramer, Larry. Extraterritorial application of American law after the Insurance Antitrust Case: a reply to
          professors Lowenfeld and Trimble. *American Journal of International Law* 89(4):750-758 (October 1995).

937. Brown v. Allen   February 9, 1953
          Coupled with Daniels v. Allen
     344 US 443   97 LEd 469   73 SCt 397, 437
          En Am Con 161, 879-886
     Bamonte, Thomas J. Supreme Court review: Habeas Corpus—limiting the availability of habeas corpus after a
          procedural default. *Journal of Criminal Law and Criminology* 73(4):1612-1640 (Winter 1982).
     Chemerinsky, Erwin. Supreme Court review: Making sense of habeas corpus. *Trial* 28(12):79-82 (December
          1992).
     Mello, Michael A. Is there a federal constitutional right to counsel in capital post-conviction proceedings?
          Journal of Criminal Law and Criminology 79(4):1065-1104 (Winter 1989).
     Weisberg, Robert. A Great writ while it lasted. *Journal of Criminal Law and Criminology* 81(1):9-36 (Spring
          1990).

938. United States v. Reynolds   March 9, 1953
     345 US 1   97 LEd 727   73 SCt 528
     White, Welsh S. Evidentiary privileges and the defendant's constitutional right to introduce evidence. *Journal*
          of Criminal Law and Criminology 80(2):377-426 (Summer 1989).

939. United States v. Rumely   March 9, 1953
     345 US 41   97 LEd 770   73 SCt 543
          Powers 207-208

940. Fowler v. Rhode Island   March 9, 1953
345 US 67   97 LEd 828   73 SCt 526
Regan, Richard J. Regulating cult activities: the limits of religious freedom. *Thought* 61(241):185-196 (June 1986).

941. Shaughnessy v. United States ex. rel. Mezei   March 16, 1953
345 US 206   97 LEd 956   73 SCt 625
En Am Con 1675

942. Poulos v. New Hampshire   April 27, 1953
345 US 395   97 LEd 1105   73 SCt 760
Regan, Richard J. Regulating cult activities: the limits of religious freedom. *Thought* 61(241):185-196 (June 1986).

943. Terry v. Adams   May 4, 1953
345 US 461   97 LEd 1152   73 SCt 809
Const (Currie) 322-325
En Am Con 727-728, 1413-1417, 1736-1738, 1879
Making 109-112+
Sup Ct Ind 113

944. Lauritzen v. Larsen   May 25, 1953
345 US 571   97 LEd 1254   73 SCt 921
Sup Ct Review (1991):179-224
Asenault, Richard J., and Richard W. Beard. Maritime personal injury on foreign waters. *Trial* 20(6):72-76 (June 1984).

945. Automatic Canteen Co. of America v. Federal Trade Commission (FTC) June 8, 1953
346 US 61   97 LEd 1454   73 SCt 1017
Werner, Ray O. Marketing and the United States Supreme Court, 1975-1981. *Journal of Marketing* 46(2):73-81 (Spring 1982).

946. Federal Communications Commission (FCC) v. RCA Communications, Inc. June 8, 1953
         Coupled with Mackay Radio and Telegraph Co. v. RCA Communications, Inc.
346 US 86   97 LEd 1470   73 SCt 998
Cohen, Dorothy. Unfairness in advertising revisited. *Journal of Marketing* 46(1):73-80 (Winter 1982).

947. Barrows v. Jackson   June 15, 1953
346 US 249   97 LEd 1586   73 SCt 1031
En Am Con 102, 1561-1562

948. Rosenberg v. United States   June 19, 1953
346 US 273   97 LEd 1607   73 SCt 1152
Antagonists 203-208
En Am Con 1611, 1903-1909
Landmark (v. 4):125-133R

949. Toolson v. New York Yankees   November 9, 1953
         Coupled with Kowalaski v. Chandler
         Coupled with Corbett v. Chandler
346 US 356   98 LEd 64   74 SCt 78
Owners 62-64+
Super 162-164+

950. Wilco v. Swan   December 7, 1953
      346 US 427   98 LEd 168   74 SCt 182
            Almanac (1989):327-328
            Sup Ct Review (1995):99-124
      Scheibla, Shirley Hobbs. Big decision: can you sue a broker? High court to say. *Barron's* 67(9):16, 32-33
            (March 2, 1987).
            ————. Final victory? Brokerages win arbitration battle, but war may go on. *Barron's* 67(24):38-39, 79 (June
            15, 1987).

951. Walder v. United States   February 1, 1954
      347 US 62   98 LEd 503   74 SCt 354
      Couleur, Terri M. The use of illegally obtained evidence to rebut the insanity defense: a new exception to the
            exclusionary rule? *Journal of Criminal Law and Criminology* 74(2):391-427 (Summer 1983).
      Hartman, Marshall J., and Sidney Bernstein. To Leon, and beyond; two commentators react. *Trial* 21(1):50-56
            (January 1985).

952. Irvine v. California   February 8, 1954
      347 US 128   98 LEd 561   74 SCt 381
            En Am Con 1002
            Super 134-138+

953. Hernandez v. Texas   May 3, 1954
      347 US 475   98 LEd 866   74 SCt 667
            En Am Con 1082-1085
            Super 138-139

954. Brown v. Board of Education of Topeka, Kansas   May 17, 1954
            Coupled with Briggs v. Elliot (See record 955)
            Coupled with Davis v. County of School Board of Prince Edward County (See record 956)
            Coupled with Gebhart v. Belton (See record 957)
      347 US 483   98 LEd 873   74 SCt 686
            Abortion (Frohock) 112, 119-122
            Abortion Pol (Rubin) 61-62, 85-86+
            Affirmative (Woods) 35-36
            Am Educators 78-79, 167
            Amending 203-213
            Antagonists 211-213, 217-221, 223-231+
            Ascent 29-30, 255-265+
            Behind Bakke 12-13, 27-29
            Burden 3-8, 84-92, 125-127, 137-150, 274-277+
            Burger Court 113-116
            Civil 20th 3, 7, 61-69R
            Const (Currie) 375-381, 416-421
            Const (Friendly) 214-215
            Const Law 482-486R+
            Court Const 254-268+
            Court Public 98-99, 101-102, 104-109R
            Culture 130-141
            Documents (v. 2):602-614R
            Editorials (1984):589-597
            En Am Con 44-45, 161-164, 273-280, 557-561, 640-647, 1040-1043, 1500-1506, 1645-1646, 1729-1736,
                  1979-1987
            Equal (Harrell) 97, 100, 102
            Eyes 35-37, 61-74R, 83-89+
            Godless 97-98+

Guide (CQ) 48-49

Guide (West) (v. 2):170-182

Landmark (v. 1):13-21R

Magic 264-265, 286-288, 322-324, 326-327

Make 15-22+

Making 150-154, 161-167, 168-186, 188-195, 209-215+

New Right (Schwartz) 22-25, 138-154, 159-162+

New Right (Whitaker) 142-168

One 387-392R

Quarrels 307-333

Reader's 33, 131-132, 177-180, 898-900, 1050-1052

Sup Ct Ind 234-235, 237+

Sup Ct Review (1986):99-134; (1988):245-267; (1995):1-43

Sup Ct Yearbook (1991-92):26-27

Super 72-127, 298-302, 704-706, 825-829+

American survey: Burger leaves the labyrinth. *Economist* 300(7454):17-22 (July 12-18, 1986).

Baker, banker, clergyman, thief. *Life* 10(10):84-88 (Fall 1987).

Barrett, Edward L. The Supreme Court: why the Constitution survives: long-term view of the Court. *Trial* 25(12):30-35 (December 1989).

Basic court ruling: the Brown decision. *Congressional Digest* 59(2):34-35, 64 (February 1981).

Bell, Derrick A. Learning from our losses: is school desegregation still feasible in the 1980s? *Phi Delta Kappan* 64(8):572-575 (April 1983).

Bennett, Lerone, Jr. The day race relations changed forever. *Ebony* 40(7):108-116 (May 1985).

Berns, Walter. Government by lawyers and judges. *Commentary* 83(6):17-24 (June 1987).

Blitzer, Charles. From the center. [Editorial] *Wilson Quarterly* 18(3):160 (Summer 1994).

Bodine, Margot R. Opening the schoolhouse door for children with AIDS: the Education for All Handicapped Children Act. *Boston College Environmental Affairs Law Review* 13(4):583-641 (Summer 1986).

Bowen, Lauren. Attorney advertising in the wake of Bates v. State Bar of Arizona (1977): a study of judicial impact. *American Politics Quarterly* 23(4):461-484 (October 1995).

Brady, Timothy Patrick. "But most of it belongs to those yet to be born": the public trust doctrine, NEPA, and the stewardship ethic. *Boston College Environmental Affairs Law Review* 17(3):621-646 (Spring 1990).

Brown, Kevin. Revisiting the Supreme Court's opinion in Brown v. Board of Education from a multiculturalist perspective. *Teachers College Record* 96(4):644-653 (Summer 1995).

Brown vs. Board of Education decision: 40 years later. *Jet* 86(5):26 (June 6, 1994).

Burns, Haywood. The activism in not affirmative. *Nation* 239(9):264-268 (September 29, 1984).

Camper, Diane, Ethel Payne, Nathaniel R. Jones, Charles Ogletree, Charles and Julius L. Chambers. To form a more perfect union. *Black Enterprise* 17(12):11, 51-66 (July 1987).

Canon, Bradley C. The Supreme Court as a cheerleader in politico-moral disputes. *Journal of Politics* 54(3):637-653 (August 1992).

Carlin, David R. As American as freeways: abortion's roots in our culture. *Commonweal* 116(13):392-393 (July 14, 1989).

Cassimere, Raphael Jr. Remembering Brown vs. Board of Education. [Editorial] *Crisis* 101(4):10 (May 1994).

Cecil, Andrew R. Moral values in a free society: Individualism and social conscience. *Vital Speeches of the Day* 60(7):204-209 (January 15, 1994).

The Civil Rights Act of 1990. *Congressional Digest* 69(8-9):196-224 (August/September 1990).

Civil rights since Brown: 1954-1984. *Center Magazine* 17(5):2-40 (September/October 1984).

Clayton, Marian. Desegregating America's public schools. *Crisis* 91(5):20-21 (May 1984).

Clinton teaches at Maryland school to commemorate Brown vs. Board of Education decision. *Jet* 86(5):25 (June 6, 1994).

Committee L on the Historically Black Institutions and the Status of Minorities in the Profession. The historically black colleges and universities: a future in the balance. *Academe* 81(1):49-58 (January/February 1995).

Cook, Stuart W. The 1954 social science statement and school desegregation: a reply to Gerard. *American Psychologist* 39(8):819-832 (August 1984).

Delon, Floyd G. The legacy of Thurgood Marshall. *Journal of Negro Education* 63(3):278-288 (Summer 1994).

Dent, David J. Brown case revisited. *Black Enterprise* 15(2):16 (September 1984).

Devins, Neal E., and Benjamin Feder. Reading the establishment clause. *Commonweal* 112(16):492-494 (September 20, 1985).

Dumas, Kitty. Will U.S. schools resegregate? *Black Enterprise* 22(10):29 (May 1992).

Erler, Edward J. Brown v. Board of Education at 30. *National Review* 36(17):26-28, 30-31, 53 (September 7, 1984).

Ethridge, Samuel B. Impact of the Brown decision on black educators. *Education Digest* 45(6):24-27 (February 1980).

Evolution of the present controversy. *Congressional Digest* 61(5):134-135, 160 (May 1982).

Farrell, Charles S. Promise of the landmark 'Brown' decision is unfulfilled after 30 years, scholars say. *Chronicle of Higher Education* 28(12):12-13 (May 16, 1984).

Fast Eddie v. Honest Abe. [Editorial] *Nation* 243(15):473 (November 8, 1986).

Feinberg, Rosa Castro. Brown and Lau: seeking the common ground. *Teachers College Record* 96(4):775-782 (Summer 1995).

Fiss, Owen M., and Charles Krauthammer. The Rehnquist Court. *New Republic* 186(10):14-16, 18 (March 10, 1982).

Five cases that changed American society. *Scholastic Update* (Teachers' Edition) 117(7):19-20 (November 30, 1984).

Frederickson, H. George. Public administration and social equity. *Public Administration Review* 50(2):228-237 (March/April 1990).

Fuerst, J. S. Time to get off the bus?: the courts, schools, and desegregation. *Commonweal* 118(12):403-405 (June 14, 1991).

Garraty, John Arthur. 101 things every college graduate should know about American history. *American Heritage* 38(1):24-32 (December 1986).

Gerard, Harold B. School desegregation: the social science role. *American Psychologist* 38(8):869-877 (August 1983).

Gest, Ted. Courts: a major battleground of social upheaval. *U.S. News and World Report* 98(3):48-50 (January 28, 1985).

———. Next stage: Court lite. *U.S. News and World Report* 111(2):16-19 (July 8, 1991).

Gordon, William M. The implementation of desegregation plans since Brown. *Journal of Negro Education* 63(3):310-322 (Summer 1994).

Graglia, Lino A. How the Constitution disappeared. *Commentary* 81(2):19-27 (February 1986).

———. Saving the Constitution: a theory of power. *National Review* 39(13):33-36 (July 17, 1987).

Grant, Carl A. Reflections on the promise of Brown and multicultural education. *Teachers College Record* 96(4):707-721 (Summer 1995).

Gresham, Jewell Handy, Michael Eric Dyson, Robert Coles, Jess Mowry, John C. Brittain, David Cecelski, Micaela di Leonardo, Gerald Horne, Robert Sherrill, Jack Greenberg, Anne Wheelock, Ben Chavis, E. Ethelbert Miller, Anne Braden, Si Kahn, Tamar Jacoby, Herbert Kohl, J. Anthony Luckas, and Haywood Burns. Symposium. Does Brown still matter? *Nation* 258(20):718-728 (May 23, 1994).

Gross, Ken. Linda Brown reopens her landmark case against racism. *People Weekly* 26(22):146, 148 (December 1, 1986).

Gunther, Gerald. Judicial review. *Society* 24(1):18-23 (November/December 1986).

Heffner, Judith C. The Constitution in court. *Scholastic Update* (Teachers' Edition) 116(5):16-18 (October 28, 1983).

Hertzberg, Hendrik. Wounds of race. *New Republic* 201(2):4, 42 (July 10, 1989).

Higginbotham, A. Leon, Jr. 45 Years in Law and Civil Rights. *Ebony* 46(1):80-86 (November 1990).

———. 50 years of civil rights. *Ebony* 51(1):148-154 (November 1995).

Hobbs, Gardner J. Public school finance and the courts. *Clearing House* 53(9):405-409 (May 1980) .

Hooks, Benjamin L. Brown vs. Board of Education—30 years later. *Crisis* 91(5):4 (May 1984).

———. Thirty years after Brown v. Board of Education. *Crisis* 91(5):24 (May 1984).

Hooks, Benjamin L., and Margaret Bush Wilson. The real NAACP stands up—NAACP v. LDF. *Crisis* 89(5):10-15 (May 1984).

Howard, A. E. Dick. Making it work. *Wilson Quarterly* 11(2):122-133 (Spring 1987).

Hyde, Alison A. School desegregation: the role of the courts and means of achievement. *NASSP Bulletin* 78(565):28-37 (November 1994).

"I didn't experience that": the world of Brown's children. *Nation* 258(20):700-703 (May 23, 1994).

Johnson, Constance. The sad way kids look at integration. *U.S. News & World Report* 116(20):33-36 (May 23, 1994).

Kahn, Michael A. Ike's hidden hand on civil rights. *Wilson Quarterly* 16(3):10-11 (Summer 1992).

Karst, Kenneth L. Equal protection of the laws. *Society* 24(1):24-30 (November/December 1986).

Katz, Stanley N. The strange birth and unlikely history of constitutional equality. *Journal of American History* 75(3):747-762 (December 1988).

Kennedy, Randall. Brown plus 35. [Editorial] *Nation* 248(21):725 (May 29, 1989).

Klarman, Michael J. How Brown changed race relations: the backlash thesis. *Journal of American History* 81(1):81-118 (June 1994).

Klein, Joe. The legacy of Summerton: Brown v. Board of Education: 40 years later, a visit to the town where it all began. *Newsweek* 123(20):26-31 (May 16, 1994).

Kozol, Jonathan. Giant steps backward: Romance of the ghetto school. *Nation* 258(20):703-706 (May 23, 1994).

Lacayo, Richard, and Alain L. Sanders. A judge's breach of confidence: did Felix Frankfurter go too far to secure a famous victory? *Time* 129(14):71 (April 6, 1987).

Lacayo, Richard, and Anne Constable. Supreme or not Supreme: that is the question, says the Attorney General. *Time* 128(18):46 (November 3, 1986).

Lamb, Charles M. Legal foundations of civil rights and pluralism America. *Annals of the American Academy of Political and Social Science* 454:13-25 (March 1981).

Landsberg, Brian K. The federal government and the promise of Brown. *Teachers College Record* 96(4):627-636 (Summer 1995).

Loftus, Elizabeth, and John Monohan. Trial by data: psychological research as legal evidence. *American Psychologist* 35(3):270-283 (March 1980).

Mathias, Charles McC., Jr. The federal courts under siege. *Annals of the American Academy of Political and Social Science* 462:26-33 (July 1982).

McDonald, Donald. The fate of school desegregation. [Editorial]. *Center Magazine* 15(4):6-8 (July/August 1982).

McDowell, Gary L. Modest remedy for judicial activism. *Public Interest* (67):3-20 (Spring 1982).

Meese, Edwin, III. Interpreting the Constitution. *USA Today* 115(2496):36-39 (September 1986).

Menacker, Julius. Review of Supreme Court reasoning in cases of expression, due process, and equal protection. *Phi Delta Kappan* 63(3):188-190 (November 1981).

Miller, LaMar P. Tracking the progress of Brown. *Teachers College Record* 96(4):609-613 (Summer 1995).

Minow, Martha. We, the family: constitutional rights and American families. *Journal of American History* 74(3):959-983 (December 1987).

Motley, Constance Baker. The legacy of Brown v. Board of Education. *Teachers College Record* 96(4):637-643 (Summer 1995).

Not quite emancipation. *National Review* 43(2):17-18 (February 11, 1991).

Olson, Tod. Barbara Johns. *Scholastic Update* 126(2):20-21 (September 17, 1993).

Orren, Karen. The primacy of labor in American constitutional development. *American Political Science Review* 89(2):377-388 (June 1995).

Parikh, Sunita. The Supreme Court, civil rights, and preference policies: judicial decision making processes in the United States and India. *Teachers College Record* 92(2):192-211 (Winter 1990).

Parker, Franklin. School desegregation since Brown: a 30-year perspective. *USA Today* 114(2486):90-91 (November 1985).

Polin, Raymond. The Supreme Court's dilemma and defense. *USA Today* 115(2496):43-45 (September 1986).

Quirk, William J. Judicial dictatorship. *Society* 31(2):34-38 (January/February 1994).

Rabinove, Samuel, William E. Johnston, Jr., Lawrence E. Mitchell, Christopher C. Faille, Wallace M. Rudolph, David A. Frolick, Ronald K. L. Collins, Herb Greer, H. Elliot Wales, Thomas A. Bustin, and Lino A. Graglia. The Constitution and the Court. [Editorial] *Commentary* 81(6):2-11 (June 1986).

Rabkin, Jeremy. The judiciary in the administrative state. *Public Interest* (71):62-84 (Spring 1983).

Reed, Adolph L. Looking back at 'Brown'. *Progressive* 58(6):20-21 (June 1994).

Rees, Grover, 3d. Constitution, the court, and the president-elect. *National Review* 32(26):1595-1602 (December 31, 1980).

Reid, Herbert O., Sr. State of the art: the law and education since 1954. *Journal of Negro Education* 52(3):234-249 (Summer 1983).

Reid, Herbert O., and Frankie M. Foster-Davis. Three decades of "all deliberate speed". *Crisis* 91(5):12-15 (May 1984).

Relin, David Oliver. Five landmark decisions. *Scholastic Update* 120(15):20 (April 8, 1988).

Reynolds, William Bradford. Affirmative action and its negative repercussions. *Annals of the American Academy of Political and Social Science* 523:38-49 (September 1992).

Rosenberg, Gerald N. Judicial independence and the reality of political power. *Review of Politics* 54(3):369-398 (Summer 1992).

Russo, Charles J., J. John Harris III, and Rosetta F. Sandidge. Brown v. Board of Education at 40: A Legal History of Equal Educational Opportunity in American Public Education. *Journal of Negro Education* 63(3):297-309 (Summer 1994).

School busing controversy. *Congressional Digest* 60(2):33 (February 1981).

Sherwin, Martin J. Brown at 40. [Editorial] *Nation* 258(20):687-688 (May 23, 1994).

Simmons, Althea T. L. From Brown to Grove City: blueprint for education. *Crisis* 91(5):6-10 (May 1984).

Spillenger, Clyde. Reading the judicial canon: Alexander Bickel and the book of Brandeis. *Journal of American History* 79(1):125-151 (June 1992).

Starr, Mark, Ann McDaniel, and Bob Cohn. Meese weighs in on abortion. *Newsweek* 106(5):60-61 (July 29, 1985).

Stefkovich, Jacqueline A., and Terrence Leas. A legal history of desegregation in higher education. *Journal of Negro Education* 63(3):406-420 (Summer 1994).

Sudo, Phil. Five "little" people who changed U.S. history. *Scholastic Update* 122(10):8-10 (January 16, 1990).

Taylor, Stuart, Jr. Meese v. Brennan. *New Republic* 194(1):17-21 (January 6-13, 1986).

Thirty years of desegregation. *America* 150(21):410 (June 2, 1984).

Thomas, Evan, Kenneth W. Banta, and Anne Constable. Court at the crossroads: the 1984 election may chart the future course of American justice. *Time* 124(15):28-35 (October 8, 1984).

Timberlake, Constance H. A historical perspective of school desegregation. *Crisis* 91(5):26-29 (1984).

Tollett, Kenneth S., Jeanette J. Leonard, and Portia P. James. A color-conscious constitution: the one pervading purpose redux. *Journal of Negro Education* 52(3):189-212 (Summer 1983).

Vile, John R. Bob Jones before the bench. *Christian Century* 100(23):707-711 (August 3-10, 1983).

Ware, Leland. Will there be a "different world" after Fordice? *Academe* 80(3):6-11 (May/June 1994).

Welsh, Robert, and Ronald K. L. Collins. Taking state constitutions seriously: the protection of civil liberties has been shifting away from the U.S. Supreme Court. *Center Magazine* 14(5):6-35, 38-43 (September/ October 1981).

White, Forrest R. Brown revisited. *Phi Delta Kappan* 76(1):12-19 (September 1994).

White, Jack E. The heirs of Oliver Brown: in Topeka, a landmark equality case is still before the courts. *Time* 130(1):88-89 (July 6, 1987).

Wilkins, Roger. The Brown decision: dream deferred, not defeated. *Education Digest* 61(2):19-23 (October 1995).

———. Dream deferred but not defeated. *Teachers College Record* 96(4):614-618 (Summer 1995).

———. Poor blacks after Brown: dream deferred but not defeated. *Nation* 258(20):714-717 (May 23, 1994).

Will, George F. From Topeka to Kansas City. [Editorial] *Newsweek* 125(26):66 (June 26, 1995).

Williams, Dennis A. A tale of two schools. *Newsweek* 103(21):85-86 (May 21, 1984).

Williams, Patricia J. Conversations about Brown: among Moses' bridge-builders. *Nation* 258(20):694-698 (May 23, 1994).

Winkler, Karen J. Who says what the Constitution means? Supreme Court's authority to decide is debated. *Chronicle of Higher Education* 34(27):A4-A7 (March 16, 1988).

955. Briggs v. Elliot   May 17, 1954
        Decided with Brown v. Board of Education of Topeka, Kansas (See record 954)
        347 US 483   98 LEd 873   74 SCt 686
            Burden 133-140+
            Equal (Harrell) 100
            Making 157-161

Brown, Kevin. Revisiting the Supreme Court's opinion in Brown v. Board of Education from a multiculturalist perspective. *Teachers College Record* 96(4):644-653 (Summer 1995).

Kempton, Murray. The high cost of victory. *New York Review of Books* 38(12):64 (June 27, 1991).

Spillenger, Clyde. Reading the judicial canon: Alexander Bickel and the book of Brandeis. *Journal of American History* 79(1):125-151 (June 1992).

White, Forrest R. Brown revisited. *Phi Delta Kappan* 76(1):12-19 (September 1994).

Williams, Dennis A. A tale of two schools. *Newsweek* 103(21):85-86 (May 21, 1984).

956. Davis v. County of School Board of Prince Edward County   May 17, 1954
     Decided with Brown v. Board of Education of Topeka, Kansas (See record 954)
     347 US 483   98 LEd 873   74 SCt 686
     Making 161-163, 177-184, 204-207+
     White, Forrest R. Brown revisited. *Phi Delta Kappan* 76(1):12-19 (September 1994).

957. Gebhart v. Belton   May 17, 1954
     Decided with Brown v. Board of Education of Topeka, Kansas (See record 954)
     347 US 483   98 LEd 873   74 SCt 686
     White, Forrest R. Brown revisited. *Phi Delta Kappan* 76(1):12-19 (September 1994).

958. Bolling v. Sharpe   May 17, 1954
     347 US 497   98 LEd 884   74 SCt 693
     Burden 9-17+
     Const (Currie) 377-381
     Const Law 465-466+
     En Am Con 132-133, 273-280, 640-647, 1500-1506
     Hard Choices 309
     Magic 322-324
     Marbury 207-211
     Sup Ct Review (1995):1-43
     Super 98-100+
     Karst, Kenneth L. Equal protection of the laws. *Society* 24(1):24-30 (November/December 1986).

     Katz, Stanley N. The strange birth and unlikely history of constitutional equality. *Journal of American History* 75(3):747-762 (December 1988).

     Lamb, Charles M. Legal foundations of civil rights and pluralism America. *Annals of the American Academy of Political and Social Science* 454:13-25 (March 1981).

     Reid, Herbert O., and Frankie M. Foster-Davis. Three decades of "all deliberate speed". *Crisis* 91(5):12-15 (May 1984).

     Russo, Charles J., J. John Harris III, and Rosetta F. Sandidge. Brown v. Board of Education at 40: a legal history of equal educational opportunity in American public education. *Journal of Negro Education* 63(3):297-309 (Summer 1994).

959. Galvan v. Press, Immigration and Naturalization Service   May 24, 1954
     347 US 522   98 LEd 911   74 SCt 737
     Sup Ct Review (1984):255-307

960. Alton v. Alton   June 1, 1954
     347 US 610   98 LEd 987   74 SCt 736
     Super 139-143+

961. Berman v. Parker   November 22, 1954
     348 US 26   99 LEd 27   75 SCt 98
     En Am Con 1489-1492, 1494, 1744-1751
     Guide (CQ) 143b
     New Right (Schwartz) 100-104+

Bobrowski, Mark. Scenic landscape protection under the police power. *Boston College Environmental Affairs Law Review* 22(4):697-746 (Summer 1995).

Cavarello, Daniel T. From Penn Central to United Artists' I and II: the rise to immunity of historic preservation designation from successful takings challenges. *Boston College Environmental Affairs Law Review* 22(3):593-622 (Spring 1995).

Note; the public use test: would a ban on the possession of firearms require just compensation? *Law and Contemporary Problems* 49(1):223-249 (Winter 1986).

Plater, Zygmunt J. B., and William Lund Norine. Through the looking glass of eminent domain: exploring the "arbitrary and capricious" test and substantive rationality review of governmental decisions. *Boston College Environmental Affairs Law Review* 16(4):661-752 (Summer 1989).

962. United States v. Shubert   January 31, 1955
     348 US 222   99 LEd 279   75 SCt 277
     Super 163-165

963. United States v. International Boxing Club of New York   January 31, 1955
     348 US 236   99 LEd 290   75 SCt 259
     Super 163-165, 213

964. Tee-Hit-Ton Indians v. United States   February 7, 1955
     348 US 272   99 LEd 314   75 SCt 313
     Orlando, Caroline L. Aboriginal title claims in the Indian Claims Commission: U.S. v. Dann and its due process limitations. *Boston College Environmental Affairs Law Review* 13(2):241-280 (Winter 1986).

965. United States v. Guy W. Capps, Inc.   February 7, 1955
     348 US 296   99 LEd 329   75 SCt 326
     Super 165-166
     Driesen, David M. The congressional role in international environmental law and its implications for statutory interpretation. *Boston College Environmental Affairs Law Review* 19(2):287-315 (Fall/Winter 1991).

966. Sicurella v. United States   March 14, 1955
     348 US 385   99 LEd 436   75 SCt 403
     McKown, Delos Banning. Deism and the Supreme Court. *Humanist* 52(2):25-28, 48 (March/April 1992).

967. Internal Revenue Commissioner v. Glenshaw Glass Co.   March 28, 1955
     348 US 426   99 LEd 483   75 SCt 473
     Sup Ct Review (1983):32-82
     O'Hara, Steven T. In search of the meaning of income. *Trusts and Estates* 127(7):50-51 (July 1988).

968. Williamson v. Lee Optical of Oklahoma Inc.   March 28, 1955
     348 US 483   99 LEd 563   75 SCt 461
     Brennan 270-273+
     En Am Con 2066

969. Regan v. New York   April 25, 1955
     349 US 58   99 LEd 883   75 SCt 585
     Super 166-168+

970. Rice v. Sioux City Memorial Park Cemetery   November, 15, 1954
     349 US 70   99 LEd 897   75 SCt 614
     Super 156-158+

971. Quinn v. United States   May 23, 1955
     349 US 155   99 LEd 964   75 SCt 668
     En Am Con 1569-1577

Just War 233-235
Powers 208-209
Super 177-179

972. Emspak v. United States   May 23, 1955
      349 US 190   99 LEd 997   75 SCt 687
         Powers 208-209
         Super 177-179

973. Brown v. Board of Education of Topeka Kansas   May 31, 1955
         Coupled with Briggs v. Elliott
         Coupled with Davis v. County School Board of Prince Edward County
         Coupled with Bolling v. Sharpe
         Coupled with Gebhart v. Belton
      349 US 294   99 LEd 1083   75 SCt 753
         Am Educators 78-79
         Burden 79-81+
         Civil 20th 3, 8, 71-75R
         Court Public 98-99, 101-102, 109-111R
         En Am Con 44-45, 161-164, 273-280, 557-561
         Eyes 95-96R
         Magic 322-324, 326-327
         Making 219-222, 224-231, 235-240+
         New Right (Schwartz) 141-145

Alter, Robert J. Shareholder's Fifth Amendment privilege bars summons of corporate records. *Journal of Taxation* 63(4):208-210 (October 1985).

Brady, Timothy Patrick. "But most of it belongs to those yet to be born:" the public trust doctrine, NEPA, and the stewardship ethic. *Boston College Environmental Affairs Law Review* 17(3):621-646 (Spring 1990).

Brown, Kevin. Revisiting the Supreme Court's opinion in Brown v. Board of Education from a multiculturalist perspective. *Teachers College Record* 96(4):644-653 (Summer 1995).

Delon, Floyd G. The legacy of Thurgood Marshall. *Journal of Negro Education* 63(3):278-288 (Summer 1994).

Evolution of court policy. *Congressional Digest* 59(2):39 (February 1981).

Gordon, William M. The implementation of desegregation plans since Brown. *Journal of Negro Education* 63(3):310-322 (Summer 1994).

Grant, Carl A. Reflections on the promise of Brown and multicultural education. *Teachers College Record* 96(4):707-721 (Summer 1995).

Hyde, Alison A. School desegregation: the role of the courts and means of achievement. *NASSP Bulletin* 78(565):28-37 (November 1994).

Lamb, Charles M. Legal foundations of civil rights and pluralism America. *Annals of the American Academy of Political and Social Science* 454:13-25 (March 1981).

Landsberg, Brian K. The federal government and the promise of Brown. *Teachers College Record* 96(4):627-636 (Summer 1995).

McDonald, Donald. The fate of school desegregation. [Editorial]. *Center Magazine* 15(4):6-8 (July/August 1982).

McDowell, Gary L. Modest remedy for judicial activism. *Public Interest* (67):3-20 (Spring 1982).

Not quite emancipation. *National Review* 43(2):17-18 (February 11, 1991).

Parker, Franklin. A 30-year perspective on school desegregation. *Education Digest* 51(7):26-28 (March 1986).

Reid, Herbert O., Sr. State of the art: the law and education since 1954. *Journal of Negro Education* 52(3):234-249 (Summer 1983).

Reynolds, William Bradford. Affirmative action and its negative repercussions. *Annals of the American Academy of Political and Social Science* 523:38-49 (September 1992).

Russo, Charles J., J. John Harris III, and Rosetta F. Sandidge. Brown v. Board of Education at 40: a legal history of equal educational opportunity in American public education. *Journal of Negro Education* 63(3):297-309 (Summer 1994).

Simmons, Althea T. L. From Brown to Grove City: blueprint for education. *Crisis* 91(5):6-10 (May 1984).

Stefkovich, Jacqueline A., and Terrence Leas. A legal history of desegregation in higher education. *Journal of Negro Education* 63(3):406-420 (Summer 1994).

Ware, Leland. Will there be a "different world" after Fordice? *Academe* 80(3):6-11 (May/June 1994).

974. Peters v. Hobby   June 6, 1955
349 US 331   99 LEd 1129   75 SCt 790
    Const (Currie) 385-386
    En Am Con 670-671
    Super 152-155

975. Williams v. Georgia   June 6, 1955
349 US 375   99 LEd 1161   75 SCt 814
    Death Penalty (Tushnet) 158

976. Federal Power Commission (FPC) v. Oregon   June 6, 1955
349 US 435   99 LEd 1215   75 SCt 832
    Am Indian (Deloria)   197-220

977. U.S. ex rel. Toth v. Quarles   November 7, 1955
350 US 11   100 LEd 8   76 SCt 1
    Const (Currie) 400-403
    En Am Con 1253-1255, 1902
    Guide (CQ) 130
    Landmark (v. 5):67-76R
    Super 179-182+

978. Corn Products Refining Co. v. Commissioner of Internal Revenue (IRS)   November 7, 1955
350 US 46   100 LEd 29   76 SCt 20
Herrmann, Gary A., and Steven C. Malvey. New rules for business hedges resolve many uncertainties of Arkansas Best. *Journal of Taxation* 80(3):132-138 (March 1994).

Swift, Kenton D. New tax court decision gives a boost to ordinary loss treatment for hedging transactions. *Taxes* 71(10):636-640 (October 1993).

Yang, Wesley. Impact of Arkansas Best on some types of investments remains uncertain. *Journal of Taxation* 70(2):106-109 (February 1989).

979. Indian Towing Co. v. United States   April 11, 1955
350 US 61   100 LEd 48   76 SCt 122
    Super 198-199
Lewis, Jan. The exchange report: discretionary function exception: an update after Berkovitz. *Trial* 26(4):93-97 (April 1990).

980. Rex Trailer Co., Inc. v. United States   January 9, 1956
350 US 148   100 LEd 149   76 SCt 219
Caginalp, O. A. Fifth Amendment privilege against self-incrimination and compulsory self-disclosure under the Clean Air and Clean Water Acts. *Boston College Environmental Affairs Law Review* 9(2):359-395 (1980-1981).

981. United States v. Green   March 26, 1956
350 US 415   100 LEd 494   76 SCt 522
    En Am Con 516-522, 576-578
    Sup Ct Review (1994):129-168

982. Ullmann v. United States   March 26, 1956
350 US 422   100 LEd 511   76 SCt 497
    En Am Con 1569-1577, 1933

Super 188-190+

983. Pennsylvania v. Nelson — April 2, 1956
350 US 497   100 LEd 640   76 SCt 477
Documents (v. 2):614-617R
En Am Con 1375-1376
Guide (CQ) 49
Super 182-183, 324-325+

984. Slochower v. Board of Higher Education of City of New York — April 9, 1956
350 US 551   100 LEd 692   76 SCt 637
Const (Currie) 386-388, 392-394, 539-540
En Am Con 1569-1577
Guide (CQ) 49
Super 183-185

985. Griffin v. Illinois — April 23, 1956
351 US 12   100 LEd 891   76 SCt 585
Const (Currie) 403-405
En Am Con 534-535, 583, 869-870, 1585-1592
Super 193-195+
Bennett, Fred Warren. Toward eliminating bargain basement justice: providing indigent defendants with expert services and an adequate defense. *Law and Contemporary Problems* 58(1):95-138 (Winter 1995).
Flygare, Thomas J. School finance a decade after Rodriguez. *Phi Delta Kappan* 64(7):477-478 (March 1983).
Harris, David A. The Constitution and truth seeking: a new theory on expert services for indigent defendants. *Journal of Criminal Law and Criminology* 83(3):469-525 (Fall 1992).

986. National Labor Relations Board (NLRB) v. Babcock and Wilcox Co. — April 30, 1956
     Coupled with National Labor Relations Board (NLRB) v. Seamprufe, Inc.
     Coupled with Ranco, Inc. v. National Labor Relations Board (NLRB)
351 US 105   100 LEd 975   76 SCt 679
Hukill, Craig. Labor and the Supreme Court: significant issues of 1991-92. *Monthly Labor Review* 115(1):34-39 (January 1992).

987. Communist Party of United States v. Subversive Activities Control Board — April 30, 1956
351 US 115   100 LEd 1003   76 SCt 663
En Am Con 1804-1807
Guide (CQ) 51
May 137-150R
Super 185-188

988. Berra v. United States — April 30, 1956
351 US 131   100 LEd 1013   76 SCt 685
Tish, Martin H. Duplicative statutes, prosecutorial discretion, and the Illinois armed violence statute. *Journal of Criminal Law and Criminology* 71(3):226-243 (Fall 1980).

989. United States v. Storer Broadcasting Co. — May 21, 1956
351 US 192   100 LEd 1081   76 SCt 763
Funk, William. The exception that approves the rule: FDF variances under the Clean Water Act. *Boston College Environmental Affairs Law Review* 13(1):1-60 (Fall 1985).

990. Railway Employees' Department, American Federation of Labor v. Hanson — May 21, 1956
351 US 225   100 LEd 1112   76 SCt 714
Sup Ct Review (1990):163-205

991. United States v. E.I. du Pont de Nemours and Co.   June 11, 1956
    351 US 377   100 LEd 1264   76 SCt 994
      Super 195-196

992. Kinsella v. Krueger   June 11, 1956
    351 US 470   100 LEd 1342   76 SCt 886
      Const (Currie) 400-403
      Sup Ct Review (1986):259-316

993. Reid v. Covert   June 11, 1956
    351 US 487   100 LEd 1352   76 SCt 880
      Const (Currie) 400-403
      En Am Con 448-454, 677-678, 1253-1255
      Sup Ct Review (1986):259-316
    Ball, Howard. The U.S. Supreme Court's glossing of the Federal Tort Claims Act: statutory construction and
    veterans' tort actions. *Western Political Quarterly* 41(3):529-552 (September 1988).

994. Cole v. Young   June 11, 1956
    351 US 536   100 LEd 1396   76 SCt 861
      Documents (v. 2):613-614R

995. Mesaroch v. United States   November 5, 1956
    352 US 1   1 LEd2d 1   77 SCt 8
      Super 208-210

996. Delli Paoli v. United States   January 14, 1957
    352 US 232   1 LEd2d 278   77 SCt 294
      Super 711-713
    Goldberg, Steven H. Harmless error: constitutional sneak thief. *Journal of Criminal Law and Criminology*
    71(4):421-442 (Winter 1980).
    Krit, Jonathan J. Supreme Court review: Sixth Amendment—confrontation and the use of interlocking
    confessions at joint trial. *Journal of Criminal Law and Criminology* 78(4):937-953 (Winter 1988).

997. La Buy v. Howes Leather Co.   January 14, 1957
    352 US 249   1 LEd2d 290   77 SCt 309
    Feldman, Stuart P. Curbing the recalcitrant polluter: post-decree judicial agents in environmental litigation.
    Boston College Environmental Affairs Law Review 18(4):809-840 (Summer 1991).

998. Butler v. Michigan   February 25, 1957
    352 US 380   1 LEd2d 412   77 SCt 524
      Documents (v. 2):619-620R
      En Am Con 187
      Super 218-219+

999. Breithaupt v. Abram   February 25, 1957
    352 US 432   1 LEd2d 448   77 SCt 408
      En Am Con 148

1000. Radovich v. National Football League (NFL)   February 25, 1957
    352 US 445   1 LEd2d 456   77 SCt 390
      Owners 243-246

1001. Roviaro v. United States   March 25, 1957
    353 US 53   1 LEd2d 639   77 SCt 623

White, Welsh S. Evidentiary privileges and the defendant's constitutional right to introduce evidence. *Journal of Criminal Law and Criminology* 80(2):377-426 (Summer 1989).

1002. National Labor Relations Board (NLRB) v. Truck Drivers Local Union, No. 449   April 1, 1957
353 US 87   1 LEd2d 676   77 SCt 643
Lissy, William E. Use of temporary replacements during a lockout. *Supervision* 43(9):18-20 (September 1981).

1003. Automobile Club of Michigan v. Commissioner of Internal Revenue   April 22, 1957
353 US 180   1 LEd2d 746   77 SCt 707
Lynch, James M. Indianapolis Power and Light Company: issues and planning opportunities where the government seeks the acceleration of income. *Taxes* 68(12):931-944 (December 1990).
Seago, W. Eugene. What chance for prepaid income deferrals based on statistical estimates after RCA? *Journal of Taxation* 54(1):16-20 (January 1981).

1004. Schware v. Board of Bar of Examiners of New Mexico   May 6, 1957
353 US 232   1 LEd2d 796   77 SCt 752
En Am Con 1627
Super 229-230

1005. Konigsberg v. State Bar of California   May 6, 1957
353 US 252   1 LEd2d 810   77 SCt 722
Const (Currie) 392-394
En Am Con 770-73, 1108
Super 229-230, 362-363+

1006. Achilli v. United States   May 27, 1957
353 US 373   1 LEd2d 918   77 SCt 995
Super 214-215

1007. United States v. E.I. du Pont de Nemours and Co.   June 3, 1957
353 US 586   1 LEd2d 1057   77 SCt 872
Super 222-224, 376-377+

1008. Jencks v. United States   June 3, 1957
353 US 657   1 LEd2d 1103   77 SCt 1007
En Am Con 1018-1019
Guide (West) (v. 6):338
Super 226-228+
Rosenberg, Gerald N. Judicial independence and the reality of political power. *Review of Politics* 54(3):369-398 (Summer 1992).

1009. Reid v. Covert   June 10, 1957
          Coupled with Kinsella v. Kreuger
354 US 1   1 LEd2d 1148   77 SCt 1222
En Am Con 1535
Sup Ct Review (1986):259-316
Super 239-247, 347-349+

1010. Watkins v. United States   June 17, 1957
354 US 178   1 LEd2d 1273   77 SCt 1173
Const (Currie) 388-390
En Am Con 1569-1577, 1659-1664, 2038
Guide (CQ) 49-50
Making 295-300
Powers 209-210

Super 234-239+

Rosenberg, Gerald N. Judicial independence and the reality of political power. *Review of Politics* 54(3):369-398 (Summer 1992).

The talk of the town: notes and comment. *New Yorker* 59(36):39-40 (October 24, 1983).

1011. Sweezy v. New Hampshire by Wyman   June 17, 1957
      354 US 234   1 LEd2d 1311   77 SCt 1203
        Const (Currie) 391-392
        En Am Con 2038
        Super 234-236, 239+

Rosenberg, Gerald N. Judicial independence and the reality of political power. *Review of Politics* 54(3):369-398 (Summer 1992).

Scales, Ann C., William W. Van Alstyne, Mary W. Gray, Joel T. Rosenthal, James O. Freedman, Elizabeth Bartholet, and Julius G. Getman. University of Pennsylvania v. EEOC and the status of peer review: a symposium. *Academe* 76(3):31-35 (May/June 1990).

Sloviter, Dolores K. Faculty in federal court: decreasing receptivity? *Academe* 68(5):19-23 (September/October 1982).

Van Alstyne, William W. Academic freedom and the First Amendment in the Supreme Court of the United States: an unhurried historical review. *Law and Contemporary Problems* 53(3):79-154 (Summer 1990).

1012. Yates v. United States   June 17, 1957
          Coupled with Schneiderman v. United States
          Coupled with Richmond v. United States
      354 US 298   1 LEd2d 1356   77 SCt 1064
        Documents (v. 2):625-626R
        En Am Con 555-556, 770-773, 1804-1807, 2082-2083
        First 145-150
        Guide (CQ) 49-50
        Sup Ct Ind 137,139+
        Super 232-234+

Fiss, Owen M., and Charles Krauthammer. The Rehnquist Court. *New Republic* 186(10):14-16, 18 (March 10, 1982.)

1013. Kingsley Books, Inc. v. Brown   June 24, 1957
      354 US 436   1 LEd2d 1469   77 SCt 1325
        Const (Currie) 398-399
        En Am Con 1105

1014. Mallory v. United States   June 24, 1957
      354 US 449   1 LEd2d 1479   77 SCt 1356
        En Am Con 1242-1243
        Guide (CQ) 49-50
        Guide (West) (v. 7):319-320
        Super 225-226+

Rosenberg, Gerald N. Judicial independence and the reality of political power. *Review of Politics* 54(3):369-398 (Summer 1992).

1015. Roth v. United States   June 24, 1957
      354 US 476   1 LEd2d 1498   77 SCt 1304
        Brennan 166-176
        Const (Currie) 396-398
        Const Law 230-234R+, 236-242
        En Am Con 1009, 1335-1337, 1612-1613
        First 283-288
        Guide (CQ) 49-50

Guide (West) (v. 9):70-71, 327-328
Landmark (v. 1):23-34R
Law 326-328
Magic 317-320
Price 8-13
Sup Ct Ind 58-59+
Sup Ct Review (1982):285-317
Super 218-221+

Hagle, Timothy M. But do they have to see it to know it? the Supreme Court's obscenity and pornography decisions. *Western Political Quarterly* 44(4):1039-1054 (December 1991).

Kobylka, Joseph F. A court-created context for group litigation: libertarian groups and obscenity. *Journal of Politics* 49(4):1061-1078 (November 1987).

McGuire, Kevin T. Obscenity, libertarian values, and decision making in the Supreme Court. *American Politics Quarterly* 18(1):47-67 (January 1990).

McGuire, Kevin T., and Gregory A. Caldeira. Lawyers, organized interests, and the law of obscenity: agenda setting in the Supreme Court. *American Political Science Review* 87(3):717-726 (September 1993).

Staal, Lorri. Supreme Court review: First Amendment—the objective standard for social value in obscenity cases. *Journal of Criminal Law and Criminology* 78(4):735-762 (Winter 1988).

Teachout, Terry. The pornography report that never was. *Commentary* 84(2):51-57 (August 1987).

Welsh, Robert, and Ronald K. L. Collins. Taking state constitutions seriously: the protection of civil liberties has been shifting away from the U.S. Supreme Court. *Center Magazine* 14(5):6-35, 38-43 (September/ October 1981).

Yen, Marianne. First Amendment watch update: 43 states now use Miller test. *Publishers' Weekly* 229(18):15 (May 2, 1986).

1016. Wilson v. Girard   July 11, 1957
354 US 524   1 LEd2d 1544   77 SCt 1409
Super 247-249

Raymond, John M., and Barbara J. Frischholz. Lawyers who established international law in the United States, 1776-1914. *American Journal of International Law* 76(4):802-829 (October 1982).

1017. Rathbun v. United States   December 9, 1957
355 US 107   2 LEd2d 134   78 SCt 161

Turley, Jonathan. The not-so-noble lie: the nonincorporation of state consensual surveillance standards in federal court. *Journal of Criminal Law and Criminology* 79(1):66-134 (Spring 1988).

1018. Rowoldt v. Perfetto, Immigration and Naturalization Service   December 9, 1957
355 US 115   2 LEd2d 140   78 SCt 180
Super 266-267

1019. Green v. United States   December 16, 1957
355 US 184   2 LEd2d 199   78 SCt 221

Pachciarek, Anne M. Supreme Court review: Fifth Amendment—extension of double jeopardy protection to sentencing. *Journal of Criminal Law and Criminology* 72(4):1276-1287 (Winter 1981).

1020. Lambert v. California   December 16, 1957
355 US 225   2 LEd2d 228   78 SCt 240
Super 307-309+

1021. Northern Pacific Railway Co. v. United States   March 10, 1958
356 US 1   2 LEd2d 545   78 SCt 514
Sup Ct Review (1984):69-148

1022. Commissioner of Internal Revenue v. Sullivan   March 17, 1958
356 US 27   2 LEd2d 559   78 SCt 512

Sup Ct Review (1983):32-82

1023. Tank Truck Rentals, Inc. v. Commissioner of Internal Revenue   March 17, 1958
     356 US 30   2 LEd2d 562   78 SCt 507
       Sup Ct Review (1983):32-82

Vile, John R. Bob Jones before the bench. *Christian Century* 100(23):707-711 (August 3-10, 1983).

1024. Perez v. Brownell   March 31, 1958
     356 US 44   2 LEd2d 603   78 SCt 568
       Const (Currie) 405-407
       En Am Con 1921
       Guide (CQ) 144, 146-147
       Super 313-319+

1025. Trop v. Dulles, Secretary of State   March 31, 1958
     356 US 86   2 LEd2d 630   78 SCt 590
       Brennan 215-220
       Const (Currie) 405-407, 547-550
       Death Penalty 154
       En Am Con 524-526, 1921
       Guide (CQ) 147
       Super 313-318+

Caginalp, O. A. Fifth Amendment privilege against self-incrimination and compulsory self-disclosure under the Clean Air and Clean Water Acts. *Boston College Environmental Affairs Law Review* 9(2):359-395 (1980-1981).

Murphy, Walter F. The Constitution and the 14th Amendment. *Center Magazine* 20(4):9-30 (July/August 1987).

Schwartz, Charles Walter. Eighth Amendment proportionality analysis and the compelling case of William Rummel. *Journal of Criminal Law and Criminology* 71(4):378-420 (Winter 1980).

1026. Nishikawa v. Dulles, Secretary of State   March 31, 1958
     356 US 129   2 LEd2d 659   78 SCt 612
       Japanese 72, 265

1027. Grimes v. Raymond Concrete Pile Co.   April 7, 1958
     356 US 252   2 LEd2d 737   78 SCt 687

Arsenault, Richard J. Seaman status: has the traditional mariner been forgotten? *Trial* 28(9):66-71 (September 1992).

1028. Sherman v. United States   May 19, 1958
     356 US 369   2 LEd2d 848   78 SCt 819
       Sup Ct Review (1981):111-155

Dripps, Donald A. Supreme Court review: the riddle of entrapment. *Trial* 28(7):97-100 (July 1992).

1029. Kent v. Dulles, Secretary of State   June 16, 1958
     357 US 116   2 LEd2d 1204   78 SCt 1113
       Burger Years 50-55
       En Am Con 747-755, 1102
       Sup Ct Review (1981):263-290
       Super 309-311+

Halperin, Morton H. Never question the president. *Nation* 239(9):285-288 (September 29, 1984).

Lewin, Nathan. Supreme Court's travel bug. *New Republic* 185(4):17-20 (July 25, 1981).

Pawelek, Dick. How the Supreme Court ruled in Dulles v. Kent. *Scholastic Update* (Teachers' Edition) 119(2):43 (September 22, 1986).

Who's free to travel? *Scholastic Update* (Teachers' Edition) 119(2):43 (September 22, 1986).

1030. Dayton v. Dulles, Secretary of State   June 16, 1958
     357 US 144   2 LEd2d 1221   78 SCt 1127
       Super 309-311

1031. Societe Internationale Pour Participations Industrielles v. Rogers   June 16, 1958
     357 US 197   2 LEd2d 1255   78 SCt 1087
     Note: beyond the rhetoric of comparative interest balancing: an alternative approach to extraterritorial discovery conflicts. *Law and Contemporary Problems* 50(3):95-115 (Summer 1987).

1032. Ivanhoe Irrigation District v. McCracken   June 23, 1958
          Coupled with Madera Irrigation District v. Steiner
          Coupled with Madera Irrigation District v. Albonico
          Coupled with Santa Barbara County Water Agency v. Balaam
     357 US 275   2 LEd2d 1313   78 SCt 1174
       Sup Ct Review (1988):85-113

1033. City of Tacoma v. Taxpayers of Tacoma   June 23, 1958
     357 US 320   2 LEd2d 1345   78 SCt 1209
     Provost, Denise. The Massachusetts Hazardous Waste Facility Siting Act: what impact on municipal power to exclude and regulate? *Boston College Environmental Affairs Law Review* 10(3):715-795 (December 1982-January 1983).

1034. Wiener v. United States   June 30, 1958
     357 US 349   2 LEd2d 1377   78 SCt 1275
       Powers 244-245
       Sup Ct Review (1986):41-97

1035. Beilan v. Board of Public Education   June 30, 1958
     357 US 399   2 LEd2d 1414   78 SCt 1317
     Menacker, Julius. Review of Supreme Court reasoning in cases of expression, due process, and equal protection. *Phi Delta Kappan* 63(3):188-190 (November 1981).

1036. National Association for the Advancement of Colored People (NAACP)   June 30, 1958
        v. Alabama ex rel. Patterson
     357 US 449   2 LEd2d 1488   78 SCt 1163
       Const (Currie) 381-385
       Documents (v. 2):630-632R
       En Am Con 770-773, 1291, 1577-1581, 1722-1724
       Freedom (Cox) 68-74
       Making 283-289
       Sup Ct Review (1982):243-284; (1983):583-626
       Super 304-305, 452-453+
     Abram, Morris B. Is "strict separation" too strict? *Public Interest* (82):81-90 (Winter 1986).
     Padgett, Gregory L. Racially-motivated violence and intimidation: inadequate state enforcement and federal civil rights remedies. *Journal of Criminal Law and Criminology* 75(1):103-138 (Spring 1984).

1037. Speiser v. Randall   June 30, 1958
     357 US 513   2 LEd2d 1460   78 SCt 1332, 1352
       En Am Con 1718

1038. First Unitarian Church v. County of Los Angeles   June 30, 1958
          Coupled with Valley Unitarian-Universalist Church, Inc. v. County of Los Angeles
     357 US 545   2 LEd2d 1484   78 SCt 1350
       Documents (v. 2):632-633R

1039. Federal Trade Commission (FTC) v. National Casualty Co.   June 30, 1958
      Coupled with Federal Trade Commission (FTC) v. American Hospital and Life Insurance Co.
357 US 560   2 LEd2d 1540   78 SCt 1260
    Weller, Charles D. McCarran Act interpretation may have been charted in Barry Case. *Best's Review*
      (Life/Health Insurance Edition) 83(2):40-42, 87-89 (June 1982).

1040. Cooper v. Aaron   September 29, 1958
    358 US 1   3 LEd2d 5, 19   78 SCt 1401
      Antagonists 227-228, 232-233+
      Civil 20th 3, 8, 77-93R
      Const (Currie) 377-381
      Documents (v. 2):633-636R
      En Am Con 448-454, 502-503, 557-561
      Guide (CQ) 49-50
      Hard Choices 305
      Magic 324-325
      Making 257-266
      May 249-261R
      Sup Ct Review (1986):259-316
      Super 289-305+
    Delon, Floyd G. The legacy of Thurgood Marshall. *Journal of Negro Education* 63(3):278-288 (Summer 1994).
    Erler, Edward J. Brown v. Board of Education at 30. *National Review* 36(17):26-28, 30-31, 53 (September 7,
      1984).
    Evolution of court policy. *Congressional Digest* 59(2):39 (February 1981).
    Fast Eddie v. Honest Abe. [Editorial] *Nation* 243(15):473 (November 8, 1986).
    Gordon, William M. The implementation of desegregation plans since Brown. *Journal of Negro Education*
      63(3):310-322 (Summer 1994).
    Gunther, Gerald. Judicial review. *Society* 24(1):18-23 (November/December 1986).
    Lacayo, Richard, and Anne Constable. Supreme or not Supreme: that is the question, says the Attorney General.
      Time 128(18):46 (November 3, 1986).
    Levinson, Sanford. Looking at the Constitution: could Meese be right this time? *Nation* 243(21):689, 704-707
      (December 20, 1986).
    Meese, Edwin, III. Saving the Constitution: the law of the Constitution. *National Review* 39(13):30-33 (July 17,
      1987).
    Russo, Charles J., J. John Harris III, and Rosetta F. Sandidge. Brown v. Board of Education at 40: a legal
      history of equal educational opportunity in American public education. *Journal of Negro Education*
      63(3):297-309 (Summer 1994).
    Simmons, Althea T. L. From Brown to Grove City: blueprint for education. *Crisis* 91(5):6-10 (May 1984).

1041. Hawkins v. United States   November 24, 1958
    358 US 74   3 LEd2d 125   79 SCt 136
    Pachciarek, Anne. Supreme Court review: Federal Rules of Evidence—testimonial privileges. *Journal of*
      Criminal Law and Criminology 71(4):593-600 (Winter 1980).

1042. Federal Housing Administration (FHA) v. Darlington, Inc.   November 24, 1958
    358 US 84   3 LEd2d 132   79 SCt 141
    Ball, Howard. The U.S. Supreme Court's glossing of the Federal Tort Claims Act: statutory construction and
      veterans' tort actions. *Western Political Quarterly* 41(3):529-552 (September 1988).

1043. Williams v. Lee   January 12, 1959
    358 US 217   3 LEd2d 251   79 SCt 269
      Am Indian (Deloria)   63-82+
      Am Indians (Wilkinson) 1-3, 123, 133+

Allen, Mark. Native American control of tribal natural resource development in the context of the federal trust and tribal self-determination. *Boston College Environmental Affairs Law Review* 16(4):857-895 (Summer 1989).

1044. Draper v. United States   January 26, 1959
      358 US 307   3 LEd2d 327   79 SCt 329
         En Am Con 584, 979-980, 1628-1635

1045. Romero v. International Terminal Operating Co.   February 24, 1959
      358 US 354   3 LEd2d 368   79 SCt 468
         Sup Ct Review (1991):179-224
      Arsenault, Richard J., and Richard W. Beard. Maritime personal injury on foreign waters. *Trial* 20(6):72-76 (June 1984).

1046. Cammarano v. United States   February 24, 1959
         Coupled with F. Strauss and Son, Inc. v. Commissioner of Internal Revenue
      358 US 498   3 LEd2d 462   79 SCt 524
         Sup Ct Review (1983):32-82

1047. Kermarec v. Compagnie Generale Transatlantique   February 24, 1959
      358 US 625   3 LEd2d 550   79 SCt 406
      Baker, Nathan. Santos decision: a positive step toward harbor workers' safety. *Trial* 17(9):26-29, 58 (September 1981).

1048. Bartkus v. Illinois   March 30, 1959
      359 US 121   3 LEd2d 684   79 SCt 676
         En Am Con 102-103, 576-578
         Super 322-324

1049. Abbate v. United States   March 30, 1959
      359 US 187   3 LEd2d 729   79 SCt 666
         En Am Con 102-103

1050. San Diego Building Trades Council v. Garmon   April 20, 1959
      359 US 236   3 LEd2d 775   79 SCt 773
         Sup Ct Review (1986):135-155
      Finkin, Matthew W. Regulation by agreement: the case of private higher education. *Academe* 67(2):67-80 (April 1981).

1051. United States v. Shirey   April 20, 1959
      359 US 255   3 LEd2d 789   79 SCt 746
         Super 330-331

1052. Frank v. Maryland   May 4, 1959
      359 US 360   3 LEd2d 877   79 SCt 804
         En Am Con 1947-1949
         Sup Ct Review (1989):87-163
         Super 326-328, 343-344+

1053. Beacon Theatres, Inc. v. Westover   May 25, 1959
      359 US 500   3 LEd2d 988   79 SCt 948
         Const (Currie) 407-410
         En Am Con 104, 1913-1920

1054. Bibb v. Navajo Freight Lines, Inc.   May 25, 1959
       359 US 520   3 LEd2d 1003   79 SCt 962
          En Am Con 109, 1751-1755

1055. Vitarelli v. Seaton, Secretary of the Interior   June 1, 1959
       359 US 535   3 LEd2d 1012   79 SCt 968
          Super 328-329

1056. Lassiter v. Northampton County Board of Election   June 8, 1959
       360 US 45   3 LEd2d 1072   79 SCt 985
          Abortion Moral 128-139
          Const (Currie) 381-385
          En Am Con 1169, 1979-1987
       Flaherty, Francis J. Abortion, the Constitution and the Human Life Statute. *Commonweal* 108(19):586-593
          (October 23, 1981).

1057. Uphaus v. Wyman   June 8, 1959
       360 US 72   3 LEd2d 1090   79 SCt 1040
          Documents (v. 2):637-642R
          En Am Con 1951-1952
          Super 324-325
       Rosenberg, Gerald N. Judicial independence and the reality of political power. *Review of Politics* 54(3):369-398
          (Summer 1992).

1058. Barenblatt v. United States   June 8, 1959
       360 US 109   3 LEd2d 1115   79 SCt 1081
          Antagonists 241-243
          Const (Currie) 392-394
          Courage 81-104, 425
          Documents (v. 2):642-647R
          En Am Con 101-102, 844, 877, 1148-1151
          Powers 209-210
       The association and the courts. *Academe* 75(3):31-33 (May/June 1989).
       Rosenberg, Gerald N. Judicial independence and the reality of political power. *Review of Politics* 54(3):369-398
          (Summer 1992).
       Van Alstyne, William W. Academic freedom and the First Amendment in the Supreme Court of the United
          States: an unhurried historical review. *Law and Contemporary Problems* 53(3):79-154 (Summer 1990).

1059. National Labor Relations Board (NLRB) v. Cabot Carbon Co.   June 8, 1959
       360 US 203   3 LEd2d 1175   79 SCt 1015
       Andresky, Jill. Just a puppet? *Forbes* 137(10):80-81 (May 5, 1986).

1060. Spano v. New York   June 22, 1959
       360 US 315   3 LEd2d 1265   79 SCt 1202
       Bahl, Martin. The Sixth Amendment as constitutional theory: does originalism require that Massiah be
          abandoned? *Journal of Criminal Law and Criminology* 82(2):423-463 (Summer 1991).
       Lundstrom, Bruce D. Supreme Court review: Sixth Amendment—right to counsel: limited postindictment use
          of jailhouse informants is permissible. *Journal of Criminal Law and Criminology* 77(3):743-774 (Fall 1986).

1061. Barr v. Matteo   June 29, 1959
       360 US 564   3 LEd2d 1434   79 SCt 1335
       Rosenbloom, David H. Public administrators' official immunity and the Supreme Court: developments during
          the 1970s. *Public Administration Review* 40(2):166-173 (March/April 1980).

1062. Kingsley International Pictures Corp. v. Regents of University of State of New York   June 29, 1959
     360 US 684   3 LEd2d 1512   79 SCt 1362
     En Am Con 1105

1063. United Steelworkers of America v. United States   November 7, 1959
     361 US 39   4 LEd2d 12, 169   80 SCt 1, 177
     Super 352-354+

1064. Smith v. California   December 14, 1959
     361 US 147   4 LEd2d 205   80 SCt 215
     Super 350-351+
     McGuire, Kevin T. Obscenity, libertarian values, and decision making in the Supreme Court. *American Politics Quarterly* 18(1):47-67 (January 1990).

1065. National Labor Relations Board (NLRB) v. Insurance Agents International Union   February 23, 1960
     361 US 477   4 LEd2d 454   80 SCt 419
     Finkin, Matthew W. Regulation by agreement: the case of private higher education. *Academe* 67(2):67-80 (April 1981).

1066. Bates v. Little Rock   February 23, 1960
     361 US 516   4 LEd2d 480   80 SCt 412
     Courage 105-127, 426
     En Am Con 844
     Eyes 97-106
     Making 257-266, 291-292
     Sup Ct Review (1983):583-626
     Brewster, Todd, and Temma Ehrenfeld. First and foremost. *Life* 14 (13 Special Issue):60-66 (Fall 1991).

1067. United States v. Raines   February 29, 1960
     362 US 17   4 LEd2d 524   80 SCt 519
     Super 355-356

1068. United States v. Parke, Davis and Co.   February 29, 1960
     362 US 29   4 LEd2d 505   80 SCt 503
     Sheffet, Mary Jane, and Debra L. Scammon. Resale price maintenance: is it safe to suggest retail prices? *Journal of Marketing* 49(4):82-92 (Fall 1985).

1069. Thompson v. City of Louisville   March 21, 1960
     362 US 199   4 LEd2d 654   80 SCt 624
     Super 402-404+

1070. Abel v. United States   March 28, 1960
     362 US 217   4 LEd2d 668   80 SCt 683
     Super 339-341
     Uviller, H. Richard. Fourth Amendment: does it protect your garbage? *Nation* 247(9):302-304 (October 10, 1988).

1071. Jones v. United States   March 28, 1960
     362 US 257   4 LEd2d 697   80 SCt 725
     Hartman, Marshall J., and Sidney Bernstein. To Leon, and beyond; two commentators react. *Trial* 21(1):50-56 (January 1985).
     Laver, Rebecca J. Supreme Court review: Fourth Amendment—the court further limits standing. *Journal of Criminal Law and Criminology* 71(4):567-578 (Winter 1980).
     Yeager, Daniel B. Search, seizure, and the positive law: expectations of privacy outside the Fourth Amendment. *Journal of Criminal Law and Criminology* 84(2):249-309 (Summer 1993).

1072. Dusky v. United States   April 18, 1960
    362 US 402   4 LEd2d 824   80 SCt 788
    Boch, Brian R. Supreme Court review: Fourteenth Amendment—the standard of mental competency to waive
       constitutional rights versus the competency standard to stand trial. *Journal of Criminal Law and Criminology*
       84(4):883-914 (Winter/Spring 1994).

1073. Huron Portland Cement Co. v. Detroit, Michigan   April 25, 1960
    362 US 440   4 LEd2d 852   80 SCt 813
    En Am Con 942
    Adams, Nancy D. Title VI of the 1990 Clean Air Act Amendments and state and local initiatives to reverse the
       stratospheric ozone crisis: an analysis of preemption. *Boston College Environmental Affairs Law Review*
       19(1):173-216 (Fall 1991).

1074. Parker v. Ellis   May 16, 1960
    362 US 574   4 LEd2d 963   80 SCt 909
    Super 341-342

1075. Parr v. United States   June 13, 1960
    363 US 370   4 LEd2d 1277   80 SCt 1171
    Maurer, Virginia G. The continuing expansion of RICO in business litigation. *Business Horizons* 33(5):80-87
       (September/October 1990).

1076. United States v. Durham Lumber Co.   June 20, 1960
    363 US 522   4 LEd2d 1371   80 SCt 1282
    Super 354-355

1077. Federal Trade Commission (FTC) v. Anheuser-Busch, Inc.   June 20, 1960
    363 US 536   4 LEd2d 1385   80 SCt 1267
    McGahan, A. M. The emergence of the national brewing oligopoly: competition in the American market, 1933-
       1958. *Business History Review* 65(2):229-284 (Summer 1991).

1078. United Steelworkers of America v. American Manufacturing Co.   June 20, 1960
    363 US 564, 569   4 LEd2d 1403, 1432   80 SCt 1343, 1363
    Hollander, Rhonda G. Injunctions against occupational hazards: toward a safe workplace environment. *Boston*
       College Environmental Affairs Law Review 9(1):133-161 (1980-1981).
    Horowitz, Donald L. The deprivatization of labor relations law; foreward. *Law and Contemporary Problems*
       49(4):1-8 (Autumn 1986).

1079. United Steelworkers of America v. Warrior and Gulf Navigation Co.   June 20, 1960
    363 US 574, 569   4 LEd2d 1409, 1432   80 SCt 1347, 1363
    Hollander, Rhonda G. Injunctions against occupational hazards: toward a safe workplace environment. *Boston*
       College Environmental Affairs Law Review 9(1):133-161 (1980-1981).
    Horowitz, Donald L. The deprivatization of labor relations law; foreward. *Law and Contemporary Problems*
       49(4):1-8 (Autumn 1986).

1080. United Steelworkers of America v. Enterprise Wheel and Car Corp.   June 20, 1960
    363 US 593, 569   4 LEd2d 1424, 1432   80 SCt 1358, 1363
    Hollander, Rhonda G. Injunctions against occupational hazards: toward a safe workplace environment. *Boston*
       College Environmental Affairs Law Review 9(1):133-161 (1980-1981).
    Horowitz, Donald L. The deprivatization of labor relations law; foreward. *Law and Contemporary Problems*
       49(4):1-8 (Autumn 1986).

1081. Flemming, Secretary of Health, Education and Welfare v. Nestor   June 20, 1960
    363 US 603   4 LEd2d 1435   80 SCt 1367

Staas, John August. Supreme Court review: Fifth Amendment—statutory dilution of the privilege against self-incrimination. *Journal of Criminal Law and Criminology* 71(4):610-621 (Winter 1980).

1082. Elkins v. United States   June 27, 1960
364 US 206   4 LEd2d 1669   80 SCt 1437
En Am Con 624, 662-665, 1628-1635, 1683
Super 344-346+
Bloom, Robert M. Judicial integrity: a call for its re-emergence in the adjudication of criminal cases. *Journal of Criminal Law and Criminology* 84(3):462-501 (Fall 1993).
Jensen, D. Lowell, and Rosemary Hart. The good faith restatement of the exclusionary rule. *Journal of Criminal Law and Criminology* 73(3):916-938 (Fall 1982).

1083. Ohio ex rel. Eaton v. Price   June 27, 1960
364 US 263   4 LEd2d 1708   80 SCt 1463
Super 342-344+

1084. Gomillion v. Lightfoot   November 14, 1960
364 US 339   5 LEd2d 110   81 SCt 125
En Am Con 839-840, 851-852
Guide (CQ) 50
Super 377-378+
Eshleman, Kenneth. Affirmative gerrymandering is a matter of justice. *National Civic Review* 69(11):608-613, 620 (December 1980).
Graham, Barbara Luck. Federal court policy-making and political equality: an analysis of judicial redistricting. *Western Political Quarterly* 44(1):101-117 (March 1991).

1085. Chaunt v. United States   November 14, 1960
364 US 350   5 LEd2d 120   81 SCt 147
Beiner, Theresa M. Due process for all? due process, the Eighth Amendment and Nazi war criminals. *Journal of Criminal Law and Criminology* 80(1):293-337 (Spring 1989).
Gerson, Allan. Beyond Nuremberg. *Commentary* 72(4):62-66 (October 1981).

1086. Boynton v. Virginia   December 5, 1960
364 US 454   5 LEd2d 206   81 SCt 182
Super 555-557

1087. Shelton v. Tucker   December 12, 1960
364 US 479   5 LEd2d 231   81 SCt 247
Documents (v. 2):651-652R
En Am Con 770-773, 1132
Making 294-295+
Van Alstyne, William W. Academic freedom and the First Amendment in the Supreme Court of the United States: an unhurried historical review. *Law and Contemporary Problems* 53(3):79-154 (Summer 1990).

1088. United States v. Mississippi Valley Generating Co.   January 9, 1961
364 US 520   5 LEd2d 268   81 SCt 294
Super 382-383

1089. Times Film Corp. v. Chicago   January 23, 1961
365 US 43   5 LEd2d 403   81 SCt 391
Const (Currie) 398-399
Const Law 209-212+
Super 216-217, 367-369+
Kobylka, Joseph F. A court-created context for group litigation: libertarian groups and obscenity. *Journal of Politics* 49(4):1061-1078 (November 1987).

1090. Eastern Railroad Presidents Conference v. Noerr Motor Freight, Inc.   February 20, 1961
     365 US 127   5 LEd2d 464   81 SCt 523
     An old antitrust defense falters. *Business Week* (2785):66-69 (April 11, 1983).

1091. Monroe v. Pape   February 20, 1961
     365 US 167   5 LEd2d 492   81 SCt 473
     Burger Years 177-188
     En Am Con 533-534, 1274, 1285-1286, 1640-1641
     Askin, Frank. Justice denied: what the conservative judiciary hath wrought. *Trial* 29(10):65-68 (October 1993).
     Groszyk, Walter S., Jr., and Thomas J. Madden. Managing without immunity: the challenge for state and local
        government officials in the 1980s. *Public Administration Review* 41(2):268-278 (March/April 1981).
     Lee, Yong S. Civil liability of state and local governments: myth and reality. *Public Administration Review*
        47(2):160-170 (March/April 1987).

1092. Green v. United States   February 27, 1961
     365 US 301   5 LEd2d 670   81 SCt 653
     Super 369-370

1093. Wilkinson v. United States   February 27, 1961
     365 US 399   5 LEd2d 633   81 SCt 567
     Super 361-362+

1094. Silverman v. United States   March 6, 1961
     365 US 505   5 LEd2d 734   81 SCt 679
     En Am Con 1682
     Super 386-387, 462+
     Webber, Dawn. Supreme Court review: Fourth Amendment—of warrants, electronic surveillance, expectations
        of privacy, and tainted fruits. *Journal of Criminal Law and Criminology* 75(3):630-652 (Fall 1984).

1095. Rogers v. Richmond, Warden   March 20, 1961
     365 US 534   5 LEd2d 760   81 SCt 735
     En Am Con 1400-1408, 1605

1096. Milanovich v. United States   March 20, 1961
     365 US 551   5 LEd2d 773   81 SCt 728
     Super 254-256, 359-360+

1097. Ferguson v. Georgia   March 27, 1961
     365 US 570   5 LEd2d 783   81 SCt 756
     Super 384-386

1098. Burton v. Wilmington Parking Authority   April 17, 1961
     365 US 715   6 LEd2d 45   81 SCt 856
     Const Law 495-498R+
     Court Public 95-96
     En Am Con 130-131, 185, 1729-1736, 1736-1738
     Super 370-371+
     Sullivan, Harold J. Privatization of public services: a growing threat to constitutional rights. *Public
        Administration Review* 47(6):461-467 (November/December 1987).

1099. Stewart v. United States   April 24, 1961
     366 US 1   6 LEd2d 84   81 SCt 941
     Super 253-257, 359-360+

1100. Konigsberg v. State Bar of California   April 24, 1961
   366 US 36   6 LEd2d 105   81 SCt 997
    En Am Con 1108

1101. McGowan v. Maryland   May 29, 1961
   366 US 420   6 LEd2d 393   81 SCt 1101, 1153, 1218
    Const (Currie) 410-412
    Const Law 100-102R+
    En Am Con 1538-1545, 1650-1658, 1809-1810
    Godless 104-106
    Original (Davis) 72-73+
    Religion 172-173
    Sup Ct Church 274-298R, 400-410
    Super 380-382+
  Regan, Richard J. Supreme Court roundup: 1986 term. *Thought* 63(251):429-441 (December 1988).

1102. Two Guys from Harrison-Allentown, Inc. v. McGinley   May 29, 1961
   366 US 582   6 LEd2d 551   81 SCt 1135
    En Am Con 1538-1545, 1809-1810
    Religion 172-174

1103. Braunfeld v. Brown   May 29, 1961
   366 US 599   6 LEd2d 563   81 SCt 1144
    Const (Currie) 410-412
    Const Law 101-105R
    En Am Con 1538-1545, 1809-1810
    Godless 105-107+
    Original (Davis) 121-122
    Religion 172-174
    Sup Ct Church 400-410R
    Sup Ct Review (1983):1-31
  Ignagni, Joseph A. U.S. Supreme Court decision-making and the free exercise clause. *Review of Politics* 55(3):511-529 (Summer 1993).
  Regan, Richard J. Supreme Court roundup: 1984 term. *Thought* 61(241):290-302 (June 1986).
  Tushnet, Mark. The Constitution of religion. *Review of Politics* 50(4):628-658 (Fall 1988).

1104. Gallagher v. Crown Kosher Super Market of Massachusetts May 29, 1961
   366 US 617   6 LEd2d 536   81 SCt 1122
    Black 31-37
    En Am Con 1538-1545, 1809-1810
    Religion 172-174

1105. Irvin v. Dowd   June 5, 1961
   366 US 717   6 LEd2d 751   81 SCt 1639
    En Am Con 1002, 1492-1494
    First 202

1106. Communist Party of the United States v. Subversive Activities Control Board June 5, 1961
   367 US 1   6 LEd2d 625   81 SCt 1357
    Const (Currie) 395-396
    En Am Con 337
    Super 363-365+

1107. Scales v. United States   June 5, 1961
   367 US 203   6 LEd2d 782   81 SCt 1469

Const (Currie) 434-438
En Am Con 770-773, 1621, 1804-1807
Super 363-364+

1108. Torcaso v. Watkins   June 19, 1961
      367 US 488   6 LEd2d 982   81 SCt 1680
         Const (Currie) 410-412
         En Am Con 1538-1545, 1546, 1902
         Godless 95-97+
         Sup Ct Church 410-414R
         Super 381-382+
      McBride, James. Tillich in an Alice-in-Wonderland world. [Editorial] *Christian Century* 104(18):519-520 (June 3-10, 1987).
      McKown, Delos Banning. Deism and the Supreme Court. *Humanist* 52(2):25-28, 48 (March/April 1992).
      Pfeffer, Leo. How religious is secular humanism? *Humanist* 48(5):13-18, 50 (September/October 1988).

1109. Poe v. Ullman, State Attorney   June 19, 1961
            Coupled with Doe v. Ullman
            Coupled with Buxton v. Ullman
      367 US 497   6 LEd2d 989   81 SCt 1752
         Abortion Am 6-7+
         Abortion Pol (Rubin) 36-39+
         Hard Choices 132, 228
         Liberty 169-200+
         Super 378-380
      Wulf, Melvin L. On the origins of privacy. *Nation* 252(20):700, 702-704 (May 27, 1991).

1110. Mapp v. Ohio   June 19, 1961
      367 US 643   6 LEd2d 1081   81 SCt 1684
         Amending 203-213
         Ascent 358-363, 402-403+
         Brennan 191-196
         Const (Currie) 407-410, 451-453, 550-555
         Const (Friendly) 129-142
         Const Law 365-370R+
         Court Const 235-240, 244-247
         En Am Con 516-522, 662-665, 1199, 1472-1479, 1562-1564, 1628-1635, 1947-1949
         Equal (Harrell) 95-97
         Guide (CQ) 50-51
         Guide (West) (v. 7):262, 265-266
         Landmark (v. 3):97-112R
         Magic 320-322
         Reader's 698-699
         Sup Ct Ind 179+
         Sup Ct Review (1984):309-358
         Super 391-399+
      American survey: Burger leaves the labyrinth. *Economist* 300(7454):17-22 (July 12-18, 1986).
      Baker, banker, clergyman, thief. *Life* 10(10):84-88 (Fall 1987).
      Bender, Louis, and Steven Bender. Is the Supreme Court's decision in Baggot retroactive in application? *Journal of Taxation* 60(3):138-144 (March 1984).
      Brandt, Charles. Let our police take on the drug dealers. *Reader's Digest* 136(813):78-82 (January 1990).
      Brewster, Todd. Law and order. *Life* 14(13 Special Issue):85-87 (Fall 1991).
      Crocker, Lawrence. Can the exclusionary rule be saved? *Journal of Criminal Law and Criminology* 84(2):310-351 (Summer 1993).
      A curb on state powers. *U.S. News and World Report* 111(25):50 (December 16, 1991).

Glennon, Michael J. State-sponsored abduction: a comment on United States v. Alvarez-Machain. *American Journal of International Law* 86(4):746-756 (October 1992).

Goldberg, Steven H. Harmless error: constitutional sneak thief. *Journal of Criminal Law and Criminology* 71(4):421-442 (Winter 1980).

Haas, Kenneth C. "New federalism" and prisoners' rights: state supreme courts in comparative perspective. *Western Political Quarterly* 34(4):552-571 (December 1981).

Halberstam, Malvina. Agora: international kidnaping—in defense of the Supreme Court decision in Alvarez-Machain. *American Journal of International Law* 86(4):736-746 (October 1992).

Hartman, Marshall J., and Sidney Bernstein. To Leon, and beyond; two commentators react. *Trial* 21(1):50-56 (January 1985).

Jacobs, Robert. The state of Miranda: the effects of the Quarles decision. *Trial* 21(1):44-48 (January 1985).

Jensen, D. Lowell, and Rosemary Hart. The good faith restatement of the exclusionary rule. *Journal of Criminal Law and Criminology* 73(3):916-938 (Fall 1982).

Junker, John M. The structure of the Fourth Amendment: the scope of the protection. *Journal of Criminal Law and Criminology* 79(4):1105-1183 (Winter 1989).

Kamisar, Yale. The swing of the pendulum. *Nation* 239(9):271-274 (September 29, 1984).

Kaye, Judith S. The Supreme Court: state constitutional law. *Trial* 25(12):57-68, 70 (December 1989).

Maltz, Earl M. Lockstep analysis and the concept of federalism. *Annals of the American Academy of Political and Social Science* 496:98-106 (March 1988).

McGuire, Kevin T., and Barbara Palmer. Issue fluidity on the U.S. Supreme Court. *American Political Science Review* 89(3):691-702 (September 1995).

Moyer, Thomas J. The Bill of rights: its origins and its keepers. *Vital Speeches of the Day* 57(12):373-376 (April 1, 1991).

Nelson, Caleb. The paradox of the exclusionary rule. *Public Interest* (96):117-130 (Summer 1989).

Schlag, Pierre J. Assaults on the exclusionary rule: good faith limitations and damage remedies. *Journal of Criminal Law and Criminology* 73(3):875-915 (Fall 1982).

Scully, Leon. Civil wrongs. *National Review* 44(10):22-24, 26-28 (May 25, 1992).

Taylor, Stuart, Jr. Meese v. Brennan. *New Republic* 194(1):17-21 (January 6-13, 1986).

Uchida, Craig D., and Timothy S. Bynum. Search warrants, motions to suppress and "lost cases": the effects of the exclusionary rule in seven jurisdictions. *Journal of Criminal Law and Criminology* 81(4):1034-1066 (Winter 1991).

Use of the exclusionary rule. *Congressional Digest* 71(4):104-105 (April 1992).

1111. American Automobile Association (AAA) v. United States   June 19, 1961
     367 US 687   6 LEd2d 1109   81 SCt 1727

     Seago, W. Eugene. What chance for prepaid income deferrals based on statistical estimates after RCA? *Journal of Taxation* 54(1):16-20 (January 1981).

1112. Marcus v. Search Warrant of Property at 104 East Tenth Street, Kansas City, Missouri   June 19, 1961
     367 US 717   6 LEd2d 1127   81 SCt 1708

     McGuire, Kevin T., and Gregory A. Caldeira. Lawyers, organized interests, and the law of obscenity: agenda setting in the Supreme Court. *American Political Science Review* 87(3):717-726 (September 1993).

1113. International Association of Machinists v. Street   June 19, 1961
     367 US 740   6 LEd2d 1141   81 SCt 1784

     Super 371-376
     Sup Ct Review (1990):163-205

     Kovach, Kenneth A., and Peter Millspaugh. Implementing the Beck and Lehnert union security agreement decisions: a study in frustration. *Business Horizons* 38(3):57-65 (May/June 1995).

1114. Lathrop v. Donohue   June 19, 1961
     367 US 820   6 LEd2d 1191   81 SCt 1826

     Sup Ct Review (1990):163-205
     Super 372-376

1115. Cafeteria and Restaurant Workers Union, Local 473, AFL-CIO v. McElroy   June 19, 1961
        367 US 886   6 LEd2d 1230   81 SCt 1743
          Super 365-366

1116. Hoyt v. Florida   November 20, 1961
        368 US 57   7 LEd2d 118   82 SCt 159
          En Am Con 1082-1085, 1666-1673
          Magic 327-329

1117. Garner v. Louisiana   December 11, 1961
          Coupled with Briscoe v. Louisiana
          Coupled with Hoston v. Louisiana
        368 US 157   7 LEd2d 207   82 SCt 248
          Const (Currie) 381-385
          Sup Ct Ind 146-148,150
          Super 402-404+

1118. Oyler v. Boles, Warden   February 19, 1962
          Coupled with Crabtree v. Boles
        368 US 448   7 LEd2d 446   82 SCt 501
        Schwartz, Charles Walter. Eighth Amendment proportionality analysis and the compelling case of William
          Rummel. *Journal of Criminal Law and Criminology* 71(4):378-420 (Winter 1980).
        Tish, Martin H. Duplicative statutes, prosecutorial discretion, and the Illinois Armed Violence Statute. *Journal
          of Criminal Law and Criminology* 71(3):226-243 (Fall 1980).

1119. Charles Dowd Box Co. v. Courtney   February 19, 1962
        368 US 502   7 LEd2d 483   82 SCt 519
          Sup Ct Review (1986):135-155

1120. Griggs v. County of Allegheny   March 5, 1962
        369 US 84   7 LEd2d 585   82 SCt 531
        Brown, Todd D. The power line plaintiff and the inverse condemnation alternative. *Boston College
          Environmental Affairs Law Review* 19(3):655-694 (Spring 1992).
        Kahn, Richard. Inverse condemnation and the highway cases: compensation for abutting landowners. *Boston
          College Environmental Affairs Law Review* 22(3):563- 591 (Spring 1995).

1121. Local 174, Teamsters Chauffeurs, Warehousemen and Helpers of America   March 5, 1962
          v. Lucas Flour Co.
        369 US 95   7 LEd2d 593   82 SCt 571
          Sup Ct Review (1986):135-155

1122. Baker v. Carr   March 26, 1962
        369 US 186   7 LEd2d 663   82 SCt 691
          Almanac (1990):510-511
          Amending 203-213
          Antagonists 246-251
          Const (Currie) 412-414, 429-434
          Const Law 608-611+
          Court Const 290-298+
          Court Public 49-73R
          Documents (v. 2):671-674R
          En Am Con 92-93, 839-840, 1420-1422, 1518-1524, 1558-1560, 1565-1566, 1979-1987
          Equal (Harrell) 100-105, 110
          Equal Rights (Kanowitz) 127-129, 133-136+
          Guide (CQ) 50, 71-73

Guide (West) (v. 2):13-16
Magic 310-312
May 7-21R
New Right (Whitaker) 142-168
Reader's 73, 446
Sup Ct Ind 120-123+
Sup Ct Review (1984):255-307; (1986):175-257
Super 398-400, 410-428, 501-503+

Alpert, Peter A. Citizen suits under the Clean Air Act: universal standing for the uninjured private attorney general? *Boston College Environmental Affairs Law Review* 16(2):283-328 (Winter 1988).

Evolution of the present controversy. *Congressional Digest* 61(5):134-135, 160 (May 1982).

Franck, Thomas M., and Clifford A. Bob. The return of Humpty-Dumpty: foreign relations law after the Chadha case. *American Journal of International Law* 79(4):912-960 (October 1985).

Gillers, Stephen. The Warren Court—it still lives. *Nation* 237(7):193, 208-210 (September 17, 1983).

Gunther, Gerald. Judicial review. *Society* 24(1):18-23 (November/December 1986).

Heffner, Judith C. The Constitution in court. *Scholastic Update* (Teachers' Edition) 116(5):16-18 (October 28, 1983).

Higginbotham, A. Leon, Jr. 45 years in law and civil rights. *Ebony* 46(1):80-86 (November 1990).

Markman, Stephen J., and Alfred S. Regnery. The mind of Justice Brennan: a 25-year tribute. *National Review* 36(9):30-33, 36-38 (May 18, 1984).

Mishler, William, and Reginald S. Sheehan. The Supreme Court as a countermajoritarian institution? The impact of public opinion on Supreme Court decisions. *American Political Science Review* 87(1):87-101 (March 1993).

Public Affairs Council of Louisiana. Reapportionment for the 1980s: good faith and court decisions. *National Civic Review* 70(11):575-582 (December 1981).

Regan, Richard J. Supreme Court roundup: 1980 term. *Thought* 56(223):491-502 (December 1981).

Rush, Mark E. In search of a coherent theory of voting rights: challenges to the Supreme Court's vision of fair and effective representation. *Review of Politics* 56(3):503-523 (Summer 1994).

Weber, Ronald E. Redistricting and the courts: judicial activism in the 1990s. *American Politics Quarterly* 23(2):204-228 (April 1995).

1123. Rusk, Secretary of State v. Cort   April 2, 1962
     369 US 367   7 LEd2d 809   82 SCt 787
       Super 404-407+

1124. Dairy Queen, Inc. v. Wood   April 30, 1962
     369 US 469   8 LEd2d 44   82 SCt 894
       Const (Currie) 407-410
       En Am Con 533, 1913-1920

1125. Carnley v. Cochran   April 30, 1962
     369 US 506   8 LEd2d 70   82 SCt 884
       Super 407-410+

1126. Goldblatt v. Town of Hempstead, New York   May 14, 1962
     369 US 590   8 LEd2d 130   82 SCt 987
       Guide (CQ) 143b
       Super 434-435

Note; the public use test: would a ban on the possession of firearms require just compensation? *Law and Contemporary Problems* 49(1):223-249 (Winter 1986).

Skelton, Harold N. Houses on the sand: taking issues surrounding statutory restrictions on the use of oceanfront property. *Boston College Environmental Affairs Law Review* 18(1):125-158 (Fall 1990).

1127. Lynch v. Overholser   May 21, 1962
     369 US 705   8 LEd2d 211   82 SCt 1063

Super 433-434

1128. United States v. Davis   June 4, 1962
      370 US 65   8 LEd2d 335   82 SCt 1190
      Gans, Mitchell M., and Jonathan G. Blattmachr. Marital-property settlements: the implications of Cook. *Trusts
          and Estates* 122(11):43-48 (November 1983).
      Hull, Addis E., James H. Feldman, and Craig R. Culbertson. ERTA's effect on property division upon marital
          dissolution. *Trusts and Estates* 121(4):21-26 (April 1982).
      Podris, Katherine D., and Gary J. Podris. Section 1041 was the cure for U.S. v. Davis: now how to fix the cure.
          Taxes 68(8):580-587 (August 1990). Discussion 69(1):37-40 (January 1991).

1129. Lanza v. New York   June 4, 1962
      370 US 139   8 LEd2d 384   82 SCt 1218
      Goring, Darlene C. Supreme Court review: Fourth Amendment—prison cells: is there a right to privacy?
          Journal of Criminal Law and Criminology 75(3):609-629 (Fall 1984).

1130. Brown Shoe Co. v. United States   June 25, 1962
      370 US 294   8 LEd2d 510   82 SCt 1502
        Super 437-438
      Demsetz, Harold. The trouble with antitrust—the enforcement agencies should serve the public. *Vital Speeches
          of the Day* 47(7):196-202 (January 15, 1981).

1131. Wood v. Georgia   June 25, 1962
      370 US 375   8 LEd2d 569   82 SCt 1364
        Super 431-433

1132. Engel v. Vitale   June 25, 1962
      370 US 421   8 LEd2d 601   82 SCt 1261
        Almanac (1984):245
        Am Educators 474-475
        Brennan 119-121+
        Burger Years 56-91
        Const (Currie) 410-412
        Const (Friendly) 118-127
        Editorials (1994):1428-1433
        En Am Con 608-612, 634, 653-655, 1537-1538, 1650-1658
        Equal (Harrell) 103-104
        First 153-160
        Godless 85-89+
        Guide (CQ) 51
        Guide (West) (v. 4):302-303
        Landmark (v. 1):35-49R
        Let Us 120-122+
        Magic 317-320
        Original (Davis) 73-75+
        Religion 79-110
        Sup Ct on Church 194-204R
        Super 439-443+
      Baker, banker, clergyman, thief. *Life* 10(10):84-88 (Fall 1987).
      Baron, Mark A., and Harold L. Bishop. Come one, come all. *American School Board Journal* 178(3):29-30
          (March 1991).
      Bowen, Lauren. Attorney advertising in the wake of Bates v. State Bar of Arizona (1977): a study of judicial
          impact. *American Politics Quarterly* 23(4):461-484 (October 1995).
      Brookhiser, Richard. Let us pray. [Editorial] *Time* 144(25):84 (December 19, 1994).
      Carter, Stephen L. Let us pray. *New Yorker* 70(40):60-74 (December 5, 1994).

Collie, William E. Schempp reconsidered: the relationship between religion and public education. *Phi Delta Kappan* 65(1):57-59 (September 1983).

Collins, Daniel V. What's a teacher to do? Teach! [Editorial] *Christian Century* 100(15):459-460 (May 11, 1983).

The court decisions. *Congressional Digest* 63(5):132-134, 160 (May 1984).

Drinan, Robert F. Those moments of silence. *America* 151(9):184-186 (October 6, 1984).

Eastland, Terry. Religion, politics and the Clintons. *Commentary* 97(1):40-43 (January 1994).

Evolution of the present controversy. *Congressional Digest* 61(5):134-135, 160 (May 1982).

Gest, Ted. Courts: a major battleground of social upheaval. *U.S. News and World Report* 98(3):48-50 (January 28, 1985).

―――. Next stage: court lite. *U.S. News and World Report* 111(2):16-19 (July 8, 1991).

Gibbs, Nancy R., David Aikman, and Richard N. Ostling. America''s holy war. *Time* 138(23):60-68 (December 9, 1991).

Hammond, Phillip E. The courts and secular humanism. *Society* 21(4):11-16 (May/June 1984).

Helms, Jesse, Edward M. Kennedy, M. William Howard, Juda Glasner, Robert P. Dugan, Jr., Daniel F. Polish, William O'Reilly, and Thomas Emerson. Should Congress adopt the Helms Amendment to limit federal courts regarding "school prayer"? *Congressional Digest* 59(12):294-313 (December 1980).

Kilpatrick, James J. What in God's name is going on? *National Review* 37(2):36, 38-39 (February 8, 1985).

Lawrence, Charise K. Your Constitution: securing your rights. *Scholastic Update* 120(9):11 (January 15, 1988).

Levicoff, Steve. Upholding students' religious freedom. [Editorial] *Christian Century* 106(36):1108-1109 (November 29, 1989).

Lines, Patricia M. The new private schools and their historic purpose. *Phi Delta Kappan* 67(5):373-379 (January 1986).

Marshall, Thomas R. Public opinion, representation, and the modern Supreme Court. *American Politics Quarterly* 16(3):296-316 (July 1988).

Methvin, Eugene H. Let us pray! *Reader's Digest* 141(847):75-79 (November 1992).

Prayer in public schools. *Congressional Digest* 74(1):3-32 (January 1995).

Rabinove, Samuel. Religious liberty and church-state separation. *Vital Speeches of the Day* 52(17):526-530 (June 15, 1986).

Rabinove, Samuel, Josef Joffe, Sheldon F. Gottlieb, Adam Simms, Stephen F. Rohde, Jeffrey Valle, and Robert H. Bork. The First Amendment. [Editorial] *Commentary* 99(5):7-15 (May 1995).

Redlich, Norman. Some cracks in the wall. *Nation* 239(9):277-280 (September 29, 1984).

Regan, Richard J. Supreme Court roundup: 1981 term. *Thought* 57(227):514-527 (December 1982).

Rose, Jonathan. Decide 10 landmark cases that define your rights. *Scholastic Update* 119(1):7-9, 21 (September 8, 1986).

Sendor, Benjamin. Heaven only knows what's next on school prayer. *American School Board Journal* 172(9):20 (September 1985).

―――. The pledge passes constitutional muster. *American School Board Journal* 180(6):10-11, 39 (June 1993).

Stephenson, D. Grier, Jr. Religion and the Constitution: the Supreme Court speaks, again. *USA Today* 118(2538):21-23 (March 1990).

Thomas, Evan, Kenneth W. Banta, and Anne Constable. Court at the crossroads: the 1984 election may chart the future course of American justice. *Time* 124(15):28-35 (October 8, 1984).

Tushnet, Mark. The Constitution of religion. *Review of Politics* 50(4):628-658 (Fall 1988).

U.S. Senate votes against Helms's school prayer measure. *Christianity Today* 29(15):44-45 (October 18, 1985).

U.S. Supreme Court decisions. *Congressional Digest* 59(12):292-293, 314 (December 1980).

Woodward, Kenneth L., and Nadine Joseph. The return of the fourth R. *Newsweek* 117(23):56-57 (June 10, 1991).

Zirkel, Perry A. A hypothetical case in the public schools. *Clearing House* 57(8)346-347 (April 1984).

1133. Manual Enterprise, Inc. v. Day, Postmaster General   June 25, 1962
370 US 478   8 LEd2d 639   82 SCt 1432
Super 435-437

Staal, Lorri. Supreme Court review: First Amendment—the objective standard for social value in obscenity cases. *Journal of Criminal Law and Criminology* 78(4):735-762 (Winter 1988).

1134. Glidden Co. v. Zdanok   June 25, 1962
    370 US 530   8 LEd2d 671   82 SCt 1459
      Abortion Moral 128-139
      En Am Con 291-292

1135. Robinson v. California   June 25, 1962
    370 US 660   8 LEd2d 758   82 SCt 1417
      Const (Currie) 407-410
      Death Penalty (Tushnet) 11-12, 155, 162
      En Am Con 524-526, 1954-1955
      Guide (CQ) 50-51
      Sup Ct Review (1986):317-393
      Super 438-439, 693-694
  Dripps, Donald A. Supreme Court review: cruel, unusual, and constitutional. *Trial* 28(5):87-89 (May 1992).
  Schwartz, Charles Walter. Eighth Amendment proportionality analysis and the compelling case of William
    Rummel. *Journal of Criminal Law and Criminology* 71(4):378-420 (Winter 1980).

1136. Continental Ore Co. v. Union Carbide and Carbon Co.   June 25, 1962
    370 US 690   8 LEd2d 777   82 SCt 1404
  Arsenault, Richard J., and Richard W. Beard. Maritime personal injury on foreign waters. *Trial* 20(6):72-76
    (June 1984).
  Kramer, Larry. Extraterritorial application of American law after the insurance antitrust case: a reply to
    professors Lowenfeld and Trimble. *American Journal of International Law* 89(4):750-758 (October 1995).

1137. National Association for the Advancement of Colored People (NAACP) v. Button   January 14, 1963
    371 US 415   9 LEd2d 405   83 SCt 328
      Const (Currie) 421-425
      En Am Con 770-773, 1291-1292
      Making 277-282
      Super 450-452+

1138. Sun v. United States   January 14, 1963
    Wong Sun v. United States
    371 US 471   9 LEd2d 441   83 SCt 407
      En Am Con 1628-1635, 2074
      Super 453-457
  Cohn, William M. Supreme Court review: Sixth Amendment—inevitable discovery: a valuable but easily
    abused exception to the exclusionary rule. *Journal of Criminal Law and Criminology* 75(3):729-754 (Fall
    1984).
  Hartman, Marshall J., and Sidney Bernstein. To Leon, and beyond; two commentators react. *Trial* 21(1):50-56
    (January 1985).
  Stratton, Brent D. The attenuation exception to the exclusionary rule: a study in attenuated principle and
    dissipated logic. *Journal of Criminal Law and Criminology* 75(1):139-165 (Spring 1984).

1139. Bantam Books, Inc. v. Sullivan   February 18, 1963
    372 US 58   9 LEd2d 584   83 SCt 631
      En Am Con 100
  Kobylka, Joseph F. A court-created context for group litigation: libertarian groups and obscenity. *Journal of
    Politics* 49(4):1061-1078 (November 1987).

1140. Schlude v. Commissioner of Internal Revenue   February 18, 1963
    372 US 128   9 LEd2d 633   83 SCt 601
  Seago, W. Eugene. What chance for prepaid income deferrals based on statistical estimates after RCA? *Journal
    of Taxation* 54(1):16-20 (January 1981).

1141. Kennedy v. Mendoza-Martinez   February 18, 1963
           Coupled with Rusk v. Cort
       372 US 144   9 LEd2d 644   83 SCt 554
         Guide (CQ) 147-148
         Super 404-407+

       Caginalp, O. A. Fifth Amendment privilege against self-incrimination and compulsory self-disclosure under the
         Clean Air and Clean Water Acts. *Boston College Environmental Affairs Law Review* 9(2):359-395 (1980-
         1981).
       Eason, Michael J. Supreme Court review: Eighth Amendment—pretrial detention: what will become of the
         innocent? *Journal of Criminal Law and Criminology* 78(4):1048-1079 (Winter 1988).
       Robbins, Ira P. Cry of "Wolfish" in the federal courts: the future of federal judicial intervention in prison
         administration. *Journal of Criminal Law and Criminology* 71(3):211-225 (Fall 1980).
       Staas, John August. Supreme Court review: Fifth Amendment—statutory dilution of the privilege against self-
         incrimination. *Journal of Criminal Law and Criminology* 71(4):610-621 (Winter 1980).
       Stahl, Marc B. Asset forfeiture, burdens of proof and the war on drugs. *Journal of Criminal Law and
         Criminology* 83(2):274-337 (Summer 1992).

1142. Edwards v. South Carolina   February 25, 1963
       372 US 229   9 LEd2d 697   83 SCt 680
         Const Law 157-162R
         En Am Con 553-554, 927

       Marcy, William R. To protect or not to protect—that is the question. *Social Education* 54(6):364-365 (October
         1990).

1143. Townsend v. Sain, Sheriff   March 18, 1963
       372 US 293   9 LEd2d 770   83 SCt 745
         En Am Con 1902-1903
         Sup Ct Yearbook (1991-92):14-16
         Super 472-474

       Smith, Jim. Federal habeas corpus—a need for reform. *Journal of Criminal Law and Criminology* 73(3):1036-
         1050 (Fall 1982).

1144. Gideon v. Wainwright   March 18, 1963
       372 US 335   9 LEd2d 799   83 SCt 792
         Amending 203-213
         Ascent 329, 331, 335-336+
         Brennan 203-209
         Const (Currie) 446-450
         Const Law 403-411R+
         Editorials (1985):291-293
         En Am Con 516-522, 683-686, 844-845, 1472-1479, 1585-1592
         Equal (Harrell) 94-95, 105, 116-117+
         Fourth 197-199+
         Guide (CQ) 50-51, 51-52
         Guide (West) (v. 5):376-377
         Landmark (v. 1):51-60R
         Law 378-380
         Magic 320-322
         May 185-198R
         Quarrels 335-350
         Reader's 449-450
         Super 457-460+

       American survey: Burger leaves the labyrinth. *Economist* 300(7454):17-22 (July 12-18, 1986).
       Baker, banker, clergyman, thief. *Life* 10(10):84-88 (Fall 1987).

Bazelon, David L. Supreme Court review: forward—the morality of the criminal law: rights of the accused. *Journal of Criminal Law and Criminology* 72(4):1143-1170 (Winter 1981).

Bernstein, Sidney, and Michael Eisenstein. 1982 Supreme Court update: the criminal law, part two. *Trial* 18(10):58-65 (October 1982).

Binion, Gayle. The Burger court and the rights of the poor. *Center Magazine* 15(2):2-7 (March/April 1982).

Brewster, Todd. Law and order. *Life* 14(13 Special Issue):85-87 (Fall 1991).

Criminal justice: Son of Gideon. *Economist* 294(7384):30 (March 9-15, 1985).

Five cases that changed American society. *Scholastic Update* (Teachers' Edition) 117(7):19-20 (November 30, 1984).

Gest, Ted. One poor man's legacy. *U.S. News and World Report* 114(11):19 (March 22, 1993).

Mello, Michael A. Is there a federal constitutional right to counsel in capital post-conviction proceedings? *Journal of Criminal Law and Criminology* 79(4):1065-1104 (Winter 1989).

Mueller, Jean West, and Wynell Burroughs Schamel. Teaching with documents; the Bill of Rights: due process and rights of the accused: Clarence Earl Gideon's Petition in forma pauperis. *Social Education* 54(6):421-424 (November/December 1990).

Rose, Jonathan. Decide 10 landmark cases that define your rights. *Scholastic Update* 119(1):7-9, 21 (September 8, 1986).

Sudo, Phil. Five "little" people who changed U.S. history. *Scholastic Update* 122(10):8-10 (January 16, 1990).

Surprise ruling on child custody. *Newsweek* 97(24):31 (June 15, 1981).

Wohleber, Curt. 1963 Twenty-five years ago. *American Heritage* 39(2):36 (March 1988).

1145. Douglas v. California   March 18, 1963
     372 US 353   9 LEd2d 811   83 SCt 814
       En Am Con 534-535, 583, 1585-1592, 2041-2042

Flygare, Thomas J. School finance a decade after Rodriguez. *Phi Delta Kappan* 64(7):477-478 (March 1983).

Mello, Michael A. Is there a federal constitutional right to counsel in capital post-conviction proceedings? *Journal of Criminal Law and Criminology* 79(4):1065-1104 (Winter 1989).

1146. Gray v. Sanders   March 18, 1963
     372 US 368   9 LEd2d 821   83 SCt 801
       Court Public 73
       En Am Con 866, 1518-1524, 1979-1987
       Guide (CQ) 50, 51-52

Gest, Ted. Courts: a major battleground of social upheaval. *U.S. News & World Report* 98(3):48-50 (January 28, 1985).

Neighbor, Howard D. Equity in the electoral/representative structure: Is the Supreme Court leaving the political thicket? *National Civic Review* 74(4):169-177, 181 (April 1985).

1147. Fay, Warden v. Noia   March 18, 1963
     372 US 391   9 LEd2d 837   83 SCt 822
       Almanac (1981):14A
       Death Penalty (Tushnet) 158
       En Am Con 688-689, 2003-2005
       Guide (CQ) 51-52
       Sup Ct Review (1989):165-193
       Sup Ct Yearbook (1990-91):58-59
       Super 470-473

Askin, Frank. Justice denied: what the conservative judiciary hath wrought. *Trial* 29(10):65-68 (October 1993).

Farber, Daniel A. Supreme Court review: Brennan's finest hour. *Trial* 26(11):18-22 (November 1990).

Halberstam, Malvina. Towards neutral principles in the administration of criminal justice: a critique of Supreme Court decisions sanctioning the plea bargaining process. *Journal of Criminal Law and Criminology* 73(1):1-49 (Spring 1982).

Smith, Jim. Federal habeas corpus—a need for reform. *Journal of Criminal Law and Criminology* 73(3):1036-1050 (Fall 1982).

White, Welsh S. Waiver and the death penalty: the implications of Estelle v. Smith. *Journal of Criminal Law and Criminology* 72(4):1522-1549 (Winter 1981).

1148. Gibson v. Florida Legislative Investigation Committee   March 25, 1963
  372 US 539   9 LEd2d 929   83 SCt 889
   Const (Currie) 434-438
   En Am Con 844, 1148-1151, 1577-1581
   Making 295-300

1149. Ferguson v. Skrupa   April 22, 1963
  372 US 726   10 LEd2d 93   83 SCt 1028
   En Am Con 720, 1744-1751
  Cox, Archibald. First Amendment. *Society* 24(1):8-15 (November/December 1986).
  Howard, A. E. Dick. Making it work. *Wilson Quarterly* 11(2):122-133 (Spring 1987).
  Kommers, Donald P. Liberalism and the Supreme Court: review essay. *Review of Politics* 49(1):112-125 (Winter 1987).

1150. Sanders v. United States   April 29, 1963
  373 US 1   10 LEd2d 148   83 SCt 1068
   Super 474-475
  Lundstrom, Bruce D. Supreme Court review: Sixth Amendment—right to counsel: limited postindictment use of jailhouse informants is permissible. *Journal of Criminal Law and Criminology* 77(3):743-774 (Fall 1986).
  Wells, Diane. Federal habeas corpus and the death penalty: a need for a return to the principles of Furman. *Journal of Criminal Law and Criminology* 80(2):427-490 (Summer 1989).

1151. Willner v. Committee on Character and Fitness   May 13, 1963
  373 US 96   10 LEd2d 224   83 SCt 1175
   Sup Ct Review (1982):85-125

1152. Florida Lime and Avocado Growers, Inc. v. Paul   May 13, 1963
  373 US 132   10 LEd2d 248   83 SCt 1210
   En Am Con 1744-1751
  Adams, Nancy D. Title VI of the 1990 Clean Air Act Amendments and state and local Initiatives to reverse the stratospheric ozone crisis: an analysis of preemption. *Boston College Environmental Affairs Law Review* 19(1):173-216 (Fall 1991).

1153. Whipple v. Commissioner of Internal Revenue   May 13, 1963
  373 US 193   10 LEd2d 288   83 SCt 1168
  Bond, James G., and Royce E. Chaffin. Can securities trading be a trade or business? *Taxes* 65(11):727-732 (November 1987).

1154. National Labor Relations Board (NLRB) v. Erie Resistor Corp.   May 13, 1963
  373 US 221   10 LEd2d 308   83 SCt 1139
  The right to strike. *Congressional Digest* 70(11):264-265 (November 1991).

1155. Peterson v. City of Greenville   May 20, 1963
  373 US 244   10 LEd2d 323   83 SCt 1119
   Super 479-486

1156. Lombard v. Louisiana   May 20, 1963
  373 US 267   10 LEd2d 338   83 SCt 1122
   Super 483-486+

1157. Silver v. New York Stock Exchange   May 20, 1963
  373 US 341   10 LEd2d 389   83 SCt 1246

Favretto, Richard J. Trade associations and antitrust laws. *Credit and Financial Management* 82(2):16-18 (February 1980).

1158. Lopez v. United States   May 27, 1963
    373 US 427   10 LEd2d 462   83 SCt 1381
    En Am Con 1179
    Webber, Dawn. Supreme Court review: Fourth Amendment—of warrants, electronic surveillance, expectations of privacy, and tainted fruits. *Journal of Criminal Law and Criminology* 75(3):630-652 (Fall 1984).

1159. Haynes v. Washington   May 27, 1963
    373 US 503   10 LEd2d 513   83 SCt 1336
    En Am Con 909

1160. Watson v. City of Memphis   May 27, 1963
    373 US 526   10 LEd2d 529   83 SCt 1314
    Sup Ct Review (1986):99-134

1161. Alabama v. United States   May 27, 1963
    373 US 545   10 LEd2d 540   83 SCt 1365
    Super 463-464

1162. Arizona v. California   June 3, 1963
    373 US 546   10 LEd2d 542   83 SCt 1468
    Am Indian (Deloria)   197-220
    Am Indians (Wilkinson) 66-67, 70-71, 124+

1163. McNeese v. Board of Education, Community Unit School District 187, Cahokia, Illinois   June 3, 1963
    373 US 668   10 LEd2d 622   83 SCt 1433
    Gordon, William M. The implementation of desegregation plans since Brown. *Journal of Negro Education* 63(3):310-322 (Summer 1994).
    Russo, Charles J., J. John Harris III, and Rosetta F. Sandidge. Brown v. Board of Education at 40: a legal history of equal educational opportunity in American public education. *Journal of Negro Education* 63(3):297-309 (Summer 1994).

1164. Goss v. Board of Education of Knoxville, Tennessee   June 3, 1963
    373 US 683   10 LEd2d 632   83 SCt 1405
    Russo, Charles J., J. John Harris III, and Rosetta F. Sandidge. Brown v. Board of Education at 40: a legal history of equal educational opportunity in American public education. *Journal of Negro Education* 63(3):297-309 (Summer 1994).

1165. Ker v. California   June 10, 1963
    374 US 23   10 LEd2d 726   83 SCt 1623
    En Am Con 1102, 1462-1464

1166. Yellin v. United States   June 17, 1963
    374 US 109   10 LEd2d 778   83 SCt 1828
    Van Alstyne, William W. Academic freedom and the First Amendment in the Supreme Court of the United States: an unhurried historical review. *Law and Contemporary Problems* 53(3):79-154 (Summer 1990).
    Vanderziel, Kathleen M. The Hatfield Riders and environmental preservation: what process is due? *Boston College Environmental Affairs Law Review* 19(2):431-479 (Fall/Winter 1991).

1167. School District of Abington Township v. Schempp   June 17, 1963
        Coupled with Murray v. Curlett (See record 1168)
    374 US 203   10 LEd2d 844   83 SCt 1560
    Almanac (1984):245

Am Educators 1-2

Brennan 119-123, 129-134

Burger Years 56-91

Const Law 73-76R

Court Const 200-204

Documents (v. 2):678-680R

En Am Con 1, 608-612, 1537-1538, 1650-1658

First 153-160, 168-169

Godless 66, 87-90+

Landmark (v. 2):67-82R

Let Us 122+

May It 61-74R

Original (Davis) 75-79, 89-90, 121-122+

Religion 86-110

Sup Ct Church 204-224R

Super 466-469+

Trial 94-98, 146-148+

Baron, Mark A., and Harold L. Bishop. Come one, come all. *American School Board Journal* 178(3):29-30 (March 1991).

Bork, Robert H. What to do about the First Amendment. *Commentary* 99(2):23-29 (February 1995).

Collie, William E. Schempp reconsidered: the relationship between religion and public education. *Phi Delta Kappan* 65(1):57-59 (September 1983).

Collins, Daniel V. What's a teacher to do? Teach! [Editorial] *Christian Century* 100(15):459-460 (May 11, 1983).

Confusion in the court. *America* 152(24):501 (June 22-29, 1985).

The Court decisions. *Congressional Digest* 63(5):132-134, 160 (May 1984).

Helms, Jesse, Edward M. Kennedy, M. William Howard, Juda Glasner, Robert P. Dugan, Jr., Daniel F. Polish, William O'Reilly, and Thomas Emerson. Should Congress adopt the Helms Amendment to limit federal courts regarding "school prayer"? *Congressional Digest* 59(12):294-313 (December 1980).

Kilpatrick, James J. What in God's name is going on? *National Review* 37(2):36, 38-39 (February 8, 1985).

Lawton, Kim A. Uncle Sam v. First Church. *Christianity Today* 35(11):38-41 (October 7, 1991).

Levicoff, Steve. Upholding students' religious freedom. [Editorial] *Christian Century* 106(36):1108-1109 (November 29, 1989).

Marshall, Thomas R. Public opinion, representation, and the modern Supreme Court. *American Politics Quarterly* 16(3):296-316 (July 1988).

Methvin, Eugene H. The Supreme Court: justice in the balance. *Reader's Digest* 125(751):96-101 (November 1984).

Newsnotes: 11th Commandment: no Ten Commandments in the classroom. *Phi Delta Kappan* 62(5):405 (January 1981).

Pfeffer, Leo. How religious is secular humanism? *Humanist* 48(5):13-18,50 (September/October 1988).

———. Religious exemptions. *Society* 21(4):17-22 (May/June 1984).

Prayer in public schools. *Congressional Digest* 74(1):3-32 (January 1995).

Rabinove, Samuel. Religious liberty and church-state separation. *Vital Speeches of the Day* 52(17):526-530 (June 15, 1986).

Regan, Richard J. Supreme Court roundup: 1984 term. *Thought* 61(241):290-302 (June 1986).

———. Supreme Court roundup: 1986 term. *Thought* 63(251):429-441 (December 1988).

Schamel, Wynell Burroughs, and Jean West Mueller. Teaching with documents: Abington v. Schempp: a study in the establishment clause. *Social Education* 53(1):61-66R (January 1989).

Sendor, Benjamin. Heaven only knows what's next on school prayer. *American School Board Journal* 172(9):20 (September 1985).

———. The pledge passes constitutional muster. *American School Board Journal* 180(6):10-11, 39 (June 1993).

Stephenson, D. Grier, Jr. Religion and the Constitution: the Supreme Court speaks, again. *USA Today* 118(2538):21-23 (March 1990).

Tarr, G. Alan. Religion under state constitutions. *Annals of the American Academy of Political and Social Science* 496:65-75 (March 1988).

U.S. Supreme Court decisions. *Congressional Digest* 59(12):292-293, 314 (December 1980).

Woods, Jimmy L. Teaching the Bible: a legal and objective approach. *Clearing House* 54(3):115-116 (November 1980).

Zirkel, Perry A. A hypothetical case in the public schools. *Clearing House* 57(8)346-347 (April 1984).

1168. Murray v. Curlett   June 17, 1963
       Decided with School District of Abington Township v. Schempp (See record 1167)
       374 US 203   10 LEd2d 844   83 SCt 1560
       First 153-160
       Let Us xiv-xvii, 24-37, 53-80, 131-132+
Five cases that changed American society. *Scholastic Update* (Teachers' Edition) 117(7):19-20 (November 30, 1984).

1169. United States v. Philadelphia National Bank   June 17, 1963
       374 US 321   10 LEd2d 915   83 SCt 1715
       Super 475-479
Bandow, Doug. The Merger Barriers Fall. *ABA Banking Journal* 78(7):46-50 (July 1986).

1170. Sherbert v. Verner   June 17, 1963
       374 US 398   10 LEd2d 965   83 SCt 1790
       Am Indian (Deloria)   221-238
       Brennan 138-142
       Burger Years 56-91
       Const (Currie) 539-540
       En Am Con 587-588, 1538-1545, 1650-1658, 1678, 1934-1935
       Establishment 159+
       Godless 30-34+
       Original (Davis) 155-156+
       Religion 172-174+
       Sup Ct Church 414-423R
       Sup Ct Review (1981):193-221; (1983):1-31; (1985):1-59; (1988):85-127; (1989):373-402;
              (1992):123-153; (1995):323-391
       Super 468-470
Cerne, Kathleen M. Honor thy creditors? The religious debtor's constitutional conflict with Section 1325(b). *Business Credit* 96(3):37-40 (March 1994).

Chemerinsky, Erwin. Supreme Court review: religion clause doctrine: potential for change. *Trial* 29(2):81-84 (February 1993).

Drinan, Robert F. The Supreme Court and religious freedom. *America* 152(12):254-255 (March 30, 1985).

———. The Supreme Court expands religious freedom. *America* 160(16):388-389 (April 29, 1989).

Gibbs, Nancy R., David Aikman, and Richard N. Ostling. America's holy war. *Time* 138(23):60-68 (December 9, 1991).

Greenlaw, Paul S., and John P. Kohl. Religious freedom and unemployment compensation benefits. *Public Personnel Management* 24(3):315-330 (Fall 1995).

Hammond, Phillip E. The courts and secular humanism. *Society* 21(4):11-16 (May/June 1984).

Jensen, Laura S. Subsidies, strings, and the courts: judicial action and conditional federal spending. *Review of Politics* 55(3):491-509 (Summer 1993).

Lawton, Kim A. Uncle Sam v. First Church. *Christianity Today* 35(11):38-41 (October 7, 1991).

Regan, Richard J. Supreme Court roundup: 1980 term. *Thought* 56(223):491-502 (December 1981).

———. Supreme Court roundup: 1984 term. *Thought* 61(241):290-302 (June 1986).

———. Supreme Court roundup: 1987 term. *Thought* 64(253):176-187 (June 1989).

Rievman, Joshua D. Judicial scrutiny of Native American free exercise rights: Lyng and the decline of the Yoder doctrine. *Boston College Environmental Affairs Law Review* 17(1):169-199 (Fall 1989).

Sullivan, Catherine Beth. Are kosher food laws constitutionally kosher? *Boston College Environmental Affairs Law Review* 21(1):201-245 (Fall 1993).

Tushnet, Mark. The Constitution of religion. *Review of Politics* 50(4):628-658 (Fall 1988).

Vile, John R. Bob Jones before the bench. *Christian Century* 100(23):707-711 (August 3-10, 1983).

1171. Head v. New Mexico Board of Examiners in Optometry   June 17, 1963
374 US 424   10 LEd2d 983   83 SCt 1759
Turley, Jonathan. The not-so-noble lie: the nonincorporation of state consensual surveillance standards in federal court. *Journal of Criminal Law and Criminology* 79(1):66-134 (Spring 1988).

1172. Fahy v. Connecticut   December 2, 1963
375 US 85   11 LEd2d 171   84 SCt 229
Goldberg, Steven H. Harmless error: constitutional sneak thief. *Journal of Criminal Law and Criminology* 71(4):421-442 (Winter 1980).

1173. Securities Exchange Commission (SEC) v. Capital Gains Research Bureau, Inc.   December 9, 1963
375 US 180   11 LEd2d 237   84 SCt 275
Cox, James D. Insider trading: regulation of activity is 'in trouble.' *Trial* 24(9):22-28, 93-96 (September 1988).

1174. Anderson v. Martin   January 13, 1964
375 US 399   11 LEd2d 430   84 SCt 454
Reynolds, William Bradford. Affirmative action and its negative repercussions. *Annals of the American Academy of Political and Social Science* 523:38-49 (September 1992).

1175. Wesberry v. Sanders   February 17, 1964
376 US 1   11 LEd2d 481   84 SCt 562
Const Law 609-613R, 618+
Court Public 73
En Am Con 1518-1524, 2045
Guide (CQ) 50
Sup Ct Review (1986):175-257
Super 501-502
Neighbor, Howard D. Equity in the electoral/representative structure: is the Supreme Court leaving the political thicket? *National Civic Review* 74(4):169-177, 181 (April 1985).
Public Affairs Council of Louisiana. Reapportionment for the 1980s: good faith and court decisions. *National Civic Review* 70(11):575-582 (December 1981).
Seligman, Daniel. In broad daylight. *Fortune* 111(2):145 (January 21, 1985).

1176. Federal Power Commission (FPC) v. Southern California Edison Co.   March 2, 1964
Coupled with Colton v. Southern California Edison Co.
376 US 205   11 LEd2d 638   84 SCt 644
Mauro, Tony. From pensions to postal rates. *Nation's Business* 70(12):38-39 (December 1982).

1177. Sears, Roebuck and Co. v. Stiffel Co.   March 9, 1964
376 US 225   11 LEd2d 661   84 SCt 784
Sup Ct Review (1983):509-581; (1989):283-309

1178. Compco Corp. v. Day-Brite Lightening, Inc.   March 9, 1964
376 US 234   11 LEd2d 669   84 SCt 779
Sup Ct Review (1983):509-581; (1989):283-309

1179. New York Times Co. v. Sullivan   March 9, 1964
Coupled with Abernathy v. Sullivan
376 US 254   11 LEd2d 686   84 SCt 710
Almanac (1990):510-511

Brennan 155-159+

Burger Court 3-6, 17-18

Burger Years 23-44

Const (Currie) 513-518

Const Law 247-255R+

En Am Con 330-331, 790-797, 797-804, 873-874, 1157-1159, 1312-1313, 1487-1488, 1930

First 241-249

Fourth 82-97, 104-105+

Freedom (Cox) 14-19

Guide (CQ) 51

Guide (West) (v. 8):39-41, 346

Jerry 65-66, 165-166, 170-171, 298-303+

Landmark (v. 4):135-157R

Law 218-222

Magic 315-317

Make 1-248, 249-328R

Sup Ct Ind 63-66+

Sup Ct Review (1980):1-25; (1991):1-46; (1994):169-208

Super 531-542, 612-616, 645-648, 650-652+

Tolerant 48-53+

Without 388-390+

Anderson, David A. Presumed harm: an item for the unfinished agenda of Times v. Sullivan. *Journalism Quarterly* 62(1):24-30 (Spring 1985).

Aronow, Geoffrey, and Owen Fiss. The High Court illusion of victory. *Nation* 235(21):647-650 (December 18, 1982).

Baker, banker, clergyman, thief. *Life* 10(10):84-88 (Fall 1987).

Bill would bar mind inquires. *Editor and Publisher* 113(5):43 (February 2, 1980).

Boedecker, Karl A., and Fred W. Morgan. The evolution of First Amendment protection for commercial speech. *Journal of Marketing* 59(1):38-47 (January 1995).

Boylan, James. How free is the press? *Columbia Journalism Review* 26(3):27-32 (September/October 1987).

———. Pleading the First. *Columbia Journalism Review* 30(4):41-43 (November/December 1991).

Brandon, George. High court accepts private figure case. *Editor and Publisher* 115[114]:10-11 (November 28, 1981).

Brief of American Psychological Association and American Association for the Advancement of Science as Amici Curiae. Ronald R. Hutchinson, Petitioner v. William Proxmire and Morton Schwartz, Respondents. *American Psychologist* 35(8):750-758 (August 1980).

Castro, Janice, Anne Constable, and Raji Samghabadi. An absence of malice: the Supreme Court rules in favor of Consumer Union. *Time* 123(20):56 (May 14, 1984).

Cuomo, Mario. Preserving freedom of the press. *USA Today* 116(2512):32-35 (January 1988).

Dworkin, Ronald. The coming battles over free speech. *New York Review of Books* 39(11):55-64 (June 11, 1992).

Eskin, Leah. Do you know your rights? *Scholastic Update* 120(15):9 (April 8, 1988).

Farber, Daniel A. Supreme Court review: Brennan's finest hour. *Trial* 26(11):18-22 (November 1990).

Fields, Howard. Court rebuffs Falwell, affirms right to spoof public figure. *Publishers' Weekly* 233(10):18-19 (March 11, 1988).

———. Court weakens protection for media in libel suits. *Publishers' Weekly* 228(2);14 (July 12, 1985).

———. High Court overturns Scalia in libel case. *Publishers' Weekly* 230(2):18 (July 11, 1986).

———. High Court sides with media in libel case. *Publishers' Weekly* 225(20):38 (May 18, 1984).

First Amendment Watch: 'Emotional distress' briefs to High Court. *Publishers' Weekly* 232(3):13 (July 17, 1987).

Freidman, Robert. Freedom of the press: how far can they go? *American Heritage* 33(6):16-26 (October/November 1982).

Garbus, Martin. Limiting our rights. *Publishers' Weekly* 236(7):21 (August 18, 1989).

———. New challenge to press freedom. *New York Times Magazine* (section 6):34, 38-41, 48-49 (January 29, 1984).

Gersh, Debra. Media lose a friend: retiring Supreme Court Justice William Brennan. *Editor and Publisher* 123(30):13, 35, 47 (July 28, 1990).

―――. Supreme Court and the media. *Editor and Publisher* 120(50):18-19 (December 12, 1987).

Gertz, Elmer. Gertz on Gertz: reflections on the landmark libel case. *Trial* 21(10):66-69, 71-75 (October 1985).

Gillers, Stephen. The Warren Court—it still lives. *Nation* 237(7):193, 208-210 (September 17, 1983).

Gruhl, John. Supreme Court's impact on the law of libel: compliance by lower federal courts. *Western Political Quarterly* 33(4):502-519 (December 1980).

Hale, F. Dennis. Constitutional libel protection narrowed—not destroyed. *Trial* 17(7):54-58, 79 (July 1981).

Heath, Robert L., and Richard Alan Nelson. Image and issue advertising: a corporate and public policy perspective. *Journal of Marketing* 49(2):58-68 (Spring 1985).

Heck, Edward V., and Albert C. Ringelstein. The Burger Court and the primacy of political expression. *Western Political Quarterly* 40(3):413-425 (September 1987).

Helle, Steven. Judging public interest in libel: the Gertz decision's contribution. *Journalism Quarterly* 61(1):117-124 (Spring 1984).

Henry, William A., III, Naushad S. Mehta, and Barrett Seaman. Jousts without winners: after a flurry of major libel cases, no one has much to crow about. *Time* 130 (1):68-70 (July 6, 1987).

Hopkins, Jay. Ex-justices criticized punitive libel awards. *Editor and Publisher* 114(39):36 (September 26, 1981).

Howard, A. E. Dick. The press in court. *Wilson Quarterly* 6(5):86-93 (Special Issue 1982).

Hoyt, Michael. Malcolm, Masson, and you. *Columbia Journalism Review* 29(6):38-44 (March/April 1991).

Hughes, Robert L. Rationalizing libel law in wake of Gertz: the problem and a proposal. *Journalism Quarterly* 62(3):540-547, 566 (Autumn 1985).

Jenkins, Jolyon. It couldn't happen in America. *New Statesman and Society* 6(243):19 (March 12, 1993).

Kebbel, Gary. The different functions of speech in defamation and privacy cases. *Journalism Quarterly* 61(3):629-633, 743 (Autumn 1984).

Kommers, Donald P. Liberalism and the Supreme Court: review essay. *Review of Politics* 49(1):112-125 (Winter 1987).

Lacayo, Richard, and Anne Constable. Libel relief: the court strengthens a shield. *Time* 128(1):55 (July 7, 1986).

―――. Taking the peril out of parody: in Falwell v. Flynt, the First Amendment won. *Time* 131(10):49 (March 7, 1988).

Langvardt, Arlen W. Defamation in the business setting: basics and practical perspectives. *Business Horizons* 33(5):66-79 (September/October 1990).

Lewis, Anthony. The Sullivan case. *New Yorker* 60(38):52-95 (November 5, 1984).

―――. Staving off the silencers. *New York Times Magazine* (section 6, part 1):72-77 (December 1, 1991).

Lewis, John B., and Bruce L. Ottley. New York Times v. Sullivan: its continuing impact on libel law. *Trial* 21(10):59-65 (October 1985).

Libel: the right to be off the wall. *Economist* 291(7340):26-27 (May 5-11, 1984).

Markman, Stephen J., and Alfred S. Regnery. The mind of Justice Brennan: a 25-year tribute. *National Review* 36(9):30-33, 36-38 (May 18, 1984).

Nimmer, Melville. Tort invasions of privacy. *Center Magazine* 15(5):46-48 (September/October 1982).

Novick, Sheldon M. Holmes, Brennan, and the flag-burning cases. *Trial* 26(11):24-29 (November 1990).

Silver, Isidore. Libel Revival: the danger of "media hunting." *Commonweal* 109(20):616-167 (November 19, 1982).

Smolla, Rodney A. Free speech afire with controversy: the Supreme Court. *Trial* 25(12):46-47, 49, 51 (December 1989).

Stein, M. L. Judge advises newspapers; Supreme Court may not be so "hospitable" this time. *Editor and Publisher* 120(11):22, 48 (March 14, 1987).

Van Alstyne, William W. Academic freedom and the First Amendment in the Supreme Court of the United States: an unhurried historical review. *Law and Contemporary Problems* 53(3):79-154 (Summer 1990).

Winter, Ralph K. Political financing and the Constitution. *Annals of the American Academy of Political and Social Science* 486:34-48 (July 1986).

1180. Preston v. United States   March 23, 1964
376 US 364   11 LEd2d 777   84 SCt 881

Nelson, Caleb. The paradox of the exclusionary rule. *Public Interest* (96):117-130 (Summer 1989).

1181. Banco Nacional de Cuba v. Sabbatino   March 23, 1964
       376 US 398   11 LEd2d 804   84 SCt 923
       En Am Con 747-755
       Sup Ct Review (1990):133-161; (1994):295-343
       Franck, Thomas M., and Clifford A. Bob. The return of Humpty-Dumpty: foreign relations law after the
          Chadha case. *American Journal of International Law* 79(4):912-960 (October 1985).
       Halberstam, Malvina. Agora: international kidnaping—in defense of the Supreme Court decision in Alvarez-
          Machain. *American Journal of International Law* 86(4):736-746 (October 1992).
       Halberstam, Malvina. Sabbatino resurrected: the act of state doctrine in the revised restatement of U.S. foreign
          relations law. *American Journal of International Law* 79(1):68-91 (January 1985).

1182. Stoner v. California   March 23, 1964
       376 US 483   11 LEd2d 856   84 SCt 889
       Goldberger, Peter. Consent, expectations of privacy, and the meaning of "searches" in the Fourth Amendment.
          Journal of Criminal Law and Criminology 75(2):319-362 (Summer 1984).
       Wieber, Michael C. The theory and practice of Illinois v. Rodriguez: why an officer's reasonable belief about a
          third party's authority to consent does not protect a criminal suspect's rights. *Journal of Criminal Law and
          Criminology* 84(3):604-641 (Fall 1993).

1183. National Labor Relations Board (NLRB)   April 20, 1964
          v. Fruit and Vegetable Packers and Warehousemen, Local 760
       377 US 58   12 LEd2d 129   84 SCt 1063
       Mount, Gregory J. Significant decisions in labor cases. *Monthly Labor Review* 103(11):46-48 (November
          1980).
       Ruben, George. High Court further defines job bias. *Monthly Labor Review* 104(6):58 (June 1981).

1184. Parden v. Terminal Railway of Alabama State Docks Department   May 18, 1964
       377 US 184   12 LEd2d 233   84 SCt 1207
       Almanac (1987)18A
       Const (Currie) 569-571
       Farber, Daniel A. Supreme Court review: litigating with the sovereign. *Trial* 28(4):85-90 (April 1992).
       ———. Supreme Court review: revival of the canons. *Trial* 28(6):82-85 (June 1992).

1185. Massiah v. United States   May 18, 1964
       377 US 201   12 LEd2d 246   84 SCt 1199
       En Am Con 1228, 1400-1408, 1585-1592
       Guide (West) (v. 7):304
       Sup Ct Yearbook (1990-91):21-23
       American Survey: Burger leaves the labyrinth. *Economist* 300(7454):17-22 (July 12-18, 1986).
       Bahl, Martin. The Sixth Amendment as constitutional theory: does originalism require that Massiah be
          abandoned? *Journal of Criminal Law and Criminology* 82(2):423-463 (Summer 1991).
       Cheap water for a lush valley. *Time* 115(26):51 (June 30, 1980).
       Erickson, William H. Pronouncements of the US Supreme Court 1979-1980. *Trial* 16(10):69-71 (October
          1980).
       Franklin, Daniel. The five dumbest Supreme Court decisions. *Washington Monthly* 26(10):12-18 (October
          1994).
       Fulton, Joy D. Supreme court review: Sixth Amendment—"Messiah" revitalized. *Journal of Criminal Law and
          Criminology* 71(4):601-609 (Winter 1980).
       Kamisar, Yale. The swing of the pendulum. *Nation* 239(9):271-274 (September 29, 1984).
       Lundstrom, Bruce D. Supreme Court review: Sixth Amendment—right to counsel: limited postindictment use
          of jailhouse informants is permissible. *Journal of Criminal Law and Criminology* 77(3):743-774 (Fall 1986).
       Regan, Richard J. Supreme Court roundup: 1980 term. *Thought* 56(223):491-502 (December 1981).

1186. Griffin v. County School Board of Prince Edward County May 25, 1964
377 US 218 12 LEd2d 256 84 SCt 1226
Burden 110-127
Const (Currie) 416-421
En Am Con 557-561, 869
Guide (CQ) 51

Deegan, Glenn E. Judicial enforcement of state and municipal compliance with the Clean Water Act: can the courts succeed? *Boston College Environmental Affairs Law Review* 19(4):765-803 (Summer 1992).

Gordon, William M. The implementation of desegregation plans since Brown. *Journal of Negro Education* 63(3):310-322 (Summer 1994).

Hyde, Alison A. School desegregation: the role of the courts and means of achievement. *NASSP Bulletin* 78(565):28-37 (November 1994).

Russo, Charles J., J. John Harris III, and Rosetta F. Sandidge. Brown v. Board of Education at 40: a legal history of equal educational opportunity in American public education. *Journal of Negro Education* 63(3):297-309 (Summer 1994).

1187. Chamberlin v. Dade County Board of Public Instruction June 1, 1964
377 US 402 12 LEd2d 407 84 SCt 1272
Drinan, Robert F. Those moments of silence. *America* 151(9):184-186 (October 6, 1984).
Prayer in public schools. *Congressional Digest* 74(1):3-32 (January 1995).
Zirkel, Perry A. A hypothetical case in the public schools. *Clearing House* 57(8)346-347 (April 1984).

1188. General Motors Corp. v. Washington June 8, 1964
377 US 436 12 LEd2d 430 84 SCt 1564
Krevitsky, Philip L. Washington: heads the state wins, tails the taxpayers lose—no refunds. *CPA Journal* 58(7):111-112 (July 1988).

1189. Reynolds, et al. v. Sims June 15, 1964
Coupled with Vann v. Baggett
Coupled with McConnell v. Baggett
377 US 533 12 LEd2d 506 84 SCt 1362
Const (Currie) 425-429
Const Law 613-618R+
Court Public 73-88R
Documents (v. 2):681-684R
En Am Con 616-617, 1344, 1518-1524, 1565-1567, 1979-1987
Equal (Harrell) 110
Guide (CQ) 50
Guide (West) (v. 9):42-44
Powers 283
Sup Ct Review (1986):175-257
Super 503-508+

Evolution of the present controversy. *Congressional Digest* 61(5):134-135, 160 (May 1982).

Graham, Barbara Luck. Federal court policy-making and political equality: an analysis of judicial redistricting. *Western Political Quarterly* 44(1):101-117 (March 1991).

Neighbor, Howard D. Equity in the electoral/representative structure: is the Supreme Court leaving the political thicket? *National Civic Review* 74(4):169-177, 181 (April 1985).

Public Affairs Council of Louisiana. Reapportionment for the 1980s: good faith and court decisions. *National Civic Review* 70(11):575-582 (December 1981).

Regan, Richard J. Supreme Court roundup: 1980 term. *Thought* 56(223):491-502 (December 1981).

Rush, Mark E. In search of a coherent theory of voting rights: challenges to the Supreme Court's vision of fair and effective representation. *Review of Politics* 56(3):503-523 (Summer 1994).

Scope of enforcement. *Congressional Digest* 60(12):296-297 (December 1981).

Trank, John P. The Burger Court—the first ten years. *Law and Contemporary Problems* 43(3):101-135 (Summer 1980).

1190. Lucas v. Forty-Fourth General Assembly of the State of Colorado   June 15, 1964
    377 US 713   12 LEd2d 632   84 SCt 1459
        Court Public 88-89
        Sup Ct Review (1986):175-257

1191. Malloy v. Hogan, Sheriff   June 15, 1964
    378 US 1   12 LEd2d 653   84 SCt 1489
        Amending 203-213
        Death Penalty 80s 98-102
        En Am Con 1197-1198, 1569-1577, 1931
        Guide (CQ) 50-51
        Hard Choices 304
        Magic 320-322
        Sup Ct Review (1991):103-142

1192. Murphy v. Waterfront Commission of New York Harbor   June 15, 1964
    378 US 52   12 LEd2d 678   84 SCt 1594
        En Am Con 1569-1577, 1931
Staas, John August. Supreme Court review: Fifth Amendment—statutory dilution of the privilege against self-incrimination. *Journal of Criminal Law and Criminology* 71(4):610-621 (Winter 1980).

1193. Aguilar v. Texas   June 15, 1964
    378 US 108   12 LEd2d 723   84 SCt 1509
        En Am Con 39-40, 979-980, 1462-1464, 1628-1635
Bernstein, Sidney. Supreme Court review. *Trial* 19(10):26,28 (October 1983).
Hartman, Marshall J., and Sidney Bernstein. To Leon, and beyond; two commentators react. *Trial* 21(1):50-56 (January 1985).
LaFave, Wayne R. Supreme Court review: Fourth Amendment vagaries (of improbable cause, imperceptible plain view, notorious privacy, and balancing askew). *Journal of Criminal Law and Criminology* 74(4):1171-1224 (Winter 1983).
Moore, Cathy E. Supreme Court review: Fourth Amendment—totality of the circumstances approach to probable cause based on informant's tips. *Journal of Criminal Law and Criminology* 74(4):1249-1264 (Winter 1983).
Regan, Richard J. Supreme Court roundup: 1982 term. *Thought* 58(231):472-483 (December 1983).

1194. Barr v. City of Columbia   June 22, 1964
    378 US 146   12 LEd2d 766   84 SCt 1734
        Super 508-509, 516-519+

1195. Robinson v. Florida   June 22, 1964
    378 US 153   12 LEd2d 771   84 SCt 1693
        Super 508-509, 512-513, 516

1196. Jacobellis v. Ohio   June 22, 1964
    378 US 184   12 LEd2d 793   84 SCt 1676
        Brennan 166-176
        En Am Con 1009
        First 288-289, 293-294
Hagle, Timothy M. But do they have to see it to know it? the Supreme Court's obscenity and pornography decisions. *Western Political Quarterly* 44(4):1039-1054 (December 1991).
Kobylka, Joseph F. A court-created context for group litigation: libertarian groups and obscenity. *Journal of Politics* 49(4):1061-1078 (November 1987).

1197. Bell v. Maryland   June 22, 1964
    378 US 226   12 LEd2d 822   84 SCt 1814

Courage 129-152, 426
Court Public 95
Documents (v. 2):686-687R
En Am Con 106, 1729-1736
Super 508-525+

Belz, Herman. Equality before the law: the Civil War amendments. *Center Magazine* 20(6):4-19 (November/December 1987).

1198. Bouie v. Columbia   June 22, 1964
     378 US 347   12 LEd 2d 894   84 SCt 1697
     Super 508-509, 516-519+

1199. Jackson v. Denno, Warden   June 22, 1964
     378 US 368   12 LEd2d 908   84 SCt 1774
Schneider, Robert Roy. Supreme Court review: Fourteenth Amendment—the last gasp of due process requirements on eyewitness identifications: the admissibility of identification evidence may be determined in the jury's presence. *Journal of Criminal Law and Criminology* 72(4):1410-1425 (Winter 1981).

1200. Escobedo v. Illinois   June 22, 1964
     378 US 478   12 LEd2d 977   84 SCt 1758
     Amending 203-213
     Const Law 376-379R+
     Documents (v. 2):684-685R
     En Am Con 652, 1400-1408, 1585-1592
     Guide (CQ) 50-51
     Guide (West) (v. 4):381-382
Gruhl, John. State supreme courts and the U.S. Supreme Court's post-Miranda rulings. *Journal of Criminal Law and Criminology* 72(3):886-913 (Fall 1981).
Regan, Richard J. Supreme Court roundup: 1980 term. *Thought* 56(223):491-502 (December 1981).

1201. Aptheker v. Secretary of State   June 22, 1964
     378 US 500   12 LEd2d 992   84 SCt 1659
     Const (Currie) 434-438
     En Am Con 70-71, 997-998, 1593-1596
     Liberty 243

1202. Cooper v. Pate   June 22, 1964
     378 US 546   12 LEd2d 1030   84 SCt 1733
Robbins, Ira P. Cry of "Wolfish" in the federal courts: the future of federal judicial intervention in prison administration. *Journal of Criminal Law and Criminology* 71(3):211-225 (Fall 1980).

1203. United States v. Powell   November 23, 1964
     379 US 48   13 LEd2d 112   85 SCt 248
Le Porte, Lawrence A. Supreme Court review: SEC investigations—SEC need not notify target of third-party subpoenas. *Journal of Criminal Law and Criminology* 75(3):940-952 (Fall 1984).

1204. Garrison v. Louisiana   November 23, 1964
     379 US 64   13 LEd2d 125   85 SCt 209
     En Am Con 730-738
     Super 566-568, 612-613
Cooper, Phillip J. The Supreme Court, the First Amendment, and freedom of information. *Public Administration Review* 46(6):622-628 (November/December 1986).
Cox, Archibald. First Amendment. *Society* 24(1):8-15 (November/December 1986).
Kebbel, Gary. The different functions of speech in defamation and privacy cases. *Journalism Quarterly* 61(3):629-633, 743 (Autumn 1984).

1205. Schlagenhauf v. Holder   November 23, 1964
      379 US 104   13 LEd2d 152   85 SCt 234
      Schroeter, Leonard W. Privacy rights can limit discovery. *Trial* 26(11):49-54 (November 1990).

1206. McLaughlin v. Florida   December 7, 1964
      379 US 184   13 LEd2d 222   85 SCt 283
        Sup Ct Review (1995):1-43

1207. Fibreboard Paper Products Corp. v. National Labor Relations Board (NLRB)   December 14, 1964
      379 US 203   13 LEd2d 233   85 SCt 398
        Burger Court 173-175
      Unions: no say on closings. *Engineering News-Record* 207(1):73 (July 2, 1981).

1208. Heart of Atlanta Motel, Inc. v. United States   December 14, 1964
      379 US 241   13 LEd2d 258   85 SCt 348
        Civil 20th 3, 10, 167-186R
        Court Public 96
        En Am Con 273-280, 284-287, 640-647, 911, 1729-1736
        Guide (CQ) 51, 95, 106
        Hard Choices 236, 308
        May It 263-276R
        Powers 149-150
        Sup Ct Ind 251-252
      Karst, Kenneth L. Equal protection of the laws. *Society* 24(1):24-30 (November/December 1986).
      O'Neill Andrew J. Retail electric rates: drawing the line between federal and state authority under the commerce
        clause. *Public Utilities Fortnightly* 112(9):52-55 (October 27, 1983).
      Orren, Karen. The primacy of labor in American constitutional development. *American Political Science
        Review* 89(2):377-388 (June 1995).
      Solimine, Michael E. Constitutionality of congressional legislation to overrule Zurcher v. Stanford daily.
        Journal of Criminal Law and Criminology 71(2):147-162 (Summer 1980).

1209. Katzenbach v. McClung   December 14, 1964
      379 US 294   13 LEd2d 290   85 SCt 377
        En Am Con 273-280, 284-287, 911
        Guide (CQ) 106
        Hard Choices 236, 308

1210. Fortson v. Dorsey   January 18, 1965
      379 US 433   13 LEd2d 401   85 SCt 498
        Sup Ct Review (1986):175-257
      Public Affairs Council of Louisiana. Reapportionment for the 1980s: good faith and court decisions. *National
        Civic Review* 70(11):575-582 (December 1981).

1211. Henry v. Mississippi   January 18, 1965
      379 US 443   13 LEd2d 408   85 SCt 564
        Super 572-575

1212. Cox v. Louisiana   January 18, 1965
      379 US 536   13 LEd2d 471   85 SCt 453
        Const Law 159-162+
        En Am Con 511
        May It 105-120R
        Super 557-559, 607-608+
      Marcy, William R. To protect or not to protect—that is the question. *Social Education* 54(6):364-365 (October
        1990).

Winter, Ralph K. Political financing and the Constitution. *Annals of the American Academy of Political and Social Science* 486:34-48 (July 1986).

1213. Cox v. Louisiana   January 18, 1965
     379 US 559   13 LEd2d 487   85 SCt 476
     Const Law 159-160
     En Am Con 511

1214. Republic Steel Corp. v. Maddox   January 25, 1965
     379 US 650   13 LEd2d 580   85 SCt 614
     Hollander, Rhonda G. Injunctions against occupational hazards: toward a safe workplace environment. *Boston College Environmental Affairs Law Review* 9(1):133-161 (1980-1981).

1215. Freedman v. Maryland   March 1, 1965
     380 US 51   13 LEd2d 649   85 SCt 734
     Const Law 209-213R
     En Am Con 769

McGuire, Kevin T., and Gregory A. Caldeira. Lawyers, organized interests, and the law of obscenity: agenda setting in the Supreme Court. *American Political Science Review* 87(3):717-726 (September 1993).

1216. United States v. Gainey   March 1, 1965
     380 US 63   13 LEd2d 658   85 SCt 754
     Super 575-577

Harris, Leslie J. Constitutional limits on criminal presumptions as an expression of changing concepts of fundamental fairness. *Journal of Criminal Law and Criminology* 77(2):308-357 (Summer 1986).

1217. Louisiana v. United States   March 8, 1961
     380 US 145   13 LEd2d 709   85 SCt 817
     Const Law 591-594R

1218. United States v. Seeger   March 8, 1965
     380 US 163   13 LEd2d 733   85 SCt 850
     Courage 153-187, 426
     Documents (v. 2):706-708R
     En Am Con 352-353, 730-738, 1538-1545, 1645
     Godless 56-60
     Super 570-572

Cox, Archibald. First Amendment. *Society* 24(1):8-15 (November/December 1986).

Demerath, N. J., III, and Rhys H. Williams. A mythical past and uncertain future. *Society* 21(4):3-10 (May/June 1984).

McBride, James. Tillich in an Alice-in-Wonderland world. [Editorial] *Christian Century* 104(18):519-520 (June 3-10, 1987).

McKown, Delos Banning. Deism and the Supreme Court. *Humanist* 52(2):25-28,48 (March/April 1992).

Regan, Richard J. Supreme Court roundup: 1980 term. *Thought* 56(223):491-502 (December 1981).

————. Supreme Court roundup: 1984 term. *Thought* 61(241):290-302 (June 1986).

1219. Swain v. Alabama   March 8, 1965
     380 US 202   13 LEd2d 759   85 SCt 824
     Almanac (1986):8A
     Editorials (1986):534-541
     En Am Con 683-686, 1082-1085, 1839, 1913-1920
     Sup Ct Review (1987):97-156
     Sup Ct Yearbook (1990-91):62

Dripps, Donald A. Supreme Court review: 'I didn't like the way he looked.' *Trial* 31(7):94-96 (July 1995).

Juries: Blacker, and pro the death penalty. *Economist* 299(7445):25-26 (May 10-16, 1986).

Kennedy, Randall. Grand Marshall. [Editorial] *Nation* 253(5):180-181 (August 12-19, 1991).

Kirk, Michael W. Supreme Court review: Sixth and Fourteenth Amendments—the Swain song of the racially discriminatory use of peremptory challenges. *Journal of Criminal Law and Criminology* 77(3):821-843 (Fall 1986).

Mosk, Stanley. The emerging agenda in state constitutional rights law. *Annals of the American Academy of Political and Social Science* 496:54-64 (March 1988).

Press, Aric, and Ann McDaniel. Integrating the jury box. *Newsweek* 107(19):70 (May 12, 1986).

Schultz, Marjorie S. Jury defined: a review of Burger court decisions. *Law and Contemporary Problems* 43(4):8-23 (Autumn 1980).

Serr, Brian J., and Mark Maney. Racism, peremptory challenges, and the democratic jury: the jurisprudence of a delicate balance. *Journal of Criminal Law and Criminology* 79(1):1-65 (Spring 1988).

1220. American Shipbuilding co. v. National Labor Relations Board (NLRB)   March 29, 1965
380 US 300   13 LEd2d 855   85 SCt 955
Lissy, William E. Use of temporary replacements during a lockout. *Supervision* 43(9):18-20 (September 1981).

1221. Pointer v. Texas   April 5, 1965
380 US 400   13 LEd2d 923   85 SCt 1065
En Am Con 658-661, 1399, 1472-1479
Guide (CQ) 339, 384, 531, 913

1222. Douglas v. Alabama   April 5, 1965
380 US 415   13 LEd2d 934   85 SCt 1074
Sup Ct Review (1995):277-321
Haddad, James B., and Richard G. Agin. A potential revolution in Bruton doctrine: is Bruton applicable where domestic evidence rules prohibit use of a codefendant's confession as evidence against a defendant although the confrontation clause would allow such use? *Journal of Criminal Law and Criminology* 81(2):235-266 (Summer 1990).

1223. American Oil Co. (AMOCO) v. Neill   April 26, 1965
380 US 451   14 LEd2d 1   85 SCt 1130
Quirk, William J. Minimizing state taxation of interstate business. *Journal of Taxation* 65(3):180-186 (September 1986).

1224. Dombrowski v. Pfister   April 26, 1965
380 US 479   14 LEd2d 22   85 SCt 1116
En Am Con 575
Guide (CQ) 51-52
Super 755-757
Askin, Frank. Justice denied: what the conservative judiciary hath wrought. *Trial* 29(10):65-68 (October 1993).

1225. Griffin v. California   April 28, 1965
380 US 609   14 LEd2d 106   85 SCt 1229
Death Penalty 80s 98-102
Death Penalty 90s 121-123
En Am Con 868-869, 1472-1479, 1569-1577
Guide (CQ) 50-51
Bernstein, Sidney, and Michael Eisenstein. 1981 Supreme Court update: the criminal law. *Trial* 17(10):54-60, 85 (October 1981).

Goldberg, Steven H. Harmless error: constitutional sneak thief. *Journal of Criminal Law and Criminology* 71(4):421-442 (Winter 1980).

Gromer, Sharon K. Supreme Court review: Fifth Amendment—the right to a no "adverse inference" jury instruction. *Journal of Criminal Law and Criminology* 72(4):1307-1325 (Winter 1981).

Methvin, Eugene H. The case of common sense vs. Miranda. *Reader's Digest* 131(784):96-100 (August 1987).

Mosk, Stanley. The emerging agenda in state constitutional rights law. *Annals of the American Academy of Political and Social Science* 496:54-64 (March 1988).

Uviller, H. Richard. Self-incrimination by inference: constitutional restrictions on the evidentiary use of a suspect's refusal to submit to a search. *Journal of Criminal Law and Criminology* 81(1):37-76 (Spring 1990).

1226. Warren Trading Post Co. v. Arizona State Tax Commission   April 29, 1965
     380 US 685   14 LEd2d 165   85 SCt 1242
     Am Indians (Wilkinson) 96-97, 124+

1227. One 1958 Plymouth Sedan v. Pennsylvania   April 29, 1965
     380 US 693   14 LEd2d 170   85 SCt 1246
     Staas, John August. Supreme Court review: Fifth Amendment—statutory dilution of the privilege against self-incrimination. *Journal of Criminal Law and Criminology* 71(4):610-621 (Winter 1980).

1228. Zemel v. Rusk, Secretary of State   May 3, 1965
     381 US 1   14 LEd2d 179   85 SCt 1271
     En Am Con 1593-1596, 2087
     Sup Ct Review (1981):263-290
     Super 563-565

     Franck, Thomas M., and Clifford A. Bob. The return of Humpty-Dumpty: foreign relations law after the Chadha case. *American Journal of International Law* 79(4):912-960 (October 1985).

1229. Lamont v. Postmaster General of United States   May 24, 1965
     Lamont, dba Basic Pamphlets v. Postmaster General
     381 US 301   14 LEd2d 398   85 SCt 1493
     En Am Con 1122-1123
     Sup Ct Review (1987):303-344
     Super 565-566

     Bleisch, N. David. The Congressional Record and the First Amendment: accuracy is the best policy. *Boston College Environmental Affairs Law Review* 12(2):341-379 (Winter 1985).

     Cooper, Phillip J. The Supreme Court, the First Amendment, and freedom of information. *Public Administration Review* 46(6):622-628 (November/December 1986).

1230. United States v. Brown   June 7, 1965
     381 US 437   14 LEd2d 484   85 SCt 1707
     En Am Con 165
     Guide (CQ) 76-77

1231. Griswold v. Connecticut   June 7, 1965
     381 US 479   14 LEd2d 510   85 SCt 1678
     Abortion (Frohock) 62-63, 66+
     Abortion Am 6-10, 30-31+
     Abortion Contr 121-123+
     Abortion Dec 130-131
     Abortion Moral 1-7, 37, 66-70
     Abortion Pol (Rubin) 35-42, 77-81+
     Abortion Quest 94-95, 97+
     Almanac (1987):272
     Ascent 294-297+
     Brennan 294-302+
     Const (Currie) 465-471
     Const (Friendly) 189-202
     Const Law 268-274R+
     Court Public 387-397R
     Documents (v. 2):702-703R

Economics 323-329+

En Am Con 4-6, 118-119, 686-688, 782-789, 870-871, 1552-1558, 1577-1581, 1796-1803

Guide (CQ) 51

Guide (West) (v. 5):401

Hard Choices 132-133+

Landmark I 61-67R

Law Governing 29-30+

Liberty 131-166, 225-269, 302-312, 338-339+

Magic 317-320

New Right (Schwartz) 36-41, 55-62

New Right (Whitaker) 142-168

Quarrels 362-364

Reader's 475-476, 951-952

Religion 235-237

Super 577-580+

Baker, banker, clergyman, thief. *Life* 10(10):84-88 (Fall 1987).

Barnum, David G. The Supreme Court and public opinion: judicial decision making in the post-New Deal period. *Journal of Politics* 47(2): 652-666 (May 1985).

Bresler, Robert J. Privacy, the courts, and social values. *USA Today* 115(2498):6-7 (November 1986).

Byrne, Harry J. A house divided: the pro-life movement. *America* 164(1):6-10 (January 5-12, 1991).

Carlin, David R. Leviathan at large: the court and the right to privacy. *Commonweal* 113(15):456-457 (September 12, 1986).

———. Two doctrines of privacy. *America* 155(3):50-51 (August 2-9, 1986).

Christopher, Maura. How the Constitution protects your "right to be let alone." *Scholastic Update* 119(1):12-13 (September 8, 1986).

Dworkin, Ronald. The great abortion case. *New York Review of Books* 36(11):49-53 (June 29, 1989).

Freeman, Alan David, and Elizabeth Mensch. The Court and the sexual revolution. *Commonweal* 121(18):19-23 (October 21, 1994).

Gillers, Stephen. The Warren Court—it still lives. *Nation* 237(7):193,208-210 (September 17, 1983).

Gillman, Howard. Preferred freedoms: the progressive expansion of state power and the rise of modern civil liberties jurisprudence. *Political Research Quarterly* 47(3):623-653 (September 1994).

Graglia, Lino. Saving the Constitution: A theory of power. *National Review* 39(13):33-36 (July 17, 1987).

Grey, Thomas C. Eros, civilization and the Burger Court. *Law and Contemporary Problems* 43(3):83-100 (Summer 1980).

Jaffa, Harry V., and Joseph Sobran. A right to privacy? *National Review* 41(5):51-52 (March 24, 1989).

Kaplan, David A. Is Roe good law? *Newsweek* 119(17):49-51 (April 27, 1992).

Leo, John. Return of the ERA. [Editorial] *U.S. News & World Report* 119(24):28 (December 18, 1995).

Linde, Hans. The Constitution and privacy. *Center Magazine* 15(6):46-50 (November/December 1982).

McDowell, Gary L. Congress and the courts. *Public Interest* (100):89-101 (Summer 1990).

Minow, Martha. We, the family: constitutional rights and American families. *Journal of American History* 74(3):959-983 (December 1987).

Orren, Karen. The primacy of labor in American constitutional development. *American Political Science Review* 89(2):377-388 (June 1995).

Polin, Raymond. The Supreme Court's dilemma and defense. *USA Today* 115(2496):43-45 (September 1986).

Reynolds, William Bradford. Power to the people. *New York Times Magazine* (section 6, part 1):116-122 (September 13, 1987).

Rosenblatt, Roger. The Bill of Rights. *Life* 14(13 Special Issue):9-30 (Fall 1991).

Schroeter, Leonard W. Privacy rights can limit discovery. *Trial* 26(11):49-54 (November 1990).

Stoner, James R., Jr. Common law and constitutionalism in the abortion case. *Review of Politics* 55(3):421-441 (Summer 1993).

Tatalovich, Raymond, and Byron W. Daynes. Trauma of abortion politics. *Commonweal* 108(21):644-649 (November 20, 1981).

Welsh, Robert, and Ronald K. L. Collins. Taking state constitutions seriously: the protection of civil liberties has been shifting away from the U.S. Supreme Court. *Center Magazine* 14(5):6-35, 38-43 (September/October 1981).

Winkler, Karen J. Who says what the Constitution means? Supreme Court's authority to decide is debated. *Chronicle of Higher Education* 34(27):A4-A7 (March 16, 1988).

Wulf, Melvin L. On the origins of privacy. *Nation* 252(20):700, 702-704 (May 27, 1991).

1232. Estes v. Texas   June 7, 1965
     381 US 532   14 LEd2d 543   85 SCt 1628
       Ascent 173-175+
       Court Public 319
       En Am Con 227, 655-656, 683-686, 805-808
       Sup Ct Review (1981):157-192
       Super 543-552+

Beach, Bennet H., and Evan Thomas. Blind justice gets a seeing eye: The Supreme Court gives a green light to televising trials. *Time* 117(6):51 (February 9, 1981).

Fulton, Joy D. Supreme Court review: Fourteenth Amendment—cameras in the courtroom: Supreme Court gives the go-ahead. *Journal of Criminal Law and Criminology* 72(4):1393-1409 (Winter 1981).

Green light for courtroom TV. *U.S. News & World Report* 90(5):6 (February 9, 1981).

Press, Aric, and Diane Camper. Giving cameras a day in court. *Newsweek* 97(6):102 (February 9, 1981).

Trials: for all to see. *Economist* 278(7170):29-30 (January 31-February 6, 1981).

Williamson, Lenora. Courtroom camera crusader elated by court's ruling. *Editor and Publisher* 114(7):7, 10 (February 14, 1981).

1233. Linkletter v. Walkers   June 7, 1965
     381 US 618   14 LEd2d 601   85 SCt 1731
       Const (Currie) 451-453
       En Am Con 1562-1564
       Sup Ct Review (1982):1-24; (1989):165-193

Bender, Louis, and Steven Bender. Is the Supreme Court's decision in Baggot retroactive in application? *Journal of Taxation* 60(3):138-144 (March 1984).

Branigan, Roger D., III. Supreme Court review: Sixth Amendment—the evolution of the Supreme Court's retroactivity doctrine: a futile search for theoretical clarity. *Journal of Criminal Law and Criminology* 80(4):1128-1153 (Winter 1990).

Jensen, D. Lowell, and Rosemary Hart. The good faith restatement of the exclusionary rule. *Journal of Criminal Law and Criminology* 73(3):916-938 (Fall 1982).

1234. WMCA, Inc. v. Lomenzo, Secretary of State of New York   October 11, 1965
     382 US 4   15 LEd2d 2   86 SCt 24

Regan, Richard J. Supreme Court roundup: 1980 term. *Thought* 56(223):491-502 (December 1981).

1235. Albertson v. Subversive Activities Control Board (SACB)   November 15, 1965
     382 US 70   15 LEd2d 165   86 SCt 194
       En Am Con 40, 991-992, 1804-1807
       Guide (CQ) 51
       Magic 314-315

Caginalp, O. A. Fifth Amendment privilege against self-incrimination and compulsory self-disclosure under the Clean Air and Clean Water Acts. *Boston College Environmental Affairs Law Review* 9(2):359-395 (1980-1981).

1236. Bradley v. School Board of Richmond   November 15, 1965
     382 US 103   15 LEd2d 187   86 SCt 224

Menacker, Julius. Review of Supreme Court reasoning in cases of expression, due process, and equal protection. *Phi Delta Kappan* 63(3):188-190 (November 1981).

Russo, Charles J., J. John Harris III, and Rosetta F. Sandidge. Brown v. Board of Education at 40: a legal history of equal educational opportunity in American public education. *Journal of Negro Education* 63(3):297-309 (Summer 1994).

Simmons, Althea T. L. From Brown to Grove City: blueprint for education. *Crisis* 91(5):6-10 (May 1984).

1237. United States v. Romano   November 22, 1965
      382 US 136   15 LEd2d 210   86 SCt 279
      Harris, Leslie J. Constitutional limits on criminal presumptions as an expression of changing concepts of
          fundamental fairness. *Journal of Criminal Law and Criminology* 77(2):308-357 (Summer 1986).

1238. Rodgers v. Paul   December 6, 1965
      382 US 198   15 LEd2d 265   86 SCt 358
      Menacker, Julius. Review of Supreme Court reasoning in cases of expression, due process, and equal
          protection. *Phi Delta Kappan* 63(3):188-190 (November 1981).
      Russo, Charles J., J. John Harris III, and Rosetta F. Sandidge. Brown v. Board of Education at 40: a legal
          history of equal educational opportunity in American public education. *Journal of Negro Education*
          63(3):297-309 (Summer 1994).

1239. Katchen v. Landy   January 17, 1966
      382 US 323   15 LEd2d 391   86 SCt 467
      En Am Con 1913-1920
      Sup Ct Review (1989):261-282

1240. Rosenblatt v. Baer   February 21, 1966
      383 US 75   15 LEd2d 597   86 SCt 669
      Super 612-617+
      Brief of American Psychological Association and American Association for the Advancement of Science as
          Amici Curiae. Ronald R. Hutchinson, Petitioner v. William Proxmire and Morton Schwartz, Respondents.
          American Psychologist 35(8):750-758 (August 1980).
      Kebbel, Gary. The different functions of speech in defamation and privacy cases. *Journalism Quarterly*
          61(3):629-633,743 (Autumn 1984).

1241. Baxstrom v. Herold   February 23, 1966
      383 US 107   15 LEd2d 620   86 SCt 760
      Steadman, Henry J., and Joseph P. Morrissey. The insanity defense: problems and prospects for studying the
          impact of legal reforms. *Annals of the American Academy of Political and Social Science* 484:115-126
          (March 1986).

1242. Brown v. Louisiana   February 23, 1966
      383 US 131   15 LEd2d 637   86 SCt 719
      Super 606-609+

1243. Carnation Co. v. Pacific Westbound Conference   February 28, 1966
      383 US 213   15 LEd2d 709   86 SCt 781
      Curley, Stephen C., and David Wawro. To what extent does deductibility of insurance premiums depend on risk
          shifting? *Journal of Taxation* 53(2):116-119 (August 1980).

1244. South Carolina v. Katzenbach   March 7, 1966
      383 US 301   15 LEd2d 769   86 SCt 803
      Abortion Moral 128-147
      Const (Currie) 425-429
      Const Law 594-597R
      Documents (v. 2):711-713R
      En Am Con 1169, 1711-1712, 1979-1987, 1987-1988
      Guide (CQ) 51, 154
      Marshall, Thomas R. Public opinion, representation, and the modern Supreme Court. *American Politics
          Quarterly* 16(3):296-316 (July 1988).
      Public Affairs Council of Louisiana. Reapportionment for the 1980s: good faith and court decisions. *National
          Civic Review* 70(11):575-582 (December 1981).

1245. A Book named "John Cleland's Memoirs of a Woman of Pleasure"   March 21, 1966
     v. Attorney General of Massachusetts
    383 US 413   16 LEd2d 1   86 SCt 975
     Brennan 166-171
     Const Law 233-234, 237-239
     En Am Con 1246
     First 289-290
     Landmark II 83-91R
     Law 327-330+
     Super 618-622+
    Kobylka, Joseph F. A court-created context for group litigation: libertarian groups and obscenity. *Journal of Politics* 49(4):1061-1078 (November 1987).
    Staal, Lorri. Supreme Court review: First Amendment—the objective standard for social value in obscenity cases. *Journal of Criminal Law and Criminology* 78(4):735-762 (Winter 1988).
    Teachout, Terry. The pornography report that never was. *Commentary* 84(2):51-57 (August 1987).
    Winter, Ralph K. Political financing and the Constitution. *Annals of the American Academy of Political and Social Science* 486:34-48 (July 1986).
    Yen, Marianne. First Amendment watch update: 43 states now use Miller test. *Publishers' Weekly* 229(18):15 (May 2, 1986).

1246. Ginzburg v. United States   March 21, 1966
    383 US 463   16 LEd2d 31   86 SCt 942
     Const Law 234-235
     Super 618-623+

1247. Mishkin v. New York   March 21, 1966
    383 US 502   16 LEd2d 56   86 SCt 958
     Super 618-623+
    McGuire, Kevin T. Obscenity, libertarian values, and decision making in the Supreme Court. *American Politics Quarterly* 18(1):47-67 (January 1990).

1248. Kent v. United States   March 21, 1966
    383 US 541   16 LEd2d 84   86 SCt 1045
     Death Penalty (Streib) 5-6+
    Feld, Barry C. The juvenile court meets the principle of the offense: legislative changes in juvenile waiver statutes. *Journal of Criminal Law and Criminology* 78(3):471-533 (Fall 1987).

1249. Harper v. Virginia State Board of Elections   March 24, 1966
    383 US 663   16 LEd2d 169   86 SCt 1079
     Const (Currie) 421-425
     Const Law 600-601R
     En Am Con 210, 464-471, 903-904, 1928
     Sup Ct Review (1986):317-393R
     Super 595-597
    Binion, Gayle. The Burger court and the rights of the poor. *Center Magazine* 15(2):2-7 (March/April 1982).
    High court hears arguments on retroactivity of Davis decision. *Taxes* 71(1):53 (January 1993).

1250. Commissioner of Internal Revenue v. Tellier   March 24, 1966
    383 US 687   16 LEd2d 185   86 SCt 1118
     Sup Ct Review (1983):32-82
    Hume, Evelyn C., and Ernest R. Larkins. Takeover expenses: national starch and the IRS add new wrinkles. *Journal of Accountancy* 174(2):87-93 (August 1992).

1251. United Mine Workers v. Gibbs   March 28, 1966
    383 US 715   16 LEd2d 218   86 SCt 1130

Brooks, Thornton H., M. Daniel McGinn, and William P. H. Cary. Second generation problems facing employers in employment discrimination cases: continuing violations, pendent state claims, and double attorneys' fees. *Law and Contemporary Problems* 49(4):26-51 (Autumn 1986).

1252. United States v. Guest   March 28, 1966
     383 US 745   16 LEd2d 239   86 SCt 1170
        En Am Con 875-876, 1593-1596, 1736-1738, 1892-1894
        Hard Choices 266
        Super 602-606

1253. United States v. Price   March 28, 1966
     383 US 787   16 LEd2d 267   86 SCt 1152
        En Am Con 1451

1254. Elfbrandt v. Russell   April 18, 1966
     384 US 11   16 LEd2d 321   86 SCt 1238
        Const (Currie) 434-438
        Courage 179-203, 427
        En Am Con 624, 1485-1487
        Sup Ct Ind 150+

1255. Burns v. Richardson   April 25, 1966
        Coupled with Cravalho v. Richardson
        Coupled with Abe v. Richardson
     384 US 73   16 LEd2d 376   86 SCt 1286
        Sup Ct Review (1986):175-257
        Super 625-627
Public Affairs Council of Louisiana. Reapportionment for the 1980s: good faith and court decisions. *National Civic Review* 70(11):575-582 (December 1981).

1256. Westbrook v. Arizona   May 2, 1966
     384 US 150   16 LEd2d 429   86 SCt 1320
Boch, Brian R. Supreme Court review: Fourteenth Amendment—the standard of mental competency to waive constitutional rights versus the competency standard to stand trial. *Journal of Criminal Law and Criminology* 84(4):883-914 (Winter/Spring 1994).

1257. Mills v. Alabama   May 23, 1966
     384 US 214   16 LEd2d 484   86 SCt 1434
        Const (Currie) 434-438
Winter, Ralph K. Political financing and the Constitution. *Annals of the American Academy of Political and Social Science* 486:34-48 (July 1986).

1258. Sheppard v. Maxwell, Warden   June 6, 1966
     384 US 333   16 LEd2d 600   86 SCt 1507
        Const Law 424-431R
        Court Public 318-328R
        En Am Con 683-686, 805-808, 831-832, 1492-1494
        First 204-207, 209
        Sup Ct Ind 72-73+
Boylan, James. How free is the press? *Columbia Journalism Review* 26(3):27-32 (September/October 1987).
Hartman, Marshall J., and Sidney Bernstein. To Leon, and beyond; two commentators react. *Trial* 21(1):50-56 (January 1985).
The legacy of the Burger Court. *U.S. News & World Report* 100(25):22 (June 30, 1986).

1259. Cheff v. Schnackenberg   June 6, 1966
     384 US 373   16 LEd2d 629   86 SCt 1523
       Law 391-395

1260. Miranda v. Arizona   June 13, 1966
         Coupled with Vignera v. New York
         Coupled with Westover v. United States
         Coupled with California v. Stewart
     384 US 436   16 LEd2d 694   86 SCt 1602
       Almanac (1981):4A; (1985):6A; (1987):6A-7A
       Amending 203-213
       Ascent 365-370, 402-403+
       Brennan 189-191
       Burger Court 66-68, 82-91, 199
       Burger Years 143-168
       Const (Currie) 446-450, 488-493, 550-555
       Const Law 376, 379-385R, 386-395+
       Documents (v. 2):713-717R
       Editorials (1985):1160-1165; (1987):88-93; (1990):1452-1455
       En Am Con 355, 1263-1264, 1264-1265, 1400-1408, 1569-1577, 1585-1592
       Equal (Harrell) 116-117
       Guide (CQ) 50-51
       Guide (West) (v. 7):349-351; (1987):60-61, 247-245; (1990):183-184
       Landmark (v. 2):95-113R
       Law 397-398
       Magic 320-322
       May It 213-227R
       Reader's 734-735
       Sup Ct Review (1991):103-142
       Super 588-595+

Altman, David B. Supreme Court review: Fifth Amendment—coercion and clarity: the Supreme Court approves altered Miranda warnings. *Journal of Criminal Law and Criminology* 80(4):1086-1111 (Winter 1990).

American survey: Burger leaves the labyrinth. *Economist* 300(7454):17-22 (July 12-18, 1986).

Baker, banker, clergyman, thief. *Life* 10(10):84-88 (Fall 1987).

Bates, David M. Supreme Court review: Fifth Amendment—the meaning of interrogation under Miranda. *Journal of Criminal Law and Criminology* 71(4):466-473 (Winter 1980).

Bazelon, David L. Supreme Court review: Forward—the morality of the criminal law: rights of the accused. *Journal of Criminal Law and Criminology* 72(4):1143-1170 (Winter 1981).

Behuniak-Long, Susan. Justice Sandra Day O'Connor and the power of maternal legal thinking. *Review of Politics* 54(3):417-444 (Summer 1992).

Bernstein, Sidney, and Michael Eisenstein. 1981 Supreme Court update: the criminal law. *Trial* 17(10):54-60, 85 (October 1981).

Bigornia, Anthony P. Supreme Court review: Habeas corpus—Fifth Amendment—the Supreme Court's cost-benefit analysis of federal habeas review of alleged Miranda violations. *Journal of Criminal Law and Criminology* 84(4):915-942 (Winter/Spring 1994).

Bitterman, Patrick J. Supreme Court review: Fifth Amendment—the applicability of the assertion of the right to counsel to unrelated investigations. *Journal of Criminal Law and Criminology* 79(3):676-700 (Fall 1988).

Bowen, Lauren. Attorney advertising in the wake of Bates v. State Bar of Arizona (1977): a study of judicial impact. *American Politics Quarterly* 23(4):461-484 (October 1995).

Brewster, Todd. Law and order. *Life* 14(13 Special Issue):85-87 (Fall 1991).

Collins, Ronald K. L., and Robert Welsh. Miranda's fate in the Burger court. *Center Magazine* 13(5):43-52 (September/October 1980).

A curb on state powers. *U.S. News & World Report* 111(25):50 (December 16, 1991).

Dripps, Donald A. Supreme Court review: Justice White and the rights of the accused. *Trial* 29(5):71-74 (May 1993).

————. Supreme Court review: 'Maybe I should talk to a lawyer': ambiguous invocations of Miranda. *Trial* 30(9):90-92 (September 1994).

————. Supreme Court review: the great writ and the right to silence. *Trial* 30(1):72-73 (January 1994).

————. Supreme Court review: Warren Burger in perspective. *Trial* 31(8):73-75 (August 1995).

Drizin, Steven Andrew. Supreme Court review: Fifth Amendment—will the public safety exception swallow the Miranda exclusionary rule? *Journal of Criminal Law and Criminology* 75(3):692-715 (Fall 1984).

Erickson, William H. Pronouncements of the US Supreme Court 1979-1980. *Trial* 16(10):69-71 (October 1980).

Farber, Daniel A. Supreme Court review: from Warren to Rehnquist. *Trial* 25(7):124-126 (July 1989).

Five cases that changed American society. *Scholastic Update* (Teachers' Edition) 117(7):19-20 (November 30, 1984).

Flaherty, Francis J. Abortion, the Constitution and the Human Life Statute. *Commonweal* 108(19):586-593 (October 23, 1981).

Gest, Ted. Courts: a major battleground of social upheaval. *U.S. News & World Report* 98(3):48-50 (January 28, 1985).

Gillers, Stephen. The Meese lie. [Editorial] *Nation* 244(7):205 (February 21, 1987).

Gruhl, John. State supreme courts and the U.S. Supreme Court's post-Miranda rulings. *Journal of Criminal Law and Criminology* 72(3):886-913 (Fall 1981).

Holtz, Larry E. Miranda in a juvenile setting: a child's right to silence. *Journal of Criminal Law and Criminology* 78(3):534-556 (Fall 1987).

Inbau, Fred E. Over-reaction—the mischief of Miranda v. Arizona. *Journal of Criminal Law and Criminology* 73(2):797-810 (Summer 1982).

Kamisar, Yale. The swing of the pendulum. *Nation* 239(9):271-274 (September 29, 1984).

Kannar, George. Liberals and crime. *New Republic* 199(25):19-23 (December 19, 1988).

Jacobs, Robert. The state of Miranda: the effects of the Quarles decision. *Trial* 21(1):44-48 (January 1985).

Jordan, Horace W., Jr. Supreme Court review: Fifth and Sixth Amendments—changing the balance of Miranda. *Journal of Criminal Law and Criminology* 77(3):666-691 (Fall 1986).

LeBoeuf, Jacques. Supreme Court review: Fifth Amendment—videotaping drunk drivers limitations on Miranda's protections. *Journal of Criminal Law and Criminology* 81(4):883-925 (Winter 1991).

The legacy of the Burger Court. *U.S. News & World Report* 100(25):22 (June 30, 1986).

Levenberg, Thomas O. Supreme Court review: Fifth Amendment—responding to ambiguous requests for counsel during custodial interrogations. *Journal of Criminal Law and Criminology* 85(4):962-988 (Spring 1995).

Lewin, Nathan. White's flight. *New Republic* 191(9):17-20 (August 27, 1984).

Link, Anne Elizabeth. Supreme Court review: Fifth Amendment—the constitutionality of custodial confessions. *Journal of Criminal Law and Criminology* 82(4):878-903 (Winter 1992).

Lupia, Lynnette L. Supreme Court review: Fifth Amendment—admissibility of confession obtained without Miranda warnings in noncustodial setting. *Journal of Criminal Law and Criminology* 75(3):673-691 (Fall 1984).

Melson, David E. Supreme Court review: Fifth Amendment—waivers of previously invoked right to counsel. *Journal of Criminal Law and Criminology* 72(4):1288-1306 (Winter 1981).

Methvin, Eugene H. The case of common sense vs. Miranda. *Reader's Digest* 131(784):96-100 (August 1987).

————. The Supreme Court: justice in the balance. *Reader's Digest* 125(751):96-101 (November 1984).

Miranda: out of the doghouse: the Supreme Court broadens defendants' pretrial rights. *Time* 117(22):64 (June 1, 1981).

Mosk, Stanley. The emerging agenda in state constitutional rights law. *Annals of the American Academy of Political and Social Science* 496:54-64 (March 1988).

Pace, Michael R. Supreme Court review: Fifth and Fourteenth Amendments—defining the protections of the Fifth and Fourteenth Amendments against self-incrimination for the mentally impaired. *Journal of Criminal Law and Criminology* 78(4):877-914 (Winter 1988).

Pizzi, William T. The privilege against self-incrimination in a rescue situation. *Journal of Criminal Law and Criminology* 76(3):567-607 (Fall 1985).

Press, Aric, and Diane Camper. God forbid excuse for the cops. *Newsweek* 95(21):93 (May 26, 1980).

————. New lease on life for Miranda. *Newsweek* 97(22):63 (June 1, 1981).

Rapp, David. The High Court and the new balance of power. *Governing* 6(8):68 (May 1993).

Regan, Richard J. Supreme Court roundup: 1979 term. *Thought* 55(219):487-455 (December 1980).

———. Supreme Court roundup: 1980 term. *Thought* 56(223):491-502 (December 1981).

———. Supreme Court roundup: 1983 term. *Thought* 60(236):99-111 (March 1985).

Rights ruling: on chatting and busing. *Time* 115(21):59 (May 26, 1980).

Songer, Donald R., and Reginald S. Sheehan. Supreme Court impact on compliance and outcomes: Miranda and *New York Times* in the United States Courts of Appeals. *Western Political Quarterly* 43(2):297-316 (June 1990).

Spitzer, Gregory E. Supreme Court review: Fifth Amendment—validity of waiver: a suspect need not know the subjects of interrogation. *Journal of Criminal Law and Criminology* 78(4):828-852 (Winter 1988).

Sudo, Phil. Five "little" people who changed U.S. History. *Scholastic Update* 122(10):8-10 (January 16, 1990).

Supreme Court: doctrine of expedient deceit. *Economist* 298(7437):23 (March 15-23 1986).

Suspects' rights: Do you remember a sin, Miranda? *Economist* 302(7483)21-24 (January 31-February 6, 1987).

The talk of the town: notes and comment. *New Yorker* 59(36):39-40 (October 24, 1983).

Thomas, Evan, Kenneth W. Banta, and Anne Constable. Court at the crossroads: the 1984 election may chart the future course of American justice. *Time* 124(15):28-35 (October 8, 1984).

Toobin, Jeffrey R. Viva Miranda. *New Republic* 196(7):11-12 (February 16, 1987).

Tucker, William. Crime victims strike back. *Reader's Digest* 126(758):51-55 (June 1985).

———. True confessions: the long road back from Miranda. *National Review* 37(20):28-33, 36 (October 18, 1985).

Ullman, Patricia. Supreme Court review: Fifth and Sixth Amendments—the right to counsel in multiple charge arraignments. *Journal of Criminal Law and Criminology* 82(4):904-919 (Winter 1992).

Weiss, Lee A. Supreme Court review: Fifth Amendment—Fifth Amendment exclusionary rule: the assertion and subsequent waiver of the right to counsel. *Journal of Criminal Law and Criminology* 74(4):1315-1333 (Winter 1983).

Welsh, Robert, and Ronald K. L. Collins. Taking state constitutions seriously: the protection of civil liberties has been shifting away from the U.S. Supreme Court. *Center Magazine* 14(5):6-35, 38-43 (September/ October 1981).

What they say it is: the justices' words instruct the nation, and often address history. *Time* 130(1):44-49 (July 6, 1987).

White, S. Welsh. Waiver and the death penalty: the implications of Estelle v. Smith. *Journal of Criminal Law and Criminology* 72(4):1522-1549 (Winter 1981).

Zirkel, Perry A., and Ivan B. Gluckman. Miranda warnings—when are they required? *NASSP Bulletin* 71(495):102-105 (January 1987).

1261. United States v. Pabst Brewing Co.   June 13, 1966
      384 US 546   16 LEd2d 765   86 SCt 1665
      McGahan, A. M. The emergence of the national brewing oligopoly: competition in the American market, 1933-1958. *Business History Review* 65(2):229-284 (Summer 1991).

1262. Katzenbach v. Morgan   June 13, 1966
            Coupled with New York City Board of Elections v. Morgan
      384 US 641   16 LEd2d 828   86 SCt 1717
      Abortion (Frohock) 114
      Abortion Moral 123-147
      Const (Currie) 425-429
      En Am Con 1097-1098, 1169, 1979-1987, 1987-1988
      Guide (CQ) 154
      Hard Choices 318
      Sup Ct Review (1995):323-391
      Super 599-602
      Abortion: readers respond. [Editorial] *Commonweal* 109(3):75-84 (February 12, 1982).

      Flaherty, Francis J. Abortion, the Constitution and the Human Life Statute. *Commonweal* 108(19):586-593 (October 23, 1981).

      Markman, Stephen J.,and Alfred S. Regnery. The mind of Justice Brennan: a 25-year tribute. *National Review* 36(9):30-33, 36-38 (May 18, 1984).

Regan, Richard J. Supreme Court roundup: 1981 term. *Thought* 57(227):514-527 (December 1982).

Sager, Lawrence. Shortcut to outlaw abortion. *New York Review of Books* 28(11):39-42 (June 25, 1981); Discussion 28(16):60 (October 22, 1981).

Solimine, Michael E. Constitutionality of congressional legislation to overrule Zurcher v. Stanford daily. *Journal of Criminal Law and Criminology* 71(2):147-162 (Summer 1980).

1263. Schmerber v. California   June 20, 1966
384 US 757   16 LEd2d 908   86 SCt 1826
     En Am Con 1472-1479, 1569-1577, 1624, 1947-1949
     Super 594-595, 657-658+

Gitles, Jay A. Supreme Court review: Fourth Amendment—reasonableness of surgical intrusions. *Journal of Criminal Law and Criminology* 76(4):972-985 (Winter 1985).

Mandell, Leonard Bruce, and L. Anita Richardson. Surgical search: removing a scar on the Fourth Amendment. *Journal of Criminal Law and Criminology* 75(3):525-552 (Fall 1984).

Welsh, Robert, and Ronald K. L. Collins. Taking state constitutions seriously: the protection of civil liberties has been shifting away from the U.S. Supreme Court. *Center Magazine* 14(5):6-35, 38-43 (September/ October 1981).

1264. Adderley v. Florida   November 14, 1966
385 US 39   17 LEd2d 149   87 SCt 242
     Const (Currie) 421-425
     Const Law 160-163R
     En Am Con 24
     Sup Ct Review (1994):129-168
     Super 631-632+

1265. Bank of Marin v. England   November 21, 1966
385 US 99   17 LEd2d 197   87 SCt 274
Weintraub, Benjamin. Legally speaking: equity—a court of conscience. *Credit & Financial Management* 82(8):11 (September 1980).

1266. Bond v. Floyd   December 5, 1966
385 US 116   17 LEd2d 235   87 SCt 339
     Const (Currie) 438-446
     En Am Con 1804-1807
     Super 666-668

1267. Fortson v. Morris   December 12, 1966
385 US 231   17 LEd2d 330   87 SCt 446
     Super 634-638

1268. Hoffa v. United States   December 12, 1966
     Coupled with Parks v. United States
     Coupled with King v. United States
385 US 293   17 LEd2d 374   87 SCt 408
     En Am Con 920

1269. Time, Inc. v. Hill   January 9, 1967
385 US 374   17 LEd2d 456   87 SCt 534
     En Am Con 1457-1458
     Make 183-199+
     Super 642-649+

Garment, Leonard. The Hill case. *New Yorker* 65(9):90-110 (April 17, 1989).

Gertz, Elmer. Gertz on Gertz: reflections on the landmark libel case. *Trial* 21(10):66-69,71-75 (October 1985).

Hopkins, Jay. Ex-justices criticized punitive libel awards. *Editor and Publisher* 114(39):36 (September 26, 1981).

Kebbel, Gary. The different functions of speech in defamation and privacy cases. *Journalism Quarterly* 61(3):629-633, 743 (Autumn 1984).

Nimmer, Melville. Tort invasions of privacy. *Center Magazine* 15(5):46-48 (September/October 1982).

Welsh, Robert, and Ronald K. L. Collins. Taking state constitutions seriously: the protection of civil liberties has been shifting away from the U.S. Supreme Court. *Center Magazine* 14(5):6-35, 38-43 (September/October 1981).

1270. Garrity v. New Jersey   January 16, 1967
    385 US 493   17 LEd2d 562   87 SCt 616
        En Am Con 835, 1569-1577

Dority, Barbara. Police powers expanded as abuses escalate. *Humanist* 51(4):35-36 (July/August 1991).

Halberstam, Malvina. Towards neutral principles in the administration of criminal justice: a critique of Supreme Court decisions sanctioning the plea bargaining process. *Journal of Criminal Law and Criminology* 73(1):1-49 (Spring 1982).

1271. Spencer v. Texas   January 23, 1967
        Coupled with Bell v. Texas
        Coupled with Reed v. Beto
    385 US 554   17 LEd2d 606   87 SCt 648

Schwartz, Charles Walter. Eighth Amendment proportionality analysis and the compelling case of William Rummel. *Journal of Criminal Law and Criminology* 71(4):378-420 (Winter 1980).

1272. Keyishian v. Board of Regents of the University of the State of New York   January 23, 1967
    385 US 589   17 LEd2d 629   87 SCt 675
        En Am Con 608-612, 1102-1103, 1485-1487
        First 38-54
        Sup Ct Ind 150+

Delon, Floyd G. The legacy of Thurgood Marshall. *Journal of Negro Education* 63(3):278-288 (Summer 1994).

Elston, Michael J. Artists and unconstitutional conditions: the Big Bad Wolf won't subsidize Little Red Riding Hood's indecent art. *Law and Contemporary Problems* 56(4):327-361 (Autumn 1993).

Kermerer, Frank R., and Stephanie Abraham Hirsch. School library censorship comes before the Supreme Court. *Phi Delta Kappan* 63(7):444-448 (March (1982).

Van Alstyne, William W. Academic freedom and the First Amendment in the Supreme Court of the United States: an unhurried historical review. *Law and Contemporary Problems* 53(3):79-154 (Summer 1990).

1273. Chapman v. California   February 20, 1967
    386 US 18   17 LEd2d 705   87 SCt 824
        Editorials (1991):358-361
        En Am Con 903
        Sup Ct Review (1989):195-211
        Sup Ct Yearbook (1990-91):61, 69

Bonebrake, James G. Supreme Court review: Sixth and Fourteenth Amendments—the lost role of the peremptory challenge in securing an accused's right to an impartial jury. *Journal of Criminal Law and Criminology* 79(3):899-920 (Fall 1988).

Dripps, Donald A. Supreme Court review: to err is harmless? *Trial* 27(7):83-86 (July 1991).

Goldberg, Steven H. Harmless error: constitutional sneak thief. *Journal of Criminal Law and Criminology* 71(4):421-442 (Winter 1980).

Koosed, Margery Malkin. Habeas corpus: where have all the remedies gone? rebuilding the Great Writ. *Trial* 29(7):70-79 (July 1993).

Welch, Sara E. Supreme Court review: Fifth Amendment—harmless error analysis applied to coerced confessions. *Journal of Criminal Law and Criminology* 82:849-877 (Winter 1992).

Yeager, Daniel B. Search, seizure and the positive law: expectations of privacy outside the Fourth Amendment. *Journal of Criminal Law and Criminology* 84(2):249-309 (Summer 1993).

1274. Giles v. Maryland   February 20, 1967
      386 US 66   17 LEd2d 737   87 SCt 793
      Super 663-664

1275. Vaca v. Sipes   February 27, 1967
      386 US 171   17 LEd2d 842   87 SCt 903
      Fox, Arthur. Showing workers who's the boss. *Nation* 239(9):295-299 (September 29, 1984).
      Hollander, Rhonda G. Injunctions against occupational hazards: toward a safe workplace environment. *Boston College Environmental Affairs Law Review* 9(1):133-161 (1980-1981).

1276. Klopfer v. North Carolina   March 13, 1967
      386 US 213   18 LEd2d 1   87 SCt 988
      En Am Con 1106, 1717-1718
      Guide (CQ) 51, 384, 529-530, 914

1277. McCray v Illinois   March 20, 1967
      386 US 300   18 LEd2d 62   87 SCt 1056
      Burger Court 64-66
      En Am Con 979-980

1278. Honda v. Clark, Attorney General   April 10, 1967
      386 US 484   18 LEd2d 244   87 SCt 1188
      Japanese 74, 266

1279. Pierson v. Ray   April 11, 1967
      386 US 547   18 LEd2d 288   87 SCt 1213
      En Am Con 1389
      Askin, Frank. Justice denied: what the conservative judiciary hath wrought. *Trial* 29(10):65-68 (October 1993).
      Ball, Howard. The U.S. Supreme Court's glossing of the Federal Tort Claims Act: statutory construction and veterans' tort actions. *Western Political Quarterly* 41(3):529-552 (September 1988).
      Plotkin, Steven R., and Carol D. Mazorol. Judicial malpractice: Pulliam is not the answer. *Trial* 20(12):24-26 (December 1984).

1280. National Woodwork Manufacturers Association v. National Labor Relations Board   April 17, 1967
      386 US 612   18 LEd2d 357   87 SCt 1250
      Burger Court 169-172
      Mounts, Gregory J. Labor and the Supreme Court: significant decisions of 1979-80. *Monthly Labor Review* 104(4):13-22 (April 1981).

1281. Anders v. California   May 8, 1967
      386 US 738   18 LEd2d 493   87 SCt 1396
      Almanac (1987):7A
      Gross, David J. Supreme Court review: Sixth and Fourteenth Amendments—appointed counsel has no constitutional duty to argue all nonfrivolous issues on appeal. *Journal of Criminal Law and Criminology* 74(4):1353-1371 (Winter 1983).

1282. National Bellas Hess, Inc. v. Department of Revenue of Illinois   May 8, 1967
      386 US 753   18 LEd2d 505   87 SCt 1389
      Almanac (1992):328
      Sup Ct Review (1989):223-259
      Biondo, John. Bellas Hess v. Quill: a Supreme Court use tax showdown. *Practical Accountant* 25(3):32-37 (March 1992).
      Colford, Steven W. High court may open ad tax. *Advertising Age* 62(44):1, 60 (October 14, 1991).
      ———. Use-tax issue moving toward day in high court. *Advertising Age* 61(21):S5, S9 (May 21, 1990).

Genetelli, Richard W., David B. Zigman, and Cesar E. Bencosme. Recent U.S. Supreme Court decisions on state and local tax issues. *CPA Journal* 62(11):38-44 (November 1992).

Hellerstein, Walter. Supreme Court says no state use tax imposed on mailorder sellers—for now. *Journal of Taxation* 77(2):120-124 (August 1992).

Levin, Gary. Direct marketers triumph in tax case. *Advertising Age* 62(26):12 (June 24, 1991).

Lucas, Joyce Ann. To collect or not to collect; a look at sales and use taxes. *Business Credit* 93(8):10-11 (September 1991).

O'Connell, Daniel. U.S. Supreme court reviews state and local taxation issues. *CPA Journal* 62(3):16-21 (March 1992).

Supreme Court upholds National Bellas Hess in Quill. *CPA Journal* 62(8):12 (August 1992).

Sylvester, Kathleen. Mail-order tax issue is back. *Governing* 4(11):14 (August 1991).

Tucker, William. Unpopularity tax. *Forbes* 147(13):88-91 (June 24, 1991).

1283. Redrup v. New York   May 8, 1967
            Coupled with Austin v. Kentucky
            Coupled with Gent v. Arkansas
        386 US 767   18 LEd2d 515   87 SCt 1414
        Fourth 93-97
        Super 652-656+

Hagle, Timothy M. But do they have to see it to know it? the Supreme Court's obscenity and pornography decisions. *Western Political Quarterly* 44(4):1039-1054 (December 1991).

Kobylka, Joseph F. A court-created context for group litigation: libertarian groups and obscenity. *Journal of Politics* 49(4):1061-1078 (November 1987).

McGuire, Kevin T., and Gregory A. Caldeira. Lawyers, organized interests, and the law of obscenity: agenda setting in the Supreme Court. *American Political Science Review* 87(3):717-726 (September 1993).

Staal, Lorri. Supreme Court review: First Amendment—the objective standard for social value in obscenity cases. *Journal of Criminal Law and Criminology* 78(4):735-762 (Winter 1988).

1284. In re Gault   May 15, 1967
        387 US 1   18 LEd2d 527   87 SCt 1428
        Amending 203-213
        Burger Court 103-104
        Death Penalty (Streib) 4-6+
        En Am Con 835-836, 1090-1093, 1585-1592
        Guide (West) (v. 5):154-159, 341-344
        Magic 320-322
        Super 672-673

Bernstein, Sidney. Supreme Court review. *Trial* 21(4):14-15 (April 1985).

Christopher, Maura. Decide seven Court cases that test teenagers' rights. *Scholastic Update* (Teachers' Edition) 120(1):16-18+ (September 4, 1987).

Feld, Barry C. The juvenile court meets the principle of the offense: legislative changes in juvenile waiver statutes. *Journal of Criminal Law and Criminology* 78(3):471-533 (Fall 1987).

————. The right to counsel in juvenile court: an empirical study of when lawyers appear and the difference they make. *Journal of Criminal Law and Criminology* 79(4):1185-1346 (Winter 1989).

Gardner, William, David Scherer, and Maya Tester. Asserting scientific authority: cognitive development and adolescent legal rights. *American Psychologist* 44(6):895-902 (June 1989).

Grant, Gerald. Children's rights and adult confusions. *Public Interest* (69):83-99 (Fall 1982).

Holtz, Larry E. Miranda in a juvenile setting: a child's right to silence. *Journal of Criminal Law and Criminology* 78(3):534-556 (Fall 1987).

Lawrence, Charise K. Your Constitution: securing your rights. *Scholastic Update* 120(9):11 (January 15, 1988).

Melton, Gary B., and Nancy Felipe Russo. Adolescent abortion: psychological perspectives on public policy. *American Psychologist* 42(1):69-72 (January 1987).

Minow, Martha. We, the family: constitutional rights and American families. *Journal of American History* 74(3):959-983 (December 1987).

Sparks, Richard K. Before you bring back school dress codes, recognize that the courts frown upon attempts to "restrict" students' rights. *American School Board Journal* 170(7):24-25 (July 1983).

1285. Dombrowski v. Eastland   May 15, 1967
    387 US 82   18 LEd2d 577   87 SCt 1425
      Super 674-676

1286. Afroyim v. Rusk, Secretary of State   May 29, 1967
    387 US 253   18 LEd2d 757   87 SCt 1660
      Documents (v. 2):719-720R
      En Am Con 36, 675, 747-755
      Guide (CQ) 148
      Guide (West) (v. 1):125-126

1287. Warden, Maryland Penitentiary v. Hayden   May 29, 1967
    387 US 294   18 LEd2d 782   87 SCt 1642
      En Am Con 1251, 1393, 1636-1637, 1637-1638, 1947-1949, 2007
      Freedom (Cox) 62-67
      Super 640-642

Bayh, Birch. Search and seizure: aftermath of Stanford daily. *Trial* 16(8):30-33,70 (August 1980).

Yeager, Daniel B. Search, seizure and the positive law: expectations of privacy outside the Fourth Amendment. *Journal of Criminal Law and Criminology* 84(2):249-309 (Summer 1993).

1288. Reitman v. Mulkey   May 29, 1967
    387 US 369   18 LEd2d 830   87 SCt 1627
      En Am Con 1535, 1729-1736, 1736-1738

1289. Commissioner of Internal Revenue v. Estate of Bosch   June 5, 1967
      Coupled with Second National Bank of New Haven v. United States
    387 US 456   18 LEd2d 886   87 SCt 1776

Gans, Mitchell M., and Jonathan G. Blattmachr. Marital-property settlements: the implications of Cook. *Trusts and Estates* 122(11):43-48 (November 1983).

1290. Camara v. Municipal Court of the City and County of San Francisco   June 5, 1967
    387 US 523   18 LEd2d 930   87 SCt 1727
      En Am Con 198, 1628-1635, 1947-1949
      Sup Ct Review (1989):87-163

Andersen, Robert M. Technology, pollution control, and EPA access to commercial property: a constitutional and policy framework. *Boston College Environmental Affairs Law Review* 17(1):1-74 (Fall 1989).

Bazarian, Stephen C. Dow Chemical Company v. United States and aerial surveillance by the EPA: an argument for post-surveillance notice to the observed. *Boston College Environmental Affairs Law Review* 15(3-4):593-626 (Spring 1988).

Bernstein, Sidney. Supreme Court review. *Trial* 21(4):14-15 (April 1985).

Guerra, Sandra. Domestic drug interdiction operations: finding the balance. *Journal of Criminal Law and Criminology* 82(4):1109-1161 (Winter 1992).

Mussio, Donna. Drawing the line between administrative and criminal searches: defining the "object of the search" in environmental inspections. *Boston College Environmental Affairs Law Review* 18(1):185-211 (Fall 1990).

Roberts, Thomas A. Supreme Court review: Fourth Amendment—warrantless administrative inspections of commercial property. *Journal of Criminal Law and Criminology* 72(4):1222-1245 (Winter 1981).

1291. See v. City of Seattle   June 5, 1967
    387 US 541   18 LEd2d 943   87 SCt 1737

Andersen, Robert M. Technology, pollution control, and EPA access to commercial property: a constitutional and policy framework. *Boston College Environmental Affairs Law Review* 17(1):1-74 (Fall 1989).

Batey, Robert. Strict construction of firearms offenses: the Supreme Court and the Gun Control Act of 1968. *Law and Contemporary Problems* 49(1):163-198 (Winter 1986).

Mussio, Donna. Drawing the line between administrative and criminal searches: defining the "object of the search" in environmental inspections. *Boston College Environmental Affairs Law Review* 18(1):185-211 (Fall 1990).

1292. Loving v. Virginia   June 12, 1967
       388 US 1   18 LEd2d 1010   87 SCt 1817
       Abortion (Frohock) 62-63
       Abortion Am 9+
       Civil 20th 3, 10, 187-197R
       Const Law 486-488R, 543
       En Am Con 572, 686-688, 1181
       Guide (CQ) 51
       Hard Choices 133-134
       Landmark (v. 3):113-123R
       May It 277-289R
       Super 668-669

Lamb, Charles M. Legal foundations of civil rights and pluralism America. *Annals of the American Academy of Political and Social Science* 454:13-25 (March 1981).

Leslie, Connie, Regina Elam, Allison Samuels, and Danzy Senna. The loving generation. *Newsweek* 125(7):72 (February 13, 1995).

Minow, Martha. We, the family: constitutional rights and American families. *Journal of American History* 74(3):959-983 (December 1987).

1293. Washington v. Texas   June 12, 1967
       388 US 14   18 LEd2d 1019   87 SCt 1920
       En Am Con 339-342
       Guide (CQ) 527, 914

White, Welsh S. The psychiatric examination and the Fifth Amendment privilege in capital cases. *Journal of Criminal Law and Criminology* 74(3):943-990 (Fall 1983).

1294. National Labor Relations Board (NLRB) v. Great Dane Trailers, Inc.   June 12, 1967
       388 US 26   18 LEd2d 1027   87 SCt 1792
       The right to strike. *Congressional Digest* 70(11):264-265 (November 1991).

1295. Berger v. New York   June 12, 1967
       388 US 41   18 LEd2d 1040   87 SCt 1873
       En Am Con 108, 618-621, 683-686

Goldsmith, Michael. The Supreme Court and Title III: rewriting the law of electronic surveillance. *Journal of Criminal Law and Criminology* 74(1):1-171 (Spring 1983).

Turley, Jonathan. The not-so-noble lie: the nonincorporation of state consensual surveillance standards in federal court. *Journal of Criminal Law and Criminology* 79(1):66-134 (Spring 1988).

1296. Curtis Publishing Co. v. Butts   June 12, 1967
          Coupled with Associated Press v. Walker
       388 US 130   18 LEd2d 1094   87 SCt 1975
       En Am Con 1157-1159, 1487-1488
       Make 183-199+
       Super 648-652+

Brief of American Psychological Association and American Association for the Advancement of Science as Amici Curiae. Ronald R. Hutchinson, Petitioner v. William Proxmire and Morton Schwartz, Respondents. *American Psychologist* 35(8):750-758 (August 1980).

Gertz, Elmer. Gertz on Gertz: reflections on the landmark libel case. *Trial* 21(10):66-69,71-75 (October 1985).

Gruhl, John. Supreme Court's impact on the law of libel: compliance by lower federal courts. *Western Political Quarterly* 33(4):502-519 (December 1980).

Hopkins, Jay. Ex-justices criticized punitive libel awards. *Editor and Publisher* 114(39):36 (September 26, 1981).

Howard, A. E. Dick. The press in court. *Wilson Quarterly* 6(5):86-93 (Special Issue 1982).

Kebbel, Gary. The different functions of speech in defamation and privacy cases. *Journalism Quarterly* 61(3):629-633,743 (Autumn 1984).

Smolla, Rodney A. Free speech afire with controversy: the Supreme Court. *Trial* 25(12):46-47,49,51 (December 1989).

1297. National Labor Relations Board (NLRB) v. Allis-Chalmers Manufacturing Co.   June 12, 1967
    388 US 175   18 LEd2d 1123   87 SCt 2001
    Super 665-666

Coleman, John J., III. Can union members resign during a strike? *Personnel Journal* 65(5):99-100, 102, 105 (May 1986).

1298. United States v. Wade   June 12, 1967
    388 US 218   18 LEd2d 1149   87 SCt 1926
    Ascent 320-322+
    Burger Court 68-72
    Burger Years 143-168
    En Am Con 1167-1168, 1585-1592, 1990
    Sup Ct Review (1991):103-142
    Super 656-663

Kamisar, Yale. The swing of the pendulum. *Nation* 239(9):271-274 (September 29, 1984).

Lane, Margaret J. Eyewitness identification: should psychologists be permitted to address the jury? *Journal of Criminal Law and Criminology* 75(4):1321-1365 (Winter 1984).

Welsh, Robert, and Ronald K. L. Collins. Taking state constitutions seriously: the protection of civil liberties has been shifting away from the U.S. Supreme Court. *Center Magazine* 14(5):6-35, 38-43 (September/ October 1981).

1299. Gilbert v. California   June 12, 1967
    388 US 263   18 LEd2d 1178   87 SCt 1951
    Burger Court 68-72
    Burger Years 143-168
    En Am Con 1167-1168
    Super 656-663

Bender, Louis, and Steven Bender. Is the Supreme Court's decision in Baggot retroactive in application? *Journal of Taxation* 60(3):138-144 (March 1984).

1300. Stovall v. Denno   June 12, 1967
    388 US 293   18 LEd2d 1199   87 SCt 1967
    Burger Years 143-168
    Const (Currie) 451-453
    En Am Con 1167-1168
    Sup Ct Review (1991):103-142
    Super 656-663

Bender, Louis, and Steven Bender. Is the Supreme Court's decision in Baggot retroactive in application? *Journal of Taxation* 60(3):138-144 (March 1984).

Lane, Margaret J. Eyewitness identification: should psychologists be permitted to address the jury? *Journal of Criminal Law and Criminology* 75(4):1321-1365 (Winter 1984).

Welsh, Robert, and Ronald K. L. Collins. Taking state constitutions seriously: the protection of civil liberties has been shifting away from the U.S. Supreme Court. *Center Magazine* 14(5):6-35, 38-43 (September/ October 1981).

1301. Walker v. Birmingham   June 12, 1967
      388 US 307   18 LEd2d 1210   87 SCt 1824
      En Am Con 2005
      Super 632-634

1302. United States v. Arnold, Schwinn and Co.   June 12, 1967
      388 US 365   18 LEd2d 1249   87 SCt 1856
      Burger Years 206-219
      Sheffet, Mary Jane, and Debra L. Scammon. Resale price maintenance: is it safe to suggest retail prices?
          Journal of Marketing 49(4):82-92 (Fall 1985).
      Werner, Ray O. Marketing and the United States Supreme Court, 1975-1981. *Journal of Marketing* 46(2):73-81
          (Spring 1982).

1303. Whitehill v. Elkins, President, University of Maryland   November 6, 1967
      389 US 54   19 LEd2d 228   88 SCt 184
      Van Alstyne, William W. Academic freedom and the First Amendment in the Supreme Court of the United
          States: an unhurried historical review. *Law and Contemporary Problems* 53(3):79-154 (Summer 1990).

1304. Burgett v. Texas   November 13, 1967
      389 US 109   19 LEd2d 319   88 SCt 258
      Feld, Barry C. The right to counsel in juvenile court: an empirical study of when lawyers appear and the
          difference they make. *Journal of Criminal Law and Criminology* 79(4):1185-1346 (Winter 1989).

1305. United States v. Robel   December 11, 1967
      389 US 258   19 LEd2d 508   88 SCt 419
      Const (Currie) 434-438
      En Am Con 1598
      Super 709-711
      Glennon, Michael J. State-sponsored abduction: a comment on United States v. Alvarez-Machain. *American
          Journal of International Law* 86(4):746-756 (October 1992).
      Halperin, Morton H. Never question the president. *Nation* 239(9):285-288 (September 29, 1984).

1306. Katz v. United States   December 18, 1967
      389 US 347   19 LEd2d 576   88 SCt 507
      Burger Court 63-64
      Const Law 274-276R+
      Economics 320-322, 343-344
      En Am Con 618-621, 1097, 1628-1635, 1947-1949, 2071-2072
      Abrams, Sharon E. Third-party consent searches, the Supreme Court, and the Fourth Amendment. *Journal of
          Criminal Law and Criminology* 75(3):963-994 (Fall 1984).
      Andersen, Robert M. Technology, pollution control, and EPA access to commercial property: a constitutional
          and policy framework. *Boston College Environmental Affairs Law Review* 17(1):1-74 (Fall 1989).
      Bazarian, Stephen C. Dow Chemical Company v. United States and aerial surveillance by the EPA: an
          argument for post-surveillance notice to the observed. *Boston College Environmental Affairs Law Review*
          15(3-4):593-626 (Spring 1988).
      Dripps, Donald A. Supreme Court review: search and seizure: finding for the Fourth Amendment. *Trial*
          29(3):95-97 (March 1993).
      Gardner, Martin R. Hudson v. Palmer—"bright lines" but dark directions for prisoner privacy rights. *Journal of
          Criminal Law and Criminology* 76(1):75-115 (Spring 1985).
      Goldberger, Peter. Consent, expectations of privacy, and the meaning of "searches" in the Fourth Amendment.
          Journal of Criminal Law and Criminology 75(2):319-362 (Summer 1984).
      Goldsmith, Michael. The Supreme Court and Title III: rewriting the law of electronic surveillance. *Journal of
          Criminal Law and Criminology* 74(1):1-171 (Spring 1983).
      Goring, Darlene C. Supreme Court review: Fourth Amendment—prison cells: is there a right to privacy?
          Journal of Criminal Law and Criminology 75(3):609-629 (Fall 1984).

Junker, John M. The structure of the Fourth Amendment: the scope of the protection. *Journal of Criminal Law and Criminology* 79(4):1105-1183 (Winter 1989).

LaFave, Wayne R. Supreme Court review: Fourth Amendment vagaries (of improbable cause, imperceptible plain view, notorious privacy, and balancing askew). *Journal of Criminal Law and Criminology* 74(4):1171-1224 (Winter 1983).

Line, Julie A. Supreme Court review: Fourth Amendment—further erosion of the warrant requirement for unreasonable searches and seizures: the warrantless trash search exception. *Journal of Criminal Law and Criminology* 79(3):623-646 (Fall 1988).

Power, Robert C. Technology and the Fourth Amendment: a proposed formulation for visual searches. *Journal of Criminal Law and Criminology* 80(1):1-113 (Spring 1989).

Rosenblatt, Roger. The Bill of Rights. *Life* 14(13 Special Issue):9-30 (Fall 1991).

Turley, Jonathan. The not-so-noble lie: the nonincorporation of state consensual surveillance standards in federal court. *Journal of Criminal Law and Criminology* 79(1):66-134 (Spring 1988).

Webber, Dawn. Supreme Court review: Fourth Amendment—of warrants, electronic surveillance, expectations of privacy, and tainted fruits. *Journal of Criminal Law and Criminology* 75(3):630-652 (Fall 1984).

Wieber, Michael C. The theory and practice of Illinois v. Rodriguez: why an officer's reasonable belief about a third party's authority to consent does not protect a criminal suspect's rights. *Journal of Criminal Law and Criminology* 84(3):604-641 (Fall 1993).

Yeager, Daniel B. Search, seizure and the positive law: expectations of privacy outside the Fourth Amendment. *Journal of Criminal Law and Criminology* 84(2):249-309 (Summer 1993).

1307. Mora v. McNamara   November 6, 1967
        389 US 934   19 LEd2d 287   88 SCt 282
        Guide (CQ) 128

1308. Marchetti v. United States   January 29, 1968
        390 US 39   19 LEd2d 889   88 SCt 697
        En Am Con 1202-1203, 1869-1871
        Super 694-701

Batey, Robert. Strict construction of firearms offenses: the Supreme Court and the Gun Control Act of 1968. *Law and Contemporary Problems* 49(1):163-198 (Winter 1986).

Caginalp, O. A. Fifth Amendment privilege against self-incrimination and compulsory self-disclosure under the Clean Air and Clean Water Acts. *Boston College Environmental Affairs Law Review* 9(2):359-395 (1980-1981).

Rosenblatt, Leonard R. The Fifth Amendment and the production of business records: and Braswell Begat Bouknight. *Taxes* 68(6):418-424 (June 1990).

1309. Grosso v. United States   January 29, 1968
        390 US 62   19 LEd2d 906   88 SCt 709
        En Am Con 1202-1203
        Super 694-701

1310. Haynes v. United States   January 29, 1968
        390 US 85   19 LEd2d 923   88 SCt 722
        En Am Con 1202-1203

Batey, Robert. Strict construction of firearms offenses: the Supreme Court and the Gun Control Act of 1968. *Law and Contemporary Problems* 49(1):163-198 (Winter 1986).

Caginalp, O. A. Fifth Amendment privilege against self-incrimination and compulsory self-disclosure under the Clean Air and Clean Water Acts. *Boston College Environmental Affairs Law Review* 9(2):359-395 (1980-1981).

1311. Smith v. Illinois   January 29, 1968
        390 US 129   19 LEd2d 956   88 SCt 748

Haddad, James B. The future of confrontation clause developments: what will emerge when the Supreme Court synthesizes the diverse lines of confrontation decisions? *Journal of Criminal Law and Criminology* 81(1):77-98 (Spring 1990).

1312. Albrecht v. Herald Co.   March 4, 1968
390 US 145   19 LEd2d 998   88 SCt 869
Graglia, Lino A. One hundred years of antitrust. *Public Interest* (104):50-66 (Summer 1991).
Werner, Ray O. Marketing and the Supreme Court in transition, 1982-1984. *Journal of Marketing* 49(3):97-105 (Summer 1985).

1313. Simmons v. United States   March 18, 1968
390 US 377   19 LEd2d 1247   88 SCt 967
Lane, Margaret J. Eyewitness identification: should psychologists be permitted to address the jury? *Journal of Criminal Law and Criminology* 75(4):1321-1365 (Winter 1984).
Uviller, H. Richard. Self-incrimination by inference: constitutional restrictions on the evidentiary use of a suspect's refusal to submit to a search. *Journal of Criminal Law and Criminology* 81(1):37-76 (Spring 1990).
White, Welsh S. The psychiatric examination and the Fifth Amendment privilege in capital cases. *Journal of Criminal Law and Criminology* 74(3):943-990 (Fall 1983).

1314. Newman v. Piggie Park Enterprises, Inc.   March 18, 1968
390 US 400   19 LEd2d 1263   88 SCt 964
Jordan, Scott J. Awarding attorney's fees to environmental plaintiffs under a private attorney general theory. *Boston College Environmental Affairs Law Review* 14(2):287-311 (Winter 1987).
O'Connor, Karen, and Lee Epstein. Bridging the gap between Congress and the Supreme Court: interest groups and the erosion of the American rule governing awards of attorneys' fees. *Western Political Quarterly* 38(2):238-249 (June 1985).

1315. Avery v. Midland County, Texas   April 1, 1968
390 US 474   20 LEd2d 45   88 SCt 1114
Court Public 93-94
En Am Con 85
Public Affairs Council of Louisiana. Reapportionment for the 1980s: good faith and court decisions. *National Civic Review* 70(11):575-582 (December 1981).

1316. United States v. Jackson   April 8, 1968
390 US 570   20 LEd2d 138   88 SCt 1209
Const (Currie) 555-559
Sup Ct Review (1980):211-279
Halberstam, Malvina. Towards neutral principles in the administration of criminal justice: a critique of Supreme Court decisions sanctioning the plea bargaining process. *Journal of Criminal Law and Criminology* 73(1):1-49 (Spring 1982).
Schultz, Marjorie S. Jury defined: a review of Burger court decisions. *Law and Contemporary Problems* 43(4):8-23 (Autumn 1980).

1317. Ginsberg v. New York   April 22, 1968
390 US 629   20 LEd2d 195   88 SCt 1274
En Am Con 846
First 295-296
Super 706-709

1318. Interstate Circuit, Inc. v. Dallas   April 22, 1968
Coupled with United Artists Corp. v. Dallas
390 US 676   20 LEd2d 225   88 SCt 1298
McGuire, Kevin T. Obscenity, libertarian values, and decision making in the Supreme Court. *American Politics Quarterly* 18(1):47-67 (January 1990).

1319. St. Amant v. Thompson April 29, 1968
390 US 727 20 LEd2d 262 88 SCt 1323
Kebbel, Gary. The different functions of speech in defamation and privacy cases. *Journalism Quarterly* 61(3):629-633, 743 (Autumn 1984).

1320. In Re Permian Basin Area Rate Cases May 1, 1968
Permian Basin Area Rate Cases
      Coupled with Continental Oil Co. v. Federal Power Commission (FPC)
      Coupled with Superior Oil Co. v. Federal Power Commission (FPC)
      Coupled with New Mexico v. Federal Power Commission (FPC)
      Coupled with Sun Oil Co. v. Federal Power Commission (FPC)
      Coupled with California v. Skelly Oil Co.
      Coupled with Hunt Oil Co. v. Federal Power Commission (FPC)
      Coupled with Pacific Gas & Electric Co. v. Skelly Oil Co.
      Coupled with Bass v. Federal Power Commission (FPC)
      Coupled with Federal Power Commission (FPC) v. Skelly Oil Co.
      Coupled with City and County of Los Angeles v. Skelly Oil Co.
      Coupled with City and County of San Francisco v. Skelly Oil Co.
      Coupled with City of San Diego v. Skelly Oil Co.
      Coupled with Standard Oil Co. of Texas v. Federal Power Commission (FPC)
      Coupled with Mobil Oil Co. v. Federal Power Commission (FPC)
390 US 747 20 LEd2d 312 88 SCt 1344
Cleaves, Robert E., IV. Constitutional protection for the utility investor: the confiscation doctrine after Cleveland Electric Illuminating Co. v. Public Utilities Commission of Ohio. *Boston College Environmental Affairs Law Review* 12(3):527-558 (Spring 1985).

1321. Levy v. Louisiana Through the Charity Hospital of Louisiana May 20, 1968
391 US 068 20 LEd2d 436 88 SCt 1509
   Brennan 282-285
   Const (Currie) 425-429
   En Am Con 947-948, 1156-1157
Abortion: readers respond. [Editorial] *Commonweal* 109(3):75-84 (February 12, 1982).
Graglia, Lino. Saving the Constitution: a theory of power. *National Review* 39(13):33-36 (July 17, 1987).

1322. Glona v. American Guarantee and Liability Insurance Co. May 20, 1968
391 US 73 20 LEd2d 441 88 SCt 1515
   En Am Con 1156-1157

1323. Bruton v. United States May 20, 1968
391 US 123 20 LEd2d 476 88 SCt 1620
   En Am Con 339-342, 658-661
   Super 711-715
Dickett, William G. Supreme Court review: Sixth Amendment—limiting the scope of Bruton. *Journal of Criminal Law and Criminology* 78(4):984-1013 (Winter 1988).
Goldberg, Steven H. Harmless error: constitutional sneak thief. *Journal of Criminal Law and Criminology* 71(4):421-442 (Winter 1980).
Haddad, James B. The future of confrontation clause developments: what will emerge when the Supreme Court synthesizes the diverse lines of confrontation decisions? *Journal of Criminal Law and Criminology* 81(1):77-98 (Spring 1990).
Haddad, James B., and Richard G. Agin. A potential revolution in Bruton doctrine: is Bruton applicable where domestic evidence rules prohibit use of a codefendant's confession as evidence against a defendant although the confrontation clause would allow such use? *Journal of Criminal Law and Criminology* 81(2):235-266 (Summer 1990).
Krit, Jonathan J. Supreme Court review: Sixth Amendment—confrontation and the use of interlocking confessions at joint trial. *Journal of Criminal Law and Criminology* 78(4):937-953 (Winter 1988).

1324. Duncan v. Louisiana   May 20, 1968
    391 US 145   20 LEd2d 491   88 SCt 1444
        En Am Con 516-522, 592, 1082-1085, 1472-1479, 1796-1803
        Guide (CQ) 50-51, 281, 339, 384, 524, 526, 914
    American survey: Burger leaves the labyrinth. *Economist* 300(7454):17-22 (July 12-18, 1986).
    Bradley, Craig M. The Sixth Amendment lives! a reply to Professor Jonakait. *Journal of Criminal Law and Criminology* 83(3):526-537 (Fall 1992).
    Goldberg, Steven H. Harmless error: constitutional sneak thief. *Journal of Criminal Law and Criminology* 71(4):421-442 (Winter 1980).
    Schultz, Marjorie S. Jury defined: a review of Burger court decisions. *Law and Contemporary Problems* 43(4):8-23 (Autumn 1980).

1325. Amalgamated Food Employees Union, Local 590 v. Logan Valley Plaza Inc.   May 20, 1968
    391 US 308   20 LEd2d 603   88 SCt 1601
        Ascent 155-156, 434
        Black 115-123
        Burger Court 167-169
        En Am Con 1378-1388, 1681, 1729-1736
    Askin, Frank. Justice denied: what the conservative judiciary hath wrought. *Trial* 29(10):65-68 (October 1993).
    Marcy, William R. To protect or not to protect—that is the question. *Social Education* 54(6):364-365 (October 1990).
    Sullivan, Harold J. Privatization of public services: a growing threat to constitutional rights. *Public Administration Review* 47(6):461-467 (November/December 1987).
    Trank, John P. The Burger Court—the first ten years. *Law and Contemporary Problems* 43(3):101-135 (Summer 1980).

1326. United States v. O'Brien   May 27, 1968
    391 US 367   20 LEd2d 672   88 SCt 1673
        Almanac (1989):309-311,313
        Brennan 86-90
        Const (Currie) 438-442
        Const Law 136-139R, 148-150
        En Am Con 583-584, 1136-1143, 1334-1335, 1843-1844
        Sup Ct Review (1982);285-317; (1990):69-103; (1993):1-36; (1994):1-56, 57-128
        Super 683-685+
        Tolerant 204-212
    Brennan, William. The United States Supreme Court: decision. *Congressional Digest* 68(8-9)196, 198, 200 (August/September 1989).
    The flag and freedom of speech. *America* 161(1):3 (July 1-8, 1989).
    Greenawalt, Kent. Free speech in the United States and Canada. *Law and Contemporary Problems* 55(1):5-33 (Winter 1992).
    Marcy, William R. To protect or not to protect—that is the question. *Social Education* 54(6):364-365 (October 1990).
    Smolla, Rodney A. Academic freedom, hate speech, and the idea of a university. *Law and Contemporary Problems* 53(3):195-225 (Summer 1990).
    Tushnet, Mark. The Constitution of religion. *Review of Politics* 50(4):628-658 (Fall 1988).

1327. Puyallup Tribe v. Department of Game of Washington   May 27, 1968
        Coupled with Kautz v. Department of Game of Washington
    391 US 392   20 LEd2d 689   88 SCt 1725
    Ott, Brian R. Indian fishing rights in the Pacific Northwest: the need for federal intervention. *Boston College Environmental Affairs Law Review* 14(2):313-343 (Winter 1987).

1328. Menominee Tribe of Indians v. United States   May 27, 1968
    391 US 404   20 LEd2d 697   88 SCt 1705

Am Indians (Wilkinson) 48-50, 75-76, 124

1329. Green v. County School Board of New Kent County, Virginia   May 27, 1968
           391 US 430   20 LEd2d 716   88 SCt 1689
               Ascent 255-256, 278-280+
               Behind Bakke 29-31
               Brennan 249-255
               Burden 7, 155-165, 274-280+
               Burger Court 114-117
               Const (Currie) 416-421
               Const Law 545-548
               Court Const 262-264
               En Am Con 557-561, 867
               Guide (CQ) 51
               Magic 326-327
               New Right (Schwartz) 145-154+
               New Right (Whitaker) 142-168
               Super 703-706
           Askin, Frank. Justice denied: what the conservative judiciary hath wrought. *Trial* 29(10):65-68 (October 1993).
           Brown, Kevin. Revisiting the Supreme Court's opinion in Brown v. Board of Education from a multiculturalist perspective. *Teachers College Record* 96(4):644-653 (Summer 1995).
           Butler, Grace L. Legal and policy issues in higher education. *Journal of Negro Education* 63(3):451-459 (Summer 1994).
           Canon, Bradley C. The Supreme Court as a cheerleader in politico-moral disputes. *Journal of Politics* 54(3):637-653 (August 1992).
           Evolution of court policy. *Congressional Digest* 59(2):39 (February 1981).
           Gordon, William M. The implementation of desegregation plans since Brown. *Journal of Negro Education* 63(3):310-322 (Summer 1994).
           Hyde, Alison A. School desegregation: the role of the courts and means of achievement. *NASSP Bulletin* 78(565):28-37 (November 1994).
           Lamb, Charles M. Legal foundations of civil rights and pluralism America. *Annals of the American Academy of Political and Social Science* 454:13-25 (March 1981).
           Landsberg, Brian K. The federal government and the promise of Brown. *Teachers College Record* 96(4):627-636 (Summer 1995).
           Markman, Stephen J., and Alfred S. Regnery. The mind of Justice Brennan: a 25-year tribute. *National Review* 36(9):30-33, 36-38 (May 18, 1984).
           Parker, Franklin. School desegregation since Brown: a 30-year perspective. *USA Today* 114(2486):90-91 (November 1985).
           Reid, Herbert O., Sr. State of the art: the law and education since 1954. *Journal of Negro Education* 52(3):234-249 (Summer 1983).
           Reid, Herbert O., and Frankie M. Foster-Davis. Three decades of "all deliberate speed." *Crisis* 91(5):12-15 (May 1984).
           Russo, Charles J., J. John Harris III, and Rosetta F. Sandidge. Brown v. Board of Education at 40: a legal history of equal educational opportunity in American public education. *Journal of Negro Education* 63(3):297-309 (Summer 1994).
           Simmons, Althea T. L. From Brown to Grove City: blueprint for education. *Crisis* 91(5):6-10 (May 1984).
           Stefkovich, Jacqueline A., and Terrence Leas. A legal history of desegregation in higher education. *Journal of Negro Education* 63(3):406-420 (Summer 1994).
           Timberlake, Constance H. A historical perspective of school desegregation. *Crisis* 91(5):26-29 (1984).

1330. Raney v. Board of Education of the Gould School District   May 27, 1968
           391 US 443   20 LEd2d 727   88 SCt 1697
           Russo, Charles J., J. John Harris III, and Rosetta F. Sandidge. Brown v. Board of Education at 40: a legal history of equal educational opportunity in American public education. *Journal of Negro Education* 63(3):297-309 (Summer 1994).

1331. Monroe v. Board of Commissioners of Jackson, Tennessee May 27, 1968
391 US 450   20 LEd2d 733   88 SCt 1700
   Const (Currie) 416-421

Russo, Charles J., J. John Harris III, and Rosetta F. Sandidge. Brown v. Board of Education at 40: a legal history of equal educational opportunity in American public education. *Journal of Negro Education* 63(3):297-309 (Summer 1994).

1332. Reading Co. v. Brown June 3, 1968
391 US 471   20 LEd2d 751   88 SCt 1759

Cistulli, Joseph P. Striking a balance between competing policies: the administrative claim as an alternative to enforce state clean-up orders in bankruptcy proceedings. *Boston College Environmental Affairs Law Review* 16(3):581-614 (Spring 1989).

1333. Witherspoon v. Illinois June 3, 1968
391 US 510   20 LEd2d 776   88 SCt 1770
   Almanac (1985):7A
   Guide (West) (v.10):398-400
   Death Penalty (Tushnet) 33-37, 116+
   Death Penalty 80s 162-167, 181-183
   Death Penalty 90s 186-207
   En Am Con 1978

Bersoff, Donald N. Social science data and the Supreme Court: Lockhart as a case in point. *American Psychologist* 42(1):52-58 (January 1987).

Callans, Patrick J. Supreme Court review: Sixth Amendment—assembling a jury willing to impose the death penalty: a new disregard for a capital defendant's right. *Journal of Criminal Law and Criminology* 76(4):1027-1050 (Winter 1985).

Ewer, Phyllis A. Supreme Court review: Eighth Amendment—the death penalty. *Journal of Criminal Law and Criminology* 71(4):538-546 (Winter 1980).

In the Supreme Court of the United States Lockhart v. McCree: Amicus Curiae Brief for the American Psychological Association. *American Psychologist* 42(1):59-68 (January 1987).

Juries: Blacker, and pro the death penalty. *Economist* 299(7445):25-26 (May 10-16, 1986).

Lake, L. B. Court stacks the deck in capital cases. [Editorial] *Christian Century* 103(20):575-576 (June 18-25, 1986).

Schultz, Marjorie S. Jury defined: a review of Burger court decisions. *Law and Contemporary Problems* 43(4):8-23 (Autumn 1980).

Schwartz, Charles Walter. Eighth Amendment proportionality analysis and the compelling case of William Rummel. *Journal of Criminal Law and Criminology* 71(4):378-420 (Winter 1980).

Wells, Diane. Federal habeas corpus and the death penalty: a need for a return to the principles of Furman. *Journal of Criminal Law and Criminology* 80(2):427-490 (Summer 1989).

Whisler, Barbara J. Supreme Court review: Sixth Amendment—death qualification of the jury: process is permissible where defendant does not face death penalty. *Journal of Criminal Law and Criminology* 78(4):954-983 (Winter 1988).

1334. Bumper v. North Carolina June 3, 1968
391 US 543   20 LEd2d 797   88 SCt 1788

Gardiner, Thomas G. Consent to search in response to police threats to seek or to obtain a search warrant: some alternatives. *Journal of Criminal Law and Criminology* 71(2):163-172 (Summer 1980).

1335. Pickering June 3, 1968
   v. Board of Education of Township High School District 205, Will County, Illinois
391 US 563   20 LEd2d 811   88 SCt 1731

Delon, Floyd G. The legacy of Thurgood Marshall. *Journal of Negro Education* 63(3):278-288 (Summer 1994).

Flygare, Thomas J. De jure: the Supreme Court adds a new twist to free speech for public employees. *Phi Delta Kappan* 65(2):144-145 (October 1983).

Menacker, Julius. Review of Supreme Court reasoning in cases of expression, due process, and equal protection. *Phi Delta Kappan* 63(3):188-190 (November 1981).

Mounts, Gregory J. Labor and the Supreme Court: significant decisions of 1978-79. *Monthly Labor Review* 103(1):14-21 (January 1980).

Van Alstyne, William W. Academic freedom and the First Amendment in the Supreme Court of the United States: an unhurried historical review. *Law and Contemporary Problems* 53(3):79-154 (Summer 1990).

Zirkel, Perry A., and Ivan B. Gluckman. Educators' free speech: new developments. *NASSP Bulletin* 68(475):127-130 (November 1984).

1336. Terry v. Ohio   June 10, 1968
          392 US 1   20 LEd2d 889   88 SCt 1868

Almanac (1983):6A
Brennan 191-196
Const Law 351-358R, 388-389+
En Am Con 72-73, 662-665, 1462-1464, 1628-1635, 1780-1782, 1879-1880
May It 199-212R
Super 685-692+

Bernstein, Sidney. Supreme Court review. *Trial* 19(10):26, 28 (October 1983).

———. Supreme Court review. *Trial* 19(11):20, 22 (November 1983).

Bernstein, Sidney, and Michael Eisenstein. 1981 Supreme Court update: the criminal law. *Trial* 17(10):54-60, 85 (October 1981).

Bernstein, Steven K. Supreme Court review: Fourth Amendment—using the drug courier profile to fight the war on drugs. *Journal of Criminal Law and Criminology* 80(4):996-1017 (Winter 1990).

Butterfoss, Edwin J. Bright line seizures: the need for clarity in determining when Fourth Amendment activity begins. *Journal of Criminal Law and Criminology* 79(2):437-482 (Summer 1988).

Carter, Jeffrey A. Supreme Court review: Fourth Amendment—airport searches and seizures: where will the Court land? *Journal of Criminal Law and Criminology* 71(4):499-517 (Winter 1980).

Devetski, Timothy J. Supreme Court review: Fourth Amendment—protection against unreasonable seizure of the person: the new (?) common law arrest test for seizure. *Journal of Criminal Law and Criminology* 82(4):747-772 (Winter 1992).

Dripps, Donald A. Supreme Court review: it might be a roust, but it isn't a 'seizure.' *Trial* 28(1):66-68 (January 1992).

———. Supreme Court review: Supreme Court trims Fourth Amendment with 'plain feel' exception. *Trial* 29(9):77-78 (September 1993).

Goldberger, Peter. Consent, expectations of privacy, and the meaning of "searches" in the Fourth Amendment. *Journal of Criminal Law and Criminology* 75(2):319-362 (Summer 1984).

Greig, William H., and Phillip S. Althoff. The constitutionality of roadblocks; the Fourth Amendment on the firing line again. *Trial* 22(2):56-62 (February 1986).

Ison, Timothy M. Supreme Court review: Fourth Amendment—officer safety and the protective automobile search: an expansion of the pat-down frisk. *Journal of Criminal Law and Criminology* 74(4):1265-1281 (Winter 1983).

Kulowiec, David J. Supreme Court review: Fourth Amendment—determining the reasonable length of a Terry stop. *Journal of Criminal Law and Criminology* 76(4):1003-1026 (Winter 1985).

LaFave, Wayne R. Supreme Court review: Fourth Amendment vagaries (of improbable cause, imperceptible plain view, notorious privacy, and balancing askew). *Journal of Criminal Law and Criminology* 74(4):1171-1224 (Winter 1983).

The legacy of the Burger Court. *U.S. News & World Report* 100(25):22 (June 30, 1986).

MacIntosh, Susanne M. Supreme Court review: Fourth Amendment—the plain touch exception to the warrant requirement. *Journal of Criminal Law and Criminology* 84(4):743-768 (Winter/Spring 1994).

Maclin, Tracey. New York v. Class: a little-noticed case with disturbing implications. *Journal of Criminal Law and Criminology* 78(1):1-86 (Spring 1987).

Pettus, Jolene D. Supreme Court review: Fourth Amendment—the expansion of the Terry doctrine to completed felonies. *Journal of Criminal Law and Criminology* 76(4):986-1002 (Winter 1985).

Sickman, Linda M. Supreme Court review: Fourth Amendment—limited luggage seizures valid on reasonable suspicion. *Journal of Criminal Law and Criminology* 74(4):1225-1248 (Winter 1983).

Sifferlen, Mark J. Supreme Court review: Fourth Amendment—protective sweep doctrine: when does the Fourth Amendment allow police officers to search the home incident to a lawful arrest? *Journal of Criminal Law and Criminology* 81(4):862-882 (Winter 1991).

Vawrinek, Jeffrey J. Supreme Court review: Fourth Amendment—detention of occupants during a premises search: the winter of discontent for probable cause. *Journal of Criminal Law and Criminology* 72(4):1246-1264 (Winter 1981).

Wall, Sandra J. Supreme Court review: Fourth Amendment—search of an individual pursuant to a warrant to search the premises. *Journal of Criminal Law and Criminology* 71(4):558-566 (Winter 1980).

Wieber, Michael C. The theory and practice of Illinois v. Rodriguez: why an officer's reasonable belief about a third party's authority to consent does not protect a criminal suspect's rights. *Journal of Criminal Law and Criminology* 84(3):604-641 (Fall 1993).

1337. Sibron v. New York   June 10, 1968
    392 US 40   20 LEd2d 917   88 SCt 1889
    En Am Con 1780-1782, 1879-1880

1338. Flast v. Cohen, Secretary of Health, Education, and Welfare   June 10, 1968
    392 US 83   20 LEd2d 947   88 SCt 1942
    Const (Currie) 442-446
    En Am Con 743-744, 1871-1872
    Equal Rights (Kanowitz) 130-133+
    Godless 68-69
    Guide (CQ) 51-52
    Religion 71, 157-159+

Alpert, Peter A. Citizen suits under the Clean Air Act: universal standing for the uninjured private attorney general? *Boston College Environmental Affairs Law Review* 16(2):283-328 (Winter 1988).

Rabinove, Samuel, Josef Joffe, Sheldon F. Gottlieb, Adam Simms, Stephen F. Rohde, Jeffrey Valle, and Robert H. Bork. The First Amendment. [Editorial] *Commentary* 99(5):7-15 (May 1995).

1339. Perma Life Mufflers, Inc. v. International Parts Corp.   June 10, 1968
    392 US 134   20 LEd2d 982   88 SCt 1981
    Sup Ct Review (1984):69-148

1340. Maryland v. Wirtz, Secretary of Labor   June 10, 1968
    392 US 183   20 LEd2d 1020   88 SCt 2017
    Ascent 100-102
    En Am Con 680-682
    Guide (CQ) 107

Johnston, Richard E., and John T. Thompson. Burger court and federalism: a revolution in 1976? *Western Political Quarterly* 33(2):197-216 (June 1980).

Johnston, Van R., and Maxine Kurtz. Handling a public policy emergency: the Fair Labor Standards Act in the public sector. *Public Administration Review* 46(5):414-422 (September/October 1986).

Stephens, Pamela J. Implementing federal energy policy at the state and local levels: "every power requisite." *Boston College Environmental Affairs Law Review* 10(4):875-904 (May 1983).

1341. Harrison v. United States   June 10, 1968
    392 US 219   20 LEd2d 1047   88 SCt 2008
Halberstam, Malvina. Towards neutral principles in the administration of criminal justice: a critique of Supreme Court decisions sanctioning the plea bargaining process. *Journal of Criminal Law and Criminology* 73(1):1-49 (Spring 1982).

1342. Board of Education of Central School District No. 1 v. Allen   June 10, 1968
    392 US 236   20 LEd2d 1060   88 SCt 1923
    Burger Years 56-91
    Const Law 76, 82-84+

En Am Con 131, 854-856, 1650-1658
First 168-174
Godless 70-71
Religion 24-26
Sup Ct Church 71-80R

Abram, Morris B. Is "strict separation" too strict? *Public Interest* (82):81-90 (Winter 1986).

Buzzard, Lynn Robert, and Samuel Ericsson. Public aid to private schools: Caesar rendering to God? *Christianity Today* 27(10):20-23 (June 17, 1983).

Flygare, Thomas J. De jure: Supreme Court permits state tax deductions for nonpublic schools. *Phi Delta Kappan* 65(1):63-64 (September 1983).

Mosk, Stanley. The emerging agenda in state constitutional rights law. *Annals of the American Academy of Political and Social Science* 496:54-64 (March 1988).

Rayer, Thomas A. The bicentennial and church-related schools. *America* 157(17):427-429, 438 (December 5, 1987).

Regan, Richard J. Supreme Court roundup: 1986 term. *Thought* 63(251):429-441 (December 1988).

1343. Jones v. Alfred H. Mayer Co.   June 17, 1968
      392 US 409   20 LEd2d 1189   88 SCt 2186
      Court Public 96
      Documents (v. 2):720-721R
      En Am Con 284-287, 640-647, 1029, 1729-1736, 1892-1894
      Guide (CQ) 51, 154
      Sup Ct Review (1989):1-51; (1988):43-60
      Super 701-703

Belz, Herman. Equality before the law: the Civil War amendments. *Center Magazine* 20(6):4-19 (November/December 1987).

Demon Runyon. [Editorial] *Commonweal* 115(10):291-292 (May 20, 1988).

Karst, Kenneth L. Equal protection of the laws. *Society* 24(1):24-30 (November/December 1986).

Lamb, Charles M. Legal foundations of civil rights and pluralism America. *Annals of the American Academy of Political and Social Science* 454:13-25 (March 1981).

Williams, Preston N. Court reviews Runyon: an unsettling move. [Editorial] *Christian Century* 105(30):919-920 (October 19, 1988).

1344. Hanover Shoe, Inc. v. United Shoe Machinery Corp.   June 17, 1968
      392 US 481   20 LEd2d 1231   88 SCt 2224

Consumer and antitrust law. *Congressional Digest* 59(2):34-64 (February 1980).

Laycock, Douglas. Continuing violations, disparate impact in compensation, and other Title VII issues. *Law and Contemporary Problems* 49(4):53-61 (Autumn 1986).

Werner, Ray O. Marketing and the United States Supreme Court, 1975-1981. *Journal of Marketing* 46(2):73-81 (Spring 1982).

1345. Powell v. Texas   June 17, 1968
      392 US 514   20 LEd2d 1254   88 SCt 2154
      Const (Friendly) 179
      En Am Con 524-526, 1954-1955
      Sup Ct Review (1986):317-393R
      Super 693-694
      Thurgood 338-353R+

Schwartz, Charles Walter. Eighth Amendment proportionality analysis and the compelling case of William Rummel. *Journal of Criminal Law and Criminology* 71(4):378-420 (Winter 1980).

1346. Epperson v. Arkansas   November 12, 1968
      393 US 97   21 LEd2d 228   89 SCt 266
      Abortion Pol (Rubin) 75-76
      Brennan 129-134

Courage 205-230, 427

En Am Con 608-612, 640, 1537-1538, 1650-1658

Establishment 151-152+

Godless 93-95+

Landmark (v. 3):125-135R

Let Us 123-124

Religion 71-77

Sup Ct Church 224-230R

Super 753-755

Trial 4, 6-7, 98-104, 108-119, 160-162, 166-167+

The court decisions. *Congressional Digest* 63(5):132-134,160 (May 1984).

Kermerer, Frank R., and Stephanie Abraham Hirsch. School library censorship comes before the Supreme Court. *Phi Delta Kappan* 63(7):444-448 (March (1982).

McKown, Delos Banning. Deism and the Supreme Court. *Humanist* 52(2):25-28,48 (March/April 1992).

O'Neil, Robert M. Creationism, curriculum, and the Constitution. *Academe* 68(2):21-26 (March/April 1982).

Ostling, Richard, Anne Constable, and Michael P. Harris. Threatening the wall: church-state separation has powerful new critics. *Time* 130(1):70-71 (July 6, 1987).

Prayer in public schools. *Congressional Digest* 74(1):3-32 (January 1995).

Regan, Richard J. Supreme Court roundup: 1986 term. *Thought* 63(251):429-441 (December 1988).

Sendor, Benjamin. Here's a closer look at that creationism decision and what it means to your schools. *American School Board Journal* 174(9):24-25 (September 1987).

Van Alstyne, William W. Academic freedom and the First Amendment in the Supreme Court of the United States: an unhurried historical review. *Law and Contemporary Problems* 53(3):79-154 (Summer 1990).

1347. Carroll v. President and Commissioners of Princess Anne County, Maryland   November 19, 1968
393 US 175   21 LEd2d 325   89 SCt 347
En Am Con 216

1348. United States v. Container Corp. of America   January 14, 1969
393 US 333   21 LEd2d 526   89 SCt 510
Favretto, Richard J. Trade associations and antitrust laws. *Credit and Financial Management* 82(2):16-18 (February 1980).

1349. Hunter v. Erickson   January 20, 1969
393 US 385   21 LEd2d 616   89 SCt 557
En Am Con 514, 941-942, 1729-1736
Sup Ct Review (1982):127-166
Binion, Gayle. The Burger court and the rights of the poor. *Center Magazine* 15(2):2-7 (March/April 1982).

Gale, Mary Ellen. Relegating minorities to the back of the courthouse. *Trial* 18(10):40-45,86 (October 1982).

1350. Spinelli v. United States   January 27, 1969
393 US 410   21 LEd2d 637   89 SCt 584
En Am Con 979-980, 1462-1464, 1628-1635, 1719
Bernstein, Sidney. Supreme Court review. *Trial* 19(10):26, 28 (October 1983).

Hartman, Marshall J., and Sidney Bernstein. To Leon, and beyond; two commentators react. *Trial* 21(1):50-56 (January 1985).

LaFave, Wayne R. Supreme Court review: Fourth Amendment vagaries (of improbable cause, imperceptible plain view, notorious privacy, and balancing askew). *Journal of Criminal Law and Criminology* 74(4):1171-1224 (Winter 1983).

Moore, Cathy E. Supreme Court review: Fourth Amendment—totality of the circumstances approach to probable cause based on informant's tips. *Journal of Criminal Law and Criminology* 74(4):1249-1264 (Winter 1983).

Regan, Richard J. Supreme Court roundup: 1982 term. *Thought* 58(231):472-483 (December 1983).

1351. Presbyterian Church in United States   January 27, 1969
      v. Mary Elizabeth Blue Hull Memorial Presbyterian Church
393 US 440   21 LEd2d 658   89 SCt 601
    Ascent 212-214
    Godless 47-48+
Taylor, Barry W. Diversion of church funds to personal use: state, federal and private sanctions. *Journal of Criminal Law and Criminology* 73(3):1204-1237 (Fall 1982).

1352. Securities and Exchange Commission (SEC) v. National Securities, Inc.   January 27, 1969
393 US 453   21 LEd2d 668   89 SCt 564
Kempler, Cecelia, and William Duffy. Insolvent reinsurers pose even greater risk. *Best's Review* (Life/Health Insurance Edition) 94(10):54-57 (April 1994).
    ———. Insolvent reinsurers pose even greater risk. *Best's Review* (Property/Casualty Insurance Edition) 94(12):42-45 (April 1994).
Tish, Martin H. Duplicative statutes, prosecutorial discretion, and the Illinois armed violence statute. *Journal of Criminal Law and Criminology* 71(3):226-243 (Fall 1980).

1353. Johnson v. Avery, Commissioner of Corrections   February 24, 1969
393 US 483   21 LEd2d 718   89 SCt 747
    En Am Con 1026-1027
Haas, Kenneth C. "New federalism" and prisoners' rights: state Supreme courts in comparative perspective. *Western Political Quarterly* 34(4):552-571 (December 1981).
Mello, Michael A. Is there a federal constitutional right to counsel in capital post-conviction proceedings? *Journal of Criminal Law and Criminology* 79(4):1065-1104 (Winter 1989).
Methvin, Eugene H. Highest court cost. *National Review* 44(5):36-38 (March 16, 1992).
Robbins, Ira P. Cry of "wolfish" in the federal courts: the future of federal judicial intervention in prison administration. *Journal of Criminal Law and Criminology* 71(3):211-225 (Fall 1980).

1354. Tinker v. Des Moines Independent Community School District   February 24, 1969
393 US 503   21 LEd2d 731   89 SCt 733
    Abortion Pol (Rubin) 132
    Am Educators 575
    Brennan 86-90
    Const Law 139-143R+
    Courage 231-252, 427
    En Am Con 608-612, 1843-1844, 1899
    First 3-9+
    May It 121-135R
    Sup Ct Review (1984):169-236
    Super 736-737
Abrams, Marc. Don't mess with the student press. *American School Board Journal* 181(9):32-35 (September 1994).
Bernstein, Sidney. Supreme Court review. *Trial* 21(4):14-15 (April 1985).
Brewster, Todd, and Temma Ehrenfeld. First and foremost. *Life* 14 (13 Special Issue):60-66 (Fall 1991).
Christopher, Maura. Decide seven Court cases that test teenagers' rights. *Scholastic Update* (Teachers' Edition) 120(1):16-18+ (September 4, 1987).
Eberlein, Larry. The teacher in the courtroom: new role expectation? *Clearing House* 53(6):287-291 (February 1980).
Eskin, Leah. Student journalists fight for free expression. *Scholastic Update* 122(1):19-21 (September 8, 1989).
Fields, Cheryl M. Supreme Court backs official who censored school newspaper, skirts issue at colleges. *Chronicle of Higher Education* 34(19):A1, A22 (January 20, 1988).
The flag and freedom of speech. *America* 161(1):3 (July 1-8, 1989).
Flygare, Thomas J. De jure: is Tinker dead? *Phi Delta Kappan* 68(2):165-166 (October 1986).
Fraser, Laura. Fallout from Hazelwood. *Columbia Journalism Review* 27(1):8-9 (May/June 1988).
Gluckman, Ivan B. Separating myth from reality. *NASSP Bulletin* 69(485):60-66 (December 1985).

Grant, Gerald. Children's rights and adult confusions. *Public Interest* (69):83-99 (Fall 1982).

Greenawalt, Kent. Free speech in the United States and Canada. *Law and Contemporary Problems* 55(1):5-33 (Winter 1992).

Hafen, Bruce C. School-backed student activities: what the courts say. *Education Digest* 54(1):29-31 (September 1988).

James, Bernard. Supreme Court docket: students' speech rights revisited. *Social Education* 52(4):243-245 (April/May 1988).

Lacayo, Richard, and Anne Constable. Stop the student presses: the Supreme Court says educators can censor school newspapers. *Time* 131(4):54 (January 25, 1988).

Lane, Kenneth E., Stanley L. Swartz, Michael D. Richardson, and Dennis W. VanBerkum. You aren't what you wear. *American School Board Journal* 181(3):64-65 (March 1994).

Lawrence, Charise K. Your Constitution: securing your rights. *Scholastic Update* 120(9):11 (January 15, 1988).

Menacker, Julius. Review of Supreme Court reasoning in cases of expression, due process, and equal protection. *Phi Delta Kappan* 63(3):188-190 (November 1981).

Menacker, Julius, Emanuel Hurwitz, and Ward Weldon. Supreme Court attitudes about school discipline compared to attitudes of urban teachers. *Journal of Negro Education* 58(1):92-101 (Winter 1989).

Methvin, Eugene H. The Supreme Court: justice in the balance. *Reader's Digest* 125(751):96-101 (November 1984).

Olson, Tod. Mary Beth Tinker. *Scholastic Update* 126(2):19-20 (September 17, 1993).

Rabban, David M. A functional analysis of "individual" and "institutional" academic freedom under the First Amendment. *Law and Contemporary Problems* 53(3):227-301 (Summer 1990).

Rose, Lowell C. 'Reasonableness'—the High Court's new standard for cases involving student rights. *Phi Delta Kappan* 69(8):589-592 (April 1988).

Schimmel, David. How the Tinker decision has affected student rights. *Education Digest* 46(2):40-43 (October 1980).

Seligmann, Jean, and Tessa Namuth. A limit on the student press. *Newsweek* 111(4):60 (January 25, 1988).

Sendor, Benjamin. A court affirms the rights of the student press. *American School Board Journal* 173(12):11 (December 1986).

———. Court to kid: sorry, Matt, you can't say that at a school assembly. *American School Board Journal* 173(10):11, 47 (October 1986).

———. Managing the student press: consider carefully before you unsheathe the censor's scissors. *American School Board Journal* 175(4):24-25 (April 1988).

Sparks, Richard K. Before you bring back school dress codes, recognize that the courts frown upon attempts to "restrict" students' rights. *American School Board Journal* 170(7):24-25 (July 1983).

Student newspapers: teachers' delight. *Economist* 306(7534):20-21 (January 23-29, 1988).

Van Alstyne, William W. Academic freedom and the First Amendment in the Supreme Court of the United States: an unhurried historical review. *Law and Contemporary Problems* 53(3):79-154 (Summer 1990).

Visser, Steve. Students and free speech: a civics lesson at Hazelwood East. *Nation* 245(13):441-442 (October 24, 1987).

1355. Allen v. State Board of Elections   March 3, 1969
     Coupled with Fairley v. Patterson
     Coupled with Bunton v. Patterson
     Coupled with Whitley v. Williams
393 US 544   22 LEd2d 1   89 SCt 817

Davis, Olethia. Tenuous interpretation: Sections 2 and 5 of the Voting Rights Act. *National Civic Review* 84(4):310-322 (Fall/Winter 1995).

Zimmerman, Joseph F. Election systems and representative democracy: reflections on the Voting Rights Act of 1965. *National Civic Review* 84(4):287-309 (Fall/Winter 1995).

1356. Citizens Publishing Co. v. United States   March 10, 1969
394 US 131   22 LEd2d 148   89 SCt 927

Parks, Michael. Fold or combine: it's a matter of dollars. *Advertising Age* 53(30):M-30 - M-33 (July 19, 1982).

1357. Alderman v. United States   March 10, 1969
        Coupled with Ivanov v. United States
        Coupled with Butenko v. United States
    394 US 165   22 LEd2d 176   89 SCt 961
     En Am Con 40-41, 1628-1635
     Super 741-752
   Goldsmith, Michael. The Supreme Court and Title III: rewriting the law of electronic surveillance. *Journal of Criminal Law and Criminology* 74(1):1-171 (Spring 1983).

1358. Kaufman v. United States   March 24, 1969
    394 US 217   22 LEd2d 227   89 SCt 1068
     Super 747-749

1359. Orozco v. Texas   March 25, 1969
    394 US 324   22 LEd2d 311   89 SCt 1095
     En Am Con 1264-1256, 1350
   Jacobs, Robert. The state of Miranda: the effects of the Quarles decision. *Trial* 21(1):44-48 (January 1985).

1360. Hadnott v. Amos   March 25, 1969
    394 US 358   22 LEd2d 336   89 SCt 1101
   Davis, Olethia. Tenuous interpretation: Sections 2 and 5 of the Voting Rights Act. *National Civic Review* 84(4):310-322 (Fall/Winter 1995).

1361. Fortner Enterprises, Inc. v. United States Steel Corp.   April 7, 1969
    394 US 495   22 LEd2d 495   89 SCt 1252
     Sup Ct Review 69-148
   Werner, Ray O. Marketing and the United States Supreme Court, 1975-1981. *Journal of Marketing* 46(2):73-81 (Spring 1982).

1362. Kirkpatrick v. Preisler   April 7, 1969
        Coupled with Heinkel v. Preisler
    394 US 526   22 LEd2d 519   89 SCt 1225
     En Am Con 616-617, 1518-1524
     Guide (CQ) 50
     Sup Ct Review (1986):175-257
   Public Affairs Council of Louisiana. Reapportionment for the 1980s: good faith and court decisions. *National Civic Review* 70(11):575-582 (December 1981).

1363. Wells v. Rockefeller   April 7, 1969
    394 US 542   22 LEd2d 535   89 SCt 1234
     Sup Ct Review (1986):175-257
     Super 752-753
   Public Affairs Council of Louisiana. Reapportionment for the 1980s: good faith and court decisions. *National Civic Review* 70(11):575-582 (December 1981).

1364. Stanley v. Georgia   April 7, 1969
    394 US 557   22 LEd2d 542   89 SCt 1243
     Const Law 276-280R+
     En Am Con 1335-1337, 1724
     Fourth 93-97
     Liberty 621-622, 657-659+
     Sup Ct Review (1987):303-344
     Sup Ct Yearbook (1989-90):65
     Thurgood 279-284R+

Cooper, Phillip J. The Supreme Court, the First Amendment, and freedom of information. *Public Administration Review* 46(6):622-628 (November/December 1986).

Fields, Howard. Supreme Court, 6-3, bans possession of child porn. *Publishers' Weekly* 237(18):10 (May 4, 1990).

Grey, Thomas C. Eros, civilization and the Burger Court. *Law and Contemporary Problems* 43(3):83-100 (Summer 1980).

Kobylka, Joseph F. A court-created context for group litigation: libertarian groups and obscenity. *Journal of Politics* 49(4):1061-1078 (November 1987).

McCoy, Frank. Justice Thurgood Marshall lays down his gavel. *Black Enterprise* 22(2):13 (September 1991).

1365. Street v. New York   April 21, 1969
     394 US 576   22 LEd2d 572   89 SCt 1354
          Almanac (1989):309-311, 313
          Jerry 227-228
          Sup Ct Review (1990):69-103
          Super 732-734

Garbus, Martin. Supreme Court retreat?: The 'crime' of flag burning. *Nation* 248(11):369-370 (March 20, 1989).

Rehnquist, William H. The United States Supreme Court: dissent. *Congressional Digest* 68(8-9):197, 199, 201 (August/September 1989).

Winter, Ralph K. Political financing and the Constitution. *Annals of the American Academy of Political and Social Science* 486:34-48 (July 1986).

1366. Shapiro v. Thompson   April 21, 1969
          Coupled with Washington v. Legrant
          Coupled with Reynolds v. Smith
     394 US 618   22 LEd2d 600   89 SCt 1322
          Ascent 282-286+
          Brennan 285-287
          Burger Court 47-50 53, 57
          Const (Currie) 425-429
          Const Law 526-529R+
          Court Const 308-311
          En Am Con 596-600, 1593-1596, 1674-1675
          Sup Ct Review (1982):167-194
          Super 725-732+

Gillers, Stephen. The Warren Court—it still lives. *Nation* 237(7):193, 208-210 (September 17, 1983).

Jensen, Laura S. Subsidies, strings, and the courts: judicial action and conditional federal spending. *Review of Politics* 55(3):491-509 (Summer 1993).

Plater, Zygmunt J. B., and William Lund Norine. Through the looking glass of eminent domain: exploring the "arbitrary and capricious" test and substantive rationality review of governmental decisions. *Boston College Environmental Affairs Law Review* 16(4):661-752 (Summer 1989).

Regan, Richard J. Supreme Court roundup: 1980 term. *Thought* 56(223):491-502 (December 1981).

Schwartz, Herman. Concern for the basic necessities. *Nation* 239(9):299-300 (September 29, 1984).

1367. National Labor Relations Board (NLRB) v. Wyman-Gordon Co.   April 23, 1969
     394 US 759   22 LEd2d 709   89 SCt 1426
          Sup Ct Review (1991):261-301

Funk, William. The exception that approves the rule: FDF variances under the Clean Water Act. *Boston College Environmental Affairs Law Review* 13(1):1-60 (Fall 1985).

1368. Leary v. United States   May 19, 1969
     395 US 6   23 LEd2d 57   89 SCt 1532
          En Am Con 1131-1132
          Landmark (v. 5):77-99R

Caginalp, O. A. Fifth Amendment privilege against self-incrimination and compulsory self-disclosure under the Clean Air and Clean Water Acts. *Boston College Environmental Affairs Law Review* 9(2):359-395 (1980-1981).

Harris, Leslie J. Constitutional limits on criminal presumptions as an expression of changing concepts of fundamental fairness. *Journal of Criminal Law and Criminology* 77(2):308-357 (Summer 1986).

Regan, Richard J. Regulating cult activities: the limits of religious freedom. *Thought* 61(241):185-196 (June 1986).

1369. United States v. Montgomery County Board of Education   June 2, 1969
        Coupled with Carr v. Montgomery County Board of Education
395 US 225   23 LEd2d 263   89 SCt 1670
Russo, Charles J., J. John Harris III, and Rosetta F. Sandidge. Brown v. Board of Education at 40: a legal history of equal educational opportunity in American public education. *Journal of Negro Education* 63(3):297-309 (Summer 1994).

1370. Boykin v. Alabama   June 2, 1969
395 US 238   23 LEd2d 274   89 SCt 1709
        Death Penalty (Tushnet) 45-46
Carr, Pitts, and Luther J. Carroll. Conboy and the plaintiff's antitrust case. *Trial* 20(3):80-82 (March 1984).

1371. Harrington v. California   June 2, 1969
395 US 250   23 LEd2d 284   89 SCt 1726
Goldberg, Steven H. Harmless error: constitutional sneak thief. *Journal of Criminal Law and Criminology* 71(4):421-442 (Winter 1980).

Krit, Jonathan J. Supreme Court review: Sixth Amendment—confrontation and the use of interlocking confessions at joint trial. *Journal of Criminal Law and Criminology* 78(4):937-953 (Winter 1988).

1372. O'Callahan v. Parker, Warden   June 2, 1969
395 US 258   23 LEd2d 291   89 SCt 1683
        En Am Con 1253-1255
        Guide (CQ) 130
        Super 745-747
Ball, Howard. The U.S. Supreme Court's glossing of the Federal Tort Claims Act: statutory construction and veterans' tort actions. *Western Political Quarterly* 41(3):529-552 (September 1988).

1373. Rodrigue v. Aetna Casualty and Surety Co.   June 9, 1969
395 US 352   23 LEd2d 360   89 SCt 1835
Arsenault, Richard J., and Richard W. Beard. Maritime personal injury on foreign waters. *Trial* 20(6):72-76 (June 1984).

Bender, Louis, and Steven Bender. Is the Supreme Court's decision in Baggot retroactive in application? *Journal of Taxation* 60(3):138-144 (March 1984).

1374. Red Lion Broadcasting Co. v. Federal Communications Commission (FCC)   June 9, 1969
        Coupled with United States v. Radio, Television News Directors Association
395 US 367   23 LEd2d 371   89 SCt 1794
        Const Law 215-218R+
        En Am Con 314, 682, 1526
        Fourth 245-248+
        Sup Ct Review (1981):223-262; (1982):195-241, 243-284; (1987):303-344; (1990):105-132;
            (1994):57-128
Barron, Jerome A. Whose First Amendment? *Vital Speeches of the Day* 46(10):313-315 (March 1, 1980).

Cooper, Phillip J. The Supreme Court, the First Amendment, and freedom of information. *Public Administration Review* 46(6):622-628 (November/December 1986).

Devins, Neal. Congress, the FCC, and the search for the public trustee. *Law and Contemporary Problems* 56(4):145-188 (Autumn 1993).

Fischer, Raymond L. The FCC and the Fairness Doctrine. *USA Today* 116(2516):40-42 (May 1988).

Hazlett, Thomas W. The Fairness Doctrine and the First Amendment. *Public Interest* (96):103-116 (Summer 1989).

Powe, L. A., Jr. Mass communications and the First Amendment: an overview. *Law and Contemporary Problems* 55(1):53-76 (Winter 1992).

Winter, Ralph K. Political financing and the Constitution. *Annals of the American Academy of Political and Social Science* 486:34-48 (July 1986).

Zoglin, Richard, and Jay Peterzell. Crying foul over fairness: should the government require that broadcasting be balanced? *Time* 130(1):80-81 (July 6, 1987).

1375. Brandenburg v. Ohio   June 9, 1969
        395 US 444   23 LEd2d 430   89 SCt 1827
        Brennan 153-155
        Const (Currie) 505-510
        Const Law 143-145R+
        En Am Con 145-146, 298-301, 514-516, 555-556, 790-797, 968-970, 1804-1807
        Fighting 367-368
        Fourth 93-97
        Jerry 221-222
        Magic 314-315
        Make 234-248+
        Sup Ct Ind 33+
        Sup Ct Review (1982):285-317; (1994):209-245

Bork, Robert H. What to do about the First Amendment. *Commentary* 99(2):23-29 (February 1995).

Ennis, Bruce J. Protecting individual rights: hate speech and the heckler's veto. *Trial* 27(12):27-30 (December 1991).

Greenawalt, Kent. Free speech in the United States and Canada. *Law and Contemporary Problems* 55(1):5-33 (Winter 1992).

Padgett, Gregory L. Racially-motivated violence and intimidation: inadequate state enforcement and federal civil rights remedies. *Journal of Criminal Law and Criminology* 75(1):103-138 (Spring 1984).

1376. Powell v. McCormack   June 16, 1969
        395 US 486   23 LEd2d 491   89 SCt 1944
        Almanac (1991):13A-14A; (1992):71; (1994):314-315
        En Am Con 1434
        Equal Rights (Kanowitz) 129-133+
        Sup Ct Yearbook (1993-94):294-297; (1994-95):40-43
        Super 757-760+

Bryant, Winston. Is it constitutional for states to limit congressional terms by restricting ballot access? *Congressional Digest* 74(4):104, 106 (April 1995).

Gunther, Gerald. Judicial review. *Society* 24(1):18-23 (November/December 1986).

Robben, Elizabeth J. Is it constitutional for states to limit congressional terms by restricting ballot access? *Congressional Digest* 74(4):105, 107 (April 1995).

1377. National Labor Relations Board (NLRB) v. Gissel Packing Co.   June 16, 1969
          Coupled with Food Store Employees Union, Local No. 347, Amalgamated Meat Cutters and Butchers
                Workermen of North America v. Gissel Packing Co.
          Coupled with Sinclair Co. v. National Labor Relations Board (NLRB)
        395 US 575   23 LEd2d 547   89 SCt 1918
        Sup Ct Review (1994):1-56

1378. Kramer v. Union Free School District, No. 15   June 16, 1969
        395 US 621   23 LEd2d 583   89 SCt 1886
        Const Law 597-599
        En Am Con 616-617, 1109

1379. North Carolina v. Pearce   June 23, 1969
   Coupled with Simpson, Warden v. Rice
 395 US 711   23 LEd2d 656   89 SCt 2072
  Almanac (1986):8A
  Brilliant, Allan S. Supreme Court review: Fifth Amendment—sentence enhancement: rethinking the Pearce prophylactic rule. *Journal of Criminal Law and Criminology* 75(3):716-728 (Fall 1984).
  Erlinder, C. Peter, and David C. Thomas. Prohibiting prosecutorial vindictiveness while protecting prosecutorial discretion: toward a principled resolution of a due process dilemma. *Journal of Criminal Law and Criminology* 76(2):341-438 (Summer 1985).
  Halberstam, Malvina. Towards neutral principles in the administration of criminal justice: a critique of Supreme Court decisions sanctioning the plea bargaining process. *Journal of Criminal Law and Criminology* 73(1):1-49 (Spring 1982).
  Kobayashi, Glenn H. Supreme Court review: Fourteenth Amendment—reexamining judicial vindictiveness. *Journal of Criminal Law and Criminology* 77(3):867-893 (Fall 1986).

1380. Chimel v. California   June 23, 1969
 395 US 752   23 LEd2d 685   89 SCt 2034
  Const Law 342-346R+
  En Am Con 250, 1628-1635, 1636-1637, 1947-1949, 2016-2019
  Bernstein, Sidney, and Michael Eisenstein. 1981 Supreme Court update: the criminal law. *Trial* 17(10):54-60, 85 (October 1981).
  Carter, Jeffrey A. Supreme Court review: Fourth Amendment—of cars, containers and confusion. *Journal of Criminal Law and Criminology* 72(4):1171-1221 (Winter 1981).
  Katz, Lewis R. United States v. Ross: evolving standards for warrantless searches. *Journal of Criminal Law and Criminology* 74(1):172-208 (Spring 1983).
  Misner, Robert L. Justifying searches on the basis of equality of treatment. *Journal of Criminal Law and Criminology* 82(3):547-578 (Fall 1991).
  Sifferlen, Mark J. Supreme Court review: Fourth Amendment—protective sweep doctrine: when does the Fourth Amendment allow police officers to search the home incident to a lawful arrest? *Journal of Criminal Law and Criminology* 81(4):862-882 (Winter 1991).

1381. Benton v. Maryland   June 23, 1969
 395 US 784   23 LEd2d 707   89 SCt 2056
  En Am Con 107-108, 576-578
  Guide (CQ) 51, 288, 339, 384, 565-566, 915

1382. Alexander v. Holmes County Board of Education October 29, 1969
 396 US 19   24 LEd2d 19   90 SCt 29
  En Am Con 41, 44-45, 557-561
  Hyde, Alison A. School desegregation: the role of the courts and means of achievement. *NASSP Bulletin* 78(565):28-37 (November 1994).
  Reid, Herbert O., and Frankie M. Foster-Davis. Three decades of "all deliberate speed." *Crisis* 91(5):12-15 (May 1984).
  Russo, Charles J., J. John Harris III, and Rosetta F. Sandidge. Brown v. Board of Education at 40: a legal history of equal educational opportunity in American public education. *Journal of Negro Education* 63(3):297-309 (Summer 1994).
  Simmons, Althea T. L. From Brown to Grove City: blueprint for education. *Crisis* 91(5):6-10 (May 1984).

1383. Nacirema Operating Co. v. Johnson   December 9, 1969
   Coupled with Traynor v. Johnson
 396 US 212   24 LEd2d 371   90 SCt 347
  Mount, Gregory J. Significant decisions in labor cases. *Monthly Labor Review* 103(3):51-52 (March 1980).

1384. Dowell v. Board of Education of Oklahoma City Public Schools   December 15, 1969
 396 US 269   24 LEd2d 414   90 SCt 415

Hyde, Alison A. School desegregation: the role of the courts and means of achievement. *NASSP Bulletin* 78(565):28-37 (November 1994).

Russo, Charles J., J. John Harris III, and Rosetta F. Sandidge. Brown v. Board of Education at 40: a legal history of equal educational opportunity in American public education. *Journal of Negro Education* 63(3):297-309 (Summer 1994).

1385. Carter v. West Feliciana Parish School Board   January 14, 1970
      Coupled with Singleton v. Jackson Municipal Separate School District
396 US 290   24 LEd2d 477   90 SCt 608
Russo, Charles J., J. John Harris III, and Rosetta F. Sandidge. Brown v. Board of Education at 40: a legal history of equal educational opportunity in American public education. *Journal of Negro Education* 63(3):297-309 (Summer 1994).

1386. Mills v. Electric Auto-Lite Co.   January 20, 1970
396 US 375   24 LEd2d 593   90 SCt 616
Jordan, Scott J. Awarding attorney's fees to environmental plaintiffs under a private attorney general theory. *Boston College Environmental Affairs Law Review* 14(2):287-311 (Winter 1987).
O'Connor, Karen, and Lee Epstein. Bridging the gap between Congress and the Supreme Court: interest groups and the erosion of the American rule governing awards of attorneys' fees. *Western Political Quarterly* 38(2):238-249 (June 1985).

1387. Turner v. United States   January 20, 1970
396 US 398   24 LEd2d 610   90 SCt 642
Harris, Leslie J. Constitutional limits on criminal presumptions as an expression of changing concepts of fundamental fairness. *Journal of Criminal Law and Criminology* 77(2):308-357 (Summer 1986).

1388. Evans v. Abney   January 26, 1970
396 US 435   24 LEd2d 634   90 SCt 628
En Am Con 656-657, 1729-1736

1389. Ross v. Bernhard   February 2, 1970
396 US 531   24 LEd2d 729   90 SCt 733
Hogan, R. Ben, III. The Seventh Amendment: the founders' views. *Trial* 23(9):76, 78, 80, 82 (September 1987).

1390. United States v. Kordel   February 24, 1970
397 US 1   25 LEd2d 1   90 SCt 763
Lupia, Lynnette L. Supreme Court review: Fifth Amendment—admissibility of confession obtained without Miranda warnings in noncustodial setting. *Journal of Criminal Law and Criminology* 75(3):673-691 (Fall 1984).

1391. Hadley v. Junior College District of Metropolitan Kansas City, Missouri   February 25, 1970
397 US 50   25 LEd2d 45   90 SCt 791
Const Law 618-620
Court Public 93-94
Sup Ct Review (1986):175-257
Graham, Barbara Luck. Federal court policy-making and political equality: an analysis of judicial redistricting. *Western Political Quarterly* 44(1):101-117 (March 1991).

1392. Colonnade Catering Corp. v. United States   February 25, 1970
397 US 72   25 LEd2d 60   90 SCt 774
Sup Ct Review (1989)87-163
Andersen, Robert M. Technology, pollution control, and EPA access to commercial property: a constitutional and policy framework. *Boston College Environmental Affairs Law Review* 17(1):1-74 (Fall 1989).
Batey, Robert. Strict construction of firearms offenses: the Supreme Court and the Gun Control Act of 1968. *Law and Contemporary Problems* 49(1):163-198 (Winter 1986).

Roberts, Thomas A. Supreme Court review: Fourth Amendment—warrantless administrative inspections of commercial property. *Journal of Criminal Law and Criminology* 72(4):1222-1245 (Winter 1981).

1393. Pike v. Bruce Church, Inc.   March 2, 1970
      397 US 137   25 LEd2d 174   90 SCt 844
      En Am Con 1751-1755
      Schwartz, Edward B. Water as an article of commerce: state embargoes spring a leak under Sporhase v. Nebraska. *Boston College Environmental Affairs Law Review* 12(1):103-169 (Fall 1985).

1394. Association of Data Processing Service Organizations, Inc. v. Camp   March 3, 1970
      397 US 150   25 LEd2d 184   90 SCt 827
      Ascent 50-52
      Burger Years 191-205
      Sup Ct Review (1981):41-47; (1993):37-64
      Morrison, Alan B. Close reins on the bureaucracy. *Nation* 239(9):290-294 (September 29, 1984).
      Perino, Michael A. Justice Scalia: standing, environmental law, and the Supreme Court. *Boston College Environmental Affairs Law Review* 15(1):135-179 (Fall 1987).

1395. Barlow v. Collins   March 3, 1970
      397 US 159   25 LEd2d 192   90 SCt 832
      Ascent 50-52

1396. Northcross v. Board of Education of the Memphis, Tennessee, City Schools   March 9, 1970
      397 US 232   25 LEd2d 246   90 SCt 891
      Russo, Charles J., J. John Harris III, and Rosetta F. Sandidge. Brown v. Board of Education at 40: a legal history of equal educational opportunity in American public education. *Journal of Negro Education* 63(3):297-309 (Summer 1994).

1397. Goldberg v. Kelly   March 23, 1970
      397 US 254   25 LEd2d 287   90 SCt 1011
      Almanac (1990):510-511
      Ascent 379-383, 387-388+
      Brennan 23-42
      Const (Currie) 539-542+
      En Am Con 119, 679-680, 849-850, 1465-1472, 1582-1583, 1704-1705
      Sup Ct Review (1982):85-125; (1987)157-200
      Fuerst, J. S., and Roy Petty. Due process—how much is enough? *Public Interest* (79):96-110 (Spring 1985).
      Groszyk, Walter S., Jr., and Thomas J. Madden. Managing without immunity: the challenge for state and local government officials in the 1980s. *Public Administration Review* 41(2):268-278 (March/April 1981).
      Robbins, Ira P. Cry of "wolfish" in the federal courts: the future of federal judicial intervention in prison administration. *Journal of Criminal Law and Criminology* 71(3):211-225 (Fall 1980).
      Trank, John P. The Burger Court—the first ten years. *Law and Contemporary Problems* 43(3):101-135 (Summer 1980).

1398. United States v. Davis   March 23, 1970
      397 US 301   25 LEd2d 323   90 SCt 1041
      Davenport, Fred B. Redeeming stock from trusts after TEFRA. *Trusts and Estates* 122(12):16-21 (December 1983).

1399. Illinois v. Allen   March 31, 1970
      397 US 337   25 LEd2d 353   90 SCt 1057
      Ascent 339-341

1400. In re Winship   March 31, 1970
      397 US 358   25 LEd2d 368   90 SCt 1068

Ascent 341-346

En Am Con 1090-1093, 1472-1479, 2071

Dennis, Anthony J. Supreme Court review: Fifth Amendment—due process rights at sentencing. *Journal of Criminal Law and Criminology* 77(3):646-665 (Fall 1986).

Harris, Leslie J. Constitutional limits on criminal presumptions as an expression of changing concepts of fundamental fairness. *Journal of Criminal Law and Criminology* 77(2):308-357 (Summer 1986).

1401. Ashe v. Swenson   April 6, 1970
     397 US 436   25 LEd2d 469   90 SCt 1189

     Const Law 453-455R

Lane, James R. Supreme Court review: Fifth Amendment—the covert narrowing of double jeopardy precedent: the Supreme Court's real reason for hearing Schiro v. Farley. *Journal of Criminal Law and Criminology* 85(4):909-935 (Spring 1995).

1402. Dandridge v. Williams   April 6, 1970
     397 US 471   25 LEd2d 491   90 SCt 1153

     Brennan 285-287

     Burger Court 47-49, 51, 56-57

     En Am Con 534-535, 2041-2042

     Hard Choices 309

     Magic 292

Binion, Gayle. The Burger Court and the rights of the poor. *Center Magazine* 15(2):2-7 (March/April 1982).

Schwartz, Herman. Concern for the basic necessities. *Nation* 239(9):299-300 (September 29, 1984).

Wilkinson, J. Harvie, III. The dimensions of American constitutional equality. *Law and Contemporary Problems* 55(1):236-251 (Winter 1992).

1403. Walz v. Tax Commission of New York City   May 4, 1970
     397 US 664   25 LEd2d 697   90 SCt 1409

     Ascent 188-190

     Burger Years 56-91

     Const (Currie) 527-528

     Const Law 76-80+

     En Am Con 854-856, 1538-1545, 1650-1658, 2006

     Godless 66-67, 111-113+

     Original (Davis) 78, 79-81+

     Religion 2-7

     Sup Ct Church 80-94R

     Sup Ct Review (1995):323-391

Byrne, Harry J. Thanksgiving Day and the Supreme Court. *America* 162(5):121-123 (February 10, 1990).

Cord, Robert L. Correcting the record. *National Review* 38(6):42 (April 11, 1986).

Hammond, Phillip E. The courts and secular humanism. *Society* 21(4):11-16 (May/June 1984).

Kelley, Dean M. The Supreme Court redefines tax exemption. *Society* 21(4):23-28 (May/June 1984).

Kobylka, Joseph F. Leadership on the Supreme Court of the United States: Chief Justice Burger and the establishment clause. *Western Political Quarterly* 42(4):545-568 (December 1989).

Lesly, Elizabeth, and Elliott Beard. Pennies from Heaven. *Washington Monthly* 23(4):40-45 (April 1991).

Pfeffer, Leo. Religious exemptions. *Society* 21(4):17-22 (May/June 1984).

Rabkin, Jeremy. Behind the tax-exempt schools debate. *Public Interest* (68):21-38 (Summer 1982).

Redlich, Norman. Some cracks in the wall. *Nation* 239(9):277-280 (September 29, 1984).

Roelofs, H. Mark. Church and state in America: toward a biblically derived reformulation of their relationship. *Review of Politics* 50(4):561-581 (Fall 1988).

Rosen, Jeff. Village people. *New Republic* 210(15):11-12,14 (April 11, 1994).

Taylor, Barry W. Diversion of church funds to personal use: state, federal and private sanctions. *Journal of Criminal Law and Criminology* 73(3):1204-1237 (Fall 1982).

Vile, John R. Bob Jones before the bench. *Christian Century* 100(23):707-711 (August 3-10, 1983).

Weber, Paul J. Excessive entanglement: a wavering First Amendment standard. *Review of Politics* 46(4):483-501 (October 1984).

1404. Rowan dba American Book Service v. United States Post Office   May 4, 1970
     397 US 728   25 LEd2d 736   90 SCt 1484
     Kobylka, Joseph F. A court-created context for group litigation: libertarian groups and obscenity. *Journal of Politics* 49(4):1061-1078 (November 1987).

1405. Brady v. United States   May 4, 1970
     397 US 742   25 LEd2d 747   90 SCt 1463
       Const (Currie) 555-559
       Sup Ct Review (1991):103-142
     Halberstam, Malvina. Towards neutral principles in the administration of criminal justice: a critique of Supreme Court decisions sanctioning the plea bargaining process. *Journal of Criminal Law and Criminology* 73(1):1-49 (Spring 1982).
     Schultz, Marjorie S. Jury defined: a review of Burger court decisions. *Law and Contemporary Problems* 43(4):8-23 (Autumn 1980).

1406. McMann v. Richardson   May 4, 1970
     397 US 759   25 LEd2d 763   90 SCt 1441
       En Am Con 809-810
       Sup Ct Review (1984):309-358
     Halberstam, Malvina. Towards neutral principles in the administration of criminal justice: a critique of Supreme Court decisions sanctioning the plea bargaining process. *Journal of Criminal Law and Criminology* 73(1):1-49 (Spring 1982).

1407. Parker v. North Carolina   May 4, 1970
     397 US 790   25 LEd2d 785   90 SCt 1458
     Halberstam, Malvina. Towards neutral principles in the administration of criminal justice: a critique of Supreme Court decisions sanctioning the plea bargaining process. *Journal of Criminal Law and Criminology* 73(1):1-49 (Spring 1982).

1408. Greenbelt Cooperative Publishing Association v. Bresler   May 18, 1970
     398 US 6   26 LEd2d 6   90 SCt 1537
       Jerry 244-249+
       Sup Ct Review (1994):169-208

1409. Boys Markets, Inc. v. Retail Clerk Union, Local 770   June 1, 1970
     398 US 235   26 LEd2d 199   90 SCt 1583
     Trank, John P. The Burger Court—the first ten years. *Law and Contemporary Problems* 43(3):101-135 (Summer 1980).

1410. Maxwell v. Bishop, Superintendent   June 1, 1970
     398 US 262   26 LEd2d 221   90 SCt 1578
       Death Penalty (Tushnet) 35-40, 163-174R
       Super 738-742

1411. Hellenic Lines, Ltd. v. Rhoditis   June 8, 1970
     398 US 306   26 LEd2d 252   90 SCt 1731
     Arsenault, Richard J., and Richard W. Beard. Maritime personal injury on foreign waters. *Trial* 20(6):72-76 (June 1984).

1412. Welsh v. United States   June 15, 1970
     398 US 333   26 LEd2d 308   90 SCt 1792
       En Am Con 352-353

Godless 59-60

Guide (West) (v. 10):355-357

Demerath, N. J., III, and Rhys H. Williams. A mythical past and uncertain future. *Society* 21(4):3-10 (May/June 1984).

Regan, Richard J. Supreme Court roundup: 1980 term. *Thought* 56(223):491-502 (December 1981).

1413. Moragne v. States Marine Lines, Inc.   June 15, 1970
    398 US 375   26 LEd2d 339   90 SCt 1772

Edelman, Paul S. Wrongful death on the high seas: Tallentire says federal law governs. *Trial* 23(4):58-61 (April 1987).

George, James A. The 'triple crown' of admiralty cases: from definitions to damages. *Trial* 27(10):46-53 (October 1991).

1414. Chambers v. Maroney, Superintendent   June 22, 1970
    399 US 42   26 LEd2d 419   90 SCt 1975
     En Am Con 226, 1628-1635
     Guide (CQ) 544

1415. Baldwin v. New York   June 22, 1970
    399 US 66   26 LEd2d 437   90 SCt 1886
     En Am Con 97, 1913-1920

1416. Williams v. Florida   June 22, 1970
    399 US 78   26 LEd2d 446   90 SCt 1893
     En Am Con 592, 1085-1086, 1086-1088, 1913-1920, 2065

Bersoff, Donald N. Social science data and the Supreme Court: Lockhart as a case in point. *American Psychologist* 42(1):52-58 (January 1987).

Goldberg, Steven H. Harmless error: constitutional sneak thief. *Journal of Criminal Law and Criminology* 71(4):421-442 (Winter 1980).

Schultz, Marjorie S. Jury defined: a review of Burger court decisions. *Law and Contemporary Problems* 43(4):8-23 (Autumn 1980).

Trank, John P. The Burger Court—the first ten years. *Law and Contemporary Problems* 43(3):101-135 (Summer 1980).

1417. California v. Green   June 23, 1970
    399 US 149   26 LEd2d 489   90 SCt 1930
     En Am Con 658-661
     Sup Ct Review (1995):277-321

1418. Gunn v. University Committee to End the War in Vietnam   June 29, 1970
    399 US 383   26 LEd2d 684   90 SCt 2013
     Sup Ct Review (1986):317-393
     Super 737-738

1419. North Carolina v. Alford   November 23, 1970
    400 US 25   27 LEd2d 162   91 SCt 160

Halberstam, Malvina. Towards neutral principles in the administration of criminal justice: a critique of Supreme Court decisions sanctioning the plea bargaining process. *Journal of Criminal Law and Criminology* 73(1):1-49 (Spring 1982).

1420. Dutton, Warden v. Evans   December 15, 1970
    400 US 74   27 LEd2d 213   91 SCt 210

Haddad, James B., and Richard G. Agin. A potential revolution in Bruton doctrine: is Bruton applicable where domestic evidence rules prohibit use of a codefendant's confession as evidence against a defendant although the confrontation clause would allow such use? *Journal of Criminal Law and Criminology* 81(2):235-266 (Summer 1990).

1421. Oregon v. Mitchell   December 21, 1970
          Coupled with Texas v. Mitchell
          Coupled with United States v. Arizona
          Coupled with United States v. Idaho
      400 US 112   27 LEd2d 272   91 SCt 260
      Abortion (Frohock) 114
      Abortion Moral 128-139
      Const (Currie) 561-563
      En Am Con 1347-1348, 1928-1929, 1979-1987
      Hard Choices 318-319
      Marshall, Thomas R. Public opinion, representation, and the modern Supreme Court. *American Politics Quarterly* 16(3):296-316 (July 1988).
      Regan, Richard J. Supreme Court roundup: 1981 term. *Thought* 57(227):514-527 (December 1982).
      Solimine, Michael E. Constitutionality of congressional legislation to overrule Zurcher v. Stanford daily. *Journal of Criminal Law and Criminology* 71(2):147-162 (Summer 1980).

1422. Wyman v. James   January 12, 1971
      400 US 309   27 LEd2d 408   91 SCt 381
      Burger Court 50-52, 94-95+
      En Am Con 1947-1949, 2078
      Rosen, Jeff. Sentimental journey. *New Republic* 210(18):13-14, 16 (May 2, 1994).

1423. Perkins v. Matthews, Mayor   January 14, 1971
      400 US 379   27 LEd2d 476   91 SCt 431
      Davis, Olethia. Tenuous interpretation: Sections 2 and 5 of the Voting Rights Act. *National Civic Review* 84(4):310-322 (Fall/Winter 1995).
      Zimmerman, Joseph F. Election systems and representative democracy: reflections on the Voting Rights Act of 1965. *National Civic Review* 84(4):287-309 (Fall/Winter 1995).

1424. Kennerly v. District Court of Ninth Judicial District of Montana   January 18, 1971
      400 US 423   27 LEd2d 507   91 SCt 480
      Am Indians (Wilkinson) 38, 125+

1425. Phillips v. Martin Marietta Corp.   January 25, 1971
      400 US 542   27 LEd2d 613   91 SCt 496
      Magic 329-330
      Hogan, Joyce, and Ann M. Quigley. Physical standards for employment and the courts. *American Psychologist* 41(11):1193-1217 (November 1986).

1426. Massachusetts v. Laird   November 9, 1970
      400 US 886   27 LEd2d 130   91 SCt 128
      En Am Con 1223-1224

1427. Baird v. State Bar of Arizona   February 23, 1971
      Baird v. Arizona State Bar
      401 US 1   27 LEd2d 639   91 SCt 702
      Baird, Peter D., Oyez, oyez, oyez. *American Heritage* 45(7):32-37 (November 1994).

1428. Younger v. Harris   February 23, 1971
      401 US 37   27 LEd2d 669   91 SCt 746
      Almanac (1986):17A
      En Am Con 2085

Guide (CQ) 52-53
Super 755-757

Rowe, Thomas D. No final victories: the incompleteness of equity's triumph in federal public law. *Law and Contemporary Problems* 56(3):105-121 (Summer 1993).

Welsh, Robert, and Ronald K. L. Collins. Taking state constitutions seriously: the protection of civil liberties has been shifting away from the U.S. Supreme Court. *Center Magazine* 14(5):6-35, 38-43 (September/October 1981).

Wise, Charles, and Rosemary O'Leary. Is federalism dead or alive in the Supreme Court?: implications for public administrators. *Public Administration Review* 52(6):559-572 (November/December 1992).

1429. Dyson, Chief of Police of Dallas v. Stein   February 23, 1971
     401 US 200   27 LEd2d 781   91 SCt 769

     Kobylka, Joseph F. A court-created context for group litigation: libertarian groups and obscenity. *Journal of Politics* 49(4):1061-1078 (November 1987).

1430. Harris v. New York   February 24, 1971
     401 US 222   28 LEd 2d 1   91 SCt 643
       Burger Court 82-86
       Burger Years 143-168
       En Am Con 662-665, 905, 1264-1265, 1400-1408
       Guide (CQ) 52-53

     Farber, Daniel A. Supreme Court review: from Warren to Rehnquist. *Trial* 25(7):124-126 (July 1989).

     Gruhl, John. State supreme courts and the U.S. Supreme Court's post-Miranda rulings. *Journal of Criminal Law and Criminology* 72(3):886-913 (Fall 1981).

     Hartman, Marshall J., and Sidney Bernstein. To Leon, and beyond; two commentators react. *Trial* 21(1):50-56 (January 1985).

     Mosk, Stanley. The emerging agenda in state constitutional rights law. *Annals of the American Academy of Political and Social Science* 496:54-64 (March 1988).

1431. Time, Inc. v. Pape   February 24, 1971
     401 US 279   28 LEd2d 45   91 SCt 633
       Sup Ct Review (1994):169-208

1432. Ocala Star-Banner Co. v. Damron   February 24, 1971
     401 US 295   28 LEd2d 57   91 SCt 628
       Price 259-265

1433. Boddie v. Connecticut   March 2, 1971
     401 US 371   28 LEd2d 113   91 SCt 780
       En Am Con 132, 572, 2041-2042

     Binion, Gayle. The Burger court and the rights of the poor. *Center Magazine* 15(2):2-7 (March/April 1982).

1434. Citizens to Preserve Overton Park, Inc.   March 2, 1971
     v. Volpe, Secretary, Department of Transportation
     401 US 402   28 LEd2d 136   91 SCt 814
       Burger Years 191-205

     Baer, Susan D. The public trust doctrine—a tool to make federal administrative agencies increase protection of public land and its resources. *Boston College Environmental Affairs Law Review* 15(2):385-436 (Winter 1988).

     Case, Charles D. Problems in judicial review arising from the use of computer models and other quantitative methodologies in environmental decisionsmaking. *Boston College Environmental Affairs Law Review* 10(2):251-364 (September 1982).

     Glicksman, Robert, and Christopher H. Schroeder. EPA and the courts: twenty years of law and politics. *Law and Contemporary Problems* 54(4):249-309 (Autumn 1991).

Hassler, Gregory L., and Karen O'Connor. Woodsy witchdoctors versus judicial guerrillas: the role and impact of competing interest groups in environmental litigation. *Boston College Environmental Affairs Law Review* 13(4):487-520 (Summer 1986).

Kelly, Paula. Judicial review of agency decisions under the National Environmental Policy Act of 1969—Strycker's Bay Neighborhood Council, Inc. v. Karlen. *Boston College Environmental Affairs Law Review* 10(1):79-109 (1982-83).

Morrison, Alan B. Close reins on the bureaucracy. *Nation* 239(9):290-294 (September 29, 1984).

Shea, Thomas E. The judicial standard for review of environmental impact statement threshold decisions. *Boston College Environmental Affairs Law Review* 9(1):63-101 (1980-1981).

1435. Griggs v. Duke Power Co.   March 8, 1971
      401 US 424   28 LEd2d 158   91 SCt 849

Affirmative (Greene) 63-71, 168-170
Affirmative (Woods) 66-68
Almanac (1989):316-317; (1991):251-261; (1994):298-299
Burger Court 114, 120-124, 145-147
Burger Years 95-108
Conflict 41-43
Culture 130-141
En Am Con 284-287, 870
Sup Ct Review (1984):1-68; (1989):1-51

Baer, Judith A. Women's rights and the limits of constitutional doctrine. *Western Political Quarterly* 44(4):821-852 (December 1991).

Bersoff, Donald N. In the Supreme Court of the United States: Clara Watson v. Fort Worth Bank & Trust. *American Psychologist* 43(12):1019-1028 (December 1988).

———. Should subjective employment devices be scrutinized? It's elementary, my dear Ms. Watson. *American Psychologist* 43(12):1016-1018 (December 1988).

Blits, Jan H., and Linda S. Gottfredson. Equality or lasting inequality? *Society* 27(3):4-11 (March/April 1990).

Burns, Haywood. The activism in not affirmative. *Nation* 239(9):264-268 (September 29, 1984).

Canon, Bradley C. The Supreme Court as a cheerleader in politico-moral disputes. *Journal of Politics* 54(3):637-653 (August 1992).

Chambers, Julius L., and Barry Goldstein. Title VII: the continuing challenge of establishing fair employment practices. *Law and Contemporary Problems* 49(4):9-23 (Autumn 1986).

The Civil Rights Act of 1990. *Congressional Digest* 69(8-9):196-224 (August/September 1990).

Eastland, Terry. Toward a real restoration of civil rights: reverse discrimination *Commentary* 88(5):25-29 (November 1989).

Farber, Daniel A. Supreme Court review: proving discrimination in Title VII cases. *Trial* 25(8):15-18 (August 1989).

Fein, Bruce. A court that obeys the law. *National Review* 41(18):50-51 (September 29, 1989).

Frederickson, H. George. Public administration and social equity. *Public Administration Review* 50(2):228-237 (March/April 1990).

Gest, Ted. Seniority vs. minorities—impact of Court ruling. *U.S. News and World Report* 96(25):22-23 (June 25, 1984).

Gray, Mary W. The halls of ivy and the halls of justice: resisting sex discrimination against faculty women. *Academe* 71(5):33-41 September/October 1985).

Hogan, Joyce, and Ann M. Quigley. Physical standards for employment and the courts. *American Psychologist* 41(11):1193-1217 (November 1986).

Hood, Stafford, and Laurence Parker. Minorities, teacher testing, and recent U.S. Supreme Court holdings: a regressive step. *Teachers College Record* 92(4):603-618 (Summer 1991).

Katz, Stanley N. The strange birth and unlikely history of constitutional equality. *Journal of American History* 75(3):747-762 (December 1988).

Kohl, John P., and David B. Stephens. Wanted: recruitment advertising that doesn't discriminate. *Personnel* 66(2):18-26 (February 1989).

Marshall, Thurgood. The Supreme Court and civil rights: has the tide turned? *USA Today* 118(2538):19-20 (March 1990).

McFeeley, Neil D. Weber versus affirmative action? *Personnel* 57(1):38-51 (January/February 1980).

Morehead, Jere W., and Peter J. Shedd. Civil rights and affirmative action: revolution or fine-tuning? *Business Horizons* 33(5):53-60 (September/October 1990).

Nalbandian, John. The U.S. Supreme Court's "consensus" on affirmative action. *Public Administration Review* 49(1):38-45 (January/February 1989).

Orenstein, Morton H. Equal opportunity: the balance changes. *Across the Board* 27(4):57-59 (April 1990).

Reid-Dove, Allyson, and Michael E. Howard. "Night has fallen on the Court . . ." *Black Enterprise* 20(2):44-45 (September 1989).

Roberts, Paul Craig. Takings by the bureaucracy: the economy, and legal and property rights. *Vital Speeches* 58(24):744-751 (October 1, 1992).

Ross, Patrick C. Are quotas making a comeback? *Personnel Journal* 69(9):42-44 (September 1990).

Scalise, David G., and Daniel J. Smith. Legal update: when are job requirements discriminatory? *Personnel* 63(3):41-48 (March 1986).

Seligman, Daniel, and David C. Kaufman. The all-purpose suit. *Fortune* 132(12):235 (December 11, 1995).

Sherwood, O. Peter. Court innocence. *Society* 27(3):24-25 (March/April 1990).

Simpson, Peggy. Constitutional crisis. *Ms.* 18(3):90-98 (September 1989).

Taylor, William L., and Susan M. Liss. Affirmative action in the 1990s: staying the course. *Annals of the American Academy of Political and Social Science* 523:30-37 (September 1992).

Vile, John R., and Kathy Ruth McCoy. The Memphis Case: another precedent? *Personnel* 62(7):72-76 (July 1985).

Zall, Milton. What to expect from the Civil Rights Act. *Personnel Journal* 71(3):46-50 (March 1992).

1436. Gillette v. United States   March 8, 1971
          Coupled with Negre v. Larsen (See record 1437)
      401 US 437   28 LEd2d 168   91 SCt 828
      Documents (v. 2):753-756R
      En Am Con 352-353, 1538-1545
      Godless 60

      Regan, Richard J. Supreme Court roundup: 1980 term. *Thought* 56(223):491-502 (December 1981).
      ————. Supreme Court roundup: 1984 term. *Thought* 61(241):290-302 (June 1986).
      Vile, John R. Bob Jones before the bench. *Christian Century* 100(23):707-711 (August 3-10, 1983).

1437. Negre v. Larsen   March 8, 1971
          Decided with Gillette v. United States (See record 1436)
      401 US 437   28 LEd2d 168   91 SCt 828
      En Am Con 730-738
      Cox, Archibald. First Amendment. *Society* 24(1):8-15 (November/December 1986).

1438. United States v. District Court in and for County of Eagle   March 24, 1971
      401 US 520   28 LEd2d 278   91 SCt 998
      Am Indian (Deloria) 197-220

1439. Labine v. Vincent   March 29, 1971
      401 US 532   28 LEd2d 288   91 SCt 1017
      Ascent 243-244, 246-247
      Drinan, Robert F. The Supreme Court and Scarsdale's crèche. *America* 151(18):377-380 (December 8, 1984).

1440. United States v. Freed   April 5, 1971
      401 US 601   28 LEd2d 356   91 SCt 1112
      Batey, Robert. Strict construction of firearms offenses: the Supreme Court and the Gun Control Act of 1968. *Law and Contemporary Problems* 49(1):163-198 (Winter 1986).

      Goldberg, Andrew M. Corporate officer liability for federal environmental statute violations. *Boston College Environmental Affairs Law Review* 18(2):357-379 (Winter 1991).

      Webber, Rebecca S. Element analysis applied to environmental crimes: what did they know and when did they know it? *Boston College Environmental Affairs Law Review* 16(1):53-93 (Fall 1988).

1441. Investment Company Institute (ICI) v. Camp   April 5, 1971
      Coupled with National Association of Securities Dealers, Inc. v. Securities Exchange Commission (SEC)
      401 US 617   28 LEd2d 367   91 SCt 1091
      Lybecker, Martin E. Investor protection, competition and capital allocation. *Trusts and Estates* 120(4):18-22
      (April 1981).

1442. United States v. United States Coin and Currency   April 5, 1971
      401 US 715   28 LEd2d 434
                                                                                       91 SCt 1041
      En Am Con 1202-1203

1443. United States v. White   April 5, 1971
      401 US 745   28 LEd2d 453   91 SCt 1122
      En Am Con 1628-1635, 2054-2055
      Dripps, Donald A. Supreme Court review: Justice White and the rights of the accused. *Trial* 29(5):71-74 (May
      1993).

1444. Swann v. Charlotte-Mecklenburg Board of Education   April 20, 1971
      402 US 1   28 LEd2d 554   91 SCt 1267
         Am Educators 556
         Ascent 14-16, 256-265, 403-404+
         Behind Bakke 29-32+
         Brennan 249-255+
         Burger Court 114-117
         Burger Years 95-108
         Civil 20th 3, 8, 95-122R
         Const (Currie) 477-482
         Const Law 544-550R+
         Court Const 263-266
         Court Public 99-102, 111-121R
         Documents (v. 2):756-760R
         En Am Con 557-561, 1040-1043, 1507-1508, 1625-1626, 1839-1840
         Guide (CQ) 52-53
         Magic 326-327
         New Right (Schwartz) 141-145, 152-154+
         New Right (Whitaker) 142-168
         Sup Ct Ind 242-243
      American survey: Burger leaves the labyrinth. *Economist* 300(7454):17-22 (July 12-18, 1986).
      Burns, Haywood. The activism in not affirmative. *Nation* 239(9):264-268 (September 29, 1984).
      Camper, Diane, Ethel Payne, Nathaniel R. Jones, Charles Ogletree, Charles and Julius L. Chambers. To form a
      more perfect union. *Black Enterprise* 17(12):11, 51-66 (July 1987).
      Canon, Bradley C. The Supreme Court as a cheerleader in politico-moral disputes. *Journal of Politics*
      54(3):637-653 (August 1992).
      Christopher, Maura. Decide seven Court cases that test teenagers' rights. *Scholastic Update* (Teachers' Edition)
      120(1):16-18+ (September 4, 1987).
      Clayton, Marian. Desegregating America's public schools. *Crisis* 91(5):20-21 (May 1984).
      Cook, Stuart W. The 1954 social science statement and school desegregation: a reply to Gerard. *American
      Psychologist* 39(8):819-832 (August 1984).
      Evolution of court policy. *Congressional Digest* 59(2):39 (February 1981).
      Evolution of the present controversy. *Congressional Digest* 61(5):134-135, 160 (May 1982).
      Frederickson, H. George. Public administration and social equity. *Public Administration Review* 50(2):228-237
      (March/April 1990).
      Gest, Ted. Courts: a major battleground of social upheaval. *U.S. News and World Report* 98(3):48-50 (January
      28, 1985).
      Gordon, William M. The implementation of desegregation plans since Brown. *Journal of Negro Education*
      63(3):310-322 (Summer 1994).

Hyde, Alison A. School desegregation: the role of the courts and means of achievement. *NASSP Bulletin* 78(565):28-37 (November 1994).

Lamb, Charles M. Legal foundations of civil rights and pluralism America. *Annals of the American Academy of Political and Social Science* 454:13-25 (March 1981).

Landsberg, Brian K. The federal government and the promise of Brown. *Teachers College Record* 96(4):627-636 (Summer 1995).

McDowell, Gary L. Modest remedy for judicial activism. *Public Interest* (67):3-20 (Spring 1982).

Pohlhaus, J. Francis. Fundamental shift seen for high court. *Crisis* 88(1):34-37 (January/February 1981).

Reid, Herbert O., Sr. State of the art: the law and education since 1954. *Journal of Negro Education* 52(3):234-249 (Summer 1983).

Reid, Herbert O., and Frankie M. Foster-Davis. Three decades of "all deliberate speed." *Crisis* 91(5):12-15 (May 1984).

Russo, Charles J., J. John Harris III, and Rosetta F. Sandidge. Brown v. Board of Education at 40: a legal history of equal educational opportunity in American public education. *Journal of Negro Education* 63(3):297-309 (Summer 1994).

Simmons, Althea T. L. From Brown to Grove City: blueprint for education. *Crisis* 91(5):6-10 (May 1984).

Timberlake, Constance H. A historical perspective of school desegregation. *Crisis* 91(5):26-29 (1984).

Trank, John P. The Burger Court—the first ten years. *Law and Contemporary Problems* 43(3):101-135 (Summer 1980).

1445. Davis v. Board of School Commissioners of Mobile County   April 20, 1971
402 US 33   28 LEd2d 577   91 SCt 1289

Gordon, William M. The implementation of desegregation plans since Brown. *Journal of Negro Education* 63(3):310-322 (Summer 1994).

Russo, Charles J., J. John Harris III, and Rosetta F. Sandidge. Brown v. Board of Education at 40: a legal history of equal educational opportunity in American public education. *Journal of Negro Education* 63(3):297-309 (Summer 1994).

1446. McDaniel v. Barresi   April 20, 1971
402 US 39   28 LEd2d 582   91 SCt 1287

Russo, Charles J., J. John Harris III, and Rosetta F. Sandidge. Brown v. Board of Education at 40: a legal history of equal educational opportunity in American public education. *Journal of Negro Education* 63(3):297-309 (Summer 1994).

1447. North Carolina State Board of Education v. Swann   April 20, 1971
402 US 43   28 LEd2d 586   91 SCt 1284

Russo, Charles J., J. John Harris III, and Rosetta F. Sandidge. Brown v. Board of Education at 40: a legal history of equal educational opportunity in American public education. *Journal of Negro Education* 63(3):297-309 (Summer 1994).

1448. United States v. Vuitch   April 21, 1971
402 US 62   28 LEd2d 601   91 SCt 1294
Abortion Am 15-16, 20, 23+
Abortion Con 90, 97-99, 117
Abortion Pol (Rubin) 43-45, 54
Abortion Quest 94-95
Hard Choices 136-137
Liberty 328-388, 417-418, 468-480, 488-491, 493-495+

1449. James v. Valtierra   April 26, 1971
   Coupled with Shaffer v. Valtierra
402 US 137   28 LEd2d 678   91 SCt 1331
En Am Con 1010

Binion, Gayle. The Burger court and the rights of the poor. *Center Magazine* 15(2):2-7 (March/April 1982).

1450. Perez v. United States   April 26, 1971
       402 US 146   28 LEd2d 686   91 SCt 1357
            En Am Con 1126-1130, 1379

Binion, Gayle. An assessment of Potter Stewart. *Center Magazine* 14(5):2-5 (September/October 1981).

O'Brien, David M. Federalism as a metaphor in the constitutional politics of public administration. *Public Administration Review* 49(5):411-419 (September/October 1989).

Solimine, Michael E. Constitutionality of congressional legislation to overrule Zurcher v. Stanford daily. *Journal of Criminal Law and Criminology* 71(2):147-162 (Summer 1980).

1451. McGautha v. California   May 3, 1971
            Coupled with Crampton v. Ohio
       402 US 183   28 LEd2d 711   91 SCt 1454
            Const (Currie) 547-550
            Court Public 237
            Death Penalty (Bedau) 247-253, 268-270.
            Death Penalty (Tushnet) 40-44, 62, 175-183R
            Death Penalty 80s 44-46
            En Am Con 201-206, 207-209
            Equal (Baldus) 10-14, 22-24+
            Sup Ct Review (1983):305-395

Bilionis, Louis D. Moral appropriateness, capital punishment, and the Lockett doctrine. *Journal of Criminal Law and Criminology* 82(2):283-333 (Summer 1991).

Cho, Susie. Capital confusion: the effect of jury instructions on the decision to impose death. *Journal of Criminal Law and Criminology* 85(2):532-561 (Fall 1994).

Dripps, Donald A. Supreme Court review: Justice White and the rights of the accused. *Trial* 29(5):71-74 (May 1993).

Schwartz, Charles Walter. Eighth Amendment proportionality analysis and the compelling case of William Rummel. *Journal of Criminal Law and Criminology* 71(4):378-420 (Winter 1980).

1452. Organization for a Better Austin v. Keefe   May 17, 1971
       402 US 415   29 LEd2d 1   91 SCt 1575
            Sup Ct Review (1994):129-168

1453. California v. Byers   May 17, 1971
       402 US 424   29 LEd2d 9   91 SCt 1535

Caginalp, O. A. Fifth Amendment privilege against self-incrimination and compulsory self-disclosure under the Clean Air and Clean Water Acts. *Boston College Environmental Affairs Law Review* 9(2):359-395 (1980-1981).

1454. United States v. International Minerals and Chemical Corp.   June 1, 1971
       402 US 558   29 LEd2d 178   91 SCt 169

Goldberg, Andrew M. Corporate officer liability for federal environmental statute violations. *Boston College Environmental Affairs Law Review* 18(2):357-379 (Winter 1991).

Webber, Rebecca S. Element analysis applied to environmental crimes: what did they know and when did they know it? *Boston College Environmental Affairs Law Review* 16(1):53-93 (Fall 1988).

1455. Nelson, Warden v. O'Neil   June 1, 1971
       402 US 622   29 LEd2d 222   91 SCt 1723
            Sup Ct Review (1995):277-321

1456. Cohen v. California   June 7, 1971
       403 US 15   29 LEd2d 284   91 SCt 1780
            Const Law 163-168R+
            En Am Con 304-305, 1843-1844
            First 305-310

Freedom (Cox) 49-52

Jerry 223-224+

Make 234-248

Sup Ct Review (1985):149-178; (1990):69-103; (1991):1-46

Kommers, Donald P. Liberalism and the Supreme Court: review essay. *Review of Politics* 49(1):112-125 (Winter 1987).

McGuire, Kevin T. Obscenity, libertarian values, and decision making in the Supreme Court. *American Politics Quarterly* 18(1):47-67 (January 1990).

McGuire, Kevin T., and Gregory A. Caldeira. Lawyers, organized interests, and the law of obscenity: agenda setting in the Supreme Court. *American Political Science Review* 87(3):717-726 (September 1993).

Winter, Ralph K. Political financing and the Constitution. *Annals of the American Academy of Political and Social Science* 486:34-48 (July 1986).

1457. Rosenbloom v. Metromedia, Inc.   June 7, 1971

403 US 29   29 LEd2d 296   91 SCt 1811

    Ascent 182-185

    Const Law 255-259, 261

    En Am Con 1157-1159

    Make 183-199+

Gertz, Elmer. Gertz on Gertz: reflections on the landmark libel case. *Trial* 21(10):66-69, 71-75 (October 1985).

Gruhl, John. Supreme Court's impact on the law of libel: compliance by lower federal courts. *Western Political Quarterly* 33(4):502-519 (December 1980).

Hale, F. Dennis. Constitutional libel protection narrowed—not destroyed. *Trial* 17(7):54-58, 79 (July 1981).

Helle, Steven. Judging public interest in libel: the Gertz decision's contribution. *Journalism Quarterly* 61(1):117-124 (Spring 1984).

Howard, A. E. Dick. The press in court. *Wilson Quarterly* 6(5):86-93 (Special Issue 1982).

Hughes, Robert L. Rationalizing libel law in wake of Gertz: the problem and a proposal. *Journalism Quarterly* 62(3):540-547, 566 (Autumn 1985).

Kebbel, Gary. The different functions of speech in defamation and privacy cases. *Journalism Quarterly* 61(3):629-633, 743 (Autumn 1984).

1458. Griffin v. Breckenridge   June 7, 1971

403 US 88   29 LEd2d 338   91 SCt 1790

    En Am Con 868, 1729-1736

    Guide (CQ) 154

    Sup Ct Review (1993):199-243

    Sup Ct Yearbook (1992-93):83

Padgett, Gregory L. Racially-motivated violence and intimidation: inadequate state enforcement and federal civil rights remedies. *Journal of Criminal Law and Criminology* 75(1):103-138 (Spring 1984).

Shepherd, William. Legal protection for freedom of religion. *Center Magazine* 15(2):30-37 (March/April 1982).

1459. Ely v. Klahr   June 7, 1971

403 US 108   29 LEd2d 352   91 SCt 1803

Public Affairs Council of Louisiana. Reapportionment for the 1980s: good faith and court decisions. *National Civic Review* 70(11):575-582 (December 1981).

1460. Whitcomb, Governor of Indiana v. Chavis   June 7, 1971

403 US 124   29 LEd2d 363   91 SCt 1858

    Sup Ct Review (1986):175-257

Neighbor, Howard D. The Supreme Court speaks, sort of, on the 1982 Voting Rights Act Amendments. *National Civic Review* 75(6):346-353 (November/December 1986).

Public Affairs Council of Louisiana. Reapportionment for the 1980s: good faith and court decisions. *National Civic Review* 70(11):575-582 (December 1981).

Scope of enforcement. *Congressional Digest* 60(12):296-297 (December 1981).

1461. Abate v. Mundt   June 7, 1971
       403 US 182   29 LEd2d 399   91 SCt 1904
           Sup Ct Review (1986):175-257
       Public Affairs Council of Louisiana. Reapportionment for the 1980s: good faith and court decisions. *National
           Civic Review* 70(11):575-582 (December 1981).

1462. Palmer v. Thompson, Mayor   June 14, 1971
       403 US 217   29 LEd2d 438   91 SCt 1940
           Ascent 16-17
           Burger Years 95-108
           En Am Con 1136-1143, 1361, 1729-1736
           May It 291-304R
       Baer, Judith A. Women's rights and the limits of constitutional doctrine. *Western Political Quarterly* 44(4):821-
           852 (December 1991).
       Burns, Haywood. The activism in not affirmative. *Nation* 239(9):264-268 (September 29, 1984).

1463. Commissioner of Internal Revenue v. Lincoln Savings and Loan Association   June 14, 1971
       403 US 345   29 LEd2d 519   91 SCt 1893
       Hume, Evelyn C., and Ernest R. Larkins. Takeover expenses: national starch and the IRS add new wrinkles.
           Journal of Accountancy 174(2):87-93 (August 1992).
       Saunders, Laura. The agents run riot. *Forbes* 150(11):144 (November 9, 1992).

1464. Graham, Commissioner v. Richardson   June 14, 1971
              Coupled with Sailor v. Leger
       403 US 365   29 LEd2d 534   91 SCt 1848
           Brennan 270-276
           Const (Currie) 500-504
           En Am Con 858
       Rosen, Jeffrey. The war on immigrants: why the courts can't save us. *New Republic* 212(5):22, 24-26 (January
           30, 1995).

1465. Bivens v. Six Unknown Named Agents of Federal Bureau of Narcotics   June 21, 1971
       403 US 388   29 LEd2d 619   91 SCt 1999
           En Am Con 119-120, 533-534
           Sup Ct Yearbook (1993-94):101
       Askin, Frank. Justice denied: what the conservative judiciary hath wrought. *Trial* 29(10):65-68 (October 1993).
       Ball, Howard. The U.S. Supreme Court's glossing of the Federal Tort Claims Act: statutory construction and
           veterans' tort actions. *Western Political Quarterly* 41(3):529-552 (September 1988).
       Hartman, Marshall J., and Sidney Bernstein. To Leon, and beyond; two commentators react. *Trial* 21(1):50-56
           (January 1985).
       Neuborne, Burt. Taking away the right to sue. *Nation* 239(9):268-271 (September 29, 1984).
       Rosenbloom, David H. Public administrators' official immunity and the Supreme Court: developments during
           the 1970s. *Public Administration Review* 40(2):166-173 (March/April 1980).
       Rowe, Thomas D. No final victories: the incompleteness of equity's triumph in federal public law. *Law and
           Contemporary Problems* 56(3):105-121 (Summer 1993).

1466. Coolidge v. New Hampshire   June 21, 1971
       403 US 443   29 LEd2d 564   91 SCt 2022
           En Am Con 502, 1393, 1628-1635, 1637-1638
       Bernstein, Sidney, and Michael Eisenstein. 1982 Supreme Court update: the criminal law. *Trial* 18(9):45-50, 81
           (September 1982).
       Bernstein, Sidney. Supreme Court review. *Trial* 19(10):26, 28 (October 1983).
       Garvey, Denise P. Supreme court review: Fourth Amendment—nonexistent home arrest entries. *Journal of
           Criminal Law and Criminology* 71(4):518-528 (Winter 1980).

Hall, Richard J. Supreme Court review: Fourth Amendment—eliminating the inadvertent discovery requirement for seizures under the plain view doctrine. *Journal of Criminal Law and Criminology* 81(4):819-840 (Winter 1991).

MacIntosh, Susanne M. Supreme Court review: Fourth Amendment—the plain touch exception to the warrant requirement. *Journal of Criminal Law and Criminology* 84(4):743-768 (Winter/Spring 1994).

Romero, Elsie. Supreme Court review: Fourth Amendment—requiring probable cause for searches and seizures under the plain view doctrine. *Journal of Criminal Law and Criminology* 78(4):763-791 (Winter 1988).

1467. McKeiver v. Pennsylvania   June 21, 1971
           Coupled with In re Burns
      403 US 528   29 LEd2d 647   91 SCt 1976
           En Am Con 1090-1093, 1238, 1913-1920

Feld, Barry C. The juvenile court meets the principle of the offense: legislative changes in juvenile waiver statutes. *Journal of Criminal Law and Criminology* 78(3):471-533 (Fall 1987).

Schultz, Marjorie S. Jury defined: a review of Burger Court decisions. *Law and Contemporary Problems* 43(4):8-23 (Autumn 1980).

1468. Lemon v. Kurtzman,   June 28, 1971
      Superintendent of Public Instruction of the Commonwealth of Pennsylvania
           Coupled with Earley v. DiCenso
           Coupled with Robinson v. DiCenso
      403 US 602   29 LEd2d 745   91 SCt 2105
           Almanac (1992):326
           Am Educators 323
           Ascent 189-194+
           Burger Years 56-91
           Const (Currie) 528-535
           Const Law 80-85R+
           Court Const 206-210
           En Am Con 854-856, 1155-1156, 1650-1658
           First 170-174
           Godless 66-67, 72, 136-139+
           Original (Davis) 79-81, 111-116, 156-162+
           Religion 26-45+
           Sup Ct Church 94-113R
           Sup Ct Review (1985):1-59; (1992):123-153; (1995):323-391
           Sup Ct Yearbook (1991-92):24-25; (1992-93):79; (1993-94):49-52

Abram, Morris B. Is "strict separation" too strict? *Public Interest* (82):81-90 (Winter 1986).

Arledge, Paula C., and Edward V. Heck. A freshman justice confronts the Constitution: Justice O'Connor and the First Amendment. *Western Political Quarterly* 45(3):761-772 (September 1992).

Baer, Judith A. Women's rights and the limits of constitutional doctrine. *Western Political Quarterly* 44(4):821-852 (December 1991).

Baron, Mark A., and Harold L. Bishop. Come one, come all. *American School Board Journal* 178(3):29-30 (March 1991).

Bates, Stephen. Ignore a menorah. *New Republic* 201(5):14-16 (July 31, 1989).

Bork, Robert H. What to do about the First Amendment. *Commentary* 99(2):23-29 (February 1995).

Buzzard, Lynn Robert, and Samuel Ericsson. Public aid to private schools: Caesar rendering to God? *Christianity Today* 27(10):20-23 (June 17, 1983).

Cerne, Kathleen M. Honor thy creditors? the religious debtor's constitutional conflict with Section 1325(b). *Business Credit* 96(3):37-40 (March 1994).

Chemerinsky, Erwin. Supreme Court review: free speech or religious freedom: revisiting the establishment clause. *Trial* 31(12):16-19 (December 1995).

———. Supreme Court review: religion clause doctrine: potential for change. *Trial* 29(2):81-84 (February 1993).

Church-state separation case to be heard. *Christian Century* 111(1):8-9 (January 5-12, 1994).

Conn, James J. Graduation prayers and the establishment clause. *America* 167(15):380-382 (November 14, 1992).

Cooke, Ronald J. The religious schools controversy. *America* 172(5):17-19 (February 18, 1995).

Cord, Robert L. Church, state, and the Rehnquist Court. *National Review* 44(16):35-37 (August 17, 1992).

Coughlin, John J. Religion, education and the First Amendment. *America* 168(17):12-15 (May 15, 1993).

The Court and the crib. *America* 150(10):182 (March 17, 1984).

Court decision on prayer. *Christian Century* 109(21):641 (July 1-8, 1992).

Court ruling favors deaf student. *Christian Century* 110(20):666-667 (June 30-July 7, 1993).

Court rulings on religion. *Christian Century* 110(19):624-625 (June 16-23, 1993).

Demerath, N. J., III, and Rhys H. Williams. A mythical past and uncertain future. *Society* 21(4):3-10 (May/June 1984).

Ferranti, Jennifer. Time to strip the lemon Pledge? *Christianity Today* 39(1):47, 49 (January 9, 1995).

Flygare, Thomas J. De jure: Supreme Court permits state tax deductions for nonpublic schools. *Phi Delta Kappan* 65(1):63-64 (September 1983).

Ford, Maurice deG. Christmas creche in July: an exchange of views. *Commonweal* 111(13):386, 412-414 (July 13, 1984).

Freid, Stephen H. The constitutionality of choice under the Establishment Clause. *Clearing House* 66(2):92-95 (November/December 1992).

Gibbs, Nancy R., David Aikman, and Richard N. Ostling. America's holy war. *Time* 138(23):60-68 (December 9, 1991).

Kilpatrick, James J. What in God's name is going on? *National Review* 37(2):36, 38-39 (February 8, 1985).

Kobylka, Joseph F. Leadership on the Supreme Court of the United States: Chief Justice Burger and the Establishment Clause. *Western Political Quarterly* 42(4):545-568 (December 1989).

Lawton, Kim A. Uncle Sam v. First Church. *Christianity Today* 35(11):38-41 (October 7, 1991).

Lesly, Elizabeth, and Elliott Beard. Pennies from Heaven. *Washington Monthly* 23(4):40-45 (April 1991).

Loconte, Joe. Will Court reshape church-state test? *Christianity Today* 38(6):50 (May 16, 1994).

McBride, James. Tillich in an Alice-in-Wonderland world. [Editorial] *Christian Century* 104(18):519-520 (June 3-10, 1987).

McCarthy, Martha M. Much ado over graduation prayer. *Phi Delta Kappan* 75(2):120-125 (October 1993).

McConnell, Michael. Why 'separation' is not the key to church-state relations. *Christian Century* 106(2):43-47 (January 18, 1989).

Monagle, Katie. What place for God? *Scholastic Update* (Teachers' Edition) 124(5):17-18 (November 1, 1991).

Ostling, Richard, Anne Constable, and Michael P. Harris. Threatening the wall: church-state separation has powerful new critics. *Time* 130(1):70-71 (July 6, 1987).

Ostling, Richard N., and Jeff Hooten. Is there a place for God in school? *Time* 143(15):60-61 (April 11, 1994).

Prayer in public schools. *Congressional Digest* 74(1):3-32 (January 1995).

Rayer, Thomas A. The bicentennial and church-related schools. *America* 157(17):427-429, 438 (December 5, 1987).

Redlich, Norman. Some cracks in the wall. *Nation* 239(9):277-280 (September 29, 1984).

Regan, Richard J. Regulating cult activities: the limits of religious freedom. *Thought* 61(241):185-196 (June 1986).

———. Supreme Court roundup: 1982 term. *Thought* 58(231):472-483 (December 1983).

———. Supreme Court roundup: 1983 term. *Thought* 60(236):99-111 (March 1985).

———. Supreme Court roundup: 1986 term. *Thought* 63(251):429-441 (December 1988).

Rosen, Jeffrey. Lemon law. *New Republic* 208(13):17-18 (March 29, 1993).

School prayer. *Christian Century* 108(13):424-425 (April 17, 1991).

Schwartz, Michael. A new direction for the courts on the school question. *America* 149(13):251-254 (October 29, 1983).

Scrap the 'Lemon test,' say Southern Baptists. *Christian Century* 111(7):219-220 (March 2, 1994).

Sendor, Benjamin. Time for a primer on commencement prayer. *American School Board Journal* 182(7):16-17 (July 1995).

———. To pray or not to pray? *American School Board Journal* 180(4):20-21 (April 1993).

———. When it comes to coercion, context is all. *American School Board Journal* 181(6):14-15 (June 1994).

Serrill, Michael S., and Anne Constable. Rebuilding Jefferson's wall: the Court recesses after an unexpected turn in church-state cases. *Time* 126(2):73 (July 15, 1985).

Spring, Beth. U.S. Supreme Court nullifies Alabama school prayer law. *Christianity Today* 29(10):52 (July 12, 1985).

Stephenson, D. Grier, Jr. Religion and the Constitution: the Supreme Court speaks, again. *USA Today* 18(2538):21-23 (March 1990).

Sullivan, Catherine Beth. Are kosher food laws constitutionally kosher? *Boston College Environmental Affairs Law Review* 21(1):201-245 (Fall 1993).

Supreme Court: Twixt church and state. *Economist* 296(7401):29-30 (July 6, 1985).

Taylor, Barry W. Diversion of church funds to personal use: state, federal and private sanctions. *Journal of Criminal Law and Criminology* 73(3):1204-1237 (Fall 1982).

Vacca, Richard S., and H. C. Hudgins, Jr. Pomp and controversy. *American School Board Journal* 181(5):29-32 (May 1994).

Weber, Paul J. Excessive entanglement: a wavering First Amendment standard. *Review of Politics* 46(4):483-501 (October 1984).

Williams, Charles F. Supreme Court docket: Court orders equal access for Bible club. *Social Education* 54(5):261 (September 1990).

Young, Roy E. Religious liberty on campus. *Commonweal* 109(7):209-210 (April 9, 1982).

Zirkel, Perry A., and Ivan B. Gluckman. Invocations and benedictions at school ceremonies. *NASSP Bulletin* 76(547):102-105 (November 1992).

1469. Tilton v. Richardson, Secretary of Department of Health, Education and Welfare   June 28, 1971
      403 US 672   29 LEd2d 790   91 SCt 2091
      Ascent 191-194
      Burger Years 56-91
      En Am Con 854-856, 1650-1658
      Godless 79-80
      Religion 53-58
      Sup Ct Church 271-273

Abram, Morris B. Is "strict separation" too strict? *Public Interest* (82):81-90 (Winter 1986).

Buzzard, Lynn Robert, and Samuel Ericsson. Public aid to private schools: Caesar rendering to God? *Christianity Today* 27(10):20-23 (June 17, 1983).

Franke, Ann H., and Jacqueline W. Mintz. Four trends in higher education law. *Academe* 73(5):57-63 (September/October 1987).

From Tilton to Ewing: some major higher-education decisions of the Burger court. *Chronicle of Higher Education* 32(17):10 (June 25, 1986).

Manion, Maureen. The impact of state aid on sectarian higher education: The case of New York State. *Review of Politics* 48(2): 264-288 (Spring 1986).

McBride, James. A decision entangling church and state. [Editorial] *Christian Century* 105(25):756-758 (August 31-September 7, 1988).

Rayer, Thomas A. The bicentennial and church-related schools. *America* 157(17):427-429, 438 (December 5, 1987).

Regan, Richard J. Supreme Court roundup: 1980 term. *Thought* 56(223):491-502 (December 1981).

————. Supreme Court roundup: 1981 term. *Thought* 57(227):514-527 (December 1982).

————. Supreme Court roundup: 1986 term. *Thought* 63(251):429-441 (December 1988).

Taylor, Barry W. Diversion of church funds to personal use: state, federal and private sanctions. *Journal of Criminal Law and Criminology* 73(3):1204-1237 (Fall 1982).

Van Alstyne, William W. Academic freedom and the First Amendment in the Supreme Court of the United States: an unhurried historical review. *Law and Contemporary Problems* 53(3):79-154 (Summer 1990).

Weber, Paul J. Excessive entanglement: a wavering First Amendment standard. *Review of Politics* 46(4):483-501 (October 1984).

1470. Muhammad Ali v. United States   June 28, 1971
      Cassius Clay v. United States
      403 US 698   29 LEd2d 810   91 SCt 2068
      Landmark (v. 4):159-166R

1471. New York Times Co. v. United States   June 30, 1971
           Coupled with United States v. Washington Post Co.
       403 US 713   29 LEd2d 822   91 SCt 2140
           Ascent 158-162
           Burger Court 11-12, 28-30, 201
           Burger Years 50-55
           Const (Currie) 505-510
           Const (Friendly) 64-65
           Const Law 195-206R
           Court Const 226-232
           Court Public 315-316
           Documents (v. 2):760-764R
           En Am Con 790-797, 797-804, 1313-1315, 1453-1456
           First 191-199+
           Fourth 97-105+
           Landmark (v. 1):69-87R
           Magic 315-317
           Make 90-102
           May It 167-180R
           Minnesota 172-179
           Sup Ct Ind 60-63
           Without 300-343+

       Boylan, James. How free is the press? *Columbia Journalism Review* 26(3):27-32 (September/October 1987).
       Dee, Juliet. Legal confrontations between press, ex-CIA agents and the government. *Journalism Quarterly* 66(2):418-426 (Summer 1989).
       Dripps, Donald A. Supreme Court review: Warren Burger in perspective. *Trial* 31(8):73-75 (August 1995).
       Ferguson, James R. Scientific freedom, national security, and the First Amendment. *Science* 221(4611):620-624 (August 12, 1983).
       Halperin, Morton H. Never question the president. *Nation* 239(9):285-288 (September 29, 1984).
       Howard, A. E. Dick. The press in court. *Wilson Quarterly* 6(5):86-93 (Special Issue 1982).
       Kaplan, David A. Still stopping the press. *Newsweek* 126(14):76 (October 2, 1995).
       The legacy of the Burger Court. *U.S. News and World Report* 100(25):22 (June 30, 1986).
       Lewin, Nathan. High court hexes free speech. *New Republic* 182(12):18-21 (March 22, 1980).
       McGuire, Kevin T. Obscenity, libertarian values, and decision making in the Supreme Court. *American Politics Quarterly* 18(1):47-67 (January 1990).
       Songer, Donald R., and Reginald S. Sheehan. Supreme Court impact on compliance and outcomes: Miranda and New York Times in the United States Courts of Appeals. *Western Political Quarterly* 43(2):297-316 (June 1990).
       Stein, M.L. Judge advises newspapers; Supreme Court may not be so "hospitable" this time. *Editor and Publisher* 120(11):22, 48 (March 14, 1987).
       Trank, John P. The Burger Court—the first ten years. *Law and Contemporary Problems* 43(3):101-135 (Summer 1980).
       Winter, Ralph K. Political financing and the Constitution. *Annals of the American Academy of Political and Social Science* 486:34-48 (July 1986).

1472. Reed v. Reed   November 22, 1971
       404 US 71   30 LEd2d 225   92 SCt 251
           Abortion Pol (Rubin) 85-86, 164
           Ascent 221-227
           Brennan 294-302+
           Burger Court 133-135
           Burger Years 109-124
           Const (Currie) 493-500
           Const Law 502-504R+, 507-510, 543
           En Am Con 1666-1673

Equal (Harrell) 105-107, 112

Magic 329-330

Aliotta, Jilda M. The unfinished feminist agenda: the shifting forum. *Annals of the American Academy of Political and Social Science* 515:140-150 (May 1991).

Baer, Judith A. Women's rights and the limits of constitutional doctrine. *Western Political Quarterly* 44(4):821-852 (December 1991).

Barnum, David G. The Supreme Court and public opinion: judicial decision making in the post-New Deal period. *Journal of Politics* 47(2): 652-666 (May 1985).

Binion, Gayle. The case for an Equal Rights Act. *Center Magazine* 16(6):2-7 (November/December 1983).

Katz, Stanley N. The strange birth and unlikely history of constitutional equality. *Journal of American History* 75(3):747-762 (December 1988).

Lamb, Charles M. Legal foundations of civil rights and pluralism America. *Annals of the American Academy of Political and Social Science* 454:13-25 (March 1981).

Segal, Jeffrey A., and Cheryl D. Reedy. The Supreme Court and sex discrimination: the role of the solicitor general. *Western Political Quarterly* 41(3):553-568 (September 1988).

Williams, Wendy W., and Judith L. Lichtman. Closing the law's gender gap. *Nation* 239(9):280-285 (September 29, 1984).

1473. Chevron Oil Co. v. Huson   December 6, 1971
404 US 97   30 LEd2d 296   92 SCt 349

Bender, Louis, and Steven Bender. Is the Supreme Court's decision in Baggot retroactive in application? *Journal of Taxation* 60(3):138-144 (March 1984).

Ervin, James M., Jr., and Giddings, Katherine E. Supreme Court distinguishes remedy and retroactivity issues affecting state taxes. *Journal of Taxation* 73(5):296-302 (November 1990).

1474. United States v. Marion   December 20, 1971
404 US 307   30 LEd2d 468   92 SCt 455

Const Law 416-417

En Am Con 1717-1718

Bernstein, Sidney, and Michael Eisenstein. 1982 Supreme Court update: the criminal law, part two. *Trial* 18(10):58-65 (October 1982).

Moore, Cathy E. Supreme Court review: Sixth Amendment—limited protection against excessive prosecutorial delay. *Journal of Criminal Law and Criminology* 73(4):1491-1506 (Winter 1982).

1475. United States v. Bass   December 20, 1971
404 US 336   30 LEd2d 488   92 SCt 515

Batey, Robert. Strict construction of firearms offenses: the Supreme Court and the Gun Control Act of 1968. *Law and Contemporary Problems* 49(1):163-198 (Winter 1986).

1476. Diffenderfer v. Central Baptist Church of Miami, Florida   January 10, 1972
404 US 412   30 LEd2d 567   92 SCt 574

Pfeffer, Leo. Religious exemptions. *Society* 21(4):17-22 (May/June 1984).

1477. United States v. Tucker   January 11, 1972
404 US 443   30 LEd2d 592   92 SCt 589

Feld, Barry C. The right to counsel in juvenile court: an empirical study of when lawyers appear and the difference they make. *Journal of Criminal Law and Criminology* 79(4):1185-1346 (Winter 1989).

1478. Federal Power Commission (FPC) v. Florida Power and Light Co.   January 12, 1972
404 US 453   30 LEd2d 600   92 SCt 637

Martin, Stanley A. Problems with PURPA: the need for state legislation to encourage cogeneration and small power production. *Boston College Environmental Affairs Law Review* 11(1):149-202 (October 1983).

1479. Haines v. Kerner   January 13, 1972
404 US 519   30 LEd2d 652   92 SCt 594

Burger Years 177-188

1480. United States v. Christian Echoes National Ministry, Inc.   January 24, 1972
      404 US 561   30 LEd2d 716   92 SCt 663
         Godless 117-119

1481. Lindsey v. Normet   February 23, 1972
      405 US 56   31 LEd2d 36   92 SCt 862
      Binion, Gayle. The Burger court and the rights of the poor. *Center Magazine* 15(2):2-7 (March/April 1982).
      Schwartz, Herman. Concern for the basic necessities. *Nation* 239(9):299-300 (September 29, 1984).

1482. Papachristou v. City of Jacksonville   February 24, 1972
      405 US 156   31 LEd2d 110   92 SCt 839
         En Am Con 1954-1955
      Batey, Robert. Strict construction of firearms offenses: the Supreme Court and the Gun Control Act of 1968.
         Law and Contemporary Problems 49(1):163-198 (Winter 1986).
      Horowitz, Carl F. Inventing homelessness. *National Review* 44(17):48-52 (August 31, 1992).
      Walking tall in California: the Supreme Court overturns the state's vagrancy law. *Time* 121(20):86 (May 16,
         1983).

1483. Federal Trade Commission (FTC) v. Sperry & Hutchinson Co.   March 1, 1972
      405 US 233   31 LEd2d 170   92 SCt 898
      Cohen, Dorothy. Unfairness in advertising revisited. *Journal of Marketing* 46(1):73-80 (Winter 1982).

1484. Hawaii v. Standard Oil Co. of California   March 1, 1972
      405 US 251   31 LEd2d 184   92 SCt 885
      Grady, Kevin T. Commonwealth of Puerto Rico v. SS Zoe Colocotroni: state actions for damage to non-
         commercial living natural resources. *Boston College Environmental Affairs Law Review* 9(2):397-429 (1980-
         1981).

1485. Cruz v. Beto, Corrections Director   March 20, 1972
      405 US 319   31 LEd2d 263   92 SCt 1079
         En Am Con 1538-1545
         Religion 159-163

1486. Dunn, Governor v. Blumstein   March 21, 1972
      405 US 330   31 LEd2d 274   92 SCt 995
         Const Law 602-605R+
         En Am Con 592
      Plater, Zygmunt J. B., and William Lund Norine. Through the looking glass of eminent domain: exploring the
         "arbitrary and capricious" test and substantive rationality review of governmental decisions. *Boston College
         Environmental Affairs Law Review* 16(4):661-752 (Summer 1989).

1487. Commissioner of Internal Revenue v. First Security Bank of Utah, N.A.   March 21, 1972
      405 US 394   31 LEd2d 318   92 SCt 1085
      Aland, Robert H. Can IRS use Section 482 to allocate income which cannot be earned under applicable law?
         Journal of Taxation 52(4):220-223 (April 1980).
      Anspach, William N., Paul L. Marlin, and Charles J. Muller III. Deferred compensation: a case study of
         purposeful negation of Supreme Court jurisdiction over income tax laws. *Taxes* 59(10):691-711 (October
         1981).

1488. Schneble v. Florida   March 21, 1972
      405 US 427   31 LEd2d 340   92 SCt 1056
      Goldberg, Steven H. Harmless error: constitutional sneak thief. *Journal of Criminal Law and Criminology*
         71(4):421-442 (Winter 1980).

1489. Eisenstadt, Sheriff v. Baird   March 22, 1972
    405 US 438   31 LEd2d 349   92 SCt 1029
        Abortion (Frohock) 63
        Abortion Am 8-9+
        Abortion Moral 35-44
        Abortion Pol (Rubin) 70, 78
        Const (Friendly) 202
        Economics 329-331
        En Am Con 615-616, 686-688, 782-789, 1552-1558, 1577-1581, 1796-1803
        Hard Choices 134
        Landmark (v. 5):101-114R
        Law Governing 32-36
        Liberty 517-520, 541-545, 620-624+

    Aliotta, Jilda M. The unfinished feminist agenda: the shifting forum. *Annals of the American Academy of Political and Social Science* 515:140-150 (May 1991).
    Blank, Robert H. Judicial decision making and biological fact: Roe v. Wade and the unresolved question of fetal viability. *Western Political Quarterly* 37(4):584-602 (December 1984).
    Freeman, Alan David, and Elizabeth Mensch. The Court and the sexual revolution. *Commonweal* 121(18):19-23 (October 21, 1994).
    Gillers, Stephen. The Warren Court—it still lives. *Nation* 237(7):193, 208-210 (September 17, 1983).
    Gordon, Sol. Unsung heroes I: Bill Baird. *Humanist* 51(4):43-44 (July/August 1991).
    Grey, Thomas C. Eros, civilization and the Burger Court. *Law and Contemporary Problems* 43(3):83-100 (Summer 1980).
    Kaplan, David A. Is Roe good law? *Newsweek* 119(17):49-51 (April 27, 1992).

1490. United States v. Topco Associates, Inc.   March 29, 1972
    405 US 596   31 LEd2d 515   92 SCt 1126
        Sup Ct Review (1982)319-349

1491. Stanley v. Illinois   April 3, 1972
    405 US 645   31 LEd2d 551   92 SCt 1208
        Burger Court 133-135
        En Am Con 1577-1581
        Hard Choices 309-310

    Minow, Martha. We, the family: constitutional rights and American families. *Journal of American History* 74(3):959-983 (December 1987).

1492. Sierra Club v. Morton   April 19, 1972
    405 US 727   31 LEd2d 636   92 SCt 1361
        En Am Con 1682, 1871-1872

    Alpert, Peter A. Citizen suits under the Clean Air Act: universal standing for the uninjured private attorney general? *Boston College Environmental Affairs Law Review* 16(2):283-328 (Winter 1988).
    Farber, Daniel A. Supreme Court review: the global environment and the Rehnquist Court. *Trial* 28(8):73-77 (August 1992).
    Hassler, Gregory L., and Karen O'Connor. Woodsy witchdoctors versus judicial guerrillas: the role and impact of competing interest groups in environmental litigation. *Boston College Environmental Affairs Law Review* 13(4):487-520 (Summer 1986).

1493. Illinois v. City of Milwaukee, Wisconsin   April 24, 1972
    406 US 91   31 LEd2d 712   92 SCt 1385

    Collins, Michael. The dilemma of the downstream state: the untimely demise of federal common law nuisance. *Boston College Environmental Affairs Law Review* 11(2):295-412 (January 1984).
    Giesser, John L. The National Park Service and external development: addressing park boundary-area threats through public nuisance. *Boston College Environmental Affairs Law Review* 20(4):761-809 (Summer 1993).

1494. Washington v. General Motors Corp.   April 24, 1972
      406 US 109   31 LEd2d 727   92 SCt 1396
      Collins, Michael. The dilemma of the downstream state: the untimely demise of federal common law nuisance. *Boston College Environmental Affairs Law Review* 11(2):295-412 (January 1984).

1495. Weber v. Aetna Casualty and Surety Co.   April 24, 1972
      406 US 164   31 LEd2d 768   92 SCt 1400
      Brennan 282-285

1496. State of Wisconsin v. Yoder   May 15, 1972
      406 US 205   32 LEd2d 15   92 SCt 1526
      Am Indian (Deloria) 221-238
      Burger Court 95-99, 204-205, 230-231
      Const (Currie) 530-531
      Const Law 62-65R
      En Am Con 608-612, 686-688, 730-738, 1538-1545, 1650-1658, 2072
      Godless 32-33
      May It 93-104R
      Religion 59-62+
      Sup Ct Church 423-445R
      Sup Ct Review (1983):1-31; (1985):1-59; (1992):123-153; (1995):323-391
      Carter, Stephen L. Let us pray. *New Yorker* 70(40):60-74 (December 5, 1994).
      Cort'es, Carlos E., and Van L. Perkins. U.S. Supreme Court decisions on diversity. *Education Digest* 46(6):21-24 (February 1981).
      Cox, Archibald. First Amendment. *Society* 24(1):8-15 (November/December 1986).
      Drinan, Robert F. The Supreme Court and religious freedom. *America* 152(12):254-255 (March 30, 1985).
      Glazer, Nathan. The Constitution and American diversity. *Public Interest* (86):10-21 (Winter 1987).
      Hammond, Phillip E. The courts and secular humanism. *Society* 21(4):11-16 (May/June 1984).
      Ignagni, Jospeh A. U.S. Supreme Court decision-making and the free exercise clause. *Review of Politics* 55(3):511-529 (Summer 1993).
      Lawton, Kim A. Uncle Sam v. First Church. *Christianity Today* 35(11):38-41 (October 7, 1991).
      Minow, Martha. We, the family: constitutional rights and American families. *Journal of American History* 74(3):959-983 (December 1987).
      Neuhaus, Richard John. Church, state, and peyote. *National Review* 42(11):40-42, 44 (June 11, 1990).
      Prayer in public schools. *Congressional Digest* 74(1):3-32 (January 1995).
      Rabkin, Jeremy. The curious case of Kiryas Joel. *Commentary* 98(5):58-61 (November 1994).
      Rayer, Thomas A. The bicentennial and church-related schools. *America* 157(17):427-429, 438 (December 5, 1987).
      Regan, Richard J. Supreme Court roundup: 1980 term. *Thought* 56(223):491-502 (December 1981).
      Rievman, Joshua D. Judicial scrutiny of Native American free exercise rights: Lyng and the decline of the Yoder doctrine. *Boston College Environmental Affairs Law Review* 17(1):169-199 (Fall 1989).
      Roelofs, H. Mark. Church and state in America: toward a biblically derived reformulation of their relationship. *Review of Politics* 50(4):561-581 (Fall 1988).
      Rose, Jonathan. Decide 10 landmark cases that define your rights. *Scholastic Update* 119(1):7-9, 21 (September 8, 1986).
      Rosen, Jeff. Village people. *New Republic* 210(15):11-12, 14 (April 11, 1994).
      Sendor, Benjamin. Advice for lawsuit-weary board members: learn these lessons about labor relations, liquor, and legislative laxity. *American School Board Journal* 170(1):34-35 (January 1983).
      Sherman, Edward F. The role of religion in school curriculum and textbooks. *Academe* 74(1):17-22 (January/February 1988).
      Sullivan, Catherine Beth. Are kosher food laws constitutionally kosher? *Boston College Environmental Affairs Law Review* 21(1):201-245 (Fall 1993).
      Tushnet, Mark. The Constitution of religion. *Review of Politics* 50(4):628-658 (Fall 1988).

1497. National Labor Relations Board (NLRB) v. Burns International Security Services, Inc.   May 15, 1972
  406 US 272   32 LEd2d 61   92 SCt 1571
  Burger Years 220-227

1498. United States v. Biswell   May 15, 1972
  406 US 311   32 LEd2d 87   92 SCt 1593
  Sup Ct Review (1989):87-163

  Andersen, Robert M. Technology, pollution control, and EPA access to commercial property: a constitutional and policy framework. *Boston College Environmental Affairs Law Review* 17(1):1-74 (Fall 1989).

  Batey, Robert. Strict construction of firearms offenses: the Supreme Court and the Gun Control Act of 1968. *Law and Contemporary Problems* 49(1):163-198 (Winter 1986).

  Roberts, Thomas A. Supreme Court review: Fourth Amendment—warrantless administrative inspections of commercial property. *Journal of Criminal Law and Criminology* 72(4):1222-1245 (Winter 1981).

1499. Johnson v. Louisiana   May 22, 1972
  406 US 356   32 LEd2d 152   92 SCt 1620
  Documents (v. 2):769-772R
  En Am Con 1027, 1086-1087

  Schultz, Marjorie S. Jury defined: a review of Burger court decisions. *Law and Contemporary Problems* 43(4):8-23 (Autumn 1980).

1500. Apodaca v. Oregon   May 22, 1972
  406 US 404   32 LEd2d 184   92 SCt 1628
  En Am Con 1027, 1082-1085, 1086-1087

  Goldberg, Steven H. Harmless error: constitutional sneak thief. *Journal of Criminal Law and Criminology* 71(4):421-442 (Winter 1980).

  Schultz, Marjorie S. Jury defined: a review of Burger court decisions. *Law and Contemporary Problems* 43(4):8-23 (Autumn 1980).

  What they say it is: the justices' words instruct the nation, and often address history. *Time* 130(1):44-49 (July 6, 1987).

1501. Kastigar v. United States   May 22, 1972
  406 US 441   32 LEd2d 212   92 SCt 1653
  Almanac (1990):535
  En Am Con 1096-1097, 1569-1577

  Carr, Pitts, and Luther J. Carroll. Conboy and the plaintiff's antitrust case. *Trial* 20(3):80-82 (March 1984).

  Lushing, Peter. Testimonial immunity and the privilege against self-incrimination: a study in isomorphism. *Journal of Criminal Law and Criminology* 73(4):1690-1739 (Winter 1982).

  Staas, John August. Supreme Court review: Fifth Amendment—statutory dilution of the privilege against self-incrimination. *Journal of Criminal Law and Criminology* 71(4):610-621 (Winter 1980).

  White, Welsh S. The psychiatric examination and the Fifth Amendment privilege in capital cases. *Journal of Criminal Law and Criminology* 74(3):943-990 (Fall 1983).

1502. Jefferson v. Hackney, Commissioner   May 30, 1972
  406 US 535   32 LEd2d 285   92 SCt 1724
  Brennan 285-287

1503. Kirby v. Illinois   June 7, 1972
  406 US 682   32 LEd2d 411   92 SCt 1877
  Burger Court 68-72, 90-91
  Burger Years 143-168
  En Am Con 1105, 1167-1168

  Welsh, Robert, and Ronald K. L. Collins. Taking state constitutions seriously: the protection of civil liberties has been shifting away from the U.S. Supreme Court. *Center Magazine* 14(5):6-35, 38-43 (September/October 1981).

1504. Jackson v. Indiana   June 7, 1972
      406 US 715   32 LEd2d 435   92 SCt 1845
        En Am Con 1247-1249

1505. First National City Bank v. Banco Nacional de Cuba   June 7, 1972
      406 US 759   32 LEd2d 466   92 SCt 1808
      Halberstam, Malvina. Sabbatino resurrected: the act of state doctrine in the revised restatement of U.S. foreign relations law. *American Journal of International Law* 79(1):68-91 (January 1985).

1506. Argersinger v. Hamlin, Sheriff   June 12, 1972
      407 US 25   32 LEd2d 530   92 SCt 2006
        Ascent 329-331, 335-336+
        Const Law 408-411+
        En Am Con 71, 683-686, 1266-1267, 1585-1592
        Law (Rembar) 380-382

1507. Fuentes v. Shevin, Attorney General   June 12, 1972
          Coupled with Parham v. Cortese
      407 US 67   32 LEd2d 556   92 SCt 1983
        Sup Ct Review (1988):129-161

1508. Colten v. Kentucky   June 12, 1972
      407 US 104   32 LEd2d 584   92 SCt 1953
      Erlinder, C. Peter, and David C. Thomas. Prohibiting prosecutorial vindictiveness while protecting prosecutorial discretion: toward a principled resolution of a due process dilemma. *Journal of Criminal Law and Criminology* 76(2):341-438 (Summer 1985).

1509. Adams v. Williams   June 12, 1972
      407 US 143   32 LEd2d 612   92 SCt 1921
        En Am Con 1780-1782
      Spitzer, Robert J. Shooting down gun myths. *America* 152(22):468-469 (June 8 1985).

1510. Moose Lodge, No. 107 v. Irvis   June 12, 1972
      407 US 163   32 LEd2d 627   92 SCt 1965
        Brennan 255-257
        Const Law 498-501R
        Court Public 96
        En Am Con 1278
        Sup Ct Review (1988):129-161
      Farber, Daniel A. Supreme Court review: picking the jury. *Trial* 27(8):69-72 (August 1991).
      Trank, John P. The Burger Court—the first ten years. *Law and Contemporary Problems* 43(3):101-135 (Summer 1980).

1511. Flower v. United States   June 12, 1972
      407 US 197   32 LEd2d 653   92 SCt 1842
      Haubner, Michael J. Military search of civilians: a commander's power. *Trial* 22(9):48-54 (September 1986).

1512. Mitchum dba Book Mart v. Foster   June 19, 1972
      407 US 225   32 LEd2d 705   92 SCt 2151
        En Am Con 1269-1270

1513. Flood v. Kuhn   June 19, 1972
      407 US 258   32 LEd2d 728   92 SCt 2099
        Almanac (1995):3-45-46
        Landmark (v. 5):115-134R

Owners 64-66, 69-70+

O'Brien, Richard. Bench player. *Sports Illustrated* 80(15):15-16 (April 18, 1994).

Ward, Geoffrey C., and Ken Burns. Take the money and run. *U.S. News and World Report* 117(9):100 (August 29-September 5, 1994).

1514. United States v. United States District Court for the Eastern District of Michigan   June 19, 1972
407 US 297   32 LEd2d 752   92 SCt 2125
Documents (v. 2):779-782R
En Am Con 491-492, 618-621, 790-797, 1299-1300, 1637-1638, 1706-1710, 1942-1943
Goldsmith, Michael. The Supreme Court and Title III: rewriting the law of electronic surveillance. *Journal of Criminal Law and Criminology* 74(1):1-171 (Spring 1983).

1515. Milton v. Wainwright, Corrections Director   June 22, 1972
407 US 371   33 LEd2d 1   92 SCt 2174
Goldberg, Steven H. Harmless error: constitutional sneak thief. *Journal of Criminal Law and Criminology* 1(4):421-442 (Winter 1980).

1516. Pipefitters Local Union, No. 562 v. United States   June 22, 1972
407 US 385   33 LEd2d 11   92 SCt 2247
Freedom (Cox) 84-86

1517. Wright v. Council of the City of Emporia   June 22, 1972
407 US 451   33 LEd2d 51   92 SCt 2196
Gordon, William M. The implementation of desegregation plans since Brown. *Journal of Negro Education* 63(3):310-322 (Summer 1994).
Russo, Charles J., J. John Harris III, and Rosetta F. Sandidge. Brown v. Board of Education at 40: a legal history of equal educational opportunity in American public education. *Journal of Negro Education* 63(3):297-309 (Summer 1994).
Trank, John P. The Burger Court—the first ten years. *Law and Contemporary Problems* 43(3):101-135 (Summer 1980).

1518. United States v. Scotland Neck City Board of Education   June 22, 1972
      Coupled with Cotton v. Scotland Neck City Board of Education
407 US 484   33 LEd2d 75   92 SCt 2214
Russo, Charles J., J. John Harris III, and Rosetta F. Sandidge. Brown v. Board of Education at 40: a legal history of equal educational opportunity in American public education. *Journal of Negro Education* 63(3):297-309 (Summer 1994).

1519. Barker v. Wingo, Warden   June 22, 1972
407 US 514   33 LEd2d 101   92 SCt 2182
Const Law 417-418
En Am Con 102, 1716-1717
Bernstein, Sidney, and Michael Eisenstein. 1982 Supreme Court update: the criminal law, part two. *Trial* 18(10):58-65 (October 1982).
Bradley, Craig M. The Sixth Amendment lives! a reply to Professor Jonakait. *Journal of Criminal Law and Criminology* 83(3):526-537 (Fall 1992).

1520. Central Hardware Co. v. National Labor Relations Board (NLRB)   June 22, 1972
407 US 539   933 LEd2d 122   92 SCt 2238
Burger Years 220-227

1521. Lloyd Corp. v. Tanner   June 22, 1972
407 US 551   33 LEd2d 131   92 SCt 2219
Ascent 155-157+
Black 115-123

Burger Court 34-37
Documents (v. 2):776-779R
En Am Con 1681
Sup Ct Review (1982):195-241

Mosk, Stanley. The emerging agenda in state constitutional rights law. *Annals of the American Academy of Political and Social Science* 496:54-64 (March 1988).

Trank, John P. The Burger Court—the first ten years. *Law and Contemporary Problems* 43(3):101-135 (Summer 1980).

Welsh, Robert, and Ronald K. L. Collins. Taking state constitutions seriously: the protection of civil liberties has been shifting away from the U.S. Supreme Court. *Center Magazine* 14(5):6-35, 38-43 (September/October 1981).

1522. Laird, Secretary of Defense v. Tatum   June 26, 1972
        408 US 1   33 LEd2d 154   92 SCt 2318
        Brennan 91-99
        En Am Con 1120, 1577-1581

Askin, Frank. Justice denied: what the conservative judiciary hath wrought. *Trial* 29(10):65-68 (October 1993).

Neuborne, Burt. Taking away the right to sue. *Nation* 239(9):268-271 (September 29, 1984).

1523. Gelbard v. United States   June 26, 1972
        Coupled with United States v. Egan
        408 US 41   33 LEd2d 179   92 SCt 2357
        En Am Con 836

Goldsmith, Michael. The Supreme Court and Title III: rewriting the law of electronic surveillance. *Journal of Criminal Law and Criminology* 74(1):1-171 (Spring 1983).

Silver, Stephen E. IRS use of wiretap evidence in civil tax proceedings in doubt despite recent case. *Journal of Taxation* 56(5):300-303 (May 1982).

1524. Police Department of Chicago v. Mosley   June 26, 1972
        408 US 92   33 LEd2d 212   92 SCt 2286
        En Am Con 856-858, 1378-1388, 1399-1400
        Freedom (Cox) 52-56
        Sup Ct Review (1992):29-77

Heath, Robert L., and Richard Alan Nelson. Image and issue advertising: a corporate and public policy perspective. *Journal of Marketing* 49(2):58-68 (Spring 1985).

Winter, Ralph K. Political financing and the Constitution. *Annals of the American Academy of Political and Social Science* 486:34-48 (July 1986).

1525. Grayned v. City of Rockford   June 26, 1972
        408 US 104   33 LEd2d 222   92 SCt 2294
        Sup Ct Review (1992):79-122; (1994):57-128
        Thurgood 285-293R+

Bernstein, Sidney, and Michael Eisenstein. 1982 Supreme Court update: the criminal law, part two. *Trial* 18(10):58-65 (October 1982).

Cohen, Dorothy. Unfairness in advertising revisited. *Journal of Marketing* 46(1):73-80 (Winter 1982).

Mehra, Achal. Iskcon court decisions: setback for proselytizing rights. *Journalism Quarterly* 61(1):109-116 (Spring 1984).

Menacker, Julius. Review of Supreme Court reasoning in cases of expression, due process, and equal protection. *Phi Delta Kappan* 63(3):188-190 (November 1981).

Sendor, Benjamin. This sidewalk dispute led to the courthouse. *American School Board Journal* 177(1):10 (January 1990).

1526. Healy v. James   June 26, 1972
        408 US 169   33 LEd2d 266   92 SCt 2338

From Tilton to Ewing: some major higher-education decisions of the Burger court. *Chronicle of Higher Education* 32(17):10 (June 25, 1986).

Marcy, William R. To protect or not to protect—that is the question. *Social Education* 54(6):364-365 (October 1990).

Van Alstyne, William W. Academic freedom and the First Amendment in the Supreme Court of the United States: an unhurried historical review. *Law and Contemporary Problems* 53(3):79-154 (Summer 1990).

1527. Kois v. Wisconsin   June 26, 1972
        408 US 229   33 LEd2d 312   92 SCt 2245

        Hagle, Timothy M. But do they have to see it to know it? the Supreme Court's obscenity and pornography decisions. *Western Political Quarterly* 44(4):1039-1054 (December 1991).

1528. Furman v. Georgia   June 29, 1972
            Coupled with Jackson v. Georgia
            Coupled with Branch v. Texas
        408 US 238   33 LEd2d 346   92 SCt 2726
        Amending 203-213
        Brennan 215-220
        Burger Years 169-176
        Capital Punish 5-13, 19-28, 87-95+
        Const (Currie) 547-550
        Const Law 439-447+
        Court Public 237-240, 242-266R
        Death Penalty (Bedau) 247-270R+
        Death Penalty (Tushnet) 46-56+, 184-190R
        Death Penalty 80s 5-8, 31-32, 113-117
        Death Penalty 90s 4-7, 22-23, 135-139, 151-147+
        Documents (v. 2):788-792R
        En Am Con 201-206, 206-207
        Equal (Baldus) 1-33+
        Equal (Harrell) 115-116
        Landmark (v. 2):115-132R
        Letting Go 76-96
        Sup Ct Review (1983):305-395
        Thurgood 354-381R+

American survey: Burger leaves the labyrinth. *Economist* 300(7454):17-22 (July 12-18, 1986).

Bernstein, Sidney, and Michael Eisenstein. 1982 Supreme Court update: the criminal law, part two. *Trial* 18(10):58-65 (October 1982).

Bilionis, Louis D. Moral appropriateness, capital punishment, and the Lockett doctrine. *Journal of Criminal Law and Criminology* 82(2):283-333 (Summer 1991).

Binion, Gayle. An assessment of Potter Stewart. *Center Magazine* 14(5):2-5 (September/October 1981).

Bowers, William J. The pervasiveness of arbitrariness and discrimination under post-Furman capital statutes. *Journal of Criminal Law and Criminology* 74(3):1067-1100 (Fall 1983).

Brown, J. Michael. Supreme Court review: Eighth Amendment—capital sentencing instructions. *Journal of Criminal Law and Criminology* 84(4):854-882 (Winter/Spring 1994).

Bynam, Anderson E. Supreme Court review: Eighth and Fourteenth Amendments—the death penalty survives. *Journal of Criminal Law and Criminology* 78(4):1080-1118 (Winter 1988).

Cho, Susie. Capital confusion: the effect of jury instructions on the decision to impose death. *Journal of Criminal Law and Criminology* 85(2):532-561 (Fall 1994).

Death penalty: soldiers out of step. *Economist* 288(7296):27 (July 2-8, 1983).

Ewer, Phyllis A. Supreme court review: Eighth Amendment—the death penalty. *Journal of Criminal Law and Criminology* 71(4):538-546 (Winter 1980).

George, Tracey E., and Lee Epstein. On the nature of Supreme Court decision making. *American Political Science Review* 86(2):323-337 (June 1992).

Gest, Ted. Courts: a major battleground of social upheaval. *U.S. News and World Report* 98(3):48-50 (January 28, 1985).

Lanza-Kaduce, Lonn. Formality, neutrality, and goal-rationality: the legacy of Weber in analyzing legal thought. *Journal of Criminal Law and Criminology* 73(2):533-560 (Summer 1982).

Meltsner, Michael. On death row, the wait is over. *Nation* 239(9):274-277 (September 29, 1984).

Murphy, Cornelius F. The Supreme Court and capital punishment: a new hands-off approach. *USA Today* 121(2574):51-52 (March 1993).

Press, Aric, Susan Agrest, Lucy Howard, and George Raine. To die or not to die. *Newsweek* 102(16):43-45 (October 17, 1983).

Rosenbaum, Ron. A tangled web for the Supreme Court. *New York Times Magazine* (section 6, part 1):60 (March 12, 1989).

Rosenblatt, Roger. The Bill of Rights. *Life* 14(13 Special Issue):9-30 (Fall 1991).

Schwartz, Charles Walter. Eighth Amendment proportionality analysis and the compelling case of William Rummel. *Journal of Criminal Law and Criminology* 71(4):378-420 (Winter 1980).

Trank, John P. The Burger Court—the first ten years. *Law and Contemporary Problems* 43(3):101-135 (Summer 1980).

Vito, Gennaro F., and Thomas J. Keil. Capital sentencing in Kentucky: an analysis of the factors influencing decision making in the post-Gregg period. *Journal of Criminal Law and Criminology* 79(2):483-503 (Summer 1988).

Wellek, Jeffrey Alan. Supreme Court review: Eighth Amendment—trial court may impose death sentence despite jury's recommendation of life imprisonment. *Journal of Criminal Law and Criminology* 75(3):813-838 (Fall 1984).

Wells, Diane. Federal habeas corpus and the death penalty: a need for a return to the principles of Furman. *Journal of Criminal Law and Criminology* 80(2):427-490 (Summer 1989).

What they say it is: the justices' words instruct the nation, and often address history. *Time* 130(1):44-49 (July 6, 1987).

1529. United States v. Brewster   June 29, 1972
        408 US 501   33 LEd2d 507   92 SCt 2531
        En Am Con 154, 1716-1717

1530. Board of Regents of State Colleges v. Roth   June 29, 1972
        408 US 564   33 LEd2d 548   92 SCt 2701
          Ascent 384-386
          Const (Currie) 540-542
          En Am Con 131-132, 1465-1472
          Sup Ct Review (1987):157-200

Davis, Sue. Federalism and property rights: an examination of Justice Rehnquist's legal positivism. *Western Political Quarterly* 39(3):250-264 (June 1986).

From Tilton to Ewing: some major higher-education decisions of the Burger court. *Chronicle of Higher Education* 32(17):10 (June 25, 1986).

Groszyk, Walter S., Jr., and Thomas J. Madden. Managing without immunity: the challenge for state and local government officials in the 1980s. *Public Administration Review* 41(2):268-278 (March/April 1981).

Jacobson, Robert L. Supreme Court, in a 4-4 vote, affirms due-process ruling. *Chronicle of Higher Education* 28(13):21, 25 (May 23, 1984).

Jaegal, Don, and N. Joseph Cayer. Public personnel administration by lawsuit: the impact of Supreme Court decisions on public employee litigiousness. *Public Administration Review* 51(3):211-221 (May/June 1991).

Sender, Benjamin. Oral contracts can leave you down in the mouth. *American School Board Journal* 171(6):21, 39 (June 1984).

Van Alstyne, William W. Academic freedom and the First Amendment in the Supreme Court of the United States: an unhurried historical review. *Law and Contemporary Problems* 53(3):79-154 (Summer 1990).

Youngblood, Stuart A., and Gary L. Tidwell. Termination at will: some changes in the wind. *Personnel* 58(3):22-33 (May/June 1981).

1531. Perry v. Sindermann   June 29, 1972
       408 US 593   33 LEd2d 570   92 SCt 2694
         Const (Currie) 540-542
         En Am Con 131-132
       The association and the courts. *Academe* 75(3):31-33 (May/June 1989).
       Davis, Sue. Federalism and property rights: an examination of Justice Rehnquist's legal positivism. *Western Political Quarterly* 39(3):250-264 (June 1986).
       Franke, Ann H., and Jacqueline W. Mintz. Four trends in higher education law. *Academe* 73(5):57-63 (September/October 1987).
       From Tilton to Ewing: some major higher-education decisions of the Burger court. *Chronicle of Higher Education* 32(17):10 (June 25, 1986).
       Jacobson, Robert L. Supreme Court, in a 4-4 vote, affirms due-process ruling. *Chronicle of Higher Education* 28(13):21, 25 (May 23, 1984).
       Sender, Benjamin. Oral contracts can leave you down in the mouth. *American School Board Journal* 171(6):21, 39 (June 1984).
       Sloviter, Dolores K. Faculty in federal court: decreasing receptivity? *Academe* 68(5):19-23 (September/October 1982).
       Youngblood, Stuart A., and Gary L. Tidwell. Termination at will: some changes in the wind. *Personnel* 58(3):22-33 (May/June 1981).

1532. Gravel v. United States   June 29, 1972
       408 US 606   33 LEd2d 583   92 SCt 2614
         En Am Con 864, 1716-1717

1533. Branzburg v. Hayes   June 29, 1972
         Coupled with In re Pappas
         Coupled with United States v. Caldwell
       408 US 665   33 LEd2d 626   92 SCt 2646
         Burger Court 15-18, 25-26
         Const (Currie) 523-527
         Const Law 222-227R
         En Am Con 146-147, 797-804, 1548-1549, 1679-1680
         First 226-233, 235-238
         Fourth 177-190+
         Freedom (Cox) 62-67
         Guide (West) (v. 2):151-152
         Sup Ct Review (1980):1-25; (1994):169-208
       Boylan, James. How free is the press? *Columbia Journalism Review* 26(3):27-32 (September/October 1987).
       ————. Pleading the First. *Columbia Journalism Review* 30(4):41-43 (November/December 1991).
       Copley, Helen K. General spirit of the people. *Vital Speeches* 46(6):169-172 (January 1, 1980).
       Fenner, G. Michael, and James L. Koley. Real meaning of the Gannett decision. *Trial* 16(1):45, 60 (January 1980).
       Frazer, Douglas H. The newsperson's privilege in grand jury proceedings: an argument for uniform recognition and application. *Journal of Criminal Law and Criminology* 75(2):413-442 (Summer 1984).
       Hale, F. Dennis. Constitutional libel protection narrowed—not destroyed. *Trial* 17(7):54-58, 79 (July 1981).
       Howard, A. E. Dick. The press in court. *Wilson Quarterly* 6(5):86-93 (Special Issue 1982).
       Maybe court will decide right to gather news. *Editor and Publisher* 113(17):28 (April 26, 1980).
       Powe, L. A., Jr. Mass communications and the First Amendment: an overview. *Law and Contemporary Problems* 55(1):53-76 (Winter 1992).
       Schulz, David A. Electronic dragnet renews: debate over protection of sources. *Editor and Publisher* 124(39)16-17 (Sepember 28, 1991).
       Solimine, Michael E. Constitutionality of congressional legislation to overrule Zurcher v. Stanford daily. *Journal of Criminal Law and Criminology* 71(2):147-162 (Summer 1980).

1534. Kleindienst v. Mandel   June 29, 1972
      408 US 753   33 LEd2d 683   92 SCt 2576
      Bleisch, N. David. The Congressional Record and the First Amendment: accuracy is the best policy. *Boston
          College Environmental Affairs Law Review* 12(2):341-379 (Winter 1985).
      Flack, Sarah. May the U.S. ban "undesirable" foreigners? *Scholastic Update* 120(3):35 (October 2, 1987).

1535. O'Brien v. Brown   July 7, 1972
          Coupled with Keane v. National Democratic Party
      409 US 1   34 LEd2d 1   92 SCt 2718
      En Am Con 1335
      Sup Ct Review (1986):259-316

1536. California v. Krivda   October 24, 1972
      409 US 33   34 LEd2d 45   93 SCt 32
      Uviller, H. Richard. Fourth Amendment: does it protect your garbage? *Nation* 247(9):302-304 (October 10,
          1988).
      Welsh, Robert, and Ronald K. L. Collins. Taking state constitutions seriously: the protection of civil liberties
          has been shifting away from the U.S. Supreme Court. *Center Magazine* 14(5):6-35, 38-43
          (September/October 1981).

1537. California v. LaRue   December 5, 1972
      409 US 109   34 LEd2d 342   93 SCt 390
      Brennan 171-176

1538. Neil, Warden v. Biggers   December 6, 1972
      409 US 188   34 LEd2d 401   93 SCt 375
      Lane, Margaret J. Eyewitness identification: should psychologists be permitted to address the jury? *Journal of
          Criminal Law and Criminology* 75(4):1321-1365 (Winter 1984).

1539. Trafficante v. Metropolitan Life Insurance Co.   December 7, 1972
      409 US 205   34 LEd2d 415   93 SCt 364
      Alpert, Peter A. Citizen suits under the Clean Air Act: universal standing for the uninjured private attorney
          general? *Boston College Environmental Affairs Law Review* 16(2):283-328 (Winter 1988).
      Chemerinsky, Erwin. Protecting individual rights: policing the police. *Trial* 27(12):32-36 (December 1991).

1540. One Lot Emerald Cut Stones and One Ring v. United States   December 11, 1972
      409 US 232   34 LEd2d 438   93 SCt 489
      Caginalp, O. A. Fifth Amendment privilege against self-incrimination and compulsory self-disclosure under the
          Clean Air and Clean Water Acts. *Boston College Environmental Affairs Law Review* 9(2):359-395 (1980-
          1981).
      Staas, John August. Supreme Court review: Fifth Amendment—statutory dilution of the privilege against self-
          incrimination. *Journal of Criminal Law and Criminology* 71(4):610-621 (Winter 1980).

1541. Executive Jet Aviation, Inc. v. Cleveland   December 18, 1972
      409 US 249   34 LEd2d 454   93 SCt 493
      Arsenault, Richard J., and Richard W. Beard. Bringing pleasure boat accidents under the admirality forum.
          Trial 18(10):66-71, 88 (October 1982).
      ————. Maritime personal injury on foreign waters. *Trial* 20(6):72-76 (June 1984).
      George, James A. The 'triple crown' of admiralty cases: from definitions to damages. *Trial* 27(10):46-53
          (October 1991).
      Mulhern, Pegeen. Marine pollution, fishes, and the pillars of the land: a tort recovery standard for pure
          economic losses. *Boston College Environmental Affairs Law Review* 18(1):85-123 (Fall 1990).

1542. Heublein, Inc. v. South Carolina Tax Commission   December 18, 1972
      409 US 275   34 LEd2d 472   93 SCt 483

O'Connell, Daniel. U.S. Supreme Court reviews state and local taxation issues. *CPA Journal* 62(3):16-21 (March 1992).

1543. Couch v. United States   January 9, 1973
   409 US 322   34 LEd2d 548   93 SCt 611
   Fifth Amendment: compulsory production of incriminating business records. *Journal of Criminal Law and Criminology* 71(1):51-55 (Spring 1980).

1544. United States v. Kras   January 10, 1973
   409 US 434   34 LEd2d 626   93 SCt 631
     En Am Con 1465-1472
   Binion, Gayle. The Burger court and the rights of the poor. *Center Magazine* 15(2):2-7 (March/April 1982).
   Schwartz, Herman. Concern for the basic necessities. *Nation* 239(9):299-300 (September 29, 1984).

1545. Ham v. South Carolina   January 17, 1973
   409 US 524   35 LEd2d 46   93 SCt 848
   Mar, Linda. Supreme Court review: Probing racial prejudice on voir dire: the Supreme Court provides illusory justice for minority defendants. *Journal of Criminal Law and Criminology* 72(4):1444-1461 (Winter 1981).
   Schultz, Marjorie S. Jury defined: a review of Burger court decisions. *Law and Contemporary Problems* 43(4):8-23 (Autumn 1980).
   Wyckoff, Maria. Supreme Court review: Sixth Amendment—right to inquire into juror's racial prejudices. *Journal of Criminal Law and Criminology* 77(3):713-742 (Fall 1986).

1546. United States v. Dionisio   January 22, 1973
   410 US 1   35 LEd2d 67   93 SCt 764
     En Am Con 564

1547. Environmental Protection Agency (EPA) v. Mink   January 22, 1973
   410 US 73   35 LEd2d 119   93 SCt 827
     Burger Years 191-205
   Morrison, Alan B. The Supreme Court and the Freedom of Information Act. *Nation* 239(9):287 (September 29, 1984).

1548. Roe v. Wade   January 22, 1973
   410 US 113   35 LEd2d 147   93 SCt 705
     Abortion (Frohock) 8, 24, 47, 59-66, 68-73, 109-114+
     Abortion Am 5-32R, 42-43, 77-79+
     Abortion Con 131-138+, 290
     Abortion Dec 2, 11-16+
     Abortion Decs 70s Introduction, 1-54R
     Abortion Moral 1-34R, 35-44, 55-62, 103-122, 238-244+
     Abortion Pol (Jaffe) 7-19, 31-43, 200-208+
     Abortion Pol (Rubin) 57-86, 115-118+
     Abortion Quest 101-110, 126-130+
     Almanac (1980):467; (1983):306-311; (1986):263-264; (1989):304-307+; (1992):398-400
     Amending 187-188+
     Ascent 34-35, 46-47, 293-294, 297-313+
     Brennan 302-304, 316-320+
     Burger Court 107-109, 147-148, 212-213, 242
     Burger Years 109-124
     Center 85-167+
     Const (Currie) 465-477
     Const (Friendly) 202-208
     Const Law 294-305R+, 310-312, 317-326
     Court Const 322-338+

Court Public 383-386, 397-411R

Editorials (1983):716-723; (1985):822-831; (1986):660-665; (1989):762-773; (1990):344-349; (1992):770-781

En Am Con 1043-1046, 1552-1558, 1577-1581, 1602-1604

Equal (Harrell) 114, 117-118

Ethics 13-22, 143-150

Guide (CQ) 56

Guide (West) (v. 9):58-60

Hard Choices 8-11, 15-19, 114-146, 149-168

Landmark (v. 1):89-125R

Law Governing 13-21+

Liberty 405-650+

Magic 317-320+

May It 343-360R

New Right (Whitaker) 142-168

Nobody's 3-46

Quarrels 351-378

Reader's 3-5, 99-103, 951-952, 1050-1052

Religion 237-244

Sup Ct Review (1995):125-215

Abortion: a march and a muddle. *Economist* 311(7598):29 (April 15-21, 1989).

Abortion: readers respond. [Editorial] *Commonweal* 109(3):75-84 (February 12, 1982).

Abortion ruling. *Christian Century* 109(22):674-675 (July 15-22, 1992).

Abortion test cases. *Time* 137(26):22-23 (July 1, 1991).

Abortion time bomb. *New Republic* 192(8):4 (February 25, 1985).

Aliotta, Jilda M. The unfinished feminist agenda: the shifting forum. *Annals of the American Academy of Political and Social Science* 515:140-150 (May 1991).

And now, a feminist full court press. *U.S. News and World Report* 105(21):12-13 (November 28, 1988).

Annas, George J. The Supreme Court, liberty, and abortion. *New England Journal of Medicine* 327(9):651-654 (August 27, 1992).

————. The Supreme Court, privacy, and abortion. *New England Journal of Medicine* 321(17):1200-1203 (October 26, 1989).

Arkes, Hadley. How to roll back Roe. *National Review* 40(21):30-31, 34-35, 59 (October 28, 1988).

Baker, banker, clergyman, thief. *Life* 10(10):84-88 (Fall 1987).

Behuniak-Long, Susan. Justice Sandra Day O'Connor and the power of maternal legal thinking. *Review of Politics* 54(3):417-444 (Summer 1992).

Benshoof, Janet. Planned Parenthood v Casey. *JAMA: The Journal of the American Medical Association* 269(17): 2249-2257 (May 5, 1993).

Bernardin, Joseph L. The consistent ethic after 'Webster:' opportunities and dangers. *Commonweal* 117(8):242-248 (April 20, 1990).

Bernstein, Sidney. Supreme Court review. *Trial* 19(12):20, 22 (December 1983).

Binion, Gayle. The Burger court and the rights of the poor. *Center Magazine* 15(2):2-7 (March/April 1982).

Blank, Robert H. Judicial decision making and biological fact: Roe v. Wade and the unresolved question of fetal viability. *Western Political Quarterly* 37(4):584-602 (December 1984).

Bork, Robert H. Beside the law. *National Review* 44(20):38, 40-43 (October 19, 1992).

Bowen, Lauren. Attorney advertising in the wake of Bates v. State Bar of Arizona (1977): a study of judicial impact. *American Politics Quarterly* 23(4):461-484 (October 1995).

Bresler, Robert J. Abortion, politics, and the Supreme Court. [Editorial] *USA Today* 118(2536):7 (January 1990).

————. Privacy, the courts, and social values. *USA Today* 115(2498):6-7 (November 1986).

Brief attack: Meese goes after abortion law. *Time* 126(4):24 (July 29, 1985).

Bryden, David P. Is the Rehnquist Court conservative? *Public Interest* (109):73-88 (Fall 1992).

Buckley, William F., Jr., Right to life breakthrough. *National Review* 33(5):313 (March 20, 1981).

Byrne, Harry J. A house divided: the pro-life movement. *America* 164(1):6-10 (January 5-12, 1991).

Canon, Bradley C. The Supreme Court as a cheerleader in politico-moral disputes. *Journal of Politics* 54(3):637-653 (August 1992).

Caplan, Lincoln. The tenth justice (II). *New Yorker* 63(26):30-62 (August 17, 1987).

Carey, Peter, Joanne Silberner, Ted Gest, Miriam Horn, and Jeffrey Sheler. Reappraising topic A. *U.S. News and World Report* 106(3):9-10 (January 23, 1989).

Carlin, David R. As American as freeways: abortion's roots in our culture. *Commonweal* 116(13):392-393 (July 14, 1989).

Carr, Baker V. Kennedy justice. *New Republic* 198(8):10, 12 (February 29, 1988).

Carter, Byrum E. Setting the political agenda. *Business Horizons* 33(1):14-19 (January/February 1990).

The case against Casey. *New Republic* 207(5):7 (July 27 1992).

Casey, Robert P. The democratic party. *Vital Speeches* 58(17)520-524 (June 15, 1992).

Cecil, Andrew R. Moral values in a free society: individualism and social conscience. *Vital Speeches* 60(7):204-209 (January 15, 1994).

Chipping away at Roe v. Wade. *Christianity Today* 34(11):37 (August 20, 1990).

Christopher, Maura. How the Constitution protects your "right to be let alone." *Scholastic Update* 119(1):12-13 (September 8, 1986).

Coalitions on abortion. *Christian Century* 109(15):447-448 (April 29, 1992).

Colt, George Howe. Save my law. *Life* 12(6):111-118 (May 1989).

Copelon, Rhonda, and Kathryn Kolbert. Our bodies, our business: imperfect justice. *Ms.* 18(1-2):42-44 (July/August 1989).

————. The gathering storm: Roe v. Wade. *Ms.* 17(10):88-92 (April 1989).

The Court and free choice. *Progressive* 47(8):11-12 (August 1983).

Cunningham, Paige Comstock. Reversing Roe vs Wade. *Christianity Today* 29(13):20-22 (September 20, 1985).

Degnan, Daniel A. When (if) 'Roe' falls. *Commonweal* 116(9):267-269 (May 5, 1989).

DiIanni, Albert. Abortion, liberalism and the law. *America* 159(18):491-494, 501 (December 10, 1988).

Doerr, Edd. Abortion rights imperiled. *Humanist* 49(4):39 (July/August 1989).

————. The end of Roe v. Wade. *Humanist* 52(3):45-46 (May/June 1992).

Donlan, Thomas G. When money talks: Justice Blackmun made a great contribution to economic liberty. [Editorial] *Barron's* 74(16):50 (April 18, 1994).

Dripps, Donald A. Supreme Court review: Warren Burger in perspective. *Trial* 31(8):73-75 (August 1995).

Dump 'Roe.' *New Republic* 206(20):7 (May 18, 1992).

Ehrlich, Elizabeth. If pro-choice is mainstream, now's the time to prove it. [Editorial] *Business Week* (Industrial/Technology Edition) (3115):64 (July 17, 1989).

The end of Roe? *National Review* 41(5):12-13 (March 24, 1989).

Evolution of the present controversy. *Congressional Digest* 61(5):134-135, 160 (May 1982).

Ewer, Phyllis A. Supreme Court review: Court upholds parental notice requirement before allowing abortions on minors. *Journal of Criminal Law and Criminology* 72(4):1461-1481 (Winter 1981).

Farber, Daniel A. Supreme Court review: from Warren to Rehnquist. *Trial* 25(7):124-126 (July 1989).

Flaherty, Francis J. Abortion, the Constitution and the Human Life Statute. *Commonweal* 108(19):586-593 (October 23, 1981).

Ford, Maurice deG. Rocking the Roe boat: hearing the Missouri case. *Commonweal* 116(11):326-328 (June 2, 1989).

Frame, Randy. Strategists work to sound the death knell for abortion. *Christianity Today* 28(8):74 (May 18, 1984).

Freeman, Alan David, and Elizabeth Mensch. The Court and the sexual revolution. *Commonweal* 121(18):19-23 (October 21, 1994).

Garraty, John Arthur. 101 things every college graduate should know about American history. *American Heritage* 38(1):24-32 (December 1986).

Gest, Ted. Abortion rights ride out an attack—for now. *U.S. News and World Report* 100(24):8 (June 23, 1986).

————. Courts: a major battleground of social upheaval. *U.S. News and World Report* 98(3):48-50 (January 28, 1985).

————. New abortion fights. *U.S. News and World Report* 106(16):22-26 (April 24, 1989).

————. Next stage: court lite. *U.S. News and World Report* 111(2):16-19 (July 8, 1991).

Gest, Ted, and Jeannye Thornton. Battle over abortion gets hot again. *U.S. News and World Report* 99(5):59 (July 29, 1985).

Gest, Ted, Mary Lord, Constance Johnson, Matthew Cooper, and Steven V. Roberts. Sound and fury signifying little. *U.S. News and World Report* 113(2):32-38 (July 13, 1992).

Glendon, Mary Ann. A world without Roe. *New Republic* 200(8):19-20 (February 20, 1989).

Goggin, Malcolm L. Understanding the new politics of abortion: a framework and agenda for research. *American Politics Quarterly* 21(1):4-30 (January 1993).

Green, Michelle. The woman behind Roe v. Wade. *People Weekly* 31(20):36-41 (May 22, 1989).

Hansen, Susan B. State implementation of Supreme Court decisions: abortion rates since Roe v. Wade. *Journal of Politics* 42(2):372-395 (May 1980).

Harrington-Lueker, Donna. Supreme Court actions push a wrenching controversy straight at you. *American School Board Journal* 176(11):20-24 (November 1989).

Heffner, Judith C. The Constitution in Court. *Scholastic Update* (Teachers' Edition) 116(5):16-18 (October 28, 1983).

Howard, A. E. Dick. Making it work. *Wilson Quarterly* 11(2):122-133 (Spring 1987).

Hunter, Nan. What Akron does/does not say. *Nation* 237(5):137-139 (August 20-27, 1983).

Isaacson, Walter, Anne Constable, and David S. Jackson. Holding firm on abortion: the Supreme Court solidly supports a woman's right to choose. *Time* 121(26):14-15 (June 27, 1983).

Kantrowitz, Barbara, and Ginny Carroll. Tipping the odds on abortion. *Newsweek* 118(2):23 (July 8, 1991).

Kaplan, David A. Is Roe good law? *Newsweek* 119(17):49-51(April 27, 1992).

Kaplan, John. Abortion as a vice crime: a "what if" story. *Law and Contemporary Problems* 51(1):151-179 (Winter 1988).

Kaus, Mickey. A world without Roe? *Newsweek* 110(11):33 (September 14, 1987).

Kelley, Dean M. "Let them eat cake," says the Supreme Court. *Christian Century* 97(27):820-824 (August 27-September 3, 1980).

Lacayo, Richard, and Julie Johnson. Abortion: inside the Court: Justice Kennedy flipped positions to uphold abortion rights. *Time* 140(2):29 (July 13, 1992).

———. Taking aim at Roe v. Wade. *Time* 139(5):16 (February 3, 1992).

Lacayo, Richard, Julie Johnson, Priscilla Painton, and Elizabeth Taylor. Abortion: the future is already here. *Time* 139(18):26-32 (May 4, 1992).

Lacayo, Richard, and Steven Holmes. A day of reckoning on Roe: the high court faces the abortion question—and asks a few. *Time* 133(19):24 (May 8, 1989).

Lacayo, Richard, Steven Holmes, Naushad S. Mehta, and Elizabeth Taylor. Whose life is it?: the long, emotional battle over abortion approaches a climax as the Supreme Court prepares for a historic challenge to Roe v. Wade. *Time* 133(18):20-24 (May 1, 1989).

LaFay, Laura, and James Earl Hardy. A court-wathcher's guide. *Scholastic Update* 124(5):13-16 (November 1, 1991).

Lawrence, Charise K. Your Constitution: securing your rights. *Scholastic Update* 120(9):11 (January 15, 1988).

Lawton, Kim A. Confrontation's stage is set. *Christianity Today* 33(11):36-38 (August 18, 1989).

———. Could this be the year? *Christianity Today* 33(6):36-38 (April 7, 1989).

———. High Court strikes down abortion restrictions, rules on handicapped infants. *Christianity Today* 30(10):38-39 (July 11, 1986).

———. Promises to keep. *Christianity Today* 33(2):44-45 (February 3, 1989).

The legacy of the Burger Court. *U.S. News and World Report* 100(25):22 (June 30, 1986).

Legislating life. [Editorial] *Nation* 232(12):355-356 (March 28, 1981).

Lehrman, Lewis E. The right to life and the restoration of the American republic. *National Review* 38(16):25-28 (August 29, 1986).

Leo, John. Lawmakers on the bench. *U.S. News and World Report* 114(13):22 (April 5, 1993).

———. The quagmire of abortion rights. [Editorial] *U.S. News and World Report* 113(2):16 (July 13, 1992).

Liberty for some. [Editorial] *Commonweal* 119(13):3 (July 17, 1992).

The longer march. [Editorial] *Commonweal* 116(9):259-260 (May 5, 1989).

McConnell, Margaret Liu. Living with Roe v. Wade. *Commentary* 90(5):34-38 (November 1990).

McCormick, Richard A., Mary Ann Glendon, Fred Siegel, Sidney Callahan, Mary C. Segers, E. J. Dionne, Daniel Callahan, Juli Loesch Wiley, Annie Lally Milhaven, and Burke J. Balch. Abortion: what does 'Webster' mean? *Commonweal* 116(14):425-428 (August 11, 1989).

McDaniel, Ann. Countdown on abortion. *Newsweek* 113(4):50 (January 23, 1989).

———. The future of abortion. *Newsweek* 114(3):14-16 (July 17, 1989).

———. Judicial flash points. *Newsweek* 116(6):18-19 (July 30, 1990).

McLoughlin, Merrill, Ted Gest, Jospeh Carey, Tracy L. Shryer, and Sandra R. Gregg. America's new civil war. *U.S. News and World Report* 105(13):22-31 (October 3, 1988).

Minow, Martha. We, the family: constitutional rights and American families. *Journal of American History* 74(3):959-983 (December 1987).

Murphy, Jamie, Laurence L. Barrett, and Anne Constable. Abortion's shrinking majority: the right-to-life movement loses a pair of controversial decisions. *Time* 127(25):30-31 (June 23, 1986).

Neuhaus, Richard John. Abortion after Akron: the contradictions are showing. *Commonweal* 110(13):388 (July 15, 1983).

———. After Roe. *National Review* 41(6):38-40 (April 7, 1989).

———. Democratic morality. *National Review* 38(13):47 (July 18, 1986).

———. Hyde and hysteria: the liberal banner has been planted on the wrong side of the abortion debates. *Christian Century* 97(28):849-852 (September 10-17, 1980).

New arguments on an old issue. *Christianity Today* 29(18):56-57 (December 13, 1985).

Novick, Sheldon M. Justice Holmes and Roe v. Wade. *Trial* 25(12):58-64, 65-66 (December 1989).

O'Hair, James P. Pulse: A brief history of abortion in the United States. *JAMA: The Journal of the American Medical Association* 262(13): 1875, 1878-1879 (October 6, 1989).

Opposing views argued in court, on the streets. *Christianity Today* 36(6):48 (May 18, 1992).

Orren, Karen. The primacy of labor in American constitutional development. *American Political Science Review* 89(2):377-388 (June 1995).

Pine, Rachael. Roe on the brink. [Editorial] *Nation* 249(4):112 (July 24-31, 1989).

Press, Aric, Ann McDaniel, Gloria Borger, Howard Fineman, and Elisa Williams. Abortion storm. *Newsweek* 107(25):26-27 (June 23, 1986).

Press, Aric, and Ann McDaniel. A Court in collision. *Newsweek* 105(2):28 (January 14, 1985).

Prolifers mark 15-year battle for unborn. *Christianity Today* 32(3):51 (February 19, 1988).

Rees, Grover, III. Constitution, the court, and the president-elect. *National Review* 32(26):1595-1602 (December 31, 1980).

Regan, Richard J. Supreme Court roundup: 1979 term. *Thought* 55(219):487-455 (December 1980).

———. Supreme Court roundup: 1980 term. *Thought* 56(223):491-502 (December 1981).

———. Supreme Court roundup: 1981 term. *Thought* 57(227):514-527 (December 1982).

———. Supreme Court roundup: 1982 term. *Thought* 58(231):472-483 (December 1983).

———. Supreme Court roundup: 1985 term. *Thought* 62(245):234-246 (June 1987).

Relin, David Oliver. Agonizing over abortion. *Scholastic Update* 122(16):2-3 (April 20, 1990).

———. Five landmark decisions. *Scholastic Update* 120(15):20 (April 8, 1988).

'Roe' must stand. *Progressive* 53(3):6-7 (March 1989).

'Roe' redux. [Editorial] *Commonweal* 119(5):3-4 (March 13, 1992).

Rosenblatt, Roger. The Bill of Rights. *Life* 14(13 Special Issue):9-30 (Fall 1991).

Rosenblum, Victor G. Letting the states set abortion policy. [Editorial] *Christian Century* 106(8):252-253 (March 8, 1989).

Sachs, Andrea, and Steven Holmes. Abortion on the ropes: is the historic Roe v. Wade ruling about to be overturned? *Time* 132(23):58-59 (December 5, 1988).

Salholz, Eloise, Vera Azar, Tony Clifton, Farai Chideya, Daniel Glick, Michael Mason, and Susan Miller. Abortion angst. *Newsweek* 120(2):16-19 (July 13, 1992).

Salholz, Eloise, and Ann McDaniel. The abortion battlefield. *Newsweek* 112(22):44 (November 28, 1988).

Salholz, Eloise, Ann McDaniel, and Andrew Murr. Answering the High Court's invitation. *Newsweek* 115(14):39 (April 2, 1990).

Salholz, Eloise, Ann McDaniel, Patricia King, Nadine Joseph, Gregory Cerio, and Ginny Carroll. The battle over abortion. *Newsweek* 113(18):28-32 (May 1, 1989).

Salholz, Eloise, Ann McDaniel, and Sue Hutchinson. Pro-choice: 'a sleeping giant' awakes. *Newsweek* 113(17):39-40 (April 24, 1989).

Seligman, Daniel. Flunking Harry. *Fortune* 122(5):111-112 (August 27, 1990).

Simpson, Peggy. The gathering storm: Politics. *Ms.* 17(10):88-89 (April 1989).

Sowell, Thomas. Hypocrisy. [Editorial] *Forbes* 156(6):80 (September 11, 1995).

Spivack, Miranda S. . . . and women's groups prepare for life after Roe. *Ms.* 2(5)91 (March/April 1992).

Spring, Beth. Harsh days at the High Court. *Christianity Today* 27(11):30-31 (July 15, 1983).

————. White House files prolife court brief. *Christianity Today* 26(14):66-70 (September 3, 1982).

Starr, Mark, Ann McDaniel, and Bob Cohn. Meese weighs in on abortion. *Newsweek* 106(5):60-61 (July 29, 1985).

State by state: what might happen if the Supreme Court overturns Roe v. Wade. *Newsweek* 113(18):38 (May 1, 1989).

Steinem, Gloria. Our bodies, our business: a basic human right. *Ms.* 18(1-2):38-41 (July/August 1989).

Stoner, James R., Jr. Common law and constitutionalism in the abortion case. *Review of Politics* 55(3):421-441 (Summer 1993).

Sudo, Phil. Five "little" people who changed U.S. history. *Scholastic Update* 122(10):8-10 (January 16, 1990).

————. Roe v. Wade, 1973. *Scholastic Update* (Teachers' Edition) 122(10):10 (January 26, 1990).

Supreme Court: reconsidering rights. *Economist* 309(7577):27-28 (November 19-25, 1988).

The talk of the town: notes and comment. [Editorial] *New Yorker* 68(21):23-24 (July 13, 1992).

Tatalovich, Raymond, and Byron W. Daynes. The limits of judicial intervention in abortion politics. *Christian Century* 99(1):16-20 (January 6-13, 1980).

————. Trauma of abortion politics. *Commonweal* 108(21):644-649 (November 20, 1981).

Thomas, Evan, Kenneth W. Banta, and Anne Constable. Court at the crossroads: the 1984 election may chart the future course of American justice. *Time* 124(15):28-35 (October 8, 1984).

A thousand cuts. [Editorial] *Nation* 255(3):76-77 (July 20-27, 1992).

Too many abortions. [Editorial] *Commonweal* 116(14):419-420 (August 11, 1989).

Trank, John P. The Burger Court—the first ten years. *Law and Contemporary Problems* 43(3):101-135 (Summer 1980).

Van Biema, David, S. C. Gwynne, and Hilary Hylton. An icon in search mode. *Time* 146(8):36 (August 21, 1995).

Waldman, Steven, and Ginny Caroll. Roe v. Roe. *Newsweek* 126(8):22-24 (August 21, 1995).

Wallis, Claudia, and Christine Gorman. Abortion, ethics and the law: advancing technology further complicates a national dilemma. *Time* 130(1):82-83 (July 6, 1987).

Wattleton, Faye. Planned Parenthood and pro choice: sexual and reproductive freedom. *Vital Speeches* 58(17):524-527 (June 15, 1992).

Whitman, David. Abortion rights are intact—so far. *U.S. News and World Report* 109(12):52-53 (September 24, 1990).

Will, George F. Splitting differences. [Editorial] *Newsweek* 113(7):86 (February 13, 1989).

Williams, Wendy W., and Judith L. Lichtman. Closing the law's gender gap. *Nation* 239(9):280-285 (September 29, 1984).

The wire next time? *Progressive* 49(9):9-10 (September 1985).

1549. Doe v. Bolton, Attorney General   January 22, 1973
      410 US 179   35 LEd2d 201   93 SCt 739
        Abortion (Frohock) 65-66
        Abortion Am 97+
        Abortion Con 138-139+, 290
        Abortion Dec 2-3, 20-29+
        Abortion Decs 70s Introduction, 55-74R
        Abortion Moral 35-44
        Abortion Pol (Jaffe) 7-19, 136-135, 185-199+
        Abortion Pol (Rubin) 61-67+
        Abortion Quest 101, 107-108
        Almanac (1980):467
        Ascent 46-47, 302-303+
        Burger Court 147-148
        Const (Currie) 471-475
        Court Public 412
        En Am Con 1552-1558, 1602-1604
        Equal (Harrell) 114, 117-118

Hard Choices 147-148, 173-174+

Law Governing 13-21+

Quarrels 366-367, 378

Arkes, Hadley. How to roll back Roe. *National Review* 40(21):30-31, 34-35, 59 (October 28, 1988).

Bernardin, Joseph L. The consistent ethic after 'Webster': opportunities and dangers. *Commonweal* 117(8):242-248 (April 20, 1990).

Blank, Robert H. Judicial decision making and biological fact: Roe v. Wade and the unresolved question of fetal viability. *Western Political Quarterly* 37(4):584-602 (December 1984).

Schwartz, Herman. Concern for the basic necessities. *Nation* 239(9):299-300 (September 29, 1984).

Tatalovich, Raymond, and Byron W. Daynes. The limits of judicial intervention in abortion politics. *Christian Century* 99(1):16-20 (January 6-13, 1980).

————. Trauma of abortion politics. *Commonweal* 108(21):644-649 (November 20, 1981).

1550. United States v. Florida East Coast Railway Co.   January 22, 1973
     410 US 224   35 LEd2d 223   93 SCt 810
     Burger Years 191-205

Morrison, Alan B. Close reins on the bureaucracy. *Nation* 239(9):290-294 (September 29, 1984).

1551. Chambers v. Mississippi   February 21, 1973
     410 US 284   35 LEd2d 297   93 SCt 1038
     Death Penalty 90s 100-101
     En Am Con 339-342, 658-661

1552. Mahan v. Howell   February 21, 1973
         Coupled with City of Virginia Beach v. Howell
         Coupled with Weinberg v. Prichard
     410 US 315   35 LEd2d 320   93 SCt 979
     Const Law 624-625R
     En Am Con 1197, 1518-1524
     Sup Ct Review (1986):175-257

Public Affairs Council of Louisiana. Reapportionment for the 1980s: good faith and court decisions. *National Civic Review* 70(11):575-582 (December 1981).

1553. United States v. Enmons   February 22, 1973
     410 US 396   35 LEd2d 379   93 SCt 1007

Striking at labor violence: business is urging Congress to undo the Supreme Court's hobbling of the Hobbs Act. *Nation's Business* 71(7):62-63 (July 1983).

1554. United States v. Basye   February 27, 1973
     410 US 441   35 LEd2d 412   93 SCt 1080

Anspach, William N., Paul L. Marlin, and Charles J. Muller III. Deferred compensation: a case study of purposeful negation of Supreme Court jurisdiction over income tax laws. *Taxes* 59(10):691-711 (October 1981).

Karjala, Dennis S. Deferred compensation and the Supreme Court. *Taxes* 60(9):684-694 (September 1982).

1555. United States v. Falstaff Brewing Corp.   February 28, 1973
     410 US 526   35 LEd2d 475   93 SCt 1096

McGahan, A. M. The emergence of the national brewing oligopoly: competition in the American market, 1933-1958. *Business History Review* 65(2):229-284 (Summer 1991).

1556. Linda R. S. v. Richard D.   March 5, 1973
     410 US 614   35 LEd2d 536   93 SCt 1146
     En Am Con 1722-1724
     Sup Ct Review (1993):37-64

O'Neill, Timothy P. The good, the bad, and the Burger Court: victims' rights and a new model of criminal review. *Journal of Criminal Law and Criminology* 75(2):363-387 (Summer 1984).

1557. Ortwein v. Schwab   March 5, 1973
     410 US 656   35 LEd2d 572   93 SCt 1172
     Binion, Gayle. The Burger court and the rights of the poor. *Center Magazine* 15(2):2-7 (March/April 1982).

1558. Papish v. Board of Curators of the University of Missouri   March 19, 1973
     410 US 667   35 LEd2d 618   93 SCt 1197
     Kobylka, Joseph F. A court-created context for group litigation: libertarian groups and obscenity. *Journal of Politics* 49(4):1061-1078 (November 1987).

1559. Salyer Land Co. v. Tulare Lake Basin Water Storage District   March 20, 1973
     410 US 719   35 LEd2d 659   93 SCt 1224
       Court Public 94

1560. Associated Enterprises v. Toltec Watershed Improvement District   March 20, 1973
     410 US 743   35 LEd2d 675   93 SCt 1237
       Court Public 94

1561. San Antonio Independent School District v. Rodriguez   March 21, 1973
     411 US 1   36 LEd2d 16   93 SCt 1278
       Am Educators 485-486
       Ascent 289-292+
       Brennan 276-282, 287-291
       Burden 220-223
       Burger Court 53-56, 219
       Const Law 529-535R+
       Courage 280-303, 428
       Court Const 311-316
       Court Public 98, 200-223R
       En Am Con 608-612, 1619-1620
       May It 321-337R
       Sup Ct Review (1982):167-194

Bersoff, Donald N., and David W. Ogden. APA amicus curiae briefs: furthering lesbian and gay male civil rights. *American Psychologist* 46(9):950-956 (September 1991).

Binion, Gayle. The Burger court and the rights of the poor. *Center Magazine* 15(2):2-7 (March/April 1982).

Bodine, Margot R. Opening the schoolhouse door for children with AIDS: the Education for All Handicapped Children Act. *Boston College Environmental Affairs Law Review* 13(4):583-641 (Summer 1986).

Camper, Diane, Ethel Payne, Nathaniel R. Jones, Charles Ogletree, Charles and Julius L. Chambers. To form a more perfect union. *Black Enterprise* 17(12):11, 51-66 (July 1987).

A decade after Rodriguez: an interview with John Coons. *Phi Delta Kappan* 64(7):479-480 (March 1983).

Delon, Floyd G. The legacy of Thurgood Marshall. *Journal of Negro Education* 63(3):278-288 (Summer 1994).

Farber, Daniel A. Supreme Court review: from Warren to Rehnquist. *Trial* 25(7):124-126 (July 1989).

Flygare, Thomas J. School finance a decade after Rodriguez. *Phi Delta Kappan* 64(7):477-478 (March 1983).

Hobbs, Gardner J. Public school finance and the courts. *Clearing House* 53(9):405-409 (May 1980) .

Kozol, Jonathan. Giant steps backward: romance of the ghetto school. *Nation* 258(20):703-706 (May 23, 1994).

Lamb, Charles M. Legal foundations of civil rights and pluralism America. *Annals of the American Academy of Political and Social Science* 454:13-25 (March 1981).

Long, David C. Rodriguez: the state courts respond. *Phi Delta Kappan* 64(7):481-484 (March 1983).

Menacker, Julius. Review of Supreme Court reasoning in cases of expression, due process, and equal protection. *Phi Delta Kappan* 63(3):188-190 (November 1981).

Mosk, Stanley. The emerging agenda in state constitutional rights law. *Annals of the American Academy of Political and Social Science* 496:54-64 (March 1988).

Natale, Jo Anna. Why the courts play Solomon with school funding. *American School Board Journal* 177(3):22-23 (March 1990).

Oakes, Jeannie. Tracking and ability grouping in American schools: some constitutional questions. *Teachers College Record* 84(4):801-819 (Summer 1983).

Regan, Richard J. Supreme Court roundup: 1980 term. *Thought* 56(223):491-502 (December 1981).

Rotunda, Ronald D. The Supreme Court: eschewing bright lines. *Trial* 25(12):52-56 (December 1989).

Schwartz, Herman. Concern for the basic necessities. *Nation* 239(9):299-300 (September 29, 1984).

Trank, John P. The Burger Court—the first ten years. *Law and Contemporary Problems* 43(3):101-135 (Summer 1980).

1562. McClanahan v. Arizona State Tax Commission   March 27, 1973
     411 US 164   36 LEd2d 129   93 SCt 1257
     Am Indian (Deloria) 197-220
     Am Indians (Wilkinson) 35-37, 59-60, 175-176+

1563. Lemon v. Kurtzman   April 2, 1973
     411 US 192   36 LEd2d 151   93 SCt 1453
     En Am Con 1155-1156

1564. Tollett v. Henderson   April 17, 1973
     411 US 258   36 LEd2d 235   93 SCt 1602
     Halberstam, Malvina. Towards neutral principles in the administration of criminal justice: a critique of Supreme court decisions sanctioning the plea bargaining process. *Journal of Criminal Law and Criminology* 73(1):1-49 (Spring 1982).

1565. Askew v. Amerian Waterways Operators, Inc.   April 18, 1973
     411 US 325   36 LEd2d 280   93 SCt 1590
     Kelly, Ambrose B. Insurance against oil pollution of the seas. *Best's Review* (Property/Casualty Insurance Edition) 82(1):24-28, 122-123 (May 1981).
     Mulhern, Pegeen. Marine pollution, fishes, and the pillars of the land: a tort recovery standard for pure economic losses. *Boston College Environmental Affairs Law Review* 18(1):85-123 (Fall 1990).

1566. Palmore v. United States   April 24, 1973
     411 US 389   36 LEd2d 342   93 SCt 1670
     Ascent 40-41
     Buckley, William F., Jr. On the question of jurisdiction. *National Review* 33(12):741 (June 26, 1981).

1567. Georgia v. United States   May 7, 1973
     411 US 526   36 LEd2d 472   93 SCt 1702
     Davis, Olethia. Tenuous interpretation: Sections 2 and 5 of the Voting Rights Act. *National Civic Review* 84(4):310-322 (Fall/Winter 1995).
     Public Affairs Council of Louisiana. Reapportionment for the 1980s: good faith and court decisions. *National Civic Review* 70(11):575-582 (December 1981).

1568. Burbank v. Lockheed Air Terminal, Inc.   May 14, 1973
     411 US 624   36 LEd2d 547   93 SCt 1854
     En Am Con 170, 637-639

1569. Frontiero v. Richardson   May 14, 1973
     411 US 677   36 LEd2d 583   93 SCt 1764
     Ascent 222-227+
     Brennan 294-302+
     Burger Court 135-136, 143-145
     Burger Years 109-124
     Const (Currie) 493-500

Const Law 504-508R, 511-512+
Court Const 318-320
Court Public 98, 101, 195-199R
En Am Con 809, 1666-1673
Equal Rights 17-42+
Magic 329-330

Cort'es, Carlos E., and Van L. Perkins. U.S. Supreme Court decisions on diversity. *Education Digest* 46(6):21-24 (February 1981).

Hogan, Joyce, and Ann M. Quigley. Physical standards for employment and the courts. *American Psychologist* 41(11):1193-1217 (November 1986).

What they say it is: the justices' words instruct the nation, and often address history. *Time* 130(1):44-49 (July 6, 1987).

Williams, Wendy W., and Judith L. Lichtman. Closing the law's gender gap. *Nation* 239(9):280-285 (September 29, 1984).

1570. McDonnell Douglas Corp. v. Green   May 14, 1973
        411 US 792   36 LEd2d 668   93 SCt 1817
          En Am Con 284-287

McFeeley, Neil D. Weber versus affirmative action? *Personnel* 57(1):38-51 (January/February 1980).

Murphy, Betty Southard, Wayne E. Barlow, and D. Diane Hatch. Supreme Court eases employer burden of proof. *Personnel Journal* 72(9):30, 33-34 (September 1993).

Sloviter, Dolores K. Faculty in federal court: decreasing receptivity? *Academe* 68(5):19-23 (September/October 1982).

1571. Hall v. Cole   May 21, 1973
        412 US 1   36 LEd2d 702   93 SCt 1943
          Burger Years 228-239

Jordan, Scott J. Awarding attorney's fees to environmental plaintiffs under a private attorney general theory. *Boston College Environmental Affairs Law Review* 14(2):287-311 (Winter 1987).

1572. Chaffin v. Stynchcombe   May 21, 1973
        412 US 17   36 LEd2d 714   93 SCt 1977

Erlinder, C. Peter, and David C. Thomas. Prohibiting prosecutorial vindictiveness while protecting prosecutorial discretion: toward a principled resolution of a due process dilemma. *Journal of Criminal Law and Criminology* 76(2):341-438 (Summer 1985).

1573. Booster Lodge No. 405 v. National Labor Relations Board (NLRB)   May 21, 1973
        412 US 84   36 LEd2d 764   93 SCt 1961

Coleman, John J., III. Can union members resign during a strike? *Personnel Journal* 65(5):99-100, 102, 105 (May 1986).

1574. Columbia Broadcasting System, Inc. (CBS) v. Democratic National Committee   May 29, 1973
            Coupled with Federal Communications Commission (FCC) v. Business Executives' Move for Vietnam
                Peace
            Coupled with Post-Newsweek Stations, Capital Area, Inc. v. Business Executives' Move for Vietnam
                Peace
            Coupled with American Broadcasting Co. (ABC) v. Democratic National Committee
        412 US 94   36 LEd2d 772   93 SCt 2080
          Burger Court 23-26
          Const (Currie) 518-522
          En Am Con 314
          Sup Ct Review (1981):223-262; (1982):195-241

1575. Schneckloth v. Bustamonte   May 29, 1973
        412 US 218   36 LEd2d 854   93 SCt 2041

Burger Court 75, 78-79, 84-86
Burger Years 143-168
En Am Con 355, 1624-1625, 1628-1625
Thurgood 317-324R

Gardiner, Thomas G. Consent to search in response to police threats to seek or to obtain a search warrant: some alternatives. *Journal of Criminal Law and Criminology* 71(2):163-172 (Summer 1980).

Goldberger, Peter. Consent, expectations of privacy, and the meaning of "searches" in the Fourth Amendment. *Journal of Criminal Law and Criminology* 75(2):319-362 (Summer 1984).

Kamisar, Yale. The swing of the pendulum. *Nation* 239(9):271-274 (September 29, 1984).

McGuire, Kevin T., and Barbara Palmer. Issue fluidity on the U.S. Supreme Court. *American Political Science Review* 89(3):691-702 (September 1995).

Wieber, Michael C. The theory and practice of Illinois v. Rodriguez: why an officer's reasonable belief about a third party's authority to consent does not protect a criminal suspect's rights. *Journal of Criminal Law and Criminology* 84(3):604-641 (Fall 1993).

1576. Cupp v. Murphy   May 29, 1973
412 US 291   36 LEd2d 900   93 SCt 2000
Const Law 347-348R

1577. Northcross v. Board of Education of Memphis City Schools   June 4, 1973
Northcross v. Memphis Board of Education
412 US 427   37 LEd2d 48   93 SCt 2201
Jordan, Scott J. Awarding attorney's fees to environmental plaintiffs under a private attorney general theory. *Boston College Environmental Affairs Law Review* 14(2):287-311 (Winter 1987).

1578. Vlandis v. Kline   June 11, 1973
412 US 441   37 LEd2d 63   93 SCt 2230
En Am Con 1977-1978

1579. Goldstein v. California   June 18, 1973
412 US 546   37 LEd2d 163   93 SCt 2303
En Am Con 504-505
Sup Ct Review (1983):509-581; (1989):283-309

1580. United States v. Students Challenging Regulatory Agency Procedures (SCRAP)   June 18, 1973
Coupled with Aberdeen and Rockfish Railroad Co. v. Students Challenging Regulatory Agency
Procedures (SCRAP)
412 US 669   37 LEd2d 254   93 SCt 2405
Burger Years 191-205
En Am Con 1722-1724, 1793
Alpert, Peter A. Citizen suits under the Clean Air Act: universal standing for the uninjured private attorney general? *Boston College Environmental Affairs Law Review* 16(2):283-328 (Winter 1988).

Farber, Daniel A. Supreme Court review: the global environment and the Rehnquist court. *Trial* 28(8):73-77 (August 1992).

McDowell, Gary L. Modest remedy for judicial activism. *Public Interest* (67):3-20 (Spring 1982).

Morrison, Alan B. Close reins on the bureaucracy. *Nation* 239(9):290-294 (September 29, 1984).

Perino, Michael A. Justice Scalia: standing, environmental law, and the Supreme Court. *Boston College Environmental Affairs Law Review* 15(1):135-179 (Fall 1987).

1581. Gaffney v. Cummings   June 18, 1973
412 US 735   37 LEd2d 298   93 SCt 2321
En Am Con 1518-1524
Sup Ct Review (1986):175-257
Engstrom, Richard L. Shaw, Miller and the districting thicket. *National Civic Review* 84(4):323-336 (Fall/Winter 1995).

Public Affairs Council of Louisiana. Reapportionment for the 1980s: good faith and court decisions. *National Civic Review* 70(11):575-582 (December 1981).

Scarrow, Howard A. Partisan gerrymandering—invidious or benevolent? Gaffney v. Cummings and its aftermath. *Journal of Politics* 44(3):810-821 (August 1982).

1582. White v. Regester   June 18, 1973
412 US 755   37 LEd2d 314   93 SCt 2332
  En Am Con 1518-1524
  Sup Ct Review (1986):175-257

Davis, Olethia. Tenuous interpretation: Sections 2 and 5 of the Voting Rights Act. *National Civic Review* 84(4):310-322 (Fall/Winter 1995).

Graham, Barbara Luck. Federal court policy-making and political equality: an analysis of judicial redistricting. *Western Political Quarterly* 44(1):101-117 (March 1991).

Neighbor, Howard D. The Supreme Court speaks, sort of, on the 1982 Voting Rights Act Amendments. *National Civic Review* 75(6):346-353 (November/December 1986).

Public Affairs Council of Louisiana. Reapportionment for the 1980s: good faith and court decisions. *National Civic Review* 70(11):575-582 (December 1981).

Zimmerman, Joseph F. Election systems and representative democracy: reflections on the Voting Rights Act of 1965. *National Civic Review* 84(4):287-309 (Fall/Winter 1995).

1583. White v. Weiser   June 18, 1973
412 US 783   37 LEd2d 335   93 SCt 2348
  Sup Ct Review (1986):175-257

Public Affairs Council of Louisiana. Reapportionment for the 1980s: good faith and court decisions. *National Civic Review* 70(11):575-582 (December 1981).

1584. Miller v. California   June 21, 1973
413 US 15   37 LEd2d 419   93 SCt 2607
  Abortion (Frohock) 10
  Brennan 171-176
  Const Law 237-241R+
  Documents (v. 2):801-804R
  En Am Con 790-797, 1258-1259, 1335-1337, 1428-1429
  First 290-294+
  Magic 317-320
  Price 8-13
  Sup Ct Ind 59
  Sup Ct Review (1982):285-317

Baer, Judith A. Women's rights and the limits of constitutional doctrine. *Western Political Quarterly* 44(4):821-852 (December 1991).

Bork, Robert H. What to do about the First Amendment. *Commentary* 99(2):23-29 (February 1995).

Brown, Sandra Zunker. Supreme Court review: First Amendment—nonobscene child pornography and its categorical exclusion from constitutional protection. *Journal of Criminal Law and Criminology* 73(4):1337-1364 (Winter 1982).

Fields, Howard. First Amendment watch: obscenity test challenged in U.S. Supreme Court. *Publishers' Weekly* 231(10):10 (March 13, 1987).

————. High Court to hear challenge to Miller. *Publishers' Weekly* 230(17):15 (October 24, 1986).

————. Supreme Court may redefine obscenity. *Publishers' Weekly* 227(10):37-38 (March 8, 1985).

Hafen, Bruce C. The First Amendment and obscenity: a sense of restraint is necessary. *Vital Speeches* 53(7):210-212 (January 15, 1987).

Hagle, Timothy M. But do they have to see it to know it? the Supreme Court's obscenity and pornography decisions. *Western Political Quarterly* 44(4):1039-1054 (December 1991).

Kobylka, Joseph F. A court-created context for group litigation: libertarian groups and obscenity. *Journal of Politics* 49(4):1061-1078 (November 1987).

McGuire, Kevin T. Obscenity, libertarian values, and decision making in the Supreme Court. *American Politics Quarterly* 18(1):47-67 (January 1990).

McGuire, Kevin T., and Gregory A. Caldeira. Lawyers, organized interests, and the law of obscenity: agenda setting in the Supreme Court. *American Political Science Review* 87(3):717-726 (September 1993).

Mosk, Stanley. The emerging agenda in state constitutional rights law. *Annals of the American Academy of Political and Social Science* 496:54-64 (March 1988).

Reuter, Madalynne. High Court to review key part of Miller test. *Publishers' Weekly* 230(25):14 (December 19, 1986).

Rosen, Jeffrey. 'Miller' time. *New Republic* 203(14):17-19 (October 1, 1990).

Spring, Beth. How harmful is pornography? *Christianity Today* 30(10):26-27 (July 11, 1986).

Staal, Lorri. Supreme Court review: First Amendment—the objective standard for social value in obscenity cases. *Journal of Criminal Law and Criminology* 78(4):735-762 (Winter 1988).

Supreme Court fine-tunes third part of 'Miller' test. *Publishers' Weekly* 231(20):20 (May 22, 1987).

Supreme Court rules against child porn. *Christianity Today* 26(13):58 (August 6, 1982).

Teachout, Terry. The pornography report that never was. *Commentary* 84(2):51-57 (August 1987).

Trank, John P. The Burger Court—the first ten years. *Law and Contemporary Problems* 43(3):101-135 (Summer 1980).

Winter, Ralph K. Political financing and the Constitution. *Annals of the American Academy of Political and Social Science* 486:34-48 (July 1986).

Yen, Marianne. First Amendment watch update: 43 states now use Miller test. *Publishers' Weekly* 229(18):15 (May 2, 1986).

1585. Paris Adult Theatre I v. Slaton   June 21, 1973
    413 US 49   37 LEd2d 446   93 SCt 2628

En Am Con 1258-1259, 1335-1337, 1955-1957

Sup Ct Review (1982):285-317

Hagle, Timothy M. But do they have to see it to know it? the Supreme Court's obscenity and pornography decisions. *Western Political Quarterly* 44(4):1039-1054 (December 1991).

Kobylka, Joseph F. A court-created context for group litigation: libertarian groups and obscenity. *Journal of Politics* 49(4):1061-1078 (November 1987).

McGuire, Kevin T. Obscenity, libertarian values, and decision making in the Supreme Court. *American Politics Quarterly* 18(1):47-67 (January 1990).

Winter, Ralph K. Political financing and the Constitution. *Annals of the American Academy of Political and Social Science* 486:34-48 (July 1986).

1586. Colgrove v. Battin   June 21, 1973
    413 US 149   37 LEd2d 522   93 SCt 2448

En Am Con 1085-1986

Bersoff, Donald N. Social science data and the Supreme Court: Lockhart as a case in point. *American Psychologist* 42(1):52-58 (January 1987).

Hogan, R. Ben, III. The Seventh Amendment: the founders' views. *Trial* 23(9):76, 78, 80, 82 (September 1987).

1587. Keyes v. Denver School District No. 1   June 21, 1973
    413 US 189   37 LEd2d 548   93 SCt 2686

Am Educators 306-307

Ascent 259-266+

Brennan 249-255

Burger Court 117-120

Burger Years 95-108

Const (Currie) 477-482

Court Public 99-100, 121-141R

En Am Con 557-561, 1102, 1625-1626

Eyes 609-611

Sup Ct Ind 236

Brown, Kevin. Revisiting the Supreme Court's opinion in Brown v. Board of Education from a multiculturalist perspective. *Teachers College Record* 96(4):644-653 (Summer 1995).

Burns, Haywood. The activisim in not affirmative. *Nation* 239(9):264-268 (September 29, 1984).

Evolution of court policy. *Congressional Digest* 59(2):39 (February 1981).

Evolution of the present controversy. *Congressional Digest* 61(5):134-135, 160 (May 1982).

Gordon, William M. The implementation of desegregation plans since Brown. *Journal of Negro Education* 63(3):310-322 (Summer 1994).

Hyde, Alison A. School desegregation: the role of the courts and means of achievement. *NASSP Bulletin* 78(565):28-37 (November 1994).

Lamb, Charles M. Legal foundations of civil rights and pluralism America. *Annals of the American Academy of Political and Social Science* 454:13-25 (March 1981).

Reid, Herbert O., Sr. State of the art: the law and education since 1954. *Journal of Negro Education* 52(3):234-249 (Summer 1983).

Reid, Herbert O., and Frankie M. Foster-Davis. Three decades of "all deliberate speed." *Crisis* 91(5):12-15 (May 1984).

Russo, Charles J., J. John Harris III, and Rosetta F. Sandidge. Brown v. Board of Education at 40: a legal history of equal educational opportunity in American public education. *Journal of Negro Education* 63(3):297-309 (Summer 1994).

Simmons, Althea T. L. From Brown to Grove City: blueprint for education. *Crisis* 91(5):6-10 (May 1984).

Sullivan, Harold J. Formula for failure: a critique of the intent requirement in school segregation litigation. *Journal of Negro Education* 52(3):270-289 (Summer 1983).

1588. Almeida-Sanchez v. United States   June 21, 1973
    413 US 266   37 LEd2d 596   93 SCt 2535
      En Am Con 46, 134-135

Greig, William H., and Phillip S. Althoff. The constitutionality of roadblocks; the Fourth Amendment on the firing line again. *Trial* 22(2):56-62 (February 1986).

Jensen, D. Lowell, and Rosemary Hart. The good faith restatement of the exclusionary rule. *Journal of Criminal Law and Criminology* 73(3):916-938 (Fall 1982).

1589. United States v. Ash   June 21, 1973
    413 US 300   37 LEd2d 619   93 SCt 2568
      Burger Court 68-72, 90-91
      Burger Years 143-168
      En Am Con 78, 1585-1592

1590. NAACP v. New York   June 21, 1973
    413 US 345   37 LEd2d 648   93 SCt 2591

Zimmerman, Joseph F. Election systems and representative democracy: reflections on the Voting Rights Act of 1965. *National Civic Review* 84(4):287-309 (Fall/Winter 1995).

1591. Pittsburgh Press Co. v. Pittsburgh Commission on Human Relations   June 21, 1973
    413 US 376   37 LEd2d 669   93 SCt 2553
      Fourth 160-167
      Price 226-228

Chemerinsky, Erwin. Supreme Court review: commercial speech: what degree of protection? *Trial* 29(8):66-68 (August 1993).

Pawelek, Dick. Put yourself on the U.S. Supreme Court. *Senior Scholastic* 113(8):12-13, 27 (December 12, 1980).

1592. Cady v. Dombrowski   June 21, 1973
    413 US 433   37 LEd2d 706   93 SCt 2523
      Brennan 191-196

Nelson, Caleb. The paradox of the exclusionary rule. *Public Interest* (96):117-130 (Summer 1989).

1593. Norwood v. Harrison   June 25, 1973
     413 US 455   37 LEd2d 723   93 SCt 2804
      Sup Ct Review (1983):1-31

1594. Levitt and Nyquist v. Committee for Public Education and Religious Liberty (PERL)   June 25, 1973
       Coupled with Anderson v. Committee for Public Education and Religious Liberty (PERL)
       Coupled with Cathedral Academy v. Committee for Public Education and Religious Liberty (PERL)
     413 US 472   37 LEd2d 736   93 SCt 2814
      Burger Years 56-91
      En Am Con 1650-1658
      Godless 73

1595. United States Department of Agriculture (USDA) v. Murray   June 25, 1973
     413 US 508   37 LEd2d 767   93 SCt 2832
      Brennan 3-22
      En Am Con 556
    Schwartz, Herman. Concern for the basic necessities. *Nation* 239(9):299-300 (September 29, 1984).

1596. United States Department of Agriculture (USDA) v. Moreno   June 25, 1973
     413 US 528   37 LEd2d 782   93 SCt 2821
      Brennan 3-22
      En Am Con 556
    Schwartz, Herman. Concern for the basic necessities. *Nation* 239(9):299-300 (September 29, 1984).
    Trank, John P. The Burger Court—the first ten years. *Law and Contemporary Problems* 43(3):101-135 (Summer 1980).

1597. United States Civil Service Commission   June 25, 1973
       v. National Association of Letter Carriers, AFL-CIO
     413 US 548   37 LEd2d 796   93 SCt 2880
      En Am Con 907
    Supreme Court rulings. *Congressional Digest* 72(8-9):201, 224 (August/September 1993).
    Winter, Ralph K. Political financing and the Constitution. *Annals of the American Academy of Political and Social Science* 486:34-48 (July 1986).

1598. Broadrick v. Oklahoma   June 25, 1973
     413 US 601   37 LEd2d 830   93 SCt 2908
      En Am Con 158-159, 907, 1352-1354, 1955-1957
      Sup Ct Review (1981):1-39

1599. Sugarman v. Dougall   June 25, 1973
     413 US 634   37 LEd2d 853   93 SCt 2842
      Ascent 233-236, 240+
      Brennan 270-276
      Const (Currie) 500-504
      En Am Con 41-43, 1808

1600. In re Griffiths   June 25, 1973
     413 US 717   37 LEd2d 910   93 SCt 2851
      Const (Currie) 500-504
      En Am Con 1808

1601. Federal Communications Commission (FCC) v. Pacifica Foundation   July 3, 1978
     413 US 726   57 LEd2d 1073   98 SCt 3026
      En Am Con 157, 694, 728-729
      Freedom (Cox) 52-56

Jerry 195-201+

Sup Ct Review (1982):285-317

Bork, Robert H. Blue boys of the airwaves. *U.S. News and World Report* 102(16)16-17 (April 27, 1987).

Hagle, Timothy M. But do they have to see it to know it? the Supreme Court's obscenity and pornography decisions. *Western Political Quarterly* 44(4):1039-1054 (December 1991).

Kobylka, Joseph F. A court-created context for group litigation: libertarian groups and obscenity. *Journal of Politics* 49(4):1061-1078 (November 1987).

1602. Hunt v. McNair, Governor   June 25, 1973
413 US 734   37 LEd2d 923   93 SCt 2868
   Burger Years 56-91
   En Am Con 1650-1658
   Religion 54-58
   Sup Ct Church 271-273

Manion, Maureen. The impact of state aid on sectarian higher education: the case of New York State. *Review of Politics* 1986 48(2): 264-288.

1603. Committee for Public Education and Religious Liberty (PEARL)   June 25, 1973
         v. Nyquist, Commissioner of Education of the State of New York
             Coupled with Anderson v. Committee for Public Education and Religious Liberty (PERL)
             Coupled with Cherry v. Committee for Public Education and Religious Literty (PERL)
   413 US 756   37 LEd2d 948   93 SCt 2955
   Ascent 194-196
   Brennan 125-129
   Burger Years 56-91
   En Am Con 331, 1650-1658
   Godless 72-77
   Religion 30-45+
   Sup Ct Church 113-141R
   Sup Ct Review (1985):61-92

Coughlin, John J. Religion, education and the First Amendment. *America* 168(17):12-15 (May 15, 1993).

Drinan, Robert F. Compensatory education in private schools. *America* 152(13):278-280 (April 6, 1985).

Flygare, Thomas J. De jure: Supreme Court permits state tax deductions for nonpublic schools. *Phi Delta Kappan* 65(1):63-64 (September 1983).

Kobylka, Joseph F. Leadership on the Supreme Court of the United States: Chief Justice Burger and the establishment clause. *Western Political Quarterly* 42(4):545-568 (December 1989).

Mosk, Stanley. The emerging agenda in state constitutional rights law. *Annals of the American Academy of Political and Social Science* 496:54-64 (March 1988).

Regan, Richard J. Supreme Court roundup: 1982 term. *Thought* 58(231):472-483 (December 1983).

Schwartz, Michael. A new direction for the courts on the school question. *America* 149(13):251-254 (October 29, 1983).

Tushnet, Mark. The Constitution of religion. *Review of Politics* 50(4):628-658 (Fall 1988).

Weber, Paul J. Excessive entanglement: a wavering First Amendment standard. *Review of Politics* 46(4):483-501 (October 1984).

1604. Sloan v. Lemon   June 25, 1973
413 US 825   37 LEd2d 939   93 SCt 2982
   En Am Con 331

1605. Department of Game of Washington v. Puyallup Tribe   November 19, 1973
413 US 44   38 LEd2d 254   94 SCt 330
   Ott, Brian R. Indian fishing rights in the Pacific Northwest: the need for federal intervention. *Boston College Environmental Affairs Law Review* 14(2):313- 343 (Winter 1987).

1606. Hess v. Indiana   November 19, 1973
       414 US 105   38 LEd2d 303   94 SCt 326
       Jerry 222-223

1607. Cupp, Superintendent v. Naughten   December 4, 1973
       414 US 141   38 LEd2d 368   94 SCt 396
       Brennan 196-199

1608. United States v. Robinson   December 11, 1973
       414 US 218   38 LEd2d 427   94 SCt 467
       Documents (v. 2):805-806R
       En Am Con 1601, 1628-1635, 1636-1637
       Bradley, Craig M. The Court's "two model" approach to the Fourth Amendment: carpe diem! *Journal of Criminal Law and Criminology* 84(3):429-461 (Fall 1993).
       Carter, Jeffrey A. Supreme Court review: Fourth Amendment—of cars, containers and confusion. *Journal of Criminal Law and Criminology* 72(4):1171-1221 (Winter 1981).
       Misner, Robert L. Justifying searches on the basis of equality of treatment. *Journal of Criminal Law and Criminology* 82(3):547-578 (Fall 1991).
       Welsh, Robert, and Ronald K. L. Collins. Taking state constitutions seriously: the protection of civil liberties has been shifting away from the U.S. Supreme Court. *Center Magazine* 14(5):6-35, 38-43 (September/October 1981).

1609. Gustafson v. Florida   December 11, 1973
       414 US 260   38 LEd2d 456   94 SCt 488
       Welsh, Robert, and Ronald K. L. Collins. Taking state constitutions seriously: the protection of civil liberties has been shifting away from the U.S. Supreme Court. *Center Magazine* 14(5):6-35, 38-43 (September/October 1981).

1610. Zahn v. International Paper Co.   December 17, 1973
       414 US 291   38 LEd2d 511   94 SCt 505
       Sup Ct Review (1983):459-507
       Rowe, Thomas D. No final victories: the incompleteness of equity's triumph in federal public law. *Law and Contemporary Problems* 56(3):105-121 (Summer 1993).

1611. United States v. Calandra   January 8, 1974
       414 US 338   38 LEd2d 561   94 SCt 613
       Burger Years 143-168
       Const (Currie) 550-555
       En Am Con 194, 662-665, 974, 1628-1635
       Crocker, Lawrence. Can the exclusionary rule be saved? *Journal of Criminal Law and Criminology* 84(2):310-351 (Summer 1993).
       Hartman, Marshall J., and Sidney Bernstein. To Leon, and beyond; two commentators react. *Trial* 21(1):50-56 (January 1985).
       Jensen, D. Lowell, and Rosemary Hart. The good faith restatement of the exclusionary rule. *Journal of Criminal Law and Criminology* 73(3):916-938 (Fall 1982).
       Kamisar, Yale. The swing of the pendulum. *Nation* 239(9):271-274 (September 29, 1984).
       Nelson, Caleb. The paradox of the exclusionary rule. *Public Interest* (96):117-130 (Summer 1989).
       Use of the exclusionary rule. *Congressional Digest* 71(4):104-105 (April 1992).

1612. Gateway Coal Co. v. United Mine Workers of America   January 8, 1974
       414 US 368   38 LEd2d 583   94 SCt 629
       Burger Years 228-239
       Hollander, Rhonda G. Injunctions against occupational hazards: toward a safe workplace environment. *Boston College Environmental Affairs Law Review* 9(1):133-161 (1980-1981).

1613. United States v. Maze   January 8, 1974
    414 US 395   38 LEd2d 603   94 SCt 645
    Maurer, Virginia G. The continuing expansion of RICO in business litigation. *Business Horizons* 33(5):80-87
        (September/October 1990).

1614. O'Shea v. Littleton   January 15, 1974
    414 US 488   38 LEd2d 674   94 SCt 669
    En Am Con 1351

1615. Lau v. Nichols   January 21, 1974
    414 US 563   39 LEd2d 1   94 SCt 786
        Almanac (1980):226, 469-470; (1987):522
        Am Educators 315
        En Am Con 608-612, 1126
        Sup Ct Review (1988):85-113
    Cort'es, Carlos E., and Van L. Perkins. U.S. Supreme Court decisions on diversity. *Education Digest* 46(6):21-
        24 (February 1981).
    Easterbrook, Gregg. English, si Spanish no. *Washington Monthly* 12(10):37-44 (December 1980).
    Feinberg, Rosa Castro. Brown and Lau: seeking the common ground. *Teachers College Record* 96(4):775-782
        (Summer 1995).
    Hobbs, Gardner J. Public school finance and the courts. *Clearing House* 53(9):405-409 (May 1980) .
    Menacker, Julius. Review of Supreme Court reasoning in cases of expression, due process, and equal
        protection. *Phi Delta Kappan* 63(3):188-190 (November 1981).
    Simmons, Althea T. L. From Brown to Grove City: blueprint for education. *Crisis* 91(5):6-10 (May 1984).
    Thernstrom, Abigail M. E pluribus plura: Congress and bilingual education. *Public Interest* (60):3-22 (Summer
        1980).

1616. Sea-Land Services, Inc. v. Gaudet   January 21, 1974
    414 US 573   39 LEd2d 9   94 SCt 806
    George, James A., and Michelle M. O'Daniels. Recoverable damages in admiralty and maritime cases: muddied
        waters after Miles v. Apex Marine. *Trial* 31(5):58-65 (May 1995).

1617. Cleveland Board of Education v. La Fleur   January 21, 1974
            Coupled with Cohen v. Chesterfield County School Board
    414 US 632   39 LEd2d 52   94 SCt 791
        Am Educators 109, 340
        Brennan 304-307
        Burger Court 149-150
        Burger Years 109-124
        Courage 305-329, 428
        En Am Con 302, 1666-1673
    Feitshans, Ilise L. Job security for pregnant employees: the model employment termination act. *Annals of the
        American Academy of Political and Social Science* 536:119-134 (November 1994).
    Friedman, Dana E. Liberty, equality, maternity! *Across the Board* 24(3):10-17 (March 1987).
    Katz, Joni F. Hazardous working conditions and fetal protection policies: women are going back to the future.
        Boston College Environmental Affairs Law Review 17(1):201-230 (Fall 1989).
    Lee, Yong S. Civil liability of state and local governments: myth and reality. *Public Administrative Review*
        47(2):160-170 (March/April 1987).
    Menacker, Julius. Review of Supreme Court reasoning in cases of expression, due process, and equal
        protection. *Phi Delta Kappan* 63(3):188-190 (November 1981).
    Plater, Zygmunt J. B., and William Lund Norine. Through the looking glass of eminent domain: exploring the
        "arbitrary and capricious" test and substantive rationality review of governmental decisions. *Boston College
        Environmental Affairs Law Review* 16(4):661-752 (Summer 1989).
    Williams, Wendy W., and Judith L. Lichtman. Closing the law's gender gap. *Nation* 239(9):280-285
        (September 29, 1984).

1618. Oneida Indian Nation of New York v. County of Oneida   January 21, 1974
      414 US 661   39 LEd2d 73   94 SCt 772
      Am Indians (Wilkinson) 40, 126+

1619. Alexander v. Gardner-Denver Co.   February 19, 1974
      415 US 36   39 LEd2d 147   94 SCt 1011
      Hollander, Rhonda G. Injunctions against occupational hazards: toward a safe workplace environment. *Boston College Environmental Affairs Law Review* 9(1):133-161 (1980-1981).

1620. United States v. Kahn   February 20, 1974
      415 US 143   39 LEd2d 225   94 SCt 977
      Goldsmith, Michael. The Supreme Court and Title III: rewriting the law of electronic surveillance. *Journal of Criminal Law and Criminology* 74(1):1-171 (Spring 1983).

1621. United States v. Matlock   February 20, 1974
      415 US 164   39 LEd2d 242   94 SCt 988
      Abrams, Sharon E. Third-party consent searches, the Supreme Court, and the Fourth Amendment. *Journal of Criminal Law and Criminology* 75(3):963-994 (Fall 1984).
      Goldberger, Peter. Consent, expectations of privacy, and the meaning of "searches" in the Fourth Amendment. *Journal of Criminal Law and Criminology* 75(2):319-362 (Summer 1984).
      Wieber, Michael C. The theory and practice of Illinois v. Rodriguez: why an officer's reasonable belief about a third party's authority to consent does not protect a criminal suspect's rights. *Journal of Criminal Law and Criminology* 84(3):604-641 (Fall 1993).

1622. Morton, Secretary of the Interior v. Ruiz   February 20, 1974
      415 US 199   39 LEd2d 270   94 SCt 1055
      Baer, Susan D. The Public Trust Doctrine—a tool to make federal adminstrative agencies increase protection of public land and its resources. *Boston College Environmental Affairs Law Review* 15(2):385-436 (Winter 1988).

1623. Memorial Hospital v. Maricopa County   February 26, 1974
      415 US 250   39 LEd2d 306   94 SCt 1076
      En Am Con 1593-1596
      Schwartz, Herman. Concern for the basic necessities. *Nation* 239(9):299-300 (September 29, 1984).

1624. Davis v. Alaska   February 27, 1974
      415 US 308   39 LEd2d 347   94 SCt 1105
      White, Welsh S. Evidentiary privileges and the defendant's constitutional right to introduce evidence. *Journal of Criminal Law and Criminology* 80(2):377-426 (Summer 1989).

1625. National Cable Television Association v. United States   March 4, 1974
      415 US 336   39 LEd2d 370   94 SCt 1146
      Gallogly, Richard J. Opening the door for Boston's poor: will "linkage" survive judicial review? *Boston College Environmental Affairs Law Review* 14(3):447-480 (Spring 1987).
      Norris, James E. The assessment of user fees to recover generic regulatory costs. *Public Utilities Fortnightly* 123(13):42-45 (June 22, 1989).

1626. Federal Power Commission (FPC) v. New England Power Co.   March 4, 1976
      415 US 345   39 LEd2d 383   94 SCt 1151
      Norris, James E. The assessment of user fees to recover generic regulatory costs. *Public Utilities Fortnightly* 123(13):42-45 (June 22, 1989).

1627. United States v. General Dynamics Corp.   March 19, 1974
      415 US 486   39 LEd2d 530   94 SCt 1186
      Burger Court 184-187

1628. Smith, Sheriff v. Goguen   March 25, 1974
    415 US 566   39 LEd2d 605   94 SCt 1242
        Almanac (1989):309-311, 313
        Brennan 159-161
        En Am Con 1955-1957
        Sup Ct Review (1990):60-103
    Rehnquist, William H. The United States Supreme Court: dissent. *Congressional Digest* 68(8-9):197, 199, 201
        (August/September 1989).
    Winter, Ralph K. Political financing and the Constitution. *Annals of the American Academy of Political and
        Social Science* 486:34-48 (July 1986).

1629. Edelman, Director of Illinois Department of Public Aid v. Jordan   March 25, 1974
    415 US 651   39 LEd2d 662   94 SCt 1347
        Burger Court 57-59
        Const (Currie) 569-571, 574-577
        En Am Con 607, 740
        Sup Ct Review (1984):149-168
    Colton, Roger D., Kathleen Uehling, and Dr. Michael F. Sheehan. Seven-cum-eleven: rolling the toxic dice in
        the U.S. Supreme Court. *Boston College Environmental Affairs Law Review* 14(3):345-379 (Spring 1987).
    Groszyk, Walter S., Jr., and Thomas J. Madden. Managing without immunity: the challenge for state and local
        government officials in the 1980s. *Public Administration Review* 41(2):268-278 (March/April 1981).
    Wise, Charles, and Rosemary O'Leary. Is federalism dead or alive in the Supreme Court?: implications for
        public administrators. *Public Administration Review* 52(6):559-572 (November/December 1992).

1630. Storer v. Brown   March 25, 1974
    415 US 724   `39 LEd2d 714   94 SCt 1274
        Sup Ct Yearbook (1993-94):294-297

1631. Village of Belle Terre v. Boraas   April 1, 1974
    Belle Terre v. Boraas
    416 US 1   39 LEd2d 797   94 SCt 1536
        Black 59-64
        En Am Con 686-688, 782-789
        Thurgood 406-411R+

1632. Arnett, Director v. Kennedy   April 16, 1974
    416 US 134   40 LEd2d 15   94 SCt 1633
        Const (Currie) 540-542
        En Am Con 71, 119, 1465-1472
        Sup Ct Review (1982):85-125
    Davis, Sue. Federalism and property rights: an examination of Justice Rehnquist's legal positivism. *Western
        Political Quarterly* 39(3):250-264 (June 1986).

1633. Scheuer, Administratix v. Rhodes, Governor   April 17, 1974
        Coupled with Krause, Administrator v. Rhodes
    416 US 232   40 LEd2d 90   94 SCt 1683
        En Am Con 1624
    Groszyk, Walter S., Jr., and Thomas J. Madden. Managing without immunity: the challenge for state and local
        government officials in the 1980s. *Public Administration Review* 41(2):268-278 (March/April 1981).
    Rosenbloom, David H. Public administrators' official immunity and the Supreme Court: developments during
        the 1970s. *Public Administration Review* 40(2):166-173 (March/April 1980).

1634. National Labor Relations Board (NLRB)   April 23, 1974
        v. Bell Aerospace Co., Division of Textron, Inc.
    416 US 267   40 LEd2d 134   94 SCt 1757

Burger Years 220-227
Sup Ct Review (1980):27-55

Funk, William. The exception that approves the rule: FDF variances under the Clean Water Act. *Boston College Environmental Affairs Law Review* 13(1):1-60 (Fall 1985).

1635. DeFunis v. Odegaard April 23, 1974
 416 US 312 40 LEd2d 164 94 SCt 1704
 Behind Bakke 32-35, 41
 Brennan 257-263
 Conflict 44-46
 Const (Friendly) 218-221
 Economics 364-386+
 En Am Con 551, 1500-1506

Gregory, David L. The continuing vitality of affirmative action diversity principles in professional and graduate school student admissions and faculty hiring. *Journal of Negro Education* 63(3):421-429 (Summer 1994).

Tollett, Kenneth S., Jeanette J. Leonard, and Portia P. James. A color-conscious Constitution: the one pervading purpose redux. *Journal of Negro Education* 52(3):189-212 (Summer 1983).

Trank, John P. The Burger Court—the first ten years. *Law and Contemporary Problems* 43(3):101-135 (Summer 1980).

Vile, John R., and Kathy Ruth McCoy. The Memphis Case: another precedent? *Personnel* 62(7):72-76 (July 1985).

1636. Kahn v. Shevin, Attorney General of Florida April 24, 1974
 416 US 351 40 LEd2d 189 94 SCt 1734
 Burger Court 136-139+
 Burger Years 109-124
 En Am Con 1666-1673
 Equal Rights 17-42, 145-153+
 Magic 329-330

Baer, Judith A. Women's rights and the limits of constitutional doctrine. *Western Political Quarterly* 44(4):821-852 (December 1991).

Williams, Wendy W., and Judith L. Lichtman. Closing the law's gender gap. *Nation* 239(9):280-285 (September 29, 1984).

1637. Procunier, Director, California Department of Corrections v. Martinez April 29, 1974
 416 US 396 40 LEd2d 224 94 SCt 1800
 En Am Con 1480
 Sup Ct Review (1984):169-236

Robbins, Ira P. Cry of "wolfish" in the federal courts: the future of federal judicial intervention in prison administration. *Journal of Criminal Law and Criminology* 71(3):211-225 (Fall 1980).

1638. Kewanee Oil Co. v. Bicron Corp. May 13, 1974
 416 US 470 40 LEd2d 315 94 SCt 1879
 Sup Ct Review (1983):509-581; (1989):283-309

1639. United States v. Giordana May 13, 1974
 416 US 505 40 LEd2d 341 94 SCt 1820

Goldsmith, Michael. The Supreme Court and Title III: rewriting the law of electronic surveillance. *Journal of Criminal Law and Criminology* 74(1):1-171 (Spring 1983).

Silver, Stephen E. IRS Use of wiretap evidence in civil tax proceedings in doubt despite recent case. *Journal of Taxation* 56(5):300-303 (May 1982).

1640. United States v. Chavez May 13, 1974
 416 US 562 40 LEd2d 380 94 SCt 1849

Goldsmith, Michael. The Supreme Court and Title III: rewriting the law of electronic surveillance. *Journal of Criminal Law and Criminology* 74(1):1-171 (Spring 1983).

Silver, Stephen E. IRS Use of wiretap evidence in civil tax proceedings in doubt despite recent case. *Journal of Taxation* 56(5):300-303 (May 1982).

1641. Bradley v. School Board of City of Richmond   May 15, 1974
    416 US 696   40 LEd2d 476   94 SCt 2006

Russo, Charles J., J. John Harris III, and Rosetta F. Sandidge. Brown v. Board of Education at 40: a legal history of equal educational opportunity in American public education. *Journal of Negro Education* 63(3):297-309 (Summer 1994).

1642. Air Pollution Variance Board of Colorado v. Western Alfalfa Corp.   May 20, 1974
    416 US 861   40 LEd2d 607   94 SCt 2114
     En Am Con 637-639

Andersen, Robert M. Technology, pollution control, and EPA access to commercial property: a constitutional and policy framework. *Boston College Environmental Affairs Law Review* 17(1):1-74 (Fall 1989).

Bazarian, Stephen C. Dow Chemical Company v. United States and aerial surveillance by the EPA: an argument for post-surveillance notice to the observed. *Boston College Environmental Affairs Law Review* 15(3-4):593-626 (Spring 1988).

1643. Blackledge, Warden v. Perry   May 20, 1974
    417 US 21   40 LEd2d 628   94 SCt 2098
     Sup Ct Review (1980):211-279

Erlinder, C. Peter, and David C. Thomas. Prohibiting prosecutorial vindictiveness while protecting prosecutorial discretion: toward a principled resolution of a due process dilemma. *Journal of Criminal Law and Criminology* 76(2):341-438 (Summer 1985).

Halberstam, Malvina. Towards neutral principles in the administration of criminal justice: a critique of Supreme Court decisions sanctioning the plea bargaining process. *Journal of Criminal Law and Criminology* 73(1):1-49 (Spring 1982).

1644. Bellis v. United States   May 28, 1974
    417 US 85   40 LEd2d 678   94 SCt 1536

Fifth Amendment: compulsory production of incriminating business records. *Journal of Criminal Law and Criminology* 71(1):51-55 (Spring 1980).

1645. Corning Glass Works v. Brennan, Secretary of Labor   June 3, 1974
    417 US 188   41 LEd2d 1   94 SCt 2223
     Landmark (v. 5):135-151R

O'Hara, Julie Underwood. Use this legal briefing to assess your board's position on comparable worth. *American School Board Journal* 172(8):26-27 (August 1985).

1646. Howard Johnson Co., Inc. v. Detroit Local Joint Executive Board,   June 3, 1974
    Hotel and Restuarant Employees and Bartenders International Union, AFL-CIO
    417 US 249   41 LEd2d 46   94 SCt 2236
     Burger Years 220-227

1647. Michigan v. Tucker   June 10, 1974
    417 US 433   41 LEd2d 182   94 SCt 2357
     Burger Court 85-86
     Burger Years 143-168
     En Am Con 1400-1408

Collins, Ronald K. L., and Robert Welsh. Miranda's fate in the Burger Court. *Center Magazine* 13(5):43-52 (September/October 1980).

Drizin, Steven Andrew. Supreme Court review: Fifth Amendment—will the public safety exception swallow the Miranda exclusionary rule? *Journal of Criminal Law and Criminology* 75(3):692-715 (Fall 1984).

Gruhl, John. State supreme courts and the U.S. Supreme Court's post-Miranda rulings. *Journal of Criminal Law and Criminology* 72(3):886-913 (Fall 1981).

Kamisar, Yale. The swing of the pendulum. *Nation* 239(9):271-274 (September 29, 1984).

Schlag, Pierre J. Assaults on the exclusionary rule: good faith limitations and damage remedies. *Journal of Criminal Law and Criminology* 73(3):875-915 (Fall 1982).

1648. Geduldig v. Aiello   June 17, 1974
        417 US 484   41 LEd2d 256   94 SCt 2485
          Brennan 307-309
          Burger Court 149-150
          Burger Years 109-124
          En Am Con 1666-1673
          Hard Choices 311

Katz, Joni F. Hazardous working conditions and fetal protection policies: women are going back to the future. *Boston College Environmental Affairs Law Review* 17(1):201-230 (Fall 1989).

Rose, Jonathan. Decide 10 landmark cases that define your rights. *Scholastic Update* 119(1):7-9, 21 (September 8, 1986).

Williams, Wendy W., and Judith L. Lichtman. Closing the law's gender gap. *Nation* 239(9):280-285 (September 29, 1984).

1649. Morton, Secretary of the Interior v. Mancari   June 17, 1974
        417 US 535   41 LEd2d 290   94 SCt 2474
          Am Indians (Wilkinson) 48-49, 79, 126+

1650. Cardwell, Warden v. Lewis   June 17, 1974
        417 US 583   41 LEd2d 325   94 SCt 2464
          Guide (CQ) 340, 545

Dripps, Donald A. Supreme Court review: search and seizure: finding for the Fourth Amendment. *Trial* 29(3):95-97 (March 1993).

1651. Ross v. Moffitt   June 17, 1974
        417 US 600   41 LEd2d 341   94 SCt 2437
          En Am Con 1585-1592, 1611-1612

Mello, Michael A. Is there a federal constitutional right to counsel in capital post-conviction proceedings? *Journal of Criminal Law and Criminology* 79(4):1065-1104 (Winter 1989).

1652. Parker, Warden v. Levy   June 19, 1974
        417 US 733   41 LEd2d 439   94 SCt 2547
          Brennan 155-159
          En Am Con 1253-1255, 1365, 1955-1957

Ball, Howard. The U.S. Supreme Court's glossing of the Federal Tort Claims Act: statutory construction and veterans' tort actions. *Western Political Quarterly* 41(3):529-552 (September 1988).

1653. Pell v. Procunier, Director, California Department of Corrections   June 24, 1974
                Coupled with Procunier v. Hillery
        417 US 817   41 LEd2d 495   94 SCt 2800
          En Am Con 1372

Bleisch, N. David. The *Congressional Record* and the First Amendment: accuracy is the best policy. *Boston College Environmental Affairs Law Review* 12(2):341-379 (Winter 1985).

Copley, Helen K. General spirit of the people. *Vital Speeches* 46(6):169-172 (January 1, 1980).

Epstein, Judith. The journalists' rights. *Center Magazine* 15(6):40-42 (November/December 1982).

Howard, A. E. Dick. The press in court. *Wilson Quarterly* 6(5):86-93 (Special Issue 1982).

Maybe court will decide right to gather news. *Editor and Publisher* 113(17):28 (April 26, 1980).

Robbins, Ira P. Cry of "wolfish" in the federal courts: the future of federal judicial intervention in prison administration. *Journal of Criminal Law and Criminology* 71(3):211-225 (Fall 1980).

1654. Saxbe, Attorney General v. Washington Post Co.   June 24, 1974
      417 US 843   41 LEd2d 514   94 SCt 2811
      Bleisch, N. David. The Congressional Record and the First Amendment: accuracy is the best policy. *Boston College Environmental Affairs Law Review* 12(2):341-379 (Winter 1985).
      Copley, Helen K. General spirit of the people. *Vital Speeches* 46(6):169-172 (January 1, 1980).
      Hale, Dennis. How retiring Supreme Court Justice White voted in First Amendment cases. *Editor and Publisher* 126(30):44, 36 (July 24, 1993).

1655. Hamling v. United States   June 24, 1974
      418 US 87   41 LEd2d 590   94 SCt 2887
      Brennan 171-176
      Kobylka, Joseph F. A court-created context for group litigation: libertarian groups and obscenity. *Journal of Politics* 49(4):1061-1078 (November 1987).

1656. Jenkins v. Georgia   June 24, 1974
      418 US 153   41 LEd2d 642   94 SCt 2750
      Hagle, Timothy M. But do they have to see it to know it? the Supreme Court's obscenity and pornography decisions. *Western Political Quarterly* 44(4):1039-1054 (December 1991).
      Kobylka, Joseph F. A court-created context for group litigation: libertarian groups and obscenity. *Journal of Politics* 49(4):1061-1078 (November 1987).

1657. United States v. Richardson   June 25, 1974
      418 US 166   41 LEd2d 678   94 SCt 2940
      Equal Rights 130-133
      Alpert, Peter A. Citizen suits under the Clean Air Act: universal standing for the uninjured private attorney general? *Boston College Environmental Affairs Law Review* 16(2):283-328 (Winter 1988).
      McDowell, Gary L. Modest remedy for judicial activism. *Public Interest* (67):3-20 (Spring 1982).
      Neuborne, Burt. Taking away the right to sue. *Nation* 239(9):268-271 (September 29, 1984).

1658. Schlesinger, Secretary of Defense v. Reservists Committee to Stop the War   June 25, 1974
      418 US 208   41 LEd2d 706   94 SCt 2925
      Alpert, Peter A. Citizen suits under the Clean Air Act: universal standing for the uninjured private attorney general? *Boston College Environmental Affairs Law Review* 16(2):283-328 (Winter 1988).
      Perino, Michael A. Justice Scalia: standing, environmental law, and the Supreme Court. *Boston College Environmental Affairs Law Review* 15(1):135-179 (Fall 1987).

1659. Miami Herald Publishing Co. v. Tornillo   June 25, 1974
      418 US 241   41 LEd2d 730   94 SCt 2831
      Burger Court 23-27
      Const (Currie) 518-522
      Const Law 218-221R
      En Am Con 682, 730-738, 797-804, 1252
      First 269-272
      Fourth 260-287+
      Make 219-233
      Sup Ct Review (1982):195-241; (1987):345-396; (1994):57-128
      Cox, Archibald. First Amendment. *Society* 24(1):8-15 (November/December 1986).
      Epstein, Judith. The journalists' rights. *Center Magazine* 15(6):40-42 (November/December 1982).
      Hale, Dennis. How retiring Supreme Court Justice White voted in First Amendment cases. *Editor and Publisher* 126(30):44, 36 (July 24, 1993).
      Powe, L. A., Jr. Mass communications and the First Amendment: an overview. *Law and Contemporary Problems* 55(1):53-76 (Winter 1992).
      Winter, Ralph K. Political financing and the Constitution. *Annals of the American Academy of Political and Social Science* 486:34-48 (July 1986).

1660. Old Dominion Branch, No. 496, National Association of Letter Carriers, AFL-CIO   June 25, 1974
        v. Austin
      418 US 264   41 LEd2d 745   94 SCt 2770
        Jerry 246-247+
        Sup Ct Review (1994):169-208

1661. Lehman v. City of Shaker Heights   June 25, 1974
      418 US 298   41 LEd2d 770   94 SCt 2714
        Sup Ct Review (1982):195-241; (1992):29-77, 79-122

1662. Gertz v. Robert Welch, Inc.   June 25, 1974
      418 US 323   41 LEd2d 789   94 SCt 2997
        Ascent 184-186+
        Const Law 256-261R
        Courage 331-378, 429
        En Am Con 591-592, 840, 873-874, 1157-1159, 1457-1458
        First 249-254
        Fourth 110-115+
        Freedom (Cox) 16-18
        Jerry 66-68+
        Make 183-199+
        Sup Ct Ind 69-70
      Anderson, David A. Presumed harm: an item for the unfinished agenda of Times v. Sullivan. *Journalism Quarterly* 62(1):24-30 (Spring 1985).
      Brandon, George. High court accepts private figure case. *Editor and Publisher* 115[114]:10-11 (November 28, 1981).
      Brief of American Psychological Association and American Association for the Advancement of Science as Amici Curiae. Ronald R. Hutchinson, Petitioner v. William Proxmire and Morton Schwartz, Respondents. *American Psychologist* 35(8):750-758 (August 1980).
      Fields, Howard. Court weakens protection for media in libel suits. *Publishers' Weekly* 228(2):14 (July 12, 1985).
      Gertz, Elmer. Gertz on Gertz: reflections on the landmark libel case. *Trial* 21(10):66-69, 71-75 (October 1985).
      Gruhl, John. Supreme Court's impact on the law of libel: compliance by lower federal courts. *Western Political Quarterly* 33(4):502-519 (December 1980).
      Hale, F. Dennis. How retiring Supreme Court Justice White voted in First Amendment cases. *Editor and Publisher* 126(30):44, 36 (July 24, 1993).
      ———. Constitutional libel protection narrowed—not destroyed. *Trial* 17(7):54-58, 79 (July 1981).
      Helle, Steven. Judging public interest in libel: the Gertz decision's contribution. *Journalism Quarterly* 61(1):117-124 (Spring 1984).
      Hopkins, Jay. Ex-justices criticized punitive libel awards. *Editor and Publisher* 114(39):36 (September 26, 1981).
      Howard, A. E. Dick. The press in court. *Wilson Quarterly* 6(5):86-93 (Special Issue 1982).
      Hughes, Robert L. Rationalizing libel law in wake of Gertz: the problem and a proposal. *Journalism Quarterly* 62(3):540-547, 566 (Autumn 1985).
      Kebbel, Gary. The different functions of speech in defamation and privacy cases. *Journalism Quarterly* 61(3):629-633, 743 (Autumn 1984).
      Langvardt, Arlen W. Defamation in the business setting: basics and practical perspectives. *Business Horizons* 33(5):66-79 (September/October 1990).
      Nimmer, Melville. Tort invasions of privacy. *Center Magazine* 15(5):46-48 (September/October 1982).
      Powe, L. A., Jr. Mass communications and the First Amendment: an overview. *Law and Contemporary Problems* 55(1):53-76 (Winter 1992).
      Radolf, Andrew. Landmark libel case? *Editor and Publisher* 122(20):9-10 (May 20, 1989).
      Smolla, Rodney A. Supreme Court review: when a quote is not a quote. *Trial* 27(1):16-21 (January 1991).

1663. Spence v. Washington
    418 US 405   41 LEd2d 842
       Almanac (1989):309-311, 313
       Ascent 145-148
       Freedom (Cox) 59-62
       Sup Ct Review (1990):69-103

June 25, 1974
94 SCt 2727

Brennan, William. The United States Supreme Court: decision. *Congressional Digest* 68(8-9)196, 198, 200 (August/September 1989).

Rehnquist, William H. The United States Supreme Court: dissent. *Congressional Digest* 68(8-9):197, 199, 201 (August/September 1989).

Rose, Jonathan. Decide 10 landmark cases that define your rights. *Scholastic Update* 119(1):7-9, 21 (September 8, 1986).

Winter, Ralph K. Political financing and the Constitution. *Annals of the American Academy of Political and Social Science* 486:34-48 (July 1986).

1664. Codispoti v. Pennsylvania
    418 US 506   41 LEd2d 912
       En Am Con 304

June 24, 1974
94 SCt 2687

1665. Wolff v. McDonnell
    418 US 539   41 LEd2d 935

June 26, 1974
94 SCt 2963

Fuerst, J. S., and Roy Petty. Due process—how much is enough? *Public Interest* (79):96-110 (Spring 1985).

Goring, Darlene C. Supreme Court review: Fourth Amendment—prison cells: is there a right to privacy? *Journal of Criminal Law and Criminology* 75(3):609-629 (Fall 1984).

Robbins, Ira P. Cry of "wolfish" in the federal courts: the future of federal judicial intervention in prison administration. *Journal of Criminal Law and Criminology* 71(3):211-225 (Fall 1980).

1666. United States v. Marine Bancorporation, Inc.
    418 US 602   41 LEd2d 978
       Burger Court 184-187

January 26, 1974
94 SCt 2856

1667. United States v. Nixon
    418 US 683   41 LEd2d 1039
       Almanac (1987):66; (1988):124
       Ascent 23-24, 81-87+
       Const (Currie) 585-588
       Documents (v. 2):807-811R
       En Am Con 454-460, 671-673, 729-730, 1323-1324, 1659-1664, 2036-2037
       Equal (Harrell) 112-115+
       Guide (CQ) 53-54
       Guide (West) (v. 8):44-45
       Landmark (v. 3):25-38R
       May It 23-37R
       Sup Ct Review (1986):259-316
       Wars 506-526+

July 24, 1974
94 SCt 3090

American survey: Burger leaves the labyrinth. *Economist* 300(7454):17-22 (July 12-18, 1986).

Baker, banker, clergyman, thief. *Life* 10(10):84-88 (Fall 1987).

Dripps, Donald A. Supreme Court review: Warren Burger in perspective. *Trial* 31(8):73-75 (August 1995).

Fisher, Louis. Foreign policy powers of the President and Congress. *Annals of the American Academy of Political and Social Science* 499:149-159 (September 1988).

The legacy of the Burger Court. *U.S. News and World Report* 100(25):22 (June 30, 1986).

Rodriguez, Leon. Constitutional and statutory limits for cost-benefit analysis pursuant to Executive Orders 12,291 and 12,498. *Boston College Environmental Affairs Law Review* 15(3-4):505-546 (Spring 1988).

Trank, John P. The Burger Court—the first ten years. *Law and Contemporary Problems* 43(3):101-135 (Summer 1980).

1668. Milliken, Governor of Michigan v. Bradley   July 25, 1974
        Coupled with Allen Park Public Schools v. Bradley
        Coupled with Grosse Point Public Schools v. Bradley
    418 US 717   41 LEd2d 1069   94 SCt 3112
      Am Educators 352
      Ascent 263-266
      Burden 217-218, 221-223+
      Burger Court 119-120, 231
      Burger Years 95-108
      Const (Currie) 477-482, 574-577
      Court Public 99-100, 141-158R
      En Am Con 557-561, 1261, 1625-1626
      Sup Ct Ind 243-246+
      Thurgood 426-450R+

Burns, Haywood. The activisim in not affirmative. *Nation* 239(9):264-268 (September 29, 1984).

Chemerinsky, Erwin. Supreme Court review: race and the Supreme Court. *Trial* 31(10):86-88 (October 1995).

Delon, Floyd G. The legacy of Thurgood Marshall. *Journal of Negro Education* 63(3):278-288 (Summer 1994).

Fuerst, J. S. Time to get off the bus?: the courts, schools and desegregation. *Commonweal* 118(12):403-405 (June 14, 1991).

Gest, Ted. Next stage: court lite. *U.S. News and World Report* 111(2):16-19 (July 8, 1991).

Gordon, William M. The implementation of desegregation plans since Brown. *Journal of Negro Education* 63(3):310-322 (Summer 1994).

Hyde, Alison A. School desegregation: the role of the courts and means of achievement. *NASSP Bulletin* 78(565):28-37 (November 1994).

Kozol, Jonathan. Giant steps backward: romance of the ghetto school. *Nation* 258(20):703-706 (May 23, 1994).

Menacker, Julius. Review of Supreme Court reasoning in cases of expression, due process, and equal protection. *Phi Delta Kappan* 63(3):188-190 (November 1981).

Reid, Herbert O., Sr. State of the art: the law and education since 1954. *Journal of Negro Education* 52(3):234-249 (Summer 1983).

Reid, Herbert O., and Frankie M. Foster-Davis. Three decades of "all deliberate speed." *Crisis* 91(5):12-15 (May 1984).

Russo, Charles J., J. John Harris III, and Rosetta F. Sandidge. Brown v. Board of Education at 40: a legal history of equal educational opportunity in American public education. *Journal of Negro Education* 63(3):297-309 (Summer 1994).

Sendor, Benjamin. Kansas City and the limits of desegregation. *American School Board Journal* 182(9):18-20 (September 1995).

Simmons, Althea T. L. From Brown to Grove City: blueprint for education. *Crisis* 91(5):6-10 (May 1984).

Trank, John P. The Burger Court—the first ten years. *Law and Contemporary Problems* 43(3):101-135 (Summer 1980).

1669. Cantrell v. Forest City Publishing Co.   December 18, 1974
    419 US 245   42 LEd2d 419   95 SCt 465
    Kebbel, Gary. The different functions of speech in defamation and privacy cases. *Journalism Quarterly* 61(3):629-633, 743 (Autumn 1984).

1670. Schick v. Reed, Chairman, United States Board of Parole   December 23, 1974
    419 US 256   42 LEd2d 430   95 SCt 379
      En Am Con 1624

1671. Linden Lumber Division, Summer & Co.   December 23, 1974
      v. National Labor Relations Board (NLRB)
        Coupled with National Labor Relations Board (NLRB) v. Truck Drivers Union Local, No. 413
    419 US 301   42 LEd2d 465   95 SCt 429
      Burger Court 167

1672. Jackson v. Metropolitan Edison Co.   December 23, 1974
     419 US 345   42 LEd2d 477   95 SCt 449
       En Am Con 1007-1008, 1729-1736, 1736-1738
       Sup Ct Review (1988):129-161
     Sullivan, Harold J. Privatization of public services: a growing threat to constitutional rights. *Public Administration Review* 47(6):461-467 (November/December 1987).

1673. Sosna v. Iowa   January 14, 1975
     419 US 393   42 LEd2d 532   95 SCt 553
       En Am Con 572, 1593-1596, 1711

1674. Schlesinger, Secretary of Defense v. Ballard   January 15, 1975
     419 US 498   42 LEd2d 610   95 SCt 572
       Burger Court 136-137, 141-142, 151-153+
       En Am Con 1666-1673
       Equal Rights 17-42+
       Magic 329-330

1675. Taylor v. Louisiana   January 21, 1975
     419 US 522   42 LEd2d 690   95 SCt 692
       Burger Court 137-140
       Death Penalty 80s 19-20
       En Am Con 1082-1085, 1873
     Goldberg, Steven H. Harmless error: constitutional sneak thief. *Journal of Criminal Law and Criminology* 71(4):421-442 (Winter 1980).
     Kull, Andrew. Racial justice. *New Republic* 207(23):17-18, 20-21 (November 30, 1992).
     Schultz, Marjorie S. Jury defined: a review of Burger court decisions. *Law and Contemporary Problems* 43(4):8-23 (Autumn 1980).

1676. United States v. Mazurie   January 21, 1975
     419 US 544   42 LEd2d 706   95 SCt 710
       Am Indians (Wilkinson) 60, 127+

1677. Goss v. Lopez   January 22, 1975
     419 US 565   42 LEd2d 725   95 SCt 729
       Abortion Pol (Rubin) 132
       Am Educators 245
       Ascent 386-388+
       Burger Court 99-101
       Const (Currie) 542-546
       En Am Con 608-612, 679-680, 854, 1465-1472
     Christopher, Maura. Decide seven court cases that test teenagers' rights. *Scholastic Update* (Teachers' Edition) 120(1):16-18+ (September 4, 1987).
     Eberlein, Larry. The teacher in the courtroom: new role expectation? *Clearing House* 53(6):287-291 (February 1980).
     Flygare, Thomas J. The hundredth column: looking back/looking forward. *Phi Delta Kappan* 67(3):229-230 (November 1985).
     ————. De jure: ten years after Goss v. Lopez: an interview with Peter D. Roos. *Phi Delta Kappan* 66(6):441-442 (February 1985).
     Lawrence, Charise K. Your Constitution: securing your rights. *Scholastic Update* 120(9):11 (January 15, 1988).
     Menacker, Julius. Review of Supreme Court reasoning in cases of expression, due process, and equal protection. *Phi Delta Kappan* 63(3):188-190 (November 1981).
     Menacker, Julius, Emanuel Hurwitz, and Ward Weldon. Supreme Court attitudes about school discipline compared to attitudes of urban teachers. *Journal of Negro Education* 58(1):92-101 (Winter 1989).

Mueller, Jean West, and Wynell Burroughs Schamel. Teaching with documents: due process and student rights: syllabus of the Goss v. Lopez decision. *Social Education* 55(3):161-163R, 168 (March 1991).

Oakes, Jeannie. Tracking and ability grouping in American schools: some constitutional questions. *Teachers College Record* 84(4):801-819 (Summer 1983).

Sendor, Benjamin. A judicial wink mustn't blind you to due process. *American School Board Journal* 176(12):12-13 (December 1989).

————. Trend: courts sustain your tough, but fair, actions. *American School Board Journal* 172(6):20-21 (June 1985).

1678. Emporium Capwell Co. v. Western Addition Community Organization   February 18, 1975
        Coupled with National Labor Relations Board (NLRB) v. Western Addition Community Organization
420 US 50   43 LEd2d 12   95 SCt 977
    Burger Court 165

1679. United States v. Bisceglia   February 19, 1975
420 US 141   43 LEd2d 88   95 SCt 915
Waldron, Dorothy, and Leslie D. Ball. The bottom line on checkless banking. *Across the Board* 17(8): 34-41 (August 1980).

1680. Antoine v. Washington   February 19, 1975
420 US 194   43 LEd2d 129   95 SCt 944
    Am Indians (Wilkinson) 64-65, 127+

1681. United States v. ITT Continental Baking Co.   February 19, 1975
420 US 223   43 LEd2d 148   95 SCt 926
Cardone, John V. Substantive standards and NEPA: mitigating environmental consequences with consent decrees. *Boston College Environmental Affairs Law Review* 18(1):159-184 (Fall 1990).

1682. National Labor Relations Board (NLRB) v. J. Weingarten, Inc.   February 19, 1975
420 US 251   43 LEd2d 171   95 SCt 959
Kruchko, John G., and Lawrence E. Dube, Jr. New right for non-union workers. *Personnel* 60(6):59-64 (November/December 1983).

Schachter, Victor. Investigating misconduct? three is not a crowd. *ABA Banking Journal* 75(6):28-30 (June 1983).

1683. Wood v. Strickland   February 25, 1975
420 US 308   43 LEd2d 214   95 SCt 992
    En Am Con 2074

Flygare, Thomas J. The hundredth column: looking back/looking forward. *Phi Delta Kappan* 67(3):229-230 (November 1985).

Rosenbloom, David H. Public administrators' official immunity and the Supreme Court: developments during the 1970s. *Public Administration Review* 40(2):166-173 (March/April 1980).

1684. DeCoteau v. District County Court for the Tenth Judicial District   March 3, 1975
        Coupled with Erickson, Warden v. Feather
420 US 425   43 LEd2d 300   95 SCt 1082
    Am Indians (Wilkinson) 50-51, 91, 127+

1685. Cox Broadcasting Corp. v. Cohn   March 3, 1975
420 US 469   43 LEd2d 328   95 SCt 1029
    En Am Con 512, 1457-1458
    Freedom (Cox) 19-20
Garneau, George. First Amendment upheld. *Editor and Publisher* 122(26):10-11 (July 1, 1989).

————. Press vs. privacy. *Editor and Publisher* 121(43):20, 53 (October 22, 1988).

Hale, Dennis. How retiring Supreme Court Justice White voted in First Amendment cases. *Editor and Publisher* 126(30):44, 36 (July 24, 1993).

Nimmer, Melville. Tort invasions of privacy. *Center Magazine* 15(5):46-48 (September/October 1982).

Rotunda, Ronald D. The Supreme Court: eschewing bright lines. *Trial* 25(12):52-56 (December 1989).

Welsh, Robert, and Ronald K. L. Collins. Taking state constitutions seriously: the protection of civil liberties has been shifting away from the U.S. Supreme Court. *Center Magazine* 14(5):6-35, 38-43 (September/October 1981).

1686. Southeastern Promotions, Ltd. v. Conrad   March 18, 1975
420 US 546   43 LEd2d 448   95 SCt 1239

Kobylka, Joseph F. A court-created context for group litigation: libertarian groups and obscenity. *Journal of Politics* 49(4):1061-1078 (November 1987).

O'Neil, Robert M. Artistic freedom and academic freedom. *Law and Contemporary Problems* 53(3):177-193 (Summer 1990).

Winter, Ralph K. Political financing and the Constitution. *Annals of the American Academy of Political and Social Science* 486:34-48 (July 1986).

1687. Weinberger v. Wiesenfeld   March 19, 1975
420 US 636   43 LEd2d 514   95 SCt 1225
Burger Court 137-139+, 141-142
En Am Con 1666-1673, 1704-1705
Equal Rights 17-42+

Baer, Judith A. Women's rights and the limits of constitutional doctrine. *Western Political Quarterly* 44(4):821-852 (December 1991).

1688. Oregon v. Hass   March 19, 1975
420 US 714   43 LEd2d 570   95 SCt 1215
Burger Court 82-83
Burger Years 143-168

Gruhl, John. State supreme courts and the U.S. Supreme Court's post-Miranda rulings. *Journal of Criminal Law and Criminology* 72(3):886-913 (Fall 1981).

Haas, Kenneth C. "New federalism" and prisoners' rights: state supreme courts in comparative perspective. *Western Political Quarterly* 34(4):552-571 (December 1981).

Hartman, Marshall J., and Sidney Bernstein. To Leon, and beyond; two commentators react. *Trial* 21(1):50-56 (January 1985).

1689. Schlesinger v. Councilman   March 25, 1975
420 US 738   43 LEd2d 591   95 SCt 1300

Ball, Howard. The U.S. Supreme Court's glossing of the Federal Tort Claims Act: statutory construction and veterans' tort actions. *Western Political Quarterly* 41(3):529-552 (September 1988).

1690. Stanton v. Stanton   April 15, 1975
421 US 7   43 LEd2d 688   95 SCt 1373
Burger Court 137-140
En Am Con 1666-1673

1691. Withrow v. Larkin   April 16, 1975
421 US 35   43 LEd2d 712   95 SCt 1456

Sendor, Benjamin. Balancing your roles as an employer. *American School Board Journal* 181(9):20-21 (September 1994).

1692. Hill v. Stone   May 12, 1975
421 US 289   44 LEd2d 172   95 SCt 1637
Court Public 94

1693. Meek v. Pittenger   May 19, 1975
     421 US 349   44 LEd2d 217   95 SCt 1753
       Ascent 196-199
       Brennan 125-129
       Burger Years 56-91
       En Am Con 1650-1658
       Establishment 128-129, 136-138+
       Godless 70-74+
       Religion 34-42+
       Sup Ct Church 141-142

Buzzard, Lynn Robert, and Samuel Ericsson. Public aid to private schools: Caesar rendering to God? *Christianity Today* 27(10):20-23 (June 17, 1983).

Doerr, Edd. Victories . . . and warnings. *Humanist* 45(5):39-40 (September/October 1985).

Drinan, Robert F. Compensatory education in private schools. *America* 152(13):278-280 (April 6, 1985).

Regan, Richard J. Supreme Court roundup: 1980 term. *Thought* 56(223):491-502 (December 1981).

Schwartz, Michael. A new direction for the courts on the school question. *America* 149(13):251-254 (October 29, 1983).

Weber, Paul J. Excessive entanglement: a wavering First Amendment standard. *Review of Politics* 46(4):483-501 (October 1984).

1694. Alyeska Pipeline Service Co. v. Wilderness Society   May 12, 1975
     421 US 420   44 LEd2d 141   95 SCt 1612

Jordan, Scott J. Awarding attorney's fees to environmental plaintiffs under a private attorney general theory. *Boston College Environmental Affairs Law Review* 14(2):287-311 (Winter 1987).

O'Connor, Karen, and Lee Epstein. Bridging the gap between Congress and the Supreme Court: interest groups and the erosion of the American rule governing awards of attorneys' fees. *Western Political Quarterly* 38(2):238-249 (June 1985).

Spurrier, Robert L., Jr. Paying the piper in federal civil rights litigation. *Public Administration Review* 43(3):199-208 (May/June 1983).

1695. Eastland v. United States Servicemen's Fund   May 27, 1975
     421 US 491   44 LEd2d 324   95 SCt 1813
       Almanac (1990):510-511

1696. Breed v. Jones   May 27, 1975
     421 US 519   44 LEd2d 346   95 SCt 1779
       Abortion Pol (Rubin) 132
       En Am Con 1091-1093

Feld, Barry C. The juvenile court meets the principle of the offense: legislative changes in juvenile waiver statutes. *Journal of Criminal Law and Criminology* 78(3):471-533 (Fall 1987).

1697. Fry v. United States   May 27, 1975
     421 US 542   44 LEd2d 363   95 SCt 1792
       Const (Currie) 563-568
       Sup Ct Review (1983):215-281

Johnston, Richard E., and John T. Thompson. Burger Court and federalism: a revolution in 1976? *Western Political Quarterly* 33(2):197-216 (June 1980).

Solimine, Michael E. Constitutionality of congressional legislation to overrule Zurcher v. Stanford daily. *Journal of Criminal Law and Criminology* 71(2):147-162 (Summer 1980).

Wise, Charles, and Rosemary O'Leary. Is federalism dead or alive in the Supreme Court?: implications for public administrators. *Public Administration Review* 52(6):559-572 (November/December 1992).

1698. Dunlop v. Bachowski   June 2, 1975
     421 US 560   44 LEd2d 377   95 SCt 1851
       Burger Years 191-205

Morrison, Alan B. Close reins on the bureaucracy. *Nation* 239(9):290-294 (September 29, 1984).

1699. Connell Construction Co. v. Plumbers and Steamfitters Local Union No. 100   June 2, 1975
     421 US 616   44 LEd2d 418   95 SCt 1830
       Burger Court 177-179
       En Am Con 1111-1112
     Court limits antitrust suits in labor disputes. *Engineering News-Record* 210(9):58 (March 3, 1983).
     Losers could win in subcontracting case. *Engineering News-Record* 208(22):58 (June 3, 1982).

1700. United States v. Park   June 9, 1975
     421 US 658   44 LEd2d 489   95 SCt 1903
     Goldberg, Andrew M. Corporate officer liability for federal environmental statute violations. *Boston College Environmental Affairs Law Review* 18(2):357-379 (Winter 1991).

1701. Mullaney v. Wilbur   June 9, 1975
     421 US 684   44 LEd2d 508   95 SCt 1881
     Dennis, Anthony J. Supreme Court review: Fifth Amendment—due process rights at sentencing. *Journal of Criminal Law and Criminology* 77(3):646-665 (Fall 1986).
     Harris, Leslie J. Constitutional limits on criminal presumptions as an expression of changing concepts of fundamental fairness. *Journal of Criminal Law and Criminology* 77(2):308-357 (Summer 1986).

1702. Blue Chip Stamps v. Manor Drug Stores   June 9, 1975
     421 US 723   44 LEd2d 539   95 SCt 1917
       Burger Years 206-219
     Coffee, John C., Jr. The unfaithful champion: the plaintiff as monitor in shareholder litigation. *Law and Contemporary Problems* 48(3):5-81 (Summer 1985).
     Cohen, Jerry A., and Herbert E. Milstein. "Efficiency" over competition. *Nation* 239(9):294-295 (September 29, 1984).
     Cox, James D. Insider trading: regulation of activity is 'in trouble.' *Trial* 24(9):22-28, 93-96 (September 1988).
     Rathjen, Gregory J., and Harold J. Spaeth. Denial of access and ideological preferences: an analysis of the voting behavior of the Burger Court Justices, 1969-1976. *Western Political Quarterly* 36(1):71-87 (March 1983).

1703. Goldfarb v. Virginia State Bar   June 16, 1975
     421 US 773   44 LEd2d 572   95 SCt 2004
       En Am Con 851
       Magic 288-289
       Sup Ct Review (1984):69-148
     Hamlin, Ross J. Application of the Sherman Act state action exemption to municipal environmental regulation: a case for broader local discretion. *Boston College Environmental Affairs Law Review* 11(3):609-664 (April 1984).
     Hite, Robert E. and Cynthia Fraser. Meta-analyses of attitudes toward advertising by profession. *Journal of Marketing* 52(3):95-103 (July 1988).
     Weller, Charles D. McCarran Act interpretation may have been charted in Barry case. *Best's Review* (Life/Health Insurance Edition) 83(2):40-42, 87-89 (June 1982).
     ———. McCarran Act interpretation may have been charted in Barry case. *Best's Review* (Property/Casualty Insurance Edition) 83(3):28-32 (July 1982).
     Werner, Ray O. Marketing and the United States Supreme Court, 1975-1981. *Journal of Marketing* 46(2):73-81 (Spring 1982).

1704. Murphy v. Florida   June 16, 1975
     421 US 794   44 LEd2d 589   95 SCt 2031
       En Am Con 1287-1288

1705. Bigelow v. Virginia   June 16, 1975
     421 US 809   44 LEd2d 600   95 SCt 2222

     Abortion Am 81-83, 97

     Const (Currie) 513-518

     Const Law 171-174R+

     Magic 315-317

     Boedecker, Karl A., and Fred W. Morgan. The evolution of First Amendment protection for commercial speech. *Journal of Marketing* 59(1):38-47 (January 1995).

     Heath, Robert L., and Richard Alan Nelson. Image and issue advertising: a corporate and public policy perspective. *Journal of Marketing* 49(2):58-68 (Spring 1985).

     Winter, Ralph K. Political financing and the Constitution. *Annals of the American Academy of Political and Social Science* 486:34-48 (July 1986).

1706. Cort v. Ash   June 17, 1975
     422 US 66   45 LEd2d 26   95 SCt 2080

     Collins, Michael. The dilemma of the downstream state: the untimely demise of federal common law nuisance. *Boston College Environmental Affairs Law Review* 11(2):295-412 (January 1984).

1707. United States v. Hale   June 23, 1975
     422 US 171   45 LEd2d 99   95 SCt 2133

     Gruhl, John. State supreme courts and the U.S. Supreme Court's post-Miranda rulings. *Journal of Criminal Law and Criminology* 72(3):886-913 (Fall 1981).

     Melson, David E. Supreme Court review: Fourteenth Amendment—criminal procedure: the impeachment use of post-arrest silence which precedes the receipt of Miranda warnings. *Journal of Criminal Law and Criminology* 73(4):1572-1594 (Winter 1982).

1708. Erznoznik v. City of Jacksonville   June 23, 1975
     422 US 205   45 LEd2d 125   95 SCt 2268

     Economics 333-337, 345-346

     En Am Con 651-652

     Freedom (Cox) 52-56

     Kobylka, Joseph F. A court-created context for group litigation: libertarian groups and obscenity. *Journal of Politics* 49(4):1061-1078 (November 1987).

     McGuire, Kevin T., and Gregory A. Caldeira. Lawyers, organized interests, and the law of obscenity: agenda setting in the Supreme Court. *American Political Science Review* 87(3):717-726 (September 1993).

1709. United States v. Nobles   June 23, 1975
     422 US 225   45 LEd2d 141   95 SCt 2160

     White, Welsh S. The psychiatric examination and the Fifth Amendment privilege in capital cases. *Journal of Criminal Law and Criminology* 74(3):943-990 (Fall 1983).

1710. Administrator, Federal Aviation Administration (FAA) v. Robertson   June 24, 1975
     422 US 255   45 LEd2d 164   95 SCt 2140

     Burger Years 191-205

     Morrison, Alan B. The Supreme Court and the Freedom of Information Act. *Nation* 239(9):287 (September 29, 1984).

1711. City of Richmond, Virginia v. United States   June 24, 1975
     422 US 358   45 LEd2d 245   95 SCt 2296

     Davis, Olethia. Tenuous interpretation: Sections 2 and 5 of the Voting Rights Act. *National Civic Review* 84(4):310-322 (Fall/Winter 1995).

     Zimmerman, Joseph F. Election systems and representative democracy: reflections on the Voting Rights Act of 1965. *National Civic Review* 84(4):287-309 (Fall/Winter 1995).

1712. Albemarle Paper Co. v. Moody   June 25, 1975
        Coupled with Halifax Local No. 425 v. Moody
      422 US 405   45 LEd2d 280   95 SCt 2362
        Affirmative (Greene) 66-71
      Chambers, Julius L., and Barry Goldstein. Title VII: the continuing challenge of establishing fair employment practices. *Law and Contemporary Problems* 49(4):9-23 (Autumn 1986).
      Reid-Dove, Allyson, and Michael E. Howard. "Night has fallen on the Court . . ." *Black Enterprise* 20(2):44-45 (September 1989).
      Vile, John R., and Kathy Ruth McCoy. The Memphis Case: another precedent? *Personnel* 62(7):72-76 (July 1985).

1713. Warth v. Seldin   June 25, 1975
      422 US 490   45 LEd2d 343   95 SCt 2197
        Burger Court 59-61
        Equal Rights 130-133
        Sup Ct Review (1981):41-47
      Alpert, Peter A. Citizen suits under the Clean Air Act: universal standing for the uninjured private attorney general? *Boston College Environmental Affairs Law Review* 16(2):283-328 (Winter 1988).
      Binion, Gayle. The Burger court and the rights of the poor. *Center Magazine* 15(2):2-7 (March/April 1982).
      Farber, Daniel A. Supreme Court review: from Warren to Rehnquist. *Trial* 25(7):124-126 (July 1989).
      Neuborne, Burt. Taking away the right to sue. *Nation* 239(9):268-271 (September 29, 1984).
      Rathjen, Gregory J., and Harold J. Spaeth. Denial of access and ideological preferences: an analysis of the voting behavior of the Burger court justices, 1969-1976. *Western Political Quarterly* 36(1):71-87 (March 1983).
      Rowe, Thomas D. No final victories: the incompleteness of equity's triumph in federal public law. *Law and Contemporary Problems* 56(3):105-121 (Summer 1993).

1714. United States v. Peltier   June 25, 1975
      422 US 531   45 LEd2d 374   95 SCt 2313
      Jensen, D. Lowell, and Rosemary Hart. The good faith restatement of the exclusionary rule. *Journal of Criminal Law and Criminology* 73(3):916-938 (Fall 1982).

1715. O'Connor v. Donaldson   June 26, 1975
      422 US 563   45 LEd2d 396   95 SCt 2486
        En Am Con 1247-1249, 1339, 1465-1472
      Kaus, Robert M. They were wrong about the brethren. [Editorial] *Washington Monthly* 13(1):32-40 (March 1981).
      Meisel, Alan. The rights of the mentally ill under state constitutions. *Law and Contemporary Problems* 45(3):7-40 (Summer 1982).

1716. Brown v. Illinois   June 26, 1975
      422 US 590   45 LEd2d 416   95 SCt 2254
        Burger Court 80-82+
      Bernstein, Sidney, and Michael Eisenstein. 1982 Supreme Court update: the criminal law. *Trial* 18(9):45-50, 81 (September 1982).
      Erickson, William H. 1981-1982 US Supreme court decisions. *Trial* 18(11):44-49, 109 (November 1982).
      Hartman, Marshall J., and Sidney Bernstein. To Leon, and beyond; two commentators react. *Trial* 21(1):50-56 (January 1985).
      Levinson, William D. Supreme Court review: Fourth Amendment—a renewed plea for relevant criteria for the admissibility of tainted confessions. *Journal of Criminal Law and Criminology* 73(4):1408-1429 (Winter 1982).
      Stratton, Brent D. The attenuation exception to the exclusionary rule: a study in attenuated principle and dissipated logic. *Journal of Criminal Law and Criminology* 75(1):139-165 (Spring 1984).

1717. United States v. National Association of Securities Dealers, Inc. (NASD)   June 26, 1975
     422 US 694   45 LEd2d 486   95 SCt 2427
     Hamlin, Ross J. Application of the Sherman Act state action exemption to municipal environmental regulation: a case for broader local discretion. *Boston College Environmental Affairs Law Review* 11(3):609-664 (April 1984).

1718. Faretta v. California   June 30, 1975
     422 US 806   45 LEd2d 562   95 SCt 2525
     En Am Con 688
     Boch, Brian R. Supreme Court review: Fourteenth Amendment—the standard of mental competency to waive constitutional rights versus the competency standard to stand trial. *Journal of Criminal Law and Criminology* 84(4):883-914 (Winter/Spring 1994).

1719. United States v. Brignoni-Ponce   June 30, 1975
     422 US 873   45 LEd2d 607   95 SCt 2574
     Bernstein, Sidney, and Michael Eisenstein. 1981 Supreme Court update: the criminal law. *Trial* 17(10):54-60, 85 (October 1981).
     Greig, William H., and Phillip S. Althoff. The constitutionality of roadblocks; the Fourth Amendment on the firing line again. *Trial* 22(2):56-62 (February 1986).
     Vawrinek, Jeffrey J. Supreme Court review: Fourth Amendment—detention of occupants during a premises search: the winter of discontent for probable cause. *Journal of Criminal Law and Criminology* 72(4):1246-1264 (Winter 1981).

1720. United States v. Ortiz   June 30, 1975
     422 US 891   45 LEd2d 623   95 SCt 2585
     Greig, William H., and Phillip S. Althoff. The constitutionality of roadblocks; the Fourth Amendment on the firing line again. *Trial* 22(2):56-62 (February 1986).

1721. Turner v. Department of Employment Security and Board   November 17, 1975
     of Review of the Industrial Commission of Utah
     423 US 44   46 LEd2d 181   96 SCt 249
     Burger Court 149-150
     En Am Con 1666-1673

1722. Michigan v. Mosley   December 9, 1975
     423 US 96   46 LEd2d 313   96 SCt 321
     Burger Court 83-84
     Bitterman, Patrick J. Supreme Court review: Fifth Amendment—the applicability of the assertion of the right to counsel to unrelated investigations. *Journal of Criminal Law and Criminology* 79(3):676-700 (Fall 1988).
     Gruhl, John. State supreme courts and the U.S. Supreme Court's post-Miranda rulings. *Journal of Criminal Law and Criminology* 72(3):886-913 (Fall 1981).
     Melson, David E. Supreme Court review: Fifth Amendment—waivers of previously invoked right to counsel. *Journal of Criminal Law and Criminology* 72(4):1288-1306 (Winter 1981).

1723. Michelin Tire Corp. v. Wages, Tax Commissioner   January 14, 1976
     423 US 276   46 LEd2d 495   96 SCt 535
     Ascent 121-123
     En Am Con 164, 966, 1253, 1349-1350

1724. Federal Power Commission (FPC) v. Transcontinental Gas Pipe Line Corp.   January 19, 1976
     423 US 326   46 LEd2d 533   96 SCt 579
     Kelly, Paula. Judicial review of agency decisions under the National Environmental Policy Act of 1969—Strycker's Bay Neighborhood Council, Inc. v. Karlen. *Boston College Environmental Affairs Law Review* 10(1):79-109 (1982-83).

1725. Rizzo v. Goode   January 21, 1976
      423 US 362   46 LEd2d 561   96 SCt 598
         Brennan 91-99
         Burger Years 3-20
         En Am Con 1598
      Aronow, Geoffrey, and Owen Fiss. The High Court illusion of victory. *Nation* 235(21):647-650 (December 18,
         1982).
      Askin, Frank. Justice denied: what the conservative judiciary hath wrought. *Trial* 29(10):65-68 (October 1993).
      Chemerinsky, Erwin. Protecting individual rights: policing the police. *Trial* 27(12):32-36 (December 1991).
      Fiss, Owen M., and Charles Krauthammer. The Rehnquist Court. *New Republic* 186(10):14-16, 18 (March 10,
         1982).
      Lee, Yong S. Civil liability of state and local governments: myth and reality. *Public Administration Review*
         47(2):160-170 (March/April 1987).
      Neuborne, Burt. Taking away the right to sue. *Nation* 239(9):268-271 (September 29, 1984).

1726. United States v. Watson   January 26, 1976
      423 US 411   46 LEd2d 598   96 SCt 820
         Ascent 324-327+
         En Am Con 73-74, 1628-1635

1727. Buckley v. Valeo   January 30, 1976
      424 US 1   46 LEd2d 659   96 SCt 612
         Almanac (1992):63-64; (1993):37, 77, 51-C
         Ascent 88-90, 143-145+
         Burger Court 31-33, 200+
         Chadha 69-71+, 233-240+
         Const (Currie) 510-512+
         Const (Friendly) 92, 99-107
         Const Law 187-188
         En Am Con 168, 198-200, 694-695, 730-738, 770-773, 856-858, 1413-1417
         Financing 37-42, 163-165+
         Fourth 249-250+
         Freedom (Cox) 68-86
         Guide (CQ) 54-55, 65
         Guide (West) (v. 2):185-187
         Sup Ct Review (1982):195-241, 243-284; (1983):583-626; (1990):105-132; (1988):1-41
      Bingham, Jonathan. Democracy or plutocracy? The case for a constitutional amendment to overturn Buckley v.
         Valeo. *Annals of the American Academy of Political and Social Science* 486:103-114 (July 1986).
      Bolling, Richard. Money in politics. *Annals of the American Academy of Political and Social Science* 486:76-85
         (July 1986).
      Cox, Archibald. First Amendment. *Society* 24(1):8-15 (November/December 1986).
      Cox, James D. Insider trading: regulation of activity is 'in trouble.' *Trial* 24(9):22-28, 93-96 (September 1988).
      Cutler, Lloyd N. Can the parties regulate campaign financing? *Annals of the American Academy of Political
         and Social Science* 486:115-120 (July 1986).
      Daugherty, Donald A. Supreme Court review: the separation of powers and abuses in prosecutorial discretion.
         Journal of Criminal Law and Criminology 79(3):953-996 (Fall 1988).
      Fox, Arthur. Showing workers who's the boss. *Nation* 239(9):295-299 (September 29, 1984).
      Franklin, Daniel. The five dumbest Supreme Court decisions. *Washington Monthly* 26(10):12-18 (October
         1994).
      Heath, Robert L., amd Richard Alan Nelson. Image and issue advertising: a corporate and public policy
         perspective. *Journal of Marketing* 49(2):58-68 (Spring 1985).
      Jensen, Laura S. Subsidies, strings, and the courts: judicial action and conditional federal spending. *Review of
         Politics* 55(3):491-509 (Summer 1993).
      Lee, William P. FLPMA's legislative veto provisions and INS v. Chadha: who controls the federal lands?
         Boston College Environmental Affairs Law Review 12(4):791-821 (Summer 1985).

McGuire, Kevin T., and Barbara Palmer. Issue fluidity on the U.S. Supreme Court. *American Political Science Review* 89(3):691-702 (September 1995).

Miller Arthur S. Buying votes: is politics the last free market? *Progressive* 46(10):43-45 (October 1982).

Oldaker, William C. Of philosophers, foxes, and finances: can the Federal Election Commission ever do an adequate job? *Annals of the American Academy of Political and Social Science* 486:132-145 (July 1986).

Powe, L. A., Jr. Mass communications and the First Amendment: an overview. *Law and Contemporary Problems* 55(1):53-76 (Winter 1992).

Trank, John P. The Burger Court—the first ten years. *Law and Contemporary Problems* 43(3):101-135 (Summer 1980).

Winter, Ralph K. Political financing and the Constitution. *Annals of the American Academy of Political and Social Science* 486:34-48 (July 1986).

1728. Mathews v. Eldridge   February 24, 1976
       424 US 319   47 LEd2d 18   96 SCt 893
       Const (Currie) 545-546
       En Am Con 1228, 1465-1472, 1704-1705
       Sup Ct Review (1980):211-279; (1982):85-125; (1987):157-200

Bennett, Fred Warren. Toward eliminating bargain basement justice: providing indigent defendants with expert services and an adequate defense. *Law and Contemporary Problems* 58(1):95-138 (Winter 1995).

Chemerinsky, Erwin. Supreme Court review: civil forfeiture: a diminishing power. *Trial* 30(4):66-68 (April 1994).

Levine, Beth. Supreme Court review: Fourteenth Amendment—due process and an indigent's right to court-appointed psychiatric assistance in state criminal proceedings. *Journal of Criminal Law and Criminology* 76(4):1065-1085 (Winter 1985).

Plater, Zygmunt J. B., and William Lund Norine. Through the looking glass of eminent domain: exploring the "arbitrary and capricious" test and substantive rationality review of governmental decisions. *Boston College Environmental Affairs Law Review* 16(4):661-752 (Summer 1989).

Shulman, Barbara S. Supreme Court review: Fourteenth Amendment—the Supreme Court's mandate for proof beyond a preponderance of the evidence in terminating parental rights. *Journal of Criminal Law and Criminology* 73(4):1595-1611 (Winter 1982).

Vanderziel, Kathleen M. The Hatfield Riders and environmental preservation: what process is due? *Boston College Environmental Affairs Law Review* 19(2):431-479 (Fall/Winter 1991).

1729. Great Atlantic and Pacific Tea Co. v. Cottrell   February 25, 1976
       A & P Tea Co. v. Cottrell
       424 US 366   47 LEd2d 55   96 SCt 923
       En Am Con 866, 1751-1755

1730. Fisher v. District Court of the Sixteenth Judicial District of Montana   March 1, 1976
       424 US 382   47 LEd2d 106   96 SCt 943
       Am Indians (Wilkinson) 38, 127+

Ott, Brian R. Indian fishing rights in the Pacific Northwest: the need for federal intervention. *Boston College Environmental Affairs Law Review* 14(2):313- 343 (Winter 1987).

1731. Imbler v. Pachtman   March 2, 1976
       424 US 409   47 LEd2d 128   96 SCt 984
       En Am Con 949, 1039-1040

Ball, Howard. The U.S. Supreme Court's glossing of the Federal Tort Claims Act: statutory construction and veterans' tort actions. *Western Political Quarterly* 41(3):529-552 (September 1988).

1732. Time, Inc. v. Firestone   March 2, 1976
       424 US 448   47 LEd2d 154   96 SCt 958
       Brennan 176-179
       En Am Con 1487-1488

Anderson, David A. Presumed harm: an item for the unfinished agenda of Times v. Sullivan. *Journalism Quarterly* 62(1):24-30 (Spring 1985).

Barron, Jerome A. Whose First Amendment? *Vital Speeches* 46(10):313-315 (March 1, 1980).

Brief of American Psychological Association and American Association for the Advancement of Science as Amici Curiae. Ronald R. Hutchinson, Petitioner v. William Proxmire and Morton Schwartz, Respondents. *American Psychologist* 35(8):750-758 (August 1980).

Gruhl, John. Supreme Court's impact on the law of libel: compliance by lower federal courts. *Western Political Quarterly* 33(4):502-519 (December 1980).

Howard, A. E. Dick. The press in court. *Wilson Quarterly* 6(5):86-93 (Special Issue 1982).

1733. Hudgens v. National Labor Relations Board (NLRB)   March 3, 1976
      424 US 507   47 LEd2d 196   96 SCt 1029
      Burger Years 220-227
      En Am Con 929, 1729-1736
      Sullivan, Harold J. Privatization of public services: a growing threat to constitutional rights. *Public Administration Review* 47(6):461-467 (November/December 1987).

1734. Hines v. Anchor Motor Freight, Inc.   March 3, 1976
      424 US 554   47 LEd2d 231   96 SCt 1048
      Burger Court 161-162
      Burger Years 228-239
      Fox, Arthur. Showing workers who's the boss. *Nation* 239(9):295-299 (September 29, 1984).

1735. Ristaino v. Ross   March 3, 1976
      424 US 589   47 LEd2d 258   96 SCt 1017
      Mar, Linda. Supreme Court review: probing racial prejudice on voir dire: the Supreme Court provides illusory justice for minority defendants. *Journal of Criminal Law and Criminology* 72(4):1444-1461 (Winter 1981).

1736. East Carroll Parish School Board v. Marshall   March 8, 1976
      424 US 636   47 LEd2d 296   96 SCt 1083
      Public Affairs Council of Louisiana. Reapportionment for the 1980s: good faith and court decisions. *National Civic Review* 70(11):575-582 (December 1981).

1737. McKinney v. Alabama   March 23, 1976
      424 US 669   47 LEd2d 387   96 SCt 1189
      Kobylka, Joseph F. A court-created context for group litigation: libertarian groups and obscenity. *Journal of Politics* 49(4):1061-1078 (November 1987).

1738. Paul v. Davis   March 23, 1976
      424 US 693   47 LEd2d 405   96 SCt 1155
      Burger Years 45-49
      Const (Currie) 542-545
      En Am Con 1369-1370
      Davis, Sue. Federalism and property rights: an examination of Justice Rehnquist's legal positivism. *Western Political Quarterly* 39(3):250-264 (June 1986).
      Zion, Sidney. A tale of two libel theories. *Nation* 239(9):288-290 (September 29, 1984).

1739. Franks v. Bowman Transportation Co.   March 24, 1976
      424 US 747   47 LEd2d 444   96 SCt 1251
      Affirmative (Greene) 63-71
      Murphy, Betty Southard, Wayne E. Barlow, and Diane D. Hatch. Supreme Court reaffirms affirmative action. *Personnel Journal* 65(9):19-22 (September 1986).
      Sherwood, O. Peter. Court innocence. *Society* 27(3):24-25 (March/April 1990).

1740. Colorado River Water Conservation District v. United States   March 24, 1976
    424 US 800   47 LEd2d 483   96 SCt 1236
      Am Indian (Deloria) 197-220

1741. Greer v. Benjamin Spock   March 24, 1976
    424 US 828   47 LEd2d 505   96 SCt 1211
      Sup Ct Review (1982):195-241; (1992):29-77
    Ball, Howard. The U.S. Supreme Court's glossing of the Federal Tort Claims Act: statutory construction and
      veterans' tort actions. *Western Political Quarterly* 41(3):529-552 (September 1988).

1742. Abbott Laboratories v. Portland Retail Druggist Association   March 24, 1976
    425 US 1   47 LEd2d 537   96 SCt 1305
    Werner, Ray O. Marketing and the United States Supreme Court, 1975-1981. *Journal of Marketing* 46(2):73-81
      (Spring 1982).

1743. Middendorf v. Henry   March 24, 1976
    425 US 25   47 LEd2d 556   96 SCt 1281
      En Am Con 1253, 1253-1255
    Ball, Howard. The U.S. Supreme Court's glossing of the Federal Tort Claims Act: statutory construction and
      veterans' tort actions. *Western Political Quarterly* 41(3):529-552 (September 1988).

1744. Geders v. United States   March 30, 1976
    425 US 80   47 LEd2d 592   96 SCt 1330
    Baer, Harold, Jr. Sequestering witnesses: does the practice interfere with the defendants' constitutional rights?
      Trial 22(7):99-102 (July 1986).

1745. Beer v. United States   March 30, 1976
    425 US 130   47 LEd2d 629   96 SCt 1357
    Davis, Olethia. Tenuous interpretation: Sections 2 and 5 of the Voting Rights Act. *National Civic Review*
      84(4):310-322 (Fall/Winter 1995).
    Public Affairs Council of Louisiana. Reapportionment for the 1980s: good faith and court decisions. *National*
      Civic Review 70(11):575-582 (December 1981).
    Weber, Ronald E. Redistricting and the courts: judicial activism in the 1990s. *American Politics Quarterly*
      23(2):204-228 (April 1995).

1746. Ernst and Ernst v. Hochfelder   March 30, 1976
    425 US 185   47 LEd2d 668   96 SCt 1375
      Burger Years 206-219
    Barnett, Andrew H., and F. Fulton Galer. Scienter since Hochfelder. *CPA Journal* 52(11):40-45 (November
      1982).
    Cohen, Jerry A., and Herbert E. Milstein. "Efficiency" over competition. *Nation* 239(9):294-295 (September
      29, 1984).
    Miller, Robert D. Governmental oversight of the role of auditors. *CPA Journal* 56(9):20-36 (September 1986).
    Strong, George V. Supreme Court review: Securities Exchange Act of 1934—restrictive application of Section
      10(b) and Rule 10b-5 in securities fraud. *Journal of Criminal Law and Criminology* 71(4):474-487 (Winter
      1980).
    Supreme Court decision backs Hochfelder case on "intent," sustains AICPA amicus brief. *Journal of*
      Accountancy 150(1):7 (July 1980).

1747. Kelley v. Johnson   April 5, 1976
    425 US 238   47 LEd2d 708   96 SCt 1440
      Abortion (Frohock) 67
      Thurgood 412-416R+

1748. Hills v. Gautreaux   April 20, 1976
     425 US 284   47 LEd2d 792   96 SCt 1538
     En Am Con 918

1749. Baxter v. Palmigiano   April 20, 1976
        Coupled with Enomoto v. Clutchette
     425 US 308   47 LEd2d 810   96 SCt 1551
     Sup Ct Review (1980):211-279

1750. Beckwith v. United States   April 21, 1976
     425 US 341   48 LEd2d 1   96 SCt 1612
Jacobs, Robert. The state of Miranda: the effects of the Quarles decision. *Trial* 21(1):44-48 (January 1985).

Lupia, Lynnette L. Supreme Court review: Fifth Amendment—admissibility of confession obtained without Miranda warnings in noncustodial setting. *Journal of Criminal Law and Criminology* 75(3):673-691 (Fall 1984).

1751. Fisher v. United States   April 21, 1976
        Coupled with United States v. Kasmir
     425 US 391   48 LEd2d 39   96 SCt 1569
Alter, Robert J. Shareholder's Fifth Amendment privilege bars summons of corporate records. *Journal of Taxation* 63(4):208-210 (October 1985).

Causey, Denzil, and Frances McNair. Protecting taxpayers privacy from the IRS. *Journal of Accountancy* 168(4):44-48 (October 1989).

Comisky, Ian M., and Matthew J. Comisky. Supreme Court in Doe limits Fifth Amendment protection, but uncertainity remains. *Journal of Taxation* 61(2):66-70 (August 1984).

Fifth Amendment: compulsory production of incriminating business records. *Journal of Criminal Law and Criminology* 71(1):51-55 (Spring 1980).

Glanzer, Seymour, and Paul R. Taskier. Attorneys before the grand jury: assertion of the attorney-client privilege to protect a client's identity. *Journal of Criminal Law and Criminology* 75(4):1070-1099 (Winter 1984).

Grogan, John M., Jr. Supreme Court review: Fifth Amendment—the act of production privilege: the Supreme Court's protrait of a dualistic record custodian. *Journal of Criminal Law and Criminology* 79(3):701-734 (Fall 1988).

Rosenblatt, Leonard R. The Fifth Amendment and the production of business records: and Braswell Begat Bouknight. *Taxes* 68(6):418-424 (June 1990).

———. The production of business records after Braswell: where we've been, where we are, where we may be going. *Taxes* 67(4):231-237 (April 1989).

1752. United States v. Miller   April 21, 1976
     425 US 435   48 LEd2d 71   96 SCt 1619
     Burger Years 143-168
     Economics 340-345

Causey, Denzil, and Frances McNair. Protecting taxpayers privacy from the IRS. *Journal of Accountancy* 168(4):44-48 (October 1989).

Goldberger, Peter. Consent, expectations of privacy, and the meaning of "searches" in the Fourth Amendment. *Journal of Criminal Law and Criminology* 75(2):319-362 (Summer 1984).

Mosk, Stanley. The emerging agenda in state constitutional rights law. *Annals of the American Academy of Political and Social Science* 496:54-64 (March 1988).

Uviller, H. Richard. Fourth Amendment: does it protect your garbage? *Nation* 247(9):302-304 (October 10, 1988).

Waldron, Dorothy, and Leslie D. Ball. The bottom line on checkless banking. *Across the Board* 17(8): 34-41 (August 1980).

1753. Moe v. Confederated Salish & Kootenai Tribes of Flathead Reservation   April 27, 1976
     425 US 463   48 LEd2d 96   96 SCt 1634

Am Indians (Wilkinson) 35-37, 127, 160-161

1754. Hynes v. Mayor and Council of the Borough of Oradell   May 19, 1976
Hynes v. Oradell
425 US 610   48 LEd2d 243   96 SCt 1755
Freedom (Cox) 56-59

1755. Alfred Dunhill of London, Inc. v. Republic of Cuba   May 24, 1976
425 US 682   48 LEd2d 301   96 SCt 1854
Halberstam, Malvina. Sabbatino resurrected: the act of state doctrine in the revised restatement of U.S. foreign relations law. *American Journal of International Law* 79(1):68-91 (January 1985).

1756. Virginia State Board of Pharmacy v. Virginia Citizens Consumer Council, Inc.   May 24, 1976
425 US 748   48 LEd2d 346   96 SCt 1817
Ascent 132-134
Const (Currie) 513-518
Const Law 174-180+
En Am Con 330-331, 596-600, 739-740, 1976-1977
Freedom (Cox) 32-38+
Sup Ct Review (1987):303-344
Bleisch, N. David. The *Congressional Record* and the First Amendment: accuracy is the best policy. *Boston College Environmental Affairs Law Review* 12(2):341-379 (Winter 1985).
Boedecker, Karl A., and Fred W. Morgan. The evolution of First Amendment protection for commercial speech. *Journal of Marketing* 59(1):38-47 (January 1995).
Bowen, Lauren. Attorney advertising in the wake of Bates v. State Bar of Arizona (1977): a study of judicial impact. *American Politics Quarterly* 23(4):461-484 (October 1995).
Camel rights. *Fortune* 125(10):120 (May 18, 1992).
Chemerinsky, Erwin. Supreme Court review: commercial speech: what degree of protection? *Trial* 29(8):66-68 (August 1993).
Colford, Steven W. Ad industry loses hero in Brennan. *Advertising Age* 61(31):1, 44 (July 30, 1990).
————. Rehnquist slams ads' 1st Amendment shield. *Advertising Age* 57(37):12 (June 30, 1986).
————. What White's court exit means. *Advertising Age* 64(13):16 (March 29, 1993).
Donlan, Thomas G. When money talks: Justice Blackmun made a great contribution to economic liberty [Editorial] *Barron's* 74(16):50 (April 18, 1994).
Lewis, Wayne K. Environmental advertising: a delicate balance of rights. *Trial* 28(10):53-56 (October 1992).
Winter, Ralph K. Political financing and the Constitution. *Annals of the American Academy of Political and Social Science* 486:34-48 (July 1986).

1757. Simon v. Eastern Kentucky Welfare Rights Organization   June 1, 1976
426 US 26   48 LEd2d 450   96 SCt 1917
Burger Years 191-205
En Am Con 1683-1684
Sup Ct Review (1993):37-64
Morrison, Alan B. Close reins on the bureaucracy. *Nation* 239(9):290-294 (September 29, 1984).
Neuborne, Burt. Taking away the right to sue. *Nation* 239(9):268-271 (September 29, 1984).

1758. Hampton v. Mow Sun Wong   June 1, 1976
426 US 88   48 LEd2d 495   96 SCt 1895
Ascent 239-242+
Const (Currie) 500-504
En Am Con 894
Sup Ct Review (1984):255-307

1759. Washington v. Davis   June 7, 1976
Mayor of Washington, D.C. v. Davis

426 US 229   48 LEd2d 597   96 SCt 2040

    Burden 219-223+

    Burger Court 121-124, 145-147

    Burger Years 95-108

    Const (Currie) 488-493

    Const Law 488-491R

    Court Public 100

    En Am Con 640-647, 1082-1085, 1500-1506, 2035-2036

    Sup Ct Review (1983):1-31

Baer, Judith A. Women's rights and the limits of constitutional doctrine. *Western Political Quarterly* 44(4):821-852 (December 1991).

Brubaker, Stanley C. Rewriting the Constitution: the mainstream according to Laurence Tribe. *Commentary* 86(6):36-42 (December 1988).

Gordon, William M. The implementation of desegregation plans since Brown. *Journal of Negro Education* 63(3):310-322 (Summer 1994).

Hood, Stafford, and Laurence Parker. Minorities, teacher testing, and recent U.S. Supreme Court holdings: a regressive step. *Teachers College Record* 92(4):603-618 (Summer 1991).

Karst, Kennth L. Equal protection of the laws. *Society* 24(1):24-30 (November/December 1986).

Katz, Stanley N. The strange birth and unlikely history of constitutional equality. *Journal of American History* 75(3):747-762 (December 1988).

Miller, Arthur S. End of the "second recontruction." *Progressive* 46(2):38-39 (February 1982).

Reid, Herbert O., Sr. State of the art: the law and education since 1954. *Journal of Negro Education* 52(3):234-249 (Summer 1983).

Reid, Herbert O., and Frankie M. Foster-Davis. Three decades of "all deliberate speed." *Crisis* 91(5):12-15 (May 1984).

Vile, John R., and Kathy Ruth McCoy. The Memphis Case: another precedent? *Personnel* 62(7):72-76 (July 1985).

1760. Federal Power Commission (FPC) v. Conway Corp.   June 7, 1976
      426 US 271   48 LEd2d 626   96 SCt 1999

      Holmes, A. Stewart. First generation price freeze policy at the FERC. *Public Utilities Fortnightly* 110(7):32-37 (September 30, 1982).

1761. United States v. MacCollom   June 10, 1976
      426 US 317   48 LEd2d 666   96 SCt 2086

      Brennan 203-209

1762. Bishop v. Wood   June 10, 1976
      426 US 341   48 LEd2d 684   96 SCt 2074

      En Am Con 119, 1465-1472

      Jaegal, Don, and N. Joseph Cayer. Public personnel administration by lawsuit: the impact of Supreme Court decisions on public employee litigiousness. *Public Administration Review* 51(3):211-221 (May/June 1991).

1763. Bryan v. Itasca County, Minnesota   June 14, 1976
      426 US 373   48 LEd2d 710   96 SCt 2102

      Am Indians (Wilkinson) 49, 128+

1764. Hortonville Joint School District No. 1 v. Hortonville Education Association   June 17, 1976
      426 US 482   49 LEd2d 1   96 SCt 2308

      Menacker, Julius. Review of Supreme Court reasoning in cases of expression, due process, and equal protection. *Phi Delta Kappan* 63(3):188-190 (November 1981).

      Sendor, Benjamin. Balancing your roles as an employer. *American School Board Journal* 181(9):20-21 (September 1994).

1765. Kleppe v. New Mexico   June 17, 1976
     426 US 529   49 LEd2d 34   96 SCt 2285

    Baer, Susan D. The Public Trust Doctrine—a tool to make federal adminstrative agencies increase protection of public land and its resources. *Boston College Environmental Affairs Law Review* 15(2):385-436 (Winter 1988).

    Shepard, Blake. The scope of Congress' constitutional power under the property clause: regulating non-federal property to further the purposes of national parks and wilderness areas. *Boston College Environmental Affairs Law Review* 11(3): 479-538 (April 1984).

1766. Federal Energy Administration v. Algonquin SNG, Inc.   June 17, 1976
     426 US 548   49 LEd2d 49   96 SCt 2295
    En Am Con 695

1767. Doyle v. Ohio   June 17, 1976
       Coupled with Wood v. Ohio
     426 US 610   49 LEd2d 91   96 SCt 2240
    Almanac (1987):7A
    Sup Ct Yearbook (1992-93):63

    Gillers, Stephen. The Meese lie. [Editorial] *Nation* 244(7):205 (February 21, 1987).

    Gruhl, John. State supreme courts and the U.S. Supreme Court's post-Miranda rulings. *Journal of Criminal Law and Criminology* 72(3):886-913 (Fall 1981).

    High Court allows blood test refusal as proof of DWI. *Trial* 19(6):13-14 (June 1983).

    Melson, David E. Supreme Court review: Fourteenth Amendment—criminal procedure: the impeachment use of post-arrest silence which precedes the receipt of Miranda warnings. *Journal of Criminal Law and Criminology* 73(4):1572-1594 (Winter 1982).

    Mosk, Stanley. The emerging agenda in state constitutional rights law. *Annals of the American Academy of Political and Social Science* 496:54-64 (March 1988).

1768. Roemer v. Board of Public Works of Maryland   June 21, 1976
     426 US 736   49 LEd2d 179   96 SCt 2337
    Burger Years 56-91
    En Am Con 1650-1658
    Sup Ct Church 271-273

    Buzzard, Lynn Robert, and Samuel Ericsson. Public aid to private schools: Caesar rendering to God? *Christianity Today* 27(10):20-23 (June 17, 1983).

    Manion, Maureen. The impact of state aid on sectarian higher education: the case of New York State. *Review of Politics* 1986 48(2): 264-288.

    Van Alstyne, William W. Academic freedom and the First Amendment in the Supreme Court of the United States: an unhurried historical review. *Law and Contemporary Problems* 53(3):79-154 (Summer 1990).

    Weber, Paul J. Excessive entanglement: a wavering First Amendment standard. *Review of Politics* 46(4):483-501 (October 1984).

1769. Flint Ridge Development Co. v. Scenic Rivers Assocation of Oklahoma   June 24, 1976
       Coupled with Hills v. Scenic Rivers Association of Oklahoma
     426 US 776   49 LEd2d 205   96 SCt 2430

    Sandler, Ross. Law: shrinking NEPA. *Environment* 22(3):43-44 (April 1980).

    Shea, Thomas E. The judicial standard for review of environmental impact statement threshold decisions. *Boston College Environmental Affairs Law Review* 9(1):63-101 (1980-1981).

    Vanderziel, Kathleen M. The Hatfield Riders and environmental preservation: what process is due? *Boston College Environmental Affairs Law Review* 19(2):431-479 (Fall/Winter 1991).

1770. Hughes v. Alexandria Scrap Corp.   June 24, 1976
     426 US 794   49 LEd2d 220   96 SCt 2488
    Ascent 118-120
    Const (Currie) 580-585

Sup Ct Review (1995):217-276

Schwartz, Edward B. Water as an article of commerce: state embargoes spring a leak under Sporhase v. Nebraska. *Boston College Environmental Affairs Law Review* 12(1):103-169 (Fall 1985).

1771. National League of Cities v. Usery   June 24, 1976
            Coupled with California v. Usery
      426 US 833   49 LEd2d 245   96 SCt 2465
      Ascent 100-110+
      Burger Court 200, 202-203, 231-232
      Const (Currie) 563-568
      En Am Con 503-504, 588-589, 680-682, 695-697, 833-834, 1112-1119, 1294-1295
      Guide (CQ) 54-55, 57, 95, 107
      Powers 151-152
      Sup Ct Review (1981):81-109; (1983):215-281; (1985):341-419; (1988):85-127; (1995):125-215

Aronow, Geoffrey, and Owen Fiss. The High Court illusion of victory. *Nation* 235(21):647-650 (December 18, 1982).

Binion, Gayle. An assessment of Potter Stewart. *Center Magazine* 14(5):2-5 (September/October 1981).

Catalano, Peter T. Balancing federal energy regulation and state sovereignty: the emerging controversy. *Public Utilities Fortnightly* 107(8):53-56 (April 9, 1981).

Collins, Deborah. The states: federal-state relations issues hit the Supreme Court agenda. *National Civic Review* 73(11):568-571 (December 1984).

Davis, Sue. Federalism and property rights: an examination of Justice Rehnquist's legal positivism. *Western Political Quarterly* 39(3):250-264 (June 1986).

Fiss, Owen M., and Charles Krauthammer. The Rehnquist Court. *New Republic* 186(10):14-16, 18 (March 10, 1982).

Hickok, Eugene W., Jr. Federalism's future before the U.S. Supreme Court. *Annals of the American Academy of Political and Social Science* 509:73-82 (May 1990).

Johnston, Richard E., and John T. Thompson. Burger court and federalism: a revolution in 1976? *Western Political Quarterly* 33(2):197-216 (June 1980).

Johnston, Van R., and Maxine Kurtz. Handling a public policy emergency: the Fair Labor Standards Act in the public sector. *Public Administration Review* 46(5):414-422 (September/October 1986).

Lee, William P. FLPMA's legislative veto provisions and INS v. Chadha: who controls the federal lands? *Boston College Environmental Affairs Law Review* 12(4):791-821 (Summer 1985).

Martin, Stanley A. Problems with PURPA: the need for state legislation to encourage cogeneration and small power production. *Boston College Environmental Affairs Law Review* 11(1):149-202 (October 1983).

Meese, Edwin, III. The attorney general's view of the Supreme Court: toward a jurisprudence of original intention. *Public Administration Review* 45(Special Issue):701-704 (November 1985).

Mount, Gregory J. Significant decisions in labor cases. *Monthly Labor Review* 103(12):63-64 (December 1980).

O'Brien, David M. Federalism as a metaphor in the constitutional politics of public administration. *Public Administration Review* 49(5):411-419 (September/October 1989).

Orren, Karen. The primacy of labor in American constitutional development. *American Political Science Review* 89(2):377-388 (June 1995).

Provost, Denise. The Massachusetts Hazardous Waste Facility Siting Act: what impact on muncipal power to exclude and regulate? *Boston College Environmental Affairs Law Review* 10(3):715-795 (December 1982/January 1983).

Ross, Douglas. Safeguarding our federalism: lessons for the states from the Supreme Court. *Public Administration Review* 45(Special Issue):723-731 (November 1985).

Schwartz, Edward B. Water as an article of commerce: state embargoes spring a leak under Sporhase v. Nebraska. *Boston College Environmental Affairs Law Review* 12(1):103-169 (Fall 1985).

Shepard, Blake. The scope of Congress's constitutional power under the property clause: regulating non-federal property to further the purposes of national parks and wilderness areas. *Boston College Environmental Affairs Law Review* 11(3): 479-538 (April 1984).

Solimine, Michael E. Constitutionality of congressional legislation to overrule Zurcher v. Stanford daily. *Journal of Criminal Law and Criminology* 71(2):147-162 (Summer 1980).

States' rights: a landmark decision is in the making. *Business Week* (Industrial/Technology Edition) (2861):130 (September 24, 1984).

Stephens, Pamela J. Implementing federal energy policy at the state and local levels: "every power requisite." *Boston College Environmental Affairs Law Review* 10(4):875-904 (May 1983).

Thomas, Charlotte E. The Cape Cod National Seashore: a case study of federal administrative control over traditionally local land use decisions. *Boston College Environmental Affairs Law Review* 12(2):225-272 (Winter 1985).

Trends in federal regulation. *Congressional Digest* 74(3):69-71 (March 1995).

Voodoo law. *National Review* 37(5):19, 21 (March 22, 1985).

Wise, Charles and Rosemary O'Leary. Is federalism dead or alive in the Supreme Court?: implications for public administrators. *Public Administration Review* 52(6):559-572 (November/December 1992).

1772. Aldinger v. Howard   June 24, 1976
     427 US 1   49 LEd2d 276   96 SCt 2413

Brooks, Thornton H., M. Daniel McGinn, and William P. H. Cary. Second generation problems facing employers in employment discrimination cases: continuing violations, pendent state claims, and double attorneys' fees. *Law and Contemporary Problems* 49(4):26-51 (Autumn 1986).

1773. United States v. Santana   June 24, 1976
     427 US 38   49 LEd2d 300   96 SCt 2406
     Ascent 324-327+

1774. Young, Mayor of Detroit v. American Mini Theatres, Inc.   June 24, 1976
     427 US 50   49 LEd2d 310   96 SCt 2440
     En Am Con 730-738, 1335-1337, 1955-1957, 2084-2085
     Freedom (Cox) 32-38+
     Sup Ct Review (1982):195-241, 285-317

Cox, Archibald. First Amendment. *Society* 24(1):8-15 (November/December 1986).

Kobylka, Joseph F. A court-created context for group litigation: libertarian groups and obscenity. *Journal of Politics* 49(4):1061-1078 (November 1987).

McGuire, Kevin T., and Gergory A. Caldeira. Lawyers, organized interests, and the law of obscenity: agenda setting in the Supreme Court. *American Political Science Review* 87(3):717-726 (September 1993).

Rehnquist, William H. The United States Supreme Court: dissent. *Congressional Digest* 68(8-9):197R, 199R, 201R (August/September 1989).

What they say it is: the justices' words instruct the nation, and often address history. *Time* 130(1):44-49 (July 6, 1987).

1775. United States v. Agurs   June 24, 1976
     427 US 97   49 LEd2d 342   96 SCt 2392
     Const Law 438-439
     En Am Con 683-686, 1449-1450

1776. Lodge 76, International Association of Machinists and Aerospace Workers   June 25, 1976
     v. Wisconsin Employment Relations Commission
     427 US 132   49 LEd2d 396   96 SCt 2548
     Sup Ct Review (1986):135-155

Finkin, Matthew W. Regulation by agreement: the case of private higher education. *Academe* 67(2):67-80 (April 1981).

1777. Runyon et ux., dba Bobbe's School v. McCrary   June 25, 1976
        Coupled with Fairfax-Brewster School v. Gonzales
        Coupled with Southern Independent School Association v. McCrary
     427 US 160   49 LEd2d 415   96 SCt 2586
     Almanac (1988):122-123; (1989):317-318
     Center 27-30, 37-42, 45-49, 55-64+

Culture 130-141

En Am Con 1616, 1729-1736

Guide (CQ) 154

Sup Ct Review (1983):1-31; (1988):43-60; (1989):1-51; (1994):429-540

Turning 187-192, 222-224+

Allen, W. B. Making our principles work: thoughts on Runyon vs McCreary. *Vital Speeches* 55(2):37-40 (November 1, 1988).

Brown, Luther. High Court's double take looms over civil rights. *Black Enterprise* 18(12):20 (July 1988).

A "conservative court" is still uncertain. *Christianity Today* 32(16):37 (November 4, 1988).

Demon Runyon. [Editorial] *Commonweal* 115(10):291-292 (May 20, 1988).

Drinan, Robert F. Protection against racial discrimination. *America* 160(3):52 (January 28, 1989).

Farber, Daniel A. Supreme Court review: debating Congress's intent in the age of statutes. *Trial* 25(12):105-110 (December 1989).

Gewirtz, Paul. Reverse discrimination. *New Republic* 199(17):13-14, 16 (October 24, 1988).

High Court gets plea not to reverse rights ruling. *Jet* 74(15):9 (July 11, 1988).

Hukill, Craig. Significant decisions in labor cases: civil rights. *Monthly Labor Review* 113(2):52-53 (February 1990).

Lacayo, Richard, and Steven Holmes. Is the Court turning right? By reopening a civil rights case, the justices send a signal. *Time* 132(17):78 (October 24, 1988).

Lacayo, Richard, Jerome Cramer, and Alain L. Sanders. Play it again, says the Court: the justices decide to reconsider a major civil rights ruling. *Time* 131(19):73 (May 9, 1988).

Marshall, Thurgood. The Supreme Court and civil rights: has the tide turned? *USA Today* 118(2538):19-20 (March 1990).

McDowell, Gary L. Congress and the courts. *Public Interest* (100):89-101 (Summer 1990).

Murphy, Betty Southard, Wayne E. Barlow, and D. Diane Hatch. Manager's newsfront: Supreme Court redefines scope of Civil Rights Acts. *Personnel Journal* 68(8):22-26 (August 1989).

Rabkin, Jeremy. Behind the tax-exempt schools debate. *Public Interest* (68):21-38 (Summer 1982).

Schwartz, Herman. Illogical force. [Editorial] *Nation* 249(2):40-41 (July 10, 1989).

————. Judgment days. [Editorial] *Nation* 261(13):452-454 (October 23, 1995).

Supreme Court: Reconsidering rights. *Economist* 309(7577):27-28 (November 19-25, 1988).

Williams, Preston N. Court reviews Runyon: an unsettling move. [Editorial] *Christian Century* 105(30):919-920 (October 19, 1988).

Wolvovitz, Barbara M. Borked after all. [Editorial] *Nation* 246(19):664-665 (May 14, 1988).

1778. Meachum v. Fano   June 25, 1976
427 US 215   49 LEd2d 451   96 SCt 2532

Baum, David P. Supreme Court review: Fourteenth Amendment—due process and interstate prison transfers. *Journal of Criminal Law and Criminology* 74(4):1387-1403 (Winter 1983).

Knochell, Keith S. Supreme Court review: Fourteenth Amendment—due process for prisoners in commitment proceedings. *Journal of Criminal Law and Criminology* 71(4):579-592 (Winter 1980).

1779. Montanye, Former Superintendent v. Haymes   June 25, 1976
427 US 236   49 LEd2d 466   96 SCt 2543

Knochell, Keith S. Supreme Court review: Fourteenth Amendment—due process for prisoners in commitment proceedings. *Journal of Criminal Law and Criminology* 71(4):579-592 (Winter 1980).

1780. Union Electric Co. v. Environmental Protection Agency (EPA)   June 25, 1976
427 US 246   49 LEd2d 474   96 SCt 2518

Colton, Roger D., Kathleen Uehling, and Dr. Michael F. Sheehan. Seven-cum-eleven: rolling the toxic dice in the U.S. Supreme Court. *Boston College Environmental Affairs Law Review* 14(3):345-379 (Spring 1987).

1781. McDonald v. Santa Fe Trail Transportation Co.   June 25, 1976
427 US 273   49 LEd2d 493   96 SCt 2574

Marshall and colleagues rap High Court decision to review rights case. *Jet* 74(7):9 (May 16, 1988).

Reynolds, William Bradford. Affirmative action and its negative repercussions. *Annals of the American Academy of Political and Social Science* 523:38-49 (September 1992).

Youngblood, Stuart A., and Gary L. Tidwell. Termination at will: some changes in the wind. *Personnel* 58(3):22-33 (May/June 1981).

1782. New Orleans v. Dukes, dba Louisiana Concessions   June 25, 1976
    427 US 297   49 LEd2d 511   96 SCt 2513
    En Am Con 859, 1310
    Sup Ct Review (1982):127-166

1783. Massachusetts Board of Retirement v. Murgia   June 25, 1976
    427 US 307   49 LEd2d 520   96 SCt 2562
    En Am Con 37, 1225

1784. North v. Russell   June 28, 1976
    427 US 328   49 LEd2d 534   96 SCt 2709
    Ascent 334-336

1785. Elrod v. Burns   June 28, 1976
    427 US 347   49 LEd2d 547   96 SCt 2673
    Const (Currie) 505-510
    En Am Con 146, 770-773
    Sup Ct Review (1988):1-41

Franklin, Daniel. The five dumbest Supreme Court decisions. *Washington Monthly* 26(10):12-18 (October 1994).

Hukill, Craig. Significant decisions in labor cases: Patronage practices. *Monthly Labor Review* 113(10)40, 41-42 (October 1990).

McFeeley, Neil D. The Supreme Court and patronage: implications for local government. *National Civic Review* 71(5):251-258 (May 1982).

Meier, Kenneth J. Ode to patronage: a critical analysis of two recent Supreme Court decisions. *Public Administration Review* 41(5):558-564 (September/October 1981).

Mounts, Gregory J. Labor and the Supreme Court: significant decisions of 1979-80. *Monthly Labor Review* 104(4):13-22 (April 1981).

————. Significant decisions in labor cases. *Monthly Labor Review* 103(8):44-46 (August 1980).

System spoiled. *Time* 115(15):71 (April 14, 1980).

Wise, Charles and Rosemary O'Leary. Is federalism dead or alive in the Supreme Court?: implications for public administrators. *Public Administration Review* 52(6):559-572 (November/December 1992).

1786. Kleppe, Secretary of the Interior v. Sierra Club   June 28, 1976
        Coupled with American Electric Power System v. Sierra Club
    427 US 390   49 LEd2d 576   96 SCt 2718

Brady, Timothy Patrick. "But most of it belongs to those yet to be born": the public trust doctrine, NEPA, and the stewardship ethic. *Boston College Environmental Affairs Law Review* 17(3):621-646 (Spring 1990).

Kelly, Paula. Judicial review of agency decisions under the National Environmental Policy Act of 1969—Strycker's Bay Neighborhood Council, Inc. v. Karlen. *Boston College Environmental Affairs Law Review* 10(1):79-109 (1982-83).

Lovely, Jeffrey M. Protecting wetlands: consideration of secondary social and economic effects by the United States Army Corps of Engineers in its wetlands permitting process. *Boston College Environmental Affairs Law Review* 17(3):647-686 (Spring 1990).

Sandler, Ross. Law: shrinking NEPA. *Environment* 22(3):43-44 (April 1980).

Shea, Thomas E. The judicial standard for review of environmental impact statement threshold decisions. *Boston College Environmental Affairs Law Review* 9(1):63-101 (1980-1981).

1787. Pasadena City Board of Education v. Spangler   June 28, 1976
    427 US 424   49 LEd2d 599   96 SCt 2697

Court Public 158-159

Hyde, Alison A. School desegregation: the role of the courts and means of achievement. *NASSP Bulletin* 78(565):28-37 (November 1994).

Reid, Herbert O., Sr. State of the art: the law and education since 1954. *Journal of Negro Education* 52(3):234-249 (Summer 1983).

Russo, Charles J., J. John Harris III, and Rosetta F. Sandidge. Brown v. Board of Education at 40: a legal history of equal educational opportunity in American public education. *Journal of Negro Education* 63(3):297-309 (Summer 1994).

Sendor, Benjamin. New lessons on desegregation. *American School Board Journal* 181(2):24-25 (February 1994).

Timberlake, Constance H. A historical perspective of school desegregation. *Crisis* 91(5):26-29 (1984).

1788. Fitzpatrick v. Bitzer, Chairman, State Employees' Retirement Commission   June 28, 1976
    427 US 445   49 LEd2d 614   96 SCt 2666
      Const (Currie) 572-574
      En Am Con 740
      Guide (CQ) 154-155

Groszyk, Walter S., Jr., and Thomas J. Madden. Managing without immunity: the challenge for state and local government officials in the 1980s. *Public Administration Review* 41(2):268-278 (March/April 1981).

Solimine, Michael E. Constitutionality of congressional legislation to overrule Zurcher v. Stanford daily. *Journal of Criminal Law and Criminology* 71(2):147-162 (Summer 1980).

Wise, Charles, and Rosemary O'Leary. Is federalism dead or alive in the Supreme Court?: implications for public administrators. *Public Administration Review* 52(6):559-572 (November/December 1992).

1789. Andresen v. Maryland   June 29, 1976
    427 US 463   49 LEd2d 627   96 SCt 2737

Fifth Amendment: compulsory production of incriminating business records. *Journal of Criminal Law and Criminology* 71(1):51-55 (Spring 1980).

1790. Mathews v. Lucas   June 29, 1976
    427 US 495   49 LEd2d 651   96 SCt 2755
      En Am Con 947-948

Melton, Gary B. Public policy and private prejudice: psychology and law on gay rights. *American Psychologist* 44(6):933-940 (June 1989).

1791. Nebraska Press Association v. Stuart   June 30, 1976
    427 US 539   49 LEd2d 683   96 SCt 2791
      Ascent 171-173+
      Const (Friendly) 145-158
      Court Public 315, 320, 328-338R
      En Am Con 797-804, 805-808, 831-832, 1305, 1453-1456, 1492-1494
      First 198-199, 207-213+
      Fourth 146-147, 160-167+
      Freedom (Cox) 19-22

Backdoor censors. [Editorial] *Nation* 251(20):720 (December 10, 1990).

Bolbach, Cynthia J. Access to information: affirming the press's right. *Christian Century* 97(29):879-883 (September 24, 1980).

Hale, Dennis. How retiring Supreme Court Justice White voted in First Amendment cases. *Editor and Publisher* 126(30):44, 36 (July 24, 1993).

Howard, A. E. Dick. The press in court. *Wilson Quarterly* 6(5):86-93 (Special Issue 1982).

The legacy of the Burger Court. *U.S. News and World Report* 100(25):22 (June 30, 1986).

1792. Planned Parenthood of Central Missouri v. Danforth, Attorney General of Missouri   July 1, 1976
    428 US 52   49 LEd2d 788   96 SCt 2831
      Abortion (Frohock) 73-74, 88

Abortion Am 83-91, 97, 198-204+
Abortion Con 177-179, 181-182, 290
Abortion Dec 4-5, 33-46+
Abortion Decs 70s Introduction, 75-104R
Abortion Moral 35-44, 74-79
Abortion Pol (Rubin) 130-136+
Abortion Quest 108-110+
Burger Court 96-99, 230
Court Public 386, 412-425R
En Am Con 4-6, 686-688, 1394, 1552-1558, 1763
Hard Choices 172-173, 175, 177-178+, 241-243, 312
Law Governing 21-25, 48-51, 53-54
Liberty 624-626+
New Right (Whitaker) 142-168

Bersoff, Donald N., Laurel Pyle Malson, and Bruce J. Ennis. APA brief in Thornburgh v. American College of Obstetricians and Gynecologists. *American Psychologist* 42(1):77-78 (January 1987).

Blank, Robert H. Judicial decision making and biological fact: Roe v. Wade and the unresolved question of fetal viability. *Western Political Quarterly* 37(4):584-602 (December 1984).

Halpern, Sue M. The fight over teen-age abortion. *New York Review of Books* 37(5):30-32 (March 29, 1990).

Melton, Gary B., and Nancy Felipe Russo. Adolescent abortion: psychological perspectives on public policy. *American Psychologist* 42(1):69-72 (January 1987).

Melton, Gary B. Legal regulation of adolscent abortion: unintended effects. *American Psychologist* 42(1):79-83 (January 1987).

Minow, Martha. We, the family: constitutional rights and American families. *Journal of American History* 74(3):959-983 (December 1987).

Regan, Richard J. Regulating cult activities: the limits of religious freedom. *Thought* 61(241):185-196 (June 1986).

———. Supreme Court roundup: 1979 term. *Thought* 55(219):487-455 (December 1980).

Spring, Beth. White House files prolife court brief. *Christianity Today* 26(14):66-70 (September 3, 1982).

1793. Singleton v. Wulff   July 1, 1976
    428 US 106   49 LEd2d 826   96 SCt 2868
      Liberty 625-626

1794. Bellotti, Attorney General of Massachusetts v. Baird   July 1, 1976
        Coupled with Hunerwadel v. Baird
    428 US 132   49 LEd2d 844   96 SCt 2857
      Abortion (Frohock) 3-7, 73-74
      Abortion Am 89-90, 97
      Abortion Dec 47-50
      Abortion Pol (Rubin) 130-136+
      Abortion Quest 110-114
      Almanac (1989):306-307; (1990):528-531
      Const Law 306-309+
      En Am Con 4-6
      Law Governing 48-51+
      Liberty 625-626+

Gardner, William, David Scherer and Maya Tester. Asserting scientific authority: cognitive development and adolescent legal rights. *American Psychologist* 44(6):895-902 (June 1989).

Halpern, Sue M. The fight over teen-age abortion. *New York Review of Books* 37(5):30-32 (March 29, 1990).

Melton, Gary B., and Nancy Felipe Russo. Adolescent abortion: psychological perspectives on public policy. *American Psychologist* 42(1):69-72 (January 1987).

Regan, Richard J. Supreme Court roundup: 1979 term. *Thought* 55(219):487-455 (December 1980).

1795. Gregg v. Georgia   July 2, 1976
      428 US 153   49 LEd2d 859   96 SCt 2909

          Brennan 220-229
          Burger Years 169-176
          Capital Punish 15-18, 112+
          Const (Currie) 547-550
          Const Law 440-447R+
          Court Public 240-241, 267-280R
          Death Penalty (Bedau) 247-253, 271-288R+
          Death Penalty (Streib) 21, 41
          Death Penalty (Tushnet) 60-64+, 191-201R
          Death Penalty 80s 5-8, 12-15, 31-32, 44-46
          Death Penalty 90s 4-11
          En Am Con 201-206, 207-209
          Equal (Baldus) 25-33+
          Magic 301-303
          May It 229-243R
          Sup Ct Review (1983):305-395

American survey: Burger leaves the labyrinth. *Economist* 300(7454):17-22 (July 12-18, 1986).

Bernstein, Sidney, and Michael Eisenstein. 1982 Supreme Court update: the criminal law, part two. *Trial* 18(10):58-65 (October 1982).

Bowers, William J. The pervasiveness of arbitrariness and discrimination under post-Furman capital statutes. *Journal of Criminal Law and Criminology* 74(3):1067-1100 (Fall 1983).

Death penalty: cruel and ever more usual punishment. *Economist* 303(7496):24-25 (May 2-8, 1987).

Dieter, Richard C. The death penalty dinosaur: capital punishment heads for extinction. *Commonweal* 115(1):11-14 (January 15, 1988).

Dripps, Donald A. Supreme Court review: Justice White and the rights of the accused. *Trial* 29(5):71-74 (May 1993).

Ewer, Phyllis A. Supreme Court review: Eighth Amendment—the death penalty. *Journal of Criminal Law and Criminology* 71(4):538-546 (Winter 1980).

George, Tracey E., and Lee Epstein. On the nature of Supreme Court decision making. *American Political Science Review* 86(2):323-337 (June 1992).

The legacy of the Burger Court. *U.S. News and World Report* 100(25):22 (June 30, 1986).

Mayell, Manvin S. Supreme Court review: Eighth Amendment—proportionality review of death sentences not required. *Journal of Criminal Law and Criminology* 75(3):839-854 (Fall 1984).

Meltsner, Michael. On death row, the wait is over. *Nation* 239(9):274-277 (September 29, 1984).

Murphy, Cornelius F. The Supreme Court and capital punishment: a new hands-off approach. *USA Today* 121(2574):51-52 (March 1993).

Norpoth, Helmut, Jeffrey A. Segal, William Mishler, and Reginald S. Sheehan. Popular influence on Supreme Court decisions. *American Political Science Review* 88(3):711-724 (September 1994).

Press, Aric, Susan Agrest, Lucy Howard, and George Raine. To die or not to die. *Newsweek* 102(16):43-45 (October 17, 1983)

Rosenblatt, Roger. The Bill of Rights. *Life* 14(13 Special Issue):9-30 (Fall 1991).

Schwartz, Charles Walter. Eighth Amendment proportionality analysis and the compelling case of William Rummel. *Journal of Criminal Law and Criminology* 71(4):378-420 (Winter 1980).

Vito, Gennaro F., and Thomas J. Keil. Capital sentencing in Kentucky: an analysis of the factors influencing decision making in the post-Gregg period. *Journal of Criminal Law and Criminology* 79(2):483-503 (Summer 1988).

Whitebread, Charles. Will counterrevolution continue? [Editorial] *USA Today* 116(2507):11 (August 1987).

1796. Proffitt v. Florida   July 2, 1976
      428 US 242   49 LEd2d 913   96 SCt 2960
          Capital Punish 19-28
          Court Public 280-281
          Death Penalty (Bedau) 247-253, 271+

En Am Con 207-209

American survey: Burger leaves the labyrinth. *Economist* 300(7454):17-22 (July 12-18, 1986).

Mayell, Manvin S. Supreme Court review: Eighth Amendment—proportionality review of death sentences not required. *Journal of Criminal Law and Criminology* 75(3):839-854 (Fall 1984).

1797. Jurek v. Texas   July 2, 1976

428 US 262   49 LEd2d 929   96 SCt 2950

Capital Punish 19-28
Court Public 280-281
Death Penalty (Bedau) 174, 247-253, 271
En Am Con 207-209

American Survey: Burger leaves the labyrinth. *Economist* 300(7454):17-22 (July 12-18, 1986).

Brown, J. Michael. Supreme Court review: Eighth Amendment—capital sentencing instructions. *Journal of Criminal Law and Criminology* 84(4):854-882 (Winter/Spring 1994).

Mayell, Manvin S. Supreme Court review: Eighth Amendment—proportionality review of death sentences not required. *Journal of Criminal Law and Criminology* 75(3):839-854 (Fall 1984).

1798. Woodson v. North Carolina   July 2, 1976

428 US 280   49 LEd2d 944   96 SCt 2978

Brennan 220-226
Burger Years 169-176
Court Public 240-241, 281-291R
Death Penalty (Bedau) 247-253, 288-293R+
Death Penalty 80s 5-8, 151-152
Death Penalty 90s 5-11+
En Am Con 207-209
Sup Ct Review (1983):305-395

Bernstein, Sidney, and Michael Eisenstein. 1982 Supreme Court update: the criminal law, part two. *Trial* 18(10):58-65 (October 1982).

Bilionis, Louis D. Moral appropriateness, capital punishment, and the Lockett doctrine. *Journal of Criminal Law and Criminology* 82(2):283-333 (Summer 1991).

Meltsner, Michael. On death row, the wait is over. *Nation* 239(9):274-277 (September 29, 1984).

Murphy, Cornelius F. The Supreme Court and capital punishment: a new hands-off approach. *USA Today* 121(2574):51-52 (March 1993).

1799. Roberts v. Louisiana   July 2, 1976

428 US 325   49 LEd2d 974   96 SCt 3001

Burger Years 169-176
Capital Punish 19-28+
Court Public 291
Death Penalty (Bedau) 293-298+
En Am Con 207-209
Sup Ct Review (1983):305-395

Dripps, Donald A. Supreme Court review: Justice White and the rights of the accused. *Trial* 29(5):71-74 (May 1993).

Meltsner, Michael. On death row, the wait is over. *Nation* 239(9):274-277 (September 29, 1984).

1800. South Dakota v. Opperman   July 6, 1976

428 US 364   49 LEd2d 1000   96 SCt 3092

Meisel, Alan. The rights of the mentally ill under state constitutions. *Law and Contemporary Problems* 45(3):7-40 (Summer 1982).

Misner, Robert L. Justifying searches on the basis of equality of treatment. *Journal of Criminal Law and Criminology* 82(3):547-578 (Fall 1991).

Mosk, Stanley. The emerging agenda in state constitutional rights law. *Annals of the American Academy of Political and Social Science* 496:54-64 (March 1988).

1801. United States v. Janis   July 6, 1976
        428 US 433   49 LEd2d 1046   96 SCt 3021
        Hartman, Marshall J., and Sidney Bernstein. To Leon, and beyond; two commentators react. *Trial* 21(1):50-56
            (January 1985).
        Jensen, D. Lowell, and Rosemary Hart. The good faith restatement of the exclusionary rule. *Journal of Criminal
            Law and Criminology* 73(3):916-938 (Fall 1982).

1802. Stone, Warden v. Powell   July 6, 1976
                Coupled with Wolff, Warden v. Rice
        428 US 465   49 LEd2d 1067   96 SCt 3037
        Burger Court 73-75
        En Am Con 1776
        Sup Ct Review (1989):165-193; (1993):64-124
        Sup Ct Yearbook (1992-93):64-65
        Bernstein, Sidney, and Michael Eisenstein. 1982 Supreme Court update: the criminal law. *Trial* 18(9):45-50, 81
            (September 1982).
        Bigornia, Anthony P. Supreme Court review: Habeas corpus—Fifth Amendment—the Supreme Court's cost-
            benefit analysis of federal habeas review of alleged Miranda violations. *Journal of Criminal Law and
            Criminology* 84(4):915-942 (Winter/Spring 1994).
        Chemerinsky, Erwin. Supreme Court review: making sense of habeas corpus. *Trial* 28(12):79-82 (December
            1992).
        Dripps, Donald A. Supreme Court review: the great writ and the right to silence. *Trial* 30(1):72-73 (January
            1994).
        Haas, Kenneth C. "New federalism" and prisoners' rights: state supreme courts in comparative perspective.
            Western Political Quarterly 34(4):552-571 (December 1981).
        Hartman, Marshall J., and Sidney Bernstein. To Leon, and beyond; two commentators react. *Trial* 21(1):50-56
            (January 1985).

1803. United States v. Martinez-Fuerte   July 6, 1976
                Coupled with Sifuentes v. United States
        428 US 543   49 LEd2d 1116   96 SCt 3074
        Greig, William H., and Phillip S. Althoff. The constitutionality of roadblocks; the Fourth Amendment on the
            firing line again. *Trial* 22(2):56-62 (February 1986).

1804. Cantor dba Selden Drugs Co. v. Detroit Edison Co.   July 6, 1976
        428 US 579   49 LEd2d 1141   96 SCt 3110
        Hamlin, Ross J. Application of the Sherman Act state action exemption to municipal environmental regulation:
            a case for broader local discretion. *Boston College Environmental Affairs Law Review* 11(3):609-664 (April
            1984).
        Werner, Ray O. Marketing and the United States Supreme Court, 1975-1981. *Journal of Marketing* 46(2):73-81
            (Spring 1982).

1805. Estelle v. Gamble   November 30, 1976
        429 US 97   50 LEd2d 251   97 SCt 285
        En Am Con 524-526
        Newman, Amy. Supreme Court review: Eighth Amendment—cruel and unusual punishment and conditions
            cases. *Journal of Criminal Law and Criminology* 82(4):979-999 (Winter 1992).

1806. General Electric Co. v. Gilbert   December 7, 1976
        429 US 125   50 LEd2d 343   97 SCt 401
        Brennan 307-309
        Burger Court 125, 149-150
        Burger Years 109-124
        En Am Con 284-287, 1666-1673
        Hard Choices 311

Turning 67-73+

Barnett, Edith. Pregnancy discrimination: the Supreme Court spells out protections for pregnant workers. *Trial* 23(7):36-38, 42 (July 1987).

Friedman, Dana E. Liberty, equality, maternity! *Across the Board* 24(3):10-17 (March 1987).

Hofmann, Mark A. Judging Ginsburg's record: high court nominee seen as pro-business on certain issues. *Business Insurance* 27(26):1, 61 (June 21, 1993).

Katz, Joni F. Hazardous Working conditions and fetal protection policies: women are going back to the future. *Boston College Environmental Affairs Law Review* 17(1):201-230 (Fall 1989).

Ruben, George. Equal insurance coverage for spouses, says court. *Monthly Labor Review* 106(8):40 (August 1983).

Tarnoff, Stephen. Court decisions or benefits increase employers' costs. *Business Insurance* 21(44):93-95 (November 2, 1987).

Williams, Wendy W., and Judith L. Lichtman. Closing the law's gender gap. *Nation* 239(9):280-285 (September 29, 1984).

1807. City of Madison, Joint School District No. 8 v.   December 8, 1976
     Wisconsin Employment Relations Commission
     429 US 167   50 LEd2d 376   97 SCt 421

Flygare, Thomas J. De jure: Supreme Court upholds exclusive role for faculty unions in "meet-and-confer" sessions. *Phi Delta Kappan* 65(10):718-719 (June 1984).

Rabban, David M. AAUP in the courts: the association's representation of faculty members and faculty causes in appellate litigation. *Academe* 69(2): 1a-12a (March/April 1983).

1808. Craig v. Boren   December 20, 1976
     429 US 190   50 LEd2d 397   97 SCt 451
     Amending 203-213+
     Ascent 226-232+
     Brennan 309-313
     Burger Court 140-141, 154
     Burger Years 109-124
     Const (Currie) 493-500
     Const Law 508-512R+
     En Am Con 512-513, 608-612, 1666-1673
     Equal Rights 57-60, 98-103+

Aliotta, Jilda M. The unfinished feminist agenda: the shifting forum. *Annals of the American Academy of Political and Social Science* 515:140-150 (May 1991).

Baer, Judith A. Women's rights and the limits of constitutional doctrine. *Western Political Quarterly* 44(4):821-852 (December 1991).

Farber, Daniel A. Supreme Court review: from Warren to Rehnquist. *Trial* 25(7):124-126 (July 1989).

Rosenbloom, David H. Public administrators and the judiciary: the "new partnership." *Public Administration Review* 47(1):75-83 (January/February 1987).

The talk of the town: men's rights. *New Yorker* 69(20):32 (July 5, 1993).

Williams, Wendy W., and Judith L. Lichtman. Closing the law's gender gap. *Nation* 239(9):280-285 (September 29, 1984).

1809. Village of Arlington Heights v. Metropolitan Housing Development Corp.   January 11, 1977
     429 US 252   50 LEd2d 450   97 SCt 555
     Court Public 100
     En Am Con 71, 1136-1143, 2088-2089

Binion, Gayle. The Burger court and the rights of the poor. *Center Magazine* 15(2):2-7 (March/April 1982).

Gordon, William M. The implementation of desegregation plans since Brown. *Journal of Negro Education* 63(3):310-322 (Summer 1994).

Sullivan, Harold J. Formula for failure: a critique of the intent requirement in school segregation litigation. *Journal of Negro Education* 52(3):270-289 (Summer 1983).

1810. Mt. Healthy City School District Board of Education v. Doyle   January 11, 1977
    429 US 274   50 LEd2d 471   97 SCt 568
    Behind Bakke 101-102, 105
    McFeeley, Neil D. The Supreme Court and patronage: implications for local government. *National Civic Review* 71(5):251-258 (May 1982).
    Mounts, Gregory J. Labor and the Supreme Court: significant decisions of 1978-79. *Monthly Labor Review* 103(1):14-21 (January 1980).
    Sendor, Benjamin. Is speaking out cause for dismissal? *American School Board Journal* 177(3):8, 46 (March 1990).
    ———. Why you might be personally liable. *American School Board Journal* 181(12):15, 47 (December 1994).
    Zirkel, Perry A., and Ivan B. Gluckman. Educators' free speech: new developments. *NASSP Bulletin* 68(475):127-130 (November 1984).

1811. Local 3489, United Steelworkers of America, AFL-CIO v. Usery, Secretary of Labor   January 12, 1977
    429 US 305   50 LEd2d 502   97 SCt 611
    Burger Court 164

1812. United States v. Donovan   January 18, 1977
    429 US 413   50 LEd2d 652   97 SCt 658
    Goldsmith, Michael. The Supreme Court and Title III: rewriting the law of electronic surveillance. *Journal of Criminal Law and Criminology* 74(1):1-171 (Spring 1983).
    Silver, Stephen E. IRS use of wiretap evidence in civil tax proceedings in doubt despite recent case. *Journal of Taxation* 56(5):300-303 (May 1982).

1813. Brunswick Corp. v. Pueblo Bowl-O-Mat, Inc.   April 25, 1977
    429 US 477   50 LEd2d 701   97 SCt 690
    Werner, Ray O. Marketing and the United States Supreme Court, 1975-1981. *Journal of Marketing* 46(2):73-81 (Spring 1982).

1814. Oregon v. Mathiason   January 25, 1977
    429 US 492   50 LEd2d 714   97 SCt 711
    Jacobs, Robert. The state of Miranda: the effects of the Quarles decision. *Trial* 21(1):44-48 (January 1985).

1815. National Labor Relations Board (NLRB) v. Enterprise Association of Steam,   February 22, 1977
    Hot Water, Hydraulic Sprinkler, Pneumatic Tube, Ice Machine and General Pipefitters of New York and Vicinity, Local Union No. 638
    429 US 507   51 LEd2d 1   97 SCt 891
    Burger Court 169-172
    Mounts, Gregory J. Labor and the Supreme Court: significant decisions of 1979-80. *Monthly Labor Review* 104(4):13-22 (April 1981).

1816. Whalen, Commissioner of Health of New York v. Roe   February 22, 1977
    429 US 589   51 LEd2d 64   97 SCt 869
    Abortion (Frohock) 67
    Abortion Moral 37
    En Am Con 1577-1581, 2047
    Toufexis, Anastasia, Christine Gorman, and Dennis Wyss. Cracking down on the victims: as AIDS spreads, civil liberties may also be at risk. *Time* 130(1):82-83 (July 6, 1987).

1817. United States Steel Corp. v. Fortner Enterprises, Inc.   February 22, 1977
    429 US 610   51 LEd2d 80   97 SCt 861
    Sup Ct Review (1984):69-148
    Werner, Ray O. Marketing and the United States Supreme Court, 1975-1981. *Journal of Marketing* 46(2):73-81 (Spring 1982).

1818. Donovan v. Penn Shipping Co., Inc.   February 22, 1977
429 US 648   51 LEd2d 112   97 SCt 835
Garcia, Diana. Remittitur in environmental cases: developing a standard of review for federal courts. *Boston College Environmental Affairs Law Review* 16(1):119-147 (Fall 1988).

1819. Gilmore v. Utah   December 13, 1976
429 US 1012   50 LEd2d 632   97 SCt 436
Death Penalty (Tushnet) 95-98
Death Penalty 80s 140-141, 145-146, 151-154
Death Penalty 90s 169-170, 176-178
Letting Go 80-83, 86-92
Urofsky, Melvin I. A right to die: termination of appeal for condemned prisoners. *Journal of Criminal Law and Criminology* 75(3):553-582 (Fall 1984).

1820. E.I. DuPont de Nemours Co. v. Train, Administrator, February 23, 1977
Environmental Protection Agency (EPA)
430 US 112   51 LEd2d 204   97 SCt 965
Funk, William. The exception that approves the rule: FDF variances under the Clean Water Act. *Boston College Environmental Affairs Law Review* 13(1):1-60 (Fall 1985).

1821. United Jewish Organization of Williamsburgh, Inc. (UJO) v. Carey   March 1, 1977
430 US 144   51 LEd2d 229   97 SCt 996
Almanac (1993):327
Behind Bakke 34-39+, 89-90
Const Law 630-633R
En Am Con 566-568, 839-840, 1518-1524, 1937
Berns, Walter. Voting rights and wrongs. *Commentary* 73(3):31-36 (March 1982).
Daly, James J., Stephen M. Baron, Jack Noble, and Carl Cohen. Affirmative action. *Commentary* 82(1):4-6 (July 1986).
Eshleman, Kenneth. Affirmative gerrymandering is a matter of justice. *National Civic Review* 69(11):608-613, 620 (December 1980).
Public Affairs Council of Louisiana. Reapportionment for the 1980s: good faith and court decisions. *National Civic Review* 70(11):575-582 (December 1981).
Zimmerman, Joseph F. Election systems and representative democracy: reflections on the Voting Rights Act of 1965. *National Civic Review* 84(4):287-309 (Fall/Winter 1995).

1822. Califano, Secretary of Health, Education and Welfare v. Goldfarb   March 2, 1977
430 US 199   51 LEd2d 270   97 SCt 1021
Burger Court 140-142
En Am Con 197-198, 1666-1673, 1704-1705
Equal Rights 17-42+
Baer, Judith A. Women's rights and the limits of constitutional doctrine. *Western Political Quarterly* 44(4):821-852 (December 1991).

1823. Nolde Brothers, Inc. v. Local No. 358,   March 7, 1977
Bakery & Confectionary Workers Union, AFL-CIO
430 US 243   51 LEd2d 300   97 SCt 1067
Lissy, William E. Arbitration obligation after expiration of union contract. *Supervision* 53(2):20-21 (February 1992).

1824. Complete Auto Transit, Inc. v. Brady   March 3, 1977
430 US 274   51 LEd2d 326   97 SCt 1076
Ascent 123-125
En Am Con 1757-1760
Sup Ct Review (1989):223-259

Dell'Isola, Mark, and Sara Ann Hull. State sales tax on interstate transportation service valid. *CPA Journal* 65(7):62-64 (August 1995).

Genetelli, Richard W., David B. Zigman, and Cesar E. Bencosme. Recent U.S. Supreme Court decisions on state and local tax issues. *CPA Journal* 62(11):38-44 (November 1992).

Lanthrop, Robert G. Armco—a narrow and puzzling test for discriminatory state taxes under the commerce clause. *Taxes* 63(8):551-561 (August 1985).

O'Connell, Daniel. U.S. Supreme court reviews state and local taxation issues. *CPA Journal* 62(3):16-21 (March 1992).

Powers, Carol L. State taxation of energy resources: affirmation of Commonwealth Edison Co. v. Montana. *Boston College Environmental Affairs Law Review* 10(2):503-564 (September 1982).

State taxation of interstate commerce: US Supreme Court update. *CPA Journal* 51(11):56-57 (November 1981).

1825. Oklahoma Publishing Co. v. District Court in and for Oklahoma County, Oklahoma   March 7, 1977
430 US 308   51 LEd2d 355   97 SCt 1045
Court Public 338-340R

1826. Califano, Secretary of Health, Education and Welfare v. Webster   March 21, 1977
430 US 313   51 LEd2d 360   97 SCt 1192
Burger Court 141-144, 152
En Am Con 197-198, 1666-1673
Equal Rights 127-42+

1827. Gardner v. Florida   March 22, 1977
430 US 349   51 LEd2d 393   97 SCt 1197
Death Penalty 80s 8-9
Murphy, Cornelius F. The Supreme Court and capital punishment: a new hands-off approach. *USA Today* 121(2574):51-52 (March 1993).

1828. Brewer v. Williams   March 23, 1977
430 US 387   51 LEd2d 424   97 SCt 1232
En Am Con 153-154, 1569-1577, 1585-1592
Bahl, Martin. The Sixth Amendment as constitutional theory: does originalism require that Massiah be abandoned? *Journal of Criminal Law and Criminology* 82(2):423-463 (Summer 1991).

Cohn, William M. Supreme Court review: Sixth Amendment—inevitable discovery: a valuable but easily abused exception to the exclusionary rule. *Journal of Criminal Law and Criminology* 75(3):729-754 (Fall 1984).

Kamisar, Yale. The swing of the pendulum. *Nation* 239(9):271-274 (September 29, 1984).

Methvin, Eugene H. The case of common sense vs. Miranda. *Reader's Digest* 131(784):96-100 (August 1987).

Regan, Richard J. Supreme Court roundup: 1980 term. *Thought* 56(223):491-502 (December 1981).

White, Welsh S. Waiver and the death penalty: the implications of Estelle v. Smith. *Journal of Criminal Law and Criminology* 72(4):1522-1549 (Winter 1981).

1829. Atlas Roofing Co., Inc. v. Occupational Safety and Health Review Commission   March 23, 1977
         Coupled with Fred Irey, Jr., Inc. v. Occupational Safety and Health Review Commission
430 US 442   51 LEd2d 464   97 SCt 1261
Ascent 376-377+
En Am Con 1913-1920
Sup Ct Review (1989):261-282
Schultz, Marjorie S. Jury defined: a review of Burger court decisions. *Law and Contemporary Problems* 43(4):8-23 (Autumn 1980).

1830. Rosebud Sioux Tribe v. Kneip   April 4, 1977
430 US 584   51 LEd2d 660   97 SCt 1361
Am Indians (Wilkinson) 42, 128+

1831. United States v. Antelope   April 19, 1977
430 US 641   51 LEd2d 701   97 SCt 1395
Cort'es, Carlos E., and Van L. Perkins. U.S. Supreme Court decisions on diversity. *Education Digest* 46(6):21-24 (February 1981).

1832. Ingraham v. Wright   April 19, 1977
430 US 651   51 LEd2d 711   97 SCt 1401
Burger Court 93-95
Const (Currie) 542-546
En Am Con 524-526, 608-612, 686-688, 981, 1465-1472
Adams, Kathleen, and Nick Catoggio. The Supreme Court: a principal's best friend. *Time* 146(2):14 (July 10, 1995).
Christopher, Maura. Decide seven court cases that test teenagers' rights. *Scholastic Update* (Teachers' Edition) 120(1):16-18+ (September 4, 1987).
Eberlein, Larry. The teacher in the courtroom: new role expectation? *Clearing House* 53(6):287-291 (February 1980).
Flygare, Thomas J. Schools and the law: corporal punishment is not yet dead as a constitutional issue. *Phi Delta Kappan* 62(1):53 (September 1980).
Menacker, Julius. Review of Supreme Court reasoning in cases of expression, due process, and equal protection. *Phi Delta Kappan* 63(3):188-190 (November 1981).
Schwartz, Charles Walter. Eighth Amendment proportionality analysis and the compelling case of William Rummel. *Journal of Criminal Law and Criminology* 71(4):378-420 (Winter 1980).
Sendor, Benjamin. Kids gain new protection from corporal punishment. *American School Board Journal* 174(11):32, 53 (November 1987).

1833. Wooley v. Maynard   April 20, 1977
430 US 705   51 LEd2d 752   97 SCt 1428
Ascent 146-148+
Const (Currie) 518-522
Kovach, Kenneth A., and Peter Millspaugh. Implementing the Beck and Lehnert union security agreement decisions: a study in frustration. *Business Horizons* 38(3):57-65 (May/June 1995).

1834. United States v. Consumer Life Insurance Co.   April 26, 1977
        Coupled with United States v. Penn Security Life Insurance Co.
430 US 725   52 LEd2d 4   97 SCt 1440
Curley, Stephen C., and David Wawro. To what extent does deductibility of insurance premiums depend on risk shifting? *Journal of Taxation* 53(2):116-119 (August 1980).

1835. Trimble v. Gordon   April 26, 1977
430 US 762   52 LEd2d 31   97 SCt 1459
Almanac (1986):10A
Ascent 246-248+
En Am Con 947-948, 1921
Original (Davis) 18-20+
Murphy, Walter F. The Constitution and the 14th Amendment. *Center Magazine* 20(4):9-30 (July/August 1987).

1836. Bounds v. Smith   April 27, 1977
430 US 817   52 LEd2d 72   97 SCt 1491
En Am Con 136
Thurgood 386-393R+
Haas, Kenneth C. "New federalism" and prisoners' rights: state supreme courts in comparative perspective. *Western Political Quarterly* 34(4):552-571 (December 1981).
Mello, Michael A. Is there a federal constitutional right to counsel in capital post-conviction proceedings? *Journal of Criminal Law and Criminology* 79(4):1065-1104 (Winter 1989).

Zeithaml, Donald P. Jr. Supreme Court review: Sixth and Fourteenth Amendments—constitutional right to state capital collateral appeal: the due process of executing a convict without attorney representation. *Journal of Criminal Law and Criminology* 80(4):1190-1210 (Winter 1990).

1837. United States Trust Co. of New York v. New Jersey   April 27, 1977
    431 US 1   52 LEd2d 92   97 SCt 1505
    En Am Con 1947

1838. Linmark Associates, Inc. v. Township of Willingboro   May 2, 1977
    431 US 85   52 LEd2d 155   97 SCt 1614
    En Am Con 1168
    Freedom (Cox) 41-48
Boedecker, Karl A., and Fred W. Morgan. The evolution of First Amendment protection for commercial speech. *Journal of Marketing* 59(1):38-47 (January 1995).

1839. Abood v. Detroit Board of Education   May 23, 1977
    431 US 209   52 LEd2d 261   97 SCt 1782
    Burger Court 32, 165-166
    Const (Currie) 518-522
    En Am Con 4
    Religion 197-199
    Sup Ct Review (1990):163-205
Flygare, Thomas J. De jure: Supreme Court upholds exclusive role for faculty unions in "meet-and-confer" sessions. *Phi Delta Kappan* 65(10):718-719 (June 1984).
From Tilton to Ewing: some major higher-education decisions of the Burger court. *Chronicle of Higher Education* 32(17):10 (June 25, 1986).
The right to choose. *National Review* 34(25):1594-1596 (December 24, 1982).
Sendor, Benjamin. High Court: give nonunion employes a fair shake. *American School Board Journal* 173(7):16 (July 1986).

1840. Douglas, Commissioner, Virginia Marine Resources Commission   May 23, 1977
    v. Seacoast Products, Inc.
    431 US 265   52 LEd2d 304   97 SCt 1740
    Guide (CQ) 87
Schwartz, Edward B. Water as an article of commerce: state embargoes spring a leak under Sporhase v. Nebraska. *Boston College Environmental Affairs Law Review* 12(1):103-169 (Fall 1985).
Winn, John. Alaska v. F/V Baranof: state regulation beyond the territorial sea after the Magnuson Act. *Boston College Environmental Affairs Law Review* 13(2):281-327 (Winter 1986).

1841. Smith, dba Intrigue v. United States   May 23, 1977
    431 US 291   52 LEd2d 324   97 SCt 1756
Kobylka, Joseph F. A court-created context for group litigation: libertarian groups and obscenity. *Journal of Politics* 49(4):1061-1078 (November 1987).

1842. International Brotherhood of Teamsters v. United States   May 31, 1977
    Coupled with T.I.M.E.-D.C., Inc. v. United States
    431 US 324   52 LEd2d 396   97 SCt 1843
    Affirmative (Greene) 63-71
    Burger Court 158-161
    Sup Ct Review (1984):1-68
A business group fights "comparable worth." *Business Week* (Industrial Edition) (2662):100, 105 (November 10, 1980).
Carmell, William A., and Dale E. Callender. Supreme Court didn't kill affirmative action. *ABA Banking Journal* 76(9):56-60 (September 1984).

Chambers, Julius L., and Barry Goldstein. Title VII: the continuing challenge of establishing fair employment practices. *Law and Contemporary Problems* 49(4):9-23 (Autumn 1986).

Hogan, Joyce, and Ann M. Quigley. Physical standards for employment and the courts. *American Psychologist* 41(11):1193-1217 (November 1986).

Mounts, Gregory J. Labor and the Supreme Court: significant decisions of 1979-80. *Monthly Labor Review* 104(4):13-22 (April 1981).

————. Significant decisions in labor cases. *Monthly Labor Review* 103(6):51-53 (June 1980).

Roberts, Paul Craig, and Lawrence M. Stratton, Jr. Color code. *National Review* 47(5):36, 51, 80 (March 20, 1995).

Vile, John R., and Kathy Ruth McCoy. The Memphis Case: another precedent? *Personnel* 62(7):72-76 (July 1985).

1843. East Texas Motor Freight System, Inc. v. Rodriguez   May 31, 1977
       Coupled with Southern Conference of Teamsters v. Rodriguez
431 US 395   52 LEd2d 453   97 SCt 1891

A business group fights "comparable worth." *Business Week* (Industrial Edition) (2662):100, 105 (November 10, 1980).

1844. Connor v. Finch   May 31, 1977
       Coupled with United States v. Finch
431 US 407   52 LEd2d 465   97 SCt 1828

Public Affairs Council of Louisiana. Reapportionment for the 1980s: good faith and court decisions. *National Civic Review* 70(11):575-582 (December 1981).

1845. Moore v. City of East Cleveland, Ohio   May 31, 1977
431 US 494   52 LEd2d 531   97 SCt 1932
      Abortion (Frohock) 67
      Brennan 282-285
      Burger Court 109-112+
      En Am Con 686-688, 1276
      Hard Choices 134
      Sup Ct Review (1982):85-125

Minow, Martha. We, the family: constitutional rights and American families. *Journal of American History* 74(3):959-983 (December 1987).

What they say it is: the justices' words instruct the nation, and often address history. *Time* 130(1):44-49 (July 6, 1987).

1846. United Air Lines, Inc. v. Evans   May 31, 1977
431 US 553   52 LEd2d 571   97 SCt 1885

Brooks, Thornton H., M. Daniel McGinn, and William P. H. Cary. Second generation problems facing employers in employment discrimination cases: continuing violations, pendent state claims, and double attorneys' fees. *Law and Contemporary Problems* 49(4):26-51 (Autumn 1986).

Gray, Mary W. The halls of ivy and the halls of justice: lightening the burden. *Academe* 73(3):61-63 (May/June 1987).

Norris, Barbara A. Multiple regression analysis in Title VII cases: a structural approach to attacks of "missing factors" and "pre-act discrimination." *Law and Contemporary Problems* 49(4):63-96 (Autumn 1986).

1847. Alabama Power Co. v. Davis   June 6, 1977
431 US 581   52 LEd2d 595   97 SCt 2002

Geisel, Jerry. Reservists on active duty to earn pension credits. *Business Insurance* 24(35):2, 38 (August 27, 1990).

Mounts, Gregory J. Labor and the Supreme Court: significant decisions of 1979-80. *Monthly Labor Review* 104(4):13-22 (April 1981).

1848. Roberts v. Louisiana   June 6, 1977
    431 US 633   52 LEd2d 637   97 SCt 1993
      Brennan 226-229
      Death Penalty (Bedau) 247-253, 293-298R

1849. Stencel Aero Engineering Corp. v. United States   June 9, 1977
    431 US 666   52 LEd2d 665   97 SCt 2054
    Ball, Howard. The U.S. Supreme Court's glossing of the Federal Tort Claims Act: statutory construction and veterans' tort actions. *Western Political Quarterly* 41(3):529-552 (September 1988).
    Justice for all. [Editorial] *Aviation Week and Space Technology* 129(1):7 (July 4, 1988).
    Mangan, Joseph F. Government contractors: their defense rests. *Best's Review* (Property/Casualty Insurance Edition) 91(2):82, 84 (June 1990).

1850. Carey v. Population Services International   June 9, 1977
    431 US 678   52 LEd2d 675   97 SCt 2010
      Abortion Am 82-83, 98
      Abortion Moral 66-70
      En Am Con 213, 1552-1558
      Hard Choices 134
      Liberty 627-628+
    Boedecker, Karl A., and Fred W. Morgan. The evolution of First Amendment protection for commercial speech. *Journal of Marketing* 59(1):38-47 (January 1995).

1851. Illinois Brick Co. v. Illinois   June 9, 1977
    431 US 720   52 LEd2d 707   97 SCt 2061
    Consumer and antitrust law. *Congressional Digest* 59(2):34-64R (February 1980).
    Werner, Ray O. Marketing and the United States Supreme Court, 1975-1981. *Journal of Marketing* 46(2):73-81 (Spring 1982).
    Witt, Elder. State-federal power at issue in High Court. *Governing* 2(6):66-67 (March 1989).

1852. Ward v. Illinois   June 9, 1977
    431 US 767   52 LEd2d 738   97 SCt 2085
      En Am Con 2006
    Hagle, Timothy M. But do they have to see it to know it? the Supreme Court's obscenity and pornography decisions. *Western Political Quarterly* 44(4):1039-1054 (December 1991).

1853. Nyquist v. Mauclet   June 13, 1977
    432 US 1   53 LEd2d 63   97 SCt 2120
      Ascent 241-242

1854. National Socialist Party of America v. Village of Skokie   June 14, 1977
    432 US 43   53 LEd2d 96   97 SCt 2205
      Const (Friendly) 81-89
      Const Law 167-168
      First 310-323

1855. Trans World AirLines, Inc. (TWA) v. Hardison   June 16, 1977
      Coupled with International Association of Machinists and Aerospace Workers v. Hardison
    432 US 63   53 LEd2d 113   97 SCt 2264
      Burger Years 56-91
      En Am Con 284-287
      Godless 50
      Religion 176-180
    Frierson, James G. Religion in the workplace—dealing in good faith? *Personnel Journal* 67(7):60-67 (July 1988).

Koen, Clifford M., Jr. The pre-employment inquiry guide. *Personnel Journal* 59(10):825-829 (October 1980).

Lissy, William E. Labor law for supervisors: accommodating employees' religious practices. *Supervision* 49(11):22-23, 7 (November 1988).

McKinney, T. Charles. Employee relations, religion and the Constitution. *Personnel Journal* 60(12):920-921 (December 1981).

Sharp, Ralph. Keep these guidelines in mind when reviewing your religious leave policy. *American School Board Journal* 173(12):42, 45 (December 1986).

1856. Manson v. Brathwaite   June 16, 1977
432 US 98   53 LEd2d 140   97 SCt 2243
    En Am Con 339-342
    Sup Ct Review (1991):103-142
Lane, Margaret J. Eyewitness identification: should psychologists be permitted to address the jury? *Journal of Criminal Law and Criminology* 75(4):1321-1365 (Winter 1984).

1857. Patterson v. New York   June 17, 1977
432 US 197   53 LEd2d 281   97 SCt 2319
Dennis, Anthony J. Supreme Court review: Fifth Amendment—due process rights at sentencing. *Journal of Criminal Law and Criminology* 77(3):646-665 (Fall 1986).

Harris, Leslie J. Constitutional limits on criminal presumptions as an expression of changing concepts of fundamental fairness. *Journal of Criminal Law and Criminology* 77(2):308-357 (Summer 1986).

1858. Northeast Marine Terminal Co., Inc. v. Caputo   June 17, 1977
        Coupled with International Terminal Operating Co., Inc. v. Blundo
432 US 249   53 LEd2d 320   97 SCt 2348
Mount, Gregory J. Significant decisions in labor cases. *Monthly Labor Review* 103(3):51-52 (March 1980).

1859. Hunt v. Washington State Apple Advertising Commission   June 20, 1977
432 US 333   53 LEd2d 383   97 SCt 2434
    En Am Con 1751-1755
Alpert, Peter A. Citizen suits under the Clean Air Act: universal standing for the uninjured private attorney general? *Boston College Environmental Affairs Law Review* 16(2):283-328 (Winter 1988).

Farber, Daniel A. Supreme Court review: litigating with the sovereign. *Trial* 28(4):85-90 (April 1992).

1860. Beal, Secretary, Department of Public Welfare of Pennsylvania v. Doe   June 20, 1977
432 US 438   53 LEd2d 464   97 SCt 2366
    Abortion (Frohock) 82-83
    Abortion Am 91, 98
    Abortion Decs 70s Introduction, 105-119R
    Abortion Pol (Rubin) 151-157
    Abortion Quest 115-118
    Almanac (1993): 636
    Court Public 386
    En Am Con 1552-1558
    Hard Choices 313
    Liberty 627-628

1861. Maher, Commissioner of Social Services of Connecticut v. Roe   June 20, 1977
432 US 464   53 LEd2d 484   97 SCt 2376
    Abortion (Frohock) 83
    Abortion Am 91-94R, 98, 233-234+
    Abortion Con 183-185+, 292
    Abortion Dec 51-57+
    Abortion Decs 70s 121-134R
    Abortion Pol (Jaffe) 127-131, 185-208

Abortion Pol (Rubin) 151-157
Abortion Quest 115-118
Almanac (1993):636
Const (Currie) 471-475
Court Public 386, 427-436R
En Am Con 904-905, 1197, 2041-2042
Hard Choices 313
Liberty 627-629, 634-638+
Nobody's 11-13

Goggin, Malcolm L. Understanding the new politics of abortion: a framework and agenda for research. *American Politics Quarterly* 21(1):4-30 (January 1993).

Regan, Richard J. Supreme Court roundup: 1979 term. *Thought* 55(219):487-455 (December 1980).

Rose, Jonathan. Decide 10 landmark cases that define your rights. *Scholastic Update* 119(1):7-9, 21 (September 8, 1986).

Schwartz, Herman. Concern for the basic necessities. *Nation* 239(9):299-300 (September 29, 1984).

1862. Poelker v. Doe   June 20, 1977
432 US 519   53 LEd2d 528   97 SCt 2391
Abortion (Frohock) 83
Abortion Am 91, 98+
Abortion Decs 70s Introduction, 135-144R
Almanac (1993):636
Hard Choices 313
Liberty 627-629

1863. United States v. Chadwick   June 21, 1977
433 US 1   53 LEd2d 538   97 SCt 2476

Carter, Jeffrey A. Supreme Court review: Fourth Amendment—of cars, containers and confusion. *Journal of Criminal Law and Criminology* 72(4):1171-1221 (Winter 1981).

Jensen, D. Lowell, and Rosemary Hart. The good faith restatement of the exclusionary rule. *Journal of Criminal Law and Criminology* 73(3):916-938 (Fall 1982).

Katz, Lewis R. United States v. Ross: evolving standards for warrantless searches. *Journal of Criminal Law and Criminology* 74(1):172-208 (Spring 1983).

LaFave, Wayne R. Supreme Court review: Fourth Amendment vagaries (of improbable cause, imperceptible plain view, notorious privacy, and balancing askew). *Journal of Criminal Law and Criminology* 74(4):1171-1224 (Winter 1983).

1864. Continental TV, Inc. v. GTE Sylvania, Inc.   June 23, 1977
433 US 36   53 LEd2d 568   97 SCt 2549
Burger Court 181-184, 190-191
Sup Ct Review (1982):319-349; (1984):69-148

Bork, Robert H. Beside the law. *National Review* 44(20):38, 40-43 (October 19, 1992).

Dolan, Michael W. Congress, the executive, and the court: the great resale price maintenance affair of 1983. *Public Administration Review* 45(Special Issue):718-722 (November 1985).

A powerful bid to rewrite the antitrust rule book. *Business Week* (Industrial Edition) (2811):84-90 (October 10, 1983).

Sheffet, Mary Jane, and Debra L. Scammon. Resale price maintenance: is it safe to suggest retail prices? *Journal of Marketing* 49(4):82-92 (Fall 1985).

Werner, Ray O. Marketing and the United States Supreme Court, 1975-1981. *Journal of Marketing* 46(2):73-81 (Spring 1982).

1865. Wainwright v. Sykes   June 23, 1977
433 US 72   53 LEd2d 594   97 SCt 2497
Brennan 199-203
En Am Con 1993, 2003-2005

Bamonte, Thomas J. Supreme Court review: habeas corpus—limiting the availability of habeas corpus after a procedural default. *Journal of Criminal Law and Criminology* 73(4):1612-1640 (Winter 1982).

Bernstein, Sidney, and Michael Eisenstein. 1982 Supreme Court update: the criminal law. *Trial* 18(9):45-50, 81 (September 1982).

Chemerinsky, Erwin. Supreme Court review: making sense of habeas corpus. *Trial* 28(12):79-82 (December 1992).

Malone, Patrick A. False statistic. [Editorial] *Nation* 237(22):685 (December 31, 1983-January 7, 1984).

Smith, Jim. Federal habeas corpus—a need for reform. *Journal of Criminal Law and Criminology* 73(3):1036-1050 (Fall 1982).

Wells, Diane. Federal habeas corpus and the death penalty: a need for a return to the principles of Furman. *Journal of Criminal Law and Criminology* 80(2):427-490 (Summer 1989).

1866. Jones v. North Carolina Prisoners' Labor Union, Inc.   June 23, 1977
   433 US 119   53 LEd2d 629   97 SCt 2532
   Robbins, Ira P. Cry of "wolfish" in the federal courts: the future of federal judicial intervention in prison administration. *Journal of Criminal Law and Criminology* 71(3):211-225 (Fall 1980).

1867. Shaffer v. Heitner   June 24, 1977
   433 US 186   53 LEd2d 683   97 SCt 2569
   Const (Currie) 580-585
   Sup Ct Review (1980):77-113
   DeMott, Deborah A. Perspectives on choice of law for corporate internal affairs. *Law and Contemporary Problems* 48(3):161-198 (Summer 1985).

1868. Wolman v. Walter   June 24, 1977
   433 US 229   53 LEd2d 714   97 SCt 2593
   Burger Years 56-91
   En Am Con 1650-1658, 2073
   Establishment 28, 127-128, 136, 213+
   Godless 71, 73-74+
   Buzzard, Lynn Robert, and Samuel Ericsson. Public aid to private schools: Caesar rendering to God? *Christianity Today* 27(10):20-23 (June 17, 1983).

   Kilpatrick, James J. What in God's name is going on? *National Review* 37(2):36, 38-39 (February 8, 1985).

   Kobylka, Joseph F. Leadership on the Supreme Court of the United States: Chief Justice Burger and the establishment clause. *Western Political Quarterly* 42(4):545-568 (December 1989).

   Rabkin, Jeremy. The curious case of Kiryas Joel. *Commentary* 98(5):58-61 (November 1994).

   Regan, Richard J. Supreme Court roundup: 1979 term. *Thought* 55(219):487-455 (December 1980).

   Weber, Paul J. Excessive entanglement: a wavering First Amendment standard. *Review of Politics* 46(4):483-501 (October 1984).

1869. Milliken, Governor of Michigan v. Bradley   June 27, 1977
   433 US 267   53 LEd2d 745   97 SCt 2749
   En Am Con 557-561, 1261
   Sup Ct Review (1984):149-168
   Delon, Floyd G. The legacy of Thurgood Marshall. *Journal of Negro Education* 63(3):278-288 (Summer 1994).

   Hyde, Alison A. School desegregation: the role of the courts and means of achievement. *NASSP Bulletin* 78(565):28-37 (November 1994).

   Russo, Charles J., J. John Harris III, and Rosetta F. Sandidge. Brown v. Board of Education at 40: a legal history of equal educational opportunity in American public education. *Journal of Negro Education* 63(3):297-309 (Summer 1994).

   Wise, Charles, and Rosemary O'Leary. Is federalism dead or alive in the Supreme Court?: implications for public administrators. *Public Administration Review* 52(6):559-572 (November/December 1992).

1870. Hazelwood School District v. United States   June 27, 1977
   433 US 299   53 LEd2d 768   97 SCt 2736

Cohen, Carl. Naked racial preference. *Commentary* 81(3):24-31 (March 1986).

Gray, Mary W. The halls of ivy and the halls of justice: lightening the burden. *Academe* 73(3):61-63 (May/June 1987).

Hogan, Joyce, and Ann M. Quigley. Physical standards for employment and the courts. *American Psychologist* 41(11):1193-1217 (November 1986).

Norris, Barbara A. Multiple regression analysis in Title VII cases: a structural approach to attacks of "missing factors" and "pre-act discrimination." *Law and Contemporary Problems* 49(4):63-96 (Autumn 1986).

Open season on the high school press. [Editorial] *Columbia Journalism Review* 26(6):18 (March/April 1988).

Ruben, George. Developments in industrial relations: High Court backs laid-off white teachers. *Monthly Labor Review* 109(7):46-47 (July 1986).

Sendor, Benjamin. Good cases make bad law, and this curriculum ruling suggests the opposite also can be true. *American School Board Journal* 175(9):7, 37 (September 1988).

1871. Dothard v. Rawlinson   June 27, 1977
     433 US 321   53 LEd2d 786   97 SCt 2720
       Burger Years 109-124
       En Am Con 284-287

Gest, Ted. Seniority vs. minorities—impact of court ruling. *U.S. News and World Report* 96(25):22-23 (June 25, 1984).

Hogan, Joyce, and Ann M. Quigley. Physical standards for employment and the courts. *American Psychologist* 41(11):1193-1217 (November 1986).

Williams, Wendy W., and Judith L. Lichtman. Closing the law's gender gap. *Nation* 239(9):280-285 (September 29, 1984).

1872. Bates v. State Bar of Arizona   June 27, 1977
     433 US 350   53 LEd2d 810   97 SCt 2691
       Ascent 133-137
       Const Law 174, 179-185R
       En Am Con 103-104, 770-773
       Magic 288-289
       Sup Ct Review (1984):69-148

Boedecker, Karl A., and Fred W. Morgan. The evolution of First Amendment protection for commercial speech. *Journal of Marketing* 59(1):38-47 (January 1995).

Bowen, Lauren. Attorney advertising in the wake of Bates v. State Bar of Arizona (1977): a study of judicial impact. *American Politics Quarterly* 23(4):461-484 (October 1995).

Colford, Steven W. Lawyer ads on high court docket. *Advertising Age* 55(80):58 (November 26, 1984).

———. Rehnquist slams ads' 1st Amendment shield. *Advertising Age* 57(37):12 (June 30, 1986).

———. Two ad cases will gauge new justice. *Advertising Age* 65(43):40 (October 10, 1994).

Hamlin, Ross J. Application of the Sherman Act state action exemption to municipal environmental regulation: a case for broader local discretion. *Boston College Environmental Affairs Law Review* 11(3):609-664 (April 1984).

High court hears arguments on lawyer ad rules. *Editor and Publisher* 114(46): 12-13 (November 14, 1981).

Hite, Robert E., and Cynthia Fraser. Meta-analyses of attitudes toward advertising by profession. *Journal of Marketing* 52(3):95-103 (July 1988).

Reed, O. Lee. Reading the tea leaves: future regulation of product-extrinsic advertising. *Business Horizons* 33(5):88-93 (September/October 1990).

Smith, Robert E., and Tiffany S. Meyer. Attorney advertising: a consumer perspective. *Journal of Marketing* 44(2):56-64 (Spring 1980).

Werner, Ray O. Marketing and the Supreme Court in transition. 1982-1984. *Journal of Marketing* 49(3):97-105 (Summer 1985).

———. Marketing and the United States Supreme Court, 1975-1981. *Journal of Marketing* 46(2):73-81 (Spring 1982).

What they say it is: the justices' words instruct the nation, and often address history. *Time* 130(1):44-49 (July 6, 1987).

Winter, Ralph K. Political financing and the Constitution. *Annals of the American Academy of Political and Social Science* 486:34-48 (July 1986).

1873. Dayton Board of Education v. Brinkman   June 27, 1977
    433 US 406   53 LEd2d 851   97 SCt 2766
        Burden 220-223+
        Burger Years 95-108
        Court Public 159
        En Am Con 314-315

    Gordon, William M. The implementation of desegregation plans since Brown. *Journal of Negro Education* 6(3):310-322 (Summer 1994).

    Reid, Herbert O., Sr. State of the art: the law and education since 1954. *Journal of Negro Education* 52(3):234-249 (Summer 1983).

    Russo, Charles J., J. John Harris III, and Rosetta F. Sandidge. Brown v. Board of Education at 40: a legal history of equal educational opportunity in American public education. *Journal of Negro Education* 63(3):297-309 (Summer 1994).

1874. Nixon v. Administrator of General Services   June 28, 1977
    433 US 425   53 LEd2d 867   97 SCt 2777
        En Am Con 1324
        Guide (CQ) 65

1875. Zacchini v. Scripps-Howard Broadcasting Co.   June 28, 1977
    433 US 562   53 LEd2d 965   97 SCt 2849
        En Am Con 1457-1458

    Hale, Dennis. How retiring Supreme Court Justice White voted in First Amendment cases. *Editor and Publisher* 126(30):44, 36 (July 24, 1993).

    Nimmer, Melville. Tort invasions of privacy. *Center Magazine* 15(5):46-48 (September/October 1982).

1876. Coker v. Georgia   June 29, 1977
    433 US 584   53 LEd2d 982   97 SCt 2861
        Court Public 236, 238, 241, 291-300R
        Death Penalty (Bedau) 299-304R+
        Death Penalty (Tushnet) 73-78
        En Am Con 309

    Dripps, Donald A. Supreme Court review: Cruel, unusual, and constitutional. *Trial* 28(5):87-89 (May 1992).

    Meltsner, Michael. On death row, the wait is over. *Nation* 239(9):274-277 (September 29, 1984).

    Murphy, Cornelius F. The Supreme Court and capital punishment: a new hands-off approach. *USA Today* 121(2574):51-52 (March 1993).

    Schwartz, Charles Walter. Eighth Amendment proportionality analysis and the compelling case of William Rummel. *Journal of Criminal Law and Criminology* 71(4):378-420 (Winter 1980).

    Wickert, John H. Supreme Court review: Eighth Amendment—the death penalty and vicarious felony murder: nontriggerman may not be executed absent a finding of an intent to kill. *Journal of Criminal Law and Criminology* 73(4):1553-1571 (Winter 1982).

1877. Califano v. Jobst   November 8, 1977
    434 US 47   54 LEd2d 228   98 SCt 95
        En Am Con 1204-1205

1878. Nashville Gas Co. v. Satty   December 6, 1977
    434 US 136   54 LEd2d 356   98 SCt 347
        Burger Court 149-150
        En Am Con 1666-1673

    Katz, Joni F. Hazardous working conditions and fetal protection policies: women are going back to the future. *Boston College Environmental Affairs Law Review* 17(1):201-230 (Fall 1989).

1879. United Air Lines, Inc. v. McMann   December 12, 1977
       434 US 192   54 LEd2d 402   98 SCt 444
       Pryor, David. New law battles age dicrimination. *Trial* 27(4):30-34 (April 1991).

1880. Pfizer, Inc. v. Government of India   January 11, 1978
       Pfizer, Inc. v. India
       434 US 308   54 LEd2d 563   98 SCt 584
          Almanac (1981):434-435
       Werner, Ray O. Marketing and the United States Supreme Court, 1975-1981. *Journal of Marketing* 46(2):73-81
          (Spring 1982).

1881. Bordenkircher v. Hayes   January 18, 1978
       434 US 357   54 LEd2d 604   98 SCt 663
          Const (Currie) 555-559
          Sup Ct Review (1980):211-279
       Erlinder, C. Peter, and David C. Thomas. Prohibiting prosecutorial vindictiveness while protecting prosecutorial
          discretion: toward a principled resolution of a due process dilemma. *Journal of Criminal Law and
          Criminology* 76(2):341-438 (Summer 1985).
       Halberstam, Malvina. Towards neutral principles in the administration of criminal justice: a critique of Supreme
          Court decisions sanctioning the plea bargaining process. *Journal of Criminal Law and Criminology* 73(1):1-
          49 (Spring 1982).
       Schwartz, Charles Walter. Eighth Amendment proportionality analysis and the compelling case of William
          Rummel. *Journal of Criminal Law and Criminology* 71(4):378-420 (Winter 1980).

1882. Zablocki v. Redhail   January 18, 1978
       434 US 374   54 LEd2d 618   98 SCt 673
          Abortion (Frohock) 67
          Ascent 286-288
          En Am Con 572, 1204-1205, 1796-1803, 2087
          Thurgood 417-425R+
       Minow, Martha. We, the family: constitutional rights and American families. *Journal of American History*
          74(3):959-983 (December 1987).

1883. Christiansburg Garment Co. v. Equal Employment Opportunity Commission (EEOC)   January 23, 1978
       434 US 412   54 LEd2d 648   98 SCt 694
       Brooks, Thornton H., M. Daniel McGinn, and William P. H. Cary. Second generation problems facing
          employers in employment discrimination cases: continuing violations, pendent state claims, and double
          attorneys' fees. *Law and Contemporary Problems* 49(4):26-51 (Autumn 1986).
       Spurrier, Robert L., Jr. Paying the piper in federal civil rights litigation. *Public Administration Review*
          43(3):199-208 (May/June 1983).

1884. Raymond Motor Transporation, Inc. v. Rice   February 21, 1978
       434 US 429   54 LEd2d 664   98 SCt 787
          Ascent 112-114
          En Am Con 1515, 1751-1755

1885. United States Steel Corp. v. Multistate Tax Commission   February 21, 1978
       434 US 452   54 LEd2d 682   98 SCt 799
       Briggett, Marlissa S. State supremacy in the federal realm: the interstate compact. *Boston College
          Environmental Affairs Law Review* 18(4):751-772 (Summer 1991).

1886. Central Illinois Public Service Co. v. United States   February 28, 1978
       435 US 21   55 LEd2d 82   98 SCt 917
       Emory, Meade, James B. Swenson, and Herbert J. Lerner. Sales course "reimbursement'" subject to
          withholding. *Journal of Taxation* 52(3):184-185 (March 1980).

Kovey, Mark H., and Peter H. Winslow. Sup. Ct. in Rowan holds "wages" excludable from income are exempt from FICA, FUTA. *Journal of Taxation* 55(3):130-136 (September 1981).

1887. Board of Curators of the University of Missouri v. Horowitz   March 1, 1978
435 US 78   55 LEd2d 124   98 SCt 948
En Am Con 131, 608-612
From Tilton to Ewing: some major higher-education decisions of the Burger court. *Chronicle of Higher Education* 32(17):10 (June 25, 1986).

1888. Ray, Governor of Washington v. Atlantic Richfield Co.   March 6, 1978
435 US 151   55 LEd2d 179   98 SCt 988
Guide (CQ) 87
Adams, Nancy D. Title VI of the 1990 Clean Air Act Amendments and state and local initiatives to reverse the stratospheric ozone crisis: an analysis of preemption. *Boston College Environmental Affairs Law Review* 19(1):173-216 (Fall 1991).

1889. Oliphant v. Suquamish Indian Tribe   March 6, 1978
435 US 191   55 LEd2d 209   98 SCt 1011
Am Indian (Deloria) 42-49+
Am Indians (Wilkinson) 43, 61, 109, 128+
Allen, Mark. Native American control of tribal natural resource development in the context of the federal trust and tribal self-determination. *Boston College Environmental Affairs Law Review* 16(4):857-895 (Summer 1989).
Hentoff, Nicholas. The natives are arrestless. *Washington Monthly* 22(11):20-24 (December 1990).

1890. Ballew v. Georgia   March 21, 1978
435 US 223   55 LEd2d 234   98 SCt 1029
En Am Con 97, 1085-1086, 1086-1087, 1913-1920
Bersoff, Donald N. Social science data and the Supreme Court: Lockhart as a case in point. *American Psychologist* 42(1):52-58 (January 1987).
In the Supreme Court of the United States Lockhart v. McCree: Amicus Curiae Brief for the American Psychological Assoication. *American Psychologist* 42(1):59-68 (January 1987).
Loftus, Elizabeth, and John Monahan. Trial by data: psychological research as legal evidence. *American Psychologist* 35(5):270-283 (March 1980).
Schultz, Marjorie S. Jury defined: a review of Burger court decisions. *Law and Contemporary Problems* 43(4):8-23 (Autumn 1980).

1891. Carey v. Piphus   March 21, 1978
435 US 247   55 LEd2d 252   98 SCt 1042
En Am Con 533-534

1892. United States v. Ceccolini   March 21, 1978
435 US 268   55 LEd2d 268   98 SCt 1054
Hartman, Marshall J., and Sidney Bernstein. To Leon, and beyond; two commentators react. *Trial* 21(1):50-56 (January 1985).
Nelson, Caleb. The paradox of the exclusionary rule. *Public Interest* (96):117-130 (Summer 1989).
Stratton, Brent D. The attenuation exception to the exclusionary rule: a study in attenuated principle and dissipated logic. *Journal of Criminal Law and Criminology* 75(1):139-165 (Spring 1984).

1893. Foley v. Connelie   March 22, 1978
435 US 291   55 LEd2d 287   98 SCt 1067
Ascent 235-238
Brennan 276-282
Const (Currie) 500-504
Const Law 535-538R

En Am Con 46, 745-746

Mounts, Gregory J. Labor and the Supreme Court: significant decisions of 1978-79. *Monthly Labor Review* 103(1):14-21 (January 1980).

1894. United States v. Wheeler   March 22, 1978
      435 US 313   55 LEd2d 303   98 SCt 1079
          Am Indian (Deloria) 22-29
          Am Indians (Wilkinson) 61-62, 128+

1895. Lakeside v. Oregon   March 22, 1978
      435 US 333   55 LEd2d 319   98 SCt 1091
      Bernstein, Sidney, and Michael Eisenstein. 1981 Supreme Court update: the criminal law. *Trial* 17(10):54-60, 85 (October 1981).
      Gromer, Sharon K. Supreme Court review: Fifth Amendment—the right to a no "adverse inference" jury instruction. *Journal of Criminal Law and Criminology* 72(4):1307-1325 (Winter 1981).

1896. Stump v. Sparkman   March 28, 1978
      435 US 349   55 LEd2d 331   98 SCt 1099
          Black 247-257
          En Am Con 1039-1040, 1793
      Neuborne, Burt. Taking away the right to sue. *Nation* 239(9):268-271 (September 29, 1984).
      Plotkin, Steven R., and Carol D. Mazorol. Judicial malpratice: Pulliam is not the answer. *Trial* 20(12):24-26 (December 1984).

1897. LaFayette v. Louisiana Power and Light Co.   March 29, 1978
      435 US 389   55 LEd2d 364   98 SCt 1123
      Chapple, Stephan. Community Communications v. City of Boulder: an intergovernmental paradox. *Public Administration Review* 45(Special Issue):732-737 (November 1985).
      Fletcher, Meg. High court bucks precedent in municipal antitrust ruling. *Business Insurance* 19(41):15 (October 14, 1985).
      Hamlin, Ross J. Application of the Sherman Act state action exemption to municipal environmental regulation: a case for broader local discretion. *Boston College Environmental Affairs Law Review* 11(3):609-664 (April 1984).
      Roberts, Robert N. Municipal antitrust immunity and the state-action exemption: Developments in the law. *State Government* 58(4):164-171 (Winter 1986).
      Ross, Douglas. Safeguarding our federalism: lessons for the states from the Supreme Court. *Public Administration Review* 45(Special Issue):723-731 (November 1985).
      Werner, Ray O. Marketing and the Supreme Court in transition. 1982-1984. *Journal of Marketing* 49(3):97-105 (Summer 1985).
      ———. Marketing and the United States Supreme Court, 1975-1981. *Journal of Marketing* 46(2):73-81 (Spring 1982).

1898. Massachusetts v. United States   March 29, 1978
      435 US 444   55 LEd2d 403   98 SCt 1153
      Johnston, Richard E., and John T. Thompson. Burger court and federalism: a revolution in 1976? *Western Political Quarterly* 33(2):197-216 (June 1980).

1899. Holloway v. Arkansas   April 3, 1978
      435 US 475   55 LEd2d 426   98 SCt 1173
      Bleiweiss, Shell J. Supreme Court review: Sixth Amendment—conflicts of interest in multiple representation of codefendants. *Journal of Criminal Law and Criminology* 71(4):529-537 (Winter 1980).

1900. Vermont Yankee Nuclear Power Corp. v. Natural Resources Defense Council (NRDC)   April 3, 1978
            Coupled with Consumer Power Co. v. Aeschliman
      435 US 519   55 LEd2d 460   98 SCt 1197

Burger Years 191-205

Bernstein, Sidney. Nuclear law: the battle over atomic power in the courts. *Trial* 16(4):28-32, 61-62 (April 1980).

Brady, Timothy Patrick. "But most of it belongs to those yet to be born": the public trust doctrine, NEPA, and the stewardship ethic. *Boston College Environmental Affairs Law Review* 17(3):621-646 (Spring 1990).

Funk, William. The exception that approves the rule: FDF variances under the Clean Water Act. *Boston College Environmental Affairs Law Review* 13(1):1-60 (Fall 1985).

Hassler, Gregory L., and Karen O'Connor. Woodsy witchdoctors versus judicial guerrillas: the role and impact of competing interest groups in environmental litigation. *Boston College Environmental Affairs Law Review* 13(4):487-520 (Summer 1986).

Kelly, Paula. Judicial review of agency decisions under the National Environmental Policy Act of 1969— Strycker's Bay Neighborhood Council, Inc. v. Karlen. *Boston College Environmental Affairs Law Review* 10(1):79-109 (1982-83).

Lovely, Jeffrey M. Protecting wetlands: consideration of secondary social and economic effects by the United States Army Corps of Engineers in its wetlands permitting process. *Boston College Environmental Affairs Law Review* 17(3):647-686 (Spring 1990).

Meyers, Gary D. Old-growth forests, the owl, and yew: environmental ethics versus traditional dispute resolution under the Endangered Species Act and other public land and resources laws. *Boston College Environmental Affairs Law Review* 18(4):623-668 (Summer 1991).

Morrison, Alan B. Close reins on the bureaucracy. *Nation* 239(9):290-294 (September 29, 1984).

Sandler, Ross. Law: Shrinking NEPA. *Environment* 22(3):43-44 (April 1980).

———. Law: Supreme Court trends in environmental law. *Environment* 23(7):4-5 (September 1981).

Shea, Thomas E. The judicial standard for review of environmental impact statement threshold decisions. *Boston College Environmental Affairs Law Review* 9(1):63-101 (1980/1981).

1901. Frank Lyon Co. v. United States   April 18, 1978
435 US 561   55 LEd2d 550   98 SCt 1291

Rosenberg, Alan S., and Herbert T. Weinstein. Applying the tax court's nontax benefit test for multiple-party sale-leasebacks. *Journal of Taxation* 54(6):366-372 (June 1981).

1902. McDaniel v. Paty   April 19, 1978
435 US 618   55 LEd2d 593   98 SCt 1322

Const (Currie) 531-533

Godless 38-39

Religion 138-139

Hammond, Phillip E. The courts and secular humanism. *Society* 21(4):11-16 (May/June 1984).

Pfeffer, Leo. Religious exemptions. *Society* 21(4):17-22 (May/June 1984).

1903. National Society of Professional Engineers v. United States   April 25, 1978
435 US 679   55 LEd2d 637   98 SCt 1355

Sup Ct Review (1982):319-349; (1984):69-148

Werner, Ray O. Marketing and the United States Supreme Court, 1975-1981. *Journal of Marketing* 46(2):73-81 (Spring 1982).

1904. Los Angeles, Department of Water and Power v. Manhart   April 25, 1978
435 US 702   55 LEd2d 657   98 SCt 1370

Almanac (1984):280

Burger Court 150-151

En Am Con 284-287, 1666-1673

Cummins, J. David. Risk classification in life insurance. *Best's Review* (Life/Health Insurance Edition) 81(5):12-14, 103-105 (September 1980).

Fields, Cheryl M. Court declares women must get equal benefits in pension plans, sends back 2 TIAA cases. *Chronicle of Higher Education* 26(20):1, 13-14 (July 13, 1983).

From Tilton to Ewing: some major higher-education decisions of the Burger court. *Chronicle of Higher Education* 32(17):10 (June 25, 1986).

Geisel, Jerry. High Court to rule if women must get equal pensions. *Business Insurance* 16(42): 2, 36 (October 18, 1982).

Kelly, Eileen P., Amy Oakes Young, and Lawrence S. Clark. Sex stereotyping in the workplace; a manager's guide. *Business Horizons* 36(2):23-29 (March/April 1993).

Laycock, Douglas. Continuing violations, disparate impact in compensation, and other Title VII issues. *Law and Contemporary Problems* 49(4):53-61 (Autumn 1986).

Lewis, Albert B. Unisex issues: what price equality? *Best's Review* (Life/Health Insurance Edition) 82(11):10-12, 115-117 (March 1982).

Rabban, David M. AAUP in the courts: the association's representation of faculty members and faculty causes in appellate litigation. *Academe* 69(2):1a-12a (March/April 1983).

———. Developments in equal periodic pension benefits. *Academe* 68(5):24-26 (September/October 1982).

Rubens, George. Supreme Court bans sex bias in pensions. *Monthly Labor Review* 106(9):36 (September 1983).

Tarnoff, Stephen. Court decisions or benefits increase employers' costs. *Business Insurance* 21(44):93-95 (November 2, 1987).

1905. First National Bank of Boston v. Bellotti   April 26, 1978
435 US 765   55 LEd2d 707   98 SCt 1407
    Ascent 139-142
    Burger Court 31-33, 205
    En Am Con 506-508, 739-740
    Fourth 249-250+
    Freedom (Cox) 68-74, 78-86
    Sup Ct Review (1982):243-284; (1987):303-344; (1990):105-132; (1994):57-128

Boedecker, Karl A., and Fred W. Morgan. The evolution of First Amendment protection for commercial speech. *Journal of Marketing* 59(1):38-47 (January 1995).

Heath, Robert L., and Richard Alan Nelson. Image and issue advertising: a corporate and public policy perspective. *Journal of Marketing* 49(2):58-68 (Spring 1985).

Miller, Arthur S. Buying votes: is politics the last free market? *Progressive* 46(10):43-45 (October 1982).

Powe, L. A., Jr. Mass communications and the First Amendment: an overview. *Law and Contemporary Problems* 55(1):53-76 (Winter 1992).

Winter, Ralph K. Political financing and the Constitution. *Annals of the American Academy of Political and Social Science* 486:34-48 (July 1986).

1906. Landmark Communications, Inc. v. Virginia   May 1, 1978
435 US 829   56 LEd2d 1   98 SCt 1535
    Freedom (Cox) 13-14, 19-20

Bunker, Matthew D. Lifting the veil: ethics bodies, the citizen-critic, and the First Amendment. *Journalism Quarterly* 70(1):98-107 (Spring 1993).

Howard, A. E. Dick. The press in court. *Wilson Quarterly* 6(5):86-93 (Special Issue 1982).

1907. Santa Clara Pueblo v. Martinez   May 15, 1978
436 US 49   56 LEd2d 106   98 SCt 1670
    Am Indians (Wilkinson) 49, 113-116, 128+

Allen, Mark. Native American control of tribal natural resource development in the context of the federal trust and tribal self-determination. *Boston College Environmental Affairs Law Review* 16(4):857-895 (Summer 1989).

1908. Scott v. United States   May 15, 1978
436 US 128   56 LEd2d 168   98 SCt 1717

Goldsmith, Michael. The Supreme Court and Title III: rewriting the law of electronic surveillance. *Journal of Criminal Law and Criminology* 74(1):1-171 (Spring 1983).

1909. Flagg Brothers, Inc. v. Brooks   May 15, 1978
       Coupled with Lefkowitz v. Brooks
       Coupled with American Warehousemen's Association v. Brooks

436 US 149   56 LEd2d 185   98 SCt 1729
  En Am Con 741, 1465-1472, 1736-1738
  Sup Ct Review (1988):129-161
Sullivan, Harold J. Privatization of public services: a growing threat to constitutional rights. *Public Administration Review* 47(6):461-467 (November/December 1987).

1910. Sears, Roebuck and Co. v. San Diego County District Council of Carpenters   May 15, 1978
  436 US 180   56 LEd2d 209   98 SCt 1745
  Sup Ct Review (1986):135-155

1911. Marshall, Secretary of Labor v. Barlow's, Inc.   May 23, 1978
  436 US 307   56 LEd2d 305   98 SCt 1816
  En Am Con 1211, 1628-1635
  Sup Ct Review (1989):87-163
Andersen, Robert M. Technology, pollution control, and EPA access to commercial property: a constitutional and policy framework. *Boston College Environmental Affairs Law Review* 17(1):1-74 (Fall 1989).
Bernstein, Sidney. Supreme Court review. *Trial* 21(4):14-15 (April 1985).
Mussio, Donna. Drawing the line between administrative and criminal searches: defining the "object of the search" in environmental inspections. *Boston College Environmental Affairs Law Review* 18(1):185-211 (Fall 1990).
Roberts, Thomas A. Supreme Court review: Fourth Amendment—warrantless administrative inspections of commercial property. *Journal of Criminal Law and Criminology* 72(4):1222-1245 (Winter 1981).

1912. Baldwin v. Fish and Game Commission of Montana May 23, 1978
  Baldwin v. Montana Fish and Game Commission
  436 US 371   56 LEd2d 354   98 SCt 1852
  Behind Bakke 123-127
  En Am Con 96, 1458-1461

1913. In re Primus   May 30, 1978
  436 US 412   56 LEd2d 417   98 SCt 1893
  Freedom (Cox) 39-41
Boedecker, Karl A., and Fred W. Morgan. The evolution of First Amendment protection for commercial speech. *Journal of Marketing* 59(1):38-47 (January 1995).
Bowen, Lauren. Attorney advertising in the wake of Bates v. State Bar of Arizona (1977): a study of judicial impact. *American Politics Quarterly* 23(4):461-484 (October 1995).

1914. Ohralik v. Ohio State Bar Association   May 30, 1978
  436 US 447   56 LEd2d 444   98 SCt 1912
  Const (Currie) 513-518
  Freedom (Cox) 39-41
  Sup Ct Yearbook (1992-93):80-81
Boedecker, Karl A., and Fred W. Morgan. The evolution of First Amendment protection for commercial speech. *Journal of Marketing* 59(1):38-47 (January 1995).
Bowen, Lauren. Attorney advertising in the wake of Bates v. State Bar of Arizona (1977): a study of judicial impact. *American Politics Quarterly* 23(4):461-484 (October 1995).
Smith, Robert E., and Tiffany S. Meyer. Attorney advertising: a consumer perspective. *Journal of Marketing* 44(2):56-64 (Spring 1980).

1915. Michigan v. Tyler   May 30, 1978
  436 US 499   56 LEd2d 486   98 SCt 1942
Mussio, Donna. Drawing the line between administrative and criminal searches: defining the "object of the search" in environmental inspections. *Boston College Environmental Affairs Law Review* 18(1):185-211 (Fall 1990).

1916. Zurcher v. Stanford Daily   May 31, 1978
       436 US 547   56 LEd2d 525   98 SCt 1970
            Almanac (1980):387
            Burger Court 18-20, 25-27
            Const Law 227-228
            En Am Con 797-804, 1251, 1548-1549, 2090
            Freedom (Cox) 62-67
       Andersen, Robert M. Technology, pollution control, and EPA access to commercial property: a constitutional
            and policy framework. *Boston College Environmental Affairs Law Review* 17(1):1-74 (Fall 1989).
       Bayh, Birch. Search and seizure: aftermath of Stanford daily. *Trial* 16(8):30-33, 70 (August 1980).
       Brown, Robert U. Shop talk at thirty: paranoid press [Editorial]. *Editor and Publisher* 113(28):66 (July 12,
            1980).
       Copley, Helen K. General spirit of the people. *Vital Speeches* 46(6):169-172 (January 1, 1980).
       Dripps, Donald A. Supreme Court review: Justice White and the rights of the accused. *Trial* 29(5):71-74 (May
            1993).
       Hale, Dennis. How retiring Supreme Court Justice White voted in First Amendment cases. *Editor and Publisher*
            126(30):44, 36 (July 24, 1993).
       Howard, A. E. Dick. The press in court. *Wilson Quarterly* 6(5):86-93 (Special Issue 1982).
       Paley, William S. Press freedom: a continuing struggle. *Vital Speeches* 46(21):670-672 (August 15, 1980).
       Radolf, Andrew. Press urged to explain First Amendment rights. *Editor and Publisher* 113(4):14 (January 26,
            1980).
       Solimine, Michael E. Constitutionality of congressional legislation to overrule Zurcher v. Stanford daily.
            Journal of Criminal Law and Criminology 71(2):147-162 (Summer 1980).
       Trank, John P. The Burger Court—the first ten years. *Law and Contemporary Problems* 43(3):101-135
            (Summer 1980).

1917. Mobil Oil Corp. v. Higginbotham   June 5, 1978
       436 US 618   56 LEd2d 581   98 SCt 2010
       Edelman, Paul S. Wrongful death on the high seas:Tallentire says federal law governs. *Trial* 23(4):58-61 (April
            1987).

1918. Monell v. Department of Social Services of the City of New York   June 6, 1978
       436 US 658   56 LEd2d 611   98 SCt 2018
            Almanac (1989):318
            En Am Con 1270, 1640-1641, 2088-2089
            Sup Ct Review (1987):249-301
       Bernstein, Sidney, and Michael Eisenstein. 1982 Supreme Court update: the criminal law, part two. *Trial*
            18(10):58-65 (October 1982).
       Chemerinsky, Erwin. Supreme Court review: reaffirmation of notice pleading. *Trial* 29(6):73-76 (June 1993).
       Groszyk, Walter S., Jr., and Thomas J. Madden. Managing without immunity: the challenge for state and local
            government officials in the 1980s. *Public Administration Review* 41(2):268-278 (March/April 1981).
       Lee, Yong S. Civil liability of state and local governments: myth and reality. *Public Administration Review*
            47(2):160-170 (March/April 1987).
       Spurrier, Robert L., Jr. Paying the piper in federal civil rights litigation. *Public Administration Review*
            43(3):199-208 (May/June 1983).
       Supreme Court further erodes municipal immunity. *American City and County* 95(6):16 (June 1980).

1919. Federal Communications Commission (FCC)   June 12, 1978
          v. National Citizens Committee for Broadcasting (NCCB)
                 Coupled with Channel Two Television, Co. v. National Citizens Committee for Broadcasting
                 Coupled with National Association of Broadcasters v. Federal Communications Commission (FCC)
                 Coupled with American Newspaper Publishers Association v. National Citizens Committee for
                    Broadcasting
                 Coupled with Illinois Broadcasting Co., Inc. v. National Citizens Committee for Broadcasting
                 Coupled with Post Co. v. National Citizens Committee for Broadcasting

436 US 775   56 LEd2d 697   98 SCt 2096

    Burger Court 23-27

    Fourth 227-229+

Barron, Jerome A. Whose First Amendment? *Vital Speeches* 46(10):313-315 (March 1, 1980).

Devins, Neal. Congress, the FCC, and the search for the public trustee. *Law and Contemporary Problems* 56(4):145-188 (Autumn 1993).

1920. National Broiler Marketing Association v. United States   June 12, 1978

    436 US 816   56 LEd2d 728   98 SCt 2122

Werner, Ray O. Marketing and the United States Supreme Court, 1975-1981. *Journal of Marketing* 46(2):73-81 (Spring 1982).

1921. Burks v. United States   June 14, 1978

    437 US 1   57 LEd2d 1   98 SCt 2141

Bernstein, Sidney, and Michael Eisenstein. 1981 Supreme Court update: the criminal law. *Trial* 17(10):54-60, 85 (October 1981).

————. 1982 Supreme Court update: the criminal law. *Trial* 18(9):45-50, 81 (September 1982).

Sikora, John J., Jr. Supreme Court review: Fifth Amendment—affording society's interest greater protection in double jeopardy analysis. *Journal of Criminal Law and Criminology* 80(4):1112-1127 (Winter 1990).

Volkert, Adam N. Supreme Court review: Fifth Amendment—double jeopardy: two-tier trial systems and the continuing jeopardy principle. *Journal of Criminal Law and Criminology* 75(3):653-672 (Fall 1984).

1922. Exxon Corp. v. Governor of Maryland   June 14, 1978

        Coupled with Shell Oil Co. v. Governor of Maryland

        Coupled with Continental Oil Co. v. Governor of Maryland

        Coupled with Gulf Oil Co. v. Governor of Maryland

        Coupled with Ashland Oil, Inc. v. Governor of Maryland

    437 US 117   57 LEd2d 91   98 SCt 2207

Werner, Ray O. Marketing and the United States Supreme Court, 1975-1981. *Journal of Marketing* 46(2):73-81 (Spring 1982).

1923. Tennessee Valley Authority v. Hill   June 15, 1978

    437 US 153   57 LEd2d 117   98 SCt 2279

    Sup Ct Yearbook (1994-95):60-63

Ball, Howard. The U.S. Supreme Court's glossing of the Federal Tort Claims Act: statutory construction and veterans' tort actions. *Western Political Quarterly* 41(3):529-552 (September 1988).

Carter, Christopher H. M. A dual track for incidental takings: reexamining Sections 7 and 10 of the Endangered Species Act. *Boston College Environmental Affairs Law Review* 19(1):135-171 (Fall 1991).

Fregeau, Jason David. Statutes and judicial discretion: against the law . . . sort of. *Boston College Environmental Affairs Law Review* 18(3):501-542 (Spring 1991).

Meyers, Gary D. Old-growth forests, the owl, and yew: environmental ethics versus traditional dispute resolution under the Endangered Species Act and other public land and resources laws. *Boston College Environmental Affairs Law Review* 18(4):623-668 (Summer 1991).

Sandler, Ross. Law: Supreme Court trends in environmental law. *Environment* 23(7):4-5 (September 1981).

Vanderziel, Kathleen M. The Hatfield Riders and environmental preservation: what process is due? *Boston College Environmental Affairs Law Review* 19(2):431-479 (Fall/Winter 1991).

1924. Moorman Manufacturing Co. v. Bair   June 15, 1978

    437 US 267   57 LEd2d 197   98 SCt 2340

    Ascent 125-127

    En Am Con 1757-1760

1925. United States v. LaSalle National Bank   June 19, 1978

    437 US 298   57 LEd2d 221   98 SCt 2357

Mussio, Donna. Drawing the line between administrative and criminal searches: defining the "object of the search" in environmental inspections. *Boston College Environmental Affairs Law Review* 18(1):185-211 (Fall 1990).

1926. Owen Equipment and Erection Co. v. Kroger   June 21, 1978
        437 US 365   57 LEd2d 274   98 SCt 2396
        Brooks, Thornton H., M. Daniel McGinn, and William P. H. Cary. Second generation problems facing
            employers in employment discrimination cases: continuing violations, pendent state claims, and double
            attorneys' fees. *Law and Contemporary Problems* 49(4):26-51 (Autumn 1986).

1927. Hicklin v. Orbeck   June 22, 1978
        437 US 518   57 LEd2d 397   98 SCt 2482
          En Am Con 914, 1458-1461
        Put yourself on the U.S. Supreme Court. *Senior Scholastic* 114(8):22-23, 27 (December 11, 1981).

1928. Parker, Acting Commissioner of Patents and Trademarks v. Flook   June 22, 1978
        437 US 584   57 LEd2d 451   98 SCt 2522
        Norman, Colin. Court broadens rules on patenting software. *Science* 211(4488):1325, 1328 (March 20, 1981).

1929. Philadelphia v. New Jersey   June 23, 1978
        437 US 617   57 LEd2d 475   98 SCt 2531
          En Am Con 1384, 1751-1755
        Waste disposal shipments upheld in two big cases. *ENR* 228(23):14 (June 8, 1992).

1930. Hutto v. Finney   June 23, 1978
        437 US 678   57 LEd2d 522   98 SCt 2565
          Const (Currie) 574-577+
          Sup Ct Review (1984):149-168
        Angelos, Claudia, and James B. Jacobs. Prison overcrowding and the law. *Annals of the American Academy of
            Political and Social Science* 478:100-112 (March 1985).
        Spurrier, Robert L., Jr. Paying the piper in federal civil rights litigation. *Public Administration Review*
            43(3):199-208 (May/June 1983).

1931. Houchins v. KQED, Inc.   June 26, 1978
        438 US 1   57 LEd2d 553   98 SCt 2588
          Ascent 162-165
          Burger Court 20-22, 25-27
          En Am Con 797-804, 1592-1593
          Sup Ct Review (1980):1-25
        Bleisch, N. David. The *Congressional Record* and the First Amendment: accuracy is the best policy. *Boston
            College Environmental Affairs Law Review* 12(2):341-379 (Winter 1985).
        Copley, Helen K. General spirit of the people. *Vital Speeches* 46(6):169-172 (January 1, 1980).
        Epstein, Judith. The journalists' rights. *Center Magazine* 15(6):40-42 (November/December 1982).
        Howard, A. E. Dick. The press in court. *Wilson Quarterly* 6(5):86-93 (Special Issue 1982).
        Maybe court will decide right to gather news. *Editor and Publisher* 113(17):28 (April 26, 1980).

1932. Duke Power Co. v. Carolina Environment Study Group, Inc.   June 26, 1978
                Coupled with United States Nuclear Regulatory Commission v. Carolina Environment Study Group, Inc.
        438 US 59   57 LEd2d 595   98 SCt 2620
          En Am Con 1597, 1722-1724
          Sup Ct Review (1981):41-47
        Bernstein, Sidney. Nuclear law: the battle over atomic power in the courts. *Trial* 16(4):28-32, 61-62 (April
            1980).
        Neuborne, Burt. Taking away the right to sue. *Nation* 239(9):268-271 (September 29, 1984).

Perino, Michael A. Justice Scalia: standing, environmental law, and the Supreme Court. *Boston College Environmental Affairs Law Review* 15(1):135-179 (Fall 1987).

Rocchio, David M. The Price-Anderson Act: allocation fo the extrordinary risk of nuclear generated electricity: a model punitive damage provision. *Boston College Environmental Affairs Law Review* 14(3): 521-560 (Spring 1987).

1933. Penn Central Transporation Co. v. New York City   June 26, 1978
438 US 104   57 LEd2d 631   98 SCt 2646
En Am Con 637-639, 1374, 1855-1857

Blackwell, Robert J. Overlay zoning, performance standards, and environmental protection after Nollan. *Boston College Environmental Affairs Law Review* 16(3):615-659 (Spring 1989).

Cavarello, Daniel T. From Penn Central to United Artists' I and II: the rise to immunity of historic preservation designation from successful takings challenges. *Boston College Environmental Affairs Law Review* 22(3):593-622 (Spring 1995).

Cohen, Jonathan E. A constitutional safety valve: the variance in zoning and land-use based environmental controls. *Boston College Environmental Affairs Law Review* 22(2):307-364 (Winter 1995).

Hanley, Thomas. A developer's dream: the United States Claims Court's new analysis of Section 404 takings challenges. *Boston College Environmental Affairs Law Review* 19(2):317-353 (Fall/Winter 1991).

Hippler, Thomas A. Reexamining 100 years of the Supreme Court regulatory taking doctrine: the principles of "noxious use," "average reciprocity of advantage," and "bundle of rights" from Mugler to Keystone Bituminous Coal. *Boston College Environmental Affairs Law Review* 14(4):653-727 (Summer 1987).

Kliman, Burton S. The Use of conservation restrictions on historic properties as charitable donations for federal income tax purposes. *Boston College Environmental Affairs Law Review* 9(3):513-547 (1981-82).

Kourtis, Jane Papademetriou. The constructive trust: equity's answer to the need for a strong deterrent to the destruction of historic landmarks. *Boston College Environmental Affairs Law Review* 16(4):793-820 (Summer 1989).

LaRusso, Joseph. "Paying for the change": First English Evangelical Lutheran Church of Glendale v. County of Los Angeles and the calculation of interim damages for regulatory takings. *Boston College Environmental Affairs Law Review* 17(3):551-583 (Spring 1990).

Note; the public use test: would a ban on the possession of firearms require just compensation? *Law and Contemporary Problems* 49(1):223-249 (Winter 1986).

Randle, Ellen M. The national reserve system and transferable development rights: is the New Jersey Pinelands plan in unconstitutional "taking"? *Boston College Environmental Affairs Law Review* 10(1):183-241 (1982-83).

Skelton, Harold N. Houses on the sand: taking issues surrounding statutory restrictions on the use of oceanfront property. *Boston College Environmental Affairs Law Review* 18(1):125-158 (Fall 1990).

Welsh, Robert, and Ronald K. L. Collins. Taking state constitutions seriously: the protection of civil liberties has been shifting away from the U.S. Supreme Court. *Center Magazine* 14(5):6-35, 38-43 (September/October 1981).

1934. Franks v. Delaware   June 26, 1978
438 US 154   57 LEd2d 667   98 SCt 2674
Burger Court 80-82+
En Am Con 1637-1638
Sup Ct Review (1984):309-358

1935. Allied Structural Steel Co. v. Spannaus   June 28, 1978
438 US 234   57 LEd2d 727   98 SCt 2716
En Am Con 45-46

1936. Regents of the University of California v. Bakke   June 28, 1978
438 US 265   57 LEd2d 750   98 SCt 2733
Affirmative (Greene) 71-80
Affirmative (Woods) 68-73
Amending 203-213

Ascent 23-27, 268-274, 276-280, 400-404+

Bakke 3-262

Behind Bakke 1-259

Brennan 257-263

Burger Court 124-131, 142-144

Burger Years 95-108

Civil 20th 3, 11, 199-229R

Conflict 44-46, 126

Const (Currie) 482-488

Const (Friendly)·211-230

Const Law 556-563+

Court Const 270-281+

Court Public 100-101, 169-193R

Culture 130-141

Documents (v. 2):830-833R

Economics 387-404, 406-407

En Am Con 273-280, 566-568, 1500-1506, 1507-1508, 1529

Equal (Harrell) 118-119

Eyes 591-596, 625-630, 631-651R, 651-655

Guide (CQ) 55

Guide (West) (v. 2):17-21, 352-353

Landmark (v. 1):127-157R

Magic 330-331

May It 305-320R

New Right (Schwartz) 154-159+

Sup Ct Ind 262

Tenth 39-48

American survey: Burger leaves the labyrinth. *Economist* 300(7454):17-22 (July 12-18, 1986).

American survey: the week the Supreme Court changed colour? *Economist* 304(7505):25-26 (July 4-10, 1987).

The association and the courts. *Academe* 75(3):31-33 (May/June 1989).

Baer, Judith A. Women's rights and the limits of constitutional doctrine. *Western Political Quarterly* 44(4):821-852 (December 1991).

Bresler, Robert J. The forgotten issue. [Editorial] *USA Today* 116(2516):7 (May 1988).

Burns, Haywood. The activisim in not affirmative. *Nation* 239(9):264-268 (September 29, 1984).

Campbell, Bebe Moore. Supreme Court challenge: laying off affirmative action. *Black Enterprise* 13(7):31 (February 1983).

Chambers, Julius L., and Barry Goldstein. Title VII: the continuing challenge of establishing fair employment practices. *Law and Contemporary Problems* 49(4):9-23 (Autumn 1986).

Daly, James J., Stephen M. Baron, Jack Noble, and Carl Cohen. Affirmative action. *Commentary* 82(1):4-6 (July 1986).

Delon, Floyd G. The legacy of Thurgood Marshall. *Journal of Negro Education* 63(3):278-288 (Summer 1994).

Dingle, Derek T. Affirmative action. *Black Enterprise* 20(2):42-48 (September 1989).

Drinan, Robert F. Another look at affirmative action. *America* 152(5):104-106 (February 9, 1985).

Eastland, Terry. Racial preference in court (again). *Commentary* 87(1):32-38 (January 1989).

Erler, Edward J. Brown v. Board of Education at 30. *National Review* 36(17):26-28, 30-31, 53 (September 7, 1984).

Eskin, Leah. Do You know your rights? *Scholastic Update* 120(15):9 (April 8, 1988).

Fields, Cheryl M. Supreme Court ruling on seniority may be blow to affirmative action. *Chronicle of Higher Education* 28(17):11, 16 (June 20, 1984).

———. 10 years after Bakke ruling, opinions on affirmative action still polarized. *Chronicle of Higher Education* 34(42):A14-A17 (June 29, 1988).

Five cases that changed American society. *Scholastic Update* (Teachers' Edition) 117(7):19-20 (November 30, 1984).

Franke, Ann H., and Jacqueline W. Mintz. Four trends in higher education law. *Academe* 73(5):57-63 (September/October 1987).

Frederickson, H. George. Public administration and social equity. *Public Administration Review* 50(2):228-237 (March/April 1990).

From Tilton to Ewing: some major higher-education decisions of the Burger court. *Chronicle of Higher Education* 32(17):10 (June 25, 1986).

Garvey, John H. Black and white images. *Law and Contemporary Problems* 56(4):189-216 (Autumn 1993).

Gest, Ted. Courts: a major battleground of social upheaval. *U.S. News and World Report* 98(3):48-50 (January 28, 1985).

———. Seniority vs. minorities—impact of Court ruling. *U.S. News and World Report* 96(25):22-23 (June 25, 1984).

Gray, Mary W. The tragic legacy of the Supreme Court's 1978 Bakke ruling is that affirmative action has been ineffectual ever since. [Editorial] *Chronicle of Higher Education* 34(42):B1-B3 (June 29, 1988).

Gregory, David L. The continuing vitality of affirmative action diversity principles in professional and graduate school student admissions and faculty hiring. *Journal of Negro Education* 63(3):421-429 (Summer 1994).

Hogan, Joyce, and Ann M. Quigley. Physical standards for employment and the courts. *American Psychologist* 41(11):1193-1217 (November 1986).

Jaschik, Scott. From Bakke to Yeshiva, Justice Powell played key role in Court's education rulings. *Chronicle of Higher Education* 33(43):16 (July 8, 1987).

———. U.S. report questions 'Bakke' defense of affirmative action. *Chronicle of Higher Education* 41(43):A20 (July 7, 1995).

Klein, Joe. The end of affirmative action. *Newsweek* 125(7):36-37 (February 13, 1995).

LaFay, Laura, and James Earl Hardy. A court-wathcher's guide. *Scholastic Update* 124(5):13-16 (November 1, 1991).

Lamb, Charles M. Legal foundations of civil rights and pluralism America. *Annals of the American Academy of Political and Social Science* 454:13-25 (March 1981).

McFeeley, Neil D. Weber versus affirmative action? *Personnel* 57(1):38-51 (January/February 1980).

Mounts, Gregory J. Labor and the Supreme Court: significant decisions of 1979-80. *Monthly Labor Review* 104(4):13-22 (April 1981).

———. Significant decisions in labor cases. *Monthly Labor Review* 103(12):63-64 (December 1980).

Mounts, Gregory J., and Kate Farrell. Constitutional quotas. *Monthly Labor Review* 103(9):53-56 (September 1980).

Nagel, Robert F. A plague of judges: the Burger court''s secret plan for America. *Washington Monthly* 12(9):20-24 (November 1980).

O'Neill, Timothy J. The language of equality in a constitutional order. *American Political Science Review* 75(3):626-635 (September 1981).

Ornstein, Allan C., and Daniel U. Levine. Schools, society, and the concept of equality. *Clearing House* 55(3):127-131 (November 1981).

Parikh, Sunita. The Supreme Court, civil rights, and preference policies: judicial decision making processes in the United States and India. *Teachers College Record* 92(2):192-211 (Winter 1990).

Press, Aric, and Ann McDaniel. A woman's day in court. *Newsweek* 109(14):58-59 (April 6, 1987).

Rabban, David M. AAUP in the courts: the association's representation of faculty members and faculty causes in appellate litigation. *Academe* 69(2):1a-12a (March/April 1983).

Regan, Richard J. Supreme Court roundup: 1979 term. *Thought* 55(219):487-455 (December 1980).

———. Supreme Court roundup: 1980 term. *Thought* 56(223):491-502 (December 1981).

Reid-Dove, Allyson, and Michael E. Howard. "Night has fallen on the Court . . ." *Black Enterprise* 20(2):44-45 (September 1989).

Rose, Jonathan. Decide 10 landmark cases that define your rights. *Scholastic Update* 119(1):7-9, 21 (September 8, 1986).

Rosen, Jeff. Is affirmative action doomed? *New Republic* 211(16):25-27 (October 17, 1994).

Sowell, Thomas. A dissenting opinion about affirmative action. *Across the Board* 18(1):64-72 (January 1981).

Stengel, Richard, and Anne Constable. Balancing act: in a sweeping decision, the high court expands affirmative action. *Time* 129(14):18-20 (April 6, 1987).

Stoper, Emily. Women's work, women's movement: taking stock. *Annals of the American Academy of Political and Social Science* 515:151-162 (May 1991).

Taylor, William L., and Susan M. Liss. Affirmative action in the 1990s: staying the course. *Annals of the American Academy of Political and Social Science* 523:30-37 (September 1992).

Thomas, Evan, Kenneth W. Banta, and Anne Constable. Court at the crossroads: the 1984 election may chart the future course of American justice. *Time* 124(15):28-35 (October 8, 1984).

Tollett, Kenneth S., Jeanette J. Leonard, and Portia P. James. A color-conscious constitution: the one pervading purpose redux. *Journal of Negro Education* 52(3):189-212 (Summer 1983).

Trank, John P. The Burger Court—the first ten years. *Law and Contemporary Problems* 43(3):101-135 (Summer 1980).

Van Alstyne, William W. Academic freedom and the First Amendment in the Supreme Court of the United States: an unhurried historical review. *Law and Contemporary Problems* 53(3):79-154 (Summer 1990).

Vile, John R., and Kathy Ruth McCoy. The Memphis case: another precedent? *Personnel* 62(7):72-76 (July 1985).

1937. United States v. United States Gypsum Co.   June 29, 1978
438 US 422   57 LEd2d 854   98 SCt 2864
Werner, Ray O. Marketing and the United States Supreme Court, 1975-1981. *Journal of Marketing* 46(2):73-81 (Spring 1982).

1938. Butz v. Economou   June 29, 1978
438 US 478   57 LEd2d 895   98 SCt 2894
En Am Con 188, 668
Rosenbloom, David H. Public administrators' official immunity and the Supreme Court: developments during the 1970s. *Public Administration Review* 40(2):166-173 (March/April 1980).

Tish, Martin H. Duplicative statutes, prosecutorial discretion, and the Illinois armed violence statute. *Journal of Criminal Law and Criminology* 71(3):226-243 (Fall 1980).

1939. St. Paul Fire and Marine Insurance Co. v. Barry   June 29, 1978
438 US 531   57 LEd2d 932   98 SCt 2923
Greenwald, Judy. Boycott charge grabs attention of High Court. *Business Insurance* 27(9):1, 29 (March 1, 1993).

———. "Boycott" definition sets stage for litigation. *Business Insurance* 27(28):101-102 (July 5, 1993).

Weller, Charles D. McCarran Act interpretation may have been charted in Barry case. *Best's Review* (Life/Health Insurance Edition) 83(2):40-42, 87-89 (June 1982).

Weller, Charles D. McCarran Act interpretation may have been charted in Barry case. *Best's Review* (Property/Casualty Insurance Edition) 83(3):28-32 (July 1982).

1940. Furnco Construction Corp. v. Waters   June 29, 1978
438 US 567   57 LEd2d 957   98 SCt 2943
Mounts, Gregory J. Labor and the Supreme Court: significant decisions of 1978-79. *Monthly Labor Review* 103(1):14-21 (January 1980).

1941. Lockett v. Ohio   July 3, 1978
Companion Case Bell v. Ohio (See record 1942).
438 US 586   57 LEd2d 973   98 SCt 2954
Brennan 226-229
Court Public 240-241, 300-310R
Death Penalty (Streib) 21-22, 130-131
Death Penalty 80s 5-12, 15-18, 51-54, 75-78
Death Penalty 90s 97-100+
En Am Con 201-206
Sup Ct Review (1983):305-395
Bernstein, Sidney, and Michael Eisenstein. 1982 Supreme Court update: the criminal law, part two. *Trial* 18(10):58-65 (October 1982).

Bilionis, Louis D. Moral appropriateness, capital punishment, and the Lockett doctrine. *Journal of Criminal Law and Criminology* 82(2):283-333 (Summer 1991).

Brown, J. Michael. Supreme Court review: Eighth Amendment—capital sentencing instructions. *Journal of Criminal Law and Criminology* 84(4):854-882 (Winter/Spring 1994).

Chan, Peter K. M. Supreme Court review: Eighth Amendment—the death penalty and the mentally retarded criminal: fairness, culpability, and death. *Journal of Criminal Law and Criminology* 80(4):1211-1235 (Winter 1990).

Cho, Susie. Capital confusion: the effect of jury instructions on the decision to impose death. *Journal of Criminal Law and Criminology* 85(2):532-561 (Fall 1994).

Murphy, Cornelius F. The Supreme Court and capital punishment: a new hands-off approach. *USA Today* 121(2574):51-52 (March 1993).

Trank, John P. The Burger Court—the first ten years. *Law and Contemporary Problems* 43(3):101-135 (Summer 1980).

1942. Bell v. Ohio   July 3, 1978
Companion Case Lockett v. Ohio (See record 1941).
438 US 637   57 LEd2d 1010   98 SCt 2977
Death Penalty (Streib) 21-22, 130-131

1943. California v. United States   July 3, 1978
438 US 645   57 LEd2d 1018   98 SCt 2985
Proctor, Michael G. Section 10 of the Rivers and Harbors Act and western water allocations—are the western states up a creek without a permit? *Boston College Environmental Affairs Law Review* 10(1):111-182 (1982-83).

1944. United States v. New Mexico   July 3, 1978
438 US 696   57 LEd2d 1052   98 SCt 3012
Proctor, Michael G. Section 10 of the Rivers and Harbors Act and western water allocations—are the western states up a creek without a permit? *Boston College Environmental Affairs Law Review* 10(1):111-182 (1982-83).

1945. Board of Trustees of Keene State College v. Sweeney   November 13, 1979
439 US 24   58 LEd2d 216   99 SCt 295
Mounts, Gregory J. Labor and the Supreme Court: significant decisions of 1978-79. *Monthly Labor Review* 103(1):14-21 (January 1980).

1946. Dougherty County, Georgia, Board of Education v. White   November 28, 1978
439 US 32   58 LEd2d 269   99 SCt 368
Mounts, Gregory J. Labor and the Supreme Court: significant decisions of 1978-79. *Monthly Labor Review* 103(1):14-21 (January 1980).

1947. Rakas v. Illinois   December 5, 1978
439 US 128   58 LEd2d 387   99 SCt 421
Hartman, Marshall J., and Sidney Bernstein. To Leon, and beyond; two commentators react. *Trial* 21(1):50-56 (January 1985).
Junker, John M. The structure of the Fourth Amendment: the scope of the protection. *Journal of Criminal Law and Criminology* 79(4):1105-1183 (Winter 1989).
Laver, Rebecca J., Supreme Court review: Fourth Amendment—the court further limits standing. *Journal of Criminal Law and Criminology* 71(4):567-578 (Winter 1980).

1948. Califano v. Aznavorian   December 11, 1978
439 US 170   58 LEd2d 435   99 SCt 471
En Am Con 1593-1596

1949. Corbitt v. New Jersey   December 11, 1978
439 US 212   58 LEd2d 466   99 SCt 492
Halberstam, Malvina. Towards neutral principles in the administration of criminal justice: a critique of Supreme Court decisions sanctioning the plea bargaining process. *Journal of Criminal Law and Criminology* 73(1):1-49 (Spring 1982).

1950. Lalli v. Lalli   December 11, 1978
    439 US 259   58 LEd2d 503   99 SCt 518
      Ascent 246-248
      En Am Con 947-948, 1121, 1666-1673

1951. Parklane Hosiery Co., Inc. v. Shore   January 9, 1979
    439 US 322   58 LEd2d 552   99 SCt 645
    Hogan, R. Ben, III. The Seventh Amendment: the founders' views. *Trial* 23(9):76, 78, 80, 82 (September 1987).

1952. Duren v. Missouri   January 9, 1979
    439 US 357   58 LEd2d 579   99 SCt 664
    Goldberg, Steven H. Harmless error: constitutional sneak thief. *Journal of Criminal Law and Criminology* 71(4):421-442 (Winter 1980).

1953. Colautti v. Franklin   January 9, 1979
    439 US 379   58 LEd2d 596   99 SCt 675
      Abortion (Frohock) 80, 87-88
      Abortion Am 98R+
      Abortion Dec 68-75+
      Abortion Decs 70s Introduction, 145-164R
      Abortion Moral 35-44
      Abortion Pol (Rubin) 134, 137
      En Am Con 1552-1558
      Hard Choice 172-175+
      Liberty 631-632
    Blank, Robert H. Judicial decision making and biological fact: Roe v. Wade and the unresolved question of fetal viability. *Western Political Quarterly* 37(4):584-602 (December 1984).
    Regan, Richard J. Supreme Court roundup: 1979 term. *Thought* 55(219):487-455 (December 1980).

1954. Givhan v. Western Line Consolidated School District   January 9, 1979
    439 US 410   58 LEd2d 619   99 SCt 693
    Flygare, Thomas J. De jure: teachers' First Amendment rights eroding. *Phi Delta Kappan* 67(5):396-397 (January 1986).
    Franke, Ann H., and Jacqueline W. Mintz. Four trends in higher education law. *Academe* 73(5):57-63 (September/October 1987).
    Mounts, Gregory J. Labor and the Supreme Court: significant decisions of 1978-79. *Monthly Labor Review* 103(1):14-21 (January 1980).
    Rabban, David M. AAUP in the courts: the association's representation of faculty members and faculty causes in appellate litigation. *Academe* 69(2):1a-12a (March/April 1983).
    Supplement II to First Amendment index. *Editor and Publisher* 113(4):17-18 (January 26, 1980).
    Zirkel, Perry A., and Ivan B. Gluckman. Educators' free speech: new developments. *NASSP Bulletin* 68(475):127-130 (November 1984).

1955. Thor Power Tool Co. v. Commissioner, Internal Revenue Service   January 16, 1979
    439 US 522   58 LEd2d 785   99 SCt 773
    Blyskal, Jeff. Thor(n) in the publishers' side. *Forbes* 127(1):255 (January 5, 1981).
    Bush, John N., Donal E. Flannery, and J. H. Dasburg. IRS' tough new rules under Thor Power: how they work; what they mean; how to cope. *Journal of Taxation* 52(4):194-201 (April 1980).
    Coughlin, Ellen K. IRS ruling is seen threatening supplies of many scholarly and professional books. *Chronicle of Higher Education* 21(6):1, 22 (September 29, 1980).
    Dahlin, Robert. Learning to live with Thor. *Publishers' Weekly* 221(10):26-29 (March 5, 1982).
    Endangered list. [Editorial] *Nation* 231(12):363-364 (October 18, 1980).
    Fischel, Daniel N. Thor's sledgehammer blow against books—the case for repealing tax law. *Publishers' Weekly* 218(5):17-18 (August 1, 1980).

Greene, Richard, and Calvin Johnson. In defense of Thor. *Forbes* 127(4):54-55 (February 16, 1981).

Inventory accounting that adds to the tax bill. *Business Week* (Industrial Edition) (2627):128 (March 10, 1980).

Lynch, James M. Indianapolis Power & Light Company: issues and planning opportunities where the government seeks the acceleration of income. *Taxes* 68(12):931-944 (December 1990).

Menachem, Neal J., and Howard B. Lucas. Thor decision puts squeeze on cash flow. *Credit and Financial Management* 82(8)30-31 (September 1980).

Metz, LeRoy, and Wesley Yang. New strategies in inventory writedowns—to avoid the impact of Thor. *Practical Accountant* 13(1):23-28 (January/February 1980).

Sheils, Merrill, Elsie B. Washington, and Jane Whitmore. Tax man cometh to publishers' row. *Newsweek* 96(16):78 (October 20, 1980).

Taxman's ax: An IRS ruling may prompt publishers to destroy stocks. *Time* 116(18):112-113 (November 3, 1980).

1956. International Brotherhood of Teamsters, Chauffeurs, Warehousemen and Helpers   January 16, 1979
of America v. Daniel
439 US 551   58 LEd2d 808   99 SCt 790

Mounts, Gregory J. Labor and the Supreme Court: significant decisions of 1978-79. *Monthly Labor Review* 103(1):14-21 (January 1980).

Tarnoff, Stephen. Court decisions or benefits increase employers' costs. *Business Insurance* 21(44):93-95 (November 2, 1987).

1957. Hisquierdo v. Hisquierdo   January 22, 1979
439 US 572   59 LEd2d 1   99 SCt 802

Mounts, Gregory J. Labor and the Supreme Court: significant decisions of 1978-79. *Monthly Labor Review* 103(1):14-21 (January 1980).

1958. Friedman v. Rogers   Feburary 21, 1979
     Coupled with Rogers v. Friedman
     Coupled with Texas Optometric Association, Inc. v. Rogers
440 US 1   59 LEd2d 100   99 SCt 887
Freedom (Cox) 39-41

Boedecker, Karl A., and Fred W. Morgan. The evolution of First Amendment protection for commercial speech. *Journal of Marketing* 59(1):38-47 (January 1995).

Chemerinsky, Erwin. Supreme Court review: commercial speech: what degree of protection? *Trial* 29(8):66-68 (August 1993).

Reed, O. Lee. Reading the tea leaves: future regulation of product-extrinsic advertising. *Business Horizons* 33(5):88-93 (September/October 1990).

Supplement II to First Amendment index. *Editor and Publisher* 113(4):17-18 (January 26, 1980).

1959. Great Atlantic & Pacific Tea, Co. v. Federal Trade Commission (FTC)   Februrary 22, 1979
440 US 69   59 LEd2d 153   99 SCt 925

Werner, Ray O. Marketing and the United States Supreme Court, 1975-1981. *Journal of Marketing* 46(2):73-81 (Spring 1982).

1960. Harrah Independent School District v. Martin   February 26, 1979
440 US 194   59 LEd2d 248   99 SCt 1062

Lisman, David. Mandatory continuing education and teachers. *Phi Delta Kappan* 62(2):125-126 (October 1980).

Mounts, Gregory J. Labor and the Supreme Court: significant decisions of 1978-79. *Monthly Labor Review* 103(1):14-21 (January 1980).

1961. Group Life and Health Insurance Co. aka Blue Shield of Texas   February 27, 1979
v. Royal Drug Co., dba Royal Pharmacy of Castle Hills
440 US 205   59 LEd2d 261   99 SCt 1067

Weller, Charles D. McCarran Act interpretation may have been charted in Barry case. *Best's Review* (Life/Health Insurance Edition) 83(2):40-42, 87-89 (June 1982).

———. McCarran Act interpretation may have been charted in Barry case. *Best's Review* (Property/Casualty Insurance Edition) 83(3):28-32 (July 1982).

Werner, Ray O. Marketing and the Supreme Court in transition. 1982-1984. *Journal of Marketing* 49(3):97-105 (Summer 1985).

———. Marketing and the United States Supreme Court, 1975-1981. *Journal of Marketing* 46(2):73-81 (Spring 1982).

1962. Aronson v. Quick Point Pencil Co.   February 28, 1979
    440 US 257   59 LEd2d 296   99 SCt 1096
      Sup Ct Review (1989):283-309

1963. Orr v. Orr   March 5, 1979
    440 US 268   59 LEd2d 306   99 SCt 1102
      Burger Court 144-145, 154
      Const Law 518-520R+
      En Am Con 686-688, 1666-1673
      Equal Rights 17-42+
      Sup Ct Review (1987):201-247
  Baer, Judith A. Women's rights and the limits of constitutional doctrine. *Western Political Quarterly* 44(4):821-852 (December 1991).

1964. Detroit Edison, Co. v. National Labor Relations Board (NLRB)   March 5, 1979
    440 US 301   59 LEd2d 333   99 SCt 1123
  Mounts, Gregory J. Labor and the Supreme Court: significant decisions of 1978-79. *Monthly Labor Review* 103(1):14-21 (January 1980).

1965. Quern v. Jordan   March 5, 1979
    440 US 332   59 LEd2d 358   99 SCt 1139
      Const (Currie) 574-577
      En Am Con 1497
      Sup Ct Review (1984):149-168

1966. Scott v. Illinois   March 5, 1979
    440 US 367   59 LEd2d 383   99 SCt 1158
      Brennan 203-209
      Const Law 408-410R
      En Am Con 1585-1592

1967. Lake Country Estates, Inc. v. Tahoe Regional Planning Agency   March 5, 1979
    440 US 391   59 LEd2d 401   99 SCt 1171
      En Am Con 1121, 1146

1968. Anders v. Floyd   March 5, 1979
    440 US 445   59 LEd2d 442   99 SCt 1200
      Abortion (Frohock) 80

1969. New Jersey v. Portash   March 20, 1979
    440 US 450   59 LEd2d 501   99 SCt 1292
  Lushing, Peter. Testimonial immunity and the privilege against self-incrimination: a study in isomorphism. *Journal of Criminal Law and Criminology* 73(4):1690-1739 (Winter 1982).

1970. National Muffler Dealers Association, Inc. v. United States   March 20, 1979
    440 US 472   59 LEd2d 519   99 SCt 1304

Knight, Lee G., and Ray A. Knight. A new approach to judicial review of interpretative regs. *Journal of Taxation* 65(5):326-331 (November 1986).

1971. National Labor Relations Board (NLRB) v. Catholic Bishop of Chicago   March 21, 1979
440 US 490   59 LEd2d 533   99 SCt 1313
Godless 52
Religion 185-196
Sup Ct Review (1980):27-55
Franke, Ann H., and Jacqueline W. Mintz. Four trends in higher education law. *Academe* 73(5):57-63 (September/October 1987).
Mounts, Gregory J. Labor and the Supreme Court: significant decisions of 1978-79. *Monthly Labor Review* 103(1):14-21 (January 1980).
Pfeffer, Leo. Religious exemptions. *Society* 21(4):17-22 (May/June 1984).
Regan, Richard J. Supreme Court roundup: 1980 term. *Thought* 56(223):491-502 (December 1981).
Weber, Paul J. Excessive entanglement: a wavering First Amendment standard. *Review of Politics* 46(4):483-501 (October 1984).

1972. New York Telephone Co. v. New York Department of Labor   March 21, 1979
440 US 519   59 LEd2d 553   99 SCt 1328
Finkin, Matthew W. Regulation by agreement: the case of private higher education. *Academe* 67(2):67-80 (April 1981).

1973. New York City Transit Authority v. Beazer   March 21, 1979
440 US 568   59 LEd2d 587   99 SCt 1355
Mounts, Gregory J. Labor and the Supreme Court: significant decisions of 1978-79. *Monthly Labor Review* 103(1):14-21 (January 1980).

1974. County of Los Angeles v. Davis   March 27, 1979
440 US 625   59 LEd2d 642   99 SCt 1379
Mounts, Gregory J. Labor and the Supreme Court: significant decisions of 1978-79. *Monthly Labor Review* 103(1):14-21 (January 1980).

1975. Delaware v. Prouse   March 27, 1979
440 US 648   59 LEd2d 660   99 SCt 1391
Burger Court 80-82
En Am Con 1628-1635
Sup Ct Review (1989):87-163
Bialosky, David L. Supreme Court review: Fourth Amendment—steering away from automobile detention precedents to justify warrantless searches of pleasure boats in inland waters. *Journal of Criminal Law and Criminology* 74(4):1282-1299 (Winter 1983).
Greig, William H., and Phillip S. Althoff. The constitutionality of roadblocks; the Fourth Amendment on the firing line again. *Trial* 22(2):56-62 (February 1986).
Kamisar, Yale. The swing of the pendulum. *Nation* 239(9):271-274 (September 29, 1984).

1976. Federal Communications Commission (FCC) v. Midwest Video Corp.   April 2, 1979
Coupled with American Civil Liberties Union v. Federal Communications Commission (FCC)
Coupled with National Black Media Coalition v. Midwest Video Corp.
440 US 689   59 LEd2d 692   99 SCt 1435
Burger Court 23-27

1977. Broadcast Music, Inc. v. Columbia Broadcasting System, Inc. (CBS)   April 17, 1979
Coupled with American Society of Composers, Authors and Publishers v. Columbia Broadcasting System, Inc. (CBS)
441 US 1   60 LEd2d 1   99 SCt 1551
Sup Ct Review (1984):69-148

Royalties' high value. *U.S. News and World Report* 112(4):46-47 (February 3, 1992).

Werner, Ray O. Marketing and the United States Supreme Court, 1975-1981. *Journal of Marketing* 46(2):73-81 (Spring 1982).

1978. Ambach v. Norwick   April 17, 1979
     441 US 68   60 LEd2d 49   99 SCt 1589
        Ascent 236-238
        En Am Con 46

Mounts, Gregory J. Labor and the Supreme Court: significant decisions of 1978-79. *Monthly Labor Review* 103(1):14-21 (January 1980).

1979. Gladstone, Realtors v. Village of Bellwood   April 17, 1979
     441 US 91   60 LEd2d 66   99 SCt 1601
        En Am Con 1345

Alpert, Peter A. Citizen suits under the Clean Air Act: universal standing for the uninjured private attorney general? *Boston College Environmental Affairs Law Review* 16(2):283-328 (Winter 1988).

1980. Burch v. Louisiana   April 17, 1979
     441 US 130   60 LEd2d 96   99 SCt 1623
        Almanac (1980):6A
        En Am Con 170, 1913-1920

Goldberg, Steven H. Harmless error: constitutional sneak thief. *Journal of Criminal Law and Criminology* 71(4):421-442 (Winter 1980).

1981. Herbert v. Lando   April 18, 1979
     441 US 153   60 LEd2d 115   99 SCt 1635
        En Am Con 797-804, 913-914, 1548-1549
        First 256-264
        Fourth 125-128+
        Freedom (Cox) 62-67
        Make 200-218+
        Sup Ct Review (1994):169-208

Barron, Jerome A. Whose First Amendment? *Vital Speeches* 46(10):313-315 (March 1, 1980).

Bill would bar mind inquires. *Editor and Publisher* 113(5):43 (February 2, 1980).

Bow, James, and Ben Silver. Effects of Herbert v. Lando on small newspapers and TV stations. *Journalism Quarterly* 61(2):414-418 (Summer 1984).

Brown, Robert U. Shop talk at thirty: paranoid press [Editorial]. *Editor and Publisher* 113(28):66 (July 12, 1980).

Copley, Helen K. General spirit of the people. *Vital Speeches* 46(6):169-172 (January 1, 1980).

Dworkin, Ronald. The coming battles over free speech. *New York Review of Books* 39(11):55-64 (June 11, 1992).

————. Is the press losing the First Amendment? *New York Review of Books* 27(19):49-57 (December 4, 1980).

Hale, Dennis. How retiring Supreme Court Justice White voted in First Amendment cases. *Editor and Publisher* 126(30):44, 36 (July 24, 1993).

Hale, F. Dennis. Constitutional libel protection narrowed—not destroyed. *Trial* 17(7):54-58, 79 (July 1981).

Howard, A. E. Dick. The press in court. *Wilson Quarterly* 6(5):86-93 (Special Issue 1982).

Supplement II to First Amendment index. *Editor and Publisher* 113(4):17-18 (January 26, 1980).

Trank, John P. The Burger Court—the first ten years. *Law and Contemporary Problems* 43(3):101-135 (Summer 1980).

1982. Dalia v. United States   April 18, 1979
     441 US 238   60 LEd2d 177   99 SCt 1682

Goldsmith, Michael. The Supreme Court and Title III: rewriting the law of electronic surveillance. *Journal of Criminal Law and Criminology* 74(1):1-171 (Spring 1983).

1983. Chrysler Corp. v. Brown   April 18, 1979
441 US 281   60 LEd2d 208   99 SCt 1705
The legal questions are still being answered. *Chemical Week* 127(4):30-31 (December 10, 1980).
Morris, Roberta A., Bruce D. Sales, and John J. Berman. Research and the Freedom of Information Act.
American Psychologist 36(8):819-826 (August 1981).
Rodriguez, Leon. Constitutional and statutory limits for costbBenefit analysis pursuant to Executive Orders
12,291 and 12,498. *Boston College Environmental Affairs Law Review* 15(3-4):505-546 (Spring 1988).

1984. Hughes v. Oklahoma   April 24, 1979
441 US 322   60 LEd2d 250   99 SCt 1727
En Am Con 1751-1755
Grady, Kevin T. Commonwealth of Puerto Rico v. SS Zoe Colocotroni: state actions for damage to non-
commercial living natural resources. *Boston College Environmental Affairs Law Review* 9(2):397-429 (1980-
1981).
Schwartz, Edward B. Water as an article of commerce: state embargoes spring a leak under Sporhase v.
Nebraska. *Boston College Environmental Affairs Law Review* 12(1):103-169 (Fall 1985).

1985. Parham v. Hughes   April 24, 1979
441 US 347   60 LEd2d 269   99 SCt 1742
Burger Years 109-124
En Am Con 947-948, 1666-1673

1986. Caban v. Mohammed   April 24, 1979
441 US 380   60 LEd2d 297   99 SCt 1760
Burger Years 109-124
En Am Con 686-688
Baer, Judith A. Women's rights and the limits of constitutional doctrine. *Western Political Quarterly* 44(4):821-
852 (December 1991).

1987. Addington v. Texas   April 30, 1979
441 US 418   60 LEd2d 323   99 SCt 1804
Burger Years 125-139
En Am Con 1247-1249
Meisel, Alan. The rights of the mentally ill under state constitutions. *Law and Contemporary Problems* 45(3):7-
40 (Summer 1982).

1988. Japan Line, Ltd. v. County of Los Angeles   April 30, 1979
441 US 434   60 LEd2d 336   99 SCt 1813
En Am Con 755-756, 1757-1760
Sup Ct Review (1994):295-343
McArthur, J. William, Jr., and Kendall L. Houghton. In Barclays, U.S. Supreme Court finds for California,
which was banking on it. *Journal of Taxation* 81(3):176-179 (September 1994).
Peters, James H. Sup. Ct.'s Mobil decision on multistate income apportionment raises new questions. *Journal of
Taxation* 53(1):36-40 (July 1980).
Unitary tax: the Supreme Court says pay. *Economist* 275(7138):84-86 (June 21, 1980).

1989. Smith v. Arkansas State Highway Employees, Local 315   April 30, 1979
441 US 463   60 LEd2d 360   99 SCt 1826
Mounts, Gregory J. Labor and the Supreme Court: significant decisions of 1978-79. *Monthly Labor Review*
103(1):14-21 (January 1980).

1990. Burks v. Lasker   May 14, 1979
441 US 471   60 LEd2d 404   99 SCt 1831
Troy, Joseph F. Dismissing D&O suits: committee can nip litigation in bud. *Business Insurance* 14(27):17 (July
7, 1980).

1991. Ford Motor Co. v. National Labor Relations Board (NLRB)   May 14, 1979
    441 US 488   60 LEd2d 420   99 SCt 1842
        Mounts, Gregory J. Labor and the Supreme Court: significant decisions of 1978-79. *Monthly Labor Review*
        103(1):14-21 (January 1980).

1992. Bell v. Wolfish   May 14, 1979
    441 US 520   60 LEd2d 447   99 SCt 1861
      Brennan 101-106
      Burger Years 177-188
      En Am Con 1450-1451, 1577-1581
        Angelos, Claudia, and James B. Jacobs. Prison overcrowding and the law. *Annals of the American Academy of
        Political and Social Science* 478:100-112 (March 1985).
        Bamonte, Thomas J. Supreme Court review: Eighth Amendment—a significant limit on federal court activism
        in ameliorating state prison conditions. *Journal of Criminal Law and Criminology* 72(4):1345-1373 (Winter
        1981).
        Eason, Michael J. Supreme Court review: Eighth Amendment—pretrial detention: what will become of the
        innocent? *Journal of Criminal Law and Criminology* 78(4):1048-1079 (Winter 1988).
        Farber, Daniel A. Supreme Court review: litigating with the sovereign. *Trial* 28(4):85-90 (April 1992).
        Goring, Darlene C. Supreme Court review: Fourth Amendment—prison cells: is there a right to privacy?
        Journal of Criminal Law and Criminology 75(3):609-629 (Fall 1984).
        Robbins, Ira P. Cry of "wolfish" in the federal courts: the future of federal judicial intervention in prison
        administration. *Journal of Criminal Law and Criminology* 71(3):211-225 (Fall 1980).
        Schwartz, Herman. Fifteen years of the Burger Court. *Nation* 239(9):262-264 (September 29, 1984).
        Staas, John August. Supreme Court review: Fifth Amendment—statutory dilution of the privilege against self-
        incrimination. *Journal of Criminal Law and Criminology* 71(4):610-621 (Winter 1980).

1993. Cannon v. University of Chicago   May 14, 1979
    441 US 677   60 LEd2d 560   99 SCt 1946
      En Am Con 607
        From Tilton to Ewing: some major higher-education decisions of the Burger court. *Chronicle of Higher
        Education* 32(17):10 (June 25, 1986).
        Kuceris, Misty. The High Court gives your employes another way to fight sex discrimination. *American School
        Board Journal* 169(8):21-24, 38 (August 1982).
        Mounts, Gregory J. Labor and the Supreme Court: significant decisions of 1978-79. *Monthly Labor Review*
        103(1):14-21 (January 1980).
        Pending civil rights legislation. *Congressional Digest* 64(1):1-32 (January 1985).
        Van Alstyne, William W. Academic freedom and the First Amendment in the Supreme Court of the United
        States: an unhurried historical review. *Law and Contemporary Problems* 53(3):79-154 (Summer 1990).
        Zirkel, Perry A. Cannons and canons: enough is enough. *Phi Delta Kappan* 70(1):74-75 (September 1988).
        ———. De jure: damages for sexual harassment. *Phi Delta Kappan* 73(10):812-813 (June 1992).

1994. Oscar Mayer and Co. v. Evans   May 21, 1979
    441 US 750   60 LEd2d 609   99 SCt 2066
        Mounts, Gregory J. Labor and the Supreme Court: significant decisions of 1978-79. *Monthly Labor Review*
        103(1):14-21 (January 1980).

1995. United States v. Naftalin   May 21, 1979
    441 US 768   60 LEd2d 624   99 SCt 2077
      Sup Ct Review (1995):99-124

1996. Kentucky v. Whorton   May 21, 1979
    441 US 786   60 LEd2d 640   99 SCt 2088
        Tushnet, Mark V. The justices decide: rule of law, or rule of five? *Nation* 257(14):497-499 (November 1,
        1993).

1997. Greenholtz v. Inmates of the Nebraska Penal and Correctional Complex   May 29, 1979
     442 US 1   60 LEd2d 668   99 SCt 2100

     Schwartz, Charles Walter. Eighth Amendment proportionality analysis and the compelling case of William Rummel. *Journal of Criminal Law and Criminology* 71(4):378-420 (Winter 1980).

1998. International Brotherhood of Electrical Workers (IBEW) v. Foust   May 29, 1979
     442 US 42   60 LEd2d 698   99 SCt 2121

     Mounts, Gregory J. Labor and the Supreme Court: significant decisions of 1978-79. *Monthly Labor Review* 103(1):14-21 (January 1980).

1999. Parker v. Randolph   May 29, 1979
     442 US 62   60 LEd2d 713   99 SCt 2132

     Goldberg, Steven H. Harmless error: constitutional sneak thief. *Journal of Criminal Law and Criminology* 71(4):421-442 (Winter 1980).

     Krit, Jonathan J. Supreme Court review: Sixth Amendment—confrontation and the use of interlocking confessions at joint trial. *Journal of Criminal Law and Criminology* 78(4):937-953 (Winter 1988).

2000. Green v. Georgia   May 29, 1979
     442 US 95   60 LEd2d 738   99 SCt 2150

     Death Penalty 80s 78-82

     Death Penalty 90s 100-104, 139-150+

     En Am Con 658-661

2001. United States v. Batchelder   June 4, 1979
     442 US 114   60 LEd2d 755   99 SCt 2198

     Tish, Martin H. Duplicative statutes, prosecutorial discretion, and the Illinois armed violence statute. *Journal of Criminal Law and Criminology* 71(3):226-243 (Fall 1980).

2002. County Court of Ulster County, New York v. Allen   June 4, 1979
     442 US 140   60 LEd2d 777   99 SCt 2213

     Harris, Leslie J. Constitutional limits on criminal presumptions as an expression of changing concepts of fundamental fairness. *Journal of Criminal Law and Criminology* 77(2):308-357 (Summer 1986).

     Ponsoldt, James F. A due process analysis of judicially authorized presumptions in federal aggravated bank robbery cases. *Journal of Criminal Law and Criminology* 74(2):363-390 (Summer 1983).

2003. Dunaway v. New York   June 5, 1979
     442 US 200   60 LEd2d 824   99 SCt 2248

     Burger Court 80-82

     En Am Con 1628-1635

     Bernstein, Sidney, and Michael Eisenstein. 1982 Supreme Court update: the criminal law. *Trial* 18(9):45-50, 81 (September 1982).

     Erickson, William H. 1981-1982 U.S. Supreme Court decisions. *Trial* 18(11):44-49, 109 (November 1982).

     Levinson, William D. Supreme Court review: Fourth Amendment—a renewed plea for relevant criteria for the admissibility of tainted confessions. *Journal of Criminal Law and Criminology* 73(4):1408-1429 (Winter 1982).

     Vawrinek, Jeffrey J. Supreme Court review: Fourth Amendment—detention of occupants during a premises search: the winter of discontent for probable cause. *Journal of Criminal Law and Criminology* 72(4):1246-1264 (Winter 1981).

2004. Davis v. Passman   June 5, 1979
     442 US 228   60 LEd2d 846   99 SCt 2264

     Almanac (1980):559; (1990):510-511

     En Am Con 119-120, 533-534, 542

Grady, Kevin T. Commonwealth of Puerto Rico v. SS Zoe Colocotroni: state actions for damage to non-commercial living natural resources. *Boston College Environmental Affairs Law Review* 9(2):397-429 (1980-1981).

Mounts, Gregory J. Labor and the Supreme Court: significant decisions of 1978-79. *Monthly Labor Review* 103(1):14-21 (January 1980).

2005. Personnel Administrator of Massachusetts v. Feeney   June 5, 1979
     442 US 256   60 LEd2d 870   99 SCt 2282
     Burger Years 109-124
     En Am Con 1382, 1666-1673
     Equal Rights 31-33+

Baer, Judith A. Women's rights and the limits of constitutional doctrine. *Western Political Quarterly* 44(4):821-852 (December 1991).

Hatch, Orrin G. Intent rather than 'disparate impact' should be the test. *Center Magazine* 16(6):13-14 (November/December 1983).

Mounts, Gregory J. Labor and the Supreme Court: significant decisions of 1978-79. *Monthly Labor Review* 103(1):14-21 (January 1980).

Williams, Wendy W., and Judith L. Lichtman. Closing the law's gender gap. *Nation* 239(9):280-285 (September 29, 1984).

2006. Babbitt v. United Farm Workers National Union   June 5, 1979
     442 US 289   60 LEd2d 895   99 SCt 2301

Mounts, Gregory J. Labor and the Supreme Court: significant decisions of 1978-79. *Monthly Labor Review* 103(1):14-21 (January 1980).

2007. Lo-Ji Sales, Inc. v. New York   June 11, 1979
     442 US 319   60 LEd2d 920   99 SCt 2319
     Sup Ct Review (1984):309-358

Bernstein, Sidney. Supreme Court review. *Trial* 19(10):26, 28 (October 1983).

Kobylka, Joseph F. A court-created context for group litigation: libertarian groups and obscenity. *Journal of Politics* 49(4):1061-1078 (November 1987).

2008. Reiter v. Sonotone Corp.   June 11, 1979
     442 US 330   60 LEd2d 931   99 SCt 2326

Werner, Ray O. Marketing and the Supreme Court in transition. 1982-1984. *Journal of Marketing* 49(3):97-105 (Summer 1985).

————. Marketing and the United States Supreme Court, 1975-1981. *Journal of Marketing* 46(2):73-81 (Spring 1982).

2009. Andrus v. Sierra Club   June 11, 1979
     442 US 347   60 LEd2d 943   99 SCt 2335

Shortsleeve, Catherine Finnegan. Andrus v. Sierra Club: no effective environmental review in the federal budget process. *Boston College Environmental Affairs Law Review* 9(1):205-243 (1980-1981).

Vanderziel, Kathleen M. The Hatfield Riders and environmental preservation: what process is due? *Boston College Environmental Affairs Law Review* 19(2):431-479 (Fall/Winter 1991).

2010. Great American Savings and Loan Assocation v. Novotny   June 11, 1979
     442 US 366   60 LEd2d 957   99 SCt 2345

Mounts, Gregory J. Labor and the Supreme Court: significant decisions of 1978-79. *Monthly Labor Review* 103(1):14-21 (January 1980).

2011. Southeastern Community College v. Davis   June 11, 1979
     442 US 397   60 LEd2d 980   99 SCt 2361
     Burger Years 125-139
     En Am Con 1532

Baer, Judith A. Burger Court and the rights of the handicapped: the case for starting all over again. *Western Political Quarterly* 35(3):339-358 (September 1982).

2012. Sandstrom v. Montana   June 18, 1979
    442 US 510   61 LEd2d 39   99 SCt 2450
        Almanac (1983):7A
    Harris, Leslie J. Constitutional limits on criminal presumptions as an expression of changing concepts of fundamental fairness. *Journal of Criminal Law and Criminology* 77(2):308-357 (Summer 1986).

2013. Touche Ross and Co. v. Redington   June 18, 1979
    442 US 560   61 LEd2d 82   99 SCt 2479
    Collins, Michael. The dilemma of the downstream state: the untimely demise of federal common law nuisance. *Boston College Environmental Affairs Law Review* 11(2):295-412 (January 1984).

2014. Parham v. J.R., a minor   June 20, 1979
    442 US 584   61 LEd2d 101   99 SCt 2493
        Abortion (Frohock) 67
        Burger Court 92-97, 102, 106-107
        Burger Years 125-139
        En Am Con 686-688, 1364-1365, 1465-1472
    Baer, Judith A. Burger court and the rights of the handicapped: the case for starting all over again. *Western Political Quarterly* 35(3):339-358 (September 1982).
    Gardner, William, David Scherer, and Maya Tester. Asserting scientific authority: cognitive development and adolescent legal rights. *American Psychologist* 44(6):895-902(June 1989).
    Meisel, Alan. The rights of the mentally ill under state constitutions. *Law and Contemporary Problems* 45(3):7-40 (Summer 1982).
    Melton, Gary B. Legal regulation of adolscent abortion: unintended effects. *American Psychologist* 42(1):79-83 (January 1987).
    Minow, Martha. We, the family: constitutional rights and American families. *Journal of American History* 74(3):959-983 (December 1987).

2015. Secretary of Public Welfare of Pennsylvania v. Institutionalized Juveniles   June 20, 1979
    442 US 640   61 LEd2d 142   99 SCt 2523
        Burger Years 125-139
    Baer, Judith A. Burger court and the rights of the handicapped: the case for starting all over again. *Western Political Quarterly* 35(3):339-358 (September 1982).

2016. Fare v. Michael C.   June 20, 1979
    442 US 707   61 LEd2d 197   99 SCt 2560
        En Am Con 1264-1265
    Collins, Ronald K. L., and Robert Welsh. Miranda's fate in the Burger Court. *Center Magazine* 13(5):43-52 (September/October 1980).

2017. Smith v. Maryland   June 20, 1979
    442 US 735   61 LEd2d 220   99 SCt 2577
        Burger Years 143-168
        En Am Con 1628-1635
    Bernstein, Sidney. Supreme Court review. *Trial* 19(10):26, 28 (October 1983).
    Goldberger, Peter. Consent, expectations of privacy, and the meaning of "searches" in the Fourth Amendment. *Journal of Criminal Law and Criminology* 75(2):319-362 (Summer 1984).
    LaFave, Wayne R. Supreme Court review: Fourth Amendment vagaries (of improbable cause, imperceptible plain view, notorious privacy, and balancing askew). *Journal of Criminal Law and Criminology* 74(4):1171-1224 (Winter 1983).

2018. Arkansas v. Sanders   June 20, 1979
    442 US 753   61 LEd2d 235   99 SCt 2586

    Bazelon, David L. Supreme Court review: Forward—the morality of the criminal law: rights of the accused. *Journal of Criminal Law and Criminology* 72(4):1143-1170 (Winter 1981).

    Bernstein, Sidney, and Michael Eisenstein. 1982 Supreme Court update: the criminal law. *Trial* 18(9):45-50, 81 (September 1982).

    Carter, Jeffrey A. Supreme Court review: Fourth Amendment—of cars, containers and confusion. *Journal of Criminal Law and Criminology* 72(4):1171-1221 (Winter 1981).

    Katz, Lewis R. United States v. Ross: evolving standards for warrantless searches. *Journal of Criminal Law and Criminology* 74(1):172-208 (Spring 1983).

    LaFave, Wayne R. Supreme Court review: Fourth Amendment vagaries (of improbable cause, imperceptible plain view, notorious privacy, and balancing askew). *Journal of Criminal Law and Criminology* 74(4):1171-1224 (Winter 1983).

2019. National Labor Relations Board (NLRB) v. Baptist Hospital, Inc.   June 20, 1979
    442 US 773   61 LEd2d 251   99 SCt 2598

    Mounts, Gregory J. Labor and the Supreme Court: significant decisions of 1978-79. *Monthly Labor Review* 103(1):14-21 (January 1980).

2020. Michigan v. DeFillippo   June 25, 1979
    443 US 31   61 LEd2d 343   99 SCt 2627

    Hartman, Marshall J., and Sidney Bernstein. To Leon, and beyond; two commentators react. *Trial* 21(1):50-56 (January 1985).

2021. Brown v. Texas   June 25, 1979
    443 US 47   61 LEd2d 357   99 SCt 2637

    Greig, William H., and Phillip S. Althoff. The constitutionality of roadblocks; the Fourth Amendment on the firing line again. *Trial* 22(2):56-62 (February 1986).

2022. Califano v. Westcott   June 25, 1979
        Coupled with Pratt v. Westcott
    443 US 76   61 LEd2d 382   99 SCt 2655
    Burger Court 52-53, 133, 144-145
    En Am Con 198, 1666-1673
    Equal Rights 43-60+

    Binion, Gayle. The Burger court and the rights of the poor. *Center Magazine* 15(2):2-7 (March/April 1982).

    Mounts, Gregory J. Labor and the Supreme Ccourt: significant decisions of 1978-79. *Monthly Labor Review* 103(1):14-21 (January 1980).

2023. Smith v. Daily Mail Publishing Co.   June 26, 1979
    443 US 97   61 LEd2d 399   99 SCt 2667
    Freedom (Cox) 19-20

    Garneau, George. First Amendment upheld. *Editor and Publisher* 122(26):10-11 (July 1, 1989).

    Powe, L. A., Jr. Mass communications and the First Amendment: an overview. *Law and Contemporary Problems* 55(1):53-76 (Winter 1992).

    Supplement II to First Amendment index. *Editor and Publisher* 113(4):17-18 (January 26, 1980).

2024. Hutchinson v. Proxmire   June 26, 1979
    443 US 111   61 LEd2d 411   99 SCt 2675
    Almanac (1990):510-511
    En Am Con 944, 1716-1717
    Freedom (Cox) 18-19
    Sup Ct Review (1994):169-208

Brief of American Psychological Association and American Association for the Advancement of Science as Amici Curiae. Ronald R. Hutchinson, Petitioner v. William Proxmire and Morton Schwartz, Respondents. *American Psychologist* 35(8):750-758 (August 1980).

Consoli, John. High Court holds: consultants to government aren't public figures. *Editor and Publisher* 114(3):9-10 (January 17, 1981).

Garbus, Martin. New challenge to press freedom. *New York Times Magazine* (section 6):34, 38-41, 48-49 (January 29, 1984).

Gregory, William H. Taste of his own fleece. *Aviation Week and Space Technology* 112(13):13 (March 31, 1980).

Helle, Steven. Judging public interest in libel: the Gertz decision's contribution. *Journalism Quarterly* 61(1):117-124 (Spring 1984).

Howard, A. E. Dick. The press in court. *Wilson Quarterly* 6(5):86-93 (Special Issue 1982).

Kebbel, Gary. The different functions of speech in defamation and privacy cases. *Journalism Quarterly* 61(3):629-633, 743 (Autumn 1984).

Kiesler, Charles A., and Robert P. Lowman. Hutchinson versus Proxmire [Editorial]. *American Psychologist* 35(8):689-690 (August 1980).

2025. Baker v. McCollan   June 29, 1979
      443 US 137   61 Led2d 433   99 SCt 2689
      Zion, Sidney. A tale of two libel theories. *Nation* 239(9):288-290 (September 29, 1984).

2026. Wolston v. Reader's Digest Association   June 26, 1979
      443 US 157   61 LEd2d 450   99 SCt 2701
         Burger Years 45-49
         First 264-268
      Barron, Jerome A. Whose First Amendment? *Vital Speeches* 46(10):313-315 (March 1, 1980).

      Brandon, George. High Court accepts private figure case. *Editor and Publisher* 115[114]:10-11 (November 28, 1981).

      Helle, Steven. Judging public interest in libel: the Gertz decision's contribution. *Journalism Quarterly* 61(1):117-124 (Spring 1984).

      Kebbel, Gary. The different functions of speech in defamation and privacy cases. *Journalism Quarterly* 61(3):629-633, 743 (Autumn 1984).

      Supplement II to First Amendment index. *Editor and Publisher* 113(4):17-18 (January 26, 1980).

      Zion, Sidney. A tale of two libel theories. *Nation* 239(9):288-290 (September 29, 1984).

2027. United Steelworkers of America v. Weber   June 27, 1979
         Coupled with Kaiser Aluminum and Chemical Corp. v. Weber
         Coupled with United States v. Weber
      443 US 193   61 LEd2d 480   99 SCt 2721
         Affirmative (Greene) 87-98
         Affirmative (Woods) 73-74
         Bakke 246-248, 250-252
         Brennan 257-263
         Burger Court 128-129
         Burger Years 95-108
         Conflict 46-49
         Court Public 100, 193-194
         Culture 130-141
         Economics 404-407
         En Am Con 670, 1947
         Guide (CQ) 55
         Guide (West): (v. 10):334-335
         Magic 330-331
         Sup Ct Ind 262-263
         Sup Ct Review (1984):1-68

Askin, Steve. Last hired, first fired? *Black Enterprise* 13(1):17 (August 1982).

Bell, Derrick. To make a nation whole. *New York Times Magazine* (section 6, part 1):43-50 (September 13, 1987).

Bresler, Robert J. The forgotten issue. [Editorial] *USA Today* 116(2516):7 (May 1988).

Burns, Haywood. The activisim in not affirmative. *Nation* 239(9):264-268 (September 29, 1984).

Campbell, Bebe Moore. Supreme Court challenge: laying off affirmative action. *Black Enterprise* 13(7):31 (February 1983).

Camper, Diane. . . . and justice for whom? *Black Enterprise* 15(8):52-55 (March 1985).

Carmell, William A., and Dale E. Callender. Supreme Court didn't kill affirmative action. *ABA Banking Journal* 76(9):56-60 (September 1984).

Chambers, Julius L., and Barry Goldstein. Title VII: the continuing challenge of establishing fair employment practices. *Law and Contemporary Problems* 49(4):9-23 (Autumn 1986).

Church, George J., and Evan Thomas. Four big decisions: High Court rules on abortions, race quotas, open trials, safety rules. *Time* 116(2):10-13 (July 14, 1980).

Fein, Bruce. A court that obeys the law. *National Review* 41(18):50-51 (September 29, 1989).

Franke, Ann H., and Jacqueline W. Mintz. Four trends in higher education law. *Academe* 73(5):57-63 (September/October 1987).

Gest, Ted. Seniority vs. minorities—impact of Court ruling. *U.S. News and World Report* 96(25):22-23 (June 25, 1984).

Hogan, Joyce, and Ann M. Quigley. Physical standards for employment and the courts. *American Psychologist* 41(11):1193-1217 (November 1986).

Job promotions: one up for women. *Economist* 303(7492):23-24 (April 4-10, 1987).

Lamb, Charles M. Legal foundations of civil rights and pluralism America. *Annals of the American Academy of Political and Social Science* 454:13-25 (March 1981).

Markman, Stephen J., and Alfred S. Regnery. The mind of Justice Brennan: a 25-year tribute. *National Review* 36(9):30-33, 36-38 (May 18, 1984).

Matusewitch, Eric. Pitfalls of informal affirmative action. *Personnel Journal* 69(1):84-90 (January 1990).

McFeeley, Neil D. Weber versus affirmative action? *Personnel* 57(1):38-51 (January/February 1980).

Moskowitz, Daniel B. High Court expands affirmative action. *ENR* 218(14):42 (April 2, 1987).

Mounts, Gregory J. Labor and the Supreme Court: significant decisions of 1978-79. *Monthly Labor Review* 103(1):14-21 (January 1980).

————. Significant decisions in labor cases. *Monthly Labor Review* 103(6):51-53 (June 1980).

————. Significant decisions in labor cases. *Monthly Labor Review* 103(12):63-64 (December 1980).

Murphy, Betty Southard, Wayne E. Barlow, and Diane D. Hatch. Supreme Court reaffirms affirmative action. *Personnel Journal* 65(9):19-22 (September 1986).

Nalbandian, John. The U.S. Supreme Court's "consensus" on affirmative action. *Public Administration Review* 49(1):38-45 (January/February 1989).

Ornstein, Allan C., and Daniel U. Levine. Schools, society, and the concept of equality. *Clearing House* 55(3):127-131 (November 1981).

Phillips, Michael J. Paradoxes of equal opportunity: "voluntary'" racial preferences and the Weber case. *Business Horizons* 23(4):41-47 (August 1980).

Press, Aric, and Ann McDaniel. A woman's day in court. *Newsweek* 109(14):58-59 (April 6, 1987).

Redeker, James R. The Supreme Court on affirmative action: conflicting opinions. *Personnel* 63(10):8-14 (October 1986).

Regan, Richard J. Supreme Court roundup: 1979 term. *Thought* 55(219):487-455 (December 1980).

————. Supreme Court roundup: 1980 term. *Thought* 56(223):491-502 (December 1981).

————. Supreme Court roundup: 1986 term. *Thought* 63(251):429-441 (December 1988).

Reid-Dove, Allyson, and Michael E. Howard. "Night has fallen on the Court . . ." *Black Enterprise* 20(2):44-45 (September 1989).

Reynolds, William Bradford. Affirmative action and its negative repercussions. *Annals of the American Academy of Political and Social Science* 523:38-49 (September 1992).

Ritter, Anne. The way it was: HR in the 1980s. *Personnel* 66(12):30-37 (December 1989).

Roberts, Paul Craig, and Lawrence M. Stratton, Jr. Color code. *National Review* 47(5):36, 51, 80 (March 20, 1995).

Sendor, Benjamin. It's okay to set affirmative action "targets." *American School Board Journal* 174(7):16-17, 40 (July 1987).

Sowell, Thomas. A dissenting opinion about affirmative action. *Across the Board* 18(1):64-72 (January 1981).

Stengel, Richard, and Anne Constable. Balancing act: in a sweeping decision, the High Court expands affirmative action. *Time* 129(14):18-20 (April 6, 1987).

Stephenson, D. Grier, Jr. Weber, affirmative action, and restorative justice. *USA Today* 108(2420):48-50 (May 1980).

Taylor, William L., and Susan M. Liss. Affirmative action in the 1990s: staying the course. *Annals of the American Academy of Political and Social Science* 523:30-37 (September 1992).

Tollett, Kenneth S., Jeanette J. Leonard, and Portia P. James. A color-conscious constitution: the one pervading purpose redux. *Journal of Negro Education* 52(3):189-212 (Summer 1983).

Tortora, Anthony. Ex parte McCardle. *National Review* 32(19):1140-1141, 1157 (September 19, 1980).

Trank, John P. The Burger Court—the first ten years. *Law and Contemporary Problems* 43(3):101-135 (Summer 1980).

Vile, John R., and Kathy Ruth McCoy. The Memphis case: another precedent? *Personnel* 62(7):72-76 (July 1985).

Villere, Maurice, and Sandra Hartman. What's affirmative about affirmative action? *Business Horizons* 32(5):22-27 (September/October 1989).

2028. Califano v. Boles   June 27, 1979
     443 US 282   61 LEd2d 541   99 SCt 2767

Mounts, Gregory J. Labor and the Supreme Court: significant decisions of 1978-79. *Monthly Labor Review* 103(1):14-21 (January 1980).

2029. Jackson v. Virginia   June 28, 1979
     443 US 307   61 LEd2d 560   99 SCt 2781

Basta, James. Supreme Court review: habeas corpus: unresolved standard of review on mixed questions for state prisoners. *Journal of Criminal Law and Criminology* 83(4):978-997 (Winter 1993).

2030. Gannett Co., Inc. v. DePasquale   July 2, 1979
     443 US 368   61 LEd2d 608   99 SCt 2898

Ascent 166-171+

Burger Court 6-11, 22, 25-27

Const (Currie) 523-527

Court Public 318-320, 340-361R

En Am Con 805-808, 833, 1453-1456, 1492-1494

First 224-226

Fourth 190-197+

Freedom (Cox) 22-32

Sup Ct Review (1980):1-25

Barron, Jerome A. Whose First Amendment? *Vital Speeches* 46(10):313-315 (March 1, 1980).

Bolbach, Cynthia J. Access to information: affirming the press's right. *Christian Century* 97(29):879-883 (September 24, 1980).

Brown, Robert U. Shop talk at thirty: paranoid press [Editorial]. *Editor and Publisher* 113(28):66 (July 12, 1980).

Copley, Helen K. General spirit of the people. *Vital Speeches* 46(6):169-172 (January 1, 1980).

Erickson, William H. Pronouncements of the U.S. Supreme Court 1979-1980. *Trial* 16(10):69-71 (October 1980).

Fenner, G. Michael, and James L. Koley. Real meaning of the Gannett decision. *Trial* 16(1):45, 60 (January 1980).

High court refuses to hear closure cases. *Editor and Publisher* 115(12):22 (March 20, 1982).

Hill, I. William. Powell absents himself from gag order hearing. *Editor and Publisher* 113(9):27 (March 1, 1980).

Howard, A. E. Dick. The press in court. *Wilson Quarterly* 6(5):86-93 (Special Issue 1982).

Jenkins, John A. A candid talk with Justice Blackmun. *New York Times Magazine* (section 6):20-29, 57, 61, 66 (February 20, 1983).

Leeper, Roy V. Richmond Newspapers, Inc. v. Virginia and the emerging right of access. *Journalism Quarterly* 61(3):615-622 (Autumn 1984).

Lubben, Craig H. Supreme Court review: First Amendment—constitutional right of access to criminal trials. *Journal of Criminal Law and Criminology* 71(4):547-557 (Winter 1980).

Malak, Michael P. Supreme Court review: First Amendment—guarantee of public access to voir dire. *Journal of Criminal Law and Criminology* 75(3):583-608 (Fall 1984).

Maybe court will decide right to gather news. *Editor and Publisher* 113(17):28 (April 26, 1980).

160 take part in forum of DePasquale rule. *Editor and Publisher* 113(1):32 (January 5, 1980).

Paley, William S. Press freedom: a continuing struggle *Vital Speeches* 46(21):670-672 (August 15, 1980).

Press, Aric, and Diane Camper. High Court's grand finale.*Newsweek* 96(2):22-25 (July 14, 1980).

Radolf, Andrew. Press urged to explain First Amendment rights. *Editor and Publisher* 113(4):14 (January 26, 1980).

Regan, Richard J. Supreme Court roundup: 1979 term. *Thought* 55(219):487-455 (December 1980).

———. Supreme Court roundup: 1980 term. *Thought* 56(223):491-502 (December 1981).

Reid, Traciel V. Judicial policy-making and implementation: an empirical examination. *Western Political Quarterly* 41(3):509-527 (September 1988).

Supplement II to First Amendment index. *Editor and Publisher* 113(4):17-18 (January 26, 1980).

Supreme Court to hear closed trial case. *Editor and Publisher* 115[114]:11 (November 28, 1981).

Welsh, Robert, and Ronald K. L. Collins. Taking state constitutions seriously: the protection of civil liberties has been shifting away from the U.S. Supreme Court. *Center Magazine* 14(5):6-35, 38-43 (September/October 1981).

2031. Columbus Board of Education v. Penick   July 2, 1979
       443 US 449   61 LEd2d 666   99 SCt 2941
       Burger Years 95-108
       Court Public 159
       En Am Con 314-315, 1625-1626

       Gordon, William M. The implementation of desegregation plans since Brown. *Journal of Negro Education* 63(3):310-322 (Summer 1994).

       Russo, Charles J., J. John Harris III, and Rosetta F. Sandidge. Brown v. Board of Education at 40: a legal history of equal educational opportunity in American public education. *Journal of Negro Education* 63(3):297-309 (Summer 1994).

2032. Dayton Board of Education v. Brinkman   July 2, 1979
       443 US 562   61 LEd2d 720   99 SCt 2971
       En Am Con 314-315

       Gordon, William M. The implementation of desegregation plans since Brown. *Journal of Negro Education* 63(3):310-322 (Summer 1994).

       Russo, Charles J., J. John Harris III, and Rosetta F. Sandidge. Brown v. Board of Education at 40: a legal history of equal educational opportunity in American public education. *Journal of Negro Education* 63(3):297-309 (Summer 1994).

2033. Jones v. Wolf   July 2, 1979
       443 US 595   61 LEd2d 775   99 SCt 3020
       Godless 48-49

       Lawton, Kim A. Uncle Sam v. First Church. *Christianity Today* 35(11):38-41 (October 7, 1991).

       Taylor, Barry W. Diversion of church funds to personal use: state, federal and private sanctions. *Journal of Criminal Law and Criminology* 73(3):1204-1237 (Fall 1982).

2034. Bellotti, Attorney General of Massachusetts v. Baird   July 2, 1979
              Coupled with Hunderwadel v. Baird
       443 US 622   61 LEd2d 797   99 SCt 3035
       Abortion Con 177-183, 291

Abortion Dec 58-67+

Abortion Decs 70s Introduction, 165-188R

Abortion Moral 66-70

Abortion Pol (Rubin) 130-136+

En Am Con 1552-1558

Hard Choices 312-313+

Liberty 631-638

Lewis, Catherine C. Minors' competence to consent to abortion. *American Psychologist* 42(1):84-88 (January 1987).

Melton, Gary B. Legal regulation of adolscent abortion: unintended effects. *American Psychologist* 42(1):79-83 (January 1987).

Melton, Gary B., and Nancy Felipe Russo. Adolescent abortion: psychological perspectives on public policy. *American Psychologist* 42(1):69-72 (January 1987).

Minow, Martha. We, the family: constitutional rights and American families. *Journal of American History* 74(3):959-983 (December 1987).

Regan, Richard J. Regulating cult activities: the limits of religious freedom. *Thought* 61(241):185-196 (June 1986).

2035. Washington v. Washington State Commercial Passenger Fishing Vessel Association   July 2, 1979

        Coupled with Washington v. United States

        Coupled with Puget Sound Gillnetters Association v. United States

443 US 658   61 LEd2d 823   99 SCt 3055

Am Indians (Wilkinson) 72-73, 129, 211+

Ott, Brian R. Indian fishing rights in the Pacific Northwest: the need for federal intervention. *Boston College Environmental Affairs Law Review* 14(2):313-343 (Winter 1987).

2036. Transamerica Mortgage Advisors, Inc. (TAMA) v. Lewis   November 13, 1979

444 US 11   62 LEd2d 146   100 SCt 242

Almanac (1980):10A

Burger Years 206-219

Collins, Michael. The dilemma of the downstream state: the untimely demise of federal common law nuisance. *Boston College Environmental Affairs Law Review* 11(2):295-412 (January 1984).

2037. Andrus v. Allard   November 27, 1979

444 US 51   62 LEd2d 210   100 SCt 318

Hippler, Thomas A. Reexamining 100 years of the Supreme Court regulatory taking doctrine: the principles of "noxious use," "average reciprocity of advantage," and "bundle of rights" from Mugler to Keystone Bituminous Coal. *Boston College Environmental Affairs Law Review* 14(4):653-727 (Summer 1987).

2038. P.C. Pfeiffer Co., Inc. v. Ford   November 27, 1979

444 US 69   62 LEd2d 225   100 SCt 328

Almanac (1980):10A

Mount, Gregory J. Significant decisions in labor cases. *Monthly Labor Review* 103(6):51-52 (March 1980).

2039. Ybarra v. Illinois   November 28, 1979

444 US 85   62 LEd2d 238   100 SCt 338

Almanac (1980):4A-5A

En Am Con 1462-1464, 2083

Erickson, William H. Pronouncements of the U.S. Supreme Court 1979-1980. *Trial* 16(10):69-71 (October 1980).

Kamisar, Yale. The swing of the pendulum. *Nation* 239(9):271-274 (September 29, 1984).

Wall, Sandra J. Supreme Court review: Fourth Amendment—search of an individual pursuant to a warrant to search the premises. *Journal of Criminal Law and Criminology* 71(4):558-566 (Winter 1980).

2040. Board of Education of the City School District of New York v. Harris　　　November 28, 1979
　　　　444 US 130　　　　　　　　　　　62 LEd2d 275　　　　　　　　　　　100 SCt 363
　　　　　Almanac (1980):7A
　　　　Mount, Gregory J. Significant decisions in labor cases. *Monthly Labor Review* 103(3):51-52 (March 1980).

2041. Kaiser Aetna v. United States　　　　　　　　　　　　　　　　　　　December 4, 1979
　　　　444 US 164　　　　　　　　　　　62 LEd2d 332　　　　　　　　　　　100 SCt 383
　　　　　Almanac (1980):9A
　　　　Cohen, Jonathan E. A constitutional safety valve: the variance in zoning and land-use based environmental controls. *Boston College Environmental Affairs Law Review* 22(2):307-364 (Winter 1995).
　　　　Hippler, Thomas A. Reexamining 100 years of the Supreme Court regulatory taking doctrine: the principles of "noxious use," "average reciprocity of advantage," and "bundle of rights" from Mugler to Keystone Bituminous Coal. *Boston College Environmental Affairs Law Review* 14(4):653-727 (Summer 1987).

2042. Ferri v. Ackerman　　　　　　　　　　　　　　　　　　　　　　　December 4, 1979
　　　　444 US 193　　　　　　　　　　　62 LEd2d 355　　　　　　　　　　　100 SCt 402
　　　　　Almanac (1980):13A
　　　　Carlson, Patricia B. Liability of government-appointed attorneys in state tort actions. *Journal of Criminal Law and Criminology* 71(2):136-146 (Summer 1980).

2043. Carbon Fuel Co. v. United Mine Workers　　　　　　　　　　　　　December 10, 1979
　　　　444 US 212　　　　　　　　　　　62 LEd2d 394　　　　　　　　　　　100 SCt 410
　　　　　Almanac (1980):3A, 11A
　　　　Mount, Gregory J. Significant decisions in labor cases. *Monthly Labor Review* 103(3):51-52 (March 1980).

2044. Strycker's Bay Neighborhood Council, Inc. v. Karlen　　　　　　　　January 7, 1980
　　　　444 US 223　　　　　　　　　　　62 LEd2d 433　　　　　　　　　　　100 SCt 497
　　　　Brady, Timothy Patrick. "But most of it belongs to those yet to be born": the public trust doctrine, NEPA, and the stewardship ethic. *Boston College Environmental Affairs Law Review* 17(3):621-646 (Spring 1990).
　　　　Kelly, Paula. Judicial review of agency decisions under the National Environmental Policy Act of 1969—Strycker's Bay Neighborhood Council, Inc. v. Karlen. *Boston College Environmental Affairs Law Review* 10(1):79-109 (1982-83).
　　　　Sandler, Ross. Law: shrinking NEPA. *Environment* 22(3):43-44 (April 1980).
　　　　———. Law: Supreme Court trends in environmental law. *Environment* 23(7):4-5 (September 1981).

2045. McLain v. Real Estate Board of New Orleans, Inc.　　January 8, 1980
　　　　444 US 232　　　　　　　　　　　62 LEd2d 441　　　　　　　　　　　100 SCt 502
　　　　　Almanac (1980):3A, 9A

2046. Martinez v. California　　　　　　　　　　　　　　　　　　　　　January 15, 1980
　　　　444 US 277　　　　　　　　　　　62 LEd2d 481　　　　　　　　　　　100 SCt 553
　　　　　Almanac (1980):13A
　　　　Groszyk, Walter S., Jr., and Thomas J. Madden. Managing without immunity: the challenge for state and local government officials in the 1980s. *Public Administration Review* 41(2):268-278 (March/April 1981).

2047. World-Wide Volkswagen Corp. v. Woodson　　　　　　　　　　　　January 21, 1980
　　　　444 US 286　　　　　　　　　　　62 LEd2d 490　　　　　　　　　　　100 SCt 559
　　　　Sup Ct Review (1980):77-113

2048. Rush v. Savchuk　　　　　　　　　　　　　　　　　　　　　　　January 21, 1980
　　　　444 US 320　　　　　　　　　　　62 LEd2d 516　　　　　　　　　　　100 SCt 571
　　　　　Sup Ct Review (1980):77-113

2049. Brown v. Glines　　　　　　　　　　　　　　　　　　　　　　　January 21, 1980
　　　　444 US 348　　　　　　　　　　　62 LEd2d 540　　　　　　　　　　　100 SCt 594

Almanac (1980):8A-9A
Sup Ct Review (1984):169-236

2050. United States v. Bailey   January 21, 1980
    444 US 394   62 LEd2d 575   100 SCt 624
    Almanac (1980):8A

2051. Norfolk and Western Railway Co. v. Liepelt   February 19, 1980
    444 US 490   62 Led2d 689   100 SCt 755
    Almanac (1980):11A
    Mount, Gregory J. Significant decisions in labor cases. *Monthly Labor Review* 103(6):51-53 (June 1980).

2052. Snepp v. United States   February 19, 1980
    444 US 507   62 LEd2d 704   100 SCt 763
    Burger Court 11-15
    Burger Years 50-55
    Court Const 231-233
    Editorials (1980):257-260
    En Am Con 797-804, 169-1700
    Fourth 147-151
    Freedom (Cox) 6-14
    Make 234-248
    Sup Ct Review (1981):309-365
    Alter, Jonathan. Slaying the message: how the Frank Snepp case hurts us all. *Washington Monthly* 13(7):43-50 (September 1981).
    Beach, Bennet H., and Evan Thomas. Nine minds of its own. *Time* 116(3):75-76 (July 21, 1980).
    Carver, George A., Jr. CIA's case against Snepp. [Editorial] *Newsweek* 95(11):21 (March 17, 1980).
    Dee, Juliet. Legal confrontations between press, ex-CIA agents and the government. *Journalism Quarterly* 66(2):418-426 (Summer 1989).
    Dong, Stella. Supreme Court says Snepp violated CIA contracts. *Publishers' Weekly* 217(9):12, 18 (March 7, 1980).
    Dworkin, Ronald. Is the press losing the First Amendment? *New York Review of Books* 27(19):49-57 (December 4, 1980).
    Ferguson, James R. Scientific freedom, national security,and the First Amendment. *Science* 221(4611):620-624 (August 12, 1983).
    Fields, Howard. Government won't use Snepp ruling against publishers. *Publishers' Weekly* 218(7):16-17 (August 15, 1980).
    ———. High Court ends Snepp's fight to keep royalties. *Publishers' Weekly* 217(16):18, 23 (April 25, 1980).
    First to show your book to Uncle Sam. *Economist* 274(7121):47-48 (February 23, 1980).
    5 Court rulings on explosive issues. *U.S. News and World Report* 88(8):6 (March 3, 1980).
    Halperin, Morton H. Never question the president. *Nation* 239(9):285-288 (September 29, 1984).
    Indecent haste. [Editorial] *Nation* 230(9):257 (March 8, 1980).
    Kourtis, Jane Papademetriou. The constructive trust: equity's answer to the need for a strong deterrent to the destruction of historic landmarks. *Boston College Environmental Affairs Law Review* 16(4):793-820 (Summer 1989).
    Lewin, Nathan. High court hexes free speech. *New Republic* 182(12):18-21 (March 22, 1980).
    Lewis, Anthony. Staving off the silencers. *New York Times Magazine* (section 6, part 1):72-77 (December 1, 1991).
    MacKenzie, Angus. The most serious threat is . . . the secrecy obsession. *Columbia Journalism Review* 30(4):51-52 (November/December 1991).
    Powers, Thomas. The good soldier system: when the CIA plays book reviewer. *Commonweal* 107(9):261-262 (May 9, 1980).
    Press, Aric, and Diane Camper. High Court hits tellers of secrets. *Newsweek* 95(9):50-51 (March 3, 1980).
    Question-ducking. [Editorial] *Nation* 234(4):100 (January 30, 1982).
    Quirk, William J. Judicial dictatorship. *Society* 31(2):34-38 (January/February 1994).

Regan, Richard J. Supreme Court roundup: 1979 term. *Thought* 55(219):487-455 (December 1980).

Schwartz, Herman. Fifteen years of the Burger Court. *Nation* 239(9):262-264 (September 29, 1984).

Snepp fallout. [Editorial] *Nation* 230(11):323-324 (March 22, 1980).

TRB from Washington: the supreme legislature. *New Republic* 182(11):2 (March 15, 1980).

Wages of faithlessness ruling. *Time* 115(9):48-49 (March 3, 1980).

2053. Stafford v. Briggs   February 20, 1980
    Coupled with Colby v. Driver
444 US 527   63 Led2d 1   100 SCt 774
 Almanac (1980)12A-13A

2054. Ford Motor Credit Co. v. Milhollin   February 20, 1980
Ford Motor Credit Co. v. Millhollin
444 US 555   63 LEd2d 22   100 SCt 790
 Almanac (1980):7A

Brandel, Roland E., and Barry A. Abbott. More battles ahead to simplify truth in lending. *ABA Banking Journal* 72(5):100-114 (May 1980).

2055. Seatrain Shipbuilding Corp. v. Shell Oil Co.   February 20, 1980
444 US 572   63 LEd2d 36   100 SCt 800
 Almanac (1980):10A

2056. California Brewers Assocation v. Bryant   February 20, 1980
444 US 598   63 LEd2d 55   100 SCt 814
 Almanac (1980):7A

Mounts, Gregory J. Labor and the Supreme Court: significant decisions of 1979-80. *Monthly Labor Review* 104(4):13-22 (April 1981).

———. Significant decisions in labor cases. *Monthly Labor Review* 103(6):51-53 (June 1980).

Nelson, Joani. Benzine tops High Court docket. *Industry Week* 204(2):19-21 (January 21, 1980).

2057. Village of Schaumburg v. Citizens for Better Environment   February 20, 1980
444 US 620   63 LEd2d 73   100 SCt 826
 Almanac (1980):8A
 Freedom (Cox) 56-59

Beach, Bennet H., and Evan Thomas. Nine minds of its own. *Time* 116(3):75-76 (July 21, 1980).

5 Court rulings on explosive issues. *U.S. News and World Report* 88(8):6 (March 3, 1980).

2058. Committee for Public Education and Religious Liberty (PEARL) v. Regan   February 20, 1980
444 US 646   63 LEd2d 94   100 SCt 840
 Almanac (1980):8A
 En Am Con 331-332, 854-856, 1650-1658

5 Court rulings on explosive issues. *U.S. News and World Report* 88(8):6 (March 3, 1980).

Rayer, Thomas A. The bicentennial and church-related schools. *America* 157(17):427-429, 438 (December 5, 1987).

Regan, Richard J. Supreme Court roundup: 1979 term. *Thought* 55(219):487-455 (December 1980).

2059. National Labor Relations Board (NLRB) v. Yeshiva University   February 20, 1980
    Coupled with Yeshiva University Faculty Association v. Yeshiva
444 US 672   63 LEd2d 115   100 SCt 856
 Almanac (1980):11A
 Religion 185-196
 Sup Ct Review (1980):27-55

Are professionals managers? *Business Week* (Industrial Edition) (2632):59-62 (April 14, 1980).

The association and the courts. *Academe* 75(3):31-33 (May/June 1989).

Blum, Debra E. 10 years after High Court limited faculty bargaining, merits of academic unionism still hotly debated.*Chronicle of Higher Education* 36(20):A15-A16 (January 31, 1990).

Brennan, William J., Jr. Text of Brennan's dissent on Yeshiva. *Chronicle of Higher Education* 19(23):8-9R (February 25, 1980).

Chill for campus unions. [Editorial] *America* 142(9):182 (March 8, 1980).

Deitsch, Clarence R., and David A. Dilts. NLRB v. Yeshiva University: a positive perspective. *Monthly Labor Review* 106(7):34-37 (July 1983).

Finkin, Matthew W. Regulation by agreement: the case of private higher education (part I & II). *Academe* 67(1):5-21 (February/March 1981).

————. Regulation by agreement: the case of private higher education. (part III). *Academe* 67(2):67-80 (April 1981).

5 Court rulings on explosive issues. *U.S. News and World Report* 88(8):6 (March 3, 1980).

Flygare, Thomas J. Schools and the law: Yeshiva University: implications for the future of college collective bargaining. *Phi Delta Kappan* 61(9):639-640 (May 1980).

Fox, Arthur. Showing workers who's the boss. *Nation* 239(9):295-299 (September 29, 1984).

From Tilton to Ewing: some major higher-education decisions of the Burger court. *Chronicle of Higher Education* 32(17):10 (June 25, 1986).

Getman, Julius G. and Ann H. Franke. The 'Yeshiva' case revisited: professors' right to bargain is entitled to statutory protection. [Editorial] *Chronicle of Higher Education* 34(21):B1-B2 (February 3, 1988).

Gorman, Robert A. The Yeshiva decision. *Academe* 66(4):188-197R (May 1980).

Jaschik, Scott. From Bakke to Yeshiva, Justice Powell played key role in Court's education rulings. *Chronicle of Higher Education* 33(43):16 (July 8, 1987).

Levy, Herman M. The Yeshiva case revisited. *Academe* 73(5):34-37 (September/October 1987).

Mangan, Katherine S. High Court's 'Yeshiva' ruling on faculty unions is starting to affect public campuses. *Chronicle of Higher Education* 33(35):16-17, 25 (May 13, 1987).

Mounts, Gregory J. Labor and the Supreme Court: significant decisions of 1979-80. *Monthly Labor Review* 104(4):13-22 (April 1981).

————. Significant decisions in labor cases. *Monthly Labor Review* 103(4):57-58 (April 1980).

Powell, Lewis F., Jr. Text of majority opinion on Yeshiva. *Chronicle of Higher Education* 19(23):7-8R (February 25, 1980).

Press, Aric, and Diane Camper. High Court hits tellers of secrets. *Newsweek* 95(9):50-51 (March 3, 1980).

Rabban, David M. AAUP in the courts: the association's representation of faculty members and faculty causes in appellate litigation. *Academe* 69(2):1a-12a (March/April 1983).

Regan, Richard J. Supreme Court roundup: 1979 term. *Thought* 55(219):487-455 (December 1980).

Wages of faithlessness ruling. *Time* 115(9):48-49 (March 3, 1980).

Watkins, Beverly T. Fallout from the Yeshiva ruling. *Chronicle of Higher Education* 20(22):3-4 (June 9, 1980).

Watkins, Beverly T. High Court calls Yeshiva faculty managers, not subject to National Labor Relations Act. *Chronicle of Higher Education* 19(23):1, 7 (February 25, 1980).

————. Supreme Court's Yeshiva decision produces uncertainty, disappointment. *Chronicle of Higher Education* 19(23):8-9 (February 25, 1980).

————. What the High Court's 'Yeshiva' decision has meant to Yeshiva University itself. *Chronicle of Higher Education* 29(23):27-28 (February 20, 1985).

2060. United States v. Euge   February 20, 1980
   444 US 707   63 LEd2d 141   100 SCt 874
   Almanac (1980):5A

Bray, John M., and David J. Curtin. IRS's power to summons handwriting: analyzing the Supreme Court's Euge decision. *Journal of Taxation* 52(5):290-292 (May 1980).

2061. Goldwater v. Carter   December 13, 1979
   444 US 996   62 LEd2d 428   100 SCt 533
   Ascent 58-60, 90, 92+
   En Am Con 460-464, 747-755, 851, 1910-1911

Fung, Teresa. Does the U.S. president have the right to cancel a treaty? *Scholastic Update* (Teachers' Edition) 120(2):40 (September 18, 1987).

2062. Whirlpool Corp. v. Marshall   February 26, 1980
    445 US 1   63 LEd2d 154   100 SCt 883
      Almanac (1980):3A,11A

Cook, Daniel D. Who decides when a job's too dangerous? *Industry Week* 204(6):23-25 (March 17, 1980).

Fox, Arthur. Showing workers who's the boss. *Nation* 239(9):295-299 (September 29, 1984).

Lissy, William E. Employees can refuse to perform hazardous jobs. *Supervision* 42(8):19-20 (August 1980).

Mounts, Gregory J. Labor and the Supreme Court: significant decisions of 1979-80. *Monthly Labor Review* 104(4):13-22 (April 1981).

———. Significant decisions in labor cases. *Monthly Labor Review* 103(4):57-58 (April 1980).

Nelson, Joani. Benzine tops High Court docket. *Industry Week* 204(2):19-21 (January 21, 1980).

OSHA protects refusal to work, court rules. *Engineering News Record* 204(10):76 (March 6, 1980).

Unsafe: workers can refuse tasks. *Business Insurance* 14(9):1, 29 (March 3, 1980).

2063. United States v. Clark   February 26, 1980
    445 US 23   63 LEd2d 171   100 SCt 895
      Almanac (1980):8A

Mounts, Gregory J. Labor and the Supreme Court: significant decisions of 1979-80. *Monthly Labor Review* 104(4):13-22 (April 1981).

———. Significant decisions in labor cases. *Monthly Labor Review* 103(6):51-53 (June 1980).

2064. Trammel v. United States   February 27, 1980
    445 US 40   63 LEd2d 186   100 SCt 906
      Almanac (1980):4A

Mate vs. mate. *Time* 115(10):49 (March 10, 1980).

Pachciarek, Anne. Supreme Court review: federal rules of evidence—testimonial privileges. *Journal of Criminal Law and Criminology* 71(4):593-600 (Winter 1980).

2065. California Retail Liquor Dealers Assocation v. Midcal Aluminum, Inc.   March 3, 1980
    445 US 97   63 LEd2d 233   100 SCt 937
      Almanac (1980):9A-10A
      Sup Ct Review (1986):157-173

Hamlin, Ross J. Application of the Sherman Act state action exemption to municipal environmental regulation: a case for broader local discretion. *Boston College Environmental Affairs Law Review* 11(3):609-664 (April 1984).

Roberts, Robert N. Municipal antitrust immunity and the state-action exemption: developments in the law. *State Government* 58(4):164-171 (Winter 1986).

Weller, Charles D. McCarran Act interpretation may have been charted in Barry case. *Best's Review* (Life/Health Insurance Edition) 83(2):40-42, 87-89 (June 1982).

———. McCarran Act interpretation may have been charted in Barry case. *Best's Review* (Property/Casualty Insurance Edition) 83(3):28-32 (July 1982).

Werner, Ray O. Marketing and the United States Supreme Court, 1975-1981. *Journal of Marketing* 46(2):73-81 (Spring 1982).

2066. United States v. Apfelbaum   March 3, 1980
    445 US 115   63 LEd2d 250   100 SCt 948
      Almanac (1980):5A

Batey, Robert. Strict construction of firearms offenses: the Supreme Court and the Gun Control Act of 1968. *Law and Contemporary Problems* 49(1):163-198 (Winter 1986).

Lushing, Peter. Testimonial immunity and the privilege against self-incrimination: a study in isomorphism. *Journal of Criminal Law and Criminology* 73(4):1690-1739 (Winter 1982).

Staas, John August. Supreme Court review: Fifth Amendment—statutory dilution of the privilege against self-incrimination. *Journal of Criminal Law and Criminology* 71(4):610-621 (Winter 1980).

2067. Kissinger v. Reporters Committee for Freedom of the Press   March 3, 1980
    445 US 136   63 LEd2d 267   100 SCt 960

Almanac (1980):13A-14A

Editorials (1980):312-314

American survey: Court continues its bamboozlement. *Economist* 276(7140):21-22 July 5, 1980.

Fields, Cheryl M. High Court limits scholars' use of Information Act. *Chronicle of Higher Education* 20(2):1, 12 (March 10, 1980).

From Tilton to Ewing: some major higher-education decisions of the Burger court. *Chronicle of Higher Education* 32(17):10 (June 25, 1986).

Hill, I. William. Top court limits media access to government papers. *Editor and Publisher* 113(10):8 (March 8, 1980).

Press, Aric, and Diane Camper. Kissinger transcripts. *Newsweek* 95(11):60 (March 17, 1980).

Regan, Richard J. Supreme Court roundup: 1979 term. *Thought* 55(219):487-455 (December 1980).

Reuter, Madalynne. Supreme Court upholds Kissinger over transcripts. *Publishers' Weekly* 217(11):19-20 (March 21, 1980).

State secrets. *Time* 115(11):51 (March 17, 1980).

2068. Forsham v. Harris   March 3, 1980

445 US 169   63 LEd2d 293   100 SCt 978

Almanac (1980):14A

From Tilton to Ewing: some major higher-education decisions of the Burger court. *Chronicle of Higher Education* 32(17):10 (June 25, 1986).

Press, Aric, and Diane Camper. Kissinger transcripts. *Newsweek* 95(11):60 (March 17, 1980).

Morris, Roberta A., Bruce D. Sales, and John J. Berman. Research and the Freedom of Information Act. *American Psychologist* 36(8):819-826 (August 1981).

2069. Costle v. Pacific Legal Foundation   March 18, 1980

445 US 198   63 LEd2d 329   100 SCt 1095

Hassler, Gregory L., and Karen O'Connor. Woodsy witchdoctors versus judicial guerrillas: the role and impact of competing interest groups in environmental litigation. *Boston College Environmental Affairs Law Review* 13(4):487-520 (Summer 1986).

Nelson, Joani. Benzine tops High Court docket. *Industry Week* 204(2):19-21 (January 21, 1980).

2070. Chiarella v. United States   March 18, 1980

445 US 222   63 LEd2d 348   100 SCt 1108

Almanac (1980):10A

Burger Years 206-219

Sup Ct Review (1981):309-365

Cohen, Jerry A., and Herbert E. Milstein. "Efficiency" over competition. *Nation* 239(9):294-295 (September 29, 1984).

Cox, James D. Insider trading: regulation of activity is 'in trouble.' *Trial* 24(9):22-28, 93-96 (September 1988).

Glaberson, William B. Insider trading: a widening net catches the small fry. *Business Week* (Industrial/Technology Edition) (2880):60-64 (February 11, 1985).

Press, Aric, and Diane Camper. Strict views of the law. *Newsweek* 95(13):49 (March 31, 1980).

Scheppele, Kim Lane. "It's just not right": the ethics of insider trading. *Law and Contemporary Problems* 56(3):123-173 (Summer 1993).

Schiffres, Manuel. What did they know—and how? *U.S. News and World Report* 101(22):48-49 (December 1, 1986).

Strong, George V. Supreme Court review: Securities Exchange Act of 1934—restrictive application of Section 10(b) and Rule 10b-5 in securities fraud. *Journal of Criminal Law and Criminology* 71(4):474-487 (Winter 1980).

2071. Rummel v. Estelle   March 18, 1980

445 US 263   63 LEd2d 382   100 SCt 1133

Almanac (1980):6A

Black 203-211

Brennan 209-211

Editorials (1980):377-379

En Am Con 524-526, 1615-1616

Bernstein, Sidney. Supreme Court review. *Trial* 19(11):20, 22 (November 1983).

Cruel, as usual. [Editorial] *Nation* 230(13):387-388 (April 5, 1980).

Dripps, Donald A. Supreme Court review: cruel, unusual, and constitutional. *Trial* 28(5):87-89 (May 1992).

Goetz, Ronald. Petty crimes, severe sentence. [Editorial] *Christian Century* 97(14):428-429 (April 16, 1980).

Mills, Elizabeth M. Supreme Court review: Eighth Amendment—cruel and unusual punishment: habitual offender's life sentence without parole is disproportionate. *Journal of Criminal Law and Criminology* 74(4):1372-1386 (Winter 1983).

Press, Aric, and Diane Camper. Strict views of the law. *Newsweek* 95(13):49 (March 31, 1980).

Schwartz, Charles Walter. Eighth Amendment proportionality analysis and the compelling case of William Rummel. *Journal of Criminal Law and Criminology* 71(4):378-420 (Winter 1980).

2072. Vance v. Universal Amusement Co.   March 18, 1980
       445 US 308   63 LEd2d 413   100 SCt 1156
       Almanac (1980):9A

McGuire, Kevin T., and Gregory A. Caldeira. Lawyers, organized interests, and the law of obscenity: agenda setting in the Supreme Court. *American Political Science Review* 87(3):717-726 (September 1993).

2073. Deposit Guaranty National Bank v. Roper   March 19, 1980
       445 US 326   63 LEd2d 427   100 SCt 1166
       Almanac (1980):13A

2074. United States v. Gillock   March 19, 1980
       445 US 360   63 LEd2d 454   100 SCt 1185
       Almanac (1980):13A
       En Am Con 1716-1717

Pachciarek, Anne. Supreme Court review: federal rules of evidence—testimonial privileges. *Journal of Criminal Law and Criminology* 71(4):593-600 (Winter 1980).

2075. GTE Sylvania, Inc. v. Consumers Union of the United States, Inc.   March 19, 1980
       445 US 375   63 LEd2d 467   100 SCt 1194
       Almanac (1980):14A

Nelson, Joani. Benzine tops High Court docket. *Industry Week* 204(2):19-21 (January 21, 1980).

Supreme Court deals blow to multinationals. *Industry Week* 204(7):18-19 (March 31, 1980).

2076. United States Parole Commission v. Geraghty   March 19, 1980
       445 US 388   63 LEd2d 479   100 SCt 1202
       Almanac (1980):13A

2077. Mobil Oil Corp. v. Commissioner of Taxes of Vermont   March 19, 1980
       445 US 425   63 LEd2d 510   100 SCt 1223
       Almanac (1980):3A,10A

Another view of the Mobil Oil case. *CPA Journal* 50(9):67-68 (September 1980).

Corporate taxes: ounce of flesh for American states. *Economist* 274(7126):110 (March 29, 1980).

Disputing a state's tax reach. *Business Week* (Industrial Edition) (2712):131-132 (November 2, 1981).

For the states, a freer hand over multinationals. *Business Week* (Industrial Edition) (2647):68H-68L (July 28, 1980).

Genetelli, Richard W., David B. Zigman, and Cesar E. Bencosme. Recent U.S. Supreme Court decisions on state and local tax issues. *CPA Journal* 62(11):38-44 (November 1992).

Jurinski, James John. A primer on the unitary business concept. *CPA Journal* 56(9):52-64 (Sepempter 1986).

———. The U.S. Supreme Court on the unitary tax. *Journal of Accountancy* 161(1):96 (January 1986).

Nelson, Joani. Benzine tops High Court docket. *Industry Week* 204(2):19-21 (January 21, 1980).

Peters, James H. Sup. Ct.'s Mobil decision on multistate income apportionment raises new questions. *Journal of Taxation* 53(1):36-40 (July 1980).

Spears, L. Stephen. Applying the unitary business concept to diverse businesses. *CPA Journal* 58(6):34-45 (June 1988).

State taxation of foreign source dividend income. *CPA Journal* 50(9):64-68 (September 1980).

State wins on foreign source dividend income. *CPA Journal* 50(6):46-47 (June 1980).

Supreme Court deals blow to multinationals. *Industry Week* 204(7):18-19 (March 31, 1980).

Wasson, Hilda C., and Robert E. Weigand. Unitary taxation: a search for fairness. *Business Horizons* 31(2):45-50 (March/April 1988).

2078. United States v. Crews   March 25, 1980
 445 US 463   63 LEd2d 537   100 SCt 1244
  En Am Con 809-810

Fagan, Terence P. Supreme Court review: Fourth Amendment—in-court identifications. *Journal of Criminal Law and Criminology* 71(4):488-498 (Winter 1980).

Halberstam, Malvina. Agora: international kidnaping—in defense of the Supreme Court decision in Alvarez-Machain. *American Journal of International Law* 86(4):736-746 (October 1992).

2079. Vitek v. Jones   March 25, 1980
 445 US 480   63 LEd2d 552   100 SCt 1254
  Almanac (1980):4A
  Sup Ct Review (1982):85-125

Fuerst, J. S., and Roy Petty. Due process—how much is enough? *Public Interest* (79):96-110 (Spring 1985).

Hartstone, Eliot, Henry J. Steadman, and John Monahan. Vitek and beyond: the empirical context of prison-to-hospital transfers. *Law and Contemporary Problems* 45(3):125-136 (Summer 1982).

Knochell, Keith S. Supreme Court review: Fourteenth Amendment—due process for prisoners in commitment proceedings. *Journal of Criminal Law and Criminology* 71(4):579-592 (Winter 1980).

2080. Branti v. Finkel   March 31, 1980
 445 US 507   63 LEd2d 574   100 SCt 1287
  Almanac (1980):4A, 8A
  Const (Currie) 505-510
  En Am Con 146

Blow against political patronage. *Newsweek* 95(15):30 (April 14, 1980).

Court throws wrench in machine politics. *U.S. News and World Report* 88(14):7 (April 14, 1980).

Franklin, Daniel. The five dumbest Supreme Court decisions. *Washington Monthly* 26(10):12-18 (October 1994).

Kaus, Robert M. Zbig for life: the way the Supreme Court is going, that's what we could be stuck with. *Washington Monthly* 12(4):25-32 (June 1980).

McFeeley, Neil D. The Supreme Court and patronage: implications for local government. *National Civic Review* 71(5):251-258 (May 1982).

Meier, Kenneth J. Ode to patronage: a critical analysis of two recent Supreme Court decisions. *Public Administration Review* 41(5):558-564 (September/October 1981).

Mounts, Gregory J. Labor and the Supreme Court: significant decisions of 1979-80. *Monthly Labor Review* 104(4):13-22 (April 1981).

———. Significant decisions in labor cases. *Monthly Labor Review* 103(8):44-46 (August 1980).

Rosenbloom, David H. Public administrators and the judiciary: the "new partnership." *Public Administration Review* 47(1):75-83 (January/February 1987).

System spoiled. *Time* 115(15):71 (April 14, 1980).

Wise, Charles, and Rosemary O'Leary. Is federalism dead or alive in the Supreme Court?: implications for public administrators. *Public Administration Review* 52(6):559-572 (November/December 1992).

2081. United States v. Mitchell   April 15, 1980
 445 US 535   63 LEd2d 607   100 SCt 1349
  Am Indians (Wilkinson) 83-84, 129+

Baer, Susan D. The Public Trust Doctrine—a tool to make federal adminstrative agencies increase protection of public land and its resources. *Boston College Environmental Affairs Law Review* 15(2):385-436 (Winter 1988).

2082. Roberts v. United States   April 15, 1980
445 US 552   63 LEd2d 622   100 SCt 1358
   Almanac (1980):6A
   Sup Ct Review (1980):211-279
New rules for police and judges. *U.S. News and World Report* 88(16):8 (April 28, 1980).

2083. Payton v. New York   April 15, 1980
         Coupled with Riddick v. New York
445 US 573   63 LEd2d 639   100 SCt 1371
   Almanac (1980):4A-5A; (1982):5A
   Editorials 1980):505-508
   En Am Con 1325, 1371, 1628-1635
   Sup Ct Review (1982):1-24
Adler, Jerry, and Diane Camper. Court guards the door. *Newsweek* 95(17):81 (April 1980).
American survey: Court continues its bamboozlement. *Economist* 276(7140):21-22 July 5, 1980.
Beach, Bennet H., and Evan Thomas. Nine minds of its own. *Time* 116(3):75-76 (July 21, 1980).
Bender, Louis, and Steven Bender. Is the Supreme Court's decision in Baggot retroactive in application? *Journal of Taxation* 60(3):138-144 (March 1984).
Bernstein, Sidney, and Michael Eisenstein. 1981 Supreme Court update: the criminal law. *Trial* 17(10):54-60, 85 (October 1981).
———. 1982 Supreme Court update: the criminal law. *Trial* 18(9):45-50, 81 (September 1982).
Civil rights: an American's home is his castle. *Economist* 275(7130):24 (April 26, 1980).
Erickson, William H. Pronouncements of the U.S. Supreme Court 1979-1980. *Trial* 16(10):69-71 (October 1980).
Garvey, Denise P. Supreme Court review: Fourth Amendment—nonexistent home arrest entries. *Journal of Criminal Law and Criminology* 71(4):518-528 (Winter 1980).
Halberstam, Malvina. Agora: international kidnaping—in defense of the Supreme Court decision in Alvarez-Machain. *American Journal of International Law* 86(4):736-746 (October 1992).
House arrests. *Time* 115(17):65 (April 28, 1980).
Kamisar, Yale. The swing of the pendulum. *Nation* 239(9):271-274 (September 29, 1984).
New rules for police and judges. *U.S. News and World Report* 88(16):8 (April 28, 1980).
Regan, Richard J. Supreme Court roundup: 1979 term. *Thought* 55(219):487-455 (December 1980).
Welsh, Robert, and Ronald K. L. Collins. Taking state constitutions seriously: the protection of civil liberties has been shifting away from the U.S. Supreme Court. *Center Magazine* 14(5):6-35, 38-43 (September/October 1981).

2084. Owen v. City of Independence, Missouri   April 16, 1980
445 US 622   63 LEd2d 673   100 SCt 1398
   Almanac (1980):4A, 13A
   En Am Con 1285-1286, 1357
Adler, Jerry, and Diane Camper. Court guards the door. *Newsweek* 95(17):81 (April 1980).
Beach, Bennet H., and Evan Thomas. Nine minds of its own. *Time* 116(3):75-76 (July 21, 1980).
Fein, Bruce. A court that obeys the law. *National Review* 41(18):50-51 (September 29, 1989).
Groszyk, Walter S., Jr., and Thomas J. Madden. Managing without immunity: the challenge for state and local government officials in the 1980s. *Public Administration Review* 41(2):268-278 (March/April 1981).
Lee, Yong S. Civil liability of state and local governments: myth and reality. *Public Administration Review* 47(2):160-170 (March/April 1987).
Marfin, Gary C., and Jerome J. Hanus. Supreme Court restraints on state and local officials. *National Civic Review* 70(2):83-89 (February 1981).
Mounts, Gregory J. Labor and the Supreme Court: significant decisions of 1979-80. *Monthly Labor Review* 104(4):13-22 (April 1981).

Neuborne, Burt. Taking away the right to sue. *Nation* 239(9):268-271 (September 29, 1984).

Supreme Court further erodes municipal immunity. *American City and County* 95(6):16 (June 1980).

2085. Whalen v. United States   April 16, 1980
445 US 684   63 LEd2d 715   100 SCt 1432

New rules for police and judges. *U.S. News and World Report* 88(16):8 (April 28, 1980).

Schmitt, Deborah. Supreme Court review: Fifth Amendment—double jeopardy: legislative intent controls in crimes and punishment. *Journal of Criminal Law and Criminology* 74(4):1300-1314 (Winter 1983).

2086. Carlson v. Green   April 22, 1980
446 US 14   64 LEd2d 15   100 SCt 1468
    Almanac (1980):4A
    Brennan 101-106

2087. City of Mobile, Alabama v. Bolden   April 22, 1980
446 US 55   64 LEd2d 47   100 SCt 1490
    Almanac (1980):4A; (1982):373-376; (1986):11A; (1989):316
    En Am Con 1270, 1500-1506, 1987-1988

Action in the current Congress. *Congressional Digest* 60(12):295, 314 (December 1981).

Aronow, Geoffrey, and Owen Fiss. The High Court illusion of victory. *Nation* 235(21):647-650 (December 18, 1982).

Beach, Bennet H., and Evan Thomas. Nine minds of its own. *Time* 116(3):75-76 (July 21, 1980).

Berns, Walter. Voting rights and wrongs. *Commentary* 73(3):31-36 (March 1982).

Burns, Haywood. The activisim in not affirmative. *Nation* 239(9):264-268 (September 29, 1984).

Graham, Barbara Luck. Federal court policy-making and political equality: an analysis of judicial redistricting. *Western Political Quarterly* 44(1):101-117 (March 1991).

Miller, Arthur S. End of the "second recontruction." *Progressive* 46(2):38-39 (February 1982).

Neighbor, Howard D. Equity in the electoral/ representative structure: is the Supreme Court leaving the political thicket? *National Civic Review* 74(4):169-177, 181 (April 1985).

———. The Supreme Court speaks, sort of, on the 1982 Voting Rights Act Amendments. *National Civic Review* 75(6):346-353 (November/December 1986).

Poole, Isaiah J., Diane Camper, and Janice Simpson. The Court: uneasy defense of minority rights. *Black Enterprise* 11:54-56 (March 1981).

Pohlhaus, J. Francis. Fundamental shift seen for high court. *Crisis* 88(1):34-37 (January/February 1981).

Press, Aric, and Diane Camper. Right to vote, not a right to win. *Newsweek* 95(18):99 (May 5, 1980).

Public Affairs Council of Louisiana. Reapportionment for the 1980s: good faith and court decisions. *National Civic Review* 70(11):575-582 (December 1981).

Schwartz, Herman. Fifteen years of the Burger Court. *Nation* 239(9):262-264 (September 29, 1984).

Scope of enforcement. *Congressional Digest* 60(12):296-297(December 1981).

The Voting Rights Act. *Congressional Digest* 60(12):291 (December 1981).

Weber, Ronald E. Redistricting and the courts: judicial activism in the 1990s. *American Politics Quarterly* 23(2):204-228 (April 1995).

Zimmerman, Joseph F. Election systems and representative democracy: reflections on the Voting Rights Act of 1965. *National Civic Review* 84(4):287-309 (Fall/Winter 1995).

2088. Wengler v. Druggists Mutual Insurance Co.   April 22, 1980
446 US 142   64 LEd2d 107   100 SCt 1540
    Almanac (1980):7A
    En Am Con 1666-1673, 2045

Mounts, Gregory J. Labor and the Supreme Court: significant decisions of 1979-80. *Monthly Labor Review* 104(4):13-22 (April 1981).

———. Significant decisions in labor cases. *Monthly Labor Review* 103(8):44-46 (August 1980).

2089. City of Rome v. United States   April 22, 1980
446 US 156   64 LEd2d 119   100 SCt 1548

Abortion Moral 128-139
Almanac (1980):9A
Burger Years 95-108
En Am Con 1979-1987

Burns, Haywood. The activisim in not affirmative. *Nation* 239(9):264-268 (September 29, 1984).

Davis, Olethia. Tenuous interpretation: Sections 2 and 5 of the Voting Rights Act. *National Civic Review* 84(4):310-322 (Fall/Winter 1995).

Neighbor, Howard D. Equity in the electoral/ representative structure: is the Supreme Court leaving the political thicket? *National Civic Review* 74(4):169-177, 181 (April 1985).

Public Affairs Council of Louisiana. Reapportionment for the 1980s: good faith and court decisions. *National Civic Review* 70(11):575-582 (December 1981).

2090. Baldasar v. Illinois   April 22, 1980
446 US 222   64 LEd2d 169   100 SCt 1585
   Almanac (1980):6A
   Sup Ct Yearbook (1993-94):84-85

Feld, Barry C. The right to counsel in juvenile court: an empirical study of when lawyers appear and the difference they make. *Journal of Criminal Law and Criminology* 79(4):1185-1346 (Winter 1989).

2091. Marshall v. Jerrico, Inc.   April 28, 1980
446 US 238   64 LEd2d 182   100 SCt 1610
   Almanac (1980):14A

Mounts, Gregory J. Labor and the Supreme Court: significant decisions of 1979-80. *Monthly Labor Review* 104(4):13-22 (April 1981).

————. Significant decisions in labor cases. *Monthly Labor Review* 103(6):51-53 (June 1980).

2092. American Export Lines, Inc. v. Alvez   May 12, 1980
446 US 274   64 LEd2d 284   100 SCt 1673

George, James A., and Michelle M. O'Daniels. Recoverable damages in admiralty and maritime cases: muddied waters after Miles v. Apex Marine. *Trial* 31(5):58-65 (May 1995).

2093. Rhode Island v. Innis   May 12, 1980
446 US 291   64 LEd2d 297   100 SCt 1682
   Almanac (1980):4A
   Burger Court 86-88, 90-91
   Burger Years 143-168
   Const Law 391-393R
   Editorials (1980): 564-566
   En Am Con 1264-1265, 1400-1408, 1568

Bates, David M. Supreme Court review: Fifth Amendment—the meaning of interrogation under Miranda. *Journal of Criminal Law and Criminology* 71(4):466-473 (Winter 1980).

Collins, Ronald K. L., and Robert Welsh. Miranda's fate in the Burger Court. *Center Magazine* 13(5):43-52 (September/October 1980).

Erickson, William H. Pronouncements of the U.S. Supreme Court 1979-1980. *Trial* 16(10):69-71 (October 1980).

Kamisar, Yale. The swing of the pendulum. *Nation* 239(9):271-274 (September 29, 1984).

Press, Aric, and Diane Camper. God forbid excuse for the cops. *Newsweek* 95(21):93 (May 26, 1980).

Regan, Richard J. Supreme Court roundup: 1979 term. *Thought* 55(219):487-455 (December 1980).

Rights ruling: on chatting and busing. *Time* 115(21):59 (May 26, 1980).

White, Welsh S. Waiver and the death penalty: the implications of Estelle v. Smith. *Journal of Criminal Law and Criminology* 72(4):1522-1549 (Winter 1981).

2094. General Telephone Co. of the Northwest, Inc.   May 12, 1980
   v. Equal Employment Opportunity Commission (EEOC)
446 US 318   64 LEd2d 319   100 SCt 1698

Mounts, Gregory J., and Kate Farrell. Significant decisions in labor cases. 103(8):44-46 (August 1980).

Ruben, George. High Court further defines job bias. *Monthly Labor Review* 104(6):58 (June 1981).

2095. Cuyler v. Sullivan   May 12, 1980
446 US 335   64 LEd2d 333   100 SCt 1708

Bleiweiss, Shell J. Supreme Court review: Sixth Amendment—conflicts of interest in multiple representation of codefendants. *Journal of Criminal Law and Criminology* 71(4):529-537 (Winter 1980).

Bleiweiss, Shell J. Supreme Court review: Sixth and Fourteenth Amendments—counsel conflicts of interest in state court and the Supreme Court's power to vacate and remand. *Journal of Criminal Law and Criminology* 72(4):1326-1344 (Winter 1981).

2096. Nachman Corp. v. Pension Benefit Guaranty Corp.   May 12, 1980
446 US 359   64 LEd2d 354   100 SCt 1723

Mounts, Gregory J. Labor and the Supreme Court: significant decisions of 1979-80. *Monthly Labor Review* 104(4):13-22 (April 1981).

Mounts, Gregory J., and Kate Farrell. Constitutional quotas. *Monthly Labor Review* 103(9):53-56 (September 1980).

2097. Busic v. United States   May 19, 1980
       Coupled with LaRocca v. United States
446 US 398   64 LEd2d 381   100 SCt 1747
Almanac (1980):5A

2098. Godfrey v. Georgia   May 19, 1980
446 US 420   64 LEd2d 398   100 SCt 1759
Almanac (1980):6A
Court Public 310-314R
Death Penalty (Tushnet) 70-71
Death Penalty 80s 8-9
En Am Con 848

Ewer, Phyllis A. Supreme Court review: Eighth Amendment—the death penalty. *Journal of Criminal Law and Criminology* 71(4):538-546 (Winter 1980).

Murphy, Cornelius F. The Supreme Court and capital punishment: a new hands-off approach. *USA Today* 121(2574):51-52 (March 1993).

2099. United States v. Mendenhall   May 27, 1980
446 US 544   64 LEd2d 497   100 SCt 1870
Almanac (1980):4A-5A

Bernstein, Sidney. Supreme Court review. *Trial* 19(10):26, 28 (October 1983).

Butterfoss, Edwin J. Bright line seizures: the need for clarity in determining when Fourth Amendment activity begins. *Journal of Criminal Law and Criminology* 79(2):437-482 (Summer 1988).

Carter, Jeffrey A. Supreme Court review: Fourth Amendment—airport searches and seizures: where will the Court land? *Journal of Criminal Law and Criminology* 71(4):499-517 (Winter 1980).

Dripps, Donald A. Supreme Court review: it might be a roust, but it isn't a 'seizure.' *Trial* 28(1):66-68 (January 1992).

Guerra, Sandra. Domestic drug interdiction operations: finding the balance. *Journal of Criminal Law and Criminology* 82(4):1109-1161 (Winter 1992).

Seligman, Daniel. Score for the crooks. *Fortune* 102(1)[101(13)]:45-46 (June 30, 1980).

2100. Andrus v. Glover Construction Co.   May 27, 1980
446 US 608   64 LEd2d 548   100 SCt 1905

Supreme Court blocks Indian set-asides. *Engineering News Record* 204(23):70 (June 5, 1980).

2101. United States v. Havens   May 27, 1980
446 US 620   64 LEd2d 559   100 SCt 1912

Almanac (1980):5A

Erickson, William H. Pronouncements of the U.S. Supreme Court 1979-1980. *Trial* 16(10):69-71 (October 1980).

Regan, Richard J. Supreme Court roundup: 1979 term. *Thought* 55(219):487-455 (December 1980).

2102. Gomez v. Toledo   May 27, 1980
     446 US 635   64 LEd2d 572   100 SCt 1920
     Almanac (1980):13A

2103. Catalano, Inc. v. Target Sales, Inc.   May 27, 1980
     446 US 643   64 LEd2d 580   100 SCt 1925
     Parsons, William J. A Court decision with credit implications. *Credit and Financial Management* 82(2):33, 39 (January 1980).

     ———. Supreme Court rules on trade credit case. *Credit and Financial Management* 82(8):32-33 (September 1980).

     Werner, Ray O. Marketing and the United States Supreme Court, 1975-1981. *Journal of Marketing* 46(2):73-81 (Spring 1982).

2104. Andrus v. Shell Oil Co.   June 2, 1980
     446 US 657   64 LEd2d 593   100 SCt 1932
     Almanac (1980):12A

2105. Aaron v. Securities Exchange Commission (SEC)   June 2, 1980
     446 US 680   64 LEd2d 611   100 SCt 1945
     Almanac (1980):10A
     Burger Years 206-219
     Supreme Court decision backs Hochfelder case on "intent," sustains AICPA amicus brief. *Journal of Accountancy* 150(1):7 (July 1980).

2106. Supreme Court of Virginia v. Consumers Union of the United States   June 2, 1980
     446 US 719   64 LEd2d 641   100 SCt 1967
     Almanac (1980):13A
     Spurrier, Robert L., Jr. Paying the piper in federal civil rights litigation. *Public Administration Review* 43(3):199-208 (May/June 1983).

2107. Hanrahan v. Hampton   June 2, 1980
     446 US 754   64 LEd2d 670   100 SCt 1987
     Spurrier, Robert L., Jr. Paying the piper in federal civil rights litigation. *Public Administration Review* 43(3):199-208 (May/June 1983).

2108. Standefer v. United States   June 9, 1980
     447 US 10   64 LEd2d 689   100 SCt 1999
     Almanac (1980):7A

2109. Lewis v. BT Investment Managers, Inc.   June 9, 1980
     447 US 27   64 LEd2d 702   100 SCt 2009
     Almanac (1980):10A
     Business is target of court rulings. *U.S. News and World Report* 88(24):11 (June 23, 1980).

2110. New York Gaslight Club, Inc. v. Carey   June 9, 1980
     447 US 54   64 LEd2d 723   100 SCt 2024
     Almanac (1980):7A
     Mounts, Gregory J. Labor and the Supreme Court: significant decisions of 1979-80. *Monthly Labor Review* 104(4):13-22 (April 1981).

2111. Pruneyard Shopping Center v. Robins .   June 9, 1980
      447 US 74   64 LEd2d 741   100 SCt 2035
      Almanac (1980):9A
      En Am Con 1484, 1681
      New Right (Schwartz) 130-136
      Sup Ct Review (1982):195-241; (1994):57-128

      Business is target of court rulings. *U.S. News and World Report* 88(24):11 (June 23, 1980).

      First Amendment rights upheld by high court. *Editor and Publisher* 113(25):20A (June 21, 1980).

      Friedman, Lawrence M. State constitutions in historical perspective. *Annals of the American Academy of Political and Social Science* 496:33-42 (March 1988).

      Hippler, Thomas A. Reexamining 100 years of the Supreme Court regulatory taking doctrine: the principles of "noxious use," "average reciprocity of advantage," and "bundle of rights" from Mugler to Keystone Bituminous Coal. *Boston College Environmental Affairs Law Review* 14(4):653-727 (Summer 1987).

      Marcy, William R. To protect or not to protect—that is the question. *Social Education* 54(6):364-365 (October 1990).

      Mosk, Stanley. The emerging agenda in state constitutional rights law. *Annals of the American Academy of Political and Social Science* 496:54-64 (March 1988).

      Press, Aric, and Diane Camper. There's still life in states' rights. *Newsweek* 95(25):88 (June 23, 1980).

      Van Alstyne, William W. The recrudescence of property rights as the foremost principle of civil liberties: the first decade of the Burger Court. *Law and Contemporary Problems* 43(3):67-82 (Summer 1980).

2112. Consumer Product Safety Commission v. GTE Sylvania, Inc.   June 9, 1980
      447 US 102   64 LEd2d 766   100 SCt 2051
      Almanac (1980):14A

      Business is target of court rulings. *U.S. News and World Report* 88(24):11 (June 23, 1980).

      First Amendment rights upheld by high court. *Editor and Publisher* 113(25):20A (June 21, 1980).

2113. Washington v. Confederated Tribes of the Colville Indian Reservation   June 10, 1980
      447 US 134   65 LEd2d 10   100 SCt 2069
      Almanac (1980):12A
      Am Indians (Wilkinson) 110, 129, 201, 211-213

2114. Coffy v. Republic Steel Corp.   June 10, 1980
      447 US 191   65 LEd2d 53   100 SCt 2100
      Almanac (1980):8A

      Mounts, Gregory J. Significant decisions in labor cases. *Monthly Labor Review* 103(11):46-48 (November 1980).

2115. Exxon Corp. v. Wisconsin Department of Revenue   June 10, 1980
      447 US 207   65 LEd2d 66   100 SCt 2109
      Almanac (1980):3A, 10A
      En Am Con 1757-1760

      Another view of the Mobil Oil case. *CPA Journal* 50(9):67-68 (September 1980).

      Business is target of court rulings. *U.S. News and World Report* 88(24):11 (June 23, 1980).

      For the states, a freer hand over multinationals. *Business Week* (Industrial Edition) (2647):68H-68L (July 28, 1980).

      Jurinski, James John. A primer on the unitary business concept. *CPA Journal* 56(9):52-64 (September 1986).

      ———. The U.S. Supreme Court on the unitary tax. *Journal of Accountancy* 161(1):96 (January 1986).

      Peters, James H. Apportioning multistate income in Exxon: analyzing the decision; the implications. *Journal of Taxation* 53(4):246-250 (October 1980).

      Spears, L. Stephen . Applying the unitary business concept to diverse businesses. *CPA Journal* 58(6):34-45 (June 1988).

      Unger, Joseph. Investment income of multistate corporations. *CPA Journal* 63(6):66 (June 1993).

      Unitary tax: the Supreme Court says pay. *Economist* 275(7138):84-86 (June 21, 1980).

2116. Jenkins v. Anderson, Warden   June 10, 1980
      447 US 231   65 LEd2d 86   100 SCt 2124
          Almanac (1980):6A
          En Am Con 1019

      Erickson, William H. Pronouncements of the U.S. Supreme Court 1979-1980. *Trial* 16(10):69-71 (October
          1980).

      Melson, David E. Supreme Court review: Fourteenth Amendment—criminal procedure: the impeachment use
          of post-arrest silence which precedes the receipt of Miranda warnings. *Journal of Criminal Law and
          Criminology* 73(4):1572-1594 (Winter 1982).

      Mosk, Stanley. The emerging agenda in state constitutional rights law. *Annals of the American Academy of
          Political and Social Science* 496:54-64 (March 1988).

2117. Agins v. City of Tiburon   June 10, 1980
      447 US 255   65 LEd2d 106   100 SCt 2138
          Almanac (1980):4A
          En Am Con 1744-1751

      Blackwell, Robert J. Overlay zoning, performance standards, and environmental protection after Nollan. *Boston
          College Environmental Affairs Law Review* 16(3):615-659 (Spring 1989).

      Business is target of court rulings. *U.S. News and World Report* 88(24):11 (June 23, 1980).

      Darnell, Tim. The land and the law. *American City and County* 103(1):38-45 (January 1988).

      Folsom, Robin E. Executive Order 12,630: a president's manipulation of the Fifth Amendment's just
          compensation clause to achieve control over executive agency regulatory decisionmaking. *Boston College
          Environmental Affairs Law Review* 20(4):639-697 (Summer 1993).

      Hippler, Thomas A. Reexamining 100 years of the Supreme Court regulatory taking doctrine: the principles of
          "noxious use," "average reciprocity of advantage," and "bundle of rights" from Mugler to Keystone
          Bituminous Coal. *Boston College Environmental Affairs Law Review* 14(4):653-727 (Summer 1987).

      Randle, Ellen M. The national reserve system and transferable development rights: is the New Jersey Pinelands
          plan in unconstitutional "taking"? *Boston College Environmental Affairs Law Review* 10(1):183-241 (1982-
          83).

      Singer, Saul Jay. Flooding the Fifth Amendment: the National Flood Insurance Program and the "takings"
          clause. *Boston College Environmental Affairs Law Review* 17(2):323-379 (Winter 1990).

      Welsh, Robert, and Ronald K. L. Collins. Taking state constitutions seriously: the protection of civil liberties
          has been shifting away from the U.S. Supreme Court. *Center Magazine* 14(5):6-35, 38-43
          (September/October 1981).

2118. United States v. Henry   June 16, 1980
      447 US 264   65 LEd2d 115   100 SCt 2183
          Almanac (1980):4A, 6A
          En Am Con 1400-1408

      Bahl, Martin. The Sixth Amendment as constitutional theory: does originalism require that Massiah be
          abandoned? *Journal of Criminal Law and Criminology* 82(2):423-463 (Summer 1991).

      Beach, Bennet H., and Evan Thomas. Nine minds of its own. *Time* 116(3):75-76 (July 21, 1980).

      Cheap water for a lush valley. *Time* 115(26):51 (June 30, 1980).

      Collins, Ronald K. L., and Robert Welsh. Miranda's fate in the Burger court. *Center Magazine* 13(5):43-52
          (September/October 1980).

      Erickson, William H. Pronouncements of the U.S. Supreme Court 1979-1980. *Trial* 16(10):69-71 (October
          1980).

      Fulton, Joy D. Supreme Court review: Sixth Amendment—"Messiah" revitalized. *Journal of Criminal Law and
          Criminology* 71(4):601-609 (Winter 1980).

      Kamisar, Yale. The swing of the pendulum. *Nation* 239(9):271-274 (September 29, 1984).

      Lundstrom, Bruce D. Supreme Court review: Sixth Amendment—right to counsel: limited postindictment use
          of jailhouse informants is permissible. *Journal of Criminal Law and Criminology* 77(3):743-774 (Fall 1986).

      Press, Aric, Diane Camper, Mary Hager, Susan Dentzer, and Mitchell Zoler. Right to patent life. *Newsweek*
          95(26):74-75 (June 30, 1980).

White, Welsh S. Waiver and the death penalty: the implications of Estelle v. Smith. *Journal of Criminal Law and Criminology* 72(4):1522-1549 (Winter 1981).

2119. Diamond, Commissioner of Patents and Trademarks v. Chakrabarty   June 16, 1980
    447 US 303   65 LEd2d 144   100 SCt 2204
    Almanac (1980):10A
    Editorials (1980):700-711
    Equal (Harrell) 119-120
    Sup Ct Review (1980):57-75
Adding life to patent law. *Science News* 117(25):387 (June 21, 1980).
American survey: Court continues its bamboozlement. *Economist* 276(7140):21-22 July 5, 1980.
Beach, Bennet H., and Evan Thomas. Nine minds of its own. *Time* 116(3):75-76 (July 21, 1980).
Brennan, William J. Justice Brennan's dissent. *Chronicle of Higher Education* 20(25):12R (June 23, 1980).
Breu, Giovanna. Illinois biochemist wins a crucial patent fight, and a new era of life in a test tube begins. *People Weekly* 14(2):37-38 (July 14, 1980).
Burger, William E. Excerpts from opinions in High Court's patent ruling. *Chronicle of Higher Education* 20(25):11-12R (June 23, 1980).
Corcoran, Elizabeth. Science and business: patent medicine. *Scientific American* 259(3):128-130 (September 1988).
DeMott, John S., and Evan Thomas. Test-tube life: Reg. U.S. Pat. Off.: the Supreme Court protects the genetic engineers. *Time* 115(26):52-53 (June 30, 1980).
Fields, Cheryl M. Supreme Court lets scientists patent new forms of life. *Chronicle of Higher Education* 20(25):1, 11 (June 23, 1980).
Genetic patents: less than meets the eye. *Business Week* (Industrial Edition) (2643):48-49 (June 30, 1980).
Kass, Leon R. Patenting life. *Commentary* 72(6):45-57 (December 1981).
New arguments on an old issue. *Christianity Today* 29(18):56-57 (December 13, 1985).
New life forms: a clear road ahead? *U.S. News and World Report* 88(25):34-35 (June 30, 1980).
O'Rourke, C. Larry. Science policy: the Chakrabarty decision. *Environment* 22(6):4-5, 42 (July/August 1980).
Out of the bottle. *Progressive* 44(8):8 (August 1980).
Patent of life. *Economist* 275(7138):18 (June 21, 1980).
Patent ruling won't shift gene R&D goals. *Chemical Week* 126(26):57 (June 25, 1980).
Patenting germs. *Nation* 230(25):772-773 (June 28, 1980).
Patenting life: split perspectives. *Science News* 118(5):71 (August 2, 1980).
Press, Aric, Diane Camper, Mary Hager, Susan Dentzer, and Mitchell Zoler. Right to patent life. *Newsweek* 95(26):74-75 (June 30, 1980).
Rosenblatt, David P. The regulation of recombinant DNA tesearch: the alternative of local control. *Boston College Environmental Affairs Law Review* 10(1):37-78 (1982-83).
Smith, Donna H., and Jonathan King. Proprietary rights & public interest: the legal and legislative background. *Environment* 24(6):24-26, 33-37 (July/August 1982).
Supreme Court rules life forms patentable. *Chemical and Engineering News* 58(25):10R (June 23, 1980).
Wade, Nicholas. Court says lab-made life can be patented. *Science* 208(4451):1445 (June 27, 1980).
———. Supreme Court hears arguments on patenting life forms. *Science* 208(4439):31-32 (April 4, 1980).

2120. Brown v. Louisiana   June 16, 1980
    447 US 323   65 LEd2d 159   100 SCt 2214
    Almanac (1980):6A

2121. Bryant v. Yellen   June 16 1980
      Coupled with California v. Yellen
      Coupled with Imperial Irrigation District v. Yellen
    447 US 352   65 LEd2d 184   100 SCt 2232
    Almanac (1980):599, 3A,12A
Cheap water for a lush valley. *Time* 115(26):51 (June 30, 1980).
Empire built on water. *Newsweek* 95(26):75 (June 30, 1980).

2122. Reeves, Inc. v. Stake   June 19, 1980
     447 US 429   65 LEd2d 244   100 SCt 2271
       Almanac (1980):10A
       Const (Currie) 580-585
       En Am Con 1751-1755
     Powers, Carol L. State taxation of energy resources: affirmation of Commonwealth Edison Co. v. Montana. *Boston College Environmental Affairs Law Review* 10(2):503-564 (September 1982).
     Schwartz, Edward B. Water as an article of commerce: state embargoes spring a leak under Sporhase v. Nebraska. *Boston College Environmental Affairs Law Review* 12(1):103-169 (Fall 1985).

2123. Carey v. Brown   June 20, 1980
     447 US 455   65 LEd2d 263   100 SCt 2286
       Almanac (1980):14A
       Brennan 185-188
     Heck, Edward V., and Albert C. Ringelstein. The Burger court and the primacy of political expression. *Western Political Quarterly* 40(3):413-425 (September 1987).
     Mounts, Gregory J. Labor and the Supreme Court: significant decisions of 1979-80. *Monthly Labor Review* 104(4):13-22 (April 1981).

2124. National Labor Relations Board (NLRB) v. International Longshoremen's Association, AFL-CIO   June 20, 1980
     447 US 490   65 LEd2fd 289   100 SCt 2305
       Almanac (1980):4A, 11A
     Mounts, Gregory J. Labor and the Supreme Court: significant decisions of 1979-80. *Monthly Labor Review* 104(4):13-22 (April 1981).
     ————. Significant decisions in labor cases. *Monthly Labor Review* 103(11):46-48 (November 1980).

2125. Consolidated Edison Co. of New York, Inc. v. Public Service Commission of New York   June 20, 1980
     447 US 530   65 LEd2d 319   100 SCt 2326
       Almanac (1980):3A, 8A
     Beach, Bennet H., and Evan Thomas. Nine minds of its own. *Time* 116(3):75-76 (July 21, 1980).
     Corporate free speech rights upheld. *Editor and Publisher* 113(26):27 (June 28, 1980).
     Heath, Robert L., and Richard Alan Nelson. Image and issue advertising: a corporate and public policy perspective. *Journal of Marketing* 49(2):58-68 (Spring 1985).
     Press, Aric, Diane Camper, Mary Hager, Susan Dentzer, and Mitchell Zoler. Right to patent life. *Newsweek* 95(26):74-75 (June 30, 1980).
     Progress of regulation: utility free speech. *Public Utilities Fortnightly* 106(4):48-51 (August 14, 1980).

2126. Central Hudson Gas and Electric Corp. v. Public Service Commission of New York   June 20, 1980
     447 US 557   65 LEd2d 341   100 SCt 2343
       Almanac (1980):3A, 8A
       Const (Currie) 513-518
       En Am Con 223, 330-331
       Freedom (Cox) 41-48
       Sup Ct Review (1986):1-17
     Boedecker, Karl A., and Fred W. Morgan. The evolution of First Amendment protection for commercial speech. *Journal of Marketing* 59(1):38-47 (January 1995).
     Chemerinsky, Erwin. Supreme Court review: commercial speech: what degree of protection? *Trial* 29(8):66-68 (August 1993).
     Colford, Steven W. Ad industry loses hero in Brennan. *Advertising Age* 61(31):1, 44 (July 30, 1990).
     ————. Court revives ad-ban worry. *Advertising Age* 60(29):1, 24 (July 3, 1989).
     ————. High court's ruling sets back ad rights. *Advertising Age* 57(38):1, 62 (July 7, 1986).
     ————. Rehnquist slams ads' 1st Amendment shield. *Advertising Age* 57(37):12 (June 30, 1986).
     Corporate free speech rights upheld. *Editor and Publisher* 113(26):27 (June 28, 1980).
     Ferguson, James R. Scientific freedom, national security, and the First Amendment. *Science* 221(4611):620-624 (August 12, 1983).

Hayes, William C. High Court affirms right of free speech: now let's use it. [Editorial] *Electrical World* 194(2):3 (July 15, 1980).

Heath, Robert L., and Richard Alan Nelson. Image and issue advertising: a corporate and public policy perspective. *Journal of Marketing* 49(2):58-68 (Spring 1985).

Hovland, Roxanne, and Ronald E. Taylor. Advertising and commercial speech since the 1986 Posadas case. *Journalism Quarterly* 67(4):1083-1089 (Winter 1990).

Ile, Michael L., and Laura A. Kroll. Tobacco advertising and the First Amendment. *JAMA: The Journal of the American Medical Association* 264(12):1593-1594 (September 26, 1990).

Lewis, Wayne K. Environmental advertising: a delicate balance of rights. *Trial* 28(10):53-56 (October 1992).

Phillips, Kevin. A careful handshake between business and the media. *Across the Board* 18(10):22-26 (November 1981).

Progress of regulation: utility free speech. *Public Utilities Fortnightly* 106(4):48-51 (August 14, 1980).

Reed, O. Lee. Reading the tea leaves: future regulation of product-extrinsic advertising. *Business Horizons* 33(5):88-93 (September/October 1990).

Wulf, Melvin L. Advertising pleads the First: the great American smoke-in. *Commonweal* 114(3):75-79 (February 13, 1987).

2127. National Labor Relations Board (NLRB) v. Retail Store Employees Union, Local 1001   June 20, 1980
447 US 607   65 LEd2d 377   100 SCt 2372
   Almanac (1980):11A
   En Am Con 1378-1388
   Freedom (Cox) 41-48

Mounts, Gregory J. Labor and the Supreme Court: significant decisions of 1979-80. *Monthly Labor Review* 104(4):13-22 (April 1981).

———. Significant decisions in labor cases. *Monthly Labor Review* 103(11):46-48 (November 1980).

2128. Beck v. Alabama   June 20, 1980
447 US 625   65 LEd2d 392   100 SCt 2382
   Almanac (1980):4A

Ewer, Phyllis A. Supreme Court review: Eighth Amendment—the death penalty. *Journal of Criminal Law and Criminology* 71(4):538-546 (Winter 1980).

2129. Walter v. United States   June 20, 1980
447 US 649   65 LEd2d 410   100 SCt 2395
   Almanac (1980):5A
   En Am Con 1628-1635

Open season on state governments. *U.S. News and World Report* 89(1):8 (July 7, 1980).

2130. United States v. Raddatz   June 23, 1980
447 US 667   65 LEd2d 424   100 SCt 2406
   Almanac (1980):12A
   Sup Ct Review (1980):211-279; (1989):261-282

2131. Sun Ship, Inc. v. Pennsylvania   June 23, 1980
447 US 715   65 LEd2d 458   100 SCt 2432
   Almanac (1980):11A

Postol, Lawrence P., and Junius C. McElveen. Anchoring longshore. *Business Insurance* 14(33):17 (August 18, 1980).

2132. United States v. Payner   June 23, 1980
447 US 727   65 LEd2d 468   100 SCt 2439
   Almanac (1980):4A-5A

Abrams, Stuart E. Doe v. United States: has the veil of foreign bank secrecy been lifted? *Taxes* 67(4):238-242 (April 1989).

Beach, Bennet H., and Evan Thomas. Nine minds of its own. *Time* 116(3):75-76 (July 21, 1980).

Erickson, William H. Pronouncements of the U.S. Supreme Court 1979-1980. *Trial* 16(10):69-71 (October 1980).

Laver Rebecca J. Supreme Court review: Fourth Amendment—the court further limits standing. *Journal of Criminal Law and Criminology* 71(4):567-578 (Winter 1980).

Nelson, Caleb. The paradox of the exclusionary rule. *Public Interest* (96):117-130 (Summer 1989).

Open season on state governments. *U.S. News and World Report* 89(1):8 (July 7, 1980).

Rothwacks, Meyer. The tax advisor as a defendant: what he faces. *Practical Accountant* 14(4):53-64 (April 1981).

Thibodeau, Joseph H. Supreme Court in Payner admits stolen third-party evidence in tax prosecutions. *Journal of Taxation* 53(3):152-154 (September 1980).

When can tainted evidence be used? *Newsweek* 96(1):70 (July 7, 1980).

2133. Roadway Express, Inc. v. Piper   June 23, 1980
    447 US 752   65 LEd2d 488   100 SCt 2455
      Almanac (1980):12A

Mounts, Gregory J. Labor and the Supreme Court: significant decisions of 1979-80. *Monthly Labor Review* 104(4):13-22 (April 1981).

Spurrier, Robert L., Jr. Paying the piper in federal civil rights litigation. *Public Administration Review* 43(3):199-208 (May/June 1983).

2134. O'Bannon v. Town Court Nursing Center   June 23, 1980
    447 US 773   65 LEd2d 506   100 SCt 2467
      Almanac (1980):14A
      En Am Con 1465-1472

Grumet, Barbara R. Who is "due" process? *Public Administration Review* 42(4):321-326 (July/August 1982).

Vanderziel, Kathleen M. The Hatfield Riders and environmental preservation: what process is due? *Boston College Environmental Affairs Law Review* 19(2):431-479 (Fall/Winter 1991).

2135. Mohasco Corp. v. Silver   June 23, 1980
    447 US 807   65 LEd2d 532   100 SCt 2486

Ruben, George. High Court further defines job bias. *Monthly Labor Review* 104(6):58 (June 1981).

2136. Maine v. Thiboutot   June 25, 1980
    448 US 1   65 LEd2d 555   100 SCt 2502
      Almanac (1980):4A, 12A

Beach, Bennet H., and Evan Thomas. Nine minds of its own. *Time* 116(3):75-76 (July 21, 1980).

Groszyk, Walter S., Jr., and Thomas J. Madden. Managing without immunity: the challenge for state and local government officials in the 1980s. *Public Administration Review* 41(2):268-278 (March/April 1981).

Jaegal, Don, and N. Joseph Cayer. Public personnel administration by lawsuit: the impact of Supreme Court decisions on public employee litigiousness. *Public Administration Review* 51(3):211-221 (May/June 1991).

Lee, Yong S. Civil liability of state and local governments: myth and reality. *Public Administration Review* 47(2):160-170 (March/April 1987).

Marfin, Gary C., and Jerome J. Hanus. Supreme Court restraints on state and local officials. *National Civic Review* 70(2):83-89 (February 1981).

Mounts, Gregory J. Labor and the Supreme Court: significant decisions of 1979-80. *Monthly Labor Review* 104(4):13-22 (April 1981).

Open season on state governments. *U.S. News and World Report* 89(1):8 (July 7, 1980).

Spurrier, Robert L., Jr., Paying the piper in federal civil rights litigation. *Public Administration Review* 43(3):199-208 (May/June 1983).

Suing a state. *Time* 116(1):72 (July 7, 1980).

2137. Adams v. Texas   June 25, 1980
    448 US 38   65 LEd2d 581   100 SCt 2521
      Death Penalty 80s 9-12
      Death Penalty 90s 39-46, 199-205

Callans, Patrick J. Supreme Court review: Sixth Amendment—assembling a jury willing to impose the death penalty: a new disregard for a capital defendant's right. *Journal of Criminal Law and Criminology* 76(4):1027-1050 (Winter 1985).

Ewer, Phyllis A. Supreme Court review: Eighth Amendment—the death penalty. *Journal of Criminal Law and Criminology* 71(4):538-546 (Winter 1980).

In the Supreme Court of the United States Lockhart v. McCree: Amicus Curiae Brief for the American Psychological Association. *American Psychologist* 42(1):59-68 (January 1987).

2138. Ohio v. Roberts   June 25, 1980
     448 US 56   65 LEd2d 597   100 SCt 2531

Dripps, Donald A. Supreme Court review: the confrontation clause and the sexual abuse of children. *Trial* 27(5):11-13 (May 1991).

Erickson, William H. Pronouncements of the U.S. Supreme Court 1979-1980. *Trial* 16(10):69-71 (October 1980).

Hanusa, Julie. Supreme Court review: Sixth Amendment—the co-conspirator exemption to the hearsay rule: the confrontation clause and preliminary factual determinations relevant to federal rule of evidence 801(d)(2)(E). *Journal of Criminal Law and Criminology* 78(4):915-936 (Winter 1988).

2139. United States v. Salvucci   June 25, 1980
     448 US 83   65 LEd2d 619   100 SCt 2547
     Almanac (1980):4A

Laver Rebecca J. Supreme Court review: Fourth Amendment—the court further limits standing. *Journal of Criminal Law and Criminology* 71(4):567-578 (Winter 1980).

2140. Rawlings v. Kentucky   June 25, 1980
     448 US 98   65 LEd2d 633   100 SCt 2556
     Almanac (1980):5A

Hartman, Marshall J., and Sidney Bernstein. To Leon, and beyond; two commentators react. *Trial* 21(1):50-56 (January 1985).

Laver, Rebecca J. Supreme Court review: Fourth Amendment—the court further limits standing. *Journal of Criminal Law and Criminology* 71(4):567-578 (Winter 1980).

2141. Maher v. Gagne   June 25, 1980
     448 US 122   65 LEd2d 653   100 SCt 2570

Groszyk, Walter S., Jr., and Thomas J. Madden. Managing without immunity: the challenge for state and local government officials in the 1980s. *Public Administration Review* 41(2):268-278 (March/April 1981).

Ruben, George. High Court further defines job bias. *Monthly Labor Review* 104(6):58 (June 1981).

Spurrier, Robert L., Jr. Paying the piper in federal civil rights litigation. *Public Administration Review* 43(3):199-208 (May/June 1983).

2142. White Mountain Apache Tribe v. Bracker   June 27, 1980
     448 US 136   65 LEd2d 665   100 SCt 2578
     Almanac (1980):12A
     Am Indians (Wilkinson) 93-94, 98, 129+

2143. Central Machinery Co. v. Arizona State Tax Commission   June 27, 1980
     448 US 160   65 LEd2d 684   100 SCt 2592
     Almanac (1980):12A
     Am Indians (Wilkinson) 96-97, 129+

2144. Dawson Chemical Co. v. Rohm and Haas Co.   June 27, 1980
     448 US 176   65 LEd2d 696   100 SCt 2601
     Almanac (1980):10A
     Sup Ct Review (1980):57-75

American patents: dog in the manger. *Economist* 276(7140):71 July 5, 1980.

Rulings from the High Court: benzene, patents for unpatentable chemicals, the Hyde Amendment. *Science News* 118(2):20-21 (July 12, 1980).

2145. United States v. Ward dba L.O. Ward Oil and Gas Operations   June 27, 1980
      448 US 242   65 LEd2d 742   100 SCt 2636
         Almanac (1980):12A
         En Am Con 637-639

         Caginalp, O. A. Fifth Amendment privilege against self-incrimination and compulsory self-disclosure under the Clean Air and Clean Water Acts. *Boston College Environmental Affairs Law Review* 9(2):359-395 (1980-1981).

         Staas, John August. Supreme Court review: Fifth Amendment—statutory dilution of the privilege against self-incrimination. *Journal of Criminal Law and Criminology* 71(4):610-621 (Winter 1980).

         Stahl, Marc B. Asset forfeiture, burdens of proof and the war on drugs. *Journal of Criminal Law and Criminology* 83(2):274-337 (Summer 1992).

2146. Thomas v. Washington Gas Light Co.   June 27, 1980
      448 US 261   65 LEd2d 757   100 SCt 2647
         Postol, Lawrence P., and Junius C. McElveen. Anchoring longshore. *Business Insurance* 14(33):17 (August 18, 1980).

2147. Harris v. McRae   June 30, 1980
      448 US 297   65 LEd2d 784   100 SCt 2671
         Abortion (Frohock) 83, 89
         Abortion Am 162-164R, 227-228+
         Abortion Dec 80s Introduction, 1-43R
         Abortion Moral 35-44
         Abortion Pol (Jaffe) 185-208
         Abortion Pol (Rubin) 157-161+
         Abortion Quest 115-118+
         Almanac (1980):4A, 7A; (1993):636
         Brennan 313-316
         Burger Years 109-124
         Const (Currie) 471-475
         Const Law 310-311+
         Court Public 385-386, 437-452R
         Editorials (1980):261-263, 762-771; (1981):503-505
         En Am Con 904-905, 944, 1552-1558
         Hard Choices 184-187, 191-192, 313+
         Liberty 634-638+
         Nobody's 11-13

Abortion and the Constitution. [Editorial] *America* 143(2):24 (July 19-26, 1980).

American survey: Court continues its bamboozlement. *Economist* 276(7140):21-22 July 5, 1980.

Beach, Bennet H., and Evan Thomas. Nine minds of its own. *Time* 116(3):75-76 (July 21, 1980).

Binion, Gayle. The Burger court and the rights of the poor. *Center Magazine* 15(2):2-7 (March/April 1982).

Blank, Robert H. Judicial decision making and biological fact: Roe v. Wade and the unresolved question of fetal viability. *Western Political Quarterly* 37(4):584-602 (December 1984).

Church, George J., and Evan Thomas. Four big decisions: High Court rules on abortions, race quotas, open trials, safety rules. *Time* 116(2):10-13 (July 14, 1980).

Cockburn, Alexander. Aborted justice: behind the Supreme Court ruling on abortion lies a history of subversion of American liberalism. *New Statesman and Society* 2(58):19-20 (July 14, 1989).

Courtship. *National Review* 32(15):877 (July 25, 1980).

Dissent of four just men. *Ms.* 9(3):24R (September 1980).

Edges of life, 2. *Commonweal* 107(14):421 (August 1, 1980).

Erickson, William H. Pronouncements of the U.S. Supreme Court 1979-1980. *Trial* 16(10):69-71 (October 1980).

Ewer, Phyllis A. Supreme Court review: Court upholds parental notice requirement before allowing abortions on minors. *Journal of Criminal Law and Criminology* 72(4):1461-1481 (Winter 1981).

5 Court rulings on explosive issues. *U.S. News and World Report* 88(8):6 (March 3, 1980).

Hyde Amendement. [Editorial] *America* 142(9):181 (March 8, 1980).

Kelley, Dean M. "Let them eat cake," says the Supreme Court. *Christian Century* 97(27):820-824 (August 27-September 3, 1980).

McDaniel, Ann. Countdown on abortion. *Newsweek* 113(4):50 (January 23, 1989).

Neuhaus, Richard John. Hyde and hysteria: the liberal banner has been planted on the wrong side of the abortion debates. *Christian Century* 97(28):849-852 (September 10-17, 1980).

Not free to choose. [Editorial] *Nation* 231(2):33 (July 12, 1980).

Press, Aric, and Diane Camper. High Court hits tellers of secrets. *Newsweek* 95(9):50-51 (March 3, 1980).

———. High Court's grand finale. *Newsweek* 96(2):22-25 (July 14, 1980).

Overkill on abortion [Editorial]. *America* 155(1) (July 5-12, 1986).

Readers' response: many sides to the abortion furor. [Editorial] *Christian Century* 97(35):1066-1068 (November 5, 1980).

Regan, Richard J. Supreme Court roundup: 1979 term. *Thought* 55(219):487-455 (December 1980).

———. Supreme Court roundup: 1980 term. *Thought* 56(223):491-502 (December 1981).

Rose, Jonathan. Decide 10 landmark cases that define your rights. *Scholastic Update* 119(1):7-9, 21 (September 8, 1986).

Rulings from the High Court: benzene, patents for unpatentable chemicals, the Hyde Amendment. *Science News* 118(2):20-21 (July 12, 1980).

Trussell, James, and Jane Menken. Two Princeton scholars cast a cold eye on the Supreme Court's abortion ruling: nobody wins. *People Weekly* 14(3):77-78, 81, 83 (July 21, 1980).

Wages of faithlessness ruling. *Time* 115(9):48-49 (March 3, 1980).

Where abortion fight goes from here. *U.S. News and World Report* 89(2):42 (July 14, 1980).

2148. Williams v. Zbaraz   June 30, 1980
      448 US 358   65 LEd2d 831   100 SCt 2694
      Abortion Pol (Rubin) 157-161+
      Almanac (1980):4A,7A
      Liberty 633-635
      Where abortion fight goes from here. *U.S. News and World Report* 89(2):42 (July 14, 1980).

2149. United States v. Sioux Nation of Indians   June 30, 1980
      448 US 371   65 LEd2d 844   100 SCt 2716
      Almanac (1980):3A
      Am Indians (Wilkinson) 79-81, 129-130+
      Chu, Daniel. About faces. *People Weekly* 36(2):68-70 (July 22, 1991).
      Cort'es, Carlos E., and Van L. Perkins. U.S. Supreme Court decisions on diversity. *Education Digest* 46(6):21-24 (February 1981).
      Norgren, Jill, and Petra T. Shattuck. Black Hills whitewash. *Nation* 230(18):557-560 (May 10, 1980).
      Press, Aric, and Diane Camper. High Court's grand finale. *Newsweek* 96(2):22-25 (July 14, 1980).

2150. Reid v. Georgia   June 30, 1980
      448 US 438   65 LEd2d 890   100 SCt 2752
      Carter, Jeffrey A. Supreme Court review: Fourth Amendment—airport searches and seizures: where will the Court land? *Journal of Criminal Law and Criminology* 71(4):499-517 (Winter 1980).

2151. Fullilove v. Klutznick   July 2, 1980
      448 US 448   65 LEd2d 902   100 SCt 2758
      Abortion Moral 128-139
      Affirmative (Greene) 80-85
      Affirmative (Woods) 74-75
      Almanac (1980):4A, 7A
      Ascent 272-274

Bakke 248-250

Behind Bakke 156-160

Burger Court 129-131

Burger Years 95-108

Const (Currie) 482-488

Const Law 568-569, 572-575

Court Public 100, 194

Culture 130-141

En Am Con 273-280, 566-568, 825, 1500-1506, 1506-1507

Guide (CQ) 55

Magic 330-331

New Right (Whitaker) 142-168

Sup Ct Ind 263

Sup Ct Review (1988):85-113; (1989):1-51; (1995):1-43

Sup Ct Yearbook (1994-95):27-32

Beach, Bennet H., and Evan Thomas. Nine minds of its own. *Time* 116(3):75-76 (July 21, 1980).

Burns, Haywood. The activisim in not affirmative. *Nation* 239(9):264-268 (September 29, 1984).

Campbell, Bebe Moore. Supreme Court challenge: laying off affirmative action. *Black Enterprise* 13(7):31 (February 1983).

Camper, Diane. . . . and justice for whom? *Black Enterprise* 15(8):52-55 (March 1985).

Church, George J., and Evan Thomas. Four big decisions: High Court rules on abortions, race quotas, open trials, safety rules. *Time* 116(2):10-13 (July 14, 1980).

Court finds MBE set-aside legal. *Engineering News Record* 204(2):12-13 (July 10, 1980).

Court speaks on quotas, trials, job risks. *U.S. News and World Report* 89(2):10 (July 14, 1980).

Eastland, Terry. Racial preference in court (again). *Commentary* 87(1):32-38 (January 1989).

———. Toward a real restoration of civil rights. *Commentary* 88(5):25-29 (November 1989).

Erickson, William H. Pronouncements of the U.S. Supreme Court 1979-1980. *Trial* 16(10):69-71 (October 1980).

Erler, Edward J. Brown v. Board of Education at 30. *National Review* 36(17):26-28, 30-31, 53 (September 7, 1984).

Frederickson, H. George. Public administration and social equity. *Public Administration Review* 50(2):228-237 (March/April 1990).

Gest, Ted. Seniority vs. minorities—impact of Court ruling. *U.S. News and World Report* 96(25):22-23 (June 25, 1984).

Hairston, Julie B. Affirmative action plans in disarray after Croson. *American City and County* 104(6):62-66 (June 1989).

Koch color bind. [Editorial] *Nation* 231(3):67-68 (July 19-26, 1980).

Korman, Richard, and Tom Ichniowski. Feds face narrower options. *ENR* 234(24):8-9 (June 19, 1995).

Lamb, Charles M. Legal foundations of civil rights and pluralism. *Annals of the American Academy of Political and Social Science* 454:13-25 (March 1981).

LaNoue, George R. Split visions: minority business set-asides. *Annals of the American Academy of Political and Social Science* 523:104-116 (September 1992).

MBE reg. war escalates. *Engineering News Record* 205(3):87-88 (July 17, 1980).

Morehead, Jere W., and Peter J. Shedd. Civil rights and affirmative action: revolution or fine-tuning? *Business Horizons* 33(5):53-60 (September/October 1990).

Mounts, Gregory J., and Kate Farrell. Constitutional quotas. *Monthly Labor Review* 103(9):53-56 (September 1980).

———. Significant decisions in labor cases. *Monthly Labor Review* 103(12):63-64 (December 1980).

Pace, Joseph M., and Zachary Smith. Understanding affirmative action: from the practitioner's perspective. *Public Personnel Management* 24(2):139-147 (Summer 1995).

Poole, Isaiah J. Saving the set-asides. *Black Enterprise* 11(2):21 (September 1980).

Poole, Isaiah J., Diane Camper, and Janice Simpson. The Court: uneasy defense of minority rights. *Black Enterprise* 11:54-56 (March 1981).

Press, Aric, and Diane Camper. High Court's grand finale. *Newsweek* 96(2):22-25 (July 14, 1980).

Press, Aric, and Ann McDaniel. A woman's day in court. *Newsweek* 109(14):58-59 (April 6, 1987).

Regan, Richard J. Supreme Court roundup: 1979 term. *Thought* 55(219):487-455 (December 1980).

―――. Supreme Court roundup: 1980 term. *Thought* 56(223):491-502 (December 1981).

Reid-Dove, Allyson, and Michael E. Howard. "Night has fallen on the Court . . ." *Black Enterprise* 20(2):44-45 (September 1989).

Reynolds, William Bradford. Affirmative action and its negative repercussions. *Annals of the American Academy of Political and Social Science* 523:38-49 (September 1992).

Rice, Mitchell F. Government set-asides, minority business enterprises, and the Supreme Court. *Public Administration Review* 51(2):114-122 (March/April 1991).

Roberts, Paul Craig, and Lawrence M. Stratton, Jr. Color code. *National Review* 47(5):36, 51, 80 (March 20, 1995).

Thomas, Evan, David Beckwith, and Anne Constable. Reagan's Mr. Right: Rehnquist is picked for the court's top job. *Time* 127(26):24-33 (June 30, 1986).

Tollett, Kenneth S., Jeanette J. Leonard, and Portia P. James. A color-conscious constitution: the one pervading purpose redux. *Journal of Negro Education* 52(3):189-212 (Summer 1983).

Tortora, Anthony. Ex parte McCardle. *National Review* 32(19):1140-1141, 1157 (September 19, 1980).

Vile, John R., and Kathy Ruth McCoy. The Memphis case: another precedent? *Personnel* 62(7):72-76 (July 1985).

2152. Richmond Newspapers, Inc. v. Virginia   July 2, 1980
    448 US 555   65 LEd2d 973   100 SCt 2814

Almanac (1980):3A, 8A
Ascent 169-171
Brennan 176-179
Burger Court 9-11, 22-23, 25-27
Const (Currie) 523-527
Const Law 431-433R
Court Public 318-319, 362-371R
En Am Con 683-686, 770-773, 781, 797-804, 1492-1494, 1569, 1592-1593
Fourth 190-199+
Freedom (Cox) 22-32+
New Right (Schwartz) 62-67+
Sup Ct Review (1980):1-25; (1981):157-192

Beach, Bennet H., and Evan Thomas. Nine minds of its own. *Time* 116(3):75-76 (July 21, 1980).

Bleisch, N. David. The *Congressional Record* and the First Amendment: accuracy is the best policy. *Boston College Environmental Affairs Law Review* 12(2):341-379 (Winter 1985).

Bolbach, Cynthia J. Access to information: affirming the press's right. *Christian Century* 97(29):879-883 (September 24, 1980).

Boylan, James. How free is the press? *Columbia Journalism Review* 26(3):27-32 (September/October 1987).

Brown, Robert U. Shop talk at thirty: paranoid press. [Editorial] *Editor and Publisher* 113(28):66 (July 12, 1980).

Burrows, Karen B. Supreme Court review: First Amendment—the right of access to criminal trials extended. *Journal of Criminal Law and Criminology* 73(4):1388-1407 (Winter 1982).

Church, George J., and Evan Thomas. Four big decisions: High Court rules on abortions, race quotas, open trials, safety rules. *Time* 116(2):10-13 (July 14, 1980).

Court speaks on quotas, trials, job risks. *U.S. News and World Report* 89(2):10 (July 14, 1980).

Dworkin, Ronald. Is the press losing the First Amendment? *New York Review of Books* 27(19):49-57 (December 4, 1980).

Erickson, William H. 1981-1982 U.S. Supreme court decisions. *Trial* 18(11):44-49, 109 (November 1982).

―――. Pronouncements of the U.S. Supreme Court 1979-1980. *Trial* 16(10):69-71 (October 1980).

Gloede, Bill. Press leaders laud Richmond ruling. *Editor and Publisher* 113(28):12, 54 (July 12, 1980).

High Court refuses to hear closure cases. *Editor and Publisher* 115(12):22 (March 20, 1982).

Hill, I. William. Closed trials ruled out by U.S. Supreme Court. *Editor and Publisher* 113(27):10 (July 5, 1980).

―――. Powell absents himself from gag order hearing. *Editor and Publisher* 113(9):27 (March 1, 1980).

Howard, A. E. Dick. The press in court. *Wilson Quarterly* 6(5):86-93 (Special Issue 1982).

Leeper, Roy V. Richmond Newspapers, Inc. v. Virginia and the emerging right of access. *Journalism Quarterly* 61(3):615-622 (Autumn 1984).

Lubben, Craig H. Supreme Court review: First Amendment—constitutional right of access to criminal trials. *Journal of Criminal Law and Criminology* 71(4):547-557 (Winter 1980).

Malak, Michael P. Supreme Court review: First Amendment—guarantee of public access to voir dire. *Journal of Criminal Law and Criminology* 75(3):583-608 (Fall 1984).

Maybe court will decide right to gather news. *Editor and Publisher* 113(17):28 (April 26, 1980).

Press, Aric, and Diane Camper. High Court's grand finale. *Newsweek* 96(2):22-25 (July 14, 1980).

Regan, Richard J. Supreme Court roundup: 1979 term. *Thought* 55(219):487-455 (December 1980).

———. Supreme Court roundup: 1980 term. *Thought* 56(223):491-502 (December 1981).

Reid, Traciel V. Judicial policy-making and implementation: an empirical examination. *Western Political Quarterly* 41(3):509-527 (September 1988).

Supreme Court to hear closed trial case. *Editor and Publisher* 115[114]:11 (November 28, 1981).

Text of Richmond v. Virginia decision. *Editor and Publisher* 113:18-20, 48-49, 52-53R (July 12, 1980).

Thomas, Evan, David Beckwith, and Anne Constable. Reagan's Mr. Right: Rehnquist is picked for the court's top job. *Time* 127(26):24-33 (June 30, 1986).

Welsh, Robert, and Ronald K. L. Collins. Taking state constitutions seriously: the protection of civil liberties has been shifting away from the U.S. Supreme Court. *Center Magazine* 14(5):6-35, 38-43 (September/October 1981).

2153. Industrial Union Department, AFL-CIO v. American Petroleum Institute   July 2, 1980
Benzene Case
        Coupled with Marshall, Secretary of Labor v. American Petroleum Institute
448 US 607   65 LEd2d 1010   100 SCt 2844
    Almanac (1980):4A, 11A-12A
    Burger Years 191-205
    Sup Ct Review (1981):291-307; (1988):1-41

American survey: Court continues its bamboozlement. *Economist* 276(7140):21-22 July 5, 1980.

Baird, Vincent C. Industrial Union Department, AFL-CIO v. American Petroleum Institute: limiting OSHA's authority to regulate workplace carcinogens under the Occupational Safety and Health Act. *Boston College Environmental Affairs Law Review* 9(3):623-685 (1981-82).

Bangser, Paul M. An inherent role for cost-benefit analysis in judicial review of agency decisions: a new perspective on OSHA rulemaking. *Boston College Environmental Affairs Law Review* 10(2):365-444 (September 1982).

Beach, Bennet H., and Evan Thomas. Nine minds of its own. *Time* 116(3):75-76 (July 21, 1980).

A blow to OSHA's benzene rules. *Chemical Week* 127(2):11-12 (July 9, 1980).

Church, George J., and Evan Thomas. Four big decisions: High Court rules on abortions, race quotas, open trials, safety rules. *Time* 116(2):10-13 (July 14, 1980).

Court leaves OSHA hanging. *Business Week* (2646):67-68 (July 21, 1980).

Court speaks on quotas, trials, job risks. *U.S. News and World Report* 89(2):10 (July 14, 1980).

Erickson, William H. Pronouncements of the U.S. Supreme Court 1979-1980. *Trial* 16(10):69-71 (October 1980).

Gadfly to the brethren. *Time* 116(3):76 (July 21, 1980).

High Court overturns OSHA benzene rule. *Chemical and Engineering News* 58(27):4-5 (July 7, 1980).

MacCarthy, Mark. A review of some normative and conceptual issues in occupational safety and health. *Boston College Environmental Affairs Law Review* 9(4):773-814 (1981-82).

McDowell, Gary L. Congress and the courts. *Public Interest* (100):89-101 (Summer 1990).

Morrison, Alan B. Close reins on the bureaucracy. *Nation* 239(9):290-294 (September 29, 1984).

Mounts, Gregory J. Labor and the Supreme Court: significant decisions of 1979-80. *Monthly Labor Review* 104(4):13-22 (April 1981).

Mounts, Gregory J., and Kate Farrell. Constitutional quotas. *Monthly Labor Review* 103(9):53-56 (September 1980).

Nelson, Joani. Benzine tops high court docket. *Industry Week* 204(2):19-21 (January 21, 1980).

OSHA standard found unjustified. *Engineering News Record* 204(2):73:73 (July 10, 1980).

Press, Aric, and Diane Camper. High Court's grand finale. *Newsweek* 96(2):22-25 (July 14, 1980).

Rulings from the High Court: benzene, patents for unpatentable chemicals, the Hyde Amendment. *Science News* 118(2):20-21 (July 12, 1980).

Smith, R. Jeffrey. Light rein falls on OSHA. *Science* 209(4456):567-568 (August 1, 1980).

Supreme Court rules against OSHA on its benzene standard. *Chemical Marketing Reporter* 218(1):3, 53 (July 7, 1980).

Verespej, Michael A., and Joani Nelson. Putting the burden of proof on OSHA. *Industry Week* 206(2):18-19, 23-24 (July 21, 1980).

2154. Hughes v. Rowe						November 10, 1980
	449 US 5				66 LEd2d 163				101 SCt 173

	Spurrier, Robert L., Jr. Paying the piper in federal civil rights litigation. *Public Administration Review* 43(3):199-208 (May/June 1983).

2155. Dennis v. Sparks						November 17, 1980
	449 US 24				66 LEd2d 185				101 SCt 183
		Almanac (1981):15A

2156. Stone v. Graham						November 17, 1980
	449 US 39				66 LEd2d 199				101 SCt 192
		Burger Years 56-91
		Const (Currie) 531-533
		En Am Con 1537-1538, 1650-1658
		Godless 98
		Original (Davis) 88-89, 145-146
		Religion 77-79, 132, 136-137+

	Bork, Robert H. What to do about the First Amendment. *Commentary* 99(2):23-29 (February 1995).

	Carols get green light, Ten Commandments get red. *Christianity Today* 24(21):59-60 (December 12, 1980).

	Church-state commandments: the justices dig in as a constitutional clash looms. *Time* 116(22):74 (December 1, 1980).

	The Court decisions. *Congressional Digest* 63(5):132-134, 160 (May 1984).

	Hammond, Phillip E. The courts and secular humanism. *Society* 21(4):11-16 (May/June 1984).

	Meese, Edwin, III. Saving the Constitution: the law of the Constitution. *National Review* 39(13):30-33 (July 17, 1987).

	Methvin, Eugene H. Let us pray! *Reader's Digest* 141(847):75-79 (November 1992).

	———. The Supreme Court: justice in the balance. *Reader's Digest* 125(751):96-101 (November 1984).

	Newsnotes: 11th Commandment: no Ten Commandments in the classroom. *Phi Delta Kappan* 62(5):405 (January 1981).

	Prayer in public schools. *Congressional Digest* 74(1):3-32 (January 1995).

	Regan, Richard J. Supreme Court roundup: 1980 term. *Thought* 56(223):491-502 (December 1981).

	Woodward, Kenneth L., and Nadine Joseph. The return of the fourth R. *Newsweek* 117(23):56-57 (June 10, 1991).

2157. County of Imperial, California v. Munoz					December 2, 1980
	449 US 54				66 LEd2d 258				101 SCt 289
		Almanac (1981):14A

2158. Environmental Protection Agency (EPA) v. National Crushed Stone Association					December 2, 1980
		Coupled with Costle v. Consolidated Coal Co.
	449 US 64				66 LEd2d 268				101 SCt 295
		Almanac (1981):12A

	Funk, William. The exception that approves the rule: FDF variances under the Clean Water Act. *Boston College Environmental Affairs Law Review* 13(1):1-60 (Fall 1985).

	Nelson-Horchler, Joani. High Court mulls regulators' reach. *Industry Week* 207(2):18-23 (October 27, 1980).

	Sandler, Ross. Law: Supreme Court trends in environmental law. *Environment* 23(7):4-5 (September 1981).

	A time for crucial rulings on job bias. *Business Week* (Industrial Edition) (2658):46-47 (October 13, 1980).

2159. Allen v. McCurry   December 9, 1980
       449 US 90   66 LEd2d 308   101 SCt 411
       Almanac (1981):14A

2160. United States v. DiFrancesco   December 9, 1980
       449 US 117   66 LE2d 328   101 SCt 426
       Almanac (1981):5A
       En Am Con 563, 576-578
       Bernstein, Sidney, and Michael Eisenstein. 1981 Supreme Court update: the criminal law. *Trial* 17(10):54-60,
            85 (October 1981).
       Pachciarek, Anne M. Supreme Court review: Fifth Amendment—extension of double jeopardy protection to
            sentencing. *Journal of Criminal Law and Criminology* 72(4):1276-1287 (Winter 1981).
       Toward more uniform sentences:despite double jeopardy, prosecutors can appeal light terms. *Time* 116(25):74
            (December 22, 1980).

2161. Webb's Fabulous Pharmacies, Inc. v. Beckwith   December 9, 1980
       449 US 155   66 LEd2d 358   101 SCt 446
       Almanac (1981):10A

2162. United States Railroad Retirement Board v. Fritz   December 9, 1980
       449 US 166   66 LEd2d 368   101 SCt 453
       Almanac (1981):7A-8A
       En Am Con 1796-1803

2163. United States v. Will   December 15, 1980
       449 US 200   66 LEd2d 392   101 SCt 471
       Almanac (1981):14A-15A
       Ascent 42-44, 425

2164. Federal Trade Commission (FTC) v. Standard Oil Co. of California   December 15, 1980
       449 US 232   66 LEd2d 416   101 SCt 488
       Almanac (1981):14A
       A time for crucial rulings on job bias. *Business Week* (Industrial Edition) (2658):46-47 (October 13, 1980).
       Werner, Ray O. Marketing and the United States Supreme Court, 1975-1981. *Journal of Marketing* 46(2):73-81
            (Spring 1982).

2165. Delaware State College v. Ricks   December 15, 1980
       449 US 250   66 LEd2d 431   101 SCt 498
       Almanac (1981):14A
       Brooks, Thornton H., M. Daniel McGinn, and William P. H. Cary. Second generation problems facing
            employers in employment discrimination cases: continuing violations, pendent state claims, and double
            attorneys' fees. *Law and Contemporary Problems* 49(4):26-51 (Autumn 1986).
       Fields, Cheryl M. High Court sets time limits on filing of bias complaints. *Chronicle of Higher Education*
            21(18):19 (Janury 12, 1981).
       Flygare, Thomas J. Schools and the law: Supreme Court decides when discrimination complaints against
            educational institutions must be filed. *Phi Delta Kappan* 62(8):597-598 (April 1981).
       Franke, Ann H., and Martha A. Toll. Legal watch: Court decisions hinder women's, minorities' rights.
            Academe 75(4):47 (July/August 1989).
       Rabban, David M. AAUP in the courts: the association's representation of faculty members and faculty causes
            in appellate litigation. *Academe* 69(2):1a-12a (March/April 1983).

2166. Potomac Electric Power Co. v. Director Office of Workers Compensation Programs,   December 15, 1980
       United States Department of Labor
       449 US 268   66 LEd2d 446   101 SCt 509
       Almanac (1981):11A

Postol, Lawrence P. Maritime industry seeks benefit relief. *Business Insurance* 15(21):21 (May 25, 1981).

2167. Allstate Insurance Co. v. Hague   January 13, 1981
      449 US 302   66 LEd2d 521   101 SCt 633
         Almanac (1981):15A
         Const (Currie) 580-585
      DeMott, Deborah A. Perspectives on choice of law for corporate internal affairs. *Law and Contemporary Problems* 48(3):161-198 (Summer 1985).

2168. Watkins v. Sowders, Warden   January 13, 1981
           Coupled with Summitt v. Sowders, Warden
      449 US 341   66 LEd2d 549   101 SCt 654
         Almanac (1981):5A
      Schneider, Robert Roy. Supreme Court review: Fourteenth Amendment—the last gasp of due process requirements on eyewitness identifications: the admissibility of identification evidence may be determined in the jury's presence. *Journal of Criminal Law and Criminology* 72(4):1410-1425 (Winter 1981).

2169. United States v. Morrison   January 13, 1981
      449 US 361   66 LEd2d 564   101 SCt 665
         Almanac (1981):6A
      Thomas, Evan. Sam's hour of glory—and agony. *Time* 117(4):78-79 (January 26, 1981).

2170. Firestone Tire and Rubber Co. v. Risjord   January 13, 1981
      449 US 368   66 LEd2d 571   101 SCt 669
         Almanac (1981):14A

2171. Upjohn Co. v. United States   January 13, 1981
      449 US 383   66 LEd2d 584   101 SCt 677
         Almanac (1981):6A
         Sup Ct Review (1981):309-365
      Bernstein, Sidney, and Michael Eisenstein. 1981 Supreme Court update: the criminal law. *Trial* 17(10):54-60, 85 (October 1981).
      Corporate law: Supreme Court extends attorney-client privilege below senior executives. *Journal of Accountancy* 151(3):22-23 (March 1981).
      Corporate secrets safe with lawyers. *Industry Week* 208(3):27 (February 9, 1981).
      Feld, Lawrence S. Sup. Ct. in Upjohn protects attorney-client privilege; upholds the work-product doctrine. *Journal of Taxation* 54(4):210-214 (April 1981).
      Glanzer, Seymour, and Paul R. Taskier. Attorneys before the grand jury: assertion of the attorney-client privilege to protect a clients identity. *Journal of Criminal Law and Criminology* 75(4):1070-1099 (Winter 1984).
      Major Supreme Court business decisions in the 1980-81 Term. *Business Week* (Industrial Edition) (2697):62 (July 20, 1981).
      Nelson-Horchler, Joani. High Court mulls regulators' reach. *Industry Week* 207(2):18-23 (October 27, 1980).
      A time for crucial rulings on job bias. *Business Week* (Industrial Edition) (2658):46-47 (October 13, 1980).
      Scheibla, Shirley Hobbs. Attorney-client privilege: the Upjohn case leaves basic issues unresolved. *Barron's* 61(7):11, 24-25, 39 (February 16, 1981).
      Weintraub, Benjamin. Creditors' committee composition: attorney/client privileges. *Credit and Finanical Management* 89(9):43-44 (October 1987).
      What secrets can company lawyers keep? *Business Week* (Industrial Edition) (2663):197-198 (November 17, 1980).

2172. United States v. Cortez   January 21, 1981
      449 US 411   66 LEd2d 621   101 SCt 690
         Almanac (1981):5A
         En Am Con 1780-1782

2173. Rubin v. United States   January 21, 1981
       449 US 424   66 LEd2d 633   101 SCt 698
           Almanac (1981):11A
       A time for crucial rulings on job bias. *Business Week* (Industrial Edition) (2658):46-47 (October 13, 1980).

2174. Cuyler v. Adams   January 21, 1981
       449 US 433   66 LEd2d 641   101 SCt 703
           Almanac (1981):8A

2175. Minnesota v. Clover Leaf Creamery Co.   January 21, 1981
       449 US 456   66 LEd2d 659   101 SCt 715
           Almanac (1981):13A
           En Am Con 1751-1755
           Sup Ct Review (1982):127-166
       Hassler, Gregory L., and Karen O'Connor. Woodsy witchdoctors versus judicial guerrillas: the role and impact
       of competing interest groups in environmental litigation. *Boston College Environmental Affairs Law Review*
       13(4):487-520 (Summer 1986).

2176. Fedorenko v. United States   January 21, 1981
       449 US 490   66 LEd2d 686   101 SCt 737
           Almanac (1981):7A
       Gerson, Allan. Beyond Nuremberg. *Commentary* 72(4):62-66 (October 1981).

2177. Sumner v. Mata   January 21, 1981
       449 US 539   66 LEd2d 722   101 SCt 764
           Almanac (1981):14A

2178. Chandler v. Florida   January 26, 1981
       449 US 560   66 LEd2d 740   101 SCt 802
           Almanac (1981):5A
           Court Public 319-320, 371-379R
           Editorials (1981):116-123
           En Am Con 227, 683-686, 797-804
           Sup Ct Review (1981):157-192
       Bass, Martin Clark. Television's day in court. *New York Times Magazine* (section 6):36-38, 40-54 (February
       15, 1981).
       Beach, Bennet H., and Evan Thomas. Blind justice gets a seeing eye: the Supreme Court gives a green light to
       televising trials. *Time* 117(6):51 (February 9, 1981).
       Fulton, Joy D. Supreme Court review: Fourteenth Amendment—cameras in the courtroom: Supreme Court
       gives the go-ahead. *Journal of Criminal Law and Criminology* 72(4):1393-1409 (Winter 1981).
       Green light for courtroom TV. *U.S. News and World Report* 90(5):6 (February 9, 1981).
       Hill, I. William. High Court upholds use of cameras in state courts. *Editor and Publisher* 114(5):7 (January 31,
       1981).
       Journalism groups praise camera ruling. *Editor and Publisher* 114(7):40 (February 14, 1981).
       Media joins state in dispute over courtroom photos. *Editor and Publisher* 113(34-35):38 (August 23-30, 1980).
       Pike, David F. Old issues never die for Supreme Court. *U.S. News and World Report* 89(15):46 (October 13,
       1980).
       Press, Aric, and Diane Camper. Court's new term. *Newsweek* 96(16):60 (October 20, 1980).
       ———. Giving cameras a day in court. *Newsweek* 97(6):102 (February 9, 1981).
       Regan, Richard J. Supreme Court roundup: 1980 term. *Thought* 56(223):491-502 (December 1981).
       Trials: for all to see. *Economist* 278(7170):29-30 (January 31-February 6, 1981).
       Williamson, Lenora. Courtroom camera crusader elated by court's ruling. *Editor and Publisher* 114(7):7, 10
       (February 14, 1981).

2179. Equal Employment Opportunity Commission (EEOC) v. Associated Dry Goods Corp.   January 26, 1981
    449 US 590   66 LEd2d 762   101 SCt 817
    Almanac (1981):6A
    Nelson-Horchler, Joani. High Court mulls regulators' reach. *Industry Week* 207(2):18-23 (October 27, 1980).
    A time for crucial rulings on job bias. *Business Week* (Industrial Edition) (2658):46-47 (October 13, 1980).

2180. Weaver v. Graham   February 24, 1981
    450 US 24   67 LEd2d 17   101 SCt 960
    Almanac (1981):8A
    En Am Con 676-677
    Bernstein, Sidney, and Michael Eisenstein. 1981 Supreme Court update: the criminal law. *Trial* 17(10):54-60, 85 (October 1981).

2181. Hudson v. Louisiana   February 24, 1981
    450 US 40   67 LEd2d 30   101 SCt 970
    Almanac (1981):5A
    Bernstein, Sidney, and Michael Eisenstein. 1981 Supreme Court update: the criminal law. *Trial* 17(10):54-60, 85 (October 1981).

2182. Board of Governors of the Federal Reserve System v. Investment Co. Institute   February 24, 1981
    450 US 46   67 LEd2d 36   101 SCt 973
    Almanac (1981):10A
    Major Supreme Court business decisions in the 1980-81 Term. *Business Week* (Industrial Edition) (2697):62 (July 20, 1981).
    A time for crucial rulings on job bias. *Business Week* (Industrial Edition) (2658):46-47 (October 13, 1980).

2183. Carson v. American Brands, Inc., t/a American Tobacco Co.   February 25, 1981
    450 US 79   67 LEd2d 59   101 SCt 993
    Almanac (1981):14A
    Nelson-Horchler, Joani. On business issues: O'Connor fits conservative mold. *Industry Week* 213(3):29, 31 (May 3, 1982).

2184. Steadman v. Securities and Exchange Commission (SEC)   February 25, 1981
    450 US 91   67 LEd2d 69   101 SCt 999
    Almanac (1981):11A
    An evidence test for regulators. *Business Week* (Industrial Edition) (2677):105 (March 2, 1981).
    Nelson-Horchler, Joani. High Court mulls regulators' reach. *Industry Week* 207(2):18-23 (October 27, 1980).
    A time for crucial rulings on job bias. *Business Week* (Industrial Edition) (2658):46-47 (October 13, 1980).
    High Court backs standard by which SEC proves fraud. *Journal of Accountancy* 151(4):8 (April 1981).

2185. Democratic Party of the United States v. Wisconsin ex. rel. LaFollette   February 25, 1981
    450 US 107   67 LEd2d 82   101 SCt 1010
    Almanac (1981):8A
    En Am Con 1413-1417, 1452-1453
    Cutler, Lloyd N. Can the parties regulate campaign financing? *Annals of the American Academy of Political and Social Science* 486:115-120 (July 1986).

2186. Commissioner of Internal Revenue v. Portland Cement Company of Utah   March 3, 1981
    450 US 156   67 LEd2d 140   101 SCt 1037
    Almanac (1981):11A
    Freidin, Richard G. Supreme Court upholds IRS on "first marketable product" for depletion purposes. *Journal of Taxation* 54(6):376 (June 1981).

2187. Diamond, Commissioner of Patents and Trademarks v. Diehr   March 3, 1981
    450 US 175   67 LEd2d 155   101 SCt 1048

Almanac (1981):10A

Major Supreme Court business decisions in the 1980-81 term. *Business Week* (Industrial Edition) (2697):62 (July 20, 1981).

Nelson-Horchler, Joani. High Court mulls regulators' reach. *Industry Week* 207(2):18-23 (October 27, 1980).

Science and society: confusing rule on computer processes. *Science News* 119 (11):171 (March 14, 1981).

A time for crucial rulings on job bias. *Business Week* (Industrial Edition) (2658):46-47 (October 13, 1980).

2188. Schweiker, Secretary of Health and Human Services v. Wilson   March 4, 1981
    450 US 221   67 LEd2d 186   101 SCt 1074
      Almanac (1981):8A

Schwartz, Herman. Concern for the basic necessities. *Nation* 239(9):299-300 (September 29, 1984).

2189. Texas Department of Community Affairs v. Burdine   March 4, 1981
    450 US 248   67 LEd2d 207   101 SCt 1089
      Almanac (1981):6A-7A

Denniston, Lyle. What the all-boys bench did last year. *Ms.* 10(4):74, 84, 87 (October 1981).

Flygare, Thomas J. De jure: Supreme Court says employer does not have burden of proof in discrimination cases. *Phi Delta Kappan* 63(4):280-281 (December 1981).

Norris, Barbara A. Multiple regression analysis in Title VII cases: a structural approach to attacks of "missing factors" and "pre-act discrimination." *Law and Contemporary Problems* 49(4):63-96 (Autumn 1986).

Ruben, George. High Court further defines job bias. *Monthly Labor Review* 104(6):58 (June 1981).

Schwartz, Herman. New term, same tilt: the Supreme Court stays hard right. *Nation* 257(13):452-454 (October 25, 1993).

2190. Wood v. Georgia   March 4, 1981
    450 US 261   67 LEd2d 220   101 SCt 1097
      Almanac (1981):6A

Bleiweiss, Shell J. Supreme Court review: Sixth and Fourteenth Amendments—counsel conflicts of interest in state court and the Supreme Court's power to vacate and remand. *Journal of Criminal Law and Criminology* 72(4):1326-1344 (Winter 1981).

2191. Carter v. Kentucky   March 9, 1981
    Carter v. Commonwealth of Kentucky
    450 US 288   67 LEd2d 241   101 SCt 1112
      Almanac (1981):5A
      Brennan 196-199

Bernstein, Sidney, and Michael Eisenstein. 1981 Supreme Court update: the criminal law. *Trial* 17(10):54-60, 85 (October 1981).

Gromer, Sharon K. Supreme Court review: Fifth Amendment—the right to a no "adverse inference" jury instruction. *Journal of Criminal Law and Criminology* 72(4):1307-1325 (Winter 1981).

2192. Chicago and North Western Transportation Co. v. Kalo Brick & Tile Co.   March 9, 1981
    450 US 311   67 LEd2d 258   101 SCt 1124
      Almanac (1981):10A

2193. Albernaz v. United States   March 9, 1981
    450 US 333   67 LEd2d 275   101 SCt 1137
      Almanac (1981):5A

Schmitt, Deborah. Supreme Court review: Fifth Amendment—double jeopardy: legislative intent controls in crimes and punishment. *Journal of Criminal Law and Criminology* 74(4):1300-1314 (Winter 1983).

2194. Delta Air Lines, Inc. v. August   March 9, 1981
    450 US 346   67 LEd2d 287   101 SCt 1146
      Almanac (1981):14A

2195. Diamond, Commissioner of Patents and Trademarks v. Bradley   March 9, 1981
    450 US 381   67 LEd2d 311   101 SCt 1495
    Nelson-Horchler, Joani. High Court mulls regulators' reach. *Industry Week* 207(2):18-23 (October 27, 1980).
    A time for crucial rulings on job bias. *Business Week* (Industrial Edition) (2658):46-47 (October 13, 1980).

2196. H.L. v. Matheson, Governor of Utah   March 23, 1981
    450 US 398   67 LEd2d 388   101 SCt 1164
    Abortion (Frohock) 73
    Abortion Am 90, 98
    Abortion Dec 5, 76-86
    Abortion Dec 80s Introduction, 45-69R
    Abortion Quest 110-114
    Almanac (1981):7A
    Editorials (1981):356-359
    Hard Choices 313
    Liberty 637-640
    Nobody's 19-22
    Denniston, Lyle. What the all-boys bench did last year. *Ms.* 10(4):74, 84, 87 (October 1981).
    Ewer, Phyllis A. Supreme Court review: Court upholds parental notice requirement before allowing abortions on minors. *Journal of Criminal Law and Criminology* 72(4):1461-1481 (Winter 1981).
    Gest, Ted. Another dark day for the feminist cause. *U.S. News and World Report* 91(1):53-54 (July 6, 1981).
    High Court on teens, trucks, airwaves. *U.S. News and World Report* 90(13):8 (April 6, 1981).
    Melton, Gary B. Legal regulation of adolscent abortion: unintended effects. *American Psychologist* 42(1):79-83 (January 1987).
    Melton, Gary B., and Nancy Felipe Russo. Adolescent abortion: psychological perspectives on public policy. *American Psychologist* 42(1):69-72 (January 1987).
    Notifying the parents. [Editorial] *America* 144(14):289-90 (April 11, 1981).
    Pike, David F. Old issues never die for Supreme Court. *U.S. News and World Report* 89(15):46 (October 13, 1980).
    Regan, Richard J. Regulating cult activities: the limits of religious freedom. *Thought* 61(241):185-196 (June 1986).
    ————. Supreme Court roundup: 1980 term. *Thought* 56(223):491-502 (December 1981).
    Sex, abortion and the Supreme Court. *Newsweek* 97(14):83 (April 6, 1981).

2197. Kirchberg v. Feenstra   March 23, 1981
    450 US 455   67 LEd2d 428   101 SCt 1195
    Almanac (1981):7A
    En Am Con 1666-1673
    Baer, Judith A. Women's rights and the limits of constitutional doctrine. *Western Political Quarterly* 44(4):821-852 (December 1991).
    Denniston, Lyle. What the all-boys bench did last year. *Ms.* 10(4):74, 84, 87 (October 1981).

2198. Michael M. v. Superior Court of Sonoma County   March 23, 1981
    450 US 464   67 LEd2d 437   101 SCt 1200
    Almanac (1981):7A
    Ascent 229-231
    Brennan 309-313
    Burger Court 153-155
    Burger Years 109-124
    Const (Currie) 493-500
    Const Law 513-516R+
    Editorials (1981):356-359
    En Am Con 1252-1253, 1666-1673
    Equal Rights 145-153

Baer, Judith A. Women's rights and the limits of constitutional doctrine. *Western Political Quarterly* 44(4):821-852 (December 1991).

Bernstein, Sidney, and Michael Eisenstein. 1981 Supreme Court update: the criminal law. *Trial* 17(10):54-60, 85 (October 1981).

Denniston, Lyle. What the all-boys bench did last year. *Ms.* 10(4):74, 84, 87 (October 1981).

For men only: the blame in statutory rape. *Time* 117(14):83 (April 6, 1981).

High Court on teens, trucks, airwaves. *U.S. News and World Report* 90(13):8 (April 6, 1981).

Lauer, Rebecca J. Supreme Court review: Fourteenth Amendment—statutory rape: protection of minor female and prosecution of minor male. *Journal of Criminal Law and Criminology* 72(4):1374-1392 (Winter 1981).

Pike, David F. Old issues never die for Supreme Court. *U.S. News and World Report* 89(15):46 (October 13, 1980).

Regan, Richard J. Supreme Court roundup: 1980 term. *Thought* 56(223):491-502 (December 1981).

Sex, abortion and the Supreme Court. *Newsweek* 97(14):83 (April 6, 1981).

Williams, Wendy W., and Judith L. Lichtman. Closing the law's gender gap. *Nation* 239(9):280-285 (September 29, 1984).

2199. Rosewell v. LaSalle National Bank, Trustee   March 24, 1981
        450 US 503   67 LEd2d 464   101 SCt 1221
            Almanac (1981):13A

2200. Montana v. United States   March 24, 1981
        450 US 544   67 LEd2d 493   101 SCt 1245
            Almanac (1981):13A
            Am Indian (Deloria) 22-29
            Am Indians (Wilkinson) 43-44, 50-51, 130+

2201. Federal Communications Commission (FCC) v. WNCN Listeners Guild   March 24, 1981
            Coupled with Insilco Broadcasting Corp. v. WNCN Listeners Guild
            Coupled with American Broadcasting Co., Inc. (ABC) v. WNCN Listeners Guild
            Coupled with National Association of Broadcasters v. WNCN Listeners Guild
        450 US 582   67 LEd2d 521   101 SCt 1266
            Almanac (1981):9A
        High Court on teens, trucks, airwaves. *U.S. News and World Report* 90(13):8 (April 6, 1981).
        Hopkins, Jay. High Court backs billboards and cable in First decisions. *Editor and Publisher* 115(1):20 (January 2, 1982).
        Pike, David F. Old issues never die for Supreme Court. *U.S. News and World Report* 89(15):46 (October 13, 1980).
        A time for crucial rulings on job bias. *Business Week* (Industrial Edition) (2658):46-47 (October 13, 1980).

2202. San Diego Gas and Electric Co. v. City of San Diego   March 24, 1981
        450 US 621   67 LEd2d 551   101 SCt 1287
            Almanac (1981):10A
            En Am Con 998-999
        Darnell, Tim. The land and the law. *American City and County* 103(1):38-45 (January 1988).
        LaRusso, Joseph. "Paying for the change": First English Evangelical Lutheran Church of Glendale v. County of Los Angeles and the calculation of interim damages for regulatory takings. *Boston College Environmental Affairs Law Review* 17(3):551-583 (Spring 1990).
        Nelson-Horchler, Joani. High Court mulls regulators' reach. *Industry Week* 207(2):18-23 (October 27, 1980).
        Pike, David F. Old issues never die for Supreme Court. *U.S. News and World Report* 89(15):46 (October 13, 1980).

2203. Kassel v. Consolidated Freightways Corp. of Delaware   March 24, 1981
        450 US 662   67 LEd2d 580   101 SCt 1309
            Almanac (1981):13A
            En Am Con 1751-1755

Gest, Ted. Supreme Court sets back from activism. *U.S. News and World Report* 91(2):52 (July 13, 1981).

High Court on teens, trucks, airwaves. *U.S. News and World Report* 90(13):8 (April 6, 1981).

Major Supreme Court business decisions in the 1980-81 term. *Business Week* (Industrial Edition) (2697):62 (July 20, 1981).

Nelson-Horchler, Joani. High Court mulls regulators' reach. *Industry Week* 207(2):18-23 (October 27, 1980).

A time for crucial rulings on job bias. *Business Week* (Industrial Edition) (2658):46-47 (October 13, 1980).

2204. Thomas v. Review Board of the Indiana Employment Security Division   April 6, 1981
      450 US 707   67 LEd2d 624   101 SCt 1425

    Almanac (1981):9A
    Brennan 138-142
    Burger Years 56-91
    En Am Con 1894
    Godless 33-34
    Original (Davis) 91-92, 120-123+
    Religion 141-142
    Sup Ct Review (1981):193-221; (1983):1-31

Bearing witness: the right not to work is upheld. *Time* 117(16):51 (April 20, 1981).

Drinan, Robert F. The Supreme Court and religious freedom. *America* 152(12):254-255 (March 30, 1985).

———. The Supreme Court expands religious freedom. *America* 160(16):388-389 (April 29, 1989).

Greenlaw, Paul S., and John P. Kohl. Religious freedom and unemployment compensation benefits. *Public Personnel Management* 24(3):315-330 (Fall 1995).

Hammond, Phillip E. The courts and secular humanism. *Society* 21(4):11-16 (May/June 1984).

Pike, David F. Old issues never die for Supreme Court. *U.S. News and World Report* 89(15):46 (October 13, 1980).

Regan, Richard J. Supreme Court roundup: 1980 term. *Thought* 56(223):491-502 (December 1981).

———. Supreme Court roundup: 1981 term. *Thought* 57(227):514-527 (December 1982).

Rievman, Joshua D. Judicial scrutiny of Native American free exercise rights: Lyng and the decline of the Yoder doctrine. *Boston College Environmental Affairs Law Review* 17(1):169-199 (Fall 1989).

2205. Barrentine v. Arkansas-Best Freight System, Inc.   April 6, 1981
      450 US 728   67 LEd2d 641   101 SCt 1437

    Almanac (1981):11A

Hoyman, Michele M., and Lamont E. Stallworth. Arbitrating discrimination grievances in the wake of Gardner-Denver: some observers believed that the Supreme Court's 1974 ruling blunted the usefulness of arbitration in resolving Title VII [Civil Rights Act of 1964]-related grievances. *Monthly Labor Review* 106(10):3-10 (October 1983).

2206. Universities Research Association, Inc. v. Coutu   April 6, 1981
      450 US 754   67 LEd2d 662   101 SCt 1451

    Almanac (1981):11A

High court sets Davis-Bacon review. *Engineering News Record* 205(14):156 (October 2, 1980).

2207. Pennhurst State School and Hospital v. Halderman   April 20, 1981
        Coupled with Mayor of City of Philadelphia v. Halderman
        Coupled with Pennsylvania Association of Retarded Citizens v. Pennhurst State School and Hospital
        Coupled with Commissioners and Mental Health/Mental Retardation Administrator for Bucks County v. Halderman
        Coupled with Pennhurst Parents-Staff Association v. Halderman
      451 US 1   67 LEd2d 694   101 SCt 1531

    Almanac (1981):8A
    Burger Years 125-139
    Const (Currie) 577-580
    En Am Con 1249-1251, 1374-1375

Baer, Judith A. Burger court and the rights of the handicapped: the case for starting all over again. *Western Political Quarterly* 35(3):339-358 (September 1982).

Court restricts rights of retarded. *Science News* 119(18):278 (May 2, 1981).

Fiss, Owen M., and Charles Krauthammer. The Rehnquist Court. *New Republic* 186(10):14-16, 18 (March 10, 1982).

Hickok, Eugene W., Jr. Federalism's future before the U.S. Supreme Court. *Annals of the American Academy of Political and Social Science* 509:73-82 (May 1990).

Mental handicap: no new dawn. *Economist* 279(7184):28 (May 9, 1981).

Neuborne, Burt. Taking away the right to sue. *Nation* 239(9):268-271 (September 29, 1984).

Patients' rights: the high court slows a trend. *Time* 117(18):44 (May 4, 1981).

Press, Aric. Pushing the law to new limits. *Newsweek* 103(6):58 (February 6, 1984).

Press, Aric, and Diane Camper. Blow to the retarded. *Newsweek* 97(18):55 (May 4, 1981).

Ross, Douglas. Safeguarding our federalism: lessons for the states from the Supreme Court. *Public Administration Review* 45(Special Issue):723-731 (November 1985).

Search my house? Where's your warrant? *U.S. News and World Report* 90(17):12 (May 4, 1981).

Stephens, Pamela J. Implementing federal energy policy at the state and local kevels: "every power requisite." *Boston College Environmental Affairs Law Review* 10(4):875-904 (May 1983).

2208. United Parcel Service, Inc. v. Mitchell   April 20, 1981
      451 US 56   67 LEd2d 732   101 SCt 1559
        Almanac (1981):11A
        Burger Years 228-239

2209. Northwest Airlines, Inc. v. Transport Workers Union of America, AFL-CIO   April 20, 1981
      451 US 77   67 LEd2d 750   101 SCt 1571
        Almanac (1981):7A

Major Supreme Court business decisions in the 1980-81 term. *Business Week* (Industrial Edition) (2697):62 (July 20, 1981).

Nelson-Horchler, Joani. High Court mulls regulators' reach. *Industry Week* 207(2):18-23 (October 27, 1980).

A time for crucial rulings on job bias. *Business Week* (Industrial Edition) (2658):46-47 (October 13, 1980).

Union not liable for job bias. *Engineering News Record* 206(18):70 (April 30, 1981).

2210. City of Memphis v. Greene   April 20, 1981
      451 US 100   67 LEd2d 769   101 SCt 1584
        Almanac (1981):6A
        En Am Con 1247

Miller, Arthur S. End of the "second recontruction." *Progressive* 46(2):38-39 (February 1982).

Search my house? Where's your warrant? *U.S. News and World Report* 90(17):12 (May 4, 1981).

2211. Scindia Steam Navigation Co., LTD. v. De Los Santos   April 21, 1981
      451 US 156   68 LEd2d 1   101 SCt 1614
        Almanac (1981):11A

Baker, Nathan. Santos decision: a postive step toward harbor workers' safety. *Trial* 17(9):26-29, 58 (September 1981).

Due, Paul H. Proof of negligence under the LHWCA. *Trial* 20(2):60-65 (February 1984).

2212. Rosales-Lopez v. United States   April 21, 1981
      451 US 182   68 LEd2d 22   101 SCt 1629
        Almanac (1981):5A-6A
        En Am Con 1978

Bernstein, Sidney, and Michael Eisenstein. 1981 Supreme Court update: the criminal law. *Trial* 17(10):54-60, 85 (October 1981).

Mar, Linda. Supreme Court review: probing racial prejudice on voir dire: the Supreme Court provides illusory justice for minority defendants. *Journal of Criminal Law and Criminology* 72(4):1444-1461 (Winter 1981).

Wyckoff, Maria. Supreme Court review: Sixth Amendment—right to inquire into juror's racial prejudices. *Journal of Criminal Law and Criminology* 77(3):713-742 (Fall 1986).

2213. Steagald v. United States   April 21, 1981
    451 US 204   68 LEd2d 38   101 SCt 1642
      Almanac (1981):5A
      En Am Con 1628-1635, 1761

Bernstein, Sidney, and Michael Eisenstein. 1981 Supreme court update: the criminal law. *Trial* 17(10):54-60, 85 (October 1981).

Regan, Richard J. Supreme Court roundup: 1980 term. *Thought* 56(223):491-502 (December 1981).

Search my house? Where's your warrant? *U.S. News and World Report* 90(17):12 (May 4, 1981).

Watson, G. Andrew. Supreme Court review: Fourth Amendment—balancing the interests in third party home arrests. *Journal of Criminal Law and Criminology* 72(4):1263-1275 (Winter 1981).

2214. Arizona v. Manypenny   April 21, 1981
    451 US 232   68 LEd2d 58   101 SCt 1657
      Almanac (1981):14A

2215. Watt v. Alaska   April 21, 1981
    451 US 259   68 LEd2d 80   101 SCt 1673
      Almanac (1981):12A

2216. California v. Sierra Club   April 28, 1981
      Coupled with Kern County Water Agency v. Sierra Club
    451 US 287   68 LEd2d 101   101 SCt 1775
      Almanac (1981):12A

Hassler, Gregory L., and Karen O'Connor. Woodsy witchdoctors versus judicial guerrillas: the role and impact of competing interest groups in environmental litigation. *Boston College Environmental Affairs Law Review* 13(4):487-520 (Summer 1986).

Proctor, Michael G. Section 10 of the Rivers and Harbors Act and western water allocations—are the western states up a creek without a permit? *Boston College Environmental Affairs Law Review* 10(1):111-182 (1982-83).

Sandler, Ross. Law: Supreme Court ousts environmental plaintiffs. *Environment* 23(6):4-5 (July/August 1981).

———. Law: Supreme Court trends in environmental law. *Environment* 23(7):4-5 (September 1981).

2217. City of Milwaukee v. Illinois and Michigan   April 28, 1981
    451 US 304   68 LEd2d 114   101 SCt 1784
      Almanac (1981):12A

Collins, Michael. The dilemma of the downstream state: the untimely demise of federal common law nuisance. *Boston College Environmental Affairs Law Review* 11(2):295-412 (January 1984).

Giesser, John L. The National Park Service and external development: addressing park boundary-area threats through public nuisance. *Boston College Environmental Affairs Law Review* 20(4):761-809 (Summer 1993).

Hassler, Gregory L., and Karen O'Connor. Woodsy witchdoctors versus judicial guerrillas: the role and impact of competing interest groups in environmental litigation. *Boston College Environmental Affairs Law Review* 13(4):487-520 (Summer 1986).

Interstate sewage battle cooled by Supreme Court: Milwaukee saves $300 million. *Engineering News Record* 206(19):12-13 (May 7, 1981).

Major Supreme Court business decisions in the 1980-81 term. *Business Week* (Industrial Edition) (2697):62 (July 20, 1981).

Sandler, Ross. Law: Supreme Court ousts environmental plaintiffs. *Environment* 23(6):4-5 (July/August 1981).

———. Law: Supreme Court trends in environmental law. *Environment* 23(7):4-5 (September 1981).

2218. Ball v. James   April 29, 1981
    451 US 355   68 LEd2d 150   101 SCt 1811
      Almanac (1981):9A

Court Public 94

Reese, Michael, Susan Agrest, and Kim Foltz. Election that wasn't. *Newsweek* 98(12):49 (September 21, 1981).

2219. University of Texas v. Camenisch   April 29, 1981
    451 US 390   68 LEd2d 175   101 SCt 1830
      Almanac (1981):8A

Fields, Cheryl M. Supreme Court sidesteps question of aid by colleges to handicapped. *Chronicle of Higher Education* 22(11):9 (May 4, 1981).

2220. Complete Auto Transit, Inc. v. Reis   May 4, 1981
    451 US 401   68 US 248   101 SCt 1836
      Almanac (1981):11A

2221. Bullington v. Missouri   May 4, 1981
    451 US 430   68 LEd2d 270   101 SCt 1852
      Almanac (1981):5A

Bernstein, Sidney, and Michael Eisenstein. 1981 Supreme Court update: the criminal law. *Trial* 17(10):54-60, 85 (October 1981).

Lane, James R. Supreme Court review: Fifth Amendment—the covert narrowing of double jeopardy precedent: the Supreme Court's real reason for hearing Schiro v. Farley. *Journal of Criminal Law and Criminology* 85(4):909-935 (Spring 1995).

Pachciarek, Anne M. Supreme Court review: Fifth Amendment—extension of double jeopardy protection to sentencing. *Journal of Criminal Law and Criminology* 72(4):1276-1287 (Winter 1981).

2222. Estelle, Corrections Director v. Smith   May 18, 1981
    451 US 454   68 LEd2d 359   101 SCt 1866
      Almanac (1981):4A, 6A
      Death Penalty 80s 9-12, 98-102
      Death Penalty 90s 19-21
      En Am Con 655, 1264-1265

Bernstein, Sidney, and Michael Eisenstein. 1981 Supreme Court update: the criminal law. *Trial* 17(10):54-60, 85 (October 1981).

It's criminal defendants 2 police 0. *U.S. News and World Report* 90(21):8 (June 1, 1981).

Miranda: out of the doghouse:the Supreme Court broadens defendants' pretrial rights. *Time* 117(22):64 (June 1, 1981).

Press, Aric, and Diane Camper. New lease on life for Miranda. *Newsweek* 97(22):63 (June 1, 1981).

Regan, Richard J. Supreme Court roundup: 1980 term. *Thought* 56(223):491-502 (December 1981).

Whisler, Barbara J. Supreme Court review: Sixth Amendment—death qualification of the jury: process is permissible where defendant does not face death penalty. *Journal of Criminal Law and Criminology* 78(4):954-983 (Winter 1988).

White, Welsh S. The psychiatric examination and the Fifth Amendment privilege in capital cases. *Journal of Criminal Law and Criminology* 74(3):943-990 (Fall 1983).

———. Waiver and the death penalty: the implications of Estelle v. Smith. *Journal of Criminal Law and Criminology* 72(4):1522-1549 (Winter 1981).

2223. Edwards v. Arizona   May 18, 1981
    451 US 477   68 LEd2d 378   101 SCt 1880
      Almanac (1981):4A, 6A; (1985):6A
      Burger Court 89-91
      Burger Years 143-168
      En Am Con 613, 1264-1265

Bernstein, Sidney, and Michael Eisenstein. 1981 Supreme Court update: the criminal law. *Trial* 17(10):54-60, 85 (October 1981).

Bitterman, Patrick J. Supreme Court review: Fifth Amendment—the applicability of the assertion of the right to counsel to unrelated investigations. *Journal of Criminal Law and Criminology* 79(3):676-700 (Fall 1988).

Dripps, Donald A. Supreme Court review: 'maybe I should talk to a lawyer': ambiguous invocations of Miranda. *Trial* 30(9):90-92 (September 1994).

Echikson, Thomas. Supreme Court review: Sixth Amendment—waiver after request for counsel. *Journal of Criminal Law and Criminology* 77(3):775-795 (Fall 1986).

It's criminal defendants 2 police 0. *U.S. News and World Report* 90(21):8 (June 1, 1981).

Link, Anne Elizabeth. Supreme Court review: Fifth Amendment—the constitutionality of custodial confessions. *Journal of Criminal Law and Criminology* 82(4):878-903 (Winter 1992).

Melson, David E. Supreme Court review: Fifth Amendment—waivers of previously invoked right to counsel. *Journal of Criminal Law and Criminology* 72(4):1288-1306 (Winter 1981).

Miranda: out of the doghouse: the Supreme Court broadens defendants' pretrial rights. *Time* 117(22):64 (June 1, 1981).

Regan, Richard J. Supreme Court roundup: 1980 term. *Thought* 56(223):491-502 (December 1981).

Ullman, Patricia. Supreme Court review: Fifth and Sixth Amendments—the right to counsel in multiple charge arraignments. *Journal of Criminal Law and Criminology* 82(4):904-919 (Winter 1992).

Weiss, Lee A. Supreme Court review: Fifth Amendment—Fifth Amendment exclusionary rule: the assertion and subsequent waiver of the right to counsel. *Journal of Criminal Law and Criminology* 74(4):1315-1333 (Winter 1983).

2224. Webb v. Webb		May 18, 1981
451 US 493	68 LEd2d 392	101 SCt 1889
Almanac (1981):15A		

2225. Alessi v. Raybestos-Manhattan, Inc.		May 18, 1981
451 US 504	68 LEd2d 402	101 SCt 1895
Almanac (1981):11A-12A		

Reich, Laurence. Sup. Ct. in Alessi upholds workers' comp. integration and ERISA state law preemption. *Journal of Taxation* 55(2):66-69 (August 1981).

Ruben, George. Supreme Court finds pension offset valid. *Monthly Labor Review* 104(7):49 (July 1981).

Tarnoff, Stephen. Court decisions or benefits increase employers' costs. *Business Insurance* 21(44):93-95 (November 2, 1987).

2226. Parratt v. Taylor		May 18, 1981
451 US 527	68 LEd2d 420	101 SCt 1908
Almanac (1981):6A; (1986):9A		

Berns, Walter. Has the Burger Court gone too far? *Commentary* 78(4):27-33 (October 1984).

Goring, Darlene C. Supreme Court review: Fourth Amendment—prison cells: is there a right to privacy? *Journal of Criminal Law and Criminology* 75(3):609-629 (Fall 1984).

2227. J. Truett Payne Co., Inc. v. Chrysler Motors Corp.		May 18, 1981
451 US 557	68 LEd2d 442	101 SCt 1923
Almanac (1981):10A		
Burger Years 206-219		

Pike, David F. Old issues never die for Supreme Court. *U.S. News and World Report* 89(15):46 (October 13, 1980).

Werner, Ray O. Marketing and the United States Supreme Court, 1975-1981. *Journal of Marketing* 46(2):73-81 (Spring 1982).

2228. United States v. Swank		May 18, 1981
451 US 571	68 LEd2d 454	101 SCt 1931
Almanac (1981):11A		

Henshaw, Harry P., III, and Laird Minor. Short-notice terminability no bar to lessee mineral depletion, says Sup. Ct. in Swank. *Journal of Taxation* 55(2):102-105 (August 1981).

2229. Rodriguez v. Compass Shipping Co., Ltd.		May 18, 1981
451 US 596	68 LEd2d 472	101 SCt 1945

Almanac (1981):11A

2230. Flynt v. Ohio   May 18, 1981
       451 US 619   68 LEd2d 489   101 SCt 1958
          Almanac (1981):8A-9A

2231. Beltran v. Myers, Director, California State Department of Health   May 18, 1981
       451 US 625   68 LEd2d 495   101 SCt 1961
          Almanac (1981):15A

2232. Texas Industries, Inc. v. Radcliff Materials, Inc.   May 26, 1981
       451 US 630   68 LEd2d 500   101 SCt 2061
          Almanac (1981):10A; (1982):381
       Major Supreme Court business decisions in the 1980-81 term. *Business Week* (Industrial Edition) (2697):62
          (July 20, 1981).
       Werner, Ray O. Marketing and the United States Supreme Court, 1975-1981. *Journal of Marketing* 46(2):73-81
          (Spring 1982).

2233. Western and Southern Life Insurance Co. v. State Board of Equalization of California   May 26, 1981
       451 US 648   68 LEd2d 514   101 SCt 2070
          Almanac (1981):13A
       Hellerstein, Walter. Supreme Ct. bars Louisiana's first use tax, upholds Calif.'s retaliatory insurance tax.
          Journal of Taxation 55(2):106-111 (August 1981).
       Hellerstein, Walter, and Ruurd Leegstra. Supreme Court in Metropolitan Life strikes down discriminatory state
          insurance tax. *Journal of Taxation* 63(2):108-111 (August 1985).
       Vinyard, Walter D., Jr. Retaliatory taxation—a crack in the foundation? *Best's Review* (Property/Casualty
          Insurance Edition) 81(12):14, 94-100 (April 1981).

2234. Clayton v. International Union, United Automobile, Aerospace and Agricultural   May 26, 1981
          Implement Workers of America
             Coupled with Gilfillan v. Clayton
       451 US 679   68 LEd2d 538   101 SCt 2088
       Fox, Arthur. Showing workers who's the boss. *Nation* 239(9):295-299 (September 29, 1984).

2235. H.A. Artists & Associates, Inc. v. Actors' Equity Association   May 26, 1981
       451 US 704   68 LEd2d 558   101 SCt 2102
          Almanac (1981):10A

2236. Maryland v. Louisiana   May 26, 1981
       451 US 725   68 LEd2d 576   101 SCt 2114
          Almanac (1981):13A
          En Am Con 816-821
       Hellerstein, Walter. Supreme Ct. bars Louisiana's first use tax, upholds Calif.'s retaliatory insurance tax.
          Journal of Taxation 55(2):106-111 (August 1981).
       Louisiana loses Supreme Court OCS tax case. *Oil and Gas Journal* 79(23):68 (June 1, 1981).
       Major Supreme Court business decisions in the 1980-81 term. *Business Week* (Industrial Edition) (2697):62
          (July 20, 1981).
       Montana: Treasure state's treasure trove. *Economist* 280(7193):41 (July 11-17, 1981).

2237. St. Martin Evangelical Lutheran Church and Northwestern Lutheran Academy v. South Dakota   May 26, 1981
       451 US 772   68 LEd2d 612   101 SCt 2142
          Almanac (1981):9A
       Regan, Richard J. Supreme Court roundup: 1980 term. *Thought* 56(223):491-502 (December 1981).

2238. Becker v. United States May 29, 1981
451 US 1306 68 LEd2d 828 101 SCt 3161
Daues, Vincent F. More on Phillip Becker. [Editorial] *America* 143(1):211 (October 11, 1980).
Riga, Peter J. Phillip Becker: another milestone. [Editorial] *America* 143(1):8-9 (July 5-12, 1980).
Will, George F. Case of Phillip Becker. [Editorial] *Newsweek* 95(15):112 (April 14, 1980).

2239. Little v. Streater June 1, 1981
452 US 1 68 LEd2d 627 101 SCt 2202
Almanac (1981):8A
Denniston, Lyle. What the all-boys bench did last year. *Ms.* 10(4):74, 84, 87 (October 1981).
Pike, David F. Old issues never die for Supreme Court. *U.S. News and World Report* 89(15):46 (October 13, 1980).

2240. Lassiter v. Department of Social Services of Durham County, North Carolina June 1, 1981
452 US 18 68 LEd2d 640 101 SCt 2153
Almanac (1981):8A
Editorials (1981):667-669
En Am Con 686-688, 1465-1472, 1585-1592
Denniston, Lyle. What the all-boys bench did last year. *Ms.* 10(4):74, 84, 87 (October 1981).
McGrath, Ellie, and Evan Thomas. Parents beware. *Time* 117(24):57 (June 15, 1981).
Pike, David F. Old issues never die for Supreme Court. *U.S. News and World Report* 89(15):46 (October 13, 1980).
Surprise ruling on child custody. *Newsweek* 97(24):31 (June 15, 1981).

2241. Schad v. Borough of Mount Ephraim June 1, 1981
452 US 61 68 LEd2d 671 101 SCt 2176
Almanac (1981):9A
En Am Con 1622
Hopkins, Jay. High Court backs billboards and cable in First decisions. *Editor and Publisher* 115(1):20 (January 2, 1982).
McGrath, Ellie, and Evan Thomas. Incongruity at the High Court: mantle for nude dancing. *Time* 117(24):56-57 (June 15, 1981).
McGuire, Kevin T., and Gregory A. Caldeira. Lawyers, organized interests, and the law of obscenity: agenda setting in the Supreme Court. *American Political Science Review* 87(3):717-726 (September 1993).
O'Rourke, William. Will the Court bare all? *Nation* 252(24):846-847 (June 24, 1991).
Regan, Richard J. Supreme Court roundup: 1980 term. *Thought* 56(223):491-502 (December 1981).

2242. Gulf Oil Co. v. Bernard June 1, 1981
452 US 89 68 LEd 2d 693 101 SCt 2193
Almanac (1981):14A

2243. Minnick v. California Department of Corrections June 1, 1981
452 US 105 68 LEd2d 706 101 SCt 2211
Almanac (1981):7A
Denniston, Lyle. What the all-boys bench did last year. *Ms.* 10(4):74, 84, 87 (October 1981).
Pike, David F. Old issues never die for Supreme Court. *U.S. News and World Report* 89(15):46 (October 13, 1980).
Poole, Isaiah J., Diane Camper, and Janice Simpson. The Court: uneasy defense of minority rights. *Black Enterprise* 11:54-56 (March 1981).
A time for crucial rulings on job bias. *Business Week* (Industrial Edition) (2658):46-47 (October 13, 1980).

2244. McDaniel v. Sanchez June 1, 1981
452 US 130 68 LEd2d 724 101 SCt 2224
Almanac (1981):10A
Reese, Michael, Susan Agrest, and Kim Foltz. Election that wasn't. *Newsweek* 98(12):49 (September 21, 1981).

2245. County of Washington, Oregon v. Gunther   June 8, 1981
      452 US 161   68 LEd 2d 751   101 SCt 2242
          Almanac (1981):7A
          Court Public 101, 224-234R
          Editorials (1981):680-683
          Equal Pay 13-14, 30-32, 99-101, 144-148, 172-176+
      Breakthrough in the wage war: the Supreme Court opens the door to more pay suits by women. *Time*
          117(25):70 (June 22, 1981).
      Carmell, William A. High Court fails to address "comparable worth" issue, but opens door a crack. *ABA*
          Banking Journal 73(9):20-25 (September 1981).
      Dellaverson, JoAnne. Comparable worth keeps brewing. *ABA Banking Journal* 76(10):140-142 (October 1984).
      Denniston, Lyle. What the all-boys bench did last year. *Ms.* 10(4):74, 84, 87 (October 1981).
      Footlick, Jerrold K., Diane Camper, and Peggy Clausen. Women's issue of the '80s. *Newsweek* 97(25):58-59
          (June 22, 1981).
      Gest, Ted. Another dark day for the feminist cause. *U.S. News and World Report* 91(1):53-54 (July 6, 1981).
      Gray, Mary W. The halls of ivy and the halls of justice: resisting sex discrimination against faculty women.
          Academe 71(5):33-41 (September/October 1985).
      Kinsley, Michael. Worthier than thou. *New Republic* 184(26):10-11 (June 27, 1981).
      Laycock, Douglas. Continuing violations, disparate impact in compensation, and other Title VII issues. *Law*
          and Contemporary Problems 49(4):53-61 (Autumn 1986).
      Lee, Yong S. Shaping judicial response to gender discrimination in employment compensation. *Public*
          Administration Review 49(5):420-430 (September/October 1989).
      Major Supreme Court business decisions in the 1980-81 term. *Business Week* (Industrial Edition) (2697):62
          (July 20, 1981).
      Nelson-Horchler, Joanie. Justices didn't resolve 'comparable worth.' *Industry Week* 209(7):29-31 (June 29,
          1981).
      A new basis for job discrimination suits. *Business Week* (Industrial Edition) (2702):90J-90M (August 24,
          1981).
      O'Hara, Julie Underwood. Use this legal briefing to assess your board's position on comparable worth.
          American School Board Journal 172(8):26-27 (August 1985).
      Regan, Richard J. Supreme Court roundup: 1980 term. *Thought* 56(223):491-502 (December 1981).
      Ruben, George. "Comparable worth" decision. *Monthly Labor Review* 104(8):61-62 (August 1981).
      Seligman, Daniel. Supreme foolishness. *Fortune* 104(1):31-32 (July 13, 1981).
      Sheler, Jeffery L. A fresh round in fight over equal pay: women still lag far behind men in earnings, but now
          the Supreme Court has opened up lawsuits on a volatile issue: "comparable worth" *U.S. News and World*
          Report 90(24):81-82 (June 22, 1981).
      Tolley, Howard B., Jr. Challenging discriminatory wages for women's work. *USA Today* 111(2456):50-52
          (May, 1983).
      Women: more work, less pay. *Economist* 279(7189):25 (June 13, 1981).
      Women's work. *Progressive* 45(8):9-10 (August 1981).

2246. Anderson Brothers Ford and Ford Motor Credit v. Valencia   June 8, 1981
      452 US 205   68 LEd2d 783   101 SCt 2266
          Almanac (1981):7A

2247. American Express Co. v. Koerner   June 8, 1981
      452 US 233   68 LEd2d 803   101 SCt 2281
          Almanac (1981):7A

2248. Rowan Companies, Inc. v. United States   June 8, 1981
      452 US 247   68 LEd 2d 814   101 SCt 2288
          Almanac (1981):11A
      Greene, Richard. Blood from a turnip? *Forbes* 128(4):82-83 (August 17, 1981).

Kovey, Mark H., and Peter H. Winslow. Supreme Court's citation of letter rulings: what does it mean to practitioners? *Journal of Taxation* 55(3):166-167 (September 1981).

———. Sup. Ct. in Rowan holds "wages" excludable from income are exempt from FICA, FUTA. *Journal of Taxation* 55(3):130-136 (September 1981).

Refund procedure for FICA and FUTA taxes paid on excludable wages announced. *Journal of Taxation* 56(3):187 (March 1982).

Refunds on overpayments. *CPA Journal* 52(6):64-66 (June 1982).

Tortorella, Robert J. Sec. 403(b) annuities and Rowan Companies' decision. *CPA Journal* 54(6):50-51 (June 1984).

2249. Hodel v. Virginia Surface Mining and Reclamation Association, Inc.   June 15, 1981
452 US 264   69 LEd2d 1   101 SCt 2352
    Almanac (1981):12A-13A
    Editorials (1981):740-743
    En Am Con 637-639, 919

Hassler, Gregory L., and Karen O'Connor. Woodsy witchdoctors versus judicial guerrillas: the role and impact of competing interest groups in environmental litigation. *Boston College Environmental Affairs Law Review* 13(4):487-520 (Summer 1986).

Johnston, Van R., and Maxine Kurtz. Handling a public policy emergency: the Fair Labor Standards Act in the public sector. *Public Administration Review* 46(5):414-422 (September/October 1986).

Major setback in fight against regulations. *U.S. News and World Report* 90(25):54 (June 29, 1981).

Major Supreme Court business decisions in the 1980-81 term. *Business Week* (Industrial Edition) (2697):62 (July 20, 1981).

Nelson-Horchler, Joani. High Court mulls regulators' reach. *Industry Week* 207(2):18-23 (October 27, 1980).

Regan, Richard J. Supreme Court roundup: 1980 term. *Thought* 56(223):491-502 (December 1981).

Shepard, Blake. The scope of Congress's constitutional power under the property clause: regulating non-federal property to further the purposes of national parks and wilderness areas. *Boston College Environmental Affairs Law Review* 11(3): 479-538 (April 1984).

Stephens, Pamela J. Implementing federal energy policy at the state and local levels: "every power requisite." *Boston College Environmental Affairs Law Review* 10(4):875-904 (May 1983).

Thomas, Charlotte E. The Cape Cod National Seashore: a case study of federal administrative control over traditionally local land use decisions. *Boston College Environmental Affairs Law Review* 12(2):225-272 (Winter 1985).

Van Alstyne, William W. Implied powers. *Society* 24(1):56-60 (November/December 1986).

2250. Hodel, Acting Secretary of the Interior v. Indiana   June 15, 1981
452 US 314   69 LEd2d 40   101 SCt 2376
    Almanac (1981):13A

Hassler, Gregory L., and Karen O'Connor. Woodsy witchdoctors versus judicial guerrillas: the role and impact of competing interest groups in environmental litigation. *Boston College Environmental Affairs Law Review* 13(4):487-520 (Summer 1986).

Major setback in fight against regulations. *U.S. News and World Report* 90(25):54 (June 29, 1981).

Major Supreme Court business decisions in the 1980-81 term. *Business Week* (Industrial Edition) (2697):62 (July 20, 1981).

Smith, R. Jeffrey. Court upholds controversial regulations. *Science* 213(4504):185, 188 (July 10, 1981).

Stephens, Pamela J. Implementing federal energy policy at the state and local levels: "every power requisite." *Boston College Environmental Affairs Law Review* 10(4):875-904 (May 1983).

Supreme Court: not the president's brethren—yet. *Economist* 279(7191):22-23 (June 27-July 3, 1981).

2251. Rhodes, Governor of Ohio v. Chapman   June 15, 1981
452 US 337   69 LEd2d 59   101 SCt 2392
    Almanac (1981):6A
    Burger Years 177-188
    Editorials (1981):744-749
    En Am Con 524-526

Angelos, Claudia, and James B. Jacobs. Prison overcrowding and the law. *Annals of the American Academy of Political and Social Science* 478:100-112 (March 1985).

Bamonte, Thomas J. Supreme Court review: Eighth Amendment—a significant limit on Federal Court activism in ameliorating state prison conditions. *Journal of Criminal Law and Criminology* 72(4):1345-1373 (Winter 1981).

Major setback in fight against regulations. *U.S. News and World Report* 90(25):54 (June 29, 1981).

Newman, Amy. Supreme Court review: Eighth Amendment—cruel and unusual punishment and conditions cases. *Journal of Criminal Law and Criminology* 82(4):979-999 (Winter 1992).

Prison rights: doubling up is O.K.. *Time* 117(26):51 (June 29, 1981).

They do a prison make. [Editorial] *Commonweal* 108(18):547-548 (October 9, 1981).

2252. National Gerimedical Hospital and Gerontology Center v. Blue Cross of Kansas City   June 15, 1981
    452 US 378   69 LEd2d 89   101 SCt 2415
      Almanac (1981):10A

Hamlin, Ross J. Application of the Sherman Act state action exemption to municipal environmental regulation: a case for broader local discretion. *Boston College Environmental Affairs Law Review* 11(3):609-664 (April 1984).

Weller, Charles D. McCarran Act interpretation may have been charted in Barry case. *Best's Review* (Life/Health Insurance Edition) 83(2):40-42, 87-89 (June 1982).

———. McCarran Act interpretation may have been charted in Barry case. *Best's Review* (Property/Casualty Insurance Edition) 83(3):28-32 (July 1982).

2253. Federated Department Stores, Inc. v. Moitie   June 15, 1981
    452 US 394   69 LEd2d 103   101 SCt 2424
      Almanac (1981):14A

2254. Jones, Warden v. Helms   June 15, 1981
    452 US 412   69 LEd2d 118   101 SCt 2434
      Almanac (1981):8A

2255. United States v. Maine   June 15, 1981
    452 US 429   69 LEd2d 132   101 SCt 3074
      Almanac (1981):15A

2256. California v. Arizona and the United States   June 15, 1981
    452 US 431   69 LEd2d 134   101 SCt 2445
      Almanac (1981):15A

2257. Maryland v. Louisiana   June 15, 1981
    452 US 456   69 LEd2d 156   101 SCt 3075
      Guide (CQ) 328

2258. Connecticut Board of Pardons v. Dumschat   June 17, 1981
    452 US 458   69 LEd2d 158   101 SCt 2460
      Almanac (1981):5A

2259. Howe v. Smith, Attorney General   June 17, 1981
    452 US 473   69 LEd2d 171   101 SCt 2468
      Almanac (1981):8A

2260. American Textile Manufacturers Institute, Inc. v. Donovan   June 17, 1981
        Coupled with National Cotton Council of America v. Donovan
    452 US 490   69 LEd2d 185   101 SCt 2478
      Almanac (1981):12A
      Burger Years 191-205

Editorials (1981):750-753

New Right (Schwartz) 168-174

Sup Ct Review (1981):291-307; (1988):1-41

Bangser, Paul M. A inherent role for cost-benefit analysis in judicial review of agency decisions: a new perspective on OSHA rulemaking. *Boston College Environmental Affairs Law Review* 10(2):365-444 (September 1982).

Cahan, Vicky. For deregulation, a detour—not a roadblock. *Business Week* (2695):26 (July 6, 1981).

Dangerous dust: Employers must pay the cost. *Time* 117(26):51 (June 29, 1981).

A defeat for deregulation. *Chemical Week* 128(25):16-17 (June 24, 1981).

Greer, Edward H. Deregulation fever hits the Supreme Court. *Nation* 231(21):666-668 (December 20, 1980).

High Court lets stand OSHA's lead standard. *Chemical and Engineering News* 59(27):6 (July 6, 1981).

MacCarthy, Mark. A review of some normative and conceptual issues in occupational safety and health. *Boston College Environmental Affairs Law Review* 9(4):773-814 (1981-82).

Major setback in fight against regulations. *U.S. News and World Report* 90(25):54 (June 29, 1981).

Major Supreme Court business decisions in the 1980-81 term. *Business Week* (Industrial Edition) (2697):62 (July 20, 1981).

Morrison, Alan B. Close reins on the bureaucracy. *Nation* 239(9):290-294 (September 29, 1984).

Nelson-Horchler, Joani. Business's year in court a disappointment *Industry Week* 210(1):19-20 (July 13, 1981).

————. High Court mulls regulators' reach. *Industry Week* 207(2):18-23 (October 27, 1980).

OSHA's latest recall of Carter era rules. *Business Week* (2685):48 (April 27, 1981).

Regan, Richard J. Supreme Court roundup: 1980 term. *Thought* 56(223):491-502 (December 1981).

Regulatory reform gets a setback. *Engineering News Record* 206(26):10-11 (June 25, 1981).

Rodriguez, Leon. Constitutional and statutory limits for cost-benefit analysis pursuant to Executive Orders 12,291 and 12,498. *Boston College Environmental Affairs Law Review* 15(3-4):505-546 (Spring 1988).

Ruben, George. Supreme Court upholds cotton dust standard. *Monthly Labor Review* 104(8):62 (August 1981).

Saasta, Timothy. Decisions on OSHA. *Nation* 233(1):5 (July 4, 1981).

Science and society: workers win in cotton-dust ruling. *Science News* 120(1):15 (July 4, 1981).

Sheils, Merrill, Diane Camper, and Peggy Clausen. High Court win for OSHA. *Newsweek* 97(26):59 (June 29, 1981).

Smith, R. Jeffrey. Court upholds controversial regulations. *Science* 213(4504):185, 188 (July 10, 1981).

Supreme Court: not the president's brethren—yet. *Economist* 279(7191):22-23 (June 27-July 3, 1981).

Verespej, Michael A. Cost-benefit decision jars OSHA reform. *Industry Week* 209(7):18-23 (June 29, 1981).

2261. Monroe v. Standard Oil Co.   June 17, 1981
      452 US 549   69 LEd2d 226   101 SCt 2510
          Almanac (1981):8A

Kirkpatrick, James J. Conservatism at the High Court. *National Review* 33(15):893-895 (August 7, 1981).

Major setback in fight against regulations. *U.S. News and World Report* 90(25):54 (June 29, 1981).

2262. United States v. Turkette   June 17, 1981
      452 US 576   69 LEd2d 246   101 SCt 2524
          Almanac (1981):6A
          Sup Ct Review (1993):157-198

Bernstein, Sidney, and Michael Eisenstein. 1981 Supreme Court update: the criminal law. *Trial* 17(10):54-60, 85 (October 1981).

Keneally, Kathryn. Partial limitation on the risk of RICO liability. *CPA Journal* 64(2):67-69 (February 1994).

Maurer, Virginia G. The continuing expansion of RICO in business litigation. *Business Horizons* 33(5):80-87 (September/October 1990).

Neuenschwander, Jan. Supreme Court review: RICO extended to apply to wholly illegitimate enterprises. *Journal of Criminal Law and Criminology* 72(4):1426-1443 (Winter 1981).

2263. Donovan v. Dewey   June 17, 1981
      452 US 594   69 LEd2d 262   101 SCt 2534
          Almanac (1981):12A
          Sup Ct Review (1989):87-163

Andersen, Robert M. Technology, pollution control, and EPA access to commercial property: a constitutional and policy framework. *Boston College Environmental Affairs Law Review* 17(1):1-74 (Fall 1989).

High court lets stand OSHA's lead standard. *Chemical and Engineering News* 59(27):6 (July 6, 1981).

High court takes cases on inspections, pensions. *Engineering News Record* 206(6):81 (February 5, 1981).

Roberts, Thomas A. Supreme Court review: Fourth Amendment—warrantless administrative inspections of commercial property. *Journal of Criminal Law and Criminology* 72(4):1222-1245 (Winter 1981).

2264. United Association of Journeymen & Apprentices of the Plumbing and Pipefitting   June 22, 1981
      Industry of the United States and Canada, AFL-CIO v. Local 334, United Assocation of Journeymen &
      Apprentices of the Plumbing and Pipefitting Industry of the United States and Canada
    452 US 615   69 LEd2d 280   101 SCt 2546
      Almanac (1981):12A

2265. Heffron v. International Society for Krishna Consciousness, Inc. (ISKCON)   June 22, 1981
    452 US 640   69 LEd2d 298   101 SCt 2559
      Almanac (1981):9A
      En Am Con 911, 1538-1545
      Godless 42-43
      Religion 218-221

Flygare, Thomas J. De jure: High Court sets standards for First Amendment time, place, and manner rules. *Phi Delta Kappan* 63(1):60-61 (September 1981).

Mehra, Achal. Iskcon court decisions: setback for proselytizing rights. *Journalism Quarterly* 61(1):109-116 (Spring 1984).

Press, Aric, and Diane Camper. Uncle Sam says "men only." *Newsweek* 98(1):64-65 (July 6, 1981)

Put yourself on the U.S. Supreme Court. *Senior Scholastic* 114(8):22-23, 27 (December 11, 1981).

Regan, Richard J. Regulating cult activities: the limits of religious freedom. *Thought* 61(241):185-196 (June 1986).

―――――. Supreme Court roundup: 1980 term. *Thought* 56(223):491-502 (December 1981).

Supreme Court draws the line. *U.S. News and World Report* 91(1):7 (July 6, 1981).

2266. First National Maintenance Corp. v. National Labor Relations Board (NLRB)   June 22, 1981
    452 US 666   69 LEd2d 318   101 SCt 2573
      Almanac (1981):4A, 12A
      Burger Years 220-227, 228-239

Draznin, Julius N. Closings and consolidations. *Personnel Journal* 60(10):764, 766 (October 1981).

Fox, Arthur. Showing workers who's the boss. *Nation* 239(9):295-299 (September 29, 1984).

Major Supreme Court business decisions in the 1980-81 term. *Business Week* (Industrial Edition) (2697):62 (July 20, 1981).

Must industry negotiate a plant-closing date? *Chemical Week* 128(8):45 (February 25, 1981).

Ruben, George. Developments in industrial relations: NLRB says operations transfer not negotiable. *Monthly Labor Review* 107(6):56 (June 1984).

―――――. Partial closing not a bargaining item. *Monthly Labor Review* 104(9):51 (September 1981).

Unions: no say on closings. *Engineering News Record* 207(1):73 (July 2, 1981).

2267. Michigan v. Summers   June 22, 1981
    452 US 692   69 LEd2d 340   101 SCt 2587
      Almanac (1981):4A, 5A
      En Am Con 1253, 1628-1635

Bernstein, Sidney, and Michael Eisenstein. 1981 Supreme Court update: the criminal law. *Trial* 17(10):54-60, 85 (October 1981).

Regan, Richard J. Supreme Court roundup: 1980 term. *Thought* 56(223):491-502 (December 1981).

Vawrinek, Jeffrey J. Supreme Court review: Fourth Amendment—detention of occupants during a premises search: the winter of discontent for probable cause. *Journal of Criminal Law and Criminology* 72(4):1246-1264 (Winter 1981).

2268. Kissinger v. Halperin   June 22, 1981
    452 US 713   69 LEd2d 367   101 SCt 3132
        Almanac (1981):15A
    Collect call: a former president must pay. *Time* 118(1):21 (July 6, 1981).
    Pike, David F. Old issues never die for Supreme Court. *U.S. News and World Report* 89(15):46 (October 13, 1980).
    Press, Aric, and Diane Camper. Court's new term. *Newsweek* 96(16):60 (October 20, 1980).
    ———. Uncle Sam says "men only." *Newsweek* 98(1):64-65 (July 6, 1981).
    Supreme Court draws the line. *U.S. News and World Report* 91(1):7 (July 6, 1981).

2269. New York State Liquor Authority v. Bellanca, dba The Main Event   June 22, 1981
    452 US 714   69 LEd2d 357   101 SCt 2599
    Regan, Richard J. Supreme Court roundup: 1980 term. *Thought* 56(223):491-502 (December 1981).

2270. United States v. Louisiana   June 22, 1981
    452 US 726   69 LEd2d 368   101 SCt 2605
        Almanac (1981):15A

2271. Middlesex County Sewerage Authority v. National Sea Clammers Association June 25, 1981
            Coupled with Joint Meeting of Essex and Union Counties v. National Sea Clammers Association
            Coupled with City of New York v. National Sea Clammers Association
            Coupled with Envirnmental Protection Agency (EPA) v. National Sea Clammers Association
    453 US 1   69 LEd2d 435   101 SCt 2615
        Almanac (1981):13A
    Collins, Michael. The dilemma of the downstream state: the untimely demise of federal common law nuisance. *Boston College Environmental Affairs Law Review* 11(2):295-412 (January 1984).
    Sandler, Ross. Law: Supreme Court trends in environmental law. *Environment* 23(7):4-5 (September 1981).
    Supreme Court draws the line. *U.S. News and World Report* 91(1):7 (July 6, 1981).

2272. Schweiker, Secretary of Health and Human Services v. Gray Panthers   June 25, 1981
    453 US 34   69 LEd2d 460   101 SCt 2633
        Almanac (1981):15A

2273. Rostker, Director of Selective Service v. Goldberg   June 25, 1981
    453 US 57   69 LEd2d 478   101 SCt 2646
        Almanac (1980):46; (1981):3A, 7A
        Burger Years 109-124
        Const (Currie) 493-500
        Const Law 516-518R
        Editorials (1981):700-707
        En Am Con 354, 1612, 1666-1673
        Equal Rights 145-153
        Guide (CQ) 130
        Magic 329-330
        Religion 144-150
    Baer, Judith A. Women's rights and the limits of constitutional doctrine. *Western Political Quarterly* 44(4):821-852 (December 1991).
    Beach, Bennett H., and Evan Thomas. Draft: for men only, women may be excluded the Supreme Court rules. *Time* 118(1):44 (July 6, 1981).
    Denniston, Lyle. What the all-boys bench did last year. *Ms.* 10(4):74, 84, 87 (October 1981).
    Draft women? The arguments for and against. *U.S. News and World Report* 90(13):30-31 (April 6, 1981).
    Eskin, Leah. Do you know your rights? *Scholastic Update* 120(15):9 (April 8, 1988).
    Gest, Ted. Another dark day for the feminist cause. *U.S. News and World Report* 91(1):53-54 (July 6, 1981).
    ———. Courts: a major battleground of social upheaval. *U.S. News and World Report* 98(3):48-50 (January 28, 1985).

Kelber, Mim. Combat in the erroneous zone. *Nation* 233(3):72-73 (July 25-August 1, 1981).

Kirkpatrick, James J. Conservatism at the High Court. *National Review* 33(15):893-895 (August 7, 1981).

Overselective service. *New Republic* 185(3):5-6, 8 (July 18, 1981).

Pike, David F. Old issues never die for Supreme Court. *U.S. News and World Report* 89(15):46 (October 13, 1980).

Press, Aric, and Diane Camper. Uncle Sam says "men only." *Newsweek* 98(1):64-65 (July 6, 1981).

Regan, Richard J. Supreme Court roundup: 1980 term. *Thought* 56(223):491-502 (December 1981).

Supreme Court: treading on thorns. *Economist* 280(7193):40-41 July 11-17, 1981.

Williams, Wendy W., and Judith L. Lichtman. Closing the law's gender gap. *Nation* 239(9):280-285 (September 29, 1984).

2274. United States Postal Service v. Council of Greenburgh Civic Associations   June 25, 1981
    453 US 114   69 LEd2d 517   101 SCt 2676
      Almanac (1981):9A
      Black 103-108
    Court rulings sow confusion. *Advertising Age* 52(29):14 (July 13, 1981).
    Supreme Court draws the line. *U.S. News and World Report* 91(1):7 (July 6, 1981).

2275. Lehman, Secretary of the Navy v. Nakshian   June 26, 1981
    453 US 156   69 LEd2d 548   101 SCt 2698
      Almanac (1981):7A

2276. California Medical Association v. Federal Election Commission (FEC)   June 26, 1981
    453 US 182   69 LEd2d 567   101 SCt 2712
      Almanac (1981):10A
      Sup Ct Review (1982):243-284
    Press, Aric, and Diane Camper. Uncle Sam says "men only." *Newsweek* 98(1):64-65 (July 6, 1981).
    Supreme Court draws the line. *U.S. News and World Report* 91(1):7 (July 6, 1981).

2277. McCarty v. McCarty   June 26, 1981
    453 US 210   69 LEd2d 589   101 SCt 2728
      Almanac (1981):4A, 10A
    Denniston, Lyle. What the all-boys bench did last year. *Ms.* 10(4):74, 84, 87 (October 1981).
    Geisel, Jerry. Court OKs strikes to force firms to join pension plans. *Business Insurance* 15(27):1, 26 (July 6, 1981).
    Kirkpatrick, James J. Conservatism at the High Court. *National Review* 33(15):893-895 (August 7, 1981).
    Quinn, Jane Bryant. Housewife's lot. [Editorial] *Newsweek* 98(11):79 (September 14, 1981).

2278. City of Newport v. Fact Concerts, Inc.   June 26, 1981
    453 US 247   69 LEd2d 616   101 SCt 2748
      Almanac (1981):15A
      En Am Con 1285-1286
    Geisel, Jerry. Court OKs strikes to force firms to join pension plans. *Business Insurance* 15(27):1, 26 (July 6, 1981).

2279. Haig, Secretary of State v. Agee   June 29, 1981
    453 US 280   69 LEd2d 640   101 SCt 2766
      Almanac (1981):9A; (1982):133-134
      Ascent 94-98+
      Burger Years 50-55
      Editorials (1981):784-793
      En Am Con 677-678, 747-755, 797-804, 888
      Fourth 173-177
      Sup Ct Review (1981):263-290

Alter, Jonathan. Slaying the message: how the Frank Snepp case hurts us all. *Washington Monthly* 13(7):43-50 (September 1981).

Brandon, George. Newspapers wait impact of high court's Agee ruling. *Editor and Publisher* 114(28):60 (July 11, 1981).

Ferguson, James R. Scientific freedom, national security, and the First Amendment. *Science* 221(4611):620-624 (August 12, 1983).

Gest, Ted. Supreme Court sets back from activism. *U.S. News and World Report* 91(2):52 (July 13, 1981).

Gillers, Stephen. Reasoning not the need. [Editorial] *Nation* 233(3):67-69 (July 25-August 1, 1981).

Grounding a critic—and others? The High Court upholds the lifting of a maverick's passport. *Time* 118(2):52 (July 13, 1981).

Halperin, Morton H. Never question the president. *Nation* 239(9):285-288 (September 29, 1984).

High Court bars spy disclosures. *Editor and Publisher* 114(27):44 (July 4, 1981).

Kirkpatrick, James J. Conservatism at the High Court. *National Review* 33(15):893-895 (August 7, 1981).

Lewin, Nathan. Supreme Court's travel bug. *New Republic* 185(4):17-20 (July 25, 1981).

Press, Aric, Diane Camper, and Christopher Ma. Court's final days. *Newsweek* 98(2):84-85 (July 13, 1981).

Regan, Richard J. Supreme Court roundup: 1980 term. *Thought* 56(223):491-502 (December 1981).

Supreme Court: treading on thorns. *Economist* 280(7193):40-41 (July 11-17, 1981).

Yankee, stay home. *Progressive* 45(9):10 (September 1981).

2280. National Labor Relations Board (NLRB) v. Amax Coal Co.   June 29, 1981
      Coupled with United Mine Workers of America v. National Labor Relations Board (NLRB)
453 US 322   69 LEd2d 672   101 SCt 2789
   Almanac (1981):12A

Geisel, Jerry. Court OKs strikes to force firms to join pension plans. *Business Insurance* 15(27):1, 26 (July 6, 1981).

High Court takes cases on inspections, pensions. *Engineering News Record* 206(6):81 (February 5, 1981).

Ruben, George. Fund trustee not bargaining agent, high court says. *Monthly Labor Review* 104(9):51 (September 1981).

2281. Columbia Broadcasting System (CBS), Inc. v. Federal Communications Commission (FCC)   July 1, 1981
      Coupled with American Broadcasting Co., Inc. v. Federal Communications Commission (FCC)
      Coupled with National Broadcasting Co., Inc. v. Federal Communications Commission (FCC)
453 US 367   69 LEd2d 706   101 SCt 2813
   En Am Con 314
   Sup Ct Review (1981):223-262; (1987):303-344

Candidates' right to air time upheld by U.S. Supreme Court. *Editor and Publisher* 114(28):22 (July 11, 1981).

Court rulings sow confusion. *Advertising Age* 52(29):14 (July 13, 1981).

Final days: the Court adjourns with a flurry. *Time* 118(2):52 (July 13, 1981).

Minow, Newton N., and Lee M. Mitchell. Putting on the candidates: the use of television in presidential elections. *Annals of the American Academy of Political and Social Science* 486:146-157 (July 1986).

Press, Aric, Diane Camper, and Christopher Ma. Court's final days. *Newsweek* 98(2):84-85 (July 13, 1981).

Regan, Richard J. Supreme Court roundup: 1980 term. *Thought* 56(223):491-502 (December 1981).

2282. Robbins v. California   July 1, 1981
453 US 420   69 LEd2d 744   101 SCt 2841
   Almanac (1981):5A; (1982):5A
   Ascent 354-357
   Editorials (1982):1441-1443

Bazelon, David L. Supreme Court review: forward—the morality of the criminal law: rights of the accused. *Journal of Criminal Law and Criminology* 72(4):1143-1170 (Winter 1981).

Bernstein, Sidney, and Michael Eisenstein. 1981 Supreme Court update: the criminal law. *Trial* 17(10):54-60, 85 (October 1981).

———. 1982 Supreme Court update: the criminal law. *Trial* 18(9):45-50, 81 (September 1982).

Carter, Jeffrey A. Supreme Court review: Fourth Amendment—of cars, containers and confusion. *Journal of Criminal Law and Criminology* 72(4):1171-1221 (Winter 1981).

Jensen, D. Lowell, and Rosemary Hart. The good faith restatement of the exclusionary rule. *Journal of Criminal Law and Criminology* 73(3):916-938 (Fall 1982).

LaFave, Wayne R. Supreme Court review: Fourth Amendment vagaries (of improbable cause, imperceptible plain view, notorious privacy, and balancing askew). *Journal of Criminal Law and Criminology* 74(4):1171-1224 (Winter 1983).

Ray, Kent S. Supreme Court review: Fourth Amendment—overextending the automobile exception to justify the warrantless search of closed containers in cars. *Journal of Criminal Law and Criminology* 73(4):1430-1451 (Winter 1982).

Regan, Richard J. Supreme Court roundup: 1980 term. *Thought* 56(223):491-502 (December 1981).

———. *Thought* 57(227):514-527 (December 1982).

2283. New York v. Belton   July 1, 1981
     453 US 454   69 LEd2d 768   101 SCt 2860
      Almanac (1981):5A
      Brennan 191-196
      Burger Years 143-168
      Editorials (1982):1441-1443
      En Am Con 1628-1635

Bazelon, David L. Supreme Court review: forward—the morality of the criminal law: rights of the accused. *Journal of Criminal Law and Criminology* 72(4):1143-1170 (Winter 1981).

Bernstein, Sidney, and Michael Eisenstein. 1981 Supreme Court update: the criminal law. *Trial* 17(10):54-60, 85 (October 1981).

Bradley, Craig M. The Court's "two model" approach to the Fourth Amendment: carpe diem! *Journal of Criminal Law and Criminology* 84(3):429-461 (Fall 1993).

Carter, Jeffrey A. Supreme Court review: Fourth Amendment—of cars, containers and confusion. *Journal of Criminal Law and Criminology* 72(4):1171-1221 (Winter 1981).

Jensen, D. Lowell, and Rosemary Hart. The good faith restatement of the exclusionary rule. *Journal of Criminal Law and Criminology* 73(3):916-938 (Fall 1982).

Katz, Lewis R. United States v. Ross: evolving standards for warrantless searches. *Journal of Criminal Law and Criminology* 74(1):172-208 (Spring 1983).

Misner, Robert L. Justifying searches on the basis of equality of treatment. *Journal of Criminal Law and Criminology* 82(3):547-578 (Fall 1991).

Regan, Richard J. Supreme Court roundup: 1980 term. *Thought* 56(223):491-502 (December 1981).

2284. Gulf Offshore Co. v. Mobil Oil Corp.   July 1, 1981
     453 US 473   69 LEd2d 784   101 SCt 2870
      Almanac (1981):14A

Due, Paul H., and David W. Robertson. Remedies for injured offshore oil workers: finding the way through the maze of applicable law. *Trial* 20(12):48-52 (December 1984).

High court upholds Montana coal tax. *Oil and Gas Journal* 79(28):42-43 (July 13, 1981).

2285. Metromedia, Inc. v. City of San Diego   July 2, 1981
     453 US 490   69 LEd2d 800   101 SCt 2882
      Almanac (1981):9A
      En Am Con 330-331, 637-639
      Magic 315-317
      Sup Ct Review (1982):195-241; (1992):29-77

Boedecker, Karl A., and Fred W. Morgan. The evolution of First Amendment protection for commercial speech. *Journal of Marketing* 59(1):38-47 (January 1995).

Court rulings sow confusion. *Advertising Age* 52(29):14 (July 13, 1981).

Final days: the Court adjourns with a flurry. *Time* 118(2):52 (July 13, 1981).

Hopkins, Jay. High Court backs billboards and cable in First decisions. *Editor and Publisher* 115(1):20 (January 2, 1982).

Regan, Richard J. Supreme Court roundup: 1980 term. *Thought* 56(223):491-502 (December 1981).

2286. Arkansas Louisiana Gas Co. v. Hall   July 2, 1981
       453 US 571   69 LEd2d 856   101 SCt 2925
         Almanac (1981):13A

2287. Commonwealth Edison Co. v. Montana   July 2, 1981
       453 US 609   69 LEd2d 884   101 SCt 2946
         Almanac (1981):13A-14A
         Documents (v. 2):846-847R
         Editorials (1981):816-821
         En Am Con 596-600
         Sup Ct Review (1989):223-259
       Drive to cap serverance taxes. *Business Week* (2698):94 (July 27, 1981).
       Final days: the Court adjourns with a flurry. *Time* 118(2):52 (July 13, 1981).
       High Court upholds Montana coal tax. *Oil and Gas Journal* 79(28):42-43 (July 13, 1981).
       Major Supreme Court business decisions in the 1980-81 term. *Business Week* (Industrial Edition) (2697):62
         (July 20, 1981).
       Montana: treasure state's treasure trove. *Economist* 280(7193):41 (July 11-17, 1981).
       Powers, Carol L. State taxation of energy resources: affirmation of Commonwealth Edison Co. v. Montana.
         Boston College Environmental Affairs Law Review 10(2):503-564 (September 1982).

2288. Dames & Moore v. Regan, Secretary of Treasury   July 2, 1981
       453 US 654   69 LEd2d 918   101 SCt 2972
         Almanac (1981):3A, 13A
         Ascent 90-94+
         Editorials (1981):800-803
         En Am Con 534
         Sup Ct Review (1986):259-316
       Arguing the hostage deal. *Newsweek* 98(1):65 (July 6, 1981).
       Driesen, David M. The congressional role in international environmental law and its implications for statutory
         interpretation. *Boston College Environmental Affairs Law Review* 19(2):287-315 (Fall/Winter 1991).
       Great Satan pays up. *Time* 118(2):31 (July 13, 1981).
       Halberstam, Malvina. Sabbatino resurrected: the act of state doctrine in the revised restatement of U.S. foreign
         relations law. *American Journal of International Law* 79(1):68-91 (January 1985).
       Major Supreme Court business decisions. *Business Week* (Industrial Edition) (2687):62 (July 20, 1981).
       Pawelek, Dick. You decide the limits of a president's power in the disputed deal with Iran. *Scholastic Update*
         (Teachers' Edition) 119(6):22-23, 27 (November 17, 1986).
       Press, Aric, Diane Camper, and Christopher Ma. Court's final days. *Newsweek* 98(2):84-85 (July 13, 1981).
       Regan, Richard J. Supreme Court roundup: 1980 term. *Thought* 56(223):491-502 (December 1981).
       Ruling on Iran may be a landmark. *Business Week* (Industrial Edition) (2697):62-64 (July 20, 1981).
       Supreme Court: treading on thorns. *Economist* 280(7193):40-41 July 11-17, 1981.

2289. Chardon v. Fernandez   November 2, 1981
       454 US 6   70 LEd2d 6   102 SCt 28
       Brooks, Thornton H., M. Daniel McGinn, and William P.H. Cary. Second generation problems facing
         employers in employment discrimination cases: continuing violations, pendent state claims, and double
         attorneys' fees. *Law and Contemporary Problems* 49(4):26-51 (Autumn 1986).

2290. Jago v. Van Curen   November 9, 1981
       454 US 14   70 LEd2d 13   102 SCt 31
       Bernstein, Sidney, and Michael Eisenstein. 1982 Supreme Court update: the criminal law, part two. *Trial*
         18(10):58-65 (October 1982).

2291. Federal Election Commission (FEC) v. Democratic Senatorial Campaign Committee   November 10, 1981
         Coupled with National Republican Senatorial Committee v. Democractic Senatorial Campaign
         Committee

454 US 27   70 LEd2d 23   102 SCt 38
   Almanac (1982):10A
   Burger Years 191-205
Morrison, Alan B. Close reins on the bureaucracy. *Nation* 239(9):290-294 (September 29, 1984).

2292. Ridgway v. Ridgway   November 10, 1981
   454 US 46   70 LEd2d 39   102 SCt 49
   Almanac (1982):15A
Quinn, Jane Bryant. Housewife's lot. [Editorial] *Newsweek* 98(11):79 (September 14, 1981).

2293. Fair Assessment in Real Estate Association, Inc. v. McNary   December 1, 1981
   454 US 100   70 LEd2d 271   102 SCt 177
   Almanac (1982):16A

2294. Weinberger, Secretary of Defense v. Catholic Action of Hawaii/Peace Education Project   December 1, 1981
   454 US 139   70 LEd2d 298   102 SCt 197
   Almanac (1982):14A
   Burger Years 50-55
Bombs, bunkers, and blind justice. *Progressive* 46(2):10-11 (February 1982).
Driesen, David M. The congressional role in international environmental law and its implications for statutory
   interpretation. *Boston College Environmental Affairs Law Review* 19(2):287-315 (Fall/Winter 1991).
Halperin, Morton H. Never question the president. *Nation* 239(9):285-288 (September 29, 1984).
Weinberger v. Catholic Action of Hawaii/Peace Education Project et al. *Boston College Environmental Affairs
   Law Review* 11(3):805-838 (December 1981).

2295. Watt, Secretary of the Interior v. Energy Action Educational Foundation   December 1, 1981
   454 US 151   70 LEd2d 309   102 SCt 205
   Almanac (1982):14A
Business issues on the Supreme Court's 1981-82 calendar. *Business Week* (2709):54 (October 12, 1981).

2296. National Labor Relations Board (NLRB) v. Hendricks County Rural Electric   December 2, 1981
   Membership Corp.
   454 US 170   70 LEd2d 323   102 SCt 216
   Almanac (1982):13A
Business issues on the Supreme Court's 1981-82 calendar. *Business Week* (2709):54 (October 12, 1981).
O'Connor has her say in dissenting opinions. *Editor and Publisher* 115(39):58 (September 25, 1982).

2297. Ralston, Warden v. Robinson   December 2, 1981
   454 US 201   70 LEd2d 345   102 SCt 233
   Almanac (1982):6A
Bernstein, Sidney, and Michael Eisenstein. 1982 Supreme Court update: the criminal law, part two. *Trial*
   18(10):58-65 (October 1982).
Mar, Linda. Supreme Court review: Federal Youth Corrections Act—YCA treatment not required during
   unexpired term of YCA inmate sentenced to consecutive adult term. *Journal of Criminal Law and
   Criminology* 73(4):1654-1677 (Winter 1982).

2298. Piper Aircraft Co. v. Reyno   December 8, 1981
   454 US 235   70 LEd2d 419   102 SCt 252
   Almanac (1982):16A
Arsenault, Richard J., and Richard W. Beard. Maritime personal injury on foreign waters. *Trial* 20(6):72-76
   (June 1984).

2299. Widmar v. Vincent   December 8, 1981
   454 US 263   70 LEd2d 440   102 SCt 269
   Almanac (1982):10A; (1983):302

Burger Years 56-91
Const (Currie) 531-533
En Am Con 1537-1538, 1546-1547, 1650-1658, 2062-2063
Godless 101+
Religion 110-111

Baron, Mark A., and Harold L. Bishop. Come one, come all. *American School Board Journal* 178(3):29-30 (March 1991).

Clapp, Rodney. Supreme Court defends religious freedom on college campuses. *Christianity Today* 26(1):46 (January 1, 1982).

The Court decisions. *Congressional Digest* 63(5):132-134, 160 (May 1984).

Drakeman, Donald L. Equal access: the continuing saga. *Christian Century* 102(10):284-285 (March 20-27, 1985).

Drinan, Robert F. The Supreme Court to review student prayer groups in high school. *America* 162(16):429-430 (April 28, 1990).

———. University funding for religious activities. *America* 172(1):16-18 (January 14-21, 1995).

Ericsson, Samuel. The Supreme Court's changing stance on religious freedom. *Christianity Today* 29(7):38-41 (April 19, 1985).

Flygare, Thomas J. De jure: worship services on campus: different standards apply to schools and universities. *Phi Delta Kappan* 63(7):487-488 (March 1982).

Hammond, Phillip E. The courts and secular humanism. *Society* 21(4):11-16 (May/June 1984).

Levicoff, Steve. Upholding students' religious freedom. [Editorial] *Christian Century* 106(36):1108-1109 (November 29, 1989).

Prayer in public schools. *Congressional Digest* 74(1):3-32 (January 1995).

Redlich, Norman. Some cracks in the wall. *Nation* 239(9):277-280 (September 29, 1984).

Regan, Richard J. Supreme Court roundup: 1981 term. *Thought* 57(227):514-527 (December 1982).

———. Supreme Court roundup: 1982 term. *Thought* 58(231):472-483 (December 1983).

Sendor, Benjamin. Equal access: courts and Congress disagree. *American School Board Journal* 171(11):7, 48 (November 1984).

———. Religious clubs gain "equal access" to schools. *American School Board Journal* 177(9):15, 41 (September 1990).

———. A school system must repent for its rent. *American School Board Journal* 181(7):5-6 (July 1994).

Smolla, Rodney A. Academic freedom, hate speech, and the idea of a university. *Law and Contemporary Problems* 53(3):195-225 (Summer 1990).

Spring, Beth. Why high school students can't discuss the Bible. *Christianity Today* 27(4):34-35 (February 18, 1983).

Swomley, John M. Public schools embattled over prayer. *Christian Century* 100(22):681-683 (July 20-27, 1983).

Tushnet, Mark. The Constitution of religion. *Review of Politics* 50(4):628-658 (Fall 1988).

Van Alstyne, William W. Academic freedom and the First Amendment in the Supreme Court of the United States: an unhurried historical review. *Law and Contemporary Problems* 53(3):79-154 (Summer 1990).

Weber, Paul J. Excessive entanglement: a wavering First Amendment standard. *Review of Politics* 46(4):483-501 (October 1984).

Young, Roy E. Religious liberty on campus. *Commonweal* 109(7):209-210 (April 9, 1982).

Zirkel, Perry A. De jure: opening the door to after-school prayer. *Phi Delta Kappan* 72(1):84-86 (September 1990).

2300. Citizens Against Rent Control/Coalition for Fair Housing v. City of Berkeley, California   December 14, 1981
454 US 290   70 LEd2d 492   102 SCt 434
     Almanac (1982):10A
     Sup Ct Review (1982):243-284

2301. Polk County v. Dodson   December 14, 1981
454 US 312   70 LEd2d 509   102 SCt 445
     Almanac (1982):17A
     En Am Con 1736-1738

Bernstein, Sidney, and Michael Eisenstein. 1982 Supreme Court update: the criminal law, part two. *Trial* 18(10):58-65 (October 1982).

2302. Tennessee v. Arkansas   December 14, 1981
      454 US 351   70 LEd2d 539   102 SCt 962
      Almanac (1982):16A

2303. Hutto v. Davis   January 11, 1982
      454 US 370   70 LEd2d 556   102 SCt 703
      Dripps, Donald A. Supreme Court review: cruel, unusual, and constitutional. *Trial* 28(5):87-89 (May 1992).

2304. Charles D. Bonanno Linen Service, Inc. v. National Labor Relations Board (NLRB)   January 12, 1982
      454 US 404   70 LEd2d 656   102 SCt 720
      Almanac (1982):13A
      Business issues on the Supreme Court's 1981-82 calendar. *Business Week* (2709):54 (October 12, 1981).
      Court faces industry issues. *Engineering News Record* 207(15):79 (October 8, 1981).
      Ruben, George. Court bans withdrawal from multiemployer talks. *Monthly Labor Review* 105(3):48 (March 1982).

2305. Cabell v. Chavez-Salido   January 12, 1982
      454 US 432   70 LEd2d 677   102 SCt 735
      Almanac (1982):8A
      Ascent 236-238+

2306. Valley Forge Christian College v. Americans United for Separation of Church and State, Inc.   January 12, 1982
      454 US 464   70 LEd2d 700   102 SCt 752
      Almanac (1982):10A
      En Am Con 1031-1038, 1958
      Godless 69-70
      Religion 42, 56-58, 135, 157-158+
      Fields, Cheryl M. High Court to decide church-state issues in 2 college cases; interns' appeal denied. *Chronicle of Higher Education* 22(2):11-12 (March 2, 1981).
      Flygare, Thomas J. De jure: Supreme Court make filling church/state lawsuits more difficult. *Phi Delta Kappan* 63(8):560-561 (April 1982).
      Lewis, Neil A. Justice O'Connor's first six months. *New Republic* 186(10):17 (March 10, 1982).
      Rathjen, Gregory J., and Harold J. Spaeth. Denial of access and ideological preferences: an analysis of the voting behavior of the Burger court justices, 1969-1976. *Western Political Quarterly* 36(1):71-87 (March 1983).

2307. Texaco, Inc. v. Short   January 12, 1982
         Coupled with Pond v. Walden
      454 US 516   70 LEd2d 738   102 SCt 781
      Almanac (1982):15A
      Sup Ct Review (1982):351-380
      High court upholds ruling on mineral interests. *Oil and Gas Journal* 80(4):110-111 (January 25, 1982).

2308. United States v. Clark   January 12, 1982
      454 US 555   70 LEd2d 768   102 SCt 805
      Almanac (1982):18A

2309. Washington v. Chrisman   January 13, 1982
      455 US 1   70 LEd2d 778   102 SCt 812
      Almanac (1982):5A

Bernstein, Sidney, and Michael Eisenstein. 1982 Supreme Court update: the criminal law. *Trial* 18(9):45-50, 81 (September 1982).

Hook, Janet, and Cheryl M. Fields. High Court upholds dorm drug seizure, skirts issue of curbs on access to campus. *Chronicle of Higher Education* 23(19):13, 18 (January 20, 1982).

2310. United States v. Vogel Fertilizer Co.   January 13, 1982
455 US 16   70 LEd2d 792   102 SCt 821
   Almanac (1982):12A

Business issues on the Supreme Court's 1981-82 calendar. *Business Week* (2709):54 (October 12, 1981).

Knight, Lee G., and Ray A. Knight. A new approach to judicial review of interpretative regs. *Journal of Taxation* 65(5):326-331 (November 1986).

Welz, Elzbieta K., and Teryl L. Minasian. Supreme Court in Vogel voids IRS's 80% brother-sister group test; wide impact seen. *Journal of Taxation* 56(4):202-205 (April 1982).

2311. Community Communications Co., Inc. v. City of Boulder, Colorado   January 13, 1982
455 US 40   70 LEd2d 810   102 SCt 835
   Almanac (1982):11A; *Almanac* (1984):257-258

Chapple, Stephan. Community Communications v. City of Boulder: an intergovernmental paradox. *Public Administration Review* 45(Special Issue):732-737 (November 1985).

Fletcher, Meg. High Court bucks precedent in municipal antitrust ruling. *Business Insurance* 19(41):15 (October 14, 1985).

Hamlin, Ross J. Application of the Sherman Act state action exemption to municipal environmental regulation: a case for broader local discretion. *Boston College Environmental Affairs Law Review* 11(3):609-664 (April 1984).

O'Connor has her say in dissenting opinions. *Editor and Publisher* 115(39):58 (September 25, 1982).

Roberts, Robert N. Municipal antitrust immunity and the state-action exemption: developments in the law. *State Government* 58(4):164-171 (Winter 1986).

Ross, Douglas. Safeguarding our federalism: lessons for the states from the Supreme Court. *Public Administration Review* 45(Special Issue):723-731 (November 1985).

A string of challenges to local regulations. *Business Week* (2709):53-54 (October 12, 1981).

Werner, Ray O. Marketing and the Supreme Court in transition, 1982-1984. *Journal of Marketing* 49(3):97-105 (Summer 1985).

2312. Kaiser Steel Corp. v. Mullins   January 13, 1982
455 US 72   70 LEd2d 833   102 SCt 851
   Almanac (1982):11A

Nelson-Horchler, Joani. On business issues: O'Connor fits conservative mold. *Industry Week* 213(3):29, 31 (May 3, 1982).

2313. Princeton University v. Schmid   January 13, 1982
455 US 100   70 LEd2d 855   102 SCt 867
   Almanac (1982):9A
   Sup Ct Review (1982):195-241

Hook, Janet, and Cheryl M. Fields. High Court upholds dorm drug seizure, skirts issue of curbs on access to campus. *Chronicle of Higher Education* 23(19):13, 18 (January 20, 1982).

Rabban, David M. AAUP in the courts: the association's representation of faculty members and faculty causes in appellate litigation. *Academe* 69(2): 1a-12a (March/April 1983).

Rabban, David M. A functional analysis of "individual" and "institutional" academic freedom under the First Amendment. *Law and Contemporary Problems* 53(3):227-301 (Summer 1990).

2314. Eddings v. Oklahoma   January 19, 1982
455 US 104   71 LEd2d 1   102 SCt 869
   Almanac (1982):6A
   Death Penalty (Streib) 21-22, 48

Death Penalty 80s 75-78

Death Penalty 90s 97-100

Bernstein, Sidney, and Michael Eisenstein. 1982 Supreme Court update: the criminal law, part two. *Trial* 18(10):58-65 (October 1982).

Erickson, William H. 1981-1982 U.S. Supreme Court decisions. *Trial* 18(11):44-49, 109 (November 1982).

Greenwald, Helene B. Supreme Court review: Eighth Amendment—minors and the death penalty. *Journal of Criminal Law and Criminology* 73(4):1525-1552 (Winter 1982).

Lewis, Neil A. Justice O'Connor's first six months. *New Republic* 186(10):17 (March 10, 1982).

Murphy, Cornelius F. The Supreme Court and capital punishment: a new hands-off approach. *USA Today* 121(2574):51-52 (March 1993).

2315. Common Cause v. Schmitt   January 19, 1982

      Coupled with Federal Elections Commission (FEC) v. American for Change

455 US 129   71 LEd2d 20   102 SCt 1266

   Almanac (1982):11A

   Sup Ct Review (1982):243-284

Money talks: free speech includes spending. *Time* 119(5):62 (February 1, 1982).

2316. Merrion, dba Merrion & Bayless v. Jicarilla Apache Tribe   January 25, 1982

      Coupled with Amoco Production Co. and Marathon Oil Co. v. Jicarilla Apache Indian Tribe

455 US 130   71 LEd2d 21   102 SCt 894

   Almanac (1982):12A

   Am Indians (Wilkinson) 39, 45-46, 130, 203+

Allen, Mark. Native American control of tribal natural resource development in the context of the federal trust and tribal self-determination. *Boston College Environmental Affairs Law Review* 16(4):857-895 (Summer 1989).

High Court allows tribal severance tax. *Oil and Gas Journal* 80(5):81-82 (February 1, 1982).

Nelson-Horchler, Joani. On business issues: O'Connor fits conservative mold. *Industry Week* 213(3):29, 31 (May 3, 1982).

2317. In Re R.M.J.   January 25, 1982

455 US 191   71 LEd2d 64   102 SCt 929

   Almanac (1982):9A

Boedecker, Karl A., and Fred W. Morgan. The evolution of First Amendment protection for commercial speech. *Journal of Marketing* 59(1):38-47 (January 1995).

Bowen, Lauren. Attorney advertising in the wake of Bates v. State Bar of Arizona (1977): a study of judicial impact. *American Politics Quarterly* 23(4):461-484 (October 1995).

Business issues on the Supreme Court's 1981-82 calendar. *Business Week* (2709):54 (October 12, 1981).

High Court hears arguments on lawyer ad rules. *Editor and Publisher* 114(46): 12-13 (November 14, 1981).

Werner, Ray O. Marketing and the Supreme Court in transition, 1982-1984. *Journal of Marketing* 49(3):97-105 (Summer 1985).

2318. Smith v. Phillips   January 25, 1982

455 US 209   71 LEd2d 78   102 SCt 940

   Almanac (1982):5A-6A

Bernstein, Sidney, and Michael Eisenstein. 1982 Supreme Court update: the criminal law, part two. *Trial* 18(10):58-65 (October 1982).

Gromer, Sharon R. Supreme Court review: Sixth Amendment—the demise of the doctrine of implied juror bias. *Journal of Criminal Law and Criminology* 73(4):1507-1524 (Winter 1982).

2319. United States v. Lee   February 23, 1982

455 US 252   71 LEd2d 127   102 SCt 1051

   Almanac (1982):17A

   En Am Con 1133, 1538-1545

   Godless 113-114

Religion 13-14
Sup Ct Review (1995):323-391

Abram, Morris B. Is "strict separation" too strict? *Public Interest* (82):81-90 (Winter 1986).

Brelis, Dean. The Amish and the law. *Time* 119(16):12-E4 (April 19, 1982).

Drinan, Robert F. The Supreme Court and religious freedom. *America* 152(12):254-255 (March 30, 1985).

Gest, Ted. The Supreme Court: a house divided: the dominant direction in the 1981-82 term was to the right. *U.S. News and World Report* 93(2)::45-46 (July 12, 1982).

Regan, Richard J. Supreme Court roundup: 1981 term. *Thought* 57(227):514-527 (December 1982).

Rose, Jonathan. Decide 10 landmark cases that define your rights. *Scholastic Update* 119(1):7-9, 21 (September 8, 1986).

Tushnet, Mark. The Constitution of religion. *Review of Politics* 50(4):628-658 (Fall 1988).

2320. Herweg v. Ray, Governor of Iowa   February 23, 1982
    455 US 265   71 LEd2d 137   102 SCt 1059
      Almanac (1982):18A

2321. City of Mesquite v. Aladdin's Castle, Inc.   February 23, 1982
    455 US 283   71 LEd2d 152   102 SCt 1070
      Almanac (1982):8A

2322. Jewett v. Commissioner of Internal Revenue   February 23, 1982
    455 US 305   71 LEd2d 170   102 SCt 1082
      Almanac (1982):12A

Interest creation starts pre-1977 disclaimer period. *Journal of Taxation* 56(5):280 (May 1982).

McCue, Howard M., III. Supreme Court to hear Irvine case—may reconsider Jewett. *Trusts and Estates* 132(12):22-24 (December 1993).

O'Connor has her say in dissenting opinions. *Editor and Publisher* 115(39):58 (September 25, 1982).

2323. New England Power Co. v. New Hampshire   February 24, 1982
         Coupled with Massachusetts v. New Hampshire
         Coupled with Roberts v. New Hampshire
    455 US 331   71 LEd2d 188   102 SCt 1096
      Almanac (1982):14A
      En Am Con 1751-1755

Hassler, Gregory L., and Karen O'Connor. Woodsy witchdoctors versus judicial guerrillas: the role and impact of competing interest groups in environmental litigation. *Boston College Environmental Affairs Law Review* 13(4):487-520 (Summer 1986).

2324. Baldrige, Secretary of Commerce v. Shapiro   February 24, 1982
         Coupled with McNichols v. Baldridge, Secretary of Commerce
    455 US 345   71 LEd2d 199   102 SCt 1103
      Almanac (1982):18A

2325. Havens Realty Corp. v. Coleman   February 24, 1982
    455 US 363   71 LEd2d 214   102 SCt 1114
      Almanac (1982):7A

Brooks, Thornton H., M. Daniel McGinn, and William P. H. Cary. Second generation problems facing employers in employment discrimination cases: continuing violations, pendent state claims, and double attorneys' fees. *Law and Contemporary Problems* 49(4):26-51 (Autumn 1986).

2326. Zipes v. Trans World Airlines, Inc. (TWA)   February 24, 1982
         Coupled with Independent Federation of Flight Attendants v. Trans World Airlines, Inc. (TWA)
    455 US 385   71 LEd2d 234   102 SCt 1127
      Almanac (1982):6A-7A

2327. G. D. Searle & Co. v. Cohn   February 24, 1982
      455 US 404   71 LEd2d 250   102 SCt 1137
        Almanac (1982):14A

      Geisel, Jerry. Supreme Court will rule on N.J. product lawsuit. *Business Insurance* 15(41):2, 81 (October 12,
        1981).

2328. Logan v. Zimmerman Brush Co.   February 24, 1982
      455 US 422   71 LEd2d 265   102 SCt 1148
        Almanac (1982):6A
        En Am Con 1465-1472
        Sup Ct Review (1982):85-125

      Plater, Zygmunt J. B., and William Lund Norine. Through the looking glass of eminent domain: exploring the
        "arbitrary and capricious" test and substantive rationality review of governmental decisions. *Boston College
        Environmental Affairs Law Review* 16(4):661-752 (Summer 1989).

2329. White v. New Hampshire Department of Employment Security   March 2, 1982
      455 US 445   71 LEd2d 325   102 SCt 1162
        Almanac (1982):16A

2330. Railway Labor Executives' Association v. Gibbons   March 2, 1982
      455 US 457   71 LEd2d 335   102 SCt 1169
        Almanac (1982):11A-12A
        Sup Ct Review (1982):25-47; (1991):143-177

2331. Murphy v. Hunt   March 2, 1982
      455 US 478   71 LEd2d 353   102 SCt 1181
        Almanac (1982):6A

2332. Village of Hoffman Estates v. Flipside, Hoffman Estates, Inc.   March 3, 1982
      455 US 489   71 LEd2d 362   102 SCt 1186
        Almanac (1982):14A
        Editorials (1982):274-279
        En Am Con 1955-1957

      Bernstein, Sidney, and Michael Eisenstein. 1982 Supreme Court update: the criminal law, part two. *Trial*
        18(10):58-65 (October 1982).
      Gest, Ted. The Supreme Court: a house divided: the dominant direction in the 1981-82 term was to the right.
        U.S. News and World Report 93(2):45-46 (July 12, 1982).
      Vawrinek, Jeffrey J. Supreme Court review: First Amendment—drug paraphernalia statutes and the
        Constitution: the court creates a legal haze. *Journal of Criminal Law and Criminology* 73(4):1365-1387
        (Winter 1982).

2333. Rose, Warden v. Lundy   March 3, 1982
      455 US 509   71 LEd2d 379   102 SCt 1198
        Almanac (1982):16A

      Bernstein, Sidney, and Michael Eisenstein. 1982 Supreme Court update: the criminal law. *Trial* 18(9):45-50, 81
        (September 1982).
      Erickson, William H. 1981-1982 U.S. Supreme Court decisions. *Trial* 18(11):44-49, 109 (November 1982).
      Neuenschwander, Jan. Supreme Court review: habeas corpus—much ado about very little: the total exhaustion
        rule. *Journal of Criminal Law and Criminology* 73(4):1641-1653 (Winter 1982).
      Wells, Diane. Federal habeas corpus and the death penalty: a need for a return to the principles of Furman.
        Journal of Criminal Law and Criminology 80(2):427-490 (Summer 1989).

2334. Marine Bank v. Weaver   March 8, 1982
      455 US 551   71 LEd2d 409   102 SCt 1220
        Almanac (1982):12A

      Business issues on the Supreme Court's 1981-82 calendar. *Business Week* (2709):54 (October 12, 1981).

Gest, Ted. The Supreme Court: a house divided: the dominant direction in the 1981-82 term was to the right. *U.S. News and World Report* 93(2):45-46 (July 12, 1982).

2335. United Mine Workers of America Health & Retirement Funds v. Robinson   March 8, 1982
     455 US 562   71 LEd2d 419   102 SCt 1226
     Almanac (1982):13A

2336. Bread Political Action Committee v. Federal Election Commission (FEC)   March 8, 1982
     455 US 577   71 LEd2d 432   102 SCt 1235
     Almanac (1982):11A

     Gest, Ted. The Supreme Court: a house divided: the dominant direction in the 1981-82 term was to the right. *U.S. News and World Report* 93(2):45-46 (July 12, 1982).

2337. Fletcher v. Weir   March 22, 1982
     455 US 603   71 LEd2d 490   102 SCt 1309
     Melson, David E. Supreme Court review: Fourteenth Amendment—criminal procedure: the impeachment use of post-arrest silence which precedes the receipt of Miranda warnings. *Journal of Criminal Law and Criminology* 73(4):1572-1594 (Winter 1982).

2338. U. S. Industries/Federal Sheet Metal, Inc.   March 23, 1982
     v. Director, Office of Workers' Compensation Programs, United States Department of Labor
     455 US 608   71 LEd2d 495   102 SCt 1312
     Almanac (1982):13A

2339. Lane v. Williams   March 23, 1982
     455 US 624   71 LEd2d 508   102 SCt 1322
     Almanac (1982):16A

     Watson, G. Andrews. Supreme Court review: mootness—contingent collateral consequences in the context of collateral challenges. *Journal of Criminal Law and Criminology* 73(4):1678-1689 (Winter 1982).

2340. McElroy v. United States   March 23, 1982
     455 US 642   71 LEd2d 522   102 SCt 1332
     Almanac (1982):6A

2341. American Medical Association (AMA) v. Federal Trade Commission (FTC)   March 23, 1982
     455 US 676   71 LEd2d 546   102 SCt 1744
     Almanac (1982):12A

     The antitrust threat to technical standards. *Business Week* (2742):31-32 (June 7, 1982).

     Business issues on the Supreme Court's 1981-82 calendar. *Business Week* (2709):54 (October 12, 1981).

2342. United Transportation Union v. Long Island Railroad Co.   March 24, 1982
     455 US 678   71 LEd2d 547   102 SCt 1349
     Almanac (1982):14A

     Gest, Ted. The Supreme Court: a house divided: the dominant direction in the 1981-82 term was to the right. *U.S. News and World Report* 93(2):45-46 (July 12, 1982).

     Orren, Karen. The primacy of labor in American constitutional development. *American Political Science Review* 89(2):377-388 (June 1995).

     Stephens, Pamela J. Implementing federal energy policy at the state and local levels: "every power requisite." *Boston College Environmental Affairs Law Review* 10(4):875-904 (May 1983).

2343. Underwriters National Assurance Co.   March 24, 1982
     v. North Carolina Life and Accident and Health Insurance Guaranty Association
     455 US 691   71 LEd2d 558   102 SCt 1357
     Almanac (1982):15A

2344. United States v. New Mexico   March 24, 1982
      455 US 720   71 LEd2d 580   102 SCt 1373
      Almanac (1982):15A

2345. Santosky v. Kramer   March 24, 1982
      455 US 745   71 LEd2d 599   102 SCt 1388
      Almanac (1982):9A
      En Am Con 686-688
      Sup Ct Review (1982):85-125
      Fuerst, J. S., and Roy Petty. Due process—how much is enough? *Public Interest* (79):96-110 (Spring 1985).
      Shulman, Barbara S. Supreme Court review: Fourteenth Amendment—the Supreme Court's mandate for proof
         beyond a preponderance of the evidence in terminating parental rights. *Journal of Criminal Law and
         Criminology* 73(4):1595-1611 (Winter 1982).

2346. United States v. MacDonald   March 31, 1982
      456 US 1   71 LEd2d 696   102 SCt 1497
      Almanac (1982):5A
      En Am Con 1189, 1717-1718
      Bernstein, Sidney, and Michael Eisenstein. 1982 Supreme Court update: the criminal law, part two. *Trial*
         18(10):58-65 (October 1982).
      Gest, Ted. The Supreme Court: a house divided: the dominant direction in the 1981-82 term was to the right.
         U.S. News and World Report 93(2):45-46 (July 12, 1982).
      Moore, Cathy E. Supreme Court review: Sixth Amendment—limited protection against excessive prosecutorial
         delay. *Journal of Criminal Law and Criminology* 73(4):1491-1506 (Winter 1982).
      Stopped clock: Dr. MacDonald jailed again. *Time* 119(15):54 (April 12, 1982).

2347. Weinberger, Secretary of Defense v. Rossi   March 31, 1982
      456 US 25   71 LEd2d 715   102 SCt 1510
      Almanac (1982):18A

2348. Brown v. Hartlage   April 5, 1982
      456 US 45   71 LEd2d 732   102 SCt 1523
      Almanac (1982):9A

2349. American Tobacco Co. v. Patterson   April 5, 1982
      456 US 63   71 LEd2d 748   102 SCt 1534
      Almanac (1982):7A
      Burger Court 160-161
      And now the Arizona twins. *Time* 119(16):49 (April 19, 1982).
      Business issues on the Supreme Court's 1981-82 calendar. *Business Week* (2709):54 (October 12, 1981).

2350. Mills v. Habluetzel   April 5, 1982
      456 US 91   71 LEd2d 770   102 SCt 1549
      Almanac (1982):8A

2351. Engle v. Isaac   April 5, 1982
      456 US 107   71 LEd2d 783   102 SCt 1558
      Almanac (1982):16A
      And now the Arizona twins. *Time* 119(16):49 (April 19, 1982).
      Bamonte, Thomas J. Supreme Court review: habeas corpus—limiting the availability of habeas corpus after a
         procedural default. *Journal of Criminal Law and Criminology* 73(4):1612-1640 (Winter 1982).
      Bernstein, Sidney, and Michael Eisenstein. 1982 Supreme Court update: the criminal law. *Trial* 18(9):45-50, 81
         (September 1982).
      Erickson, William H. 1981-1982 U.S. Supreme court decisions. *Trial* 18(11):44-49, 109 (November 1982).

2352. United States v. Frady   April 5, 1982
      456 US 152   71 LEd2d 816   102 SCt 1584
        Almanac (1982):16A

        Bamonte, Thomas J. Supreme Court review: habeas corpus—limiting the availability of habeas corpus after a procedural default. *Journal of Criminal Law and Criminology* 73(4):1612-1640 (Winter 1982).

        Bernstein, Sidney, and Michael Eisenstein. 1982 Supreme Court update: the criminal law. *Trial* 18(9):45-50, 81 (September 1982).

        Erickson, William H. 1981-1982 U.S. Supreme Court decisions. *Trial* 18(11):44-49, 109 (November 1982).

2353. Schweiker, Secretary of Health and Human Services v. McClure   April 20, 1982
      456 US 188   72 LEd2d 1   102 SCt 1665
        Almanac (1982):18A

2354. United States v. Erika, Inc.   April 20, 1982
      456 US 201   72 LEd2d 12   102 SCt 1650
        Almanac (1982):18A

2355. International Longshoremen's Association, AFL-CIO v. Allied International, Inc.   April 20, 1982
      456 US 212   72 LEd2d 21   102 SCt 1656
        Almanac (1982):13A
        Black 125-132

2356. Larson v. Valente   April 21, 1982
      456 US 228   72 LEd2d 33   102 SCt 1673
        Almanac (1982):10A
        En Am Con 527-538, 1125
        Godless 110-111
        Sup Ct Review (1995):323-391

        Gest, Ted. The Supreme Court: a house divided: the dominant direction in the 1981-82 term was to the right. *U.S. News and World Report* 93(2):45-46 (July 12, 1982).

        Regan, Richard J. Regulating cult activities: the limits of religious freedom. *Thought* 61(241):185-196 (June 1986).

        ———. Supreme Court roundup: 1981 term. *Thought* 57(227):514-527 (December 1982).

        Taylor, Barry W. Diversion of church funds to personal use: state, federal and private sanctions. *Journal of Criminal Law and Criminology* 73(3):1204-1237 (Fall 1982).

2357. Pullman-Standard v. Swint   April 27, 1982
          Coupled with United Steelworkers v. Swint
      456 US 273   72 LEd2d 66   102 SCt 1781
        Almanac (1982):7A

        Askin, Steve. Last hired, first fired? *Black Enterprise* 13(1):17 (August 1982).

        Business issues on the Supreme Court's 1981-82 calendar. *Business Week* (2709):54 (October 12, 1981).

2358. Weinberger, Secretary of Defense v. Romero-Barcelo   April 27, 1982
      456 US 305   72 LEd2d 91   102 SCt 1798
        Almanac (1982):14A

        Collins, Michael. The dilemma of the downstream state: the untimely demise of federal common law nuisance. *Boston College Environmental Affairs Law Review* 11(2):295-412 (January 1984).

        Fregeau, Jason David. Statutes and judicial discretion: against the law . . . sort of. *Boston College Environmental Affairs Law Review* 18(3):501-542 (Spring 1991).

        Jordan, Scott J. Awarding attorney's fees to environmental plaintiffs under a private attorney general theory. *Boston College Environmental Affairs Law Review* 14(2):287-311 (Winter 1987).

2359. Southern Pacific Transportation Co. v. Commercial Metals Co.   April 27, 1982
      456 US 336   72 LEd2d 114   102 SCt 1815

Almanac (1982):12A

2360. Merrill Lynch, Pierce, Fenner and Smith, Inc. v. Curran   May 3, 1982
            Coupled with New York Mercantile Exchange v. Leist
            Coupled with Clayton Brokerage Co. of St. Louis v. Leist
            Coupled with Heinhold Commodities, Inc. v. Leist
    456 US 353   72 LEd2d 182   102 SCt 1825
      Almanac (1982):12A

Business issues on the Supreme Court's 1981-82 calendar. *Business Week* (2709):54 (October 12, 1981).

Gest, Ted. The Supreme Court: a house divided: the dominant direction in the 1981-82 term was to the right.
    U.S. News and World Report 93(2):45-46 (July 12, 1982).

Schwartz, Herman. A scorecard for the new Court term. *Nation* 235(12):353, 367-370 (October 16, 1982).

2361. Zant, Warden v. Stephens   May 3, 1982
    456 US 410   72 LEd2d 222   102 SCt 1856
      Almanac (1982):6A

Mayell, Manvin S. Supreme Court review: Eighth Amendment—proportionality review of death sentences not
    required. *Journal of Criminal Law and Criminology* 75(3):839-854 (Fall 1984).

Murphy, Cornelius F. The Supreme Court and capital punishment: a new hands-off approach. *USA Today*
    121(2574):51-52 (March 1993).

2362. O'Dell v. Espinoza   May 3, 1982
    456 US 430   72 LEd2d 237   102 SCt 1865
      Almanac (1982):7A-8A

2363. Finnegan v. Leu   May 17, 1982
    456 US 431   72 LEd2d 239   102 SCt 1867
      Almanac (1982):13A
      Burger Years 228-239

Bernstein, Jules, and Laurence E. Gold. Should the courts determine policy? *Nation* 234(21):654-655 (May 29,
    1982).

Fox, Arthur. Showing workers who's the boss. *Nation* 239(9):295-299 (September 29, 1984).

2364. Greene v. Lindsey   May 17, 1982
    456 US 444   72 LEd2d 249   102 SCt 1874
      Almanac (1982):9A

2365. Kremer v. Chemical Construction Corp.   May 17, 1982
    456 US 461   72 LEd2d 262   102 SCt 1883
      Almanac (1982):7A

2366. North Haven Board of Education v. Bell, Secretary of Education   May 17, 1982
    456 US 512   72 LEd2d 299   102 SCt 1912
      Almanac (1982):7A
      En Am Con 607

Erickson, William H. 1981-1982 U.S. Supreme Court decisions. *Trial* 18(11):44-49, 109 (November 1982).

Fields, Cheryl M. High Court to decide church-state issues in 2 college cases; interns' appeal denied. *Chronicle
    of Higher Education* 22(2):11-12 (March 2, 1981).

————. Justices rule Maryland cannot charge out-of-state tuition to certain aliens. *Chronicle of Higher
    Education* 24(19):11, 14 (July 7, 1982).

————. Supreme Court lets sex-bias ruling stand and acts on other college cases. *Chronicle of Higher
    Education* 24(9):13 (April 28, 1982).

Flygare, Thomas J. De jure: Supreme Court says Title IX covers employment but raises a serious question
    about the future impact of the law. *Phi Delta Kappan* 64(2):134-136 (October 1982).

From Tilton to Ewing: some major higher-education decisions of the Burger Court. *Chronicle of Higher Education* 32(17):10 (June 25, 1986).

Kuceris, Misty. The High Court gives your employees another way to fight sex discrimination. *American School Board Journal* 169(8):21-24, 38 (August 1982).

O'Hara, Julie Underwood. Use this legal briefing to assess your board's position on comparable worth. *American School Board Journal* 172(8):26-27 (August 1985).

Pending Civil Rights Legislation. *Congressional Digest* 64(1):1-32 (January 1985).

Regan, Richard J. Supreme Court roundup: 1981 term. *Thought* 57(227):514-527 (December 1982).

Ruben, George. High Court finds two schools guilty of job bias. *Monthly Labor Review* 105(7):55 (July 1982).

Simmons, Althea T. L. From Brown to Grove City: blueprint for education. *Crisis* 91(5):6-10 (May 1984).

Sloviter, Dolores K. Faculty in federal court: decreasing receptivity? *Academe* 68(5):19-23 (September/October 1982).

2367. American Society of Mechanical Engineers, Inc. v. Hydrolevel Corp.   May 17, 1982
        456 US 556   72 LEd2d 330   102 SCt 1935
        Almanac (1982):11A

        Court faces industry issues. *Engineering News Record* 207(15):79 (October 8, 1981).

        Hydrolevel wins case: standard-setters stunned but won't fold up shop. *Engineering News Record* 208(21):11-12 (May 27, 1982).

        Societies liable for codes set by members. *Chemical and Engineering News* 60(21):7 (May 24, 1982).

        Werner, Ray O. Marketing and the Supreme Court in transition, 1982-1984. *Journal of Marketing* 49(3):97-105 (Summer 1985).

2368. United States Department of State v. Washington Post Co.   May 17, 1982
        456 US 595   72 LEd2d 358   102 SCt 1957
        Almanac (1982):18A

2369. Hopper v. Evans   May 24, 1982
        456 US 605   72 LEd2d 367   102 SCt 2049
        Almanac (1982):6A

2370. Federal Bureau of Investigation (FBI) v. Abramson   May 24, 1982
        456 US 615   72 LEd2d 376   102 SCt 2054
        Almanac (1982):18A

        Hale, F. Dennis. Shop talk at thirty: the Powell seat on the U.S. Supreme Court. [Editorial] *Editor and Publisher* 120(35):56, 44 (August 29, 1987).

        O'Connor has her say in dissenting opinions. *Editor and Publisher* 115(39):58 (September 25, 1982).

2371. Woelke & Romero Framing, Inc. v. National Labor Relations Board (NLRB)   May 24, 1982
            Coupled with Pacific Northwest Chapter of the Associated Builders and Contractors, Inc. v. National Labor Relations Board (NLRB)
            Coupled with Oregon-Columbia Chapter, Associated General Contractors of America v. National Labor Relations Board (NLRB)
        456 US 645   72 LEd2d 398   102 SCt 2071
        Almanac (1982):13A

        Court faces industry issues. *Engineering News Record* 207(15):79 (October 8, 1981).

        Losers could win in subcontracting case. *Engineering News Record* 208(22):58 (June 3, 1982).

2372. Oregon v. Kennedy   May 24, 1982
        456 US 667   72 LEd2d 416   102 SCt 2083
        Almanac (1982):5A

        Bernstein, Sidney, and Michael Eisenstein. 1982 Supreme Court update: the criminal law. *Trial* 18(9):45-50, 81 (September 1982).

Schmitt, Deborah L. Supreme Court review: Fifth Amendment—twice jeopardizing the rights of the accused: the Supreme Court's Tibbs and Kennedy decisions. *Journal of Criminal Law and Criminology* 73(4):1474-1490 (Winter 1982).

2373. Insurance Corp. of Ireland, Ltd. v. Compagnie des Bauxites de Guinee   June 1, 1982
    456 US 694   72 LEd2d 492   102 SCt 2099
        Almanac (1982):16A

2374. Summit Valley Industries, Inc. v. Local 112, United Brotherhood of Carpenters and   June 1, 1982
    Joiners of America
    456 US 717   72 LEd2d 511   102 SCt 2112
        Almanac (1982):13A
    Bomster, Mark. Say High Court slants toward business. *Electronic News* 28(1401):6 (July 12, 1982).

2375. Army and Air Force Exchange Service v. Sheehan   June 1, 1982
    456 US 728   72 LEd2d 520   102 SCt 2118
        Almanac (1982):16A

2376. Federal Energy Regulatory Commission (FERC) v. Mississippi   June 1, 1982
    456 US 742   72 LEd2d 532   102 SCt 2126
        Almanac (1982):14A
        En Am Con 637-639
    Business issues on the Supreme Court's 1981-82 calendar. *Business Week* (2709):54 (October 12, 1981).
    Howe, Shippen. The Mississippi PURPA case: states' rights revisited. *Public Utilities Fortnightly* 110(3):58-62 (August 5, 1982).
    Iwler, Louis. States back Purpa ruling by U.S. Supreme Court. *Electrical World* 198(3):19-20 (March 1984).
    ———. Supreme Court rules Purpa is constitutional. *Electrical World* 196(7):25-26 (July 1982).
    Martin, Stanley A. Problems with PURPA: the need for state legislation to encourage cogeneration and small power production. *Boston College Environmental Affairs Law Review* 11(1):149-202 (October 1983).
    O'Neill, Andrew J. Retail electric rates: drawing the line between federal and state authority under the commerce clause. *Public Utilities Fortnightly* 112(9):52-55 (October 27, 1983).
    Stephens, Pamela J. Implementing federal energy policy at the state and local levels: "every power requisite." *Boston College Environmental Affairs Law Review* 10(4):875-904 (May 1983).
    Thomas, Charlotte E. The Cape Cod National Seashore: a case study of federal administrative control over traditionally local land use decisions. *Boston College Environmental Affairs Law Review* 12(2):225-272 (Winter 1985).

2377. United States v. Ross   June 1, 1982
    456 US 798   72 LEd2d 572   102 SCt 2157
        Almanac (1982):5A; (1985):5A
        Const Law 359-362R
        Editorials (1982):636-645, 1441-1443
        En Am Con 1611, 1628-1635
    Bernstein, Sidney, and Michael Eisenstein. 1982 Supreme Court update: the criminal law. *Trial* 18(9):45-50, 81 (September 1982).
    Bobber, Bernard J. Supreme Court review: Fourth Amendment—warrantless search of packages seized from an automobile. *Journal of Criminal Law and Criminology* 76(4):933-954 (Winter 1985).
    Cops' new ally: Supreme Court. *U.S. News and World Report* 92(23):8 (June 14, 1982).
    The Court's ruling on auto searches. *Newsweek* 99(24):64 (June 14, 1982).
    Katz, Lewis R. United States v. Ross: evolving standards for warrantless searches. *Journal of Criminal Law and Criminology* 74(1):172-208 (Spring 1983).
    Lochhead, George S. Supreme Court review: Fourth Amendment—expanding the scope of automobile consent searches. *Journal of Criminal Law and Criminology* 82(4):773-796 (Winter 1992).

Ray, Kent S. Supreme Court review: Fourth Amendment—overextending the automobile exception to justify the warrantless search of closed containers in cars. *Journal of Criminal Law and Criminology* 73(4):1430-1451 (Winter 1982).

Regan, Richard J. Supreme Court roundup: 1981 term. *Thought* 57(227):514-527 (December 1982).

Searching cars: court gives police more power. *Time* 119(24):70 (June 14, 1982).

2378. Inwood Laboratories, Inc. v. Ives Laboratories, Inc. June 1, 1982
    456 US 844   72 LEd2d 606   102 SCt 2182
      Almanac (1982):12A-13A

High court: few CPI cases. *Chemical Week* 129(15):15-16 (October 7, 1981).

High court says drug firms not responsible for pharmacists. *Chemical Marketing Reporter* 221:3, 61 (June 7, 1982).

Now the generic drugs can be look-alikes, too. *Chemical Week* 130(26):41-42 (June 30, 1982).

2379. Rivera-Rodriguez v. Popular Democratic Party   June 7, 1982
    457 US 1   72 LEd2d 628   102 SCt 2194
      Almanac (1982):11A
      En Am Con 616-617

2380. Jackson Transit Authority   June 7, 1982
      v. Local Division 1285, Amalgamated Transit Union, AFL-CIO-CLC
    457 US 15   72 LEd2d 639   102 SCt 2211
      Almanac (1982):13

2381. Tibbs v. Florida   June 7, 1982
    457 US 31   72 LEd2d 652   102 SCt 2211
      Almanac (1982):5A

Bernstein, Sidney, and Michael Eisenstein. 1982 Supreme Court update: the criminal law. *Trial* 18(9):45-50, 81 (September 1982).

Schmitt, Deborah L. Supreme Court review: Fifth Amendment—twice jeopardizing the rights of the accused: the Supreme Court's Tibbs and Kennedy decisions. *Journal of Criminal Law and Criminology* 73(4):1474-1490 (Winter 1982).

2382. Zobel v. Williams, Commissioner of Revenue, and Alaska   June 14, 1982
    457 US 55   72 LEd2d 672   102 SCt 2309
      Almanac (1982):9A
      Const (Currie) 580-585
      En Am Con 1458-1461, 1593-1596

Alaska: misplaced generosity. *Economist* 283(7242):47-48 (June 19-25, 1982).

2383. Cory, Controller of the State of California v. White, Attorney General of Texas   June 14, 1982
    457 US 85   72 LEd2d 694   102 SCt 2325
      Almanac (1982):14A

Bomster, Mark. Say High Court slants toward business. *Electronic News* 28(1401):6 (July 12, 1982).

2384. United Steelworkers of America, AFL-CIO-CLC v. Sadlowski   June 14, 1982
    457 US 102   72 LEd2d 707   102 SCt 2339
      Almanac (1982):13A
      Burger Court 163-164
      Burger Years 228-239

Barnes, Alan. What role for outsiders? *Nation* 234 (21):639, 652 (May 29, 1982).

Bernstein, Jules, and Laurence E. Gold. Should the courts determine policy? *Nation* 234(21):654-655 (May 29, 1982).

Bomster, Mark. Say High Court slants toward business. *Electronic News* 28(1401):6 (July 12, 1982).

Fox, Arthur. Showing workers who's the boss. *Nation* 239(9):295-299 (September 29, 1984).

Hentoff, Nat. Talkin' union. *Progressive* 46(11):41-43 (November 1982).

Ruben, George. Court bans "nonunion" contributors to campaigns. *Monthly Labor Review* 105(8):58 (August 1982).

2385. Blum v. Bacon   June 14, 1982
457 US 132   72 LEd2d 728   102 SCt 2355
Almanac (1982):17A-18A

2386. General Telephone Co. of the Southwest v. Falcon   June 14, 1982
457 US 147   72 LEd2d 740   102 SCt 2364
Almanac (1982):7A

Bomster, Mark. Say High Court slants toward business. *Electronic News* 28(1401):6 (July 12, 1982).

Gray, Mary W. The halls of ivy and the halls of justice: resisting sex discrimination against faculty women. *Academe* 71(5):33-41 (September/October 1985).

2387. Sumitomo Shoji America, Inc. v. Avagliano   June 15, 1982
457 US 176   72 LEd2d 765   102 SCt 2374
Almanac (1982):7A

Bomster, Mark. Ruling extends hire law to subs. *Electronic News* 28(1399):Supp J (June 28, 1982).

———. Say High Court slants toward business. *Electronic News* 28(1401):6 (July 12, 1982).

Breslin, Catherine. The Sumitomo thirteen. *Ms.* 16(8):30-31 (February 1988).

2388. Diedrich v. Commissioner of Internal Revenue   June 15, 1982
        Coupled with United Missouri Bank of Kansas v. Commissioner of Internal Revenue
457 US 191   72 LEd2d 777   102 SCt 2414
Almanac (1982):12A

Braunstein, Samuel L. Net gift still a valuable planning technique despite Supreme Court's decision in Diedrich. *Practical Accountant* 15(9):41-42 (September 1982).

Bromberg, Barbara Schwartz. Trust taxes. *Trusts and Estates* 121(8):56 (August 1982).

Duhl, Stuart, and Jeffrey L. Kwall. Supreme Court holds that net gift triggers income to donor: an analysis of Diedrich. *Journal of Taxation* 57(3):130-134 (September 1982).

2389. Plyler, Superintendent v. Doe   June 15, 1982
        Coupled with Texas v. Certain Named and Unnamed Undocumented Alien Children
457 US 202   72 LEd2d 786   102 SCt 2382
Almanac (1982):8A
Brennan 244-246
Const (Currie) 500-504
Const (Friendly) 239-247
Const Law 538-543R
Documents (v. 2):849-852R
Editorials (1982):698-705
En Am Con 608-612, 1398
Sup Ct Review (1982):167-194

Aliens in school: Court upholds their rights. *Time* 119(26):77 (June 28, 1982).

American survey: the west comes to court. *Economist* 284(7245):21-22 (July 10-16 1982).

Aronow, Geoffrey, and Owen Fiss. The High Court illusion of victory. *Nation* 235(21):647-650 (December 18, 1982).

The children of illegal aliens. [Editorial] *America* 147(1):2-3 (June 26-July 3, 1982).

Delon, Floyd G. The legacy of Thurgood Marshall. *Journal of Negro Education* 63(3):278-288 (Summer 1994).

Flygare, Thomas J. De jure: ten years after Goss v. Lopez: an interview with Peter D. Roos. *Phi Delta Kappan* 66(6):441-442 (February 1985).

Gest, Ted. The Supreme Court: a house divided: the dominant direction in the 1981-82 term was to the right. *U.S. News and World Report* 93(2):45-46 (July 12, 1982).

Gillers, Stephen. The Warren Court—it still lives. *Nation* 237(7):193, 208-210 (September 17, 1983).

Illegal aliens: a right to learn. *Economist* 283(7242):46-47 (June 19-25, 1982).

Mosk, Stanley. The emerging agenda in state constitutional rights law. *Annals of the American Academy of Political and Social Science* 496:54-64 (March 1988).

Newsfront: last-minute ruling by Powell opens door to Texas schools for illegal aliens. *Phi Delta Kappan* 62(2):83 (October 1980).

Oakes, Jeannie. Tracking and ability grouping in American schools: some constitutional questions. *Teachers College Record* 84(4):801-819 (Summer 1983).

Reagan's reverse in school policy. *Newsweek* 98(12):73 (September 21, 1981).

Regan, Richard J. Supreme Court roundup: 1981 term. *Thought* 57(227):514-527 (December 1982).

Rosen, Jeffrey. The war on immigrants: why the courts can't save us. *New Republic* 212(5):22, 24-26 (January 30, 1995).

School is in for illegal aliens. *Newsweek* 99(26):47 (June 28, 1982).

Schwartz, Herman. Concern for the basic necessities. *Nation* 239(9):299-300 (September 29, 1984).

Stone, Marvin. Help for illegals—how much? [Editorial] *U.S. News and World Report* 93(7):74 (August 16, 1982).

2390. Hathorn v. Lovorn   June 15, 1982
      457 US 255   72 LEd2d 824   102 SCt 2421
         Almanac (1982):10A

2391. California ex rel State Lands Commission v. United States   June 18, 1982
      457 US 273   73 LEd2d 1   102 SCt 2432
         Almanac (1982):16A

2392. Mills v. Rogers   June 18, 1982
      457 US 291   73 LEd2d 16   102 SCt 2442
         Almanac (1982):9A

Aliens in school: Court upholds their rights. *Time* 119(26):77 (June 28, 1982).

Herbert, Wray. Court bolsters mental patients' rights. *Science News* 121(26):420 (June 26, 1982).

Meisel, Alan. The rights of the mentally ill under state constitutions. *Law and Contemporary Problems* 45(3):7-40 (Summer 1982).

Refusing medication: legal battle goes on. *Science News* 119(15):230 (April 11, 1981).

2393. Youngberg v. Romeo   June 18, 1982
      457 US 307   73 LEd2d 28   102 SCt 2452
         Almanac (1982):9A
         Burger Years 125-139
         En Am Con 1247-1249, 1249-1251
         Sup Ct Review (1982):85-125

Aliens in school: Court upholds their rights. *Time* 119(26):77 (June 28, 1982).

Herbert, Wray. Court bolsters mental patients' rights. *Science News* 121(26):420 (June 26, 1982).

Meisel, Alan. The rights of the mentally ill under state constitutions. *Law and Contemporary Problems* 45(3):7-40 (Summer 1982).

Regan, Richard J. Supreme Court roundup: 1981 term. *Thought* 57(227):514-527 (December 1982).

2394. Arizona v. Maricopa County Medical Society   June 18, 1982
      457 US 332   73 LEd2d 48   102 SCt 2466
         Almanac (1982):11A
         Sup Ct Review (1982):319-349

Aliens in school: Court upholds their rights. *Time* 119(26):77 (June 28, 1982).

Dolan, Michael W. Congress, the executive, and the court: the great resale price maintenance affair of 1983. *Public Administration Review* 45(Special Issue):718-722 (November 1985).

Werner, Ray O. Marketing and the Supreme Court in transition, 1982-1984. *Journal of Marketing* 49(3):97-105 (Summer 1985).

2395. United States v. Goodwin   June 18, 1982
      457 US 368   73 LEd2d 74   102 SCt 2485
        Almanac (1982):5A
        Loud 224-228

        Erlinder, C. Peter, and David C. Thomas. Prohibiting prosecutorial vindictiveness while protecting prosecutorial discretion: toward a principled resolution of a due process dilemma. *Journal of Criminal Law and Criminology* 76(2):341-438 (Summer 1985).

        Mills, Elizabeth M. Supreme Court review: Fifth Amendment—prosecutor not presumed vindictive in pretrial charge increases after defendant's request for jury trial. *Journal of Criminal Law and Criminology* 73(4):1452-1473 (Winter 1982).

2396. California v. Grace Brethren Church   June 18, 1982
           Coupled with United States v. Grace Brethren Church
      457 US 393   73 LEd2d 93   102 SCt 2498
        Almanac (1982):16A-17A

2397. Middlesex County Ethics Committee v. Garden State Bar Association   June 21, 1982
      457 US 423   73 LEd2d 116   102 SCt 2515
        Almanac (1982):17A

2398. Connecticut v. Teal   June 21, 1982
      457 US 440   73 LEd2d 130   102 SCt 2525
        Almanac (1982):7A

        Bomster, Mark. Say High Court slants toward business. *Electronic News* 28(1401):6 (July 12, 1982).

        The Civil Rights Act of 1990. *Congressional Digest* 69(8-9):196-224 (August/September 1990).

        Fields, Cheryl M. Supreme Court rules in 2 job-bias cases that have implications for colleges. *Chronicle of Higher Education* 24(18):9, 12 (June 30, 1982).

        ———. Supreme Court to consider single-sex-college case. *Chronicle of Higher Education* 23(11):16 (November 11, 1981).

        Hogan, Joyce, and Ann M. Quigley. Physical standards for employment and the courts. *American Psychologist* 41(11):1193-1217 (November 1986).

2399. Blue Shield of Virginia v. McCready   June 21, 1982
      457 US 465   73 LEd2d 149   102 SCt 2540
        Almanac (1982):11A

        Fields, Cheryl M. Supreme Court lets sex-bias ruling stand and acts on other college cases. *Chronicle of Higher Education* 24(9):13 (April 28, 1982).

        ———. Supreme Court to consider single-sex-college case. *Chronicle of Higher Education* 23(11):16 (November 11, 1981).

        Werner, Ray O. Marketing and the Supreme Court in transition, 1982-1984. *Journal of Marketing* 49(3):97-105 (Summer 1985).

2400. Patsy v. Board of Regents of the State of Florida   June 21, 1982
      457 US 496   73 LEd2d 172   102 SCt 2557
        Almanac (1982):8A
        En Am Con 673-674

        Fields, Cheryl M. Supreme Court lets sex-bias ruling stand and acts on other college cases. *Chronicle of Higher Education* 24(9):13 (April 28, 1982).

        ———. Supreme Court rules in 2 job-bias cases that have implications for colleges. *Chronicle of Higher Education* 24(18):9, 12 (June 30, 1982).

        ———. U. of Missouri's ban on worship services challenged, defended at Supreme Court. *Chronicle of Higher Education* 23(7):11, 16 (October 14, 1981).

2401. United States v. Johnson   June 21, 1982
      457 US 537   73 LEd2d 202   102 SCt 2579

Almanac (1982):5A

Sup Ct Review (1982):1-24

Bender, Louis, and Steven Bender. Is the Supreme Court's decision in Baggot retroactive in application? *Journal of Taxation* 60(3):138-144 (March 1984).

2402. Schweiker, Secretary of Health and Human Services v. Hogan   June 21, 1982
     457 US 569   73 LEd2d 227   102 SCt 2597
     Almanac (1982):18A

2403. Globe Newspaper Co. v. Superior Court for the County of Norfolk   June 23, 1982
     457 US 596   73 LEd2d 248   102 SCt 2613
     Almanac (1982):10A
     En Am Con 848

American survey: the west comes to court. *Economist* 284(7245):21-22 (July 10-16 1982).

Arledge, Paula C., and Edward V. Heck. A freshman justice confronts the Constitution: Justice O'Connor and the First Amendment. *Western Political Quarterly* 45(3):761-772 (September 1992).

Bleisch, N. David. The *Congressional Record* and the First Amendment: accuracy is the best policy. *Boston College Environmental Affairs Law Review* 12(2):341-379 (Winter 1985).

Burrows, Karen B. Supreme Court review: First Amendment—the right of access to criminal trials extended. *Journal of Criminal Law and Criminology* 73(4):1388-1407 (Winter 1982).

Erickson, William H. 1981-1982 U.S. Supreme Court decisions. *Trial* 18(11):44-49, 109 (November 1982).

Leeper, Roy V. Richmond Newspapers, Inc. v. Virginia and the emerging right of access. *Journalism Quarterly* 61(3):615-622 (Autumn 1984).

Malak, Michael P. Supreme Court review: First Amendment—guarantee of public access to voir dire. *Journal of Criminal Law and Criminology* 75(3):583-608 (Fall 1984).

O'Connor has her say in dissenting opinions. *Editor and Publisher* 115(39):58 (September 25, 1982).

Press, Aric, Lucy Howard, and Diane Camper. You can't sue the president. *Newsweek* 100(1):80 (July 5, 1982).

Supreme Court reaffirms access to criminal trials. *Editor and Publisher* 115(27-28):11 (July 3-10, 1982).

Supreme Court to hear closed trial case. *Editor and Publisher* 115[114]:11 (November 28, 1981).

2404. Edgar v. MITE Corp.   June 23, 1982
     457 US 624   73 LEd2d 269   102 SCt 2629
     Almanac (1982):15A; (1987):15A
     En Am Con 1641-1642
     Sup Ct Review (1987):47-95

American survey: the west comes to court. *Economist* 284(7245):21-22 (July 10-16 1982).

Bomster, Mark. Say High Court slants toward business. *Electronic News* 28(1401):6 (July 12, 1982).

Business issues on the Supreme Court's 1981-82 calendar. *Business Week* (2709):54 (October 12, 1981).

DeMott, Deborah A. Perspectives on choice of law for corporate internal affairs. *Law and Contemporary Problems* 48(3):161-198 (Summer 1985).

Hofmann, Mark A. Courts, laws change boundaries of liability for corporate officers. *Business Insurance* 22(44):77-79 (October 31, 1988).

Kaufman, Allen, and Lawrence Zacharias. From trust to contract: the legal language of managerial ideology, 1920-1980. *Business History Review* 66(3):523-572 (Autumn 1992).

2405. Foremost Insurance Co. v. Richardson   June 23, 1982
     457 US 668   73 LEd2d 300   102 SCt 2654
     Almanac (1982):17A

Arsenault, Richard J., and Richard W. Beard. Bringing pleasure boat accidents under the admirality forum. *Trial* 18(10):66-71, 88 (October 1982).

George, James A. The 'triple crown' of admiralty cases: from definitions to damages. *Trial* 27(10):46-53 (October 1991).

2406. Taylor v. Alabama   June 23, 1982
     457 US 687   73 LEd2d 314   102 SCt 2664

Almanac (1982):5A

Burger Court 80-82+

Bernstein, Sidney, and Michael Eisenstein. 1982 Supreme Court update: the criminal law. *Trial* 18(9):45-50, 81 (September 1982).

Erickson, William H. 1981-1982 U.S. Supreme Court decisions. *Trial* 18(11):44-49, 109 (November 1982).

Levinson, William D. Supreme Court review: Fourth Amendment—a renewed plea for relevant criteria for the admissibility of tainted confessions. *Journal of Criminal Law and Criminology* 73(4):1408-1429 (Winter 1982).

2407. Jacksonville Bulk Terminals, Inc. v. International Longshoremen's Association   June 24, 1982
457 US 702   73 LEd2d 327   102 SCt 2673

    Almanac (1982):13A

Bomster, Mark. Say High Court slants toward business. *Electronic News* 28(1401):6 (July 12, 1982).

Gest, Ted. The Supreme Court: a house divided: the dominant direction in the 1981-82 term was to the right. *U.S. News and World Report* 93(2):45-46 (July 12, 1982).

2408. Nixon v. Fitzgerald   June 24, 1982
457 US 731   73 LEd2d 349   102 SCt 2690

    Almanac (1982):17A

    Editorials (1982):774-781

    En Am Con 668, 1324-1325

American survey: the west comes to court. *Economist* 284(7245):21-22 (July 10-16 1982).

Beach, Bennett H. Shielding the president: the Supreme Court upholds his immunity from suits. *Time* 120(1):48 (July 5, 1982).

Collect call: a former president must pay. *Time* 118(1):21 (July 6, 1981).

Court rules: you can't sue the president. *U.S. News and World Report* 93(1):66 (July 5, 1982).

Erickson, William H. 1981-1982 U.S. Supreme Court decisions. *Trial* 18(11):44-49, 109 (November 1982).

Press, Aric. Lucy Howard, and Diane Camper. You can't sue the president. *Newsweek* 100(1):80 (July 5, 1982).

Regan, Richard J. Supreme Court roundup: 1981 term. *Thought* 57(227):514-527 (December 1982).

2409. Harlow v. Fitzgerald   June 24, 1982
457 US 800   73 LEd2d 396   102 SCt 2727

    Almanac (1982):17A

    En Am Con 1324-1325

American survey: the west comes to court. *Economist* 284(7245):21-22 (July 10-16 1982).

Chemerinsky, Erwin. Stunting the Constitution's growth. *Trial* 26(11):36-40 (November 1990).

Erickson, William H. 1981-1982 U.S. Supreme Court decisions. *Trial* 18(11):44-49, 109 (November 1982).

Sendor, Benjamin. Why you might be personally liable. *American School Board Journal* 181(12):15, 47 (December 1994).

2410. Rendell-Baker v. Kohn   June 25, 1982
457 US 830   73 LEd2d 418   102 SCt 2764

    Almanac (1982):8A

    En Am Con 130-131, 1736-1738

Sullivan, Harold J. Privatization of public services: a growing threat to constitutional rights. *Public Administration Review* 47(6):461-467 (November/December 1987).

2411. Board of Education, Island Trees Union Free School District No. 26 v. Pico   June 25, 1982
457 US 853   73 LEd2d 435   102 SCt 2799

    Almanac (1982):9A-10A

    Brennan 179-184

    En Am Con 131, 608-612, 856-858

    Landmark (v. 1):159-179R

    Sup Ct Review (1987):303-344

American survey: the west comes to court. *Economist* 284(7245):21-22 (July 10-16 1982).

Balton, David A. Human rights in the classroom: teaching the convention on the rights of the child. *Social Education* 56(4):210-212 (April/May 1992).

Cole, Robert W., Jr. Editor's page: whose are the schools? [Editorial] *Phi Delta Kappan* 63(7):434 (March 1982).

Epley, B. Glen, and Kay M. Moore. Censorship in the schools: the responsibilities of courts, boards, and administrators. *NASSP Bulletin* 69(485):54-60 (December 1985).

Erickson, William H. 1981-1982 U.S. Supreme Court decisions. *Trial* 18(11):44-49, 109 (November 1982).

Fields, Howard. Authors League files brief in Island Trees case. *Publishers' Weekly* 221(1):14-16 (January 22, 1982).

———. High Court hears arguments on Island Trees suit. *Publishers' Weekly* 221(12):10, 18 (March 19, 1982).

———. Island Trees decision, though split, is hailed. *Publishers' Weekly* 222(2):10, 14-15 (July 9, 1982).

Flygare, Thomas J. De jure: Supreme Court perpetuates confusion in school library censorship case. *Phi Delta Kappan* 64(3):208-209 (November 1982).

Gluckman, Ivan B. Separating myth from reality. *NASSP Bulletin* 69(485):60-66 (December 1985).

Island Trees: no decision. [Editorial] *America* 147(2): 24 (July 10-17, 1982).

Kermerer, Frank R., and Stephanie Abraham Hirsch. School library censorship comes before the Supreme Court. *Phi Delta Kappan* 63(7):444-448 (March 1982).

Kobylka, Joseph F. A court-created context for group litigation: libertarian groups and obscenity. *Journal of Politics* 49(4):1061-1078 (November 1987).

Kraus, Larry L. Censorship: what Island Trees v. Pico means to schools. *Clearing House* 57(8):343-345 (April 1984).

Leeper, Roy V. Richmond Newspapers, Inc. v. Virginia and the emerging right of access. *Journalism Quarterly* 61(3):615-622 (Autumn 1984).

Newsnotes: High Court rules trial must be held in school board censorship case. *Phi Delta Kappan* 64(1):73 (September 1982).

Nocera, Joseph. The big book-banning brawl. *New Republic* 187(11):20-25 (September 13, 1982).

O'Connor has her say in dissenting opinions. *Editor and Publisher* 115(39):58 (September 25, 1982).

Press, Aric, and Diane Camper. Can schools ban books? *Newsweek* 99(11):82 (March 15, 1982).

Press, Aric, Lucy Howard, and Diane Camper. You can't sue the president. *Newsweek* 100(1):80 (July 5, 1982).

Regan, Richard J. Supreme Court roundup: 1981 term. *Thought* 57(227):514-527 (December 1982).

Reuter, Madalynne. Island Trees board restores banned books to libraries. *Publishers' Weekly* 222(9):260 (August 27, 1982).

The right to read. [Editorial] *Nation* 235(3):65 (July 24-July 31, 1982).

Rose, Jonathan. Decide 10 landmark cases that define your rights. *Scholastic Update* 119(1):7-9, 21 (September 8, 1986).

Schwartz, Herman. A scorecard for the new Court term. *Nation* 235(12):353, 367-370 (October 16, 1982).

Sendor, Benjamin. Good cases make bad law, and this curriculum ruling suggests the opposite also can be true. *American School Board Journal* 175(9)7, 37 (September 1988).

Van Alstyne, William W. Academic freedom and the First Amendment in the Supreme Court of the United States: an unhurried historical review. *Law and Contemporary Problems* 53(3):79-154 (Summer 1990).

2412. Lugar v. Edmondson Oil Co.   June 25, 1982
      457 US 922   73 LEd2d 482   102 SCt 2744
      Almanac (1982):8A
      En Am Con 1736-1738

      Josephs, Mark L. Supreme Court review: Fourteenth Amendment—peremptory challenges and the equal protection clause. *Journal of Criminal Law and Criminology* 82(4):1000-1028 (Winter 1992).

2413. Clements, Governor of Texas v. Fashing   June 25, 1982
      457 US 957   73 LEd2d 508   102 SCt 2836
      Almanac (1982):14A-15A
      Sup Ct Yearbook (1993-94):294-297

2414. Blum, Commissioner of the New York State Department of Social Services v. Yaretsky   June 25, 1982
      457 US 991   73 LEd2d 534   102 SCt 2777

Almanac (1982):8A

En Am Con 130-131, 1736-1738

Sullivan, Harold J. Privatization of public services: a growing threat to constitutional rights. *Public Administration Review* 47(6):461-467 (November/December 1987).

2415. Toll, President, University of Maryland v. Moreno   June 28, 1982
   458 US 1   73 LEd2d 563   102 SCt 2977

   Almanac (1982):8A

Fields, Cheryl M. High Court to decide church-state issues in 2 college cases; interns' appeal denied. *Chronicle of Higher Education* 22(2):11-12 (March 2, 1981).

———. Justices rule Maryland cannot charge out-of-state tuition to certain aliens. *Chronicle of Higher Education* 24(19):11, 14 (July 7, 1982).

———. Supreme Court lets sex-bias ruling stand and acts on other college cases. *Chronicle of Higher Education* 24(9):13 (April 28, 1982).

———. Supreme Court rejects university's ban on services by student religious group. *Chronicle of Higher Education* 23(16):1, 14 (December 16, 1981).

———. Supreme Court sidesteps question of aid by colleges to handicapped. *Chronicle of Higher Education* 22(11):9 (May 4, 1981).

———. U. of Missouri's ban on worship services challenged, defended at Supreme Court. *Chronicle of Higher Education* 23(7):11, 16 (October 14, 1981).

2416. Northern Pipeline Construction Co. v. Marathon Pipe Line Co.   June 28, 1982
         Coupled with United States v. Marathan Pipe Line Co.
   458 US 50   73 LEd2d 598   102 SCt 2858

   Almanac (1982):389-390, 12A; (1984):265-266

   Const (Currie) 593-596

   Editorials (1982):1192-1195

   En Am Con 100, 367, 1046-1054, 1327

   Guide (CQ) 65

   Sup Ct Review (1982):1-24, 25-47; (1988):1-41; (1991):225-260

Cerne, Kathleen M. Honor thy creditors? The religious debtor's constitutional conflict with Section 1325(b). *Business Credit* 96(3):37-40 (March 1994).

Court session ends with a rush. *U.S. News and World Report* 93(2):11 (July 12, 1982).

Feldman, Stuart P. Curbing the recalcitrant polluter: post-decree judicial agents in environmental litigation. *Boston College Environmental Affairs Law Review* 18(4):809-840 (Summer 1991).

Fisher, Louis. The administrative world of Chadha and Bowsher. *Public Administration Review* 47(3):213-219 (May/June 1987).

Gross, Karen. Recent bankruptcy developments: do they take away with the right what they give with the left? *Credit and Finanical Management* 88(5):9-14 (May 1986).

Nelson, Lester. What you should know about bankruptcy code amendments and the Federal Judgeship Act of 1984. *Credit and Finanical Management* 86(9):14-17 (October 1984).

Status of bankruptcy act could affect case. *Business Insurance* 16(37):31 (September 6, 1982).

Supreme court declares bankruptcy code unconstitutional. *Credit and Finanical Management* 84:49 (September 1982).

Weintraub, Benjamin. Legally speaking: is the bankruptcy court still open? *Credit and Finanical Management* 85(4):10, 43 (April 1983).

2417. Union Labor Life Insurance Co. v. Pireno   June 28, 1982
   458 US 119   73 LEd2d 647   102 SCt 3002

   Almanac (1982):11A

Kempler, Cecelia, and William Duffy. Insolvent reinsurers pose even greater risk. *Best's Review* (Life/Health Insurance Edition) 94(10):54-57 (April 1994).

———. Insolvent reinsurers pose even greater risk. *Best's Review* (Property/Casualty Insurance Edition) 94(12):42-45 (April 1994).

Weller, Charles D. McCarran Act interpretation may have been charted in Barry case. *Best's Review* (Life/Health Insurance Edition) 83(2):40-42, 87-89 (June 1982).

———. McCarran Act interpretation may have been charted in Barry case. *Best's Review* (Property/Casualty Insurance Edition) 83(3):28-32 (July 1982).

Werner, Ray O. Marketing and the Supreme Court in transition, 1982-1984. *Journal of Marketing* 49(3):97-105 (Summer 1985).

2418. Fidelity Federal Savings & Loan Association v. De La Cuesta   June 28, 1982
    458 US 141   73 LEd2d 664   102 SCt 3014

    Almanac (1982):46, 11A

    Editorials (1982):804-807

Beach, Bennett H. The Court's final flurry: decisions on child pornography, busing, other thorny issues. *Time* 120(2):52-53 (July 12, 1982).

Court session ends with a rush. *U.S. News and World Report* 93(2):11 (July 12, 1982).

A mortgage windfall that will help S&Ls. *Business Week* (2747):32 (July 12, 1982).

Pauly, Diane. Mortgages aren't for sale. *Newsweek* 100(2):56 (July 12, 1982).

Regan, Richard J. Supreme Court roundup: 1981 term. *Thought* 57(227):514-527 (December 1982).

Wise, Charles, and Rosemary O'Leary. Is federalism dead or alive in the Supreme Court?: implications for public administrators. *Public Administration Review* 52(6):559-572 (November/December 1992).

2419. Board of Education of the Hendrick Hudson Central School District v. Rowley   June 28, 1982
    458 US 176   73 LEd2d 690   102 SCt 3034

    Almanac (1982):9A

    Burger Years 125-139

    Editorials (1982):1186-1191

    En Am Con 612-613

Beach, Bennett H. The Court's final flurry: decisions on child pornography, busing, other thorny issues. *Time* 120(2):52-53 (July 12, 1982).

Butler, Daniel P., and Timothy M. Cook. After Rowley: an effective education for handicapped children. *Trial* 18(9):71-75, 84 (September 1982).

Fields, Cheryl M. Justices rule Maryland cannot charge out-of-state tuition to certain aliens. *Chronicle of Higher Education* 24(19):11, 14 (July 7, 1982).

———. Supreme Court lets sex-bias ruling stand and acts on other college cases. *Chronicle of Higher Education* 24(9):13 (April 28, 1982).

Flygare, Thomas J. De jure: Supreme Court holds that P.L. 94-142 does not require sign-language interpreters for deaf students. *Phi Delta Kappan* 64(1):62-63 (September 1982).

Gest, Ted. The Supreme Court: a house divided: the dominant direction in the 1981-82 term was to the right. *U.S. News and World Report* 93(2):45-46 (July 12, 1982).

Kehoe, Sharon M. Looking back on Rowley: are school districts overserving the disabled under the Individuals with Disabilities Education Act? *Clearing House* 68(1):19-21 (September/October 1994).

McCarthy, Martha M. Education for the handicapped: lawyers and judges will decide what your schools can and can't do for students. *American School Board Journal* 168(7):24-25 (July 1981).

Press, Aric. The Court's hectic finale. *Newsweek* 100(2):77 (July 12, 1982).

Regan, Richard J. Supreme Court roundup: 1981 term. *Thought* 57(227):514-527 (December 1982).

2420. Ford Motor Co. v. Equal Employment Opportunity Commmission (EEOC)   June 28, 1982
    458 US 219   73 LEd2d 721   102 SCt 3057

    Almanac (1982):7A

Bomster, Mark. Say High Court slants toward business. *Electronic News* 28(1401):6 (July 12, 1982).

Fields, Cheryl M. Justices rule Maryland cannot charge out-of-state tuition to certain aliens. *Chronicle of Higher Education* 24(19):11, 14 (July 7, 1982).

Murphy, Betty Southard, Wayne E. Barlow, and D. Diane Hatch. Limiting back pay liability. *Personnel Journal* 66(2):16-17 (February 1987).

2421. United States v. Hollywood Motor Car Co., Inc.   June 28, 1982
     458 US 263   73 LEd2d 754   102 SCt 3081
      Loud 224-228

2422. Williams v. United States   June 29, 1982
     458 US 279   73 LEd2d 767   102 SCt 3088
      Almanac (1982):6A
     Kaufman, Richard F. Do you know a kite when you see one? *ABA Banking Journal* 79(11):88, 92-94 (November 1987).

2423. ASARCO Inc. v. Idaho State Tax Commission   June 29, 1982
     458 US 307   73 LEd2d 787   102 SCt 3103
      Almanac (1982):15A
     Bomster, Mark. Say High Court slants toward business. *Electronic News* 28(1401):6 (July 12, 1982).
     ————. Weaken state role in corp. taxation. *Electronic News* 28(1402):Supp L (July 19, 1982).
     Genetelli, Richard W., David B. Zigman, and Cesar E. Bencosme. Recent U.S. Supreme Court decisions on state and local tax issues. *CPA Journal* 62(11):38-44 (November 1992).
     Jurinski, James John. A primer on the unitary business concept. *CPA Journal* 56(9):52-64 (September 1986).
     ————. The U.S. Supreme Court on the unitary tax. *Journal of Accountancy* 161(1):96 (January 1986).
     Peters, James H. Supreme Court requires unitary relationship before states can tax investment income. *Journal of Taxation* 57(5):314-318 (November 1982).
     Recent Supreme Court decisions in ASARCO and Woolworth. *CPA Journal* 53(1):56-58 (January 1983).
     Unger, Joseph. Investment income of multistate corporations. *CPA Journal* 63(6):66 (June 1993).

2424. F.W. Woolworth Co. v. Taxation and Revenue Department of the State of New Mexico   June 29, 1982
     458 US 354   73 LEd2d 819   102 SCt 3128
      Almanac (1982):15A-16A
     Bomster, Mark. Say High Court slants toward business. *Electronic News* 28(1401):6 (July 12, 1982).
     ————. Weaken state role in corp. taxation. *Electronic News* 28(1402):Supp L (July 19, 1982).
     Jurinski, James John. A primer on the unitary business concept. *CPA Journal* 56(9):52-64 (September 1986).
     ————. The U.S. Supreme Court on the unitary tax. *Journal of Accountancy* 161(1):96 (January 1986).
     Recent Supreme Court decisions in ASARCO and Woolworth. *CPA Journal* 53(1):56-58 (January 1983).
     Spragins, Ellyn. Out of state, out of pocket. *Forbes* 130(5):135 (August 30, 1982).
     Wasson, Hilda C., and Robert E. Weigand. Unitary taxation: a search for fairness. *Business Horizons* 31(2):45-50 (March/April 1988).

2425. General Building Contractors Association, Inc. v. Pennsylvania   June 29, 1982
        Coupled with United Engineers and Construction, Inc. v. Pennsylvania
        Coupled with Contractors Association of Eastern Pennsylvania v. Pennsylvania
        Coupled with Glasgow, Inc. v. Pennsylvania
        Coupled with Bechtel Power Corp. v. Pennsylvania
     458 US 375   73 LEd2d 835   102 SCt 3141
      Almanac (1982):8A

2426. Loretto v. Teleprompter Manhattan CATV Corp.   June 30, 1982
     458 US 419   73 LEd2d 868   102 SCt 3164
      Almanac (1982):15A
      En Am Con 1179
      Sup Ct Review (1982):195-241, 351-380
     Andersen, Robert M. Technology, pollution control, and EPA access to commercial property: a constitutional and policy framework. *Boston College Environmental Affairs Law Review* 17(1):1-74 (Fall 1989).
     Bomster, Mark. Say High Court slants toward business. *Electronic News* 28(1401):6 (July 12, 1982).
     Cohen, Jonathan E. A constitutional safety valve: the variance in zoning and land-use based environmental controls. *Boston College Environmental Affairs Law Review* 22(2):307-364 (Winter 1995).

Hippler, Thomas A. Reexamining 100 years of the Supreme Court regulatory taking doctrine: the principles of "noxious use," "average reciprocity of advantage," and "bundle of rights" from Mugler to Keystone Bituminous Coal. *Boston College Environmental Affairs Law Review* 14(4):653-727 (Summer 1987).

2427. Washington v. Seattle School District No. 1   June 30, 1982
      458 US 457   73 LEd2d 896   102 SCt 3187

        Almanac (1982):6A

        En Am Con 514

        Sup Ct Review (1982):127-166

American survey: the west comes to court. *Economist* 284(7245):21-22 (July 10-16 1982).

Aronow, Geoffrey, and Owen Fiss. The High Court illusion of victory. *Nation* 235(21):647-650 (December 18, 1982).

Beach, Bennett H. The Court's final flurry: decisions on child pornography, busing, other thorny issues. *Time* 120(2):52-53 (July 12, 1982).

Court session ends with a rush. *U.S. News and World Report* 93(2):11 (July 12, 1982).

Gale, Mary Ellen. Relegating minorities to the back of the courthouse. *Trial* 18(10):40-45, 86 (October 1982).

Press, Aric. The Court's hectic finale. *Newsweek* 100(2):77 (July 12, 1982).

Reagan's reverse in school policy. *Newsweek* 98(12):73 (September 21, 1981).

Russo, Charles J., J. John Harris III, and Rosetta F. Sandidge. Brown v. Board of Education at 40: a legal history of equal educational opportunity in american public education. *Journal of Negro Education* 63(3):297-309 (Summer 1994).

Schwartz, Herman. A scorecard for the new Court term. *Nation* 235(12):353, 367-370 (October 16, 1982).

Spurrier, Robert L., Jr. Paying the piper in federal civil rights litigation. *Public Administration Review* 43(3):199-208 (May/June 1983).

2428. Lehman v. Lycoming County Children's Service Agency   June 30, 1982
      458 US 502   73 LEd2d 928   102 SCt 3231

        Almanac (1982):17A

Beach, Bennett H. The Court's final flurry: decisions on child pornography, busing, other thorny issues. *Time* 120(2):52-53 (July 12, 1982).

2429. Crawford v. Board of Education of the City of Los Angeles   June 30, 1982
      458 US 527   73 LEd2d 948   102 SCt 3211

        Almanac (1982):6A

        En Am Con 514, 557-561

        Sup Ct Review (1982):127-166

American survey: the west comes to court. *Economist* 284(7245):21-22 (July 10-16 1982).

Beach, Bennett H. The Court's final flurry: decisions on child pornography, busing, other thorny issues. *Time* 120(2):52-53 (July 12, 1982).

Court session ends with a rush. *U.S. News and World Report* 93(2):11 (July 12, 1982).

Gale, Mary Ellen. Relegating minorities to the back of the courthouse. *Trial* 18(10):40-45, 86 (October 1982).

Press, Aric. The Court's hectic finale. *Newsweek* 100(2):77 (July 12, 1982).

Regan, Richard J. Supreme Court roundup: 1981 term. *Thought* 57(227):514-527 (December 1982).

Russo, Charles J., J. John Harris III, and Rosetta F. Sandidge. Brown v. Board of Education at 40: a legal history of equal educational opportunity in American public education. *Journal of Negro Education* 63(3):297-309 (Summer 1994).

2430. Griffin v. Oceanic Contractors, Inc.   June 30, 1982
      458 US 564   73 LEd2d 973   102 SCt 3245

        Almanac (1982):12A

Bomster, Mark. Say High Court slants toward business. *Electronic News* 28(1401):6 (July 12, 1982).

Fregeau, Jason David. Statutes and judicial discretion: against the law . . . sort of. *Boston College Environmental Affairs Law Review* 18(3):501-542 (Spring 1991).

2431. Velde v. National Black Police Association, Inc.   June 30, 1982
      458 US 591   73 LEd2d 994   102 SCt 3503
         Almanac (1982):17A

2432. Alfred L. Snapp & Son, Inc. v. Puerto Rico   July 1, 1982
      458 US 592   73 LEd2d 995   102 SCt 3260
         Almanac (1982):15A

2433. Rogers v. Lodge   July 1, 1982
      458 US 613   73 LEd2d 1012   102 SCt 3272
         Almanac (1982):10A
         Const Law 627-630R
         En Am Con 1604-1605
      Supreme Court rules that voting rights law covers the election of judges. *Jet* 80(13):33 (July 15, 1991).

2434. Rice, Director, Department of Alcoholic Beverage Control of California v. Norman Williams Co.   July 1, 1982
      458 US 654   73 LEd2d 1042   102 SCt 3294
             Coupled with Bohemian Distributing Co. v. Norman Williams Co.
             Coupled with Wine and Spirits Wholesalers of California v. Norman Williams Co.
         Almanac (1982):15A

2435. Florida Department of State v. Treasure Salvors, Inc. July 1, 1982
      458 US 670   73 LEd2d 1057
         Almanac (1982):15A   102 SCt 3304

2436. Mississippi University for Women v. Hogan   July 1, 1982
      458 US 718   73 LEd2d 1090   102 SCt 3331
         Almanac (1982):7A
         Burger Court 155-156
         Burger Years 109-124
         Const (Currie) 493-504
         Const Law 520-525R
         En Am Con 608-612, 1267, 1666-1673
      American survey: the west comes to court. *Economist* 284(7245):21-22 (July 10-16 1982).
      Avner, Judith I. The Amendment must come before, not after, a Rights Act. *Center Magazine* 16(6):14-15
         (November/December 1983).
      Beach, Bennett H. The Court's final flurry: decisions on child pornography, busing, other thorny issues. *Time*
         120(2):52-53 (July 12, 1982).
      Blackmun, Harry A. Text of dissent: Justice Blackmun. *Chronicle of Higher Education* 24(20):15R (July 14,
         1982).
      Burger, William E. Text of dissent: Chief Justice Burger. *Chronicle of Higher Education* 24(20):14R (July 14,
         1982).
      Court session ends with a rush. *U.S. News and World Report* 93(2):11 (July 12, 1982).
      Erickson, William H. 1981-1982 U.S. Supreme Court decisions. *Trial* 18(11):44-49, 109 (November 1982).
      Fields, Cheryl M. Supreme Court lets sex-bias ruling stand and acts on other college cases. *Chronicle of Higher
         Education* 24(9):13 (April 28, 1982).
      ———. Supreme Court to consider single-sex-college case. *Chronicle of Higher Education* 23(11):16
         (November 11, 1981).
      From Tilton to Ewing: some major higher-education decisions of the Burger court. *Chronicle of Higher
         Education* 32(17):10 (June 25, 1986).
      McDonald, Kim. State nursing school may not bar men; Supreme Court rules in 5-to-4 vote. *Chronicle of
         Higher Education* 24(20):1, 12 (July 14, 1982).
      O'Connor, Sandra, William J. Brennan, Jr., Thurgood Marshall, John Paul Stevens, and Byron R. White. Text
         of the Supreme Court's majority opinion in the Mississippi case. *Chronicle of Higher Education* 24(20):12-
         13R (July 14, 1982).

Powell, Lewis F., Jr., and William H. Rehnquist. Text of dissent: Justice Powell. *Chronicle of Higher Education* 24(20):13-15R (July 14, 1982).

Press, Aric. The Court's hectic finale. *Newsweek* 100(2):77 (July 12, 1982).

Rosen, Jeffrey. Boys and girls. *New Republic* 210(7):14, 16 (February 14, 1994).

Williams, Wendy W., and Judith L. Lichtman. Closing the law's gender gap. *Nation* 239(9):280-285 (September 29, 1984).

2437. New York v. Ferber   July 2, 1982
      458 US 747   73 LEd2d 1113   102 SCt 3348
        Almanac (1982):10A
        Const Law 241-245R
        Editorials (1982):782-787
        En Am Con 1310-1311
        Sup Ct Review (1982):285-317

American survey: the west comes to court. *Economist* 284(7245):21-22 (July 10-16 1982).

Beach, Bennett H. The Court's final flurry: decisions on child pornography, busing, other thorny issues. *Time* 120(2):52-53 (July 12, 1982).

Brown, Sandra Zunker. Supreme Court review: First Amendment—nonobscene child pornography and its categorical exclusion from constitutional protection. *Journal of Criminal Law and Criminology* 73(3):1337-1364 (Winter 1982).

Court session ends with a rush. *U.S. News and World Report* 93(2):11 (July 12, 1982).

Erickson, William H. 1981-1982 U.S. Supreme Court decisions. *Trial* 18(11):44-49, 109 (November 1982).

Fields, Howard. Coping with the Reagan years. *Publishers' Weekly* 237(1):30-31 (January 5, 1990).

———. High Court hears N.Y. child pornography case. *Publishers' Weekly* 221(20):114 (May 14, 1982).

———. Supreme Court, 6-3, bans possession of child porn. *Publishers' Weekly* 237(18):10 (May 4, 1990).

———. Supreme Court upholds N.Y. kiddie porn law. *Publishers' Weekly* 222(4):66-68 (July 23, 1982).

Kobylka, Joseph F. A court-created context for group litigation: libertarian groups and obscenity. *Journal of Politics* 49(4):1061-1078 (November 1987).

McGuire, Kevin T. Obscenity, libertarian values, and decision making in the Supreme Court. *American Politics Quarterly* 18(1):47-67 (January 1990).

Regan, Richard J. Supreme Court roundup: 1981 term. *Thought* 57(227):514-527 (December 1982).

Reuter, Madalynne. St. Martin's joins new action in N.Y. kiddie porn law. *Publishers' Weekly* 222(14):33 (October 1, 1982).

Supreme Court rules against child porn. *Christianity Today* 26(13):58 (August 6, 1982).

2438. Enmund v. Florida   July 2, 1982
      458 US 782   73 LEd2d 1140   102 SCt 3368
        Almanac (1982):6A; (1987):8A
        Court Public 310
        Death Penalty (Tushnet) 74-78
        En Am Con 634-635

Beach, Bennett H. The Court's final flurry: decisions on child pornography, busing, other thorny issues. *Time* 120(2):52-53 (July 12, 1982).

Bernstein, Sidney. Supreme Court review. *Trial* 19(11):20, 22 (November 1983).

Bernstein, Sidney, and Michael Eisenstein. 1982 Supreme Court update: the criminal law, part two. *Trial* 18(10):58-65 (October 1982).

Erickson, William H. 1981-1982 U.S. Supreme Court decisions. *Trial* 18(11):44-49, 109 (November 1982).

Press, Aric. The Court's hectic finale. *Newsweek* 100(2):77 (July 12, 1982).

Wickert, John H. Supreme Court review: Eighth Amendment—the death penalty and vicarious felony murder: nontriggerman may not be executed absent a finding of an intent to kill. *Journal of Criminal Law and Criminology* 73(4):1553-1571 (Winter 1982).

2439. Ramah Navajo School Board, Inc. v. Bureau of Revenue of New Mexico   July 2, 1982
      458 US 832   73 LEd2d 1174   102 SCt 3394
        Almanac (1982):16A

Am Indians (Wilkinson) 98-99, 130+

2440. United States v. Valenzuela-Bernal   July 2, 1982
      458 US 858   73 LEd2d 1193   102 SCt 3440
         Almanac (1982):5A
      American survey: the west comes to court. *Economist* 284(7245):21-22 (July 10-16 1982).
      White, Welsh S. Evidentiary privileges and the defendant's constitutional right to introduce evidence. *Journal
         of Criminal Law and Criminology* 80(2):377-426 (Summer 1989).

2441. National Association for the Advancement of Colored People (NAACP) v. Claiborne Hardware Co. July 2, 1982
      458 US 886   73 LEd2d 1215   102 SCt 3409
         Almanac (1982):10A
         Sup Ct Review (1994):129-168
      American survey: the west comes to court. *Economist* 284(7245):21-22 (July 10-16 1982).
      Aronow, Geoffrey, and Owen Fiss. The High Court illusion of victory. *Nation* 235(21):647-650 (December 18,
         1982).
      Beach, Bennett H. The Court's final flurry: decisions on child pornography, busing, other thorny issues. *Time*
         120(2):52-53 (July 12, 1982).
      Camper, Diane, Ethel Payne, Nathaniel R. Jones, Charles Ogletree, Charles and Julius L. Chambers. To form a
         more perfect union. *Black Enterprise* 17(12):11, 51-66 (July 1987).
      Carter, Charles E. Port Gibson, Mississippi, revisited. *Crisis* 89(7):24-25 (August/September 1982).
      Court session ends with a rush. *U.S. News and World Report* 93(2):11 (July 12, 1982).
      Higgins, Chester A. Boycott decision has wrought miracle changes in Port Gibson. *Crisis* 89(8):19-22 (October
         1982).
      Press, Aric. The Court's hectic finale. *Newsweek* 100(2):77 (July 12, 1982).
      Schwartz, Herman. A scorecard for the new Court term. *Nation* 235(12):353, 367-370 (October 16, 1982).
      Supplement: Supreme Court of the United States, decision. *Crisis* 89(7):59-74R (August/September 1982).

2442. Sporhase v. Nebraska ex rel. Douglas, Attorney General   July 2, 1982
      458 US 941   73 LEd2d 1254   102 SCt 3456
         Almanac (1982):15A
         En Am Con 1751-1755
      Court session ends with a rush. *U.S. News and World Report* 93(2):11 (July 12, 1982).
      Schwartz, Edward B. Water as an article of commerce: state embargoes spring a leak under Sporhase v.
         Nebraska. *Boston College Environmental Affairs Law Review* 12(1):103-169 (Fall 1985).

2443. Board of Education of Rogers, Arkansas v. McCluskey   July 2, 1982
      458 US 966   73 LEd2d 1273   102 SCt 3469
      Flygare, Thomas J. De jure: minor school discipline case reveals sharp disagreements on Supreme Court. *Phi
         Delta Kappan* 64(4):282-283 (December 1982).
      Sendor, Benjamin. Advice for lawsuit-weary board members: learn these lessons about labor relations, liquor,
         and legislative laxity. *American School Board Journal* 170(1):34-35 (January 1983).

2444. Landon, District Director of the Immigration and Naturalization Service v. Plasencia   November 15, 1982
      459 US 21   74 LEd2d 21   103 SCt 321
         Almanac (1983):11A

2445. Griggs v. Provident Consumer Discount Co.   November 29, 1982
      459 US 56   74 LEd2d 225   103 SCt 400
      Werner, Ray O. Marketing and the Supreme Court in transition, 1982-1984. *Journal of Marketing* 49(3):97-
         105 (Summer 1985).

2446. United States v. Security Industrial Bank   November 30, 1982
      459 US 70   74 LEd2d 235   103 SCt 407
         Almanac (1983):14A

2447. Brown v. Socialist Workers '74 Campaign Committee (Ohio)   December 8, 1982
    459 US 87   74 LEd2d 250   103 SCt 416
     Almanac (1983):13A
     En Am Con 165
     Sup Ct Review (1983):583-626

2448. Larkin v. Grendel's Den, Inc.   December 13, 1982
    459 US 116   74 LEd2d 297   103 SCt 505
     Almanac (1983):12A
     Burger Years 56-91
     En Am Con 1124
     Establishment 157-158, 216+
     Godless 109-110

Regan, Richard J. Supreme Court roundup: 1982 term. *Thought* 58(231):472-483 (December 1983).

Sullivan, Catherine Beth. Are kosher food laws constitutionally kosher? *Boston College Environmental Affairs Law Review* 21(1):201-245 (Fall 1993).

Weber, Paul J. Excessive entanglement: a wavering First Amendment standard. *Review of Politics* 46(4):483-501 (October 1984).

2449. Burlington Northern Inc. v. United States   December 13, 1982
    459 US 131   74 LEd2d 311   103 SCt 514
     Almanac (1983):14A

2450. Xerox Corp. v. County of Harris, Texas   December 13, 1982
    459 US 145   74 LEd2d 323   103 SCt 523
     Almanac (1983):18A

Adams, Nancy D. Title VI of the 1990 Clean Air Act Amendments and state and local initiatives to reverse the stratospheric ozone crisis: an analysis of preemption. *Boston College Environmental Affairs Law Review* 19(1):173-216 (Fall 1991).

Customs warehouses revived. *CPA Journal* 53(4):73 (April 1983).

2451. City of Port Arthur, Texas v. United States   December 13, 1982
    459 US 159   74 LEd2d 334   103 SCt 530
     Almanac (1983):13A

2452. Colorado v. New Mexico   December 13, 1982
    459 US 176   74 LEd2d 348   103 SCt 539
     Almanac (1983):18A-19A

Beach, Bennett H., and David S. Jackson. Back to business—and lots of it. *Time* 120(16):102 (October 18, 1982).

2453. Federal Election Commission (FEC) v. National Right to Work Committee   December 13, 1982
    459 US 197   74 LEd2d 364   103 SCt 552
     Almanac (1983):13A

The case for recasting the High Court's role. *Business Week* (2760):33-34 (October 11, 1982).

2454. Bowen v. United States Postal Service   January 11, 1983
    459 US 212   74 LEd2d 402   103 SCt 588
     Almanac (1983):15A
     Burger Years 228-239

Compensation statute murky despite ruling. *Engineering News Record* 210(3):149 (January 20, 1983).

Draznin, Julius N. Grievance arbitration. *Personnel Journal* 62(4):284 (April 1983).

Fox, Arthur. Showing workers who's the boss. *Nation* 239(9):295-299 (September 29, 1984).

Ruben, George. Supreme Court says union liable for back wages. *Monthly Labor Review* 106(3):45 (March 1983).

2455. Pillsbury Co. v. Conboy   January 11, 1983
    459 US 248   74 LEd2d 430   103 SCt 608
      Almanac (1983):7A

Bernstein, Sidney. Supreme Court review. *Trial* 19(12):20, 22 (December 1983).

Carr, Pitts, and Luther J. Carroll. Conboy and the plaintiff's antitrust case. *Trial* 20(3):80-82 (March 1984).

Lushing, Peter. Testimonial immunity and the privilege against self-incrimination: a study in isomorphism. *Journal of Criminal Law and Criminology* 73(4):1690-1739 (Winter 1982).

Werner, Ray O. Marketing and the Supreme Court in transition, 1982-1984. *Journal of Marketing* 49(3):97-105 (Summer 1985).

2456. Director, Office of Workers' Compensation Programs,   January 11, 1983
    United States Department of Labor v. Perini North River Associates
    459 US 297   74 LEd2d 465   103 SCt 634
      Almanac (1983):16A

Compensation statute murky despite ruling. *Engineering News Record* 210(3):149 (January 20, 1983).

2457. Shepard v. National Labor Relations Board (NLRB) January 18, 1983
    459 US 344   74 LEd2d 523   103 SCt 665
      Almanac (1983):15A

2458. Missouri v. Hunter   January 19, 1983
    459 US 359   74 LEd2d 535   103 SCt 673
      Almanac (1983):7A

Bernstein, Sidney. Supreme Court review. *Trial* 19(11):20, 22 (November 1983).

Schmitt, Deborah. Supreme Court review: Fifth Amendment—double jeopardy: legislative intent controls in crimes and punishment. *Journal of Criminal Law and Criminology* 74(4):1300-1314 (Winter 1983).

2459. Herman and MacLean v. Huddleston   January 24, 1983
    459 US 375   74 LEd2d 548   103 SCt 683
      Almanac (1983):14A

Szockyj, Elizabeth. Insider trading: the SEC meets Carl Karcher. *Annals of the American Academy of Political and Social Science* 525:46-58 (January 1993).

2460. Memphis Bank & Trust Co. v. Garner   January 24, 1983
    459 US 392   74 LEd2d 562   103 SCt 692
      Almanac (1983):18A

2461. Energy Reserves Group, Inc. v. Kansas Power and Light Co.   January 24, 1983
    459 US 400   74 LEd2d 569   103 SCt 697
      Almanac (1983):16A

Gransee, Marsha. A year of regulatory decisions in review. *Public Utilities Fortnightly* 113(1):51-55 (January 5, 1984).

High Court due pipeline gas output price cases. *Oil and Gas Journal* 80(42):58 (October 18, 1982).

Several energy cases on Supeme Court docket. *Oil and Gas Journal* 80(45):120 (November 8, 1982).

2462. Marshall, Superintendent, Southern Ohio Correctional Facility v. Lonberger   February 22, 1983
    459 US 422   74 LEd2d 646   103 SCt 843
      Almanac (1983):7A

2463. Hewitt v. Helms   February 22, 1983
    459 US 460   74 LEd2d 675   103 SCt 864
      Almanac (1983):11A

Vanderziel, Kathleen M. The Hatfield Riders and environmental preservation: what process is due? *Boston College Environmental Affairs Law Review* 19(2):431-479 (Fall/Winter 1991).

2464. Community Television of Southern California v. Gottfried   February 22, 1983
       Coupled with Federal Communications Commission (FCC) v. Gottfried
    459 US 498   74 LEd2d 705   103 SCt 885
     Almanac (1983):11A

Fields, Cheryl M. Bias cases among first on Supreme Court docket. *Chronicle of Higher Education* 25(6):13-14
    (October 6, 1982).

2465. Associated General Contractors of California, Inc. v. California State Council of Carpenters   February 22, 1983
    459 US 519   74 LEd2d 723   103 SCt 897
     Almanac (1983):13A

Bomster, Mark. Court faces busy term. *Electronic News* 28(1414):Supp W (October 11, 1982).

Court limits antitrust suits in labor disputes. *Engineering News Record* 210(9):58 (March 3, 1983).

Gest, Ted. A bulging agenda for Supreme Court. *U.S. News and World Report* 93(15):82 (October 11, 1982).

Nelson-Horchler, Joani. Term begins: Supreme Court centers on job bias, labor law. *Industry Week* 215(1):22,
    24 (October 4, 1982).

2466. South Dakota v. Neville   February 22, 1983
    459 US 553   74 LEd2d 748   103 SCt 916
     Almanac (1983):7A
     Editorials (1983):212-215
     En Am Con 1713

Flunked tests: drunks and trademarks lose. *Time* 121(10):75 (March 7, 1983).

Gest, Ted. A bulging agenda for Supreme Court. *U.S. News and World Report* 93(15):82 (October 11, 1982).

————. The justices take a turn to activism. *U.S. News and World Report* 95(2):33 (July 11, 1983).

High Court allows blood test refusal as proof of DWI. *Trial* 19(6):13-14 (June 1983).

Maltz, Earl M. Lockstep analysis and the concept of federalism. *Annals of the American Academy of Political
    and Social Science* 496:98-106 (March 1988).

O'Neill, Timothy P. The good, the bad, and the Burger court: victims' rights and a new model of criminal
    review. *Journal of Criminal Law and Criminology* 75(2):363-387 (Summer 1984).

Uviller, H. Richard. Self-incrimination by inference: constitutional restrictions on the evidentiary use of a
    suspect's refusal to submit to a search. *Journal of Criminal Law and Criminology* 81(1):37-76 (Spring 1990).

2467. Carmen v. Idaho   October 4, 1982
       Coupled with National Organization of Women (NOW) v. Idaho
    459 US 809   74 LEd2d 39   103 SCt 22
     Almanac (1982):377-378
     Powers 291, 294-295

Lewin, Nathan. Judgment time for ERA. *New Republic* 186(6):8, 10-13 (February 10, 1982).

2468. Moses H. Cone Memorial Hospital v. Mercury Construction Corp.   February 23, 1983
    460 US 1   74 LEd2d 765   103 SCt 927
     Almanac (1983):19A

Court limits antitrust suits in labor disputes. *Engineering News Record* 210(9):58 (March 3, 1983).

2469. Perry Education Association v. Perry Local Educators' Association   February 23, 1983
    460 US 37   74 LEd2d 794   103 SCt 948
     Almanac (1983):12A
     En Am Con 506, 1380, 1488-1489
     Sup Ct Review (1992):79-122

Fields, Cheryl M. Bias cases among first on Supreme Court docket. *Chronicle of Higher Education* 25(6):13-14
    (October 6, 1982).

Flygare, Thomas J. De jure: Supreme Court holds that teachers' mailboxes are not a public forum. *Phi Delta
    Kappan* 64(9):659-660 (May 1983).

2470. Connecticut v. Johnson February 23, 1983
460 US 73 74 LEd2d 823 103 SCt 969
Almanac (1983):7A
Bernstein, Sidney. Supreme Court review. *Trial* 19(11):20, 22 (November 1983).
Harris, Leslie J. Constitutional limits on criminal presumptions as an expression of changing concepts of fundamental fairness. *Journal of Criminal Law and Criminology* 77(2):308-357 (Summer 1986).

2471. Dickerson, Director, Bureau of Alcohol, Tobacco and Firearms v. New Banner Institute, Inc. February 23, 1983
460 US 103 74 LEd2d 845 103 SCt 986
Almanac (1983):8A

2472. City of Lockhart v. United States February 23, 1983
460 US 125 74 LEd2d 863 103 SCt 998
Almanac (1983):13A

2473. Jefferson County Pharmaceutical Association, Inc. v. Abbott Laboratories February 23, 1983
460 US 150 74 LEd2d 882 103 SCt 1011
Almanac (1983):13A
Werner, Ray O. Marketing and the Supreme Court in transition, 1982-1984. *Journal of Marketing* 49(3):97-105 (Summer 1985).
What the High Court may decide. *Chemical Week* 131(14):10-11 (October 6, 1982).

2474. Lockheed Aircraft Corp. v. United States February 23, 1983
460 US 190 74 LEd2d 911 103 SCt 1033
Almanac (1983):20A
Nelson-Horchler, Joani. Term begins: Supreme Court centers on job bias, labor law. *Industry Week* 215(1):22, 24 (October 4, 1982).

2475. White v. Massachusetts Council of Construction Employers, Inc. February 28, 1983
460 US 204 75 LEd2d 1 103 SCt 1042
Almanac (1983):17A
Const (Currie) 580-585
The case for recasting the High Court's role. *Business Week* (2760):33-34 (October 11, 1982).
Court boosts local-hire rules. *Engineering News Record* 210(10):59-60 (March 10, 1983).
Mauro, Tony. From pensions to postal rates. *Nation's Business* 70(12):38-39 (December 1982).

2476. Equal Employment Opportunity Commission (EEOC) v. Wyoming March 2, 1983
460 US 226 75 LEd2d 18 103 SCt 1054
Almanac (1983):5A, 17A
En Am Con 640
Sup Ct Review (1983):215-281
Fields, Cheryl M. Bias cases among first on Supreme Court docket. *Chronicle of Higher Education* 25(6):13-14 (October 6, 1982).
Hook, Janet. Supreme Court and faculty rights: retirement, sex bias, and tenure. *Chronicle of Higher Education* 25(7):25-26 (October 13, 1982).
Regan, Richard J. Supreme Court roundup: 1982 term. *Thought* 58(231):472-483 (December 1983).
Shepard, Blake. The scope of Congress's constitutional power under the property clause: regulating non-federal property to further the purposes of national parks and wilderness areas. *Boston College Environmental Affairs Law Review* 11(3): 479-538 (April 1984).

2477. United States v. Knotts March 2, 1983
460 US 276 75 LEd2d 55 103 SCt 1081
Almanac (1983):6A
Burger Years 143-168

Bazarian, Stephen C. Dow Chemical Company v. United States and aerial surveillance by the EPA: an argument for post-surveillance notice to the observed. *Boston College Environmental Affairs Law Review* 15(3-4):593-626 (Spring 1988).

Bernstein, Sidney. Supreme Court review. *Trial* 19(10):26, 28 (October 1983).

Junker, John M. The structure of the Fourth Amendment: the scope of the protection. *Journal of Criminal Law and Criminology* 79(4):1105-1183 (Winter 1989).

Kamisar, Yale. The swing of the pendulum. *Nation* 239(9):271-274 (September 29, 1984).

LaFave, Wayne R. Supreme Court review: Fourth Amendment vagaries (of improbable cause, imperceptible plain view, notorious privacy, and balancing askew). *Journal of Criminal Law and Criminology* 74(4):1171-1224 (Winter 1983).

Webber, Dawn. Supreme Court review: Fourth Amendment—of warrants, electronic surveillance, expectations of privacy, and tainted fruits. *Journal of Criminal Law and Criminology* 75(3):630-652 (Fall 1984).

2478. Block, Secretary of Agriculture v. Neal   March 7, 1983
       460 US 289   75 LEd2d 67   103 SCt 1089
       Almanac (1983):20A

Uncle Sam's bad-dream house. *Business Week* (2773):116 (January 17, 1983).

2479. North Dakota v. United States   March 7, 1983
       460 US 300   75 LEd2d 77   103 SCt 1095
       Almanac (1983):17A

Hassler, Gregory L., and Karen O'Connor. Woodsy witch doctors versus judicial guerrillas: the role and impact of competing interest groups in environmental litigation. *Boston College Environmental Affairs Law Review* 13(4):487-520 (Summer 1986).

2480. Briscoe v. LaHue   March 7, 1983
       460 US 325   75 LEd2d 96   103 SCt 1108
       Almanac (1983):8A-9A

2481. Hillsboro National Bank v. Commissioner of Internal Revenue   March 7, 1983
            Coupled with United States v. Bliss Dairy
       460 US 370   75 LEd2d 130   103 SCt 1134
       Almanac (1983):14A

Blum, Walter J. The role of the Supreme Court in federal income tax controversies—Hillsboro National Bank and Bliss Dairy, Inc. *Taxes* 61(6):363-369 (June 1983).

Landau, Zev. Redefinition of tax benefit rule by Supreme Court. *CPA Journal* 53(9):48-52 (September 1983).

Supreme Court holds that tax benefit rule applies in otherwise tax-free liquidation. *Journal of Taxation* 58(5):297-298 (May 1983).

Yin, George K. Supreme Court's tax benefit rule decision: unanswered questions invite future litigation. *Journal of Taxation* 59(3):130-133 (September 1983).

2482. Falls City Industries, Inc. v. Vanco Beverage, Inc.   March 22, 1983
       460 US 428   75 LEd2d 174   103 SCt 1282
       Almanac (1983):13A

Werner, Ray O. Marketing and the Supreme Court in transition, 1982-1984. *Journal of Marketing* 49(3):97-105 (Summer 1985).

2483. United States v. Generix Drug Corp.   March 22, 1983
       460 US 453   75 LEd2d 198   103 SCt 1298
       Almanac (1983):14A

Raloff, Janet. High Court requires generic-drug tests. *Science News* 123(14):214 (April 2, 1983).

What the High Court may decide. *Chemical Week* 131(14):10-11 (October 6, 1982).

2484. District of Columbia Court of Appeals v. Feldman   March 23, 1983
       460 US 462   75 LEd2d 206   103 SCt 1303

Almanac (1983):19A

2485. Florida v. Royer   March 23, 1983
        460 US 491   75 LEd2d 229   103 SCt 1319
        Almanac (1983):6A
        En Am Con 1628-1635
    Bernstein, Sidney. Supreme Court review. *Trial* 19(10):26, 28 (October 1983).
    Bernstein, Steven K. Supreme Court review: Fourth Amendment—using the drug courier profile to fight the
        war on drugs. *Journal of Criminal Law and Criminology* 80(4):996-1017 (Winter 1990).
    Butterfoss, Edwin J. Bright line seizures: the need for clarity in determining when Fourth Amendment activity
        begins. *Journal of Criminal Law and Criminology* 79(2):437-482 (Summer 1988).
    Guerra, Sandra. Domestic drug interdiction operations: finding the balance. *Journal of Criminal Law and
        Criminology* 82(4):1109-1161 (Winter 1992).
    Kamisar, Yale. The swing of the pendulum. *Nation* 239(9):271-274 (September 29, 1984).
    LaFave, Wayne R. Supreme Court review: Fourth Amendment vagaries (of improbable cause, imperceptible
        plain view, notorious privacy, and balancing askew). *Journal of Criminal Law and Criminology* 74(4):1171-
        1224 (Winter 1983).

2486. Washington v. United States   March 29, 1983
        460 US 536   75 LEd2d 264   103 SCt 1344
        Almanac (1983):18A

2487. Illinois v. Abbott & Associates, Inc.   March 29, 1983
        460 US 557   75 LEd2d 281   103 SCt 1356
        Almanac (1983):13A
    The case for recasting the High Court's role. *Business Week* (2760):33-34 (October 11, 1982).
    Werner, Ray O. Marketing and the Supreme Court in transition, 1982-1984. *Journal of Marketing* 49(3):97-105
        (Summer 1985).

2488. Minneapolis Star & Tribune Co. v. Minnesota Commissioner of Revenue   March 29, 1983
        460 US 575   75 LEd2d 295   103 SCt 1365
        Almanac (1983):12A
    Kalette, Denise. Several press cases on High Court's docket. *Editor and Publisher* 115(40-41):13 (October 2-9,
        1982).
    Regan, Richard J. Supreme Court roundup: 1982 term. *Thought* 58(231):472-483 (December 1983).
    Roper, James E. Supreme Court to hear major libel cases in '84. *Editor and Publisher* 117(1):16, 21, 27
        (January 7, 1984).
    Tofel, Richard J. Is differential taxation of press entities by states constitutional? *Journal of Taxation* 73(1):42-
        45 (July 1990).

2489. Arizona v. California   March 30, 1983
        460 US 605   75 LEd2d 318   103 SCt 1382
        Almanac (1983):19A
        Am Indians (Wilkinson) 42-43, 130+

2490. Tuten v. United States   March 30, 1983
        460 US 660   75 LEd2d 359   103 SCt 1412
        Almanac (1983):8A

2491. Local 926, International Union of Operating Engineers, AFL-CIO v. Jones   April 4, 1983
        460 US 669   75 LEd2d 368   103 SCt 1453
        Almanac (1983):18A

2492. Metropolitan Edison Co. v. National Labor Relations Board (NLRB)   April 4, 1983
        460 US 693   75 LEd2d 387   103 SCt 1467

Almanac (1983):15A

The case for recasting the High Court's role. *Business Week* (2760):33-34 (October 11, 1982).

Nelson-Horchler, Joani. Term begins: Supreme Court centers on job bias, labor law. *Industry Week* 215(1):22, 24 (October 4, 1982).

Zippo, Mary. Roundup: Supreme Court decision erodes managerial rights under the NLRA. *Personnel* 60(6):47-49 (November/December 1983).

2493. United States Postal Service, Board of Governors v. Aikens   April 4, 1983
460 US 711   75 LEd2d 403   103 SCt 1478
Almanac (1983):9A

Fields, Cheryl M. High Court rules that job-bias plaintiffs need not prove direct discrimination. *Chronicle of Higher Education* 26(7):9-10 (April 13, 1983).

Mauro, Tony. From pensions to postal rates. *Nation's Business* 70(12):38-39 (December 1982).

2494. Kush v. Rutledge   April 4, 1983
460 US 719   75 LEd2d 413   103 SCt 1483
Almanac (1983):9A

2495. Texas v. Brown   April 19, 1983
460 US 730   75 LEd2d 502   103 SCt 1535
Almanac (1983):6A
En Am Con 1884

Bernstein, Sidney. Supreme Court review. *Trial* 19(10):26, 28 (October 1983).

LaFave, Wayne R. Supreme Court review: Fourth Amendment vagaries (of improbable cause, imperceptible plain view, notorious privacy, and balancing askew). *Journal of Criminal Law and Criminology* 74(4):1171-1224 (Winter 1983).

2496. United States v. Rylander   April 19, 1983
460 US 752   75 LEd2d 521   103 SCt 1548
Almanac (1983):14A-15A

Ritholz, Jules, and Elliot Silverman. Supreme Court's Rylander decision contains a message for corporate records custodians. *Journal of Taxation* 59(1):16-17 (July 1983).

2497. Metropolitan Edison Co. v. People Against Nuclear Energy (PANE)   April 19, 1983
Coupled with United States Nuclear Regulatory Commission (NRC) v. People Against Nuclear Energy (PANE)
460 US 766   75 LEd2d 534   103 SCt 1556
Almanac (1983):16A

Gest, Ted. A bulging agenda for Supreme Court. *U.S. News and World Report* 93(15):82 (October 11, 1982).

———. The justices take a turn to activism. *U.S. News and World Report* 95(2):33 (July 11, 1983).

Hartsough, Don M., and Jeffrey C. Savitsky. Three Mile Island: psychology and environmental policy at a crossroads. *American Psychologist* 39(10):1113-1122 (October 1984).

Lovely, Jeffrey M. Protecting wetlands: consideration of secondary social and economic effects by the United States Army Corps of Engineers in its wetlands permitting process. *Boston College Environmental Affairs Law Review* 17(3):647-686 (Spring 1990).

Marshall, Eliot. Nuclear industry, 1, nuclear critics, 1. *Science* 220(4597):587 (May 6, 1983).

Nuke moratorium upheld. *Engineering News Record* 210(18[17]):27 (April 28, 1983).

Press, Aric, Diane Camper, Mary Lord, and Frank Gibney, Jr. A blow to nuclear power. *Newsweek* 101(18):67-68 (May 2, 1983).

Raloff, Janet. Two high-court rulings could affect nuclear power's future. *Science News* 123(18):279 (April 30, 1983).

Sandler, Ross. Mixed rulings on nuclear power. *Environment* 25(6):2-3 (July/August 1983).

Top court rules for, against nuclear industry. *Chemical and Engineering News* 61(18):35 (May 2, 1983).

2498. Anderson v. Celebrezze, Secretary of State of Ohio   April 19, 1983
    460 US 780   75 LEd2d 547   103 SCt 1564
      Almanac (1983):13A
      Sup Ct Review (1986):259-316
    A boost for third parties. *Newsweek* 101(18):33 (May 2, 1983).
    Gest, Ted. A bulging agenda for Supreme Court. *U.S. News and World Report* 93(15):82 (October 11, 1982).

2499. Bowsher, Comptroller General of the United States v. Merck & Co., Inc.   April 19, 1983
    460 US 824   75 LEd2d 580   103 SCt 1587
      Almanac (1983):20A
    Bomster, Mark. Antitrust, bankruptcy rulings highlight Supreme Court term. *Electronic News* 29(1455):Supp E
      (July 25, 1983).
    ———. Court faces busy term. *Electronic News* 28(1414):Supp W (October 11, 1982).
    The case for recasting the High Court's role. *Business Week* (2760):33-34 (October 11, 1982).

2500. Morris, Warden v. Slappy   April 20, 1983
    461 US 1   75 LEd2d 610   103 SCt 1610
      Almanac (1983):7A
    Bernstein, Sidney. Supreme Court review. *Trial* 19(11):20, 22 (November 1983).
    Hardy, Melinda. Supreme Court review: Sixth Amendment—applicability of right to counsel of choice to
      forfeiture of attorney's fees. *Journal of Criminal Law and Criminology* 80(4):1154-1189 (Winter 1990).

2501. Smith v. Wade   April 20, 1983
    461 US 30   75 LEd2d 632   103 SCt 1625
      Almanac (1983):9A
    Siegel, Michael S. High Court rules inmates may seek punitive damages. *Trial* 19(7):14, 16-17 (July 1983).

2502. City of Los Angeles v. Lyons   April 20, 1983
    461 US 95   75 LEd2d 675   103 SCt 1660
      Almanac (1983):19A
      Burger Years 3-20
    Chemerinsky, Erwin. Protecting individual rights: policing the police. *Trial* 27(12):32-36 (December 1991).
    ———. Stunting the Constitution's growth. *Trial* 26(11):36-40 (November 1990).
    Gest, Ted. A bulging agenda for Supreme Court. *U.S. News and World Report* 93(15):82 (October 11, 1982).
    Neuborne, Burt. Taking away the right to sue. *Nation* 239(9):268-271 (September 29, 1984).
    Rowe, Thomas D. No final victories: the incompleteness of equity's triumph in federal public law. *Law and
      Contemporary Problems* 56(3):105-121 (Summer 1993).

2503. Connick, District Attorney v. Myers   April 20, 1983
    461 US 138   75 LEd2d 708   103 SCt 1684
      Almanac (1983):5A,12A
    Flygare, Thomas J. De jure: teachers' First Amendment rights eroding. *Phi Delta Kappan* 67(5):396-397
      (January 1986).
    Franke, Ann H., and Jacqueline W. Mintz. Four trends in higher education law. *Academe* 73(5):57-63
      (September/October 1987).
    Palmer, Stacy E. Free-speech ruling seen having little effect on college teachers. *Chronicle of Higher Education*
      26(10):30 (May 4, 1983).
    Regan, Richard J. Supreme Court roundup: 1982 term. *Thought* 58(231):472-483 (December 1983).
    Ruben, George. Public workers not protected by "free speech." *Monthly Labor Review* 106(6):48 (June 1983).
    Sendor, Benjamin. The chain of command may be broken—sometimes. *American School Board Journal*
      173(1):11 (January 1986).
    ———. Is speaking out cause for dismissal? *American School Board Journal* 177(3):8, 46 (March 1990).
    ———. Two rulings define when staff members may bad-mouth your schools. *American School Board Journal*
      171(7):11 (July 1984).

————. Why you might be personally liable. *American School Board Journal* 181(12):15, 47 (December 1994).

2504. United States v. Grace   April 20, 1983
461 US 171   75 LEd2d 736   103 SCt 1702
Almanac (1983):12A
En Am Con 858
Regan, Richard J. Supreme Court roundup: 1982 term. *Thought* 58(231):472-483 (December 1983).

2505. Pacific Gas and Electric Co. v. State Energy Resources Conservation   April 20, 1983
    and Development Commission
461 US 190   75 LEd2d 752   103 SCt 1713
Almanac (1983):16A
Editorials (1983):444-453
Adams, Nancy D. Title VI of the 1990 Clean Air Act Amendments and state and local initiatives to reverse the stratospheric ozone crisis: an analysis of preemption. *Boston College Environmental Affairs Law Review* 19(1):173-216 (Fall 1991).
Bernstein, Sidney. Supreme Court review. *Trial* 19(12):20, 22 (December 1983).
Brown, Omer F., and Edward M. Davis. The implications of the Supreme Court's California nuclear moratorium decision. *Public Utilities Fortnightly* 111(11):35-38 (May 26, 1983).
The case for recasting the High Court's role. *Business Week* (2760):33-34 (October 11, 1982).
Egan, Thomas E. Wrongful discharge and federal preemption: nuclear whistleblower protection under state law and section 210 of the Energy Reorganization Act. *Boston College Environmental Affairs Law Review* 17(2):405-440 (Winter 1990).
Gest, Ted. A bulging agenda for Supreme Court. *U.S. News and World Report* 93(15):82 (October 11, 1982).
Gransee, Marsha. A year of regulatory decisions in review. *Public Utilities Fortnightly* 113(1):51-55 (January 5, 1984).
Hassler, Gregory L., and Karen O'Connor. Woodsy witchdoctors versus judicial guerrillas: the role and impact of competing interest groups in environmental litigation. *Boston College Environmental Affairs Law Review* 13(4):487-520 (Summer 1986).
Marshall, Eliot. Nuclear industry, 1, nuclear critics, 1. *Science* 220(4597):587 (May 6, 1983).
————. Supreme Court to review California nuclear ban. *Science* 217(4555):134 (July 9, 1982).
Moskowitz, Daniel B. How the Supreme Court is redistributing power. [Editorial] *Business Week* (Industrial Edition) (2799):55 (July 18, 1983).
Nuclear industry takes it on the chin again. *U.S. News and World Report* 94(17):8 (May 2, 1983).
Nuke moratorium upheld. *Engineering News Record* 210(18[17]):27 (April 28, 1983).
Raloff, Janet. Two high-court rulings could affect nuclear power's future. *Science News* 123(18):279 (April 30, 1983).
Rocchio, David M. The Price-Anderson Act: allocation for the extraordinary risk of nuclear generated electricity: a model punitive damage provision. *Boston College Environmental Affairs Law Review* 14(3): 521-560 (Spring 1987).
Ross, Douglas. Safeguarding our federalism: lessons for the states from the Supreme Court. *Public Administration Review* 45(Special Issue):723-731 (November 1985).
Sherman, RuthAnn. Chemical warfare agent research regulation: the conflict between federal and local control. *Boston College Environmental Affairs Law Review* 14(1):131-163 (Fall 1986).
Short circuit: a setback for nuclear power. *Time* 121(18):26 (May 2, 1983).
Top court rules for, against nuclear industry. *Chemical and Engineering News* 61(18):35 (May 2, 1983).

2506. Olim v. Wakinekona   April 26, 1983
461 US 238   75 LEd2d 813   103 SCt 1741
Almanac (1983):11A
Baum, David P. Supreme Court review: Fourteenth Amendment—due process and interstate prison transfers. *Journal of Criminal Law and Criminology* 74(4):1387-1403 (Winter 1983).
Ross, Douglas. Safeguarding our federalism: lessons for the states from the Supreme Court. *Public Administration Review* 45(Special Issue):723-731 (November 1985).

2507. Jim McNeff, Inc. v. Todd   April 27, 1983
     461 US 260   75 LEd2d 830   103 SCt 1753
     Almanac (1983):15A

2508. Block, Secretary of Agriculture v. North Dakota ex rel. Board of University and School Lands   May 2, 1983
     461 US 273   75 LEd2d 840   103 SCt 1811
     Almanac (1983):17A

2509. Commissioner of Internal Revenue v. Tufts   May 2, 1983
     461 US 300   75 LEd2d 863   103 SCt 1826
     Almanac (1983):15A

     Bolling, Rodger A., and Philip P. Storrer. The Supreme Court's second look at Crane: what should it do? *Taxes* 61(2):138-144 (February 1983).

     Dorr, Patrick B., and Melvin E. Lacy. Crane after Tufts: still some unanswered questions. *Taxes* 62(3):162-169 (March 1984).

     Protass, Steven, and Gary Albert. Supreme Court decides Crane controversy. *CPA Journal* 53(11):64-65 (November 1983).

     Sanders, Michael I. Supreme Court ending Crane controversy, says nonrecourse debt is always part of sales price. *Journal of Taxation* 59(1):2-5 (July 1983).

     Yang, Wesley. Tufts: footnote to Crane. *Taxes* 62(2):118-124 (Febraury 1984).

2510. Martinez, as Next Friend of Morales v. Bynum   May 2, 1983
     461 US 321   75 LEd2d 879   103 SCt 1838
     Almanac (1983):17A

     Delon, Floyd G. The legacy of Thurgood Marshall. *Journal of Negro Education* 63(3):278-288 (Summer 1994).

2511. Kolender v. Lawson   May 2, 1983
     461 US 352   75 LEd2d 903   103 SCt 1855
     Almanac (1983):11A
     Editorials (1983):553-556
     En Am Con 1107-1108, 1955-1957

     Bernstein, Sidney. Supreme Court review. *Trial* 19(11):20, 22 (November 1983).

     The California walkman wins. *Newsweek* 101(20:63 (May 16, 1983).

     Court: loiterers have their rights. *U.S. News and World Report* 94(19):8 (May 16, 1983).

     Gest, Ted. A bulging agenda for Supreme Court. *U.S. News and World Report* 93(15):82 (October 11, 1982).

     ———. The justices take a turn to activism. *U.S. News and World Report* 95(2):33 (July 11, 1983).

     Jaynes, Gregory. This is against my rights!: three who felt wronged—and determined to battle for redress. *Time* 130(1):40-42 (July 6, 1987).

     Nelson, Jill. A case of anonymity. *Black Enterprise* 13(8):26 (March 1983).

     Press, Aric, and Richard Sandza. The California walkman. *Newsweek* 100(3):58 (July 19, 1982).

     Seligman, Daniel. Vagrancy unlimited. *Fortune* 107(12):55 (June 13, 1983).

     Walking tall in California: the Supreme Court overturns the state's vagrancy law. *Time* 121(20):86 (May 16, 1983).

2512. Arkansas Electric Cooperative Corp. v. Arkansas Public Service Commission   May 16, 1983
     461 US 375   76 LEd2d 1   103 SCt 1905
     Almanac (1983):16A

     O'Neill, Andrew J. Retail electic rates: drawing the line between federal and state authority under the commerce clause. *Public Utilities Fortnightly* 112(9):52-55 (October 27, 1983).

2513. American Paper Institute, Inc. v. American Electric Power Service Corp.   May 16, 1983
     Coupled with Federal Energy Regulatory Commission (FERC) v. American Electric Power Service Corp.
     461 US 402   76 LEd2d 22   103 SCt 1921
     Almanac (1983):16A

Court lifts shadow over small power projects. *Engineering News Record* 210(21):26-27 (May 26, 1983).

Gransee, Marsha. A year of regulatory decisions in review. *Public Utilities Fortnightly* 113(1):51-55 (January 5, 1984).

Howe, Shippen. Cogeneration rates: the aftermath of the American Electric Power case. *Public Utilities Fortnightly* 110(11):51-54 (November 25, 1982).

Iwler, Louis. States back Purpa ruling by U.S. Supreme Court. *Electrical World* 198(3):19-20 (March 1984).

———. Supreme Court rules Purpa is constitutional. *Electrical World* 196(7):25-26 (July 1982).

2514. Hensley v. Eckerhart   May 16, 1983
461 US 424   76 LEd2d 40   103 SCt 1933
   Almanac (1983):9A

Brooks, Thornton H., M. Daniel McGinn, and William P.H. Cary. Second generation problems facing employers in employment discrimination cases: continuing violations, pendent state claims, and double attorneys' fees. *Law and Contemporary Problems* 49(4):26-51 (Autumn 1986).

Conte, Alba. Public interest lawyers deserve risk multipliers. *Trial* 30(12):36-42 (December 1994).

O'Connor, Karen, and Lee Epstein. Bridging the gap between Congress and the Supreme Court: interest groups and the erosion of the American rule governing awards of attorneys' fees. *Western Political Quarterly* 38(2):238-249 (June 1985).

2515. Heckler, Secretary of Health and Human Services v. Campbell   May 16, 1983
461 US 458   76 LEd2d 66   103 SCt 1952
   Almanac (1983):20A

2516. Boston Firefighters Union, Local 718 v. Boston Chapter, NAACP   May 16, 1983
   Coupled with Boston Police Patrolmen's Association v. Castro
   Coupled with Beecher v. Boston Chapter, NAACP
461 US 477   76 LEd2d 330   103 SCt 2076
   Almanac (1983):9A

Campbell, Bebe Moore. Supreme Court challenge: laying off affirmative action. *Black Enterprise* 13(7):31 (February 1983).

Camper, Diane. Blacks and the Supreme Court. *Black Enterprise* 13(8):48 (March 1983).

Gest, Ted. The justices take a turn to activism. *U.S. News and World Report* 95(2):33 (July 11, 1983).

High Court sidesteps a civil-rights case. *Newsweek* 101(22):101 (May 30, 1983).

Press, Aric, Phylis Malamud, Diane Camper, and Peggy Clausen. Quotas under attack. *Newsweek* 101(17):95-96 (April 25, 1983).

Regan, Richard J. Supreme Court roundup: 1982 term. *Thought* 58(231):472-483 (December 1983).

Seniority rights. [Editorial] *Nation* 236(11):324-325 (March 19, 1983).

2517. Verlinden B. V. v. Central Bank of Nigeria   May 23, 1983
461 US 480   76 LEd2d 81   103 SCt 1962
   Almanac (1983):19A

2518. United States v. Hasting   May 23, 1983
461 US 499   76 LEd2d 96   103 SCt 1974
   Almanac (1983):7A

2519. Pallas Shipping Agency, Ltd. v. Duris   May 23, 1983
461 US 529   76 LEd2d 120   103 SCt 1991
   Almanac (1983):16A

2520. Regan, Secretary of the Treasury v. Taxation with Representation of Washington   May 23, 1983
461 US 540   76 LEd2d 129   103 SCt 1997
   Almanac (1983):12A

Kelley, Dean M. The Supreme Court redefines tax exemption. *Society* 21(4):23-28 (May/June 1984).

Supreme Court decision. *Congressional Digest* 70(8-9)197-199 (August/September 1991).

Supreme Court upholds U.S. limits on lobbying by nonprofit groups. *Chronicle of Higher Education* 26(14):16 (June 1, 1983).

2521. United States v. Eight Thousand Eight Hundred   May 23, 1983
     and Fifty Dollars ($8,850) in United States Currency
    461 US 555   76 LEd2d 143   103 SCt 2005
     Almanac (1983):11A

2522. Bob Jones University v. United States   May 24, 1983
     Coupled with Goldsboro Christian School District v. United States
    461 US 574   76 LEd2d 157   103 SCt 2017
     Almanac (1982):276, 397-399; (1983):4A, 10A
     Burger Years 95-108
     Const Law 55-56R
     Documents (v. 2):852-855R
     Editorials (1982):12-19; (1983):576-586
     En Am Con 132
     Godless 119-120
     Original (Davis) 86-88
     Religion 8-11
     Sup Ct Review (1983):1-82
     Tenth 51-64

Arkes, Hadley. Principled playfulness: case study I. *National Review* 43(11):26-27 (June 24, 1991).

Ball, Howard. The U.S. Supreme Court's glossing of the Federal Tort Claims Act: statutory construction and veterans' tort actions. *Western Political Quarterly* 41(3):529-552 (September 1988).

Bernstein, Sidney. Supreme Court review. *Trial* 19(12):20, 22 (December 1983).

Black magic. *National Review* 35(12):736-737 (June 24, 1983).

The Bob Jones case. *National Review* 34(20):1262, 1264 (October 15, 1982).

Camper, Diane. Blacks and the Supreme Court. *Black Enterprise* 13(8):48 (March 1983).

Civil rights caper. *New Republic* 188(24):9-10 (June 20, 1983).

Collision course. *Christian Century* 103(16):456-457 (May 7, 1986).

Excerpts from the Supreme Court's opinions in Bob Jones U. case. *Chronicle of Higher Education* 26(14):10, 12-16R (June 1, 1983).

Fields, Cheryl M. Bias cases among first on Supreme Court docket. *Chronicle of Higher Education* 25(6):13-14 (October 6, 1982).

———. Tax exemption denied schools practicing bias. *Chronicle of Higher Education* 26(14):1, 10 (June 1, 1983).

Flygare, Thomas J. De jure: Supreme Court hears arguments on tax breaks for racially discriminatory private schools. *Phi Delta Kappan* 64(5):369 (January 1983).

From Tilton to Ewing: some major higher-education decisions of the Burger court. *Chronicle of Higher Education* 32(17):10 (June 25, 1986).

Gest, Ted. A bulging agenda for Supreme Court. *U.S. News and World Report* 93(15):82 (October 11, 1982).

High Court hears Jones case. *Christianity Today* 26(18):92 (November 12, 1982).

Kantzer, Kenneth S. The Bob Jones decision: a dangerous precedent. [Editorial] *Christianity Today* 27(13):14-15 (September 2, 1983).

Kelley, Dean M. The Supreme Court redefines tax exemption. *Society* 21(4):23-28 (May/June 1984).

Neuborne, Burt. Taking away the right to sue. *Nation* 239(9):268-271 (September 29, 1984).

Off the hook: the court tackles school taxes. *Time* 119(18):60 (May 3, 1982).

Pious racists for tax exemption. *Economist* 287(7292):26 (June 4-10, 1983).

Press, Aric, and Diane Camper. Religion, race and taxes. *Newsweek* 100(17):102 (October 25, 1982).

Rabkin, Jeremy. Behind the tax-exempt schools debate. *Public Interest* (68):21-38 (Summer 1982).

Reagan and blacks—the lines harden. *U.S. News and World Report* 94(22):8 (June 6, 1983).

A Reagan defeat. *Christian Century* 100(19):577 (June 8-15, 1983).

Redlich, Norman. Some cracks in the wall. *Nation* 239(9):277-280 (September 29, 1984).

Regan, Richard J. Supreme Court roundup: 1982 term. *Thought* 58(231):472-483 (December 1983).

Reid, Herbert O., and Frankie M. Foster-Davis. Three decades of "all deliberate speed." *Crisis* 91(5):12-15 (May 1984).

Rosen, Jeffrey. Boys and girls. *New Republic* 210(7):14, 16 (February 14, 1994).

Shapiro, Walter, and Diane Camper. Reagan's civil-rights woes. *Newsweek* 101(23):38 (June 6, 1983).

Simmons, Althea T. L. From Brown to Grove City: blueprint for education. *Crisis* 91(5):6-10 (May 1984).

Spring, Beth. The ominous implications of the Bob Jones decision. *Christianity Today* 27(11):32-35 (July 15, 1983).

Stefkovich, Jacqueline A., and Terrence Leas. A legal history of desegregation in higher education. *Journal of Negro Education* 63(3):406-420 (Summer 1994).

Tifft, Susan E., and Douglas Brew. In trouble with blacks: trying to cut his losses, Reagan looks for votes elsewhere. *Time* 121(23):28 (June 6, 1983).

Truesch, Paul E. Bob Jones—where now? *Taxes* 62(1):43-54 (January 1984).

Vile, John R. Bob Jones before the bench. *Christian Century* 100(23):707-711 (August 3-10, 1983).

Williams, Dennis A. No tax breaks for racism. *Black Enterprise* 14(2):17 (September 1983).

2523. Morrison-Knudsen Construction Co. v. Director,   May 24, 1983
      Office of Workers' Compensation Programs, United States Department of Labor
    461 US 624   76 LEd2d 194   103 SCt 2045
    Almanac (1983):16A

2524. General Motors Corp. v. Devex Corp.   May 24, 1983
    461 US 648   76 LEd2d 211   103 SCt 2058
    Almanac (1983):14A

2525. Bearden v. Georgia   May 24, 1983
    461 US 660   76 LEd2d 221   103 SCt 2064
    Almanac (1983):8A

2526. United States v. Rodgers   May 31, 1983
    461 US 677   76 LEd2d 236   103 SCt 2132
    Almanac (1983):11A

Conrad, Victor, and Christopher S. Cole. Tax liens and the homestead: a fortress falls. *Taxes* 64(9):555-559 (September 1986).

Two new Supreme Court decisions define the priority of the government's liens. *Journal of Taxation* 59(2):120-121 (August 1983).

2527. Bill Johnson's Restaurants, Inc. v. National Labor Relations Board (NLRB)   May 31, 1983
    461 US 731   76 LEd2d 277   103 SCt 2161
    Almanac (1983):15A
    Burger Years 228-239

Fox, Arthur. Showing workers who's the boss. *Nation* 239(9):295-299 (September 29, 1984).

Hentoff, Nat. Libel and labor. *Progressive* 47(11);25-27 (November 1983).

2528. W.R. Grace and Co. v. Local Union 759,   May 31, 1983
      International Union of the United Rubber, Cork, Linoleum & Plastic Workers of America
    461 US 757   76 LEd2d 298   103 SCt 2177
    Almanac (1983):15A

2529. Bell, Secretary of Education v. New Jersey and Pennsylvania   May 31, 1983
    461 US 773   76 LEd2d 312   103 SCt 2187
    Almanac (1983):17A

2530. Pickett v. Brown   June 6, 1983
    462 US 1   76 LEd2d 372   103 SCt 2199
    Almanac (1983):11A

2531. Federal Trade Commission (FTC) v. Grolier, Inc.   June 6, 1983
    462 US 19   76 LEd2d 387   103 SCt 2209
      Almanac (1983):20A

    Werner, Ray O. Marketing and the Supreme Court in transition, 1982-1984. *Journal of Marketing* 49(3):97-105
      (Summer 1985).

2532. Watt, Secretary of the Interior v. Western Nuclear, Inc.   June 6, 1983
    462 US 36   76 LEd2d 400   103 SCt 2218
      Almanac (1983):17A

    Four key rulings from Supreme Court. *U.S. News and World Report* 94(24):12 (June 20, 1983).

2533. United States v. Ptasynski   June 6, 1983
    462 US 74   76 LEd2d 427   103 SCt 2239
      Almanac (1983):15A

    Hassler, Gregory L., and Karen O'Connor. Woodsy witch doctors versus judicial guerrillas: the role and impact
      of competing interest groups in environmental litigation. *Boston College Environmental Affairs Law Review*
      13(4):487-520 (Summer 1986).

    High Court leaves windfall profits tax in place. *Oil and Gas Journal* 81(24):54-55 (June 13, 1983).

    Supreme Court mulls windfall profits tax case. *Oil and Gas Journal* 81(18):99 (May 2, 1983).

    Supreme Court upholds windfall profits tax as constitutional. *Journal of Taxation* 59(2):105-106 (August
      1983).

    Windfall profits tax upheld by court in unanimous ruling. *Chemical Marketing Reporter* 223:4, 17 (June 13,
      1983).

2534. Baltimore Gas and Electric Co. v. Natural Resources Defense Council, Inc. (NRDC)   June 6, 1983
      Coupled with United States Nuclear Regulatory Commission (NRC) v. Natural Resources Defense
        Council, Inc. (NRDC)
      Coupled with Commonwealth of Edison, Co. v. Natural Resources Defense Council, Inc. (NRDC)
    462 US 87   76 LEd2d 437   103 SCt 2246
      Almanac (1983):16A

    Brady, Timothy Patrick. "But most of it belongs to those yet to be born:" the public trust doctrine, NEPA, and
      the Stewardship ethic. *Boston College Environmental Affairs Law Review* 17(3):621-646 (Spring 1990).

    Hassler, Gregory L. and Karen O'Connor. Woodsy witch doctors versus judicial guerrillas: the role and impact
      of competing interest groups in environmental litigation. *Boston College Environmental Affairs Law Review*
      13(4):487-520 (Summer 1986).

2535. BankAmerica Corp. v. United States   June 8, 1983
    462 US 122   76 LEd2d 456   103 SCt 2266
      Almanac (1983):14A

    Four key rulings from Supreme Court. *U.S. News and World Report* 94(24):12 (June 20, 1983).

    Gest, Ted. The justices take a turn to activism. *U.S. News and World Report* 95(2):33 (July 11, 1983).

    Werner, Ray O. Marketing and the Supreme Court in transition, 1982-1984. *Journal of Marketing* 49(3):97-105
      (Summer 1985).

2536. DelCostello v. International Brotherhood of Teamsters   June 8, 1983
      Coupled with United Steelworkers of America v. Flowers
    462 US 151   76 LEd2d 476   103 SCt 2281
      Almanac (1983):15A
      Burger Years 228-239

    Ruben, George. Harsher penalties for union officers banned. *Monthly Labor Review* 106(6):47-48 (June 1983).

2537. Exxon Corp. v. Eagerton, Commissioner of Revenue of Alabama   June 8, 1983
      Coupled with Exchange Oil and Gas Co. v. Eagerton
    462 US 176   76 LEd2d 497   103 SCt 2296
      Almanac (1983):18A

Four key rulings from Supreme Court. *U.S. News and World Report* 94(24):12 (June 20, 1983).

Gest, Ted. The justices take a turn to activism. *U.S. News and World Report* 95(2):33 (July 11, 1983).

High Court won't speed WPT case. *Oil and Gas Journal* 81(4):34-35 (January 24, 1983).

Nelson-Horchler, Joani. Term begins: Supreme Court centers on job bias, labor law. *Industry Week* 215(1):22, 24 (October 4, 1982).

Several energy cases on Supeme Court docket. *Oil and Gas Journal* 80(45):120 (November 8, 1982).

State ban on severance tax passthrough okayed. *Oil and Gas Journal* 81(24):53 (June 13, 1983).

Supreme Court's okay doesn't make selective taxation by states good law. [Editorial] *Oil and Gas Journal* 81(25):55 (June 20, 1983).

2538. United States v. Whiting Pools, Inc.   June 8, 1983
      462 US 198   76 LEd2d 515   103 SCt 2309
      Almanac (1983):14A

Two new Supreme Court decisions define the priority of the government's liens. *Journal of Taxation* 59(2):120-121 (August 1983).

2539. Illinois v. Gates   June 8, 1983
      462 US 213   76 LEd2d 527   103 SCt 2317
      Almanac (1983):5A-6A
      Burger Years 143-168
      Const Law 339-342R
      Editorials (1982):1441-1443; (1983):757-760
      En Am Con 948-949, 979-980, 1462-1464, 1628-1635, 1637-1638
      Sup Ct Review (1983):283-304; (1984):309-358

Beach, Bennett H., and David S. Jackson. When the police blunder a little: the court considers a major exception to the exclusionary rule. *Time* 121(11):56-61 (March 14, 1983).

Bernstein, Sidney. Supreme Court review. *Trial* 19(10):26, 28 (October 1983).

Dripps, Donald A. Supreme Court review: Justice White and the rights of the accused. *Trial* 29(5):71-74 (May 1993).

Easier searches: but "apologies to all." *Time* 121(25):64 (June 20, 1983).

Four key rulings from Supreme Court. *U.S. News and World Report* 94(24):12 (June 20, 1983).

Kamisar, Yale. The swing of the pendulum. *Nation* 239(9):271-274 (September 29, 1984).

LaFave, Wayne R. Supreme Court review: Fourth Amendment vagaries (of improbable cause, imperceptible plain view, notorious privacy, and balancing askew). *Journal of Criminal Law and Criminology* 74(4):1171-1224 (Winter 1983).

Moore, Cathy E. Supreme Court review: Fourth Amendment—totality of the circumstances approach to probable cause based on informate's tips. *Journal of Criminal Law and Criminology* 74(4):1249-1264 (Winter 1983).

Mussio, Donna. Drawing the line between administrative and criminal searches: defining the "object of the search" in environmental inspections. *Boston College Environmental Affairs Law Review* 18(1):185-211+ (Fall 1990).

Regan, Richard J. Supreme Court roundup: 1982 term. *Thought* 58(231):472-483 (December 1983).

The Supreme Court: apologies to all. *Newsweek* 101(25):65 (June 20, 1983).

2540. Chappell v. Wallace   June 13, 1983
      462 US 296   76 LEd2d 586   103 SCt 2362
      Almanac (1983):9A

Ball, Howard. The U.S. Supreme Court's glossing of the Federal Tort Claims Act: statutory construction and veterans' tort actions. *Western Political Quarterly* 41(3):529-552 (September 1988).

Sour apples: The Supreme Court bites back. *Time* 121(26):61 (June 27, 1983).

2541. Haring, Lieutenant, Arlington County Police Department v. Prosise   June 13, 1983
      462 US 306   76 LEd2d 595   103 SCt 2368
      Almanac (1983):9A

Sour apples: the Supreme Court bites back. *Time* 121(26):61 (June 27, 1983).

2542. New Mexico v. Mescalero Apache Tribe   June 13, 1983
      462 US 324   76 LEd2d 611   103 SCt 2378
        Almanac (1983):17A
        Am Indians (Wilkinson) 98, 130

2543. Crown, Cork & Seal Co., Inc. v. Parker   June 13, 1983
      462 US 345   76 LEd2d 628   103 SCt 2392
        Almanac (1983):9A

2544. Bell v. United States   June 13, 1983
      462 US 356   76 LEd2d 638   103 SCt 2398
        Almanac (1983):8A

2545. Bush v. Lucas   June 13, 1983
      462 US 367   76 LEd2d 648   103 SCt 2404
        Almanac (1983):12A
      Sour apples: the Supreme Court bites back. *Time* 121(26):61 (June 27, 1983).

2546. National Labor Relations Board (NLRB) v. Transportation Management Corp.   June 15, 1983
      462 US 393   76 LEd2d 667   103 SCt 2469
        Almanac (1983):15A

2547. Philko Aviation, Inc. v. Shacket et ux.   June 15, 1983
      462 US 406   76 LEd2d 678   103 SCt 2476
        Almanac (1983):17A-18A

2548. City of Akron v. Akron Center for Reproductive Health, Inc.   June 15, 1983
      462 US 416   76 LEd2d 687   103 SCt 2481
        Abortion Am 84-87R, 90-91, 98-99, 185-187+
        Abortion Con 256-260, 292
        Abortion Dec 90-99+
        Abortion Dec 80s Introduction, 71-104R
        Abortion Quest 110-114, 118-122, 125-126+
        Almanac (1982):403-404; (1983)306-308, 10A
        Burger Years 109-124
        Editorials (1982):1438-1440; (1983):716-723
        En Am Con 1552-1558
        Hard Choices 173-174, 312-313+
        Liberty 640-643, 690-691+
      Abortion: court unmoved. *Economist* 287(7295):32-33 (June 25-July 1, 1983).
      The abortion perplex. *New Republic* 189(2):7-8 (July 11, 1983).
      Aliotta, Jilda M. The unfinished feminist agenda: the shifting forum. *Annals of the American Academy of
         Political and Social Science* 515:140-150 (May 1991).
      Behuniak-Long, Susan. Justice Sandra Day O'Connor and the power of maternal legal thinking. *Review of
         Politics* 54(3):417-444 (Summer 1992).
      Bernstein, Sidney. Supreme Court review. *Trial* 19(12):20, 22 (December 1983).
      Blank, Robert H. Judicial decision making and biological fact: Roe v. Wade and the unresolved question of
         fetal viability. *Western Political Quarterly* 37(4):584-602 (December 1984).
      Copelon, Rhonda, and Kathryn Kolbert. The gathering storm: Roe v. Wade. *Ms.* 17(10):88-92 (April 1989).
      The Court and free choice. *Progressive* 47(8):11-12 (August 1983).
      Doerr, Edd. Good news, bad news. *Humanist* 43(5):36, 43 (September/October 1983).
      Gest, Ted. Anti-abortion groups have a bad day in Court. *U.S. News and World Report* 94(25):31 (June 27,
         1983).
      ———. A bulging agenda for Supreme Court. *U.S. News and World Report* 93(15):82 (October 11, 1982).

———. What the Supreme Court heard on abortion. *U.S. News and World Report* 93(24):83 (December 13, 1982).

Hunter, Nan. What Akron does/does not say. *Nation* 237(5):137-139 (August 20-27, 1983).

Isaacson, Walter, Anne Constable, and David S. Jackson. Holding firm on abortion: The Supreme Court solidly supports a woman's right to choose. *Time* 121(26):14-15 (June 27, 1983).

It's up to Congress now. *National Review* 35(13):793 (July 8, 1983).

McDaniel, Ann. Countdown on abortion. *Newsweek* 113(4):50 (January 23, 1989).

Melton, Gary B. Legal regulation of adolescent abortion: unintended effects. *American Psychologist* 42(1):79-83 (January 1987).

Melton, Gary B., and Nancy Felipe Russo. Adolescent abortion: psychological perspectives on public policy. *American Psychologist* 42(1):69-72 (January 1987).

Neuhaus, Richard John. Abortion after Akron: the contradictions are showing. *Commonweal* 110(13):388 (July 15, 1983).

Press, Aric, and Diane Camper. The Court stands by abortion. *Newsweek* 101(26):62-63 (June 27, 1983).

Regan, Richard J. Supreme Court roundup: 1982 term. *Thought* 58(231):472-483 (December 1983).

Spring, Beth. Harsh days at the High Court. *Christianity Today* 27(11):30-31 (July 15, 1983).

———. White House files prolife court brief. *Christianity Today* 26(14):66-70 (September 3, 1982).

Starr, Mark, Ann McDaniel, and Bob Cohn. Meese weighs in on abortion. *Newsweek* 106(5):60-61 (July 29, 1985).

Stoner, James R., Jr. Common law and constitutionalism in the abortion case. *Review of Politics* 55(3):421-441 (Summer 1993).

Two cheers for the Court. *National Review* 35(16):983 (August 19, 1983).

Vetoes and votes. [Editorial] *Nation* 237(2):35-36 (July 9-16, 1983).

2549. Planned Parenthood Association of Kansas City, Missouri, Inc.   June 15, 1983
    v. Ashcroft, Attorney General of Missouri
462 US 476   76 LEd2d 733   103 SCt 2517
    Abortion Am 90-91, 99, 199-201+
    Abortion Dec 102-109+
    Abortion Dec 80s Introduction, 105-121R
    Almanac (1982):403-404; (1983)306-308, 10A
    Editorials (1982):1438-1440; (1983):716-723
    En Am Con 1552-1558
    Hard Choices 176, 313
    Liberty 640-643+

Abortion: court unmoved. *Economist* 287(7295):32-33 (June 25-July 1, 1983).

The abortion perplex. *New Republic* 189(2):7-8 (July 11, 1983).

Blank, Robert H. Judicial decision making and biological fact: Roe v. Wade and the unresolved question of fetal viability. *Western Political Quarterly* 37(4):584-602 (December 1984).

The Court and free choice. *Progressive* 47(8):11-12 (August 1983).

Doerr, Edd. Good news, bad news. *Humanist* 43(5):36, 43 (September/October 1983).

Gest, Ted. Anti-abortion groups have a bad day in Court. *U.S. News and World Report* 94(25):31 (June 27, 1983).

———. A bulging agenda for Supreme Court. *U.S. News and World Report* 93(15):82 (October 11, 1982).

———. What the Supreme Court heard on abortion. *U.S. News and World Report* 93(24):83 (December 13, 1982).

Isaacson, Walter, Anne Constable, and David S. Jackson. Holding firm on abortion: the Supreme Court solidly supports a woman's right to choose. *Time* 121(26):14-15 (June 27, 1983).

McDaniel, Ann. Countdown on abortion. *Newsweek* 113(4):50 (January 23, 1989).

Melton, Gary B. Legal regulation of adolescent abortion: unintended effects. *American Psychologist* 42(1):79-83 (January 1987).

Press, Aric, and Diane Camper. The Court stands by abortion. *Newsweek* 101(26):62-63 (June 27, 1983).

Regan, Richard J. Supreme Court roundup: 1982 term. *Thought* 58(231):472-483 (December 1983).

Spring, Beth. White House files prolife court brief. *Christianity Today* 26(14):66-70 (September 3, 1982).

Starr, Mark, Ann McDaniel, and Bob Cohn. Meese weighs in on abortion. *Newsweek* 106(5):60-61 (July 29, 1985).

2550. Simopoulos v. State of Virginia   June 15, 1983
      462 US 506   76 LEd2d 755   103 SCt 2532
        Abortion Am 80, 99
        Abortion Dec 110-114
        Abortion Dec 80s Introduction, 123-133R
        Almanac (1982):403-404; (1983)306-308, 10A-11A
        Editorials (1982):1438-1440; (1983):716-723
        En Am Con 1552-1558
        Liberty 640-641

      Blank, Robert H. Judicial decision making and biological fact: Roe v. Wade and the unresolved question of fetal viability. *Western Political Quarterly* 37(4):584-602 (December 1984).

      The Court and free choice. *Progressive* 47(8):11-12 (August 1983).

      Doerr, Edd. Good news, bad news. *Humanist* 43(5):36, 43 (September/October 1983).

      Gest, Ted. Anti-abortion groups have a bad day in Court. *U.S. News and World Report* 94(25):31 (June 27, 1983).

      ————. A bulging agenda for Supreme Court. *U.S. News and World Report* 93(15):82 (October 11, 1982).

      ————. What the Supreme Court heard on abortion. *U.S. News and World Report* 93(24):83 (December 13, 1982).

      Press, Aric, and Diane Camper. The Court stands by abortion. *Newsweek* 101(26):62-63 (June 27, 1983).

      Regan, Richard J. Supreme Court roundup: 1982 term. *Thought* 58(231):472-483 (December 1983).

      Spring, Beth. White House files prolife court brief. *Christianity Today* 26(14):66-70 (September 3, 1982).

2551. Jones & Laughlin Steel Corp. v. Pfeifer   June 15, 1983
      462 US 523   76 LEd2d 768   103 SCt 2541
        Almanac (1983):16A

      Formuzis, Peter, and Joyce Pickersgill. Present value of economic loss: a guide to Jones & Laughlin v. Pfeifer. *Trial* 21(2):22-27 (February 1985).

2552. Texas v. New Mexico   June 17, 1983
      462 US 554   77 LEd2d 1   103 SCt 2558
        Almanac (1983):19A

      Bomster, Mark. Court faces busy term. *Electronic News* 28(1414):Supp W (October 11, 1982).

2553. United States v. Villamonte-Marquez   June 17, 1983
      462 US 579   77 LEd2d 22   103 SCt 2573
        Almanac (1983):6A

      Bernstein, Sidney. Supreme Court review. *Trial* 19(10):26, 28 (October 1983).

      Bialosky, David L. Supreme Court review: Fourth Amendment—steering away from automobile detention precedents to justify warrantless searches of pleasure boats in inland waters. *Journal of Criminal Law and Criminology* 74(4):1282-1299 (Winter 1983).

      Greig, William H., and Phillip S. Althoff. The constitutionality of roadblocks; the Fourth Amendment on the firing line again. *Trial* 22(2):56-62 (February 1986).

      LaFave, Wayne R. Supreme Court review: Fourth Amendment vagaries (of improbable cause, imperceptible plain view, notorious privacy, and balancing askew). *Journal of Criminal Law and Criminology* 74(4):1171-1224 (Winter 1983).

      Press, Aric, and Diane Camper. The Court stands by abortion. *Newsweek* 101(26):62-63 (June 27, 1983).

2554. First National City Bank v. Banco Para El Comercio Exterior De Cuba   June 17, 1983
      462 US 611   77 LEd2d 46   103 SCt 2591
        Almanac (1983):14A

2555. Florida v. Casal   June 17, 1983
     462 US 637   77 LEd2d 277   103 SCt 3100
       Almanac (1983):6A

Press, Aric, and Diane Camper. The Court stands by abortion. *Newsweek* 101(26):62-63 (June 27, 1983).

2556. Illinois v. Lafayette   June 20, 1983
     462 US 640   77 LEd2d 65   103 SCt 2605
       Almanac (1983):6A
       En Am Con 1636-1637

LaFave, Wayne R. Supreme Court review: Fourth Amendment vagaries (of improbable cause, imperceptible plain view, notorious privacy, and balancing askew). *Journal of Criminal Law and Criminology* 74(4):1171-1224 (Winter 1983).

2557. Chardon v. Fumero Soto   June 20, 1983
     462 US 650   77 LEd2d 74   103 SCt 2611
       Almanac (1983):9A

2558. Newport News Shipbuilding and Dry Dock Co.   June 20, 1983
       v. Equal Employment Opportunity Commission (EEOC)
     462 US 669   77 LEd2d 89   103 SCt 2622
       Almanac (1983):10A
       En Am Con 1666-1673

Barnett, Edith. Pregnancy discrimination: the Supreme Court spells out protections for pregnant workers. *Trial* 23(7):36-38, 42 (July 1987).

Bomster, Mark. Antitrust, bankruptcy rulings highlight Supreme Court term. *Electronic News* 29(1455):Supp E (July 25, 1983).

Geisel, Jerry. Pregnancy benefits retroactively covering spouses' deliveries will cost shipbuilder more than $1 million. *Business Insurance* 18:3+ (January 16, 1984).

———. High Court to decide on longshore ruling. *Business Insurance* 16(41):1, 75 (October 11, 1982).

Other rulings by the Justices. *U.S. News and World Report* 95(1):15 (July 4, 1983).

Perry, Suzanne. Court orders equal benefits for costs of pregnancy. *Chronicle of Higher Education* 26(18):23-24 (June 29, 1983).

Ruben, George. Equal insurance coverage for spouses, says court. *Monthly Labor Review* 106(8):40 (August 1983).

Tarnoff, Stephen. Court decisions or benefits increase employers' costs. *Business Insurance* 21(44):93-95 (November 2, 1987).

2559. United States v. Place   June 20, 1983
     462 US 696   77 LEd2d 110   103 SCt 2637
       Almanac (1983):6A

Junker, John M. The structure of the Fourth Amendment: the scope of the protection. *Journal of Criminal Law and Criminology* 79(4):1105-1183 (Winter 1989).

Kamisar, Yale. The swing of the pendulum. *Nation* 239(9):271-274 (September 29, 1984).

LaFave, Wayne R. Supreme Court review: Fourth Amendment vagaries (of improbable cause, imperceptible plain view, notorious privacy, and balancing askew). *Journal of Criminal Law and Criminology* 74(4):1171-1224 (Winter 1983).

Regan, Richard J. Supreme Court roundup: 1982 term. *Thought* 58(231):472-483 (December 1983).

Sickman, Linda M. Supreme Court review: Fourth Amendment—limited luggage seizures valid on reasonable suspicion. *Journal of Criminal Law and Criminology* 74(4):1225-1248 (Winter 1983).

2560. Karcher, Speaker, New Jersey Assembly v. Daggett June 22, 1983
     462 US 725   77 LEd2d 133   103 SCt 2653
       Almanac (1983):12A-13A
       Const Law 620-623R+
       En Am Con 1518-1524
       Sup Ct Review (1986):175-257

Congressional districts: tyranny of arithmetic. *Economist* 288(7296):23-24 (July 2-8, 1983).

Gest, Ted. A bulging agenda for Supreme Court. *U.S. News and World Report* 93(15):82 (October 11, 1982).

Other rulings by the justices. *U.S. News and World Report* 95(1):15 (July 4, 1983).

Regan, Richard J. Supreme Court roundup: 1982 term. *Thought* 58(231):472-483 (December 1983).

Rush, Mark E. In search of a coherent theory of voting rights: challenges to the Supreme Court's vision of fair and effective representation. *Review of Politics* 56(3):503-523 (Summer 1994).

Seligman, Daniel. In broad daylight. *Fortune* 111(2):145 (January 21, 1985).

Wells, David I. The 1983 redistricting decisions: what people think the court said; what the court really said . *National Civic Review* 73(4):181-188 (April 1984).

2561. Mennonite Board of Missions v. Adams   June 22, 1983
        462 US 791   77 LEd2d 180   103 SCt 2706
            Almanac (1983):11A

2562. National Association of Greeting Card Publishers v. United States Postal Service   June 22, 1983
        462 US 810   77 LEd2d 195   103 SCt 2717
            Almanac (1983):20A

        The case for recasting the High Court's role. *Business Week* (2760):33-34 (October 11, 1982).

        Fields, Howard. High Court to rule USPS suit over library rate. *Publishers' Weekly* 222(25):19 (December 24, 1982).

        Gordon, Richard L. Ad leaders laud court veto ruling. *Advertising Age* 54(27):2, 83 (June 27, 1983).

        Kalette, Denise. Several press cases on High Court's docket. *Editor and Publisher* 115(40-41):13 (October 2-9, 1982).

2563. Brown v. Thomson, Secretary of State of Wyoming June 22, 1983
        462 US 835   77 LEd2d 214   103 SCt 2690
            Almanac (1983):13A

        Wells, David I. The 1983 redistricting decisions: what people think the court said; what the court really said . *National Civic Review* 73(4):181-188 (April 1984).

2564. Zant, Warden v. Stephens   June 22, 1983
        462 US 862   77 LEd2d 235   103 SCt 2733
            Almanac (1983):8A
            Sup Ct Review (1983):305-395

2565. Immigration and Naturalization Service (INS) v. Chadha   June 23, 1983
        462 US 919   77 LEd2d 317   103 SCt 2764
            Almanac (1983):565-573, 4A, 19A-22AR; (1984):192-193; (1986):49-53; (1988):125; (1995):(3)14-(3)15
            Ascent 76-81+
            Burger Years 191-205
            Chadha 3-35, 115-147, 188-232
            Const (Currie) 588-593
            Editorials (1983):704-715
            En Am Con 460-464, 628-629, 951-952, 1153-1154, 1659-1664
            Guide (CQ) 56-57, 65, 79-80
            Sup Ct Review (1983):1-31, 125-176; (1984):255-307; (1986):19-40; (1988):1-41

        American survey: Congress learns how to talk without saying no. *Economist* 288(7296):21-22 (July 2-9, 1983).

        Andersen, Kurt, David S. Jackson, and Neil MacNeil. An epic Court decision: out of an obscure case, a reshaping to the powers of Congress and president. *Time* 122(1):12-14 (July 4, 1983).

        Barrett, Edward L. The Supreme Court: why the Constitution survives: long-term view of the Court. *Trial* 25(12):30-35 (December 1989).

        Baruch, Jeremiah. Vetoing the veto. *Commonweal* 110(14):421-424 (August 12, 1983).

        Bernstein, Sidney. Supreme Court review. *Trial* 19(12):20, 22 (December 1983).

        Beyond the legislative veto. *Fortune* 108(3):28, 32 (August 8, 1983).

Bomster, Mark. Antitrust, bankruptcy rulings highlight Supreme Court term. *Electronic News* 29(1455):Supp E (July 25, 1983).

———. Court faces busy term. *Electronic News* 28(1414):Supp W (October 11, 1982).

The case for recasting the High Court's role. *Business Week* (2760):33-34 (October 11, 1982).

Controversy over the legislative veto. *Congressional Digest* 62(12):291-314 (December 1983).

The court is supreme: America's Supreme Court strikes down nearly 200 laws, as it shifts back power from Congress to the president. *Economist* 288(7296):16 (July 2-8, 1983).

Daugherty, Donald A. Supreme Court review: the separation of powers and abuses in prosecutorial discretion. *Journal of Criminal Law and Criminology* 79(3):953-996 (Fall 1988).

Fields, Cheryl M. Bias cases among first on Supreme Court docket. *Chronicle of Higher Education* 25(6):13-14 (October 6, 1982).

Fisher, Louis. The administrative world of Chadha and Bowsher. *Public Administration Review* 47(3):213-219 (May/June 1987).

———. Judicial misjudgments about the lawmaking process: the legislative veto case. *Public Administration Review* 45(Special Issue):705-711 (November 1985).

———. The legislative veto: invalidated, it survives. *Law and Contemporary Problems* 56(4):273-292 (Autumn 1993).

Franck, Thomas M., and Clifford A. Bob. The return of Humpty-Dumpty: foreign relations law after the Chadha case. *American Journal of International Law* 79(4):912-960 (October 1985).

Gest, Ted. A bulging agenda for Supreme Court. *U.S. News and World Report* 93(15):82 (October 11, 1982).

Hanson, David. Legislative veto decision: modest effect on chemical industry. *Chemical and Engineering News* 61(28):13-14 (July 11, 1983).

High Court ruling hits N-waste law. *Electrical World* 197(8):23 (August 1983).

High Court rulings impact industry. *Oil and Gas Journal* 81(27):64-66 (July 4, 1983).

High Court strikes down another legislative veto. *Oil and Gas Journal* 81(28):36 (July 11, 1983).

Hook, Janet. Supreme Court's prohibition of 'legislative veto' may limit Congress's control over rule making. *Chronicle of Higher Education* 26(18):13 (June 29, 1983).

How Congress may replace the legislative veto. *Business Week* (2798):29-30 (July 11, 1983).

Johnson, Stephen F. The legislative veto in the states. *State Government* 56(3):99-102 (Fall 1983).

Justices detail regulatory reform. *Engineering News Record* 211(1):58 (July 7, 1983).

Justices rein in Congress. *Chemical Week* 133(1):11-12 (July 6, 1983).

Kaus, Robert. Vetoed veto. *New Republic* 189(6):10-11 (August 8, 1983).

Kirwan, Kent A. The use and abuse of power: the Supreme Court and separation of powers. *Annals of the American Academy of Political and Social Science* 537:76-84 (January 1995).

Lee, William P. FLPMA's legislative veto provisions and INS v.Chadha: who controls the federal lands? *Boston College Environmental Affairs Law Review* 12(4):791-821 (Summer 1985).

The legacy of the Burger Court. *U.S. News and World Report* 100(25):22 (June 30, 1986).

Let Congress be Congress. *Progressive* 47(9):10 (September 1983).

Mann, Paul. Authority on arms sales survives Court decision. *Aviation Week and Space Technology* 119(1):22-24 (July 4, 1983).

Mauro, Tony. A controversial decision's silver lining. *Nation's Business* 71(8):44-46 (August 1983).

———. Will Congress's veto power be vetoed? *Nation's Business* 71(2):42-43 (February 1983).

Memo claims Court rulings alter congressional arms procedures. *Aviation Week and Space Technology* 123(16):71 (October 21, 1985).

Morrison, Alan B. Close reins on the bureaucracy. *Nation* 239(9):290-294 (September 29, 1984).

Parker, Alan A. Legislative veto. *Trial* 24(2):15-17 (February 1988).

Press, Aric, Diane Camper, John Lindsay, Gloria Borger, and Howard Fineman. The Court vetoes the veto. *Newsweek* 102(1):16-18 (July 4, 1983).

Regan, Richard J. Supreme Court roundup: 1982 term. *Thought* 58(231):472-483 (December 1983).

Rosenbloom, David H. Public administrators and the judiciary: the "new partnership." *Public Administration Review* 47(1):75-83 (January/February 1987).

Silverstein, Gordon. Statutory interpretation and the balance of institutional power. *Review of Politics* 56(3):475-501 (Summer 1994).

Supreme Court decision that stunned Congress. *U.S. News and World Report* 95(1):14-15 (July 4, 1983).

Vetoes and votes. [Editorial] *Nation* 237(2):35-36 (July 9-16, 1983).

Vetoing the legislative veto. *Public Utilities Fortnightly* 112(5):44-45 (September 1, 1983).

Werner, Ray O. Marketing and the Supreme Court in transition, 1982-1984. *Journal of Marketing* 49(3):97-105 (Summer 1985).

Will, George F. More government, less control. [Editorial] *Newsweek* 102(1):84 (July 4, 1983).

2566. Idaho ex rel. Evans, Governor of Idaho v. Oregon and Washington   June 23, 1983
    462 US 1017   77 LEd2d 387   103 SCt 2817
      Almanac (1983):19A

2567. Oregon v. Bradshaw   June 23, 1983
    462 US 1039   77 LEd2d 405   103 SCt 2830
      Almanac (1983):7A
      En Am Con 613

Kamisar, Yale. The swing of the pendulum. *Nation* 239(9):271-274 (September 29, 1984).

Weiss, Lee A. Supreme Court review: Fifth Amendment—Fifth Amendment exclusionary rule: the assertion and subsequent waiver of the right to counsel. *Journal of Criminal Law and Criminology* 74(4):1315-1333 (Winter 1983).

2568. Franchise Tax Board of California v. Construction Laborers Vacation   June 24, 1983
    Trust For Southern California
    463 US 1   77 LEd2d 420   103 SCt 2841
      Almanac (1983):19A

2569. Motor Vehicle Manufacturers Association of the United States, Inc. v. State Farm Mutual   June 24, 1983
    Automobile Insurance Co.
          Coupled with Consumer Alert v. State Farm
          Coupled with Department of Transportation v. State Farm
    463 US 29   77 LEd2d 443   103 SCt 2856
      Almanac (1983):14A
      Burger Years 191-205
      Editorials (1983):789-802
      Magic 304-308
      Sup Ct Review (1983):177-213

American survey: another puff for the air bag. *Economist* 288(7296):22 (July 2-8, 1983).

Justices detail regulatory reform. *Engineering News Record* 211(1):58 (July 7, 1983).

Morrison, Alan B. Close reins on the bureaucracy. *Nation* 239(9):290-294 (September 29, 1984).

Moskowitz, Daniel B. How the Supreme Court is redistributing power. [Editorial] *Business Week* (2799):55 (July 18, 1983).

No end in sight for the air bag blowup. *Business Week* (2798):30 (July 11, 1983).

Other rulings by the justices. *U.S. News and World Report* 95(1):15 (July 4, 1983).

Plater, Zygmunt J. B., and William Lund Norine. Through the looking glass of eminent domain: exploring the "arbitrary and capricious" test and substantive rationality review of governmental decisions. *Boston College Environmental Affairs Law Review* 16(4):661-752 (Summer 1989).

Regan, Richard J. Supreme Court roundup: 1982 term. *Thought* 58(231):472-483 (December 1983).

2570. Bolger v. Youngs Drug Products Corp.   June 24, 1983
    463 US 60   77 LEd2d 469   103 SCt 2875
      Almanac (1983):12A
      En Am Con 1552-1558

Boedecker, Karl A., and Fred W. Morgan. The evolution of First Amendment protection for commercial speech. *Journal of Marketing* 59(1):38-47 (January 1995).

Gordon, Richard L. Ad leaders laud court veto ruling. *Advertising Age* 54(27):2, 83 (June 27, 1983).

Heath, Robert L., and Richard Alan Nelson. Image and issue advertising: a corporate and public policy perspective. *Journal of Marketing* 49(2):58-68 (Spring 1985).

High court strikes down ad circular ban. *Advertising Age* 53(22):73 (May 24, 1982).

Kalette, Denise. Several press cases on High Court's docket. *Editor and Publisher* 115(40-41):13 (October 2-9, 1982).

Lewis, Wayne K. Environmental advertising: a delicate balance of rights. *Trial* 28(10):53-56 (October 1992).

Roper, James E. Supreme Court to hear major libel cases in '84. *Editor and Publisher* 117(1):16, 21, 27 (January 7, 1984).

Top court upholds right to advertise condoms. *Editor and Publisher* 116(27):34 (July 2, 1983).

2571. Shaw, Acting Commissioner, New York State Division of Human Rights v. Delta Air Lines, Inc. June 24, 1983
    463 US 85   77 LEd2d 490   103 SCt 2890
    Almanac (1983):18A

Adams, Nancy D. Title VI of the 1990 Clean Air Act Amendments and state and local initiatives to reverse the stratospheric ozone crisis: an analysis of preemption. *Boston College Environmental Affairs Law Review* 19(1):173-216 (Fall 1991).

2572. Nevada v. United States   June 24, 1983
        Coupled with Truckee-Carson Irrigation District v. United States
        Coupled with Pyramid Lake Paiute Tribe of Indians v. Truckee-Carson Irrigation District
    463 US 110   77 LEd2d 509   103 SCt 2906
    Almanac (1983):17A
    Am Indians (Wilkinson) 42-43, 83-85, 130, 165-166+

Hassler, Gregory L., and Karen O'Connor. Woodsy witchdoctors versus judicial guerrillas: the role and impact of competing interest groups in environmental litigation. *Boston College Environmental Affairs Law Review* 13(4):487-520 (Summer 1986).

Press, Aric, and Diane Camper. Arguing life and death. *Newsweek* 102(3):56-57 (July 18, 1983).

2573. Edward J. DeBartolo Corp. v. National Labor Relations Board (NLRB)   June 24, 1983
    463 US 147   77 LEd2d 535   103 SCt 2926
    Almanac (1983):15A-16A

Courts make it tougher for secondary boycotts. *Engineering News Record* 211(1):58-59 (July 7, 1983).

Murphy, Betty Southard, Wayne E. Barlow, and D. Diane Hatch. Supreme Court upholds peaceful handbilling. *Personnel Journal* 67(10):22, 24 (October 1988).

2574. Container Corp. of America v. California Franchise Tax Board   June 27, 1983
    463 US 159   77 LEd2d 545   103 SCt 2933
    Almanac (1983):18A
    Sup Ct Review (1989):223-259

Bark, Melvin M. U.S. Supreme Court allows unitary business concept. *CPA Journal* 53(11):66-67, 70 (November 1983).

Bomster, Mark. Antitrust, bankruptcy rulings highlight Supreme Court term. *Electronic News* 29(1455):Supp E (July 25, 1983).

———. Court faces busy term. *Electronic News* 28(1414):Supp W (October 11, 1982).

The case for recasting the High Court's role. *Business Week* (2760):33-34 (October 11, 1982).

Gotlinger, Jeffrey B., and Benjamin P. Kraisky. Amendments to temp regs.—allocation of state income taxes against foreign source income. *CPA Journal* 59(8):72-74 (August 1989).

The High Court defers to state regulators. *Business Week* (2747):30-32 (July 12, 1982).

High Court rulings impact industry. *Oil and Gas Journal* 81(27):64-66 (July 4, 1983).

How latest Supreme Court rulings affect people. *U.S. News and World Report* 95(2):32 (July 11, 1983).

Jurinski, James John. A primer on the unitary business concept. *CPA Journal* 56(9):52-64 (September 1986).

———. The U.S. Supreme Court on the unitary tax. *Journal of Accountancy* 161(1):96 (January 1986).

McArthur, J. William, Jr., and Kendall L. Houghton. In Barclays, U.S. Supreme Court finds for California, which was banking on it. *Journal of Taxation* 81(3):176-179 (September 1994).

Nelson-Horchler, Joani. Term begins: Supreme Court centers on job bias, labor law. *Industry Week* 215(1):22, 24 (October 4, 1982).

Now states can really put the bite on business. *Business Week* (2798):90 (July 11, 1983).

Peters, James H. Supreme Ct. in container upholds state's broad power under unitary taxation method. *Journal of Taxation* 59(5):300-307 (November 1983).

Saunders, Laura. Containing container. *Forbes* 132(4):85 (August 15, 1983).

Taxation: unite and soak. *Economist* 288(7296):22-23 (July 2-8, 1983).

Unger, Joseph. Investment income of multistate corporations. *CPA Journal* 63(6):66 (June 1993).

Unitary tax: the Supreme Court says pay. *Economist* 275(7138):84-86 (June 21, 1980).

2575. United States v. Mitchell   June 27, 1983
      463 US 206   77 LEd2d 580   103 SCt 2961
        Almanac (1983):20A
        Am Indians (Wilkinson) 83-84, 130

Allen, Mark. Native American control of tribal natural resource development in the context of the federal trust and tribal self-determination. *Boston College Environmental Affairs Law Review* 16(4):857-895 (Summer 1989).

Baer, Susan D. The Public Trust Doctrine—a tool to make federal adminstrative agencies increase protection of public land and its resources. *Boston College Environmental Affairs Law Review* 15(2):385-436 (Winter 1988).

Fox, Arthur. Showing workers who's the boss. *Nation* 239(9):295-299 (September 29, 1984).

2576. City of Revere v. Massachusetts General Hospital   June 27, 1983
      463 US 239   77 LEd2d 605   103 SCt 2979
        Almanac (1983):17A

2577. Lehr v. Robertson   June 27, 1983
      463 US 248   77 LEd2d 614   103 SCt 2985
        Almanac (1983):11A
        Burger Years 109-124

Minow, Martha. We, the family: constitutional rights and American families. *Journal of American History* 74(3):959-983 (December 1987).

2578. Solem, Warden, South Dakota State Penitentiary v. Helm   June 28, 1983
      463 US 277   77 LEd2d 637   103 SCt 3001
        Almanac (1983):8A
        Editorials (1983):807-810
        En Am Con 524-526, 1706

Bernstein, Sidney. Supreme Court review. *Trial* 19(11):20, 22 (November 1983).

Dripps, Donald A. Supreme Court review: cruel, unusual, and constitutional. *Trial* 28(5):87-89 (May 1992).

Gest, Ted. A bulging agenda for Supreme Court. *U.S. News and World Report* 93(15):82 (October 11, 1982).

Gibbs, Margaret R. Supreme Court review: Eighth Amendment—narrow proportionality requirement preserves deference to legislative judgment. *Journal of Criminal Law and Criminology* 82(4):955-978 (Winter 1992).

How latest Supreme Court rulings affect people. *U.S. News and World Report* 95(2):32 (July 11, 1983).

Mayell, Manvin S. Supreme Court review: Eighth Amendment—proportionality review of death sentences not required. *Journal of Criminal Law and Criminology* 75(3):839-854 (Fall 1984).

Mills, Elizabeth M. Supreme Court review: Eighth Amendment—cruel and unusual punishment: habitual offender's life sentence without parole is disapproportionate. *Journal of Criminal Law and Criminology* 74(4):1372-1386 (Winter 1983).

Nevares-Muniz, Dora. The Eighth Amendment revisited: a model of weighted punishments. *Journal of Criminal Law and Criminology* 75(1):272-289 (Spring 1984).

Press, Aric, and Diane Camper. Sometimes 'life' can be cruel. *Newsweek* 102(2):54 (July 11, 1983).

Toufexis, Anastasia, Marc Hequet, and David S. Jackson. A green light, with conditions: the justices okay tax aid for parochial school education. *Time* 122(2):42-43 (July 11, 1983).

2579. Public Service Commission of the State of New York v. Mid-Louisiana Gas Co.   June 28, 1983
        Coupled with Arizona Electric Power Cooperative v. Mid-Louisiana Gas Co.
        Coupled with Michigan v. Mid-Louisiana Gas Co.

Coupled with Federal Energy Regulatory Commission v. Mid-Louisiana Gas Co.

463 US 319   77 LEd2d 668   103 SCt 3024

    Almanac (1983):17A

High Court due pipeline gas output price cases. *Oil and Gas Journal* 80(42):58 (October 18, 1982).

High Court rulings impact industry. *Oil and Gas Journal* 81(27):64-66 (July 4, 1983).

How latest Supreme Court rulings affect people. *U.S. News and World Report* 95(2):32 (July 11, 1983).

Several energy cases on Supeme Court docket. *Oil and Gas Journal* 80(45):120 (November 8, 1982).

2580. Jones v. United States   June 29, 1983

463 US 354   77 LEd2d 694   103 SCt 3043

    Almanac (1983):7A

    En Am Con 1247-1249

Bernstein, Sidney. Supreme Court review. *Trial* 19(11):20, 22 (November 1983).

How latest Supreme Court rulings affect people. *U.S. News and World Report* 95(2):32 (July 11, 1983).

Papadakis, Ellen M. Supreme Court review: Fourteenth Amendment—the continued confinement of insanity acquittees. *Journal of Criminal Law and Criminology* 83(4):944-977 (Winter 1993).

Shralow, Donna R. Supreme Court review: Fifth Amendment—indefinite commitment of insanity acquittees and due process considerations. *Journal of Criminal Law and Criminology* 74(4):1334-1352 (Winter 1983).

Singer, Richard The aftermath of an insanity acquittal: the Supreme Court's recent decision in Jones v. United States. *Annals of the American Academy of Political and Social Science* 477:114-124R (January 1985).

Toufexis, Anastasia, Marc Hequet, and David S. Jackson. A green light, with conditions: the justices okay tax aid for parochial school education. *Time* 122(2):42-43 (July 11, 1983).

2581. Mueller v. Allen   June 29, 1983

463 US 388   77 LEd2d 721   103 SCt 3062

    Almanac (1983):395, 3A-4A, 12A

    Ascent 195-197

    Burger Years 56-91

    Const (Currie) 534-535

    Documents (v. 2):858-859R

    Editorials (1983):776-783

    En Am Con 1282-1283, 1650-1658

    Establishment 134-136+

    Godless 76-78

    Religion 32-53, 70-71+

    Sup Ct Church 142

All or nothing: the Minnesota school aid case. *America* 149(2):22 (July 9-16, 1983)

Card, Robert L. Church-state relations: where is the Supreme Court going? *Vital Speeches* 51(24):752-755 (October 1, 1985).

Court decision seen as aid to Reagan's tuition tax credit plan. *Christianity Today* 27(12):51 (August 5, 1983).

Doerr, Edd. Good news, bad news. *Humanist* 43(5):36, 43 (September/October 1983).

Fields, Cheryl M. State tax break school tuition upheld by Supreme Court. *Chronicle of Higher Education* 26(19):1, 8 (July 6, 1983).

Flygare, Thomas J. De jure: Supreme Court permits state tax deductions for nonpublic schools. *Phi Delta Kappan* 65(1):63-64 (September 1983).

Freid, Stephen H. The constitutionality of choice under the establishment clause. *Clearing House* 66(2):92-95 (November/December 1992).

Gest, Ted. Next stage: Court lite. *U.S. News and World Report* 111(2):16-19 (July 8, 1991).

Hook, Janet. Supreme Court starts its term, agrees to rule in tax-credit case. *Chronicle of Higher Education* 25(7):15 (October 13, 1982).

How latest Supreme Court rulings affect people. *U.S. News and World Report* 95(2):32 (July 11, 1983).

Palmer, Stacy E. Church-state separation not always violated by aid to ministry students, High Court says. *Chronicle of Higher Education* 31(21):12, 14 (February 5, 1986).

Press, Aric, Diane Camper, and Lucy Howard. A new turn on tuition credits. *Newsweek* 102(2):26 (July 11, 1983).

Rabinove, Samuel. Religious liberty and church-state separation. *Vital Speeches* 52(17):526-530 (June 15, 1986).

Redlich, Norman. Some cracks in the wall. *Nation* 239(9):277-280 (September 29, 1984).

Regan, Richard J. Supreme Court roundup: 1982 term. *Thought* 58(231):472-483 (December 1983).

———. Supreme Court roundup: 1984 term. *Thought* 61(241):290-302 (June 1986).

Schwartz, Michael. A new direction for the courts on the school question. *America* 149(13):251-254 (October 29, 1983)

Rayer, Thomas A. The bicentennial and church-related schools. *America* 157(17):427-429, 438 (December 5, 1987).

Toufexis, Anastasia, Sheila Gribben, and David S. Jackson. Going thisaway and thataway: a mature Burger Court is more umpire than ideological player. *Time* 122(3):39 (July 18, 1983).

Toufexis, Anastasia, Marc Hequet, and David S. Jackson. A green light, with conditions: the justices okay tax aid for parochial school education. *Time* 122(2):42-43 (July 11, 1983).

Tuition tax deductible. *Christian Century* 100(23):706 (August 3-10, 1983).

Tushnet, Mark. The Constitution of religion. *Review of Politics* 50(4):628-658 (Fall 1988).

Weber, Paul J. Excessive entanglement: a wavering First Amendment standard. *Review of Politics* 46(4):483-501 (October 1984).

Zirkel, Perry A. De jure: is the 'wall of separation' like the Walls of Jericho? *Phi Delta Kappan* 75(1):88-90 (September 1993).

2582. United States v. Sells Engineering, Inc.   June 30, 1983
       463 US 418   77 LEd2d 743   103 SCt 3133
       Almanac (1983):19A

       Bender, Louis, and Steven Bender. Is the Supreme Court's decision in Baggot retroactive in application? *Journal of Taxation* 60(3):138-144 (March 1984).

       Berge, Tammy Jo. Supreme Court review: grand jury—disclosure of grand jury materials to government attorneys for civil use under federal rule of criminal procedure 6(e). *Journal of Criminal Law and Criminology* 74(4):1425-1445 (Winter 1983).

2583. United States v. Baggot   June 30, 1983
       463 US 476   77 LEd2d 785   103 SCt 3164
       Almanac (1983):19A

2584. Belknap, Inc. v. Hale   June 30, 1983
       463 US 491   77 LEd2d 798   103 SCt 3172
       Almanac (1983):16A

       The right to strike. *Congressional Digest* 70(11):264-265 (November 1991).

2585. Arizona v. San Carlos Apache Tribe of Arizona   July 1, 1983
            Coupled with Montana v. North Cheyenne Tribe
            Coupled with Arizona v. Navajo Tribe of Indians
       463 US 545   77 LEd2d 837   103 SCt 3201
       Almanac (1983):18A
       Am Indian (Deloria) 197-220

2586. Guardians Association v. Civil Service Commission of the City of New York   July 1, 1983
       463 US 582   77 LEd2d 866   103 SCt 3221
       Almanac (1983):9A-10A

       The case for recasting the High Court's role. *Business Week* (2760):33-34 (October 11, 1982).

       Nelson-Horchler, Joani. Term begins: Supreme Court centers on job bias, labor law. *Industry Week* 215(1):22, 24 (October 4, 1982).

2587. Dirks v. Securities and Exchange Commission (SEC)   July 1, 1983
       463 US 646   77 LEd2d 911   103 SCt 3255
       Almanac (1983):14A

Burger Years 206-219

Cox, James D. Insider trading: regulation of activity is 'in trouble.' *Trial* 24(9):22-28, 93-96 (September 1988).

Dentzer, Susan, Connie Leslie, and Hope Lambert. Attacking insider trading. *Newsweek* 102(3):66-68 (July 18, 1983).

Press, Aric, and Diane Camper. Sometimes 'life' can be cruel. *Newsweek* 102(2):54 (July 11, 1983).

Ray Dirks gets his day in court. *Business Week* (2782):130 (March 21, 1983).

Scheppele, Kim Lane. "It's just not right": the ethics of insider trading. *Law and Contemporary Problems* 56(3):123-173 (Summer 1993).

Schiffres, Manuel. What did they know—and how? *U.S. News and World Report* 101(22):48-49 (December 1, 1986).

When it's O.K. to use an inside stock tip. *Business Week* (2799):55-56 (July 18, 1983).

2588. Ruckelshaus, Administrator, Environmental Protection Agency (EPA) v. Sierra Club   July 1, 1983
463 US 680   77 LEd2d 938   103 SCt 3274
Almanac (1983):17A

O'Connor, Karen, and Lee Epstein. Bridging the gap between Congress and the Supreme Court: interest groups and the erosion of the American rule governing awards of attorneys' fees. *Western Political Quarterly* 38(2):238-249 (June 1985).

2589. Rice, Director, Department of Alcoholic Beverage Control of California v. Rehner   July 1, 1983
463 US 713   77 LEd2d 961   103 SCt 3291
Almanac (1983):18A
Am Indians (Wilkinson) 97, 130+

2590. Jones, Superintendent, Great Meadow Correctional Facility v. Barnes   July 5, 1983
463 US 745   77 LEd2d 987   103 SCt 3308
Almanac (1983):8A

Bernstein, Sidney. Supreme Court review. *Trial* 19(11):20, 22 (November 1983).

Gross, David J. Supreme Court review: Sixth and Fourteenth Amendments—appointed counsel has no constitutional duty to argue all nonfrivolous issues on appeal. *Journal of Criminal Law and Criminology* 74(4):1353-1371 (Winter 1983).

2591. Illinois v. Andreas   July 5, 1983
463 US 765   77 LEd2d 1003   103 SCt 3319
Almanac (1983):6A

LaFave, Wayne R. Supreme Court review: Fourth Amendment vagaries (of improbable cause, imperceptible plain view, notorious privacy, and balancing askew). *Journal of Criminal Law and Criminology* 74(4):1171-1224 (Winter 1983).

2592. Marsh, Nebraska State Treasurer v. Chambers   July 5, 1983
463 US 783   77 LEd2d 1019   103 SCt 3330
Almanac (1983):12A
Brennan 134-138
Burger Years 56-91
Const (Currie) 535-538
Const Law 86-87
En Am Con 1205, 1650-1658
Establishment 160-162+
Godless 107-109+
Hard Choices 122
Original (Davis) 114-115
Religion 93, 158, 163-170+
Sup Ct Yearbook (1991-92):25

Bates, Stephen. Ignore a menorah. *New Republic* 201(5):14-16 (July 31, 1989).

Doerr, Edd. Good news, bad news. *Humanist* 43(5):36, 43 (September/October 1983).

Drakeman, Donald L. New ruling on school prayer. [Editorial] *Christian Century* 102(21):604-605 (June 19-26, 1985).

Drinan, Robert F. Paying for prayers before the legislatures. *America* 148(4):66-68 (January 29, 1983).

Ford, Maurice deG. Christmas creche in July: an exchange of views. *Commonweal* 111(13):386, 412-414 (July 13, 1984).

Garcia, Guy, and Anne Constable. Turning the sexual tables: equal premiums must buy equal retirement benefits. *Time* 122(3):34 (July 18, 1983).

Hook, Janet. Supreme Court reaffirms earlier ruling, outlaws 'two-house' legislative veto. *Chronicle of Higher Education* 26(20):7 (July 13, 1983).

Kilpatrick, James J. What in God's name is going on? *National Review* 37(2):36, 38-39 (February 8, 1985).

Lawton, Kim A. Uncle Sam v. First Church. *Christianity Today* 35(11):38-41 (October 7, 1991).

Pfeffer, Leo. Religious exemptions. *Society* 21(4):17-22 (May/June 1984).

Prayer in public schools. *Congressional Digest* 74(1):3-32 (January 1995).

Redlich, Norman. Some cracks in the wall. *Nation* 239(9):277-280 (September 29, 1984).

Regan, Richard J. Supreme Court roundup: 1982 term. *Thought* 58(231):472-483 (December 1983).

State-paid chaplaincies. *Christian Century* 100(23):705 (August 3-10, 1983).

Stephenson, D. Grier, Jr. Religion and the Constitution: the Supreme Court speaks, again. *USA Today* 118(2538):21-23 (March 1990).

Two cheers for the Court. *National Review* 35(16):983 (August 19, 1983).

2593. United Brotherhood of Carpenters & Joiners of America, Local 610, AFL-CIO v. Scott   July 5, 1983
     463 US 825   77 LEd2d 1049   103 SCt 3352
        Almanac (1983):9A
        Sup Ct Review (1993):199-243

2594. American Bank & Trust Co. v. Dallas County   July 5, 1983
        Coupled with Bank of Texas v. Childs
        Coupled with Wynnewood Bank & Trust Co. v. Childs
     463 US 855   77 LEd2d 1072   103 SCt 3369
        Almanac (1983):18A; (1985):17A

2595. Barefoot v. Estelle, Director, Texas Department of Corrections   July 6, 1983
     463 US 880   77 LEd2d 1090   103 SCt 3383
        Almanac (1983):5A, 8A
        Death Penalty 80s 12-18, 79-82
        Death Penalty 90s 8-11
        Editorials (1983):803-806
        En Am Con 101
        Sup Ct Review (1983):305-395

Bernstein, Sidney. Supreme Court review. *Trial* 20(3):26-29 (March 1984).

Garcia, Guy and Anne Constable. Turning the sexual tables: equal premiums must buy equal retirement benefits. *Time* 122(3):34 (July 18, 1983).

Gest, Ted. The noose gets tighter on death row. *U.S. News and World Report* 95(3):21 (July 18, 1983).

Giannelli, Paul C. "Junk science": the criminal cases. *Journal of Criminal Law and Criminology* 84(1):105-128 (Spring 1993).

Herbert, Wray. High Court OKs testimony on future violence. *Science News* 124(3):38 (July 16, 1983).

Ita, Timothy A. Supreme Court review: habeas corpus—expedited appellate review of habeas corpus petitions brought by death-sentenced state prisoners. *Journal of Criminal Law and Criminology* 74(4):1404-1424 (Winter 1983).

McDonald, Kim. Supreme Court says psychiatrists may testify on a defendant's 'future dangerousness.' *Chronicle of Higher Education* 26(20):2 (July 13, 1983).

Press, Aric, and Diane Camper. Arguing life and death. *Newsweek* 102(3):56-57 (July 18, 1983).

Wells, Diane. Federal habeas corpus and the death penalty: a need for a return to the principles of Furman. *Journal of Criminal Law and Criminology* 80(2):427-490 (Summer 1989).

2596. Barclay v. Florida | July 6, 1983
463 US 939 77 LEd2d 1134 103 SCt 3446
Almanac (1983):8A
Sup Ct Review (1983):305-395

2597. California v. Ramos | July 6, 1983
463 US 992 77 LEd2d 1171 103 SCt 3446
Almanac (1983):8A
Sup Ct Review (1983):305-395

O'Neill, Timothy P. The good, the bad, and the Burger court: victims' rights and a new model of criminal review. *Journal of Criminal Law and Criminology* 75(2):363-387 (Summer 1984).

2598. Michigan v. Long | July 6, 1983
463 US 1032 77 LEd2d 1201 103 SCt 3469
Almanac (1983):6A
En Am Con 178-1782

Ison, Timothy M. Supreme Court review: Fourth Amendment—officer safety and the protective automobile search: an expansion of the pat-down frisk. *Journal of Criminal Law and Criminology* 74(4):1265-1281 (Winter 1983).

Kamisar, Yale. The swing of the pendulum. *Nation* 239(9):271-274 (September 29, 1984).

LaFave, Wayne R. Supreme Court review: Fourth Amendment vagaries (of improbable cause, imperceptible plain view, notorious privacy, and balancing askew). *Journal of Criminal Law and Criminology* 74(4):1171-1224 (Winter 1983).

Maltz, Earl M. Lockstep analysis and the concept of federalism. *Annals of the American Academy of Political and Social Science* 496:98-106 (March 1988).

O'Neill, Timothy P. The good, the bad, and the Burger court: victims' rights and a new model of criminal review. *Journal of Criminal Law and Criminology* 75(2):363-387 (Summer 1984).

Ross, Douglas. Safeguarding our federalism: lessons for the states from the Supreme Court. *Public Administration Review* 45(Special Issue):723-731 (November 1985).

2599. Arizona Governing Committee for Tax Deferred Annuity and Deferred Compensation Plans | July 6, 1983
v. Norris
463 US 1073 77 LEd2d 1236 103 SCt 3492
Almanac (1983):280, 10A
Editorials (1983):784-789

Bomster, Mark. Antitrust, bankruptcy rulings highlight Supreme Court term. *Electronic News* 29(1455):Supp E (July 25, 1983).

Fields, Cheryl M. Bias cases among first on Supreme Court docket. *Chronicle of Higher Education* 25(6):13-14 (October 6, 1982).

———. Court declares women must get equal benefits in pension plans, sends back 2 TIAA cases. *Chronicle of Higher Education* 26(20):1, 13-14 (July 13, 1983).

From Tilton to Ewing: some major higher-education decisions of the Burger court. *Chronicle of Higher Education* 32(17):10 (June 25, 1986).

Garcia, Guy, and Anne Constable. Turning the sexual tables: equal premiums must buy equal retirement benefits. *Time* 122(3):34 (July 18, 1983).

Geisel, Jerry. Employers may not offer group annuity benefits. *Business Insurance* 17(32):1, 6 (August 8, 1983).

———. High Court to rule if women must get equal pensions. *Business Insurance* 16(42): 2, 36 (October 18, 1982).

Gest, Ted. When pension plans go unisex. *U.S. News and World Report* 95(3):62 (July 18, 1983).

Marshall, Thurgood. The Supreme Court's opinions in case challenging sex-based pensions. *Chronicle of Higher Education* 26(20):14-16R (July 13, 1983).

Mauro, Tony. From pensions to postal rates. *Nation's Business* 70(12):38-39 (December 1982).

Nicholson, Tom, and Penny Wang. A bow to unisex pensions. *Newsweek* 102(3):66 (July 18, 1983).

O'Connor, Sandra Day. Justice O'Connor's opinion. *Chronicle of Higher Education* 26(20):17R (July 13, 1983).

Pensions: the other gender gap. *Economist* 288(7298):33-34 (July 16-22, 1983).

Powell, Lewis F., Jr. Justice Powell's opinion. *Chronicle of Higher Education* 26(20):16-17R (July 13, 1983).

Rabban, David M. AAUP in the courts: the association's representation of faculty members and faculty causes in appellate litigation. *Academe* 69(2): 1a-12a (March/April 1983).

Regan, Richard J. Supreme Court roundup: 1982 term. *Thought* 58(231):472-483 (December 1983).

Rubens, George. Supreme Court bans sex bias in pensions. *Monthly Labor Review* 106(9):36 (September 1983).

2600. Autry v. Estelle, Director, Texas Department of Corrections   October 3, 1983
     464 US 1   78 LEd2d 1   104 SCt 20
      Editorials (1983):1181-1184; (1984):348-351

The death penalty: a sense of proportion. *Economist* 290(7326):25-26 (January 28-February 4, 1984).

Press, Aric, Susan Agrest, Lucy Howard, and George Raine. To die or not to die. *Newsweek* 102(16):43-73 (October 17, 1983).

Rejected again: death and proportionality. *Time* 123(6):55 (February 6, 1984).

Serrill, Michael S., Hays Gorey, and David S. Jackson. Thirty-one minutes from death: are legal procedures in capital cases lethally arbitrary? *Time* 122(17):52 (October 17, 1983).

A step closer to death. *Newsweek* 103(6):58 (February 6, 1984).

Supreme Court: red, green, amber. *Economist* 289(7311:25-26 (October 15-21, 1983)

Supreme Court's death-row dilemma. *U.S. News and World Report* 95(16):17 (October 17, 1983).

2601. Aloha Airlines, Inc. v. Director of Taxation of Hawaii   November 1, 1983
        Coupled with Hawaiian Airlines, Inc. v. Director of Taxation of Hawaii
     464 US 7   78 LEd2d 10   104 SCt 291
      Almanac (1984):14A

Adams, Nancy D. Title VI of the 1990 Clean Air Act Amendments and state and local initiatives to reverse the stratospheric ozone crisis: an analysis of preemption. *Boston College Environmental Affairs Law Review* 19(1):173-216 (Fall 1991).

Collins, Deborah. The states: federal-state relations issues hit the Supreme Court agenda. *National Civic Review* 73(11):568-571 (December 1984).

Supreme Court bans state tax on gross receipts of airlines. *Aviation Week and Space Technology* 119(7):30-31 (November 7, 1983).

2602. Russello v. United States   November 1, 1983
     464 US 16   78 LEd2d 17   104 SCt 296
      Almanac (1984):8A

Ita, Timothy A. Supreme Court review: RICO—criminal forfeiture of proceeds of racketeering activity under RICO. *Journal of Criminal Law and Criminology* 75(3):893-939 (Fall 1984).

2603. Norfolk Redevelopment and Housing Authority v. Chesapeake & Potomac Telephone   November 1, 1983
     Co. of Virginia
     464 US 30   78 LEd2d 29   104 SCt 304
      Almanac (1984):14A

2604. Maggio, Warden v. Williams   November 7, 1983
     464 US 46   78 LEd2d 43   104 SCt 311
     Bernstein, Sidney. Supreme Court review. *Trial* 20(3):26-29 (March 1984).

2605. Wainwright v. Goode   November 28, 1983
     464 US 78   78 LEd2d 187   104 Sct 378
     Bernstein, Sidney. Supreme Court review. *Trial* 20(3):26-29 (March 1984).

2606. Bureau of Alcohol, Tobacco and Firearms v. Federal Labor Relations Authority   November 29, 1983
     464 US 89   78 LEd2d 195   104 SCt 439

Almanac (1984):15A

2607. Sullivan v. Wainwright   November 29, 1983
       464 US 109   78 LEd2d 210   104 SCt 450
          Editorials (1983):1444-1448
       Bernstein, Sidney. Supreme Court review. *Trial* 20(3):26-29 (March 1984).
       Malone, Patrick A. False statistic. [Editorial] *Nation* 237(22):685 (December 31, 1983-January 7, 1984).

2608. United States v. Mendoza   January 10, 1984
       464 US 154   78 LEd2d 379   104 SCt 568
          Almanac (1984):18A

2609. United States v. Stauffer Chemical Co.   January 10, 1984
       464 US 165   78 LEd2d 388   104 SCt 575
          Almanac (1984):18A

2610. Immigration and Naturalization Service (INS) v. Phinpathya   January 10, 1984
       464 US 183   78 LEd2d 401   104 SCt 584
          Almanac (1984):10A

2611. Commissioner of Internal Revenue v. Engle et ux.   January 10, 1984
       464 US 206   78 LEd2d 420   104 SCt 597
          Almanac (1984):14A
       IPAA presses for early decision on excise tax. *Oil and Gas Journal* 81(3):54-55 (January 17, 1983).
       Offshore leasing wins in High Court. *Oil and Gas Journal* 82(3):60, 62 (January 16, 1984).
       Production not required for depletion, says Supreme Court. *Journal of Taxation* 60(3):192 (March 1984).

2612. Silkwood, Administrator of the Estate of Silkwood v. Kerr-McGee Corp.   January 11, 1984
       464 US 238   78 LEd2d 443   104 SCt 615
          Almanac (1984):15A
       Collins, Deborah. The states: federal-state relations issues hit the Supreme Court agenda. *National Civic Review*
          73(11):568-571 (December 1984).
       Egan, Thomas E. Wrongful discharge and federal preemption: nuclear whistleblower protection under state law
          and section 210 of the Energy Reorganization Act. *Boston College Environmental Affairs Law Review*
          17(2):405-440 (Winter 1990).
       Gest, Ted. Old issues come home to roost at Supreme Court. *U.S. News and World Report* 95(15):70 (October
          10, 1983).
       High Court upholds nuclear injury award. *Electrical World* 198(3):20-21 (March 1984).
       Rocchio, David M. The Price-Anderson Act: allocation for the extraordinary risk of nuclear generated
          electricity: a model punitive damage provision. *Boston College Environmental Affairs Law Review* 14(3):
          521-560 (Spring 1987).
       Ross, Douglas. Safeguarding our federalism: lessons for the states from the Supreme Court. *Public
          Administration Review* 45(Special Issue):723-731 (November 1985).
       Sherman, RuthAnn. Chemical warfare agent research regulation: the conflict between federal and local control.
          Boston College Environmental Affairs Law Review 14(1):131-163 (Fall 1986).
       Sponseller, Diane. Utility liability; the trend toward damages awards. *Public Utilities Fortnightly* 119(12):47-
          50 (June 11, 1987).

2613. Michigan v. Clifford   January 11, 1984
       464 US 287   78 LEd2d 477   104 SCt 641
          Almanac (1984):5A
       Mussio, Donna. Drawing the line between administrative and criminal searches: defining the "object of the
          search" in environmental inspections. *Boston College Environmental Affairs Law Review* 18(1):185-211 (Fall
          1990).

2614. Secretary of the Interior v. California   January 11, 1984
      Coupled with Western Oil and Gas Association v. California
464 US 312   78 LEd2d 496   104 SCt 656
    Almanac (1984):335-336, 15A; (1990):154, 288-289
Collins, Deborah. The states: federal-state relations issues hit the Supreme Court agenda. *National Civic Review* 73(11):568-571 (December 1984).
Fitzgerald, Edward A. Secretary of Interior v. California: should continental shelf lease sales be subject to consistency review? *Boston College Environmental Affairs Law Review* 12(3):425-471 (Spring 1985).
Gest, Ted. Old issues come home to roost at Supreme Court. *U.S. News and World Report* 95(15):70 (October 10, 1983).
Golden, Frederic, Jay Branegan, and William R. Doerner. Pouring oil on troubled waters: the new interior chief launches a policy of compromise. *Time* 123(5):81 (January 30, 1984).
Hassler, Gregory L., and Karen O'Connor. Woodsy witch doctors versus judicial guerrillas: the role and impact of competing interest groups in environmental litigation. *Boston College Environmental Affairs Law Review* 13(4):487-520 (Summer 1986).
High Court to decide state role in OCS sales. *Oil and Gas Journal* 81(21):47 (May 23, 1983).
Offshore leasing wins in high court. *Oil and Gas Journal* 82(3):60, 62 (January 16, 1984).
Sandler, Ross. Reversals for the environment. *Environment* 26(9):44-45 (November 1984).
Supreme Court hears federal-state OCS case. *Oil and Gas Journal* 81(45):71 (November 7, 1983).

2615. Badaracco v. Commissioner of Internal Revenue   January 17, 1984
      Coupled with Deleet Merchandising Corp. v. United States
464 US 386   78 LEd2d 549   104 SCt 756
    Almanac (1984):14A

2616. Donovan, Secretary of Labor v. Lone Steer, Inc.   January 17, 1984
464 US 408   78 LEd2d 567   104 SCt 769
    Almanac (1984):15A
It's High Court conspiracy time. *Industry Week* 219(1):25-26 (October 3, 1983).
Mauro, Tony. Government vs. business privacy. *Nation's Business* 71(9):64-66 (September 1983).
A powerful bid to rewrite the antitrust rule book. *Business Week* (Industrial Edition) (2811):84-90 (October 10, 1983).

2617. Sony Corp. of America v. Universal City Studios, Inc.   January 17, 1984
464 US 417   78 LEd2d 574   104 SCt 774
    Almanac (1982):402; (1984):4A, 13A
    Editorials (1984):82-91
    Guide (West): (v.9):304-305
    Sup Ct Review (1984):237-253
Bernstein, Sidney. Supreme Court review. *Trial* 20(3):26-29 (March 1984).
Bomster, Mark. Antitrust, bankruptcy rulings highlight Supreme Court term. *Electronic News* 29(1455):Supp E (July 25, 1983).
———. Court faces busy term. *Electronic News* 28(1414):Supp W (October 11, 1982).
———. Supreme Court hears Sony home videotaping case. *Electronic News* 29(1430):41 (January 31, 1983).
The case against VCRs will be long-playing. *Business Week* (2826):30 (January 30, 1984).
The case for recasting the High Court's role. *Business Week* (2760):33-34 (October 11, 1982).
Fields, Cheryl M. Bias cases among first on Supreme Court docket. *Chronicle of Higher Education* 25(6):13-14 (October 6, 1982).
———. New Supreme Court session starts Monday; scope of anti-sex-bias law a major issue. *Chronicle of Higher Education* 27(6):15, 19 (September 28, 1983).
Fields, Howard. AAP authors urge Court to retain Betamax ruling. *Publishers' Weekly* 222(19):23 (November 5, 1982).
———. ALA urges Supreme Court to overturn Betamax ruling. *Publishers' Weekly* 222(13):13-14 (September 24, 1982).
———. Betamax ruling widens fair-use interpretation. *Publishers' Weekly* 225(5):290-291 (February 3, 1984).

————. Supreme Court cites books in Betamax arguments. *Publishers' Weekly* 223(5):271, 274-275 (February 4, 1983).

————. Supreme Court hears new Betamax arguments. *Publishers' Weekly* 224(16):17 (October 14, 1983).

Gest, Ted. Old issues come home to roost at Supreme Court. *U.S. News and World Report* 95(15):70 (October 10, 1983).

Goddy, David. The Court's broad impact on our economic life. *Scholastic Update* (Teachers' Edition) 117(7):17-18 (November 30, 1984).

Gordon, Richard L. Advertiser interest in Sony case blasted. *Advertising Age* 55(4):3, 77 (January 23, 1984).

High Court rules for Sony, holds home taping is legal. *Electronic News* 30(1481):37 (January 23, 1984).

Home TV taping gets all-clear. *U.S. News and World Report* 96(4):10 (January 30, 1984).

It's OK to videotape TV programs. *Editor and Publisher* 117(3):26 (January 21, 1984).

Kalette, Denise. Several press cases on High Court's docket. *Editor and Publisher* 115(40-41):13 (October 2-9, 1982).

Lardner, James. The Betamax case (II). *New Yorker* 63(8):60-81 (April 13, 1987).

Mutter, John. Publishers comment. *Publishers' Weekly* 225(5):290 (February 3, 1984).

Newsnotes: High Court rules 5-4 that videotaping for home use is legal. *Phi Delta Kappan* 65(7):507 (March 1984).

Palmer, Stacy E. Court delays ruling in videotaping case that concerns educators and librarians. *Chronicle of Higher Education* 26(20):13 (July 13, 1983).

————. Videotaping for education aided by Court's ruling. *Chronicle of Higher Education* 27(20):21, 23 (January 25, 1984).

A powerful bid to rewrite the antitrust rule book. *Business Week* (Industrial Edition) (2811):84-90 (October 10, 1983).

Press, Aric, and Lucy Howard. A blank tape for Hollywood. *Newsweek* 103(5):57-58 (January 30, 1984).

Regan, Richard J. Supreme Court roundup: 1983 term. *Thought* 60(236):99-111 (March 1985).

Roper, James E. Supreme Court to hear major libel cases in '84. *Editor and Publisher* 117(1):16, 21, 27 (January 7, 1984).

Stengel, Richard, and Anne Constable. Decision: tape it to the max: the Supreme Court says a VCR switch in time is not a crime. *Time* 123(5):67 (January 30, 1984).

2618. Press-Enterprise Co. v. Superior Court of California, Riverside County   January 18, 1984
464 US 501   78 LEd2d 629   104 SCt 819
Almanac (1984):11A
Editorials (1984):92-95

Chandler, Logan Munroe. Supreme Court review: Sixth Amendment—public trial guarantee applies to pretrial supression hearings. *Journal of Criminal Law and Criminology* 75(3):802-812 (Fall 1984).

Malak, Michael P. Supreme Court review: First Amendment—guarantee of public access to voir dire. *Journal of Criminal Law and Criminology* 75(3):583-608 (Fall 1984).

Open trials win a High-Court verdict. *U.S. News and World Report* 96(4):10 (January 30, 1984).

Plamondon, Ann L. Recent developments in law of access. *Journalism Quarterly* 63(1):61-68 (Spring 1986).

Reid, Traciel V. Judicial policy-making and implementation: an empirical examination. *Western Political Quarterly* 41(3):509-527 (September 1988).

Roper, James E. Supreme Court to hear major libel cases in '84. *Editor and Publisher* 117(1):16, 21, 27 (January 7, 1984).

2619. Daily Income Fund, Inc. v. Fox   January 18, 1984
464 US 523   78 LEd2d 645   104 SCt 831
Almanac (1984):14A

2620. McDonough Power Equipment, Inc. v. Greenwood   January 18, 1984
464 US 548   78 LEd2d 663   104 SCt 845
Almanac (1984):18A

2621. Southland Corp. v. Keating   January 23, 1984
465 US 1   79 LEd2d 1   104 SCt 852

Almanac (1984):16A

Adams, Nancy D. Title VI of the 1990 Clean Air Act Amendments and state and local initiatives to reverse the stratospheric ozone crisis: an analysis of preemption. *Boston College Environmental Affairs Law Review* 19(1):173-216 (Fall 1991).

Collins, Deborah. The states: federal-state relations issues hit the Supreme Court agenda. *National Civic Review* 73(11):568-571 (December 1984).

2622. Pulley, Warden v. Harris   January 23, 1984
      465 US 37   79 LEd2d 29   104 SCt 871
         Almanac (1984):7A
         Brennan 229-238
         Burger Years 169-176
         Death Penalty (Tushnet) 106-111

      Bernstein, Sidney. Supreme Court review. *Trial* 20(3):26-29 (March 1984).

      The death penalty: a sense of proportion. *Economist* 290(7326):25-26 (January 28-February 4, 1984).

      Gest, Ted. Death penalty again haunts Supreme Court. *U.S. News and World Report* 95(20):54 (November 14, 1983).

      Mayell, Manvin S. Supreme Court review: Eighth Amendment—proportionality review of death sentences not required. *Journal of Criminal Law and Criminology* 75(3):839-854 (Fall 1984).

      Meltsner, Michael. On death row, the wait is over. *Nation* 239(9):274-277 (September 29, 1984).

      Rejected again: death and proportionality. *Time* 123(6):55 (February 6, 1984).

2623. Migra v. Warren City School District Board of Education   January 23, 1984
      465 US 75   79 LEd2d 56   104 SCt 892
         Almanac (1984):17A

2624. Pennhurst State School and Hospital v. Halderman   January 23, 1984
      465 US 89   79 LEd2d 67   104 SCt 900
         Almanac (1984):18A
         Burger Years 125-139
         Sup Ct Review (1984):149-168

      Press, Aric. Pushing the law to new limits. *Newsweek* 103(6):58 (February 6, 1984).

2625. McKaskle, Acting Director, Texas Department of Corrections v. Wiggins   January 23, 1984
      465 US 168   79 LEd2d 122   104 SCt 944
         Almanac (1984):7A

2626. United Building & Construction Trades Council of Camden   February 21, 1984
         County and Vicinity v. Mayor and Council of the City of Camden
      465 US 208   79 LEd2d 249   104 SCt 1020
         Almanac (1984):17A
         Const (Currie) 580-585
         En Am Con 1458-1461

      Collins, Deborah. The states: federal-state relations issues hit the Supreme Court agenda. *National Civic Review* 73(11):568-571 (December 1984).

      Ross, Douglas. Safeguarding our federalism: lessons for the states from the Supreme Court. *Public Administration Review* 45(Special Issue):723-731 (November 1985).

2627. McCain v. Lybrand   February 21, 1984
      465 US 236   79 LEd2d 271   104 SCt 1037
         Almanac (1984):12A

2628. Flanagan v. United States   February 21, 1984
      465 US 259   79 LEd2d 288   104 SCt 1051
         Almanac (1984):7A

2629. Minnesota State Board for Community Colleges v. Knight   February 21, 1984
        Coupled with Minnesota Community Collge Faculty Association v. Knight
        465 US 271   79 LEd2d 299   104 SCt 1058
            Almanac (1984):11A

Collins, Deborah. The states: federal-state relations issues hit the Supreme Court agenda. *National Civic Review*
    73(11):568-571 (December 1984).

Fields, Cheryl M. New Supreme Court session starts Monday; scope of anti-sex-bias law a major issue.
    Chronicle of Higher Education 27(6):15, 19 (September 28, 1983).

Flygare, Thomas J. De jure: Supreme Court upholds exclusive role for faculty unions in "meet-and-confer"
    sessions. *Phi Delta Kappan* 65(10):718-719 (June 1984).

From Tilton to Ewing: some major higher-education decisions of the Burger court. *Chronicle of Higher
    Education* 32(17):10 (June 25, 1986).

O'Connor, Sandra Day, Thurgood Marshall, John Paul Stevens, and William J. Brennan. Excerpts from High
    Court's opinions in Minn. community-college case. *Chronicle of Higher Education* 28(1):18-22R (February
    29, 1984).

The right to choose. *National Review* 34(25):1594-1596 (December 24, 1982).

Watkins, Beverly T. Justices approve curb on role of teachers. *Chronicle of Higher Education* 28(1):1, 8
    (February 29, 1984).

2630. Colorado v. Nunez   February 21, 1984
        465 US 324   79 LEd2d 338   104 SCt 1257
            Almanac (1984):5A

2631. Dickman v. Commissioner of Internal Revenue   February 22, 1984
        465 US 330   79 LEd2d 343   104 SCt 1086
            Almanac (1984):14A

Andresky, Jill. The Court has spoken, but what did it say? *Forbes* 133(12):107 (May 21, 1984).

Dunn, Donald H. You can still capitalize on your youngsters' low tax rate. *Business Week*
    (Industrial/Technology Edition) (2832):123-124 (March 12, 1984).

Edwards, Mark B. Interest-free loans are held to be gifts in Supreme Court's recent Dickman decision. *Journal
    of Taxation* 60(5):266-268 (May 1984).

Loutos, William A. Interest-free loans: an endangered species. *Taxes* 62(7):445-450 (July 1984).

Mauro, Tony. The tax collector and the family loan. *Nation's Business* 71(8):42-43 (August 1983).

Padwe, Gerald W. Those interest-free loans. *Nation's Business* 72(5):13 (May 1984).

A powerful bid to rewrite the antitrust rule book. *Business Week* (Industrial Edition) (2811):84-90 (October 10,
    1983).

2632. United States v. One Assortment of 89 Firearms   February 22, 1984
        465 US 354   79 LEd2d 361   104 SCt 1099
            Almanac (1984):8A

2633. South Carolina v. Regan, Secretary of the Treasury   February 22, 1984
        465 US 367   79 LEd2d 372   104 SCt 1107
            Almanac (1984):17A-18A

Collins, Deborah. The states: federal-state relations issues hit the Supreme Court agenda. *National Civic Review*
    73(11):568-571 (December 1984).

A powerful bid to rewrite the antitrust rule book. *Business Week* (Industrial Edition) (2811):84-90 (October 10,
    1983).

2634. Minnesota v. Murphy   February 22, 1984
        465 US 420   79 LEd2d 409   104 SCt 1136
            Almanac (1984):6A

Lupia, Lynnette L. Supreme Court review: Fifth Amendment—admissibility of confession obtained without
    Miranda warnings in noncustodial setting. *Journal of Criminal Law and Criminology* 75(3):673-691 (Fall
    1984).

2635. Solem, Warden, South Dakota State Penitentiary v. Bartlett   February 22, 1984
        465 US 463   79 LEd2d 443   104 SCt 1161
            Almanac (1984):17A

2636. Dixson v. United States   February 22, 1984
            Coupled with Hinton v. United States
        465 US 482   79 LEd2d 458   104 SCt 1172
            Almanac (1984):8A
        Peters, Charles. Supreme Court review: bribery, graft, and conflicts of interest: the scope of "public official."
            Journal of Criminal Law and Criminology 75(3):875-892 (Fall 1984).

2637. National Labor Relations Board (NRLB) v. Bildisco and Bildisco   February 22, 1984
            Coupled with Local 408, International Brotherhood of Teamsters v. National Labor Relations Board
                (NLRB)
        465 US 513   79 LEd2d 482   104 SCt 188
            Almanac (1984):266, 13A
            Burger Years 220-227, 228-239
            Editorials (1984):176-181
        Another body blow for big labor. *Newsweek* 103(10):76 (March 5, 1984).
        Bankruptcy as an escape hatch: the high court permits troubled firms to cancel union pacts. *Time* 123(10):14
            (March 5, 1984).
        Bomster, Mark. Rule union pacts dismissible in bankruptcy. *Electronic News* 30(1488):77 (February 27, 1984).
        ———. Supreme Court: mixed bag for business. *Electronic News* 30(1506):15 (July 16, 1984).
        Cramer, Jerome. School bankruptcy is risky business. *American School Board Journal* 171(5):41 (May 1984).
        Fox, Arthur. Showing workers who's the boss. *Nation* 239(9):295-299 (September 29, 1984).
        Gest, Ted. Old issues come home to roost at Supreme Court. *U.S. News and World Report* 95(15):70 (October
            10, 1983).
        Gross, Karen. Recent bankruptcy developments: do they take away with the right what they give with the left?
            Credit and Finanical Management 88(5):9-14 (May 1986).
        Hukill, Craig. Significant decisions in labor cases: bankrupt employers. *Monthly Labor Review* 113(7):46-48
            (July 1990).
        Mauro, Tony. Government vs. business privacy. *Nation's Business* 71(9):64-66 (September 1983).
        Muller, John F. How to organize and operate a creditors' committee. *Credit and Finanical Management*
            86(9):31-36 (October 1984).
        Nelson, Lester. What you should know about bankruptcy code amendments and the Federal Judgeship Act of
            1984. *Credit and Finanical Management* 86(9):14-17 (October 1984).
        A powerful bid to rewrite the antitrust rule book. *Business Week* (Industrial Edition) (2811):84-90 (October 10,
            1983).
        Regan, Richard J. Supreme Court roundup: 1983 term. *Thought* 60(236):99-111 (March 1985).
        Ruben, George. Developments in industrial relations: Court says companies can alter contracts. *Monthly Labor
            Review* 107(4):48-49 (April 1984).
        Weintraub, Benjamin. Bargaining agreements—balancing the equities: 1. *Credit and Finanical Management*
            88(3):36 (March 1986).

2638. Grove City College v. Bell, Secretary of Education   February 28, 1984
        465 US 555   79 LEd2d 516   104 SCt 1211
            Abortion Am 148-149+
            Almanac (1983):300, 397; (1984):239-243, 9A; (1986):27; (1987):23, 281-282; (1988):61, 63-68;
            (1989):316
            Burger Years 95-108
            Editorials (1984):272-279, 774-779
            Sup Ct Review (1985):61-92
        Aliotta, Jilda M. The unfinished feminist agenda: the shifting forum. *Annals of the American Academy of
            Political and Social Science* 515:140-150 (May 1991).
        Brown, Luther. High Court's double take looms over civil rights. *Black Enterprise* 18(12):20 (July 1988).

Change of course on sex-bias rules. *U.S. News and World Report* 96(10):13 (March 12, 1984).

Civil rights v. freedom. *National Review* 36(7):19 (April 20, 1984).

Desruisseaux, Paul. Grove City is proud of independence that led it to Supreme Court. *Chronicle of Higher Education* 28(2):20 (March 7, 1984).

A double-edged decision by the Court on Grove City College. *Christianity Today* 28(6):70-72 (April 6, 1984).

Engelgau, Donna. House backs bill to counter Supreme Court ruling in Grove City case; Senate unit postpones action. *Chronicle of Higher Education* 28(19):13-14 (July 5, 1984).

Fields, Cheryl M. Bias cases among first on Supreme Court docket. *Chronicle of Higher Education* 25(6):13-14 (October 6, 1982).

———. Bill to reverse High Court's Grove City decision gets bipartisan support. *Chronicle of Higher Education* 28(8):21 (April 18, 1984).

———. Civil-rights groups will seek law to reverse Grove City decision. *Chronicle of Higher Education* 28(3):1, 24 (March 14, 1984).

———. Grove City ruling has produced erratic anti-bias probes, critics charge. *Chronicle of Higher Education* 30(1):28 (March 6, 1985).

———. High Court hears Grove City's challenge to scope of U.S. law barring sex bias. *Chronicle of Higher Education* 27(15):19, 21 (December 7, 1983).

———. New Supreme Court session starts Monday; scope of anti-sex-bias law a major issue. *Chronicle of Higher Education* 27(6):15, 19 (September 28, 1983).

———. Strong anti-sex-bias policies of universities and states are seen dampening the effect of Grove City ruling. *Chronicle of Higher Education* 28(3):24 (March 14, 1984).

———. Supreme Court rules anti-sex-bias law covers only college programs that get direct U.S. aid: lawmakers move to clarify intent of Congress to construe law broadly. *Chronicle of Higher Education* 28(2):1, 19 (March 7, 1984).

———. 2 House panels back conflicting measures to nullify High Court's Grove City ruling. *Chronicle of Higher Education* 30(13)19, 21 (May 29, 1985).

Flygare, Thomas J. De jure: the Supreme Court's Title IX decision: who won? *Phi Delta Kappan* 65(9):640-641 (May 1984).

From Tilton to Ewing: some major higher-education decisions of the Burger court. *Chronicle of Higher Education* 32(17):10 (June 25, 1986).

Gender slap: trimming U.S. oversight. *Time* 123(11):59 (March 12, 1984).

Gest, Ted. A new civil-rights debate. *U.S. News and World Report* 108(6):26-27 (February 12, 1990).

———. Old issues come home to roost at Supreme Court. *U.S. News and World Report* 95(15):70 (October 10, 1983).

Goddy, David. The Court's broad impact on our economic life. *Scholastic Update* (Teachers' Edition) 117(7):17-18 (November 30, 1984).

Graves, Earl G. The erosion of civil rights by the Supreme Court. [Editorial] *Black Enterprise* 15(2):9 (September 1984).

Gray, Mary W. The halls of ivy and the halls of justice: resisting sex discrimination against faculty women. *Academe* 71(5):33-41 (September/October 1985).

Jaschik, Scott. From Bakke to Yeshiva, Justice Powell played key role in Court's education rulings. *Chronicle of Higher Education* 33(43):16 (July 8, 1987).

Leatherman, Courtney. House votes 315-98 to widen scope of anti-bias laws at institutions that receive federal funds. *Chronicle of Higher Education* 34(26):A1, A26 (March 9, 1988).

Lewin, Nathan. White's flight. *New Republic* 191(9):17-20 (August 27, 1984).

Maguire, Daniel C. Can a university be catholic? *Academe* 74(1):12-16 (January/February 1988).

McDowell, Gary L. Congress and the courts. *Public Interest* (100):89-101 (Summer 1990).

Murphy, Betty Southard, Wayne E. Barlow, and D. Diane Hatch. New Civil Rights Act passed. *Personnel Journal* 67(5):19-20 (May 1988).

Neff, Craig. Equality at last, part II. *Sport Illustrated* 68(12):70-71 (March 21, 1988).

Negative action. [Editorial] *Nation* 238(25):788-789 (June 30, 1984).

Newsnotes: Bell says Grove City won't divert ED from enforcement of antidiscrimination laws. *Phi Delta Kappan* 65(9):650 (May 1984).

1984: the legislation. *National Review* 36(19):19-20 (October 5, 1984).

Pending civil rights legislation. *Congressional Digest* 64(1):1-32R (January 1985).

Press, Aric, and Ann McDaniels. A civil-rights reversal. *Newsweek* 103(11):86 (March 12, 1984).

Press, Aric, and Lucy Howard. No hiding place this term. *Newsweek* 102(15):61 (October 10, 1983).

Regan, Richard J. Supreme Court roundup: 1983 term. *Thought* 60(236):99-111 (March 1985).

Roche, George. The federal squeeze. *National Review* 36(18):38, 61 (September 21, 1984).

Sex discrimination. *National Review* 35(18):1117 (September 16, 1983).

Simmons, Althea T. L. From Brown to Grove City: blueprint for education. *Crisis* 91(5):6-10 (May 1984).

Sullivan, Robert. A law that needs new muscle. *Sport Illustrated* 62(9):9 (March 4, 1985).

Supreme Court ruling is civil rights roadblock. *Jet* 70(3):8 (April 7, 1986).

Trends in federal regulation. *Congressional Digest* 74(3):69-71 (March 1995).

Universities: is segregation a sin? *Economist* 290(7332):28-29 (March 10-18, 1984).

Vance, N. Scott. Supreme Court rules anti-sex-bias law covers only college programs that get direct U.S. aid: sports scholarships may still be covered by Title IX, NCAA cautions members. *Chronicle of Higher Education* 28(2):1, 26 (March 7, 1984).

Weldon, Ward. Effects of the 1987 civil rights restoration act on educational policy and practice. *Journal of Negro Education* 59(2):155-164 (Spring 1990).

White, Byron R., Lewis F. Powell, Jr., William J. Brennan, Jr., and John Paul Stevens. Texts of opinions by Supreme Court in case of Grove City College v. Bell. *Chronicle of Higher Education* 28(2):19-25R (March 7, 1984).

2639. United States v. Doe   February 28, 1984
  465 US 605   79 LEd2d 552   104 SCt 1237
    Almanac (1984):6A

Alter, Robert J. Shareholder's Fifth Amendment privilege bars summons of corporate records. *Journal of Taxation* 63(4):208-210 (October 1985).

Causey, Denzil,and Frances McNair. Protecting taxpayers privacy from the IRS. *Journal of Accountancy* 168(4):44-48 (October 1989).

Grogan, John M. Jr. Supreme Court review: Fifth Amendment—the act of production privilege: the Supreme Court's protrait of a dualistic record custodian. *Journal of Criminal Law and Criminology* 79(3):701-734 (Fall 1988).

Rosenblatt, Leonard R. The Fifth Amendment and the production of business records: and Braswell Begat Bouknight. *Taxes* 68(6):418-424 (June 1990).

———. The production of business records after Braswell: where we've been, where we are, where we may be going. *Taxes* 67(4):231-237 (April 1989).

Supreme Court holds that production of business records may be privileged. *Journal of Taxation* 60(5):324 (May 1984).

2640. Consolidated Rail Corp. v. Darrone, Administratrix of the Estate of LeStrange February 28, 1984
  465 US 624   79 LEd2d 568   104 SCt 1248
    Almanac (1984):9A
    Burger Years 125-139

Engelgau, Donna. Supreme Court rules anti-sex-bias law covers only college programs that get direct U.S. aid: High Court backs right of disabled to sue employers. *Chronicle of Higher Education* 28(2):1, 26 (March 7, 1984).

Fields, Cheryl M. High court hears Grove City's challenge to scope of U.S. law barring sex bias. *Chronicle of Higher Education* 27(15):19, 21 (December 7, 1983).

———. New Supreme Court session starts Monday; scope of anti-sex-bias law a major issue. *Chronicle of Higher Education* 27(6):15, 19 (September 28, 1983).

Pending civil rights legislation. *Congressional Digest* 64(1):1-32 (January 1985).

2641. Solem, Warden, South Dakota State Penitentiary v. Stumes February 29, 1984
  465 US 638   79 LEd2d 579   104 SCt 1338
    Almanac (1984):7A

2642. Lynch, Mayor of Pawtucket v. Donnelly March 5, 1984
  465 US 668   79 LEd 2d 604   104 SCt 1355

Almanac (1984):11A

Brennan 134-138

Burger Years 56-91

Center 241-246+

Const (Currie) 535-538

Const Law 86, 95-100

Documents (v. 2):860-862R

Editorials (1984):262-271

En Am Con 1186-1187, 1546-1547, 1650-1658

Establishment 156-157, 216

Godless 123-125+

Original (Davis) 114-115

Religion 113-128+

Sup Ct Church 317-345R

Sup Ct Review (1995):323-391

Turning 248-251+, 296-297

Abram, Morris B. Is "strict separation" too strict? *Public Interest* (82):81-90 (Winter 1986).

Arledge, Paula C., and Edward V. Heck. A freshman justice confronts the Constitution: Justice O'Connor and the First Amendment. *Western Political Quarterly* 45(3):761-772 (September 1992).

Away with a manger. *New Republic* 189(18):4 (October 31, 1983).

Bates, Stephen. Ignore a menorah. *New Republic* 201(5):14-16 (July 31, 1989).

Berns, Walter. Has the Burger Court gone too far? *Commentary* 78(4):27-33 (October 1984).

Bork, Robert H. What to do about the First Amendment. *Commentary* 99(2):23-29 (February 1995).

Carlin, David R. Pawtucket & its nativity scene. *Commonweal* 110(22):682-684 (December 16, 1983).

Castelli, Jim. Creche on the plaza? There are no clear rules. *Governing* 3(3):56-57 (December 1989).

Cerne, Kathleen M. Honor thy creditors? The religious debtor's constitutional conflict with Section 1325(b). *Business Credit* 96(3):37-40 (March 1994).

Collins, Deborah. The states: federal-state relations issues hit the Supreme Court agenda. *National Civic Review* 73(11):568-571 (December 1984).

The Court and the crib. *America* 150(10):182 (March 17, 1984).

Court OK's crieche. *Christian Century* 101(10):297 (March 21-28, 1984).

Drinan, Robert F. The creche and the Constitution. *America* 149(14):265-268 (November 5, 1983).

———. Do creches violate the Constitution? *America* 159(16):428-429 (November 26, 1988).

———. Is a Christmas creche legal in 1986? [Editorial] *America* 155(18)375-376 (December 13, 1986).

———. The Supreme Court and Scarsdale's creche. *America* 151(18):377-380 (December 8, 1984).

Ford, Maurice deG. Christmas creche in July: an exchange of views. *Commonweal* 111(13):386, 412-414 (July 13, 1984).

———. Creche landing. *Commonweal* 111(7):202 (April 6, 1984).

Gaffney, Edward McGlynn, Jr. O'Connor fumbles 'Christian nation' case. [Editorial] *Christian Century* 106(12):373-375 (April 12, 1989).

Garvey, John. That old civil religion: to creche or not to creche. *Commonweal* 110(19):583-584 (November 4, 1983).

Gest, Ted. Old issues come home to roost at Supreme Court. *U.S. News and World Report* 95(15):70 (October 10, 1983).

Heard, Alex. God rest ye merry gentlemen—and women, and blacks, and Hispanics, and Jews, and Scientologists, and Lithuanians, and Eskimos, and Tastafarians, and . . . [Editorial] *Washington Monthly* 15(9):30-32 (December 1983).

High Court shifts church-state stance. *U.S. News and World Report* 96(11):10 (March 19, 1984).

Kilpatrick, James J. A tangled separation. [Editorial] *Nation's Business* 73(11):5 (November 1985).

———. What in God's name is going on? *National Review* 37(2):36, 38-39 (February 8, 1985).

Lacayo, Richard, and Anne Constable. Establishing her independence: Sandra Day O'Connor is still conservative, but on her own terms. *Time* 127(19):85 (May 12, 1986).

Lewin, Nathan. White's flight. *New Republic* 191(9):17-20 (August 27, 1984).

Marty, Martin E. Diocesan lawn displays. [Editorial] *Christian Century* 101(12):383 (April 11, 1984).

McKown, Delos Banning. Deism and the Supreme Court. *Humanist* 52(2):25-28, 48 (March/April 1992).

Methvin, Eugene H. The Supreme Court: justice in the balance. *Reader's Digest* 125(751):96-101 (November 1984).

Morris, Richard Brandon. The wall of separation. *American Heritage* 35(5):77-79 (August/September 1984).

Negative action. [Editorial] *Nation* 238(25):788-789 (June 30, 1984).

Press, Aric, and Ann McDaniel. The Lord's day in Court. *Newsweek* 104(26):57 (December 17, 1984).

————. A Reagan Court? *Newsweek* 106(3):69-71 (July 15, 1985).

Press, Aric, and Lucy Howard. No hiding place this term. *Newsweek* 102(15):61 (October 10, 1983).

Rabinove, Samuel. Religious liberty and church-state separation. *Vital Speeches* 52(17):526-530 (June 15, 1986).

Redlich, Norman. Some cracks in the wall. *Nation* 239(9):277-280 (September 29, 1984).

Regan, Richard J. Supreme Court roundup: 1983 term. *Thought* 60(236):99-111 (March 1985).

Rotunda, Ronald D. The Supreme Court: eschewing bright lines. *Trial* 25(12):52-56 (December 1989).

Ruling on a creche. *Newsweek* 103(18):33 (March 19, 1984).

Sendor, Benjamin. Deck the halls, but skip the creche and angels. *American School Board Journal* 176(10): 12-13 (October 1989).

————. Oral contracts can leave you down in the mouth. *American School Board Journal* 171(6):21, 39 (June 1984).

Spring, Beth. Is it illegal for the government to keep Christ in Christmas? *Christianity Today* 27(17):52 (November 11, 1983).

————. Supreme Court speaks up for religion in American life. *Christianity Today* 28(6):68-69 (April 6, 1984).

Stephenson, D. Grier, Jr. Religion and the Constitution: the Supreme Court speaks, again. *USA Today* 118(2538):21-23 (March 1990).

Tarr, G. Alan. Religion under state constitutions. *Annals of the American Academy of Political and Social Science* 496:65-75 (March 1988).

Thomas, Evan, David Beckwith, and Anne Constable. Reagan's Mr. Right: Rehnquist is picked for the Court's top job. *Time* 127(26):24-33 (June 30, 1986).

Tushnet, Mark. The Constitution of religion. *Review of Politics* 50(4):628-658 (Fall 1988).

Weber, Paul J. Excessive entanglement: a wavering First Amendment standard. *Review of Politics* 46(4):483-501 (October 1984).

Zakariya, Sally Banks. Celebrate the holiday season by teaching kids about their world. *American School Board Journal* 171(12):40-41 (December 1984).

2643. Heckler, Secretary of Health and Human Services v. Mathews   March 5, 1984
      465 US 728   79 LEd2d 646   104 SCt 1387
         Almanac (1984):16A
      Baer, Judith A. Women's rights and the limits of constitutional doctrine. *Western Political Quarterly* 44(4):821-852 (December 1991).

2644. Monsanto Co. v. Spray-Rite Service Corp.   March 20, 1984
      465 US 752   79 LEd2d 775   104 SCt 1464
         Almanac (1984):12A; (1987):280-281; (1988):131-132; (1989):286; (1990):539-540; (1991):291-292
         Burger Years 206-219
         Sup Ct Review (1984):69-148
      Bomster, Mark. Supreme Court: mixed bag for business. *Electronic News* 30(1506):15 (July 16, 1984).

      Dolan, Michael W. Congress, the executive, and the Court: the great resale price maintenance affair of 1983. *Public Administration Review* 45(Special Issue):718-722 (November 1985).

      It's High Court conspiracy time. *Industry Week* 219(1):25-26 (October 3, 1983).

      A powerful bid to rewrite the antitrust rule book. *Business Week* (Industrial Edition) (2811):84-90 (October 10, 1983).

      Price-fixing decision: High Court rules against Monsanto. *Chemical and Engineering News* 62(13):5 (March 26, 1984).

      Sheffet, Mary Jane, and Debra L. Scammon. Resale price maintenance: is it safe to suggest retail prices? *Journal of Marketing* 49(4):82-92 (Fall 1985).

Werner, Ray O. Marketing and the Supreme Court in transition, 1982-1984. *Journal of Marketing* 49(3):97-105 (Summer 1985).

2645. Keeton v. Hustler Magazine, Inc.   March 20, 1984
    465 US 770   79 LEd2d 790   104 SCt 1473
     Almanac (1984):11A
Fields, Howard. High Court rules on libel suit venues. *Publishers' Weekly* 225(15):17 (April 13, 1984).
————. Supreme Court hears three libel cases. *Publishers' Weekly* 224(22):22-23 (November 25, 1983).
Gersh, Debra. Media lose a friend: retiring Supreme Court justice William Brennan. *Editor and Publisher* 123(30):13, 35, 47 (July 28, 1990).
Liability for libel. *Newsweek* 103(14):91 (April 2, 1984).

2646. Calder v. Jones   March 20, 1984
    465 US 783   79 LEd2d 804   104 SCt 1482
     Almanac (1984):11A-12A

2647. United States v. Weber Aircraft Corp.   March 20, 1984
    465 US 792   79 LEd2d 814   104 SCt 1488
     Almanac (1984):18A

2648. United States v. Arthur Young & Co.   March 21, 1984
    465 US 805   79 LEd2d 826   104 SCt 1495
     Almanac (1984):14A
Buchholz, David L., and Joseph F. Moraglio. IRS access to auditors' work papers: the Supreme Court decision. *Journal of Accountancy* 158(3):91-100 (September 1984).
Caplin, Mortimer. Accountants lose tax work-product privilege. *Taxes* 62(6):373-379 (June 1984).
Dungan, Christopher W., G. Thomas Friedlob, and Robert W. Rouse. The Supreme Court on tax accrual workpapers. *CPA Journal* 55(2):20-26 (February 1985).
McGrath, Anne. Lawyers v. CPAs. *Forbes* 133(9):158 (April 23, 1984).
Miller, Robert D. Governmental oversight of the role of auditors. *CPA Journal* 56(9):20-36 (September 1986).
Padwe, Gerald W. Those interest-free loans. *Nation's Business* 72(5):13 (May 1984).
Professional: U.S. Supreme Court decision on tax accrual work papers draws response by IRS, profession. *Journal of Accountancy* 157(5):11-12 (May 1984).
Saltzman, Michael I. The Arthur Young decision—and what it means to accountants. *Practical Accountant* 17(8):37-39 (July 1984).

2649. National Labor Relations Board (NLRB) v. City Disposal Systems, Inc.   March 21, 1984
    465 US 822   79 LEd2d 839   104 SCt 1505
     Almanac (1984):15A
     Burger Years 228-239
Fox, Arthur. Showing workers who's the boss. *Nation* 239(9):295-299 (September 29, 1984).

2650. Kosak v. United States   March 21, 1984
    465 US 848   79 LEd2d 860   104 SCt 1519
     Almanac (1984):18A

2651. Heckler, Secretary of Health and Human Services v. Edwards   March 21, 1984
    465 US 870   79 LEd2d 878   104 SCt 1532
     Almanac (1984):18A

2652. Blum, Commissioner, New York State Department of Social Services v. Stenson   March 21, 1984
    465 US 886   79 LEd2d 891   104 SCt 1541
     Almanac (1984):9A-10A
Conte, Alba. Public interest lawyers deserve risk multipliers. *Trial* 30(12):36-42 (December 1994).

Press, Aric, Peggy Clausen, and Nikki Finke Greenberg. Can lawyers sue for equal pay? *Newsweek* 102(14):86 (October 3, 1983).

Woods, Jeanne M. Fight for legal fees. *Black Enterprise* 14(11):50 (June 1984).

2653. Koehler, Warden v. Engle   March 26, 1984
    466 US 1   80 LEd2d 1   104 SCt 1673
     Almanac (1984):6A

2654. Jefferson Parish Hospital District No. 2 v. Hyde   March 27, 1984
    466 US 2   80 LEd2d 2   104 SCt 1551
     Almanac (1984):12A
     Sup Ct Review (1984):69-148
Bomster, Mark. Supreme Court: mixed bag for business. *Electronic News* 30(1506):15 (July 16, 1984).
A powerful bid to rewrite the antitrust rule book. *Business Week* (Industrial Edition) (2811):84-90 (October 10, 1983).

2655. Escambia County, Florida v. McMillan   March 27, 1984
    466 US 48   80 LEd2d 36   104 SCt 1577
     Almanac (1984):12A

2656. Equal Employment Opportunity Commission (EEOC) v. Shell Oil Co.   April 2, 1984
    466 US 54   80 LEd2d 41   104 SCt 1621
     Almanac (1984):8A
Fields, Cheryl M. New Supreme Court session starts Monday; scope of anti-sex-bias law a major issue. *Chronicle of Higher Education* 27(6):15, 19 (September 28, 1983).
It's High Court conspiracy time. *Industry Week* 219(1):25-26 (October 3, 1983).
Mauro, Tony. Government vs. business privacy. *Nation's Business* 71(9):64-66 (September 1983).

2657. Louisiana v. Mississippi   April 2, 1984
    466 US 96   80 LEd2d 74   104 SCt 1645
     Almanac (1984):16A

2658. United States v. Jacobsen   April 2, 1984
    466 US 109   80 LEd2d 85   104 SCt 1652
     Almanac (1984):5A
Dripps, Donald A. Supreme Court review: search and seizure: finding for the Fourth Amendment. *Trial* 29(3):95-97 (March 1993).
Junker, John M. The structure of the Fourth Amendment: the scope of the protection. *Journal of Criminal Law and Criminology* 79(4):1105-1183 (Winter 1989).

2659. Oliver v. United States   April 17, 1984
      Coupled with Maine v. Thornton
    466 US 170   80 LEd2d 214   104 SCt 1735
     Almanac (1984):234, 5A
     En Am Con 1341
Bazarian, Stephen C. Dow Chemical Company v. United States and aerial surveillance by the EPA: an argument for post-surveillance notice to the observed. *Boston College Environmental Affairs Law Review* 15(3-4):593-626 (Spring 1988).
The boundaries of privacy: a court O.K. for police searches of factories and fields. *Time* 123(18):64 (April 30, 1984).
Junker, John M. The structure of the Fourth Amendment: the scope of the protection. *Journal of Criminal Law and Criminology* 79(4):1105-1183 (Winter 1989).
Police power wins anew in High Court. *U.S. News and World Report* 96(17):20 (April 30, 1984).
Regan, Richard J. Supreme Court roundup: 1983 term. *Thought* 60(236):99-111 (March 1985).

Yeager, Daniel B. Search, seizure and the positive law: expectations of privacy outside the Fourth Amendment. *Journal of Criminal Law and Criminology* 84(2):249-309 (Summer 1993).

2660. Summa Corp. v. California ex rel. State Lands Commission   April 17, 1984
466 US 198   80 LEd2d 237   104 SCt 1751
Almanac (1984):16A

2661. Immigration and Naturalization Service (INS) v. Delgado   April 17, 1984
466 US 210   80 LEd2d 247   104 SCt 1758
Almanac (1984):5A

The boundaries of privacy: a court O.K. for police searches of factories and fields. *Time* 123(18):64 (April 30, 1984).

Guerra, Sandra. Domestic drug interdiction operations: finding the balance. *Journal of Criminal Law and Criminology* 82(4):1109-1161 (Winter 1992).

Police power wins anew in High Court. *U.S. News and World Report* 96(17):20 (April 30, 1984).

A question of seizure. *Newsweek* 103(18):81 (April 30, 1984).

Regan, Richard J. Supreme Court roundup: 1983 term. *Thought* 60(236):99-111 (March 1985).

2662. Trans World Airlines, Inc. (TWA) v. Franklin Mint Corp.   April 17, 1984
466 US 243   80 LEd2d 273   104 SCt 1776
Almanac (1984):13A

A powerful bid to rewrite the antitrust rule book. *Business Week* (Industrial Edition) (2811):84-90 (October 10, 1983).

2663. McDonald v. City of West Branch, Michigan   April 18, 1984
466 US 284   80 LEd2d 302   104 SCt 1799
Almanac (1984):10A

Ruben, George. Developments in industrial relations: arbitration not equal to judicial factfinding. *Monthly Labor Review* 107(6):57 (June 1984).

2664. Justices of Boston Municipal Court v. Lydon   April 18, 1984
466 US 294   80 LEd2d 311   104 SCt 1805
Almanac (1984):6A

Volkert, Adam N. Supreme Court review: Fifth Amendment—double jeopardy: two-tier trial systems and the continuing jeopardy principle. *Journal of Criminal Law and Criminology* 75(3):653-672 (Fall 1984).

2665. James v. Kentucky   April 18, 1984
466 US 341   80 LEd2d 346   104 SCt 1830
Almanac (1984):6A

2666. Limbach, Tax Commissioner of Ohio v. Hooven & Allison Co.   April 18, 1984
466 US 353   80 LEd2d 356   104 SCt 1837
Almanac (1984):14A

2667. Schneider Moving & Storage Co. v. Robbins   April 18, 1984
     Coupled with Prosser's Moving & Storage Co. v. Robbins
466 US 364   80 LEd2d 366   104 SCt 1844
Almanac (1984):13A

2668. Board of Education of Paris Union School District No. 95 v. Vail   April 23, 1984
466 US 377   80 LEd2d 377   104 SCt 2144
Almanac (1984):10A

Flygare, Thomas J. De jure: Supreme Court agrees to hear case that could alter probation in public school employment. *Phi Delta Kappan* 65(6):427-428 (Febrary 1984).

Jacobson, Robert L. Supreme Court, in a 4-4 vote, affirms due-process ruling. *Chronicle of Higher Education* 28(13):21, 25 (May 23, 1984).

2669. Westinghouse Electric Corp. v. Tully   April 24, 1984
    466 US 388   80 LEd2d 388   104 SCt 1856
      Almanac (1984):14A
Bomster, Mark. High Court weigh franchise tax claim. *Electronic News* 29(1430): Supp B (January 31, 1983).

2670. Helicopteros Nacionales de Colombia, S.A. v. Hall   April 24, 1984
    466 US 408   80 LEd2d 404   104 SCt 1868
      Almanac (1984):17A

2671. Palmore v. Sidoti   April 25, 1984
    466 US 429   80 LEd2d 421   104 SCt 1879
      Almanac (1984):10A
      En Am Con 572, 1362
      Sup Ct Review (1986):99-134
Court awards custody to Fla. interracial couple. *Jet* 66(8):30 (May 14, 1984).
Melton, Gary B. Public policy and private prejudice: psychology and law on gay rights. *American Psychologist* 44(6):933-940 (June 1989).

2672. Ellis v. Brotherhood of Railway, Airline & Streamship Clerks,   April 25, 1984
      Freight Handlers, Express & Station Employes
    466 US 435   80 LEd2d 428   104 SCt 1883
      Almanac (1984):15A
      Sup Ct Review (1990):163-205
The right to choose. *National Review* 34(25):1594-1596 (December 24, 1982).
Ruben, George. Developments in industrial relations: Supreme Court rules on agency shop fees. *Monthly Labor Review* 107(7):46 (July 1984).

2673. Federal Communications Commission (FCC) v. ITT World Communications, Inc.   April 30, 1984
    466 US 463   80 LEd2d 480   104 SCt 1936
      Almanac (1984):18A

2674. United States v. Rodgers   April 30, 1984
    466 US 475   80 LEd2d 492   104 SCt 1942
      Almanac (1984):7A

2675. Bose Corp. v. Consumers Union of United States, Inc.   April 30, 1984
    466 US 485   80 LEd2d 502   104 SCt 1949
      Almanac (1984):12A
      Fourth 110-113
Castro, Janice, Anne Constable, and Raji Samghabadi. An absence of malice: the Supreme Court rules in favor of Consumer Union. *Time* 123(20):56 (May 14, 1984).
Fields, Howard. High Court sides with media in libel case. *Publishers' Weekly* 225(20):38 (May 18, 1984).
———. Supreme Court hears three libel cases. *Publishers' Weekly* 224(22):22-23 (November 25, 1983).
Gloede, Bill. The courts and the press: 'things may get a lot worse.' *Editor and Publisher* 116(48):10-11 (November 26, 1983).
A High-Court vote for press rights. *Newsweek* 103(20):81 (May 14, 1984).
Libel: the right to be off the wall. *Economist* 291(7340):26-27 (May 5-11, 1984).
Media lawyers talk shop at ANPA clinic. *Editor and Publisher* 117(18):44 (May 5, 1984).
Regan, Richard J. Supreme Court roundup: 1983 term. *Thought* 60(236):99-111 (March 1985).
Roper, James E. Supreme Court rules on libel. *Editor and Publisher* 117(18):15 (May 5, 1984).
———. Supreme Court to hear major libel cases in '84. *Editor and Publisher* 117(1):16, 21, 27 (January 7, 1984).

Smolla, Rodney A. Free speech afire with controversy: the Supreme Court. *Trial* 25(12):46-47, 49, 51 (December 1989).

2676. Pulliam, Magistrate for the County of Culpeper, Virginia v. Allen   May 14, 1984
     466 US 522   80 LEd2d 565   104 SCt 1970
         Almanac (1984):17A
         En Am Con 1039-1040

Brooks, Thornton H., M. Daniel McGinn, and William P. H. Cary. Second generation problems facing employers in employment discrimination cases: contiuing violations, pendent state claims, and double attorneys' fees. *Law and Contemporary Problems* 49(4):26-51 (Autumn 1986).

Plotkin, Steven R., and Carol D. Mazorol. Judicial malpratice: Pulliam is not the answer. *Trial* 20(12):24-26 (December 1984).

Serrill, Michael S., and Alain L. Sanders. Guidelines from the Supreme Court: the justices rule on lawyer competency and other matters. *Time* 123(22):72-77 (May 28, 1984).

2677. Hoover v. Ronwin   May 14, 1984
     466 US 558   80 LEd2d 590   104 SCt 1989
         Almanac (1984):17A
         Sup Ct Review (1984):69-148

Collins, Deborah. The states: federal-state relations issues hit the Supreme Court agenda. *National Civic Review* 73(11):568-571 (December 1984).

2678. Heckler, Secretary of Health and Human Services v. Ringer   May 14, 1984
     466 US 602   80 LEd2d 622   104 SCt 2013
         Almanac (1984):16A

2679. United States v. Cronic   May 14, 1984
     466 US 648   80 LEd2d 657   104 SCt 2039
         Almanac (1984):7A

2680. Strickland, Superintendent, Florida State Prison v. Washington   May 14, 1984
     466 US 668   80 LEd2d 674   104 SCt 2052
         Almanac (1984):7A
         Death Penalty (Tushnet) 126-127

Beckman, David L., Jr. Supreme Court review: Sixth Amendment—effective assistance of counsel: a defense attorney's right to refuse cooperation in defendant's perjured testimony. *Journal of Criminal Law and Criminology* 77(3):692-712 (Fall 1986).

Gross, David J. Supreme Court review: Sixth Amendment—defendant's dual burden in claims of ineffective assistance of counsel. *Journal of Criminal Law and Criminology* 75(3):755-778 (Fall 1984).

Jonakait, Randolph N. Supreme Court review: foreword: notes for a consistent and meaningful Sixth Amendment. *Journal of Criminal Law and Criminology* 82(4):713-746 (Winter 1992).

Lukoff, Roger M. Constitutional scholars appraise Supreme Court. *Trial* 20(11):65-66, 68 (November 1984).

Pettegrew, Hillary L. Supreme Court review: Sixth and Eighth Amendments—erosion of defendant's right to an impartial jury and a fundamentally fair trial. *Journal of Criminal Law and Criminology* 77(3):796-820 (Fall 1986).

Serrill, Michael S., and Alain L. Sanders. Guidelines from the Supreme Court: the justices rule on lawyer competency and other matters. *Time* 123(22):72-77 (May 28, 1984).

Wells, Diane. Federal habeas corpus and the death penalty: a need for a return to the principles of Furman. *Journal of Criminal Law and Criminology* 80(2):427-490 (Summer 1989).

2681. Welsh v. Wisconsin   May 15, 1984
     466 US 740   80 LEd2d 732   104 SCt 2091
         Almanac (1984):5A
         En Am Con 2045

Regan, Richard J. Supreme Court roundup: 1983 term. *Thought* 60(236):99-111 (March 1985).

Serrill, Michael S., and Alain L. Sanders. Guidelines from the Supreme Court: the justices rule on lawyer competency and other matters. *Time* 123(22):72-77 (May 28, 1984).

2682. Escondido Mutual Water Co.   May 15, 1984
          v. La Jolla Rincon, San Pasqual, Pauma and Pala Band of Mission Indians
          466 US 765   80 LEd2d 753   104 SCt 2105
             Almanac (1984):15A

        Hassler, Gregory L., and Karen O'Connor. Woodsy witchdoctors versus judicial guerrillas: the role and impact of competing interest groups in environmental litigation. *Boston College Environmental Affairs Law Review* 13(4):487-520 (Summer 1986).

2683. Members of the City Council of the City of Los Angeles v. Taxpayers for Vincent   May 15, 1984
          466 US 789   80 LEd2d 772   104 SCt 2118
             Almanac (1984):11A
             En Am Con 260

        Collins, Deborah. The states: federal-state relations issues hit the Supreme Court agenda. *National Civic Review* 73(11):568-571 (December 1984).

        Regan, Richard J. Supreme Court roundup: 1983 term. *Thought* 60(236):99-111 (March 1985).

        Serrill, Michael S., and Alain L. Sanders. Guidelines from the Supreme Court: the justices rule on lawyer competency and other matters. *Time* 123(22):72-77 (May 28, 1984).

2684. Kirby Forest Industries, Inc. v. United States   May 21, 1984
          467 US 1   81 LEd2d 1   104 SCt 2187
             Almanac (1984):13A

2685. Seattle Times Co., dba The Seattle Times v. Rhinehart   May 21, 1984
          467 US 20   81 LEd2d 17   104 SCt 2199
             Almanac (1984):12A
             Fourth 160-167+
             Sup Ct Review (1984):169-236

        Coben, Larry E. Protective orders: manufacturers hide behind them. *Trial* 22(8):34-37 (August 1986).

        Fields, Howard. Supreme Court rules on prior restraint. *Publishers' Weekly* 225(24);24-25 (June 15, 1984).

        Plamondon, Ann L. Recent developments in law of access. *Journalism Quarterly* 63(1):61-68 (Spring 1986).

        Powe, L. A., Jr. Mass communications and the First Amendment: an overview. *Law and Contemporary Problems* 55(1):53-76 (Winter 1992).

        Roper, James E. High Court OK's pretrial data curb. *Editor and Publisher* 117(21):34, 25 (May 26, 1984).

        ———. Supreme Court agrees to hear several media cases. *Editor and Publisher* 116(41):11, 37 (October 8, 1983).

        ———. Supreme Court to hear major libel cases in '84. *Editor and Publisher* 117(1):16, 21, 27 (January 7, 1984).

2686. Waller v. Georgia   May 21, 1984
             Coupled with Cole v. Georgia
          467 US 39   81 LEd2d 31   104 SCt 2210
             Almanac (1984):6A

        Chandler, Logan Munroe. Supreme Court review: Sixth Amendment—public trial guarantee applies to pretrial supression hearings. *Journal of Criminal Law and Criminology* 75(3):802-812 (Fall 1984).

        Plamondon, Ann L. Recent developments in law of access. *Journalism Quarterly* 63(1):61-68 (Spring 1986).

        Roper, James E. High Court OK's pretrial data curb. *Editor and Publisher* 117(21):34, 25 (May 26, 1984).

        ———. Supreme Court to hear major libel cases in '84. *Editor and Publisher* 117(1):16, 21, 27 (January 7, 1984).

2687. Heckler, Secretary of Health and Human Services v. Community Health Services   May 21, 1984
             of Crawford County, Inc.
          467 US 51   81 LEd2d 42   104 SCt 2218

Almanac (1984):16A

2688. Hishon v. King and Spalding   May 22, 1984
467 US 69   81 LEd2d 59   104 SCt 2229
    Almanac (1984):9A
    Editorials (1984):584-588

Are partnerships immune to sex-bias laws? *Business Week* (Industrial Edition) (2815):52 (November 7, 1983).

Dent, David J. Forging partnerships. *Black Enterprise* 15(1):20 (August 1984).

Fiske, Susan T., Donald N. Bersoff, Eugene Borgida, Kay Deaux, and Madeline E. Heilman. Social science research on trial: use of sex stereotyping research in Price Waterhouse v. Hopkins. *American Psychologist* 46(10):1049-1060 (October 1991).

Gest, Ted. Old issues come home to roost at Supreme Court. *U.S. News and World Report* 95(15):70 (October 10, 1983).

Getting a piece of the power: Women barred from partnerships can not go to court. *Time* 123(23):63 (June 4, 1984).

Hermanson, Roger H., and Tad D. Ransopher. What the Hishon case means to CPA firms: partnership selections and the Civil Rights Act. *Journal of Accountancy* 159(2):78-80 (February 1985).

Mauro, Tony. Government vs. business privacy. *Nation's Business* 71(9):64-66 (September 1983).

Press, Aric, Ann McDaniel, Alexander Stille, and Nadine Joseph. With justice for some. *Newsweek* 103(23):85-86 (June 4, 1984).

Red-letter day for working women. *U.S. News and World Report* 96(22):16 (June 4, 1984).

Ruben, George. Developments in industrial relations: law firms not exempt from Title VII. *Monthly Labor Review* 107(7):46-47 (July 1984).

Supreme Court decision makes bias rules apply to business partnerships. *Jet* 66(12):4 (June 11, 1984).

2689. South-Central Timber Development, Inc. v. Wunnicke,   May 22, 1984
    Commissioner, Department of Natural Resources of Alaska
467 US 82   81 LEd2d 71   104 SCt 2237
    Almanac (1984):17A

Collins, Deborah. The states: federal-state relations issues hit the Supreme Court agenda. *National Civic Review* 73(11):568-571 (December 1984).

2690. Heckler, Secretary of Health and Human Services v. Day   May 22, 1984
467 US 104   81 LEd2d 88   104 SCt 2249
    Almanac (1984):16A

2691. Three Affiliated Tribes of the Fort Berthold Reservation v. Wold Engineering, P.C.   May 29, 1984
467 US 138   81 LEd2d 113   104 SCt 2267
    Almanac (1984):17A
    Am Indians (Wilkinson) 106, 131, 199, 211-212

2692. United States v. Lorenzetti   May 29, 1984
467 US 167   81 LEd2d 134   104 SCt 2284
    Almanac (1984):19A

2693. United States v. Gouveia   May 29, 1984
467 US 180   81 LEd2d 146   104 SCt 2292
    Almanac (1984):7A

Yalowitz, Deborah L. Supreme Court review: Sixth Amendment—right to counsel of prisoners isolated in administrative detention. *Journal of Criminal Law and Criminology* 75(3):779-801 (Fall 1984).

2694. Arizona v. Rumsey   May 29, 1984
467 US 203   81 LEd2d 164   104 SCt 2305
    Almanac (1984):6A

2695. Bernal v. Fainter, Secretary of State of Texas — May 30, 1984
467 US 216 — 81 LEd2d 175 — 104 SCt 2312
> *Almanac* (1984):10A
>
> Collins, Deborah. The states: federal-state relations issues hit the Supreme Court agenda. *National Civic Review* 73(11):568-571 (December 1984).

2696. Hawaii Housing Authority v. Midkiff — May 30, 1984
467 US 229 — 81 LEd2d 186 — 104 SCt 2321
> *Almanac* (1984):16A
>
> *Editorials* (1984):648-651
>
> *En Am Con* 908
>
> *New Right* (Schwartz) 130-136
>
> Collins, Deborah. The states: federal-state relations issues hit the Supreme Court agenda. *National Civic Review* 73(11):568-571 (December 1984).
>
> Folsom, Robin E. Executive Order 12,630: a president's manipulation of the Fifth Amendment's just compensation clause to achieve control over executive agency regulatory decisionmaking. *Boston College Environmental Affairs Law Review* 20(4):639-697 (Summer 1993).
>
> Gallogly, Richard J. Opening the door for Boston's poor: will "linkage" survive judicial review? *Boston College Environmental Affairs Law Review* 14(3):447-480 (Spring 1987).
>
> Goddy, David. The Court's broad impact on our economic life. *Scholastic Update* (Teachers' Edition) 117(7):17-18 (November 30, 1984).
>
> The High Court: this property is condemned. *Newsweek* 103(24):69 (June 11, 1984).
>
> Note; the public use test: would a ban on the possession of firearms require just compensation? *Law and Contemporary Problems* 49(1):223-249 (Winter 1986).
>
> Plater, Zygmunt J. B., and William Lund Norine. Through the looking glass of eminent domain: exploring the "arbitrary and capricious" test and substantive rationality review of governmental decisions. *Boston College Environmental Affairs Law Review* 16(4):661-752 (Summer 1989).
>
> Regan, Richard J. Supreme Court roundup: 1983 term. *Thought* 60(236):99-111 (March 1985).
>
> Ross, Douglas. Safeguarding our federalism: lessons for the states from the Supreme Court. *Public Administration Review* 45(Special Issue):723-731 (November 1985).
>
> State's right: Hawaii's land reform is upheld. *Time* 123(24):27 (June 11, 1984).

2697. New York v. Uplinger — May 30, 1984
467 US 246 — 81 LEd2d 201 — 104 SCt 2332
> *Almanac* (1984):8A
>
> *Liberty* 644-649+
>
> Bersoff, Donald N., and David W. Ogden. APA amicus curiae briefs: furthering lesbian and gay male civil rights. *American Psychologist* 46(9):950-956 (September 1991).

2698. Schall, Commissioner of New York City Department of Juvenile Justice v. Martin — June 4, 1984
467 US 253 — 81 LEd2d 207 — 104 SCt 2403
> *Almanac* (1984):8A
>
> *Editorials* (1984):644-647
>
> *En Am Con* 1622
>
> Negative action. [Editorial] *Nation* 238(25):788-789 (June 30, 1984).
>
> Press, Aric, Ann McDaniel, and Alexander Stille. Juveniles: a holding action. *Newsweek* 103(25):84 (June 18, 1984).
>
> Regan, Richard J. Supreme Court roundup: 1983 term. *Thought* 60(236):99-111 (March 1985).
>
> Serrill, Michael S., and Anne Constable. Reining in juveniles and aliens: the High Court rules on preventive detention and deportation. *Time* 123(25):76 (June 18, 1984).
>
> Weiss, Lee A. Supreme Court review: Fourteenth Amendment—due process and the preventive detention of juveniles. *Journal of Criminal Law and Criminology* 75(3):855-874 (Fall 1984).

2699. Colorado v. New Mexico — June 4, 1984
467 US 310 — 81 LEd2d 247 — 104 SCt 2433

Almanac (1984):18A

2700. Block, Secretary of Agriculture v. Community Nutrition Institution   June 4, 1984
467 US 340   81 LEd2d 270   104 SCt 2450
Almanac (1984):12A
Burger Years 191-205
Light, Alfred R. The importance of "being taken": to clarify and confirm the litigative reconstruction of CERCLA's text. *Boston College Environmental Affairs Law Review* 18(1):1-52 (Fall 1990).
Morrison, Alan B. Close reins on the bureaucracy. *Nation* 239(9):290-294 (September 29, 1984).

2701. Interstate Commerce Commission (ICC) v. American Trucking Associations, Inc.   June 5, 1984
467 US 354   81 LEd2d 282   104 SCt 2458
Almanac (1984):14A

2702. Aluminum Co. of America v. Central Lincoln Peoples' Utility District   June 5, 1984
467 US 380   81 LEd2d 301   104 SCt 2472
Almanac (1984):15A

2703. Immigration and Naturalization Service (INS) v. Stevic   June 5, 1984
467 US 407   81 LEd2d 321   104 SCt 2489
Almanac (1984):10A

2704. Nix, Warden of the Iowa State Penitentiary v. Williams   June 11, 1984
467 US 431   81 LEd2d 377   104 SCt 2501
Editorials (1984):638-643
En Am Con 809-810, 1320, 1628-1635
Cohn, William M. Supreme Court review: Sixth Amendment—inevitable discovery: a valuable but easily abused exception to the exclusionary rule. *Journal of Criminal Law and Criminology* 75(3):729-754 (Fall 1984).
Nelson, Caleb. The paradox of the exclusionary rule. *Public Interest* (96):117-130 (Summer 1989).
Regan, Richard J. Supreme Court roundup: 1983 term. *Thought* 60(236):99-111 (March 1985).
Serrill, Michael S., Anne Constable, and John E. Yang. Much ado about a shift to the right: the Court favors seniority over minority, police over defendants. *Time* 123(26):63-64 (June 25, 1984).
Supreme Court: Liberals recoil. *Economist* 291(7346):22-23 (June 16-22, 1984).

2705. Michigan Canners & Freezers Association, Inc.   June 11, 1984
v. Agricultural Marketing and Bargaining Board
467 US 461   81 LEd2d 399   104 SCt 2518
Almanac (1984):16A
Collins, Deborah. The states: federal-state relations issues hit the Supreme Court agenda. *National Civic Review* 73(11):568-571 (December 1984).

2706. California v. Trombetta   June 11, 1984
467 US 479   81 LEd2d 413   104 SCt 2528
Almanac (1984):8A
Regan, Richard J. Supreme Court roundup: 1983 term. *Thought* 60(236):99-111 (March 1985).

2707. Ohio v. Johnson   June 11, 1984
467 US 493   81 LEd2d 425   104 SCt 2536
Almanac (1984):6A

2708. Mabry, Commissioner, Arkansas Department of Correction v. Johnson   June 11, 1984
467 US 504   81 LEd2d 437   104 SCt 2543
Almanac (1984):8A

2709. Franchise Tax Board of California v. United States Postal Service   June 11, 1984
   467 US 512   81 LEd2d 446   104 SCt 2549
    Almanac (1984):19A

2710. Local No. 82, Furniture & Piano Moving, Furniture Store Drivers,   June 12, 1984
    Helpers, Warehousemen & Packers v. Crowley
   467 US 526   81 LEd2d 457   104 SCt 2557
    Almanac (1984):15A
    Burger Years 228-239
  Fox, Arthur. Showing workers who's the boss. *Nation* 239(9):295-299 (September 29, 1984).

2711. Firefighters Local Union No. 1784 v. Stotts   June 12, 1984
    Coupled with Memphis Fire Department v. Stotts
   467 US 561   81 LEd2d 483   104 SCt 2576
    Affirmative (Greene) 98-107
    Affirmative (Woods) 75-76
    Almanac (1984):8A
    Burger Years 95-108
    Conflict 104-108
    Editorials (1984):630-637
    En Am Con 730
    Sup Ct Ind 263-264
    Sup Ct Review (1984):1-68
  Affirmative confusion. *New Republic* 191(3-4):4, 42 (July 16-23, 1984).
  American survey: the long right arm of the law. *Economist* 292(7350):21-22 (July 14-20, 1984).
  As Reagan tries to roll back quotas—. *U.S. News and World Report* 98(14):12 (April 15, 1985).
  Authority rules. [Editorial] *Nation* 239(2):36-37 (July 21-28, 1984).
  Berns, Walter. Has the Burger Court gone too far? *Commentary* 78(4):27-33 (October 1984).
  Bomster, Mark. Supreme Court: mixed bag for business. *Electronic News* 30(1506):15 (July 16, 1984).
  Brown, Frank Dexter. High Court reviews civil rights. *Black Enterprise* 16(6):31 (January 1986).
  Burns, Haywood. The activisim in not affirmative. *Nation* 239(9):264-268 (September 29, 1984).
  Camper, Diane. . . . and justice for whom? *Black Enterprise* 15(8):52-55 (March 1985).
  Camper, Diane, Ethel Payne, Nathaniel R. Jones, Charles Ogletree, Charles, and Julius L. Chambers. To form a
   more perfect union. *Black Enterprise* 17(12):11, 51-66 (July 1987).
  Capozzola, John M. Affirmative action alive and well under Courts' strict scrutiny. *National Civic Review*
   75(6):354-362 (November/December 1986).
  Carmell, William A., and Dale E. Callender. Supreme Court didn't kill affirmative action. *ABA Banking
   Journal* 76(9):56-60 (September 1984).
  Chambers, Julius L., and Barry Goldstein. Title VII: the continuing challenge of establishing fair employment
   practices. *Law and Contemporary Problems* 49(4):9-23 (Autumn 1986).
  Cifelli, Anna. Quotas live on. *Fortune* 110(2):95-96 (July 23, 1984).
  Dingle, Derek T. Affirmative action. *Black Enterprise* 20(2):42-48 (September 1989).
  Drinan, Robert F. Another look at affirmative action. *America* 152(5):104-106 (February 9, 1985).
  End to quotas? Court ruling prompts look at race-bias remedies. *Engineering News Record* 212(25):163 (June
   21, 1984).
  Fields, Cheryl M. Supreme Court ruling on seniority may be blow to affirmative action. *Chronicle of Higher
   Education* 28(17):11, 16 (June 20, 1984).
  Gest, Ted. Old issues come home to roost at Supreme Court. *U.S. News and World Report* 95(15):70 (October
   10, 1983).
  ———. Seniority vs. minorities—impact of Court ruling. *U.S. News and World Report* 96(25):22-23 (June 25,
   1984).
  Graves, Earl G. The erosion of civil rights by the Supreme Court. [Editorial] *Black Enterprise* 15(2):9
   (September 1984).
  High Court to tackle race bias. *Engineering News Record* 215(16):76 (October 17, 1985).

Hogan, Joyce, and Ann M. Quigley. Physical standards for employment and the courts. *American Psychologist* 41(11):1193-1217 (November 1986).

Lacayo, Richard, and Jay Branegan. Accent on the affirmative: the Supreme Court says yes and no on racial preferences. *Time* 127(22):66 (June 2, 1986).

Lukoff, Roger M. Constitutional scholars appraise Supreme Court. *Trial* 20(11):65-66, 68 (November 1984).

Mauro, Tony. Negative on affirmative action plan. *Nation's Business* 72(9):40 (September 1984).

Methvin, Eugene H. The Supreme Court: justice in the balance. *Reader's Digest* 125(751):96-101 (November 1984).

Moskowitz, Daniel B. Court OKs affirmative action. *Engineering News Record* 217(4):52 (July 10, 1986).

Murphy, Betty Southard, Wayne E. Barlow, and Diane D. Hatch. Supreme Court reaffirms affirmative action. *Personnel Journal* 65(9):19-22 (September 1986).

Negative action. [Editorial] *Nation* 238(25):788-789 (June 30, 1984).

Press, Aric, and Lucy Howard. No hiding place this term. *Newsweek* 102(15):61 (October 10, 1983).

Press, Aric, and Ann McDaniels. A right turn on race? *Newsweek* 103(26):29-31 (June 25, 1984).

————. A woman's day in court. *Newsweek* 109(14):58-59 (April 6, 1987).

Redeker, James R. The Supreme Court on affirmative action: conflicting opinions. *Personnel* 63(10):8-14 (October 1986).

Regan, Richard J. Supreme Court roundup: 1983 term. *Thought* 60(236):99-111 (March 1985).

Reid-Dove, Allyson, and Michael E. Howard. "Night has fallen on the Court . . ." *Black Enterprise* 20(2):44-45 (September 1989).

Ritter, Anne. The way it was: HR in the 1980s. *Personnel* 66(12):30-37 (December 1989).

Ruben, George. Developments in industrial relations: seniority determines layoffs, justices rule. *Monthly Labor Review* 107(8):39 (August 1984).

A ruling that could roll back affirmative action. *Business Week* (Industrial/Technology Edition) (2849):31 (July 2, 1984).

Seniority and civil rights. *America* 150(24):23-30 (June 23-30, 1984).

Sendor, Benjamin. Seniority versus affirmative action: what the High Court ruling portends for schools. *American School Board Journal* 171(9):23 (September 1984).

————. Trend: Courts sustain your tough, but fair, actions. *American School Board Journal* 172(6):20-21 (June 1985).

Serrill, Michael S., Anne Constable, and John E. Yang. Much ado about a shift to the right: the Court favors seniority over minority, police over defendants. *Time* 123(26):63-64 (June 25, 1984).

Starr, Mark, Ann McDaniel, and Patricia King. Attacking affirmative action. *Newsweek* 105(19):39 (May 13, 1985).

Supreme Court: liberals recoil. *Economist* 291(7346):22-23 (June 16-22, 1984).

Vile, John R., and Kathy Ruth McCoy. The Memphis case: another precedent? *Personnel* 62(7):72-76 (July 1985).

Villere, Maurice, and Sandra Hartman. What's affirmative about affirmative action? *Business Horizons* 32(5):22-27 (September/October 1989).

Woods, Jeanne M. Municipal about face. *Black Enterprise* 15(2):16 (September 1984).

2712. Hayfield Northern Railroad Co., Inc. v. Chicago & North Western Transportation Co.   June 12, 1984
467 US 622   81 LEd2d 527   104 SCt 2610
    Almanac (1984):16A

Collins, Deborah. The states: federal-state relations issues hit the Supreme Court agenda. *National Civic Review* 73(11):568-571 (December 1984).

2713. Armco Inc. v. Hardesty, Tax Commissioner of West Virginia   June 12, 1984
467 US 638   81 LEd2d 540   104 SCt 2620
    Almanac (1984):18A

Bernstein, Seymour F. West Virginia gross receipts tax on wholesales held unconstitutional. *CPA Journal* 54(12):64-65 (December 1984).

Collins, Deborah. The states: federal-state relations issues hit the Supreme Court agenda. *National Civic Review* 73(11):568-571 (December 1984).

Krevitsky, Philip L. Washington: heads the state wins, tails the taxpayers lose—no refunds. *CPA Journal* 58(7):111-112 (July 1988).

Lanthrop, Robert G. Armco—a narrow and puzzling test for discriminatory state taxes under the commerce clause. *Taxes* 63(8):551-561 (August 1985).

2714. New York v. Quarles   June 12, 1984
467 US 649   81 LEd2d 550   104 SCt 2626
Almanac (1984):6A
Burger Years 143-168
Const Law 393-394
Editorials (1984):638-643
En Am Con 1264-1265, 1311, 1400-1408
Equal (Harrell) 92-95, 101
Thurgood 325-337R+

Behuniak-Long, Susan. Justice Sandra Day O'Connor and the power of maternal legal thinking. *Review of Politics* 54(3):417-444 (Summer 1992).

Drizin, Steven Andrew. Supreme Court review: Fifth Amendment—will the public safety exception swallow the Miranda exclusionary rule? *Journal of Criminal Law and Criminology* 75(3):692-715 (Fall 1984).

Jacobs, Robert. The state of Miranda: the effects of the Quarles decision. *Trial* 21(1):44-48 (January 1985).

Kamisar, Yale. The swing of the pendulum. *Nation* 239(9):271-274 (September 29, 1984).

Methvin, Eugene H. The Supreme Court: justice in the balance. *Reader's Digest* 125(751):96-101 (November 1984).

Pizzi, William T. The privilege against self-incrimination in a rescue situation. *Journal of Criminal Law and Criminology* 76(3):567-607 (Fall 1985).

Press, Aric, and Ann McDaniels. A right turn on race? *Newsweek* 103(26):29-31 (June 25, 1984).

Regan, Richard J. Supreme Court roundup: 1983 term. *Thought* 60(236):99-111 (March 1985).

Serrill, Michael S., Anne Constable, and John E. Yang. Much ado about a shift to the right: the Court favors seniority over minority, police over defendants. *Time* 123(26):63-64 (June 25, 1984).

2715. Capital Cities Cable, Inc. v. Crisp, Director, Oklahoma Alcoholic Beverage Control Board   June 18, 1984
467 US 691   81 LEd2d 580   104 SCt 2694
Almanac (1984):287, 17A
Editorials (1984):725-727

Cohen, Stanley E. Cable ruling leaves issues unanswered. *Advertising Age* 55(35):1, 47 (June 21, 1984).

Collins, Deborah. The states: federal-state relations issues hit the Supreme Court agenda. *National Civic Review* 73(11):568-571 (December 1984).

McGuire, Kevin T., and Barbara Palmer. Issue fluidity on the U.S. Supreme Court. *American Political Science Review* 89(3):691-702 (September 1995).

Roper, James E. Supreme Court agrees to hear several media cases. *Editor and Publisher* 116(41):11, 37 (October 8, 1983).

———. Supreme Court to hear major libel cases in '84. *Editor and Publisher* 117(1):16, 21, 27 (January 7, 1984).

Supreme Court tangles the web. [Editorial] *Advertising Age* 55(36):18 (June 25, 1984).

2716. Pension Benefit Guaranty Corp. v. R. A. Gray & Co. June 18, 1984
Coupled with Oregon-Washington Carpenters Employers Pension Trust Fund v. R. A. Gray & Co.
467 US 717   81 LEd2d 601   104 SCt 2709
Almanac (1984):13A-14A

Bomster, Mark. Supreme Court: mixed bag for business. *Electronic News* 30(1506):15 (July 16, 1984).

Geisel, Jerry. Supreme Court to rule on multiemployer law. *Business Insurance* 17(43):2, 32 (October 24, 1983).

Pension liability clarified. *Engineering News Record* 212(26):68 (June 28, 1984).

Tarnoff, Stephen. Court decisions or benefits increase employers' costs. *Business Insurance* 21(44):93-95 (November 2, 1987).

2717. Securities and Exchange Commission (SEC) v. Jerry T. O'Brien, Inc.   June 18, 1984
    467 US 735   81 LEd2d 615   104 SCt 2720
      Almanac (1984):14A

Le Porte, Lawrence A. Supreme Court review: SEC investigations—SEC need not notify target of third-party subpoenas. *Journal of Criminal Law and Criminology* 75(3):940-952 (Fall 1984).

2718. Copperweld Corp. v. Independence Tube Corp.   June 19, 1984
    467 US 752   81 LEd2d 628   104 SCt 2731
      Almanac (1984):12A-13A
      Burger Years 206-219
      Sup Ct Review (1984):69-148

Bomster, Mark. Company, subs. incapable of conspiring: High Court. *Electronic News* 30(1503):4 (June 25, 1984).

———. Supreme Court: mixed bag for business. *Electronic News* 30(1506):15 (July 16, 1984).

———. Two antitrust suits head issues before Supreme Court. *Electronic News* 29(1470):Supp N (November 7, 1983).

It's High Court conspiracy time. *Industry Week* 219(1):25-26 (October 3, 1983).

Mauro, Tony. Government vs. business privacy. *Nation's Business* 71(9):64-66 (September 1983).

A powerful bid to rewrite the antitrust rule book. *Business Week* (Industrial Edition) (2811):84-90 (October 10, 1983).

2719. United States v. S.A. Empresa De Viacao Aerea Rio Grandense (VARIG Airlines)   June 19, 1984
    467 US 797   81 LEd2d 660   104 SCt 2755
      Almanac (1984):18A-19A

Court case may alter certification process. *Aviation Week and Space Technology* 120(17):147 (April 23, 1984).

Court finds functions of FAA immune from negligence suits. *Aviation Week and Space Technology* 120(26):36 (June 25, 1984).

A powerful bid to rewrite the antitrust rule book. *Business Week* (Industrial Edition) (2811):84-90 (October 10, 1983).

2720. United States v. Morton   June 19, 1984
    467 US 822   81 LEd2d 680   104 SCt 2769
      Almanac (1984):19A

2721. Chevron U.S.A. Inc. v. Natural Resources Defense Council, Inc. (NRDC)   June 25, 1984
      Coupled with Environmental Protection Agency (EPA) v. Natural Resources Defense Council, Inc.
      Coupled with American Iron and Steel Institute v. Natural Resources Defense Council, Inc.
    467 US 837   81 LEd2d 694   104 SCt 2778
      Almanac (1984):341, 15A
      Burger Years 191-205
      Editorials (1984):771-773
      Sup Ct Review (1988):1-41; (1991):261-301; (1994):429-540
      Sup Ct Yearbook (1990-91):192-193

Cohen, Linda R., and Matthew L. Spitzer. Solving the Chevron puzzle. *Law and Contemporary Problems* 57(1-2):65-110 (Winter/Spring 1994).

Dellinger, Walter. Gag me with a rule. *New Republic* 206(1-2):14-16 (January 6-13, 1992).

Driesen, David M. The congressional role in international environmental law and its implications for statutory interpretation. *Boston College Environmental Affairs Law Review* 19(2):287-315 (Fall/Winter 1991).

Funk, William. The exception that approves the rule: FDF variances under the Clean Water Act. *Boston College Environmental Affairs Law Review* 13(1):1-60 (Fall 1985).

Gest, Ted. Old issues come home to roost at Supreme Court. *U.S. News and World Report* 95(15):70 (October 10, 1983).

Glicksman, Robert, and Christopher H. Schroeder. EPA and the courts: twenty years of law and politics. *Law and Contemporary Problems* 54(4):249-309 (Autumn 1991).

Hanson, David. High Court review of environmental ruling sought. *Chemical and Engineering News* 71(5):25 (February 1, 1993).

Hassler, Gregory L., and Karen O'Connor. Woodsy witch doctors versus judicial guerrillas: the role and impact of competing interest groups in environmental litigation. *Boston College Environmental Affairs Law Review* 13(4):487-520 (Summer 1986).

A powerful bid to rewrite the antitrust rule book. *Business Week* (Industrial Edition) (2811):84-90 (October 10, 1983).

Regan, Richard J. Supreme Court roundup: 1983 term. *Thought* 60(236):99-111 (March 1985).

Regulatory policy: High Court backs two EPA efforts. *Chemical and Engineering News* 62(27):4-5 (July 2, 1984).

Sandler, Ross. Reversals for the environment. *Environment* 26(9):44-45 (November 1984).

Serrill, Michael S., Anne Constable, and Don Winbush. Taking away the N.C.A.A.'s ball: and the other Court decisions, three administration victories. *Time* 124(2):77 (July 9, 1984).

Sheehan, Reginald S. Federal agencies and the Supreme Court: an analysis of litigation outcomes, 1953-1988. *American Politics Quarterly* 20(4):478-500 (October 1992).

Silverstein, Gordon. Statutory interpretation and the balance of institutional power. *Review of Politics* 56(3):475-501 (Summer 1994).

Sun, Marjorie. High Court upholds EPA's "bubble" concept. *Science* 225(4658):150 (July 13, 1984).

Supreme Court upholds EPA bubble concept. *Oil and Gas Journal* 82(27):29 (July 2, 1984).

U.S. Supreme Court v. the environment? *Environment* 34(2):23-24 (March 1992).

2722. Cooper v. Federal Reserve Bank of Richmond   June 25, 1984
467 US 867   81 LEd2d 718   104 SCt 2794
Almanac (1984):9A

2723. Sure-Tan, Inc. v. National Labor Relations Board (NLRB)   June 25, 1984
467 US 883   81 LEd2d 732   104 SCt 2803
Almanac (1984):10A

2724. Tower, Public Defender of Douglas County, Oregon v. Glover   June 25, 1984
467 US 914   81 LEd2d 758   104 SCt 2820
Almanac (1984):10A

2725. Washington Metropolitan Area Transit Authority v. Johnson   June 26, 1984
467 US 925   81 LEd2d 768   104 SCt 2827
Almanac (1984):15A

2726. Secretary of State of Maryland v. Joseph H. Munson Co., Inc.   June 26, 1984
467 US 947   81 LEd2d 786   104 SCt 2839
Almanac (1984):11A

Collins, Deborah. The states: federal-state relations issues hit the Supreme Court agenda. *National Civic Review* 73(11):568-571 (December 1984).

Edel, Richard. Direct marketing: fund raising comes under scrutiny. *Advertising Age* 57(18):22 (March 6, 1986).

Regan, Richard J. Supreme Court roundup: 1983 term. *Thought* 60(236):99-111 (March 1985).

2727. Ruckelshaus, Administrator,   June 26, 1984
United States Environmental Protection Agency (EPA) v. Monsanto Co.
467 US 986   81 LEd2d 815   104 SCt 2862
Almanac (1984):14A

Bomster, Mark. Two antitrust suits head issues before Supreme Court. *Electronic News* 29(1470):Supp N (November 7, 1983).

Confidentiality—will government give away company secrets? *Chemical Week* 127(24):28-33 (December 10, 1980).

Gest, Ted. Old issues come home to roost at Supreme Court. *U.S. News and World Report* 95(15):70 (October 10, 1983).

Hanley, Thomas. A developer's dream: the United States Claims Court's new analysis of Section 404 takings challenges. *Boston College Environmental Affairs Law Review* 19(2):317-353 (Fall/Winter 1991).

Hassler, Gregory L., and Karen O'Connor. Woodsy witch doctors versus judicial guerrillas: the role and impact of competing interest groups in environmental litigation. *Boston College Environmental Affairs Law Review* 13(4):487-520 (Summer 1986).

Regulatory policy: High Court backs two EPA efforts. *Chemical and Engineering News* 62(27):4-5 (July 2, 1984).

Smith, R. Jeffrey. Supreme Court orders pesticide data released. *Science* 225(4658):150 (July 13, 1984).

Windfall profits tax upheld by court in unanimous ruling. *Chemical Marketing Reporter* 223:4, 17 (June 13, 1983).

2728. Patton v. Yount   June 26, 1984
467 US 1025   81 LEd2d 847   104 SCt 2885
Almanac (1984):6A-7A

2729. Reed v. Ross   June 27, 1984
468 US 1   82 LEd2d 1   104 SCt 2901
Almanac (1984):7A

2730. Thigpen, Commissioner, Mississippi Department of Corrections v. Roberts   June 27, 1984
468 US 27   82 LEd2d 23   104 SCt 2916
Almanac (1984):8A

Erlinder, C. Peter, and David C. Thomas. Prohibiting prosecutorial vindictiveness while protecting prosecutorial discretion: toward a principled resolution of a due process dilemma. *Journal of Criminal Law and Criminology* 76(2):341-438 (Summer 1985).

2731. Burnett v. Grattan   June 27, 1984
468 US 42   82 LEd2d 36   104 SCt 2924
Almanac (1984):9A

2732. United States v. Yermian   June 27, 1984
468 US 63   82 LEd2d 53   104 SCt 2936
Almanac (1984):7A

2733. National Collegiate Athletic Association (NCAA)   June 27, 1984
    v. Board of Regents of the University of Oklahoma
468 US 85   82 LEd2d 70   104 SCt 2948
Almanac (1984):13A
Editorials (1984):728-731
Sup Ct Review (1984):69-148

The Court's playbook for college football. *Newsweek* 104(2):62 (July 9, 1984).

Farrell, Charles S. Supreme Court strikes down NCAA control of football on television: colleges free to negotiate own contracts: High Court's action. *Chronicle of Higher Education* 28(19):1, 22 (July 5, 1984).

————. Supreme Court strikes down NCAA control of football on television: colleges free to negotiate own contracts: High Court's action: contract negotiations. *Chronicle of Higher Education* 28(19):1, 24 (July 5, 1984).

Fields, Cheryl M. New Supreme Court session starts Monday; scope of anti-sex-bias law a major issue. *Chronicle of Higher Education* 27(6):15, 19 (September 28, 1983).

Flygare, Thomas J. De jure: the end of NCAA control over college football television rights. *Phi Delta Kappan* 66(2):148-150 (October 1984).

From Tilton to Ewing: some major higher-education decisions of the Burger court. *Chronicle of Higher Education* 32(17):10 (June 25, 1986).

Goddy, David. The Court's broad impact on our economic life. *Scholastic Update* (Teachers' Edition) 117(7):17-18 (November 30, 1984).

The NCAA's goal-line stand on TV rights. *Business Week* (Industrial/Technology Edition) (2837):105 (April 9, 1984).

Regan, Richard J. Supreme Court roundup: 1983 term. *Thought* 60(236):99-111 (March 1985).

Serrill, Michael S., Anne Constable, and Don Winbush. Taking away the N.C.A.A.'s ball: and the other Court decisions, three administration victories. *Time* 124(2):77 (July 9, 1984).

Stevens, John Paul. Text of Supreme Court's majority opinion striking down NCAA's control of college football telecasts. *Chronicle of Higher Education* 28(19):22-25R (July 5, 1984).

Taaffe, William. The Supreme Court's TV ruling: will the viewer benefit most? *Sport Illustrated* 61(2):9 (July 9, 1984).

———. A supremely unsettling smorgasbord. *Sport Illustrated* 61(12 Special Issue):150-151 (September 5, 1984).

Vance, N. Scott. Supreme Court will weigh challenge to NCAA's TV football pact. *Chronicle of Higher Education* 27(9):26 (October 26, 1983).

White, Byron R. Justice White's dissent from Court's ruling on NCAA control of football telecasts. *Chronicle of Higher Education* 28(19):25-26, 28R (July 5, 1984).

2734. Securities Industry Association v. Board of Governors of the Federal Reserve System   June 28, 1984
468 US 137   82 LEd2d 107   104 SCt 2979
 Almanac (1984):13A
 Burger Years 191-205
Morrison, Alan B. Close reins on the bureaucracy. *Nation* 239(9):290-294 (September 29, 1984).

2735. Davis v. Scherer   June 28, 1984
468 US 183   82 LEd2d 139   104 SCt 3012
 Almanac (1984):10A

2736. Securities Industry Association v. Board of Governors of the Federal Reserve System   June 28, 1984
468 US 207   82 LEd2d 158   104 SCt 3003
 Almanac (1984):13A
Bisky, Tom. Strategy of a front-runner. *ABA Banking Journal* 80(11):57-60 (November 1988).

2737. Regan, Secretary of the Treasury v. Wald   June 28, 1984
468 US 222   82 LEd2d 171   104 SCt 3026
 Almanac (1984):4A, 9A
 Burger Years 50-55
 Editorials (1984):756-759
 En Am Con 1528
American survey: the long right arm of the law. *Economist* 292(7350):21-22 (July 14-20, 1984).

Authority rules. [Editorial] *Nation* 239(2):36-37 (July 21-28, 1984).

Halperin, Morton H. Never question the president. *Nation* 239(9):285-288 (September 29, 1984).

Regan, Richard J. Supreme Court roundup: 1983 term. *Thought* 60(236):99-111 (March 1985).

Schwartz, Herman. Fifteen years of the Burger Court. *Nation* 239(9)262-264 (September 29, 1984).

Serrill, Michael S., Anne Constable, and Don Winbush. Taking away the N.C.A.A.'s ball: and the other Court decisions, three administration victories. *Time* 124(2):77 (July 9, 1984).

Silverstein, Gordon. Statutory interpretation and the balance of institutional power. *Review of Politics* 56(3):475-501 (Summer 1994).

2738. Bacchus Imports, LTD. v. Dias, Director of Taxation of Hawaii   June 29, 1984
468 US 263   82 LEd2d 200   104 SCt 3049
 Almanac (1984):18A
 Sup Ct Yearbook (1990-91):50
Collins, Deborah. The states: federal-state relations issues hit the Supreme Court agenda. *National Civic Review* 73(11):568-571 (December 1984).

Hellerstein, Walter. Supreme Court settles some state tax issues while creating other problems. *Journal of Taxation* 75(3):180-186 (September 1991).

2739. Clark, Secretary of the Interior v. Community for Creative Non-Violence   June 29, 1984
       468 US 288   82 LEd2d 221   104 SCt 3065
           Almanac (1984):4A, 11A
           Const Law 168-169
           Sup Ct Review (1992):79-122
           Thurgood 294-304R+
       Berns, Walter. Has the Burger Court gone too far? *Commentary* 78(4):27-33 (October 1984).
       The Court's playbook for college football. *Newsweek* 104(2):62 (July 9, 1984).
       Marcy, William R. To protect or not to protect—that is the question. *Social Education* 54(6):364-365 (October 1990).
       Regan, Richard J. Supreme Court roundup: 1983 term. *Thought* 60(236):99-111 (March 1985).
       Roper, James E. Supreme Court to hear major libel cases in '84. *Editor and Publisher* 117(1):16, 21, 27 (January 7, 1984).
       Serrill, Michael S., Anne Constable, and Don Winbush. Taking away the N.C.A.A.'s ball: and the other Court decisions, three administration victories. *Time* 124(2):77 (July 9, 1984).

2740. Richardson v. United States   June 29, 1984
       468 US 317   82 LEd2d 242   104 SCt 3081
           Almanac (1984):6A

2741. Hobby v. United States   July 2, 1984
       468 US 339   82 LEd2d 260   104 SCt 3093
           Almanac (1984):8A

2742. Federal Communications Commission (FCC) v. League of Women Voters of California   July 2, 1984
       468 US 364   82 LEd2d 278   104 SCt 3106
           Almanac (1984):11A
           Editorials (1984):768-770
           Sup Ct Review (1987):303-344
       Elston, Michael J. Artists and unconstitutional conditions: the Big Bad Wolf won't subsidize Little Red Riding Hood's indecent art. *Law and Contemporary Problems* 56(4):327-361 (Autumn 1993).
       Fields, Cheryl M. Court ends ban on public-broadcasting editorials. *Chronicle of Higher Education* 28(20):13 (July 11, 1984).
       ———. New Supreme Court session starts Monday; scope of anti-sex-bias law a major issue. *Chronicle of Higher Education* 27(6):15, 19 (September 28, 1983).
       Hale, F. Dennis. Shop talk at thirty: the Powell seat on the U.S. Supreme Court. [Editorial] *Editor and Publisher* 120(35):56, 44 (August 29, 1987).
       Press, Aric, and Ann McDaniel. Reagan's days in Court. *Newsweek* 104(3):57-60 (July 16, 1984).
       Regan, Richard J. Supreme Court roundup: 1983 term. *Thought* 60(236):99-111 (March 1985).
       Supreme Court decision. *Congressional Digest* 70(8-9)197-199 (August/September 1991).

2743. Berkemer, Sheriff of Franklin County, Ohio v. McCarty   July 2, 1984
       468 US 420   82 LEd2d 317   104 SCt 3138
           Almanac (1984):6A
           Const Law 386-390R
       American survey: the long right arm of the law. *Economist* 292(7350):21-22 (July 14-20, 1984).
       Jacobs, Robert. The state of Miranda: the effects of the Quarles decision. *Trial* 21(1):44-48 (January 1985).
       Maltz, Earl M. Lockstep analysis and the concept of federalism. *Annals of the American Academy of Political and Social Science* 496:98-106 (March 1988).
       Regan, Richard J. Supreme Court roundup: 1983 term. *Thought* 60(236):99-111 (March 1985).

2744. Spaziano v. Florida   July 2, 1984
       468 US 447   82 LEd2d 340   104 SCt 3154
          Almanac (1984):7A
          Death Penalty (Tushnet) 68-69
       Farber, Daniel A. Supreme Court review: capital punishment and the Rehnquist court. *Trial* 27(4):13-15 (April
          1991).
       Press, Aric, Linda Prout, and Ann McDaniel. Second-guessing the jury. *Newsweek* 103(18):81 (April 30, 1984).
       Wellek, Jeffrey Alan. Supreme Court review: Eighth Amendment—trial court may impose death sentence
          despite jury's recommendation of life imprisonment. *Journal of Criminal Law and Criminology* 75(3):813-
          838 (Fall 1984).

2745. Brown, Director, Department of Law and Public Safety,   July 2, 1984
          Division of Gaming Enforcement, State of New Jersey v. Hotel & Restaurant Employees & Bartenders
       International Union, Local 54
             Coupled with Danzinger, Acting Chairman, Casino Control Commission of New Jersey v. Hotel &
                Restaurant Employees & Bartenders International Union, Local 54
       468 US 491   82 LEd2d 373   104 SCt 3179
          Almanac (1984):16A
       Collins, Deborah. The states: federal-state relations issues hit the Supreme Court agenda. *National Civic Review*
          73(11):568-571 (December 1984).

2746. Hudson v. Palmer   July 3, 1984
       468 US 517   82 LEd2d 393   104 SCt 3194
          Almanac (1984):5A
       American survey: the long right arm of the law. *Economist* 292(7350):21-22 (July 14-20, 1984).
       Gardner, Martin R. Hudson v. Palmer—"bright lines" but dark directions for prisoner privacy rights. *Journal of
          Criminal Law and Criminology* 76(1):75-115 (Spring 1985).
       Goring, Darlene C. Supreme Court review: Fourth Amendment—prison cells: is there a right to privacy?
          Journal of Criminal Law and Criminology 75(3):609-629 (Fall 1984).
       Regan, Richard J. Supreme Court roundup: 1983 term. *Thought* 60(236):99-111 (March 1985).
       Serrill, Michael S., and Anne Constable. A matter of good faith: the Court ends a busy term with a major ruling
          on police searches. *Time* 124(3):57-59 (July 16, 1984).

2747. Wasman v. United States   July 3, 1984
       468 US 559   82 LEd2d 424   104 SCt 3217
          Almanac (1984):8A
       Brilliant, Allan S. Supreme Court review: Fifth Amendment—sentence enhancement: rethinking the Pearce
          prophylactic rule. *Journal of Criminal Law and Criminology* 75(3):716-728 (Fall 1984).
       Erlinder, C. Peter, and David C. Thomas. Prohibiting prosecutorial vindictiveness while protecting
          prosecutorial discretion: toward a principled resolution of a due process dilemma. *Journal of Criminal Law
          and Criminology* 76(2):341-438 (Summer 1985).

2748. Block, Sheriff of the County of Los Angeles v. Rutherford   July 3, 1984
       468 US 576   82 LEd2d 438   104 SCt 3227
          Almanac (1984):11A
       American survey: the long right arm of the law. *Economist* 292(7350):21-22 (July 14-20, 1984).
       Authority rules. [Editorial] *Nation* 239(2):36-37 (July 21-28, 1984).
       Press, Aric, and Ann McDaniel. Reagan's days in Court. *Newsweek* 104(3):57-60 (July 16, 1984).
       Regan, Richard J. Supreme Court roundup: 1983 term. *Thought* 60(236):99-111 (March 1985).

2749. Roberts, Acting Commissioner, Minnesota Department of Human Rights v. United States Jaycees   July 3, 1984
       468 US 609   82 LEd2d 462   104 SCt 3244
          Almanac (1984):12A
          Const Law 552-556R
          Editorials (1984):750-755

En Am Con 782-789
Price 226-228

Arledge, Paula C., and Edward V. Heck. A freshman justice confronts the Constitution: Justice O'Connor and the First Amendment. *Western Political Quarterly* 45(3):761-772 (September 1992).

Collins, Deborah. The states: federal-state relations issues hit the Supreme Court agenda. *National Civic Review* 73(11):568-571 (December 1984).

Last-minute decisions—and their impact. *U.S. News and World Report* 97(3):34 (July 16, 1984).

Press, Aric, and Ann McDaniel. Reagan's days in Court. *Newsweek* 104(3):57-60 (July 16, 1984).

Regan, Richard J. Supreme Court roundup: 1983 term. *Thought* 60(236):99-111 (March 1985).

Sendor, Benjamin. How far can boards go in regulating students' off-campus behavior? *American School Board Journal* 178(6):5, 38 (June 1991).

Serrill, Michael S., and Anne Constable. A matter of good faith: the Court ends a busy term with a major ruling on police searches. *Time* 124(3):57-59 (July 16, 1984).

2750. Regan, Secretary of the Treasury v. Time, Inc.   July 3, 1984
468 US 641   82 LEd2d 487   104 SCt 3262
     Almanac (1984):12A

A powerful bid to rewrite the antitrust rule book. *Business Week* (Industrial Edition) (2811):84-90 (October 10, 1983).

Roper, James E. Supreme Court to hear major libel cases in '84. *Editor and Publisher* 117(1):16, 21, 27 (January 7, 1984).

Serrill, Michael S.,and Anne Constable. A matter of good faith: the Court ends a busy term with a major ruling on police searches. *Time* 124(3):57-59 (July 16, 1984).

2751. United States v. Karo   July 3, 1984
468 US 705   82 LEd2d 530   104 SCt 3296
     Almanac (1984):5A

Junker, John M. The structure of the Fourth Amendment: the scope of the protection. *Journal of Criminal Law and Criminology* 79(4):1105-1183 (Winter 1989).

Regan, Richard J. Supreme Court roundup: 1983 term. *Thought* 60(236):99-111 (March 1985).

Webber, Dawn. Supreme Court review: Fourth Amendment—of warrants, electronic surveillance, expectations of privacy, and tainted fruits. *Journal of Criminal Law and Criminology* 75(3):630-652 (Fall 1984).

2752. Allen v. Wright   July 3, 1984
468 US 737   82 LEd2 556   104 SCt 3315
     Almanac (1984):10A
     Burger Years 95-108; 191-205
     En Am Con 45, 1722-1724
     Sup Ct Review (1993):37-64

Fields, Cheryl M. New Supreme Court session starts Monday; scope of anti-sex-bias law a major issue. *Chronicle of Higher Education* 27(6):15, 19 (September 28, 1983).

Morrison, Alan B. Close reins on the bureaucracy. *Nation* 239(9):290-294 (September 29, 1984).

Neuborne, Burt. Taking away the right to sue. *Nation* 239(9):268-271 (September 29, 1984).

Rowe, Thomas D. No final victories: the incompleteness of equity's triumph in federal public law. *Law and Contemporary Problems* 56(3):105-121 (Summer 1993).

2753. Segura v. United States   July 5, 1984
468 US 796   82 LEd2d 599   104 SCt 3380
     Almanac (1984):5A-6A

Serrill, Michael S., and Anne Constable. A matter of good faith: the Court ends a busy term with a major ruling on police searches. *Time* 124(3):57-59 (July 16, 1984).

2754. Selective Service System v. Minnesota Public Interest Research Group   July 5, 1984
468 US 841   82 LEd2d 632   104 SCt 3348
     Almanac (1984):9A

Editorials (1983):811-813; (1984):764-767

Berns, Walter. Has the Burger Court gone too far? *Commentary* 78(4):27-33 (October 1984).

Brennan, William J., Jr. Justice Brennan's dissent. *Chronicle of Higher Education* 28(20):19R (July 11, 1984).

Burger, Warren E. Text of the Supreme Court's opinions in the selective service system case. *Chronicle of Higher Education* 28(20):14, 16-17R (July 11, 1984).

Fields, Cheryl M. New Supreme Court session starts Monday; scope of anti-sex-bias law a major issue. *Chronicle of Higher Education* 27(6):15, 19 (September 28, 1983).

From Tilton to Ewing: some major higher-education decisions of the Burger court. *Chronicle of Higher Education* 32(17):10 (June 25, 1986).

Hook, Janet. U.S. told it can enforce law linking draft registration to eligibility for student aid. *Chronicle of Higher Education* 26(19):1, 9 (July 6, 1983).

Last-minute decisions—and their impact. *U.S. News and World Report* 97(3):34 (July 16, 1984).

Lukoff, Roger M. Constitutional scholars appraise Supreme Court. *Trial* 20(11):65-66, 68 (November 1984).

Marshall, Thurgood. Justice Marshall's dissent. *Chronicle of Higher Education* 28(20):18-19R (July 11, 1984).

Palmer, Stacy E. High Court upholds ban on aid to students who shun the draft. *Chronicle of Higher Education* 28(20):1, 14 (July 11, 1984).

Powell, Lewis F., Jr. Justice Powell's dissent. *Chronicle of Higher Education* 28(20):17-18R (July 11, 1984).

Press, Aric, and Ann McDaniel. Reagan's days in Court. *Newsweek* 104(3):57-60 (July 16, 1984).

Regan, Richard J. Supreme Court roundup: 1983 term. *Thought* 60(236):99-111 (March 1985).

Sacrificing for the military. *Progressive* 48(9):12 (September 1984).

Serrill, Michael S., and Anne Constable. A matter of good faith: the Court ends a busy term with a major ruling on police searches. *Time* 124(3):57-59 (July 16, 1984).

2755. Irving Independent School District v. Tatro   July 5, 1984
      468 US 883   82 LEd2d 664   104 SCt 3371
         Almanac (1984):9A
         Burger Years 125-139

Flygare, Thomas J. De jure: High Court requires schools to provide catheterization services under 94-142. *Phi Delta Kappan* 66(3):216-217 (November 1984).

Press, Aric, and Ann McDaniel. Reagan's days in Court. *Newsweek* 104(3):57-60 (July 16, 1984).

Sendor, Benjamin. Now "related services" are your responsibility. *American School Board Journal* 171(10): 18, 42 (October 1984).

White, Eileen. P.L. 94-142's touchiest topics: health care, discipline, summer school. *American School Board Journal* 168(2):19-23 (February 1981).

2756. United States v. Leon   July 5, 1984
      468 US 897   82 LEd2d 677   104 SCt 3405
         Almanac (1984):228, 5A; (1989):260; (1995):6-5
         Ascent 360-362
         Burger Years 143-168
         Const (Currie) 550-555
         Const Law 370-375R
         Editorials (1984):760-763
         En Am Con 1628-1635
         Magic 320-322
         Sup Ct Review (1984):309-358

American survey: the long right arm of the law. *Economist* 292(7350):21-22 (July 14-20, 1984).

Forbes, Malcolm S., Jr. Good intentions, bad results. [Editorial] *Forbes* 131(5):23 (February 28, 1983).

Gest, Ted. Old issues come home to roost at Supreme Court. *U.S. News and World Report* 95(15):70 (October 10, 1983).

Hartman, Marshall J., and Sidney Bernstein. To Leon, and beyond; two commentators react. *Trial* 21(1):50-56 (January 1985).

Haubner, Michael J. Military search of civilians: a commander's power. *Trial* 22(9):48-54 (September 1986).

Kamisar, Yale. The swing of the pendulum. *Nation* 239(9):271-274 (September 29, 1984).

Last-minute decisions—and their impact. *U.S. News and World Report* 97(3):34 (July 16, 1984).

Lukoff, Roger M. Constitutional scholars appraise Supreme Court. *Trial* 20(11):65-66, 68 (November 1984).

Maltz, Earl M. Lockstep analysis and the concept of federalism. *Annals of the American Academy of Political and Social Science* 496:98-106 (March 1988).

Meese, Edwin, III. The attorney general's view of the Supreme Court: toward a jurisprudence of original intention. *Public Administration Review* 45(Special Issue):701-704 (November 1985).

Misner, Robert L. Limiting Leon: a mistake of law analogy. *Journal of Criminal Law and Criminology* 77(3):507-545 (Fall 1986).

Mosk, Stanley. The emerging agenda in state constitutional rights law. *Annals of the American Academy of Political and Social Science* 496:54-64 (March 1988).

Nelson, Caleb. The paradox of the exclusionary rule. *Public Interest* (96):117-130 (Summer 1989).

Press, Aric, and Ann McDaniel. Reagan's days in Court. *Newsweek* 104(3):57-60 (July 16, 1984).

Regan, Richard J. Supreme Court roundup: 1983 term. *Thought* 60(236):99-111 (March 1985).

Serrill, Michael S., and Anne Constable. A matter of good faith: the Court ends a busy term with a major ruling on police searches. *Time* 124(3):57-59 (July 16, 1984).

Uchida, Craig D., and Timothy S. Bynum. Search warrants, motions to suppress and "lost cases": the effects of the exclusionary rule in seven jurisdictions. *Journal of Criminal Law and Criminology* 81(4):1034-1066 (Winter 1991).

2757. Massachusetts v. Sheppard — July 5, 1984
468 US 981   82 LEd2d 737   104 SCt 3424
    Almanac (1984):5A
    Ascent 360-362
    Burger Years 143-168
    Sup Ct Review (1984):309-358

American survey: the long right arm of the law. *Economist* 292(7350):21-22 (July 14-20, 1984).

Berns, Walter. Has the Burger Court gone too far? *Commentary* 78(4):27-33 (October 1984).

Forbes, Malcolm S., Jr. Good intentions, bad results. [Editorial] *Forbes* 131(5):23 (February 28, 1983).

Gest, Ted. Old issues come home to roost at Supreme Court. *U.S. News and World Report* 95(15):70 (October 10, 1983).

Lukoff, Roger M. Constitutional scholars appraise Supreme Court. *Trial* 20(11):65-66, 68 (November 1984).

Methvin, Eugene H. The Supreme Court: justice in the balance. *Reader's Digest* 125(751):96-101 (November 1984).

Misner, Robert L. Limiting Leon: a mistake of law analogy. *Journal of Criminal Law and Criminology* 77(3):507-545 (Fall 1986).

Nelson, Caleb. The paradox of the exclusionary rule. *Public Interest* (96):117-130 (Summer 1989).

Press, Aric, and Ann McDaniel. Reagan's days in Court. *Newsweek* 104(3):57-60 (July 16, 1984).

Serrill, Michael S., and Anne Constable. A matter of good faith: the Court ends a busy term with a major ruling on police searches. *Time* 124(3):57-59 (July 16, 1984).

Uchida, Craig D., and Timothy S. Bynum. Search warrants, motions to suppress and "lost cases": the effects of the exclusionary rule in seven jurisdictions. *Journal of Criminal Law and Criminology* 81(4):1034-1066 (Winter 1991).

2758. Smith v. Robinson, Rhode Island Associate Commissioner of Education — July 5, 1984
468 US 992   82 LEd2d 746   104 SCt 3457
    Almanac (1984):9A; (1986):19, 271-272

Bodine, Margot R. Opening the schoolhouse door for children with AIDS: the Education for All Handicapped Children Act. *Boston College Environmental Affairs Law Review* 13(4):583-641 (Summer 1986).

Flygare, Thomas J. De jure: Supreme Court decides attorney fees not available in special education cases. *Phi Delta Kappan* 66(1):66-67 (September 1984).

Sendor, Benjamin. Now "related services" are your responsibility. *American School Board Journal* 171(10):18, 42 (October 1984).

2759. Immigration and Naturalization Service (INS) v. Lopez-Mendoza — July 5, 1984
468 US 1032   82 LEd2d 778   104 SCt 3479
    Almanac (1984):10A-11A

Ascent 362-364, 390-394
Burger Years 143-168
Const (Currie) 550-555
New Right (Schwartz) 176-181

Gest, Ted. Old issues come home to roost at Supreme Court. *U.S. News and World Report* 95(15):70 (October 10, 1983).

Kamisar, Yale. The swing of the pendulum. *Nation* 239(9):271-274 (September 29, 1984).

Lukoff, Roger M. Constitutional scholars appraise Supreme Court. *Trial* 20(11):65-66, 68 (November 1984).

Press, Aric, and Ann McDaniel. Reagan's days in Court. *Newsweek* 104(3):57-60 (July 16, 1984).

2760. United States Department of Justice v. Provenzano   November 26, 1984
      Coupled with Shapiro v. Drug Enforcement Administration (DEA)
    469 US 14   83 LEd2d 242   105 SCt 413
    Almanac (1985):19A

2761. United States v. 50 Acres of Land   December 4, 1984
    469 US 24   83 LEd2d 376   105 SCt 451
    Almanac (1985):18A

Collins, Deborah. The states: federal-state relations issues hit the Supreme Court agenda. *National Civic Review* 73(11):568-571 (December 1984).

2762. Luce v. United States   December 10, 1984
    469 US 38   83 LEd2d 443   105 SCt 460
    Almanac (1985):6A

2763. United States v. Abel   December 10, 1984
    469 US 45   83 LEd2d 450   105 SCt 465
    Almanac (1985):6A

2764. United States v. Powell   December 10, 1984
    469 US 57   83 LEd2d 461   105 SCt 471
    Almanac (1985):7A

2765. Garcia et al. v. United States   December 10, 1984
    469 US 70   83 LEd2d 472   105 SCt 479
    Almanac (1985):7A-8A

2766. Trans World Airlines, Inc. (TWA) v. Thurston   January 8, 1985
      Coupled with Air Line Pilots Association International v. Thurston
    469 US 111   83 LEd2d 523   105 SCt 613
    Almanac (1985):4A, 8A

Gest, Ted. For High Court, a full plate of tough cases. *U.S. News and World Report* 97(15):52 (October 8, 1984).

Greene, Jan. Business gains legal ground in Court term. *Electronic News* 31(1557):10 (July 8, 1985).

Handicapped need not prove intentional bias by employers or colleges, Supreme Court rules. *Chronicle of Higher Education* 29(18):25 (January 16, 1985).

Murphy, Betty Southard, Wayne E. Barlow, and D. Diane Hatch. Supreme Court restricts blanket retirement. *Personnel Journal* 65(1):26, 28 (January 1986).

Ruben, George. Developments in industrial relations: TWA discrimination against older pilots. *Monthly Labor Review* 108(3):49 (March 1985).

The Supreme Court is narrowing its focus. *Business Week* (Industrial/Technology Edition) (2862): 40-41 (October 1, 1984).

2767. Paulsen et ux. v. Commissioner of Internal Revenue January 8, 1985
    469 US 131   83 LEd2d 540   105 SCt 627

Almanac (1985):14A

Hite, Peggy A., and Denis J. Rice. The continuity of interest doctrine. *CPA Journal* 56(11):72-79 (November 1986).

Knight, Lee G., Ray A. Knight, and Jep Robertson. Tax status of hybrid securities. *CPA Journal* 58(9):44-50 (September 1988).

Taxation: half-century tax policy, is reversed by high court in S&L merger decision. *Journal of Accountancy* 159(3):14, 18 (March 1985).

2768. Mills Music, Inc. v. Snyder   January 8, 1985
     469 US 153   83 LEd2d 556   105 SCt 638
     Almanac (1985):14A

Fields, Howard. Congress bills would reverse Mills decision. *Publishers' Weekly* 228(23):17 (December 6, 1985).

———. Supreme Court to decide on derivative works. *Publishers' Weekly* 225(15):19 (April 13, 1984).

2769. Park 'N Fly, Inc. v. Dollar Park and Fly, Inc.   January 8, 1985
     469 US 189   83 LEd2d 582   105 SCt 658
     Almanac (1985):14A

Borchard, William M. "Olympics" not fair game. *Advertising Age* 59(24):46 (June 6, 1988).

2770. United States v. Hensley   January 8, 1985
     469 US 221   83 LEd2d 604   105 SCt 675
     Almanac (1985):5A
     En Am Con 1780-1782

Justice that panders. *Progressive* 49(3):10 (March 1985).

Pettus, Jolene D. Supreme Court review: Fourth Amendment—the expansion of the Terry doctrine to completed felonies. *Journal of Criminal Law and Criminology* 76(4):986-1002 (Winter 1985).

2771. Board of License Commissioners of the Town of Tiverton   January 8, 1985
      v. Pastore, Liquor Control Administrator of Rhode Island
     469 US 238   83 LEd2d 618   105 SCt 685
     Almanac (1985):6A

2772. United States v. Boyle, Executor of the Estate of Boyle   January 9, 1985
     469 US 241   83 LEd2d 622   105 SCt 687
     Almanac (1985):14A

Fiore, Nicholas J. Executors of decedents' estates: what CPAs should know. *Journal of Accountancy* 161(6):12 (June 1986).

Harris, Steven M., and Warner, Richard E. Boyle and beyond: recent trends for excusing the late filing penalty. *Taxes* 67(5):301-309 (May 1989).

2773. Lawrence County v. Lead-Deadwood School District No. 40-1   January 9, 1985
     469 US 256   83 LEd2d 635   105 SCt 695
     Almanac (1985):16A

2774. Ohio v. Kovacs, dba B & W Enterprises   January 9, 1985
     469 US 274   83 LEd2d 649   105 SCt 105
     Almanac (1985):15A

Berman, Mark N. Environmental cleanup: who pays the price? *Business Credit* 94(9):14-15 (October 1992).

Cistulli, Joseph P. Striking a balance between competing policies: the administrative claim as an alternative to enforce state clean-up orders in bankruptcy proceedings. *Boston College Environmental Affairs Law Review* 16(3):581-614 (Spring 1989).

Collins, Deborah. The states: federal-state relations issues hit the Supreme Court agenda. *National Civic Review* 73(11):568-571 (December 1984).

Colton, Roger D., Kathleen Uehling, and Michael F. Sheehan. Seven-cum-eleven: rolling the toxic dice in the U.S. Supreme Court. *Boston College Environmental Affairs Law Review* 14(3):345-379 (Spring 1987).

Dade County set-aside stands. *Engineering News Record* 213(15):58 (October 11, 1984).

Greene, Jan. Business gains legal ground in Court term. *Electronic News* 31(1557):10 (July 8, 1985).

Kellett, Catherine A. The future of the environmental enforcement injunction after Ohio v. Kovacs. *Boston College Environmental Affairs Law Review* 13(3):397-438 (Spring 1986).

Moskowitz, Dan, and Joseph F. Dunphy. An agenda of chemical cases goes to court. *Chemical Week* 137(15):6-7 (October 9, 1985).

The Supreme Court is narrowing its focus. *Business Week* (Industrial/Technology Edition) (2862): 40-41 (October 1, 1984).

Wein, Howard J., and James D. Morris. Emerging issues in bankruptcy and environmental law. *Environment* 27(5):4-5, 43 (June 1985).

2775. Alexander, Governor of Tennessee v. Choate   January 9, 1985
469 US 287   83 LEd2d 661   105 SCt 712
    Almanac (1985):8A-9A
    Burger Years 125-139

Handicapped need not prove intentional bias by employers or colleges, Supreme Court rules. *Chronicle of Higher Education* 29(18):25 (January 16, 1985).

2776. Tiffany Fine Arts, Inc. v. United States   January 9, 1985
469 US 310   83 LEd2d 678   105 SCt 725
    Almanac (1985):14A

2777. New Jersey v. T.L.O.   January 15, 1985
469 US 325   83 LEd2d 720   105 SCt 733
    Almanac (1985):4A
    Editorials (1984):868-871; (1985):72-81
    En Am Con 608-612, 1308
    Sup Ct Review (1989):87-163

Adams, Kathleen, and Nick Catoggio. The Supreme Court: a principal's best friend. *Time* 146(2):14 (July 10, 1995).

Aizenstein, Neal I. Supreme Court review: Fourth Amendment—searches by public school officials valid on "reasonable grounds." *Journal of Criminal Law and Criminology* 76(4):898-932 (Winter 1985).

Balton, David A. Human rights in the classroom: teaching the convention on the rights of the child. *Social Education* 56(4):210-212 (April/May 1992).

Bartlett, Larry D. Don't be in a rush to search students. *Clearing House* 59(6):252-253 (February 1986).

Bernstein, Sidney. Supreme Court review. *Trial* 21(4):14-15 (April 1985).

Bowen, Ezra, Patricia Delaney, and Timothy Loughran. Search rules: the court sets a standard. *Time* 125(4):77 (January 28, 1985).

Christopher, Maura. Decide seven Court cases that test teenagers' rights. *Scholastic Update* (Teachers' Edition) 120(1):16-18+ (September 4, 1987).

———. A sampler of the 1984-85 docket. *Scholastic Update* (Teachers' Edition) 117(7):6 (November 30, 1984).

Courtside: drug test passes Court test. *Phi Delta Kappan* 77(2):187-188 (October 1995).

Dictates of common sense. *America* 152(5):98-99 (Feburary 9, 1985).

Dripps, Donald A. Supreme Court review: Justice White and the rights of the accused. *Trial* 29(5):71-74 (May 1993).

Eskin, Leah. Do you know your rights? *Scholastic Update* 120(15):9 (April 8, 1988).

Flygare, Thomas J. De jure: High Court approves searches of students but ducks many tough issues. *Phi Delta Kappan* 66(7):504-505 (March 1985).

———. De jure: U.S. Supreme Court volunteers to decide New Jersey student search-and-seizure case. *Phi Delta Kappan* 66(4):294-295 (December 1984).

Gest, Ted. For High Court, a full plate of tough cases. *U.S. News and World Report* 97(15):52 (October 8, 1984).

Justice that panders. *Progressive* 49(3):10 (March 1985).

Lawrence, Charise K. Your Constitution: securing your rights. *Scholastic Update* 120(9):11 (January 15, 1988).

Lincoln, Eugene A. Searches and seizures in public schools: going beyond the Supreme Court's ruling in New Jersey v. T.L.O. *Journal of Negro Education* 57(1):3-10 (Winter 1988).

Meese, Edwin, III. The attorney general's view of the Supreme Court: toward a jurisprudence of original intention. *Public Administration Review* 45(Special Issue):701-704 (November 1985).

Menacker, Julius, Emanuel Hurwitz, and Ward Weldon. Supreme Court attitudes about school discipline compared to attitudes of urban teachers. *Journal of Negro Education* 58(1):92-101 (Winter 1989).

Misner, Robert L. Justifying searches on the basis of equality of treatment. *Journal of Criminal Law and Criminology* 82(3):547-578 (Fall 1991).

New student search rule will prove hard on blacks. *Jet* 67(20):37 (February 4, 1985).

Regan, Richard J. Supreme Court roundup: 1984 term. *Thought* 61(241):290-302 (June 1986).

Repa, Barbara Kate. Supreme Court docket: did the Fourth Amendment go up in smoke? Supreme Court rules on searches in schools. *Social Education* 49(20):266 (April 1985).

Repa, Barbara Kate, and Joseph L. Daly. A Supreme Court case preview. Does the Fourth Amendment belong in school? *Social Education* 49(1):76-78 (January 1985).

Rose, Jonathan. Decide 10 landmark cases that define your rights. *Scholastic Update* 119(1):7-9, 21 (September 8, 1986).

Rose, Lowell C. 'Reasonableness'—the High Court's new standard for cases involving student rights. *Phi Delta Kappan* 69(8):589-592 (April 1988).

Sendor, Benjamin. Good news: courts uphold "reasonable" searches. *American School Board Journal* 173(3):24 (March 1986).

———. A hunch is no substitute for reasonable suspicion. *American School Board Journal* 182(8):18, 47 (August 1995).

———. Learn when you may (and may not) search students. *American School Board Journal* 172(5):26 (May 1985).

———. Now you can search students' lockers, too. *American School Board Journal* 173(11):23 (November 1986).

———. Searching for guidance on student searches. *American School Board Journal* 180(2):20-21 (February 1993).

———. Student drug searches: can you risk the frisk? *American School Board Journal* 171(3):27, 54 (March 1984).

———. That heralded High Court ruling on student searches leaves crucial questions unanswered. *American School Board Journal* v172(4):24-25 (April 1985).

———. Trend: courts sustain your tough, but fair, actions. *American School Board Journal* 172(6):20-21 (June 1985).

———. Two new cases shed a little more light on searches of students and employees. *American School Board Journal* 174(8):14-15 (August 1987).

———. Will the real conservative please stand up? *American School Board Journal* 182(10):22, 44 (October 1995).

———. Wounded pride and the right to search. *American School Board Journal* 182(4):18-20 (April 1995).

———. Your frustrating student search dilemma: catching the guilty, but protecting the innocent. *American School Board Journal* 174(10):28, 47 (October 1987).

Sudo, Philip. Constitutional rights: a casualty of the drug war? *Scholastic Update* (Teachers' Edition) 122(6):17-18 (November 17, 1989).

The Supreme Court on the student's right to privacy. *Center Magazine* 18(5):23-34 (September/October 1985).

Supreme Court: the lingering liberals. *Economist* 293(7362):29-30 (October 6, 1984).

Zirkel, Perry A., and Ivan B. Gluckman. Student searches revisited—what is the proper standard? *NASSP Bulletin* 69(481):117-120 (May 1985).

2778. Evitts, Superintendent, Blackburn Correctional Complex v. Lucey   January 21, 1985
    469 US 387   83 LEd2d 821   105 SCt 830
    Almanac (1985):6A
    Brennan 203-209
    En Am Con 662

2779. Wainwright, Secretary, Florida Department of Corrections v. Witt   January 21, 1985
      469 US 412   83 LEd2d 841   105 SCt 844
         Almanac (1985):7A
         Death Penalty (Tushnet) 34-35
         Death Penalty 80s 20-22
         En Am Con 1978
      Callans, Patrick J. Supreme Court review: Sixth Amendment—assembling a jury willing to impose the death
         penalty: a new disregard for a capital defendant's right. *Journal of Criminal Law and Criminology*
         76(4):1027-1050 (Winter 1985).
      In the Supreme Court of the United States Lockhart v. McCree: Amicus Curiae Brief for the American
         Psychological Association. *American Psychologist* 42(1):59-68 (January 1987).
      Justice that panders. *Progressive* 49(3):10 (March 1985).
      Wells, Diane. Federal habeas corpus and the death penalty: a need for a return to the principles of Furman.
         Journal of Criminal Law and Criminology 80(2):427-490 (Summer 1989).

2780. Brandon v. Holt, Director of Police for the City of Memphis   January 21, 1985
      469 US 464   83 LEd2d 878   105 SCt 873
         Almanac (1985):9A-10A

2781. United States v. Johns   January 21, 1985
      469 US 478   83 LEd2d 890   105 SCt 881
         Almanac (1985):5A
         En Am Con 1019-1020
      Bobber, Bernard J. Supreme Court review: Fourth Amendment—warrantless search of packages seized from an
         automobile. *Journal of Criminal Law and Criminology* 76(4):933-954 (Winter 1985).
      Meese, Edwin, III. The attorney general's view of the Supreme Court: toward a jurisprudence of original
         intention. *Public Administration Review* 45(Special Issue):701-704 (November 1985).

2782. National Labor Relations Board (NLRB) v. Action Automotive, Inc.   February 19, 1985
      469 US 490   83 LEd2d 986   105 SCt 984
         Almanac (1985):15A
      The Supreme Court is narrowing its focus. *Business Week* (Industrial/Technology Edition) (2862): 40-41
         (October 1, 1984).

2783. United States v. Maine et al.   February 19, 1985
      469 US 504   83 LEd2d 998   105 SCt 992
         Almanac (1985):19A

2784. Garcia v. San Antonio Metropolitan Transit Authority   February 19, 1985
               Coupled with Donovan v. San Antonio Metropolitan Transit Authority
      469 US 528   83 LEd2d 1016   105 SCt 1005
         Almanac (1985):16A
         Ascent 61-63, 103-110+
         Const (Currie) 563-568
         Documents (v. 2):862-864R
         En Am Con 503-504, 680-682, 833-834
         Guide (CQ) 95, 107
         Hard Choices 319
         Sup Ct Review (1985):341-419; (1988):85-127
      American survey: nine for the seesaw. *Economist* 294(7383):21 (March 2-8, 1985).
      Bilik, Al. Union viewpoint: Amendments send the wrong message. *Journal of State Government* 63(1):8-9
         (January/March 1990).
      Collins, Deborah. The states: federal-state relations issues hit the Supreme Court agenda. *National Civic Review*
         73(11):568-571 (December 1984).

Crane, Stacey. Treasurers urge remedy: public works financing endangered. *Journal of State Government* 62(1):34-35 (January/February 1989).

Dripps, Donald A. Supreme Court review: don't make a federal case out of it. *Trial* 31(1):90-92 (January 1995).

Farber, Daniel A. Supreme Court review: the return of federalism. *Trial* 27(10):63-65 (October 1991).

Gest, Ted. For High Court, a full plate of tough cases. *U.S. News and World Report* 97(15):52 (October 8, 1984).

———. Reining in citizens' rights: Rehnquist Court will reinterpret the 200-year-old Bill of Rights. *U.S. News and World Report* 111(25):49-53 (December 16, 1991).

———. Supreme Court shows independent streak. *U.S. News and World Report* 99(3):43-44 (July 15, 1985).

Gunther, Gerald. Judicial review. *Society* 24(1):18-23 (November/December 1986).

Hawkins, Robert B., Jr. An ode to the 10th Amendment (may federalism rest in peace). [Editorial] *Governing* 1(10):74 (July 1988).

———. Linking constitutional reform to local self-governance. *Journal of State Government* 62(1):31-33 (January/February 1989).

Henry, Douglas, Jr. Liberty and sophistication. *Journal of State Government* 62(1):28-30 (January/February 1989).

Hickok, Eugene W., Jr. Federalism's future before the U.S. Supreme Court. *Annals of the American Academy of Political and Social Science* 509:73-82 (May 1990).

Howard, A. E. Dick. A historical view: federalism at the bicentennial. *Journal of State Government* 62(1):12-19 (January/February 1989).

Howard, S. Kenneth. A message from Garcia. *Public Administration Review* 45(Special Issue):738-741 (November 1985).

Johnston, Van R., and Maxine Kurtz. Handling a public policy emergency: the Fair Labor Standards Act in the public sector. *Public Administration Review* 46(5):414-422 (September/October 1986).

Kincaid, John. A proposal to strengthen federalism. *Journal of State Government* 62(1):36-45 (January/February 1989).

Lee, William P. FLPMA's legislative veto provisions and INS v. Chadha: who controls the federal lands? *Boston College Environmental Affairs Law Review* 12(4):791-821 (Summer 1985).

McDowell, Gary L. Congress and the courts. *Public Interest* (100):89-101 (Summer 1990).

Meese, Edwin, III. The attorney general's view of the Supreme Court: toward a jurisprudence of original intention. *Public Administration Review* 45(Special Issue):701-704 (November 1985).

Moskowitz, Daniel B. The Court sends mixed signals on free speech. *Business Week* (Industrial/Technology Edition) (2903):40 (July 15, 1985).

O'Brien, David M. Federalism as a metaphor in the constitutional politics of public administration. *Public Administration Review* 49(5):411-419 (September/October 1989).

Orren, Karen. The primacy of labor in American constitutional development. *American Political Science Review* 89(2):377-388 (June 1995).

Press, Aric, and Ann McDaniel. Reversing new federalism. *Newsweek* 105(9):20 (March 4, 1985).

Rapp, David. States' rights and Sandra Day O'Connor. *Governing* 6(3):59 (December 1992).

Reynolds, William Bradford. Power to the people. *New York Times Magazine* (section 6, part 1):116-122 (September 13, 1987).

Ross, Douglas. Safeguarding our federalism: lessons for the states from the Supreme Court. *Public Administration Review* 45(Special Issue):723-731 (November 1985).

Ruben, George. Labor and management continue to combat mutual problems in 1985. *Monthly Labor Review* 109(1):3-15 (January 1986).

The ruling that rocked city hall. *U.S. News and World Report* 98(8):12 (March 4, 1985).

Serrill, Michael S., David Beckwith, and Raji Samghabadi. Court flip-flop: a redefinition of states' rights. *Time* 125(9):73 (March 4, 1985).

States' rights: a landmark decision is in the making. *Business Week* (Industrial/Technology Edition) (2861):130 (September 24, 1984).

Sununu, John. The spirit of federalism: restoring the balance. *Journal of State Government* 62(1):25-27 (January/February 1989).

The Supreme Court is narrowing its focus. *Business Week* (Industrial/Technology Edition) (2862): 40-41 (October 1, 1984).

Trends in federal regulation. *Congressional Digest* 74(3):69-71 (March 1995).

Voodoo law. *National Review* 37(5):19, 21 (March 22, 1985).

What they say it is: the justices' words instruct the nation, and often address history. *Time* 130(1):44-49 (July 6, 1987).

Wise, Charles, and Rosemary O'Leary. Is federalism dead or alive in the Supreme Court?: implications for public administrators. *Public Administration Review* 52(6):559-572 (November/December 1992).

Witt, Elder. Will the Supreme Court relax the federal grip on state and local government? *Governing* 3(1):21-23, 25-29 (October 1989).

2785. Skillern v. Procunier, Director, Texas Department of Corrections   January 15, 1985
469 US 1182   83 LEd2d 956   105 SCt 945
Kaplan, David A. The tumbrels roll. [Editorial] *Nation* 240(6):165 (February 16, 1985).

2786. United States v. Young   February 20, 1985
470 US 1   84 LEd2d 1   105 SCt 1038
     Almanac (1985):6A

2787. United States v. Dann   February 20, 1985
470 US 39   84 LEd2d 28   105 SCt 1058
     Almanac (1985):18A
Orlando, Caroline L. Aboriginal title claims in the Indian Claims Commission: U.S. v. Dann and its due process limitations. *Boston College Environmental Affairs Law Review* 13(2):241-280 (Winter 1986).

2788. Shea v. Louisiana   February 20, 1985
470 US 51   84 LEd 38   105 SCt 1065
     Almanac (1985):6A

2789. Ake v. Oklahoma   February 26, 1985
470 US 68   84 LEd2d 53   105 SCt 1087
     Almanac (1985):6A-7A
     Brennan 196-199
     Death Penalty 80s 15-18
     Editorials (1985):291-293
     En Am Con 40, 1247-1249
     Thurgood 394-405R+
Bennett, Fred Warren. Toward eliminating bargain basement justice: providing indigent defendants with expert services and an adequate defense. *Law and Contemporary Problems* 58(1):95-138 (Winter 1995).

Criminal justice: son of Gideon. *Economist* 294(7384):30 (March 9-15, 1985).

Giannelli, Paul C. "Junk science": the criminal cases. *Journal of Criminal Law and Criminology* 84(1):105-128 (Spring 1993).

Harris, David A. The Constitution and truth seeking: a new theory on expert services for indigent defendants. *Journal of Criminal Law and Criminology* 83(3):469-525 (Fall 1992).

Levine, Beth. Supreme Court review: Fourteenth Amendment—due process and an indigent's right to court-appointed psychiatric assistance in state criminal proceedings. *Journal of Criminal Law and Criminology* 76(4):1065-1085 (Winter 1985).

Psychiatric help: new tools for poor defendants. *Time* 125(10):55 (March 11, 1985).

2790. United States v. Louisiana   February 26, 1985
470 US 93   84 LEd2d 73   105 SCt 1074
     Almanac (1985):19A

2791. Chemical Manufacturers Association v. Natural Resources Defense Council (NRDC)   February 27, 1985
       Coupled with Environmental Protection Agency (EPA) v. Natural Resources Defense Council
470 US 116   84 LEd2d 90   105 SCt 1102
     Almanac (1985):15A

Funk, William. The exception that approves the rule: FDF variances under the Clean Water Act. *Boston College Environmental Affairs Law Review* 13(1):1-60 (Fall 1985).

Greene, Jan. Business gains legal ground in Court term. *Electronic News* 31(1557):10 (July 8, 1985).

Hassler, Gregory L., and Karen O'Connor. Woodsy witch doctors versus judicial guerrillas: the role and impact of competing interest groups in environmental litigation. *Boston College Environmental Affairs Law Review* 13(4):487-520 (Summer 1986).

Moskowitz, Daniel B. The Court sends mixed signals on free speech. *Business Week* (Industrial/Technology Edition) (2903):40 (July 15, 1985).

The Supreme Court is narrowing its focus. *Business Week* (Industrial/Technology Edition) (2862): 40-41 (October 1, 1984).

What the High Court may decide. *Chemical Week* 131(14):10-11 (October 6, 1982).

2792. National Association for the Advancement of Colored People   February 27, 1985
     (NAACP) v. Hampton County Election Commission
     470 US 166   84 LEd2d 124   105 SCt 1128
     Almanac (1985):9A

2793. Heckler, Secretary of Health and Human Services v. Turner   February 27, 1985
     470 US 184   84 LEd2d 138   105 SCt 1138
     Almanac (1985):15A-16A

2794. Dean Witter Reynolds Inc. v. Byrd   March 4, 1985
     470 US 213   84 LEd2d 158   105 SCt 1238
     Almanac (1985):14A

Luxenberg, Stan. Who's churning whom? *Forbes* 136(16):73 (December 30, 1985).

Scheibla, Shirley Hobbs. Big decision: can you sue a broker? High Court to say. *Barron's* 67(9):16, 32-33 (March 2, 1987).

2795. County of Oneida, New York v. Oneida Indian Nation of New York State   March 5, 1985
       Coupled with New York v. Oneida Indian Nation of New York
     470 US 226   84 LEd2d 169   105 SC 1245
     Almanac (1895):18A
     Am Indians (Wilkinson) 41, 49-50, 131+

Christopher, Maura. A sampler of the 1984-85 docket. *Scholastic Update* (Teachers' Edition) 117(7):6 (November 30, 1984).

2796. Supreme Court of New Hampshire v. Piper   March 4, 1985
     470 US 274   84 LEd2d 205   105 SCt 1272
     Almanac (1985):16A
     En Am Con 1308, 1458-1461

Meese, Edwin, III. The attorney general's view of the Supreme Court: toward a jurisprudence of original intention. *Public Administration Review* 45(Special Issue):701-704 (November 1985).

Ross, Douglas. Safeguarding our federalism: lessons for the states from the Supreme Court. *Public Administration Review* 45(Special Issue):723-731 (November 1985).

2797. Oregon v. Elstad   March 4, 1985
     470 US 298   84 LEd2d 222   105 SCt 1285
     Almanac (1985):6A
     Burger Years 143-168
     En Am Con 1264-1265, 1347, 1400-1408

Gest, Ted. For High Court, a full plate of tough cases. *U.S. News and World Report* 97(15):52 (October 8, 1984).

Meese, Edwin, III. The attorney general's view of the Supreme Court: toward a jurisprudence of original intention. *Public Administration Review* 45(Special Issue):701-704 (November 1985).

Serrill, Michael S., and David Beckwith. Chip-chip-chipping away: a new exception to Miranda's "bright line."
Time 125(11):67 (March 18, 1985).

2798. Marrese v. American Academy of Orthopaedic Surgeons   March 4, 1985
470 US 373   84 LEd2d 274   105 SCt 1327
Almanac (1985):13A

2799. Air France v. Saks   March 4, 1985
470 US 392   84 LEd2d 289   105 SCt 1338
Almanac (1985):13A

2800. Herb's Welding, Inc. v. Gray   March 18, 1985
470 US 414   84 LEd2d 406   105 SCt 1421
Almanac (1985):15A

2801. National Railroad Passenger Corp. v. Atchison, Topeka & Santa Fe Railway Co. March 18, 1985
470 US 451   84 LEd2d 432   105 SCt 1441
Almanac (1985):14A

2802. Federal Elections Commission (FEC) v. National Conservative Political Action Committee   March 18, 1985
          Coupled with Democratic Party of the United States v. National Conservative Political Action
          Committee
470 US 480   84 LEd2d 455   105 SCt 1459
Almanac (1985):3A, 10A-11A
Editorials (1985):326-335
Askin, Frank. Free speech for the rich. *Nation* 251(20):728, 730 (December 10, 1990).
Gest, Ted. For High Court, a full plate of tough cases. *U.S. News and World Report* 97(15):52 (October 8,
1984).
———. Supreme Court shows independent streak. *U.S. News and World Report* 99(3):43-44 (July 15, 1985).
Oldaker, William C. Of philosophers, foxes, and finances: can the Federal Election Commission ever do an
adequate job? *Annals of the American Academy of Political and Social Science* 486:132-145 (July 1986).
Unequal speech. [Editorial] *Nation* 240(12):356-357 (March 30, 1985).
Winter, Ralph K. Political financing and the Constitution. *Annals of the Academy of Political and Social
Science* 486:34-48 (July 1986).

2803. Cleveland Board of Education v. Loudermill   March 19, 1985
470 US 532   84 LEd2d 494   105 SCt 1487
Almanac (1985):10A
Sup Ct Review (1987):157-200
Fields, Cheryl M. High Court upholds public employees' right to hearing before dismissal. *Chronicle of Higher
Education* 30(4):19 (March 27, 1985).
Ross, Douglas. Safeguarding our federalism: lessons for the states from the Supreme Court. *Public
Administration Review* 45(Special Issue):723-731 (November 1985).
Ruben, George. Developments in industrial relations: public employees entitled to respond to dismissals.
Monthly Labor Review 108(5):46 (May 1985).
Sendor, Benjamin. Now, your schools' dismissal procedures must protect the rights of all tenured employees.
American School Board Journal 172(8):15 (August 1985).
———. Your frustrating student search dilemma: catching the guilty, but protecting the innocent. *American
School Board Journal* 174(10):28, 47 (October 1987).

2804. Anderson v. City of Bessemer City, North Carolina   March 19, 1985
470 US 564   84 LEd2d 518   105 SCt 1504
Almanac (1985):9A
The Supreme Court is narrowing its focus. *Business Week* (Industrial/Technology Edition) (2862): 40-41
(October 1, 1984).

2805. First National Bank of Atlanta v. Bartow County Board of Tax Assessors   March 19, 1985
470 US 583   84 LEd2d 535   105 SCt 1516
Almanac (1985):17A

Blasi, Ronald W., and C. James Judson. Supreme Court provides guideline for taxing of federal securities by states. *Journal of Taxation* 64(1):42-45 (January 1986).

The Supreme Court is narrowing its focus. *Business Week* (Industrial/Technology Edition) (2862): 40-41 (October 1, 1984).

2806. Wayte v. United States   March 19, 1985
470 US 598   84 LEd2d 547   105 SCt 1524
Almanac (1985):11A
En Am Con 2040-2041
Religion 146-148

Christopher, Maura. A sampler of the 1984-85 docket. *Scholastic Update* (Teachers' Edition) 117(7):6 (November 30, 1984).

Gest, Ted. For High Court, a full plate of tough cases. *U.S. News and World Report* 97(15):52 (October 8, 1984).

Palmer, Stacy E. Government policy on draft resisters upheld by Court. *Chronicle of Higher Education* 30(4):19 (March 27, 1985).

Sarles, Gary D. Supreme Court review: First Amendment and equal protection—selective service or prosecution for the "vocal" nonregistrants? *Journal of Criminal Law and Criminology* 76(4):856-874 (Winter 1985).

2807. Bennett, Secretary of Education v. New Jersey   March 19, 1985
470 US 632   84 LEd2d 572   105 SCt 1555
Almanac (1985):16A

2808. Bennett, Secretary of Education v. Kentucky Department of Education   March 19, 1985
470 US 656   84 LEd2d 590   105 SCt 1544
Almanac (1985):16A

2809. United States v. Sharpe   March 20, 1985
470 US 675   84 LEd2d 605   105 SCt 1568
Almanac (1985):5A
En Am Con 1780-1782

Kulowiec, David J. Supreme Court review: Fourth Amendement—determining the reasonable length of a Terry stop. *Journal of Criminal Law and Criminology* 76(4):1003-1026 (Winter 1985).

Meese, Edwin, III. The attorney general's view of the Supreme Court: toward a jurisprudence of original intention. *Public Administration Review* 45(Special Issue):701-704 (November 1985).

2810. Florida Power & Light Co. v. Lorion, dba Center for Nuclear Responsibility   March 20, 1985
Coupled with United States Nuclear Regulatory Commission v. Lorion, dba Center for Nuclear
Responsibility
470 US 729   84 LEd2d 643   105 SCt 1598
Almanac (1985):17A

Dade County set-aside stands. *Engineering News Record* 213(15):58 (October 11, 1984).

2811. Winston, Sheriff v. Lee   March 20, 1985
470 US 753   84 LEd2d 662   105 SCt 1611
Almanac (1985):4A-5A
En Am Con 1947-1949

Christopher, Maura. A sampler of the 1984-85 docket. *Scholastic Update* (Teachers' Edition) 117(7):6 (November 30, 1984).

Gitles, Jay A. Supreme Court review: Fourth Amendment—reasonableness of surgical intrusions. *Journal of Criminal Law and Criminology* 76(4):972-985 (Winter 1985).

Mandell, Leonard Bruce, and L. Anita Richardson. Surgical search: removing a scar on the Fourth Amendment. *Journal of Criminal Law and Criminology* 75(3):525-552 (Fall 1984).

2812. Lindahl v. Office of Personnel Management (OPM) March 20, 1985
    470 US 768   84 LEd2d 674   105 SCt 1620
       Almanac (1985):17A-18A

2813. Hayes v. Florida   March 20, 1985
    470 US 811   84 LEd2d 705   105 SCt 1643
       Almanac (1985):5A

2814. Heckler, Secretary of Health and Human Services v. Chaney   March 20, 1985
    470 US 821   84 LEd2d 714   105 SCt 1649
       Almanac (1985):17A
       Burger Years 191-205

2815. Ball v. United States   March 26, 1985
    470 US 856   84 LEd2d 740   105 SCt 1668
       Almanac (1985):8A

2816. Metropolitan Life Insurance Co. v. Ward   March 26, 1985
    470 US 869   84 LEd2d 715   105 SCt 1676
       Almanac (1985):17A
       En Am Con 1251
Hellerstein, Walter, and Ruurd Leegstra. Supreme Court in Metropolitan Life strikes down discriminatory state insurance tax. *Journal of Taxation* 63(2):108-111 (August 1985).
Insurance: national insurance companies win major tax victory in Alabama. *Journal of Accountancy* 159(6):28 (June 1985).
Meese, Edwin, III. The attorney general's view of the Supreme Court: toward a jurisprudence of original intention. *Public Administration Review* 45(Special Issue):701-704 (November 1985).
Merkel, Philip L. Going national: the life insurance industry's campaign for federal regulation after the Civil War. *Business History Review* 65(3):528-553 (Autumn 1991).
Supreme Court overturns Alabama premium tax law. *Best's Review* (Life/Health Insurance Edition) 85(12):6 (April 1985).

2817. Board of Education of Oklahoma City v. National Gay Task Force   March 26, 1985
    470 US 903   84 LEd2d 776   105 SCt 1858
       Almanac (1985):11A
Press, Aric, and Ann McDaniel. The afterhours question. *Newsweek* 105(3):68 (January 21, 1985).
Serrill, Michael S., and David Beckwith. An illness ties up the justices: the second oldest Court shows the first signs of age. *Time* 125(14):59 (April 8, 1985).
The Supreme Court rules on deadly force. *Newsweek* 105(14):87 (April 8, 1985).

2818. Fugate v. New Mexico   March 26, 1985
    470 US 904   84 LEd2d 777   105 SCt 1858
       Almanac (1985):6A

2819. Tennessee v. Garner   March 27, 1985
       Coupled with Memphis Police Department v. Garner
    471 US 1   85 LEd2d 1   105 SCt 1694
       Almanac (1985):4A-5A
       En Am Con 1874
Court to police: "Cease fire!" *U.S. News and World Report* 98(13):13 (April 8, 1985).
Deadly force. *America* 152(14):294 (April 13, 1985).

Gest, Ted. For High Court, a full plate of tough cases. *U.S. News and World Report* 97(15):52 (October 8, 1984).

Press, Aric, and Ann McDaniels. Open on stage right. *Newsweek* 104(15):75-76 (October 8, 1984).

Regan, Richard J. Supreme Court roundup: 1984 term. *Thought* 61(241):290-302 (June 1986).

The Supreme Court rules on deadly force. *Newsweek* 105(14):87 (April 8, 1985).

Tennenbaum, Abraham N. The influence of the Garner decision on police use of deadly force. *Journal of Criminal Law and Criminology* 85(4):241-260 (Summer 1994).

2820. Town of Hallie v. City of Eau Claire   March 27, 1985
    471 US 34   85 LEd2d 24   105 SCt 1713
    Almanac (1985):13A

Chapple, Stephan. Community Communications v. City of Boulder: an intergovernmental paradox. *Public Administration Review* 45(Special Issue):732-737 (November 1985).

Dade County set-aside stands. *Engineering News Record* 213(15):58 (October 11, 1984).

Fletcher, Meg. High Court bucks precedent in municipal antitrust ruling. *Business Insurance* 19(41):15 (October 14, 1985).

Meese, Edwin, III. The attorney general's view of the Supreme Court: toward a jurisprudence of original intention. *Public Administration Review* 45(Special Issue):701-704 (November 1985).

Roberts, Robert N. Municipal antitrust immunity and the state-action exemption: developments in the law. *State Government* 58(4):164-171 (Winter 1986).

Ross, Douglas. Safeguarding our federalism: lessons for the states from the Supreme Court. *Public Administration Review* 45(Special Issue):723-731 (November 1985).

2821. Southern Motor Carriers Rate Conference, Inc. v. United States   March 27, 1985
    471 US 48   85 LEd2d 36   105 SCt 1721
    Almanac (1985):13A

Chapple, Stephan. Community Communications v. City of Boulder: an intergovernmental paradox. *Public Administration Review* 45(Special Issue):732-737 (November 1985).

Meese, Edwin, III. The attorney general's view of the Supreme Court: toward a jurisprudence of original intention. *Public Administration Review* 45(Special Issue):701-704 (November 1985).

Ross, Douglas. Safeguarding our federalism: lessons for the states from the Supreme Court. *Public Administration Review* 45(Special Issue):723-731 (November 1985).

2822. Cory v. Western Oil & Gas Assn.   March 27, 1985
    471 US 81   85 LEd2d 061   105 SCt 1859
    Almanac (1985):17A

2823. Spencer et ux. v. South Carolina Tax Commission   March 27, 1985
    471 US 82   85 LEd2d 62   105 SCt 1859
    Almanac (1985):16A

2824. Board of Trustees of the Village of Scarsdale v. McCreary   March 27, 1985
    471 US 83   85 LEd2d 063   105 SCt 1859
    Almanac (1985):12A
    Establishment 156-157, 177-179

Christopher, Maura. A sampler of the 1984-85 docket. *Scholastic Update* (Teachers' Edition) 117(7):6 (November 30, 1984).

Confusion in the Court. *America* 152(24):501 (June 22-29, 1985).

Drinan, Robert F. Do creches violate the Constitution? *America* 159(16):428-429 (November 26, 1988).

———. Is a Christmas creche legal in 1986? [Editorial] *America* 155(18):375-376 (December 13, 1986).

———. The Supreme Court and Scarsdale's creche. *America* 151(18):377-380 (December 8, 1984).

Ericsson, Samuel. The Supreme Court's changing stance on religious freedom. *Christianity Today* 29(7):38-41 (April 19, 1985).

The great creche fizzle. *America* 152(14):293 (April 13, 1985).

Kilpatrick, James J. A tangled separation. [Editorial] *Nation's Business* 73(11):5 (November 1985).

Press, Aric, and Ann McDaniel. The Lord's day in Court. *Newsweek* 104(26):57 (December 17, 1984).

————. A Reagan Court? *Newsweek* 106(3):69-71 (July 15, 1985).

Serrill, Michael S., and David Beckwith. An illness ties up the justices: the second oldest Court shows the first signs of age. *Time* 125(14):59 (April 8, 1985).

The Supreme Court rules on deadly force. *Newsweek* 105(14):87 (April 8, 1985).

Supreme Court upholds appeals court ruling allowing creche on public land. *Christianity Today* 29(7):67 (April 19, 1985).

2825. United States v. Locke   April 1, 1985
     471 US 84   85 LEd2d 64   105 SCt 1785
       Almanac (1985):15A

Hassler, Gregory L., and Karen O'Connor. Woodsy witchdoctors versus judicial guerrillas: the role and impact of competing interest groups in environmental litigation. *Boston College Environmental Affairs Law Review* 13(4):487-520 (Summer 1986).

2826. United States v. Miller   April 1, 1985
     471 US 130   85 LEd2d 99   105 SCt 1811
       Almanac (1985):6A

2827. Oklahoma v. Castleberry   April 1, 1985
     471 US 146   85 LEd2d 112   105 SCt 1859
       Almanac (1985):5A

2828. Ramirez v. Indiana   April 1, 1985
     471 US 147   85 LEd2d 113   105 SCt 1860
       Almanac (1985):8A

2829. Central Intelligence Agency (CIA) v. Sims   April 16, 1985
     471 US 159   85 LEd2d 173   105 SCt 1881
       Almanac (1985):19A
       Burger Years 191-205

Mackenzie, Angus. Welcome reversal. *Nation* 240(16):485 (April 27, 1985).

Palmer, Stacy E. Supreme Court upholds CIA's authority to withhold data from public. *Chronicle of Higher Education* 30(8):21 (April 24, 1985).

A setback to the public's right to know. *Editor and Publisher* 118(16):9 (April 20, 1985).

Smith, R. Jeffrey. Court gives CIA broad secrecy rights. *Science* 228(4699):566 (May 3, 1985).

2830. Kerr-McGee Corp. v. Navajo Tribe of Indians   April 16, 1985
     471 US 195   85 LEd2d 200   105 SC 1900
       Almanac (1985):18A
       Am Indians (Wilkinson) 68, 114-115, 131

Allen, Mark. Native American control of tribal natural resource development in the context of the federal trust and tribal self-determination. *Boston College Environmental Affairs Law Review* 16(4):857-895 (Summer 1989).

Neumann, Rita. Taxation of natural resource production on tribal lands. *Taxes* 63(11):813-819 (November 1985).

2831. Allis-Chalmers Corp. v. Lueck   April 16, 1985
     471 US 202   85 LEd2d 206   105 SCt 1904
       Almanac (1985):15A
       Burger Years 228-239

Fed law governs labor suit. *Engineering News Record* 214(18):50 (May 2, 1985).

2832. Hunter v. Underwood   April 16, 1985
     471 US 222   85 LEd2d 222   105 SCt 1916

Almanac (1985):9A

2833. Webb v. County Board of Education of Dyer County, Tennessee   April 17, 1985
      471 US 234   85 LEd2d 233   105 SCt 1923
      Almanac (1985):9A

2834. Wilson v. Garcia   April 17, 1985
      471 US 261   85 LEd2d 254   105 SCt 1938
      Almanac (1985):10A

2835. Springfield Township School District v. Knoll   April 17, 1985
      471 US 288   85 LEd2d 275   105 SCt 2065
      Almanac (1985):10A

2836. Tony and Susan Alamo Foundation v. Secretary of Labor   April 23, 1985
      471 US 290   85 LEd2d 278   105 SCt 1953
      Almanac (1985):12A

      Ericsson, Samuel. The Supreme Court's changing stance on religious freedom. *Christianity Today* 29(7):38-41
          (April 19, 1985).
      McConnell, Michael. Why 'separation' is not the key to church-state relations. *Christian Century* 106(2):43-47
          (January 18, 1989).
      Regan, Richard J. Supreme Court roundup: 1984 term. *Thought* 61(241):290-302 (June 1986).
      "Vexing to my soul." *America* 152(18):381 (May 11, 1985).
      Wages and religion. *Christian Century* 102(16):464 (May 8, 1985).

2837. Francis, Warden v. Franklin   April 29, 1985
      471 US 307   85 LEd2d 344   105 SCt 1965
      Almanac (1985):7A

      Harris, Leslie J. Constitutional limits on criminal presumptions as an expression of changing concepts of
          fundamental fairness. *Journal of Criminal Law and Criminology* 77(2):308-357 (Summer 1986).

2838. Commodity Futures Trading Commission v. Weintraub   April 29, 1985
      471 US 343   85 LEd2d 372   105 SCt 1986
      Almanac (1985):13A-14A

2839. School Committee of the Town of Burlington, Massachusetts   April 29, 1985
          v. Department of Education of Massachusetts
      471 US 359   85 LEd2d 385   105 SCt 1996
      Almanac (1985):9A

2840. California v. Carney   May 13, 1985
      471 US 386   85 LEd2d 406   105 SCt 2066
      Almanac (1985):5A

      Meese, Edwin, III. The attorney general's view of the Supreme Court: toward a jurisprudence of original
          intention. *Public Administration Review* 45(Special Issue):701-704 (November 1985).
      Mobile castle. [Editorial] *Nation* 240(20):612 (May 25, 1985).
      Mobile homes: new rules of the road. *Newsweek* 105(21):89 (May 27, 1985).
      Nugent, Shane V. Supreme Court review: Fourth Amendment—function over form: the automobile exception
          applied to motor homes. *Journal of Criminal Law and Criminology* 76(4):955-971 (Winter 1985).
      Regan, Richard J. Supreme Court roundup: 1984 term. *Thought* 61(241):290-302 (June 1986).

2841. Tennessee v. Street   May 13, 1985
      471 US 409   85 LEd2d 425   105 SCt 2078
      Almanac (1985):7A

2842. Liparota v. United States   May 13, 1985
    471 US 419   85 LEd2d 434   105 SCt 2084
      Almanac (1985):8A

Goldberg, Andrew M. Corporate officer liability for federal environmental statute violations. *Boston College Environmental Affairs Law Review* 18(2):357-379 (Winter 1991).

Webber, Rebecca S. Element analysis applied to environmental crimes: what did they know and when did they know it? *Boston College Environmental Affairs Law Review* 16(1):53-93 (Fall 1988).

2843. Immigration and Naturalization Service (INS) v. Rios-Pineda   May 13, 1985
    471 US 444   85 LEd2d 452   105 SCt 2098
      Almanac (1985):9A

2844. Burger King Corp. v. Rudzewicz   May 20, 1985
    471 US 462   85 LEd2d 528   105 SCt 2174
      Almanac (1985):18A
      Sup Ct Review (1989):223-259

O'Connell, Daniel. U.S. Supreme Court reviews state and local taxation issues. *CPA Journal* 62(3):16-21 (March 1992).

2845. Ponte, Superintendent, Massachusetts Correctional Institution v. Real   May 20, 1985
    471 US 491   85 LEd2d 553   105 SCt 2192
      Almanac (1985):10A

2846. Connecticut Department of Income Maintenance v. Heckler,   May 20, 1985
    Secretary of Health and Human Services
    471 US 524   85 LEd2d 577   105 SCt 2210
      Almanac (1985):16A

2847. Harper & Row, Publishers, Inc., v. Nation Enterprises   May 20, 1985
    471 US 539   85 LEd2d 588   105 SCt 2218
      Almanac (1985):3A, 11A-12A

AAP joins Harper & Row in Nation case. *Publishers' Weekly* 226(5):17 (August 3, 1984).

All the news that's fit to copyright. *Newsweek* 105(22):81 (June 3, 1985).

Copyright is now truly a grave issue. *U.S. News and World Report* 108(9):15 (March 5, 1990).

Fields, Howard. High Court hears Nation case arguments. *Publishers' Weekly* 226(21):15-16 (November 23, 1984).

————. High Court, 6-3, sustains Ford memoir copyright. *Publishers' Weekly* 227(22):17 (May 31, 1985).

————. High Court to hear H & R-Nation case. *Publishers' Weekly* 225(24):26 (June 15, 1984).

Freedom to read? [Editorial] *Nation* 237(2):36-37 (July 9-16, 1983).

Gest, Ted. For High Court, a full plate of tough cases. *U.S. News and World Report* 97(15):52 (October 8, 1984).

Knoll, Erwin. A profit without honor. [Editorial] *Progressive* 49(7):4 (July 1985).

Litman, Jessica. Copyright and information policy. *Law and Contemporary Problems* 55(2):185-209 (Spring 1992).

Monopolizing the news. [Editorial] *Nation* 240(21):657 (June 1, 1985).

Reviewing the Nation case. *Nation* 238(22):693 (June 9, 1984).

Roper, James E. A copyright infringement. *Editor and Publisher* 118(21):9, 61 (May 25, 1985).

Serrill, Michael S., and David Beckwith. When a scoop is "piracy": the Supreme Court balances copyright against press rights. *Time* 125(22):64 (June 3, 1985).

Supreme Court holds 'The Nation' violated copyright laws in printing Ford excerpts. *Chronicle of Higher Education* 30(13):21 (May 29, 1985).

2848. Black, Director, Missouri Department of Corrections and Human Resources v. Romano   May 20, 1985
    471 US 606   85 LEd2d 636   105 SCt 2254
      Almanac (1985):7A

2849. Zauderer v. Office of Disciplinary Counsel of the Supreme Court of Ohio   May 28, 1985
    471 US 626   85 LEd2d 652   105 SCt 2265
    Almanac (1985):11A

Bowen, Lauren. Attorney advertising in the wake of Bates v. State Bar of Arizona (1977): a study of judicial impact. *American Politics Quarterly* 23(4):461-484 (October 1995).

Colford, Steven W. High Court backs lawyer on ads' art, pitch. *Advertising Age* 56(43):12 (June 3, 1985).

———. Lawyer ads on High Court docket. *Advertising Age* 55(80):58 (November 26, 1984).

Meyers, Janet. Direct-mail win: Court ruling good sign for ad industry. *Advertising Age* 59(26):99 (June 20, 1988).

Moskowitz, Daniel B. The Court sends mixed signals on free speech. *Business Week* (Industrial/Technology Edition) (2903):40 (July 15 1985).

———. Lawyers learn the hard sell—and companies shudder. *Business Week* (Industrial/Technology Edition) (2898):70-71 (June 10, 1985).

Reed, O. Lee. Reading the tea leaves: future regulation of product-extrinsic advertising. *Business Horizons* 33(5):88-93 (September/October 1990).

Serrill, Michael S., and Cathy Booth. Less dignity, more hustle: lawyers ads get a boost from high tech. *Time* 125(23):66-67 (June 10, 1985).

2850. Landreth Timber Co. v. Landreth   May 28, 1985
    471 US 681   85 LEd2d 692   105 SCt 2297
    Almanac (1985):14A
    Sup Ct Review (1995):99-124

Moskowitz, Daniel B. The Court sends mixed signals on free speech. *Business Week* (Industrial/Technology Edition) (2903):40 (July 15 1985).

Moskowitz, Daniel B., and William B. Glaberson. The not-so-long arm of federal securities law. *Business Week* (Industrial/Technology Edition) (2876):138 (January 14, 1985).

Quinlivan, Stephen M. What every accountant should know about securities law. *Journal of Accountancy* 174(1):109-112 (July 1992).

2851. Hillsborough County, Florida v. Automated Medical Laboratories, Inc.   June 3, 1985
    471 US 707   85 LEd2d 714   105 SCt 2371
    Almanac (1985):16A

Rutrick, Elena S. Local pesticide regulation since Wisconsin Public Intervenor v. Mortier. *Boston College Environmental Affairs Law Review* 20(1):65-97 (Fall 1992).

2852. Metropolitan Life Insurance Co. v. Massachusetts   June 3, 1985
      Coupled with Travelers Insurance Co. v. Massachusetts
    471 US 724   85 LEd2d 728   105 SCt 2380
    Almanac (1985):16A

Geisel, Jerry. State can mandate benefits offered by health insurers. *Business Insurance* 19(23):1, 4 (June 10, 1985).

Locke, Adrienne C. National health plan debated. *Business Insurance* 23(43):21 (October 23, 1989).

Moskowitz, Daniel B. The Court sends mixed signals on free speech. *Business Week* (Industrial/Technology Edition) (2903):40 (July 15 1985).

———. Health benefits: now states call the shots. *Business Week* (Industrial/Technology Edition) (2899):39-40 (June 17, 1985).

Ruben, George. Developments in industrial relations: Court rules on employee-sponsored health plans. *Monthly Labor Review* 108(8):51 (August 1985).

States can dictate benefits. *Engineering News Record* 214(24):56-57 (June 13, 1985).

States can require certain coverages, High Court says. *Best's Review* (Life/Health Insurance Edition) 86(2):5 (June 1985).

Supreme Court rules states can mandate benefits. *Business Insurance* 19(52):12-13 (December 30, 1985).

Tarnoff, Stephen. Court decisions or benefits increase employers' costs. *Business Insurance* 21(44):93-95 (November 2, 1987).

2853. Montana v. Blackfeet Tribe of Indians June 3, 1985
    471 US 759   85 LEd2d 753   105 SCt 2399
      Almanac (1985):18A
      Am Indians (Wilkinson) 50, 131, 203

2854. Garrett v. United States June 3, 1985
    471 US 773   85 LEd2d 764   105 SCt 2407
      Almanac (1985):6A

2855. City of Oklahoma City v. Tuttle June 3, 1985
    471 US 808   85 LEd2d 791   105 SCt 2427
      Almanac (1985):10A
  Meese, Edwin, III. The attorney general's view of the Supreme Court: toward a jurisprudence of original intention. *Public Administration Review* 45(Special Issue):701-704 (November 1985).

2856. National Farmers Union Insurance Cos. v. Crow Tribe of Indians June 3, 1985
    471 US 845   85 LEd2d 818   105 SCt 2447
      Almanac (1985):18A
      Am Indians (Wilkinson) 114, 116, 132+

2857. Russell v. United States June 3, 1985
    471 US 858   85 LEd2d 829   105 SCt 2455
      Almanac (1985):8A

2858. Schreiber v. Burlington Northern, Inc. June 4, 1985
    472 US 1   86 LEd2d 1   105 SCt 2458
      Almanac (1985):14A
  Jereski, Laura. Empty gesture. *Forbes* 136(12):66 (November 4, 1985).

2859. Williams v. Vermont June 4, 1985
    472 US 14   86 LEd2d 11   105 SCt 2465
      Almanac (1985):17A
      En Am Con 2066

2860. George C. Wallace, Governor of Alabama v. Jaffree June 4, 1985
        Coupled with Smith v. Jaffree
    472 US 38   86 LEd2d 29   105 SCt 2479
      Almanac (1984):247, 496; (1985):3A,12A
      Ascent 200-202
      Brennan 123-125, 129-134
      Burger Years 56-91
      Const (Currie) 535-538
      Const Law 87-89R
      Courage 355-378, 429
      Court Const 206-210
      Editorials (1985):650-661; (1994):1428-1433
      En Am Con 1537-1538, 1650-1658, 2006
      Establishment 154-156+
      Godless 90-91+
      Let Us 124-126
      New Right (Schwartz) 25-34
      Original (Davis) 98, 114-117, 145-146+
      Sup Ct Church 230-255R
      Sup Ct Review (1985):1-59; (1995):323-391
  Abram, Morris B. Is "strict separation" too strict? *Public Interest* (82):81-90 (Winter 1986).

Arledge, Paula C., and Edward V. Heck. A freshman justice confronts the Constitution: Justice O'Connor and the First Amendment. *Western Political Quarterly* 45(3):761-772 (September 1992).

Card, Robert L. Church-state relations: where is the Supreme Court going? *Vital Speeches* 51(24):752-755 (October 1, 1985).

Carter, Stephen L. Let us pray. *New Yorker* 70(40):60-74 (December 5, 1994).

Christopher, Maura. A sampler of the 1984-85 docket. *Scholastic Update* (Teachers' Edition) 117(7):6 (November 30, 1984).

Confusion in the Court. *America* 152(24):501 (June 22-29, 1985).

Cord, Robert L. Church, state, and the Rehnquist Court. *National Review* 44(16):35-37 (August 17, 1992).

————. Correcting the record. *National Review* 38(6):42 (April 11, 1986).

Doerr, Edd. Victories . . . and warnings. *Humanist* 45(5):39-40 (September/October 1985).

Drakeman, Donald L. The new Court and church-state issues. [Editorial] *Christian Century* 103(21):607-608 (July 2-9, 1986).

————. New ruling on school prayer. [Editorial] *Christian Century* 102(21):604-605 (June 19-26, 1985).

Drinan, Robert F. Those moments of silence. *America* 151(9):184-186 (October 6, 1984).

Ericsson, Samuel. The Supreme Court's changing stance on religious freedom. *Christianity Today* 29(7):38-41 (April 19, 1985).

Flygare, Thomas J. De jure: Supreme Court reinforces the 'wall of separation.' *Phi Delta Kappan* 67(2):157-158 (October 1985).

Gaffney, Edward McGlynn, Jr. Prayer at commencement. *Christian Century* 110(18):590-591 (June 2-9, 1993).

Gest, Ted. For High Court, a full plate of tough cases. *U.S. News and World Report* 97(15):52 (October 8, 1984).

————. Supreme Court shows independent streak. *U.S. News and World Report* 99(3):43-44 (July 15, 1985).

————. What High Court heard about school prayer. *U.S. News and World Report* 97(25):71 (December 17, 1984).

Glazer, Nathan. Church-state bargain. *New Republic* 193(17):16-18 (October 21, 1985).

Kilpatrick, James J. What in God's name is going on? *National Review* 37(2):36, 38-39 (February 8, 1985).

Leviton, Joyce. A former child evangelist wins a Supreme Court fight against prayer in public schools. *People Weekly* 23(25):36-38 (June 24, 1985).

Lukoff, Roger M. Constitutional scholars appraise Supreme Court. *Trial* 20(11):65-66, 68 (November 1984).

Meese, Edwin, III. The attorney general's view of the Supreme Court: toward a jurisprudence of original intention. *Public Administration Review* 45(Special Issue):701-704 (November 1985).

Ostling, Richard, Anne Constable, and Michael P. Harris. Threatening the wall: church-state separation has powerful new critics. *Time* 130(1):70-71 (July 6, 1987).

Pfeffer, Leo. How religious is secular humanism? *Humanist* 48(5):13-18, 50 (September/October 1988).

Prayer in public schools. *Congressional Digest* 74(1):3-32 (January 1995).

Prayer in the schools. *Newsweek* 105(24):28 (June 17, 1985).

Press, Aric, and Ann McDaniel. Intent of the framers. *Newsweek* 106(18):97-98 (October 28, 1985).

————. The Lord's day in Court. *Newsweek* 104(26):57 (December 17, 1984).

————. Open on stage right. *Newsweek* 104(15):75-76 (October 8, 1984).

————. A Reagan Court? *Newsweek* 106(3):69-71 (July 15, 1985).

Rabinove, Samuel, Josef Joffe, Sheldon F. Gottlieb, Adam Simms, Stephen F. Rohde, Jeffrey Valle, and Robert H. Bork. The First Amendment. [Editorial] *Commentary* 99(5):7-15 (May 1995).

Regan, Richard J. Supreme Court roundup: 1984 term. *Thought* 61(241):290-302 (June 1986).

————. Supreme Court roundup: 1986 term. *Thought* 63(251):429-441 (December 1988).

Religious leaders support High Court prayer ruling. *Jet* 68(14)13 (June 24, 1985).

School prayer's bad day in court. *U.S. News and World Report* 98(23):9 (June 17, 1985).

Sendor, Benjamin. Heaven only knows what's next on school prayer. *American School Board Journal* 172(9):20 (Sepember 1985).

Serrill, Michael S., and Anne Constable. Uproar over silence: the Court again stirs the school-prayer debate. *Time* 125(24):52 (June 17, 1985).

Silent prayer. *Christian Century* 101(13):394 (April 18, 1984).

Spring, Beth. Can states allow prayer in public schools when some citizens believe it is wrong? *Christianity Today* 29(1):55-57 (January 18, 1985).

————. Supreme Court will rule on moment-of-silence law. *Christianity Today* 31(5):56-58 (March 20, 1987).

————. U.S. Supreme Court nullifies Alabama school prayer law. *Christianity Today* 29(10):52 (July 12, 1985).

Stephenson, D. Grier, Jr. Religion and the Constitution: the Supreme Court speaks, again. *USA Today* 118(2538):21-23 (March 1990).

Supreme Court: the lingering liberals. *Economist* 2937362):29-30 (October 6, 1984).

Supreme Court: twixt church and state. *Economist* 296(7401):29-30 (July 6, 1985).

Tushnet, Mark. The Constitution of religion. *Review of Politics* 50(4):628-658 (Fall 1988).

U.S. Senate votes against Helms's school prayer measure. *Christianity Today* 29(15):44-45 (October 18, 1985).

Woodward, Kenneth L., and Nadine Joseph. The return of the fourth R. *Newsweek* 117(23):56-57 (June 10, 1991).

Zirkel, Perry A. A hypothetical case in the public schools. *Clearing House* 57(8)346-347 (April 1984).

2861. Atkins, Commissioner of the Massachusetts Department of Public Welfare v. Parker   June 4, 1985
            Coupled with Parker v. Block
      472 US 115   86 LEd2d 81   105 SCt 2520
          Almanac (1985):10A

2862. Northeast Bancorp, Inc. v. Board of Governors of the Federal Reserve System   June 10, 1985
      472 US 159   86 LEd2d 112   105 SCt 2545
          Almanac (1985):13A
          Editorials (1985):662-665
          Sup Ct Review (1985):179-225
      American banks: stopped on the interstate. *Economist* 295(7398):92 (June 15-21, 1985).

Gest, Ted. Supreme Court shows independent streak. *U.S. News and World Report* 99(3):43-44 (July 15, 1985).

Moskowitz, Daniel B. The Court sends mixed signals on free speech. *Business Week* (Industrial/Technology Edition) (2903):40 (July 15 1985).

Much, Marilyn. The road to nationwide banking. *Industry Week* 226(4):43-46 (August 19, 1985).

Scherschel, Patricia M. Green light is on for regional banks. *U.S. News and World Report* 98(24):50 (June 24, 1985).

Toufexis, Anastasia, Christopher Redman, and Frederick Ungeheuer. Muscling up to the big guys: the Supreme Court boosts regional banks. *Time* 125(25):59 (June 24, 1985).

Wallace, David, Blanc Riemer, and Lois Therrien. Nationwide banking: a welcome mat—not a slammed door. *Business Week* (Industrial/Technology Edition): 90-91 (June 24, 1985).

2863. Lowe v. Securities and Exchange Commission (SEC)   June 10, 1985
      472 US 181   86 LEd2d 130   105 SCt 2557
          Almanac (1985):11A
          En Am Con 1641-1642
          Sup Ct Review (1985):93-148
      Cox, James D. Insider trading: regulation of activity is 'in trouble.' *Trial* 24(9):22-28, 93-96 (September 1988).

Does the First Amendment protect investor tip sheets? *Business Week* (Industrial/Technology Edition) (2868):65, 68 (November 12, 1984).

Fields, Howard. AAP files amicus brief against SEC. *Publishers' Weekly* 226(23):18 (December 7, 1984).

————. Supreme Court roundup. *Publishers' Weekly* 228(3):14 (July 19, 1985).

Moskowitz, Daniel B. The Court sends mixed signals on free speech. *Business Week* (Industrial/Technology Edition) (2903):40 (July 15 1985).

Roper, James E. High Court: ex-investment advisor can publish newsletter. *Editor and Publisher* 118(24):11 (June 15, 1985).

Tip tiff: newsletters vs. the SEC. *Time* 125(3):51 (January 21, 1985).

2864. Mountain States Telephone and Telegraph Co. v. Pueblo of Santa Ana   June 10, 1985
      472 US 237   86 LEd2d 168   105 SCt 2587
          Almanac (1985):18A

2865. Northwest Wholesale Stationers, Inc. v. Pacific Stationery & Printing Co.   June 11, 19
          472 US 284   86 LEd2d 202   105 SCt 2613
          Almanac (1985):13A

2866. Bateman Eichler, Hill Richards, Inc. v. Berner   June 11, 1985
          472 US 299   86 LEd2d 215   105 SCt 2622
          Almanac (1985):14A
       Glaberson, William B. Insider trading: a widening net catches the small fry. *Business Week*
          (Industrial/Technology Edition) (2880):60-61 (February 11, 1985).

2867. Caldwell v. Mississippi   June 11, 1985
          472 US 320   86 LEd2d 231   105 SCt 2633
          Almanac (1985):7A
          Death Penalty 80s 9-12, 15-18, 20-22, 90-98
          Death Penalty 90s 112-114, 117-121, 129-130
       Bennett, Fred Warren. Toward eliminating bargain basement justice: providing indigent defendants with expert
          services and an adequate defense. *Law and Contemporary Problems* 58(1):95-138 (Winter 1995).
       Gest, Ted. Supreme Court shows independent streak. *U.S. News and World Report* 99(3):43-44 (July 15, 1985).
       A jury's burden: taking death seriously. *Time* 125(25):64 (June 24, 1985).
       Schultz, Michael L. Supreme Court review: Eighth Amendment—references to appellate review in capital
          sentencing determinations. *Journal of Criminal Law and Criminology* 76(4):1051-1064 (Winter 1985).

2868. Johnson v. Mayor and City Council of Baltimore   June 17, 1985
             Coupled with Equal Employment Opportunity Commission (EEOC) v. Mayor and City Council of
             Baltimore
          472 US 353   86 LEd2d 286   105 SCt 2717
          Almanac (1985):4A, 8A
       Serrill, Michael S., and Anne Constable. Cockpit gray: a broad ruling on age bias. *Time* 125(26):45 (July 1,
          1985).

2869. Baldwin v. Alabama   June 17, 1985
          472 US 372   86 LEd2d 300   105 SCt 2727
          Almanac (1985):7A

2870. Western Air Lines, Inc. v. Criswell   June 17, 1985
          472 US 400   86 LEd2d 321   105 SCt 2743
          Almanac (1985):4A,8A
       Moskowitz, Daniel B. The Court sends mixed signals on free speech. *Business Week* (Industrial/Technology
          Edition) (2903):40 (July 15, 1985).
       Murphy, Betty Southard, Wayne E. Barlow, and D. Diane Hatch. Supreme Court restricts blanket retirement.
          Personnel Journal 65(1):26, 28 (January 1986).
       Ruben, George. Developments in industrial relations: Court rules on mandatory retirement in airlines. *Monthly
          Labor Review* 108(8):51 (August 1985).
       Serrill, Michael S., and Anne Constable. Cockpit gray: a broad ruling on age bias. *Time* 125(26):45 (July 1,
          1985).

2871. Richardson-Merrell, Inc. v. Koller, an infant, by and through Koller et ux.,   June 17, 1985
          her natural guardians
          472 US 424   86 LEd2d 340   105 SCt 2757
          Almanac (1985):18A

2872. Superintendent, Massachusetts Correctional Institution at Walpole v. Hill   June 17, 1985
          472 US 445   86 LEd2d 356   105 SCt 2768
          Almanac (1985):10A

2873. Maryland v. Macon   June 17, 1985
      472 US 463   86 LEd2d 370   105 SCt 2778
           Almanac (1985):5A

      Fields, Howard. Supreme Court roundup. *Publishers' Weekly* 228(3):14 (July 19, 1985).

      Giampietro, Nicholas L. Supreme Court review: First and Fourth Amendments—obscenity and police
           purchases: a purchase is a purchase is a seizure? *Journal of Criminal Law and Criminology* 76(4):875-897
           (Winter 1985).

      Supreme Court: the lingering liberals. *Economist* 2937362):29-30 (October 6, 1984).

2874. Jensen, Director, Department of Motor Vehicles of Nebraska v. Quaring   June 17, 1985
      472 US 478   86 LEd2d 383   105 SCt 3492
           Almanac (1985):12A

      Christopher, Maura. A sampler of the 1984-85 docket. *Scholastic Update* (Teachers' Edition) 117(7):6
           (November 30, 1984).

      Confusion in the Court. *America* 152(24):501 (June 22-29, 1985).

      Drinan, Robert F. The Supreme Court and religious freedom. *America* 152(12):254-255 (March 30, 1985).

      Ericsson, Samuel. The Supreme Court's changing stance on religious freedom. *Christianity Today* 29(7):38-41
           (April 19, 1985).

      Kilpatrick, James J. A tangled separation. [Editorial] *Nation's Business* 73(11):5 (November 1985).

      Press, Aric, and Ann McDaniel. The Lord's day in Court. *Newsweek* 104(26):57 (December 17, 1984).

2875. McDonald v. Smith   June 19, 1985
      472 US 479   86 LEd2d 384   105 SCt 2787
           Almanac (1985):12A

2876. Brockett v. Spokane Arcades, Inc.   June 19, 1985
      472 US 491   86 LEd2d 394   105 SCt 2794
           Almanac (1985):13A
           En Am Con 159, 1352-1354

      Fields, Howard. High Court to hear challenge to Miller. *Publishers' Weekly* 230(17):15 (October 24, 1986).

      ———. Supreme Court may redefine obscenity. *Publishers' Weekly* 227(10):37-38 (March 8, 1985).

      ———. Supreme Court roundup. *Publishers' Weekly* 228(3):14 (July 19, 1985).

      Gest, Ted. Supreme Court shows independent streak. *U.S. News and World Report* 99(3):43-44 (July 15, 1985).

      Serrill, Michael S., and Anne Constable. Cockpit gray: a broad ruling on age bias. *Time* 125(26):45 (July 1,
           1985).

      Supreme Court: the lingering liberals. *Economist* 293(7362):29-30 (October 6, 1984).

2877. Mitchell v. Forsyth   June 19, 1985
      472 US 511   86 LEd2d 411   105 SCt 2806
           Almanac (1985):19A

      Gest, Ted. Supreme Court shows independent streak. *U.S. News and World Report* 99(3):43-44 (July 15, 1985).

      Serrill, Michael S., and Anne Constable. Cockpit gray: a broad ruling on age bias. *Time* 125(26):45 (July 1,
           1985).

2878. Central States, Southeast & Southwest Areas Pension Fund v. Central Transport, Inc.   June 19, 1985
      472 US 559   86 LEd2d 447   105 SCt 2833
           Almanac (1985):15A

      Dade County set-aside stands. *Engineering News Record* 213(15):58 (October 11, 1984).

      Kallen, Barbara. Teamster calculation. *Forbes* 136(12):184 (November 4, 1985).

      Ruben, George. Developments in industrial relations: pension fund trustees can see payroll records. *Monthly
           Labor Review* 108(8):51 (August 1985).

      The Supreme Court is narrowing its focus. *Business Week* (Industrial/Technology Edition) (2862): 40-41
           (October 1, 1984).

2879. Aspen Skiing Co. v. Aspen Highlands Skiing Corp.   June 19, 1985
       472 US 585   86 LEd2d 467   105 SCt 2847
            Almanac (1985):13A

2880. Hooper v. Bernalillo County Assessor   June 24, 1985
       472 US 612   86 LEd2d 487   105 SCt 2862
            Almanac (1985):17A

2881. In re Snyder   June 24, 1985
       472 US 634   86 LEd2d 504   105 SCt 2874
            Almanac (1985):11A

2882. Cornelius, Acting Director, Office of Personnel Management v. Nutt   June 24, 1985
       472 US 648   86 LEd2d 515   105 SCt 2882
            Almanac (1985):15A

2883. United States v. Albertini   June 24, 1985
       472 US 675   86 LEd2d 536   105 SCt 2897
            Almanac (1985):11A

Arledge, Paula C., and Edward V. Heck. A freshman justice confronts the Constitution: Justice O'Connor and the First Amendment. *Western Political Quarterly* 45(3):761-772 (September 1992).

Haubner, Michael J. Military search of civilians: a commander's power. *Trial* 22(9):48-54 (September 1986).

2884. Estate of Donald E. Thornton v. Caldor, Inc.   June 26, 1985
       472 US 703   86 LEd2d 557   105 SCt 2914
            Almanac (1985):3A, 12A
            Burger Years 56-91
            En Am Con 1650-1658, 1809-1810, 1897
            Establishment 159+
            Godless 106-107
            Religion 178-182
            Sup Ct Review (1985):1-59; (1995):323-391

As High Court goes into home stretch—. *U.S. News and World Report* 99(2):12 (July 8, 1985).

Collins, Deborah. The states: federal-state relations issues hit the Supreme Court agenda. *National Civic Review* 73(11):568-571 (December 1984).

The Connecticut Sabbath law. *America* 153(1):1 (July 6-13, 1985).

Drinan, Robert F. The Supreme Court and religious freedom. *America* 152(12):254-255 (March 30, 1985).

Ericsson, Samuel. The Supreme Court's changing stance on religious freedom. *Christianity Today* 29(7):38-41 (April 19, 1985).

Gest, Ted. For High Court, a full plate of tough cases. *U.S. News and World Report* 97(15):52 (October 8, 1984).

———. Supreme Court shows independent streak. *U.S. News and World Report* 99(3):43-44 (July 15, 1985).

Labor loses a major round. *Nation's Business* 73(10):37 (October 1985).

Mauro, Tony. The dictates of work and worship. *Nation's Business* 72(9):38-39 (September 1984).

Meese, Edwin, III. The attorney general's view of the Supreme Court: toward a jurisprudence of original intention. *Public Administration Review* 45(Special Issue):701-704 (November 1985).

Press, Aric, and Ann McDaniels. Open on stage right. *Newsweek* 104(15):75-76 (October 8, 1984).

Regan, Richard J. Supreme Court roundup: 1984 term. *Thought* 61(241):290-302 (June 1986).

Serrill, Michael S., and Anne Constable. Rebuilding Jefferson's wall: the Court recesses after an unexpected turn in church-state cases. *Time* 126(2):73 (July 15, 1985).

The Supreme Court is narrowing its focus. *Business Week* (Industrial/Technology Edition) (2862): 40-41 (October 1, 1984).

Supreme Court: twixt church and state. *Economist* 296(7401):29-30 (July 6, 1985).

2885. United States v. National Bank of Commerce   June 26, 1985
     472 US 713   86 LEd2d 565   105 SCt 2919
       Almanac (1985):14A

2886. Dun & Bradstreet, Inc. v. Greenmoss Builders, Inc.   June 26, 1985
     472 US 749   86 LEd2d 593   105 SCt 2939
       Almanac (1985):11A
       En Am Con 591-592
       Make 219-233

As High Court goes into home stretch—. *U.S. News and World Report* 99(2):12 (July 8, 1985).

Burke, John R. Five votes shy of a load: reflections on the mass media today. *Vital Speeches* 51(22):700-704 (Sepetmber 1, 1985).

Contractor wins libel suit. *Engineering News Record* 215(4):58 (July 25, 1985).

Fields, Howard. Court weakens protection for media in libel suits. *Publishers' Weekly* 228(2):14 (July 12, 1985).

Geisel, Jerry. Supreme Court will decide on insurance, benefit cases. *Business Insurance* 18:1+ (October 8, 1984).

Gertz, Elmer. Gertz on Gertz: reflections on the landmark libel case. *Trial* 21(10):66-69, 71-75 (October 1985).

Gest, Ted. For High Court, a full plate of tough cases. *U.S. News and World Report* 97(15):52 (October 8, 1984).

Hale, F. Dennis. Shop talk at thirty: the Powell seat on the U.S. Supreme Court. [Editorial] *Editor and Publisher* 120(35):56, 44 (August 29, 1987).

Langvardt, Arlen W. Defamation in the business setting: basics and practical perspectives. *Business Horizons* 33(5):66-79 (September/October 1990).

Moskowitz, Daniel B. The Court sends mixed signals on free speech. *Business Week* (Industrial/Technology Edition) (2903):40 (July 15, 1985).

Powe, L. A., Jr. Mass communications and the First Amendment: an overview. *Law and Contemporary Problems* 55(1):53-76 (Winter 1992).

Press, Aric, and Ann McDaniels. Open on stage right. *Newsweek* 104(15):75-76 (October 8, 1984).

Roper, James E. Supreme Court to hear major libel cases in '84. *Editor and Publisher* 117(1):16, 21, 27 (January 7, 1984).

Weiss, Gary. Absence of malice: the Supreme Court to hear a key libel case. *Barron's* 64(33):26-29 (August 13, 1984).

2887. Phillips Petroleum Co. v. Shutts   June 26, 1985
     472 US 797   86 LEd2d 628   105 SCt 2965
       Almanac (1985):17A
       Const (Currie) 580-585

DeMott, Deborah A. Perspectives on choice of law for corporate internal affairs. *Law and Contemporary Problems* 48(3):161-198 (Summer 1985).

Glaberson, William B. A class action that could backfire in a big way. *Business Week* (2871): 160-161 (December 3, 1984).

2888. Jean v. Nelson, Commissioner, Immigration and Naturalization Service (INS)   June 26, 1985
     472 US 846   86 LEd2d 664   105 SCt 2992
       Almanac (1985):9A

Help for Haitians. [Editorial] *Nation* 240(13):388 (April 6, 1985).

2889. Marek v. Chesny, Indvidually, and as Administrator of the Estate of Chesny   June 27, 1985
     473 US 1   87 LEd2d 1   105 SCt 3012
       Almanac (1985):9A

As High Court goes into home stretch—. *U.S. News and World Report* 99(2):12 (July 8, 1985).

The Civil Rights Act of 1990. *Congressional Digest* 69(8-9):196-224 (August/September 1990).

2890. United States v. Shearer, Individually and as Administratrix for the Estate of Shearer   June 27, 1985
473 US 52   87 LEd2d 38   105 SCt 3039
Almanac (1985):18A-19A

2891. National Labor Relations Board (NLRB) v. International Longshoremen's Association, AFL-CIO June 27, 1985
473 US 61   87 LEd2d 47   105 SCt 3045
Almanac (1985):15A

Serrill, Michael S., and Anne Constable. Rebuilding Jefferson's wall: the Court recesses after an unexpected turn in church-state cases. *Time* 126(2):73 (July 15, 1985).

2892. Pattern Makers' League of North America, AFL-CIO v. National Labor Relations Board   June 27, 1985
473 US 95   87 LEd2d 68   105 SCt 3064
Almanac (1985):4A, 15A
Burger Years 220-227

As High Court goes into home stretch—. *U.S. News and World Report* 99(2):12 (July 8, 1985).

Coleman, John J., III. Can union members resign during a strike? *Personnel Journal* 65(5):99-100, 102, 105 (May 1986).

Dade County set-aside stands. *Engineering News Record* 213(15):58 (October 11, 1984).

Gest, Ted. Supreme Court shows independent streak. *U.S. News and World Report* 99(3):43-44 (July 15, 1985).

Greene, Jan. Business gains legal ground in Court term. *Electronic News* 31(1557):10 (July 8, 1985).

Lissy, William E. Election of "financial core" union membership. *Supervision* 51(9):22-23 (September 1990).

————. Union members' right to resign from union. *Supervision* 47(12):19-20, 11 (December 1985).

Palmer, Stacy E. High Court lets stand a university ban on selling wares in dormitory rooms. *Chronicle of Higher Education* 30(19):1, 18 (July 10, 1985).

Pollock, Michael A. Unions are getting clobbered in the courts. *Business Week* (Industrial/Technology Edition) (2904):106A (July 22, 1985).

2893. Massachusetts Mutual Life Insurance Co. v. Russell June 27, 1985
473 US 134   87 LEd2d 96   105 SCt 3085
Almanac (1985):15A

Benefits brouhaha: High Court to decide state health coverage. *Engineering News Record* 213(19):69 (November 8, 1984).

Morrison, John M. ERISA and the loss of just remedies. *Trial* 31(3):18-25 (March 1995).

2894. Kentucky, dba Bureau of State Police v. Graham   June 28, 1985
473 US 159   87 LEd2d 114   105 SCt 3099
Almanac (1985):9A

2895. Williamson County Regional Planning Commission v. Hamilton Bank of Johnson City   June 28, 1985
473 US 172   87 LEd2d 126   105 SCt 3108
Almanac (1985):17A

Darnell, Tim. The land and the law. *American City and County* 103(1):38-45 (January 1988).

2896. Dowling v. United States   June 28, 1985
473 US 207   87 LEd2d 152   105 SCt 3127
Almanac (1985):8A

2897. Atascadero State Hospital v. Scanlon   June 28, 1985
473 US 234   87 LEd2d 171   105 SCt 3142
Almanac (1985):16A-17A; (1986):272-273
En Am Con 79-80

Meese, Edwin, III. The attorney general's view of the Supreme Court: toward a jurisprudence of original intention. *Public Administration Review* 45(Special Issue):701-704 (November 1985).

Palmer, Stacy E. High Court lets stand a university ban on selling wares in dormitory rooms. *Chronicle of Higher Education* 30(19):1, 18 (July 10, 1985).

Wise, Charles, and Rosemary O'Leary. Is federalism dead or alive in the Supreme Court?: implications for public administrators. *Public Administration Review* 52(6):559-572 (November/December 1992).

2898. Harry N. Walters, Administrator of Veterans' Affairs v. National Association of   June 28, 1985
     Radiation Survivors
     473 US 305   87 LEd2d 220   105 SCt 3180
        Almanac (1985):3A-4A, 13A
        Black 231-237

2899. School District of the City of Grand Rapids v. Ball   July 1, 1985
     473 US 373   87 LEd2d 267   105 SCt 3216
        Almanac (1985):3A, 12A
        Brennan 125-129
        Burger Years 56-91
        Const (Currie) 531-533
        Editorials (1985):778-785
        En Am Con 39
        Establishment 139-140
        Godless 74
        Religion 68-71
        Sup Ct Church 142-159R
        Sup Ct Review (1985):61-92

Arledge, Paula C., and Edward V. Heck. A freshman justice confronts the Constitution: Justice O'Connor and the First Amendment. *Western Political Quarterly* 45(3):761-772 (September 1992).

Carlin, David R. Negative liberty: cheering for the good old clause. *Commonweal* 112(15):455 (September 6, 1985).

Christopher, Maura. A sampler of the 1984-85 docket. *Scholastic Update* (Teachers' Edition) 117(7):6 (November 30, 1984).

Cooke, Ronald J. The religious schools controversy. *America* 172(5):17-19 (February 18, 1995).

Court builds higher church-state wall. *U.S. News and World Report* 99(3):11 (July 15, 1985).

Doerr, Edd. Victories . . . and warnings. *Humanist* 45(5):39-40 (September/October 1985).

Does the Constitution allow private-school students to receive public assistance? *Christianity Today* 29(2):60-61 (February 1, 1985).

Drinan, Robert F. The Supreme Court confronts shared time. *America* 151(7):148-150 (September 22, 1984).

Flygare, Thomas J. De jure: Supreme Court reinforces the 'wall of separation.' *Phi Delta Kappan* 67(2):157-158 (October 1985).

Gest, Ted. For High Court, a full plate of tough cases. *U.S. News and World Report* 97(15):52 (October 8, 1984).

———. Supreme Court shows independent streak. *U.S. News and World Report* 99(3):43-44 (July 15, 1985).

———. What High Court heard about school prayer. *U.S. News and World Report* 97(25):71 (December 17, 1984).

Glazer, Nathan. Church-state bargain. *New Republic* 193(17):16-18 (October 21, 1985).

Kilpatrick, James J. A tangled separation. [Editorial] *Nation's Business* 73(11):5 (November 1985).

McConnell, Michael. Why 'separation' is not the key to church-state relations. *Christian Century* 106(2):43-47 (January 18, 1989).

McDaniels, Ann. Judicial flash points. *Newsweek* 116(5):18-19.

Meese, Edwin, III. The attorney general's view of the Supreme Court: toward a jurisprudence of original intention. *Public Administration Review* 45(Special Issue):701-704 (November 1985).

Press, Aric, and Ann McDaniel. The Lord's day in Court. *Newsweek* 104(26):57 (December 17, 1984).

———. Open on stage right. *Newsweek* 104(15):75-76 (October 8, 1984).

———. A Reagan Court? *Newsweek* 106(3):69-71 (July 15, 1985).

Rabinove, Samuel. Religious liberty and church-state separation. *Vital Speeches* 52(17):526-530 (June 15, 1986).

Rayer, Thomas A. The bicentennial and church-related schools. *America* 157(17):427-429, 438 (December 5, 1987).

Regan, Richard J. Supreme Court roundup: 1984 term. *Thought* 61(241):290-302 (June 1986).

Sendor, Benjamin. In a showdown before the Supreme Court, public aid to private schools gets picked off. *American School Board Journal* 172(10):20 (October 1985).

Serrill, Michael S., and Anne Constable. Rebuilding Jefferson's wall: the Court recesses after an unexpected turn in church-state cases. *Time* 126(2):73 (July 15, 1985).

The sidewalk of separation. *America* 153(2):21 (July 20-27, 1985).

Spring, Beth. U.S. Supreme Court restates its commitment to separation of church and state. *Christianity Today* 29(11):44-45 (August 9, 1985).

Supreme Court: twixt church and state. *Economist* 296(7401):29-30 (July 6, 1985).

Thomas, Evan, Kenneth W. Banta, and Anne Constable. Court at the crossroads: the 1984 election may chart the future course of American justice. *Time* 124(15):28-35 (October 8, 1984).

Wall, James M. A wise decision in a complex case. [Editorial] *Christian Century* 102(23):667-668 (July 17-24, 1985).

Zirkel, Perry A. De jure: is the 'wall of separation' like the Walls of Jericho? *Phi Delta Kappan* 75(1):88-90 (September 1993).

2900. Aguilar v. Felton   July 1, 1985
     Coupled with Secretary, United States Department of Education v. Felton
     Coupled with Chancellor of the Board of Education of the City of New York v. Felton
473 US 402   87 LEd2d 290   105 SCt 3232

Almanac (1985):3A, 12A
Am Educators 17
Burger Years 56-91
Editorials (1985):778-785
En Am Con 39
Establishment 140-143
Godless 74
Sup Ct Church 142-143, 159-172R
Sup Ct Review (1985):1-59, 61-92; (1995):323-391

Arledge, Paula C., and Edward V. Heck. A freshman justice confronts the Constitution: Justice O'Connor and the First Amendment. *Western Political Quarterly* 45(3):761-772 (September 1992).

Byrne, Harry J. Tragic paranoia: the Supreme Court and parochial schools. *America* 153(8):185-189 (October 5, 1985).

Carlin, David R. Negative liberty: cheering for the good old clause. *Commonweal* 112(15):455 (September 6, 1985).

Christopher, Maura. A sampler of the 1984-85 docket. *Scholastic Update* (Teachers' Edition) 117(7):6 (November 30, 1984).

Cooke, Ronald J. The religious schools controversy. *America* 172(5):17-19 (February 18, 1995).

Court builds higher church-state wall. *U.S. News and World Report* 99(3):11 (July 15, 1985).

Doerr, Edd. Parochiaid challenged again. *Humanist* 47(4):43-4 (July/August 1987).

———. Victories . . . and warnings. *Humanist* 45(5):39-40 (September/October 1985).

Drinan, Robert F. Compensatory education in private schools. *America* 152(13):278-280 (April 6, 1985).

Ericsson, Samuel. The Supreme Court's changing stance on religious freedom. *Christianity Today* 29(7):38-41 (April 19, 1985).

Flygare, Thomas J. De jure: Supreme Court reinforces the 'wall of separation.' *Phi Delta Kappan* 67(2):157-158 (October 1985).

Gest, Ted. Supreme Court shows independent streak. *U.S. News and World Report* 99(3):43-44 (July 15, 1985).

Glazer, Nathan. Church-state bargain. *New Republic* 193(17):16-18 (October 21, 1985).

Kiryas Joel: victory from defeat. [Editorial] *America* 171(2):3 (July 16-23, 1994).

Loconte, Joe. Will Court reshape church-state test? *Christianity Today* 38(6):50 (May 16, 1994).

McConnell, Michael. Why 'separation' is not the key to church-state relations. *Christian Century* 106(2):43-47 (January 18, 1989).

Meese, Edwin, III. The attorney general's view of the Supreme Court: toward a jurisprudence of original intention. *Public Administration Review* 45(Special Issue):701-704 (November 1985).

Press, Aric, and Ann McDaniel. The Lord's day in Court. *Newsweek* 104(26):57 (December 17, 1984).

————. Open on stage right. *Newsweek* 104(15):75-76 (October 8, 1984).

————. A Reagan Court? *Newsweek* 106(3):69-71 (July 15, 1985).

Rayer, Thomas A. The bicentennial and church-related schools. *America* 157(17):427-429, 438 (December 5, 1987).

Regan, Richard J. Supreme Court roundup: 1984 term. *Thought* 61(241):290-302 (June 1986).

Sendor, Benjamin. In a showdown before the Supreme Court, public aid to private schools gets picked off. *American School Board Journal* 172(10):20 (October 1985).

Serrill, Michael S., and Anne Constable. Rebuilding Jefferson's wall: the Court recesses after an unexpected turn in church-state cases. *Time* 126(2):73 (July 15, 1985).

The sidewalk of separation. *America* 153(2):21 (July 20-27, 1985).

Spring, Beth. U.S. Supreme Court restates its commitment to separation of church and state. *Christianity Today* 29(11):44-45 (August 9, 1985).

Supreme Court: twixt church and state. *Economist* 296(7401):29-30 (July 6, 1985).

Wall, James M. A wise decision in a complex case. [Editorial] *Christian Century* 102(23):667-668 (July 17-24, 1985).

2901. City of Cleburne, Texas v. Cleburne Living Center, Inc.   July 1, 1985
473 US 432   87 LEd2d 313   105 SCt 3249
    Almanac (1985):10A
    Burger Years 125-139
    En Am Con 608-612, 1249-1251, 2088-2089

Court builds higher church-state wall. *U.S. News and World Report* 99(3):11 (July 15, 1985).

Gest, Ted. Supreme Court shows independent streak. *U.S. News and World Report* 99(3):43-44 (July 15, 1985).

Lauber, Daniel. Mainstreaming group homes: a recent U.S. Supreme Court decision put some new twists on zoning for group homes. *Planning* 51(12):14-18 (December 1985).

Melton, Gary B. Public policy and private prejudice: psychology and law on gay rights. *American Psychologist* 44(6):933-940 (June 1989).

Press, Aric, and Ann McDaniel. Where will the retarded live? *Newsweek* 105(17):76 (April 29, 1985).

Serrill, Michael S., and Anne Constable. Rebuilding Jefferson's wall: the Court recesses after an unexpected turn in church-state cases. *Time* 126(2):73 (July 15, 1985).

2902. Sedima, S.P.R.L. v. Imrex Co., Inc.   July 1, 1985
473 US 479   87 LEd2d 346   105 SCt 3275
    Almanac (1985):8A; (1989)319-321; (1990):536-538
    Sup Ct Review (1993):157-198

Boucher, Frederick C. Why civil RICO must be reformed: RICO hits hard: treble damages and destroyed reputations. *Journal of Accountancy* 160(6):102-108 (December 1985).

Canade, Terrence P. Supreme Court review: Civil RICO—incentive to litigate: the court's rejection of standing requirements. *Journal of Criminal Law and Criminology* 76(4):1086-1102 (Winter 1985).

Court builds higher church-state wall. *U.S. News and World Report* 99(3):11 (July 15, 1985).

Gest, Ted. Supreme Court shows independent streak. *U.S. News and World Report* 99(3):43-44 (July 15, 1985).

Jacks, Ronald A. Decisions revolutionize RICO: Supreme Court opinions change the rules for fraud litigation. *Business Insurance* 19(31):19 (August 5, 1985).

Maurer, Virginia G. The continuing expansion of RICO in business litigation. *Business Horizons* 33(5):80-87 (September/October 1990).

McLeod, Douglas. Supreme Court overturns ruling limiting use of RICO. *Business Insurance* 19(27):2, 26 (July 8, 1985).

Moskowitz, Daniel B. The Court sends mixed signals on free speech. *Business Week* (Industrial/Technology Edition) (2903):40 (July 15 1985).

Supreme Court overturns decision curbing RICO. *Best's Review* (Life/Health Insurance Edition) 86(4):5 (August 1985).

Supreme Court okays racketeering lawsuits. *Engineering News Record* 215(2):70 (July 11, 1985).

Supreme Court overturns decision curbing RICO. *Best's Review* (Property/Casualty Insurance Edition) 86(4):5 (August 1985).

Wright, Jay Kelly. The RICO decision: what it means. *Best's Review* (Life/Health Insurance Edition) 86(7):26-32 (November 1985).

2903. United States v. Montoya de Hernandez   July 1, 1985
    473 US 531   87 LEd2d 381   105 SCt 3304
      Almanac (1985):5A-6A

2904. Thomas, Administrator, United States Environmental Protection Agency (EPA)   July 1, 1985
      v. Union Carbide Agricultural Products Co.
    473 US 568   87 LEd2d 409   105 SCt 3325
      Almanac (1985):14A
      En Am Con 1894-1895
      Sup Ct Review (1988):1-41

2905. American Natonal Bank & Trust Co. of Chicago v. Haroco, Inc.   July 1, 1985
    473 US 606   87 LEd2d 437   105 SCt 3291
      Almanac (1985):8A; (1989):319-321

Greene, Jan. Business gains legal ground in Court term. *Electronic News* 31(1557):10 (July 8, 1985).

Jacks, Ronald A. Decisions revolutionize RICO: Supreme Court opinions change the rules for fraud litigation. *Business Insurance* 19(31):19 (August 5, 1985).

Supreme Court overturns decision curbing RICO. *Best's Review* (Life/Health Insurance Edition) 86(4):5 (August 1985).

2906. Mitsubishi Motors Corp. v. Soler Chrysler-Plymouth, Inc.   July 2, 1985
    473 US 614   87 LEd2d 444   105 SCt 3346
      Almanac (1985):13A
      Burger Years 206-219

Veach, James. The arbitration tug-of-war. *Best's Review* (Property/Casualty Insurance Edition) 93(11):38-42, 80-83 (March 1993).

2907. United States v. Bagley   July 2, 1985
    473 US 667   87 LEd2d 481   105 SCt 3375
      Almanac (1985):7A

2908. Carchman, Mercer County Prosecutor v. Nash   July 2, 1985
    473 US 716   87 LEd2d 516   105 SCt 3401
      Almanac (1985):7A

2909. Oregon Department of Fish and Wildlife v. Klamath Indian Tribe   July 2, 1985
    473 US 753   87 LEd2d 542   105 SCt 3420
      Almanac (1985):18A

2910. Cornelius, Acting Director, Office of Personnel Management   July 2, 1985
      v. NAACP Legal Defense and Educational Fund, Inc.
    473 US 788   87 LEd2d 567   105 SCt 3439
      Almanac (1985):11A
      En Am Con 506
      Sup Ct Review (1992):79-122

Arledge, Paula C., and Edward V. Heck. A freshman justice confronts the Constitution: Justice O'Connor and the First Amendment. *Western Political Quarterly* 45(3):761-772 (September 1992).

High Court ruling hinders NAACP legal defense fund effort to raise monies. *Jet* 68(19):33 (July 29, 1985).

2911. Pennsylvania Bureau of Correction v. United States Marshals Service   November 18, 1985
    474 US 34   88 LEd2d 189   106 SCt 355
      Almanac (1986):16A

2912. Hill v. Lockhart, Director, Arkansas Department of Correction   November 18, 1985
      474 US 52   88 LEd2d 203   106 SCt 366
         Almanac (1986):6A

2913. Green v. Mansour, Director, Michigan Department of Social Services   December 3, 1985
      474 US 64   88 LEd2d 371   106 SCt 423
         Almanac (1986):16A

2914. Heath v. Alabama   December 3, 1985
      474 US 82   88 LEd2d 387   106 SCt 433
         Almanac (1986):5A
      Allen, Ronald J., and John P. Ratnaswamy. Heath v. Alabama: a case study of doctrine and rationality in the
         Supreme Court. *Journal of Criminal Law and Criminology* 76(4):801-831 (Winter 1985).
      Berry, Sean Richard. Supreme Court review: Fifth Amendment—the double jeopardy clause and successive
         state prosecutions: if at first you don't succeed, try, try again. *Journal of Criminal Law and Criminology*
         77(3):632-645 (Fall 1986).

2915. Miller v. Fenton, Superintendent, Rahway State Prison   December 3, 1985
      474 US 104   88 LEd2d 405   106 SCt 445
         Almanac (1986):5A

2916. United States v. Riverside Bayview Homes, Inc.   December 4, 1985
      474 US 121   88 LEd2d 419   106 SCt 455
         Almanac (1986):14A
      Labor loses a major round. *Nation's Business* 73(10):37 (October 1985).
      Lovely, Jeffrey M. Protecting wetlands: consideration of secondary social and economic effects by the United
         States Army Corps of Engineers in its wetlands permitting process. *Boston College Environmental Affairs
         Law Review* 17(3):647-686 (Spring 1990).
      Wetlands protection: court, Senate affirms Corps' role as guardian of swamps. *Engineering News Record*
         215(24):13 (December 12, 1985).

2917. Thomas v. Arn   December 4, 1985
      474 US 140   88 LEd2d 435   106 SCt 466
         Almanac (1986):16A-17A

2918. Maine v. Moulton   December 10, 1985
      474 US 159   88 LEd2d 481   106 SCt 477
         Almanac (1986):6A
      Bahl, Martin. The Sixth Amendment as constitutional theory: does originalism require that Massiah be
         abandoned? *Journal of Criminal Law and Criminology* 82(2):423-463 (Summer 1991).
      Regan, Richard J. Supreme Court roundup: 1985 term. *Thought* 62(245):234-246 (June 1987).
      Taking the sixth: Brennan short-circuits a wire. *Time* 126(25):56 (December 23, 1985).

2919. Cleavinger v. Saxner   December 10, 1985
      474 US 193   88 LEd2d 507   106 SCt 496
         Almanac (1986):9A

2920. Eastern Air Lines, Inc. v. Mahfoud   December 10, 1985
      474 US 213   88 LEd2d 522   106 SCt 586
         Almanac (1986):13A

2921. Regents of University of Michigan v. Ewing   December 12, 1985
      474 US 214   88 LEd2d 523   106 SCt 507
         Almanac (1986):16A

Flygare, Thomas J. De jure: U.S. Supreme Court reaffirms role of educators in making academic decisions. *Phi Delta Kappan* 67(7):537-538 (March 1986).

Franke, Ann H. Legal watch. *Academe* 72(1):60 (January/February 1986).

From Tilton to Ewing: some major higher-education decisions of the Burger court. *Chronicle of Higher Education* 32(17):10 (June 25, 1986).

Jaschik, Scott. From Bakke to Yeshiva, Justice Powell played key role in Court's education rulings. *Chronicle of Higher Education* 33(43):16 (July 8, 1987).

Palmer, Stacy E. Supreme Court curbs judges' right to overturn academic decisions. *Chronicle of Higher Education* 31(16)1, 33 (December 18, 1985).

Stevens, John Paul, and Lewis F. Powell, Jr. Text of High Court's ruling on judges' right to upset academic decisions. *Chronicle of Higher Education* 31(16):32-33R (December 18, 1985).

Van Alstyne, William W. Academic freedom and the First Amendment in the Supreme Court of the United States: an unhurried historical review. *Law and Contemporary Problems* 53(3):79-154 (Summer 1990).

2922. United States v. Rojas-Contreras   December 16, 1985
474 US 231   88 LEd2d 537   106 SCt 555
Almanac (1986):6A

2923. United States v. Von Neumann   January 14, 1986
474 US 242   88 LEd2d 587   106 SCt 610
Almanac (1986):10A

2924. Vasquez v. Hillery   January 14, 1986
474 US 254   88 LEd2d 598   106 SCt 617
Almanac (1986):8A

Lacayo, Richard, and Paul A. Witteman. Seeing justice never done: the case that would not end torments a California town. *Time* 127(7):73 (February 17, 1986).

Regan, Richard J. Supreme Court roundup: 1985 term. *Thought* 62(245):234-246 (June 1987).

2925. Wainwright v. Greenfield   January 14, 1986
474 US 284   88 LEd2d 623   106 SCt 634
Almanac (1986):5A

2926. United States v. Loud Hawk   January 21, 1986
474 US 302   88 LEd2d 640   106 SCt 648
Almanac (1986):6A
Loud 246-259+

2927. Daniels v. Williams   January 21, 1986
474 US 327   88 LEd2d 662   106 SCt 662
Almanac (1986):9A

2928. Davidson v. Cannon   January 21, 1986
474 US 344   88 LEd2d 677   106 SCt 668
Almanac (1986):9A

2929. Board of Governors of Federal Reserve System v. Dimension Financial Corp.   January 22, 1986
474 US 361   88 LEd2d 691   106 SCt 681
Almanac (1986):12A

The Court versus the Fed. *Forbes* 137(4):12 (February 24, 1986).

Dwyer, Paula. The Burger Court put the brakes on Reagan's federalism. *Business Week* (Industrial/Technology Edition) (2956):67 (July 21, 1986).

———. Reagan's 'new federalism' is about to have its day in court. *Business Week* (Industrial/Technology Edition) (2915):59-62 (October 7, 1985).

Ellis, James E., Vicky Cahan, Mark Ivey, and Sarah Bartlett. Nonbanks: who's getting the bucks—and who's not. *Business Week* (Industrial/Technology Edition) (2932):67-68 (February 10, 1986).

Gamble, Richard H. Trust company play historic role in interstate banking. *Trusts and Estates* 125(4):48-49 (April 1986).

High court strikes down Fed nonbank bank ruling. *Best's Review* (Life/Health Insurance Edition) 86(10):5 (February 1986).

Non-bank banks supreme moments. *Economist* 298(7431):76-77 (February 1-7, 1986).

Riemer, Blanca. The Fed's lawyer turns a backwater into a battlefield. *Business Week* (Industrial/Technology Edition) (2931):68 (February 10, 1986).

Scheibla, Shirley Hobbs. New dimension in banking: the nonbank bank gets the green light. *Barron's* 66(10):30-32 (March 10, 1986).

What does the new High Court mean to banks? *ABA Banking Journal* 78(8):28-30 (August 1986).

2930. Cabana v. Bullock   January 22, 1986
       474 US 376   88 LEd2d 704   106 SCt 689
          Almanac (1986):7A

2931. Transcontinental Gas Pipe Line Corp. v. State Oil and Gas Board of Mississippi   January 22, 1986
       474 US 409   88 LEd2d 732   106 SCt 709
          Almanac (1986):15A

2932. United States v. Lane   January 27, 1986
       474 US 438   88 LEd2d 814   106 SCt 725
          Almanac (1986):8A

2933. Larry Witters v. Washington Department of Services for the Blind   January 27, 1986
       474 US 481   88 LEd2d 846   106 SCt 748
          Almanac (1986):4A, 11A
          Godless 77-78+

Decision for choice. [Editorial] *America* 154(8):149-150 (March 1, 1986).

Flygare, Thomas J. De jure: establishment clause case reveals flaws in the court system. *Phi Delta Kappan* 67(8):613-614 (April 1986).

Freid, Stephen H. The constitutionality of choice under the establishment clause. *Clearing House* 66(2):92-95 (November/December 1992).

Gest, Ted. Burger Court: imprint of its last year. *U.S. News and World Report* 101(3):15 (July 21, 1986).

————. Issues Supreme Court must rule on now. *U.S. News and World Report* 99(16):66 (October 14, 1985).

————. Now, Meese takes lead on social policy. *U.S. News and World Report* 99(12):27 (August 12 1985).

Kilpatrick, James J. A tangled separation. [Editorial] *Nation's Business* 73(11):5 (November 1985).

Marshall, Thurgood, Lewis F. Powell, Byron R. White, and Sandra Day O'Connor. Text of 4 justices' opinions in Supreme Court's ruling on government aid. *Chronicle of Higher Education* 31(21)14-15R (February 5, 1986).

Palmer, Stacy E. Church-state separation not always violated by aid to ministry students, High Court says. *Chronicle of Higher Education* 31(21):12, 14 (February 5, 1986).

Rayer, Thomas A. The bicentennial and church-related schools. *America* 157(17)427-429, 438 (December 5, 1987).

Regan, Richard J. Supreme Court roundup: 1985 term. *Thought* 62(245):234-246 (June 1987).

Three Court cases. *Christian Century* 106(32):976 (November 1, 1989).

Wylie, Pete. U.S. Supreme Court prepares to hear right-to life and religious freedom cases. *Christianity Today* 29(14):64-66 (October 4, 1985).

Zirkel, Perry A. De jure: is the 'wall of separation' like the Walls of Jericho? *Phi Delta Kappan* 75(1):88-90 (September 1993).

2934. Midlantic National Bank v. New Jersey Department of Environmental Protection   January 27, 1986
             Coupled with O'Neill v. New Jersey Department of Environmental Protection
       474 US 494   88 LEd2d 859   106 SCt 755

Almanac (1986):14A-15A

Cistulli, Joseph P. Striking a balance between competing policies: the administrative claim as an alternative to enforce state clean-up orders in bankruptcy proceedings. *Boston College Environmental Affairs Law Review* 16(3):581-614 (Spring 1989).

Colton, Roger D., Kathleen Uehling, and Michael F. Sheehan. Seven-cum-eleven: rolling the toxic dice in the U.S. Supreme Court. *Boston College Environmental Affairs Law Review* 14(3):345-379 (Spring 1987).

Labor loses a major round. *Nation's Business* 73(10):37 (October 1985).

Moskowitz, Dan, and Joseph F. Dunphy. An agenda of chemical cases goes to court. *Chemical Week* 137(15):6-7 (October 9, 1985).

2935. Parsons Steel, Inc. v. First Alabama Bank of Montgomery, N.A.   January 27, 1986
474 US 518   88 LEd2d 877   106 SCt 768
Almanac (1986):17A

2936. Pacific Gas and Electric Co. v. Public Utilities Commission   February 25, 1986
475 US 1   89 LEd2d 1   106 SCt 903
Almanac (1986):11A
Sup Ct Review (1987):303-344

Hayes, William C. Freedom can come to an envelope. [Editorial] *Electrical World* 200(4):7 (April 1986).

2937. City of Renton v. Playtime Theatres, Inc.   February 25, 1986
475 US 41   89 LEd2d 29   106 SCt 925
Almanac (1986):16A
Brennan 171-176
Sup Ct Review (1994):1-56

Gest, Ted. Burger Court: imprint of its last year. *U.S. News and World Report* 101(3):15 (July 21, 1986).

Hagle, Timothy M. But do they have to see it to know it? The Supreme Court's obscenity and pornography decisions. *Western Political Quarterly* 44(4):1039-1054 (December 1991).

Lacayo, Richard, David Beckwith, and Meg Grant. Give-and-take on pornography: after two court actions, still tough to ban but easier to banish. *Time* 127(10):67 (March 10, 1986).

Porn wars: do's and don'ts. *U.S. News and World Report* 100(9):8 (March 10, 1986).

Redlining the red lights. *Newsweek* 107(10):69 (March 10, 1986).

2938. United States v. Mechanik   February 25, 1986
475 US 66 89   LEd2d 50   106 SCt 938
Almanac (1986):8A

2939. United States v. Maine   February 25, 1986
475 US 89   89 LEd2d 68   106 SCt 951
Almanac (1986):16A

2940. New York v. Class   February 25, 1986
475 US 106   89 LEd2d 81   106 SCt 960
Almanac (1986):5A

Maclin, Tracey. New York v. Class: a little-noticed case with disturbing implications. *Journal of Criminal Law and Criminology* 78(1):1-86 (Spring 1987).

Regan, Richard J. Supreme Court roundup: 1985 term. *Thought* 62(245):234-246 (June 1987).

2941. Texas v. McCullough   February 26, 1986
475 US 134   89 LEd2d 104   106 SCt 976
Almanac (1986):8A

Kobayashi, Glenn H. Supreme Court review: Fourteenth Amendment—reexamining judicial vindictiveness. *Journal of Criminal Law and Criminology* 77(3):867-893 (Fall 1986).

2942. Nix v. Whiteside   February 26, 1986
     475 US 157   89 LEd2d 123   106 SCt 988
        Almanac (1986):6A
     Beckman, David L., Jr. Supreme Court review: Sixth Amendment—effective assistance of counsel: a defense
        attorney's right to refuse cooperation in defendant's perjured testimony. *Journal of Criminal Law and
        Criminology* 77(3):692-712 (Fall 1986).
     Lawyer's dilemma: when the client lies. *Newsweek* 106(21):89 (November 18, 1985).
     Liars and lawyers. *New Republic* 193(25):4, 49 (December 16, 1985).
     Supreme Court: doctrine of expedient deceit. *Economist* 298(7437):23 (March 15-23 1986).

2943. National Labor Relations Board (NLRB) v. Financial Institution Employees, Local 1182   February 26, 1986
           Coupled with Seattle-First National Bank v. Financial Institution Employees, Local 1182
     475 US 192   89 LEd2d 151   106 SCt 1007
        Almanac (1986):14A
     Dwyer, Paula. Reagan's 'new federalism' is about to have its day in court. *Business Week*
        (Industrial/Technology Edition) (2915):59-62 (October 7, 1985).
     Moskowitz, Daniel B. Pension penalties upheld. *Engineering News Record* 216(10):51 (March 6, 1986).

2944. Connolly v. Pension Benefit Guaranty Corp.   February 26, 1986
           Coupled with Woodward Sand Co., Inc. v. Pension Benefit Guaranty Corp.
     475 US 211   89 LEd2d 166   106 SCt 1018
        Almanac (1986):14A
     Moskowitz, Daniel B. Pension penalties upheld. *Engineering News Record* 216(10):51 (March 6, 1986).
     Pension Act Amendments upheld by Supreme Court. *Best's Review* (Life/Health Insurance Edition) 86(12):5
        (April 1986).
     Tarnoff, Stephen. Court decisions or benefits increase employers' costs. *Business Insurance* 21(44):93-95
        (November 2, 1987).
     Tax dispute among cases to be heard by High Court. *Best's Review* (Life/Health Insurance Edition) 87(9):5-6
        (January 1987).

2945. Morris v. Mathews   February 26, 1986
     475 US 237   89 LEd2d 187   106 SCt 1032
        Almanac (1986):5A

2946. Fisher v. City of Berkeley   February 26, 1986
     475 US 260   89 LEd2d 206   106 SCt 1045
        Almanac (1986):12A
        Sup Ct Review (1986):157-173
     Supreme Court says O.K. to city rent controls. *Jet* 70(1):30 (March 24, 1986).
     Dwyer, Paula. The Burger Court put the brakes on Reagan's federalism. *Business Week* (Industrial/Technology
        Edition) (2956):67 (July 21, 1986).
        ———. Reagan's 'new federalism' is about to have its day in court. *Business Week* (Industrial/Technology
        Edition) (2915):59-62 (October 7, 1985).

2947. Wisconsin Department of Industry, Labor and Human Relations v. Gould, Inc.   February 26, 1986
     475 US 282   89 LEd2d 223   106 SCt 1057
        Almanac (1986):15A
     Dwyer, Paula. The Burger Court put the brakes on Reagan's federalism. *Business Week* (Industrial/Technology
        Edition) (2956):67 (July 21, 1986).
        ———. Reagan's 'new federalism' is about to have its day in court. *Business Week* (Industrial/Technology
        Edition) (2915):59-62 (October 7, 1985).

2948. Chicago Teachers Union, Local No. 1 v. Hudson   March 4, 1986
     475 US 292   89 LEd2d 232   106 SCt 1066
        Almanac (1986):14A

Kovach, Kenneth A., and Peter Millspaugh. Implementing the Beck and Lehnert union security agreement decisions: a study in frustration. *Business Horizons* 38(3):57-65 (May/June 1995).

Labor loses a major round. *Nation's Business* 73(10):37 (October 1985).

Sendor, Benjamin. High Court: give nonunion employees a fair shake. *American School Board Journal* 173(7):16 (July 1986).

2949. Whitley v. Albers   March 4, 1986
475 US 312   89 LEd2d 251   106 SCt 1078
Almanac (1986):7A

2950. Malley v. Briggs   March 5, 1986
475 US 335   89 LEd2d 271   106 SCt 1092
Almanac (1986):9A

Supreme Court: Doctrine of expedient deceit. *Economist* 298(7437):23 (March 15-23 1986).

2951. Exxon Corp. v. Hunt   March 10, 1986
475 US 355   89 LEd2d 364   106 SCt 1103
Almanac (1986):15A

Court OKs state cleanup tax. *Engineering News Record* 216(12):43-44 (March 20, 1986).

Dwyer, Paula. Reagan's 'new federalism' is about to have its day in court. *Business Week* (Industrial/Technology Edition) (2915):59-62 (October 7, 1985).

Light, Alfred R. The importance of "being taken": to clarify and confirm the litigative reconstruction of CERCLA's text. *Boston College Environmental Affairs Law Review* 18(1):1-52 (Fall 1990).

Moskowitz, Dan, and Joseph F. Dunphy. An agenda of chemical cases goes to court. *Chemical Week* 137(15):6-7 (October 9, 1985).

Supreme Court considers state tax's application to hazardous waste cleanups fund. *Journal of Accountancy* 161(2):22 (Febraury 1986).

2952. United States v. Inadi   March 10, 1986
475 US 387   89 LEd2d 390   106 SCt 1121
Almanac (1986):6A

Haddad, James B. The future of confrontation clause developments what will emerge when the Supreme Court synthesizes the diverse lines of confrontation decisions? *Journal of Criminal Law and Criminology* 81(1):77-98 (Spring 1990).

Porcelli, Anthony C. Supreme Court review: Sixth Amendment—right to confront one's accuser when the victim does not testify. *Journal of Criminal Law and Criminology* 83(4):868-893 (Winter 1993).

2953. Moran v. Burbine   March 10, 1986
475 US 412   89 LEd2d 410   106 SCt 1135
Almanac (1986):5A
Burger Years 143-168

Jordan, Horace W., Jr. Supreme Court review: Fifth and Sixth Amendments—changing the balance of Miranda. *Journal of Criminal Law and Criminology* 77(3):666-691 (Fall 1986).

Regan, Richard J. Supreme Court roundup: 1985 term. *Thought* 62(245):234-246 (June 1987).

2954. Pembaur v. City of Cincinnati   March 25, 1986
475 US 469   89 LEd2d 425   106 SCt 1292
Almanac (1986):9A
Sup Ct Review (1987):249-301

2955. S. Simcha Goldman v. Weinberger   March 25, 1986
475 US 503   89 LEd2d 163   106 SCt 1313
Almanac (1986):477, 4A,11A; (1987):238
Ascent 209-211+
Const (Currie) 531-533
Godless 40

Sup Ct Review (1995):323-391

Arledge, Paula C., and Edward V. Heck. A freshman justice confronts the Constitution: Justice O'Connor and the First Amendment. *Western Political Quarterly* 45(3):761-772 (September 1992).

Ball, Howard. The U.S. Supreme Court's glossing of the Federal Tort Claims Act: statutory construction and veterans' tort actions. *Western Political Quarterly* 41(3):529-552 (September 1988).

Chemerinsky, Erwin. Supreme Court review: religion clause doctrine: potential for change. *Trial* 29(2):81-84 (February 1993).

Drinan, Robert F. The Supreme Court, religious freedom and the yarmulke. *America* 155(1):9-11 (July 5-12, 1986).

Gest, Ted. Burger Court: imprint of its last year. *U.S. News and World Report* 101(3):15 (July 21, 1986).

Lacayo, Richard, and Anne Constable. Establishing her independence: Sandra Day O'Connor is still conservative, but on her own terms. *Time* 127(19):85 (May 12, 1986).

Regan, Richard J. Supreme Court roundup: 1985 term. *Thought* 62(245):234-246 (June 1987).

2956. Bender v. Williamsport Area School District   March 25, 1986
       475 US 534   89 LEd2d 501   106 SCt 1326
       Almanac (1986):11A

Baron, Mark A., and Harold L. Bishop. Come one, come all. *American School Board Journal* 178(3):29-30 (March 1991).

Drakeman, Donald L. Equal access: the continuing saga. *Christian Century* 102(10):284-285 (March 20-27, 1985).

Drinan, Robert F. Will the Supreme Court permit prayer groups in public high schools? *America* 154(1):8-10 (January 4-11, 1986).

Ericsson, Samuel. The Supreme Court's changing stance on religious freedom. *Christianity Today* 29(7):38-41 (April 19, 1985).

Flygare, Thomas J. De jure: Supreme Court reinforces the 'wall of separation.' *Phi Delta Kappan* 67(2):157-158 (October 1985).

Gest, Ted. Burger Court: imprint of its last year. *U.S. News and World Report* 101(3):15 (July 21, 1986).

———. Issues Supreme Court must rule on now. *U.S. News and World Report* 99(16):66 (October 14, 1985).

Kilpatrick, James J. A tangled separation. [Editorial] *Nation's Business* 73(11):5 (November 1985).

Lacayo, Richard, and Anne Constable. Establishing her independence: Sandra Day O'Connor is still conservative, but on her own terms. *Time* 127(19):85 (May 12, 1986).

Levicoff, Steve. Upholding students' religious freedom. [Editorial] *Christian Century* 106(36):1108-1109 (November 29, 1989).

Peach, Lucinda. Supreme Court docket: does religion belong in the schools? *Social Education* 50(3):166-169 (March 1986).

Rabinove, Samuel. Religious liberty and church-state separation. *Vital Speeches* 52(17):526-530 (June 15, 1986).

Regan, Richard J. Supreme Court roundup: 1985 term. *Thought* 62(245):234-246 (June 1987).

Rossow, Lawrence F. Conflicting directives from Congress and the courts put you in the hot seat. *American School Board Journal* 174(2):38-39 (February 1987).

Sendor, Benjamin. Equal access: courts and Congress disagree. *American School Board Journal* 171(11):7, 48 (November 1984).

———. Even after the Supreme Court ruling, we're still in the dark about religion clubs at school. *American School Board Journal* 173(8):17 (August 1986).

Spring, Beth. High Court hears arguments in equal access case. *Christianity Today* 29(17):56-57 (November 22, 1985).

———. Students regain the right to hold Bible meetings in public high schools. *Christianity Today* 30(8):45-46 (May 16, 1986).

———. Why high school students can't discuss the Bible. *Christianity Today* 27(4):34-35 (February 18, 1983).

Wylie, Pete. U.S. Supreme Court prepares to hear right-to life and religious freedom cases. *Christianity Today* 29(14):64-66 (October 4, 1985).

Zakariya, Sally Banks. Here's how boards are coping with the Equal Access Act. *American School Board Journal* 172(5):37-39 (May 1985).

2957. Paulussen v. Herion   March 25, 1986
     475 US 557   89 LEd2d 521   106 SCt 1339
        Almanac (1986):10A

2958. Holbrook v. Flynn   March 26, 1986
     475 US 560   89 LEd2d 525   106 SCt 1340
        Almanac (1986):6A

2959. Matsushita Electric Industrial Co. v. Zenith Radio Corp.   March 26, 1986
     475 US 574   89 LEd2d 538   106 SCt 1348
        Almanac (1986):12A

Bork, Robert H. Beside the law. *National Review* 44(20):38, 40-43 (October 19, 1992).

Dwyer, Paula. Reagan's 'new federalism' is about to have its day in court. *Business Week* (Industrial/Technology Edition) (2915):59-62 (October 7, 1985).

Gest, Ted. Burger Court: imprint of its last year. *U.S. News and World Report* 101(3):15 (July 21, 1986).

Kallen, Barbara. Down the tube? *Forbes* 135(12):186, 189 (June 3, 1985).

Kramer, Larry. Extraterritorial application of American law after the insurance antitrust case: a reply to professors Lowenfeld and Trimble. *American Journal of International Law* 89(4):750-758 (October 1995).

Nelson-Horchler, Joani. Supreme Court: keep a hand on your wallet. *Industry Week* 226(5):28-29, 31 (September 2, 1985).

2960. Golden State Transit Corp. v. Los Angeles   April 1, 1986
     475 US 608   89 LEd2d 616   106 SCt 1395
        Almanac (1986):15A
        Guide (West): (1991):266-267

Dwyer, Paula. The Burger Court put the brakes on Reagan's federalism. *Business Week* (Industrial/Technology Edition) (2956):67 (July 21, 1986).

Dwyer, Paula. Reagan's 'new federalism' is about to have its day in court. *Business Week* (Industrial/Technology Edition) (2915):59-62 (October 7, 1985).

Hukill, Craig. Labor and the Supreme Court: significant issues of 1989-90. *Monthly Labor Review* 113(1):30-34 (January 1990).

2961. Michigan v. Jackson   April 1, 1986
        Coupled with Michigan v. Bladel
     475 US 625   89 LEd2d 631   106 SCt 1404
        Almanac (1986):6A

Echikson, Thomas. Supreme Court review: Sixth Amendment—waiver after request for counsel. *Journal of Criminal Law and Criminology* 77(3):775-795 (Fall 1986).

Regan, Richard J. Supreme Court roundup: 1985 term. *Thought* 62(245):234-246 (June 1987).

Ullman, Patricia. Supreme Court review: Fifth and Sixth Amendments—the right to counsel in multiple charge arraignments. *Journal of Criminal Law and Criminology* 82(4):904-919 (Winter 1992).

2962. AT&T Technologies, Inc. v. Communication Workers of America   April 7, 1986
     475 US 643   89 LEd2d 648   106 SCt 1415
        Almanac (1986):14A

2963. United States v. City of Fulton   April 7, 1986
     475 US 657   89 LEd2d 661   106 SCt 1422
        Almanac (1986):15A

2964. Delaware v. Van Arsdall   April 7, 1986
     475 US 673   89 LEd2d 674   106 SCt 1431
        Almanac (1986):7A

2965. Icicle Seafoods, Inc. v. Worthington   April 21, 1986
    475 US 709   89 LEd2d 739   106 SCt 1527
    Almanac (1986):17A

2966. Evans v. Jeff D.   April 21, 1986
    475 US 717   89 LEd2d 747   106 SCt 1531
    Almanac (1986):9A

The Civil Rights Act of 1990. *Congressional Digest* 69(8-9):196-224 (August/September 1990).

2967. Philadelphia Newspapers, Inc. v. Hepps   April 21, 1986
    475 US 767   89 LEd2d 783   106 SCt 1558
    Almanac (1986):12A

Arledge, Paula C., and Edward V. Heck. A freshman justice confronts the Constitution: Justice O'Connor and the First Amendment. *Western Political Quarterly* 45(3):761-772 (September 1992).

Gest, Ted. Burger Court: imprint of its last year. *U.S. News and World Report* 101(3):15 (July 21, 1986).

Hale, F. Dennis. How retiring Supreme Court Justice White voted in First Amendment cases. *Editor and Publisher* 126(30):44, 36 (July 24, 1993).

———. Shop the Powell seat on the U.S. Supreme Court. [Editorial] *Editor and Publisher* 120(35):56, 44 (August 29, 1987).

Supreme Court shifts burden of libel proof. *Publishers' Weekly* 229(19):118 (May 9, 1986).

Truth and libel: the press gets more protection. *Time* 127(18):45 (May 5, 1986).

2968. United States v. Quinn   April 21, 1986
    475 US 791   89 LEd2d 803   106 SCt 1623
    Almanac (1986):5A

2969. Aetna Life Insurance Co. v. Lavoie   April 22, 1986
    475 US 813   89 LEd2d 823   106 SCt 1580
    Almanac (1986):10A

Barger, Richard D., and Royal F. Oakes. Judicial reform on hold; Supreme Court changes stance on restrictions for punitive awards. *Business Insurance* 26(9):19-20 (March 2, 1992).

Dwyer, Paula. The right's legal ace is in the hot seat. *Business Week* (Industrial/Technology Edition) (2946):32 (May 12, 1986).

Dwyer, Paula, and William B. Glaberson. Punitive damages: cruel and unusual punishment? *Business Week* (Industrial/Technology Edition) (2944):56-59 (April 28, 1986).

Geisel, Jerry. Court hears arguments on punitive damages. *Business Insurance* 20(46):2, 4 (December 9, 1986).

Luxenberg, Stan. Taking the Eighth. *Forbes* 137(4):73, 75 (February 24, 1986).

2970. United States v. American College of Physicians   April 22, 1986
    475 US 834   89 LEd2d 841   106 SCt 1591
    Almanac (1986):13A

ABE loses on tax status of insurance program. *Journal of Taxation* 65(3):204 (September 1986).

Dwyer, Paula. Reagan's 'new federalism' is about to have its day in court. *Business Week* (Industrial/Technology Edition) (2915):59-62 (October 7, 1985).

Huffaker, John B., and Erica L. Gut. Supreme Court holds advertising revenue was not substantially related income. *Journal of Taxation* 65(1):2-5 (July 1986).

Shillingburg, J. Edward. American College of Physicians v. United States: an ending—a beginning—or? *Taxes* 64(9):539-547 (September 1986).

Wilson, Robin. High Court orders medical journal to pay taxes on ad revenues; ruling may set new standard. *Chronicle of Higher Education* 32(9):18 (April 30, 1986).

2971. Sorenson v. Secretary of the Treasury   April 22, 1986
    475 US 851   89 LEd2d 855   106 SCt 1600
    Almanac (1986):13A

2972. New York v. P.J. Video, Inc.   April 22, 1986
    475 US 868   89 LEd2d 871   106 SCt 1610
    Almanac (1986):5A
    Fields, Howard. First Amendment watch: High Court eases seizure of X-rated materials. *Publishers' Weekly*
        229(7):114 (May 9, 1986).
    Gest, Ted. Burger Court: imprint of its last year. *U.S. News and World Report* 101(3):15 (July 21, 1986).
    Regan, Richard J. Supreme Court roundup: 1985 term. *Thought* 62(245):234-246 (June 1987).

2973. Skipper v. South Carolina   April 29, 1986
    476 US 1   90 LEd2d 1   106 SCt 1669
    Almanac (1986):7A
    Death Penalty 80s 15-18, 75-78
    Death Penalty 90s 97-100+
    Gest, Ted. Burger Court: imprint of its last year. *U.S. News and World Report* 101(3):15 (July 21, 1986).

2974. McLaughlin v. United States   April 29, 1986
    476 US 16   90 LEd2d 15   106 SCt 1677
    Almanac (1986):8A

2975. Equal Employment Opportunity Commission (EEOC) v. Federal Labor Relations Authority   April 29, 1986
    476 US 19   90 LEd2d 19   106 SCt 1678
    Almanac (1986):14A

2976. Turner v. Murray   April 30, 1986
    476 US 28   90 LEd2d 27   106 SCt 1683
    Almanac (1986):7A
    Gest, Ted. Burger Court: imprint of its last year. *U.S. News and World Report* 101(3):15 (July 21, 1986).
    Juries: blacker, and pro the death penalty. *Economist* 299(7445):25-26 (May 10-16, 1986).
    Jurors and racial bias. *Time* 127(19):85 (May 12, 1986).
    Wyckoff, Maria. Supreme Court review: Sixth Amendment—right to inquire into juror's racial prejudices.
        Journal of Criminal Law and Criminology 77(3):713-742 (Fall 1986).

2977. Diamond v. Charles   April 30, 1986
    476 US 54   90 LEd2d 48   106 SCt 1697
    Almanac (1986):263-264, 8A
    Tenth 135-150
    Choice vs. life. *People Weekly* 24(5):70-72 (August 5, 1985).
    Doerr, Edd. Abortion rights at the crossroads. *Humanist* 45(6):39-40 (November/December 1985).

2978. Batson v. Kentucky   April 30, 1986
    476 US 79   90 LEd2d 69   106 SCt 1712
    Almanac (1986):8A; (1994):312
    Ascent 336-338+
    Const Law 419-422R
    Editorials (1986):534-541; (1994):486-491
    En Am Con 1082-1085
    Sup Ct Review (1987):97-156; (1989):165-193
    Sup Ct Yearbook (1990-91):26-28, 62-63; (1993-94):37 (1994-95):88
    Blacks' new key to the jury box. *U.S. News and World Report* 100(18):9 (May 12, 1986).
    Brown, Frank Dexter. High Court reviews civil rights. *Black Enterprise* 16(6):31 (January 1986).
    Chemerinsky, Erwin. Supreme Court review: the end of gender-based peremptory challenges. *Trial* 30(8):69,
        72-73 (August 1994).
    Dripps, Donald A. Supreme Court review: 'I didn't like the way he looked.' *Trial* 31(7):94-96 (July 1995).
    Farber, Daniel A. Supreme Court review: picking the jury. *Trial* 27(8):69-72 (August 1991).

Gemskie, Michele A. Supreme Court review: Fourteenth Amendment—peremptory challenges by defendants and the equal protection clause. *Journal of Criminal Law and Criminology* 83(4):920-943 (Winter 1993).

Gest, Ted. Burger Court: imprint of its last year. *U.S. News and World Report* 101(3):15 (July 21, 1986).

Josephs, Mark L. Supreme Court review: Fourteenth Amendment—peremptory challenges and the equal protection clause. *Journal of Criminal Law and Criminology* 82(4):1000-1028 (Winter 1992).

Jurors and racial bias. *Time* 127(19):85 (May 12, 1986).

Kaye, Judith S. The Supreme Court: state constitutional law. *Trial* 25(12):57-68, 70 (December 1989).

Kennedy, Randall. Grand marshall. [Editorial] *Nation* 253(5):180-181 (August 12-19, 1991).

Kirk, Michael W. Supreme Court review: Sixth and Fourteenth Amendments—the Swain song of the racially discriminatory use of peremptory challenges. *Journal of Criminal Law and Criminology* 77(3):821-843 (Fall 1986).

Lacayo, Richard, and Anne Constable. Establishing her independence: Sandra Day O'Connor is still conservative, but on her own terms. *Time* 127(19):85 (May 12, 1986).

Mosk, Stanley. The emerging agenda in state constitutional rights law. *Annals of the American Academy of Political and Social Science* 496:54-64 (March 1988).

Press, Aric, and Ann McDaniel. Integrating the jury box. [Mentioned as Baxton v. Kentucky] *Newsweek* 107(19):70 (May 12, 1986).

Regan, Richard J. Supreme Court roundup: 1985 term. *Thought* 62(245):234-246 (June 1987).

Serr, Brian J., and Mark Maney. Racism, peremptory challenges, and the democratic jury: the jurisprudence of a delicate balance. *Journal of Criminal Law and Criminology* 79(1):1-65 (Spring 1988).

2979. Smalis v. Pennsylvania   May 5, 1986
       476 US 140   90 LEd2d 116   106 SCt 1745
       Almanac (1986):5A-6A

2980. Poland v. Arizona   May 5, 1986
       476 US 147   90 LEd2d 123   106 SCt 1749
       Almanac (1986):7A

2981. Lockhart v. McCree   May 5, 1986
       476 US 162   90 LEd2d 137   106 SCt 1758
       Almanac (1986):4A, 7A
       Burger Years 169-176
       Death Penalty 80s 162, 167-183
       Death Penalty 90s 11-14, 186-187, 191-207

Bersoff, Donald N. Social science data and the Supreme Court: Lockhart as a case in point. *American Psychologist* 42(1):52-58 (January 1987).

Death penalty: a barrier falls. *Newsweek* 107(20:68 (May 19, 1986).

In the Supreme Court of the United States Lockhart v. McCree: Amicus Curiae Brief for the American Psychological Assoication. *American Psychologist* 42(1):59-68 (January 1987).

Lake, L. B. Court stacks the deck in capital cases. [Editorial] *Christian Century* 103(20):575-576 (June 18-25, 1986).

Whisler, Barbara J. Supreme Court review: Sixth Amendment—death qualification of the jury: process is permissible where defendant does not face death penalty. *Journal of Criminal Law and Criminology* 78(4):954-983 (Winter 1988).

Will, George F. 'The F word.' [Editorial] *Newsweek* 107(21):80 (May 26, 1986).

2982. California v. Ciraolo   May 19, 1986
       476 US 207   90 LEd2d 210   106 SCt 1809
       Almanac (1986):5A

Gest, Ted. Burger Court: imprint of its last year. *U.S. News and World Report* 101(3):15 (July 21, 1986).

High Court's 5-way verdict. *U.S. News and World Report* 100(21):6 (June 2, 1986).

Junker, John M. The structure of the Fourth Amendment: the scope of the protection. *Journal of Criminal Law and Criminology* 79(4):1105-1183 (Winter 1989).

Krakovec, Laura L. Supreme Court review: Fourth Amendment—the constitutionality of warrantless aerial surveillance. *Journal of Criminal Law and Criminology* 77(3):602-631 (Fall 1986).

Lacayo, Richard, and Jay Branegan. Accent on the affirmative: the Supreme Court says yes and no on racial preferences. *Time* 127(22):66 (June 2, 1986).

Regan, Richard J. Supreme Court roundup: 1985 term. *Thought* 62(245):234-246 (June 1987).

2983. Dow Chemical Co. v. United States   May 19, 1986
476 US 227   90 LEd2d 226   106 SCt 1819
Almanac (1986):5A

Andersen, Robert M. Technology, pollution control, and EPA access to commercial property: a constitutional and policy framework. *Boston College Environmental Affairs Law Review* 17(1):1-74 (Fall 1989).

Bazarian, Stephen C. Dow Chemical Company v. United States and aerial surveillance by the EPA: an argument for post-surveillance notice to the observed. *Boston College Environmental Affairs Law Review* 15(3-4):593-626 (Spring 1988).

Dow loses flyover case. *Chemical Marketing Reporter* 229(21):3, 19 (May 26, 1986).

Dwyer, Paula. The Burger Court put the brakes on Reagan's federalism. *Business Week* (Industrial/Technology Edition) (2956):67 (July 21, 1986).

———. The EPA's eye in the sky has companies seeing red. *Business Week* (Industrial/Technology Edition) (2918):90 (October 28, 1985).

———. Reagan's 'new federalism' is about to have its day in court. *Business Week* (Industrial/Technology Edition) (2915):59-62 (October 7, 1985).

EPA's aerial scrutiny of Dow plant held legal. *Chemical and Engineering News* 64(21):5 (May 26 1986).

Gest, Ted. Burger Court: imprint of its last year. *U.S. News and World Report* 101(3):15 (July 21, 1986).

High Court's 5-way verdict. *U.S. News and World Report* 100(21):6 (June 2, 1986).

Junker, John M. The structure of the Fourth Amendment: the scope of the protection. *Journal of Criminal Law and Criminology* 79(4):1105-1183 (Winter 1989).

Lacayo, Richard, and Jay Branegan. Accent on the affirmative: the Supreme Court says yes and no on racial preferences. *Time* 127(22):66 (June 2, 1986).

Mauro, Tony. Federal prying from the sky. *Nation's Business* 73(10):34, 36 (October 1985).

Nelson-Horchler, Joani. Supreme Court: keep a hand on your wallet. *Industry Week* 226(5):28-29, 31 (September 2, 1985).

Regan, Richard J. Supreme Court roundup: 1985 term. *Thought* 62(245):234-246 (June 1987).

2984. Brock v. Pierce County   May 19, 1986
476 US 253   90 LEd2d 248   106 SCt 1834
Almanac (1986):14A

2985. Wygant v. Jackson Board of Education   May 19, 1986
476 US 267   90 LEd2d 260   106 SCt 1842
Affirmative (Greene) 107-120
Affirmative (Woods) 76-78
Almanac (1986):9A
Ascent 274-278+
Behind Bakke 160-162
Burger Years 95-108
Conflict 108-110+
Const (Currie) 482-488
Court Const 282-287, 366-367
Editorials (1986):584-589
Sup Ct Ind 263-264
Sup Ct Review (1989):1-51
Tenth 201-209

Bresler, Robert J. The forgotten issue. [Editorial] *USA Today* 116(2516):7 (May 1988).

Brown, Frank Dexter. High Court reviews civil rights. *Black Enterprise* 16(6):31 (January 1986).

Capozzola, John M. Affirmative action alive and well under Courts' strict scrutiny. *National Civic Review* 75(6):354-362 (November/December 1986).

Cohen, Carl. Naked racial preference. *Commentary* 81(3):24-31 (March 1986).

The Court: back to the future. *Newsweek* 106(16):74 (October 14, 1985).

Daly, James J., Stephen M. Baron, Jack Noble, and Carl Cohen. Affirmative action. *Commentary* 82(1):4-6 (July 1986).

Did Court flash red, green or amber? [Editorial] *U.S. News and World Report* 100(22):82 (June 9, 1986).

Dometrius, Nelson C., and Lee Sigelman. Modeling the impact of Court decisions: Wygant v. Board. *Journal of Politics* 50(1):131-149 (February 1988).

Dwyer, Paula. Clearing the confusion over affirmative action. *Business Week* (Industrial/Technology Edition) (2955):26-27 (July 14, 1986).

———. Reagan's 'new federalism' is about to have its day in court. *Business Week* (Industrial/Technology Edition) (2915):59-62 (October 7, 1985).

Eastland, Terry. Racial preference in court (again). *Commentary* 87(1):32-38 (January 1989).

———. Toward a real restoration of civil rights. *Commentary* 88(5):25-29 (November 1989).

Fields, Cheryl M. High Court backs affirmative action in certain forms. *Chronicle of Higher Education* 32(13):1, 15 (May 28 1986).

———. Justice Dept. officials says High-Court ruling requires repeal of affirmative-action order. *Chronicle of Higher Education* 32(14):10 (June 4, 1986).

Flygare, Thomas J. De jure: Supreme Court confused by reverse discrimination. *Phi Delta Kappan* 68(1):77-78 (September 1986).

Franke, Ann H., and Jacqueline W. Mintz. Four trends in higher education law. *Academe* 73(5):57-63 (September/October 1987).

Gest, Ted. Issues Supreme Court must rule on now. *U.S. News and World Report* 99(16):66 (October 14, 1985).

———. Now, Meese takes lead on social policy. *U.S. News and World Report* 99(12):27 (August 12 1985).

Greenlaw, Paul S. Reverse discrimination: the Supreme Court's dilemma. *Personnel Journal* 67(1):84-89 (January 1988).

High Court to tackle race bias. *Engineering News Record* 215(16):76 (October 17, 1985).

High Court's 5-way verdict. *U.S. News and World Report* 100(21):6 (June 2, 1986).

Hogan, Joyce, and Ann M. Quigley. Physical standards for employment and the courts. *American Psychologist* 41(11):1193-1217 (November 1986).

Justice Thurgood Marshall differs in Supreme Court case. *Jet* 70(12):25 (June 9, 1986).

Lacayo, Richard, and Jay Branegan. Accent on the affirmative: the Supreme Court says yes and no on racial preferences. *Time* 127(22):66 (June 2, 1986).

Martin, Bob. The Supreme Court's new era: what's ahead for labor law? *Personnel Journal* 65(10):92-98 (October 1986).

Mauro, Tony. The High Court: what it's up to. *Nation's Business* 74(9):57-60 (September 1986).

Moskowitz, Daniel B., and Steven W. Setzer. High Court backs racial quotas. *ENR* 218(10):42 (March 5, 1987).

Murphy, Betty Southard, Wayne E. Barlow, and Diane D. Hatch. Supreme Court reaffirms affirmative action. *Personnel Journal* 65(9):19-22 (September 1986).

Nelson-Horchler, Joani. Supreme Court: keep a hand on your wallet. *Industry Week* 226(5):28-29, 31 (September 2, 1985).

Powell, Lewis F., Jr., Sandra Day O'Connor, Byron R. White, Thurgood Marshall, and John Paul Stevens. Excerpts from 5 opinions issued by U.S. Supreme Court in affirmative-action case. *Chronicle of Higher Education* 32(13):15-18 (May 28, 1986).

Press, Aric, and Ann McDaniel. Mixed signal in Court. *Newsweek* 107(22):65 (June 2, 1986).

———. A woman's day in court. *Newsweek* 109(14):58-59 (April 6, 1987).

Redeker, James R. The Supreme Court on affirmative action: conflicting opinions. *Personnel* 63(10):8-14 (October 1986).

Regan, Richard J. Supreme Court roundup: 1985 term. *Thought* 62(245):234-246 (June 1987).

Reid-Dove, Allyson, and Michael E. Howard. "Night has fallen on the Court . . ." *Black Enterprise* 20(2):44-45 (September 1989).

Rotunda, Ronald D. The Supreme Court: eschewing bright lines. *Trial* 25(12):52-56 (December 1989).

Ruben, George. Developments in industrial relations: High Court backs laid-off white teachers. *Monthly Labor Review* 109(7):46-47 (July 1986).

Seligman, Daniel. Dubious distinctions. *Fortune* 113(13):127 (June 23, 1986).

Sendor, Benjamin. The High Court splits on race-based layoff policies. *American School Board Journal* 173(9):20, 47 (September 1986).

———. Trend: Courts sustain your tough, but fair, actions. *American School Board Journal* 172(6):20-21(June 1985).

Starr, Mark, Ann McDaniel, and Bob Cohn. Meese weighs in on abortion. *Newsweek* 106(5):60-61 (July 29, 1985).

Supreme Court: jolt for justice. *Economist* 299(7448):21-22 (May 31-June 6, 1986).

Supreme Court: reaffirmative action? *Economist* 297(7421):28 (November 23-30, 1985).

Villere, Maurice, and Sandra Hartman. What's affirmative about affirmative action? *Business Horizons* 32(5):22-27 (September/October 1989).

2986. Henderson v. United States   May 19, 1986
476 US 321   90 LEd2d 299   106 SCt 1871
Almanac (1986):6A

2987. Bowen v. Owens   May 19, 1986
476 US 340   90 LEd2d 316   106 SCt 1881
Almanac (1986):10A

2988. Louisiana Public Service Commission v. Federal Communications Commission (FCC)   May 27, 1986
        Coupled with Florida Public Services Commission v. Federal Communications Commission (FCC)
        Coupled with California Public Services Commission v. Federal Communications Commission (FCC)
        Coupled with Public Utilities Commission of Ohio v. Federal Communications Commission (FCC)
476 US 355   90 LEd2d 369   106 SCt 1890
Almanac (1986):13A

Andresky, Jill. A telephonic tower of Babel. *Forbes* 139(7):92 (April 6, 1987).

Cross, Phillip S. Telephone rate refunds not guaranteed after High Court's depreciation ruling. *Public Utilities Fortnightly* 118(10):51-54 (November 13, 1986).

Dwyer, Paula. The Burger Court put the brakes on Reagan's federalism. *Business Week* (Industrial/Technology Edition) (2956):67 (July 21, 1986).

Mason, Charles. High Court rejects FCC rule on phone depreciation regs. *Electronic News* 32(1604):30 (June 2, 1986).

Matthews, Douglas T., and Joseph S. Kraemer. An expanded role for the states in prescribing telephone company depreciation rates. *Public Utilities Fortnightly* 118(7):42-44 (October 2, 1986).

Miller, Edythe S. Ideology, jurisdiction, and deregulation of the telephone network. *Public Utilities Fortnightly* 118(7):14-18 (October 2, 1986).

Radford, Bruce W. A Memorial Day sunburn. [Editorial] *Public Utilities Fortnightly* 117(13):4-5 (June 26, 1986).

Supreme Court overturns FCC position on telephone depreciation. *Public Utilities Fortnightly* 118(1):47 (July 10, 1986).

Wilke, John. An accounting clash that may boost local phone bills. *Business Week* (Industrial/Technology Edition) (2930):46-48 (January, 27 1986).

2989. International Longshoremen's Association, AFL-CIO v. Davis   May 27, 1986
476 US 380   90 LEd2d 389   106 SCt 1904
Almanac (1986):14A
Sup Ct Review (1986):135-155

2990. Square D Co. v. Niagara Frontier Tariff Bureau, Inc. May 27, 1986
476 US 409   90 LEd2d 413   106 SCt 1922
Almanac (1986):12A

Moskowitz, Daniel B. Breaking down immunity to antitrust. *Business Week* (Industrial/Technology Edition) (2936):34-36 (March 10, 1986).

2991. Federal Deposit Insurance Corp. v. Philadelphia Gear Corp.   May 27, 1986
476 US 426   90 LEd2d 428   106 SCt 1931
     Almanac (1986):12A-13A
What does the new High Court mean to banks? *ABA Banking Journal* 78(8):28-30 (August 1986).

2992. Federal Trade Commission (FTC) v. Indiana Federation of Dentists   June 2, 1986
476 US 447   90 LEd2d 445   106 SCt 2009
     Almanac (1986):12A

2993. Bowen v. City of New York   June 2, 1986
476 US 467   90 LEd2d 462   106 SCt 2022
     Almanac (1986):15A

2994. Los Angeles v. Preferred Communications, Inc.   June 2, 1986
476 US 488   90 LEd2d 480   106 SCt 2034
     Almanac (1986):11A-12A
Dwyer, Paula. The Burger Court put the brakes on Reagan's federalism. *Business Week* (Industrial/Technology Edition) (2956):67 (July 21, 1986).

2995. South Carolina v. Catawba Indian Tribe   June 2, 1986
476 US 498   90 LEd2d 490   106 SCt 2039
     Almanac (1986):17A
     Am Indians (Wilkinson) 132, 166

2996. Lee v. Illinois   June 3, 1986
476 US 530   90 LEd2d 514   106 SCt 2056
     Almanac (1986):7A
Haddad, James B., and Richard G. Agin. A potential revolution in Bruton doctrine: is Bruton applicable where domestic evidence rules prohibit use of a codefendant's confession as evidence against a defendant although the confrontation clause would allow such use? *Journal of Criminal Law and Criminology* 81(2):235-266 (Summer 1990).
Krit, Jonathan J. Supreme Court review: Sixth Amendment—confrontation and the use of interlocking confessions at joint trial. *Journal of Criminal Law and Criminology* 78(4):937-953 (Winter 1988).

2997. United States v. Hemme   June 3, 1986
476 US 558   90 LEd2d 538   106 SCt 2071

2998. Brown-Forman Distillers Corp. v. New York State Liquor Authority   June 3, 1986
476 US 573   90 LEd2d 552   106 SCt 2080
     Almanac (1986):16A

2999. United States v. Hughes Properties   June 3, 1986
476 US 593   90 LEd2d 569   106 SCt 292
     Almanac (1986):13A
Seligman, Daniel. Playing the slots on an accrual basis. *Fortune* 114(1):100 (July 7, 1986).
Supreme Court: High Court upholds casino's accrual method. *Journal of Accountancy* 162(2):30 (August 1986).

3000. Bowen, Secretary of Health and Human Services v. American Hospital Association   June 9, 1986
476 US 610   90 LEd2d 584   106 SCt 2101
     Almanac (1986):263-265, 10A
Drinan, Robert F. The Supreme Court and Baby Jane Doe. *America* 154(9):180-182 (March 8, 1986).

Gest, Ted. Abortion rights ride out an attack—for now. *U.S. News and World Report* 100(24):8 (June 23, 1986).

———. Burger Court: imprint of its last year. *U.S. News and World Report* 101(3):15 (July 21, 1986).

———. Issues Supreme Court must rule on now. *U.S. News and World Report* 99(16):66 (October 14, 1985).

———. Now, Meese takes lead on social policy. *U.S. News and World Report* 99(12):27 (August 12 1985).

Holden, Constance. High Court says no to administration's Baby Doe rules. *Science* 232(4758):1595-1596 (June 27, 1986).

If not that way, what way? [Editorial] *America* 155(2):21 (July 19-26, 1986).

Lawton, Kim A. High Court strikes down abortion restrictions, rules on handicapped infants. *Christianity Today* 30(10):38-39 (July 11, 1986).

Murphy, Jamie, Laurence L. Barrett, and Anne Constable. Abortion's shrinking majority: the right-to-life movement loses a pair of controversial decisions. *Time* 127(25):30-31 (June 23, 1986).

Science and society: old Baby Doe rule struck down, but . . . *Science News* 129(25):395 (June 21, 1986).

Wylie, Pete. U.S. Supreme Court prepares to hear right-to life and religious freedom cases. *Christianity Today* 29(14):64-66 (October 4, 1985).

3001. Bowen v. Michigan Academy of Family Physicians June 9, 1986
476 US 667 90 LEd2d 623 106 SCt 2133
Almanac (1986):15A

3002. Crane v. Kentucky June 9, 1986
476 US 683 90 LEd2d 636 106 SCt 2142
Almanac (1986):6A

3003. Bowen v. Roy June 11, 1986
476 US 693 90 LEd2d 735 106 SCt 2147
Almanac (1986):4A, 11A
Godless 41-42

Regan, Richard J. Supreme Court roundup: 1985 term. *Thought* 62(245):234-246 (June 1987).

———. Supreme Court roundup: 1987 term. *Thought* 64(253):176-187 (June 1989).

Rievman, Joshua D. Judicial scrutiny of Native American free exercise rights: Lyng and the decline of the Yoder doctrine. *Boston College Environmental Affairs Law Review* 17(1):169-199 (Fall 1989).

3004. United States v. Dion June 11, 1986
476 US 734 90 LEd2d 767 106 SCt 2216
Almanac (1986):17A
Am Indians (Wilkinson) 50-52, 132

3005. Thornburgh, Governor of Pennsylvania v. American College of Obstetricians & Gynecologists June 11, 1986
476 US 747 90 LEd2d 779 106 SCt 2169
Abortion Am 62-63, 99, 187, 204-211, 333-334, 337-338+
Abortion Dec 123-146+
Abortion Dec 80s Introduction, 135-174R
Abortion Quest 122-125
Almanac (1986):263-264, 8A-9A; (1989):306-307
Brennan 316-318
Burger Years 109-124
Editorials (1986):660-665
Hard Choices 176-181
Liberty 661-662, 667-691+
Nobody's 13-17
Tenth 135-150
Turning 260-266

Aliotta, Jilda M. The unfinished feminist agenda: the shifting forum. *Annals of the American Academy of Political and Social Science* 515:140-150 (May 1991).

Behuniak-Long, Susan. Justice Sandra Day O'Connor and the power of maternal legal thinking. *Review of Politics* 54(3):417-444 (Summer 1992).

Bersoff, Donald N., Laurel Pyle Malson, and Bruce J. Ennis. APA brief in Thornburgh v. American College of Obstetricians and Gynecologists. *American Psychologist* 42(1):77-78 (January 1987).

Carey, Peter, Joanne Silberner, Ted Gest, Miriam Horn, and Jeffrey Sheler. Reappraising topic A. *U.S. News and World Report* 106(3):9-10 (January 23, 1989).

The Court: back to the future. *Newsweek* 106(16):74 (October 14, 1985).

Doerr, Edd. Abortion rights at the crossroads. *Humanist* 45(6):39-40 (November/December 1985).

Gest, Ted. Abortion rights ride out an attack—for now. *U.S. News and World Report* 100(24):8 (June 23, 1986).

———. Burger Court: imprint of its last year. *U.S. News and World Report* 101(3):15 (July 21, 1986).

———. Now, Meese takes lead on social policy. *U.S. News and World Report* 99(12):27 (August 12 1985).

Lawton, Kim A. High Court strikes down abortion restrictions, rules on handicapped infants. *Christianity Today* 30(10):38-39 (July 11, 1986).

McDaniel, Ann. Countdown on abortion. *Newsweek* 113(4):50 (January 23, 1989).

Melton, Gary B. Legal regulation of adolscent abortion: unintended effects. *American Psychologist* 42(1):79-83 (January 1987).

Melton, Gary B., and Nancy Felipe Russo. Adolescent abortion: psychological perspectives on public policy. *American Psychologist* 42(1):69-72 (January 1987).

Murphy, Jamie, Laurence L. Barrett, and Anne Constable. Abortion's shrinking majority: the right-to-life movement loses a pair of controversial decisions. *Time* 127(25):30-31 (June 23, 1986).

Neuhaus, Richard John. Democratic morality. *National Review* 38(13):47 (July 18, 1986).

New arguments on an old issue. *Christianity Today* 29(18):56-57 (December 13, 1985).

Overkill on abortion. [Editorial] *America* 155(1):1-2 (July 5-12, 1986).

Press, Aric, Ann McDaniel, Gloria Borger, Howard Fineman, and Elisa Williams. Abortion storm. *Newsweek* 107(25):26-27 (June 23, 1986).

Regan, Richard J. Supreme Court roundup: 1985 term. *Thought* 62(245):234-246 (June 1987).

Rosenblum, Victor G. Letting the states set abortion policy. [Editorial] *Christian Century* 106(8):252-253 (March 8, 1989).

Stoner, James R., Jr. Common law and constitutionalism in the abortion case. *Review of Politics* 55(3):421-441 (Summer 1993).

Thomas, Evan, David Beckwith, and Anne Constable. Reagan's Mr. Right: Rehnquist is picked for the Court's top job. *Time* 127(26):24-33 (June 30, 1986).

Wylie, Pete. U.S. Supreme Court prepares to hear right-to life and religious freedom cases. *Christianity Today* 29(14):64-66 (October 4, 1985).

3006. United States v. Mottaz		June 11, 1986
476 US 834	90 LEd2d 841	106 SCt 2224
Almanac (1986):17A		

3007. Reed v. Campbell		June 11, 1986
476 US 852	90 LEd2d 858	106 SCt 2234
Almanac (1986):10A		

3008. East River Steamship Corp. v. Transamerica Delaval Inc.		June 16, 1986
476 US 858	90 LEd2d 865	106 SCt 2295
Almanac (1986):13A		

3009. Three Affiliated Tribes of the Fort Berthold Reservation v. Wold Engineering, P.C.		June 16, 1986
476 US 877	90 LEd2d 881	106 SCt 2267
Almanac (1986):17A		
Am Indians (Wilkinson) 132, 178, 199		

3010. Attorney General of New York v. Soto-Lopez		June 17, 1986
476 US 898	90 LEd2d 899	106 SCt 2317
Almanac (1986):10A-11A		

3011. Lyng v. Payne   June 17, 1986
476 US 926   90 LEd2d 921   106 SCt 2333
Almanac (1986):10A

3012. Nantahala Power & Light Co. v. Thornburg   June 17, 1986
476 US 953   90 LEd2d 943   106 SCt 2349
Almanac (1986):15A
FERC power allocations binding on states, Supreme Court rules. *Public Utilities Fortnightly* 118(1):46 (July
10, 1986).
Ray, Mel. The preemption muddle. [Editorial] *Electrical World* 200(12):8 (December 1986).

3013. Young v. Community Nutrition Institute   June 17, 1986
476 US 974   90 LEd2d 959   106 SCt 2360
Almanac (1986):13A
Burger Years 191-205
Gest, Ted. Burger Court: imprint of its last year. *U.S. News and World Report* 101(3):15 (July 21, 1986).

3014. Wardair Canada, Inc. v. Florida Department of Revenue   June 18, 1986
477 US 1   91 LEd2d 1   106 SCt 2369
Almanac (1986):16A
Justice Dept. asked to check legality of Florida aviation fuel tax. *Aviation Week and Space Technology*
122(14):35 (April 8, 1985).

3015. Schiavone v. Fortune, aka Time, Inc.   June 18, 1986
477 US 21   91 LEd2d 18   106 SCt 2379
Almanac (1986):17A
Gest, Ted. Burger Court: imprint of its last year. *U.S. News and World Report* 101(3):15 (July 21, 1986).

3016. Bowen v. Public Agencies Opposed to Social Security Entrapment   June 19, 1986
477 US 41   91 LEd2d 35   106 SCt 2390
Almanac (1983):219; (1986):15A
Palmer, Stacy E. High Court says rights laws apply to sexual harassment. *Chronicle of Higher Education*
32(17):11 (June 25, 1986).
Tarnoff, Stephen. Court decisions or benefits increase employers' costs. *Business Insurance* 21(44):93-95
(November 2, 1987).

3017. Meritor Savings Bank, FSB v. Mechelle Vinson   June 19, 1986
477 US 57   91 LEd2d 49   106 SCt 2399
Almanac (1986):11A
Burger Years 109-124
Editorials (1993):1366-1373
Landmark (v. 3):151-167R
Price 226-228
Sup Ct Review (1994):1-56
Barnett, Edith. Sexual harassment: a continuing source of litigation in the workplace. *Trial* 25(6):34-38 (June
1989).
Champagne, Paul J., and R. Bruce McAfee. Auditing sexual harassment. *Personnel Journal* 68(6):124-139
(June 1989).
Christopher, Maurine. Latest ruling bolsters harassment fighters. *Advertising Age* 57(37):30 (June 30, 1986).
Dworkin, Terry Morehead. Harassment in the 1990s. *Business Horizons* 36(2):52-58 (March/April 1993).
Dwyer, Paula. Sexual harassment: companies could be liable. *Business Week* (Industrial/Technology Edition)
(2939):35 (March 31, 1986).
A first on women's rights. *U.S. News and World Report* 100(25):10 (June 30, 1986).
Flaxman, Howard R., and Brian F. Jackson. New considerations for hostile working environment. *HR Focus*
71(3):18-19 (March 1994).

Ford, Robert C., and Frank S. McLaughlin. Sexual harassment at work. *Business Horizons* 31(6):14-19 (November/December 1988).

Galen, Michele, Zachary Schiller, Joan O'C. Hamilton, and Keith H. Hammonds. Ending sexual harassment: business is getting the message. *Business Week* (Industrial/Technology Edition) (3204):98-100 (March 18, 1991).

Garland, Susan B., and Troy Segal. Thomas vs. Hill: the lessons for corporate America. [Editorial] *Business Week* (Industrial/Technology Edition) (3236):32 (October 21, 1991).

Gest, Ted. Burger Court: imprint of its last year. *U.S. News and World Report* 101(3):15 (July 21, 1986).

Greene, Richard. "A pattern of fornication." *Forbes* 137(13):66 (June 16, 1986).

Koen, Clifford M., Jr. Sexual harassment claims stem from a hostile work environment. *Personnel Journal* 69(8):88-99 (August 1990).

Langevin, Judith Bevis. Sexual harassment: Vinson is just the beginning. *Trial* 22(12):35-36, 38 (December 1986).

Leo, John, Anne Constable, and Jeanne McDowell. Retreat for advances?: the fight against sexual harrassment reaches the Supreme Court. *Time* 127(14):62-63 (April 7, 1986).

Lissy, William E. Supreme Court rules on sexual harassment. *Supervision* 48(11):21-22 (November 1986).

Marczely, Bernadette. A legal update on sexual harassment in the public schools. *Clearing House* 66(6):329-331 (July/August 1993).

Martin, Bob. The Supreme Court's new era: what's ahead for labor law? *Personnel Journal* 65(10):92-98 (October 1986).

Mauro, Tony. The High Court: what it's up to. *Nation's Business* 74(9):57-60 (September 1986).

Moskowitz, Daniel B. High Court hits sex bias. *Engineering News Record* 216(26):59-60 (June 26, 1986).

Murphy, Betty Southard, Wayne E. Barlow, and Diane D. Hatch. High Court rules on sexual harassment. *Personnel Journal* 65(9):22-24 (September 1986).

Palmer, Stacy E. High Court says rights laws apply to sexual harassment. *Chronicle of Higher Education* 32(17):11 (June 25, 1986).

Regan, Richard J. Supreme Court roundup: 1985 term. *Thought* 62(245):234-246 (June 1987).

Ritter, Anne. The way it was: HR in the 1980s. *Personnel* 66(12):30-37 (December 1989).

Ruben, George. Developments in industrial relations: Supreme Court hears sexual harassment case. *Monthly Labor Review* 109(9):39 (September 1986).

Seligman, Daniel. Affairs of the heart. *Fortune* 114(6):137, 139 (September 15, 1986).

Smolowe, Jill, D. Blake Hallanan and Melissa Ludtke. Those 24 words are back: ERA surfaces once more amid doubts about its urgency. *Time* 130(1):91 (July 6, 1987).

Sullivan, Frederick L. Sexual harassment: the Supreme Court's ruling. *Personnel* 63(12):37-44 (December 1986).

Woods, Maureen P., and Walter J. Flynn. Heading off sexual harassment. *Personnel* 66(11):45-49 (November 1989).

Woolsey, Christine. Court struggles to define sexual harassment. *Business Insurance* 27(43):2, 80 (October 18, 1993).

3018. McMillan v. Pennsylvania   June 19, 1986
       477 US 79   91 LEd2d 67   106 SCt 2411
            Almanac (1986):8A

       Dennis, Anthony J. Supreme Court review: Fifth Amendment—due process rights at sentencing. *Journal of Criminal Law and Criminology* 77(3):646-665 (Fall 1986).

3019. United States v. American Bar Endowment   June 23, 1986
       477 US 105   91 LEd2d 89   106 SCt 2426
            Almanac (1986):13A-14A

       ABE loses on tax status of insurance program. *Journal of Taxation* 65(3):204 (September 1986).

3020. Maine v. Taylor   June 23, 1986
       477 US 131   91 LEd2d 110   106 SCt 2440
            Almanac (1986):16A

3021. Atkins v. Rivera   June 23, 1986
  477 US 154   91 LEd2d 131   106 SCt 2356
  Almanac (1986):15A

3022. Darden v. Wainwright, Secretary, Florida Department of Corrections June 23, 1986
  477 US 168   91 LEd2d 144   106 SCt 2464
  Almanac (1986):7A
  Pettegrew, Hillary L. Supreme Court review: Sixth and Eighth Amendments—erosion of defendant's right to an impartial jury and a fundamentally fair trial. *Journal of Criminal Law and Criminology* 77(3):796-820 (Fall 1986).

3023. Offshore Logistics, Inc. v. Tallentire June 23, 1986
  477 US 207   91 LEd2d 174   106 SCt 2485
  Almanac (1986):14A
  Edelman, Paul S. Wrongful death on the high seas: Tallentire says federal law governs. *Trial* 23(4):58-61 (April 1987).
  George, James A. The 'triple crown' of admiralty cases: from definitions to damages. *Trial* 27(10):46-53 (October 1991).

3024. Anderson v. Liberty Lobby, Inc. June 25, 1986
  477 US 242   91 LEd2d 202   106 SCt 2505
  Almanac (1986):12A
  Fields, Howard. High Court overturns Scalia in libel case. *Publishers' Weekly* 230(2):18 (July 11, 1986).
  Gest, Ted. Burger Court: imprint of its last year. *U.S. News and World Report* 101(3):15 (July 21, 1986).
  Lacayo, Richard, and Anne Constable. Libel relief: the court strengthens a shield. *Time* 128(1):55 (July 7, 1986).
  Roper, James E. Congress and the Court. *Editor and Publisher* 120(1):20 (January 3, 1987).

3025. International Union, United Automobile, Aerospace and Agricultural Implement June 25, 1986
   Workers of America v. Brock
  477 US 274   91 LEd2d 228   106 SCt 2523
  Almanac (1986):14A
  Burger Years 191-205

3026. Memphis Community School District v. Stachura June 25, 1986
  477 US 299   91 LEd2d 249   106 SCt 2537
  Almanac (1986):9A
  Flygare, Thomas J. De jure: Supreme Court restricts damages for constitutional violations. *Phi Delta Kappan* 68(4)[3]:246-248 (November 1986).
  Palmer, Stacy E. Supreme Court voids jury award to teacher for rights violation. *Chronicle of Higher Education* 32(18):11 (July 2, 1986).
  Sendor, Benjamin. Fairness is the key to balancing your authority with teachers' academic freedom. *American School Board Journal* 172(11):26, 48 (November 1985).

3027. Celotex Corp. v. Catrett June 25, 1986
  477 US 317   91 LEd2d 265   106 SCt 2548
  Almanac (1986):17A
  Tarnoff, Stephen. Punitive damages acquired with firm. *Business Insurance* 20(23):3, 24 (June 9, 1986).
  Tarnoff, Stephen. Supreme Court asked to rule on punitive damages issues. *Business Insurance* 19(48):1+ (December 2, 1985).

3028. MacDonald, Sommer and Frates v. County of Yolo June 25, 1986
  477 US 340   91 LEd2d 285   106 SCt 2561
  Almanac (1986):13A
  Darnell, Tim. The land and the law. *American City and County* 103(1):38-45 (January 1988).

Farber, Daniel A. 'Taking' liberties. *New Republic* 198(26):19-20, 22 (June 27, 1988).

3029. Kimmelman v. Morrison   June 26, 1986
    477 US 365   91 LEd2d 305   106 SCt 2574
       Almanac (1986):6A

3030. Ford v. Wainwright, Secretary, Florida Department of Corrections   June 26, 1986
    477 US 399   91 LEd2d 335   106 SCt 2595
       Almanac (1986):7A
       Death Penalty 80s 15-18
Entin, Jonathan L. Psychiatry, insanity, and the death penalty: a note on implementing Supreme Court decisions. *Journal of Criminal Law and Criminology* 79(1):218-239 (Spring 1988).
Lacayo, Richard, and Anne Constable. Libel relief: the court strengthens a shield. *Time* 128(1):55 (July 7, 1986).
Pastroff, Sanford M. Supreme Court review: Eighth Amendment—the constitutional rights of the insane on death row. *Journal of Criminal Law and Criminology* 77(3):844-866 (Fall 1986).
Press, Aric, and Ann McDaniel. A Supreme Court stay of death. *Newsweek* 108(1):63 (July 7, 1986).
Updates. *Nation* 243(2):37 (July 19-26, 1986).

3031. Kuhlmann v. Wilson   June 26, 1986
    477 US 436   91 LEd2d 364   106 SCt 2616
       Almanac (1986):6A
Lundstrom, Bruce D. Supreme Court review: Sixth Amendment—right to counsel: limited postindictment use of jailhouse informants is permissible. *Journal of Criminal Law and Criminology* 77(3):743-774 (Fall 1986).
Wells, Diane. Federal habeas corpus and the death penalty: a need for a return to the principles of Furman. *Journal of Criminal Law and Criminology* 80(2):427-490 (Summer 1989).

3032. Murray v. Carrier   June 26, 1986
    477 US 478   91 LEd2d 397   106 SCt 2639
       Almanac (1986):6A
       Sup Ct Yearbook (1994-95):86-87
Chemerinsky, Erwin. Supreme Court review: making sense of habeas corpus. *Trial* 28(12):79-82 (December 1992).
Wells, Diane. Federal habeas corpus and the death penalty: a need for a return to the principles of Furman. *Journal of Criminal Law and Criminology* 80(2):427-490 (Summer 1989).

3033. Smith v. Murray   June 26, 1986
    477 US 527   91 LEd2d 434   106 SCt 2661
       Almanac (1986):7A-8A
       Death Penalty 90s 17-18

3034. Department of Treasury v. Galioto   June 27, 1986
    477 US 556   91 LEd2d 459   106 SCt 2683
       Almanac (1986):8A

3035. City of Riverside v. Rivera   June 27, 1985
    477 US 561   91 LEd2d 466   106 SCt 2686
       Almanac (1986):9A

3036. United States Department of Transportation v. Paralyzed Veterans of America   June 27, 1986
    477 US 597   91 LEd2d 494   106 SCt 2705
       Almanac (1986):291, 10A
Lacayo, Richard, and Anne Constable. Libel relief: the court strengthens a shield. *Time* 128(1):55 (July 7, 1986).
Press, Aric, and Ann McDaniel. A Supreme Court stay of death. *Newsweek* 108(1):63 (July 7, 1986).

Supreme Court rules airlines may discriminate against disabled. *Aviation Week and Space Technology* 125(2):45 (July 14, 1986).

3037. Ohio Civil Rights Commission v. Dayton Christian Schools, Inc.   June 27, 1986
    477 US 619   91 LEd2d 512   106 SCt 2718
    Almanac (1986):17A
    Original (Davis) 85-86

Collision course. *Christian Century* 103(16):456-457 (May 7, 1986).

Drinan, Robert F. The Supreme Court examines fundamentalist Christian schools. *America* 154(14):306-308 (April 12, 1986).

Fields, Cheryl M. 2 new Supreme Court rulings support affirmative action to remedy past bias. *Chronicle of Higher Education* 32(19):9, 13 (July 9, 1986).

Golphin, Vincent. Supreme Court to hear oral arguments in Dayton Christian Schools case. *Christianity Today* 30(5):56-57 (March 21, 1986).

Maguire, Daniel C. Can a university be Catholic? *Academe* 74(1):12-16 (January/February 1988).

3038. Lyng v. Castillo   June 27, 1986
    477 US 635   91 LEd2d 527   106 SCt 2727
    Almanac (1986):10A

Melton, Gary B. Public policy and private prejudice: psychology and law on gay rights. *American Psychologist* 44(6):933-940 (June 1989).

3039. Press-Enterprise Co. v. Superior Court of Riverside County   June 30, 1986
    478 US 1   92 SCt 1   106 SCt 2735
    Almanac (1986):12A
    En Am Con 1978

Gest, Ted. Burger Court: imprint of its last year. *U.S. News and World Report* 101(3):15 (July 21, 1986).

Press, Aric, and Ann McDaniel. A Supreme Court stay of death. *Newsweek* 108(1):63 (July 7, 1986).

Reid, Traciel V. Judicial policy-making and implementation: an empirical examination. *Western Political Quarterly* 41(3):509-527 (September 1988).

Roper, James E. Congress and the Court. *Editor and Publisher* 120(1):20 (January 3, 1987).

———. Pretrial hearings must be opened. *Editor and Publisher* 119(27):14, 29 (July 5, 1986).

3040. Thornburgh v. Gingles   June 30, 1986
    478 US 30   92 LEd2d 25   106 SCt 2752
    Almanac (1986):11A; (1993):325-326, 22A-23A; (1994):312; (1995):6-39-40
    Tenth 240-244

American survey: Burger leaves the labyrinth. *Economist* 300(7454):17-22 (July 12-18, 1986).

American survey: up to a point, Governor Gerry. *Economist* 300(7454):22 (July 12-18, 1986).

Barnes, Fred. Gerrymeandering. *New Republic* 193(16):11-12 (October 14, 1985).

Brown, Frank Dexter. High Court reviews civil rights. *Black Enterprise* 16(6):31 (January 1986).

Caplan, Lincoln. The tenth justice (II). *New Yorker* 63(26):30-62 (August 17, 1987).

Court protects voter rights in Durham, N.C. *Jet* 70(17):6 (July 28, 1986).

Davis, Olethia. Tenuous interpretation: Sections 2 and 5 of the Voting Rights Act. *National Civic Review* 84(4):310-322 (Fall/Winter 1995).

Dent, David J. New ballot battles. *Black Enterprise* 16(7):28 (February 1986).

Forbes, Malcolm S., Jr. Pornographic-like quagmire. [Editorial] *Forbes* 135(11):31 (May 20, 1985).

Gerrymandering by the Court? *National Review* 38(14):12 (August 1, 1986).

Gest, Ted. Affirmative verdict on racial hiring. *U.S. News and World Report* 101(2):17-18 (July 14, 1986).

———. Now, Meese takes lead on social policy. *U.S. News and World Report* 99(12):27 (August 12 1985).

Graham, Barbara Luck. Federal Court policy-making and political equality: an analysis of judicial redistricting. *Western Political Quarterly* 44(1):101-117 (March 1991).

Heath, C. Robert. Thornburg v. Gingles: the unresolved issues. *National Civic Review* 79(1):50-71 (January/February 1990).

Lemov, Penelope. High Court lowers a barrier to state health care reform. *Governing* 8(10):59 (July 1995).

Neighbor, Howard D. The Supreme Court speaks, sort of, on the 1982 Voting Rights Act Amendments. *National Civic Review* 75(6):346-353 (November/December 1986).

Regan, Richard J. Supreme Court roundup: 1985 term. *Thought* 62(245):234-246 (June 1987).

Rush, Mark E. In search of a coherent theory of voting rights: challenges to the Supreme Court's vision of fair and effective representation. *Review of Politics* 56(3):503-523 (Summer 1994).

Seligman, Daniel. The 67% solution. *Fortune* 124(5):120 (August 26, 1991).

Weber, Ronald E. Redistricting and the courts: judicial activism in the 1990s. *American Politics Quarterly* 23(2):204-228 (April 1995).

3041. Davis v. Bandemer   June 30, 1986
    478 US 109   92 LEd2d 85   106 SCt 2797
      Almanac (1986):4A, 11A
      Const Law 634-637R
      Guide (CQ) 57
      Sup Ct Review (1986):175-257

American survey: Burger leaves the labyrinth. *Economist* 300(7454):17-22 (July 12-18, 1986).

Brace, Kimball W., and John P. Katosh. From the political thicket to a political swamp. *Journal of State Government* 59(3):104-105 (September/October 1986).

Regan, Richard J. Supreme Court roundup: 1985 term. *Thought* 62(245):234-246 (June 1987).

Rush, Mark E. In search of a coherent theory of voting rights: challenges to the Supreme Court's vision of fair and effective representation. *Review of Politics* 56(3):503-523 (Summer 1994).

Weber, Ronald E. Redistricting and the courts: judicial activism in the 1990s. *American Politics Quarterly* 23(2):204-228 (April 1995).

3042. Bowers v. Hardwick   June 30, 1986
    478 US 186   92 LEd2d 140   106 SCt 2841
      Almanac (1986):10A
      Ascent 314-319
      Black 65-74
      Const (Currie) 475-477
      Const Law 278-280R+
      Courage 379-403, 429-430
      Documents (v. 2):864-867R
      Editorials (1986):766-775
      Hard Choices 217
      Liberty 654-667, 686-687+
      Magic 317-320
      May It 361-375R
      Nobody's 121-142

Bersoff, Donald N. Social science data and the Supreme Court: Lockhart as a case in point. *American Psychologist* 42(1):52-58 (January 1987).

Bersoff, Donald N., and David W. Ogden. APA amicus curiae briefs: furthering lesbian and gay male civil rights. *American Psychologist* 46(9):950-956 (September 1991).

Bork, Robert H. Beside the law. *National Review* 44(20):38, 40-43 (October 19, 1992).

Bresler, Robert J. Privacy, the courts, and social values. *USA Today* 115(2498):6-7 (November 1986).

Caplan, Gary S. Supreme Court review: Fourteenth Amendment—the Supreme Court limits the right to privacy. *Journal of Criminal Law and Criminology* 77(3):894-930 (Fall 1986).

Carlin, David R., Jr. Two doctrines of privacy. *America* 155(3):50-51 (August 2-9, 1986).

Church, George J., and Anne Constable. Knocking on the bedroom door: the High Court hands a defeat to homosexuals—and privacy rights. *Time* 128(2):23-24 (July 14, 1986).

Colson, Charles W. What the sodomy ruling really means. [Editorial] *Christianity Today* 30(13):72 (September 19, 1986).

Copelon, Rhonda, and Kathryn Kolbert. The gathering storm: Roe v. Wade. *Ms.* 17(10):88-92 (April 1989).

Dark day in court for homosexuals. *U.S. News and World Report* 101(2):18 (July 14, 1986).

Dripps, Donald A. Supreme Court review: Warren Burger in perspective. *Trial* 31(8):73-75 (August 1995).

The final days. [Editorial] *Nation* 243(2):35-36 (July 19-26, 1986).

Franklin, Daniel. The five dumbest Supreme Court decisions. *Washington Monthly* 26(10):12-18 (October 1994).

Freeman, Alan David, and Elizabeth Mensch. The Court & the sexual revolution. *Commonweal* 121(18):19-23 (October 21, 1994).

Gieringer, Dale, Maynard F. Thomson, James A. Webber, Robert Carlen, and David Robinson, Jr. AIDS & the law. *Commentary* 83(2):2-6 (February 1987).

Grogan, David. Homosexuals get short shrift from the Supreme Court, but an expert says history tells a different tale. *People Weekly* 26(3):85-87 (July 21, 1986).

Melton, Gary B. Public policy and private prejudice: psychology and law on gay rights. *American Psychologist* 44(6):933-940 (June 1989).

Minow, Martha. We, the family: constitutional rights and American families. *Journal of American History* 74(3):959-983 (December 1987).

Morley, Jefferson. Shoving time. *New Republic* 195(4):11-13 (July 28, 1986).

Neuhaus, Richard John. God save this vulnerable Court. *National Review* 38(15):40 (August 15, 1986).

Old rights, new rights. [Editorial] *America* 155(3):41 (August 2-9, 1986).

Press, Aric, and Ann McDaniel. A law that dares not say its name. *Newsweek* 107(14):74 (April 7, 1986).

Press, Aric, Ann McDaniel, George Raine, and Ginny Carroll. A government in the bedroom. *Newsweek* 108(2):36-38 (July 14, 1986).

The purpose of privacy. *New Republic* 195(4):4 (July 28, 1986).

Regan, Richard J. Supreme Court roundup: 1985 term. *Thought* 62(245):234-246 (June 1987).

Robinson, David, Jr. Sodomy and the Supreme Court. *Commentary* 82(4):57-61 (October 1986).

Rosenblatt, Roger. The Bill of Rights. *Life* 14(13 Special Issue):9-30 (Fall 1991).

Sodomy: limits to privacy. *Economist* 300(7453):28 (July 5-11, 1986).

Stoner, James R., Jr. Common law and constitutionalism in the abortion case. *Review of Politics* 55(3):421-441 (Summer 1993).

Supreme Court upholds Ga. law making sodomy illicit. *Jet* 70(17):6 (July 14, 1986).

3043. Japan Whaling Association v. American Cetacean Society   June 30, 1986
          Coupled with Baldridge v. American Cetacean Society
    478 US 221   92 LEd2d 166   106 SCt 2860
      Almanac (1986):15A

    Driesen, David M. The congressional role in international environmental law and its implications for statutory interpretation. *Boston College Environmental Affairs Law Review* 19(2):287-315 (Fall/Winter 1991).

    Fisher, Louis. Foreign policy powers of the president and Congress. *Annals of the American Academy of Political and Social Science* 499:149-159 (September 1988).

    Silverstein, Gordon. Statutory interpretation and the balance of institutional power. *Review of Politics* 56(3):475-501 (Summer 1994).

    Zimmerman, James Michael. Baldrige/Murazumi agreement: the Supreme Court gives credence to an aberration in American Cetacean Society III. *Boston College Environmental Affairs Law Review* 14(2):257-285 (Winter 1987).

3044. Papasan v. Allain, Governor of Mississippi   July 1, 1986
    478 US 265   92 LEd2d 289   106 SCt 2932
      Almanac (1986):16A

    Mosk, Stanley. The emerging agenda in state constitutional rights law. *Annals of the American Academy of Political and Social Science* 496:54-64 (March 1988).

3045. Library of Congress v. Shaw   July 1, 1986
    478 US 310   92 LEd2d 250   106 SCt 2957
      Almanac (1986):9A; (1991):255-257
    The Civil Rights Act of 1990. *Congressional Digest* 69(8-9):196-224 (August/September 1990).

3046. Posadas de Puerto Rico Associates, dba Condado Holiday Inn v. Tourism Co. of Puerto Rico   July 1, 1986
    478 US 328   92 LEd2d 266   106 SCt 2968

Almanac (1986):12A

Const (Currie) 513-518

Sup Ct Review (1986):1-17; (1987):303-344

Boedecker, Karl A., and Fred W. Morgan. The evolution of First Amendment protection for commercial speech. *Journal of Marketing* 59(1):38-47 (January 1995).

Bovard, James. Beer bust: censorship of commercial speech blocks the pursuit of happiness. [Editorial] *Barron's* 74(47):66 (November 21, 1994).

Brody, Michael. The Supreme Court shakes the ad biz. *Fortune* 114(3):152 (August 4, 1986).

Camel rights. *Fortune* 125(10):120 (May 18, 1992).

Colford, Steven W. Ad industry loses hero in Brennan. *Advertising Age* 61(31):1, 44 (July 30, 1990).

———. High Court's ruling sets back ad rights. *Advertising Age* 57(38):1, 62 (July 7, 1986).

———. What White's court exit means. *Advertising Age* 64(13):16 (March 29, 1993).

Commercial Break. *Time* 128(2):24 (July 14, 1986).

Dwyer, Paula. The Burger Court put the brakes on Reagan's federalism. *Business Week* (Industrial/Technology Edition) (2956):67 (July 21, 1986).

Hovland, Roxanne, and Ronald E. Taylor. Advertising and commercial speech since the 1986 Posadas Case. *Journalism Quarterly* 67(4):1083-1089 (Winter 1990).

Reed, O. Lee. Reading the tea leaves: future regulation of product-extrinsic advertising. *Business Horizons* 33(5):88-93 (September/October 1990).

Roper, James E. Congress and the Court. *Editor and Publisher* 120(1):20 (January 3, 1987).

Stengel, Richard, Howard G. Chua-Eoan, Anne Constable, and Elizabeth Taylor. Sex busters: a Meese commission and the Supreme Court echo a new moral militancy. *Time* 128(3):12-21 (July 21, 1986).

3047. Allen v. Illinois   July 1, 1986
         478 US 364   92 LEd2d 296   106 SCt 2988
             Almanac (1986):5A

3048. Bazemore v. Friday   July 1, 1986
         478 US 385   92 LEd2d 315   106 SCt 3000
             Almanac (1986):10A

Butler, Grace L. Legal and policy issues in higher education. *Journal of Negro Education* 63(3):451-459 (Summer 1994).

Fields, Cheryl M. 2 new Supreme Court rulings support affirmative action to remedy past bias. *Chronicle of Higher Education* 32(19):9, 13 (July 9, 1986).

Gray, Mary W. The halls of ivy and the halls of justice: lightening the burden. *Academe* 73(3):61-63 (May/June 1987).

Lee, Yong S. Shaping judicial response to gender discrimination in employment compensation. *Public Administration Review* 49(5):420-430 (September/October 1989).

Norris, Barbara A. Multiple regression analysis in Title VII cases: a structural approach to attacks of "missing factors" and "pre-act discrimination." *Law and Contemporary Problems* 49(4):63-96 (Autumn 1986).

Stefkovich, Jacqueline A., and Terrence Leas. A legal history of desegregation in higher education. *Journal of Negro Education* 63(3):406-420 (Summer 1994).

3049. Local 28 of Sheet Metal Workers' International Association   July 2, 1986
             v. Equal Employment Opportunity Commission (EEOC)
         478 US 421   92 LEd2d 344   106 SCt 3019
             Affirmative (Greene) 120-131
             Affirmative (Woods) 78-79
             Almanac (1986):9A
             Burger Years 95-108
             Editorials (1986):756-765

Bresler, Robert J. The forgotten issue. [Editorial] *USA Today* 116(2516):7 (May 1988).

Brown, Frank Dexter. High Court reviews civil rights. *Black Enterprise* 16(6):31 (January 1986).

Capozzola, John M. Affirmative action alive and well under Courts' strict scrutiny. *National Civic Review* 75(6):354-362 (November/December 1986).

Dwyer, Paula. Clearing the confusion over affirmative action. *Business Week* (Industrial/Technology Edition) (2955):26-27 (July 14, 1986).

Fields, Cheryl M. 2 new Supreme Court rulings support affirmative action to remedy past bias. *Chronicle of Higher Education* 32(19):9, 13 (July 9, 1986).

Fineman, Howard, and Ann McDaniel. A 'yes' for affirmative action. *Newsweek* 108(2):74 (July 14, 1986).

Flygare, Thomas J. De jure: Supreme Court confused by reverse discrimination. *Phi Delta Kappan* 68(1):77-78 (September 1986).

Greenlaw, Paul S. Reverse discrimination: The Supreme Court's dilemma. *Personnel Journal* 67(1)84-89 (January 1988).

High Court to tackle race bias. *Engineering News Record* 215(16):76 (October 17, 1985).

Louis, Errol T. Affirmative reaction. *Black Enterprise* 17(3):21 (October 1986).

Lowe, Frederick H. Steel suits are settled. *Black Enterprise* 17(4):22 (November 1986).

Mauro, Tony. The High Court: what it's up to. *Nation's Business* 74(9):57-60 (September 1986).

Moskowitz, Daniel B. Court OKs affirmative action. *Engineering News Record* 217(4):52 (July 10, 1986).

———. Pension penalties upheld. *Engineering News Record* 216(10):51 (March 6, 1986).

Murphy, Betty Southard, Wayne E. Barlow, and Diane D. Hatch. Supreme Court reaffirms affirmative action. *Personnel Journal* 65(9):19-22 (September 1986).

Press, Aric, and Ann McDaniel. A woman's day in court. *Newsweek* 109(14):58-59 (April 6, 1987).

Redeker, James R. The Supreme Court on affirmative action: conflicting opinions. *Personnel* 63(10):8-14 (October 1986).

Regan, Richard J. Supreme Court roundup: 1985 term. *Thought* 62(245):234-246 (June 1987).

Sendor, Benjamin. The High Court splits on race-based layoff policies. *American School Board Journal* 173(9):20, 47 (September 1986).

Trippett, Frank, and Anne Constable. A solid yes to affirmative action: two rulings add up to a stinging repudiation of the Justice Department. *Time* 128(2):22-23 (July 14, 1986).

3050. Local 93, International Association of Firefighters, etc. v. Cleveland   July 2, 1986
478 US 501   92 LEd2d 405   106 SCt 3063

Affirmative (Greene) 131-138
Affirmative (Woods) 79
Almanac (1986):9A
Brennan 257-263, 326-330
Burger Years 95-108
Editorials (1986):756-775

Brown, Frank Dexter. High Court reviews civil rights. *Black Enterprise* 16(6):31 (January 1986).

Capozzola, John M. Affirmative action alive and well under Courts' strict scrutiny. *National Civic Review* 75(6):354-362 (November/December 1986).

Cardone, John V. Substantive standards and NEPA: mitigating environmental consequences with consent decrees. *Boston College Environmental Affairs Law Review* 18(1):159-184 (Fall 1990).

Dwyer, Paula. Clearing the confusion over affirmative action. *Business Week* (Industrial/Technology Edition) (2955):26-27 (July 14, 1986).

Fields, Cheryl M. 2 new Supreme Court rulings support affirmative action to remedy past bias. *Chronicle of Higher Education* 32(19):9, 13 (July 9, 1986).

Fineman, Howard, and Ann McDaniel. A 'yes' for affirmative action. *Newsweek* 108(2):74 (July 14, 1986).

Flygare, Thomas J. De jure: Supreme Court confused by reverse discrimination. *Phi Delta Kappan* 68(1):77-78 (September 1986).

Gest, Ted. Affirmative verdict on racial hiring. *U.S. News and World Report* 101(2):17-18 (July 14, 1986).

Greenlaw, Paul S. Reverse discrimination: The Supreme Court's dilemma. *Personnel Journal* 67(1)84-89 (January 1988).

High Court to tackle race bias. *Engineering News Record* 215(16):76 (October 17, 1985).

Louis, Errol T., Affirmative reaction. *Black Enterprise* 17(3):21 (October 1986).

Lowe, Frederick H. Steel suits are settled. *Black Enterprise* 17(4):22 (November 1986).

Mauro, Tony. The High Court: what it's up to. *Nation's Business* 74(9):57-60 (September 1986).

Murphy, Betty Southard, Wayne E. Barlow, and Diane D. Hatch. Supreme Court reaffirms affirmative action. *Personnel Journal* 65(9):19-22 (September 1986).

Press, Aric, and Ann McDaniel. A woman's day in court. *Newsweek* 109(14):58-59 (April 6, 1987).

Redeker, James R. The Supreme Court on affirmative action: conflicting opinions. *Personnel* 63(10):8-14 (October 1986).

Regan, Richard J. Supreme Court roundup: 1985 term. *Thought* 62(245):234-246 (June 1987).

Reid-Dove, Allyson, and Michael E. Howard. "Night has fallen on the Court . . ." *Black Enterprise* 20(2):44-45 (September 1989).

Sendor, Benjamin. The High Court splits on race-based layoff policies. *American School Board Journal* 173(9):20, 47 (September 1986).

Trippett, Frank, and Anne Constable. A solid yes to affirmative action: two rulings add up to a stinging repudiation of the Justice Department. *Time* 128(2):22-23 (July 14, 1986).

Villere, Maurice, and Sandra Hartman. What's affirmative about affirmative action? *Business Horizons* 32(5):22-27 (September/October 1989).

Zimmerman, Joseph F., and Thomas D. Wilson. Local government: court-approved affirmative action decrees upheld for local hiring and promotion. *National Civic Review* 75(5):306-307 (September/October 1986).

3051. Pennsylvania v. Delaware Valley Citizens' Council for Clean Air   July 2, 1986
478 US 546   92 LEd2d 439   106 SCt 3088
Almanac (1986):15A

Conte, Alba. Public interest lawyers deserve risk multipliers. *Trial* 30(12):36-42 (December 1994).

3052. Rose v. Clark   July 2, 1986
478 US 570   92 LEd2d 460   106 SCt 3101
Almanac (1986):6A
Sup Ct Review (1989):195-211

Harris, Leslie J. Constitutional limits on criminal presumptions as an expression of changing concepts of fundamental fairness. *Journal of Criminal Law and Criminology* 77(2):308-357 (Summer 1986).

3053. United States v. James   July 2, 1986
478 US 597   92 LEd2d 483   106 SCt 3116
Almanac (1986):16A

3054. Baker v. General Motors Corp.   July 2, 1986
478 US 621   92 LEd2d 504   106 SCt 3129
Almanac (1986):15A-16A

3055. Randall v. Loftsgaarden   July 2, 1986
478 US 647   92 LEd2d 525   106 SCt 3134
Almanac (1986):13A

Banoff, Sheldon I. Supreme Court holds tax shelter benefits do not offset rescission damages. *Journal of Taxation* 65(4):210-215 (October 1986).

Palmer, Kevin A. Securities fraud: Supreme Court says that tax benefits do not reduce rescissionary recoveries: Randall v. Loftsgaarden. *Taxes* 65(3):147-153 (March 1987).

Supreme Court: High Court reaches tax-offset rule decision. *Journal of Accountancy* 162(3):14 (September 1986).

3056. Bethel School District No. 403 v. Fraser   July 7, 1986
478 US 675   92 LEd2d 549   106 SCt 3159
Almanac (1986):4A,12A

Adams, Kathleen, and Nick Catoggio. The Supreme Court: a principal's best friend. *Time* 146(2):14 (July 10, 1995).

Fields, Cheryl M. Rulings handed down in cases on race bias and on free speech in high schools. *Chronicle of Higher Education* 32(20):11, 17 (July 16, 1986).

Flygare, Thomas J. De jure: is Tinker dead? *Phi Delta Kappan* 68(2):165-166 (October 1986).

———. De jure: Supreme Court agrees to reconsider First Amendment rights of students. *Phi Delta Kappan* 67(4):312-313 (December 1985).

Gest, Ted. Burger Court: imprint of its last year. *U.S. News and World Report* 101(3):15 (July 21, 1986).

Hafen, Bruce C. School-backed student activities: what the courts say. *Education Digest* 54(1):29-31 (September 1988).

James, Bernard. Supreme Court docket: students' speech rights revisited. *Social Education* 52(4):243-245 (April/May 1988).

Marczely, Bernadette A. Student freedom of expression in the wake of Hazelwood and Bethel. *Clearing House* 65(5):269-271 (May/June 1992).

Marshall, majority differ on student vulgarity case. *Jet* 70(19):22 (July 28, 1986).

Regan, Richard J. Supreme Court roundup: 1985 term. *Thought* 62(245):234-246 (June 1987).

Roper, James E. Congress and the Court. *Editor and Publisher* 120(1):20 (January 3, 1987).

Rose, Lowell C. 'Reasonableness'—the High Court's new standard for cases involving student rights. *Phi Delta Kappan* 69(8):589-592 (April 1988).

Safire, William. With all deliberate vulgarity. *New York Times Magazine* (section 6, part 1):8, 10 (August 24, 1986).

Sendor, Benjamin. A court affirms the rights of the student press. *American School Board Journal* 173(12):11 (December 1986).

———. Court to kid: sorry, Matt, you can't say that at a school assembly. *American School Board Journal* 173(10):11, 47 (October 1986).

Stengel, Richard, Howard G. Chua-Eoan, Anne Constable, and Elizabeth Taylor. Sex busters: a Meese commission and the Supreme Court echo a new moral militancy. *Time* 128(3):12-21 (July 21, 1986).

Will, George F. Fine-tuning from the bench. [Editorial] *Newsweek* 108(3):68 (July 21, 1986).

3057. Arcara v. Cloud Books   July 7, 1986
478 US 697   92 LEd2d 568   106 SCt 3172
  Almanac (1986):4A,12A

Fields, Howard. First Amendment watch: High Court OKs closing bookstore for health laws. *Publishers' Weekly* 230(4):97 (July 25, 1986).

Gest, Ted. Burger Court: imprint of its last year. *U.S. News and World Report* 101(3):15 (July 21, 1986).

Regan, Richard J. Supreme Court roundup: 1985 term. *Thought* 62(245):234-246 (June 1987).

Roper, James E. Congress and the Court. *Editor and Publisher* 120(1):20 (January 3, 1987).

Stengel, Richard, Howard G. Chua-Eoan, Anne Constable, and Elizabeth Taylor. Sex busters: a Meese commission and the Supreme Court echo a new moral militancy. *Time* 128(3):12-21 (July 21, 1986).

Will, George F. Fine-tuning from the bench. [Editorial] *Newsweek* 108(3):68 (July 21, 1986).

3058. Bowsher v. Synar   July 7, 1986
       Coupled with Senate v. Synar
       Coupled with O'Neill v. Synar
478 US 714   92 LEd2d 583   106 SCt 3181
  Almanac (1986):18, 579-580, 17A-20AR; (1988):125
  Ascent 64-76+
  Chadha 237-240
  Const (Currie) 588-593
  Editorials (1986):854-859
  En Am Con 858-859
  Guide (CQ) 56-57, 65, 124b
  New Right (Schwartz) 201-213+
  Sup Ct Review (1986):19-40, 41-97; (1988):1-41

American survey: Gramm-Rudman wounded. *Economist* 300(7454):18 (July 12-18, 1986).

Crawford, Mark. Justices kill key part of budget deficit act. *Science* 233(4761):279 (July 18, 1986).

Daugherty, Donald A. Supreme Court review: the separation of powers and abuses in prosecutorial discretion. *Journal of Criminal Law and Criminology* 79(3):953-996 (Fall 1988).

DeMott, John S., Neil MacNeil, and John E. Yang. Handing Congress a hot potato: the Supreme Court nullifies a key budget-balancing provision. *Time* 128(3):24 (July 21, 1986).

Donnybrook over the deficit. *Fortune* 114(3):9-10 (August 4, 1986).

Dwyer, Paula. The Burger Court put the brakes on Reagan's federalism. *Business Week* (Industrial/Technology Edition) (2956):67 (July 21, 1986).

Fisher, Louis. The administrative world of Chadha and Bowsher. *Public Administration Review* 47(3):213-219 (May/June 1987).

Gleckman, Howard. The budget is Congress's problem again. *Business Week* (Industrial/Technology Edition) (2956): 68 (July 21, 1986).

Gramm-Rudman, cont'd. *National Review* 38(15):16 (August 15, 1986).

Grover, Ronald. Tax-bill euphoria won't cure the budget-cutting blues. *Business Week* (Industrial/Technology Edition) (2953):34-35 (June 30, 1986).

Grover, Ronald, Richard Fly, and Howard Gleckman. A Gramm-Rudman deadline passes—and Congress yawns. *Business Week* (Industrial/Technology Edition) (2944):35 (April 28, 1986).

Lacayo, Richard, and Anne Constable. Who controls the comptroller?: the justices prepare to rule on the budget-deficit law. *Time* 127(18):45 (May 5, 1986).

Mann, Paul. Gramm-Rudman ruling intensifying pressure on space budget. *Aviation Week and Space Technology* 125(2):26-27 (July 14, 1986).

Methvin, Eugene H. A Texas tornado hits the Senate. *Reader's Digest* 130(780):17-24 (April 1987).

Palmer, Stacy E. Court strikes down part of budget law; cuts in college funds are likely to stand. *Chronicle of Higher Education* 32(20):11, 17 (July 16, 1986).

Pawelek, Dick. Call five cases that shaped Congress. *Scholastic Update* (Teachers' Edition) 119(9):12-14 (January 12, 1987).

Power lines. *New Republic* 194(20):4 (May 19, 1986).

Raloff, Janet. High Court hits key part of budget law. *Science News* 130(2):22-23 (July 12, 1986).

Regan, Richard J. Supreme Court roundup: 1985 term. *Thought* 62(245):234-246 (June 1987).

Russell, George, Laurence I. Barrett, and Jay Branegan. A case of the downturn jitters: slow growth complicates the work of Congress on tax reform and deficits. *Time* 128(5):50-51 (August 4, 1986).

Shapiro, Walter, Ann McDaniel, and Gloria Borger. The budget bill goes on trial. *Newsweek* 107(18):25 (May 5, 1986).

Sheler, Jeffery L., Monroe W. Karmin, Richard Alm, Robert J. Morse, and Ricardo Elbo. Jump-starting the economy. *U.S. News and World Report* 101(3):12-14 (July 21, 1986).

Will, George F. 'The F word.' [Editorial] *Newsweek* 107(21):80 (May 26, 1986).

3059. University of Tennesse v. Elliott   July 7, 1986
       478 US 788   92 LEd2d 635   106 SCt 3220
       Almanac (1986):11A

Fields, Cheryl M. Rulings handed down in cases on race bias and on free speech in high schools. *Chronicle of Higher Education* 32(20):11, 17 (July 16, 1986).

3060. Merrell Dow Pharmaceuticals, Inc. v. Thompson   July 7, 1986
       478 US 804   92 LEd2d 650   106 SCt 3229
       Almanac (1986):17A

3061. Commodity Futures Trading Commission v. Schor   July 7, 1986
       478 US 833   92 LEd2d 675   106 SCt 3245
       Almanac (1986):13A
       Sup Ct Review (1988):1-41

Fisher, Louis. The administrative world of Chadha and Bowsher. *Public Administration Review* 47(3):213-219 (May/June 1987).

3062. North Carolina Department of Transporation v. Crest Street Community Council, Inc.   November 4, 1986
       479 US 6   93 LEd2d 188   107 SCt 336
       Almanac (1987):10A

3063. O'Connor v. United States   November 4, 1986
       479 US 27   93 LEd2d 206   107 SCt 347
       Almanac (1987):17A

3064. Kelly v. Robinson   November 17, 1986
        479 US 36   93 LEd2d 216   107 SCt 353
        Almanac (1987):12A-13A

3065. Ansonia Board of Education v. Philbrook   November 17, 1986
        479 US 60   93 LEd2d 305   107 SCt 367
        Almanac (1987):9A-10A
        Godless 50-51
        Frierson, James G. Religion in the workplace—dealing in good faith? *Personnel Journal* 67(7):60-67 (July
        1988).
        Lawton, Kim A. High Court accepts cases on abortion, obscenity, and church hiring practices. *Christianity
        Today* 30(18):53-55 (December 12, 1986).
        Lissy, William E. Labor law for supervisors: accommodating employees' religious practices. *Supervision*
        49(11):22-23, 7 (November 1988).
        Murphy, Betty Southard, Wayne E. Barlow, and D. Diane Hatch. Supreme Court clarifies reasonable
        accommodation. *Personnel Journal* 66(2):14, 16 (February 1987).
        Regan, Richard J. Supreme Court roundup: 1986 term. *Thought* 63(251):429-441 (December 1988).
        Ruben, George. Developments in industrial relations: Court rules on accommodating religious holidays.
        Monthly Labor Review 110(3):44 (March 1987).
        Sendor, Benjamin. Your paid leave policy can't exclude religion. *American School Board Journal* 174(3):20
        (March 1987).

3066. Cargill, Inc. v. Monfort of Colorado, Inc.   December 9, 1986
        479 US 104   93 LEd2d 427   107 SCt 484
        Almanac (1987):12A
        Dwyer, Paula. Meese wants a monopoly on antitrust challenges. *Business Week* (Industrial/Technology Edition)
        (2968):44-45 (October 13, 1986).
        ———. Women's-rights cases may show where the Court is headed. *Business Week* (Industrial/Technology
        Edition) (2967):55-56 (October 6, 1986).
        Litigation: labor, mergers high on Supreme Court's agenda. *Industry Week* 231(1):32 (October 13, 1986).

3067. R.J. Reynolds Tobacco Co. v. Durham County, North Carolina   December 9, 1986
        479 US 130   93 LEd2d 449   107 SCt 499
        Almanac (1987):16A

3068. Colorado v. Connelly   December 10, 1986
        479 US 157   93 LEd2d 473   107 SCt 515
        Almanac (1987):6A
        Pace, Michael R. Supreme Court review: Fifth and Fourteenth Amendments—defining the protections of the
        Fifth and Fourteenth Amendments against self-incrimination for the mentally impaired. *Journal of Criminal
        Law and Criminology* 78(4):877-914 (Winter 1988).

3069. Munro v. Socialist Workers Party   December 10, 1986
        479 US 189   93 LEd2d 499   107 SCt 533
        Almanac (1987):3A,11A

3070. Tashjian v. Republican Party of Connecticut   December 10, 1986
        479 US 208   93 LEd2d 514   107 SCt 544
        Almanac (1987):3A, 11A
        Cutler, Lloyd N. Can the parties regulate campaign financing? *Annals of the American Academy of Political
        and Social Science* 486:115-120 (July 1986).

3071. Federal Elections Committee (FEC) v. Massachusetts Citizens for Life, Inc.   December 15, 1986
        479 US 238   93 LEd2d 539   107 SCt 616
        Almanac (1987):3A, 11A-12A; (1990):61

Dwyer, Paula. Women's-rights cases may show where the Court is headed. *Business Week* (Industrial/ Technology Edition) (2967):55-56 (October 6, 1986).

3072. California Federal Savings and Loan Association v. Mark Guerra,   January 13, 1987
      Director of Fair Employment and Housing
    479 US 272   93 LEd2d 613   107 SCt 683
      Almanac (1987):6A, 10A
      Sup Ct Review (1987):201-247
      Turning 70-73, 79-80

Baker, Jasmin C. Court rules for women. *Black Enterprise* 17(8):20 (April 1987).

Barnett, Edith. Pregnancy discrimination: the Supreme Court spells out protections for pregnant workers. *Trial* 23(7):36-38, 42 (July 1987).

Bernstein, Aaron. Business and pregnancy: good will is no longer good enough. *Business Week* (Industrial/Technology Edition) (2983):37 (Feburary 2, 1987).

Bird, Kai, and Max Holland. The Garland case. *Nation* 243(1):8 (July 5-12, 1986).

Brophy, Beth. Supreme Court gives motherhood its legal due. *U.S. News and World Report* 102(3):12 (January 26, 1987).

Brower, Montgomery. A working mother's fight for job security goes to the last round—in the U.S. Supreme Court. *People Weekly* 25(6):40-41 (February 10, 1986).

Dwyer, Paula. The Burger Court put the brakes on Reagan's federalism. *Business Week* (Industrial/Technology Edition) (2956):67 (July 21, 1986).

Feitshans, Ilise L. Job security for pregnant employees: the model employment termination act. *Annals of the American Academy of Political and Social Science* 536:119-134 (November 1994).

Fields, Cheryl M. Supreme Court upholds Cal. law requiring maternity leaves. *Chronicle of Higher Education* 33(19):19, 23 (January 21, 1987).

Friedman, Dana E. Liberty, equality, maternity! *Across the Board* 24(3):10-17 (March 1987).

Kantrowitz, Barbara. The parental-leave debate. *Newsweek* 107(7):64 (February 17, 1986).

Martin, Bob. The Supreme Court's new era: what's ahead for labor law? *Personnel Journal* 65(10):92-98 (October 1986).

Mauro, Tony. The High Court: what it's up to. *Nation's Business* 74(9):57-60 (September 1986).

Nobile, Robert J. Leaving no doubt about employee leaves. *Personnel* 67(5):54-60 (May 1990).

Pregnancy job protection upheld by Supreme Court. *Jet* 71(19):5 (February 2, 1987).

Press, Aric, Ann McDaniel, and Ginny Carroll. The Rehnquist era begins. *Newsweek* 108(15)94-98 (October 13 1986).

Press, Aric, Ann McDaniel, and Lynda Wright. A new family issue. *Newsweek* 109(4):22-24 (January 26, 1987).

Ruben, George. Developments in industrial relations: High Court rulings affect pregnant workers. *Monthly Labor Review* 110(3):43-44 (March 1987).

Sendor, Benjamin. Court okays special leave for pregnant workers. *American School Board Journal* 174(5):18 (May 1987).

Smolowe, Jill, D. Blake Hallanan, and Melissa Ludtke. Those 24 words are back: ERA surfaces once more amid doubts about its urgency. *Time* 130(1):91 (July 6, 1987).

Stoper, Emily. Women's work, women's movement: taking stock. *Annals of the American Academy of Political and Social Science* 515:151-162 (May 1991).

Wilentz, Amy, Anne Constable, and Jon D. Hull. Garland's bouquet: a landmark Supreme Court ruling supports pregnancy leave. *Time* 129(4):14-15 (January 26, 1987).

3073. West Virginia v. United States   January 13, 1987
    479 US 305   93 LEd2d 639   107 SCt 702
      Almanac (1987):15A

3074. Griffith v. Kentucky   January 13, 1987
      Coupled with Brown v. United States
    479 US 314   93 LEd2d 649   107 SCt 708
      Almanac (1987):7A

3075. 324 Liquor Corp. v. Duffy   January 13, 1987
479 US 335   93 LEd2d 667   107 SCt 720
Almanac (1987):15A

3076. Burke v. Barnes   January 14, 1987
479 US 361   93 LEd2d 732   107 SCt 734
Almanac (1987):40, 5A,17A

3077. Colorado v. Bertine   January 14, 1987
479 US 367   93 LEd2d 739   107 SCt 738
Almanac (1987):6A

King, Clayton E. Supreme Court review: Fourth Amendment—toward police discretion in determining the scope of administrative searches. *Journal of Criminal Law and Criminology* 81(4):841-861 (Winter 1991).

Misner, Robert L. Justifying searches on the basis of equality of treatment. *Journal of Criminal Law and Criminology* 82(3):547-578 (Fall 1991).

3078. Clarke v. Securities Industry Association   January 14, 1987
479 US 388   93 LEd2d 757   107 SCt 750
Almanac (1987):12A

Dwyer, Paula. Women's-rights cases may show where the Court is headed. *Business Week* (Industrial/Technology Edition) (2967):55-56 (October 6, 1986).

3079. Wright v. City of Roanoke Redevelopment and Housing Authority   January 14, 1987
479 US 418   93 LEd2d 781   107 SCt 766
Almanac (1987):11A

3080. Jersey Shore State Bank v. United States   January 20, 1987
479 US 442   93 LEd2d 800   107 SCt 782
Almanac (1987):13A

3081. Interstate Commerce Commission (ICC) v. Texas   January 20, 1987
        Coupled with Missouri-Kansas-Texas Railroad Co. v. Texas
479 US 450   93 LEd2d 809   107 SCt 787
Almanac (1987):13A

3082. City of Pleasant Grove v. United States   January 21, 1987
479 US 462   93 LEd2d 866   107 SCt 794
Almanac (1987):10A
Supreme Court: Scalia's scalpel. *Economist* 302(7489):28-31 (March 14-20, 1987).

3083. International Paper Co. v. Ouellette   January 21, 1987
479 US 481   93 LEd2d 883   107 SCt 805
Almanac (1987):14A

Giesser, John L. The National Park Service and external development: addressing park boundary-area threats through public nuisance. *Boston College Environmental Affairs Law Review* 20(4):761-809 (Summer 1993).

3084. Wimberly v. Labor and Industrial Relations Commission of Missouri   January 21, 1987
479 US 511   93 LEd2d 909   107 SCt 821
Almanac (1987):10A
Sup Ct Review (1987):201-247

Barnett, Edith. Pregnancy discrimination: the Supreme Court spells out protections for pregnant workers. *Trial* 23(7):36-38, 42 (July 1987).

Moskowitz, Daniel B. Job bias issues dominate calendar of High Court. *Engineering News Record* 217(14):82 (October 2, 1986).

Ruben, George. Developments in industrial relations: High Court rulings affect pregnant workers. *Monthly Labor Review* 110(3):43-44 (March 1987).

Wilson, Robin. Women who leave jobs to bear children not entitled to benefits, Court rules. *Chronicle of Higher Education* 33(20):22 (January 28, 1987).

3085. Connecticut v. Barrett   January 27, 1987
    479 US 523   93 LEd2d 920   107 SCt 828
      Almanac (1987):6A-7A

3086. California v. Brown   January 27, 1987
    479 US 538   93 LEd2d 934   107 SCt 837
      Almanac (1987):8A

3087. Colorado v. Spring   January 27, 1987
    479 US 564   93 LEd2d 954   107 SCt 851
      Almanac (1987):6A

Spitzer, Gregory E. Supreme Court review: Fifth Amendment—validity of waiver: a suspect need not know the subjects of interrogation. *Journal of Criminal Law and Criminology* 78(4):828-852 (Winter 1988).

3088. Burlington Northern Railroad Co. v. Woods   February 24, 1987
    480 US 1   94 LEd2d 1   107 SCt 967
      Almanac (1987):17A

Dwyer, Paula. Women's-rights cases may show where the Court is headed. *Business Week* (Industrial/Technology Edition) (2967):55-56 (October 6, 1986).

3089. Iowa Mutual Insurance Co. v. LaPlante   February 24, 1987
    480 US 9   94 LEd2d 10   107 SCt 971
      Almanac (1987):18A

3090. Commissioner v. Groetzinger   February 24, 1987
    480 US 23   94 LEd2d 25   107 SCt 980
      Almanac (1987):13A

August, Jerald D., and Steven J. Levine. Goods and services test for trade or business rejected by Supreme Court. *Journal of Taxation* 66(5):298-302 (May 1987).

Bond, James G., and Royce E. Chaffin. Can securities trading be a trade or business? *Taxes* 65(11):727-732 (November 1987).

Gulledge, Dexter E., and Zoel W. Daughtrey. Gambling—a trade or business? *CPA Journal* 58(3):12-20 (March 1988).

Supreme Court says gambler is in trade or business. *Practical Accountant* 20(5):8 (May 1987).

3091. Pennsylvania v. Ritchie   February 24, 1987
    480 US 39   94 LEd2d 40   107 SCt 989
      Almanac (1987):7A

Bradley, Craig M. The Sixth Amendment lives! a reply to Professor Jonakait. *Journal of Criminal Law and Criminology* 83(3):526-537 (Fall 1992).

Galkin, Jeffrey M. Supreme Court review: Sixth and Fourteenth Amendments—a defendant's right to disclosure of a state's confidential child abuse records. *Journal of Criminal Law and Criminology* 78(4):1014-1047 (Winter 1988).

White, Welsh S. Evidentiary privileges and the defendant's constitutional right to introduce evidence. *Journal of Criminal Law and Criminology* 80(2):377-426 (Summer 1989).

3092. Maryland v. Garrison   February 24, 1987
    480 US 79   94 LEd2d 72   107 SCt 1013
      Almanac (1987):6A

Mosk, Stanley. The emerging agenda in state constitutional rights law. *Annals of the American Academy of Political and Social Science* 496:54-64 (March 1988).

Press, Aric, and Ann McDaniel. A racial quota for Alabama. *Newsweek* 109(10):55 (March 9, 1987).

Supreme Court: Scalia's scalpel. *Economist* 302(7489):28-31 (March 14-20, 1987).

3093. Asahi Metal Industry Co. v. Superior Court of California								February 24, 1987
    480 US 102   94 LEd2d 92   107 SCt 1026
      Almanac (1987):17A

Tarnoff, Stephen. Foreign firm not subject to state law. *Business Insurance* 21(9):2, 4 (March 2, 1987).

3094. Western Air Lines v. Board of Equalization									February 24, 1987
    480 US 123   94 LEd2d 112   107 SCt 1038
      Almanac (1987):16A

3095. Paula A. Hobbie v. Unemployment Appeals Commission of Florida and Lawton & Co.   February 25, 1987
    480 US 136   94 LEd2d 190   107 SCt 1046
      Almanac (1987):3A, 12A
      Brennan 138-142
      Godless 34

Drinan, Robert F. The Supreme Court expands religious freedom. *America* 160(16):388-389 (April 29, 1989).

Greenlaw, Paul S., and John P. Kohl. Religious freedom and unemployment compensation benefits. *Public Personnel Management* 24(3):315-330 (Fall 1995).

Moskowitz, Daniel B. Job bias issues dominate calendar of High Court. *Engineering News Record* 217(14):82 (October 2, 1986).

Regan, Richard J. Supreme Court roundup: 1986 term. *Thought* 63(251):429-441 (December 1988).

Rievman, Joshua D. Judicial scrutiny of Native American free exercise rights: Lyng and the decline of the Yoder doctrine. *Boston College Environmental Affairs Law Review* 17(1):169-199 (Fall 1989).

3096. United States v. Paradise										February 25, 1987
    480 US 149   94 LEd2d 203   107 SCt 1053
      Affirmative (Greene) 138-147
      Affirmative (Woods) 79-81
      Almanac (1986):4A; (1987):4A-5A, 9A
      Brennan 257-263
      Magic 330-331
      Sup Ct Ind 264

Bresler, Robert J. The forgotten issue. [Editorial] *USA Today* 116(2516):7 (May 1988).

Camper, Diane. Court upholds racial quota. *Black Enterprise* 17(10) (May 1987).

Camper, Diane, Ethel Payne, Nathaniel R. Jones, Charles Ogletree, and Julius L. Chambers. To form a more perfect union. *Black Enterprise* 17(12):11, 51-66 (July 1987).

Dingle, Derek T. Affirmative action. *Black Enterprise* 20(2):42-48 (September 1989).

Dwyer, Paula. Women's-rights cases may show where the Court is headed. *Business Week* (Industrial/Technology Edition) (2967):55-56 (October 6, 1986).

Fields, Cheryl M. Rulings handed down in cases on race bias and on free speech in high schools. *Chronicle of Higher Education* 32(20):11, 17 (July 16, 1986).

————. Supreme Court upholds use of numerical quotas in promoting members of minority groups. *Chronicle of Higher Education* 33(25):17, 22 (March 4, 1987).

Gest, Ted. A one-white, one-black quota for promotions. *U.S. News and World Report* 102(9):8 (March 9, 1987).

Greenlaw, Paul S. Reverse discrimination: the Supreme Court's dilemma. *Personnel Journal* 67(1)84-89 (January 1988).

High Court to tackle MBE case. *ENR* 221(13):10-11 (September 29, 1988).

Job promotions: one up for women. *Economist* 303(7492):23-24 (April 4-10, 1987).

Lacayo, Richard, Joseph N. Boyce, and Joseph J. Kane. Replying in the affirmative: for the first time, the court approves promotion quotas. *Time* 129(10):66 (March 9, 1987).

Martin, Bob. The Supreme Court's new era: what's ahead for labor law? *Personnel Journal* 65(10):92-98 (October 1986).

Moskowitz, Daniel B. Job bias issues dominate calendar of High Court. *Engineering News Record* 217(14):82 (October 2, 1986).

Moskowitz, Daniel B., and Steven W. Setzer. High Court backs racial quotas. *ENR* 218(10):42 (March 5, 1987).

Nalbandian, John. The U.S. Supreme Court's "consensus" on affirmative action. *Public Administration Review* 49(1):38-45 (January/February 1989).

Press, Aric, and Ann McDaniel. A racial quota for Alabama. *Newsweek* 109(10):55 (March 9, 1987).

———. A woman's day in court. *Newsweek* 109(14):58-59 (April 6, 1987).

Regan, Richard J. Supreme Court roundup: 1986 term. *Thought* 63(251):429-441 (December 1988).

Ruben, George. Developments in industrial relations: Supreme Court upholds promotion quotas. *Monthly Labor Review* 110(5):41 (May 1987).

Sendor, Benjamin. It's okay to set affirmative action "targets." *American School Board Journal* 174(7):16-17, 40 (July 1987).

Villere, Maurice, and Sandra Hartman. What's affirmative about affirmative action? *Business Horizons* 32(5):22-27 (September/October 1989).

3097. California v. Cabazon Band of Mission Indians   February 25, 1987
       480 US 202   94 LEd2d 244   107 SCt 1083
         Almanac (1986):334; (1987):18A; (1988):622
       Press, Aric, and Ann McDaniel. A racial quota for Alabama. *Newsweek* 109(10):55 (March 9, 1987).

3098. Martin v. Ohio   February 25, 1987
       480 US 228   94 LEd2d 267   107 SCt 1098
         Almanac (1987):8A

3099. Federal Communications Commission (FCC) v. Florida Power Corp.   Februrary 25, 1987
       480 US 245   94 LEd2d 282   107 SCt 1107
         Almanac (1987):13A

3100. School Board of Nassau County, Florida and Craig Marsh,   March 3, 1987
          Superintendent of Schools of Nassau County, Florida v. Arline
       480 US 273   94 LEd2d 307   107 SCt 1123
         Almanac (1986):261; (1987):4A-5A, 9A; (1988):302
       Dwyer, Paula. Women's-rights cases may show where the Court is headed. *Business Week* (Industrial/Technology Edition) (2967):55-56 (October 6, 1986).

       Fields, Cheryl M. High Court rules that law bars bias against persons with contagious ills. *Chronicle of Higher Education* 33(26):23, 25 (March 11, 1987).

       Flygare, Thomas J. De jure: Supreme Court holds that contagious diseases are handicaps. *Phi Delta Kappan* 68(9):705-706 (May 1987).

       Gostin, Lawrence O. Health law. *JAMA: The Journal of the American Medical Association* 268(3): 364-366 (July 15, 1992).

       Lacayo, Richard, and Anne Constable. Handicap rights: even AIDS seems covered. *Time* 129(11):66 (March 16, 1987).

       Litigation: labor, mergers high on Supreme Court's agenda. *Industry Week* 231(1):32 (October 13, 1986).

       Martin, Bob. The Supreme Court's new era: what's ahead for labor law? *Personnel Journal* 65(10):92-98 (October 1986).

       Mauro, Tony. The High Court: what it's up to. *Nation's Business* 74(9):57-60 (September 1986).

       McLoughlin, Merrill. Grand tests for a grand document. *U.S. News and World Report* 101(26):18-21 (December 29, 1986-January 5, 1987).

       On unwarranted fears. *America* 156(13):266-267 (April 4, 1987).

       Press, Aric, and Ann McDaniel. Renaissance of an octogenarian liberal. *Newsweek* 110(1):18 (July 6, 1987).

       ———. A victory for AIDS victims. *Newsweek* 109(11):33 (March 16, 1987).

Press, Aric, Ann McDaniel, and Ginny Carroll. The Rehnquist era begins. *Newsweek* 108(15)94-98 (October 13, 1986).

Roe, Richard L. Supreme Court docket: should persons with contagious diseases be barred from school? *Social Education* 51(4):238-241 (April/May 1987).

Ruben, George. Developments in industrial relations: "contagiousness" is a handicap, says High Court. *Monthly Labor Review* 110(5):42 (May 1987).

Seligman, Daniel. Handicapped thinkers. *Fortune* 115(8):110 (April 13, 1987).

Sendor, Benjamin. High Court's TB ruling probably applies to AIDS. *American School Board Journal* 174(6):11, 40 (June 1987).

Witkin, Gordon, and Joseph Carey. AIDS: a job-rights victory. *U.S. News and World Report* 102(10):10-11 (March 16, 1987).

3101. United States v. Dunn   March 3, 1987
480 US 294   94 LEd2d 326   107 SCt 1134
Almanac (1987):6A

3102. Arizona v. Hicks   March 3, 1987
480 US 321   94 LEd2d 347   107 SCt 1149
Almanac (1987):6A
Sup Ct Review (1989):87-163

Romero, Elsie. Supreme Court review: Fourth Amendment—requiring probable cause for searches and seizures under the plain view doctrine. *Journal of Criminal Law and Criminology* 78(4):763-791 (Winter 1988).

Supreme Court: Scalia's scalpel. *Economist* 302(7489):28-31 (March 14-20, 1987).

3103. Illinois v. Krull   March 9, 1987
480 US 340   94 LEd2d 364   107 SCt 1160
Almanac (1987):6A

3104. Stringfellow v. Concerned Neighbors in Action   March 9, 1987
480 US 370   94 LEd2d 389   107 SCt 1177
Almanac (1987):17A

3105. Town of Newton v. Rumery   March 9, 1987
480 US 386   94 LEd2d 405   107 SCt 1187
Almanac (1987):10A

Fielkow, Brian L. Supreme Court review: 42 U.S.C. § 1983—buying justice: the role of release-dismissal agreements in the criminal justice system. *Journal of Criminal Law and Criminology* 78(4):1119-1144 (Winter 1988).

3106. Immigration and Naturalization Service (INS) v. Cardoza-Fonseca   March 9, 1987
480 US 421   94 LEd2d 434   107 SCt 1207
Almanac (1987):5A, 10A
Editorials (1987):326-329

El Norte's sheltering arms. *U.S. News and World Report* 102(11):13 (March 23, 1987).

Frame, Randy. Supreme Court eases rules on political asylum. *Christianity Today* 31(7):45 (April 17, 1987).

Lacayo, Richard, Anne Constable, and Peter Stoler. Gimme shelter: a wider opening for refugees. *Time* 129(12):70 (March 23, 1987).

Supreme Court: Scalia's scalpel. *Economist* 302(7489):28-31 (March 14-20, 1987).

3107. Keystone Bituminous Coal Assocation v. DeBenedictis   March 9, 1987
480 US 470   94 LEd2d 472   107 SCt 1232
Almanac (1987):14A
New Right (Schwartz) 116-120+
Sup Ct Review (1987):1-46

Cohen, Jonathan E. A constitutional safety valve: the variance in zoning and land-use based environmental controls. *Boston College Environmental Affairs Law Review* 22(2):307-364 (Winter 1995).

Darnell, Tim. The land and the law. *American City and County* 103(1):38-45 (January 1988).

Folsom, Robin E. Executive Order 12,630: a president's manipulation of the Fifth Amendment's just compensation clause to achieve control over executive agency regulatory decisionmaking. *Boston College Environmental Affairs Law Review* 20(4):639-697 (Summer 1993).

Hanley, Thomas. A developer's dream: the United States Claims Court's new analysis of Section 404 takings challenges. *Boston College Environmental Affairs Law Review* 19(2):317-353 (Fall/Winter 1991).

Hippler, Thomas A. Reexamining 100 years of the Supreme Court regulatory taking doctrine: the principles of "noxious use," "average reciprocity of advantage," and "bundle of rights" from Mugler to Keystone Bituminous Coal. *Boston College Environmental Affairs Law Review* 14(4):653-727 (Summer 1987).

Kaplan, David A., and Bob Cohn. Pay me, or get off my land. *Newsweek* 119(10)70 (March 9, 1992).

Singer, Saul Jay. Flooding the Fifth Amendment: the National Flood Insurance Program and the "takings" clause. *Boston College Environmental Affairs Law Review* 17(2):323-379 (Winter 1990).

Skelton, Harold N. Houses on the sand: taking issues surrounding statutory restrictions on the use of oceanfront property. *Boston College Environmental Affairs Law Review* 18(1):125-158 (Fall 1990).

3108. Amoco Production Co. v. Village of Gambell, Alaska   March 24, 1987
           Coupled with Hodel v. Village of Grambell, Alaska
      480 US 531   94 LEd2d 542   107 SCt 1396
      Almanac (1987):15A

Dwyer, Paula. Women's-rights cases may show where the Court is headed. *Business Week* (Industrial/Technology Edition) (2967):55-56 (October 6, 1986).

Fregeau, Jason David. Statutes and judicial discretion: against the law . . . sort of. *Boston College Environmental Affairs Law Review* 18(3):501-542 (Spring 1991).

3109. Atchison, Topeka and Santa Fe Railroad Co. v. Buell March 24, 1987
      480 US 557   94 LEd2d 563   107 SCt 1410
      Almanac (1987):13A

3110. California Coastal Commission v. Granite Rock Co. March 24, 1987
      480 US 572   94 LEd2d 577   107 SCt 1419
      Almanac (1987):5A, 15A

Wise, Charles, and Rosemary O'Leary. Is federalism dead or alive in the Supreme Court?: implications for public administrators. *Public Administration Review* 52(6):559-572 (November/December 1992).

3111. Johnson v. Transportation Agency, Santa Clara County   March 25, 1987
      480 US 616   94 LEd2d 615   107 SCt 1442
      Affirmative (Greene) 147-160
      Affirmative (Woods) 81-82
      Almanac (1986):4A; (1987):4A-5A, 9A
      Conflict 1-241R
      Const Law 564-568+
      Editorials (1987):330-337
      Magic 330-331
      Sup Ct Ind 264-265
      Sup Ct Review (1987):201-247
      Turning 56-62, 65-67+

Baker, Jasmin C. Court ruling affirmative. *Black Enterprise* 17(12):20 (July 1987).

Becker, Gary Stanley. Productivity is the best affirmative action plan. *Business Week* (Industrial/Technology Edition) (2996):18 (April 27, 1987).

Bresler, Robert J. The forgotten issue. [Editorial] *USA Today* 116(2516):7 (May 1988).

Camper, Diane, Ethel Payne, Nathaniel R. Jones, Charles Ogletree, and Julius L. Chambers. To form a more perfect union. *Black Enterprise* 17(12):11, 51-66 (July 1987).

Dingle, Derek T. Affirmative action. *Black Enterprise* 20(2):42-48 (September 1989).

Dwyer, Paula. Affirmative action: after the debate, opportunity. *Business Week* (Industrial/Technology Edition) (2993):37 (April 13, 1987).

———. Women's-rights cases may show where the Court is headed. *Business Week* (Industrial/Technology Edition) (2967):55-56 (October 6, 1986).

Faludi, Susan. Diane Joyce. *Ms.* 16(7):62-65, 90-92 (January 1988).

———. Paul Johnson: in defense of the white male. *Ms.* 16(7):65 (January 1988).

Farber, Daniel A. Supreme Court review: debating Congress's intent in the age of statutes. *Trial* 25(12):105-110 (December 1989).

Fein, Bruce. A court that obeys the law. *National Review* 41(18):50-51 (September 29, 1989).

Fields, Cheryl M. Rulings handed down in cases on race bias and on free speech in high schools. *Chronicle of Higher Education* 32(20):11, 17 (July 16, 1986).

———. Supreme Court upholds affirmative-action plans in its first explicit ruling on voluntary goals. *Chronicle of Higher Education* 33(29):1, 20 (April 1, 1987).

———. Supreme Court upholds use of numerical quotas in promoting members of minority groups. *Chronicle of Higher Education* 33(25):17, 22 (March 4, 1987).

Franke, Ann H., and Jacqueline W. Mintz. Four trends in higher education law. *Academe* 73(5):57-63 (September/October 1987).

Gest, Ted. Hear ye: the Rehnquist Court is now in session. *U.S. News and World Report* 101(15):10 (October 13, 1986).

Gest, Ted, and Elisabeth Blaug. The women win—again. *U.S. News and World Report* 102(13):18-19 (April 6, 1987).

Greenlaw, Paul S. Reverse discrimination: The Supreme Court's dilemma. *Personnel Journal* 67(1):84-89 (January 1988).

Higgerson, Mary Lou, and Richard G. Higgerson. The Supreme Court's decision on affirmative action: progress . . . and pitfalls. [Editorial] *Chronicle of Higher Education* 33(42):68 (July 1, 1987).

Jaschik, Scott. From Bakke to Yeshiva, Justice Powell played key role in Court's education rulings. *Chronicle of Higher Education* 33(43):16 (July 8, 1987).

Job promotions: one up for women. *Economist* 303(7492):23-24 (April 4-10, 1987).

Litigation: labor, mergers high on Supreme Court's agenda. *Industry Week* 231(1):32 (October 13, 1986).

Martin, Bob. The Supreme Court's new era: what's ahead for labor law? *Personnel Journal* 65(10):92-98 (October 1986).

Martin, Bob, and Stephanie Lawrence. Personnel executives respond to reaffirmation of affirmative action. *Personnel Journal* 66(5):9-15 (May 1987).

Mauro, Tony. The High Court: what it's up to. *Nation's Business* 74(9):57-60 (September 1986).

McLoughlin, Merrill. Grand tests for a grand document. *U.S. News and World Report* 101(26):18-21 (December 29, 1986-January 5, 1987).

Moskowitz, Daniel B. High Court expands affirmative action. *ENR* 218(14):42 (April 2, 1987).

———. Job bias issues dominate calendar of High Court. *Engineering News Record* 217(14):82 (October 2, 1986).

Plummer, William. The Supreme Court puts the mike in Diane Joyce's hands, giving feminists a major victory. *People Weekly* 27(15):49-50, 52 (April 13, 1987).

Press, Aric, and Ann McDaniel. A woman's day in court. *Newsweek* 109(14):58-59 (April 6, 1987).

Press, Aric, Ann McDaniel, and Lynda Wright. A new family issue. *Newsweek* 109(4):22-24 (January 26, 1987).

Regan, Richard J. Supreme Court roundup: 1986 term. *Thought* 63(251):429-441 (December 1988).

Roberts, Paul Craig, and Lawrence M. Stratton, Jr. Color code. *National Review* 47(5):36, 51, 80 (March 20, 1995).

Ruben, George. Developments in industrial relations: gender-based hiring and promotions approved. *Monthly Labor Review* 110(5):41-42 (May 1987).

Segal, Jeffrey A., and Cheryl D. Reedy. The Supreme Court and sex discrimination: the role of the solicitor general. *Western Political Quarterly* 41(3):553-568 (September 1988).

Seligman, Daniel. Brennanism. *Fortune* 115(9):283+ (April 27, 1987).

Sendor, Benjamin. It's okay to set affirmative action "targets." *American School Board Journal* 174(7):16-17, 40 (July 1987).

Simpson, Peggy. Constitutional crisis. *Ms.* 18(3):90-98 (September 1989).

Smolowe, Jill, D. Blake Hallanan, and Melissa Ludtke. Those 24 words are back: ERA surfaces once more amid doubts about its urgency. *Time* 130(1):91 (July 6, 1987).

Stengel, Richard, and Anne Constable. Balancing act: in a sweeping decision, the High Court expands affirmative action. *Time* 129(14):18-20 (April 6, 1987).

Stoper, Emily. Women's work, women's movement: taking stock. *Annals of the American Academy of Political and Social Science* 515:151-162 (May 1991).

TBR from Washington: Ladies' day. *New Republic* 196(16):4, 42 (April 20, 1987).

Tribal justice. *National Review* 39(7):17-18 (April 24, 1987).

Villere, Maurice, and Sandra Hartman. What's affirmative about affirmative action? *Business Horizons* 32(5):22-27 (September/October 1989).

What they say it is: the justices' words instruct the nation, and often address history. *Time* 130(1):44-49 (July 6, 1987).

3112. Alaska Airlines, Inc. v. Brock   March 25, 1987
        480 US 678   94 LEd2d 661   107 SCt 1476
        Almanac (1986):49, 53, 577; (1987):40-41, 13A
        Guide (CQ) 80

3113. United States v. Cherokee Nation of Oklahoma   March 31, 1987
        480 US 700   94 LEd2d 704   107 SCt 1487
        Almanac (1987):18A

3114. O'Connor v. Ortega   March 31, 1987
        480 US 709   94 LEd2d 714   107 SCt 1492
        Almanac (1987):6A
        Sup Ct Review (1989):87-163

Flygare, Thomas J. De jure: High Court splits on search of public employee's office. *Phi Delta Kappan* 68(10):792-794 (June 1987).

Kilburn, E. Miles. Supreme Court review: Fourth Amendment—work-related searches by government employers valid on "reasonable" grounds. *Journal of Criminal Law and Criminology* 78(4):792-827 (Winter 1988).

Ruben, George. Developments in industrial relations: Supreme Court upholds workplace searches. *Monthly Labor Review* 110(6):58 (June 1987).

Sendor, Benjamin. Two new cases shed a little more light on searches of students and employees. *American School Board Journal* 174(8):14-15 (August 1987).

3115. Pennzoil Co. v. Texaco, Inc.   April 6, 1987
        481 US 1   95 LEd2d 1   107 SCt 1519
        Almanac (1987):5A,17A

Crovitz, L. Gordon. Clarence Thomas for justice: his views on economic freedom command respect and support. [Editorial] *Barron's* 71(34):10 (August 26, 1991).

Dwyer, Paula. The Burger Court put the brakes on Reagan's federalism. *Business Week* (Industrial/Technology Edition) (2956):67 (July 21, 1986).

———. Women's-rights cases may show where the Court is headed. *Business Week* (Industrial/Technology Edition) (2967):55-56 (October 6, 1986).

Hagar, Rick. Texaco case to stay in Texas—for now. *Oil and Gas Journal* 85(15):25-26 (April 13, 1987).

Helm, Leslie, and Paula Dwyer. Meet Larry Tribe, Pennzoil's hole card. *Business Week* (Industrial/Technology Edition) (2995):78-79 (April 20, 1987).

Tell, Lawrence J. David Boies: the ace litigator playing Texaco's hand. *Business Week* (Industrial/Technology Edition) (2995):79 (April 20, 1987).

Thompson, Terri, Lawrence J. Tell, and Jo Ellen Davis. Texaco takes a knockdown punch. *Business Week* (Industrial/Technology Edition) (2995):27 (April 20, 1987).

Vogel, Todd, Lawrence J. Tell, and Mimi Bluestone. Texaco vs. Pennzoil: next stop, Washington. *Business Week* (Industrial/Technology Edition) (3026):68 (November 16, 1987).

3116. West v. Conrail   April 6, 1987
     481 US 35   95 LEd2d 32   107 SCt 1538

Almanac (1987):13A-14A

Martin, Bob. The Supreme Court's new era: what's ahead for labor law? *Personnel Journal* 65(10):92-98 (October 1986).

3117. Pilot Life Insurance Co. v. Everate W. Dedeaux   April 6, 1987
     481 US 41   95 LEd2d 39   107 SCt 1549

Almanac (1987):14A; (1992):362-363

Morrison, John M. ERISA and the loss of just remedies. *Trial* 31(3):18-25 (March 1995).

Ruben, George. Developments in industrial relations: disability, retirement suits subject to ERISA. *Monthly Labor Review* 110(6):58 (June 1987).

Supreme Court to decide disability benefits case. *Best's Review* (Life/Health Insurance Edition) 87(4):6 (August 1986).

3118. Metropolitan Life Insurance Co. v. Taylor   April 6, 1987
     481 US 58   95 LEd2d 55   107 SCt 1542

Almanac (1987):14A

Ruben, George. Developments in industrial relations: disability, retirement suits subject to ERISA. *Monthly Labor Review* 110(6):58 (June 1987).

3119. CTS Corp. v. Dynamics Corp. of America   April 21, 1987
     481 US 69   95 LEd2d 67   107 SCt 1637

Almanac (1987):5A, 15A

Sup Ct Review (1987):47-95

American takeovers: judged against. *Economist* 303(7495):75-76 (April 25-May 1, 1987).

The brethren battle takeovers. *Fortune* 115(11):9 (May 25, 1987).

Dwyer, Paula, Vicky Cahan, and Zachary Schiller. Takeover artists take a direct hit. *Business Week* (Industrial/Technology Edition) (2997):35 (May 4, 1987).

Forbes, Malcolm S., Jr. The Supreme Court. [Editorial] *Forbes* 139(11):33 (May 18, 1987).

Goldbaum, Ellen. A burst of takeover laws sparks many challenges. *Chemical Week* 142(12):29, 31 (March 23, 1988).

Hickok, Eugene W., Jr. Federalism's future before the U.S. Supreme Court. *Annals of the American Academy of Political and Social Science* 509:73-82 (May 1990).

Hofmann, Mark A. Courts, laws change boundaries of liability for corporate officers. *Business Insurance* 22(44):77-79 (October 31, 1988).

Ruling may hinder DCA bid to boost CTS stake to 35%. *Electronic News* 33:7 (April 27, 1987).

Takeover hurdle: a ruling backs state regulation. *Time* 129(18):74 (May, 4 1987).

3120. United States v. John Doe   April 21, 1987
     481 US 102   95 LEd2d 94   107 SCt 1656

Almanac (1987):9A

3121. Granberry v. Greer   April 21, 1987
     481 US 129   95 LEd2d 119   107 SCt 1671

Almanac (1987):9A

Wells, Diane. Federal habeas corpus and the death penalty: a need for a return to the principles of Furman. *Journal of Criminal Law and Criminology* 80(2):427-490 (Summer 1989).

3122. Tison v. Arizona   April 21, 1987
     481 US 137   95 LEd2d 127   107 SCt 1676

Almanac (1987):8A

Death Penalty (Tushnet) 75-77

Death penalty: cruel and ever more usual punishment. *Economist* 303(7496):24-25 (May 2-8, 1987).

3123. Cruz v. New York   April 21, 1987
        481 US 186   95 LEd2d 162   107 SCt 1714
           Almanac (1987):7A

        Krit, Jonathan J. Supreme Court review: Sixth Amendment—confrontation and the use of interlocking
           confessions at joint trial. *Journal of Criminal Law and Criminology* 78(4):937-953 (Winter 1988).

3124. Richardson v. Marsh   April 21, 1987
        481 US 200   95 LEd2d 176   107 SCt 1702
           Almanac (1987):7A

        Dickett, William G. Supreme Court review: Sixth Amendment—limiting the scope of Bruton. *Journal of
           Criminal Law and Criminology* 78(4):984-1013 (Winter 1988).

3125. Arkansas Writers' Project, Inc. v. Charles O. Ragland   April 22, 1987
        481 US 221   95 LEd2d 209   107 SCt 1722
           Almanac (1987):16A
           Sup Ct Review (1992):29-77

        Roper, James E. Congress and the Court. *Editor and Publisher* 120(1):20 (January 3, 1987).
        Tofel, Richard J. Is differential taxation of press entities by states constitutional? *Journal of Taxation* 73(1):42-
           45 (July 1990).

3126. United States v. General Dynamics Corp.   April 22, 1987
        481 US 239   95 LEd2d 226   107 SCt 1732
           Almanac (1987):13A

        Brooke, Beth A., Timothy R. Dirig, and Michael A. Yuhas. Taxation of HMOs after Section 461(h) and
           General Dynamics. *Journal of Taxation* 68(6):358-363 (June 1988).
        High Court to consider employer reimbursement plan deductions. *Journal of Accountancy* 162(2):32-34
           (August 1986).
        Horvitz, Jerome S., and Nicholas D. Endres. The General Dynamics decision. *CPA Journal* 57(12):75-77
           (December 1987).
        Kupfer, T. Milton, and Daniel F. Kruger. Medical expense reserve fails all-events test. *Journal of Taxation*
           67(1):61 (July 1987).
        Saunders, Laura. Light on the horizon. *Forbes* 137(6):120 (March 24, 1986).

3127. Brock v. Roadway Express, Inc.   April 22, 1987
        481 US 252   95 LEd2d 239   107 SCt 1740
           Almanac (1987):13A
           Sup Ct Review (1987):157-200

        Martin, Bob. The Supreme Court's new era: what's ahead for labor law? *Personnel Journal* 65(10):92-98
           (October 1986).

3128. Warren McCleskey v. Kemp, Superintendent, Georgia Diagnostic and Classification Center   April 22, 1987
        481 US 279   95 LEd2d 262   107 SCt 1756
           Almanac (1986):4A; (1987):4A-5A, 8A; (1989):261-262; (1990):490-491
           Brennan 232-238
           Center 173-181, 183-189
           Const Law 447, 449-452R
           Death Penalty (Tushnet) 81-85, 128, 202-217R
           Death Penalty 80s 113-114, 129-136
           Death Penalty 90s 22-23, 135-139, 151-159, 199-207+
           Documents (v. 2):869-871R
           Editorials (1987):452-459
           Equal (Baldus) 1-6, 306-312, 340, 370-387+
           Turning 82-88, 94-99+

        The bench and the chair. *National Review* 39(9):15 (May 22, 1987).

Bersoff, Donald N. Social science data and the Supreme Court: Lockhart as a case in point. *American Psychologist* 42(1):52-58 (January 1987).

Bynam, Anderson E. Supreme Court review: Eighth and Fourteenth Amendments—the death penalty survives. *Journal of Criminal Law and Criminology* 78(4):1080-1118 (Winter 1988).

Death penalty: cruel and ever more usual punishment. *Economist* 303(7496):24-25 (May 2-8, 1987).

Dieter, Richard C. The death penalty dinosaur: capital punishment heads for extinction. *Commonweal* 115(1):11-14 (January 15, 1988).

Finkelstein, Michael O. A shared fate. *Nation* 244(18):599 (May 9, 1987).

Gest, Ted. Black-and-white issue?: Supreme Court wrestles with the death penalty and race. *U.S. News and World Report* 101(16):24-25 (October 20, 1986).

———. Hear ye: the Rehnquist Court is now in session. *U.S. News and World Report* 101(15):10 (October 13, 1986).

———. Open door to the execution chamber? *U.S. News and World Report* 102(17):25 (May 4, 1987).

Horgan, John. Science and the citizen: the death penalty. *Scientific American* 263(1):17-18, 20 (July 1990).

Kaplan, David A. New rules on death row. *Newsweek* 117(17):68 (April 29, 1991).

Kempton, Murray. The appointment of death. *New York Review of Books* 34(9):40 (May 28, 1987).

Lacayo, Richard, Anne Constable, and Daniel S. Levy. Clearing a path to the chair: the Supreme Court rejects a key legal challenge to the death penalty. *Time* 129(18):80 (May 4, 1987).

Murphy, Cornelius F. The Supreme Court and capital punishment:a new hands-off approach. *USA Today* 121(2574):51-52 (March 1993).

Press, Aric, Ann McDaniel, Erik Calonius, George Raine, Vern E. Smith, Andrew Murr, and Daniel Shapiro. Gridlock on death row. *Newsweek* 109(18):60-61 (May 4, 1987).

Press, Aric, Ann McDaniel, and Ginny Carroll. The Rehnquist era begins. *Newsweek* 108(15):94-98 (October 13 1986).

Press, Aric, Ann McDaniel, Daniel Pedersen, and Linda R. Prout. Death row: last skirmish. *Newsweek* 108(16):34 (October 20, 1986).

Russell, Katheryn K. A critical view from the inside: an application of critical legal studies to criminal law. *Journal of Criminal Law and Criminology* 85(1):222-240 (Summer 1994).

Smolowe, Jill, Jonathan Beaty, Cathy Booth, and Julie Johnson. Race and the death penalty: a high-court move to halt repeated appeals stirs concern about an arbitrary process. *Time* 137(17):68-69 (April 29, 1991).

Thinking about the death penalty. *America* 156(19):393 (May 16, 1987).

Vito, Gennaro F., and Thomas J. Keil. Capital sentencing in Kentucky: an analysis of the factors influencing decision making in the post-Gregg period. *Journal of Criminal Law and Criminology* 79(2):483-503 (Summer 1988).

3129. Lukhard v. Reed   April 22, 1987
481 US 368   95 LEd2d 328   107 SCt 1807
Almanac (1987):16A

3130. Hitchcock v. Dugger   April 22, 1987
481 US 393   95 LEd2d 347   107 SCt 1821
Almanac (1987):8A

Death penalty: cruel and ever more usual punishment. *Economist* 303(7496):24-25 (May 2-8, 1987).

3131. Tull v. United States   April 28, 1987
481 US 412   95 LEd2d 365   107 SCt 1831
Almanac (1987):15A

3132. Burlington Northern Railroad Co. v. Brotherhood of Maintenance of Way Employees   April 28, 1987
481 US 429   95 LEd2d 381   107 SCt 1841
Almanac (1987):14A

3133. Burlington Northern Railroad v. Oklahoma Tax Commission   April 28, 1987
481 US 454   95 LEd2d 404   107 SCt 1855
Almanac (1987):16A

3134. Meese v. Keene   April 28, 1987
     481 US 465   95 LEd2d 415   107 SCt 1862
        Almanac (1987):3A,12A
     Keeping the word. *Time* 129(19):49 (May 11, 1987).

3135. Pope v. Illinois   May 4, 1987
     481 US 497   95 LEd2d 439   107 SCt 1918
        Almanac (1987):3A-4A, 12A
        Sup Ct Review (1989):195-211
     Fields, Howard. First Amendment watch: obscenity test challenged in U.S. Supreme Court. *Publishers' Weekly* 231(10):10 (March 13, 1987).
     ————. High Court to hear challenge to Miller. *Publishers' Weekly* 230(17):15 (October 24, 1986).
     Rembar, Charles. Debunking the 'reasonable man' rule. [Editorial] *Publishers' Weekly* 231(25):16 (June 26, 1987).
     Reuter, Madalynne. High Court to review key part of Miller test. *Publishers' Weekly* 230(25):14 (December 19, 1986).
     ————. Supreme Court rejects Indianapolis porn law. *Publishers' Weekly* 229(10):26 (March 7, 1986).
     Rosen, Jeffrey. 'Miller' time. *New Republic* 203(14):17-19 (October 1, 1990).
     Staal, Lorri. Supreme Court review: First Amendment—the objective standard for social value in obscenity cases. *Journal of Criminal Law and Criminology* 78(4):735-762 (Winter 1988).
     Supreme Court fine-tunes third part of 'Miller' test. *Publishers' Weekly* 231(20):20 (May 22, 1987).

3136. Arizona v. Mauro   May 4, 1987
     481 US 520   95 LEd2d 458   107 SCt 1931
        Almanac (1987):7A

3137. Board of Directors of Rotary International v. Rotary Club of Duarte   May 4, 1987
     481 US 537   95 LEd2d 474   107 SCt 1940
        Almanac (1987):3A, 10A
     Regan, Richard J. Supreme Court roundup: 1986 term. *Thought* 63(251):429-441 (December 1988).
     Rosellini, Lynn, and Lisa J. Moore. Tap, tap, tap on the clubhouse door. *U.S. News and World Report* 102(18):72-74 (May 11, 1987).
     Rotary action. *Time* 129(20):62 (May 18, 1987).
     Rotary: women's turn comes round. *U.S. News and World Report* 102(19):14 (May 18, 1987).
     Seligmann, Jean, Andrew Murr, and Erik Himmelsback. Ruckus over Rotary women. *Newsweek* 109(20):47 (May 18, 1987).
     Smolowe, Jill, D. Blake Hallanan, and Melissa Ludtke. Those 24 words are back: ERA surfaces once more amid doubts about its urgency. *Time* 130(1):91 (July 6, 1987).

3138. Pennsylvania v. Finley   May 18, 1987
     481 US 551   95 LEd2d 539   107 SCt 1990
        Almanac (1987):7A
     Mello, Michael A. Is there a federal constitutional right to counsel in capital post-conviction proceedings? *Journal of Criminal Law and Criminology* 79(4):1065-1104 (Winter 1989).

3139. National Labor Relations Board (NLRB) v. International Brotherhood of Electrical Workers,   May 18, 1987
     Local 340
     481 US 573   95 LEd2d 557   107 SCt 2002
        Almanac (1987):14A
     Court widens civil rights law. *ENR* 218(22):52 (May 28, 1987).

3140. Saint Francis College v. Al-Khazraji, aka Allan   May 18, 1987
     481 US 604   95 LEd2d 582   107 SCt 2022
        Almanac (1987):10A
     Court widens civil rights law. *ENR* 218(22):52 (May 28, 1987).

Fields, Cheryl M. High Court opens civil-rights suits to all ethnic groups. *Chronicle of Higher Education* 33(37):1, 22 (May 27, 1987).

Gest, Ted. Rules on 1866 statute: an old anti-bias law's widened bite. *U.S. News and World Report* 102(21):10-11 (June 1, 1987).

Supreme Court: reconsidering rights. *Economist* 309(7577):27-28 (November 19-25, 1988).

3141. Shaare Tefila Congregation v. Cobb   May 18, 1987
481 US 615   95 LEd2d 594   107 SCt 2019
Almanac (1987):5A, 10A-11A

Court widens civil rights law. *ENR* 218(22):52 (May 28, 1987).

Fields, Cheryl M. High Court opens civil-rights suits to all ethnic groups. *Chronicle of Higher Education* 33(37):1, 22 (May 27, 1987).

Supreme Court: reconsidering rights. *Economist* 309(7577):27-28 (November 19-25, 1988).

3142. Rose v. Rose   May 18, 1987
481 US 619   95 LEd2d 599   107 SCt 2029
Almanac (1987):11A

3143. Gray v. Mississippi   May 18, 1987
481 US 648   95 LEd2d 622   107 SCt 2045
Almanac (1987):8A

Bonebrake, James G. Supreme Court review: Sixth and Fourteenth Amendments—the lost role of the peremptory challenge in securing an accused's right to an impartial jury. *Journal of Criminal Law and Criminology* 79(3):899-920 (Fall 1988).

3144. United States v. Johnson   May 18, 1987
481 US 681   95 LEd2d 648   107 SCt 2063
Almanac (1987):15A
Turning 103-108+

Ball, Howard. The U.S. Supreme Court's glossing of the Federal Tort Claims Act: statutory construction and veterans' tort actions. *Western Political Quarterly* 41(3):529-552 (September 1988).

Mecham, Michael. Supreme Court extends limits on suits by military personnel. *Aviation Week and Space Technology* 126(21):26 (May 25, 1987).

3145. Hodel v. Irving   May 18, 1987
481 US 704   95 LEd2d 668   107 SCt 2076
Almanac (1987):18A
New Right (Schwartz) 130-136

3146. Pension Benefit Guaranty Corp. v. Yahn & McDonnnell, Inc.   May 18, 1987
Coupled with United Retail and Wholesale Employees Teamsters Union, Local No. 115 Pension Plan v. Yahn & McDonnell, Inc.
481 US 735   95 LEd2d 692   107 SCt 2171
Almanac (1987):14A

3147. Ray v. United States   May 18, 1987
481 US 736   95 LEd2d 693   107 SCt 2093
Almanac (1987):9A

3148. United States v. Salerno   May 26, 1987
481 US 739   95 LEd2d 697   107 SCt 2095
Almanac (1987):8A
Black 213-220
Brennan 99-101
Const Law 412-415R

Documents (v. 2):867-869R

Editorials (1987):582-589

Eason, Michael J. Supreme Court review: Eighth Amendment—pretrial detention: what will become of the innocent? *Journal of Criminal Law and Criminology* 78(4):1048-1079 (Winter 1988).

First jail, then a trial. *Newsweek* 109(23):19 (June 8, 1987).

Gest, Ted. No bail for the baddest. *U.S. News and World Report* 102(22):12 (June 8, 1987).

Lacayo, Richard, and Anne Constable. First the sentence, then the trial: the Supreme Court approves no bail for dangerous defendants. *Time* 129(23):69 (June 8, 1987).

Rosen, Cathryn Jo, and John S. Goldkamp. The constitutionality of drug testing at the bail stage. *Journal of Criminal Law and Criminology* 80(1):114-176 (Spring 1989).

3149. Hilton v. Braunskill   May 26, 1987

     481 US 770   95 LEd2d 724   107 SCt 2113

       Almanac (1987):8A

3150. Young v. United States ex rel Vuitton et Fils S.A.   May 26, 1987

           Coupled with Klayminc v. United States

     481 US 787   95 LEd2d 740   107 SCt 2124

       Almanac (1987):17A

Andresky, Jill. Be your own prosecuting attorney. *Forbes* 138(5):72 (September 8, 1986).

3151. United States v. Mendoza-Lopez   May 26, 1987

     481 US 828   95 LEd2d 772   107 SCt 2148

       Almanac (1987):10A

3152. International Brotherhood of Electrical Workers v. Hechler   May 26, 1987

     481 US 851   95 LEd2d 791   107 SCt 2161

       Almanac (1987):14A

Hukill, Craig. Significant decisions in labor cases: union liability. *Monthly Labor Review* 113(5):53-54 (May 1990).

Labor law overrides union safety liability. *ENR* 224(22x):13-14 (May 31, 1990).

Martin, Bob. The Supreme Court's new era: what's ahead for labor law? *Personnel Journal* 65(10):92-98 (October 1986).

Mauro, Tony. The High Court: what it's up to. *Nation's Business* 74(9):57-60 (September 1986).

3153. Fort Halifax Packing Co. Inc. v. Coyne   June 1, 1987

     482 US 1   96 LEd2d 1   107 SCt 2211

       Almanac (1987):14A

Morrison, John M. ERISA and the loss of just remedies. *Trial* 31(3):18-25 (March 1995).

Ruben, George. Developments in industrial relations: employers in Maine must pay severance benefits. *Monthly Labor Review* 110(9):74 (September 1987).

3154. Fall River Dyeing and Finishing Corp. v. National Labor Relations Board (NLRB)   June 1, 1987

     482 US 27   96 LEd2d 22   107 SCt 2225

       Almanac (1987):14A

Litigation: labor, mergers high on Supreme Court's agenda. *Industry Week* 231(1):32 (October 13, 1986).

Martin, Bob. The Supreme Court's new era: what's ahead for labor law? *Personnel Journal* 65(10):92-98 (October 1986).

Ruben, George. Developments in industrial relations: Court upholds decision on incumbent unions. *Monthly Labor Review* 110(9):74 (September 1987).

3155. United States v. Hohri   June 1, 1987

     482 US 64   96 LEd2d 51   107 SCt 2246

       Almanac (1987):278, 17A; (1988):80

Pawelek, Dick. Your Constitution: Japanese-Americans vs. the U.S. *Scholastic Update* (Teachers' Edition) 119(15):18 (April 6, 1987).

3156. Turner v. Safley   June 1, 1987
482 US 78   96 LEd2d 64   107 SCt 2254
    Almanac (1987):11A

3157. Commissioner v. Asphalt Products Co.   June 1, 1987
482 US 117   96 LEd2d 97   107 SCt 2275
    Lore, Martin M., and Marvin J. Garbis. Negligence penalty of 5% on total deficiency, Supreme Court says [Section 6653(a)(1)]. *Journal of Taxation* 67(2):118 (August 1987).

3158. Texas v. New Mexico   June 8, 1987
482 US 124   96 LEd2d 105   107 SCt 2279
    Almanac (1987):16A

3159. Bowen v. Yuckert   June 8, 1987
482 US 137   96 LEd2d 119   107 SCt 2287
    Almanac (1987):16A

3160. Rockford Life Insurance Co. v. Illinois Department of Revenue   June 8, 1987
482 US 182   96 LEd2d 152   107 SCt 2312
    Almanac (1987):16A
Grillo, Alfred T. Ginnie Maes are not exempt from state taxation. *CPA Journal* 58(1):75-76 (January 1988).
State taxes: High Court rules Ginnie Maes not exempt from state taxation. *Journal of Accountancy* 164(2):35-36 (August 1987).
Tax dispute among cases to be heard by High Court. *Best's Review* (Life/Health Insurance Edition) 87(9):5-6 (January 1987).

3161. Utah Division of State Lands v. United States   June 8, 1987
482 US 193   96 LEd2d 162   107 SCt 2318
    Almanac (1987):15A

3162. Shearson/American Express, Inc. v. McMahon   June 8, 1987
482 US 220   96 LEd2d 185   107 SCt 2332
    Almanac (1987):13A
Rescigno, Richard. Court of last resort: is arbitration better for brokers or their customers? *Barron's* 71(28):16-17, 26-27 (July 15, 1991).
Scheibla, Shirley Hobbs. Big decision: can you sue a broker? High Court to say. *Barron's* 67(9):16, 32-33 (March 2, 1987).
———. Final victory? Brokerages win arbitration battle, but war may go on. *Barron's* 67(24):38-39, 79 (June 15, 1987).
———. See you in Court: compulsory arbitration under fire. *Barron's* 69(23):13, 28-30 (June 5, 1989).
Stern, Richard L. We wuz robbed. *Forbes* 140(14):60-61 (December 28, 1987).
Weiss, Stuart. Sue your stockbroker? You can't, you know. *Business Week* (Industrial/Technology Edition) (2987):75-76 (March 2, 1987).
Wiener, Daniel P. Battling your broker gets harder. *U.S. News and World Report* 102(24):51 (June 22, 1987).
Zigas, David. Can't sue your broker? It's no big loss. *Business Week* (Industrial/Technology Edition) (3004):128 (June 22, 1987).

3163. Interstate Commerce Commission (ICC) v. Brotherhood of Locomotive Engineers   June 8, 1987
       Coupled with Missouri-Kansas-Texas Railroad Co. v. Brotherhood
482 US 270   96 LEd2d 222   107 SCt 2360
    Almanac (1987):13A

3164. First English Evangelical Lutheran Church of Glendale v. County of Los Angeles   June 9, 1987
      482 US 304   96 LEd2d 250   107 SCt 2378
        Almanac (1987):16A
        Sup Ct Review (1987):1-46
      Blackwell, Robert J. Overlay zoning, performance standards, and environmental protection after Nollan. *Boston College Environmental Affairs Law Review* 16(3):615-659 (Spring 1989).
      Cohen, Jonathan E. A constitutional safety valve: the variance in zoning and land-use based environmental controls. *Boston College Environmental Affairs Law Review* 22(2):307-364 (Winter 1995).
      Darnell, Tim. The land and the law. *American City and County* 103(1):38-45 (January 1988).
      Folsom, Robin E. Executive Order 12,630: a president's manipulation of the Fifth Amendment's just compensation clause to achieve control over executive agency regulatory decision making. *Boston College Environmental Affairs Law Review* 20(4):639-698 (Summer 1993).
      Guskind, Robert. Takings stir up a storm: yet despite the tempest, this summer's two Supreme Court land-use decisions may not be as lopsided as some experts had feared. *Planning* 53(9):5-9 (September 1987).
      LaRusso, Joseph. "Paying for the change": First English Evangelical Lutheran Church of Glendale v. County of Los Angeles and the calculation of interim damages for regulatory takings. *Boston College Environmental Affairs Law Review* 17(3):551-583 (Spring 1990).
      Moskowitz, Daniel B. Court orders payment for some land use bans. *ENR* 218(25):25, 29 (June 18, 1987).
      Sanders, Alain L., and Anne Constable. No taking without paying: from the Supreme Court, a sweeping decision on confiscation. *Time* 129(25):64-65 (June 22, 1987).
      Singer, Saul Jay. Flooding the Fifth Amendment: the National Flood Insurance Program and the "takings" clause. *Boston College Environmental Affairs Law Review* 17(2):323-379 (Winter 1990).
      Walters, Jonathan. Tightening the screws on 'takings.' *Governing* 7(11):18-20 (August 1994).

3165. O'Lone v. Estate of Shabazz   June 9, 1987
      482 US 342   96 LEd2d 282   107 SCt 2400
        Almanac (1987):11A
        Godless 40-41
      Regan, Richard J. Supreme Court roundup: 1986 term. *Thought* 63(251):429-441 (December 1988).

3166. Board of Pardons v. Allen   June 9, 1987
      482 US 369   96 LEd2d 303   107 SCt 2415
        Almanac (1987):9A

3167. Caterpillar, Inc. v. Williams   June 9, 1987
      482 US 386   96 Led2d 318   107 SCt 2425
        Almanac (1987):14A

3168. California v. Superior Court of California   June 9, 1987
      482 US 400   96 LEd2d 332   107 SCt 2433
        Almanac (1987):9A

3169. Miller v. Florida   June 9, 1987
      482 US 423   96 LEd2d 351   107 SCt 2446
        Almanac (1987):9A

3170. Crawford Fitting Co. v. J.T. Gibbons, Inc.   June 15, 1987
            Coupled with Champion International Corp. v. International Woodworkers of America
      482 US 437   96 LEd2d 385   107 SCt 2494
        Almanac (1987):17A; (1991):255-257
      The Civil Rights Act of 1990. *Congressional Digest* 69(8-9):196-224 (August/September 1990).

3171. City of Houston v. Hill   June 15, 1987
      482 US 451   96 LEd2d 398   107 SCt 2502
        Almanac (1987):4A, 12A

3172. Perry v. Thomas   June 15, 1987
    482 US 483   96 LEd2d 426   107 SCt 2520
        Almanac (1987):14A

3173. Booth v. Maryland   June 15, 1987
    482 US 496   96 LEd2d 440   107 SCt 2529
        Almanac (1987):4A-5A, 8A
        Sup Ct Review (1991):77-102
        Sup Ct Yearbook (1990-91):35-37
        Turning 403-408, 418-419+
    Boudreaux, Paul. Booth v. Maryland and the individual vengeance rationale for criminal punishment. *Journal of Criminal Law and Criminology* 80(1):177-196 (Spring 1989).
    Newman, Eric S. Supreme Court review: Eighth Amendment—prosecutorial comment regarding the victim's personal qualities should not be permitted at the sentencing phase of a capital trial. *Journal of Criminal Law and Criminology* 80(4):1236-1255 (Winter 1990).
    Sanders, Alain L., Anne Constable, and Don Winbush. Memories of the monkey trial: the Supreme Court reaffirms the barrier between church and state. *Time* 129(26):54 (June 29, 1987).
    Sargeant, Georgia. Victim impact testimony allowed by Supreme Court in death penalty hearings. *Trial* 27(10):11-14, 85 (October 1991).

3174. Societe Nationale Industrielle Aerospatiale v. United States District Court   June 15, 1987
    or Southern District of Iowa
    482 US 522   96 LEd2d 461   107 SCt 2542
        Almanac (1987):17A-18A
    Boeschoten, Cornelis D. van. Hague Conference conventions and the United States: a European view. *Law and Contemporary Problems* 57(3):47-58 (Summer 1994).
    Born, Gary B. The Hague Evidence Convention revisited: reflections on its role in U.S. civil procedure. *Law and Contemporary Problems* 57(3):77-102 (Summer 1994).
    Feldman, Mark B. Foreign discovery: a new complication; compliance with the Hague Evidence Convention may be required. *Trial* 24(3):67-69 (March 1988).
    Note: beyond the rhetoric of comparative interest balancing: an alternative approach to extraterritorial discovery conflicts. *Law and Contemporary Problems* 50(3):95-115 (Summer 1987).

3175. Board of Airport Commissioners of the City of Los Angeles v. Jews for Jesus, Inc.   June 15, 1987
    482 US 569   96 LEd2d 500   107 SCt 2568
        Almanac (1987):4A, 12A
        Godless 43
    Lawton, Kim A. A look at Robert Bork and rulings affecting the church. *Christianity Today* 31(11):42-43 (August 7, 1987).
    Sanders, Alain L., Anne Constable, and Don Winbush. Memories of the monkey trial: the Supreme Court reaffirms the barrier between church and state. *Time* 129(26):54 (June 29, 1987).
    Spring, Beth. Can Christians hand out gospel tracts in airports? *Christianity Today* 31(6):43-44 (April 3, 1987).

3176. Edwards v. Aguillard   June 19, 1987
    482 US 578   96 LEd 2d 510   107 SCt 2593
        Almanac (1987):3A-4A, 12A
        Am Educators 18
        Brennan 129-134
        Const Law 89-94R
        Editorials (1987):722-731
        Godless 95
        May It 75-91R
        Sup Ct Church 255-270R
        Sup Ct Review (1995):323-391; (1988):61-84
        Turning 116-123

Creation science: High Court to hear case. *Christianity Today* 30(9):42 (June 13, 1986).

Doerr, Edd. Nobelists attack creationism law. *Humanist* 46(6):42 (November/December 1986).

Fields, Howard. Supreme Court abolishes Louisiana creationism law. *Publishers' Weekly* 232(1):13 (July 3, 1987).

———. Supreme Court questions creationism theory. *Publishers' Weekly* 230(26):16 (December 26, 1986).

Flygare, Thomas J. De jure: Supreme Court strikes down Louisiana creationism act. *Phi Delta Kappan* 69(1):77-79 (September 1987).

Fundamentalists: apes and apostates. *Economist* 303(7504):33-34 (June 27-July 3, 1987).

Gest, Ted. Hear ye: the Rehnquist Court is now in session. *U.S. News and World Report* 101(15):10 (October 13, 1986).

Gest, Ted, and Lucia Solorzano. High Court: the day God and Darwin collided. *U.S. News and World Report* 102(25):12 (June 29, 1987).

Gould, Stephen Jay. The verdict on creationism. *New York Times Magazine* (section 6, part 1):32, 34 (July 19, 1987).

Jaffa, Harry V. The Supreme Court monkeys around. *National Review* 40(2):46, 61 (February 5, 1988).

Johnson, Phillip E. Academic freedom and the religious professor. *Academe* 81(5):16-19 (September/October 1995).

Larson, Edward J. The creation-science case: is it science or religion? *Christianity Today* 31(2):50-51 (January 16, 1987).

Lawton, Kim A. High Court accepts cases on abortion, obscenity, and church hiring practices. *Christianity Today* 30(18):53-55 (December 12, 1986).

———. A look at Robert Bork and rulings affecting the church. *Christianity Today* 31(11):42-43 (August 7, 1987).

Lewin, Roger. Creationism case argued before Supreme Court. *Science* 235(4784):22-23 (January 2, 1987).

Martz, Larry, and Ann McDaniel. Keeping God out of the classroom. *Newsweek* 109(26):23-24 (June 29, 1987).

McDonald, Kim. Pervasive belief in "creation science" dismays and perplexes researchers. *Chronicle of Higher Education* 33(15):6-7, 10 (December 10, 1986).

McKown, Delos Banning. Deism and the Supreme Court. *Humanist* 52(2):25-28, 48 (March/April 1992).

McLoughlin, Merrill. Grand tests for a grand document. *U.S. News and World Report* 101(26):18-21 (December 29, 1986-January 5, 1987).

Mondak, Jeffery J. Policy legitimacy and the Supreme Court: the sources and contexts of legitimation. *Political Research Quarterly* 47(3):675-692 (September 1994).

Norman, Colin. Creationism case goes to Supreme Court. *Science* 232(4753):928 (May 23, 1986).

———. Nobelists unite against "creation science." *Science* 233(4767):935 (August 29, 1986).

———. Supreme Court strikes down "creation science" law as promotion of religion. *Science* 236(4809):1620 (June 26, 1987).

One case: a step-by-step account of its progress through the Supreme Court. *Life* 10(10):114-115 (Fall 1987).

Ostling, Richard, Anne Constable, and Michael P. Harris. Threatening the wall: church-state separation has powerful new critics. *Time* 130(1):70-71 (July 6, 1987).

Palmer, Stacy E. High Court's overturn of La. 'creation science' law is applauded; more demands by creationists seen. *Chronicle of Higher Education* 33(42):19 (July 1, 1987).

Prayer in public schools. *Congressional Digest* 74(1):3-32 (January 1995).

Press, Aric and Ann McDaniel. Renaissance of an octogenarian liberal. *Newsweek* 110(1):18 (July 6, 1987).

Press, Aric, Ann McDaniel, and Ginny Carroll. The Rehnquist era begins. *Newsweek* 108(15)94-98 (October 13, 1986).

Raloff, Janet. High Court rejects creationism law. *Science News* 131(26):404 (June 27, 1987).

Regan, Richard J. Supreme Court roundup: 1986 term. *Thought* 63(251):429-441 (December 1988).

Sanders, Alain L., Anne Constable, and Don Winbush. Memories of the monkey trial: the Supreme Court reaffirms the barrier between church and state. *Time* 129(26):54 (June 29, 1987).

Science and the citizen: born again. *Scientific American* 255(4):76-78 (October 1986).

Science and the citizen: science, 7; creationism, 2. *Scientific American* 257(2):14 (August 1987).

Scientists urge court to reject creationism law. *Chemical and Engineering News* 64(34):5-6 (August 25, 1986).

Sendor, Benjamin. Here's a closer look at that creationism decision and what it means to your schools. *American School Board Journal* 174(9):24-25 (September 1987).

Sherman, Edward F. The role of religion in school curriculum and textbooks. *Academe* 74(1):17-22 (January/February 1988).

Stephenson, D. Grier, Jr. Religion and the Constitution: the Supreme Court speaks, again. *USA Today* 118(2538):21-23 (March 1990).

Van Alstyne, William W. Academic freedom and the First Amendment in the Supreme Court of the United States: an unhurried historical review. *Law and Contemporary Problems* 53(3):79-154 (Summer 1990).

Wall, James M. Supreme Court on 'flat souls.' [Editorial] *Christian Century* 104(20):579 (July 1-8, 1987).

Yen, Marianne. Nobel scientists file brief against creationism. *Publishers' Weekly* 230(10):22 (September 5, 1986).

Zimmerman, Michael. Although politics and science are often entwined, there are times when the two must be separated. *Chronicle of Higher Education* 34(12):B1 (November 18, 1987).

3177. Frazier v. Heebe   June 19, 1987
    482 US 641   96 LEd2d 557   107 SCt 2607
      Almanac (1987):18A

3178. Goodman v. Lukens Steel Co.   June 19, 1987
      Coupled with United Steelworkers of America v. Goodman
    482 US 656   96 LEd2d 572   107 SCt 2617
      Almanac (1987):11A

3179. New York v. Burger   June 19, 1987
    482 US 691   96 LEd2d 601   107 SCt 2636
      Almanac (1987):16A
      Sup Ct Review (1989):87-163

Andersen, Robert M. Technology, pollution control, and EPA access to commercial property: a constitutional and policy framework. *Boston College Environmental Affairs Law Review* 17(1):1-74 (Fall 1989).

Mussio, Donna. Drawing the line between administrative and criminal searches: defining the "object of the search" in environmental inspections. *Boston College Environmental Affairs Law Review* 18(1):185-211 (Fall 1990).

3180. Kentucky v. Stincer   June 19, 1987
    482 US 730   96 LEd2d 631   107 SCt 2658
      Almanac (1987):7A

3181. Hewitt v. Helms   June 19, 1987
    482 US 755   96 LEd2d 654   107 SCt 2672
      Almanac (1987):10A

Ross, Douglas. Safeguarding our federalism: lessons for the states from the Supreme Court. *Public Administration Review* 45(Special Issue):723-731 (November 1985).

3182. Ricketts v. Adamson   June 22, 1987
    483 US 1   97 LEd2d 1   107 SCt 2680
      Almanac (1987):7A
      Death Penalty (Tushnet) 122-123

3183. Citicorp Industrial Credit Inc. v. Brock   June 22, 1987
    483 US 27   97 LEd2d 23   107 SCt 2694
      Almanac (1987):14A

3184. Rock v. Arkansas   June 22, 1987
    483 US 44   97 LEd2d 37   107 SCt 2704
      Almanac (1987):7A

Kuplicki, Francis P. Supreme Court review: Fifth, Sixth, and Fourteenth Amendments—a constitutional paradigm for determining the admissibility of hypnotically refreshed testimony. *Journal of Criminal Law and Criminology* 78(4):853-876 (Winter 1988).

3185. Sumner v. Shuman   June 22, 1987
    483 US 66   97 LEd2d 56   107 SCt 2716
      Almanac (1987):4A-5A, 8A
      Death Penalty (Tushnet) 59, 70, 75

3186. Commissioner of Internal Revenue v. Fink   June 22, 1987
    483 US 89   97 LEd2d 74   107 SCt 2729
      Almanac (1987):13A
    August, Jerald David, and Steven J. Levine. Supreme Court in Fink holds non-pro rata stock surrenders are capital contributions. *Journal of Taxation* 67(3):130- 135 (September 1987).

3187. Tanner v. United States   June 22, 1987
    483 US 107   97 LEd2d 90   107 SCt 2739
      Almanac (1987):7A-8A

3188. Agency Holding Corp. v. Malley-Duff and Associates, Inc.   June 22, 1987
      Coupled with Crown Life Insurance v. Mallery-Duff and Associates, Inc.
    483 US 143   97 LEd2d 121   107 SCt 2759
      Almanac (1987):13A
    Tax dispute among cases to be heard by High Court. *Best's Review* (Life/Health Insurance Edition) 87(9):5-6 (January 1987).

3189. Bourjaily v. United States   June 23, 1987
    483 US 171   97 LEd2d 144   107 SCt 2775
      Almanac (1987):8A
    Haddad, James B. The future of confrontation clause developments what will emerge when the Supreme Court synthesizes the diverse lines of confrontation decisions? *Journal of Criminal Law and Criminology* 81(1):77-98 (Spring 1990).
    Hanusa, Julie. Supreme Court review: Sixth Amendment—the co-conspirator exemption to the hearsay rule: the confrontation clause and preliminary factual determinations relevant to federal rule of evidence 801(d)(2)(E). *Journal of Criminal Law and Criminology* 78(4):915- 936 (Winter 1988).

3190. South Dakota v. Dole   June 23, 1987
    483 US 203   97 LEd2d 171   107 SCt 2793
      Almanac (1987):4A, 17A
      Guide (CQ) 118-119
      Sup Ct Review (1995):125-215; (1988):85-127
    Hickok, Eugene W., Jr. Federalism's future before the U.S. Supreme Court. *Annals of the American Academy of Political and Social Science* 509:73-82 (May 1990).
    Jensen, Laura S. Subsidies, strings, and the courts: judicial action and conditional federal spending. *Review of Politics* 55(3):491-509 (Summer 1993).
    Tax dispute among cases to be heard by High Court. *Best's Review* (Life/Health Insurance Edition) 87(9):5-6 (January 1987).
    Wise, Charles, and Rosemary O'Leary. Is federalism dead or alive in the Supreme Court?: implications for public administrators. *Public Administration Review* 52(6):559-572 (November/December 1992).

3191. Puerto Rico v. Branstad   June 23, 1987
    483 US 219   97 LEd2d 187   107 SCt 2802
      Almanac (1987):18A

3192. Tyler Pipe Industries v. Washington State Department of Revenue   June 23, 1987
    483 US 232   97 LEd2d 199   107 SCt 2810
      Almanac (1987):16A

3193. American Trucking Association v. Scheiner   June 23, 1987
    483 US 266   97 LEd2d 226   107 SCt 2829
      Almanac (1987):16A

3194. California v. Rooney   June 23, 1987
    483 US 307   97 LEd2d 258   107 SCt 2852
      Almanac (1987):6A

3195. Corp. of the Presiding Bishop of the Church of Jesus Christ of Latter-Day Saints v. Amos   June 24, 1987
      Coupled with United States v. Amos
    483 US 327   97 LEd2d 273   107 SCt 2862
      Almanac (1987):3A, 12A
      Godless 51-52
      Sup Ct Review (1989):373-402; (1992):123-153
    Drinan, Robert F. Should a Mormon-owned corporation be able to fire a Mormon who does not tithe? *America* 156(18):375-376 (May 9, 1987).
    In brief: the Supreme Court: use of religion in hiring is upheld. *Chronicle of Higher Education* 33(42):19 (July 1, 1987).
    Kelley, Dean M., and Michael W. McConnell. Statism, not separationism, is the problem. *Christian Century* 106(2):48-52 (January 18, 1989).
    Larson, Edward J. Supreme Court hears challenge to church hiring policies. *Christianity Today* 31(8):49-50 (May 15, 1987).
    Lawton, Kim A. A look at Robert Bork and rulings affecting the church. *Christianity Today* 31(11):42-43 (August 7, 1987).
    Maguire, Daniel C. Can a university be Catholic? *Academe* 74(1):12-16 (January/February 1988).
    Regan, Richard J. Supreme Court roundup: 1986 term. *Thought* 63(251):429-441 (December 1988).

3196. McNally v. United States   June 24, 1987
      Coupled with Gray v. United States
    483 US 350   97 LEd2d 292   107 SCt 2875
      Almanac (1987):9A; (1988):92, 110-111
    Bradley, Craig M. Supreme Court review: foreward: mail fraud after McNally and Carpenter: the essence of fraud. *Journal of Criminal Law and Criminology* 79(3):573-622 (Fall 1988).
    Dwyer, Paula, and Stan Crock. Did the good guys go too far? *Business Week* (Industrial/Technology Edition) (3014):29 (August 31, 1987).
    Maurer, Virginia G. The continuing expansion of RICO in business litigation. *Business Horizons* 33(5):80-87 (September/October 1990).

3197. Rankin v. McPherson   June 24, 1987
    483 US 378   97 LEd2d 315   107 SCt 2891
      Almanac (1987):4A, 12A
      Const Law 152-153

3198. Buchanan v. Kentucky   June 24, 1987
    483 US 402   97 LEd2d 336   107 SCt 2906
      Almanac (1987):8A
    Whisler, Barbara J. Supreme Court review: Sixth Amendment—death qualification of the jury: process is permissible where defendant does not face death penalty. *Journal of Criminal Law and Criminology* 78(4):954-983 (Winter 1988).

3199. Solorio v. United States   June 25, 1987
       483 US 435   97 LEd2d 364   107 SCt 2924
          Almanac (1987):3A, 15A
       American survey: The week the Supreme Court changed colour? *Economist* 304(7505):25-26 (July 4-10, 1987).
       Ball, Howard. The U.S. Supreme Court's glossing of the Federal Tort Claims Act: statutory construction and
          veterans' tort actions. *Western Political Quarterly* 41(3):529-552 (September 1988).

3200. Welch v. Texas Department of Highways and Public Transporation   June 25, 1987
       483 US 468   97 LEd2d 389   107 SCt 2941
          Almanac (1987):18A
       Farber, Daniel A. Supreme Court review: litigating with the sovereign. *Trial* 28(4):85-90 (April 1992).

3201. San Francisco Arts and Athletics, Inc. (SFAA) v. United States Olympic Committee   June 25, 1987
       483 US 522   97 LEd2d 427   107 SCt 2971
          Almanac (1987):12A
       Boedecker, Karl A., and Fred W. Morgan. The evolution of First Amendment protection for commercial
          speech. *Journal of Marketing* 59(1):38-47 (January 1995).
       Borchard, William M. "Olympics" not fair game. *Advertising Age* 59(24):46 (June 6, 1988).
       Hovland, Roxanne, and Ronald E. Taylor. Advertising and commercial speech since the 1986 Posadas case.
          Journalism Quarterly 67(4):1083-1089 (Winter 1990).
       Notes and comment. [Editorial] *New Yorker* 63(27):19-20 (August 24, 1987).

3202. Rivera v. Minnich   June 25, 1987
       483 US 574   97 LEd2d 473   107 SCt 3001
          Almanac (1987):11A

3203. Bowen v. Gilliard   June 25, 1987
       483 US 587   97 LEd2d 485   107 SCt 3008
          Almanac (1987):17A

3204. Anderson v. Creighton   June 25, 1987
       483 US 635   97 LEd2d 523   107 SCt 3034
          Almanac (1987):11A
          Black 223-230
       Chemerinsky, Erwin. Stunting the Constitution's growth. *Trial* 26(11):36-40 (November 1990).

3205. United States v. Stanley   June 25, 1987
       483 US 669   97 LEd2d 550   107 SCt 3054
          Almanac (1987):15A
          Black 237-245
          Turning 99-108+
       Ball, Howard. The U.S. Supreme Court's glossing of the Federal Tort Claims Act: statutory construction and
          veterans' tort actions. *Western Political Quarterly* 41(3):529-552 (September 1988).
       Press, Aric, Ann McDaniel, Margaret Garrard Warner, Howard Fineman, and Tessa Namuth. Will the Court
          turn right? *Newsweek* 110(1):16-18 (July 6, 1987).

3206. Pennsylvania v. Delaware Valley Citizens' Council for Clean Air   June 26, 1987
       483 US 711   97 LEd2d 585   107 SCt 3078
          Almanac (1987):18A
       Conte, Alba. Public interest lawyers deserve risk multipliers. *Trial* 30(12):36-42 (December 1994).

3207. Greer v. Miller   June 26, 1987
       483 US 756   97 LEd2d 618   107 SCt 3102
          Almanac (1987):7A

3208. Burger v. Kemp   June 26, 1987
    483 US 776   97 LEd2d 638   107 SCt 3114
        Almanac (1987):7A

3209. Nollan v. California Coastal Commission   June 26, 1987
    483 US 825   97 LEd2d 677   107 SCt 3141
        Almanac (1987):4A-5A, 16A
        Sup Ct Review (1987):1-46
        Sup Ct Yearbook (1993-94):39-41
    Blackwell, Robert J. Overlay zoning, performance standards, and environmental protection after Nollan. *Boston College Environmental Affairs Law Review* 16(3):615-659 (Spring 1989).
    Chemerinsky, Erwin. Looking ahead to the new term. *Trial* 30(12):81-83 (December 1994).
    Cohen, Jonathan E. A constitutional safety valve: the variance in zoning and land-use based environmental controls. *Boston College Environmental Affairs Law Review* 22(2):307-364 (Winter 1995).
    Darnell, Tim. The land and the law. *American City and County* 103(1):38-45 (January 1988).
    Farber, Daniel A. 'Taking' liberties. *New Republic* 198(26):19-22 (June 27, 1988).
    Hanley, Thomas. A developer's dream: the United States Claims Court's new analysis of Section 404 takings challenges. *Boston College Environmental Affairs Law Review* 19(2):317-353 (Fall/Winter 1991).
    High Court reins zones. *ENR* 219(1):51 (July 2, 1987).
    Plater, Zygmunt J. B., and William Lund Norine. Through the looking glass of eminent domain: exploring the "arbitrary and capricious" test and substantive rationality review of governmental decisions. *Boston College Environmental Affairs Law Review* 16(4):661-752 (Summer 1989).
    Singer, Saul Jay. Flooding the Fifth Amendment: the National Flood Insurance Program and the "takings" clause. *Boston College Environmental Affairs Law Review* 17(2):323-379 (Winter 1990).
    Walters, Jonathan. Tightening the screws on 'takings.' *Governing* 7(11):18-20 (August 1994).

3210. Griffin v. Wisconsin   June 26, 1987
    483 US 868   97 LEd2d 709   107 SCt 3164
        Almanac (1987):6A
        En Am Con 2041-2042
        Sup Ct Review (1989):87-163
    Press, Aric, Ann McDaniel, and Ginny Carroll. The Rehnquist era begins. *Newsweek* 108(15):94-98 (October 13, 1986).

3211. Ronald Reagan v. Abourezk   October 19, 1987
    484 US 1   98 LEd2d 1   108 SCt 252
    The association and the courts. *Academe* 75(3):31-33 (May/June 1989).
    Fields, Cheryl M. High Court to weigh denials of visas to college guests, union's use of mail. *Chronicle of Higher Education* 34(6):A26 (October 7, 1987).
    Garneau, George. Government's ability to bar foreigners with Communist ties is limited. *Editor and Publisher* 120(44):17 (October 31, 1987).
    Palmer, Stacy E. High Court deadlocks on denial of visas to aliens; lower-court ruling stands, limiting president. *Chronicle of Higher Education* 34(9):A25-A26 (October 28, 1987).
    Press, Aric, Ann McDaniel, Margaret Garrard Warner, Howard Fineman, and Tessa Namuth. Will the Court turn right? *Newsweek* 110(1):16-18 (July 6, 1987).

3212. Church of Scientology of California v. Internal Revenue Service (IRS)   November 10, 1987
    484 US 9   98 LEd2d 228   108 SCt 271
    Supreme Court expands definition of return information. *Journal of Taxation* 68(1):58-59 (January 1988).

3213. Carpenter v. United States   November 16, 1987
    484 US 19   98 LEd2d 275   108 SCt 316
    Bradley, Craig M. Supreme Court review: foreward: mail fraud after McNally and Carpenter: the essence of fraud. *Journal of Criminal Law and Criminology* 79(3):573-622 (Fall 1988).

Castro, Janice, Jerome Cramer, and Raji Samghabadi. Of loose lips and stock tips: vitory in the Winans case will help in snaring insider traders. *Time* 130(22):63 (November 30, 1987).

Cox, James D. Insider trading: regulation of activity is 'in trouble.' *Trial* 24(9):22-28, 93-96 (September 1988).

Dwyer, Paula, and Stan Crock. Did the good guys go too far? *Business Week* (Industrial/Technology Edition) (3014):29 (August 31, 1987).

Dwyer, Paula, and Catherine Yang. Deadlock at the Court: weighty decisions may have to wait until Bork—or someone—is seated. *Business Week* (Industrial/Technology Edition) (3020):36-37 (October 12, 1987).

Garneau, George. High Court upholds conviction of ex-Wall Street journal reporter. *Editor and Publisher* 120(47):12, 33 (November 21, 1987).

————. 1987 legal review—press won some, lost some. *Editor and Publisher* 121(1):24, 58-59 (January 2, 1988).

Lazare, Daniel. What's riding on the Winans case. [Editorial] *Columbia Journalism Review* 26(5):4-5 (January/February 1988).

Maurer, Virginia G. The continuing expansion of RICO in business litigation. *Business Horizons* 33(5):80-87 (September/October 1990).

Not rain, nor snow, nor insider trading must stop the U.S. mail. *Economist* 305(7525):77-78 (November 21-27, 1987).

Scheppele, Kim Lane. "It's just not right": the ethics of insider trading. *Law and Contemporary Problems* 56(3):123-173 (Summer 1993).

Weiss, Gary. The SEC isn't clearing up anything. *Business Week* (Industrial/Technology Edition) (3013):22 (August 24, 1987).

Yang, Catherine. Insider trading: the High Court hasn't ended the confusion. *Business Week* (3028):34 (November 30, 1987).

3214. United Paperworkers International Union v. Misco, Inc.   December 1, 1987
484 US 29   98 LEd2d 286   108 SCt 364
Clean water ruling: suits by citizens are curtailed for pollution damage in the past. *ENR* 219(24):16 (December 10, 1987).

Lissy, William E. Labor law: Supreme Court limits reversal of arbitration awards. *Supervision* 49(6):21-22 (June 1988).

Murphy, Betty Southard, Wayne E. Barlow, and D. Diane Hatch. Federal courts' jurisdiction on arbitration awards. *Personnel Journal* 67(2):30 (February 1988).

3215. Gwaltney of Smithfield, Ltd. v. Chesapeake Bay Foundation, Inc.   December 1, 1987
484 US 49   98 LEd2d 306   108 SCt 376
Clean water ruling: suits by citizens are curtailed for pollution damage in the past. *ENR* 219(24):16 (December 10, 1987).

Dwyer, Paula, and Catherine Yang. Deadlock at the Court: weighty decisions may have to wait until Bork—or someone—is seated. *Business Week* (Industrial/Technology Edition) (3020):36-37 (October 12, 1987).

Hanson, David. Supreme Court ruling affects water pollution suits. *Chemical and Engineering News* 65(50):13-14 (December 14, 1987).

Moskowitz, Daniel B. Industry issues to fill High Court's calendar. *ENR* 219(14):10-11 (October 1, 1987).

3216. Karcher v. May   December 1, 1987
484 US 72   98 LEd2d 327   108 SCt 388
Editorials (1987):1440-1441
Lacayo, Richard, and Anne Constable. Is eight enough? *Time* 130(15):20 (October 12, 1987).

Spring, Beth. Supreme Court will rule on moment-of-silence law. *Christianity Today* 31(5):56-58 (March 20, 1987).

Supreme Court considers a second moment-of-silence law. *Christianity Today* 31(16):56 (November 6, 1987).

3217. National Labor Relations Board (NLRB) v. United Food & Commercial   December 14, 1987
      Workers Union, Local 23
484 US 112   98 LEd2d 429   108 SCt 413
Moskowitz, Daniel B. Industry issues to fill High Court's calendar. *ENR* 219(14):10-11 (October 1, 1987).

3218. Hartigan v. Zbaraz   December 14, 1987
       484 US 171   98 LEd2d 478   108 SCt 479

       Almanac (1989):306-307; (1990):528-531
       Turning 151

Abortion law complications. *Christianity Today* 31(18):47, 49 (December 11, 1987).

Can states restrict a minor's access to abortion? *Christianity Today* 31(6):44, 46 (April 3, 1987).

Gardner, William, David Scherer, and Maya Tester. Asserting scientific authority: cognitive development and adolescent legal rights. *American Psychologist* 44(6):895-902 (June 1989).

Lacayo, Richard, and Anne Constable. Is eight enough? *Time* 130(15):20 (October 12, 1987).

LaFay, Laura, and James Earl Hardy. A court-watcher's guide. *Scholastic Update* 124(5):13-16 (November 1, 1991).

Melton, Gary B., and Nancy Felipe Russo. Adolescent abortion: psychological perspectives on public policy. *American Psychologist* 42(1):69-72 (January 1987).

3219. Hazelwood School District v. Kuhlmeier   January 13, 1988
       484 US 260   98 LEd2d 592   108 SCt 562

       Am Educators 258
       Brennan 179-184
       Const Law 206-208R
       Editorials (1988):84-91
       Fourth 200-201
       Turning 164-166

Abrams, Marc. Don't mess with the student press. *American School Board Journal* 181(9):32-35 (September 1994).

Adams, Kathleen, and Nick Catoggio. The Supreme Court: a principal's best friend. *Time* 146(2):14 (July 10, 1995).

Civics or censorship: it's your choice. *American School Board Journal* 175(4):12 (April 1988).

Court to student editors: teacher knows best. *U.S. News and World Report* 104(3):10 (January 25, 1988).

Eskin, Leah. Student journalists fight for free expression. *Scholastic Update* 122(1):19-21 (September 8, 1989).

Excerpts from Justice White's opinion on censorship of high-school paper. *Chronicle of Higher Education* 34(19):A22, 24R (January 20, 1988).

Fields, Cheryl M. High Court to weigh denials of visas to college guests, union's use of mail. *Chronicle of Higher Education* 34(6):A26 (October 7, 1987).

———. Supreme Court backs official who censored school newspaper, skirts issue at colleges. *Chronicle of Higher Education* 34(19):A1, A22 (January 20, 1988).

Fitzgerald, Mark. Editorials support censorship decision. *Editor and Publisher* 121(4):11-12 (January 23, 1988).

Fraser, Laura. Fallout from Hazelwood. *Columbia Journalism Review* 27(1):8-11 (May/June 1988).

Garneau, George. A "First Amendment disaster." *Editor and Publisher* 121(3):12 (January 16, 1988).

———. 1987 legal review—press won some, lost some. *Editor and Publisher* 121(1):24, 58-59 (January 2, 1988).

Goodman, Mark. Student press freedom: one view of the Hazelwood decision. *NASSP Bulletin* 72(511):38-44 (November 1988).

Gough, Pauline B. Needed: more Mitch Charnleys. [Editorial] *Phi Delta Kappan* 69(8):546 (April 1988).

Gow, Haven Bradford. U.S. Supreme Court curbs student press rights. [Editorial] *Clearing House* 63(6):244 (February 1990).

Gynn, Ann. Supreme Court deals blow to student journalists. *Social Education* 53(3):175 (March 1989).

Hafen, Bruce C. School-backed student activities: what the courts say. *Education Digest* 54(1):29-31 (September 1988).

Hernandez, Debra Gersh. Censorship in the schools. *Editor and Publisher* 128(37):12-14 (September 16, 1995).

High Court backs censorship of high school newspapers. *Jet* 73(18):38 (February 1, 1988).

James, Bernard. Supreme Court docket: students' speech rights revisited. *Social Education* 52(4):243-245 (April/May 1988).

Jaschik, Scott. Supreme Court action seen as strengthening professors' First Amendment protections. *Chronicle of Higher Education* 37(15):A1, A21 (December 12, 1990).

Jones, Rebecca. Interpreting the law on the student press. *American School Board Journal* 181(9):33 (September 1994).

Kaplan, Joel. Hazelwood decision continues to haunt high school journalists. *Editor and Publisher* 127(19):48, 38 (May 7, 1994).

Lacayo, Richard, and Anne Constable. Is eight enough? *Time* 130(15):20 (October 12, 1987).

———. Stop the student presses: the Supreme Court says educators can censor school newspapers. *Time* 131(4):54 (January 25, 1988).

Levicoff, Steve. Upholding students' religious freedom. [Editorial] *Christian Century* 106(36):1108-1109 (November 29, 1989).

Marcy, William R. To protect or not to protect—that is the question. *Social Education* 54(6):364-365 (October 1990).

Marczely, Bernadette A. Student freedom of expression in the wake of Hazelwood and Bethel. *Clearing House* 65(5):269-271 (May/June 1992).

Mondak, Jeffery J. Policy legitimacy and the Supreme Court: the sources and contexts of legitimation. *Political Research Quarterly* 47(3):675-692 (September 1994).

Patten, Jim. High school confidential. *Columbia Journalism Review* 29(3):8-10 (September/October 1990).

Regan, Richard J. Supreme Court roundup: 1987 term. *Thought* 64(253):176-187 (June 1989).

Repa, Barbara Kate. Supreme Court docket: schools now have a broad right to censor student wrongs. *Social Education* 52(4):245 (April/May 1988).

Rose, Lowell C. 'Reasonableness'—the High Court's new standard for cases involving student rights. *Phi Delta Kappan* 69(8):589-592 (April 1988).

Salomone, Rosemary C. The impact of Hazelwood v. Kuhlmeier on local policy and practice. *NASSP Bulletin* 78(566):47-61 (December 1994).

Seligmann, Jean, and Tessa Namuth. A limit on the student press. *Newsweek* 111(4):60 (January 25, 1988).

Sendor, Benjamin. A court affirms the rights of the student press. *American School Board Journal* 173(12):11 (December 1986).

———. Don't stop the presses! *American School Board Journal* 182(3):20 (March 1995).

———. Managing the student press: consider carefully before you unsheath the censor's scissors. *American School Board Journal* 175(4):24-25 (April 1988).

Student newspapers: Teachers' delight. *Economist* 306(7534):20-21 (January 23-29, 1988).

Uhlig, Mark A. From Hazelwood to the High Court. *New York Times Magazine* (section 6, part 1):100-107 (September 13, 1987).

Visser, Steve. Students and free speech: a civics lesson at Hazelwood East. *Nation* 245(13):441-442 (October 24, 1987).

Whitford, Ellen. Decide two cases that affect teens. *Scholastic Update* 120(15):21-22 (April 8, 1988).

Whitson, James Anthony. Supreme Court docket: "special characteristics" and realities of schooling. *Social Education* 52(4):245-246 (April/May 1988).

Why Johnny can't speak. [Editorial] *Nation* 246(4):109 (January 30, 1988).

Wolper, Allan. California students protected from censorship. *Editor and Publisher* 121(6):17, 51 (February 6, 1988).

Zirkel, Perry A. De jure: narrowing the spectrum of student expression. *Phi Delta Kappan* 69(8):608-610 (April 1988).

3220. Westfall v. Erwin
484 US 292
Almanac (1988):119

98 LEd2d 619

January 13, 1988
108 SCt 580

3221. Honing v. Doe
484 US 305
Almanac (1988):128-129

98 LEd2d 686

January 20, 1988
108 SCt 592

Sendor, Benjamin. You can't act unilaterally in disciplining the disabled. *American School Board Journal* 175(5):24-25 (May 1988).

Zirkel, Perry A. Disciplining handicapped students: Jack and John went up the hill. *Phi Delta Kappan* 69(10):771-772 (June 1988).

3222. United Savings Association of Texas v. Timbers of Inwood Forest Associates, Ltd. January 20, 1988
484 US 365   98 LEd2d 740   108 SCt 636
Powlen, David M., and Arnold H. Wuhrman. Good news, bad news for creditors. *ABA Banking Journal* 80(6): 42, 45 (June 1988).
Weintraub, Benjamin. No compensation for delay: part I. *Business Credit* 90(7):60 (July/August 1988).
———. No compensation for delay. *Business Credit* 90(9):60-61 (October 1988).

3223. Taylor v. Illinois   January 25, 1988
484 US 400   98 LEd2d 798   108 SCt 646
Stocker, John. Supreme Court review: Sixth Amendment—preclusion of defense witnesses and the Sixth Amendment's compulsory process clause right to present a defense. *Journal of Criminal Law and Criminology* 79(3):835-865 (Fall 1988).

3224. Phillips Petroleum Co. v. Mississippi   February 23, 1988
484 US 469   98 LEd2d 877   108 SCt 791
Suits disallowed on pensions. *ENR* 220(9):13-14 (March 3, 1988).

3225. Laborers Health & Welfare Trust Fund for Northern California v. Advanced Lightweight   February 23, 1988
Concrete Co.
484 US 539   98 LEd2d 936   108 SCt 830
Moskowitz, Daniel B. Industry issues to fill High Court's calendar. *ENR* 219(14):10-11 (October 1, 1987).
Ruben, George. Developments in industrial relations: Supreme Court rules on multiemployer benefit plans. *Monthly Labor Review* 111(6):62 (June 1988).
Suits disallowed on pensions. *ENR* 220(9):13-14 (March 3, 1988).

3226. United States v. Owens   February 23, 1988
484 US 554   98 LEd2d 951   108 SCt 838
Sup Ct Review (1995):277-321
Seltz, Claire L. Supreme Court review: Sixth Amendment—the confrontation clause, witness memory loss and hearsay exceptions: what are the defendant's constitutional and evidentiary guarantees—procedure or substance? *Journal of Criminal Law and Criminology* 79(3):866-898 (Fall 1988).

3227. Pennell v. City of San Jose   February 24, 1988
485 US 1   99 LEd2d 1   108 SCt 849
New Right (Schwartz) 130-136+
Donlan, Thomas G. First Monday in October: justices face some key business cases. *Barron's* 67(40):51-52 (October 5, 1987).
Dwyer, Paula, and Catherine Yang. Deadlock at the Court: weighty decisions may have to wait until Bork—or someone—is seated. *Business Week* (Industrial/Technology Edition) (3020):36-37 (October 12, 1987).
Hoff, Jeffrey. Landlords disappointed by High Court's ruling on rent control. *Barron's* 68(9):63 (February 29, 1988).

3228. Hustler Magazine, Inc. and Larry C. Flynt v. Jerry Falwell   February 24, 1988
485 US 46   99 LEd2d 41   108 SCt 876
Brennan 179-184
Const Law 261-265R
Editorials (1988):172-181
Jerry 291-303R, 314-321R
Landmark (v. 2):145-154R
Make 219-233
Sup Ct Review (1994):57-128, 169-208
Turning 152-163
The Court denies a 'distress' call. *Newsweek* 111(10):8 (March 7, 1988).
Fields, Howard. Author and publisher groups make filings in two Supreme Court cases. *Publishers' Weekly* 232(10):12 (September 4, 1987).

———. Court rebuffs Falwell, affirms right to spoof public figure. *Publishers' Weekly* 233(10):18-19 (March 11, 1988).

———. High Court queries leave outcome of 'Hustler'-Falwell case uncertain. *Publishers' Weekly* 232(25):15 (December 18, 1987).

———. Supreme Court upholds public figure libel charge. *Publishers' Weekly* 236(2):12 (July 14, 1989).

First Amendment watch: 'emotional distress' briefs to High Court. *Publishers' Weekly* 232(3):13 (July 17, 1987).

Garneau, George. First Amendment victory. *Editor and Publisher* 121(9):9, 45 (February 27, 1988).

———. 1987 legal review—press won some, lost some. *Editor and Publisher* 121(1):24, 58-59 (January 2, 1988).

Hale, F. Dennis. Free expression: the first five years of the Rehnquist Court. *Journalism Quarterly* 69(1):89-104 (Spring 1992).

Hovland, Roxanne, and Ronald E. Taylor. Advertising and commercial speech since the 1986 Posadas case. *Journalism Quarterly* 67(4):1083-1089 (Winter 1990).

Lacayo, Richard, and Anne Constable. Taking the peril out of parody: in Falwell v. Flynt, the First Amendment won. *Time* 131(10):49 (March 7, 1988).

Lawton, Kim A. Which way will the new justice vote? *Christianity Today* 32(7):37-38 (April 22, 1988).

Lewis, Anthony. Staving off the silencers. *New York Times Magazine* (section 6, part 1):72-77 (December 1, 1991).

Over the line. *America* 158(12):316-317 (March 26, 1988).

Press, Aric, and Ann McDaniel. Jerry Falwell vs. Larry Flynt. *Newsweek* 110(24):76 (December 14, 1987).

The Rehnquist Court smiles on satire. *U.S. News and World Report* 104(9):11-12 (March 7, 1988).

Schwartz, Lynne Sharon. Falwell's mother. [Editorial] *Nation* 246(1):5, 20 (January 9, 1988).

Smolla, Rodney A. Academic freedom, hate speech, and the idea of a university. *Law and Contemporary Problems* 53(3):195-225 (Summer 1990).

———. Free speech afire with controversy: the Supreme Court. *Trial* 25(12):46-47, 49, 51 (December 1989).

Sneed, Don. Shop talk at thirty: the Falwell case—a quirky type of lawsuit. [Editorial] *Editor and Publisher* 121(3):52 (January 16, 1988).

3229. City of St. Louis v. Praprotnik   March 2, 1988
485 US 112   84 LEd2d 107   108 SCt 915
Wise, Charles, and Rosemary O'Leary. Is federalism dead or alive in the Supreme Court?: implications for public administrators. *Public Administration Review* 52(6):559-572 (November/December 1992).

3230. K Mart Corp. v. Cartier, Inc.   March 7, 1988
        Coupled with 47th Street Photo, Inc. v. Coalition to Preserve the Integrity of American Trademarks
        Coupled with United States v. Coalition to Preserve the Integrity of American Trademarks
485 US 176   99 LEd2d 151   108 SCt 950
Almanac (1988):129-130

Dwyer, Paula, and Amy Dunkin. A red-letter day for gray marketeers. *Business Week* (Industrial/Technology Edition) (3056):30 (June 13, 1988).

Engardio, Pete, Antonio Fins, Bettina Baudoin, and Lawrence J. Tell. There's nothing black-and-white about the gray market. *Business Week* (Industrial/Technology Edition) (3078):172-180 (November 7, 1988).

The 'gray market' gets a green light. *U.S. News and World Report* 104(23):8 (June 13, 1988).

LaRussa, Robert. High Court hears "gray market" case. *Electronic News* 33(1677):42 (October 19, 1987).

McCausland, Richard. Gray market ruling: semicon markers reaction mixed. *Electronic News* 34(1709):1, 30 (June 6, 1988).

3231. Norwest Bank of Worthington v. Ahlers   March 7, 1988
485 US 197   99 LEd2d 169   108 SCt 963
Powlen, David M., and Arnold H. Wuhrman. Good news, bad news for creditors. *ABA Banking Journal* 80(6): 42, 45 (June 1988).

3232. Arkansas Best Corp. v. Commissioner   March 7, 1988
485 US 212   99 LEd2d 183   108 SCt 971

Boyles, Jesse V. The Supreme Court kills the Corn Products Doctrine—but will it rest in peace? *Taxes* 66(10):723-735 (October 1988).

Breed, Richard P., III, and Andrew M. Curtis. The Arkansas Best decision: the Supreme Court knocks the starch out of Corn Products. *Practical Accountant* 21(6):96-100 (June 1988).

Briggs, Virginia L., and H. Ward Classen. Corn Products and its progeny: where do we go from here? *Taxes* 66(1):74-88 (January 1988).

Herrmann, Gary A., and Steven C. Malvey. New rules for business hedges resolve many uncertainties of Arkansas Best. *Journal of Taxation* 80(3):132-138 (March 1994).

Maydew, Gary L. Capital assets—the Arkansas Best and Circle K cases. *CPA Journal* 61(11):56-61 (November 1991).

Millman, Gregory J. The tale of Arkansas Best; when markets move faster than laws. [Editorial] *Barron's* 72(45):10 (November 9, 1992).

Swift, Kenton D. New tax court decision gives a boost to ordinary loss treatment for hedging transactions. *Taxes* 71(10):636-640 (October 1993).

Tatz, Reuben. Foreign currency hedges after Arkansas Best decision. *CPA Journal* 58(11):131-132 (November 1988).

Yang, Wesley. Impact of Arkansas Best on some types of investments remains uncertain. *Journal of Taxation* 70(2):106-109 (February 1989).

3233. Basic, Inc. v. Levinson   March 7, 1988
       485 US 224   99 LEd2d 194   108 SCt 978

Court rules on merger talks. *Business Insurance* 22(11):2, 37 (March 14, 1988).

Dwyer, Paula, and Catherine Yang. Deadlock at the Court: weighty decisions may have to wait until Bork—or someone—is seated. *Business Week* (Industrial/Technology Edition) (3020):36-37 (October 12, 1987).

Hofmann, Mark A. Mergers pose risk for company officers. *Business Insurance* 22(41):10-11 (October 10, 1988).

———. Ruling won't affect D&O market: experts. *Business Insurance* 22(20)19-20 (May 16, 1988).

Moskowitz, Daniel B. Supreme Court rulings that affect the CPI. *Chemical Week* 143(1):12-13 (July 6, 1988).

Norris, Floyd. A basic truth: Supreme Court rules companies shouldn't lie. *Barron's* 68(11):16-17, 20 (March 14, 1988).

———. Is it okay to lie? That's the basic issue the Supreme Court must decide. *Barron's* 67(32):13-14, 37-38 (August 10, 1987).

Supreme Court rules companies cannot deny merger talks. *Journal of Accountancy* 165(5):14 (May 1988).

3234. Schneidewind v. ANR Pipeline Co.   March 22, 1988
       485 US 293   99 LEd2d 316   108 SCt 1145

Adams, Nancy D. Title VI of the 1990 Clean Air Act Amendments and state and local initiatives to reverse the stratospheric ozone crisis: an analysis of preemption. *Boston College Environmental Affairs Law Review* 19(1):173-216 (Fall 1991).

Wise, Charles, and Rosemary O'Leary. Is federalism dead or alive in the Supreme Court?: implications for public administrators. *Public Administration Review* 52(6):559-572 (November/December 1992).

3235. Boos v. Barry   March 22, 1988
       485 US 312   99 LEd2d 333   108 SCt 1157
       Brennan 185-188
       Turning 163-164

Boedecker, Karl A., and Fred W. Morgan. The evolution of First Amendment protection for commercial speech. *Journal of Marketing* 59(1):38-47 (January 1995).

Brennan, William. The United States Supreme Court: decision. *Congressional Digest* 68(8-9):196, 198, 200 (August/September 1989).

3236. Commissioner v. Bollinger   March 22, 1988
       485 US 340   99 LEd2d 357   108 SCt 1173

Moskowitz, Daniel B. Industry issues to fill High Court's calendar. *ENR* 219(14):10-11 (October 1, 1987).

Nominee corporation issue to get Supreme Court attention. *Journal of Taxation* 67(5):310 (November 1987).

Seto, Theodore P., and Susan D. Glimcher. When will a related corporate nominee be a partnership's agent? *Journal of Taxation* 68(6):380-385 (June 1988).

Turner, Mark A. Agent vs. nominee: a suspended decision for dummy corporations. *Taxes* 67(4):263-268 (April 1989).

3237. United States v. Wells Fargo Bank   March 23, 1988
        485 US 351   99 LEd2d 368   108 SCt 1179
        Saunders, Laura. Constitutional wrongs. *Forbes* 140(6):154 (September 21, 1987).

3238. Lyng v. International Union, Automobile, Aerospace and Agricultural Implement   March 23, 1988
            Workers of America, UAW
        485 US 360   99 LEd2d 380   108 SCt 1184
            Almanac (1988):131
        Bid protest case taken up. *ENR* 220(13):22 (March 31, 1988).

3239. Lyng v. Northwest Indian Cemetery Protective Association   April 19, 1988
        485 US 439   99 LEd2d 534   108 SCt 1319
            Godless 42
            Sup Ct Review (1995):323-391
        Boggs, James P. NEPA in the domain of federal Indian policy: social knowledge and the negotiation of meaning. *Boston College Environmental Affairs Law Review* 19(1):31-72 (Fall 1991).
        Regan, Richard J. Supreme Court roundup: 1987 term. *Thought* 64(253):176-187 (June 1989).
        Rievman, Joshua D. Judicial scrutiny of Native American free exercise rights: Lyng and the decline of the Yoder doctrine. *Boston College Environmental Affairs Law Review* 17(1):169-199 (Fall 1989).

3240. South Carolina v. Baker   April 20, 1988
        485 US 505   99 LEd2d 592   108 SCt 1355
            Almanac (1988):133
            Guide (CQ) 118
        Collins, Stephen H. Supreme Court says Congress can tax municipal bonds. *Journal of Accountancy* 166(1):102-103 (July 1988).
        Crane, Stacey. Treasurers urge remedy: public works financing endangered. *Journal of State Government* 62(1):34-35 (January/February 1989).
        Gleckman, Howard, and David Zigas. It's open season on tax-exempt bonds. *Business Week* (Industrial/Technology Edition) (3050):38-40 (May 2, 1988).
        Greenwald, Judy. No bust for municipal bond insurance. *Business Insurance* 22(19):27 (May 9, 1988).
        Gunyon, John. Public finance: Supreme Court ruling threatens future status of tax exempt bonds. *National Civic Review* 77(4):381 (July/August 1988).
        ———. Public finance: tax immunity constitutional amendment. *National Civic Review* 77(5):485 (September/October 1988).
        Handbilling rights upheld. *ENR* 220(17):16-19 (April 28, 1988).
        Hawkins, Robert B., Jr. An ode to the 10th Amendment (may federalism rest in peace). [Editorial] *Governing* 1(10):74 (July 1988).
        ———. Linking constitutional reform to local self-governance. *Journal of State Government* 62(1):31-33 (January/February 1989).
        Henry, Douglas, Jr. Liberty and sophistication. *Journal of State Government* 62(1):28-30 (January/February 1989).
        Hickok, Eugene W., Jr. Federalism's future before the U.S. Supreme Court. *Annals of the American Academy of Political and Social Science* 509:73-82 (May 1990).
        Kincaid, John. A proposal to strengthen federalism. *Journal of State Government* 62(1):36-45 (January/February 1989).
        Kreger, Donald J. Municipal bond decision is no suprise. *American City and County* 103(6):16 (June 1988).
        Smith, Ray F. Judicial decision affects local finances. *American City and County* 103(10):10 (October 1988).
        State taxes: High Court rules Ginnie Maes not exempt from state taxation. *Journal of Accountancy* 164(2):35-36 (August 1987).

Sununu, John. The spirit of federalism: restoring the balance. *Journal of State Government* 62(1):25-27 (January/February 1989).

Wise, Charles, and Rosemary O'Leary. Is federalism dead or alive in the Supreme Court?: implications for public administrators. *Public Administration Review* 52(6):559-572 (November/December 1992).

3241. Traynor v. Turnage   April 20, 1988
485 US 535   99 LEd2d 618   108 SCt 1372
   Almanac (1988):132

Alcoholics lose some VA benefits. *Science News* 133(18):284 (April 30, 1988).

Drink and disability. *Time* 131(18):64 (May 2, 1988).

Fields, Cheryl M. High Court to weigh denials of visas to college guests, union's use of mail. *Chronicle of Higher Education* 34(6):A26 (October 7, 1987).

Holden, Constance. Is alcoholism a disease? The Supreme Court is reviewing a case challenging the VA's concept of alcoholism as willful misconduct. *Science* 238(4834):1647 (December 18, 1987).

————. Supreme Court denies plea of alcoholic vets. *Science* 240(4852):597 (April 29, 1988).

Kirn, Timothy F. Supreme Court case, federal 'initiative' put focus on alcoholism. *JAMA: The Journal of the American Medical Association* 258(23):3357 (December 18, 1987).

Lord, Lewis J., Erica E. Goode, Ted Gest, Kathleen McAuliffe, Lisa Moore, Robert F. Black, and Nancy Linnon. Coming to grips with alcoholism. *U.S. News and World Report* 103(22):56-63 (November 30, 1987).

Marwick, Charles. Court ruling expected soon in alcoholism case. *JAMA: The Journal of the American Medical Association* 259(10): 1436-1441 (March 11, 1988).

Seessel, Thomas V. Beyond the Supreme Court ruling on alcoholism as willful misconduct: it is up to Congress to act. [Editorial] *JAMA: The Journal of the American Medical Association* 260(2): 248 (July 8, 1988).

VA can deny educational benefits to veterans who were alcoholics, Supreme Court rules. *Chronicle of Higher Education* 34(33):A25, A30 (April 27, 1988).

3242. Edward J. DeBartolo Corp. v. Florida Gulf Coast Building and Construction Trades Council   April 20, 1988
485 US 568   99 LEd2d 645   108 SCt 1392
   Sup Ct Review (1995):71-98

Bernstein, Aaron, and Paul Angiolillo. The secondary boycott gets a second wind. *Business Week* (Industrial/Technology Edition) (3058):82 (June 27, 1988).

Handbilling rights upheld. *ENR* 220(17):16-19 (April 28, 1988).

Moskowitz, Daniel B. Industry issues to fill High Court's calendar. *ENR* 219(14):10-11 (October 1, 1987).

3243. Regents of the University of California v. Public Employment Relations Board   April 20, 1988
485 US 589   99 LEd2d 664   108 SCt 1404

Fields, Cheryl M. High Court to weigh denials of visas to college guests, union's use of mail. *Chronicle of Higher Education* 34(6):A26 (October 7, 1987).

In brief: the Supreme Court: Cal. union's right to use mail to be reviewed. *Chronicle of Higher Education* 33(42):19 (July 1, 1987).

Union plea to use university mail rejected. *Chronicle of Higher Education* 34(33):A30 (April 27, 1988).

Zirkel, Perry A. De jure: mail bias? *Phi Delta Kappan* 74(9):734-735 (May 1993).

3244. United States v. Providence Journal Co.   May 2, 1988
485 US 693   99 LEd2d 785   108 SCt 1502

Garneau, George. Attempt to reinstate contempt charges KO'd by Supreme Court. *Editor and Publisher* 121(19):13 (May 7, 1988).

————. High Court upholds *Washington Post* in libel case. *Editor and Publisher* 120(41):28 (October 10, 1987).

————. 1987 legal review—press won some, lost some. *Editor and Publisher* 121(1):24, 58-59 (January 2, 1988).

3245. Business Electronics Corp. v. Sharp Electronics Corp.   May 2, 1988
485 US 717   99 LEd2d 808   108 SCt 1515
   Almanac (1988):131-132; (1989):286; (1990):539-540; (1991):291-292

Bork, Robert H. Keep antitrust pro-consumer. *Fortune* 118(1):143-144 (July 4, 1988).

Dwyer, Paula. A red flag for red tags. *Business Week* (Industrial/Technology Edition) (3052):38 (May 16, 1988).

Dwyer, Paula, and Amy Dunkin. A red-letter day for gray marketeers. *Business Week* (Industrial/Technology Edition) (3056):30 (June 13, 1988).

Dwyer, Paula, and Catherine Yang. Deadlock at the Court: weighty decisions may have to wait until Bork—or someone—is seated. *Business Week* (Industrial/Technology Edition) (3020):36-37(October 12, 1987).

Taylor, Hal. Urge law to protect discounter. *Electronic News* 34(1706):34 (May 16, 1988).

3246. Kungys v. United States   May 2, 1988
485 US 759   99 LEd2d 839   108 SCt 1537
Beiner, Theresa M. Due process for all? Due process, the Eighth Amendment and Nazi war criminals. *Journal of Criminal Law and Criminology* 80(1):293-337 (Spring 1989).

3247. California v. Greenwood   May 16, 1988
486 US 35   100 LEd2d 30   108 SCt 1625
Const Law 280-281R+

Dripps, Donald A. Supreme Court review: Justice White and the rights of the accused. *Trial* 29(5):71-74 (May 1993).

Kincaid, John, and Robert F. Williams. The new judicial federalism: the states' lead in rights protection. *Journal of State Government* 65(2):50-52 (April/June 1992).

The last rights for garbage. *U.S. News and World Report* 104(21):9 (May 30, 1988).

Line, Julie A. Supreme Court review: Fourth Amendment—further erosion of the warrant requirement for unreasonable searches and seizures: the warrantless trash search exception. *Journal of Criminal Law and Criminology* 79(3):623-646 (Fall 1988).

Mondak, Jeffery J. Policy legitimacy and the Supreme Court: the sources and contexts of legitimation. *Political Research Quarterly* 47(3):675-692 (September 1994).

Regan, Richard J. Supreme Court roundup: 1987 term. *Thought* 64(253):176-187 (June 1989).

The rights of trash. *Newsweek* 111(22):58 (May 30, 1988).

Sanders, Alain L., Anne Constable, and James Willwerth. Lifting the lid on garbage: the High Court gives police broad power to search trash. *Time* 131(22):54 (May 30, 1988).

Seligman, Daniel. Secrets of trash. *Fortune* 117(13):119 (June 20, 1988).

Uviller, H. Richard. Fourth Amendment: does it protect your garbage? *Nation* 247(9):302-304 (October 10, 1988).

3248. City of New York v. Federal Communications Commission (FCC)   May 16, 1988
486 US 57   100 LEd2d 48   108 SCt 1637
Wise, Charles, and Rosemary O'Leary. Is federalism dead or alive in the Supreme Court?: implications for public administrators. *Public Administration Review* 52(6):559-572 (November/December 1992).

3249. Bankers Life & Casualty Co. v. Crenshaw   May 16, 1988
486 US 71   100 LEd2d 62   108 SCt 1645
Barger, Richard D., and Royal F. Oakes. Judicial reform on hold; Supreme Court changes stance on restrictions for punitive awards. *Business Insurance* 26(9):19-20 (March 2, 1992).

Dwyer, Paula, and Catherine Yang. Deadlock at the Court: weighty decisions may have to wait until Bork—or someone—is seated. *Business Week* (Industrial/Technology Edition) (3020):36-37 (October 12, 1987).

Fanning, Deirdre. Damage control. *Forbes* 139(14):84 (June 29, 1987).

3250. Patrick v. Burget   May 16, 1988
486 US 94   100 LEd2d 83   108 SCt 1658
Policing doctors. *Time* 131(22):54 (May 30, 1988).

3251. Wheat v. United States   May 23, 1988
486 US 153   100 LEd2d 140   108 SCt 1692

Hardy, Melinda. Supreme Court review: Sixth Amendment—applicability of right to counsel of choice to forfeiture of attorney's fees. *Journal of Criminal Law and Criminology* 80(4):1154-1189 (Winter 1990).

Klein, Randall L. Supreme Court review: Sixth Amendment—paternalistic override of waiver of right to conflict-free counsel at expense of right to counsel of one's choice. *Journal of Criminal Law and Criminology* 79(3):735-758 (Fall 1988).

3252. Satterwhite v. Texas   May 31, 1988
486 US 249   100 LEd2d 284   108 SCt 1792
Sup Ct Review (1989):195-211

3253. New Energy Co. of Indiana v. Limbach   May 31, 1988
486 US 269   100 LEd2d 302   108 SCt 1803
Sup Ct Review (1991):143-177

3254. Monessen Southwestern Railway Co. v. Morgan   June 6, 1988
486 US 330   100 LEd2d 349   108 SCt 1837
Sup Ct Review (1994):429-540

3255. Mills v. Maryland   June 6, 1988
486 US 367   100 LEd2d 384   108 SCt 1860
Death Penalty (Tushnet) 65-66

3256. Lingle v. Norge Division of Magic Chef, Inc.   June 6, 1988
486 US 399   100 LEd2d 410   108 SCt 1877
Moskowitz, Daniel B., and Hazel Bradford. Landmark decision in worker firing. *ENR* 220(24):19-20 (June 16, 1988).

Murphy, Betty Southard, Wayne E. Barlow, and D. Diane Hatch. Union employees may sue for wrongful discharge. *Personnel Journal* 67(9):20 (September 1988).

3257. Shapero v. Kentucky Bar Association   June 13, 1988
486 US 466   100 LEd2d 475   108 SCt 1916
Boedecker, Karl A., and Fred W. Morgan. The evolution of First Amendment protection for commercial speech. *Journal of Marketing* 59(1):38-47 (January 1995).

Bowen, Lauren. Attorney advertising in the wake of Bates v. State Bar of Arizona (1977): a study of judicial impact. *American Politics Quarterly* 23(4):461-484 (October 1995).

Hovland, Roxanne, and Ronald E. Taylor. Advertising and commercial speech since the 1986 Posadas case. *Journalism Quarterly* 67(4):1083-1089 (Winter 1990).

Mapother, William R. Supreme Court rules on lawyer advertising. *Business Credit* 91(3):50-51 (March 1989).

Meyers, Janet. Direct-mail win: Court ruling good sign for ad industry. *Advertising Age* 59(26):99 (June 20, 1988).

3258. Berkovitz v. United States   June 13, 1988
486 US 531   100 LEd2d 531   108 SCt 1958
Gest, Ted. Where have all the conservatives gone? *U.S. News and World Report* 105(2):15-16 (July 11, 1988).

Lewis, Jan. The exchange report: discretionary function exception: an update after Berkovitz. *Trial* 26(4):93-97 (April 1990).

Marshall opinion holds U.S. liable for product safety. *Jet* 74(14):24 (July 4, 1988).

Weiss, Rick. Polio policy: a bitter pill to swallow. *Science News* 134(3):43 (July 16, 1988).

3259. Johnson v. Mississippi   June 13, 1988
486 US 578   100 LEd2d 575   108 SCt 1981
Jacoby, Tamar. Caught between two states. *Newsweek* 111(18):67 (May 2, 1988).

3260. Webster v. Doe   June 15, 1988
486 US 592   100 LEd2d 632   108 SCt 2047

Gest, Ted. Where have all the conservatives gone? *U.S. News and World Report* 105(2):15-16 (July 11, 1988).

3261. Pinter v. Dahl   June 15, 1988
      486 US 622   100 LEd2d 658   108 SCt 2063
         Sup Ct Review (1995):99-124
      Quinlivan, Stephen M. What every accountant should know about securities law. *Journal of Accountancy*
         174(1):109-112 (July 1992).

3262. Arizonia v. Roberson   June 15, 1988
      486 US 675   100 LEd2d 704   108 SCt 2093
      Bitterman, Patrick J. Supreme Court review: Fifth Amendment—the applicability of the assertion of the right to
         counsel to unrelated investigations. *Journal of Criminal Law and Criminology* 79(3):676-700 (Fall 1988).
      Gest, Ted. Where have all the conservatives gone? *U.S. News and World Report* 105(2):15-16 (July 11, 1988).

3263. Volkswagenwerk Aktiengesellschaft v. Schlunk   June 15, 1988
      486 US 694   100 LEd2d 722   108 SCt 2104
      Boeschoten, Cornelis D. van. Hague Conference conventions and the United States: a European view. *Law and
         Contemporary Problems* 57(3):47-58 (Summer 1994).

3264. Sun Oil Co. v. Wortman   June 15, 1988
      486 US 717   100 LEd2d 743   108 SCt 2117
         Sup Ct Review (1994):295-343

3265. City of Lakewood v. Plain Dealer Publication Co.   June 17, 1988
      486 US 750   100 LEd2d 771   108 SCt 2138
      Garneau, George. 1987 legal review—press won some, lost some. *Editor and Publisher* 121(1):24, 58-59
         (January 2, 1988).
      ———. Rack ruling favorable to newspapers. *Editor and Publisher* 121(26):11 (June 25, 1988).
      Hale, F. Dennis. How retiring Supreme Court Justice White voted in First Amendment cases. *Editor and
         Publisher* 126(30):44, 36 (July 24, 1993).

3266. Immigration and Naturalization Service (INS) v. Pangilinan   June 17, 1988
         Coupled with Immigration and Naturalization Service (INS) v. Manzano
      486 US 875   100 LEd2d 882   108 SCt 2210
         Almanac (1989):283

3267. New York State Club Association v. New York   June 20, 1988
      487 US 1   101 Led2d 1   108 SCt 2225
      The clubhouse doors open for women. *Economist* 307(7556):29 (June 25-July 1, 1988).
      FitzGerald, Nora, and Peter M. Jones. Five key cases to watch for. *Scholastic Update* 120(15):22 (April 8,
         1988).
      Jacoby, Tamar. Blackballing the men's club. *Newsweek* 112(1):62 (July 4, 1988).
      Lacayo, Richard, Mary Cronin, and Steven Holmes. Storming the last male bastion: the Supreme Court ushers
         women into the private club. *Time* 132(1):43 (July 4, 1988).
      Robbins, Carla Anne, Ted Gest, Kenneth T. Walsh, William J. Cook, Joseph Carey, Gillian Sandford, and
         Louise Lief. The handwriting on the clubhouse wall. *U.S. News and World Report* 105(1):11 (July 4, 1988).

3268. United States Catholic Conference v. Abortion Rights Mobilization, Inc. (ARM)   June 20, 1988
      487 US 72   101 LEd2d 69   108 SCt 2268
      Jacoby, Tamar, and Tessa Namuth. New fronts in an old war. *Newsweek* 111(14):64 (April 4, 1988).
      Lawton, Kim A. A clean sweep for religious groups. *Christianity Today* 32(11):54 (August 12, 1988).
      ———. Which way will the new justice vote? *Christianity Today* 32(7):37-38 (April 22, 1988).
      Legal attack by bishops. *Christian Century* 104(29):881-882 (October 14, 1987).
      Regan, Richard J. Supreme Court roundup: 1987 term. *Thought* 64(253):176-187 (June 1989).
      Tax-exempt status upheld. *Christian Century* 107(17):521-522 (May 16-23, 1990).

3269. Ross v. Oklahoma   June 22, 1988
     487 US 81   101 LEd2d 80   108 SCt 2273
     Bonebrake, James G. Supreme Court review: Sixth and Fourteenth Amendments—the lost role of the peremptory challenge in securing an accused's right to an impartial jury. *Journal of Criminal Law and Criminology* 79(3):899-920 (Fall 1988).

3270. Braswell v. United States   June 22, 1988
     487 US 99   101 LEd2d 98   108 SCt 2284
     Causey, Denzil, and Frances McNair. Protecting taxpayers privacy from the IRS. *Journal of Accountancy* 168(4):44-48 (October 1989).
     Grogan, John M., Jr. Supreme Court review: Fifth Amendment—the act of production privilege: the Supreme Court's protrait of a dualistic record custodian. *Journal of Criminal Law and Criminology* 79(3):701-734 (Fall 1988).
     Moskowitz, Daniel B. Supreme Court rulings that affect the CPI. *Chemical Week* 143(1):12-13 (July 6, 1988).
     Rosenblatt, Leonard R. The Fifth Amendment and the production of business records: and Braswell Begat Bouknight. *Taxes* 68(6):418-424 (June 1990).
     ———. The production of business records after Braswell: where we've been, where we are, where we may be going. *Taxes* 67(4):231-237 (April 1989).

3271. Doe v. United States   June 22, 1988
     487 US 201   101 LEd2d 184   108 SCt 2341
     Abrams, Stuart E. Doe v. United States: has the veil of foreign bank secrecy been lifted? *Taxes* 67(4):238-242 (April 1989).
     Causey, Denzil, and Frances McNair. Protecting taxpayers privacy from the IRS. *Journal of Accountancy* 168(4):44-48 (October 1989).

3272. Bank of Nova Scotia v. United States   June 22, 1988
        Coupled with Kilpatrick v. United States
     487 US 250   101 LEd2d 228   108 SCt 2369
     Mitchells, Rebecca Ann. Supreme Court review: supervisory power meets the harmless error rule in Federal Grand Jury proceedings. *Journal of Criminal Law and Criminology* 79(3):1037-1063 (Fall 1988).

3273. Patterson v. Illinois   June 24, 1988
     487 US 285   101 LEd2d 261   108 SCt 2389
     Banas, John S. III. Supreme Court review: Sixth Amendment—waiver of the Sixth Amendment right to counsel at post-indictment interrogation. *Journal of Criminal Law and Criminology* 79(3):795-834 (Fall 1988).

3274. United States v. Taylor   June 24, 1988
     487 US 326   101 LEd2d 297   108 SCt 2413
     Isaacson, Suzanne. Supreme Court review: Speedy Trial Act of 1974—dismissal sanction for noncompliance with the act: defining the range of district courts' discretion to dismiss cases with prejudice. *Journal of Criminal Law and Criminology* 79(3):997-1036 (Fall 1988).

3275. Mississippi Power and Light Co. v. Mississippi   June 24, 1988
     487 US 354   101 LEd2d 322   108 SCt 2428
     Norris, James E. The shrinking of state rate-making power—lessons from Grand Gulf. *Public Utilities Fortnightly* 122(3):45-47 (August 4, 1988).
     Supreme Court bars state review of Grand Gulf costs. *Public Utilities Fortnightly* 122(3):47-48 (August 4, 1988).

3276. Schweiker v. Chilicky   June 24, 1988
     487 US 412   101 LEd2d 370   108 SCt 2460
     Rowe, Thomas D. No final victories: the incompleteness of equity's triumph in federal public law. *Law and Contemporary Problems* 56(3):105-121 (Summer 1993).

3277. Kadrmas v. Dickinson Public Schools   June 24, 1988
      487 US 450   101 LEd2d 399   108 SCt 2481
          Turning 194

3278. Frisby v. Schultz   June 27, 1988
      487 US 474   101 LEd2d 420   108 SCt 2495
          Brennan 185-188
      Gest, Ted. Where have all the conservatives gone? *U.S. News and World Report* 105(2):15-16 (July 11, 1988).
      Jacoby, Tamar, and Tessa Namuth. New fronts in an old war. *Newsweek* 111(14):64 (April 4, 1988).
      Lacayo, Richard, and Steven Holmes. "A slam-dunk decision": the Court proves again that it will not do a
          president's bidding. *Time* 132(3):16-17 (July 11, 1988).
      Regan, Richard J. Supreme Court roundup: 1987 term. *Thought* 64(253):176-187 (June 1989).

3279. Boyle v. United Technologies Corp.   June 27, 1988
      487 US 500   101 LEd2d 442   108 SCt 2510
          Turning 192-194
      Adler, Stacy. High Court expands federal contractors' liability protection. *Business Insurance* 22(27):1, 30
          (July 4, 1988).
      ———. Trial bar chips away at a defense bulwark. *Business Insurance* 25(31):19 (August 5, 1991).
      Agent Orange pact cleared by top court. *Chemical Marketing Reporter* 234:5, 26 (July 4, 1988).
      Dwyer, Paula, and Catherine Yang. Deadlock at the Court: weighty decisions may have to wait until Bork—or
          someone—is seated. *Business Week* (Industrial/Technology Edition) (3020):36-37 (October 12, 1987).
      FitzGerald, Nora, and Peter M. Jones. Five key cases to watch for. *Scholastic Update* 120(15):22 (April 8,
          1988).
      Justice for all. [Editorial] *Aviation Week and Space Technology* 129(1):7 (July 4, 1988).
      Larussa, Robert. Supreme Court decision eases pressure on DOD contractors. *Electronic News* 34(1713):19
          (July 4, 1988).
      Lewis, Jan. Government contractor defense: post-Boyle update. *Trial* 25(12):95-98 (December 1989).
      Mangan, Joseph F. Government contractors: their defense rests. *Best's Review* (Property/Casualty Insurance
          Edition) 91(2):82, 84 (June 1990).
      Mecham, Michael. High Court's reasoning in Sikorsky suit may provide unexpected benefits. *Aviation Week
          and Space Technology* 129(2):129-130 (July 11, 1988).
      ———. Supreme Court extends limits on suits by military personnel. *Aviation Week and Space Technology*
          126(21):26 (May 25, 1987).
      ———. Supreme Court weighs liability in military contractor suit. *Aviation Week and Space Technology*
          127(17):81-82 (October 26, 1987).
      Moskowitz, Daniel B. Industry issues to fill High Court's calendar. *ENR* 219(14):10-11 (October 1, 1987).
      Schwarz, Stephen G. The government contractor defense after Boyle: it can still be overcome. *Trial* 24(9):88-
          92 (September 1988).
      Supreme Court rules contractors immune from negligence lawsuits. *Aviation Week and Space Technology*
          129(1):21 (July 4, 1988).

3280. Murray v. United States   June 27, 1988
          Coupled with Carter v. United States
      487 US 533   101 LEd2d 472   108 SCt 2529
      Graveline, Bradley C. Supreme Court review: Fourth Amendment—an acceptable erosion of the exclusionary
          rule. *Journal of Criminal Law and Criminology* 79(3):647-675 (Fall 1988).
      Regan, Richard J. Supreme Court roundup: 1987 term. *Thought* 64(253):176-187 (June 1989).

3281. Otis R. Bowen, Secretary of Health and Human Services v. Chan Kendrick   June 29, 1988
          Coupled with Kendrick v. Bowen
          Coupled with United Families of America v. Kendrick
      487 US 589   101 LEd2d 520   108 SCt 2562
          Sup Ct Review (1995):323-391
      Advising teen-agers to say no. *America* 158(16):421 (April 23, 1988).

Carr, Baker V. Kennedy justice. *New Republic* 198(8):10+ (February 29, 1988).

Freid, Stephen H. The constitutionality of choice under the establishment clause. *Clearing House* 66(2):92-95 (November/December 1992).

Gest, Ted. Where have all the conservatives gone? *U.S. News and World Report* 105(2):15-16 (July 11, 1988).

Jacoby, Tamar. Limits on the presidency. *Newsweek* 112(2):30 (July 11, 1988).

Jacoby, Tamar, and Tessa Namuth. New fronts in an old war. *Newsweek* 111(14):64 (April 4, 1988).

Lacayo, Richard, and Steven Holmes. "A slam-dunk decision": the Court proves again that it will not do a president's bidding. *Time* 132(3):16-17 (July 11, 1988).

Lawton, Kim A. A clean sweep for religious groups. *Christianity Today* 32(11):54 (August 12, 1988).

———. Which way will the new justice vote? *Christianity Today* 32(7):37-38 (April 22, 1988).

McBride, James. A decision entangling church and state. [Editorial] *Christian Century* 105(25):756-758 (August 31-September 7, 1988).

Regan, Richard J. Supreme Court roundup: 1987 term. *Thought* 64(253):176-187 (June 1989).

Sex, not separation. *America* 159(2):27-28 (July 9-16, 1988).

Stephenson, D. Grier, Jr. Religion and the Constitution: the Supreme Court speaks, again. *USA Today* 118(2538):21-23 (March 1990).

The talk of the town: notes and comment. [Editorial] *New Yorker* 67(18):21-22 (June 24, 1991).

Whitford, Ellen. Decide two cases that affect teens. *Scholastic Update* 120(15):21-22 (April 8, 1988).

3282. Morrison v. Olson   June 29, 1988
487 US 654   101 LEd2d 569   108 SCt 2597

Almanac (1988):123-127; (1992):315-316
Editorials (1988):705-707
Guide (CQ) 56-57, 65
New Right (Schwartz) 213-217+
Sup Ct Review (1988):1-41; (1991):225-260
Turning 194-200, 435-436+

Daugherty, Donald A. Supreme Court review: the separation of powers and abuses in prosecutorial discretion. *Journal of Criminal Law and Criminology* 79(3):953-996 (Fall 1988).

FitzGerald, Nora, and Peter M. Jones. Five key cases to watch for. *Scholastic Update* 120(15):22 (April 8, 1988).

Gest, Ted. Where have all the conservatives gone? *U.S. News and World Report* 105(2):15-16 (July 11, 1988).

Jacoby, Tamar. Can a man be his own judge? *Newsweek* 111(17):57 (April 25, 1988).

———. Limits on the presidency. *Newsweek* 112(2):30 (July 11, 1988).

Kirwan, Kent A. The use and abuse of power: the Supreme Court and separation of powers. *Annals of the American Academy of Political and Social Science* 537:76-84 (January 1995).

Lacayo, Richard, and Steven Holmes. "A slam-dunk decision": the Court proves again that it will not do a president's bidding. *Time* 132(3):16-17 (July 11, 1988).

McDowell, Gary L. Congress and the courts. *Public Interest* (100):89-101 (Summer 1990).

Morley, Jefferson. Reagan v. Walsh. [Editorial] *Nation* 246(16):556-557 (April 23, 1988).

Regan, Richard J. Supreme Court roundup: 1987 term. *Thought* 64(253):176-187 (June 1989).

Rohr, John A., and Rosemary O'Leary. Public administration, executive power, and constitutional confusion; response to John Rohr. *Public Administration Review* 49(2):108-115 (March/April 1989).

3283. Communications Workers of America v. Beck   June 29, 1988
487 US 735   101 LEd2d 634   108 SCt 2641

Blum, Debra E. Little effect on faculty unions seen in Court ruling. *Chronicle of Higher Education* 34(44):A16 (July 13, 1988).

Buckley, William F., Jr. Will Bush rediscover Beck? *National Review* 44(9):63 (May 11, 1992).

Cimini, Michael H., and Susan L. Behrmann. Developments in industrial relations: presidential executive order. *Monthly Labor Review* 115(9):46 (September 1992).

Dwyer, Paula, and Catherine Yang. Deadlock at the Court: weighty decisions may have to wait until Bork—or someone—is seated. *Business Week* (Industrial/Technology Edition) (3020):36-37 (October 12, 1987).

Garneau, George. Dues ruling. *Editor and Publisher* 121(28):12-13 (July 9, 1988).

Kovach, Kenneth A., and Peter Millspaugh. Implementing the Beck and Lehnert union security agreement decisions: a study in frustration. *Business Horizons* 38(3):57-65 (May/June 1995).

Moskowitz, Daniel B. Industry issues to fill High Court's calendar. *ENR* 219(14):10-11 (October 1, 1987).

Reynolds, Larry. Review of security clauses may spell financial doom for unions. *Personnel* 68(8):19 (August 1991).

———. Right-to-work groups are suspicious of NLRB rule-making plans. *HR Focus* 69(7):1-2 (July 1992).

The right to choose. *National Review* 34(25):1594-1596 (December 24, 1982).

Seligman, Daniel. The latest threat to the unions. *Fortune* 123(13):136 (June 17, 1991).

———. Party time. *Fortune* 117(5):28, 32 (February 29, 1988).

3284. Riley v. National Federation of the Blind of North Carolina, Inc.   June 29, 1988
      487 US 781   101 LEd2d 669   108 SCt 2667

Bailey, Anne Lowrey. College fund-raising practices may be restricted by charities laws that many states are adopting. *Chronicle of Higher Education* 34(17):A29-A30 (January 6, 1988).

McMillen, Liz. Court overturns a law requiring disclosure of fund-raising costs. *Chronicle of Higher Education* 34(43):A18 (July 6, 1988).

Palmer, Stacy E. High Court deadlocks on denial of visas to aliens; lower-court ruling stands, limiting president. *Chronicle of Higher Education* 34(9):A25-A26 (October 28, 1987).

3285. Thompson v. Oklahoma   June 29, 1988
      487 US 815   101 LEd2d 702   108 SCt 2687
      Death Penalty (Tushnet) 77-78
      Sup Ct Review (1994):295-343
      Turning 204-205

Behuniak-Long, Susan. Justice Sandra Day O'Connor and the power of maternal legal thinking. *Review of Politics* 54(3):417-444 (Summer 1992).

Christopher, Maura. Decide seven Court cases that test teenagers' rights. *Scholastic Update* (Teachers' Edition) 120(1):16-18+ (September 4, 1987).

Fraust, Leslie. The ultimate price. *Scholastic Update* (Teachers' Edition) 123(14):13 (April 5, 1991).

Goi, Simona. The final verdict. *Scholastic Update* (Teachers' Edition) 123(2):11 (September 21, 1990).

Jacoby, Tamar. Limits on the presidency. *Newsweek* 112(2):30 (July 11, 1988).

Regan, Richard J. Supreme Court roundup: 1987 term. *Thought* 64(253):176-187 (June 1989).

Ricotta, Dominic J. Supreme Court review: Eighth Amendment—the death penalty for juveniles: a state's right or a child's injustice? *Journal of Criminal Law and Criminology* 79(3):921-952 (Fall 1988).

Still sweet 16. *Time* 132(3):16 (July 11, 1988).

Whitford, Ellen. How a family tragedy may lead to a landmark court ruling. *Scholastic Update* 120(15):10-12 (April 8, 1988).

———. When Thompson's case came before the court. *Scholastic Update* 120(15):12 (April 8, 1988).

3286. United States v. Kozminski   June 29, 1988
      487 US 931   101 LEd2d 788   108 SCt 2751
      Sup Ct Review (1994):345-428

3287. Clara Watson v. Fort Worth Bank and Trust   June 29, 1988
      487 US 977   101 LEd2d 827   108 SCt 2777
      Affirmative (Woods) 113-114
      Almanac (1989):316-317

Bersoff, Donald N. In the Supreme Court of the United States: Clara Watson v. Fort Worth Bank & Trust. *American Psychologist* 43(12):1019-1028 (December 1988).

———. Should subjective employment devices be scrutinized? It's elementary, my dear Ms. Watson. *American Psychologist* 43(12):1016-1018 (December 1988).

Dwyer, Paula, and Catherine Yang. Deadlock at the Court: weighty decisions may have to wait until Bork—or someone—is seated. *Business Week* (Industrial/Technology Edition) (3020):36-37 (October 12, 1987).

Jacoby, Tamar. Limits on the presidency. *Newsweek* 112(2):30 (July 11, 1988).

Jaschik, Scott. Supreme Court ruling may make it easier for faculty members to win bias lawsuits. *Chronicle of Higher Education* 34(43):A1, A12 (July 6, 1988).

Murphy, Betty Southard, Wayne E. Barlow, and D. Diane Hatch. Subjective employment practices under Title VII. *Personnel Journal* 67(9):20, 23 (September 1988).

Regan, Richard J. Supreme Court roundup: 1987 term. *Thought* 64(253):176-187 (June 1989).

Seligman, Daniel. The latest bad news about bias. *Fortune* 118(9):234 (October 24, 1988).

Sinai, Lauren. Subjectivity may trigger bias suits. *Business Insurance* 22(38):16, 18 (September 19, 1988).

Woman's bias suit to set job promotion precedent. *Jet* 73(21):16-17 (February 22, 1988).

3288. Coy v. Iowa   June 29, 1988
    487 US 1012   101 LEd2d 857   108 SCt 2798
    Turning 329-330

Dripps, Donald A. Supreme Court review: the confrontation clause and the sexual abuse of children. *Trial* 27(5):11-13 (May 1991).

Regan, Richard J. Supreme Court roundup: 1987 term. *Thought* 64(253):176-187 (June 1989).

Wollitzer, Rachel I. Supreme Court review: Sixth Amendment—defendant's right to confront witnesses: constitutionality of protective measures in child sexual assault cases. *Journal of Criminal Law and Criminology* 79(3):759-794 (Fall 1988).

3289. Town of Huntington, New York v. Huntington Branch, NACCP   November 7, 1988
    488 US 15   102 LEd2d 180   109 SCt 276

Cracking the walls of white enclaves. *U.S. News and World Report* 105(20):17-18 (November 21, 1988).

3290. Shell Oil Co. v. Iowa Department of Revenue   November 8, 1988
    488 US 19   102 LEd2d 186   109 SCt 278

Hellerstein, Walter, and James H. Peters. Recent Supreme Court decisions have far-reaching implications. *Journal of Taxation* 70(5):306-310 (May 1989).

Supreme Court approves state's unitary tax. *Oil and Gas Journal* 86(46):30 (November 14, 1988).

Witt, Elder. News briefs: Iowa wins tax fight with Shell. *Governing* 2(4):12 (January 1989).

———. State-federal power at issue in High Court. *Governing* 2(6):66-67 (March 1989).

3291. Lockhart v. Nelson   November 14, 1988
    488 US 33   102 LEd2d 265   109 SCt 285

Sikora, John J. Jr. Supreme Court review: Fifth Amendment—affording society's interest greater protection in double jeopardy analysis. *Journal of Criminal Law and Criminology* 80(4):1112-1127 (Winter 1990).

3292. Arizona v. Youngblood   November 29, 1988
    488 US 51   102 LEd2d 281   109 SCt 333

Bernstein, Sarah M. Supreme Court review: Fourteenth Amendment—police failure to preserve evidence and erosion of the due process right to a fair trial. *Journal of Criminal Law and Criminology* 80(4):1256-1280 (Winter 1990).

Schwartz, Herman. The Court next term: consolidating the new majority. *Nation* 249(11):380-383 (October 9, 1989).

3293. Pittston Coal Group v. Sebben   December 6, 1988
        Coupled with McLaughlin, Secretary of Labor v. Sebben
        Coupled with Director, Office of Workers' Compensation Programs v. Broyles
    488 US 105   102 LEd2d 408   109 SCt 414

Fanning, Deirdre. First Monday next October. *Forbes* 141(9):110[Annual Directory] (April 25, 1988).

Glaberson, William B. Determined to be heard: four Americans and their journeys to the Supreme Court. *New York Times Magazine* (section 6, part 1):32-40 (October 2, 1988).

3294. National Collegiate Athletic Association v. Tarkanian   December 12, 1988
    488 US 179   102 LEd2d 469   109 SCt 454

Lederman, Douglas.   Supreme Court agrees to review case of Nevada coach; will focus on role of the NCAA as a governmental body. *Chronicle of Higher Education* 34(25):A31-A32 (March 2, 1988).

———. Supreme Court rejects coach's plea, exempts NCAA from Constitution's due-process requirement. *Chronicle of Higher Education* 35(17):A35-A36 (January 4, 1989).

Text of High Court's majority and minority opinions in NCAA case. *Chronicle of Higher Education* 35(17):A35-A38R (January 4, 1989).

3295. Olden v. Kentucky   December 12, 1988
    488 US 227   102 LEd2d 513   109 SCt 480

Haddad, James B. The future of confrontation clause developments: what will emerge when the Supreme Court synthesizes the diverse lines of confrontation decisions? *Journal of Criminal Law and Criminology* 81(1):77-98 (Spring 1990).

3296. Goldberg v. Sweet, Director of Illinois Department of Revenue   January 10, 1989
                Coupled with GTE Sprint Communications Corp. v. Sweet
    488 US 252   102 LEd2d 607   109 SCt 582
    Sup Ct Review (1989):223-259

Hellerstein, Walter, and James H. Peters. Recent Supreme Court decisions have far-reaching implications. *Journal of Taxation* 70(5):306-310 (May 1989).

Lucas, Joyce Ann. To collect or not to collect; a look at sales and use taxes. *Business Credit* 93(8):10-11 (September 1991).

Wise, Charles, and Rosemary O'Leary. Is federalism dead or alive in the Supreme Court?: implications for public administrators. *Public Administration Review* 52(6):559-572 (November/December 1992).

Witt, Elder. High Court faces issues from A to Z. *Governing* 2(1):23 (October 1988).

———. The last Court term: a mixed bag. *Governing* 3(1):24 (October 1989).

———. State-federal power at issue in High Court. *Governing* 2(6):66-67 (March 1989).

Zemsky, Kenneth T., and Joan S. Faber. New frontiers in state taxation. *CPA Journal* 60(12):12-22 (December 1990).

3297. Duquesne Light Co. v. Barasch   January 11, 1989
    488 US 299   102 LEd2d 646   109 SCt 609

Court nixes nuke rates. *ENR* 222(3):15 (January 19, 1989).

Tye, William B., and A. Lawrence Kolbe. The Supreme Court's Duquesne opinion—practical implications for regulated industries. *Public Utilities Fortnightly* 126(5):19-22 (August 30, 1990).

Witt, Elder. High Court faces issues from A to Z. *Governing* 2(1):23 (October 1988).

———. The last Court term: a mixed bag. *Governing* 3(1):24 (October 1989).

———. State-federal power at issue in High Court. *Governing* 2(6):66-67 (March 1989).

3298. Allegheny Pittsburgh Coal Co. v. County Commissioner of Webster County, West Virginia   January 18, 1989
                Coupled with East Kentucky Energy Corp. v. County Commission of Webster County, West Virginia
    488 US 336   102 LEd2d 688   109 SCt 633
    Sup Ct Review (1989):223-259

Hellerstein, Walter, and James H. Peters. Recent Supreme Court decisions have far-reaching implications. *Journal of Taxation* 70(5):306-310 (May 1989).

High Court to review California Propostion 13. *Taxes* 69(7):437 (July 1991).

O'Connell, Daniel. U.S. Supreme Court reviews state and local taxation issues. *CPA Journal* 62(3):16-21 (March 1992).

Rusher, William A. Fair or foul? *National Review* 44(4):22-24 (March 2, 1992).

Wise, Charles, and Rosemary O'Leary. Is federalism dead or alive in the Supreme Court?: implications for public administrators. *Public Administration Review* 52(6):559-572 (November/December 1992).

Witt, Elder. High Court faces issues from A to Z. *Governing* 2(1):23 (October 1988).

———. The last Court term: a mixed bag. *Governing* 3(1):24 (October 1989).

3299. Sheet Metal Workers International Association v. Lynn   January 18, 1989
    488 US 347   102 LEd2d 700   109 SCt 639

Hukill, Craig. Significant decisions in labor cases: union affairs. *Monthly Labor Review* 112(11):76-77 (November 1989).

Ruben, George. Collective bargaining in 1989: old problems, new issues. *Monthly Labor Review* 113(1):19-29 (January 1990).

3300. Mistretta v. United States — January 18, 1989
488 US 361   102 LEd2d 714   109 SCt 647

    Almanac (1988):127-128; (1989):293
    Guide (CQ) 65

Crime: Procrustes as judge. *Economist* 308(7569):30 (Sepember 24-30, 1988).

Esayian, Lisa G. Supreme Court review: separation of powers—the federal sentencing commission: unconstitutional delegation and threat to judicial impartiality? *Journal of Criminal Law and Criminology* 80(4):944-967 (Winter 1990).

An eye for an eye in the courts. *U.S. News and World Report* 106(4):11-12 (January 30, 1989).

Farber, Daniel A. The winter thaw. *Trial* 25(4):101-105 (April 1989).

Jacoby, Tamar. An end to judicial roulette. *Newsweek* 113(5):76 (January 30, 1989).

Nagel, Ilene H. Supreme Court review: structuring sentencing discretion: the new federal sentencing guidelines. *Journal of Criminal Law and Criminology* 80(4):883-943 (Winter 1990).

Ostling, Richard N., Steven Holmes, and Andrea Sachs. Let punishment fit the crime: a controversial sentencing scheme gets a go-ahead. *Time* 133(5):63 (January 30, 1989).

3301. Argentina Republic v. Amerada Hess Shipping Corp. — January 23, 1989
488 US 428   102 LEd2d 818   109 SCt 683

    Sup Ct Review (1990):133-161

3302. Florida v. Riley — January 23, 1989
488 US 445   102 LEd2d 835   109 SCt 693

Dripps, Donald A. Supreme Court review: Justice White and the rights of the accused. *Trial* 29(5):71-74 (May 1993).

Eyes in the sky: low-level searches pass muster. *Time* 133(6):60 (February 6, 1989).

FitzGerald, Nora, and Peter M. Jones. Five key cases to watch for. *Scholastic Update* 120(15):22 (April 8, 1988).

Schwartz, Herman. The Court next term: consolidating the new majority. *Nation* 249(11):380-383 (October 9, 1989).

3303. City of Richmond v. J.A. Croson Co. — January 23, 1989
488 US 469   102 LEd2d 854   109 SCt 706

    Affirmative (Woods) 114
    Almanac (1988):130-131; (1989):293
    Const Law 569-575R
    Culture 130-141
    Editorials (1989):78-85; (1995):664-673
    Guide (CQ) 57-58
    Sup Ct Review (1989):1-51; (1995):1-43, 45-70
    Sup Ct Yearbook (1994-95):27-32
    Thurgood 451-479R+
    Turning 217-221, 239-251+, 296-297

Benson, Christopher. Equal justice under siege: coping with the runaway Supreme Court. *Ebony* 45(2):54-58 (December 1989).

The *Black Enterprise* 100s: the 19th annual report on black business. *Black Enterprise* 21(11):89-102 (June 1991).

Brimmer, Andrew F. A Croson to bear. *Black Enterprise* 22(10):43-44 (May 1992).

A build-down for black contractors. *U.S. News and World Report* 106(5):13 (February 6, 1989).

Chemerinsky, Erwin. Supreme Court review: race and the Supreme Court. *Trial* 31(10):86-88 (October 1995).

Court in the middle. *National Review* 41(3):14 (February 24, 1989).

Courting disaster. *Progressive* 53(8):7-8 (August 1989).

Crock, Stan, and Michele Galen. 'A thunderous impact' on equal opportunity. *Business Week* (3430):37 (June 26, 1995).

Croson impact assessed. *ENR* 224(20):9-10 (May 17, 1990).

Dimeo, Jean. Minority contracting. *American City and County* 107(8):54-58 (July 1992).

Dingle, Derek T. Affirmative action. *Black Enterprise* 20(2):42-48 (September 1989).

———. Affirmative reaction: overturning the High Court. *Black Enterprise* 20(9):18 (April 1990).

Dwyer, Paula. The blow to affirmative action may not hurt that much. *Business Week* (Industrial/Technology Edition) (3113):61-62 (July 3, 1989).

———. A right turn, but no free ride for business. *Business Week* (Industrial/Technology Edition) (3114):27 (July 10, 1989).

Eastland, Terry. Racial preference in court (again). *Commentary* 87(1):32-38 (January 1989).

———. Toward a real restoration of civil rights. *Commentary* 88(5):25-29 (November 1989).

Fanning, Deirdre. First Monday next October. *Forbes* 141(9):110[Annual Directory] (April 25, 1988).

Farber, Daniel A. The winter thaw. *Trial* 25(4):101-105 (April 1989).

Farnham, Alan. Holding firm on affirmative action. *Fortune* 119(6):87-88 (March 13, 1989).

Fein, Bruce. A court that obeys the law. *National Review* 41(18):50-51 (September 29, 1989).

FitzGerald, Nora, and Peter M. Jones. Five key cases to watch for. *Scholastic Update* 120(15):22 (April 8, 1988).

Gest, Ted. A new civil-rights debate. *U.S. News and World Report* 108(6):26-27 (February 12, 1990).

Hairston, Julie B. Affirmative action plans in disarray after Croson. *American City and County* 104(6):62-66 (June 1989).

High court to tackle MBE case. *ENR* 221(13):10-11 (September 29, 1988).

High court upholds race-based programs. *ENR* 224(27)[225(1)]:9-10 (July 5, 1990).

Ichniowski, Tom. Supreme Court rejects Richmond MBE plan. *ENR* 222(4):8-9 (January 26, 1989).

Ichniowski, Tom, and Mary Powers. Croson's impact widens. *ENR* 223(24):17-18 (December 14, 1989).

Jacoby, Tamar. 'Now we're on our own.' *Newsweek* 113(6):64-65 (February 6, 1989).

Kinsley, Michael. Invidious distinction. *New Republic* 202(6):4, 42 (February 5, 1990).

Korman, Richard, and Tom Ichniowski. Feds face narrower options. *ENR* 234(24):8-9 (June 19, 1995).

———. Is Randy Pech the next Croson? *ENR* 234(3):10 (January 23, 1995).

Korman, Richard, Steven W. Setzer, Tom Ichniowski, and Mary Buckner Powers. Justice, by the numbers. *ENR* 227(9):26-31 (September 2, 1991).

Kraker, Jay, F. Housley Carr, and Michael Lawson. Governments withstand assault on MBE programs, at least for now. *ENR* 222(5):12-13 (February 2, 1989).

Lacayo, Richard, and Steven Holmes. Is the Court turning right? By reopening a civil rights case, the justices send a signal. *Time* 132(17):78 (October 24, 1988).

LaNoue, George R. Social science and minority "set-asides." *Public Interest* (110):49-62 (Winter 1993).

———. Split visions: minority business set-asides. *Annals of the American Academy of Political and Social Science* 523:104-116 (September 1992).

LaNoue, George R., and John C. Sullivan. Race neutral programs in public contracting. *Public Administration Review* 55(4):348-356 (July/August 1995).

Marshall, Thurgood. The Supreme Court and civil rights: has the tide turned? *USA Today* 118(2538):19-20 (March 1990).

McCall, Nathan. Atlanta holds fund-raiser to save MBE programs. *Black Enterprise* 19(2):16 (September 1988).

———. Ruling delivers hard blow to set-asides. *Black Enterprise* 19(9):17-18 (April 1989).

McDaniel, Ann. The Court spins right. *Newsweek* 113(26):16-18 (June 26, 1989).

Morehead, Jere W., and Peter J. Shedd. Civil rights and affirmative action: revolution or fine-tuning? *Business Horizons* 33(5):53-60 (September/October 1990).

Nelson-Horchler, Joani. Supreme Court job bias tops case list. *Industry Week* 237(6):20, 22 (September 19, 1988).

Olson, Elizabeth Grillo. The workplace is high on the High Court's docket. *Business Week* (Industrial/Technology Edition) (3073):88-92 (October 10, 1988).

Orren, Karen. The primacy of labor in American constitutional development. *American Political Science Review* 89(2):377-388 (June 1995).

Pace, Joseph M., and Zachary Smith. Understanding affirmative action: from the practitioner's perspective. *Public Personnel Management* 24(2):139-147 (Summer 1995).

Painter, Therese Eve. Scholars, judge debate contemporary constitutional issues. *Trial* 25(12):103-104 (December 1989).

Reid-Dove, Allyson, and Michael E. Howard. "Night has fallen on the Court . . ." *Black Enterprise* 20(2):44-45 (September 1989).

Rice, Mitchell F. Government set-asides, minority business enterprises, and the Supreme Court. *Public Administration Review* 51(2):114-122 (March/April 1991).

————. Justifying state and local government set-aside programs through disparity studies in the post-Croson era. *Public Administration Review* 52(5):482-490 (September/October 1992).

Rosen, Jeffrey. The leader of the opposition. *New Republic* 208(3):20-21, 24, 26-27 (January 18, 1993).

Ruben, George. Collective bargaining in 1989: old problems, new issues. *Monthly Labor Review* 113(1):19-29 (January 1990).

————. Developments in industrial relations: Court rules against minority set asides. *Monthly Labor Review* 112(5):60 (May 1989).

Sachs, Andrea, and Jerome Cramer. A blow to affirmative action: the Court strikes down a plan to aid minority businesses.*Time* 133(6):60 (February 6, 1989).

Scanlan, James P. The curious case of affirmative action for women. *Society* 29(2):36-41 (January/February 1992).

Schriener, Judy. AGC celebrates Croson, promises to help DBEs. *ENR* 222(13):15-16 (March 30, 1989).

Schwartz, Herman. New term, same tilt: the Supreme Court stays hard right. *Nation* 257(13):452-454 (October 25 1993).

Simms, Margaret C. Economic perspectives: rebuilding set aside program. *Black Enterprise* 21(2):33 (September 1990).

Simpson, Peggy. Supreme Court scoreboard. *Ms.* 18(3):94 (September 1989).

'Stigmatic harm.' [Editorial] *Nation* 248(6):183-184 (February 13, 1989).

Stodghill, Ron, and Paula Dwyer. A negative on affirmative action. *Business Week* (Industrial/Technology Edition) (3090):40 (February 6, 1989).

Supreme Court: Making it clear. *Economist* 310(7587):20-21 (January 28-February 3, 1989).

Supreme Court set aside ruling not 'devastating' blow to black businesses. *Jet* 75(19):4 (February 13, 1989).

Taylor, William L., and Susan M. Liss. Affirmative action in the 1990s: staying the course. *Annals of the American Academy of Political and Social Science* 523:30-37 (September 1992).

Thomas, Ralph C., III. Muscular MBE plans to rise in Croson era. *ENR* 222(15):27 (April 13, 1989).

Ward, James D. Response to Croson. *Public Administration Review* 54(5):483-485 (September/October 1994).

Witt, Elder. High Court faces issues from A to Z. *Governing* 2(1):23 (October 1988).

————. The last Court term: a mixed bag. *Governing* 3(1):24 (October 1989).

————. State-federal power at issue in High Court. *Governing* 2(6):66-67 (March 1989).

3304. Texas Monthly v. Bullock   February 21, 1989
        489 US 1   103 LEd2d 1   109 SCt 890
        Godless 114-115
        Sup Ct Review (1989):373-402
Lesly, Elizabeth, and Elliott Beard. Pennies from Heaven. *Washington Monthly* 23(4):40-45 (April 1991).

3305. Fort Wayne Books, Inc. v. Indiana   February 21, 1989
           Coupled with Sappenfield v. Indiana
        489 US 46   103 LEd2d 34   109 SCt 916
A "conservative Court" is still uncertain. *Christianity Today* 32(16):37 (November 4, 1988).

Dwyer, Paula. Will the High Court help defang RICO? *Business Week* (Industrial/Technology Edition) (3084):61-66 (December 19, 1988).

Fields, Howard. High Court bars pretrial RICO seizure of books. *Publishers' Weekly* 235[236](9):19 (March 10, 1989).

————. High Court hears arguments in Indiana bookstore case. *Publishers' Weekly* 234(17):14 (October 21, 1988).

———. Supreme Court to hear RICO case against Indiana bookstore. *Publishers' Weekly* 233(11):10 (March 18, 1988).

High Court asked to rule on RICO bookstore case. *Publishers' Weekly* 232(20):10 (November 13, 1987).

Lawton, Kim A. Could this be the year? *Christianity Today* 33(6):36-38 (April 7, 1989).

Maurer, Virginia G. The continuing expansion of RICO in business litigation. *Business Horizons* 33(5):80-87 (September/October 1990).

Witt, Elder. High Court faces issues from A to Z. *Governing* 2(1):23 (October 1988).

3306. Blanchard v. Bergeron   February 21, 1989
       489 US 87   103 LEd2d 67   109 SCt 939
         Almanac (1990):54, 55

Farber, Daniel A. Supreme Court review: debating Congress's intent in the age of statutes. *Trial* 25(12):105-110 (December 1989).

3307. Firestone Tire and Rubber Co. v. Richard Bruch   February 21, 1989
       489 US 101   103 LEd2d 80   109 SCt 948
         Sup Ct Review (1990):207-229

High Court takes case on fight over benefits. *ENR* 220(15):13-14 (April 14, 1988).

3308. Bonito Boats, Inc. v. Thunder Craft Boats, Inc.   February 21, 1989
       489 US 141   103 LEd2d 118   109 SCt 971
         Sup Ct Review (1989):283-309; (1991):143-177; (1992) 195-234

3309. DeShaney v. Winnebago County Department of Social Services   February 22, 1989
       489 US 189   103 LEd2d 249   109 SCt 998
         Almanac (1989):293
         Brennan 106-109
         Guide (West): (1991):101-103, 515-530R
         Landmark (v. 5):153-163R
         May It 39-56R
         Sup Ct Review (1989):53-86

The battered child. *New Republic* 200(12):7-8 (March 20, 1989).

Fein, Bruce. A court that obeys the law. *National Review* 41(18):50-51 (September 29, 1989).

Franklin, Daniel. The five dumbest Supreme Court decisions. *Washington Monthly* 26(10):12-18 (October 1994).

Glaberson, William B. Determined to be heard: four Americans and their journeys to the Supreme Court. *New York Times Magazine* (section 6, part 1):32-40 (October 2, 1988).

Painter, Therese Eve. Scholars, judge debate contemporary constitutional issues. *Trial* 25(12):103-104 (December 1989).

"Poor Joshua!": the Supreme Court absolves states in child-abuse cases. *Time* 133(10):56 (March 6, 1989).

Savage, David D. The High Court considers two important cases. *Phi Delta Kappan* 70(4):306-307 (December 1988).

Sendor, Benjamin. How far must schools go to protect kids? *American School Board Journal* 181(10):20-21 (October 1994).

———. Why the liability limits established in this tragic case might not shelter your schools. *American School Board Journal* 176(7):11, 42 (July 1989).

Witt, Elder. The last Court term: a mixed bag. *Governing* 3(1):24 (October 1989).

Zirkel, Perry A. De jure: poor Joshua. *Phi Delta Kappan* 70(10):828-829 (June 1989).

3310. Eu v. San Francisco County Democratic Central Committee   February 22, 1989
       489 US 214   103 LEd2d 271   109 SCt 1013

Weber, Ronald E. Redistricting and the courts: judicial activism in the 1990s. *American Politics Quarterly* 23(2):204-228 (April 1995).

3311. United States v. Ron Pair Enterprises   February 22, 1989
489 US 235   103 LEd2d 290   109 SCt 1026

Fanning, Deirdre. First Monday next October. *Forbes* 141(9):110[Annual Directory] (April 25, 1988).

Rice, John D. Ron Pair Enterprises, postpetition interest and other bankruptcy-related tax development *Taxes* 67(11):779-785 (November 1989).

3312. Teague v. Lane   February 22, 1989
489 US 288   103 LEd2d 334   109 SCt 1060

Almanac (1990):488-489

Death Penalty 90s 19-21

Sup Ct Review (1989):165-193; (1993):65-124

Sup Ct Yearbook (1989-90):45-46; (1991-92):14-16; (1992-93):63-64

Basta, James. Supreme Court review: habeas corpus: unresolved standard of review on mixed questions for state prisoners. *Journal of Criminal Law and Criminology* 83(4):978-997 (Winter 1993).

Branigan, Roger D., III. Supreme Court review: Sixth Amendment—the evolution of the Supreme Court's retroactivity doctrine: a futile search for theoretical clarity. *Journal of Criminal Law and Criminology* 80(4):1128-1153 (Winter 1990).

Chemerinsky, Erwin. Stunting the Constitution's growth. *Trial* 26(11):36-40 (November 1990).

―――. Supreme Court review: making sense of habeas corpus. *Trial* 28(12):79-82 (December 1992).

Finley, Timothy. Supreme Court review: habeas corpus—retroactivity of post-conviction rulings: finality at the expense of justice. *Journal of Criminal Law and Criminology* 84(4):975-1005 (Winter/Spring 1994).

Glaberson, William B. Determined to be heard: four Americans and their journeys to the Supreme Court. *New York Times Magazine* (section 6, part 1):32-40 (October 2, 1988).

Hyde, Henry J. Should the Omnibus Crime Control Act of 1991 be approved? *Congressional Digest* 71(4):111, 113, 155 (April 1992).

Rosen, Jeffrey. Bad noose. *New Republic* 209(14):13-15 (October 4, 1993).

Weisberg, Robert. A great writ while it lasted. *Journal of Criminal Law and Criminology* 81(1):9-36 (Spring 1990).

3313. United States v. Stuart   February 28, 1989
489 US 353   103 LEd2d 388   109 SCt 1183

Vagts, Detlev F. Senate materials and treaty interpretation: some research hints for the Supreme Court. [Editorial] *American Journal of International Law* 83(3):546-550 (July 1989).

3314. City of Canton v. Harris   February 28, 1989
489 US 378   103 LEd2d 412   109 SCt 1197

Chemerinsky, Erwin. Supreme Court review: reaffirmation of notice pleading. *Trial* 29(6):73-76 (June 1993).

Greenwald, Judy. Cities face new training liability. *Business Insurance* 23(10):3, 46 (March 6, 1989).

Hukill, Craig. Labor and the Supreme Court: significant issues of 1991-92. *Monthly Labor Review* 115(1):34-39 (January 1992).

Ruben, George. Collective bargaining in 1989: old problems, new issues. *Monthly Labor Review* 113(1):19-29 (January 1990).

Shumate, Richard. Lethal weapon. *Washington Monthly* 23(6):25-28 (June 1991).

Witt, Elder. The last Court term: a mixed bag. *Governing* 3(1):24 (October 1989).

3315. Trans World Airlines, Inc. (TWA) v. Independent Federation of Flight Attendants (IFFA)   February 28, 1989
489 US 426   103 LEd2d 456   109 SCt 1225

Dohahue, Thomas R. AFL-CIO, should the Senate approve S.55, the Workplace Fairness Act? *Congressional Digest* 72(6-7):184, 186, 188, 190 (June 1993).

Fanning, Deirdre. First Monday next October. *Forbes* 141(9):110[Annual Directory] (April 25, 1988).

Ford, William D., Marge Roukema, Harris W. Fawell, and Howard L. Berman. Should the House approve H.R. 5, the Workplace Fairness Act? *Congressional Digest* 70(11):270-273, 275, 277-280 (November 1991).

Mecham, Michael. Supreme Court ruling lets airlines assure jobs to strike breakers. *Aviation Week and Space Technology* 130(10):67 (March 6, 1989).

The right to strike. *Congressional Digest* 70(11):264-265 (November 1991).

Ruben, George. Collective bargaining in 1989: old problems, new issues. *Monthly Labor Review* 113(1):19-29 (January 1990).

Verespej, Michael A. Striking out. *Industry Week* 238(6):72 (March 20, 1989).

3316. Blanton v. North Las Vegas   March 6, 1989
    489 US 538   103 LEd2d 550   109 SCt 1289
    Witt, Elder. High Court faces issues from A to Z. *Governing* 2(1):23 (October 1988).
    ———. The last Court term: a mixed bag. *Governing* 3(1):24 (October 1989).

3317. Samuel L. Skinner v. Railway Labor Executives' Association   March 21, 1989
    489 US 602   103 LEd2d 639   109 SCt 1402
       Almanac (1989):293, 325-327
       Editorials (1989):308-317
       Guide (CQ) 57-58
       Sup Ct Review (1989):87-163
       Turning 227-233
    Are privacy rights in peril? *USA Today* 119(2547):8 (December 1990).

    Dripps, Donald A. Supreme Court review: will the real Fourth Amendment please stand up? *Trial* 31(11):80-82(November 1995).

    Farber, Daniel A. Supreme Court review: drug-testing cases. *Trial* 25(6):14, 16 (June, 1989).

    High court to tackle MBE case. *ENR* 221(13):10-11 (September 29, 1988).

    The High Court weighs drug tests. *Newsweek* 113(14):8 (April 3, 1989).

    Hukill, Craig. Significant decisions in labor cases: Employee drug testing. *Monthly Labor Review* 112(11):75-76 (November 1989).

    Jacoby, Tamar. Drug testing in the dock. *Newsweek* 112(20):66 (November 14, 1988).

    Mallory, Heidi P. Supreme Court review: Fourth Amendment—the "reasonablenss" of suspicionless drug testing of railroad employees. *Journal of Criminal Law and Criminology* 80(4):1052-1085 (Winter 1990).

    Misner, Robert L. Justifying searches on the basis of equality of treatment. *Journal of Criminal Law and Criminology* 82(3):547-578 (Fall 1991).

    Murphy, Betty Southard, Wayne E. Barlow, and D. Diane Hatch. Supreme Court drug testing cases. *Personnel Journal* 68(6):22 (June 1989).

    Payne, Seth, and Aaron Bernstein. Uncle Sam puts drug testing to the test. *Business Week* (Industrial/Technology Edition) (3079):58 (November 14, 1988).

    Olson, Elizabeth Grillo. The workplace is high on the High Court's docket. *Business Week* (Industrial/Technology Edition) (3073):88-92 (October 10, 1988).

    Proctor, Paul. Supreme Court decisions set precedent for pilot drug testing. *Aviation Week and Space Technology* 130(13):30 (March 27, 1989).

    Ruben, George. Collective bargaining in 1989: old problems, new issues. *Monthly Labor Review* 113(1):19-29 (January 1990).

    ———. Developments in industrial relations: Supreme Court drug test rulings. *Monthly Labor Review* 112(6):43 (June 1989).

    Sanders, Alain L., Steven Holmes, and Andrea Sachs. A boost for drug testing: the Supreme Court upholds screening employees in the lab. *Time* 133(14):62 (April 3, 1989).

    Sender, Benjamin. Passing the test on drug testing. *American School Board Journal* 180(3):23-24 (March 1993).

    White, Charles, and Charles Williams. Supreme Court docket: Court upholds drug tests for custom service, railway workers. *Social Education* 53(5):272 (September 1989).

3318. National Treasury Employees Union v. William Von Raab   March 21, 1989
    489 US 656   103 LEd2d 685   109 SCt 1384
       Almanac (1988):132; (1989):293, 325-327
       Const Law 281-285R
       Editorials (1989):308-317
       Guide (CQ) 57-58
       Sup Ct Review (1989):87-163

Turning 228-233, 238-239+

Are privacy rights in peril? *USA Today* 119(2547):8 (December 1990).

Betts, Kenneth C. Supreme Court review: Fourth Amendment—suspicionless urinalysis testing: a constitutionally "reasonable" weapon in the nation's war on drugs? *Journal of Criminal Law and Criminology* 80(4):1018-1051 (Winter 1990).

Farber, Daniel A. Supreme Court review: drug-testing cases. *Trial* 25(6):14, 16 (June, 1989).

High court to tackle MBE case. *ENR* 221(13):10-11 (September 29, 1988).

The High Court weighs drug tests. *Newsweek* 113(14):8 (April 3, 1989).

Hukill, Craig. Significant decisions in labor cases: employee drug testing. *Monthly Labor Review* 112(11):75-76 (November 1989).

Jacoby, Tamar. Drug testing in the dock. *Newsweek* 112(20):66 (November 14, 1988).

Mandell, Leonard B. Supreme Court docket: drug testing and the Fourth Amendment: testing in the public sector. *Social Education* 53(4):230-232 (April/May 1989).

Misner, Robert L. Justifying searches on the basis of equality of treatment. *Journal of Criminal Law and Criminology* 82(3):547-578 (Fall 1991).

Murphy, Betty Southard, Wayne E. Barlow, and D. Diane Hatch. Supreme Court drug testing cases. *Personnel Journal* 68(6):22 (June 1989).

Proctor, Paul. Supreme Court decisions set precedent for pilot drug testing. *Aviation Week and Space Technology* 130(13):30 (March 27, 1989).

Ruben, George. Collective bargaining in 1989: old problems, new issues. *Monthly Labor Review* 113(1):19-29 (January 1990).

———. Developments in industrial relations: Supreme Court drug test rulings. *Monthly Labor Review* 112(6):43 (June 1989).

Schwartz, Herman. The Court next term: consolidating the new majority. *Nation* 249(11):380-383 (October 9, 1989).

Sender, Benjamin. Passing the test on drug testing. *American School Board Journal* 180(3):23-24 (March 1993).

White, Charles, and Charles Williams. Supreme Court docket: Court upholds drug tests for custom service, railway workers. *Social Education* 53(5):272 (September 1989).

Witt, Elder. High Court faces issues from A to Z. *Governing* 2(1):23 (October 1988).

3319. New York City Board of Estimate v. Morris Board of Estimate v. Morris   March 22, 1989
         Coupled with Ponterio v. Morris
       489 US 688   103 LEd2d 717   109 SCt 1433
       Witt, Elder. High Court faces issues from A to Z. *Governing* 2(1):23 (October 1988).
       ———. The last Court term: a mixed bag. *Governing* 3(1):24 (October 1989).

3320. Schmuck v. United States   March 22, 1989
       489 US 705   103 LEd2d 734   109 SCt 1443
       Maurer, Virginia G. The continuing expansion of RICO in business litigation. *Business Horizons* 33(5):80-87 (September/October 1990).

3321. Commissioner of Internal Revenue v. Clark   March 22, 1989
       489 US 726   103 LEd2d 753   109 SCt 1455
       Cuddy, Michael J., Marblestone, Philip K., and Barry Friedman. Tax treatment of cash 'boots' addressed by High Court. *Best's Review* (Property/Casualty Insurance Edition) 90(4):94-98, 112 (August 1989).

3322. United States Department of Justice v. Reporters Committee for Freedom of the Press   March 22, 1989
       489 US 749   103 LEd2d 774   109 SCt 1468
       Garneau, George. Locked away from public view. *Editor and Publisher* 122(13):9, 40 (April 1, 1989).

3323. Paul S. Davis v. Michigan Department of Treasury   March 28, 1989
       489 US 803   103 LEd2d 891   109 SCt 1500
       Sup Ct Review (1989):223-259
       Sup Ct Yearbook (1992-93):94-95

High Court hears arguments on retroactivity of Davis decision. *Taxes* 71(1):53 (January 1993).

Rapp, David, The High Court and the new balance of power. *Governing* 6(8):68 (May 1993).

Retroactive relief presumed when state tax held unconstitutional. *Practical Accountant* 26(8):14 (August 1993).

Ruben, George. Collective bargaining in 1989: old problems, new issues. *Monthly Labor Review* 113(1):19-29 (January 1990).

Supreme Court says Davis (and maybe every case) applies retroactively. *Journal of Taxation* 79(2):66 (August 1993).

Witt, Elder. High Court faces issues from A to Z. *Governing* 2(1):23 (October 1988).

———. The last Court term: a mixed bag. *Governing* 3(1):24 (October 1989).

3324. William A. Frazee v. Illinois Department of Employment Security   March 29, 1989
    489 US 829   103 LEd2d 914   109 SCt 1514
       Godless 34-35, 107+

       Sup Ct Review (1989):373-402

Court rules on clergy malpractice, Sabbath. *Christianity Today* 33(8):51-52 (May 12, 1989).

Drinan, Robert F. The Supreme Court expands religious freedom. *America* 160(16):388-389 (April 29, 1989).

Farber, Daniel A. Supreme Court review: religion: establishment and free exercise clauses. *Trial* 25(10):22-25 (October 1989).

Free exercise. *Fortune* 118(11):216 (November 7, 1988).

Greenlaw, Paul S., and John P. Kohl. Religious freedom and unemployment compensation benefits. *Public Personnel Management* 24(3):315-330 (Fall 1995).

Lawton, Kim A. Could this be the year? *Christianity Today* 33(6):36-38 (April 7, 1989).

Ruben, George. Collective bargaining in 1989: old problems, new issues. *Monthly Labor Review* 113(1):19-29 (January 1990).

3325. United States v. Sokolow   April 3, 1989
    490 US 1   104 LEd2d 1   109 SCt 1581
       Almanac (1989):327

       Guide (West): (1995):318-319

Are privacy rights in peril? *USA Today* 119(2547):8 (December 1990).

Bernstein, Steven K. Supreme Court review: Fourth Amendment—using the drug courier profile to fight the war on drugs. *Journal of Criminal Law and Criminology* 80(4):996-1017 (Winter 1990).

The case of the conspicuous dealer. *Newsweek* 113(16):64 (April 17, 1989).

Painter, Therese Eve. Scholars, judge debate contemporary constitutional issues. *Trial* 25(12):103-104 (December 1989).

Sanders, Alain L., Dan Cray, and Steven Holmes. Judging a book by its cover: drug-courier profiles get a favorable nod from the Court. *Time* 133(16):52 (April 17, 1989).

Seligman, Daniel. Thurgood's way. *Fortune* 119(10):165, (May 8, 1989).

3326. City of Dallas v. Stanglin   April 3, 1989
    490 US 19   104 LEd2d 18   109 SCt 1591

Painter, Therese Eve. Scholars, judge debate contemporary constitutional issues. *Trial* 25(12):103-104 (December 1989).

Sendor, Benjamin. How far can boards go in regulating students' off-campus behavior? *American School Board Journal* 178(6):5, 38 (June 1991).

3327. Amerada Hess Corp. v. Division, Director of Taxation, New Jersey Department of Treasury   April 3, 1989
      Coupled with Texaco, Inc. and Tenneco Oil Co. v. Director, Division of Taxation,
        New Jersey Department of Treasury
    490 US 66   104 LEd2d 58   109 SCt 1617
       Sup Ct Review (1989):223-259

Olson, Elizabeth Grillo. The workplace is high on the High Court's docket. *Business Week* (Industrial/Technology Edition) (3073):88-92 (October 10, 1988).

U.S. Supreme Court upholds Jersey decision on oil tax. *Chemical Marketing Reporter* 235:9, 22 (April 10, 1989).

3328. California v. ARC America Corp.   April 18, 1989
      490 US 93   104 LEd2d 86   109 SCt 1661
      Dwyer, Paula. A right turn, but no free ride for business. *Business Week* (Industrial/Technology Edition)
         (3114):27 (July 10, 1989).
      Olson, Elizabeth G. Justices hear DBE case. *ENR* 221(15):18-20 (October 13, 1988).
      Sesser, Gary D. Just who's in charge here? [Editorial] *Across the Board* 28(7-8):11-13 (July/August 1991).
      Witt, Elder. The last Court term: a mixed bag. *Governing* 3(1):24 (October 1989).

3329. Massachusetts v. Morash   April 18, 1989
      490 US 107   104 LEd2d 98   109 SCt 1668
      Murphy, Betty Southard, Wayne E. Barlow, and D. Diane Hatch. Accrued vacation pay not preempted under
         ERISA. *Personnel Journal* 68(12):18, 22 (December 1989).

3330. Elisa Chan v. Korean Air Lines, Ltd. (KAL)   April 18, 1989
      490 US 122   104 LEd2d 113   109 SCt 1676
      Shapiro, Stacy. Supreme Court to review liability limit for KAL crash. *Business Insurance* 22(15):3, 12 (April
         11, 1988).
      Smart, Tim. A shot at shooting down punitive damages. *Business Week* (Industrial/Technology Edition) (3169):
         62, 66 (July 16, 1990).
      Supreme Court to rule on limits of international air ticket liability. *Aviation Week and Space Technology* 128
         (15):133 (April 11, 1988).

3331. American Foreign Service Association v. Garfinkel   April 18, 1989
      490 US 153   104 LEd2d 139   109 SCt 1693
      Almanac (1989):328-329

3332. Price Waterhouse v. Ann Hopkins   May 1, 1989
      490 US 228   104 LEd2d 268   109 SCt 1775
      Almanac (1989):293, 314-319; (1990):462-465; (1991):251-261
      Barnes, Fred. Last laugh. *New Republic* 205(25):9-10, 12 (December 16, 1991).
      Bersoff, Donald N., and Donald B. Verrilli, Jr. In the Supreme Court of the United States Price Waterhouse v.
         Ann B. Hopkihns: Amicus Curiae Brief for the American Psychological Association. *American Psychologist*
         46(10):1061-1070 (October 1991).
      The Civil Rights Act of 1990. *Congressional Digest* 69(8-9):196-224 (August/September 1990).
      Dwyer, Paula. The blow to affirmative action may not hurt that much. *Business Week* (Industrial/Technology
         Edition) (3113):61-62 (July 3, 1989).
      Farber, Daniel A. Supreme Court review: proving discrimination in Title VII cases. *Trial* 25(8):15-18 (August
         1989).
      Fiske, Susan T. Court's ruling against sex stereotyping in employment decisions will make it easier for
         professors to win discrimination lawsuits. [Editorial] *Chronicle of Higher Education* 35(38):B1-B3 (May 31,
         1989).
      Fiske, Susan T., Donald N. Bersoff, Eugene Borgida, Kay Deaux, and Madeline E. Heilman. Social science
         research on trial: use of sex stereotyping research in Price Waterhouse v. Hopkins. *American Psychologist*
         46(10):1049-1060 (October 1991).
      Fitzpatrick, Robert B. Stereotyping in the workplace: evidence of discrimination? *Trial* 26(1):76-81 (January
         1990).
      Franke, Ann H., and Martha A. Toll. Legal watch: Court decisions hinder women's, minorities' rights.
         Academe 75(4):47 (July/August 1989).
      Fritz, Norma R. Unsafe sex discrimination. *Personnel* 66(7):4 (July 1989).
      Glaberson, William B. Determined to be heard: four Americans and their journeys to the Supreme Court. *New
         York Times Magazine* (section 6, part 1):32-40 (October 2, 1988).
      High Court ruling helps plaintiffs of job bias. *Jet* 76(7):19 (May 22, 1989).
      Jaschik, Scott. Court's bias ruling seen having little effect on colleges. *Chronicle of Higher Education*
         35(40):A28 (June 14, 1989).

———. Ruling seen helping professors bring discrimination cases. *Chronicle of Higher Education* 35(35):A1, A22 (May 10, 1989).

Kelly, Eileen P., Amy Oakes Young, and Lawrence S. Clark. Sex stereotyping in the workplace; a manager's guide. *Business Horizons* 36(2):23-29 (March/April 1993).

Lacayo, Richard, Steven Holmes, and Andrea Sachs. A hard nose and a short skirt: two cases raise questions about a woman's on-the-job style. *Time* 132(20):98 (November 14, 1988).

Lee, Barbara A. Recent Supreme Court rulings could disrupt or halt affirmative-action recruiting and hiring in academe. [Editorial] *Chronicle of Higher Education* 35(42):B1, B3 (June 28, 1989).

Lissy, William E. Avoiding discrimination liability. *Supervision* 51(8):18-19 (August 1990).

Morehead, Jere W., and Peter J. Shedd. Civil rights and affirmative action: revolution or fine-tuning? *Business Horizons* 33(5):53-60 (September/October 1990).

Murphy, Betty Southard, Wayne E. Barlow, and D. Diane Hatch. Supreme Court decisions impact Title VII and ADEA claims. *Personnel Journal* 70(6):30, 32 (June 1991).

———. Supreme Court rules on gender stereotypes under Title VII. *Personnel Journal* 68(7):12 (July 1989).

Myth America in the workplace. *U.S. News and World Report* 106(19):14 (May 15, 1989).

Olson, Elizabeth Grillo. The workplace is high on the High Court's docket. *Business Week* (Industrial/Technology Edition) (3073):88-92 (October 10, 1988).

Orenstein, Morton H. Equal opportunity: the balance changes. *Across the Board* 27(4):57-59 (April 1990).

Reid-Dove, Allyson, and Michael E. Howard. "Night has fallen on the Court . . ." *Black Enterprise* 20(2):44-45 (September 1989).

Ritter, Anne. The way it was: HR in the 1980s. *Personnel* 66(12):30-37 (December 1989).

Ruben, George. Collective bargaining in 1989: old problems, new issues. *Monthly Labor Review* 113(1):19-29 (January 1990).

———. Developments in industrial relations: Court rules on "sex stereotyping." *Monthly Labor Review* 112(7):45 (July 1989).

Sachs, Andrea, and Steven Holmes. A slap at sex stereotypes: the Supreme Court clears the way for discrimination suits. *Time* 133(20):66 (May 15, 1989).

Seligman, Daniel. Price Waterhouse gets a partner. *Fortune* 121(14):133-134 (June 18, 1990).

———. Wrestling with bias. *Fortune* 119(12):339 (June 5, 1989).

Shaw, Bill. Employee appraisals, discrimination cases, and objective evidence. *Business Horizons* 33(5):61-65 (September/October 1990).

Simpson, Peggy. Supreme Court scoreboard. *Ms.* 18(3):94 (September 1989).

Spivack, Miranda S. Courting disaster. *Ms.* 17(7-8):138 (January/February 1989).

Zall, Milton. What to expect from the Civil Rights Act. *Personnel Journal* 71(3):46-50 (March 1992).

3333. John E. Mallard v. United States District Court for Southern District of Iowa — May 1, 1989
490 US 296   104 LEd2d 318   109 SCt 1814
Sup Ct Review (1989):213-222

3334. Robertson v. Methow Valley Citizens Council — May 1, 1989
490 US 332   104 LEd2d 351   109 SCt 1835

Cardone, John V. Substantive standards and NEPA: mitigating environmental consequences with consent decrees. *Boston College Environmental Affairs Law Review* 18(1):159-184 (Fall 1990).

Meyers, Gary D. Old-growth forests, the owl, and yew: environmental ethics versus traditional dispute resolution under the Endangered Species Act and other public land and resources laws. *Boston College Environmental Affairs Law Review* 18(4):623-668 (Summer 1991).

3335. Thornburgh v. Abbott — May 15, 1989
490 US 401   104 LEd2d 459   109 SCt 1874

Schwartz, Herman. The Court next term: consolidating the new majority. *Nation* 249(11):380-383 (October 9, 1989).

3336. United States v. Halper — May 15, 1989
490 US 435   104 LEd2d 487   109 SCt 1892

Hildy, John. Supreme Court review: Fifth Amendment—double jeopardy and the dangerous drug tax. *Journal of Criminal Law and Criminology* 85(4):936-961 (Spring 1995).

Lieber, David. Supreme Court review: Eighth Amendment—the excessive fines clause. *Journal of Criminal Law and Criminology* 84(4):805-826 (Winter/Spring 1994).

Morenberg, Paul W. Environmental fraud by government contractors: a new application of the False Claims Act. *Boston College Environmental Affairs Law Review* 22(3):623-669 (Spring 1995).

3337. Kentucky Department of Corrections v. Thompson   May 15, 1989
490 US 454   104 LEd2d 506   109 SCt 1904

Schwartz, Herman. The Court next term: consolidating the new majority. *Nation* 249(11):380-383 (October 9, 1989).

3338. Rodriguez de Quijas v. Shearson/American Express, Inc.   May 15, 1989
490 US 477   104 LEd2d 526   109 SCt 1917

    Almanac (1989):293, 327-328
    Sup Ct Review (1995):99-124

Olson, Elizabeth G. Justices hear DBE case. *ENR* 221(15):18-20 (October 13, 1988).

Scheibla, Shirley Hobbs. See you in Court: compulsory arbitration under fire. *Barron's* 69(23):13, 28-30 (June 5, 1989).

3339. Finley v. United States   May 22, 1989
490 US 545   104 LEd2d 593   109 SCt 2003

Rowe, Thomas D. No final victories: the incompleteness of equity's triumph in federal public law. *Law and Contemporary Problems* 56(3):105-121 (Summer 1993).

3340. Mansell v. Mansell   May 30, 1989
490 US 581   104 LEd2d 675   109 SCt 2023

Court limits sharing of Army pension in divorce; Marshall pens decision. *Jet* 76(11):8 (June 19, 1989).

Ruben, George. Collective bargaining in 1989: old problems, new issues. *Monthly Labor Review* 113(1):19-29 (January 1990).

Spivack, Miranda S. Courting disaster. *Ms.* 17(7-8):138 (January/February 1989).

3341. Hildwin v. Florida   May 30, 1989
490 US 638   104 LEd2d 728   109 SCt 2005

George, Tracey E., and Lee Epstein. On the nature of Supreme Court decision making. *American Political Science Review* 86(2):323-337 (June 1992).

3342. Ward's Cove Packing Co. v. Atonio   June 5, 1989
490 US 642   104 LEd2d 733   109 SCt 2115

    Almanac (1989):293, 314-319; (1990):462-466; (1991):251-261; (1993):317; (1994):298-299
    Culture 130-141
    Editorials (1991):622-631
    Sup Ct Review (1989):1-51
    Turning 272-277+

Baer, Judith A. Women's rights and the limits of constitutional doctrine. *Western Political Quarterly* 44(4):821-852 (December 1991).

Barone, Michael, and Ted Gest. Letting the people decide. *U.S. News and World Report* 107(2):18-19 (July 10, 1989).

Benson, Christopher. Equal justice under siege: coping with the runaway Supreme Court. *Ebony* 45(2):54-58 (December 1989).

Biddle, Richard E. Wards Cove Packing vs. Atonio redefines EEO analyses. *Personnel Journal* 69(6):56-65 (June 1990).

Blits, Jan H., and Linda S. Gottfredson. Equality or lasting inequality? *Society* 27(3):4-11 (March/April 1990).

The Civil Rights Act of 1990. *Congressional Digest* 69(8-9):196-224 (August/September 1990).

Courting disaster. *Progressive* 53(8):7-8 (August 1989).

Dingle, Derek T. Affirmative action. *Black Enterprise* 20(2):42-48 (September 1989).

———. Affirmative reaction: overturning the High Court. *Black Enterprise* 20(9):18 (April 1990).

Dwyer, Paula. The blow to affirmative action may not hurt that much. *Business Week* (Industrial/Technology Edition) (3113):61-62 (July 3, 1989).

———. A right turn, but no free ride for business. *Business Week* (Industrial/Technology Edition) (3114):27 (July 10, 1989).

Eastland, Terry. Toward a real restoration of civil rights. *Commentary* 88(5):25-29 (November 1989).

Farber, Daniel A. Supreme Court review: proving discrimination in Title VII cases. *Trial* 25(8):15-18 (August 1989).

Fein, Bruce. A court that obeys the law. *National Review* 41(18):50-51 (September 29, 1989).

Fritz, Norma R. Supreme Court decision: easier on employers. *Personnel* 66(8):4 (August 1989).

Gest, Ted. A new civil-rights debate. *U.S. News and World Report* 108(6):26-27 (February 12, 1990).

Hood, Stafford, and Laurence Parker. Minorities, teacher testing, and recent U.S. Supreme Court holdings: a regressive step. *Teachers College Record* 92(4):603-618 (Summer 1991).

Hukill, Craig. Significant decisions in labor cases: civil rights. *Monthly Labor Review* 113(2):52-53 (February 1990).

Jacoby, Tamar. A question of statistics. *Newsweek* 113(25):58 (June 19, 1989).

Lee, Barbara A. Recent Supreme Court rulings could disrupt or halt affirmative-action recruiting and hiring in academe. [Editorial] *Chronicle of Higher Education* 35(42):B1, B3 (June 28, 1989).

Marshall, Thurgood. The Supreme Court and civil rights: has the tide turned? *USA Today* 118(2538):19-20 (March 1990).

McDaniel, Ann. The Court spins right. *Newsweek* 113(26):16-18 (June 26, 1989).

———. Judicial flash points. *Newsweek* 116(5):18-19 (July 30, 1990).

Morehead, Jere W., and Peter J. Shedd. Civil rights and affirmative action: revolution or fine-tuning? *Business Horizons* 33(5):53-60 (September/October 1990).

Murphy, Betty Southard, Wayne E. Barlow, and D. Diane Hatch. Supreme Court decisions impact Title VII and ADEA claims. *Personnel Journal* 70(6):30, 32 (June 1991).

———. Manager's newsfront: Supreme Court redefines scope of Civil Rights Acts. *Personnel Journal* 68(8):22-26 (August 1989).

Orenstein, Morton H. Equal opportunity: the balance changes. *Across the Board* 27(4):57-59 (April 1990).

Orren, Karen. The primacy of labor in American constitutional development. *American Political Science Review* 89(2):377-388 (June 1995).

Real rights. *National Review* 41(13):15-16 (July 14, 1989).

Reid-Dove, Allyson, and Michael E. Howard. "Night has fallen on the Court . . ." *Black Enterprise* 20(2):44-45 (September 1989).

Ritter, Anne. The way it was: HR in the 1980s. *Personnel* 66(12):30-37 (December 1989).

Roberts, Paul Craig, and Lawrence M. Stratton, Jr. Color code. *National Review* 47(5):36, 51, 80 (March 20, 1995).

Ross, Patrick C. Are quotas making a comeback? *Personnel Journal* 69(9):42-44 (September 1990).

Ruben, George. Collective bargaining in 1989: old problems, new issues. *Monthly Labor Review* 113(1):19-29 (January 1990).

Schwartz, Herman. Illogical force. [Editorial] *Nation* 249(2):40-41 (July 10, 1989).

Simpson, Peggy. Constitutional crisis. *Ms.* 18(3):90-98 (September 1989).

———. Supreme Court scoreboard. *Ms.* 18(3):94 (September 1989).

Stodghill, Ron, and Paula Dwyer. A negative on affirmative action. *Business Week* (Industrial/Technology Edition) (3090):40 (February 6, 1989).

Stoper, Emily. Women's work, women's movement: taking stock. *Annals of the American Academy of Political and Social Science* 515:151-162 (May 1991).

Supreme Court: negative on affirmative action. *Economist* 311(7607):36 (June 17-23, 1989).

Weisberger, Bernard A. Dreams deferred. *American Heritage* 41(2):24-26 (March 1990).

Zall, Milton. What to expect from the Civil Rights Act. *Personnel Journal* 71(3):46-50 (March 1992).

3343. Hernandez v. Commissioner of Internal Revenue   June 5, 1989
       Coupled with Graham v. Commissioner of Internal Revenue
    490 US 680   104 LEd2d 766   109 SCt 2136

Godless 120-122

Court upholds prayer ban before games. *Christianity Today* 33(10):55 (July 14, 1989).

Farber, Daniel A. Supreme Court review: religion: establishment and free exercise clauses. *Trial* 25(10):22-25 (October 1989).

Is IRS informal guidance valid authority? *Journal of Taxation* 71(3):199 (September 1989).

Lawton, Kim A. Could this be the year? *Christianity Today* 33(6):36-38 (April 7, 1989).

Teitell, Conrad. Will fixed gifts to all religions become nondeductable? *Trusts and Estates* 131(3):63-64 (March 1992).

3344. Mead Corp. v. B.E. Tilley   June 5, 1989
      490 US 714   104 LEd2d 796   109 SCt 2156

Geisel, Jerry. Court gives employers plan termination victory. *Business Insurance* 23(24):2, 7 (June 12, 1989).

———. Pension reversion threat. *Business Insurance* 25(12):2, 10 (March 25, 1991).

Shalowitz, Deborah, and Stacy Adler. High Court agrees to review dispute over asset reversion. *Business Insurance* 22(41):2, 92 (October 10, 1988).

3345. Community for Non-Violence v. Reid   June 5, 1989
      490 US 730   104 LEd2d 811   109 SCt 2166

Fields, Howard. Court aids freelancers in work-for-hire ruling. *Publishers' Weekly* 235(24):11 (June 16, 1989).

———. High Court to hear work-for-hire case. *Publishers' Weekly* 234(22):10 (November 25, 1988).

———. Supreme Court hears work-for-hire arguments. *Publishers' Weekly* 235(15):14 (April 14, 1989).

———. Lawyers see little impact from High Court's work-for-hire ruling. *Publishers' Weekly* 235(25):10-11 (June 23, 1989).

3346. Martin v. Wilks   June 12, 1989
      490 US 755   104 LEd2d 835   109 SCt 2180

Affirmative (Woods) 114

Almanac (1989):293, 314-319; (1990):462-466; (1991):251-261

Culture 130-141

Editorials (1989):690-697

Turning 277-278, 301+

Barone, Michael, and Ted Gest. Letting the people decide. *U.S. News and World Report* 107(2):18-19 (July 10, 1989).

Benson, Christopher. Equal justice under siege: coping with the runaway Supreme Court. *Ebony* 45(2):54-58 (December 1989).

Birmingham firehouse. [Editorial] *Commonweal* 116(13):387-388 (July 14, 1989).

The Civil Rights Act of 1990. *Congressional Digest* 69(8-9):196-224 (August/September 1990).

Courting disaster. *Progressive* 53(8):7-8 (August 1989).

Dingle, Derek T. Affirmative reaction: overturning the High Court. *Black Enterprise* 20(9):18 (April 1990).

Dwyer, Paula. The blow to affirmative action may not hurt that much. *Business Week* (Industrial/Technology Edition) (3113):61-62 (July 3, 1989).

———. A right turn, but no free ride for business. *Business Week* (Industrial/Technology Edition) (3114):27 (July 10, 1989).

Dyson, Michael Eric. Deaffirmation. [Editorial] *Nation* 249(1):4-5 (July 3, 1989).

Eastland, Terry. Toward a real restoration of civil rights. *Commentary* 88(5):25-29 (November 1989).

Fein, Bruce. A court that obeys the law. *National Review* 41(18):50-51 (September 29, 1989).

Gest, Ted. A new civil-rights debate. *U.S. News and World Report* 108(6):26-27 (February 12, 1990).

Hertzberg, Hendrik. Wounds of race. *New Republic* 201(2):4, 42 (July 10, 1989).

Hukill, Craig. Significant decisions in labor cases: civil rights. *Monthly Labor Review* 112(11):76 (November 1989).

Jaschik, Scott. High Court's ruling may make colleges wary of hiring plans. *Chronicle of Higher Education* 35(41):A1, A16 (June 21, 1989).

Lacayo, Richard, and Steven Holmes. Is the Court turning right? By reopening a civil rights case, the justices send a signal. *Time* 132(17):78 (October 24, 1988).

Lee, Barbara A. Recent Supreme Court rulings could disrupt or halt affirmative-action recruiting and hiring in academe. [Editorial] *Chronicle of Higher Education* 35(42):B1, B3 (June 28, 1989).

McDaniel, Ann. The Court spins right. *Newsweek* 113(26):16-18 (June 26, 1989).

Morehead, Jere W., and Peter J. Shedd. Civil rights and affirmative action: revolution or fine-tuning? *Business Horizons* 33(5):53-60 (September/October 1990).

Murphy, Betty Southard, Wayne E. Barlow, and D. Diane Hatch. Manager's newsfront: Supreme Court redefines scope of Civil Rights Acts. *Personnel Journal* 68(8):22-26 (August 1989).

Nelson-Horchler, Joani. A surprise whipping. *Industry Week* 238(14):52 (July 17, 1989).

Real rights. *National Review* 41(13):15-16 (July 14, 1989).

Reid-Dove, Allyson, and Michael E. Howard. "Night has fallen on the Court . . ." *Black Enterprise* 20(2):44-45 (September 1989).

Ritter, Anne. The way it was: HR in the 1980s. *Personnel* 66(12):30-37 (December 1989).

Ruben, George. Collective bargaining in 1989: old problems, new issues. *Monthly Labor Review* 113(1):19-29 (January 1990).

Sanders, Alain L., Steven Holmes, and Priscilla Painton. Chipping away at civil rights: with two key rulings, the court confirms its rightward shift. *Time* 133(26):63-66 (June 26, 1989).

Schwartz, Herman. Illogical force. [Editorial] *Nation* 249(2):40-41 (July 10, 1989).

Sendor, Benjamin. Affirmative action just got harder for you. *American School Board Journal* 176(9):8 (September 1989).

Simpson, Peggy. Constitutional crisis. *Ms.* 18(3):90-98 (September 1989).

———. Supreme Court scoreboard. *Ms.* 18(3):94 (September 1989).

Spivack, Miranda S. Courting disaster. *Ms.* 17(7-8):138 (January/February 1989).

Stoper, Emily. Women's work, women's movement: taking stock. *Annals of the American Academy of Political and Social Science* 515:151-162 (May 1991).

Supreme Court: negative on affirmative action. *Economist* 311(7607):36 (June 17-23, 1989).

Supreme Court splits on two landmark bias cases. *Jet* 76(13):4-5 (July 3, 1989).

Weisberger, Bernard A. Dreams deferred. *American Heritage* 41(2):24-26 (March 1990).

Wise, Charles, and Rosemary O'Leary. Is federalism dead or alive in the Supreme Court?: implications for public administrators. *Public Administration Review* 52(6):559-572 (November/December 1992).

Witt, Elder. High Court faces issues from A to Z. *Governing* 2(1):23 (October 1988).

———. The last Court term: a mixed bag. *Governing* 3(1):24 (October 1989).

Zall, Milton. What to expect from the Civil Rights Act. *Personnel Journal* 71(3):46-50 (March 1992).

3347. South Carolina v. Gathers   June 12, 1989
       490 US 805   104 LEd2d 876   109 SCt 2207
       Sup Ct Review (1991):77-102
       Sup Ct Yearbook (1990-91):35-37

Newman, Eric S. Supreme Court review: Eighth Amendment—prosecutorial comment regarding the victim's personal qualities should not be permitted at the sentencing phase of a capital trial. *Journal of Criminal Law and Criminology* 80(4):1236-1255 (Winter 1990).

Sargeant, Georgia. Victim impact testimony allowed by Supreme Court in death penalty hearings. *Trial* 27(10):11-14, 85 (October 1991).

3348. Lorance v. AT&T Technologies, Inc.   June 12, 1989
       490 US 900   104 LEd2d 961   109 SCt 2261
       Almanac (1989):293, 314-319; (1990):462-464; (1991):251-261
       Culture 130-141
       Turning 277-278, 301+

The Civil Rights Act of 1990. *Congressional Digest* 69(8-9):196-224 (August/September 1990).

Dingle, Derek T. Affirmative action. *Black Enterprise* 20(2):42-48 (September 1989).

———. Affirmative reaction: overturning the High Court. *Black Enterprise* 20(9):18 (April 1990).

Lee, Barbara A. Recent Supreme Court rulings could disrupt or halt affirmative-action recruiting and hiring in academe. [Editorial] *Chronicle of Higher Education* 35(42):B1,B3 (June 28, 1989).

McGuire, Kevin T., and Barbara Palmer. Issue fluidity on the U.S. Supreme Court. *American Political Science Review* 89(3):691-702 (September 1995).

Morehead, Jere W., and Peter J. Shedd. Civil rights and affirmative action: revolution or fine-tuning? *Business Horizons* 33(5):53-60 (September/October 1990).

Murphy, Betty Southard, Wayne E. Barlow, and D. Diane Hatch. Manager's newsfront: Supreme Court redefines scope of Civil Rights Acts. *Personnel Journal* 68(8):22-26 (August 1989).

Ritter, Anne. The way it was: HR in the 1980s. *Personnel* 66(12):30-37 (December 1989).

Ross, Patrick C. Are quotas making a comeback? *Personnel Journal* 69(9):42-44 (September 1990).

Ruben, George. Collective bargaining in 1989: old problems, new issues. *Monthly Labor Review* 113(1):19-29 (January 1990).

Schwartz, Herman. Illogical force. [Editorial] *Nation* 249(2):40-41 (July 10, 1989).

Simpson, Peggy. Constitutional crisis. *Ms.* 18(3):90-98 (September 1989).

———. One step forward, two steps back. *Ms.* 18(3):96 (September 1989).

———. Supreme Court scoreboard. *Ms.* 18(3):94 (September 1989).

Zall, Milton. What to expect from the Civil Rights Act. *Personnel Journal* 71(3):46-50 (March 1992).

3349. Pennsylvania v. Union Gas Co.   June 15, 1989
491 US 1   105 LEd2d 1   109 SCt 2273

Fields, Howard. 11th Amendment ruling by High Court is 'hopeful' for copyright. *Publishers' Weekly* 236(1):9 (July 7, 1989).

Light, Alfred R. The importance of "being taken": to clarify and confirm the litigative reconstruction of CERCLA's text. *Boston College Environmental Affairs Law Review* 18(1):1-52 (Fall 1990).

Olson, Elizabeth Grillo. Industry eyes a new court session. *Chemical Week* 143(14):19 (October 5, 1988).

Wise, Charles, and Rosemary O'Leary. Is federalism dead or alive in the Supreme Court?: implications for public administrators. *Public Administration Review* 52(6):559-572 (November/December 1992).

Witt, Elder. The last Court term: a mixed bag. *Governing* 3(1):24 (October 1989).

3350. Will v. Michigan Department of State Police   June 15, 1989
491 US 58   105 LEd2d 45   109 SCt 2304
Almanac (1989):318

Barone, Michael, and Ted Gest. Letting the people decide. *U.S. News and World Report* 107(2):18-19 (July 10, 1989).

Fein, Bruce. A Court that obeys the law. *National Review* 41(18):50-51 (September 29, 1989).

Murphy, Betty Southard, Wayne E. Barlow, and D. Diane Hatch. Supreme Court narrows scope of civil rights claims. *Personnel Journal* 68(10):19, 22 (October 1989).

Notes and comment. [Editorial] *New Yorker* 65(24):21-22 (July 31, 1989).

Schwartz, Herman. Illogical force. [Editorial] *Nation* 249(2):40-41 (July 10, 1989).

Wise, Charles, and Rosemary O'Leary. Is federalism dead or alive in the Supreme Court?: implications for public administrators. *Public Administration Review* 52(6):559-572 (November/December 1992).

Witt, Elder. The last Court term: a mixed bag. *Governing* 3(1):24 (October 1989).

3351. Quinn v. Millsap   June 15, 1989
491 US 95   105 LEd2d 74   109 SCt 2324

Witt, Elder. The last Court term: a mixed bag. *Governing* 3(1):24 (October 1989).

3352. Michael H. v. Gerald D.   June 15, 1989
491 US 110   105 LEd2d 91   109 SCt 2333
Hard Choices 135, 220
Sup Ct Yearbook (1991-92):4-5

Nagel, Robert F. Constitutional doctrine and political direction: the Supreme Court. *Trial* 25(12):72-77 (December 1989).

Spivack, Miranda S. Courting disaster. *Ms.* 17(7-8):138 (January/February 1989).

Stoner, James R., Jr. Common law and constitutionalism in the abortion case. *Review of Politics* 55(3):421-441 (Summer 1993).

3353. Patterson v. McLean Credit Union   June 15, 1989
491 US 164   105 LEd2d 132   109 SCt 2363

Almanac (1988):122; (1989):293-295;314-319; (1990):462-464; (1991):251-261

Center 19-81+

Culture 130-141

Editorials (1988):450-455

Sup Ct Review (1988):43-60; (1989):1-51; (1994):429-540

Turning 184, 188-192, 221-222, 280-282+, 476

Benson, Christopher. Equal justice under siege: coping with the runaway Supreme Court. *Ebony* 45(2):54-58 (December 1989).

The Civil Rights Act of 1990. *Congressional Digest* 69(8-9):196-224 (August/September 1990).

Courting disaster. *Progressive* 53(8):7-8 (August 1989).

Demon Runyon. [Editorial] *Commonweal* 115(10):291-292 (May 20, 1988).

Dingle, Derek T. Affirmative action. *Black Enterprise* 20(2):42-48 (September 1989).

———. Affirmative reaction: overturning the High Court. *Black Enterprise* 20(9):18 (April 1990).

Dwyer, Paula. The blow to affirmative action may not hurt that much. *Business Week* (Industrial/Technology Edition) (3113):61-62 (July 3, 1989).

———. A right turn, but no free ride for business. *Business Week* (Industrial/Technology Edition) (3114):27 (July 10, 1989).

Farber, Daniel A. Supreme Court review: debating Congress's intent in the age of statutes. *Trial* 25(12):105-110 (December 1989).

Fein, Bruce. A court that obeys the law. *National Review* 41(18):50-51 (September 29, 1989).

Franke, Ann H., and Martha A. Toll. Legal watch: Court decisions hinder women's, minorities' rights. *Academe* 75(4):47 (July/August 1989).

Gest, Ted. A new civil-rights debate. *U.S. News and World Report* 108(6):26-27 (February 12, 1990).

———. Where have all the conservatives gone? *U.S. News and World Report* 105(2):15-16 (July 11, 1988).

Higginbotham, A. Leon, Jr. 45 years in law and civil rights. *Ebony* 46(1):80-86 (November 1990).

Hukill, Craig. Significant decisions in labor cases: civil rights. *Monthly Labor Review* 113(2):52-53 (February 1990).

Jacoby, Tamar, and Ann McDaniel. Why reopen a closed case?: upheaval in the court. *Newsweek* 111(19):69 (May 9, 1988).

Lacayo, Richard, Jerome Cramer, and Alain L. Sanders. Play it again, says the Court: the justices decide to reconsider a major civil rights ruling. *Time* 131(19):73 (May 9, 1988).

Lacayo, Richard, and Steven Holmes. "A slam-dunk decision": the court proves again that it will not do a president's bidding. *Time* 132(3):16-17 (July 11, 1988).

Lee, Barbara A. Recent Supreme Court rulings could disrupt or halt affirmative-action recruiting and hiring in academe. [Editorial] *Chronicle of Higher Education* 35(42):B1, B3 (June 28, 1989).

Marshall and colleagues rap High Court decision to review rights case. *Jet* 74(7):9 (May 16, 1988).

Marshall, Thurgood. The Supreme Court and civil rights: has the tide turned? *USA Today* 118(2538):19-20 (March 1990).

McDaniel, Ann. The Court spins right. *Newsweek* 113(26):16-18 (June 26, 1989).

McDowell, Gary L. Congress and the courts. *Public Interest* (100):89-101 (Summer 1990).

Morehead, Jere W., and Peter J. Shedd. Civil rights and affirmative action: revolution or fine-tuning? *Business Horizons* 33(5):53-60 (September/October 1990).

Murphy, Betty Southard, Wayne E. Barlow, and D. Diane Hatch. 1991 Civil Rights Act not retroactive. *Personnel Journal* 73(7):24 (July 1994).

———. Manager's newsfront: Supreme Court redefines scope of Civil Rights Acts. *Personnel Journal* 68(8): 22- 26 (August 1989).

Notes and comment. [Editorial] *New Yorker* 65(24):21-22 (July 31, 1989).

Olson, Elizabeth Grillo. The workplace is high on the High Court's docket. *Business Week* (Industrial/ Technology Edition) (3073):88-92 (October 10, 1988).

Orenstein, Morton H. Equal opportunity: the balance changes. *Across the Board* 27(4):57-59 (April 1990).

Orren, Karen. The primacy of labor in American constitutional development. *American Political Science Review* 89(2):377-388 (June 1995).

Real rights. *National Review* 41(13):15-16 (July 14, 1989).

Regan, Richard J. Supreme Court roundup: 1987 term. *Thought* 64(253):176-187 (June 1989).

Reid-Dove, Allyson, and Michael E. Howard. "Night has fallen on the Court . . ." *Black Enterprise* 20(2):44-45 (September 1989).

Ritter, Anne. The way it was: HR in the 1980s. *Personnel* 66(12):30-37 (December 1989).

Sanders, Alain L., Steven Holmes, and Priscilla Painton. Chipping away at civil rights: with two key rulings, the court confirms its rightward shift. *Time* 133(26):63-66 (June 26, 1989).

Schwartz, Herman. The Court next term: consolidating the new majority. *Nation* 249(11):380-383 (October 9, 1989).

———. Illogical force. [Editorial] *Nation* 249(2):40-41 (July 10, 1989).

Simpson, Peggy. Supreme Court scoreboard. *Ms.* 18(3):94 (September 1989).

Suddenly, the conservatives start stirring. *U.S. News and World Report* 104(18):11-12 (May 9, 1988).

Supreme Court splits on two landmark bias cases. *Jet* 76(13):4-5 (July 3, 1989).

TBR from Washington: the fifth man. *New Republic* 198(20):4, 42 (May 16, 1988).

Weisberger, Bernard A. Dreams deferred. *American Heritage* 41(2):24-26 (March 1990).

Witt, Elder. High Court faces issues from A to Z. *Governing* 2(1):23 (October 1988).

Wolvovitz, Barbara M. Borked after all. [Editorial] *Nation* 246(19):664-665 (May 14, 1988).

Zall, Milton. What to expect from the Civil Rights Act. *Personnel Journal* 71(3):46-50 (March 1992).

3354. Dellmuth v. Muth   June 15, 1989
    491 US 223   105 LEd2d 181   109 SCt 2397
    Almanac (1989):198; (1990):54-55, 616-617
    Culture 130-141

Schwartz, Herman. Illogical force. [Editorial] *Nation* 249(2):40-41 (July 10, 1989).

Trends in federal regulation. *Congressional Digest* 74(3):69-71 (March 1995).

Wise, Charles, and Rosemary O'Leary. Is federalism dead or alive in the Supreme Court?: implications for public administrators. *Public Administration Review* 52(6):559-572 (November/December 1992).

Zirkel, Perry A. De jure: the latest Supreme Court special education case: not moot but Muth. *Phi Delta Kappan* 71(3):250-251 (November 1989).

3355. Colonial American Life Insurance Co. v. Commissioner   June 15, 1989
    491 US 244   105 LEd2d 199   109 SCt 2408

Cuddy, Michael J., Philip K. Marbelstone, and George Paz. IRS limits Court's decision to reinsuring existing business. *Best's Review* (Life/Health Insurance Edition) 92(5):110-116 (September 1991).

Lenrow, Gerald I., Stephen S. Olds, and John M. O'Bryan. Colonial American Life: a landmark Supreme Court decision. *Best's Review* (Life/Health Insurance Edition) 90(6):110-114 (October 1989).

———. Colonial American Life: a landmark Supreme Court decision. *Best's Review* (Property/Casualty Insurance Edition) 90(6):108-110 (October 1989).

Stodghill, Ron, and Paula Dwyer. A negative on affirmative action. *Business Week* (Industrial/Technology Edition) (3090):40 (February 6, 1989).

3356. Consolidated Rail Corp. v. Railway Labor Executives' Association   June 19, 1989
    Conrail v. Railway Labor Executives' Association
    491 US 299   105 LEd2d 250   109 SCt 2477

Murphy, Betty Southard, Wayne E. Barlow, and D. Diane Hatch. Drug testing subject to union bargaining. *Personnel Journal* 68(9):23-24 (September 1989).

Ruben, George. Collective bargaining in 1989: old problems, new issues. *Monthly Labor Review* 113(1):19-29 (January 1990).

3357. Texas v. Gregory Lee Johnson   June 21, 1989
    491 US 397   105 LEd2d 342   109 SCt 2533
    Almanac (1989):293, 307-314, 60C-63CR; (1990):52, 510-511, 524-528
    Amending 188-193+
    Brennan 161-165
    Center 257-281+
    Const Law 147-153R, 664-665
    Editorials (1989):700-709, 710-715

Guide (CQ) 57-58
Landmark (v. 1):175-194R
Make 234-248
May It 151-166R
Sup Ct Review (1990):69-103
Turning 251-260, 284-285+

Ackerson, Merlin J., John W. Burkhart, Dawyer D. Gross, Peter S. Sawtell, Donald J. Montgomery, W. Paul Jones, and James M. Wall. Faith and flag-burning. *Christian Century* 106(24):757-759 (August 16-23, 1989).

American survey: flag burning and flag waving. *Economist* 312(7609):19 (July 1-7, 1989).

Barone, Michael. Behind the flag-burning firestorm. *U.S. News and World Report* 107(1):28 (July 3, 1989).

Barone, Michael, and Ted Gest. Letting the people decide. *U.S. News and World Report* 107(2):18-19 (July 10, 1989).

Berns, Walter. Flag-burning and other modes of expression. *Commentary* 88(4):37-41 (October 1989).

Bork, Robert H. An end to political judging? *National Review* 42(25);30-32 (December 31, 1990).

———. What to do about the First Amendment. *Commentary* 99(2):23-29 (February 1995).

Brennan, William. The United States Supreme Court: decision. *Congressional Digest* 68(8-9)196, 198, 200R (August/September 1989).

Buckley, William F., Jr. The Court and the flag decision. *National Review* 41(14):54 (August 4, 1989).

———. Hooray for the amendment. *National Review* 41(14):54-55 (August 4, 1989).

Congress: the flag boosters get burned. *Newsweek* 116(1):24 (July 2, 1990).

A fiery furor over the flag. *Life* 12(9):106-110 (August 1989).

The flag and freedom of speech. *America* 161(1):3 (July 1-8, 1989).

Flag desecration legislation. *Congressional Digest* 68(8-9):193-194, 224 (August/September 1989).

Garbus, Martin. Supreme Court retreat?: the 'crime' of flag burning. *Nation* 248(11):369-370 (March 20, 1989).

Garneau, George. Friends of the First Amendment. *Editor and Publisher* 122(26):9 (July 1, 1989).

Greenawalt, Kent. Free speech in the United States and Canada. *Law and Contemporary Problems* 55(1):5-33 (Winter 1992).

Grogan, David, Kent Demaret, and Bob Stewart. Unimpressed by the freedom to burn Old Glory, Joey Johnson still wants a revolution. *People Weekly* 32(2):98-100 (July 10, 1989).

Hertzberg, Hendrik. Flagellation. *New Republic* 201(3-4):4 (July 17-24, 1989).

The High Court stands 5-4 on a burning issue. *U.S. News and World Report* 107(1):8 (July 3, 1989).

Isaacson, Walter, Laurence I. Barrett, and Nancy Traver. Hiding in the flag: Washington has more important things to do than posture about Old Glory. *Time* 135(26):16-17 (June 25, 1990).

Isaacson, Walter, and Steven Holmes. O'er the land of the free: a decision upholding the right to burn the flag is the best reason not to. *Time* 134(1):14-15 (July 3, 1989).

Jacoby, Tamar, and Eleanor Clift. Congress rallies around the flag. *Newsweek* 114(2):19 (July 10, 1989).

Jacoby, Tamar, Ann McDaniel, and Peter McKillop. A fight for Old Glory. *Newsweek* 114(1):18-20 (July 3, 1989).

McDaniel, Ann. A burning constitutional issue. *Newsweek* 115(21):78 (May 21, 1990).

———. Judicial flash point. *Newsweek* 116(5):18-19 (July 30, 1990).

Miller, Mark C. Congressional committees and the federal courts: a neo-institutional perspective. *Western Political Quarterly* 45(4):949-970 (December 1992).

Novick, Sheldon M. Holmes, Brennan, and the flag-burning cases. *Trial* 26(11):24-29 (November 1990).

Rehnquist, William H. The United States Supreme Court: dissent. *Congressional Digest* 68(8-9):197, 199, 201R (August/September 1989).

Relin, David Oliver. A burning question. *Scholastic Update* 123(2):16-18 (September 21, 1990).

Schwartz, Herman. The Court next term: consolidating the new majority. *Nation* 249(11):380-383 (October 9, 1989).

Seligman, Daniel. The speech market. *Fortune* 120(5):135 (August 28, 1989).

Smolla, Rodney A. Free speech afire with controversy: the Supreme Court. *Trial* 25(12):46-47, 49, 51 (December 1989).

———. Supreme Court review: flag burning: round two. *Trial* 26(9):20-23 (September 1990).

Waiving the flag. *New Republic* 200(4):7-8 (January 23, 1989).

Wall, James M. The dynamics of flag-burning. [Editorial] *Christian Century* 106(21):643-644 (July 5-12, 1989).

―――――. Protecting speech, protecting symbols. *Christian Century* 107(20):619-620 (June 27-July 4, 1990).

What price Old Glory?: to protect the flag, Bush calls for an amendment. *Time* 134(2):23 (July 10, 1989).

Wulf, Melvin L. Flag-saving. [Editorial] *Nation* 249(7):229-230 (September 4-11, 1989).

3358. Public Citizen v. United States Department of Justice   June 21, 1989
      Coupled with Washington Legal Foundation v. United States Department of Justice (USDOJ)
    491 US 440   105 LEd2d 377   109 SCt 2558
    Almanac (1989):321-324

Farber, Daniel A. Supreme Court review: debating Congress's intent in the age of statutes. *Trial* 25(12):105-110 (December 1989).

3359. Pittsburgh & Lake Erie Railroad Co. v. Railway Labor Executives' Association   June 21, 1989
    491 US 490   105 LEd2d 415   109 SCt 2584

Ruben, George. Collective bargaining in 1989: old problems, new issues. *Monthly Labor Review* 113(1):19-29 (January 1990).

3360. Florida Star v. B.J.F.   June 21, 1989
    491 US 524   105 LEd2d 443   109 SCt 2603
    Thurgood 305-316R+
    Turning 285

Garneau, George. First Amendment upheld. *Editor and Publisher* 122(26):10-11 (July 1, 1989).

―――――. Friends of the First Amendment. *Editor and Publisher* 122(26):9 (July 1, 1989).

―――――. Press vs. privacy. *Editor and Publisher* 121(43):20, 53 (October 22, 1988).

Gersh, Debra. Media lose another friend. *Editor and Publisher* 124(27):14-15 (July 6, 1991).

Hale, Dennis. How retiring Supreme Court Justice White voted in First Amendment cases. *Editor and Publisher* 126(30):44, 36 (July 24, 1993).

Levine, Lee, and David L. Perry. No way to celebrate the Bill of Rights. *Columbia Journalism Review* 29(2):38-39 (July/August 1990).

Powe, L. A., Jr. Mass communications and the First Amendment: an overview. *Law and Contemporary Problems* 55(1):53-76 (Winter 1992).

Rotunda, Ronald D. The Supreme Court: eschewing bright lines. *Trial* 25(12):52-56 (December 1989).

Sanders, Alain L., Steven Holmes, and Andrea Sachs. Dial-a-porn, find-a-lawyer: the court defends free speech but reins in criminal defendants. *Time* 134(1):56 (July 3, 1989).

3361. Massachusetts v. Oakes   June 21, 1989
    491 US 576   105 LEd2d 493   109 SCt 2633

Witt, Elder. High Court faces issues from A to Z. *Governing* 2(1):23 (October 1988).

3362. United States v. Monsanto   June 22, 1989
    491 US 600   105 LEd2d 512   109 SCt 2657
    Almanac (1989):293, 324

Dwyer, Paula. Will the High Court help defang RICO? *Business Week* (Industrial/Technology Edition) (3084):61-66 (December 19, 1988).

Fein, Bruce. A court that obeys the law. *National Review* 41(18):50-51 (September 29, 1989).

Hardy, Melinda. Supreme Court review: Sixth Amendment—applicability of right to counsel of choice to forfeiture of attorney's fees. *Journal of Criminal Law and Criminology* 80(4):1154-1189 (Winter 1990).

Sanders, Alain L., Steven Holmes, and Andrea Sachs. Dial-a-porn, find-a-lawyer: the Court defends free speech but reins in criminal defendants. *Time* 134(1):56 (July 3, 1989).

3363. Caplin and Drysdale, Chartered v. United States   June 22, 1989
    491 US 617   105 LEd2d 528   109 SCt 2646, 2667
    Almanac (1989):293, 324

Dwyer, Paula. Will the High Court help defang RICO? *Business Week* (Industrial/Technology Edition) (3084):61-66 (December 19, 1988).

Hardy, Melinda. Supreme Court review: Sixth Amendment—applicability of right to counsel of choice to forfeiture of attorney's fees. *Journal of Criminal Law and Criminology* 80(4):1154-1189 (Winter 1990).

Sanders, Alain L., Steven Holmes, and Andrea Sachs. Dial-a-porn, find-a-lawyer: the Court defends free speech but reins in criminal defendants. *Time* 134(1):56 (July 3, 1989).

Schwartz, Herman. The Court next term: consolidating the new majority. *Nation* 249(11):380-383 (October 9, 1989).

3364. Harte-Hanks Communications, Inc. v. Connaughton   June 22, 1989
491 US 657   105 LEd2d 562   109 SCt 2678

Dill, Barbara. The most serious threat is . . . warrior lawyers. *Columbia Journalism Review* 30(4):54-55 (November/December 1991).

Garneau, George. Silver lining in libel loss. *Editor and Publisher* 122(26):11, 20 (July 1, 1989).

Hale, F. Dennis. Free expression: the first five years of the Rehnquist Court. *Journalism Quarterly* 69(1):89-104 (Spring 1992).

Sanders, Alain L., Steven Holmes, and Andrea Sachs. Dial-a-porn, find-a-lawyer: the court defends free speech but reins in criminal defendants. *Time* 134(1):56 (July 3, 1989).

Smolla, Rodney A. Free speech afire with controversy: the Supreme Court. *Trial* 25(12):46-47, 49, 51 (December 1989).

3365. Jett v. Dallas Independent School District   June 22, 1989
491 US 701   105 LEd2d 598   109 SCt 2702
    Almanac (1989):293, 314-319

Dingle, Derek T. Affirmative action. *Black Enterprise* 20(2):42-48 (September 1989).

Murphy, Betty Southard, Wayne E. Barlow, and D. Diane Hatch. Supreme Court narrows scope of civil rights claims. *Personnel Journal* 68(10):19, 22 (October 1989).

Notes and comment. [Editorial] *New Yorker* 65(24):21-22 (July 31, 1989).

3366. Independent Federation of Flight Attendants v. Zipes   June 22, 1989
491 US 754   105 LEd2d 639   109 SCt 2732
    Almanac (1989):314-319; (1990):462-466; (1991):251-261

The Civil Rights Act of 1990. *Congressional Digest* 69(8-9):196-224 (August/September 1990).

3367. Murray v. Giarratano   June 23, 1989
492 US 1   106 LEd2d 1   109 SCt 2765
    Death Penalty (Tushnet) 101-104

Murphy, Cornelius F. The Supreme Court and capital punishment: a new hands-off approach. *USA Today* 121(2574):51-52 (March 1993).

Schwartz, Herman. The Court next term: consolidating the new majority. *Nation* 249(11):380-383 (October 9, 1989).

Zeithaml, Donald P., Jr. Supreme Court review: Sixth and Fourteenth Amendments—constitutional right to state capital collateral appeal: the due process of executing a convict without attorney representation. *Journal of Criminal Law and Criminology* 80(4):1190-1210 (Winter 1990).

3368. Granfinanciera, S.A. v. Paul C. Nordberg   June 23, 1989
492 US 33   106 LEd2d 26   109 SCt 2782
    Sup Ct Review (1989):261-282

3369. Sable Communications of California, Inc. v. Federal Communications Commission (FCC)   June 23, 1989
492 US 115   106 LEd2d 93   109 SCt 2829
    Almanac (1989):293, 324, 382
    Turning 285

Court orders: dealing with porn and drugs. *Newsweek* 114(1):20 (July 3, 1989).

Day care, porn cases heard by High Court. *Christianity Today* 33(4):53 (March 3, 1989).

Garneau, George. Friends of the First Amendment. *Editor and Publisher* 122(26):9 (July 1, 1989).

Lawton, Kim A. Confrontation's stage is set. *Christianity Today* 33(11):36-38 (August 18, 1989).

Miller, Mark C. Congressional committees and the federal courts: a neo-institutional perspective. *Western Political Quarterly* 45(4):949-970 (December 1992).

O'Rourke, William. Will the Court bare all? *Nation* 252(24):846-847 (June 24, 1991).

Rubens, Suzanne D. Supreme Court review: First Amendment—disconnecting dial-a-porn: section 223(b)'s two pronged challenge to First Amendment rights. *Journal of Criminal Law and Criminology* 80(4):968-995 (Winter 1990).

Sanders, Alain L., Steven Holmes, and Andrea Sachs. Dial-a-porn, find-a-lawyer: the Court defends free speech but reins in criminal defendants. *Time* 134(1):56 (July 3, 1989).

3370. Public Employees Retirement System of Ohio v. Betts   June 23, 1989
     492 US 158   106 LEd2d 134   109 SCt 2854
       Almanac (1989):315; (1990):54, 362-364

Hukill, Craig. Significant decisions in labor cases: age discrimination. *Monthly Labor Review* 113(2):53-54 (February 1990).

Mackey, Bruce C., and Scott F. Uhler. How to take an early out. *American School Board Journal* 177(3):27, 42 (March 1990).

Morehead, Jere W., and Peter J. Shedd. Civil rights and affirmative action: revolution or fine-tuning? *Business Horizons* 33(5):53-60 (September/October 1990).

Murphy, Betty Southard, Wayne E. Barlow, and D. Diane Hatch. Employee benefit plans under ADEA. *Personnel Journal* 68(9):22-23 (September 1989).

———. Supreme Court decisions impact Title VII and ADEA claims. *Personnel Journal* 70(6):30, 32 (June 1991).

Pryor, David. New law battles age discrimination. *Trial* 27(4):30-34 (April 1991).

Ruben, George. Collective bargaining in 1989: old problems, new issues. *Monthly Labor Review* 113(1):19-29 (January 1990).

Trends in federal regulation. *Congressional Digest* 74(3):69-71 (March 1995).

3371. Duckworth v. Eagan   June 26, 1989
     492 US 195   106 LEd2d 166   109 SCt 2875

Altman, David B. Supreme Court review: Fifth Amendment—coercion and clarity: the Supreme Court approves altered Miranda warnings. *Journal of Criminal Law and Criminology* 80(4):1086-1111 (Winter 1990).

Chemerinsky, Erwin. Supreme Court review: making sense of habeas corpus. *Trial* 28(12):79-82 (December 1992).

Painter, Therese Eve. Scholars, judge debate contemporary constitutional issues. *Trial* 25(12):103-104 (December 1989).

Schwartz, Herman. The Court next term: consolidating the new majority. *Nation* 249(11):380-383 (October 9, 1989).

3372. H.J. Inc. v. Northwestern Bell Telephone Co.   June 26, 1989
     492 US 229   106 LEd2d 195   109 SCt 2893
       Almanac (1989):293, 319-321; (1990):536-538
       Sup Ct Review (1993):157-198; (1994):129-168

Adler, Stacy. U.S. Supreme Court leaves RICO intact. *Business Insurance* 23(27):21 (July 3, 1989).

Dwyer, Paula. A right turn, but no free ride for business. *Business Week* (Industrial/Technology Edition) (3114):27 (July 10, 1989).

———. Will the High Court help defang RICO? *Business Week* (Industrial/Technology Edition) (3084):61-66 (December 19, 1988).

Fields, Howard. Supreme Court upholds broad use of RICO. *Publishers' Weekly* 236(1):7 (July 7, 1989).

Maurer, Virginia G. The continuing expansion of RICO in business litigation. *Business Horizons* 33(5):80-87 (September/October 1990).

Olson, Elizabeth Grillo. The workplace is high on the High Court's docket. *Business Week* (Industrial/Technology Edition) (3073):88-92 (October 10, 1988).

3373. Browning-Ferris Industries, Inc. v. Kelco Disposal Inc.   June 26, 1989
    492 US 257   106 LEd2d 219   109 SCt 2909

Almanac (1989):293, 325

Sup Ct Yearbook (1989-90):74-75

Adler, Stacy. Punitive damage challenge rejected. [Editorial] *Business Insurance* 23(52):37 (December 25, 1989).

————. Punitive damages: no relief now, but High Court opens door for future review. *Business Insurance* 23(27):1, 21 (July 3, 1989).

Barger, Richard D., and Royal F. Oakes. Judicial reform on hold; Supreme Court changes stance on restrictions for punitive awards. *Business Insurance* 26(9):19-20 (March 2, 1992).

Chemerinsky, Erwin. Supreme Court review: punitive damages and the Constitution. *Trial* 30(10):90-92 (October 1994).

Dwyer, Paula. A right turn, but no free ride for business. *Business Week* (Industrial/Technology Edition) (3114):27 (July 10, 1989).

Farber, Daniel A. Supreme Court review: punitive damages. *Trial* 27(6):62-66 (June 1991).

Fields, Howard. High Court hears arguments on large punitive damage awards. *Publishers' Weekly* 235(18):18 (May 5, 1989).

————. High Court refuses to place limits on jury awards in civil suits. *Publishers' Weekly* 236(2):12 (July 14, 1989).

————. Supreme Court, 7-1, refuses to cap punitive damages awards by juries. *Publishers' Weekly* 238(16):1-3, 105 (April 5, 1991).

Geisel, Jerry. Punitive damage before Supreme Court. *Business Insurance* 22(50):3, 11 (December 12, 1988).

Lieber, David. Supreme Court review: Eighth Amendment—the excessive fines clause. *Journal of Criminal Law and Criminology* 84(4):805-826 (Winter/Spring 1994).

Nelson-Horchler, Joani. A surprise whipping. *Industry Week* 238(14):52 (July 17, 1989).

Olson, Elizabeth Grillo. Punitive damages: how much is too much? the Supreme Court could soon curb runaway jury awards. *Business Week* (Industrial/Technology Edition) (3097):54-56 (March 27, 1989).

Punishment through the pocketbook. *U.S. News and World Report* 105(24):13 (December 19, 1988).

Radolf, Andrew. The chilling effect. *Editor and Publisher* 122(29):11-12 (July 22, 1989).

————. Landmark libel case? *Editor and Publisher* 122(20):9-10 (May 20, 1989).

Rapp, David. The punitive damage battle is moving to the state capitols. *Governing* 4(9):62 (June 1991).

Spencer, Leslie. Troubling days for trial lawyers. *Forbes* 145(12):108, 112 (June 11, 1990).

3374. Penry v. Lynaugh   June 26, 1989
    492 US 302   106 LEd2d 256   109 SCt 2934

Almanac (1989):293; (1991):264-265

Sup Ct Review (1989):165-193

Turning 243-245, 285-288

Barone, Michael, and Ted Gest. Letting the people decide. *U.S. News and World Report* 107(2):18-19 (July 10, 1989).

Behuniak-Long, Susan. Justice Sandra Day O'Connor and the power of maternal legal thinking. *Review of Politics* 54(3):417-444 (Summer 1992).

Brown, J. Michael. Supreme Court review: Eighth Amendment—capital sentencing instructions. *Journal of Criminal Law and Criminology* 84(4):854-882 (Winter/Spring 1994).

Chan, Peter K. M. Supreme Court review: Eighth Amendment—the death penalty and the mentally retarded criminal: fairness, culpability, and death. *Journal of Criminal Law and Criminology* 80(4):1211-1235 (Winter 1990).

Drinan, Robert F. Execute an 8-year-old? The Johnny Penry case. [Editorial] *Christian Century* 106(6):199-200 (February 22, 1989).

McDaniel, Ann. The Court: Reagan's legal legacy. *Newsweek* 114(2):19-20 (July 10, 1989).

————. Judicial flash points. *Newsweek* 116(5):18-19 (July 30, 1990).

Murphy, Cornelius F. The Supreme Court and capital punishment: a new hands-off approach. *USA Today* 121(2574):51-52 (March 1993).

Norpoth, Helmut, Jeffrey A. Segal, William Mishler, and Reginald S. Sheehan. Popular influence on Supreme Court decisions. *American Political Science Review* 88(3):711-724 (September 1994).

3375. Stanford v. Kentucky   June 26, 1989
          Coupled with Wilkins v. Missouri
      492 US 361   106 LEd2d 306   109 SCt 2969
          Almanac (1989):262, 293
          Turning 245-248, 285-288
      Fraust, Leslie. The ultimate price. *Scholastic Update* (Teachers' Edition) 123(14):13 (April 5, 1991).
      McDaniel, Ann. The Court: Reagan's legal legacy. *Newsweek* 114(2):19-20 (July 10, 1989).
      Murphy, Cornelius F. The Supreme Court and capital punishment: a new hands-off approach. *USA Today*
          121(2574):51-52 (March 1993).
      Rosenbaum, Ron. Too young to die? *New York Times Magazine* (section 6, part 1):32-35, 58-61 (March 12,
          1989).
      Sanders, Alain L., Steven Holmes, and Andrea Sachs. Bad news for death row: the Court okays execution of
          teenage and retarded criminals. *Time* 134(2):48-49 (July 10, 1989).
      Witt, Elder. High Court faces issues from A to Z. *Governing* 2(1):23 (October 1988).
      ———. The last Court term: a mixed bag. *Governing* 3(1):24 (October 1989).

3376. Brendale v. Confederate Tribes & Bands of Yakima Indian Nation   June 29, 1989
          Coupled with Wilkinson v. Confederated Tribes and Bands of Yakima Indian Nation
          Coupled with County of Yakima v. Confederated Tribes and Bands of Yakima Indian Nation
      492 US 408   106 LEd2d 343   109 SCt 2994
      Witt, Elder. High Court faces issues from A to Z. *Governing* 2(1):23 (October 1988).
      ———. The last Court term: a mixed bag. *Governing* 3(1):24 (October 1989).

3377. Board of Trustees of the State University of New York (SUNY) v. Fox   June 29, 1989
      492 US 469   106 LEd2d 388   109 SCt 3028
      Boedecker, Karl A., and Fred W. Morgan. The evolution of First Amendment protection for commercial
          speech. *Journal of Marketing* 59(1):38-47 (January 1995).
      Colford, Steven W. Ad industry loses hero in Brennan. *Advertising Age* 61(31):1, 44 (July 30, 1990).
      ———. Court revives ad-ban worry. *Advertising Age* 60(29):1, 24 (July 3, 1989).
      Hovland, Roxanne, and Ronald E. Taylor. Advertising and commercial speech since the 1986 Posadas case.
          Journalism Quarterly 67(4):1083-1089 (Winter 1990).
      Jaschik, Scott. High Court gives colleges more leeway to regulate commerce on campuses. *Chronicle of Higher
          Education* 35(43):A1,A16 (July 5, 1989).
      Lewis, Wayne K. Environmental advertising: a delicate balance of rights. *Trial* 28(10):53-56 (October 1992).
      Reed, O. Lee. Reading the tea leaves: future regulation of product-extrinsic advertising. *Business Horizons*
          33(5):88-93 (September/October 1990).

3378. William L. Webster, Attorney General of Missouri v. Reproductive Health Services   July 3, 1989
      492 US 490   106 LEd2d 410   109 SCt 3040
          Abortion Am 63, 99, 232-242R, 342-349+
          Abortion Con 10, 293, 256-259, 260-261+
          Abortion Dec 162-198+
          Abortion Dec 80s Introduction, 175-219R
          Almanac (1989):293, 296-299, 63C-73CR; (1990):528-531; (1992):398-400
          Brennan 316-318
          Center 127-143+
          Const Law 312-326R
          Editorials (1989):374-383, 762-773; (1992):770-781
          Ethics 151-169R
          Guide (CQ) 57-58
          Hard Choices 12-19, 172-173, 190-199, 212-221, 244-245, 314
          Liberty 673-681, 691-692+
          Nobody's 3-46
          Sup Ct Yearbook (1991-92):30-34
          Turning 227-228, 266-272+, 288-295, 297-298, 307-311+

Abortion: a march and a muddle. *Economist* 311(7598):29 (April 15-21, 1989).

Abortion on the line. *National Review* 41(14):12-13 (August 4, 1989).

Abortion: rage over Roe. *Economist* 323(7756):22-23 (April 25-May 1, 1992).

Abortion: sparring on the bench. *Newsweek* 114(24):49 (December 11, 1989).

Aliotta, Jilda M. The unfinished feminist agenda: the shifting forum. *Annals of the American Academy of Political and Social Science* 515:140-150 (May 1991).

Allen, Ann E, and Warren H. Pearse. The implications of Webster for practicing physicians. *JAMA: The Journal of the American Medical Association* 262(11): 1510-1511 (September 15, 1989).

And now, a feminist full Court press. *U.S. News and World Report* 105(21):12-13 (November 28, 1988).

Annas, George J. The Supreme Court, privacy, and abortion. *New England Journal of Medicine* 321(17):1200-1203 (October 26, 1989).

Anti-abortion U.S.-style. [Editorial] *New Statesman and Society* 2(57):5 (July 7, 1989).

Baer, Donald. The politics of abortion takes an unexpected turn. *U.S. News and World Report* 107(5):26 (July 31, 1989).

Barone, Michael, and Ted Gest. Letting the people decide. *U.S. News and World Report* 107(2):18-19 (July 10, 1989).

Behuniak-Long, Susan. Justice Sandra Day O'Connor and the power of maternal legal thinking. *Review of Politics* 54(3):417-444 (Summer 1992).

Bernardin, Joseph L. The consistent ethic after 'Webster': opportunities and dangers. *Commonweal* 117(8):242-248 (April 20, 1990).

Bresler, Robert J. Abortion, politics, and the Supreme Court. [Editorial] *USA Today* 118(2536):7 (January 1990).

Canon, Bradley C. The Supreme Court as a cheerleader in politico-moral disputes. *Journal of Politics* 54(3):637-653 (August 1992).

Carey, Peter, Joanne Silberner, Ted Gest, Miriam Horn, and Jeffrey Sheler. Reappraising topic A. *U.S. News and World Report* 106(3):9-10 (January 23, 1989).

Carlson, Margaret, Jerome Cramer, Melissa Ludtke, and Elizabeth Taylor. Abortion's hardest cases. *Time* 136(2):22-26 (July 9, 1990).

Carlson, Margaret B., and Steven Holmes. The battle over abortion: a bitterly divided Supreme Court sets the stage for the most corrosive political fight since the debate over Viet Nam. *Time* 134(3):62-63 (July 17, 1989).

Cockburn, Alexander. Aborted justice: behind the Supreme Court ruling on abortion lies a history of subversion of American liberalism. *New Statesman and Society* 2(58):19-20 (July 14, 1989).

A "conservative Court" is still uncertain. *Christianity Today* 32(16):37 (November 4, 1988).

Copelon, Rhonda, and Kathryn Kolbert. Our bodies, our business: imperfect justice. *Ms.* 18(1-2):42-44 (July/August 1989).

————. The gathering storm: Roe v. Wade. *Ms.* 17(10):88-92 (April 1989).

Courting disaster. *Progressive* 53(8):7-8 (August 1989).

Cowden-Guido, Richard. The post-Webster press. *National Review* 42(22):36, 38-39 (November 19, 1990).

Dellinger, Walter. Day in court. *New Republic* 200(19):11-12 (May 8, 1989).

Dingle, Derek T. Affirmative action. *Black Enterprise* 20(2):42-48 (September 1989).

Doerr, Edd. Abortion rights after Webster. *Humanist* 50(1):41-42 (January/February 1990).

————. Abortion rights imperiled. *Humanist* 49(4):39 (July/August 1989).

————. Black Monday. *Humanist* 49(5):39 (September/October 1989).

————. The end of Roe v. Wade. *Humanist* 52(3):45-46 (May/June 1992).

————. Fundamental rights in danger. *Humanist* 49(3):39-40 (May/June 1989).

————. Looking back, looking forward. [Editorial] *Humanist* 51(5):41-42 (September/October 1991).

Dworkin, Ronald. The future of abortion. *New York Review of Books* 36(14):47-51 (September 28 1989).

————. The great abortion case. *New York Review of Books* 36(11):49-53 (June 29, 1989).

Ehrlich, Elizabeth. If pro-choice is mainstream, now's the time to prove it. [Editorial] *Business Week* (Industrial/Technology Edition) (3115):64 (July 17, 1989).

The end of Roe? *National Review* 41(5):12-13 (March 24, 1989).

Farber, Daniel A. Supreme Court review: the abortion decision. *Trial* 25(9):22-25 (September 1989).

Fein, Bruce. A court that obeys the law. *National Review* 41(18):50-51 (September 29, 1989).

The first march. *National Review* 41(8):9-10 (May 5, 1989).

Ford, Maurice deG. Rocking the Roe boat: hearing the Missouri case. *Commonweal* 116(11):326-328 (June 2, 1989).

Fowler, Jack. Abortion: law & politics: the war within the states. *National Review* 41(14):35-36 (August 4, 1989).

Goggin, Malcolm L. Understanding the new politics of abortion: a framework and agenda for research. *American Politics Quarterly* 21(1):4-30 (January 1993).

Gest, Ted. New abortion fights. *U.S. News and World Report* 106(16):22-26 (April 24, 1989).

Glendon, Mary Ann. A world without Roe. *New Republic* 200(8):19-20 (February 20, 1989).

Good news on abortion. *New Republic* 201(5):5-6 (July 31, 1989).

Grogan, David, Giovanna Breu, and Civia Tamarkin. Amid a raging debate, one woman chooses abortion. *People Weekly* 32(23):89-90, 92 (July 24, 1989).

Halpern, Sue M. The fight over teen-age abortion. *New York Review of Books* 37(5):30-32 (March 29, 1990).

Harrington-Lueker, Donna. The Supreme Court, abortion, and schools. *Education Digest* 55(7):40-42 (March 1990).

————. Supreme Court actions push a wrenching controversy straight at you. *American School Board Journal* 176(11):20-24 (November 1989).

Heim, David. Beyond rights in abortion politics. [Editorial] *Christian Century* 106(22):675-676 (July 19-26, 1989).

Holmes, Steven. Pro-choicers gird for battle: the Court prepares to hear a key abortion case. *Time* 133(4):55 (January 23, 1989).

Jacoby, Tamar, and Ann McDaniel. A new majority ticks off the Reagan agenda. *Newsweek* 114(3):26-27 (July 17, 1989).

Jaschik, Scott. Supreme Court ruling clears the way for states to limit abortions in hospitals affiliated with public universities. *Chronicle of Higher Education* 35(44):A1, A25 (July 12, 1989).

Johnson, Kirk. Webster v. Reproductive Health Services: the AMA position. *JAMA: The Journal of the American Medical Association* 262(11):1522 (September 15, 1989).

Kelly, James R. Winning Webster v. Reproductive Health Services: the crisis of the pro-life movement. *America* 161(4):79-83 (August 12-19, 1989).

Kondracke, Morton. The new abortion wars. *New Republic* 201(9):17-19 (August 28, 1989).

Lacayo, Richard, and Steven Holmes. A day of reckoning on Roe: the high court faces the abortion question—and asks a few. *Time* 133(19):24 (May 8, 1989).

Lacayo, Richard, Steven Holmes, Naushad S. Mehta, and Elizabeth Taylor. Whose life is it?: the long, emotional battle over abortion approaches a climax as the Supreme Court prepares for a historic challenge to Roe v. Wade. *Time* 133(18):20-24 (May 1, 1989).

LaFay, Laura, and James Earl Hardy. A court-watcher's guide. *Scholastic Update* 124(5):13-16 (November 1, 1991).

Last days of Roe? *National Review* 41(10):14, 16 (June 2, 1989).

Lawton, Kim A. Confrontation's stage is set. *Christianity Today* 33(11):36-38 (August 18, 1989).

————. Could this be the year? *Christianity Today* 33(6):36-38 (April 7, 1989).

————. Promises to keep. *Christianity Today* 33(2):44-45 (February 3, 1989).

Leo, John. The quagmire of abortion rights. [Editorial] *U.S. News and World Report* 113(2):16 (July 13, 1992).

The longer march. [Editorial] *Commonweal* 116(9):259-260 (May 5, 1989).

Marwick, Charles. Court backs states on abortion. *JAMA: The Journal of the American Medical Association* 262(4):451-452 (July 28, 1989).

McCormick, Richard A., Mary Ann Glendon, Fred Siegel, Sidney Callahan, Mary C. Segers, E. J. Dionne, Daniel Callahan, Juli Loesch Wiley, Annie Lally Milhaven, and Burke J. Balch. Abortion: what does 'Webster' mean? *Commonweal* 116(14):425-428 (August 11, 1989).

McDaniel, Ann. Countdown on abortion. *Newsweek* 113(4):50 (January 23, 1989).

————. The Court: Reagan's legal legacy. *Newsweek* 114(2):19-20 (July 10, 1989).

————. The future of abortion. *Newsweek* 114(3):14-16 (July 17, 1989).

————. Judicial flash points. *Newsweek* 116(5):18-19 (July 30, 1990).

McGuire, Kevin T., and Barbara Palmer. Issue fluidity on the U.S. Supreme Court. *American Political Science Review* 89(3):691-702 (September 1995).

Neff, David. Life after Webster. [Editorial] *Christianity Today* 33(11):14 (August 18, 1989).

Neuhaus, Richard John. After Roe. *National Review* 41(6):38-40 (April 7, 1989).

O'Hair, James P. Pulse: A brief history of abortion in the United States. *JAMA: The Journal of the American Medical Association* 262(13): 1875, 1878-1879 (October 6, 1989).

Pine, Rachael. Roe on the brink. [Editorial] *Nation* 249(4):112 (July 24-31, 1989).

Ponnuru, Ramesh. Aborting history. *National Review* 47(20):29-32 (October 23, 1995).

Rees, Grover Joseph. Abortion: law & politics: scourage or plot? *National Review* 41(14):34-35 (August 4, 1989).

Relin, David Oliver. Agonizing over abortion. *Scholastic Update* 122(16):2-3 (April 20, 1990).

'Roe' must stand. *Progressive* 53(3):6-7 (March 1989).

Rosenblum, Victor G. Letting the states set abortion policy. [Editorial] *Christian Century* 106(8):252-253 (March 8, 1989).

Rotunda, Ronald D. The Supreme Court: eschewing bright lines. *Trial* 25(12):52-56 (December 1989).

Sachs, Andrea, and Steven Holmes. Abortion on the ropes: is the historic Roe v. Wade ruling about to be overturned? *Time* 132(23):58-59 (December 5, 1988).

Salholz, Eloise, and Ann McDaniel. The abortion battlefield. *Newsweek* 112(22):44 (November 28, 1988).

Salholz, Eloise, Ann McDaniel, and Andrew Murr. Answering the High Court's invitation. *Newsweek* 115(14):39 (April 2, 1990).

Salholz, Eloise, Ann McDaniel, Patricia King, Nadine Joseph, Gregory Cerio, and Ginny Carroll. The battle over abortion. *Newsweek* 113(18):28-32 (May 1, 1989).

Salholz, Eloise, Ann McDaniel, and Sue Hutchinson. Pro-choice: 'a sleeping giant' awakes. *Newsweek* 113(17):39-40 (April 24, 1989).

Salholz, Eloise, Patricia King, Clara Bingham, and Nonny DeLa Pena. The right-to-lifers' new tactics. *Newsweek* 116(2):23 (July 9, 1990).

Salholz, Eloise, Patricia King, Kate Robins, Nadine Joseph, Nonny de la Pena, Lucille Beachy, and Gregory Cerio. Teenagers and abortion. *Newsweek* 115(2):32-36 (January 8, 1990).

Salholz, Eloise, Ann McDaniel, Patricia King, Erik Calonius, David L. Gonzalez, and Nadine Joseph. Voting in curbs and confusion. *Newsweek* 114(3):16-20 (July 17, 1989).

Schwartz, Herman. Sandra's day. [Editorial] *Nation* 249(5):156-157 (August 7-14, 1989).

Smart, Tim. Speak softly and carry a big right-wing agenda. *Business Week* (Industrial/Technology Edition) (3135):115-118 (November 27, 1989).

Spivack, Miranda S. Courting disaster. *Ms.* 17(7-8):138 (January/February 1989).

————. . . . and women's groups prepare for life after Roe. *Ms.* 2(5)91 (March/April 1992).

Supreme Court: reconsidering rights. *Economist* 309(7577):27-28 (November 19-25, 1988).

The thread and the cloth: arguments in the Supreme Court's abortion case. *Newsweek* 113(19):19 (May 8, 1989).

Too many abortions. [Editorial] *Commonweal* 116(14):419-420 (August 11, 1989).

Whitman, David. Abortion rights are intact—so far. *U.S. News and World Report* 109(12):52-53 (September 24, 1990).

Whitman, David, Ted Gest, and Ann E. Andrews. The abortion hype: alarmists were wrong; not much has changed since Webster. *U.S. News and World Report* 108(13):20-22 (April 2, 1990).

Will, George F. Splitting differences. [Editorial] *Newsweek* 113(7):86 (February 13, 1989).

Witt, Elder. On issues of state power, the Supreme Court seems to be of two minds. *Governing* 4(1):54-59, 63-64 (October 1990).

Woodman, Sue. Reproductive rights. *New Statesman and Society* 2(63):20-21 (August 18, 1989).

3379. County of Allegheny v. American Civil Liberties Union of Greater Pittsburgh Chapter   July 3, 1989
     Coupled with Chabad v. American Civil Liberties Union
     Coupled with City of Pittsburgh v. American Civil Liberties Union of Greater Pittsburgh Chapter
492 US 573   106 LEd2d 472   109 SCt 3086
Brennan 134-138
Center 235-256+
Const Law 94-100R
Godless 137, 139-140
Editorials (1989):774-779
Guide (CQ) 57-58
Landmark (v. 3):169-194R

Original (Davis) 161-162

Sup Ct Review (1989):373-402; (1992):123-153

Turning 248-251+, 296-297

Bates, Stephen. Ignore a menorah. *New Republic* 201(5):14-16 (July 31, 1989).

Byrne, Harry J. Thanksgiving Day and the Supreme Court. *America* 162(5):121-123 (February 10, 1990).

Castelli, Jim. Crèche on the plaza? There are no clear rules. *Governing* 3(3):56-57 (December 1989).

Chemerinsky, Erwin. Supreme Court review: free speech or religious freedom: revisiting the establishment clause. *Trial* 31(12):16-19 (December 1995).

―――. Supreme Court review: religion clause doctrine: potential for change. *Trial* 29(2):81-84 (February 1993).

Christmas in July. *America* 161(2):27 (July 15-22, 1989).

Conn, James J. Graduation prayers and the establishment clause. *America* 167(15):380-382 (November 14, 1992).

Court and crèche. *Christian Century* 106(23):713 (August 2-9, 1989).

Drinan, Robert F. Do crèches violate the Constitution? *America* 159(16):428-429 (November 26, 1988).

Lawton, Kim A. Confrontation's stage is set. *Christianity Today* 33(11):36-38 (August 18, 1989).

Leo, John. A secular Christmas to all! *U.S. News and World Report* 113(25):31 (December 28, 1992-January 4, 1993).

McGough, Michael. Menorah wars. *New Republic* 202(6):12-14 (February 5, 1990).

Ostling, Richard N., Steven Holmes, and Andrea Sachs. Is the Court hostile to religion?: a conservative bloc of justices speaks out on church and state. *Time* 134(3):80 (July 17, 1989).

Rotunda, Ronald D. The Supreme Court: eschewing bright lines. *Trial* 25(12):52-56 (December 1989).

Sendor, Benjamin. Deck the halls, but skip the creche and angels. *American School Board Journal* 176(10):12-13 (October 1989).

Stephenson, D. Grier, Jr. Religion and the Constitution: the Supreme Court speaks, again. *USA Today* 118(2538):21-23 (March 1990).

Sullivan, Catherine Beth. Are kosher food laws constitutionally kosher? *Boston College Environmental Affairs Law Review* 21(1):201-245 (Fall 1993).

3380. Northbrook National Insurance Co. v. Brewer   November 7, 1989
493 US 6   107 LEd2d 223   110 SCt 297

Sup Ct Yearbook (1989-90):38

Collins, Linda J. Supreme Court ruling boon to comp insurers. *Business Insurance* 23(46):2, 41 (November 13, 1989).

3381. Hallstrom v. Tillamook County   November 17, 1989
493 US 20   107 LEd2d 237   110 SCt 304

Sup Ct Yearbook (1989-90):58-59

3382. Michigan Citizens for an Independent Press v. Thornburgh   November 13, 1989
493 US 38   107 LEd2d 277   110 SCt 398

Fourth 212-221

Sup Ct Yearbook (1989-90):28-29

Barnett, Stephen R. The most serious threat is . . . the JOA scam. *Columbia Journalism Review* 30(4):47-48 (November/December 1991).

―――. Preserving newspapers or monopoly? *Nation* 249(15):513, 530-532 (November 6, 1989).

Fitzgerald, Mark. Detroit JOA was barely approved. *Editor and Publisher* 126(26):11 (June 26, 1993).

Fitzgerald, Mark, and George Garneau. Detroit JOA can go ahead—but will it? *Editor and Publisher* 122(12):17, 53 (March 25, 1989).

Garneau, George. JOA OK'd. *Editor and Publisher* 122(46):9, 34 (November 18, 1989).

―――. Supreme Court hears JOA arguments. *Editor and Publisher* 122(44):29, 41 (November 4, 1989).

―――. U.S. Supreme Court to hear Detroit JOA case. *Editor and Publisher* 122(18):10 (May 6, 1989).

High court rejects time-sharing for JOA hearing. *Editor and Publisher* 122(43):33 (October 28, 1989).

3383. Chesapeake and Ohio Railway Co. v. Schwalb   November 28, 1989
          Coupled with Norfolk and Western Railway Co. v. Goode
        493 US 40   107 LEd2d 278
                                                                                110 SCt 381
          Sup Ct Yearbook (1989-90):57

3384. United States v. Sperry Corp.   November 28, 1989
        493 US 52   107 LEd2d 290   110 SCt 387
          Sup Ct Yearbook (1989-90):68

3385. Breininger v. Sheet Metal Workers International Association, Local Union No. 6   December 5, 1989
        493 US 67   107 LEd2d 388   110 SCt 424
          Sup Ct Yearbook (1989-90):54
        Hukill, Craig. Labor and the Supreme Court: significant issues of 1989-90. *Monthly Labor Review* 113(1):30-
          34 (January 1990).
        ———. Significant decisions in labor cases: traditional labor relations. *Monthly Labor Review* 113(3):50-61
          (March 1990).

3386. Golden State Transit Corp. v. City of Los Angeles   December 5, 1989
        493 US 103   107 LEd2d 420   110 SCt 444
          Guide (West): (1991):266-267
          Sup Ct Yearbook (1989-90):55
        Cimini, Michael H. Developments in industrial relations: Supreme Court decisions. *Monthly Labor Review*
          113(4):45-46 (April 1990).
        Hukill, Craig. Significant decisions in labor cases: traditional labor relations. *Monthly Labor Review* 113(3):50-
          61 (March 1990).

3387. Pavelic and LeFlore v. Marvel Entertainment Group   December 5, 1989
        493 US 120   107 LEd2d 438   110 SCt 456
          Sup Ct Review (1990):231-256
          Sup Ct Yearbook (1989-90):30
        Joseph, Gregory P. Supreme Court shapes Rule 11: guidance to lower courts. *Trial* 26(9):65-67 (September
          1990).

3388. United States v. Goodyear Tire & Rubber Co.   December 11, 1989
        493 US 132   107 LEd2d 449   110 SCt 462
          Sup Ct Yearbook (1989-90):36
        Henrey, Robert. Goodyear affirms supremacy of U.S. tax accounting rules. *Journal of Taxation* 72(3):164-170
          (March 1990).

3389. John Doe Agency and John Doe Government Agency v. John Doe Corporation   December 11, 1989
        493 US 146   107 LEd2d 462   110 SCt 471
          Sup Ct Yearbook (1989-90):64
        Garneau, George. Supreme Court expands government's authority to withhold records under FoIA. *Editor and
          Publisher* 122(50):16, 37 (December 16, 1989).

3390. Hoffmann-La Roche, Inc. v. Sperling   December 11, 1989
        493 US 165   107 LEd2d 480   110 SCt 482
          Sup Ct Yearbook (1989-90):52
        Cimini, Michael H. Developments in industrial relations: Supreme Court decisions. *Monthly Labor Review*
          113(4):45-46 (April 1990).
        Hukill, Craig. Labor and the Supreme Court: significant issues of 1989-90. *Monthly Labor Review* 113(1):30-
          34 (January 1990).

3391. University of Pennsylvania v. Equal Employment Opportunity Commission   January 9, 1990
        493 US 182   107 LEd2d 571   110 SCt 577

Almanac (1990):53, 623

Sup Ct Yearbook (1989-90):52-53

Blum, Debra E. Supreme Court rejects privacy claim for tenure files, says university must disclose information in bias case. *Chronicle of Higher Education* 36(18):A1, A17 (January 17, 1990).

Galle, William P., Jr., Clifford M. Koen, Jr., and Mary W. Gray. Tenure and promotion after Penn vs. EEOC. *Academe* 79(5):19-26 (September/October 1993).

Hanson, David. Supreme Court allows subpoena of tenure files. *Chemical and Engineering News* 68(3):5 (January 15, 1990).

Hukill, Craig. Significant decisions in labor cases: tenure decisions. *Monthly Labor Review* 113(5):52-53, 54 (May 1990).

Lee, Barbara A. The Supreme Court's U. of Pennsylvania ruling does not sound the death knell for peer review. [Editorial] *Chronicle of Higher Education* 36(19):B1, B3 (January 24, 1990).

Mooney, Carolyn J. Academics are divided over High-Court ruling on tenure documents. *Chronicle of Higher Education* 36(19):A1, A18 (January 24, 1990).

Murphy, Betty Southard, Wayne E. Barlow, and D. Diane Hatch. Tenure decisions under Title VII. *Personnel Journal* 69(4):27-28, 31 (April 1990).

Rabban, David M. A functional analysis of "individual" and "institutional" academic freedom under the First Amendment. *Law and Contemporary Problems* 53(3):227-301 (Summer 1990).

Sanders, Alain L., Jerome Cramer, and Andrea Sachs. A controversial quartet: the court tackles tenure, sex, housing and criminal law. *Time* 135(4):53 (January 22, 1990).

Scales, Ann C., William W. Van Alstyne, Mary W. Gray, Joel T. Rosenthal, James O. Freedman, Elizabeth Bartholet, and Julius G. Getman. University of Pennsylvania v. EEOC and the status of peer review: a symposium. *Academe* 76(3):31-35 (May/June 1990).

Sendor, Benjamin. Temper evaluation candor with discretion. *American School Board Journal* 177(4):8 (April 1990).

Text of Court's decision upholding federal agency's right to examine tenure files. *Chronicle of Higher Education* 36(18):A17-A21R (January 17, 1990).

3392. Commissioner of Internal Revenue v. Indianapolis Power & Light Co.   January 9, 1990
        493 US 203   107 LEd2d 591   110 SCt 589

        Sup Ct Yearbook (1989-90):34

Lynch, James M. Indianapolis Power & Light Company: issues and planning opportunities where the government seeks the acceleration of income. *Taxes* 68(12):931-944 (December 1990).

Persellin, Mark B., and Brian R. Greenstein. Supreme Court's ruling in Indianapolis Power clarifies security deposit issue. *Taxes* 68(6):426-433 (June 1990).

Seago, W. Eugene. Supreme Court adopts loan vs. advance payment test for customer deposits. *Journal of Taxation* 72(4):204-208 (April 1990).

Supreme Court rules that deposits paid to utility were not taxable income. *Practical Accountant* 23(4):6, (April 1990).

3393. F.W./PBS, Inc. dba Paris Adult Bookstores II v. City of Dallas   January 9, 1990
            Coupled with M.J.R., Inc. v. City of Dallas
            Coupled with Berry v. City of Dallas
        493 US 215   107 LEd2d 603   110 SCt 596

        Sup Ct Yearbook (1989-90):64

Sanders, Alain L., Jerome Cramer, and Andrea Sachs. A controversial quartet: the court tackles tenure, sex, housing and criminal law. *Time* 135(4):53 (January 22, 1990).

Witt, Elder. Will the Supreme Court relax the federal grip on state and local government? *Governing* 3(1):21-23, 25-29 (October 1989).

3394. Spallone v. United States   January 10, 1990
            Coupled with Chema v. United States
            Coupled with Longo v. United States
        493 US 265   107 LEd2d 644   110 SCt 625
        Almanac (1990):53

Sup Ct Yearbook (1989-90):7-10, 22-24, 63, 77-88R

Deegan, Glenn E. Judicial enforcement of state and municipal compliance with the Clean Water Act: can the courts succeed? *Boston College Environmental Affairs Law Review* 19(4):765-803 (Summer 1992).

Metro trends: High Court: sanction city first. *National Civic Review* 79(1):79-80 (January/February 1990).

Sanders, Alain L., Jerome Cramer, and Andrea Sachs. A controversial quartet: the court tackles tenure, sex, housing and criminal law. *Time* 135(4):53 (January 22, 1990).

Taking the activist bench down a peg. *U.S. News and World Report* 108(3):13-14 (January 22, 1990).

Wise, Charles,and Rosemary O'Leary. Is federalism dead or alive in the Supreme Court?: implications for public administrators. *Public Administration Review* 52(6):559-572 (November/December 1992).

Witt, Elder. On issues of state power, the Supreme Court seems to be of two minds. *Governing* 4(1):54-59, 63-64 (October 1990).

————. Will the Supreme Court relax the federal grip on state and local government? *Governing* 3(1):21-23, 25-29 (October 1989).

3395. James v. Illinois   January 10, 1990
       493 US 307   107 LEd2d 676   110 SCt 648
       Sup Ct Yearbook (1989-90):44

Justice Marshall dissents in ruling that jurors may be excluded by race. *Jet* 77(19):28 (February 19, 1990).

O'Sullivan, John. The swinging Court. *National Review* 42(2):10 (February 5, 1990).

Sanders, Alain L., Jerome Cramer, and Andrea Sachs. A controversial quartet: the court tackles tenure, sex, housing and criminal law. *Time* 135(4):53 (January 22, 1990).

3396. Franchise Tax Board v. Alcan Aluminium, Ltd.   January 10, 1990
       493 US 331   107 LEd2d 696   110 SCt 661
       Sup Ct Yearbook (1989-90):35

Witt, Elder. Threatening tax cases. *Governing* 3(1):26 (October 1989).

3397. Dowling v. United States   January 10, 1990
       493 US 342   107 LEd2d 708   110 SCt 668
       Sup Ct Yearbook (1989-90):43

3398. Guidry v. Sheet Metal Workers National Pension Fund   January 17, 1990
       493 US 365   107 LEd2d 782   110 SCt 680
       Sup Ct Yearbook (1989-90):56

Hukill, Craig. Labor and the Supreme Court: significant issues of 1989-90. *Monthly Labor Review* 113(1):30-34 (January 1990).

3399. Jimmy Swaggart Ministries v. Board of Equaliziation of California   January 17, 1990
       493 US 378   107 LEd2d 796   110 SCt 688
       Godless 115-116
       Sup Ct Review (1990):1-68
       Sup Ct Yearbook (1989-90):35

Gest, Ted. The Court's new catechism. *U.S. News and World Report* 108(24):22 (June 18, 1990).

Lesly, Elizabeth, and Elliott Beard. Pennies from Heaven. *Washington Monthly* 23(4):40-45 (April 1991).

Praise the Lord but render unto Caesar. *Newsweek* 115(5):75 (January 29, 1990).

Right to life, church-state cases before Court. *Christianity Today* 33(14):44-46 (October 6, 1989).

States may tax Bible sales. *Christianity Today* 34(3):37 (February 19, 1990).

Supreme Court upholds California sales tax on religious items. *Taxes* 68(6):161 (February 1990).

3400. W.S. Kirkpatrick and Co. v. Environmental Tectonics Corp., International   January 17, 1990
       493 US 400   107 LEd2d 816   110 SCt 701
       Sup Ct Review (1990):133-161
       Sup Ct Yearbook (1989-90):37-38

3401. Federal Trade Commission (FTC) v. Superior Court Trial Lawyers Association
        January 22, 1990
    493 US 411   107 LEd2d 394   110 SCt 768
    Sup Ct Yearbook (1989-90):28

3402. Tafflin v. Levitt   January 22, 1990
    493 US 455   107 LEd2d 887   110 SCt 792
    Sup Ct Yearbook (1989-90):38

3403. Holland v. Illinois   January 22, 1990
    493 US 474   107 LEd2d 905   110 SCt 803
    Sup Ct Yearbook (1989-90):41-42

3404. Sullivan, Secretary of Health and Human Services v. Zebley   February 20, 1990
    493 US 521   107 LEd2d 967   110 SCt 885
    Sup Ct Yearbook (1989-90):61

3405. Baltimore City Department of Social Services v. Bouknight   February 20, 1990
            Coupled with Maurice M. v. Bouknight
    493 US 549   107 LEd2d 992   110 SCt 900
    Guide (West): (1991):350-352, 719-733R
    Sup Ct Yearbook (1989-90):50-51
Marshall dissents in High Court's ruling on woman's right to withhold info. *Jet* 77(22):18 (March 12, 1990).
Rosenblatt, Leonard R. The Fifth Amendment and the production of business records: and Braswell Begat
    Bouknight. *Taxes* 68(6):418-424 (June 1990).
Ruffing, Elizabeth J. Supreme Court review: Fifth Amendment—preventing an abusive parent from hiding
    behind the self-incrimination privilege. *Journal of Criminal Law and Criminology* 81(4):926-951 (Winter
    1991).
Witt, Elder. Will the Supreme Court relax the federal grip on state and local government? *Governing* 3(1):21-
    23, 25-29 (October 1989).

3406. Preseault v. Interstate Commerce Commission (ICC) February 21, 1990
    494 US 1   108 LEd2d 1   110 SCt 914
    Sup Ct Yearbook (1989-90):67-68

3407. Dole v. United Steelworkers of America   February 21, 1990
    494 US 26   108 LEd2d 23   110 SCt 929
    Almanac (1990):53, 412; (1994):154-155; (1995):3-20-21
    Sup Ct Yearbook (1989-90):59-60
Court revives haz com rules. *ENR* 224(9):12 (March 1, 1990).
Hukill, Craig. Labor and the Supreme Court: significant issues of 1989-90. *Monthly Labor Review* 113(1):30-
    34 (January 1990).

3408. Reves v. Ernst and Young   February 21, 1990
    494 US 56   108 LEd2d 47   110 SCt 945
    Sup Ct Yearbook (1989-90):33

3409. Sullivan, Secretary of Health and Human Services v. Everhart   February 21, 1990
    494 US 83   108 LEd2d 72   110 SCt 960
    Sup Ct Yearbook (1989-90):60

3410. Zinermon v. Burch   February 27, 1990
    494 US 113   108 LEd2d 100   110 SCt 975
    Sup Ct Yearbook (1989-90):63
Farber, Daniel A. Supreme Court review: rights of the mentally ill. *Trial* 26(5):18+ (May 1990).

3411. Lawrence H. Crandon v. United States   February 27, 1990
    494 US 152   108 LEd2d 132   110 SCt 997
    Almanac (1990):53
    Sup Ct Yearbook (1989-90):53-54
    Hukill, Craig. Labor and the Supreme Court: significant issues of 1989-90. *Monthly Labor Review* 113(1):30-34 (January 1990).
    ———. Significant decisions in labor cases: severance payments. *Monthly Labor Review* 113(6):65-66 (June 1990).
    Supreme Court rules Boeing severance payments were legal. *Aviation Week and Space Technology* 132(10):33 (March 5, 1990).

3412. Carden v. Arkoma Associates   February 27, 1990
    494 US 185   108 LEd2d 157   110 SCt 1015
    Sup Ct Yearbook (1989-90):36-37

3413. Washington v. Walter Harper   February 27, 1990
    494 US 210   108 LEd2d 178   110 SCt 1028
    Almanac (1990):53
    Sup Ct Yearbook (1989-90):43
    Bersoff, Donald N., and David W. Ogden. APA amicus curiae briefs: furthering lesbian and gay male civil rights. *American Psychologist* 46(9):950-956 (September 1991).
    Farber, Daniel A. Supreme Court review: rights of the mentally ill. *Trial* 26(5):18+ (May 1990).
    Sainsbury, Jeffrey. Moral meltdown. *New Statesman and Society* 4(153):20 (May 31, 1991).
    Sindel, Patricia E. Supreme Court review: Fourteenth Amendment—the right to refuse antipsychotic drugs masked by prison bars. *Journal of Criminal Law and Criminology* 81(4):952-980 (Winter 1991).

3414. United States v. Rene Martin Verdugo-Urquidez   February 28, 1990
    494 US 259   108 LEd2d 222   110 SCt 1056
    Sup Ct Review (1990):133-161
    Sup Ct Yearbook (1989-90):50
    Turning 318-320
    Rosenberg, Leonard X. Supreme Court review: Fourth Amendment—search and seizure of property abroad: erosion of the rights of aliens. *Journal of Criminal Law and Criminology* 81(4):779-799 (Winter 1991).

3415. Blystone v. Pennsylvania   Febrary 28, 1990
    494 US 299   108 LEd2d 255   110 SCt 1078
    Death Penalty (Tushnet) 59-60, 71-72
    Death Penalty 90s 11-14
    Sup Ct Yearbook (1989-90):39
    Murphy, Cornelius F. The Supreme Court and capital punishment: a new hands-off approach. *USA Today* 121(2574):51-52 (March 1993).

3416. Maryland v. Buie   February 28, 1990
    494 US 325   108 LEd2d 276   110 SCt 1093
    Sup Ct Yearbook (1989-90):48-49
    Sifferlen, Mark J. Supreme Court review: Fourth Amendment—protective sweep doctrine: when does the Fourth Amendment allow police officers to search the home incident to a lawful arrest? *Journal of Criminal Law and Criminology* 81(4):862-882 (Winter 1991).

3417. Michigan v. Harvey   March 5, 1990
    494 US 344   108 LEd2d 293   110 SCt 1176
    Sup Ct Yearbook (1989-90):42

3418. Boyde v. Califonria   March 5, 1990
    494 US 370   108 LEd2d 316   110 SCt 1190

Sup Ct Yearbook (1989-90):39

3419. Butler v. McKellar
    494 US 407   108 LEd2d 347
March 5, 1990
110 SCt 1212
    Almanac (1990):488-489
    Brennan 238-240
    Death Penalty 90s 19-21
    Sup Ct Yearbook (1989-90):45
    Weisberg, Robert. A great writ while it lasted. *Journal of Criminal Law and Criminology* 81(1):9-36 (Spring 1990).

3420. Dock McKoy, Jr. v. North Carolina
    494 US 433   108 LEd2d 369
March 5, 1990
110 SCt 1227
    Sup Ct Yearbook (1989-90):40
    George, Tracey E., and Lee Epstein. On the nature of Supreme Court decision making. *American Political Science Review* 86(2):323-337 (June 1992).
    Murphy, Cornelius F. The Supreme Court and capital punishment: a new hands-off approach. *USA Today* 121(2574):51-52 (March 1993).
    Setting ahead the clock on death row. *U.S. News and World Report* 108(11):14-15 (March 19, 1990).

3421. Lewis, Comptroller of the State of Florida v. Continental Bank Corp.
    494 US 472   108 LEd2d 400
March 5, 1990
110 SCt 1249
    Sup Ct Yearbook (1989-90):32

3422. Saffle v. Parks
    494 US 484   108 LEd2d 415
March 5, 1990
110 SCt 1257
    Almanac (1990):488-489
    Sup Ct Yearbook (1989-90):45-46
    Weisberg, Robert. A great writ while it lasted. *Journal of Criminal Law and Criminology* 81(1):9-36 (Spring 1990).

3423. Ferens v. John Deere Co.
    494 US 516   108 LEd2d 443
March 5, 1990
110 SCt 1274
    Sup Ct Yearbook (1989-90):37

3424. Lytle v. Household Manufacturing, Inc., Schwitzer Turbo-chargers
    494 US 545   108 LEd2d 504
March 20, 1990
110 SCt 1331
    Sup Ct Yearbook (1989-90):52

3425. Chauffeurs, Teamsters and Helpers, Local No. 391 v. Terry
March 20, 1990
    Chauffeurs, Local No. 391 v. Terry
    494 US 558   108 LEd2d 519
110 SCt 1339
    Sup Ct Yearbook (1989-90):54
    Hukill, Craig. Labor and the Supreme Court: significant issues of 1989-90. *Monthly Labor Review* 113(1):30-34 (January 1990).

3426. United States v. Dalm
    494 US 596   108 LEd2d 548
March 20, 1990
110 SCt 1361
    Sup Ct Yearbook (1989-90):36
    Kafka, Gerald A. Equitable recoupment after Dalm: sustained, but clarified and narrowed. *Journal of Taxation* 72(6):340-344 (June 1990).
    Stein, Ronald A. Will equitable tolling of the statute of limitations gain wider acceptance in tax cases? *Journal of Taxation* 81(6):370-375 (December 1994).

3427. Butterworth v. Smith   March 21, 1990
      494 US 624   108 LEd2d 572   110 SCt 1376
        Sup Ct Yearbook (1989-90):64
      Garneau, George. Reporter gets High Court approval: U.S. Supreme Court strikes down part of Florida law that
        prevented him from reporting on his testimony to a grand jury. *Editor and Publisher* 123(13):27 (March 31,
        1990).

3428. Adams Fruit Co. v. Ramsford Barrett   March 21, 1990
      494 US 638   108 LEd2d 585   110 SCt 1384
        Almanac (1992):638; (1995):8-5-6
        Sup Ct Yearbook (1989-90):57
      Fletcher, Meg. High Court says migrant workers can sue firms for work injuries. *Business Insurance* 24(15):3,
        7 (April 9, 1990).
      Hukill, Craig. Labor and the Supreme Court: significant issues of 1989-90. *Monthly Labor Review* 113(1):30-
        34 (January 1990).
      ———. Significant decisions in labor cases: migrant labor. *Monthly Labor Review* 113(7):47-49 (July 1990).
      Sachs, Andrea, and Jerome Cramer. A victory for integration: the court rules on civil rights, privacy and labor
        relations. *Time* 135(18):85 (April 30, 1990).

3429. Austin, Michigan Secretary of State v. Michigan State Chamber of Commerce   March 27, 1990
      494 US 652   108 LEd2d 652   110 SCt 1391
        Almanac (1990):52-53, 61
        Sup Ct Review (1990):105-132
        Sup Ct Yearbook (1989-90):63-64
        Turning 328-329
      Bork, Robert H. An end to political judging? *National Review* 42(25);30-32 (December 31, 1990).
      Kinsley, Michael. Are companies people? *New Republic* 202(19):6 (May 7, 1990).
      Powe, L. A., Jr. Mass communications and the First Amendment: an overview. *Law and Contemporary
        Problems* 55(1):53-76 (Winter 1992).

3430. United States Department of Labor v. Triplett   March 27, 1990
      494 US 715   108 LEd2d 701   110 SCt 1428
        Sup Ct Yearbook (1989-90):51

3431. Clemons v. Mississippi   March 28, 1990
      494 US 738   108 Led2d 725   110 SCt 1441
        Sup Ct Yearbook (1989-90):39-40
      Gest, Ted. The new Supreme Court term may disappoint conservatives. *U.S. News and World Report* 107(13):
        31 (October 2, 1989).

3432. National Labor Relations Board (NLRB) v. Curtin Matheson Scientific, Inc.   April 17, 1990
      494 US 775   108 LEd2d 801   110 SCt 1542
        Sup Ct Yearbook (1989-90):55
      Cimini, Michael H. Developments in industrial relations: strike replacements. *Monthly Labor Review* 113(6):56
        (July 1990).
      Hukill, Craig. Significant decisions in labor cases: replacement workers. *Monthly Labor Review* 113(7):46, 48
        (July 1990).
      ———. Labor and the Supreme Court: significant issues of 1989-90. *Monthly Labor Review* 113(1):30-34
        (January 1990).

3433. Yellow Freight System, Inc. v. Donnelly   April 17, 1990
      494 US 820   108 LEd2d 834   110 SCt 1566
        Sup Ct Yearbook (1989-90):53
      Smart, Tim. The verdict on the last term: 'generally, business lost.' *Business Week* (Industrial/Technology
        Edition) (3169):30 (July 16, 1990).

3434. Kaiser Aluminum and Chemical Corp. v. Bonjorno   April 17, 1990
    494 US 827   108 LEd2d 842   110 SCt 1570
    Sup Ct Yearbook (1989-90):37

3435. Employment Division, Department of Human Resources of Oregon v. Alfred L. Smith   April 17, 1990
    494 US 872   108 LEd2d 876   110 SCt 1595
    Almanac (1992):332; (1993):315, 331; (1994):378-379
    Const Law 52-54
    Godless 129-133+
    Let Us 140-146
    Original (Davis) xii-xiv, 123-128, 155-156+
    Sup Ct Review (1990):1-68; (1992):123-153; (1995):1-43, 323-391
    Sup Ct Yearbook (1989-90):7-10, 15-17, 66, 88-102R; (1991-92):179-181; (1992-93):78-79
    Turning 321-326

Animal sacrifice case. *Christian Century* 109(13):393-394 (April 15, 1992).

Cerne, Kathleen M. Honor thy creditors? The religious debtor's constitutional conflict with Section 1325(b). *Business Credit* 96(3):37-40 (March 1994).

Chemerinsky, Erwin. Supreme Court review: religion clause doctrine: potential for change. *Trial* 29(2):81-84 (February 1993).

Church and state: necessary sacrifice? *Economist* 325(7785):28 (November 14-20, 1992).

Court considers animal sacrifice, airport witnessing. *Christianity Today* 36(5):46-47 (April 27, 1992).

Drinan, Robert F. A glimmer of hope for aid to Catholic schools. *America* 169(7):4-5 (September 18, 1993).

———. Religious freedom and the incoming Congress. *America* 163(20):512-514 (December 22-29, 1990).

Eastland, Terry. Religion, politics & the Clintons. *Commentary* 97(1):40-43 (January 1994).

Gaffney, Edward McGlynn, Jr. Animal sacrifice and religious freedom. [Editorial] *Christian Century* 109(15):508-510 (May 13, 1992).

———. Pass the peyote. *Commonweal* 121(2):5-6 (January 28, 1994).

Gest, Ted. The Court's new catechism. *U.S. News and World Report* 108(24):22 (June 18, 1990).

———. Next stage: Court lite. *U.S. News and World Report* 111(2):16-19 (July 8, 1991).

———. Reining in citizens' rights: Rehnquist Court will reinterpret the 200-year-old Bill of Rights. *U.S. News and World Report* 111(25):49-53 (December 16, 1991).

Gibbs, Nancy R., David Aikman, and Richard N. Ostling. America's holy war. *Time* 138(23):60-68 (December 9, 1991).

Greenawalt, Kent. Free speech in the United States and Canada. *Law and Contemporary Problems* 55(1):5-33 (Winter 1992).

Greenlaw, Paul S., and John P. Kohl. Religious freedom and unemployment compensation benefits. *Public Personnel Management* 24(3):315-330 (Fall 1995).

Hentoff, Nat. A blow to freedom of religion. *Progressive* 54(12):16-17 (December 1990).

Indian religion: must say no. *Economist* 317(7675):25-26 (October 6-12, 1990).

Laycock, Douglas. Peyote, wine and the First Amendment. *Christian Century* 106(28):876-880 (October 4, 1989).

———. Watering down the free-exercise clause. [Editorial] *Christian Century* 107(17):518-519 (May 16-23, 1990).

Neuhaus, Richard John. Church, state, and peyote. *National Review* 42(11):40-42, 44 (June 11, 1990).

O'Brien, David M. The framers' muse on republicanism, the Supreme Court, and pragmatic constitutional interpretivism. *Review of Politics* 53(2):251-288 (Spring 1991).

Rabkin, Jeremy. The curious case of Kiryas Joel. *Commentary* 98(5):58-61 (November 1994).

Regan, Richard J. Supreme Court roundup: 1987 term. *Thought* 64(253):176-187 (June 1989).

Religion and the 103rd Congress. *Christian Century* 110(1):7-8 (January 6-13, 1993).

Rosen, Jeffrey. Blood ritual. *New Republic* 207(19):9-10 (November 2, 1992).

———. The leader of the opposition. *New Republic* 208(3):20-21, 24, 26-27 (January 18, 1993).

Sachs, Andrea, and Jerome Cramer. A victory for integration: the court rules on civil rights, privacy and labor relations. *Time* 135(18):85 (April 30, 1990).

Schwartz, Herman. The Souter factor: the majority at the Supreme Court. *Nation* 251(12):410-413 (October 15, 1990).

Sendor, Benjamin. Congress steps in where the Court fears to tread. *American School Board Journal* 181(1):12-13 (January 1994).

Sullivan, Catherine Beth. Are kosher food laws constitutionally kosher? *Boston College Environmental Affairs Law Review* 21(1):201-245 (Fall 1993).

3436. Department of Treasury, Internal Revenue Service v. Federal Labor Relations Authority   April 17, 1990
   494 US 922   108 LEd2d 914   110 SCt 1623
   Sup Ct Yearbook (1989-90):54-55
   Hukill, Craig. Labor and the Supreme Court: significant issues of 1989-90. *Monthly Labor Review* 113(1):30-34 (January 1990).

3437. Florida v. Wells   April 18, 1990
   495 US 1   109 LEd2d 1   110 SCt 1632
   Sup Ct Yearbook (1989-90):48
   King, Clayton E. Supreme Court review: Fourth Amendment—toward police discretion in determining the scope of administrative searches. *Journal of Criminal Law and Criminology* 81(4):841-861 (Winter 1991).
   Misner, Robert L. Justifying searches on the basis of equality of treatment. *Journal of Criminal Law and Criminology* 82(3):547-578 (Fall 1991).

3438. New York v. Bernard Harris   April 18, 1990
   495 US 14   109 LEd2d 13   110 SCt 1640
   Sup Ct Yearbook (1989-90):44
   Halberstam, Malvina. Agora: international kidnaping—in defense of the Supreme Court decision in Alvarez-Machain. *American Journal of International Law* 86(4):736-746 (October 1992).

3439. Missouri v. Jenkins   April 18, 1990
   495 US 33   105 LEd2d 229   109 SCt 2463
   Almanac (1990):53
   Guide (West): (1991):317-329, 687-715R, 716-718
   Sup Ct Yearbook (1989-90):7-10, 20-21, 62, 102-112R
   Bork, Robert H. An end to political judging? *National Review* 42(25):30-32 (December 31, 1990).
   The Court as interior decorator. *National Review* 42(1):18 (January 22, 1990).
   Courting trouble. *National Review* 47(13):16-18 (July 10, 1995).
   Deegan, Glenn E. Judicial enforcement of state and municipal compliance with the Clean Water Act: can the courts succeed? *Boston College Environmental Affairs Law Review* 19(4):765-803 (Summer 1992).
   Frederickson, H. George. Public administration and social equity. *Public Administration Review* 50(2):228-237 (March/April 1990).
   Hukill, Craig. Labor and the Supreme Court: significant issues of 1990-91. *Monthly Labor Review* 114(1):34-40 (January 1991).
   Hyde, Alison A. School desegregation: the role of the courts and means of achievement. *NASSP Bulletin* 78(565):28-37 (November 1994).
   Judicial taxation. *National Review* 42(9):18-19 (May 14, 1990).
   Kansas City rights leaders praise Court's decision. *Jet* 78(4):4 (May 7, 1990).
   Kaplan, David A. Byron White leads the Court to a pair of tough rulings: judge-ordered taxes—yes; kiddie porn—no. *Newsweek* 115(18):62 (April 30, 1990).
   Levitan, Donald. Public finance: move over state and local governments—here comes the Supreme Court! *National Civic Review* 79(4):387-388 (July/August 1990).
   O'Leary, Rosemary, and Charles R. Wise. Public managers, judges, and legislators: redefining the "new partnership." *Public Administration Review* 51(4):316-327 (July/August 1991).
   Rapp, David. The High Court and the new balance of power. *Governing* 6(8):68 (May 1993).
   Russo, Charles J., J. John Harris III, and Rosetta F. Sandidge. Brown v. Board of Education at 40: a legal history of equal educational opportunity in American public education. *Journal of Negro Education* 63(3):297-309 (Summer 1994).
   Sachs, Andrea, and Jerome Cramer. A victory for integration: the Court rules on civil rights, privacy and labor relations. *Time* 135(18):85 (April 30, 1990).

Sanders, Alain L., Jerome Cramer, and Janice C. Simpson. Enter, stage right: cast conservatively, the Court returns for a busy new session. *Time* 134(15):83-85 (October 9, 1989).

Wise, Charles, and Rosemary O'Leary. Is federalism dead or alive in the Supreme Court?: implications for public administrators. *Public Administration Review* 52(6):559-572 (November/December 1992).

Witt, Elder. On issues of state power, the Supreme Court seems to be of two minds. *Governing* 4(1):54-59, 63-64 (October 1990).

————. Will the Supreme Court relax the federal grip on state and local government? *Governing* 3(1):21-23, 25-29 (October 1989).

3440. Venegas v. Mitchell		April 18, 1990
495 US 82	109 LEd2d 74	110 SCt 1679
Sup Ct Yearbook (1989-90):31		

3441. Minnesota v. Olson		April 18, 1990
495 US 91	109 LEd2d 85	110 SCt 1684
Sup Ct Yearbook (1989-90):49		

3442. Osborne v. Ohio		April 18, 1990
495 US 103	109 LEd2d 98	110 SCt 1691
Almanac (1990):53		
Sup Ct Yearbook (1989-90):65		

Fields, Howard. Supreme Court, 6-3, bans possession of child porn. *Publishers' Weekly* 237(18):10 (May 4, 1990).

Kaplan, David A. Byron White leads the Court to a pair of tough rulings: judge-ordered taxes—yes; kiddie porn—no. *Newsweek* 115(18):62 (April 30, 1990).

Reuter, Madalynne. Give and take. *Publishers' Weekly* 238(1):33 (January 4, 1991).

Sachs, Andrea, and Jerome Cramer. A victory for integration: the Court rules on civil rights, privacy and labor relations. *Time* 135(18):85 (April 30, 1990).

Sanders, Alain L., Jerome Cramer, and Janice C. Simpson. Enter, stage right: cast conservatively, the court returns for a busy new session. *Time* 134(15):83-85 (October 9, 1989).

3443. Whitmore v. Arkansas		April 24, 1990
495 US 149	109 LEd2d 135	110 SCt 1717
Letting Go 76-78		
Sup Ct Yearbook (1989-90):40		

Brown, Paul F. Supreme Court review: third party standing—"next friends" as enemies: third party petitions for capital defendants wishing to waive appeal. *Journal of Criminal Law and Criminology* 81(4):981-1001 (Winter 1991).

3444. Ngiraingas v. Sanchez		Apil 24, 1990
495 US 182	109 LEd2d 163	110 SCt 1737
Sup Ct Yearbook (1989-90):63		

3445. Stewart v. Abend, Authors Research Co.		April 24, 1990
495 US 207	109 LEd2d 184	110 SCt 1750
Sup Ct Yearbook (1989-90):33-34		

3446. United States v. Ojeda Rios		April 30, 1990
495 US 257	109 LEd2d 224	110 SCt 1845
Sup Ct Yearbook (1989-90):42-43		

3447. California v. American Stores Co.		April 30, 1990
495 US 271	109 LEd2d 240	110 SCt 1853
Sup Ct Yearbook (1989-90):27-28		

Foust, Dean, and Tim Smart. The merger parade runs into a brick wall. *Business Week* (Industrial/Technology Edition) (3159):38 (May 14, 1990).

Sesser, Gary D. Just who's in charge here? [Editorial] *Across the Board* 28(7-8):11-13 (July/August 1991).

Smart, Tim. The verdict on the last term: 'generally, business lost.' *Business Week* (Industrial/Technology Edition) (3169):30 (July 16, 1990).

Smart, Tim, and Grover, Ronald. Pumping up a state's power to bust trusts. *Business Week* (Industrial/Technology Edition) (3141):25 (January 15, 1990).

3448. Port Authority Trans-Hudson Corp. v. Feeney | April 30, 1990
   Coupled with Port Authority Trans-Hudson Corp. v. Foster
   495 US 299 | 109 LEd2d 264 | 110 SCt 1868
   Sup Ct Yearbook (1989-90):68

3449. United Steelworkers v. Rawson | May 14, 1990
   495 US 326 | 109 LEd2d 362 | 110 SCt 1904
   Sup Ct Yearbook (1989-90):55-56

Hukill, Craig. Significant decisions in labor cases: union liability. *Monthly Labor Review* 113(5):53-54 (May 1990).

3450. Atlantic Richfield Co. v. USA Petroleum Co. | May 4, 1990
   495 US 328 | 109 LEd2d 333 | 110 SCt 1884
   Sup Ct Yearbook (1989-90):21

3451. United States v. Munoz-Flores | May 21, 1990
   495 US 385 | 109 LEd2d 384 | 110 SCt 1964
   Sup Ct Yearbook (1989-90):38

3452. Hughey v. United States | May 21, 1990
   495 US 411 | 109 LEd2d 408 | 110 SCt 1979
   Sup Ct Yearbook (1989-90):47

3453. North Dakota v. United States | May 21, 1990
   495 US 423 | 109 LEd2d 420 | 110 SCt 1986
   Sup Ct Yearbook (1989-90):68

3454. Davis v. United States | May 21, 1990
   495 US 472 | 109 LEd2d 457 | 110 SCt 2014
   Sup Ct Yearbook (1989-90):34-35

Teitell, Conrad. The Supreme Court rules that parents cannot deduct living expenses for their missionary children. *Trusts and Estates* 129(9):54-57, 60 (September 1990).

3455. California v. Federal Energy Regulatory Commission (FERC) | May 21, 1990
   495 US 490 | 109 LEd2d 474 | 110 SCt 2024
   Sup Ct Yearbook (1989-90):59

3456. Grady v. Corbin | May 29, 1990
   495 US 508 | 109 LEd2d 548 | 110 SCt 2084
   Sup Ct Yearbook (1989-90):43-44; (1992-93):60

Donofrio, Anthony J. Supreme Court review: the double jeopardy clause of the Fifth Amendment—the Supreme Court's cursory treatment of underlying conduct in successive prosecutions. *Journal of Criminal Law and Criminology* 83(4):773-803 (Winter 1993).

Dripps, Donald A. Supreme Court review: final jeopardy for Grady v. Corbin. *Trial* 30(3):78-81 (March 1994).

———. Supreme Court review: double jeopardy: what is the 'same offense'? *Trial* 28(11):90-91 (November 1992).

Pace, Kirstin. Supreme Court review: Fifth Amendment—the adoption of the "same elements" test: the Supreme Court's failure to adequately protect defendants from double jeopardy. *Journal of Criminal Law and Criminology* 84(4):769-804 (Winter/Spring 1994).

3457. United States v. Energy Resources Co., Inc.   May 29, 1990
495 US 545   109 LEd2d 580   110 SCt 2139
Sup Ct Yearbook (1989-90):32
Kauffman, Stephen P. The impact of energy resources and Begier on IRS Policy Statement P-5-60. *Taxes* 69(1):31-35 (January 1991).

3458. Pennsylvania Department of Public Welfare v. Davenport   May 29, 1990
495 US 552   109 LEd2d 588   110 SCt 2126
Sup Ct Yearbook (1989-90):31-32

3459. Taylor v. United States   May 29, 1990
495 US 575   109 LEd2d 607   110 SCt 2143
Sup Ct Yearbook (1989-90):51

3460. Burnham v. Superior Court of California   May 29, 1990
495 US 604   109 LEd2d 631   110 SCt 2105
Sup Ct Review (1994):295-343
Sup Ct Yearbook (1989-90):51

3461. Fort Stewart Schools v. Federal Labor Relations Authority (FLRA)   May 29, 1990
495 US 641   109 LEd2d 659   110 SCt 2043
Sup Ct Yearbook (1989-90):55
Hukill, Craig. Labor and the Supreme Court: significant issues of 1989-90. *Monthly Labor Review* 113(1):30-34 (January 1990).

3462. Citibank, N.A. v. Wells Fargo Asia Ltd.   May 29, 1990
495 US 660   109 LEd2d 677   110 SCt 2034
Sup Ct Yearbook (1989-90):32

3463. Duro v. Reina, Chief of Police   May 29, 1990
495 US 676   109 LEd2d 693   110 SCt 2053
Sup Ct Yearbook (1989-90):67
Hentoff, Nicholas. The natives are arrestless. *Washington Monthly* 22(11):20-24 (December 1990).

3464. United States v. Montalvo-Murillo   May 29, 1990
495 US 711   109 LEd2d 720   110 SCt 2072
Sup Ct Yearbook (1989-90):42

3465. Keller v. State Bar of California   June 4, 1990
496 US 1   110 LEd2d 1   110 SCt 2228
Sup Ct Review (1990):163-205
Sup Ct Yearbook (1989-90):30

3466. McKesson Corp. v. Florida Division of Alcoholic Beverages and Tobacco   June 4, 1990
McKesson Corp. v. Division of Alcoholic Beverages and Tobacco
496 US 18   110 LEd2d 17   110 SCt 2238
Sup Ct Yearbook (1989-90):35, 34
Ervin, James M., Jr., and Katherine E. Giddings. Supreme Court distinguishes remedy and retroactivity issues affecting state taxes. *Journal of Taxation* 73(5):296-302 (November 1990).
Smart, Tim. The verdict on the last term: 'generally, business lost.' *Business Week* (Industrial/Technology Edition) (3169):30 (July 16, 1990).

Witt, Elder. State-federal power at issue in High Court. *Governing* 2(6):66-67 (March 1989).

———. Threatening tax cases. *Governing* 3(1):26 (October 1989).

3467. Begier, Trustee v. Internal Revenue Service (IRS)　　　　　　　　　June 4, 1990
496 US 53　　　　　　　　　　110 LEd2d 46　　　　　　　　　　110 Sct 2258
　　Sup Ct Yearbook (1989-90):31

Kauffman, Stephen P. The impact of energy resources and Begier on IRS Policy Statement P-5-60. *Taxes* 69(1):31-35 (January 1991).

3468. English v. General Electric Co.　　　　　　　　　　　　　　　　June 4, 1990
496 US 72　　　　　　　　　　110 LEd2d 65　　　　　　　　　　110 SCt 2270
　　Sup Ct Yearbook (1989-90):58

Court whistles a different tune. *Personnel* 67(9):HR Focus Supp 3 (September 1990).

Egan, Thomas E. Wrongful discharge and federal preemption: nuclear whistleblower protection under state law and Section 210 of the Energy Reorganization Act. *Boston College Environmental Affairs Law Review* 17(2):405-440 (Winter 1990).

Hukill, Craig. Significant decisions in labor cases: whistleblowers. *Monthly Labor Review* 113(10):41 (October 1990).

Kowitt, Arthur J., and Donna Panich. Whistleblower litigation: a potential explosion in the nuclear industry. *Public Utilities Fortnightly* 126(1):15-16, 54 (July 5, 1990).

Unanimous Supreme Court finds for actions by whistleblowers. *Public Utilities Fortnightly* 126(2):50 (July 19, 1990).

3469. Peel v. Attorney Registration and Disciplinary Commission of Illinois　　　June 4, 1990
496 US 91　　　　　　　　　　110 LEd2d 83　　　　　　　　　　110 SCt 2281
　　Sup Ct Yearbook (1989-90):30-31

Boedecker, Karl A., and Fred W. Morgan. The evolution of First Amendment protection for commercial speech. *Journal of Marketing* 59(1):38-47 (January 1995).

3470. Horton v. California　　　　　　　　　　　　　　　　　　　　　June 4, 1990
496 US 128　　　　　　　　　　110 LEd2d 112　　　　　　　　　　110 SCt 2301
　　Sup Ct Yearbook (1989-90):48

Dripps, Donald A. Supreme Court review: search and seizure: finding for the Fourth Amendment. *Trial* 29(3):95-97 (March 1993).

Hall, Richard J. Supreme Court review: Fourth Amendment—eliminating the inadvertent discovery requirement for seizures under the plain view doctrine. *Journal of Criminal Law and Criminology* 81(4):819-840 (Winter 1991).

3471. Commissioner, Immigration and Naturalization Service (INS) v. Jean　　　June 4, 1990
496 US 154　　　　　　　　　　110 LEd2d 134　　　　　　　　　　110 SCt 2316
　　Sup Ct Yearbook (1989-90):29

3472. American Trucking Association v. Smith, Director, Arkansas Highway　　　June 4, 1990
　　and Transportation Department
496 US 167　　　　　　　　　　110 LE2d 148　　　　　　　　　　110 SCt 2323
　　Sup Ct Yearbook (1989-90):34

Ervin, James M., Jr., and Katherine E. Giddings. Supreme Court distinguishes remedy and retroactivity issues affecting state taxes. *Journal of Taxation* 73(5):296-302 (November 1990).

Witt, Elder. State-federal power at issue in High Court. *Governing* 2(6):66-67 (March 1989).

———. Threatening tax cases. *Governing* 3(1):26 (October 1989).

3473. Board of Education of the Westside Community Schools (Dist.66) v. Mergens　June 4, 1990
496 US 226　　　　　　　　　　110 LEd2d 191　　　　　　　　　　110 SCt 2356
　　Almanac (1990):52-53, 618
　　Editorials (1990):660-665

Godless 98-102

Sup Ct Yearbook (1989-90):7-10, 24-25, 66, 112-127R

Baron, Mark A., and Harold L. Bishop. Come one, come all. *American School Board Journal* 178(3):29-30 (March 1991).

Confusion in the Court. *Christianity Today* 34(10):48 (July 16, 1990).

Court OKs religious clubs. *Christian Century* 107(19):593 (June 13-20, 1990).

Doerr, Edd. Looking back, looking forward. [Editorial] *Humanist* 51(5):41-42 (September/October 1991).

Drinan, Robert F. The Supreme Court to review student prayer groups in high school. *America* 162(16):429-430 (April 28, 1990).

Gaffney, Edward McGlynn, Jr. Prayer at commencement. *Christian Century* 110(18):590-591 (June 2-9, 1993).

Gest, Ted. The new Supreme Court term may disappoint conservatives. *U.S. News and World Report* 107(13):31 (October 2, 1989).

God and cheerleaders: equal access. [Editorial] *America* 162(23):595 (June 16-23, 1990).

Goi, Simona. The final verdict. *Scholastic Update* (Teachers' Edition) 123(2):11 (September 21, 1990).

Hewitt, Bill. Bridget Mayhew's desire for a Bible club in school redrew the boundary between church and state. *People Weekly* 33(25):67-68 (June 25, 1990).

James, Bernard. Religious speech in public high schools. *Social Education* 54(5):261-263 (September 1990).

Lawton, Kim A. Uncle Sam v. First Church. *Christianity Today* 35(11):38-41 (October 7, 1991).

Levicoff, Steve. Upholding students' religious freedom. [Editorial] *Christian Century* 106(36):1108-1109 (November 29, 1989).

Neff, David. Free speech, sometimes. [Editorial] *Christianity Today* 34(10):13 (July 16, 1990).

Prayer in public schools. *Congressional Digest* 74(1):3-32 (January 1995).

Right to life, church-state cases before Court. *Christianity Today* 33(14):44-46 (October 6, 1989).

Sachs, Andrea, and Jerome Cramer. A victory for integration: the Court rules on civil rights, privacy and labor relations. *Time* 135(18):85 (April 30, 1990).

———. Let us pray: the Court okays religious clubs in public high schools. *Time* 135(25):72 (June 18, 1990).

Sanders, Alain L., Jerome Cramer, and Janice C. Simpson. Enter, stage right: cast conservatively, the Court returns for a busy new session. *Time* 134(15):83-85 (October 9, 1989).

Sanders, Alain L., Jerome Cramer, and Andrea Sachs. Prayers in the schoolhouse?: the Court weighs the constitutionality of student religious groups. *Time* 135(3):51 (January 15, 1990).

Sendor, Benjamin. "Equal access" means just what it says. *American School Board Journal* 181(5):8-9 (May 1994).

———. Religious clubs gain "equal access" to schools. *American School Board Journal* 177(9):15, 41 (September 1990).

Sullivan, Catherine Beth. Are kosher food laws constitutionally kosher? *Boston College Environmental Affairs Law Review* 21(1):201-245 (Fall 1993).

Tarshis, Lauren. From high school to the High Court. *Scholastic Update* 122(10):5-7 (January 26, 1990).

Williams, Charles F. Supreme Court docket: Court orders equal access for Bible club. *Social Education* 54(5):261 (September 1990).

Witt, Elder. Will the Supreme Court relax the federal grip on state and local government? *Governing* 3(1):21-23, 25-29 (October 1989).

Woodward, Kenneth L., and Nadine Joseph. The return of the fourth R. *Newsweek* 117(23):56-57 (June 10, 1991).

Zirkel, Perry A. De jure: opening the door to after-school prayer. *Phi Delta Kappan* 72(1):84-86 (September 1990).

3474. Illinois v. Perkins   June 4, 1990

496 US 292   110 LEd2d 243   110 SCt 2394

Sup Ct Review (1991):103-142

Sup Ct Yearbook (1989-90):46

3475. United States v. Eichman   June 11, 1990

Coupled with United States v. Haggerty

496 US 310   110 LEd2d 287   110 SCt 2404

Almanac (1990):52-53, 55-56, 524-528

Amending 188-193

Center 278-281

Editorials (1990):652-659

Sup Ct Review (1990):69-103

Sup Ct Yearbook (1989-90):7-10, 22-24, 65, 128-134R

Turning 326-327

Bork, Robert H. An end to political judging? *National Review* 42(25):30-32 (December 31, 1990).

Congress: the flag boosters get burned. *Newsweek* 116(1):24 (July 2, 1990).

The flag: flammable again. *Economist* 315(7659):26 (June 16-22, 1990).

Gersh, Debra. Media lose a friend: retiring Supreme Court Justice William Brennan. *Editor and Publisher* 123(30):13, 35, 47 (July 28, 1990).

Greenawalt, Kent. Free speech in the United States and Canada. *Law and Contemporary Problems* 55(1):5-33 (Winter 1992).

Kaplan, David A., and Gregory Cerio. Tinkering with the Constitution. *Newsweek* 115(26):18 (June 25, 1990).

Kinsley, Michael. Stars and snipes. *New Republic* 203(2-3):4 (July 9-16, 1990).

McDaniel, Ann. A burning constitutional issue. *Newsweek* 115(21):78 (May 21, 1990).

————. Judicial flash points. *Newsweek* 116(5):18-19 (July 30, 1990).

Muck, Terry C. Star-spangled clamor. [Editorial] *Christianity Today* 33(13):11 (September 22, 1989).

Salholz, Eloise, Eleanor Clift, Ann McDaniel, and Spencer Reiss. Value judgments. *Newsweek* 115(26):16-18 (June 25, 1990).

Smolla, Rodney A. Supreme Court review: flag burning: round two. *Trial* 26(9):20-23 (September 1990).

Supreme Court: counterintuitive again. *Economist* 315(7661):28-29 (June 30-July 6, 1990).

Wilson, Robin. Court's flag ruling could affect policies against harassment. *Chronicle of Higher Education* 36(40):A33, A35 (June 20, 1990).

3476. Alabama v. White   June 11, 1990
       496 US 325   110 LEd2d 301   110 SCt 2412
       Sup Ct Yearbook (1989-90):47-48

Shifrin, Orrin S. Supreme Court review: Fourth Amendment—protection against unreasonable search and seizure: the inadequacies of using an anonymous tip to provide reasonable suspicion for an investigatory stop. *Journal of Criminal Law and Criminology* 81(4):760-778 (Winter 1991).

3477. Perpich v. Department of Defense   June 11, 1990
       496 US 334   110 LEd2d 312   110 SCt 2418
       Almanac (1990):52-53, 694
       Sup Ct Yearbook (1989-90):60

3478. Howlett v. Rose, as Superintendent of Schools for Pinellas County, Florida   June 11, 1990
       496 US 356   110 LEd2d 332   110 SCt 2430
       Sup Ct Yearbook (1989-90):62

3479. Cooter & Gell v. Hartmarx Corp.   June 11, 1990
       496 US 384   110 LEd2d 359   110 SCt 2447
       Sup Ct Yearbook (1989-90):29-30

Joseph, Gregory P. Supreme Court shapes Rule 11: guidance to lower courts. *Trial* 26(9):65-67 (September 1990).

3480. Office of Personnel Management v. Richmond   June 11, 1990
       496 US 414   110 LEd2d 387   110 SCt 2465
       Sup Ct Yearbook (1989-90):60

3481. Michigan Department of State Police v. Rick Sitz   June 14, 1990
       496 US 444   110 LEd2d 412   110 SCt 2481
       Almanac (1990):53
       Sup Ct Yearbook (1989-90):49

Turning 320-321

Blade, Bryan Scott. Supreme Court review: Fourth Amendment—the constitutionality of a sobriety checkpoint program. *Journal of Criminal Law and Criminology* 81(4):800-818 (Winter 1991).

3482. Sullivan, Secretary of Health and Human Services v. Stroop — June 14, 1990
496 US 478   110 LEd2d 438   110 SCt 2499
Sup Ct Yearbook (1989-90):61

3483. Wilder v. Virginia Hospital Association — June 14, 1990
496 US 498   110 LEd2d 455   110 SCt 2510
Almanac (1990):53, 571
Sup Ct Yearbook (1989-90):61-62; (1991-92):3-4

Rapp, David. Washington and the states: the politics of distrust. *Governing* 5(12):67 (September 1992).

Smart, Tim. The verdict on the last term: 'generally, business lost.' *Business Week* (Industrial/Technology Edition) (3169):30 (July 16, 1990).

Wise, Charles, and Rosemary O'Leary. Is federalism dead or alive in the Supreme Court?: implications for public administrators. *Public Administration Review* 52(6):559-572 (November/December 1992).

3484. General Motors Corp. v. United States — June 14, 1990
496 US 530   110 LEd2d 480   110 SCt 2528
Sup Ct Yearbook (1989-90):58

3485. Texaco Inc. v. Hasbrouck — June 14, 1990
496 US 543   110 LEd2d 492   110 SCt 2535
Sup Ct Yearbook (1989-90):29

3486. Pennsylvania v. Muniz — June 14, 1990
496 US 582   110 LEd2d 528   110 SCt 2638
Editorials (1990):730-735
Sup Ct Yearbook (1989-90):46-47

LeBoeuf, Jacques. Supreme Court review: Fifth Amendment—videotaping drunk drivers limitations on Miranda's protections. *Journal of Criminal Law and Criminology* 81(4):883-925 (Winter 1991).

3487. Sullivan, Secretary of Health and Human Services v. Finkelstein — June 18, 1990
496 US 617   110 LEd2d 563   110 SCt 2658
Sup Ct Yearbook (1989-90):61

3488. Pension Benefit Guaranty Corp. v. LTV Corp. — June 18, 1990
496 US 633   110 LEd2d 579   110 SCt 2668
Almanac (1990):53, 368
Sup Ct Yearbook (1989-90):56-57

Geisel, Jerry. Justices question LTV's motives in PBGC dispute. *Business Insurance* 24(10):3, 22 (March 5, 1990).

———. Legislation to protect PBGC pondered. *Business Insurance* 24(38):20 (September 17, 1990).

———. Supreme Court sides with PBGC: pension plans returned to LTV. *Business Insurance* 24(26):1, 32 (June 25, 1990).

Geisel, Jerry, and Michael Schachner. Supreme Court to rule on LTV pension plans. *Business Insurance* 23(45):2, 98 (November 6, 1989).

Hukill, Craig. Significant decisions in labor cases: pension plans. *Monthly Labor Review* 113(10):40-41 (October 1990).

Locke, Adrienne C. PBGC vows to fight latest LTV ruling. *Business Insurance* 24(23):50 (June 4, 1990).

Smart, Tim. The verdict on the last term: 'generally, business lost.' *Business Week* (Industrial/Technology Edition) (3169):30 (July 16, 1990).

3489. Eli Lilly and Co. v. Medtronic, Inc.   June 18, 1990
       496 US 661   110 LEd2d 605   110 SCt 2683
           Sup Ct Yearbook (1989-90):33

3490. Milkovich v. Lorain Journal Co.   June 21, 1990
       497 US 1   111 LEd2d 1   110 SCt 2695
           Almanac (1990):53
           Sup Ct Review (1991):1-46
           Sup Ct Yearbook (1989-90):65
       Attorneys: don't worry about Milkovich ruling. *Editor and Publisher* 123(36):26-27 (September 8, 1990).
       Cose, Ellis. Matters of fact: the Court considers whether untrue opinions are libelous. *Time* 135(24):62-67 (June
           11, 1990).
       Dill, Barbara. The most serious threat is . . . warrior lawyers. *Columbia Journalism Review* 30(4):54-55
           (November/December 1991).
       Fields, Howard. High Court puts limits on libel law 'opinion.' *Publishers' Weekly* 237(27):10-11 (July 6,
           1990).
       ———. High Court questions unverifiable facts as 'opinion' in libel case. *Publishers' Weekly* 237(21):11 (May
           25, 1990).
       ———. High Court to hear libel case turning on 'opinion.' *Publishers' Weekly* 237(6):10 (February 9, 1990).
       ———. Supreme Court upholds public figure libel charge. *Publishers' Weekly* 236(2):12 (July 14, 1989).
       Fox, Cynthia. How scary is Milkovich? [Editorial] *Columbia Journalism Review* 31(1):19-21 (May/June
           1992).
       Garbus, Martin. Courting libel. [Editorial] *Nation* 251(16):548 (November 12, 1990).
       ———. Limiting our rights. *Publishers' Weekly* 236(7):21 (August 18, 1989).
       Gersh, Debra. Opinion no exception: U.S. Supreme Court rules that published opinion has no greater protection
           than regular speech under the First Amendment. *Editor and Publisher* 123(26):12, 43 (June 30, 1990).
       Hale, F. Dennis. Free expression: the first five years of the Rehnquist Court. *Journalism Quarterly* 69(1):89-
           104 (Spring 1992).
       Reuter, Madalynne. Give and take. *Publishers' Weekly* 238(1):33 (January 4, 1991).
       Schulz, David A. Aftermath of the Mikovich case: pure opinion still protected. *Editor and Publisher* 124(5):20,
           40 (Februrary 2, 1991).
       Smolla, Rodney A. Supreme Court review: when a quote is not a quote. *Trial* 27(1):16-21 (January 1991).

3491. Collins, Director, Texas Department of Criminal Justice v. Youngblood   June 21, 1990
       497 US 37   111 LEd2d 30   110 SCt 2715
           Sup Ct Yearbook (1989-90):41

3492. Rutan v. Replublication Party of Illinois   June 21, 1990
       497 US 62   111 LEd2d 52   110 SCt 2729
           Almanac (1990):52-54, 933
           Sup Ct Yearbook (1989-90):7-10, 19-20, 56, 134-144R
       Bork, Robert H. An end to political judging? *National Review* 42(25);30-32 (December 31, 1990).
       City Hall must stop hacking around. *U.S. News and World Report* 109(1):10-11 (July 2, 1990).
       Hamilton, David K. The staffing function in Illinois state government after Rutan. *Public Administration
           Review* 53(4):381-386 (July/August 1993).
       Katz, Jeffrey L. The slow death of political patronage. *Governing* 4(7):58-62 (April 1991).
       Patronage, please. *New Republic* 203(4):9-10 (July 23, 1990).
       Supreme Court: counterintuitive again. *Economist* 315(7661):28-29 (June 30-July 6, 1990).
       Wise, Charles, and Rosemary O'Leary. Is federalism dead or alive in the Supreme Court?: implications for
           public administrators. *Public Administration Review* 52(6):559-572 (November/December 1992).

3493. Maislin Industries, U.S., Inc. v. Primary Steel, Inc.   June 21, 1990
       497 US 116   111 LEd2d 94   110 SCt 2759
           Sup Ct Yearbook (1989-90):32; (1993-94):91-92

Sanders, George D., Rene Sacasas, and Paul Munter. The search for unrecorded liabilities—the implications of Maislin. *CPA Journal* 61(2):48-51 (February 1991).

3494. Portland Golf Club v. Commissioner of Internal Revenue   June 21, 1990
     497 US 154   111 LEd2d 12   110 SCt 2780
     Sup Ct Yearbook (1989-90):35-36

Actual P&L computation method required to prove UBI profit motive. *Journal of Taxation* 73(2):66 (August 1990).

Chiechi, Carolyn P., and Jeffrey W. Munk. When can social clubs offset investment income with losses from nonmember activities? *Journal of Taxation* 73(3):184-187 (September 1990).

Supreme Court denies social club loss deduction from nonmember sales where fixed costs block profit motive. *Practical Accountant* 23(9):9-10 (September 1990).

3495. Illinois v. Rodriguez   June 21, 1990
     497 US 177   111 LEd2d 148   110 SCt 2793
     Sup Ct Yearbook (1989-90):48

Wieber, Michael C. The theory and practice of Illinois v. Rodriguez: why an officer's reasonable belief about a third party's authority to consent does not protect a criminal suspect's rights. *Journal of Criminal Law and Criminology* 84(3):604-641 (Fall 1993).

3496. Kansas v. Utilicorp United Inc.   June 21, 1990
     497 US 199   111 LEd2d 169   110 SCt 2807
     Sup Ct Yearbook (1989-90):28

3497. Sawyer v. Smith, Interim Warden   June 21, 1990
     497 US 227   111 LEd2d 193   110 SCt 2822
     Almanac (1990):488-489
     Sup Ct Yearbook (1989-90):46

3498. Cruzan v. Harmon, Director, Missouri Department of Health   June 25, 1990
     Cruzan v. Director, Missouri Department of Health
     497 US 261   111 LEd2d 224   110 SCt 2841
     Almanac (1990):53-55, 566-567
     Brennan 109-112
     Const Law 286-293R+
     Editorials (1990):724-729, 1510-1515
     Guide (West): (1991):66-74, 421-472R; (1992):321-324
     Hard Choices 315
     Landmark (v. 2):155-175R
     Letting Go 47-54+
     Nobody's 155-163+
     Sup Ct Review (1991):47-76
     Sup Ct Yearbook (1989-90):7-12, 66, 144-155R; (1991-92):2
     Turning 313-317, 339-342+

Angell, Marcia. Prisoners of technology: the case of Nancy Cruzan. [Editorial] *New England Journal of Medicine* 322(17):1226-1228 (April 26, 1990).

Annas, George J. Sounding board: Nancy Cruzan and the right to die. [Editorial] *New England Journal of Medicine* 323(10):670-673 (September 6, 1990).

Behuniak-Long, Susan. Justice Sandra Day O'Connor and the power of maternal legal thinking. *Review of Politics* 54(3):417-444 (Summer 1992).

Brower, Montgomery, and Giovanna Breu. Nancy Cruzan's parents want to let her die—and are taking the case to the Supreme Court. *People Weekly* 32(23):135-138 (December 4, 1989).

Chopko, Mark. Quinn's sins. [Editorial] *Commonweal* 117(13):402, 426-427 (July 13, 1990).

Drinan, Robert F. The right to die reaches the U.S. Supreme Court. *America* 162(3):60-61 (January 27, 1990).

Dworkin, Ronald. The right to death. *New York Review of Books* 38(3):14-17 (January 31, 1991).

Farber, Daniel A. Supreme Court review: constitutional right to die? *Trial* 26(1):22 (January 1990).

Friedrich, Otto, Jerome Cramer, and Staci D. Kramer. A limited right to die: the court affirms the principle, but not for Nancy Cruzan. *Time* 136(2):59 (July 9, 1990).

Gest, Ted. The new Supreme Court term may disappoint conservatives. *U.S. News and World Report* 107(13):31 (October 2, 1989).

———. Reining in citizens' rights: Rehnquist Court will reinterpret the 200-year-old Bill of Rrights. *U.S. News and World Report* 111(25):49-53 (December 16, 1991).

Gest, Ted, and Sarah Burke. Is there a right to die? *U.S. News and World Report* 107(23):35-37 (December 11, 1989).

Gest, Ted, Steven Findlay, Dorian R. Friedman, and Richard Z. Chesnoff. Changing the rules on dying. *U.S. News and World Report* 109(2):22-24 (July 9, 1990).

Gibbs, Nancy R., Priscilla Painton, and Elizabeth Taylor. Love and let die. *Time* 135(12):62-71 (March 19, 1990).

Glick, Henry R. The impact of permissive judicial policies: the U.S. Supreme Court and the right to die. *Political Research Quarterly* 47(1):207-222 (March 1994).

Goi, Simona. The final verdict. *Scholastic Update* (Teachers' Edition) 123(2):11 (September 21, 1990).

Gostin, Lawrence O. Health law. *JAMA: The Journal of the American Medical Association* 268(3): 364-366 (July 15, 1992).

———. Law and medicine. *JAMA: The Journal of the American Medical Association* 273(21): 1688-1689 (June 7, 1995).

Harvey, John Collins. When should the state step aside?: terminating treatment for PVS victims. *Commonweal* 117(9):286-288 (May 4, 1990).

Johnson, Sandra H. The state as parent. *Commonweal* 117(9):292-294 (May 4, 1990).

Justices consider abortion, right-to-die cases. *Christianity Today* 34(1):55 (January 15, 1990).

Kaplan, David A., and Ann McDaniels. The family vs. the state. *Newsweek* 116(2):22-23 (July 9, 1990).

Kinsley, Michael. To be or not to be. *New Republic* 201(22):6, 42 (November 27, 1989).

McDaniel, Ann. The Court and the right to privacy. *Newsweek* 114(15):36 (October 9, 1989).

———. Judicial flash points. *Newsweek* 116(5):18-19 (July 30, 1990).

Orentlicher, David. Cruzan v. Director of Missouri Department of Health. *JAMA: The Journal of the American Medical Association* 262(20):2928-2930 (November 24, 1989).

———. The right to die after Cruzan. *JAMA: The Journal of the American Medical Association* 264(18):2444-2446 (November 14, 1990).

Quinn, Kevin P. The bishops misstep. *Commonweal* 117(9):288-292 (May 4, 1990).

Relin, David Oliver. Between life and death. *Scholastic Update* 122(10):20-22 (January 26, 1990).

Right to die: will the judges let her? *Economist* 313(7631):28-29 (December 2-8, 1989).

Right to life, church-state cases before Court. *Christianity Today* 33(14):44-46 (October 6, 1989).

Sanders, Alain L., Jerome Cramer, and Janice C. Simpson. Enter, stage right: cast conservatively, the court returns for a busy new session. *Time* 134(15):83-85 (October 9, 1989).

Sanders, Alain L., Jerome Cramer, and Elizabeth Taylor. Whose right to die?: the Supreme Court will wrestle with the ultimate question. *Time* 134(24):80 (December 11, 1989).

Schwartz, Herman. The Souter factor: the majority at the Supreme Court. *Nation* 251(12):410-413 (October 15, 1990).

Smart, Tim. Speak softly and carry a big right-wing agenda. *Business Week* (Industrial/Technology Edition) (3135):115-118 (November 27, 1989).

Spillenger, Clyde. Reading the judicial canon: Alexander Bickel and the book of Brandeis. *Journal of American History* 79(1):125-151 (June 1992).

Supreme Court: counterintuitive again. *Economist* 315(7661):28-29 (June 30-July 6, 1990).

Wheeler, David L. Supreme Court's 'Cruzan' decision triggers renewed scholarly debate over patients' rights to die. *Chronicle of Higher Education* 37(4):A14 (September 26, 1990).

Wise, Charles, and Rosemary O'Leary. Is federalism dead or alive in the Supreme Court?: implications for public administrators. *Public Administration Review* 52(6):559-572 (November/December 1992).

Witt, Elder. On issues of state power, the Supreme Court seems to be of two minds. *Governing* 4(1):54-59, 63-64 (October 1990).

———. Will the Supreme Court relax the federal grip on state and local government? *Governing* 3(1):21-23, 25-29 (October 1989).

3499. Sisson v. Ruby
June 25, 1990

497 US 358
111 LEd2d 292
110 SCt 2892

Sup Ct Yearbook (1989-90):66-67; (1994-95):68-69

George, James A. The 'triple crown' of admiralty cases: from definitions to damages. *Trial* 27(10):46-53 (October 1991).

3500. Georgia v. South Carolina
June 25, 1990

497 US 378
111 LEd2d 309
110 SCt 2903

Sup Ct Yearbook (1989-90):67

3501. Hodgson v. Minnesota
June 25, 1990

497 US 417
111 LEd2d 344
110 SCt 2926

Abortion Am 91, 100+

Abortion Dec 199-200

Abortion Dec 90s Introduction, 1-43R

Almanac (1989):304-307; (1990):53, 55, 528-531

Center 144-151+

Courage 253-279, 427-428

Editorials (1989):762-773; (1990):718-723

Hard Choices 183, 200-203, 315

Liberty 681-684

Nobody's 19-22

Sup Ct Yearbook (1989-90):7-10, 12-15, 66, 155-165R

Turning 311-313+, 342-344+

Abortion: sparring on the bench. *Newsweek* 114(24):49 (December 11, 1989).

Behuniak-Long, Susan. Justice Sandra Day O'Connor and the power of maternal legal thinking. *Review of Politics* 54(3):417-444 (Summer 1992).

Canon, Bradley C. The Supreme Court as a cheerleader in politico-moral disputes. *Journal of Politics* 54(3):637-653 (August 1992).

Chipping away at Roe v. Wade. *Christianity Today* 34(11):37 (August 20, 1990).

Goi, Simona. The final verdict. *Scholastic Update* (Teachers' Edition) 123(2):11 (September 21, 1990).

Halpern, Sue M. The fight over teen-age abortion. *New York Review of Books* 37(5):30-32 (March 29, 1990).

Harrington-Lueker, Donna. Supreme Court actions push a wrenching controversy straight at you. *American School Board Journal* 176(11):20-24 (November 1989).

Kaplan, David A., and Ann McDaniels. The family vs. the state. *Newsweek* 116(2):22-23 (July 9, 1990).

Justices consider abortion, right-to-die cases. *Christianity Today* 34(1):55 (January 15, 1990).

Lawton, Kim A. Confrontation's stage is set. *Christianity Today* 33(11):36-38 (August 18, 1989).

McDaniel, Ann. The Court and the right to privacy. *Newsweek* 114(15):36 (October 9, 1989).

————. Judicial flash points. *Newsweek* 116(6):18-19 (July 30, 1990).

Right to life, church-state cases before Court. *Christianity Today* 33(14):44-46 (October 6, 1989).

Salholz, Eloise, Patricia King, Kate Robins, Nadine Joseph, Nonny de la Pena, Lucille Beachy, and Gregory Cerio. Teenagers and abortion. *Newsweek* 115(2):32-36 (January 8, 1990).

Sanders, Alain L., Jerome Cramer, and Janice C. Simpson. Enter, stage right: cast conservatively, the court returns for a busy new session. *Time* 134(15):83-85 (October 9, 1989).

Schwartz, Herman. The Souter factor: the majority at the Supreme Court. *Nation* 251(12):410-413 (October 15, 1990).

Supreme Court: counterintuitive again. *Economist* 315(7661):28-29 (June 30-July 6, 1990).

Whitman, David. When pregnant girls face mom and dad. *U.S. News and World Report* 107(22):25-26 (December 4, 1989).

Witt, Elder. Will the Supreme Court relax the federal grip on state and local government? *Governing* 3(1):21-23, 25-29 (October 1989).

3502. Ohio v. Akron Center for Reproductive Health
June 25, 1990

497 US 502
111 LEd2d 405
110 SCt 2972

Abortion Am 100

Abortion Dec 199-200

Abortion Dec 90s Introduction, 45-71R

Almanac (1989):304-307; (1990):53, 55, 528-531

Center 117-119, 150-151+

Const Law 306-309R

Editorials (1989):762-773; (1990):718-723

Hard Choices 203-206

Liberty 681-684+

Nobody's 19-22

Sup Ct Yearbook (1989-90):7-10, 12-15, 66, 166-176R

Turning 343-344+

Behuniak-Long, Susan. Justice Sandra Day O'Connor and the power of maternal legal thinking. *Review of Politics* 54(3):417-444 (Summer 1992).

Chipping away at Roe v. Wade. *Christianity Today* 34(11):37 (August 20, 1990).

Goi, Simona. The final verdict. *Scholastic Update* (Teachers' Edition) 123(2):11 (September 21, 1990).

Halpern, Sue M. The fight over teen-age abortion. *New York Review of Books* 37(5):30-32 (March 29, 1990).

Harrington-Lueker, Donna. Supreme Court actions push a wrenching controversy straight at you. *American School Board Journal* 176(11):20-24 (November 1989).

Justices consider abortion, right-to-die cases. *Christianity Today* 34(1):55 (January 15, 1990).

Kaplan, David A., and Ann McDaniels. The family vs. the state. *Newsweek* 116(2):22-23 (July 9, 1990).

Lawton, Kim A. Confrontation's stage is set. *Christianity Today* 33(11):36-38 (August 18, 1989).

Right to life, church-state cases before Court. *Christianity Today* 33(14):44-46 (October 6, 1989).

Salholz, Eloise, Patricia King, Kate Robins, Nadine Joseph, Nonny de la Pena, Lucille Beachy, and Gregory Cerio. Teenagers and abortion. *Newsweek* 115(2):32-36 (January 8, 1990).

Salholz, Eloise, Ann McDaniel, Patricia King, Erik Calonius, David L. Gonzalez, and Nadine Joseph. Voting in curbs and confusion. *Newsweek* 114(3):16-20 (July 17, 1989).

Sanders, Alain L., Jerome Cramer, and Janice C. Simpson. Enter, stage right: cast conservatively, the court returns for a busy new session. *Time* 134(15):83-85 (October 9, 1989).

Supreme Court: counterintuitive again. *Economist* 315(7661):28-29 (June 30-July 6, 1990).

Witt, Elder. Will the Supreme Court relax the federal grip on state and local government? *Governing* 3(1):21-23, 25-29 (October 1989).

3503. Metro Broadcasting, Inc. v. Federal Communications Commission (FCC)   June 27, 1990
       Coupled with Astroline Communications Co. Limited Partnership v. Shurberg Broadcasting of Hartford, Inc.

497 US 547   111 LEd2d 445   110 SCt 2997

Almanac (1990):52-53, 379, 510-511

Const Law 575-580R

Editorials (1995):664-673

Sup Ct Review (1990):105-132; (1995):1-43

Sup Ct Yearbook (1989-90):7-10, 17-19, 62, 176-191R; (1994-95):27-32; (1994-95):106-107

Turning 334-339, 346-348

Affirmative action watch: new threats to FCC minority ownership policies. *Black Enterprise* 20(9):28 (April 1990).

Bork, Robert H. An end to political judging? *National Review* 42(25);30-32 (December 31, 1990).

Chemerinsky, Erwin. Looking ahead to the new term. *Trial* 30(12):81-83 (December 1994).

———. Supreme Court review: race and the Supreme Court. *Trial* 31(10):86-88 (October 1995).

Devins, Neal. Congress, the FCC, and the search for the public trustee. *Law and Contemporary Problems* 56(4):145-188 (Autumn 1993).

Garvey, John H. Black and white images. *Law and Contemporary Problems* 56(4):189-216 (Autumn 1993).

High Court upholds race-based programs. *ENR* 224(27)[225(1)]:9-10 (July 5, 1990).

Kinsley, Michael. Invidious distinction. *New Republic* 202(6):4, 42 (February 5, 1990).

LaNoue, George R. Split visions: minority business set-asides. *Annals of the American Academy of Political and Social Science* 523:104-116 (September 1992).

A little license for racial preference. *U.S. News and World Report* 109(2):13 (July 9, 1990).

Rice, Mitchell F. Government set-asides, minority business enterprises, and the Supreme Court. *Public Administration Review* 51(2):114-122 (March/April 1991).

Scanlan, James P. The curious case of affirmative action for women. *Society* 29(2):36-41 (January/February 1992).

Schwartz, Herman. The Souter factor: the majority at the Supreme Court. *Nation* 251(12):410-413 (October 15, 1990).

Supreme Court affirms FCC minority remedies; white's rights not violated. *Jet* 78(14):27 (July 16, 1990).

Supreme Court: counterintuitive again. *Economist* 315(7661):28-29 (June 30-July 6, 1990).

Taking the activist bench down a peg. *U.S. News and World Report* 108(3):13-14 (January 22, 1990).

Taylor, William L., and Susan M. Liss. Affirmative action in the 1990s: staying the course. *Annals of the American Academy of Political and Social Science* 523:30-37 (September 1992).

Wronging rights. *National Review* 42(14):14 (July 23, 1990).

3504. Walton v. Arizona   June 27, 1990
      497 US 639   111 LEd2d 511   110 SCt 3047
       Sup Ct Yearbook (1989-90):40

Allen, Ronald J. Supreme Court review: forward—evidence, inference, rules, and judgment in constitutional adjudication: the intriguing case of Walton v. Arizona. *Journal of Criminal Law and Criminology* 81(4):727-759 (Winter 1991).

3505. United States v. Marsha B. Kokinda   June 27, 1990
      497 US 720   111 LEd2d 571   110 SCt 3115
       Sup Ct Review (1992):79-122
       Sup Ct Yearbook (1989-90):65

3506. Lewis, Director, Arizona Department of Corrections v. Jimmie Wayne Jeffers   June 27, 1990
      497 US 764   111 LEd2d 606   110 SCt 3092
       Sup Ct Yearbook (1989-90):45

Farber, Daniel A. Supreme Court review: capital punishment and the Rehnquist court. *Trial* 27(4):13-15 (April 1991).

George, Tracey E., and Lee Epstein. On the nature of Supreme Court decision making. *American Political Science Review* 86(2):323-337 (June 1992).

3507. Idaho v. Laura Lee Wright   June 27, 1990
      497 US 805   111 LEd2d 638   110 SCt 3139
       Almanac (1990):53
       Sup Ct Yearbook (1989-90):41
       Turning 332-333

Dripps, Donald A. Supreme Court review: the confrontation clause and the sexual abuse of children. *Trial* 27(5):11-13 (May 1991).

3508. Maryland v. Sandra Ann Craig   June 27, 1990
      497 US 836   111 LEd2d 666   110 SCt 3157
       Almanac (1990):53
       Const Law 434-439R
       Sup Ct Yearbook (1989-90):41
       Turning 330-332

Behuniak-Long, Susan. Justice Sandra Day O'Connor and the power of maternal legal thinking. *Review of Politics* 54(3):417-444 (Summer 1992).

Dripps, Donald A. Supreme Court review: the confrontation clause and the sexual abuse of children. *Trial* 27(5):11-13 (May 1991).

O'Sullivan, John. Court disorder. [Editorial] *National Review* 42(15):6 (August 6, 1990).

Supreme Court: counterintuitive again. *Economist* 315(7661):28-29 (June 30-July 6, 1990).

3509. Lujan, Secretary of the Interior v. National Wildlife Federation   June 27, 1990
      497 US 871   111 LEd2d 695   110 SCt 3177
      Sup Ct Yearbook (1989-90):59

3510. Miles v. Apex Marine Corp.   November 6, 1990
      498 US 19   112 LEd2d 275   111 SCt 317
      Sup Ct Yearbook (1990-91):89
      George, James A. The 'triple crown' of admiralty cases: from definitions to damages. *Trial* 27(10):46-53
          (October 1991).
      George, James A., and Michelle M. O'Daniels. Recoverable damages in admiralty and maritime cases:
          muddied waters after Miles v. Apex Marine. *Trial* 31(5):58-65 (May 1995).

3511. Perry v. Louisiana   November 13, 1990
      498 US 38   112 LEd2d 338   111 SCt 449
      Sainsbury, Jeffrey. Moral meltdown. *New Statesman and Society* 4(153):20 (May 31, 1991).

3512. Cage v. Louisiana   November 13, 1990
      498 US 39   112 LEd2d 339   111 SCt 328
      Kenney, Shelagh. Supreme Court review: Fifth Amendment—upholding the constitutional merit of misleading
          reasonable doubt jury instructions. *Journal of Criminal Law and Criminology* 85(4):989-1027 (Spring 1995).

3513. FMC Corp. v. Holliday   November 27, 1990
      498 US 52   112 LEd2d 356   111 SCt 403
      Sup Ct Yearbook (1990-91):70
      Hukill, Craig. Labor and the Supreme Court: significant issues of 1990-91. *Monthly Labor Review* 114(1):34-
          40 (January 1991).
      Minichello, Dennis. Recouping health care costs. *Business Insurance* 26(50):32 (December 7, 1992).

3514. Arcadia, Ohio v. Ohio Power Co.   November 27, 1990
      498 US 73   112 LEd2d 374   111 SCt 415
      Sup Ct Yearbook (1990-91):69-70

3515. Irwin v. Department of Veterans Affairs   December 3, 1990
      498 US 89   112 LEd2d 435   111 SCt 453
      Sup Ct Yearbook (1990-91):78-79
      Stein, Ronald A. Will equitable tolling of the statute of limitations gain wider acceptance in tax cases? *Journal
          of Taxation* 81(6):370-375 (December 1994).

3516. Moskal v. United States   December 3, 1990
      498 US 103   112 LEd2d 449   111 SCt 461
      Sup Ct Review (1994):345-428
      Sup Ct Yearbook (1990-91):68-69

3517. Ingersoll-Rand Co. v. McClendon   December 3, 1990
      498 US 133   112 LEd2d 474   111 SCt 478
      Sup Ct Yearbook (1989-90):75; (1990-91):70
      Garland, Susan B., and Tim Smart. Pension squabbles battle lines may be shifting. *Business Week* (3188):110-
          111 (November 19, 1990).
      Hukill, Craig. Labor and the Supreme Court: significant issues of 1990-91. *Monthly Labor Review* 114(1):34-
          40 (January 1991).
      Morrison, John M. ERISA and the loss of just remedies. *Trial* 31(3):18-25 (March 1995).
      Smart, Tim, and Dean Foust. The Supreme Court: 'leave it to the states.' *Business Week* (Industrial/Technology
          Edition) (3221):32 (July 8, 1991).

3518. Minnick v. Mississippi — December 3, 1990

498 US 146   112 LEd2d 489   111 SCt 485

Editorials (1990):1452-1455

Guide (West): (1992):113-115

Sup Ct Yearbook (1990-91):61-62

Link, Anne Elizabeth. Supreme Court review: Fifth Amendment—the constitutionality of custodial confessions. *Journal of Criminal Law and Criminology* 82(4):878-903 (Winter 1992).

3519. Groves v. Ring Screw Workers, Ferndale Division — December 10, 1990

498 US 168   112 LEd2d 508   111 SCt 498

Sup Ct Yearbook (1990-91):84

Hukill, Craig. Labor and the Supreme Court: significant issues of 1990-91. *Monthly Labor Review* 114(1):34-40 (January 1991).

Murphy, Betty Southard, Wayne E. Barlow, and D. Diane Hatch. Federal courts can resolve labor grieances. *Personnel Journal* 70(2):16-17 (February 1991).

3520. Damarest v. Manspeaker — January 8, 1991

498 US 184   112 LEd2d 608   111 SCt 599

Sup Ct Yearbook (1990-91):56-57

Kaplan, David A., and Bob Cohn. These clients aren't fools. *Newsweek* 117(14):66-67 (April 22, 1991).

3521. Cheek v. United States — January 8, 1991

498 US 192   112 LEd2d 617   111 SCt 604

Guide (West): (1992):400-401

Sup Ct Yearbook (1990-91):47-48

Ritholz, Jules, and David M. Kohane. Supreme Court finds subjective ignorance of the law a defense to criminal tax fraud. *Journal of Taxation* 74(4):254-258 (April 1991).

Silverman, Elliot. Turning the other cheek: tax fraud, tax protest, and the willfulness requirement. *Taxes* 69(5):302-307 (May 1991).

Winings, Mark C. Ignorance is bliss, especially for the tax evader. *Journal of Criminal Law and Criminology* 84(3):575-603 (Fall 1993).

3522. Mobil Oil Exploration & Producing Southeast, Inc. v. United Distribution Co. — January 8, 1991

Coupled with Federal Energy Regulatory Commission v. United Distribution Co.

498 US 211   112 LEd2d 636   111 SCt 615

Sup Ct Yearbook (1990-91):73

Supreme Court upholds FERC Order 451. *Oil and Gas Journal* 89(2):25 (January 14, 1991).

3523. Board of Education of Oklahoma City Public Schools, — January 15, 1991

Independent School District No. 89, Okalahoma County, Oklahoma v. Dowell

498 US 237   112 LEd2d 715   111 SCt 630

Brennan 249-255

Guide (West): (1992):311-313

Sup Ct Yearbook (1989-90):73-74; (1990-91):76-77

Turning 364-367, 397-398

Brown, Kevin. Revisiting the Supreme Court's opinion in Brown v. Board of Education from a multiculturalist perspective. *Teachers College Record* 96(4):644-653 (Summer 1995).

Chemerinsky, Erwin. Supreme Court review: race and the Supreme Court. *Trial* 31(10):86-88 (October 1995).

Cramer, Jerome. Judging where the bus can stop: the Supreme Court finds a "good-faith" limit for desegregation. *Time* 137(4):87 (January 28, 1991).

———. Mr. Souter comes to town: the frugal bachelor sets up housekeeping after his confirmation. *Time* 136(16):67 (October 15, 1990).

Delon, Floyd G. The legacy of Thurgood Marshall. *Journal of Negro Education* 63(3):278-288 (Summer 1994).

Dumas, Kitty. Will U.S. schools resegregate? *Black Enterprise* 22(10):29 (May 1992).

Fuerst, J. S. Time to get off the bus?: the courts, schools and desegregation. *Commonweal* 118(12):403-405 (June 14, 1991).

Gest, Ted. Next stage: Court lite. *U.S. News and World Report* 111(2):16-19 (July 8, 1991).

Marshall dissent in busing ruling joined by support from civil rights experts. *Jet* 79(16):12 (February 4, 1991).

Not quite emancipation. *National Review* 43(2):17-18 (February 11, 1991).

Russo, Charles J., J. John Harris III, and Rosetta F. Sandidge. Brown v. Board of Education at 40: a legal history of equal educational opportunity in American public education. *Journal of Negro Education* 63(3):297-309 (Summer 1994).

Schwartz, Herman. The Souter factor: the majority at the Supreme Court. *Nation* 251(12):410-413 (October 15, 1990).

Sendor, Benjamin. How long must court-ordered desegregation last? The Supreme Court addresses that question. *American School Board Journal* 178(4):12-13 (April 1991).

———. New lessons on desegregation. *American School Board Journal* 181(2):24-25 (February 1994).

Ward, Janet. Tipping the scales of justice. [Editorial] *American City and County* 105(9):6 (September 1990).

Wilkinson, J. Harvie, III. The dimensions of American constitutional equality. *Law and Contemporary Problems* 55(1):236-251 (Winter 1992).

Witt, Elder. Something old, something new. *Governing* 4(1):60 (October 1990).

3524. FirsTier Mortgage Co., aka Realbanc, Inc. v. Investors Mortgage Insurance Co.   January 15, 1991
498 US 269   112 LEd2d 743   111 SCt 648
Sup Ct Yearbook (1990-91):53

3525. Grogan v. Garner   January 15, 1991
498 US 279   112 LEd2d 755   111 SCt 654
Sup Ct Yearbook (1990-91):42

3526. United States v. R. Enterprises, Inc.   January 22, 1991
498 US 292   112 LEd2d 795   111 SCt 722
Sup Ct Yearbook (1990-91):58

Chefitz, Daniel E. Supreme Court review: Fourth Amendment—the presumption of reasonableness of a subpoena duces tecum issued by a grand jury. *Journal of Criminal Law and Criminology* 82(4):829-848 (Winter 1992).

3527. Parker v. Dugger, Secretary, Florida Department of Corrections   January 22, 1991
498 US 308   112 LEd2d 812   111 SCt 731
Sup Ct Yearbook (1990-91):55

Farber, Daniel A. Supreme Court review: capital punishment and the Rehnquist court. *Trial* 27(4):13-15 (April 1991).

Sudo, Philip, and James Earl Hardy. Tomorrow's news. *Scholastic Update* (Teachers' Edition) 123(16):24-25 (May 3, 1991).

3528. McDermott International, Inc. v. Wilander   February 19, 1991
498 US 337   112 LEd2d 866   111 SCt 807
Sup Ct Yearbook (1990-91):89

Arsenault, Richard J. Seaman status: has the traditional mariner been forgotten? *Trial* 28(9):66-71 (September 1992).

George, James A. The 'triple crown' of admiralty cases: from definitions to damages. *Trial* 27(10):46-53 (October 1991).

Hukill, Craig. Labor and the Supreme Court: significant issues of 1990-91. *Monthly Labor Review* 114(1):34-40 (January 1991).

3529. Trinova Corp. v. Michigan Department of Treasury   February 19, 1991
498 US 358   112 LEd2d 884   111 SCt 818
Sup Ct Yearbook (1990-91):51

Faber, Joan, and Brian D. Spillane. Supreme Court upholds Michigan single business tax formula in Trinova decision. *CPA Journal* 61(6):69 (June 1991).

Smart, Tim, and Howard Gleckman. A VAT brews trouble for corporate America: upheld on appeal, Michigan's value-added tax now begs imitation. *Business Week* (Industrial/Technology Edition) (3203):24 (March 4, 1991).

Witt, Elder. Something old, something new. *Governing* 4(1):60 (October 1990).

3530. Gozlon-Peretz v. United States		February 19, 1991
498 US 395	112 LEd2d 919	111 SCt 840
Sup Ct Yearbook (1990-91):67		

3531. Ford v. Georgia   February 19, 1991
498 US 411   112 LEd2d 935   111 SCt 850
Sup Ct Yearbook (1990-91):62

3532. Dennis v. Higgins, Director, Nebraska Department of Motor Vehicles   February 20, 1991
498 US 439   112 LEd2d 969   111 SCt 865
Sup Ct Yearbook (1990-91):49

Wise, Charles, and Rosemary O'Leary. Is federalism dead or alive in the Supreme Court?: implications for public administrators. *Public Administration Review* 52(6):559-572 (November/December 1992).

3533. International Organization of Masters, Mates & Pilots v. Brown   February 20, 1991
Masters, Mates & Pilots v. Brown
498 US 466   112 LEd2d 991   111 SCt 880
Sup Ct Yearbook (1990-91):84, 86

Hukill, Craig. Labor and the Supreme Court: significant issues of 1990-91. *Monthly Labor Review* 114(1):34-40 (January 1991).

3534. McNary, Commissioner of Immigration and Naturalization v. Haitian Refugee Center, Inc.   February 20, 1991
498 US 479   112 LEd2d 1005   111 SCt 888
Sup Ct Yearbook (1990-91):88

Kirtley, Jane E. The most serious threat is . . . the cloak of privacy. *Columbia Journalism Review* 30(4):46-47 (November/December 1991).

3535. Oklahoma Tax Commission v. Citizen Band Potawatomi Indian Tribe of Oklahoma   February 26, 1991
498 US 505   112 LEd2d 1112   111 SCt 905
Sup Ct Yearbook (1990-91):50-51

3536. Air Courier Conference of America v. American Postal Workers Union, AFL-CIO   February 26, 1991
498 US 517   112 LEd2d 1125   111 SCt 913
Sup Ct Yearbook (1990-91):83

3537. Business Guides, Inc. v. Chromatic Communications Enterprises, Inc.   February 26, 1991
498 US 533   112 LEd2d 1140   111 SCt 922
Sup Ct Yearbook (1990-91):51-52

3538. Pacific Mutual Insurance Co. v. Haslip   March 4, 1991
499 US 1   113 LEd2d 1   111 SCt 1032
Almanac (1991):287
Sup Ct Yearbook (1989-90):74-75; (1990-91):9-13, 13-16, 45, 91-101R; (1992-93):98-99
Turning 367-372, 400-401

Adler, Stacy. High Court to hear case that contests punitive damages. *Business Insurance* 24(15):1, 4 (April 9, 1990).

———. High Courts review punitive damages: justices to consider award limits. *Business Insurance* 24(40):1, 38 (October 1, 1990).

———. High Court reviews punitive damages. *Business Insurance* 24(53):20-21 (December 31, 1990).

———. Justices mull juries' role in setting punitive awards. *Business Insurance* 24(41):1, 103 (October 8, 1990).

———. Lower courts to review punitive damages. *Business Insurance* 25(12):1, 37 (March 25, 1991).

———. Punitive damage ruling mixed bag for business. *Business Insurance* 25(10):1, 29 (March 11, 1991).

Barger, Richard D., and Royal F. Oakes. Judicial reform on hold; Supreme Court changes stance on restrictions for punitive awards. *Business Insurance* 26(9):19-20 (March 2, 1992).

Bernius, Robert C., and Robb M. Jones. Punitive damages and the media: the battle against big monetary awards is far from over. *Editor and Publisher* 124(26):24-25 (June 29, 1991).

Chemerinsky, Erwin. Supreme Court review: punitive damages and the Constitution. *Trial* 30(10):90-92 (October 1994).

Cramer, Jerome. Mr. Souter comes to town: the frugal bachelor sets up housekeeping after his confirmation. *Time* 136(16):67 (October 15, 1990).

Farber, Daniel A. Supreme Court review: punitive damages. *Trial* 27(6):62-66 (June 1991).

Fields, Howard. Media groups seek ban on punitive libel awards. *Publishers' Weekly* 237(24):13 (June 22, 1990).

———. Supreme Court, 7-1, refuses to cap punitive damages awards by juries. *Publishers' Weekly* 238(16):1-3, 105 (April 5, 1991).

Gibbins, Bob. Post-Haslip cases approve state punitive damage laws: watershed opinion has little effect on lower courts. *Trial* 28(11):54-58 (November 1992).

Gordon, Stacy A. Punitive damage judgment affirmed despite Haslip ruling. *Business Insurance* 25(46):1, 70 (November 18, 1991).

High Court refuses to limit punitive damages. *Best's Review* (Property/Casualty Insurance Edition) 91(12):6 (April 1991).

Hofmann, Mark A. Court refuses to impose cap on punitive damages. *Business Insurance* 27(27):1, 21 (June 28, 1993).

———. Punitive damages back before court. *Business Insurance* 29(41):1, 70-71 (October 9, 1995).

———. Supreme Court may not give clear ruling on punitive awards. *Business Insurance* 27(15):1, 29 (April 5, 1993).

Levine, Lee, and David L. Perry. No way to celebrate the Bill of Rights. *Columbia Journalism Review* 29(2):38-39 (July/August 1990).

Rapp, David. The punitive damage battle is moving to the state capitols. *Governing* 4(9):62 (June 1991).

Sachs, Andrea, and Jerome Cramer. A blow to big business: the Supreme Court upholds a punitive damage jury verdict. *Time* 137(11):71 (March 18, 1991).

Smart, Tim. The jury keeps its big stick. *Business Week* (Industrial/Technology Edition) 3204):38 (March 18, 1991).

———. A shot at shooting down punitive damages. *Business Week* (Industrial/Technology Edition) (3169):62, 66 (July 16, 1990).

———. This term, the business of the High Court is business. *Business Week* (Industrial/Technology Edition) (3180):31(October 1, 1990).

Smart, Tim, and Dean Foust. The Supreme Court: 'leave it to the states.' *Business Week* (Industrial/Technology Edition) (3221):32 (July 8, 1991).

Spencer, Leslie. The 14th Amendment lives. *Forbes* 147(10):10 (May 13, 1991).

———. Troubling days for trial lawyers. *Forbes* 145(12):108, 112 (June 11, 1990).

Witt, Elder. Something old, something new. *Governing* 4(1):60 (October 1990).

Wojcik, Joanne. High Court affirms limits on punitive awards. *Business Insurance* 28(27):3, 10 (July 4, 1994).

———. Punitive damage awards; Supreme Court's review of new case may clarify Haslip guidance. *Business Insurance* 26(50):1, 53 (December 7, 1992).

———. Two Supreme letdowns: failure to set punitive rules may fuel state tort reform drive. *Business Insurance* 27(28):2, 98 (July 5, 1993).

3539. Air Line Pilots Association, International v. O'Neill   March 19, 1991
499 US 65   113 LEd2d 51   111 SCt 1127
Sup Ct Yearbook (1990-91):83-84

Hukill, Craig. Labor and the Supreme Court: significant issues of 1990-91. *Monthly Labor Review* 114(1):34-40 (January 1991).

Lissy, William E. Unions have wide latitude to negotiate labor pacts. *Supervision* 53(1):21-22 (January 1992).

3540. West Virginia University Hospital, Inc. v. Casey   March 19, 1991
499 US 83   113 LEd2d 68   111 SCt 1138
   Almanac (1991):255-257
   Sup Ct Yearbook (1990-91):41-42, 194-196
   Hukill, Craig. Labor and the Supreme Court: significant issues of 1990-91. *Monthly Labor Review* 114(1):34-40 (January 1991).

3541. Norfolk & Western Railway Co. v. American Train Dispatchers Association   March 19, 1991
        Coupled with CSX Transportation, Inc. v. Brotherhood of Railway Carmen
499 US 117   113 LEd2d 95   111 SCt 1156
   Sup Ct Yearbook (1990-91):40

3542. Martin, Secretary of Labor v. Occupational Safety and Health Review Commission   March 20, 1991
499 US 144   113 LEd2d 117   111 SCt 1171
   Sup Ct Yearbook (1990-91):70, 72
   Hukill, Craig. Labor and the Supreme Court: significant issues of 1990-91. *Monthly Labor Review* 114(1):34-40 (January 1991).

3543. United States v. Smith   March 20, 1991
499 US 160   113 LEd2d 134   111 SCt 1180
   Sup Ct Yearbook (1990-91):89

3544. International Union, United Automobile, Aerospace and Agricultural Implement Workers   March 20, 1991
        of America, UAW v. Johnson Controls Inc.
499 US 187   113 LEd2d 158   111 SCt 1196
   Almanac (1991):287-288
   Guide (West): (1992):355-357, 543-564R
   Sup Ct Yearbook (1989-90):69-71; (1990-91):9-13, 16-18, 78, 102-111R; (1991-92):2
   Turning 373-378, 435
   Annas, George J. Fetal protection and employment discrimination—the Johnson Controls case. *New England Journal of Medicine* 325(10):740-743 (September 5, 1991).
   Becker, Mary E. Can employers exclude women to protect children? *JAMA: The Journal of the American Medical Association* 264(16):2113-2117 (October 24, 1990).
   Behuniak-Long, Susan. Justice Sandra Day O'Connor and the power of maternal legal thinking. *Review of Politics* 54(3):417-444 (Summer 1992).
   Cramer, Jerome. Mr. Souter comes to town: the frugal bachelor sets up housekeeping after his confirmation. *Time* 136(16):67 (October 15, 1990).
   Feitshans, Ilise L. Job security for pregnant employees: the model employment termination act. *Annals of the American Academy of Political and Social Science* 536:119-134 (November 1994).
   Fetal exposure to toxics: ruling poses problems. *Chemical Marketing Reporter* 239:3+ (March 25, 1991).
   Flaherty, Francis. Who decides what's safe?: fetal protection in the workplace. *Commonweal* 118(21):713-715 (December 6, 1991).
   Fletcher, Meg. Court sets tough test for fetal protection rule. *Business Insurance* 24(33A):2, 100 (August 13, 1990).
   ———. Employers face legal issues. *Business Insurance* 26(18):18-19 (May 4, 1992).
   ———. Fetal protection policies: High Court may limit application. *Business Insurance* 24(42):3, 45 (October 15, 1990).
   ———. Fetal protection ruling spurs employee education efforts. *Business Insurance* 27(54):2, 28-29 (December 27, 1993).
   ———. Businesses' week in court: Supreme Court strikes down workplace fetal protection rule. *Business Insurance* 25(12):1, 4 (March 25, 1991).

Gest, Ted. Next stage: Court lite. *U.S. News and World Report* 111(2):16-19 (July 8, 1991).

Huber, Peter W. Equal opportunity versus the universal nanny. [Editorial] *Forbes* 146(12):276 (November 26, 1990).

Hukill, Craig. Labor and the Supreme Court: significant issues of 1990-91. *Monthly Labor Review* 114(1):34-40 (January 1991).

———. Significant decisions in labor cases: fetal protection. *Monthly Labor Review* 113(3):59-61 (March 1990).

Kaplan, David A., Bob Cohn, and Karen Springen. Equal rights, equal risks. *Newsweek* 117(13):56-59 (April 1, 1991).

Lead case is argued in top court. *Chemical Marketing Reporter* 238:7+ (October 15, 1990).

Lissy, William E. Employers' fetal protection policies barred. *Supervision* 52(10):18 (October 1991).

Long, Janice. Court overturns fetal protection policies. *Chemical and Engineering News* 69(12):5-6 (March 25, 1991).

McClenahen, John S., and Joseph F. McKenna. A leaden decision for industry? *Industry Week* 240(8):76-79 (April 15, 1991).

Murphy, Betty Southard, Wayne E. Barlow, and D. Diane Hatch. Fetal protection policy invalidated. *Personnel Journal* 70(5):33-34 (May 1991).

———. Supreme Court to decide fetal protection conflicts. *Personnel Journal* 69(5):12, 14 (May 1990).

Peak, Marhta H. It's not just a women's issue. *Personnel* 68(6):15 (June 1991).

Shoop, Julie Gannon. Supreme Court accepts fetal protection case. *Trial* 26(8):12-14 (August 1990).

Souter: the new justice remains a mystery. *Christianity Today* 34(15):62-63 (October 22, 1990).

Smart, Tim. This term, the business of the High Court is business. *Business Week* (Industrial/Technology Edition) (3180):31 (October 1, 1990).

Smart, Tim, and Dean Foust. The Supreme Court: 'leave it to the states.' *Business Week* (Industrial/Technology Edition) (3221):32 (July 8, 1991).

Smolowe, Jill, Marc Hequet, and Julie Johnson. Weighing some heavy metal: the Supreme Court rules that potential health risks to fetus are no excuse to discriminate against women in the workplace. *Time* 137(13):60 (April 1, 1991).

Spivack, Miranda S. Johnson Controls: unanimous ruling, multiple effects. *Ms.* 1(6):92 (May/June 1991).

———. Supreme Court: double trouble for repro rights? *Ms.* 1(3):89 (November/December 1990).

3545. Salve Regina College v. Russell								March 21, 1991
499 US 225					113 LEd2d 190					111 SCt 1217
	Sup Ct Yearbook (1990-91):54

3546. Equal Employment Opportunity Commission v. Arabian American Oil Co. (ARAMCO)			March 26, 1991
			Coupled with Bourseslan v. Arabian American Oil Co. and Aramco Services (ARAMCO)
499 US 244					113 LEd2d 274					111 SCt 1227
	Almanac (1991):255-257, 287
	Guide (West): (1992):315-317
	Sup Ct Review (1991):179-224
	Sup Ct Yearbook (1990-91):77

Garland, Susan B. Were civil rights laws meant to travel? *Business Week* (3196):36 (January 21, 1991).

Hukill, Craig. Labor and the Supreme Court: significant issues of 1990-91. *Monthly Labor Review* 114(1):34-40 (January 1991).

———. Significant Decisions in labor cases: discrimination abroad. *Monthly Labor Review* 113(6):64-66 (June 1990).

Kramer, Larry. Extraterritorial application of American law after the insurance antitrust case: a reply to professors Lowenfeld and Trimble. *American Journal of International Law* 89(4):750-758 (October 1995).

Murphy, Betty Southard, Wayne E. Barlow, and D. Diane Hatch. No overseas application of Title VII. *Personnel Journal* 70(6):33, 35 (June 1991).

Smart, Tim, and Dean Foust. The Supreme Court: 'leave it to the states.' *Business Week* (Industrial/Technology Edition) (3221):32 (July 8, 1991).

Zall, Milton. What to expect from the Civil Rights Act. *Personnel Journal* 71(3):46-50 (March 1992).

3547. Arizona v. Fulminante
                                                                    March 26, 1991
      499 US 279   113 LEd2d 302   111 SCt 1246

> *Almanac* (1991):264-265, 287
> *Center* 190-194, 196-200
> *Editorials* (1991):358-361
> *Guide* (West): (1992):84-87, 521-542R
> *Sup Ct Review* (1991):103-142
> *Sup Ct Yearbook* (1990-91):9-13, 18-20, 61, 111-119R
> *Turning* 378-383, 402-403

Cohn, Bob. Coerced confessions: no harm done? *Newsweek* 117(14):52 (April 8, 1991).

Dority, Barbara. Police powers expanded as abuses escalate. *Humanist* 51(4):35-36 (July/August 1991).

Dripps, Donald A. Supreme Court review: to err is harmless? *Trial* 27(7):83-86 (July 1991).

Gest, Ted. The battle over criminal law. *U.S. News and World Report* 110(13):14 (April 8, 1991).

Hyde, Henry J. Should the Omnibus Crime Control Act of 1991 be approved? *Congressional Digest* 71(4):111, 113, 155 (April 1992).

Lacayo, Richard, Julie Johnson, and Elaine Lafferty. Confessions that were taboo are now just a technicality: the Supreme Court's conservative majority delivers a big blow to the rights of defendants in a 5-to-4 decision. *Time* 137(14):26-27 (April 8, 1991).

The loud majority: the Rehnquist Supreme Court is asserting the rights of majorities; that is not its job. *Economist* 320(7714):15 (July 6-12, 1991).

Public enemy number one. *Progressive* 55(8):8-9 (August 1991).

Sudo, Philip, and James Earl Hardy. Tomorrow's news. *Scholastic Update* (Teachers' Edition) 123(16):24-25 (May 3, 1991).

Supreme Court: the silent majoritarian. *Economist* 319(7709):20-21 (June 1-7, 1991).

Welch, Sara E. Supreme Court review: Fifth Amendment—harmless error analysis applied to coerced confessions. *Journal of Criminal Law and Criminology* 82:849-877 (Winter 1992).

3548. United States v. Gaubert
                                                                    March 26, 1991
      499 US 315   113 LEd2d 335   111 SCt 1267

> *Sup Ct Yearbook* (1990-91):73

Smart, Tim. This term, the business of the High Court is business. *Business Week* (Industrial/Technology Edition) (3180):31 (October 1, 1990).

3549. Feist Publications, Inc. v. Rural Telephone Services Co., Inc.
                                                                    March 27, 1991
      499 US 340   113 LEd2d 358   111 SCt 1282

> *Guide* (West): (1992):97-99
> *Sup Ct Review* (1991):143-177; (1992):195-234
> *Sup Ct Yearbook* (1990-91):45

Abrams, Howard B. Originality and creativity in copyright law. *Law and Contemporary Problems* 55(2):3-44 (Spring 1992).

Celedonia, Baila H. From copyright to copycat: open season on data. *Publishers' Weekly* 238(37):34-35 (August 16, 1991).

Fields, Howard. Supreme Court justices question copyrighting compilation data. *Publishers' Weekly* 238(6):14 (February 1, 1991).

————. Supreme Court rules original compilations may be copyrighted. *Publishers' Weekly* 238(17)[16]:13 (April 12, 1991).

————. U.S. Supreme Court to hear three publishing cases in January. *Publishers' Weekly* 238(2):12 (January 11, 1991).

Hale, F. Dennis. Support drops for media and free expression. *Editor and Publisher* 124(38):60, 53 (September 21, 1991).

Litman, Jessica. Copyright and information policy. *Law and Contemporary Problems* 55(2):185-209 (Spring 1992).

McGrath, William T. White pages not entitled to copyright protection. *Editor and Publisher* 124(24):54-55 (June 15, 1991).

3550. Columbia v. Omni Outdoor Advertising, Inc.   April 1, 1991
      City of Columbia v. Omni Outdoor Advertising, Inc.
      499 US 365   113 LEd2d 382   111 SCt 1344
          Sup Ct Yearbook (1990-91):39-40
      Ward, Janet. Tipping the scales of justice. [Editorial] *American City and County* 105(9):6 (September 1990).
      Witt, Elder. Something old, something new. *Governing* 4(1):60 (October 1990).

3551. Powers v. Ohio   April 1, 1991
      499 US 400   113 LEd2d 411   111 SCt 1364
          Guide (West): (1992):307-309, 313-315
          Editorials (1991):424-427
          Sup Ct Yearbook (1990-91):63

3552. Kay v. Ehrler   April 16, 1991
      499 US 432   113 LEd2d 486   111 SCt 1435
          Sup Ct Yearbook (1990-91):41

3553. Leathers, Commissioner or Revenues of Arkansas v. Medlock   April 16, 1991
      499 US 439   113 LEd2d 494   111 SCt 1438
          Sup Ct Yearbook (1990-91):50
      Colford, Steven W. High court ruling hurts industry stand on taxes. *Advertising Age* 62(17):4 (April 22, 1991).
      Gersh, Debra. Singling out one medium for taxation allowable. *Editor and Publisher* 124(18):62, 94-95 (May 4, 1991).
      Hale, F. Dennis. Support drops for media and free expression. *Editor and Publisher* 124(38):60, 53 (September 21, 1991).
      Weidner, James B. Some First Amendment economies. *Editor and Publisher* 124(10):24 (March 9, 1991).

3554. McCleskey v. Zant, Superintendent, Georgia Diagnostic and Classification Center   April 16, 1991
      499 US 467   113 LEd2d 517   111 SCt 1454
          Almanac (1991):264-265, 287-288
          Center 201-204, 219-222
          Editorials (1991):474-479
          Guide (West): (1992):109-111
          Sup Ct Yearbook (1990-91):9-13, 21-23, 59, 120-132R; (1991-92):14-16, 111, 116
          Turning 413-414
      Chemerinsky, Erwin. Supreme Court review: making sense of habeas corpus. *Trial* 28(12):79-82 (December 1992).
      Kaplan, David A. New rules on death row. *Newsweek* 117(17):68 (April 29, 1991).
      Lacayo, Richard, Julie Johnson, and Andrea Sachs. Right face!: in the final stretch of the term, a conservative majority solidifies its hold on the Supreme Court and prepares an assault on the Warren legacy. *Time* 137(26):20-23 (July 1, 1991).
      The loud majority: the Rehnquist Supreme Court is asserting the rights of majorities; that is not its job. *Economist* 320(7714):15 (July 6-12, 1991).
      McLoughlin, Merrill. Grand tests for a grand document. *U.S. News and World Report* 101(26):18-21 (December 29, 1986-January 5, 1987).
      Partners in crime. *National Review* 43(9):16-18 (May 27, 1991).
      Public enemy number one. *Progressive* 55(8):8-9 (August 1991).
      Smolowe, Jill, Jonathan Beaty, Cathy Booth, and Julie Johnson. Race and the death penalty: a High-Court move to halt repeated appeals stirs concern about an arbitrary process. *Time* 137(17):68-69 (April 29, 1991).

3555. Eastern Airlines, Inc. v. Floyd   April 17, 1991
      499 US 530   113 LEd2d 569   111 SCt 1489
          Sup Ct Yearbook (1990-91):87
      Gest, Ted. Unhurt, but suing anyway. *U.S. News and World Report* 109(18):38 (November 5, 1990).

3556. Cottage Savings Assocation v. Commissioner of Internal Revenue   April 17, 1991
499 US 554   113 LEd2d 589   111 SCt 1503
Sup Ct Yearbook (1990-91):48-49, 51

Evans, Thomas L. The realization doctrine after Cottage Savings. *Taxes* 70(12):897-911 (December 1992).

Mortgage exchange losses deductible. *Taxes* 69(6):330 (June 1991).

Sax, Paul J. Supreme Court decides fundamental debt discharge, loss realization issues. *Journal of Taxation* 75(1):54-59 (July 1991).

Segal, Mark A. Recent Supreme Court decisions clarify recognition of loss concepts. *Taxes* 69(9):533-539 (September 1991).

Willens, Robert. IRS broadens the definition of wash sales: can Cottage Savings carry the day? *CPA Journal* 62(7):48-51 (July 1992).

3557. United States v. Centennial Savings Bank FSB (Resolution Trust Corporation, Receiver)   April 17, 1991
499 US 573   113 LEd2d 608   111 SCt 1512
Sup Ct Yearbook (1990-91):51

Mortgage exchange losses deductible. *Taxes* 69(6):330 (June 1991).

Sax, Paul J. Supreme Court decides fundamental debt discharge, loss realization issues. *Journal of Taxation* 75(1):54-59 (July 1991).

Segal, Mark A. Recent Supreme Court decisions clarify recognition of loss concepts. *Taxes* 69(9):533-539 (September 1991).

3558. Carnival Cruise Lines, Inc. v. Shute   April 17, 1991
499 US 585   113 LEd2d 622   111 SCt 1522
Sup Ct Yearbook (1990-91):52

Smart, Tim. This term, the business of the High Court is business. *Business Week* (Industrial/Technology Edition) (3180):31 (October 1, 1990).

3559. American Hospital Association v. National Labor Relations Board (NLRB)   April 23, 1991
499 US 606   113 LEd2d 675   111 SCt 1539
Sup Ct Yearbook (1990-91):84

Cimini, Michael H. Developments in industrial relations: Supreme Court decision. *Monthly Labor Review* 114 (8):42 (August 1991).

Hukill, Craig. Labor and the Supreme Court: significant issues of 1990-91. *Monthly Labor Review* 114(1):34-40 (January 1991).

Murphy, Betty Southard, Wayne E. Barlow, and D. Diane Hatch. Supreme Court upholds health care bargaining unit rule. *Personnel Journal* 70(7):22-23 (July 1991).

3560. California v. Hodari D.   April 23, 1991
499 US 621   113 LEd2d 690   111 SCt 1547
Guide (West): (1992):115-116
Sup Ct Yearbook (1990-91):64-65

Devetski, Timothy J. Supreme Court review: Fourth Amendment—protection against unreasonable seizure of the person: the new(?) common law arrest test for seizure. *Journal of Criminal Law and Criminology* 82(4):747-772 (Winter 1992).

Dority, Barbara. Police powers expanded as abuses escalate. *Humanist* 51(4):35-36 (July/August 1991).

Dripps, Donald A. Supreme Court review: it might be a roust, but it isn't a 'seizure,' *Trial* 28(1):66-68 (January 1992).

Public enemy number one. *Progressive* 55(8):8-9 (August 1991).

3561. Stevens v. Department of Treasury   April 24, 1991
500 US 1   114 LEd2d 1   111 SCt 1562
Guide (West): (1992):17-18
Sup Ct Yearbook (1990-91):79-80

3562. Gilmer v. Interstate/Johnson Lane Corp.   May 13, 1991
500 US 20   114 LEd2d 26   111 SCt 1647
Guide (West): (1992):16-17
Sup Ct Yearbook (1990-91):77-78
Hukill, Craig. Labor and the Supreme Court: significant issues of 1990-91. *Monthly Labor Review* 114(1):34-40 (January 1991).
———. Significant decisions in labor cases: arbitration. *Monthly Labor Review* 113(6):64, 66 (June 1990).
Murphy, Betty Southard, Wayne E. Barlow, and D. Diane Hatch. Arbitration agreements applied to age bias claims. *Personnel Journal* 70(7):22 (July 1991).
Verespej, Michael A. Arbitration: the newest legal option. *Industry Week* 240(14):56, 58 (July 15, 1991).

3563. County of Riverside, California v. McLaughlin   May 13, 1991
500 US 44   114 LEd2d 49   111 SCt 1661
Almanac (1991):264-265
Guide (West): (1992):107-109
Sup Ct Yearbook (1990-91):65-66
NBA prexy says High Court 48-hour ruling will subject minorities 'to harassment.' *Jet* 80(9):8 (June 17, 1991).
Public enemy number one. *Progressive* 55(8):8-9 (August 1991).
Tushnet, Mark V. The justices decide: rule of law, or rule of five? *Nation* 257(14):497-499 (November 1, 1993).

3564. International Primate Protection League v. Administrators of Tulane Educational Fund   May 20, 1991
500 US 72   114 LEd2d 134   111 SCt 1700
Sup Ct Yearbook (1990-91):53-54
Jaschik, Scott. Supreme Court decision could help efforts to block animal research. *Chronicle of Higher Education* 37(37):A17 (May 29, 1991).

3565. Kamen v. Kemper Financial Services, Inc.   May 20, 1991
500 US 90   114 LEd2d 152   111 SCt 1711
Sup Ct Yearbook (1990-91):46
Smart, Tim, and Dean Foust. The Supreme Court: 'leave it to the states.' *Business Week* (Industrial/Technology Edition) (3221):32 (July 8, 1991).

3566. Lankford v. Idaho   May 20, 1991
500 US 110   114 LEd2d 173   111 SCt 1723
Guide (West): (1992):68-69
Sup Ct Yearbook (1990-91):54-55

3567. McCarthy v. Bronson   May 20, 1991
500 US 136   114 LEd2d 194   111 SCt 1737
Sup Ct Yearbook (1990-91):60
Kaplan, David A., and Bob Cohn. These clients aren't fools. *Newsweek* 117(14):66-67 (April 22, 1991).

3568. Michigan v. Lucas   May 20, 1991
500 US 145   114 LEd2d 205   111 SCt 1743
Sup Ct Yearbook (1990-91):64

3569. Touby v. United States   May 20, 1991
500 US 160   114 LEd2d 219   111 SCt 1752
Sup Ct Yearbook (1990-91):58

3570. Rust v. Sullivan, Secretary of Health and Human Services   May 23, 1991
500 US 173   114 LEd2d 233   111 SCt 1759
Abortion Am 315, 318-321, 331-332R+
Abortion Con 293, 263-266+

Abortion Dec 90s Introduction, 73-107R

Almanac (1991):286-287, 340-343

Editorials (1991):606-615

Guide (West): (1992):2-8, 325-332, 489-519R

Hard Choices 207-211+, 271-272

Liberty 684-686+

Sup Ct Review (1992):29-77

Sup Ct Yearbook (1989-90):71-73; (1990-91):9-13, 23-26, 76, 132-147R,192

Turning 383-388, 409-411+

Alexander, David. From the editor: Supreme Court to federally fund health-careworkers: shut up! [Editorial] *Humanist* 51(4):2 (July/August 1991).

Annas, George J. Restricting doctor-patient conversations in federally funded clinics. *New England Journal of Medicine* 325(5):362-364 (August 1, 1991).

Canon, Bradley C. The Supreme Court as a cheerleader in politico-moral disputes. *Journal of Politics* 54(3):637-653 (August 1992).

Cockburn, Alexander. Nixon's revenge. *New Statesman and Society* 4(160):16 (July 19, 1991).

Court moves closer to Roe v. Wade showdown. *Christianity Today* 35(7):50 (June 24, 1991).

Doerr, Edd. Looking back, looking forward. [Editorial] *Humanist* 51(5):41-42 (September/October 1991).

Elmer-Dewitt, Philip, Barbara Dolan, Melissa Ludtke, and Dick Thompson. The doctors take on Bush. *Time* 138(5):52-53 (August 5, 1991).

Elston, Michael J. Artists and unconstitutional conditions: the Big Bad Wolf won't subsidize Little Red Riding Hood's indecent art. *Law and Contemporary Problems* 56(4):327-361 (Autumn 1993).

Fields, Howard. Justice Department says 'Rust' decision could affect arts grants. *Publishers' Weekly* 238(37):9 (August 16, 1991).

The First goes to Rust. *Progressive* 55(9):8 (July 1991).

Fitzpatrick, James F. The most serious threat is . . . the spread of Rust. *Columbia Journalism Review* 30(4):53 (November/December 1991).

Goggin, Malcolm L. Understanding the new politics of abortion: a framework and agenda for research. *American Politics Quarterly* 21(1):4-30 (January 1993).

Gostin, Lawrence O. Health law. *JAMA: The Journal of the American Medical Association* 268(3): 364-366 (July 15, 1992).

Hale, F. Dennis. Support drops for media and free expression. *Editor and Publisher* 124(38):60, 53 (September 21, 1991).

Hentoff, Nat. Abortion gag rule. *Progressive* 55(2):16-17 (February 1991).

Horgan, John. Science and the citizen: exporting misery. *Scientific American* 265(2):16, 18 (August 1991).

Jensen, Laura S. Subsidies, strings, and the courts: judicial action and conditional federal spending. *Review of Politics* 55(3):491-509 (Summer 1993).

Kantrowitz, Barbara, and Ginny Carroll. Tipping the odds on abortion. *Newsweek* 118(2):23 (July 8, 1991).

Kaplan, David A., Ann McDaniel, Daniel Glick, and Lauren Picker. Abortion: just say no advice: the Supreme Court upholds limits on counseling. *Newsweek* 117(22):18 (June 3, 1991).

Kaplan, David A., and Bob Cohn. Good for the left, now good for the right. *Newsweek* 118(2):20-23 (July 8, 1991).

———. Take the money and shut up! *Newsweek* 119(3):55 (January 20, 1992).

Lacayo, Richard, Julie Johnson, and Andrea Sachs. Right face!: in the final stretch of the term, a conservative majority solidifes its hold on the Supreme Court and prepares an assault on the Warren legacy. *Time* 137(26):20-23 (July 1, 1991).

Myers, Christopher. Opinion split on abortion ruling's impact on government's power to restrict grants. *Chronicle of Higher Education* 37(38):A15-A16 (June 5, 1991).

Packwood, Robert W., John C. Danforth, Thad Cochran, David Durenberger, and Jeff Bingaman. Should the Senate approve S. 323, the Title X Pregnancy Counseling Act? *Congressional Digest* 70(8-9):204-208, 213, 215, 217, 219-223 (August/September 1991).

Parachini, Allan. Widening Rust. [Editorial] *Nation* 253(13):468 (October 21, 1991).

Planned Parenthood prexy blasts High Court ruling on abortion information. *Jet* 80(9):6 (June 17, 1991).

Public enemy number one. *Progressive* 55(8):8-9 (August 1991).

Quindlen, Anna. The most serious threat is . . . Rust v. Sullivan. *Columbia Journalism Review* 30(4):52-53 (November/December 1991).

Rust v. Sullivan: a better debate. [Editorial] *America* 164(22):611 (June 8, 1991).

Schwartz, Herman. Second opinion. [Editorial] *Nation* 252(23):801 (June 17, 1991).

Sidey, Kenneth H. Money talks (and squelches). [Editorial] *Christianity Today* 35(8):12 (July 22, 1991).

Simon, Todd F. The indeterminate future of the First Amendment. *Journalism Quarterly* 69(1):28-36 (Spring 1992).

Smolowe, Jill, Tim Curry, and Julie Johnson. Gagging the clinics: the justices did not disturb the constitutional right to an abortion but made it illegal to discuss the procedure in federally funded centers. *Time* 137(22):16-17 (June 3, 1991).

Souter: the new justice remains a mystery. *Christianity Today* 34(15):62-63 (October 22, 1990).

Spivack, Miranda S. Supreme Court: double trouble for repro rights? *Ms.* 1(3):89 (November/December 1990).

Strossen, Nadine. Academic and artistic freedom. *Academe* 78(6):8-15 (November/December 1992).

Sugarman, Jeremy, and Madison Power. How the doctor got gagged: the disintegrating right of privacy in the physician-patient relationship. *JAMA: The Journal of the American Medical Association* 266(23):3323-3327 (December 18, 1991).

Supreme Court decision. *Congressional Digest* 70(8-9)197-199 (August/September 1991).

Supreme Court: the silent majoritarian. *Economist* 319(7709):20-21 (June 1-7, 1991).

The talk of the town: notes and comment. [Editorial] *New Yorker* 67(18):21-22 (June 24, 1991).

Witt, Elder. Something old, something new. *Governing* 4(1):60 (October 1990).

3571. Siegert v. Gilley   May 23, 1991
       500 US 226   111 SCt 1789
                                            114 LEd2d 277
       Sup Ct Yearbook (1990-91):75

3572. Florida v. Jimeno   May 23, 1991
       500 US 248   111 SCt 1801
                                            114 LEd2d 297
       Sup Ct Yearbook (1990-91):66

       Gest, Ted. Next stage: Court lite. *U.S. News and World Report* 111(2):16-19 (July 8, 1991).

       Lochhead, George S. Supreme Court review: Fourth Amendment—expanding the scope of automobile consent searches. *Journal of Criminal Law and Criminology* 82(4):773-796 (Winter 1992).

3573. McCormick v. United States   May 23, 1991
       500 US 257   111 SCt 1807
                                            114 LEd2d 307
       Almanac (1991):287
       Sup Ct Yearbook (1990-91):74; (1991-92):60

3574. Farrey v. Sanderfoot   May 21, 1991
       500 US 291   111 SCt 1825
                                            114 LEd2d 337
       Sup Ct Yearbook (1990-91):42

3575. Owen v. Owen   May 23, 1991
       500 US 305   111 SCt 1833
                                            114 LEd2d 350
       Sup Ct Yearbook (1990-91):44

3576. Summit Health, Ltd. v. Pinhas   May 28, 1991
       500 US 322   111 SCt 1842
                                            114 LEd2d 366
       Sup Ct Yearbook (1990-91):40-41

3577. Braxton v. United States   May 28, 1991
       500 US 344   111 SCt 1854
                                            114 LEd2d 385
       Sup Ct Yearbook (1990-91):66

3578. Hernandez v. New York   May 28, 1991
       500 US 352   111 SCt 1859
                                            114 LEd2d 395

Sup Ct Yearbook (1990-91):62-63

Dripps, Donald A. Supreme Court review: 'I didn't like the way he looked.' *Trial* 31(7):94-96 (July 1995).

Farber, Daniel A. Supreme Court review: picking the jury. *Trial* 27(8):69-72 (August 1991).

Rosen, Jeffrey. Jurymandering. *New Republic* 207(23):15-17 (November 30, 1992).

3579. Illinois v. Kentucky   May 28, 1991
500 US 380   114 LEd2d 420   111 SCt 1877
Sup Ct Yearbook (1990-91):87

3580. Yates v. Evatt, Commissioner, South Carolina Department of Corrections   May 28, 1991
500 US 391   114 LEd2d 432   111 SCt 1884
Sup Ct Yearbook (1990-91):69

3581. Mu'Min v. Virginia   May 30, 1991
500 US 415   114 LEd2d 493   111 SCt 1899
Sup Ct Yearbook (1990-91):63

Bradley, Craig M. The Sixth Amendment lives! a reply to Professor Jonakait. *Journal of Criminal Law and Criminology* 83(3):526-537 (Fall 1992).

Farber, Daniel A. Supreme Court review: picking the jury. *Trial* 27(8):69-72 (August 1991).

Friedman, Sophia R. Supreme Court review: Sixth Amendment—the right to an impartial jury: how extensive must voir dire questioning be? *Journal of Criminal Law and Criminology* 82(4):920-954 (Winter 1992).

Jonakait, Randolph N. Supreme Court review: foreword: notes for a consistent and meaningful Sixth Amendment. *Journal of Criminal Law and Criminology* 82(4):713-746 (Winter 1992).

Kaplan, David A., and Bob Cohn. These clients aren't fools. *Newsweek* 117(14):66-67 (April 22, 1991).

3582. Chapman v. United States   May 30, 1991
500 US 453   114 LEd2d 524   111 SCt 1919
Sup Ct Yearbook (1990-91):67

Meier, Thomas J. A proposal to resolve the interpretation of "mixture or substance" under the federal sentencing guidelines. *Journal of Criminal Law and Criminology* 84(2):377-409 (Summer 1993).

3583. Burns v. Reed   May 30, 1991
500 US 478   114 LEd2d 547   111 SCt 1934
Sup Ct Yearbook (1990-91):68

3584. Lehnert v. Ferris Faculty Assocation   May 30, 1991
500 US 507   114 LEd2d 572   111 SCt 1950
Sup Ct Yearbook (1990-91):86

Blum, Debra E. Both sides see gain in Court's decision on union fees. *Chronicle of Higher Education* 37(38):A11, A14 (June 5, 1991).

Cockburn, Alexander. Nixon's revenge. *New Statesman and Society* 4(160):16 (July 19, 1991).

Hale, F. Dennis. Support drops for media and free expression. *Editor and Publisher* 124(38):60, 53 (September 21, 1991).

Hukill, Craig. Labor and the Supreme Court: significant issues of 1990-91. *Monthly Labor Review* 114(1):34-40 (January 1991).

Kovach, Kenneth A., and Peter Millspaugh. Implementing the Beck and Lehnert union security agreement decisions: a study in frustration. *Business Horizons* 38(3):57-65 (May/June 1995).

Reynolds, Larry. Right-to-work groups are suspicious of NLRB rule-making plans. *HR Focus* 69(7):1-2 (July 1992).

3585. California v. Acevedo   May 30, 1991
500 US 565   114 LEd2d 619   111 SCt 1982
Almanac (1991):264-265
Guide (West): (1992):103-105
Sup Ct Yearbook (1990-91):64

Bradley, Craig M. The Court's "two model" approach to the Fourth Amendment: carpe diem! *Journal of Criminal Law and Criminology* 84(3):429-461 (Fall 1993).

Gest, Ted. Next stage: Court lite. *U.S. News and World Report* 111(2):16-19 (July 8, 1991).

Public enemy number one. *Progressive* 55(8):8-9 (August 1991).

3586. Exxon Corp. v. Central Gulf Lines, Inc.		June 3, 1991
500 US 603	114 LEd2d 649	111 SCt 2071
Sup Ct Yearbook (1990-91):88-89		

3587. Edmonson v. Leesville Concrete Co.		June 3, 1991
500 US 614	114 LEd2d 660	111 SCt 2077
Editorials (1991):650-653		
Guide (West): (1992):313-315		
Sup Ct Yearbook (1990-91):9-13, 26-28, 52-53, 62, 147-155R; (1993-94):37		

Farber, Daniel A. Supreme Court review: picking the jury. *Trial* 27(8):69-72 (August 1991).

Gemskie, Michele A. Supreme Court review: Fourteenth Amendment—peremptory challenges by defendants and the equal protection clause. *Journal of Criminal Law and Criminology* 83(4):920-943 (Winter 1993).

Josephs, Mark L. Supreme Court review: Fourteenth Amendment—peremptory challenges and the equal protection clause. *Journal of Criminal Law and Criminology* 82(4):1000-1028 (Winter 1992).

3588. Clark v. Roemer, Governor of Louisiana		June 3, 1991
500 US 646	114 LEd2d 691	111 SCt 2096
Sup Ct Yearbook (1990-91):82-83		

3589. Connecticut v. Doehr		June 6, 1991
501 US 1	115 LEd2d 1	111 SCt 2105
Sup Ct Yearbook (1990-91):52		

3590. Chambers, NASCO, Inc.		June 6, 1991
501 US 32	115 LEd2d 27	111 SCt 2123
Sup Ct Yearbook (1990-91):41		

3591. Johnson v. Home State Bank		June 10, 1991
501 US 78	115 LEd2d 66	111 SCt 2150
Sup Ct Yearbook (1990-91):43-44		

3592. Melkonyan v. Sullivan, Secretary of Health and Human Services		June 10, 1991
501 US 89	115 LEd2d 78	111 SCt 2157
Sup Ct Yearbook (1990-91):72		

3593. Astoria Federal Savings and Loan Association v. Solimino		June 10, 1991
501 US 104	115 LEd2d 96	111 SCt 2166
Sup Ct Yearbook (1990-91):76		

3594. Gollust v. Mendell		June 10, 1991
501 US 115	115 LEd2d 109	111 SCt 2173
Sup Ct Yearbook (1990-91):45-46		

3595. Burns v. United States		June 13, 1991
501 US 129	115 LEd2d 123	111 SCt 2182
Sup Ct Yearbook (1990-91):66-67		

Gilson, Thomas. Supreme Court review: federal sentencing guidelines—the requirement of notice for upward departure. *Journal of Criminal Law and Criminology* 82(4):1029-1053 (Winter 1992).

3596. Toibb v. Radloff   June 13, 1991
    501 US 157   115 LEd2d 145   111 SCt 2197
    Sup Ct Yearbook (1990-91):44-45
    Smart, Tim, and Dean Foust. The Supreme Court: 'leave it to the states.' *Business Week* (Industrial/Technology Edition) (3221):32 (July 8, 1991).

3597. McNeil v. Wisconsin   June 13, 1991
    501 US 171   115 LEd2d 158   111 SCt 2204
    Sup Ct Yearbook (1990-91):61
    Ullman, Patricia. Supreme Court review: Fifth and Sixth Amendments—the right to counsel in multiple charge arraignments. *Journal of Criminal Law and Criminology* 82(4):904-919 (Winter 1992).

3598. Litton Financial Printing Division v. National Labor Relations Board (NLRB)   June 13, 1991
    501 US 190   115 LEd2d 177   111 SCt 2215
    Sup Ct Yearbook (1990-91):86
    Lissy, William E. Arbitration obligation after expiration of union contract. *Supervision* 53(2):20-21 (February 1992).
    Murphy, Betty Southard, Wayne E. Barlow, and D. Diane Hatch. Duty to arbitrate expires with contract. *Personnel Journal* 70(10):32 (October 1991).

3599. Oklahoma v. New Mexico   June 17, 1991
    501 US 221   115 LEd2d 207   111 SCt 2281
    Sup Ct Yearbook (1990-91):88

3600. Metropolitan Washington Airports Authority v. Citizens for Abatement of Aircraft Noise, Inc.   June 17, 1991
    501 US 252   115 LEd2d 236   111 SCt 2298
    Almanac (1995):3-73-74
    Sup Ct Review (1991):225-260
    Sup Ct Yearbook (1990-91):72-73
    Court rejects review board over Washington airports. *Aviation Week and Space Technology* 134(25):34 (June 24, 1991).

3601. Wilson v. Seiter   June 17, 1991
    501 US 294   115 LEd2d 271   111 SCt 2321
    Guide (West): (1992):290-291
    Sup Ct Yearbook (1990-91):60-61; (1993-94):82-83
    Cockburn, Alexander. Nixon's revenge. *New Statesman and Society* 4(160):16 (July 19, 1991).
    Lacayo, Richard, Julie Johnson, and Andrea Sachs. Right face!: in the final stretch of the term, a conservative majority solidifes its hold on the Supreme Court and prepares an assault on the Warren legacy. *Time* 137(26):20-23 (July 1, 1991).
    Newman, Amy. Supreme Court review: Eighth Amendment—cruel and unusual punishment and conditions cases. *Journal of Criminal Law and Criminology* 82(4):979-999 (Winter 1992).
    Public enemy number one. *Progressive* 55(8):8-9 (August 1991).

3602. Renne, San Francisco City Attorney v. Geary   June 17, 1991
    501 US 312   115 LEd2d 288   111 SCt 2331
    Sup Ct Yearbook (1990-91):74
    Hale, F. Dennis. Support drops for media and free expression. *Editor and Publisher* 124(38):60, 53 (September 21, 1991).

3603. Lampf, Pleva, Lipkind, Prupis & Petigrow v. Gilbertson   June 20, 1991
    501 US 350   115 LEd2d 321   111 SCt 2773
    Sup Ct Yearbook (1990-91):46-47; (1993-94):67; (1994-95):71

3604. Chisom v. Roemer, Governor of Louisiana   June 20, 1991
        Coupled with United States v. Roemer, Governor of Louisiana
   501 US 380   115 LEd2d 348   111 SCt 2354
    Almanac (1991):287
    Guide (West): (1992):413-415
    Sup Ct Yearbook (1990-91):9-13, 28-30, 82, 155-163R
  Davis, Olethia. Tenuous interpretation: Sections 2 and 5 of the Voting Rights Act. *National Civic Review* 84(4):310-322 (Fall/Winter 1995).
  Farber, Daniel A. Supreme Court review: the return of federalism. *Trial* 27(10):63-65 (October 1991).
  Supreme Court: a quota by any other name? *Economist* 320(7713):23 (June 29-July 5, 1991).

3605. Houston Lawyers' Assocation v. Texas   June 20, 1991
        Coupled with League of United Latin American Citizens v. Attorney General of Texas
   501 US 419   115 LEd2d 379   111 SCt 2376
    Almanac (1991):287
    Sup Ct Yearbook (1990-91):9-13, 28-30, 82
  Kaplan, David A., and Bob Cohn. The annual rush to judgment. *Newsweek* 118(1):67 (July 1, 1991).
  Lacayo, Richard, Julie Johnson, and Andrea Sachs. Right face!: in the final stretch of the term, a conservative majority solidifes its hold on the Supreme Court and prepares an assault on the Warren legacy. *Time* 137(26):20-23 (July 1, 1991).
  Robinson, Lauren. Affirmative-action watch. *Black Enterprise* 22(3):20 (October 1991).
  Will, George F. The Conan Doyle school of law. [Editorial] *Newsweek* 118(1):70 (July 1, 1991).

3606. Florida v. Bostick   June 20, 1991
   501 US 429   115 LEd2d 389   111 SCt 2382
    Almanac (1991):264-265
    Guide (West): (1992):133-135
    Sup Ct Yearbook (1990-91):66
    Turning 415
  Cockburn, Alexander. Nixon's revenge. *New Statesman and Society* 4(160):16 (July 19, 1991).
  Goodman, Melissa. A long journey. *Life* 14(13 Special Issue):76-83 (Fall 1991).
  Guerra, Sandra. Domestic drug interdiction operations: finding the balance. *Journal of Criminal Law and Criminology* 82(4):1109-1161 (Winter 1992).
  Kaplan, David A., and Bob Cohn. The annual rush to judgment. *Newsweek* 118(1):67 (July 1, 1991).
  Lacayo, Richard, Julie Johnson, and Elaine Lafferty. Confessions that were taboo are now just a technicality: the Supreme Court's conservative majority delivers a big blow to the rights of defendants in a 5-to-4 decision. *Time* 137(14):26-27 (April 8, 1991).
  Lacayo, Richard, Julie Johnson, and Andrea Sachs. Right face!: in the final stretch of the term, a conservative majority solidifies its hold on the Supreme Court and prepares an assault on the Warren legacy. *Time* 137(26):20-23 (July 1, 1991).
  Lewis, Shawn V. Supreme Court review: Fourth Amendment—protection against unreasonable seizures of the person: the intrusiveness of dragnet styled drug sweeps. *Journal of Criminal Law and Criminology* 82(4):797-828 (Winter 1992).
  Public enemy number one. *Progressive* 55(8):8-9 (August 1991).

3607. Gregory v. Ashcroft   June 20, 1991
   501 US 452   115 LEd2d 410   111 SCt 2395
    Guide (West): (1992):19-21
    Sup Ct Review (1995):125-215
    Sup Ct Yearbook (1990-91):78
  Farber, Daniel A. Supreme Court review: litigating with the sovereign. *Trial* 28(4):85-90 (April 1992).
  ———. Supreme Court review: the return of federalism. *Trial* 27(10):63-65 (October 1991).
  Wise, Charles, and Rosemary O'Leary. Is federalism dead or alive in the Supreme Court?: implications for public administrators. *Public Administration Review* 52(6):559-572 (November/December 1992).

3608. Masson v. New Yorker Magazine   June 20, 1991
Masson v. The New Yorker
501 US 496   115 LEd2d 447   111 SCt 2419

> *Almanac* (1991):287
> *Guide* (West): (1992):264-265; (1994):322-326; (1995):248-250
> *Sup Ct Review* (1991):1-46
> *Sup Ct Yearbook* (1990-91):81-82

Fields, Howard. Supreme Court rules in Masson-Malcolm action. *Publishers' Weekly* 238(29):13 (July 5, 1991).

———. U.S. Supreme Court to hear three publishing cases in January. *Publishers' Weekly* 238(2):12 (January 11, 1991).

Garbus, Martin. Courting libel. [Editorial] *Nation* 251(16):548 (November 12, 1990).

Gersh, Debra. Not many press cases reaching the Supreme Court. *Editor and Publisher* 125(1):17, 30-31 (January 4, 1992).

———. Quote alterations and libel: U.S. Supreme Court says altering quote is libelous only if it changes the meaning of the statement made by the quoted person. *Editor and Publisher* 124(26):7-8 (June 29, 1991).

———. Supreme Court to hear two major media cases: press group feels they should not have been accepted. *Editor and Publisher* 124(1):20, 83 (January 5, 1991).

Gest, Ted. Next stage: Court lite. *U.S. News and World Report* 111(2):16-19 (July 8, 1991).

Gray, Paul, Georgia Harbison, and Julie Johnson. Justice comes in quotes: journalists can tinker with the words of interview subjects—but reckless falsity can be libelous. *Time* 137(26):68 (July 1, 1991).

Hale, F. Dennis. Support drops for media and free expression. *Editor and Publisher* 124(38):60, 53 (September 21, 1991).

Himmelfarb, Gertrude. The right to misquote. *Commentary* 91(4):31-34 (April 1991).

Hoyt, Michael. Malcolm, Masson, and you. *Columbia Journalism Review* 29(6):38-44 (March/April 1991).

Kaplan, David A., and Bob Cohn. The annual rush to judgment. *Newsweek* 118(1):67 (July 1, 1991).

———. When is a quote not a quote? *Newsweek* 117(3):49 (January 21, 1991).

Kinsley, Michael. Please don't quote me. [Editorial] *Time* 137(19):82 (May 13, 1991).

Libel law: don't quote me. *Economist* 318(7690):27-28 (January 19-25, 1991).

Sargeant, Georgia. Get the gist? Court okays rewritten quotes. *Trial* 25(12):19-23 (December 1989).

Smolla, Rodney A. Supreme Court review: when a quote is not a quote. *Trial* 27(1):16-21 (January 1991).

Winfield, Richard N. Altered quotes: holding the line on the First Amendment. *Editor and Publisher* 124(14):24, 26 (April 6, 1991).

3609. James B. Beam Distilling Co. v. Georgia   June 20, 1991
501 US 529   115 LEd2d 481   111 SCt 2439

> *Sup Ct Yearbook* (1990-91):50

Hellerstein, Walter. Supreme Court settles some state tax issues while creating other problems. *Journal of Taxation* 75(3):180-186 (September 1991).

Smart, Tim. This term, the business of the High Court is business. *Business Week* (Industrial/Technology Edition) (3180):31(October 1, 1990).

Supreme Court says Davis (and maybe every case) applies retroactively. *Journal of Taxation* 79(2):66 (August 1993).

Witt, Elder. Something old, something new. *Governing* 4(1):60 (October 1990).

3610. Barnes, Prosecuting Attorney of St. Joseph County, Indiana v. Glen Theatre, Inc.   June 21, 1991
501 US 560   115 LEd2d 504   111 SCt 2456

> *Almanac* (1991):287
> *Guide* (West): (1992):170-172
> *Sup Ct Yearbook* (1990-91):9-13, 31-33, 80, 163-171R
> *Turning* 394-397, 415-417+

Bare any burden. *Economist* 320(7713):22 (June 29-July 5, 1991).

Bork, Robert H. What to do about the First Amendment. *Commentary* 99(2):23-29 (February 1995).

Cockburn, Alexander. Nixon's revenge. *New Statesman and Society* 4(160):16 (July 19, 1991).

Gest, Ted. Reining in citizens' rights: Rehnquist Court will reinterpret the 200-year-old Bill of Rights. *U.S. News and World Report* 111(25):49-53 (December 16, 1991).

Hale, F. Dennis. Support drops for media and free expression. *Editor and Publisher* 124(38):60, 53 (September 21, 1991).

Kaplan, David A., and Bob Cohn. The annual rush to judgment. *Newsweek* 118(1):67 (July 1, 1991).

————. Good for the left, now good for the right. *Newsweek* 118(2):20-23 (July 8, 1991).

Lacayo, Richard, Julie Johnson, and Andrea Sachs. Right face!: in the final stretch of the term, a conservative majority solidifes its hold on the Supreme Court and prepares an assault on the Warren legacy. *Time* 137(26):20-23 (July 1, 1991).

O'Rourke, William. Will the Court bare all? *Nation* 252(24):846-847 (June 24, 1991).

Safire, William. Ode on a G-string. *New York Times Magazine* (section 6, part 1):12 (August 4, 1991).

Seligman, Daniel. Naked in Indiana. *Fortune* 123(9):116 (May 6, 1991).

Simon, Todd F. The indeterminate future of the First Amendment. *Journalism Quarterly* 69(1):28-36 (Spring 1992).

Strossen, Nadine. Academic and artistic freedom. *Academe* 78(6):8-15 (November/December 1992).

Tushnet, Mark V. The justices decide: rule of law, or rule of five? *Nation* 257(14):497-499 (November 1, 1993).

Wise, Charles, and Rosemary O'Leary. Is federalism dead or alive in the Supreme Court?: implications for public administrators. *Public Administration Review* 52(6):559-572 (November/December 1992).

3611. Wisconsin Public Intervenor and Town of Casey June 21, 1991
     v. Mortier Wisconsin Forestry/Right-of-Way/Turf Coalition
501 US 597   115 LEd2d 532   111 SCt 2476
    Sup Ct Yearbook (1990-91):73, 191-197

FIFRA pre-emption opposed by EPA. *Chemical Marketing Reporter* 241:5+ (March 9, 1992).

Hanson, David. Agricultural chemical makers face tough issues. *Chemical and Engineering News* 69(46):21-22 (November 18, 1991).

Hoffman, John. Farm chemicals '92: threats and opportunities. *Chemical Marketing Reporter* 241(20):SR16-SR17 (May 18, 1992).

Kemezis, Paul. High Court puts pest control under local control. *Chemical Week* 148(25):9 (July 3-10, 1991).

Long, Janice. High Court allows local regulation of pesticides. *Chemical and Engineering News* 69(26):6 (July 1, 1991).

Rapp, David. Casey turns mighty in Court; outslugs pesticide industry, 9-0. *Governing* 4(12):69 (September 1991).

Rutrick, Elena S. Local pesticide regulation since Wisconsin Public Intervenor v. Mortier. *Boston College Environmental Affairs Law Review* 20(1):65-97 (Fall 1992).

Smallwood, Carla. A struggle for control. *American City and County* 108(1):60-71 (January 1993).

Smart, Tim, and Dean Foust. The Supreme Court: 'leave it to the states.' *Business Week* (Industrial/Technology Edition) (3221):32 (July 8, 1991).

Smoger, Gerson H., Andrews N. Wolf, and Martin J. Hoffman. How to fight FIFRA preemption. *Trial* 31(7):34-37, (July 1995).

Wise, Charles, and Rosemary O'Leary. Is federalism dead or alive in the Supreme Court?: implications for public administrators. *Public Administration Review* 52(6):559-572 (November/December 1992).

3612. Schad v. Arizona June 21, 1991
501 US 624   115 LEd2d 555   111 SCt 2491
    Sup Ct Yearbook (1990-91):56

3613. Cohen v. Cowles Media Inc., dba Minneapolis Star & Tribune Co. June 24, 1991
501 US 663   115 LEd2d 586   111 SCt 2513
    Almanac (1991):287
    Sup Ct Review (1994):57-128
    Sup Ct Yearbook (1990-91):9-13, 33-35, 80-81, 171-175R

Fields, Howard. Court rules authors may be sued for breaking confidence promise. *Publishers' Weekly* 238(21):10 (July 19, 1991).

Gersh, Debra. Implied contract with sources upheld: divided U.S. Supreme Court says newspapers were wrong to divulge the name of a source after reporters had promised confidentiality. *Editor and Publisher* 124(26):9, 37 (June 29, 1991).

———. Not many press cases reaching the Supreme Court. *Editor and Publisher* 125(1):17, 30-31 (January 4, 1992).

———. Supreme Court to hear two major media cases: press group feels they should not have been accepted. *Editor and Publisher* 124(1):20, 83 (January 5, 1991).

Gest, Ted. Next stage: Court lite. *U.S. News and World Report* 111(2):16-19 (July 8, 1991).

Hale, F. Dennis. How retiring Supreme Court Justice White voted in First Amendment cases. *Editor and Publisher* 126(30):44, 36 (July 24, 1993).

———. Support drops for media and free expression. *Editor and Publisher* 124(38):60, 53 (September 21, 1991).

Simon, Todd F. The indeterminate future of the First Amendment. *Journalism Quarterly* 69(1):28-36 (Spring 1992).

Sommers, Louise. Clarifying confidentiality. *Editor and Publisher* 124(36):29 (September 7, 1991).

———. Confidential sources: protection and prevention. *Editor and Publisher* 124(11):32 (March 16, 1991).

Ullmann, John. The Cohen case—why the press should win. [Editorial] *Editor and Publisher* 124(14):60, 51 (April 6, 1991).

3614. Pauley, Survivor of Pauley v. BethEnergy Mines, Inc.   June 24, 1991
     Coupled with Clinchfield Coal Co. v. Director, Office of Workers' Compensation Programs, United States Department of Labor
     Coupled with Consolidation Coal Co. v. Director, Office of Workers' Compensation Programs, United States Department of Labor
     501 US 680   115 LEd2d 604   111 SCt 2524
         Sup Ct Yearbook (1990-91):87

3615. Coleman v. Thompson, Warden   June 24, 1991
     501 US 722   115 LEd2d 640   111 SCt 2546
         Almanac (1991):287-288
         Guide (West): (1992):111-113
         Sup Ct Yearbook (1990-91):58-59, 60; (1991-92):14-16, 111, 116

Chemerinsky, Erwin. Supreme Court review: making sense of habeas corpus. *Trial* 28(12):79-82 (December 1992).

Cockburn, Alexander. Nixon's revenge. *New Statesman and Society* 4(160):16 (July 19, 1991).

Farber, Daniel A. Supreme Court review: the return of federalism. *Trial* 27(10):63-65 (October 1991).

Public enemy number one. *Progressive* 55(8):8-9 (August 1991).

Supreme Court: non habeas corpus. *Economist* 323(7759):28 (May 16-22, 1992).

Tucker, John. Dead end. *New Republic* 206(18):21, 24-25 (May 4, 1992).

3616. Blatchford, Commissioner, Department of Community and   June 24, 1991
     Regional Affairs of Alaska v. Native Village of Noatak
     501 US 775   115 LEd2d 686   111 SCt 2578
         Sup Ct Yearbook (1990-91):74-75

3617. Ylst, Warden v. Nunnemaker   June 24, 1991
     501 US 797   115 LEd2d 706   111 SCt 2590
         Guide (West): (1992):111-113
         Sup Ct Yearbook (1990-91):59-60

3618. Payne v. Tennessee   June 27, 1991
     501 US 808   115 LEd2d 720   111 SCt 2597
         Almanac (1991):287
         Death Penalty (Tushnet) 86-88, 218-227R
         Guide (West): (1992):101-103

Sup Ct Review (1991):77-102
Sup Ct Yearbook (1990-91):9-13, 35-37, 55-56, 175-189R
Turning 418-419

Kaplan, David A., and Bob Cohn. Good for the left, now good for the right. *Newsweek* 118(2):20-23 (July 8, 1991).

Public enemy number one. *Progressive* 55(8):8-9 (August 1991).

Sargeant, Georgia. Victim impact testimony allowed by Supreme Court in death penalty hearings. *Trial* 27(10):11-14, 85 (October 1991).

Shapiro, Walter, and Julie Johnson. What say should victims have? *Time* 137(21):61 (May 27, 1991).

Smolowe, Jill, Jonathan Beaty, Cathy Booth, and Julie Johnson. Race and the death penalty: a High-Court move to halt repeated appeals stirs concern about an arbitrary process. *Time* 137(17):68-69 (April 29, 1991).

3619. Freytag v. Commissioner of Internal Revenue   June 27, 1991
501 US 868   115 LEd2d 764   111 SCt 2631
    Sup Ct Review (1991):225-260
    Sup Ct Yearbook (1990-91):49

3620. Peretz v. United States   June 27, 1991
501 US 923   115 LEd2d 808   111 SCt 2661
    Sup Ct Yearbook (1990-91):57-58

3621. Harmelin v. Michigan   June 27, 1991
501 US 957   115 LEd2d 836   111 SCt 2680
    Almanac (1991):287
    Guide (West): (1992):135-137
    Sup Ct Yearbook (1989-90):75-76; (1990-91):67-68
    Turning 388-393, 418+

Dripps, Donald A. Supreme Court review: cruel, unusual, and constitutional. *Trial* 28(5):87-89 (May 1992).

Gibbs, Margaret R. Supreme Court review: Eighth Amendment—narrow proportionality requirement preserves deference to legislative judgment. *Journal of Criminal Law and Criminology* 82(4):955-978 (Winter 1992).

Public enemy number one. *Progressive* 55(8):8-9 (August 1991).

3622. Gentile v. State Bar of Nevada   June 27, 1991
501 US 1030   115 LEd2d 888   111 SCt 2720
    Sup Ct Yearbook (1990-91):81

Gersh, Debra. Not many press cases reaching the Supreme Court. *Editor and Publisher* 125(1):17, 30-31 (January 4, 1992).

Hentoff, Nat. Free speech for lawyers, too? *Progressive* 55(8):12-13 (August 1991).

Weisberg, Lynn. On a constitutional collision course: attorney no-comment rules and the right of access to information. *Journal of Criminal Law and Criminology* 83(3):644-683 (Fall 1992).

3623. Virginia Bankshares, Inc. v. Sandberg   June 27, 1991
501 US 1083   115 LEd2d 929   111 SCt 2749
    Sup Ct Yearbook (1990-91):47

3624. Hafer v. Melo   November 5, 1991
502 US 21   116 LEd2d 301   112 SCt 358
    Sup Ct Yearbook (1991-92):73

3625. Board of Governors of the Federal Reserve System v. MCorp Financial, Inc.   December 3, 1991
502 US 32   116 LEd2d 358   112 SCt 459
    Sup Ct Yearbook (1991-92):66

3626. Griffin v. United States   December 3, 1991
502 US 46   116 LEd2d 371   112 SCt 466

Sup Ct Yearbook (1991-92):49

3627. Estelle, Warden v. McGuire   December 4, 1991
       502 US 62   116 LEd2d 385   112 SCt 475
       Sup Ct Yearbook (1991-92):48
       Doyle, David J. Supreme Court review: Fourteenth Amendment—admitting evidence of battered child
       syndrome to prove intent. *Journal of Criminal Law and Criminology* 83(4):894-919 (Winter 1993).

3628. Southwest Marine, Inc. v. Gizoni   December 4, 1991
       502 US 81   116 LEd2d 405   112 SCt 486
       Sup Ct Yearbook (1991-92):79-80
       Greenwald, Judy, Michael Bradford, Stacy Adler Gordon, and Jerry Geisel. ESOP fraud suits upheld; Supreme
       Court rules on benefit, risk management issues. *Business Insurance* 25:2, 61 (December 9, 1991).
       Hukill, Craig. Labor and the Supreme Court: significant issues of 1991-92. *Monthly Labor Review* 115(1):34-
       39 (January 1992).

3629. Wooddell v. International Brotherhood of Electrical Workers, Local 71   December 4, 1991
       502 US 93   116 LEd2d 419   112 SCt 494
       Sup Ct Yearbook (1991-92):80
       Hukill, Craig. Labor and the Supreme Court: significant issues of 1991-92. *Monthly Labor Review* 115(1):34-
       39 (January 1992).

3630. Simon & Schuster, Inc. v. Members of New York State Crime Victims Board   December 10, 1991
       502 US 105   116 LEd2d 476   112 SCt 501
       Almanac (1992):329
       Guide (West): (1992):169-170
       Landmark (v. 5):165-182R
       Sup Ct Review (1992):195-234
       Sup Ct Yearbook (1990-91):197; (1991-92):10-12, 78, 85-96R,124-126
       Dripps, Donald A. Supreme Court review: 'Son-of-Sam laws' and the First Amendment. *Trial* 28(3):74-76
       (March 1992).
       Fields, Howard. High Court to hear S & S appeal of 'Son of Sam' law. *Publishers' Weekly* 238(12):12 (March
       8, 1991).
       ———. Supreme Court hears arguments on 'Son of Sam' law. *Publishers' Weekly* 238(48):15 (November 1,
       1991).
       ———. U.S. Supreme Court strikes down N.Y. State's 'Son of Sam' law. *Publishers' Weekly* 239(1):16-17
       (January 1, 1992).
       Gersh, Debra. Not many press cases reaching the Supreme Court. *Editor and Publisher* 125(1):17, 30-31
       (January 4, 1992).
       ———. 'Son of Sam' law struck down. *Editor and Publisher* 124(50):13 (December 14, 1991).
       Gest, Ted. Next stage: Court lite. *U.S. News and World Report* 111(2):16-19 (July 8, 1991).
       Hale, F. Dennis. Mass media organizations avoid Supreme Court. *Editor and Publisher* 125(37):60, 51
       (September 12, 1992).
       Reid, Calvin. After 'Son of Sam' ruling: new victim laws? More crime books? *Publishers' Weekly* 239(1):16-
       17 (January 1, 1992).
       Sargeant, Georgia. 'Son-of-Sam law' appealed to Supreme Court. *Trial* 27(2):82-84 (February 1991).

3631. Ardestani v. Immigration and Naturalization Service (INS)   December 10, 1991
       502 US 129   116 LEd2d 496   112 SCt 515
       Sup Ct Yearbook (1991-92):69-70
       Farber, Daniel A. Supreme Court review: litigating with the sovereign. *Trial* 28(4):85-90 (April 1992).

3632. Union Bank v. Wolas   December 11, 1991
       502 US 151   116 LEd2d 514   112 SCt 527
       Sup Ct Yearbook (1991-92):38-39

3633. United States Department of State v. Ray   December 16, 1991
    502 US 164   116 LEd2d 526   112 SCt 541
       Sup Ct Yearbook (1991-92):69
    Gersh, Debra. Government information protected. *Editor and Publisher* 124(51):24 (December 21, 1991).
    ———. Not many press cases reaching the Supreme Court. *Editor and Publisher* 125(1):17, 30-31 (January 4,
    1992).
    Hale, F. Dennis. Mass media organizations avoid Supreme Court. *Editor and Publisher* 125(37):60, 51
    (September 12, 1992).

3634. Immigration and Naturalization Service v. National Center for Immigrants' Rights, Inc.   December 16, 1991
    502 US 183   116 LEd2d 546   112 SCt 551
       Sup Ct Yearbook (1991-92):71

3635. Hilton v. South Carolina Public Railways Commission   December 16, 1991
    502 US 197   116 LEd2d 560   112 SCt 560
       Sup Ct Yearbook (1991-92):67
    Farber, Daniel A. Supreme Court review: litigating with the sovereign. *Trial* 28(4):85-90 (April 1992).
    ———. Supreme Court review: revival of the canons. *Trial* 28(6):82-85 (June 1992).

3636. King v. St. Vincent's Hospital   December 16, 1991
    502 US 215   116 LEd2d 578   112 SCt 570
       Sup Ct Yearbook (1991-92):81-82
    Hukill, Craig. Labor and the Supreme Court: significant issues of 1991-92. *Monthly Labor Review* 115(1):34-
    39 (January 1992).

3637. Smith v. Barry   January 14, 1992
    502 US 244   116 LEd2d 678   112 SCt 678
       Sup Ct Yearbook (1991-92):46

3638. County of Yakima v. Confederated Tribes and Bands of the Yakima Indian Nation   January 14, 1992
    502 US 251   116 LEd2d 687   112 SCt 683
       Sup Ct Yearbook (1991-92):41

3639. Norman v. Reed   November 14, 1991
       Coupled with Cook County Officers Electoral Board v. Reed
    502 US 279   116 LEd2d 711   112 SCt 698
       Sup Ct Yearbook (1991-92):77

3640. Molzof, Personal Representative of the Estate of Molzof v. United States   January 14, 1992
    502 US 301   116 LEd2d 731   112 SCt 711
       Sup Ct Yearbook (1991-92):83-84
    Farber, Daniel A. Supreme Court review: litigating with the sovereign. *Trial* 28(4):85-90 (April 1992).

3641. Immigration and Naturalization Service (INS) v. Doherty   January 15, 1992
    502 US 314   116 LEd2d 823   112 SCt 719
       Guide (West): (1993):165-167
       Sup Ct Yearbook (1991-92):70-71
    Kelly, Keith J. Supreme Court knockout: one-two punch for political asylum. *Nation* 254(8):272-273 (March 2,
    1992).

3642. White v. Illinois   January 15, 1992
    502 US 346   116 LEd2d 848   112 SCt 736
       Sup Ct Yearbook (1991-92):52-53
       Turning 462-463

Porcelli, Anthony C. Supreme Court review: Sixth Amendment—right to confront one's accuser when the victim does not testify. *Journal of Criminal Law and Criminology* 83(4):868-893 (Winter 1993).

3643. Rufo, Sheriff of Suffolk County v. Inmates of the Suffolk County Jail   January 15, 1992
      Coupled with Rapone, Commissioner of Corrections of Massachusetts v. Inmates of the Suffolk County Jail
502 US 367   116 LEd2d 867   112 SCt 748
   Sup Ct Yearbook (1991-92):45-46
Farber, Daniel A. Supreme Court review: litigating with the sovereign. *Trial* 28(4):85-90 (April 1992).
Fieweger, Michael J. Supreme Court review: consent decrees in prison and jail reform—relaxed standard of review for government motions to modify consent decrees. *Journal of Criminal Law and Criminology* 83(4):1024-1054 (Winter 1993).
Methvin, Eugene H. Highest Court cost. *National Review* 44(5):36-38 (March 16, 1992).

3644. Dewsnup v. Timm   January 15, 1992
502 US 410   116 LEd2d 903   112 SCt 773
   Sup Ct Yearbook (1991-92):37

3645. Wyoming v. Oklahoma   January 22, 1992
502 US 437   117 LEd2d 1   112 SCt 789
   Sup Ct Yearbook (1991-92):81
Farber, Daniel A. Supreme Court review: litigating with the sovereign. *Trial* 28(4):85-90 (April 1992).

3646. Immigration and Naturalization Service (INS) v. Elias-Zacarias   January 22, 1992
502 US 478   117 LEd2d 38   112 SCt 812
   Sup Ct Yearbook (1991-92):71
Kelly, Keith J. Supreme Court knockout: one-two punch for political asylum. *Nation* 254(8):272-273 (March 2, 1992).
Newspeak at the High Court. *Progressive* 56(3):10 (March 1992).

3647. Presley v. Etowah County Commission   January 27, 1992
      Coupled with Mack v. Russell County Commission
502 US 491   117 LEd2d 51   112 SCt 820
   Almanac (1992):329
   Sup Ct Yearbook (1991-92):61
Davis, Olethia. Tenuous interpretation: Sections 2 and 5 of the Voting Rights Act. *National Civic Review* 84(4):310-322 (Fall/Winter 1995).
Rush, Mark E. In search of a coherent theory of voting rights: challenges to the Supreme Court's vision of fair and effective representation. *Review of Politics* 56(3):503-523 (Summer 1994).
Sancton, Thomas, Julie Johnson, and Andrea Sachs. Judging Thomas. *Time* 140(2):30-31 (July 13, 1992).

3648. Lechmere, Inc. v. National Labor Relations Board (NLRB)   January 27, 1992
502 US 527   117 LEd2d 79   112 SCt 841
   Sup Ct Yearbook (1991-92):79
Cimini, Michael H., and Susan L. Behrmann. Developments in industrial relations: Supreme Court rules on organizing. *Monthly Labor Review* 115(4):46 (April 1992).
Hale, F. Dennis. Mass media organizations avoid Supreme Court. *Editor and Publisher* 125(37):60, 51 (September 12, 1992).
Hukill, Craig. Labor and the Supreme Court: significant issues of 1991-92. *Monthly Labor Review* 115(1):34-39 (January 1992).
Lissy, William E. Access of non-employee union organizers to employers' property. *Supervision* 53(10):19-20 (October 1992).
Murphy, Betty Southard, Wayne E. Barlow, and D. Diane Hatch. Handbilling not permitted in privately owned malls. *Personnel Journal* 71(4):26, 28, 31 (April 1992).
Verespej, Michael A. Business's dirty laundry may get an airing. *Industry Week* 241(6):63 (March 16, 1992).

3649. Keith J. Hudson v. Jack McMillian   February 25, 1992
      503 US 1   117 LEd2d 156   112 SCt 995
          Guide (West): (1993):310-312
          Sup Ct Yearbook (1992-93):66
          Sup Ct Yearbook (1991-92):55
          Turning 463-464
      Jordan, Patrick. Clarence T & Camp J.: harden not your hearts. [Editorial] *Commonweal* 119(6):5-6 (March 27, 1992).
      Rosen, Jeffrey. Never mind. *New Republic* 207(13):18, 20-22 (September 21, 1992).
      Sancton, Thomas, Julie Johnson, and Andrea Sachs. Judging Thomas. *Time* 140(2):30-31 (July 13, 1992).
      Sowell, Thomas. Accomplices. [Editorial] *Forbes* 149(7):56 (March 30, 1992).
      The talk of the town: notes and comment. [Editorial] *New Yorker* 68(7):23-24 (April 6, 1992).

3650. United States v. Nordic Village, Inc.   February 25, 1992
      503 US 30   117 LEd2d 181   112 SCt 1011
          Sup Ct Yearbook (1991-92):39
      Farber, Daniel A. Supreme Court review: revival of the canons. *Trial* 28(6):82-85 (June 1992).
      IRS wins two bankruptcy cases in the Supreme Court. *Journal of Taxation* 76(4):194-195 (April 1992).

3651. Holywell Corp. v. Smith   February 25, 1992
          Coupled with United States v. Smith
      503 US 47   117 LEd2d 196   112 SCt 1021
          Sup Ct Yearbook (1991-92):37-38
      Culp, William R., Jr. Liquidating trustee must file returns and pay tax for debtors, Supreme Court says. *Journal of Taxation* 76(6):342-345 (June 1992).
      IRS wins two bankruptcy cases in the Supreme Court. *Journal of Taxation* 76(4):194-195 (April 1992).

3652. Franklin v. Gwinnett County Public Schools   February 26, 1992
      503 US 60   117 LEd2d 208   112 SCt 1028
          Guide (West): (1993):343-345
          Sup Ct Yearbook (1991-92):2, 72-73
      Lederman, Douglas. Supreme Court rules that victims of intentional sex bias can sue colleges for punitive damages under Title IX. *Chronicle of Higher Education* 38(26):A39 (March 4, 1992).
      Marczely, Bernadette. A legal update on sexual harassment in the public schools. *Clearing House* 66(6):329-331 (July/August 1993).
      Spivack, Miranda S. The Court of last resort. *Ms.* 2(4):90-91 (January/February 1992).
      Zirkel, Perry A. De jure: damages for sexual harassment. *Phi Delta Kappan* 73(10):812-813 (June 1992).

3653. INDOPCO, Inc. v. Commissioner Internal Revenue Service   February 26, 1992
      503 US 79   117 LEd2d 226   112 SCt 1039
          Sup Ct Yearbook (1991-92):41-42
      Greenstein, Brian R., and Mark B. Persellin. Supreme Court's ruling in Indopco limits deductibility of takeover expenses. *Taxes* 70(8):570-576 (August 1992).
      Hume, Evelyn C., and Ernest R. Larkins. Takeover expenses: National Starch and the IRS add new wrinkles. *Journal of Accountancy* 174(2):87-93 (August 1992).
      Lipton, Richard M., Lynne A. Schewe, and Michael C. Fondo. Supreme Court approves focus on long-term benefit in takeover expense controversy. *Journal of Taxation* 76(6):324-329 (June 1992).
      Norris, James E. The 1992 Utility Tax Conference. *Public Utilities Fortnightly* 130(11):36-38 (December 1, 1992).
      Saunders, Laura. The agents run riot. *Forbes* 150(11):144 (November 9, 1992).
      Schlessinger, Michael R. Indopco & Newark: defining the intangible "asset" in the larger cost recovery context. *Taxes* 70(12):929-947 (December 1992).
      Smart, Tim, and Howard Gleckman. The High Court has business holding its breath. *Business Week* (Industrial/Technology Edition) (3234):36, 38 (October 7, 1991).
      Supreme Court hostile to deduction of fees in friendly takeovers. *Journal of Taxation* 76(4):194 (April 1992).

Yancey, Thomas H. Emerging doctrines in the tax treatment of environmental cleanup costs. *Taxes* 70(12):948-973 (December 1992).

3654. Arkansas v. Oklahoma   February 26, 1992
    Coupled with Environmental Protection Agency (EPA) v. Oklahoma
503 US 91   117 LEd2d 239   112 SCt 1046
  Sup Ct Yearbook (1991-92):63

Kemezis, Paul. Court backs sewage plant in discharge dispute. *ENR* 228(10):14 (March 9, 1992).

Smart, Tim. The next war between the states could be over clean water. *Business Week* (Industrial/Technology Edition) (3244):32 (December 16, 1991).

Smart, Tim, and Howard Gleckman. The High Court has business holding its breath. *Business Week* (Industrial/Technology Edition) (3234):36, 38 (October 7, 1991).

Walters, Jonathan. Muddying a clean-water issue. *Governing* 5(8):16 (May 1992).

3655. Collins v. City of Harker Heights, Texas   February 26, 1992
503 US 115   117 LEd2d 261   112 SCt 1061
  Guide (West): (1993):154-156
  Sup Ct Yearbook (1991-92):4, 72

Hukill, Craig. Labor and the Supreme Court: significant issues of 1991-92. *Monthly Labor Review* 115(1):34-39 (January 1992).

3656. Willy v. Coastal Corp.   March 3, 1992
503 US 131   117 LEd2d 280   112 SCt 1076
  Sup Ct Yearbook (1991-92):47

3657. McCarthy v. Madigan   March 4, 1992
503 US 140   117 LEd2d 291   112 SCt 1081
  Sup Ct Yearbook (1991-92):55-56

3658. Dawson v. Delaware   March 9, 1992
503 US 159   117 LEd2d 309   112 SCt 1093
  Death Penalty (Tushnet) 113-114, 119
  Guide (West): (1993):92-94
  Sup Ct Yearbook (1991-92):57

Brooks, Thomas D. Supreme Court review: First Amendment—penalty enhancement for hate crimes: content regulation, questionable state interests and non-traditional sentencing. *Journal of Criminal Law and Criminology* 84(4):703-742 (Winter/Spring 1994).

Rosen, Jeffrey. Never mind. *New Republic* 207(13):18, 20-22 (September 21, 1992).

3659. General Motors Corp. v. Romein   March 9, 1992
503 US 181   117 LEd2d 328   112 SCt 1105
  Sup Ct Yearbook (1991-92):78-79

Hukill, Craig. Labor and the Supreme Court: significant issues of 1991-92. *Monthly Labor Review* 115(1):34-39 (January 1992).

3660. Williams v. United States   March 9, 1992
503 US 193   117 LEd2d 341   112 SCt 1112
  Sup Ct Yearbook (1991-92):59

3661. Stringer v. Black, Commissioner, Mississippi Department of Corrections   March 9, 1992
503 US 222   117 LEd2d 367   112 SCt 1130
  Death Penalty (Tushnet) 114-115, 119
  Sup Ct Yearbook (1991-92):54

Chemerinsky, Erwin. Supreme Court review: making sense of habeas corpus. *Trial* 28(12):79-82 (December 1992).

3662. Connecticut National Bank
    v. Germain, Trustee for the Estate of O'Sullivan's Fuel Oil Co., Inc.
    503 US 249   117 LEd2d 391
       Sup Ct Yearbook (1991-92):37

March 9, 1992

112 SCt 1146

Farber, Daniel A. Supreme Court review: revival of the canons. *Trial* 28(6):82-85 (June 1992).

3663. Holmes v. Securities Investor Protection Corp.
    503 US 258   117 LEd2d 532
       Sup Ct Review (1993):157-198
       Sup Ct Yearbook (1991-92):39

March 24, 1992

112 SCt 1311

3664. United States v. R.L.C.
    503 US 291   117 LEd2d 559
       Guide (West): (1993):94-96
       Sup Ct Yearbook (1991-92):58

March 24, 1992

112 SCt 1329

Farber, Daniel A. Supreme Court review: revival of the canons. *Trial* 28(6):82-85 (June 1992).

3665. Nationwide Mutual Insurance Co. v. Darden
    503 US 318   117 LEd2d 581
       Sup Ct Yearbook (1991-92):68

March 24, 1992

112 SCt 1344

Farber, Daniel A. Supreme Court review: revival of the canons. *Trial* 28(6):82-85 (June 1992).

Hukill, Craig. Labor and the Supreme Court: significant issues of 1991-92. *Monthly Labor Review* 115(1):34-39 (January 1992).

3666. United States v. Wilson
    503 US 329   117 LEd2d 593
       Sup Ct Yearbook (1991-92):58

March 24, 1992

112 SCt 1351

3667. Suter v. Artist M.
    503 US 347   118 LEd2d 1
       Almanac (1993):382
       Sup Ct Yearbook (1991-92):3-4, 74

March 25, 1992

112 SCt 1360

Rapp, David. Washington and the states: the politics of distrust. *Governing* 5(12):67 (September 1992).

3668. United States v. Felix
    503 US 378   118 LEd2d 25
       Guide (West): (1993):112-114
       Sup Ct Yearbook (1991-92):47-48

March 25, 1992

112 SCt 1377

Donofrio, Anthony J. Supreme Court review: the double jeopardy clause of the Fifth Amendment—the Supreme Court's cursory treatment of underlying conduct in successive prosecutions. *Journal of Criminal Law and Criminology* 83(4):773-803 (Winter 1993).

3669. Barnhill v. Johnson, Trustee
    503 US 393   118 LEd2d 39
       Sup Ct Yearbook (1991-92):36-37

March 25, 1992

112 SCt 1103

3670. National Railroad Passenger Corp. v. Boston and Maine Corp.
    Coupled with Interstate Commerce Commission (ICC) v. Boston and Maine Corp.
    503 US 407   118 LEd2d 52
       Sup Ct Yearbook (1991-92):68

March 25, 1992

112 SCt 1394

3671. Robertson v. Seattle Audubon Society
    503 US 429   118 LEd2d 73
       Guide (West): (1993):160-162
       Sup Ct Yearbook (1990-91):198-199; (1991-92):65

March 25, 1992

112 SCt 1407

3672. United States Department of Commerce v. Montana March 31, 1992
Department of Commerce v. Montana
503 US 442   118 LEd2d 87   112 SCt 1415
  Guide (West): (1993):34-36
  Sup Ct Yearbook (1991-92):62-63

3673. Freeman v. Pitts   March 31, 1992
503 US 467   118 LEd2d 108   112 SCt 1430
  Almanac (1992):329
  Guide (West): (1993):127-129
  Sup Ct Yearbook (1990-91):200; (1991-92):73
Brown, Kevin. Revisiting the Supreme Court's opinion in Brown v. Board of Education from a multiculturalist perspective. *Teachers College Record* 96(4):644-653 (Summer 1995).
Chemerinsky, Erwin. Supreme Court review: race and the Supreme Court. *Trial* 31(10):86-88 (October 1995).
Coughlin, Ellen K. Amid challenges to classic remedies for race discrimination, researchers argue merits of mandatory school desegregation. *Chronicle of Higher Education* 38(7):A9, A11 (October 9, 1991).
Dumas, Kitty. Will U.S. schools resegregate? *Black Enterprise* 22(10):29 (May 1992).
High Court eases rules on school desegregation. *Jet* 81(26):22 (April 20, 1992).
Hyde, Alison A. School desegregation: the role of the courts and means of achievement. *NASSP Bulletin* 78(565):28-37 (November 1994).
Kaplan, David A., and Bob Cohn. The hands-off Court. *Newsweek* 120(1):32-36 (July 6, 1992).
LaFay, Laura, and James Earl Hardy. A court-watcher's guide. *Scholastic Update* 124(5):13-16 (November 1, 1991).
Landsberg, Brian K. The federal government and the promise of Brown. *Teachers College Record* 96(4):627-636 (Summer 1995).
Russo, Charles J., J. John Harris III, and Rosetta F. Sandidge. Brown v. Board of Education at 40: a legal history of equal educational opportunity in American public education. *Journal of Negro Education* 63(3):297-309 (Summer 1994).
Sendor, Benjamin. New lessons on desegregation. *American School Board Journal* 181(2):24-25 (February 1994).
Taylor, William L. Segregation is (not equal). [Editorial] *Nation* 254(18):633 (May 11, 1992).
Whitman, David, and Dorian R. Friedman. Busing's unheralded legacy. *U.S. News and World Report* 112(14):63-65 (April 13, 1992).

3674. Yee v. City of Escondido, California   April 1, 1992
503 US 519   118 LEd2d 153   112 SCt 1522
  Sup Ct Yearbook (1991-92):80-81
Kinsley, Michael. Taking exception. *New Republic* 206(1-2):6 (January 6-13, 1992).
McGuire, Kevin T., and Barbara Palmer. Issue fluidity on the U.S. Supreme Court. *American Political Science Review* 89(3):691-702 (September 1995).

3675. Jacobson v. United States   April 6, 1992
503 US 540   118 LEd2d 174   112 SCt 1535
  Editorials (1992):408-413
  Guide (West): (1993):299-301
  Sup Ct Yearbook (1991-92):12-14, 50, 96-108R
Camp, Damon D. Out of the quagmire after Jacobson v. United States: towards a more balanced entrapment standard. *Journal of Criminal Law and Criminology* 83(4):1055-1097 (Winter 1993).
Dripps, Donald A. Supreme Court review: the riddle of entrapment. *Trial* 28(7):97-100 (July 1992).
Hale, F. Dennis. Mass media organizations avoid Supreme Court. *Editor and Publisher* 125(37):60, 51 (September 12, 1992).
High Court to hear abortion, porn cases. *Christianity Today* 35(11):50 (October 7, 1991).

3676. Joe Mario Trevino v. Texas   April 6, 1992
503 US 562   118 LEd2d 193   112 SCt 1547

Guide (West): (1993):103-105

3677. United States v. Alaska   April 21, 1992
     503 US 569   118 LEd2d 222   112 SCt 1606
     Sup Ct Yearbook (1991-92):68-69

3678. Barker v. Kansas   April 21, 1992
     503 US 594   118 LEd2d 243   112 SCt 1619
     Guide (West): (1993):358-360
     Sup Ct Yearbook (1991-92):41

3679. United States Department of Energy v. Ohio   April 21, 1992
     503 US 607   118 LEd2d 255   112 SCt 1627
     Sup Ct Yearbook (1991-92):63-64

3680. Taylor v. Freeland & Krontz   April 21, 1992
     503 US 638   118 LEd2d 280   112 SCt 1644
     Guide (West): (1993):47-48
     Sup Ct Yearbook (1991-92):38

3681. Keeney, Superintendent, Oregon State Penitentiary v. Tamayo-Reyes   May 4, 1992
     504 US 1   118 LEd2d 318   112 SCt 1715
     Editorials (1992):562-565
     Guide (West): (1993):211-213
     Sup Ct Yearbook (1991-92):14-16, 53, 109-116R
  Chemerinsky, Erwin. Supreme Court review: making sense of habeas corpus. *Trial* 28(12):79-82 (December
    1992).
  Kaplan, David A., and Bob Cohn. A decision of limited appeal. *Newsweek* 119(20):63 (May 18, 1992).
  Supreme Court: non habeas corpus. *Economist* 323(7759):28 (May 16-22, 1992).
  What's the rush? [Editorial] *Commonweal* 119(11):3-4 (June 5, 1992).

3682. Denton, Director of Corrections of California v. Hernandez   May 4, 1992
     504 US 25   118 LEd2d 340   112 SCt 1728
     Guide (West): (1993):312-313
     Sup Ct Yearbook (1991-92):54-55

3683. United States v. Williams   May 4, 1992
     504 US 36   118 LEd2d 352   112 SCt 1735
     Guide (West): (1993):206-208
     Sup Ct Yearbook (1991-92):52
  Bowman, Gregory W. Supreme Court review: Fifth Amendment—substantial exculpatory evidence,
    prosecutorial misconduct and grand jury proceedings: a broadening of prosecutorial discretion. *Journal of
    Criminal Law and Criminology* 83(4):718-743 (Winter 1993).

3684. Foucha v. Louisiana   May 18, 1992
     504 US 71   118 LEd2d 437   112 SCt 1780
     Guide (West): (1993):308-310
     Sup Ct Yearbook (1991-92):48-49
  Dripps, Donald A. Supreme Court review: exploring the exclusivity of the criminal sanction. *Trial* 29(1):89-91
    (January 1993).
  Papadakis, Ellen M. Supreme Court review: Fourteenth Amendment—the continued confinement of insanity
    acquittees. *Journal of Criminal Law and Criminology* 83(4):944-977 (Winter 1993).
  Robinson, Paul H. Supreme Court review: foreword: the criminal-civil distinction and dangerous blameless
    offenders. *Journal of Criminal Law and Criminology* 83(4):693-717 (Winter 1993).
  Rosen, Jeffrey. Never mind. *New Republic* 207(13):18, 20-22 (September 21, 1992).

3685. Riggins v. Nevada   May 18, 1992
    504 US 127   118 LEd2d 479   112 SCt 1810
      Death Penalty (Tushnet) 115, 119
      Guide (West): (1993):63-65
      Sup Ct Yearbook (1991-92):60
    Rosen, Jeffrey. Never mind. *New Republic* 207(13):18, 20-22 (September 21, 1992).
    Ziegelmueller, William P. Supreme Court review: Sixth Amendment—due process on drugs: the implications
      of forcibly medicating pretrial detainees with antipsychotic drugs. *Journal of Criminal Law and Criminology*
      83(4):836-867 (Winter 1993).

3686. Wyatt v. Cole   May 18, 1992
    504 US 158   118 LEd2d 504   112 SCt 1827
      Sup Ct Yearbook (1991-92):82

3687. Wade v. United States   May 18, 1992
    504 US 181   118 LEd2d 524   112 SCt 1840
      Sup Ct Yearbook (1991-92):58-59
    Fisher, David. Supreme Court review: Fifth Amendment—prosecutorial discretion not absolute: constitutional
      limits on decision not to file substantial assistance motions. *Journal of Criminal Law and Criminology*
      83(4):744-772 (Winter 1993).

3688. Coleman v. Thompson   May 20, 1992
    504 US 188   119 LEd2d 1   112 SCt 1845
      Death Penalty (Tushnet) 104-106
      Sup Ct Yearbook (1991-92):15, 111, 116
    Hertzberg, Hendrik. Premeditated execution: the Supreme Court is the death penalty's final arbiter, but the U.S.
      must decide what it achieves. *Time* 139(20):49 (May 18, 1992).
    Kaplan, David A., and Bob Cohn. Hung on a technicality. *Newsweek* 119(14):56-58 (April 6, 1992).
    Ratliff, Brenda. The crimes of Roger Coleman. *Reader's Digest* 142(849):51-56 (January 1993).
    Smolowe, Jill, and Julie Johnson. Must this man die?: Roger Keith Coleman says he didn't kill anybody, but the
      courts are tired of listening. *Time* 139(20):41-44 (May 18, 1992).
    Tucker, John. Dead end. *New Republic* 206(18):21, 24-25 (May 4, 1992).

3689. Burson, Attorney General and Reporter for Tennessee v. Freeman   May 26, 1992
    504 US 191   119 LEd2d 5   112 SCt 1846
      Almanac (1992):329
      Sup Ct Review (1992):79-122
      Sup Ct Yearbook (1991-92):75
    Hale, F. Dennis. Mass media organizations avoid Supreme Court. *Editor and Publisher* 125(37):60, 51
      (September 12, 1992).

3690. United States v. Burke   May 26, 1992
    504 US 229   119 LEd2d 34   112 SCt 1867
      Guide (West): (1993):360-361
      Sup Ct Yearbook (1991-92):43
    Back pay awards ruled includible in income. *CPA Journal* 62(8):13 (August 1992).
    Discrimination settlement awards not excludable from income. *Taxes* 70(6):397- (June 1992).
    Elwood, Robert M. Supreme Court's ruling on taxation of discrimination damages provides little resolution.
      Journal of Taxation 83(3):148-152 (September 1995).
    Helleloid, Richard T., and Lucretia S.W. Mattson. Has the scope of the personal injury exclusion been changed
      by the Supreme Court? *Journal of Taxation* 77(2):82-87 (August 1992).
    Hukill, Craig. Labor and the Supreme Court: significant issues of 1991-92. *Monthly Labor Review* 115(1):34-
      39 (January 1992).

Jaeger, David G. Taxation of back pay awards under Title VII: Supreme Court decides U.S. v. Burke. *Taxes* 70(8):523-530 (August 1992).

Palmer, Kevin A. Revisiting the tax treatment of discrimination awards and settlements after Burke. *Taxes* 71(10):642- (October 1993).

Supreme Court rules back pay award for sex discrimination is taxable. *Practical Accountant* 25(8):8-9 (August 1992).

Tax cases: back-pay award for (pre-1991 Title VII) discrimination is taxable. *Journal of Accountancy* 174(2):35-36 (August 1992).

3691. Evans v. United States   May 26, 1992
       504 US 255   119 LEd2d 57   112 SCt 1881
          Guide (West): (1993):163-165
          Sup Ct Yearbook (1991-92):60
       Rosen, Jeffrey. Never mind. *New Republic* 207(13):18, 20-22 (September 21, 1992).

3692. Quill Corp. v. North Dakota   May 26, 1992
       504 US 298   119 LEd2d 91   112 SCt 1904
          Almanac (1992):328-329
          Guide (West): (1993):364-366
          Sup Ct Yearbook (1991-92):42-43
       Biondo, John. The aftermath of Quill: are we still in a fog? *Practical Accountant* 25(9):56-60 (September 1992).

       ———. Bellas Hess v. Quill: a Supreme Court use tax showdown. *Practical Accountant* 25(3):32-37 (March 1992).

       Cain, Rita Marie. Quill Corporation v. North Dakota: an answer to the taxing problem surrounding mail-order sales. *Taxes* 71(1):3-10 (January 1993).

       Colford, Steven W. Direct marketers, states huddle on tax. *Advertising Age* 63(22):49 (June 1, 1992).

       ———. High Court may open ad tax. *Advertising Age* 62(44):1, 60 (October 14, 1991).

       ———. Use-tax issue moving toward day in High Court. *Advertising Age* 61(21):S5, S9 (May 21, 1990).

       Genetelli, Richard W., David B. Zigman, and Cesar E. Bencosme. Recent U.S. Supreme Court decisions on state and local tax issues. *CPA Journal* 62(11):38-44 (November 1992).

       Hellerstein, Walter. Supreme Court says no state use tax imposed on mailorder sellers—for now. *Journal of Taxation* 77(2):120-124 (August 1992).

       High Court says North Dakota still cannot force use tax collection by out-of-state company. *Practical Accountant* 25(8):8 (August 1992).

       Houston, M. A., and S. K. Skinner. Special report: what the Quill Decision means for business owners. *Journal of Accountancy* 174(2):34-35 (August 1992).

       Levin, Gary. Direct marketers triumph in tax case. *Advertising Age* 62(26):12 (June 24, 1991).

       O'Connell, Daniel. U.S. Supreme Court reviews state and local taxation issues. *CPA Journal* 62(3):16-21 (March 1992).

       Peters, Jeffrey S., and William D. Ault. Update on state tax issues before the U.S. Supreme Court. *CPA Journal* 62(4):73-74 (April 1992).

       Plus shipping & handling—and now taxes? *Newsweek* 119(23):64 (June 8, 1992).

       Rosen, Arthur R. Supreme Court clarifies perimeters of state tax jurisdiction. *Taxes* 70(8):559-569 (August 1992).

       Supreme Court upholds National Bellas Hess in Quill. *CPA Journal* 62(8):12 (August 1992).

       Sylvester, Kathleen. Mail-order tax issue is back. *Governing* 4(11):14 (August 1991).

       Tucker, William. Unpopularity tax. *Forbes* 147(13):88-91 (June 24, 1991).

       Walters, Jonathan. There may yet be a bonanza in taxing mail-order sales. *Governing* 5(10):17 (July 1992).

       Washington administrative rule invalidated by Quill case. *Taxes* 70(12):1052 (December 1992).

       Yang, Catherine. The bench gives business a break. *Business Week* (Industrial/Technology Edition) (3273):32 (July 6, 1992).

3693. Chemical Waste Management, Inc. v. Hunt   June 1, 1992
       504 US 334   119 LEd2d 121   112 SCt 2009

Almanac (1992):274

Sup Ct Review (1995):217-276

Sup Ct Yearbook (1991-92):63

Chemical plus seen in rule on fee on waste shipments. *Chemical Marketing Reporter* 241(23):3, 17 (June 8, 1992).

Court still shuns waste case. *ENR* 227(21):30 (November 25, 1991).

Genetelli, Richard W., David B. Zigman, and Cesar E. Bencosme. Recent U.S. Supreme Court decisions on state and local tax issues. *CPA Journal* 62(11):38-44 (November 1992).

Hanson, David. High Court kills state waste disposal limits. *Chemical and Engineering News* 70(23):5 (June 8, 1992).

Kemezis, Paul. Among the states: free trade: High Court opens the doors for waste imports. *Chemical Week* 151(7):50-52 (August 19, 1992).

————. Waste not wanted, but Alabama must take it. *Chemical Week* 148(23):9 (June 19, 1991).

Loesel, Andrew. Waste management '91: border battles: states are hoping to gain greater contorl of waste crossing their borders, and Congress may be willing to let them. *Chemical Marketing Reporter* 240(21):7 (November 18, 1991).

————. Waste management '92: mired in gridlock. *Chemical Marketing Reporter* 242(20):SR3-SR8 (November 16, 1992).

Lyons, James. The garbage war between the states. *Forbes* 146(8):92, 96 (October 15, 1990).

Put an end to the civil wars. [Editorial] *ENR* 228(3):90 (January 20, 1992).

Rosen, Arthur R. Supreme Court clarifies perimeters of state tax jurisdiction. *Taxes* 70(8):559-569 (August 1992).

Singletary, Lynda. Waste management '92: interstate—closely watched borders. *Chemical Marketing Reporter* 242(20):SR22 (November 16, 1992).

Springer, Neil. Waste management '92: plenty of room at the inn. *Chemical Marketing Reporter* 242(20):SR8-SR10 (November 16, 1992).

Waste disposal shipments upheld in two big cases. *ENR* 228(23):14 (June 8, 1992).

Yang, Catherine. The bench gives business a break. *Business Week* (Industrial/Technology Edition) (3273):32 (July 6, 1992).

3694. Fort Gratiot Sanitary Landfill, Inc. v. Michigan Department of Natural Resources — June 1, 1992

Fort Gratiot Landfill v. Michigan Department of Natural Resources

504 US 353   119 LEd2d 139   112 SCt 2019

Almanac (1992):274; (1994):261; (1995):5-17

Sup Ct Yearbook (1991-92):64

Waste disposal shipments upheld in two big cases. *ENR* 228(23):14 (June 8, 1992)

3695. Morales, Attorney General of Texas v. Trans World Airlines, Inc. — June 1, 1992

504 US 374   119 LEd2d 157   112 SCt 2031

Sup Ct Yearbook (1991-92): 67-68 (1993-94):297; (1994-95):67

Fotos, Christopher P. Court blocks state laws on airline advertising. *Aviation Week and Space Technology* 136(23):33 (June 8, 1992).

Gersh, Debra. Not many press cases reaching the Supreme Court. *Editor and Publisher* 125(1):17, 30-31 (January 4, 1992).

————. Shifting legal focus in the Supreme Court: legal action involving news media in 1992 dealt more with commercial speech, subpoenas for phone record than on libel. *Editor and Publisher* 126(1):24-25 (January 2, 1993).

————. Supreme Court rules on airline ad regulation. *Editor and Publisher* 125(24):47, 53 (June 13, 1992).

Hale, F. Dennis. Mass media organizations avoid Supreme Court. *Editor and Publisher* 125(37):60, 51 (September 12, 1992).

Yang, Catherine. The bench gives business a break. *Business Week* (Industrial/Technology Edition) (3273):32 (July 6, 1992).

3696. Burdick v. Takushi, Director of Elections of Hawaii June 8, 1992

504 US 428   119 LEd2d 245   112 SCt 2059

Almanac (1992):328-329
Guide (West): (1993):148-151
Sup Ct Yearbook (1991-92):61

3697. Eastman Kodak Co. v. Image Technical Services, Inc.   June 8, 1992
        504 US 451   119 LEd2d 265   112 SCt 2072
        Guide (West): (1993):32-34
        Sup Ct Yearbook (1991-92):35-36
        Bork, Robert H. Beside the law. *National Review* 44(20):38, 40-43 (October 19, 1992).
        Coy, Peter. High-tech repairs: are giants hogging the pie? *Business Week* (Industrial/Technology Edition)
            (3227):108 (August 19, 1991).
        Frum, David. Whom should the law protect? *Forbes* 150(11):72-73 (November 9, 1992).
        Gannon, Virginia. Ask High Court to alter CPU marketing ruling. *Electronic News* 37(1862):37 (June 3, 1991).
        Servicing manufactured goods: take it back, son. *Economist* 323(7764):69 (June 20-26, 1992).
        Smart, Tim, Gary McWilliams, and Alice Z. Cunco. Kodak takes a shot in the mug. *Business Week*
            (Industrial/Technology Edition) (3271):40 (June 22 1992).
        Smart, Tim, and Howard Gleckman. The High Court has business holding its breath. *Business Week*
            (Industrial/Technology Edition) (3234):36, 38 (October 7, 1991).
        Yang, Catherine. The bench gives business a break. *Business Week* (Industrial/Technology Edition) (3273):32
            (July 6, 1992).

3698. United States v. Thompson/Center Arms Co.   June 8, 1992
        504 US 505   119 LEd2d 308   112 SCt 2102
        Sup Ct Yearbook (1991-92):43

3699. Sochor v. Florida   June 8, 1992
        504 US 527   119 LEd2d 326   112 SCt 2114
        Death Penalty (Tushnet) 115, 116-119
        Sup Ct Yearbook (1991-92):57-58

3700. Lujan, Secretary of the Interior v. Defenders of Wildlife   June 12, 1992
        504 US 555   119 LEd2d 351   112 SCt 2130
        Sup Ct Review (1993):37-64; (1995):217-276
        Sup Ct Yearbook (1991-92):64-65
        Chemerinsky, Erwin. Supreme Court review: a bad year for environmental protection. *Trial* 28(10):83-86
            (October 1992).
        Farber, Daniel A. Supreme Court review: the global environment and the Rehnquist court. *Trial* 28(8):73-77
            (August 1992).
        ————. Supreme Court review: litigating with the sovereign. *Trial* 28(4):85-90 (April 1992).
        Rosen, Jeffrey. The leader of the opposition. *New Republic* 208(3):20-21, 24, 26-27 (January 18, 1993).
        Schmahmann, David R., and Lori J. Polacheck. The case against rights for animals. *Boston College
            Environmental Affairs Law Review* 22(4):747-781 (Summer 1995).
        Standing to sue limited in some cases. *ENR* 228(25):12-14 (June 22, 1992).

3701. Republic of Argentina v. Weltover, Inc.   June 12, 1992
        504 US 607   119 LEd2d 394   112 SCt 2160
        Sup Ct Yearbook (1991-92):82-83

3702. Federal Trade Commission (FTC) v. Ticor Title Insurance Co.   June 12, 1992
        504 US 621   119 LEd2d 410   112 SCt 2169
        Sup Ct Yearbook (1991-92):36
        Dwyer, Paula. The right's legal ace is in the hot seat. *Business Week* (Industrial/Technology Edition) (2946):32
            (May 12, 1986).
        Gordon, Stacy Adler. Other antitrust litigation; justices' opinion in Ticor case closely watched by P/C industry.
            Business Insurance 26(3):37 (January 20, 1992).

Gordon, Stacy, and Judy Greenwald. Antitrust protection under fire: ruling could affect pending industry litigation. *Business Insurance* 26(25):1, 23 (June 22, 1992).

Greenwald, Judy. Antitrust review debated *Business Insurance* 26(3):2, 35 (January 20, 1992).

———. Antitrust showdown set. *Business Insurance* 26(41):1, 48 (October 12, 1992).

Lemov, Penelope. Health care costs and the High Court. *Governing* 6(3):12 (December 1992).

Yang, Catherine. The bench gives business a break. *Business Week* (Industrial/Technology Edition) (3273):32 (July 6, 1992).

3703. Burlington Northern Railroad Co. v. Ford   June 12, 1992
     504 US 648   119 LEd2d 432   112 SCt 2184
       Sup Ct Yearbook (1991-92):45

3704. United States v. Alvarez-Machain   June 15, 1992
     504 US 655   119 LEd2d 441   112 SCt 2188
       Almanac (1992):329
       Editorials (1992):726-731
       Guide (West): (1993):125-126, 167-169
       Sup Ct Yearbook (1991-92):17-18, 83, 116-124R

Bloom, Robert M. Judicial integrity: a call for its re-emergence in the adjudication of criminal cases. *Journal of Criminal Law and Criminology* 84(3):462-501 (Fall 1993).

Cohn, Bob, and Tim Padgett. Nabbed in the name of the law. *Newsweek* 119(26):68 (June 29, 1992).

Dripps, Donald A. Supreme Court review: making right of two wrongs. *Trial* 28(9):81-83 (September 1992).

Fighting words. [Editorial] *Nation* 255(2):39-40 (July 13, 1992).

Glennon, Michael J. State-sponsored abduction: a comment on United States v. Alvarez-Machain. *American Journal of International Law* 86(4):746-756 (October 1992).

Halberstam, Malvina. Agora: international kidnaping—in defense of the Supreme Court decision in Alvarez-Machain. *American Journal of International Law* 86(4):736-746 (October 1992).

Kaplan, David A., and Bob Cohn. The hands-off Court. *Newsweek* 120(1):32-36 (July 6, 1992).

Long arm of the law: a decision to uphold an international kidnapping alarms Latin America. *Time* 139(26):30-31 (June 29, 1992).

Lonner, Jonathan A. Supreme Court review: official government abductions in the presence of extradition treaties. *Journal of Criminal Law and Criminology* 83(4):998-1023 (Winter 1993).

Trimble, Phillip R. The Supreme Court and international law: the demise of restatement section 403. [Editorial] *American Journal of International Law* 89(1):53-57 (January 1995).

United States and Mexico: a hunch too far. *Economist* 325(7790):25-28 (December 19-25, 1992).

3705. Ankenbrandt, as Next Friend and Mother of L.R. v. Richards   June 15, 1992
     504 US 689   119 LEd2d 468   112 SCt 2206
       Guide (West): (1993):110-112
       Sup Ct Yearbook (1991-92):45

3706. Morgan v. Illinois   June 15, 1992
     504 US 719   119 LEd2d 492   112 SCt 2222
       Death Penalty (Tushnet) 116, 119
       Guide (West): (1993):61-63
       Sup Ct Yearbook (1991-92):56-57

Kaplan, David A., and Bob Cohn. The hands-off Court. *Newsweek* 120(1):32-36 (July 6, 1992).

3707. Patterson, Trustee v. Shumate   June 15, 1992
     504 US 753   119 LEd2d 519   112 SCt 2242
       Sup Ct Yearbook (1991-92):38

Geisel, Jerry. Bankruptcy law vs. ERISA: Supreme Court to decide if creditors can tap pensions. *Business Insurance* 26(15):2, 82 (April 13, 1992).

Supreme Court rules on ERISA/bankruptcy issues. *Taxes* 70(7):426 (July 1992).

3708. Allied-Signal, Inc. v. Director, Division of Taxation   June 15, 1992
    504 US 768   119 LEd2d 533   112 SCt 2251
Sup Ct Yearbook (1991-92):40

Corporate: Supreme Court affirms unitary business principle. *Journal of Accountancy* 174(3):35-36 (September 1992).

Genetelli, Richard W., David B. Zigman, and Cesar E. Bencosme. Recent U.S. Supreme Court decisions on state and local tax issues. *CPA Journal* 62(11):38-44 (November 1992).

Peters, James H. Gain was not unitary income subject to state apportionment. *Journal of Taxation* 77(3):180-181 (September 1992).

Rosen, Arthur R. Supreme Court clarifies perimeters of state tax jurisdiction. *Taxes* 70(8):559-569 (August 1992).

Supreme Court reaffirms unitary business principle. *Practical Accountant* 25(9):59 (September 1992).

Unger, Joseph. Investment income of multistate corporations. *CPA Journal* 63(6):66 (June 1993).

3709. Nordlinger v. Hahn   June 18, 1992
    505 US 1   120 LEd2d 1   112 SCt 2326
Guide (West): (1993):362-365
Sup Ct Yearbook (1991-92):42

Genetelli, Richard W., David B. Zigman, and Cesar E. Bencosme. Recent U.S. Supreme Court decisions on state and local tax issues. *CPA Journal* 62(11):38-44 (November 1992).

Kinsley, Michael. Santa clause. *New Republic* 206(13):6 (March 30, 1992).

O'Connell, Daniel. U.S. Supreme Court reviews state and local taxation issues. *CPA Journal* 62(3):16-21 (March 1992).

Rosen, Arthur R. Supreme Court clarifies perimeters of state tax jurisdiction. *Taxes* 70(8):559-569 (August 1992).

Rusher, William A. Fair or foul? *National Review* 44(4):22-24 (March 2, 1992).

3710. Georgia v. McCollum   June 18, 1992
    505 US 42   120 LEd2d 33   112 SCt 2348
Almanac (1992):329
Guide (West): (1993):99-103
Sup Ct Yearbook (1991-92):56; (1993-94):37

A bar to peremptory jury challenges: the top court is divided by racial issues as the term winds down. *Time* 139(26):30 (June 29, 1992).

Gemskie, Michele A. Supreme Court review: Fourteenth Amendment—peremptory challenges by defendants and the equal protection clause. *Journal of Criminal Law and Criminology* 83(4):920-943 (Winter 1993).

Rosen, Jeffrey. Never mind. *New Republic* 207(13):18, 20-22 (September 21, 1992).

Sancton, Thomas, Julie Johnson, and Andrea Sachs. Judging Thomas. *Time* 140(2):30-31 (July 13, 1992).

3711. Kraft General Foods, Inc. v. Iowa Department of Revenue and Finance   June 18, 1992
    505 US 71   120 LEd2d 59   112 SCt 2365
Sup Ct Yearbook (1991-92):42

Genetelli, Richard W., David B. Zigman, and Cesar E. Bencosme. Recent U.S. Supreme Court decisions on state and local tax issues. *CPA Journal* 62(11):38-44 (November 1992).

Rosen, Arthur R. Supreme Court clarifies perimeters of state tax jurisdiction. *Taxes* 70(8):559-569 (August 1992).

3712. Gade, Director, Illinois Environmental Protection Agency   June 18, 1992
      v. National Solid Wastes Management Association
    505 US 88   120 LEd2d 73   112 SCt 2374
Sup Ct Yearbook (1991-92):64

3713. Forsyth County, Georgia v. Nationalist Movement   June 19, 1992
    505 US 123   120 LEd2d 101   112 SCt 2395
Guide (West): (1993):198-200

Sup Ct Review (1992):79-122

Sup Ct Yearbook (1991-92):75-76

A bar to peremptory jury challenges: the top court is divided by racial issues as the term winds down. *Time* 139(26):30 (June 29, 1992).

Cohn, Bob. Free speech that's costly. *Newsweek* 119(26):69 (June 29, 1992).

Hale, F. Dennis. Mass media organizations avoid Supreme Court. *Editor and Publisher* 125(37):60, 51 (September 12, 1992).

3714. New York v. United States   June 19, 1992

        Coupled with County of Allegany, New York v. United States

        Coupled with County of Cortland, New York v. United States

  505 US 144   120 LEd2d 120   112 SCt 2408

   Almanac (1992):329

   Hard Choices 319

   Sup Ct Review (1995):125-215

   Sup Ct Yearbook (1991-92):65

Chemerinsky, Erwin. Supreme Court review: a bad year for environmental protection. *Trial* 28(10):83-86 (October 1992).

————. Looking ahead to the new term. *Trial* 30(12):81-83 (December 1994).

Greenberger, Leonard S., and Kristen Smyth. Supreme Court weakens low-level waste law. *Public Utilities Fortnightly* 130(26-28):26-28 (August 1, 1992).

High Court to hear waste storage challenge. *ENR* 228(3):12 (January 20, 1992).

Put an end to the civil wars. [Editorial] *ENR* 228(3):90 (January 20, 1992).

Rapp, David. States' rights and Sandra Day O'Connor. *Governing* 6(3):59 (December 1992).

Wise, Charles, and Rosemary O'Leary. Is federalism dead or alive in the Supreme Court?: implications for public administrators. *Public Administration Review* 52(6):559-572 (November/December 1992).

3715. Wisconsin Department of Revenue v. William Wrigley Jr.   June 19, 1992

  505 US 214   120 LEd2d 174   112 SCt 2447

   Sup Ct Yearbook (1991-92):44

Genetelli, Richard W., David B. Zigman, and Cesar E. Bencosme. Recent U.S. Supreme Court decisions on state and local tax issues. *CPA Journal* 62(11):38-44 (November 1992).

O'Connell, Daniel. U.S. Supreme Court reviews state and local taxation issues. *CPA Journal* 62(3):16-21 (March 1992).

Peters, Jeffrey S., and William D. Ault. Update on state tax issues before the U.S. Supreme Court. *CPA Journal* 62(4):73-74 (April 1992).

Rosen, Arthur R. Supreme Court clarifies perimeters of state tax jurisdiction. *Taxes* 70(8):559-569 (August 1992).

Supreme Court rules on states' ability to impose a corporate income tax on out-of-state company. *Practical Accountant* 25(9):58 (September 1992).

3716. American National Red Cross v. S.G.   June 19, 1992

  505 US 247   120 LEd2d 201   112 SCt 2465

   Sup Ct Yearbook (1991-92):44-45

3717. Wright, Warden v. West   June 19, 1992

  505 US 277   120 LEd2d 225   112 SCt 2482

   Sup Ct Yearbook (1991-92):54

Basta, James. Supreme Court review: habeas corpus: unresolved standard of review on mixed questions for state prisoners. *Journal of Criminal Law and Criminology* 83(4):978-997 (Winter 1993).

Chemerinsky, Erwin. Supreme Court review: making sense of habeas corpus. *Trial* 28(12):79-82 (December 1992).

Rosen, Jeffrey. Never mind. *New Republic* 207(13):18, 20-22 (September 21, 1992).

3718. United States v. Salerno   June 19, 1992
      505 US 317   120 LEd2d 255   112 SCt 2503
          Sup Ct Yearbook (1991-92):50, 52

3719. Sawyer v. Whitley, Warden   June 22, 1992
      505 US 333   120 LEd2d 269   112 SCt 2514
          Death Penalty (Tushnet) 117-119, 122, 128
          Guide (West): (1993):209-211
          Sup Ct Yearbook (1991-92):53-54; (1994-95):86-87
      Chemerinsky, Erwin. Supreme Court review: innocence and habeas corpus. *Trial* 31(4):79-81 (April 1995).
      ———. Supreme Court review: making sense of habeas corpus. *Trial* 28(12):79-82 (December 1992).

3720. R.A.V. v. City of St. Paul, Minnesota   June 22, 1992
      505 US 377   120 LEd2d 305   112 SCt 2538
          Almanac (1992):326-327, 329; (1993):354
          Editorials (1992):732-737; (1993):730-733
          Guide (West): (1993):193-198
          Landmark (v. 4):167-177R
          Price 8-13, 27-31, 114-121, 169-175, 194-198, 244-248
          Sup Ct Review (1992):29-77; (1993):1-36; (1994):1-56
          Sup Ct Yearbook (1990-91):197; (1991-92):18-20, 77-78, 124-130R
      Boedecker, Karl A., and Fred W. Morgan. The evolution of First Amendment protection for commercial speech. *Journal of Marketing* 59(1):38-47 (January 1995).
      Breaking the codes. *New Republic* 205(2):7-8 (July 8, 1991).
      Brooks, Thomas D. Supreme Court review: First Amendment—penalty enhancement for hate crimes: content regulation, questionable state interests and non-traditional sentencing. *Journal of Criminal Law and Criminology* 84(4):703-742 (Winter/Spring 1994).
      Chin, Paula. A crime of hate. *People Weekly* 37(1):66-68 (January 13, 1992).
      Cohn, Bob, and David A. Kaplan. Supreme conservatism. *Newsweek* 118(16):56-57 (October 14, 1991).
      Ennis, Bruce J. Protecting individual rights: hate speech and the heckler's veto. *Trial* 27(12):27-30 (December 1991).
      Fighting words. [Editorial] *Nation* 255(2):39-40 (July 13, 1992).
      Freedom to hate. *Economist* 327(7810):33 (May 8-14, 1993).
      Gersh, Debra. Shifting legal focus in the Supreme Court: legal action involving news media in 1992 dealt more with commercial speech, subpoenas for phone record than on libel. *Editor and Publisher* 126(1):24-25 (January 2, 1993).
      Gest, Ted. The not yet totally conservative Court. *U.S. News and World Report* 113(1):16 (July 6, 1992).
      ———. Reining in citizens' rights: Rehnquist Court will reinterpret the 200-year-old Bill of Rights. *U.S. News and World Report* 111(25):49-53 (December 16, 1991).
      Hale, F. Dennis. Mass media organizations avoid Supreme Court. *Editor and Publisher* 125(37):60, 51 (September 12, 1992).
      Hentoff, Nat. Multiculturalism and free speech. *Progressive* 56(11):15-17 (November 1992).
      Jaschik, Scott. Campus 'hate speech' codes in doubt after High Court rejects a city ordinance. *Chronicle of Higher Education* 38(43):A19, A22 (July 1, 1992).
      Kaplan, David A., and Bob Cohn. The hands-off Court. *Newsweek* 120(1):32-36 (July 6, 1992).
      Leo, John. A sensible judgment on hate. [Editorial] *U.S. News and World Report* 113(1):25 (July 6, 1992).
      Meyer, Peter, and Jack Hayes. The case for hate. *Life* 14 (13 Special Issue):88-91 (Fall 1991).
      Rosen, Jeffrey. The leader of the opposition. *New Republic* 208(3):20-21, 24, 26-27 (January 18, 1993).
      ———. Never mind. *New Republic* 207(13):18, 20-22 (September 21, 1992).
      Speech therapy. *New Republic* 207(3-4):7 (July 13-20, 1992).
      Strossen, Nadine. Academic and artistic freedom. *Academe* 78(6):8-15 (November/December 1992).
      A surprising display of centrist thinking: the Supreme Court shuns extremes in four major cases. *Time* 140(1):16-17 (July 6, 1992).

3721. Medina v. California   June 22, 1992
    505 US 437   120 LEd2d 353   112 SCt 2572
      Death Penalty (Tushnet) 116-117, 119
      Guide (West): (1993):89-92
      Sup Ct Yearbook (1991-92):49-50

3722. Estate of Cowart v. Nicklos Drilling Co.   June 22, 1992
    505 US 469   120 LEd2d 379   112 SCt 2589
      Sup Ct Yearbook (1991-92):78
    Gordon, Stacy Adler. Court to hear comp case; refuses damages review. *Business Insurance* 25(50):2, 71 (December 16, 1991).

3723. Cipollone v. Liggett Group, Inc.   June 24, 1992
    505 US 504   120 LEd2d 407   112 SCt 2608
      Almanac (1992):327-329
      Guide (West): (1992):300-302; (1993):317-319
      Sup Ct Yearbook (1990-91):195-198; (1991-92):20-23, 66-67, 130-137R
    Adler, Stacy. High Court considers tobacco suit: cigarette firms say labeling law pre-empts most liability actions. *Business Insurance* 25(41):1, 40-41 (October 14, 1991).
    Are warnings good enough? *U.S. News and World Report* 110(13):55 (April 8, 1991).
    Butt out. *Washington Monthly* 25(1-2):13-19 (January 1993).
    Coben, Larry E. Protective orders: manufacturers hide behind them. *Trial* 22(8):34-37 (August 1986).
    ———. The tide has turned: federal preemption cannot defeat motor vehicle design claims. *Trial* 29(1):75-79 (January 1993).
    Colford, Steven W. What High Court ruling means for local tobacco ads. *Advertising Age* 63(26):3, 49 (June 29, 1992).
    Galen, Michele. When the smoke clears, cigarette makers may get burned. [Editorial] *Business Week* (3293):89 (November 23, 1992).
    Gordon, Stacy Adler. Cigarette liability case again before High Court. *Business Insurance* 26(3):37 (January 20, 1992).
    ———. Tobacco ruling's impact may be felt by other firms. *Business Insurance* 26(27):3, 22 (July 6, 1992).
    Gostin, Larry O, Allan M. Brandt, and Paul D. Cleary. Tobacco liability and public health policy. *JAMA: The Journal of the American Medical Association* 266(22): 3178-3182 (December 11, 1991).
    Greene, Norman L. Cigarette case may burn other firms. *Business Insurance* 25(47):26 (November 25, 1991).
    Konrad, Walecia. RJR can't seem to find a spot in the shade. *Business Week* (Industrial/Technology Edition) (3275):70-71 (July 20, 1992).
    Konrad, Walecia, and Catherine Yang. This decision may be hazardous to tobacco's health: the High Court leaves the industry open to suits charging concealment. *Business Week* (Industrial/Technology Edition) (3273):33 (July 6, 1992).
    Mabry, Marcus, and Bruce Shenitz. Suing cigarette makers. *Newsweek* 120(1):61 (July 6, 1992).
    Mangan, Joseph F. Warning: hazard warnings may be an unsafe defense. *Best's Review* (Property/Casualty Insurance Edition) 93(6):67-68 (October 1992).
    McLeod, Douglas. Supreme Court reverses tobacco liability rulings. *Business Insurance* 26(26):1, 103-104 (June 29, 1992).
    Smart, Tim. It takes more than black robes to scare tobacco companies. *Business Week* (Industrial/Technology Edition) (3208):34 (April 8, 1991).
    Smart, Tim, and Dean Foust. The Supreme Court: 'leave it to the states.' *Business Week* (Industrial/Technology Edition) (3221):32 (July 8, 1991).
    Smart, Tim, and Howard Gleckman. The High Court has business holding its breath. *Business Week* (Industrial/Technology Edition) (3234):36, 38 (October 7, 1991).
    Smith, Todd A. Toxic tort litigation: federal preemption in a post-Cipollone world. *Trial* 28(12):58-63 (December 1992).
    Smoger, Gerson H., Andrews N. Wolf, and Martin J. Hoffman. How to fight FIFRA preemption. *Trial* 31(7):34-37, (July 1995).
    Spencer, Leslie. Just smoke. *Forbes* 148(14):41-42 (December 23, 1991).

A surprising display of centrist thinking: the Supreme Court shuns extremes in four major cases. *Time* 140(1):16-17 (July 6, 1992).

3724. Lee v. Weisman   June 24, 1992
    505 US 577   120 LEd2d 467   112 SCt 2649
    Almanac (1992):326, 329
    Brennan 129-134
    Center 281-293
    Editorials (1992):720-725
    Godless 91-93
    Guide (West): (1992):172-174; (1993):186-189
    Let Us 126-128
    Sup Ct Review (1990-91):197; (1991-92):23-26, 76-77, 137-144R,179; (1992):123-153; (1995):323-391
    Turning 452-454, 468+

Bork, Robert H. Beside the law. *National Review* 44(20):38, 40-43 (October 19, 1992).

———. What to do about the First Amendment. *Commentary* 99(2):23-29 (February 1995).

Carter, Stephen L. Let us pray. *New Yorker* 70(40):60-74 (December 5, 1994).

Chemerinsky, Erwin. Supreme Court review: free speech or religious freedom: revisiting the establishment clause. *Trial* 31(12):16-19 (December 1995).

———. Supreme Court review: religion clause doctrine: potential for change. *Trial* 29(2):81-84 (February 1993).

Cohn, Bob. Supreme but not final. *Newsweek* 120(15):78-79 (October 12, 1992).

Conn, James J. Graduation prayers and the establishment clause. *America* 167(15):380-382 (November 14, 1992).

Cord, Robert L. Church, state, and the Rehnquist Court. *National Review* 44(16):35-37 (August 17, 1992).

Court decision on prayer. *Christian Century* 109(21):641 (July 1-8, 1992).

Court hears prayer case. *Christianity Today* 35(15):59-60 (December 16, 1991).

Court rulings on religion. *Christian Century* 110(19):624-625 (June 16-23, 1993).

Doerr, Edd. Looking back, looking forward. [Editorial] *Humanist* 51(5):41-42 (September/October 1991).

Drinan, Robert F. Do invocations at graduations violate the First Amendment? *America* 165(5):114-118 (August 31-September 7 1991).

Frame, Randy. Key Court rulings offer mixed blessings. *Christianity Today* 36(9):44-45 (August 17, 1992).

Freid, Stephen H. The constitutionality of choice under the establishment clause. *Clearing House* 66(2):92-95 (November/December 1992).

Gaffney, Edward McGlynn, Jr. Prayer at commencement. *Christian Century* 110(18):590-591 (June 2-9, 1993).

Gest, Ted. Next stage: Court lite. *U.S. News and World Report* 111(2):16-19 (July 8, 1991).

———. The not yet totally conservative Court. *U.S. News and World Report* 113(1):16 (July 6, 1992).

———. The Supreme Court: a reluctant referee. *U.S. News and World Report* 117(12):84 (September 26, 1994).

Gibbs, Nancy R., David Aikman, and Richard N. Ostling. America's holy war. *Time* 138(23):60-68 (December 9, 1991).

Harrington-Lueker, Donna. Putting prayer to a vote. *American School Board Journal* 181(5):30-31 (May 1994).

Kaplan, David A., and Bob Cohn. The hands-off Court. *Newsweek* 120(1):32-36 (July 6, 1992).

Lawton, Kim A. Do students have a prayer? *Christianity Today* 37(7):45 (June 21, 1993).

———. Uncle Sam v. First Church. *Christianity Today* 35(11):38-41 (October 7, 1991).

McCarthy, Martha M. Much ado over graduation prayer. *Phi Delta Kappan* 75(2):120-125 (October 1993).

Methvin, Eugene H. Let us pray! *Reader's Digest* 141(847):75-79 (November 1992).

———. Will the U.S. Supreme Court pardon Robert E. Lee?: a declaration of duty. *Vital Speeches* 58(14):437-440 (May 1, 1992).

Mishler, William, and Reginald S. Sheehan. The Supreme Court as a countermajoritarian institution? The impact of public opinion on Supreme Court decisions. *American Political Science Review* 87(1):87-101 (March 1993).

Monagle, Katie. What place for God? *Scholastic Update* (Teachers' Edition) 124(5):17-18 (November 1, 1991).

Novak, Michael. Judicial tyranny. [Editorial] *Forbes* 150(10):238 (October 26, 1992).

Prayer in public schools. *Congressional Digest* 74(1):3-32 (January 1995).

Rabinove, Samuel, Josef Joffe, Sheldon F. Gottlieb, Adam Simms, Stephen F. Rohde, Jeffrey Valle, and Robert H. Bork. The First Amendment. [Editorial] *Commentary* 99(5):7-15 (May 1995).

Rosen, Jeffrey. The leader of the opposition. *New Republic* 208(3):20-21, 24, 26-27 (January 18, 1993).

School prayer. *Christian Century* 108(13):424-425 (April 17, 1991).

Scrap the 'Lemon test,' say Southern Baptists. *Christian Century* 111(7):219-220 (March 2, 1994).

Sendor, Benjamin. The pledge passes constitutional muster. *American School Board Journal* 180(6):10-11, 39 (June 1993).

———. Time for a primer on commencement prayer. *American School Board Journal* 182(7):16-17 (July 1995).

———. To pray or not to pray? *American School Board Journal* 180(4):20-21 (April 1993).

Slafsky, Ted. One day, the rabbi gave a prayer. *U.S. News and World Report* 112(24):26 (June 22, 1992).

Sudo, Philip, and James Earl Hardy. Tomorrow's news. *Scholastic Update* (Teachers' Edition) 123(16):24-25 (May 3, 1991).

A surprising display of centrist thinking: the Supreme Court shuns extremes in four major cases. *Time* 140(1):16-17 (July 6, 1992).

Vacca, Richard S., and H. C. Hudgins, Jr. Pomp and controversy. *American School Board Journal* 181(5):29-32 (May 1994).

Woodward, Kenneth L., and Nadine Joseph. The return of the fourth R. *Newsweek* 117(23):56-57 (June 10, 1991).

Zirkel, Perry A. De jure: a bedeviling message from Providence. *Phi Delta Kappan* 74(2):183-184 (October 1992).

———. De jure: Is the 'wall of separation' like the Walls of Jericho? *Phi Delta Kappan* 75(1):88-90 (September 1993).

Zirkel, Perry A., and Ivan B. Gluckman. Invocations and benedictions at school ceremonies. *NASSP Bulletin* 76(547):102-105 (November 1992).

3725. City of Burlington v. Dague   June 24, 1992

505 US 624   120 LEd2d 449   112 SCt 2638

    Sup Ct Yearbook (1991-92):36

Conte, Alba. Public interest lawyers deserve risk multipliers. *Trial* 30(12):36-42 (December 1994).

3726. Doggett v. United States   June 24, 1992

505 US 647   120 LEd2d 520   112 SCt 2686

    Guide (West): (1993):96-98

    Sup Ct Yearbook (1991-92):59-60

Rosenblatt, Roger. The Bill of Rights. *Life* 14(13 Special Issue):9-30 (Fall 1991).

Wernikoff, Steven M. Supreme Court review: Sixth Amendment—extending Sixth Amendment speedy trial protection to defendants unaware of their indictments. *Journal of Criminal Law and Criminology* 83(4):804-835 (Winter 1993).

3727. International Society for Krishna Consciousness, Inc. and Brian Rumbaugh v. Lee   June 26, 1992

Society for Krishna Consciousness v. Lee, Superintendent of Port Authority Police

505 US 672   120 LEd2d 541   112 SCt 2701, 2711

    Godless 43-44

    Guide (West): (1993):201-203

    Let Us 129

    Sup Ct Review (1992):79-122; (1994):57-128

    Sup Ct Yearbook (1991-92):76

Court considers animal sacrifice, airport witnessing. *Christianity Today* 36(5):46-47 (April 27, 1992).

Hale, F. Dennis. Mass media organizations avoid Supreme Court. *Editor and Publisher* 125(37):60, 51 (September 12, 1992).

3728. United States v. Fordice, Governor of Mississippi   June 26, 1992
            Coupled with Ayers v. Fordice, Governor of Mississippi
        505 US 717   120 LEd2d 575   112 SCt 2727
            Almanac (1992):329
            Guide (West): (1993):129-132
            Sup Ct Yearbook (1990-91):200; (1991-92):26-27, 74, 144-154R
        Blumenstyk, Goldie. Justice dept. affirms federal backing for black colleges. *Chronicle of Higher Education*
            38(8):A41, A44 (October 16, 1991).
            ———. Ruling by Supreme Court appears to back immunity of college officials in student-dismissal cases.
            Chronicle of Higher Education 38(8):A44 (October 16, 1991).
        Butler, Grace L. Legal and policy issues in higher education. *Journal of Negro Education* 63(3):451-459
            (Summer 1994).
        Committee L on the Historically Black Institutions and the Status of Minorities in the Profession. The
            historically black colleges and universities: a future in the balance. *Academe* 81(1):49-58 (January/February
            1995).
        Cunningham, Kitty. Are black public colleges turning white? *Black Enterprise* 24(1):29 (August 1993).
        Gest, Ted. The not yet totally conservative Court. *U.S. News and World Report* 113(1):16 (July 6, 1992).
        Halpern, Stephen C. A bedeviling and worrisome court ruling on black colleges. [Editorial] *Chronicle of
            Higher Education* 39(11):B1-B2 (November 4, 1992).
        Jaschik, Scott. Education Dept. to use 1992 Supreme Court case in judging formerly segregated state systems.
            Chronicle of Higher Education 40(23):A36 (February 9, 1994).
            ———. High-Court ruling transforms battles over desegregation at colleges in 19 states. *Chronicle of Higher
            Education* 38(44):A16-A18 (July 8, 1992).
            ———. Whither desegregation? *Chronicle of Higher Education* 40(21):A33, A37 (January 26, 1994).
        Johnson, Julie. Are black colleges worth saving?: the Supreme Court will consider whether the states should
            pay publicly funded institutions for the neglect caused by decades of discrimination. *Time* 138(19):81
            (November 11, 1991).
        Mercer, Joye. Black alumni groups spurred to action by Supreme Court's desegregation decision. *Chronicle of
            Higher Education* 39(6):A25-A26 (September 30, 1992).
            ———. Black college would be closed in Mississippi plan to comply with court's ruling on desegregation.
            Chronicle of Higher Education 39(10):A29 (October 28, 1992).
        Sancton, Thomas, Julie Johnson, and Andrea Sachs. Judging Thomas. *Time* 140(2):30-31 (July 13, 1992).
        Stefkovich, Jacqueline A., and Terrence Leas. A legal history of desegregation in higher education. *Journal of
            Negro Education* 63(3):406-420 (Summer 1994).
        Supreme Court to hear Miss. state univ. system desegregation argument. *Jet* 80(3):4 (May 6, 1991).
        A surprising display of centrist thinking: the Supreme Court shuns extremes in four major cases. *Time*
            140(1):16-17 (July 6, 1992).
        Text of opinions in Supreme Court's decision on Mississippi desegregation. *Chronicle of Higher Education*
            38(44):A19-A24R (July 8, 1992).
        Ware, Leland. Will there be a "different world" after Fordice? *Academe* 80(3):6-11 (May/June 1994).

3729. Two Pesos, Inc. v. Taco Cabana, Inc.   June 26, 1992
        505 US 763   120 LEd2d 615   112 SCt 2753
            Sup Ct Yearbook (1991-92):44

3730. Franklin, Secretary of Commerce v. Massachusetts   June 26, 1992
        505 US 788   120 LEd2d 636   112 SCt 2767
            Almanac (1992):328
            Sup Ct Yearbook (1991-92):61

3731. Lee v. International Society for Krishna Consciousness, Inc.   June 26, 1992
        505 US 830   120 LEd2d 669   112 Sct 2709
            Godless 43-44
            Sup Ct Yearbook (1991-92):76

3732. Planned Parenthood of Southeastern Pennsylvania v. Casey, Governor of Pennsylvania   June 29, 1992
    505 US 833   120 LEd2d 674   112 SCt 2791

 Abortion Am 315, 325-330, 337-346R+
 Abortion Con xxii+, 256-259, 261-263, 246, 293
 Abortion Dec 90s Introduction, 109-211R
 Almanac (1992):329, 398-400, 30E-34ER
 Brennan 318-320
 Center 154-158, 163-167+
 Editorials (1992):86-93, 770-781
 Guide (West): (1993):5-7, 11-18, 381-475R
 Hard Choices 8-11+, 224-243
 Liberty 689-701+
 Sup Ct Review (1992):1-28; (1995):125-215+
 Sup Ct Yearbook (1991-92):30-34, 71-72, 159-178R
 Turning 454-461, 466-471+

Abortion: rage over Roe. *Economist* 323(7756):22-23 (April 25-May1, 1992).

Abortion ruling. *Christian Century* 109(22):674-675 (July 15-22, 1992).

Abortion test cases. *Time* 137(26):22-23 (July 1, 1991).

American survey: the high and middle ground. *Economist* 324(7766):25-26 (July 4-10, 1992).

Annas, George J. The Supreme Court, liberty, and abortion. *New England Journal of Medicine* 327(9):651-654 (August 27, 1992).

Barrett, Laurence I., and Julie Johnson. Abortion: the issue Bush hopes will go away. *Time* 140(2):28-29 (July 13, 1992).

A battle echoes from the street to the Court: the justices hear arguments over abortion rights and the death penalty. *Time* 139(18):14-15 (May 4, 1992).

Benshoof, Janet. Planned Parenthood v Casey. *JAMA: The Journal of the American Medical Association* 269(17): 2249-2257 (May 5, 1993).

Bork, Robert H. Beside the law. *National Review* 44(20):38, 40-43 (October 19, 1992).

Bryden, David P. Is the Rehnquist Court conservative? *Public Interest* (109):73-88 (Fall 1992).

The case against Casey. *New Republic* 207(5):7 (July 27 1992).

Casey, Robert P. The Democratic Party. *Vital Speeches* 58(17)520-524 (June 15, 1992).

Chemerinsky, Erwin. Looking ahead to the new term. *Trial* 30(12):81-83 (December 1994).

A close call: despite restrictions, the landmark Roe v. Wade ruling is upheld. *Time* 140(2):15-16 (July 13, 1992).

Coalitions on abortion. *Christian Century* 109(15):447-448 (April 22, 1992).

Cockburn, Alexander. Almost free to choose. *New Statesman and Society* 5(209):16-17 (July 3, 1992).

Cohn, Bob. The Court's case of nerves. *Newsweek* 119(18):26 (May 4, 1992).

Colson, Charles W. Casey strikes out. [Editorial] *Christianity Today* 38(11):104 (October 3, 1994).

Copelon, Rhonda. What's missing from the abortion debate. *Ms.* 3(2):86-87 (September/October 1992).

Dellinger, Walter. Gag me with a rule. *New Republic* 206(1-2):14-16 (January 6-13, 1992).

Doerr, Edd. The end of Roe v. Wade. *Humanist* 52(3):45-46 (May/June 1992).

Douglas, Susan J. The year of what woman? *Progressive* 56(9):11 (September 1992).

Dump 'Roe.' *New Republic* 206(20):7 (May 18, 1992).

Dworkin, Ronald. The center holds! *New York Review of Books* 39(14):29-33 (August 13, 1992).

Frame, Randy. Key Court rulings offer mixed blessings. *Christianity Today* 36(9):44-45 (August 17, 1992).

Freeman, Alan David, and Elizabeth Mensch. The Court & the sexual revolution. *Commonweal* 121(18):19-23 (October 21, 1994).

Gest, Ted. Why Roe v. Wade isn't yet in danger. *U.S. News and World Report* 112(16):38-39 (April 27, 1992).

Gest, Ted, Mary Lord, Constance Johnson, Matthew Cooper, and Steven V. Roberts. Sound and fury signifying little. *U.S. News and World Report* 113(2):32-38 (July 13, 1992).

Gillman, Howard. Preferred freedoms: the progressive expansion of state power and the rise of modern civil liberties jurisprudence. *Political Research Quarterly* 47(3):623-653 (September 1994).

Gostin, Lawrence O. Health law. *JAMA: The Journal of the American Medical Association* 268(3): 364-366 (July 15, 1992).

———. Law and medicine. *JAMA: The Journal of the American Medical Association* 273(21): 1688-1689 (June 7, 1995).

Justice Souter, out from the egg. *Economist* 324(7766):30 (July 4-10, 1992).

Kantrowitz, Barbara, and Ginny Carroll. Tipping the odds on abortion. *Newsweek* 118(2):23 (July 8, 1991).

Kaplan, David A. Is Roe good law? *Newsweek* 119(17):49-51 (April 27, 1992).

Kaplan, David A., and Bob Cohn. The hands-off Court. *Newsweek* 120(1):32-36 (July 6, 1992).

———. "Nine scorpions in a bottle." *Newsweek* 120(2):20 (July 13, 1992).

Lacayo, Richard, and Julie Johnson. Abortion: inside the Court: Justice Kennedy flipped positions to uphold abortion rights. *Time* 140(2):29 (July 13, 1992).

———. Taking aim at Roe v. Wade. *Time* 139(5):16 (February 3, 1992).

Lacayo, Richard, Julie Johnson, Priscilla Painton, and Elizabeth Taylor. Abortion: the future is already here. *Time* 139(18):26-32 (May 4, 1992).

Leo, John. The quagmire of abortion rights. [Editorial] *U.S. News and World Report* 113(2):16 (July 13, 1992).

Liberty for some. [Editorial] *Commonweal* 119(13):3 (July 17, 1992).

Mishler, William, and Reginald S. Sheehan. The Supreme Court as a countermajoritarian institution? The impact of public opinion on Supreme Court decisions. *American Political Science Review* 87(1):87-101 (March 1993).

Novak, Michael. Judicial tyranny. [Editorial] *Forbes* 150(10):238 (October 26, 1992).

Opposing views argued in court, on the streets. *Christianity Today* 36(6):48 (May 18, 1992).

Orren, Karen. The primary of labor in American constitutional development. *American Political Science Review* 89(2):377-388 (June 1995).

Ponnuru, Ramesh. Empty Souter. *National Review* 47(17):24-26 (September 11, 1995).

'Roe' redux. [Editorial] *Commonweal* 119(5):3-4 (March 13, 1992).

Rosen, Jeffrey. The leader of the opposition. *New Republic* 208(3):20-21, 24, 26-27 (January 18, 1993).

Salholz, Eloise, Vera Azar, Tony Clifton, Farai Chideya, Daniel Glick, Michael Mason, and Susan Miller. Abortion angst. *Newsweek* 120(2):16-19 (July 13, 1992).

Schwartz, Herman. New term, same tilt: The Supreme Court stays hard right. *Nation* 257(13):452-454 (October 25, 1993).

Sowell, Thomas. Court politicians. [Editorial] *Forbes* 150(3):76-77 (August 3, 1992).

Spivack, Miranda S. . . . and women's groups prepare for life after Roe. *Ms.* 2(5)91 (March/April 1992).

Stoner, James R., Jr. Common law and constitutionalism in the abortion case. *Review of Politics* 55(3):421-441 (Summer 1993).

The talk of the town: notes and comment. [Editorial] *New Yorker* 68(21):23-24 (July 13, 1992).

Talking sensibly about abortion. [Editorial]. *America* 166(16):399 (May 9, 1992).

Thanks, Governor Casey. [Editorial]. *America* 167(3):51 (August 1-8, 1992).

A thousand cuts. [Editorial] *Nation* 255(3):76-77 (July 20-27, 1992).

Wattleton, Faye. Planned Parenthood and pro choice: sexual and reproductive freedom. *Vital Speeches* 58(17):524-527 (June 15, 1992).

Whitman, David. Cracking the frenzied code of abortionspeak. *U.S. News and World Report* 112(4):10-11 (February 3, 1992).

3733. Lucas v. South Carolina Coastal Council   June 29, 1992
       505 US 1003   120 LEd2d 798   112 SCt 2886
       Guide (West): (1993):320-321
       Sup Ct Yearbook (1991-92):27-30, 80, 155-159R

Carpenter, Betsy. This land is my land: environmentalism is colliding with the rights of property owners. *U.S. News and World Report* 116(10):65-69 (March 14, 1994).

Cavarello, Daniel T. From Penn Central to United Artists' I and II: the rise to immunity of historic preservation designation from successful takings challenges. *Boston College Environmental Affairs Law Review* 22(3):593-622 (Spring 1995).

Chemerinsky, Erwin. Supreme Court review: a bad year for environmental protection. *Trial* 28(10):83-86 (October 1992).

Cohen, Jonathan E. A constitutional safety valve: the variance in zoning and land-use based environmental controls. *Boston College Environmental Affairs Law Review* 22(2):307-364 (Winter 1995).

Court to weigh property takings. *ENR* 227(22):11-12 (December 2, 1991).

Folsom, Robin E. Executive Order 12,630: a president's manipulation of the Fifth Amendment's just compensation clause to achieve control over executive agency regulatory decisionmaking. *Boston College Environmental Affairs Law Review* 20(4):639-697 (Summer 1993).

Gest, Ted. Reining in citizens' rights: Rehnquist Court will reinterpret the 200-year-old Bill of Rights. *U.S. News and World Report* 111(25):49-53 (December 16, 1991).

Gest, Ted, and Lisa J. Moore. The tide turns for property owners. *U.S. News and World Report* 113(2):57 (July 13, 1992).

Halper, Louise A. Law: A new view of regulatory takings? *Environment* 36(1):2-5, 39-40 (January/February 1994).

Kaplan, David A., and Bob Cohn. Pay me, or get off my land. *Newsweek* 119(10)70 (March 9, 1992).

Kens, Paul. Liberty and the public ingredient of private property. *Review of Politics* 55(1):85-116 (Winter 1993).

Lewis, Sylvia. Goodbye, Ramapo. Hello, Yakima and Isle of Palms. *Planning* 58(7):9-16 (July 1992).

Property rights: fight them on the beaches. *Economist* 322(7748):28 (February 29-March 6, 1992).

Rosen, Jeffrey. The leader of the opposition. *New Republic* 208(3):20-21, 24, 26-27 (January 18, 1993).

U.S. Supreme Court v. the environment? *Environment* 34(2):23-24 (March 1992).

Yang, Catherine, and Peter Hong. The grass is looking greener for landowners. *Business Week* (Industrial/Technology Edition) (3274):31 (July 13, 1992).

3734. Reynolds v. International Amateur Athletic Federation (IAAF)   June 20, 1992
        505 US 1301   120 LEd2d 861   112 SCt 2512
        Running wild. *Economist* 323(7765):28 (June 27-July 3, 1992).

3735. Church of Scientology of California v. United States   November 16, 1992
        506 US 9   121 LEd2d 313   113 SCt 447
        Sup Ct Yearbook (1992-93):54

3736. Parke, Warden v. Raley   December 1, 1992
        506 US 20   121 LEd2d 391   113 SCt 517
        Sup Ct Yearbook (1992-93):68

3737. Richmond v. Lewis, Director, Arizona Department of Corrections December 1, 1992
        506 US 40   121 LEd2d 411   113 SCt 528
        Sup Ct Yearbook (1992-93):57-58

3738. Soldal v. Cook County, Illinois   December 8, 1992
        506 US 56   121 LEd2d 450   113 SCt 538
        Guide (West): (1994):69-71
        Sup Ct Yearbook (1992-93):87
        Dripps, Donald A. Supreme Court review: search and seizure: finding for the Fourth Amendment. *Trial* 29(3):95-97 (March 1993).

3739. Mississippi v. Louisiana   December 14, 1992
        506 US 73   121 LEd2d 466   113 SCt 549
        Sup Ct Yearbook (1992-93):93-94

3740. Republic National Bank of Miami v. United States   December 14, 1992
        506 US 80   121 LEd2d 474   113 SCt 554
        Sup Ct Yearbook (1992-93):62

3741. Farrar and Smith, Co-Administrators of Estate of Joseph D. Farrar v. Hobby   December 14, 1992
        506 US 103   121 LEd2d 494   113 SCt 566
        Guide (West): (1994):67-69
        Sup Ct Yearbook (1992-93):84-85

Cameron, Christopher D. Order in the court: labor and employment issues. *HR Focus* 69(12):8-9 (December 1992).

3742. District of Columbia v. Greater Washington Board of Trade   December 14, 1992
506 US 125   121 LEd2d 513   113 SCt 580
    Sup Ct Yearbook (1992-93):91
Hofmann, Mark A. ERISA issues in 3 cases before High Court. *Business Insurance* 26(41):49 (October 12, 1992).
———. Health costs are big worry for small business. *Business Insurance* 26(18):32-33 (May 4, 1992).
———. Supreme Court strikes comp law; claimants not guaranteed group health cover. *Business Insurance* 26(52):1, 46 (December 21, 1992).
Miller, William H. Legal affairs: beware of your friends. *Industry Week* 241(21):63 (November 2, 1992).

3743. Puerto Rico Aqueduct and Sewer Authority v. Metcalf & Eddy, Inc.   January 12, 1993
506 US 139   121 LEd2d 605   113 SCt 684
    Sup Ct Yearbook (1992-93):94

3744. Bath Iron Works Corp. v. Director, Office of Workers' Compensation Programs   January 12, 1993
506 US 153   121 LEd2d 619   113 SCt 692
    Sup Ct Yearbook (1992-93):93

3745. Commissioner, Internal Revenue Service v. Soliman   January 12, 1993
506 US 168   121 LEd2d 634   113 SCt 701
    Guide (West): (1994):452-454
    Sup Ct Yearbook (1991-92):183-184; (1992-93):51
Barton, Peter, and Clayton Sager. U.S. Supreme Court limits home-office deduction. *CPA Journal* 63(4):16-20 (April 1993).
Black, Pamela J., Amy Dunkin, and Catherine Yang. An intruder just got into your home office: the IRS. *Business Week* (Industrial/Technology Edition) (3302):79 (January 25, 1993).
DeMott, John S. Hardening the rules on home offices. *Nation's Business* 81(3):66-67 (March 1993).
Gest, Ted. The Court: deciding less, writing more. *U.S. News and World Report* 114(25):24-26 (June 28, 1993).
High Court knocks down tax court's home-office test. *Practical Accountant* 26(2):10 (Februrary 1993).
Koppel, Michael D. "Soliman" gets wiser. *Business Credit* 96(9):5 (October 1994).
Megaard, Michael M., and Susan L. Megaard. Supreme Court narrows home office deducations in Soliman. *Journal of Taxation* 78(3):132-138 (March 1993).
Miller, Sandra K. Com. v. Soliman: Supreme Court unduly restricts home office deductions. *Taxes* 71(3):52-62 (March 1993).
Not deductible: a High Court ruling should bring the house down on home offices. *Time* 141(4):22 (January 25, 1993).
Supreme Court denies home office deduction. *Taxes* 71(2):66 (February 1993).
Tax cases: Supreme Court gets tough with home-office deductions. *Journal of Accountancy* 175(3):26 (March 1993).
Warren Steve E. The home office deduction. *Taxes* 72(7):355-363 (July 1994).
Wood, Robert W. Home-office deductions still alive after Soliman. *Practical Accountant* 26(4):32-36 (April 1993).
Yang, Catherine. The taxman's day in court. *Business Week* (3284):34 (September 21, 1992).

3746. Rowland, Former Director, California Department of Corrections   January 12, 1993
    v. California Men's Colony, Unit II Men's Advisory Council
Rowland v. California Men's Colony
Rowland v. California Men's Advistory Council
506 US 194   121 LEd2d 656   113 SCt 716
    Guide (West): (1994):362-364
    Sup Ct Yearbook (1992-93):54-55

3747. Nixon v. United States   January 13, 1993
    506 US 224   112 LEd2d 1   113 SCt 732
       Almanac (1993):328, 329-330
       Guide (West): (1994):296-298
       Sup Ct Review (1993):125-155
       Sup Ct Yearbook (1991-92):182; (1992-93):75-76
    Kaplan, David A., Bob Cohn, Karen Springen, and Donna Foote. A clear path to a barricade. *Newsweek* 121(4):50-51 (January 25, 1993).

3748. Crosby v. United States   January 13, 1993
    506 US 255   122 LEd2d 25   113 SCt 748
       Sup Ct Yearbook (1992-93):58

3749. Bray v. Alexandria Women's Health Clinic   January 13, 1993
    506 US 263   122 LEd2d 34   113 SCt 753
       Abortion Am 315-316
       Abortion Con 287, 293
       Abortion Dec 90s Introduction, 213-247R
       Almanac (1992):329; (1993):327-328, 354; (1994):355
       Guide (West): (1994):4-6
       Hard Choices 264-270
       Liberty 688-689+
       Sup Ct Review (1993):199-243
       Sup Ct Yearbook (1990-91):194-197, 198-199; (1991-92):30-34, 181, 182; (1992-93):23-25, 83, 101-118R
    Abortion: of racketeers and Klansmen. *Economist* 326(7795):29 (January 23-29, 1993).
    Back to the barricades: Operation Rescue is handed a victory by a divided Supreme Court. *Time* 141(4):22-23 (January 25, 1993).
    Chemerinsky, Erwin. Supreme Court review: a difficult year for civil rights. *Trial* 29(10):76-79 (October 1993).
    High Court to hear abortion, porn cases. *Christianity Today* 35(11):50 (October 7, 1991).
    Kaplan, David A., Bob Cohn, Karen Springen, and Donna Foote. A clear path to a barricade. *Newsweek* 121(4):50-51 (January 25, 1993).
    Lawton, Kim A. Church, abortion issues fill docket. *Christianity Today* 36(13):46, 66 (November 9, 1992).
    The row over Roe goes on, 20 years later. *U.S. News and World Report* 114(3):17 (January 25, 1993).
    Schwartz, Herman. New term, same tilt: the Supreme Court stays hard right. *Nation* 257(13):452-454 (October 25 1993).
    Spivack, Miranda S. The Court of last resort. *Ms.* 2(4):90-91 (January/February 1992).
    Tune in next term: the Supreme Court bumps an abortion-clinic case. *Time* 139(25):25 (June 22, 1992).
    Wattleton, Faye. Planned Parenthood and pro choice: sexual and reproductive freedom. *Vital Speeches* 58(17):524-527 (June 15, 1992).

3750. Lockhart, Director, Arkansas Department of Corrections v. Fretwell   January 25, 1993
    506 US 364   122 LEd2d 180   113 SCt 838
       Almanac (1993):330
       Sup Ct Yearbook (1992-93):67

3751. Herrera v. Collins, Director, Texas Department of Criminal Justice   January 25, 1993
    506 US 390   122 LEd2d 203   113 SCt 853
       Almanac (1993):328, 330
       Guide (West): (1994):49-52
       Sup Ct Yearbook (1991-92):181-182; (1992-93):35-38, 56-57, 118-133R
    Breuer, Jennifer. Supreme Court review: habeas corpus—limited review for actual innocence. *Journal of Criminal Law and Criminology* 84(4):943-974 (Winter/Spring 1994).
    Chemerinsky, Erwin. Supreme Court review: Innocence and habeas corpus. *Trial* 31(4):79-81 (April 1995).
    ———. Supreme Court review: making sense of habeas corpus. *Trial* 28(12):79-82 (December 1992).
    Dripps, Donald A. Supreme Court review: the importance of being innocent. *Trial* 29(7):80-83 (July 1993).

Koosed, Margery Malkin. Habeas corpus: where have all the remedies gone? rebuilding the great writ. *Trial* 29(7):70-79 (July 1993).

Tightening noose: the Court limits death-row appeals based on late claims of innocence. *Time* 141(6):23 (February 8, 1993).

3752. Spectrum Sports v. McQuillan, dba Sorboturf Enterprises   January 25, 1993
    506 US 447   122 LEd2d 247   113 SCt 884
      Sup Ct Yearbook (1992-93):45-46
    Frum, David. Whom should the law protect? *Forbes* 150(11):72-73 (November 9, 1992).

3753. Graham v. Collins, Director, Texas Department of Criminal Justice   January 25, 1993
    506 US 461   122 LEd2d 260   113 SCt 892
      Almanac (1993):330
      Guide (West): (1994):47-49
      Sup Ct Yearbook (1992-93):64, 57
    Cho, Susie. Capital confusion: the effect of jury instructions on the decision to impose death. *Journal of Criminal Law and Criminology* 85(2):532-561 (Fall 1994).

3754. Bufferd v. Commissioner of Internal Revenue Service   January 25, 1993
    506 US 523   122 LEd2d 306   113 SCt 927
      Sup Ct Yearbook (1992-93):50-51
    Becker, Joyce K. Supreme Court resolves the S/L controversy regarding pass-through items in IRS's favor. *Journal of Taxation* 78(5):288-291 (May 1993).
    Howe, Victoria M. High Court settles limitations period for S corp items. *Practical Accountant* 26(5):41-43 (May 1993).
    Supreme Court hands IRS double victory. *Journal of Taxation* 78(3):130 (March 1993).
    Tax cases: Supreme Court: IRS wins S corporation limitations-period issue. *Journal of Accountancy* 175(4):23 (April 1993).

3755. Zafiro v. United States   January 25, 1993
    506 US 534   122 LEd2d 317   113 SCt 933
      Sup Ct Yearbook (1992-93):59

3756. United States v. Hill   January 25, 1993
    506 US 546   122 LEd2d 330   113 SCt 941
      Sup Ct Yearbook (1992-93):52
    Burkhart, Lori A. High Court limits tax deduction for depletion. *Public Utilities Fortnightly* 131(5):43 (March 1, 1993).
    Hennessee, Patrick A. Depletion preference cannot be reduced by cost of tangibles, says Supreme Court. *Journal of Taxation* 78(4):236-238 (April 1993).
    Supreme Court hands IRS double victory. *Journal of Taxation* 78(3):130 (March 1993).

3757. Growe, Secretary of State of Minnesota v. Emison   February 23, 1993
    507 US 25   122 LEd2d 388   113 SCt 1075
      Sup Ct Review (1993):245-287
      Sup Ct Yearbook (1991-92):185; (1992-93):70-71
    Weber, Ronald E. Redistricting and the courts: judicial activism in the 1990s. *American Politics Quarterly* 23(2):204-228 (April 1995).

3758. Fex v. Michigan   February 23, 1993
    507 US 43   122 LEd2d 406   113 SCt 1085
      Sup Ct Yearbook (1992-93):58-59

3759. Itel Containers International Corp. v. Huddleston, Commissioner of Revenue of Tennessee   February 23, 1993
    507 US 60   122 LEd2d 421   113 SCt 1095

Sup Ct Yearbook (1992-93):95

Miller, William H. Legal affairs: beware of your friends. *Industry Week* 241(21):63 (November 2, 1992).

Supreme Court upholds sales tax on containers leased for international shipping. *Journal of Taxation* 78(4):194 (April 1993).

3760. United States v. Dunningan		February 23, 1993
507 US 87	122 LEd2d 445	113 SCt 1111

    Guide (West): (1994):399-401
    Sup Ct Yearbook (1992-93):69-70

3761. Negonsott v. Samuels, Warden		February 24, 1993
507 US 99	122 LEd2d 457	113 SCt 1119

    Sup Ct Yearbook (1992-93):70

3762. United States v. 92 Buena Vista Avenue, Rumson, New Jersey		February 24, 1993
United States v. A Parcel of Land		
507 US 111	122 LEd2d 469	113 SCt 1126, 1137

    Almanac (1993):332
    Guide (West): (1994):114-116
    Sup Ct Yearbook (1992-93):62-63

Chemerinsky, Erwin. Supreme Court review: civil forfeiture: a diminishing power. *Trial* 30(4):66-68 (April 1994).

3763. Voinovich, Governor of Ohio v. Quilter,		March 2, 1993
Speaker Pro Tempore of Ohio House of Representatives		
507 US 146	122 LEd2d 500	113 SCt 1149

    Sup Ct Review (1993):245-287
    Sup Ct Yearbook (1991-92):185; (1992-93):72

Weber, Ronald E. Redistricting and the courts: judicial activism in the 1990s. *American Politics Quarterly* 23(2):204-228 (April 1995).

3764. Leatherman v. Tarrant County Narcotics Intelligence and Coordination Unit		March 3, 1993
507 US 163	122 LEd2d 517	113 SCt 1160

    Sup Ct Yearbook (1992-93):86-87

Chemerinsky, Erwin. Supreme Court review: reaffirmation of notice pleading. *Trial* 29(6):73-76 (June 1993).

3765. Reves v. Ernst & Young		March 3, 1993
507 US 170	122 LEd2d 525	113 SCt 1163

    Sup Ct Review (1993):157-198; (1994):129-168
    Sup Ct Yearbook (1992-93):99

Bergstrom, Richard J., and Jeanne Lunsford Morrison. Special Report: RICO: has the "ultimate weapon" been crushed? *Journal of Accountancy* 175(6):17 (June 1993).

Bunim, Mark J., and Andrea B. Jacobson. RICO: the threat is lifted. *Journal of Accountancy* 178(4):119-120 (October 1994).

Clolery, Paul. High Court limits RICO use against accountants. *Practical Accountant* 26(4):7-8 (April 1993).

Keneally, Kathryn. Partial limitation on the risk of RICO liability. *CPA Journal* 64(2):67-69 (February 1994).

Legal scene: Supreme Court limits RICO. *Journal of Accountancy* 175(5):24 (May 1993).

McLeod, Douglas. RICO ruling wins applause. *Business Insurance* 27(11):1, 28 (March 1993).

Pagnani, Frederick J. Jr. Recent Court rulings aid professional liability. *Best's Review* (Property/Casualty Insurance Edition) 96(1):52-55 (May 1995).

Quinlivan, Stephen M. What every accountant should know about securities law. *Journal of Accountancy* 174(1):109-112 (July 1992).

3766. Smith v. United States		March 8, 1993
507 US 197	122 LEd2d 548	113 SCt 1178

Sup Ct Yearbook (1992-93):98

3767. Building Trades Council v. Associated Builders   March 8, 1993
  Building and Construction Trades of the Metropolitan District v. Associated Builders and Contractors of
    Massachusetts/Rhode Island, Inc.
      Coupled with Massachusetts Water Resources Authority v. Associated Builders and Contractors of
        Massachusetts/Rhode Island, Inc.
  507 US 218   122 LEd2d 565   113 SCt 1190
    Sup Ct Yearbook (1992-93):89-90
  Bradford, Hazel. High Court hears union-only case. *ENR* 229(25):8A (December 21, 1992).
  ———. High Court OK's Boston labor pact. *ENR* 230(11):8 (March 15, 1993).
  Cameron, Christopher D. Order in the court: labor and employment issues. *HR Focus* 69(12):8-9 (December
    1992).
  Miller, William H. Legal affairs: beware of your friends. *Industry Week* 241(21):63 (November 2, 1992).
  Murphy, Betty Southard, Wayne E. Barlow, and D. Diane Hatch. New public works/union developments.
    Personnel Journal 72(5):30, 32 (May 1993).
  The Supreme Court should speak clearly on Boston labor pact. [Editorial] *ENR* 228(21):148 (May 25, 1992).

3768. Ortega-Rodriguez v. United States   March 8, 1993
  507 US 234   122 LEd2d 581   113 SCt 1199
    Sup Ct Yearbook (1992-93):55-56
  Joseph, Jason W. Supreme Court review: the fugitive dismissal rule applied to pre-appeal fugitivity. *Journal of
    Criminal Law and Criminology* 84(4):1086-1108 (Winter/Spring 1994).

3769. Reiter v. Cooper   March 8, 1993
  507 US 258   122 LEd2d 604   113 SCt 1213
    Sup Ct Yearbook (1992-93):74-75
  Augello, William J. Collection interests dealt a devastating blow on undercharge issue. *Business Credit*
    95(6):47-48 (June 1993).
  Miller, William H. Legal affairs: beware of your friends. *Industry Week* 241(21):63 (November 2, 1992).

3770. Reno, Attorney General v. Flores   March 23, 1993
  507 US 292   123 LEd2d 1   113 SCt 1439
    Guide (West): (1994):250-252
    Sup Ct Yearbook (1992-93):82

3771. Saudi Arabia v. Nelson   March 23, 1993
  507 US 349   123 LEd2d 47   113 SCt 1471
    Guide (West): (1994):434-436
    Sup Ct Yearbook (1992-93):88-89

3772. Pioneer Investment Services Co. v. Brunswick Associates Limited Partnership   March 24, 1993
  507 US 380   123 LEd2d 074   113 SCt 1489
    Sup Ct Yearbook (1992-93):47

3773. City of Cincinnati v. Discovery Network, Inc.   March 24, 1993
  507 US 410   123 LEd2d 99   113 SCt 1505
    Guide (West): (1994):163-165
    Sup Ct Yearbook (1992-93):80
  Boedecker, Karl A., and Fred W. Morgan. The evolution of First Amendment protection for commercial
    speech. *Journal of Marketing* 59(1):38-47 (January 1995).
  Chemerinsky, Erwin. Supreme Court review: commercial speech: what degree of protection? *Trial* 29(8):66-68
    (August 1993).
  Colford, Steven W. Big win for commercial speech. *Advertising Age* 64(13):1, 47 (March 29, 1993).
  ———. High Court to mull commercial speech. *Advertising Age* 63(46):33 (November 9, 1992).

Frum, David. How about free speech for business, too? *Forbes* 150(8):108-109 (October 12, 1992).

Gersh, Debra. High Court: city can't selectively ban commercial racks. *Editor and Publisher* 126(14):18 (April 3, 1993).

————. Shifting legal focus in the Supreme Court: legal action involving news media in 1992 dealt more with commercial speech, subpoenas for phone record than on libel. *Editor and Publisher* 126(1):24-25 (January 2, 1993).

Hernandez, Debra Gersh. Commercial speech cases fill the Supreme Court. *Editor and Publisher* 127(1):24-25, 68 (January 1, 1994).

Seligman, Daniel. Free speech for realtors. *Fortune* 126(14):108 (December 28, 1992).

Yang, Catherine. Legally, at least, 'business is no worse off.' *Business Week* (Industrial/Technology Edition) (3327):34 (July 12, 1993).

————. The taxman's day in court. *Business Week* (3284):34 (September 21, 1992).

3774. United States by and through Internal Revenue Service (IRS) v. McDermott   March 24, 1993
507 US 447   123 LEd2d 128   113 SCt 1526
Sup Ct Yearbook (1992-93):53

3775. Arave, Warden v. Creech   March 30, 1993
507 US 463   123 LEd2d 188   113 SCt 1534
Guide (West): (1994):45-47
Sup Ct Yearbook (1992-93):56

Kessler, Daryl. Supreme Court review: Eighth Amendment—sentencer discretion in capital sentencing schemes. *Journal of Criminal Law and Criminology* 84(4):827-853 (Winter/Spring 1994).

3776. Delaware v. New York   March 30, 1993
507 US 490   123 LEd2d 211   113 SCt 1550
Almanac (1993):332
Sup Ct Yearbook (1992-93):97

3777. Conroy v. Aniskoff   March 31, 1993
507 US 511   123 LEd2d 229   113 SCt 1562
Guide (West): (1994):329-331
Sup Ct Yearbook (1992-93):76-77

3778. United States v. Texas   April 5, 1993
507 US 529   123 LEd2d 245   113 SCt 1631
Sup Ct Yearbook (1992-93):78

3779. Newark Morning Ledger Co. v. United States   April 20, 1993
507 US 546   123 LEd2d 288   113 SCt 1670
Sup Ct Yearbook (1992-93):51-52

Corporate: Newark Morning Ledger: a clear but narrow victory. *Journal of Accountancy* 175(7):29 (July 1993).

Cuddy, Michael J., and Jonathan J. Davies. Taxpayer wins intangible assets case. *Best's Review* (Life/Health Insurance Edition) 943):103-104 (July 1993).

————. Taxpayer wins intangible assets case. *Best's Review* (Property/Casualty Insurance Edition) 94(3):73-74 (July 1993).

Depreciation permitted for list of paid subscribers. *Taxes* 71(5):274 (May 1993).

Fields, Howard. Court rules intangibles can be depreciated. *Publishers' Weekly* 240(18):15 (May 3, 1993).

Gersh, Debra. Newspaper subscribers can be used as depreciable assets. *Editor and Publisher* 126(17):12 (April 24, 1993).

————. Shifting legal focus in the Supreme Court: legal action involving news media in 1992 dealt more with commercial speech, subpoenas for phone record than on libel. *Editor and Publisher* 126(1):24-25 (January 2, 1993).

Hernandez, Debra Gersh. Commercial speech cases fill the Supreme Court. *Editor and Publisher* 127(1):24-25, 68 (January 1, 1994).

How will the taxpayer victory in Newark Morning Ledger affect pending legislation? *Journal of Taxation* 78(6):322 (June 1993).

Huffman, Richard L., and Manuel Quintana. Depreciation of subscriber lists. *Editor and Publisher* 126(21):5, 42 (May 22, 1993).

Jaeger, David G. Supreme Court decides Newark Morning Ledger Co. *Taxes* 71(7):406-413 (July 1993).

Levy, Marc D., C. Ellen MacNeil, and Barbara J. Young. Supreme Court's decision on amortizing intangibles removes one barrier. *Journal of Taxation* 79(1):4-10 (July 1993).

Schlessing, Michael R. Indopco & Newark: defining the intangible "asset" in the larger cost recovery context. *Taxes* 70(12):929-947 (December 1992).

Wolosky, Howard W. Depreciating customer bases after Newark. *Practical Accountant* 26(7):34-39 (July 1993).

Yang, Catherine. The taxman's day in court. *Business Week* (3284):34 (September 21, 1992).

3780. Nebraska v. Wyoming   April 20, 1993
       507 US 584   123 LEd2d 317   113 SCt 1689
          Sup Ct Yearbook (1992-93):96

3781. Hazen Paper Co. v. Biggins   April 20, 1993
       507 US 604   -   123 LEd2d 338   113 SCt 1701
          Almanac (1993):331-332
          Guide (West): (1994):22-24
          Sup Ct Yearbook (1992-93):84
       Cameron, Christopher D. Order in the court: labor and employment issues. *HR Focus* 69(12):8-9 (December 1992).

       Miller, William H. Legal affairs: beware of your friends. *Industry Week* 241(21):63 (November 2, 1992).

       Yang, Catherine. The taxman's day in court. *Business Week* (3284):34 (September 21, 1992).

3782. Brecht v. Abrahamson, Superintendent, Dodge Correctional Institution   April 21, 1993
       507 US 619   123 LEd2d 353   113 SCt 1710
          Guide (West): (1994):192-194
          Sup Ct Yearbook (1992-93):63
       Chemerinsky, Erwin. Supreme Court review: making sense of habeas corpus. *Trial* 28(12):79-82 (December 1992).

       'Harmless error.' [Editorial] *Nation* 252(14):471-472 (April 15, 1991).

       Koosed, Margery Malkin. Habeas corpus: where have all the remedies gone? rebuilding the great writ. *Trial* 29(7):70-79 (July 1993).

       Liebman, James S., and Randy Hertz. Brecht v. Abrahamson: harmful error in habeas corpus law. *Journal of Criminal Law and Criminology* 84(4):1109-1056 (Winter/Spring 1994).

       Rosen, Jeffrey. Bad noose. *New Republic* 209(14):13-15 (October 4, 1993).

3783. CSX Transportation, Inc. v. Easterwood   April 21, 1993
       507 US 658   123 LEd2d 387   113 SCt 1732
          Sup Ct Yearbook (1992-93):73

3784. Withrow v. Williams   April 21, 1993
       507 US 680   123 LEd2d 407   113 SCt 1745
          Guide (West): (1994):190-192
          Sup Ct Yearbook (1991-92):183; (1992-93):64-65
       Bigornia, Anthony P. Supreme Court review: habeas corpus—Fifth Amendment—the Supreme Court's cost-benefit analysis of federal habeas review of alleged Miranda violations. *Journal of Criminal Law and Criminology* 84(4):915-942 (Winter/Spring 1994).

       Chemerinsky, Erwin. Supreme Court review: making sense of habeas corpus. *Trial* 28(12):79-82 (December 1992).

       Dripps, Donald A. Supreme Court review: the great writ and the right to silence. *Trial* 30(1):72-73 (January 1994).

3785. United States v. Olano   April 26, 1993
     507 US 725   123 LEd2d 508   113 SCt 1770
       Sup Ct Yearbook (1992-93):65-66
     Lowry, Jeffrey L. Supreme Court review: plain error rule—clarifying plain error analysis under Rule 52(b) of the Federal Rules of Criminal Procedure. *Journal of Criminal Law and Criminology* 84(4):1065-1085 (Winter/Spring 1994).

3786. United States v. California   April 26, 1993
     507 US 746   123 LEd2d 528   113 SCt 1748
       Sup Ct Yearbook (1992-93):96

3787. Edenfield v. Fane   April 26, 1993
     507 US 761   123 LEd2d 543   113 SCt 1792
       Guide (West): (1994):165-167
       Sup Ct Yearbook (1992-93):80-81
     Boedecker, Karl A., and Fred W. Morgan. The evolution of First Amendment protection for commercial speech. *Journal of Marketing* 59(1):38-47 (January 1995).
     Chemerinsky, Erwin. Supreme Court review: commercial speech: what degree of protection? *Trial* 29(8):66-68 (August 1993).
     Clolery, Paul. Fane too busy to solicit business despite Supreme Court's approval. *Practical Accountant* 26(6):7 (June 1993).
     Colford, Steven W. Big win for commercial speech. *Advertising Age* 64(13):1, 47 (March 29, 1993).
     DePree, Chauncey M., Jr., and Rebecca Kathryn Jude. Constitutionally of in-person solicitations. *Journal of Accountancy* 176(3):81-82 (September 1993).
     Lantry, Terry. Supreme Court allows in-person solicitations by CPAs. *CPA Journal* 63(10):72-76 (October 1993).
     Legal scene: Supreme Court ends CPA solicitation ban. *Journal of Accountancy* 176(3):28 (September 1993).
     Levinson, L. Harold. Supreme Court says CPAs can solicit business clients. *Practical Accountant* 26(7):41-43 (July 1993).

3788. Fargo Women's Health Organization v. Schafer   April 2, 1993
     507 US 1013   123 LEd2d 285   113 SCt 1668
       Almanac (1993):328

3789. United States v. Idaho ex rel. Director, Idaho Department of Water Resources   May 3, 1993
     508 US 1   123 LEd2d 563   113 SCt 1893
       Sup Ct Yearbook (1992-93):97

3790. Cisneros, Secretary of Housing and Urban Developmment v. Alpine Ridge Group   May 3, 1993
     508 US 10   123 LEd2d 572   113 SCt 1898
       Sup Ct Yearbook (1992-93):72-73

3791. Moreau v. Klevenhagen, Sheriff of Harris County, Texas   May 3, 1993
     508 US 22   123 LEd2d 584   113 SCt 1905
       Sup Ct Yearbook (1992-93):92-93
     Walters, Jonathan. Work rules: a win for governments. *Governing* 6(11):14 (August 1993).

3792. Stinson v. United States   May 3, 1993
     508 US 36   123 LEd2d 598   113 SCt 1913
       Guide (West): (1994):397-399
       Sup Ct Yearbook (1992-93):69

3793. Professional Real Estate Investors, Inc. v. Columbia Pictures Industries, Inc.   May 3, 1993
     508 US 49   123 LEd2d 611   113 SCt 1920
       Sup Ct Yearbook (1992-93):45

3794. United States v. Padilla
    508 US 77   123 LEd2d 635
       Sup Ct Yearbook (1992-93):68

May 3, 1993
113 SCt 1936

3795. Cardinal Chemical Co. v. Morton International, Inc. May 17, 1993
    508 US 83   124 LEd2d 1
       Sup Ct Yearbook (1992-93):49-50

113 SCt 1967

3796. McNeil v. United States
    508 US 106   124 LEd2d 21
       Sup Ct Yearbook (1992-93):98

May 17, 1993
113 SCt 1980

3797. Oklahoma Tax Commission v. Sac and Fox Nation
    508 US 114   124 LEd2d 30
       Guide (West): (1994):459-461
       Sup Ct Yearbook (1992-93):95-96

May 17, 1993
113 SCt 1985

3798. Deal v. United States
    508 US 129   124 LEd2d 44
       Guide (West): (1994):396-397
       Sup Ct Yearbook (1992-93):68

May 17, 1993
113 SCt 1993

Apostolides, George P. Supreme Court review: 18 U.S.C. § 924(c)(1)—the Court's construction of "use" and "second or subsequent conviction." *Journal of Criminal Law and Criminology* 84(4):1006-1040 (Winter/Spring 1994).

3799. Commissioner of Internal Revenue v. Keystone Consolidated Industries, Inc.
    508 US 152   124 LEd2d 71
       Sup Ct Yearbook (1992-93):90

May 24, 1993
113 SCt 589

Cimini, Michael H., Susan L. Behrmann, and Eric M. Johnson. Labor-management bargaining in 1993. *Monthly Labor Review* 117(1):20-35 (January 1994).

Contributing unencumbered property to plan can't avoid excise tax, Supreme Court rules. *Journal of Taxation* 79(1):2 (July 1993).

Doering, James A. Property contributions may constitute prohibited transactions: an analysis of Keystone. *Taxes* 71(9):555-564 (September 1993).

High Court rules contribution of unencumbered property to plan was taxable. *Practical Accountant* 26(7):14 (July 1993).

Hofmann, Mark A. ERISA issues in 3 cases before High Court. *Business Insurance* 26(41):49 (October 12, 1992).

3800. United States Department of Justice v. Landano
    508 US 165   124 LEd2d 84
       Guide (West): (1994):146-149
       Sup Ct Yearbook (1992-93):75

May 24, 1993
113 SCt 2014

Gersh, Debra. High Court rules FBI records not confidential per se. *Editor and Publisher* 126(23):40 (June 5, 1993).

Hernandez, Debra Gersh. Commercial speech cases fill the Supreme Court. *Editor and Publisher* 127(1):24-25, 68 (January 1, 1994).

Salzman, Matthew J. Supreme Court review: exemption 7(D) of the Freedom of Information Act—the evidentiary showing the government must make to establish that a source is confidential. *Journal of Criminal Law and Criminology* 84(4):1041-1064 (Winter/Spring 1994).

3801. Lincoln, Acting Director, Indian Health Service v. Vigil
    508 US 182   124 LEd2d 101
       Sup Ct Yearbook (1992-93):77

May 24, 1993
113 SCt 2024

3802. Keene Corp. v. United States   May 24, 1993
  508 US 200   124 LEd2d 118   113 SCt 2035
  Sup Ct Yearbook (1992-93):54

3803. Smith v. United States   June 1, 1993
  508 US 223   124 LEd2d 138   113 SCt 2050
  Guide (West): (1994):101-103
  Sup Ct Yearbook (1992-93):69

Apostolides, George P. Supreme Court review: 18 U.S.C. § 924(c)(1)—the Court's construction of "use" and "second or subsequent conviction." *Journal of Criminal Law and Criminology* 84(4):1006-1040 (Winter/Spring 1994).

3804. Mertens v. Hewitt Associates   June 1, 1993
  508 US 248   124 LEd2d 161   113 SCt 2063
  Almanac (1993):398; (1994):404
  Sup Ct Yearbook (1992-93):92

Cimini, Michael H., Susan L. Behrmann, and Eric M. Johnson. Labor-management bargaining in 1993. *Monthly Labor Review* 117(1):20-35 (January 1994).

Geisel, Jerry. Congress eyes benefit proposals. *Business Insurance* 27(32):2, 30 (August 2, 1993).

Hofmann, Mark A. Clinton seeks Mertens reversal. *Business Insurance* 27(33):3, 21 (August 9, 1993).

———. ERISA issues in 3 cases before High Court. *Business Insurance* 26(41):49 (October 12, 1992).

———. Pension adviser can't be sued, High Court rules. *Business Insurance* 27(24):2, 47 (June 7, 1993).

Morrison, John M. ERISA and the loss of just remedies. *Trial* 31(3):18-25 (March 1995).

3805. Sullivan v. Louisiana   June 1, 1993
  508 US 275   124 LEd2d 182   113 SCt 2078
  Guide (West): (1994):97-99
  Sup Ct Yearbook (1992-93):65

3806. Musick, Peeler & Garrett v. Employers Insurance of Wausau   June 1, 1993
  508 US 286   124 LEd2d 194   113 SCt 2085
  Guide (West): (1994):392-393
  Sup Ct Yearbook (1992-93):50

3807. Federal Communications Commission (FCC) v. Beach Communications, Inc.   June 1, 1993
  508 US 307   124 LEd2d 211   113 SCt 2096
  Sup Ct Yearbook (1992-93):74

3808. Nobelman v. American Savings Bank   June 1, 1993
  508 US 324   124 LEd2d 228   113 SCt 2106
  Sup Ct Yearbook (1992-93):47

3809. Gilmore v. Taylor   June 7, 1993
  508 US 333   124 LEd2d 306   113 SCt 2112
  Sup Ct Yearbook (1992-93):63-64

Chemerinsky, Erwin. Supreme Court review: making sense of habeas corpus. *Trial* 28(12):79-82 (December 1992).

Finley, Timothy. Supreme Court review: habeas corpus—retroactivity of post-conviction rulings: finality at the expense of justice. *Journal of Criminal Law and Criminology* 84(4):975-1005 (Winter/Spring 1994).

3810. Minnesota v. Dickerson   June 7, 1993
  508 US 366   124 LEd2d 334   113 SCt 2130
  Guide (West): (1994):99-101
  Sup Ct Yearbook (1992-93):67-68

Dripps, Donald A. Supreme Court review: Supreme Court trims Fourth Amendment with 'plain feel' exception. *Trial* 29(9):77-78 (September 1993).

MacIntosh, Susanne M. Supreme Court review: Fourth Amendment—the plain touch exception to the warrant requirement. *Journal of Criminal Law and Criminology* 84(4):743-768 (Winter/Spring 1994).

3811. Lamb's Chapel and John Steigerwald v. Center Moriches Union Free School District   June 7, 1993
508 US 384   124 LEd2d 352   113 SCt 2141
Almanac (1993):328, 331
Editorials (1993):666-673
Godless 102
Guide (West): (1994):161-163
Sup Ct Yearbook (1992-93):31-33, 79, 133-140R
Chemerinsky, Erwin. Supreme Court review: free speech or religious freedom: revisiting the establishment clause. *Trial* 31(12):16-19 (December 1995).
———. Supreme Court review: religion clause doctrine: potential for change. *Trial* 29(2):81-84 (February 1993).
Coughlin, John J. Religion, education and the First Amendment. *America* 168(17):12-15 (May 15, 1993).
Court rulings on religion. *Christian Century* 110(19):624-625 (June 16-23, 1993).
Equal rights for religion. [Editorial] *America* 169(2):3 (July 17-24, 1993).
Establishment clause issues examined. *Christianity Today* 37(4):71 (April 5, 1993).
Johnson, Phillip E. Academic freedom and the religious professor. *Academe* 81(5):16-19 (September/October 1995).
Lawton, Kim A. Church, abortion issues fill docket. *Christianity Today* 36(13):46, 66 (November 9, 1992).
———. Trio of rulings clarifies religious-liberty rights. *Christianity Today* 37(8):56 (July 19, 1993).
Prayer in public schools. *Congressional Digest* 74(1):3-32 (January 1995).
Sendor, Benjamin. Religion rulings: too soon to say amen. *American School Board Journal* 180(8):14, 39 (August 1993).
———. A school system must repent for its rent. *American School Board Journal* 181(7):5-6 (July 1994).

3812. Good Samaritan Hospital v. Shalala, Secretary of Health and Human Services   June 7, 1993
508 US 402   124 LEd2d 368   113 SCt 2151
Sup Ct Yearbook (1992-93):74

3813. Antoine v. Byers & Anderson, Inc.   June 7, 1993
508 US 429   124 LEd2d 391   113 SCt 2167
Guide (West): (1994):298-300
Sup Ct Yearbook (1992-93):85-86

3814. United States National Bank of Oregon v. Independent Insurance Agents of America, Inc.   June 7, 1993
Coupled with Ludwig v. Independent Insurance Agents of America, Inc.
508 US 439   124 LEd2d 402   113 SCt 2173
Sup Ct Yearbook (1992-93):46
Christensen, Burke A. Issue of banks in insurance business is far from settled. *Trusts and Estates* 132(5):55-56 (May 1993).
1993 litigation scorecard. *Best's Review* (Life/Health Insurance Edition) 94(10):32 (February 1994).
Mazzuca, Laura. Supreme Court to decide if banks can sell insurance. *Business Insurance* 26(52):45 (December 21, 1992).

3815. Rake v. Wade, Trustee   June 7, 1993
508 US 464   124 LEd2d 424   113 SCt 2187
Sup Ct Yearbook (1992-93):46-47

3816. Wisconsin v. Mitchell   June 11, 1993
508 US 476   124 LEd2d 436   113 SCt 2194
Almanac (1993):328, 331, 354

Editorials (1993):730-733

Guide (West): (1994):194-196

Landmark (v. 4):179-186R

Price 8-13, 151-156

Sup Ct Review (1993):1-36

Sup Ct Yearbook (1992-93):38-39, 70, 140-144R

Brooks, Thomas D. Supreme Court review: First Amendment—penalty enhancement for hate crimes: content regulation, questionable state interests and non-traditional sentencing. *Journal of Criminal Law and Criminology* 84(4):703-742 (Winter/Spring 1994).

Freedom to hate. *Economist* 327(7810):33 (May 8-14, 1993).

Jaschik, Scott. High Court's ruling on bias crimes may permit 'hate speech' penalties. *Chronicle of Higher Education* 39(42):A22 (June 23, 1993).

Knoll, Erwin. A matter of intent. [Editorial] *Progressive* 57(8):4 (August 1993).

Rosen, Jeffrey. Bad thoughts. *New Republic* 209(1):15-16, 18 (July 5, 1993).

3817. United States Department of Treasury v. Fabe, Superintendent of Insurance of Ohio   June 11, 1993
508 US 491   124 LEd2d 449   113 SCt 2202

Sup Ct Yearbook (1992-93):49

Fletcher, Meg. Policyholders before feds: High Court clarifies payment priority in insurer liquidations. *Business Insurance* 27(27):2, 11 (June 28, 1993).

Greenwald, Judy. Antitrust case review opposed by government. *Business Insurance* 26(33):1, 67 (August 17, 1992).

Kempler, Cecelia, and William Duffy. Insolvent reinsurers pose even greater risk. *Best's Review* (Life/Health Insurance Edition) 94(10):54-57 (April 1994).

———. Insolvent reinsurers pose even greater risk. *Best's Review* (Property/Casualty Insurance Edition) 94(12):42-45 (April 1994).

Veach, James. The arbitration tug-of-war. *Best's Review* (Property/Casualty Insurance Edition) 93(11):38-42, 80-83 (March 1993).

3818. Church of the Lukumi Babalu Aye, Inc. v. City of Hialeah   June 11, 1993
508 US 520   123 LEd2d 472   113 SCt 2217

Almanac (1993):331

Editorials (1993):734-735

Godless 38-39

Guide (West): (1994):154-157

Sup Ct Review (1993):1-36; (1995):323-391

Sup Ct Yearbook (1991-92):179, 181-182; (1992-93):78-79

Animal sacrifice case. *Christian Century* 109(13):393-394 (April 15, 1992).

Chemerinsky, Erwin. Supreme Court review: religion clause doctrine: potential for change. *Trial* 29(2):81-84 (February 1993).

Church and state: necessary sacrifice? *Economist* 325(7785):28 (November 14-20, 1992).

Cohn, Bob, and David A. Kaplan. A chicken on every altar? *Newsweek* 120(19):79 (November 9, 1992).

Court considers animal sacrifice, airport witnessing. *Christianity Today* 36(5):46-47 (April 27, 1992).

Drinan, Robert F. A glimmer of hope for aid to Catholic schools. *America* 169(7):4-5 (September 18, 1993).

Equal rights for religion. [Editorial] *America* 169(2):3 (July 17-24, 1993).

Gaffney, Edward McGlynn, Jr. Animal sacrifice and religious freedom. [Editorial] *Christian Century* 109(15):508-510 (May 13, 1992).

Lawton, Kim A. Church, abortion issues fill docket. *Christianity Today* 36(13):46, 66 (November 9, 1992).

Ostling, Richard N., and Greg Aunapu. Shedding blood in sacred bowls. *Time* 140(16):60 (October 19, 1992).

Rosen, Jeffrey. Blood ritual. *New Republic* 207(19):9-10 (November 2, 1992).

Schmahmann, David R., and Lori J. Polacheck. The case against rights for animals. *Boston College Environmental Affairs Law Review* 22(4):747-781 (Summer 1995).

3819. Local 144 Nursing Home Pension Fund v. Demisay   June 13, 1993
508 US 581   124 LEd2d 522   113 SCt 2252

Sup Ct Yearbook (1992-93):91

3820. Concrete Pipe and Products of California, Inc.   June 14, 1993
      v. Construction Laborers Pension Trust for Southern California
    508 US 602   124 LEd2d 539   113 SCt 264
      Sup Ct Yearbook (1992-93):90-91
    Geisel, Jerry. Withdrawal liability found constitutional. *Business Insurance* 27(26):58 (June 21, 1993).

3821. Northeastern Florida Chapter of the Associated General Contractors of America   June 14, 1993
      v. City of Jacksonville, Florida
    508 US 656   124 LEd2d 586   113 SCt 2297
      Sup Ct Review (1993):37-64
      Sup Ct Yearbook (1992-93):83-84
    Court makes suits easier. *ENR* 230(26):7 (June 28, 1993).

3822. South Dakota v. Bourland   June 14, 1993
    508 US 679   124 LEd2d 606   113 SCt 2309
      Guide (West): (1994):335-337
      Sup Ct Yearbook (1992-93):77

3823. Zobrest V. Catalina Foothills School District   June 18, 1993
    509 US 1   125 LEd2d 1   113 SCt 2462
      Almanac (1993):328, 331
      Godless 78
      Guide (West): (1994):159-161
      Sup Ct Yearbook (1992-93):29-31, 79-80, 144-153R
    Chemerinsky, Erwin. Supreme Court review: religion clause doctrine: potential for change. *Trial* 29(2):81-84
      (February 1993).
    Coughlin, John J. Religion, education and the First Amendment. *America* 168(17):12-15 (May 15, 1993).
    Court ruling favors deaf student. *Christian Century* 110(20):666-667 (June 30-July 7, 1993).
    Court rulings on religion. *Christian Century* 110(19):624-625 (June 16-23, 1993).
    Drinan, Robert F. Are profoundly handicapped children in Catholic schools entitled to government assistance?
      America 168(3):16-18 (January 30, 1993).
    ————. The Constitution and handicapped Hasidim children. *America* 170(7):8-11 (February 26, 1994).
    ————. A glimmer of hope for aid to Catholic schools. *America* 169(7):4-5 (September 18, 1993).
    Establishment clause issues examined. *Christianity Today* 37(4):71 (April 5, 1993).
    Lawton, Kim A. Church, abortion issues fill docket. *Christianity Today* 36(13):46, 66 (November 9, 1992).
    ————. Trio of rulings clarifies religious-liberty rights. *Christianity Today* 37(8):56 (July 19, 1993).
    Rosen, Jeffrey. Lemon law. *New Republic* 208(13):17-18 (March 29, 1993).
    Zirkel, Perry A. De jure: is the 'wall of separation' like the Walls of Jericho? *Phi Delta Kappan* 75(1):88-90
      (September 1993).

3824. Helling v. McKinney   June 18, 1993
    509 US 25   125 LEd2d 22   113 SCt 2475
      Guide (West): (1994):357-359
      Sup Ct Yearbook (1991-92):184-185; (1992-93):66

3825. Reno, Attorney General v. Catholic Social Services, Inc.   June 18, 1993
    509 US 43   125 LEd2d 38   113 SCt 2485
      Sup Ct Yearbook (1992-93):81-82

3826. Harper v. Virginia Department of Taxation   June 18, 1993
    509 US 86   125 LEd2d 74   113 SCt 2510
      Guide (West): (1994):456-457
      Sup Ct Yearbook (1992-93):94-95

Gest, Ted. The Court: deciding less, writing more. *U.S. News and World Report* 114(25):24-26 (June 28, 1993).

High Court hears arguments on retroactivity of Davis decision. *Taxes* 71(1):53 (January 1993).

Rapp, David, The High Court and the new balance of power. *Governing* 6(8):68 (May 1993).

Supreme Court says Davis (and maybe every case) applies retroactively. *Journal of Taxation* 79(2):66 (August 1993).

Yang, Catherine. The taxman's day in court. *Business Week* (3284):34 (September 21, 1992).

3827. Darby v. Cisneros, Secretary of Housing and Urban Development   June 21, 1993
    509 US 137   125 LEd2d 113   113 SCt 2539
     Sup Ct Yearbook (1992-93):73

3828. Sale, Acting Commissioner, Immigration and Naturalization Service   June 21, 1993
     v. Haitian Centers Council, Inc.
    509 US 155   125 LEd2d 128   113 SCt 2549
     Almanac (1993):328-329, 499-500
     Editorials (1993):720-729; (1994):904-907
     Guide (West): (1994):254-256
     Sup Ct Yearbook (1992-93):27-29, 82, 153-166R
Hold the wretched refuse. *Progressive* 57(8):10 (August 1993).

3829. Brooke Group Ltd. v. Brown and Williamson Tobacco Corp.   June 21, 1993
    509 US 209   125 LEd2d 168   113 SCt 2578
     Sup Ct Yearbook (1992-93):44-45

3830. Buckley v. Fitzsimmons   June 24, 1993
    509 US 259   125 LEd2d 209   113 SCt 2606
     Guide (West): (1994):370-372
     Sup Ct Yearbook (1992-93):86

3831. Shalala, Secretary of Health and Human Services v. Schaefer   June 24, 1993
    509 US 292   125 LEd2d 239   113 SCt 2625
     Sup Ct Yearbook (1992-93):85

3832. Heller, Secretary, Kentucky Cabinet for Human Resources v. Doe   June 24, 1993
    509 US 312   125 LEd2d 257   113 SCt 2637
     Guide (West): (1994):132-134
     Sup Ct Yearbook (1992-93):87-88
Chemerinsky, Erwin. Supreme Court review: a difficult year for civil rights. *Trial* 29(10):76-79 (October 1993).

3833. Johnson v. Texas   June 24, 1993
    509 US 350   125 LEd2d 290   113 SCt 2658
     Sup Ct Yearbook (1992-93):57, 64
Brown, J. Michael. Supreme Court review: Eighth Amendment—capital sentencing instructions. *Journal of Criminal Law and Criminology* 84(4):854-882 (Winter/Spring 1994).

3834. Godinez, Warden v. Moran   June 24, 1993
    509 US 389   125 LEd2d 321   113 SCt 2680
     Guide (West): (1994):188-190
     Sup Ct Yearbook (1992-93):59
Boch, Brian R. Supreme Court review: Fourteenth Amendment—the standard of mental competency to waive constitutional rights versus the competency standard to stand trial. *Journal of Criminal Law and Criminology* 84(4):883-914 (Winter/Spring 1994).

3835. United States v. Edge Broadcasting Co.   June 25, 1993
    509 US 418   125 LEd2d 345   113 SCt 2696

Guide (West): (1994):167-169

Sup Ct Yearbook (1992-93):81

Boedecker, Karl A., and Fred W. Morgan. The evolution of First Amendment protection for commercial speech. *Journal of Marketing* 59(1):38-47 (January 1995).

Chemerinsky, Erwin. Supreme Court review: commercial speech: what degree of protection? *Trial* 29(8):66-68 (August 1993).

Colford, Steven W. Big win for commercial speech. *Advertising Age* 64(13):1, 47 (March 29, 1993).

———. High Court hits commercial speech hard. *Advertising Age* 64(27):1 (June 28, 1993).

Fisher, Christy. High Court ruling could bring more ad limits. *Advertising Age* 64(9):1, 44 (March 1, 1993).

3836. TXO Production Corp. v. Alliance Resources Corp. June 25, 1993

509 US 443   125 LEd2d 366   113 SCt 2711

Almanac (1993):328, 332

Guide (West): (1994):107-110

Sup Ct Yearbook (1992-93):98-99

Chemerinsky, Erwin. Supreme Court review: punitive damages and the Constitution. *Trial* 30(10):90-92 (October 1994).

Hofmann, Mark A. Court refuses to impose cap on punitive damages. *Business Insurance* 27(27):1, 21 (June 28, 1993).

———. Punitive damages back before Court. *Business Insurance* 29(41):1, 70-71 (October 9, 1995).

———. Supreme Court may not give clear ruling on punitive awards. *Business Insurance* 27(15):1, 29 (April 5, 1993).

Massey, Jonathan S. TXO and the future of punitive damages: the battle continues. *Trial* 29(12):53-57 (December 1993).

Murphy, Betty Southard, Wayne E. Barlow, and D. Diane Hatch. Supreme Court refuses to limit punitive damages. *Personnel Journal* 72(9):33 (September 1993).

Wojcik, Joanne. High Court affirms limits on punitive awards. *Business Insurance* 28(27):3, 10 (July 4, 1994).

———. Punitive damage awards; Supreme Court's review of new case may clarify Haslip guidance. *Business Insurance* 26(50):1, 53 (December 7, 1992).

———. Two Supreme letdowns: failure to set punitive rules may fuel state tort reform drive. *Business Insurance* 27(28):2, 98 (July 5, 1993).

Yang, Catherine. Legally, at least, 'business is no worse off.' *Business Week* (Industrial/Technology Edition) (3327):34 (July 12, 1993).

———. Will the High Court make damages less punitive? calling awards too high, business wants caps, national standards. *Business Week* (Industrial/Technology Edition) (3309):83-84 (March 15, 1993).

3837. St. Mary's Honor Center v. Hicks   June 25, 1993

509 US 502   125 LEd2d 407   113 SCt 2742

Almanac (1993):328, 331-332

Guide (West): (1994):377-379; (1995):304-306

Sup Ct Yearbook (1992-93):25-27, 88, 167-174R

Chemerinsky, Erwin. Supreme Court review: a difficult year for civil rights. *Trial* 29(10):76-79 (October 1993).

Cimini, Michael H., Susan L. Behrmann, and Eric M. Johnson. Labor-management bargaining in 1993. *Monthly Labor Review* 117(1):20-35 (January 1994).

Hofmann, Mark A. Justices reject tighter standards for expert testimony. *Business Insurance* 27(28):2, 99 (July 5, 1993).

Kaplan, David A. A whimper and a bang. *Newsweek* 122(2):53-55 (July 12, 1993).

Murphy, Betty Southard, Wayne E. Barlow, and D. Diane Hatch. Supreme Court eases employer burden of proof. *Personnel Journal* 72(9):30, 33-34 (September 1993).

Schwartz, Herman. New term, same tilt: the Supreme Court stays hard right. *Nation* 257(13):452-454 (October 25 1993).

Sendor, Benjamin. A chink in the armor against discrimination. *American School Board Journal* 180(9): 24, 54 (September 1993).

Yang, Catherine. Legally, at least, 'business is no worse off.' *Business Week* (Industrial/Technology Edition) (3327):34 (July 12, 1993).

3838. Alexander v. United States   June 28, 1993
    509 US 544   125 LEd2d 441   113 SCt 2766

      Almanac (1993):332

      Guide (West): (1994):91-93

      Sup Ct Yearbook (1991-92):185; (1992-93):35, 61

Gersh, Debra. High Court OKs porno confiscation. *Editor and Publisher* 126(33):14-15 (August 14, 1993).

Hernandez, Debra Gersh. Commercial speech cases fill the Supreme Court. *Editor and Publisher* 127(1):24-25, 68 (January 1, 1994).

Schwartz, Herman. New term, same tilt: the Supreme Court stays hard right. *Nation* 257(13):452-454 (October 25 1993).

3839. Daubert v. Merrell Dow Pharmaceuticals, Inc.   June 28, 1993
    509 US 579   125 LEd2d 469   113 SCt 2786

      Almanac (1993):229-230, 330

      Guide (West): (1994):134-136

      Sup Ct Yearbook (1992-93):40-41, 53, 205-214R

Allen, Ronald J. Expertise and the Daubert decision. *Journal of Criminal Law and Criminology* 84(4):1157-1175 (Winter/Spring 1994).

Annas, George J. Scientific evidence in the courtroom: the death of the Frye rule. *New England Journal of Medicine* 330(14):1018-1021 (April 7, 1994).

Begley, Sharon. The meaning of junk. *Newsweek* 121(12):62-64 (March 22, 1993).

Burd, Stephen. High Court bars strict limit on use of scientific evidence. *Chronicle of Higher Education* 39(44):A34-A35 (July 7, 1993).

Cordes, Renee. High Court takes closer look at expert testimony. *Trial* 29(1):13-14 (January 1993).

Court picks Bendectin case to decide on junk science. *Chemical Marketing Reporter* 242(45):5, 31 (October 19, 1992).

Foster, Kenneth R., David E. Bernstein, and Peter W. Huber. Science and the toxic tort. *Science* 261(5119):1509 (September 17, 1993).

Gold, Jay A., Mile J. Zaremski, Elaine Rappaport, and Deborah H. Shefrin. Daubert v. Merrell Dow: the Supreme Court tackles scientific evidence in the courtroom. *JAMA: The Journal of the American Medical Association* 270(24): 2964-2967 (December 22, 1993).

Hanson, David. Supreme Court gives more latitude on admitting scientific evidence. *Chemical and Engineering News* 71(28):20-21 (July 12, 1993).

High Court hears views on Bendection. *Chemical Marketing Reporter* 243(14):13 (April 5, 1993).

Hofmann, Mark A. Justices reject tighter standards for expert testimony. *Business Insurance* 27(28):2, 99 (July 5, 1993).

————. Supreme Court to define expert witness testimony. *Business Insurance* 26(42):3, 39 (October 19, 1992).

Imwinkelried, Edward J. The Daubert decision: Frye is dead, long live the Federal Rules of Evidence. *Trial* 29(9):60-65 (September 1993).

Johnson, Nancy P. High Court reviews "junk science" case. *Business Insurance* 27(15):29 (April 5, 1993).

Judges as science gatekeepers. *Chemical Marketing Reporter* 244(1):7, 14 (July 5, 1993).

Long, Janice. High Court ponders use of scientific evidence. *Chemical and Engineering News* 71(5):7-8 (February 1, 1993).

————. Scientific evidence in court retains validity. *Chemical and Engineering News* 72(13):22-23 (March 28, 1994).

Mack, Thomas J. Scientific testimony after Daubert: some early returns from lower courts. *Trial* 30(8):23-25, 28-31 (August 1994).

Marshall, Eliot. Supreme Court to weigh science. *Science* 259(5110):588-590 (January 29, 1993).

Marwick, Charles. Court ruling on 'junk science' gives judges more say about what expert witness testimony to allow. *JAMA: The Journal of the American Medical Association* 270(4): 423 (July 28, 1993).

————. What constitutes an expert witness? *JAMA: The Journal of the American Medical Association* 269(16): 2057 (April 28, 1993).

Mervis, Jeffrey. Expert testimony: Supreme Court to judges: start thinking like scientists. *Science* 261(5117):22 (July 2, 1993).

Nace, Barry J. Daubert: victory for the jury. [Editorial] *Trial* 29(10):7 (October 1993).

Plishner, Emily S. High Court to define evidence rules. *Chemical Week* 152(13):9 (April 7, 1993).

Product liability reform backed by industry study. *Chemical Marketing Reporter* 242(11):9, 18 (September 14, 1992).

Reisch, Marc. Lawsuits raise issues of scientific credibility. *Chemical and Engineering News* 73(30):27-28 (July 24, 1995).

Science and society: what science is admissible in court? *Science News* 144(4):63 (July 24, 1993).

Yang, Catherine. Legally, at least, 'business is no worse off.' *Business Week* (Industrial/Technology Edition) (3327):34 (July 12, 1993).

———. Under attack: testimony for hire. *Business Week* (3301):60-61 (January 18, 1993).

3840. Austin v. United States   June 28, 1993
        509 US 602   125 LEd2d 488   113 SCt 2801
           Almanac (1993):328, 332
           Guide (West): (1994):113-114
           Sup Ct Yearbook (1992-93):33-35, 61-62, 196-205R

Dripps, Donald A. Supreme Court review: civil forfeiture: a glimmer of hope for property owners. *Trial* 29(11):70-74 (November 1993).

Lieber, David. Supreme Court review: Eighth Amendment—the excessive fines clause. *Journal of Criminal Law and Criminology* 84(4):805-826 (Winter/Spring 1994).

3841. Shaw v. Reno, Attorney General   June 28, 1993
        509 US 630   125 LEd2d 511   113 SCt 2816
           Almanac (1993):325-328, 22-A-23-B; (1994):312, 591-592; (1995):6-39-40, 12-3-4
           Guide (West): (1994):473-475
           Sup Ct Review (1993):245-287; (1995):45-70
           Sup Ct Yearbook (1992-93):20-23, 71, 174-196R; (1994-95):32-36; (1994-95):88

Along racial lines. [Editorial] *New Yorker* 70(7):6-8 (April 4, 1994).

Barone, Michael. Race decisions that backfire. *U.S. News and World Report* 115(2):34 (July 12, 1993).

Bolick, Clint. Bad fences. *National Review* 47(6):51-53 (April 3, 1995).

Chemerinsky, Erwin. Supreme Court review: a difficult year for civil rights. *Trial* 29(10):76-79 (October 1993).

———. Supreme Court review: race and the Supreme Court. *Trial* 31(10):86-88 (October 1995).

Davis, Olethia. Tenuous interpretation: Sections 2 and 5 of the Voting Rights Act. *National Civic Review* 84(4):310-322 (Fall/Winter 1995).

Engstrom, Richard L. Shaw, Miller and the districting thicket. *National Civic Review* 84(4):323-336 (Fall/Winter 1995).

Gerrymandering: whither shall it wander? *Economist* 328(7819):18-19 (July 10-16, 1993).

Hernandez, Roger E. Gerrymandering decision is out of bounds. [Editorial] *Crisis* 100(6):45 (August/September 1993).

High Court ruling puts U.S. minority voting districts in jeopardy. *Jet* 84(12):9 (July 19, 1993).

Kaplan, David A. A whimper and a bang. *Newsweek* 122(2):53-55 (July 12, 1993).

Karlan, Pamela S. Minority reps. [Editorial] *Nation* 256(9):292 (March 8, 1993).

———. Voting rights and the Court: end of the second reconstruction? *Nation* 258(20):698-700 (May 23, 1994).

Lemov, Penelope. High Court lowers a barrier to state health care reform. *Governing* 8(10):59 (July 1995).

McCoy, Frank. Racial politics and the High Court. *Black Enterprise* 24(3):25 (November 1993).

———. Under Supreme attack. *Black Enterprise* 26(3):24 (October 1995).

Moore, Acel. A voting rights threat? Yes, but it's really about sharing power. [Editorial] *Crisis* 100(6):44 (August/September 1993).

Rabkin, Jeremy. The curious case of Kiryas Joel. *Commentary* 98(5):58-61 (November 1994).

Raskin, Jamin B. Gerrymander hypocrisy: Supreme Court's double standard. *Nation* 260(5):167-168 (February 6, 1995).

Rosen, Jeffrey. Gerrymandered. *New Republic* 209(17):12, 14 (October 25, 1993).

Rush, Mark E. In search of a coherent theory of voting rights: challenges to the Supreme Court's vision of fair and effective representation. *Review of Politics* 56(3):503-523 (Summer 1994).

Schwartz, Herman. Judgment days. [Editorial] *Nation* 261(13):452-454 (October 23, 1995).

————. New term, same tilt: the Supreme Court stays hard right. *Nation* 257(13):452-454 (October 25 1993).

Van Biema, David, Wendy Cole, and Michael Riley. Snakes or ladders?: a controversial Supreme Court decision on racial redistricting uncovers a can of worms. *Time* 142(2):30-31 (July 12, 1993).

Weber, Ronald E. Redistricting and the courts: judicial activism in the 1990s. *American Politics Quarterly* 23(2):204-228 (April 1995).

Will, George F. Districting by pigmentation. [Editorial] *Newsweek* 122(2):72 (July 12, 1993).

Zimmerman, Joseph F. Election systems and representative democracy: reflections on the Voting Rights Act of 1965. *National Civic Review* 84(4):287-309 (Fall/Winter 1995).

3842. United States v. Dixon and Foster		June 28, 1993
509 US 688	125 LEd2d 556	113 SCt 2849

Guide (West): (1994):103-105

Sup Ct Yearbook (1992-93):60

Dripps, Donald A. Supreme Court review: final jeopardy for Grady v. Corbin. *Trial* 30(3):78-81 (March 1994).

Pace, Kirstin. Supreme Court review: Fifth Amendment—the adoption of the "same elements" test: the Supreme Court's failure to adequately protect defendants from double jeopardy. *Journal of Criminal Law and Criminology* 84(4):769-804 (Winter/Spring 1994).

3843. Hartford Fire Insurance Co. v. California		June 28, 1993
Coupled with Merrett Underwriting Agency Management Ltd. v. California		
509 US 764	125 LEd2d 612	113 SCt 2891

Guide (West): (1994):22-24

Sup Ct Review (1993):289-328

Sup Ct Yearbook (1992-93):48-49

Frum, David. Blaming the victim. *Forbes* 151(13):48 (June 21, 1993).

Greenwald, Judy. Antitrust case review opposed by government. *Business Insurance* 26(33):1, 67 (August 17, 1992).

————. Antitrust decision would wreak havoc: defendants. *Business Insurance* 26(48):2, 63 (November 23, 1992).

————. Antitrust review debated. *Business Insurance* 26(3):2, 35 (January 20, 1992).

————. Antitrust review opposed; attorneys general say reinstatement of case follows precedent. *Business Insurance* 26(8):2, 37 (February 24, 1992).

————. Boycott charge grabs attention of High Court. *Business Insurance* 27(9):1, 29 (March 1, 1993).

————. "Boycott" definition sets stage for litigation. *Business Insurance* 27(28):101-102 (July 5, 1993).

————. Briefs support defendants: U.K. government, others favor review. *Business Insurance* 26(8):37 (February 24, 1992).

————. Industry defendants ask justices to review antitrust decision. *Business Insurance* 26(2):2, 37 (January 13, 1992).

————. Insurers see victory in antitrust ruling. *Business Insurance* 27(28):1, 101 (July 5, 1993).

————. Non-U.S. parties seek Court review of separate issues. *Business Insurance* 26(3):35-36 (January 20, 1992).

————. States file antitrust briefs with U.S. Supreme Court. *Business Insurance* 26(54):2, 39 (December 28, 1992).

Kramer, Larry. Extraterritorial application of American law after the insurance antitrust case: a reply to professors Lowenfeld and Trimble. *American Journal of International Law* 89(4):750-758 (October 1995).

Lowenfeld, Andreas F. Conflict, balancing of interests, and the exercise of jurisdiction to prescribe: reflections on the insurance antitrust case. [Editorial] *American Journal of International Law* 89(1):42-53 (January 1995).

Shapiro, Stacy. Ruling a disappointing non-event in London. *Business Insurance* 27(28):101 (July 5, 1993).

Sylvester, Kathleen. The states vs. big insurance. *Governing* 6(6):14 (March 1993).

Trimble, Phillip R. The Supreme Court and international law: the demise of restatement section 403. [Editorial] *American Journal of International Law* 89(1):53-57 (January 1995).

Yang, Catherine. Legally, at least, 'business is no worse off.' *Business Week* (Industrial/Technology Edition) (3327):34 (July 12, 1993).

3844. DeBoer, aka Baby Girl Clausen v. DeBoer   July 26, 1993
         Coupled with DeBoer v. Schmidt
      509 US 1301   125 LEd2d 755   114 SCt 1
         Guide (West): (1994):15-18

3845. Florence County School District Four v. Carter by and Through Carter   November 9, 1993
      510 US 7   126 LEd2d 284   114 SCt 361
         Sup Ct Yearbook (1992-93):224; (1993-94):102
      Zirkel, Perry A. A somewhat ironic decision. *Phi Delta Kappan* 75(6):497-499 (February 1994).

3846. Harris v. Forklift Systems, Inc.   November 9, 1993
      510 US 17   126 LEd2d 295   114 SCt 367
         Almanac (1994):312
         Editorials (1993):1366-1373
         Guide (West): (1995):341-343, 565-572R
         Sup Ct Review (1994):1-56
         Sup Ct Yearbook (1992-93):224; (1993-94):104-105
      Chemerinsky, Erwin. Supreme Court review: the Court confronts sexual harassment. *Trial* 30(2):72-73
         (February 1994).
      Flaxman, Howard R., and Brian F. Jackson. New considerations for hostile working environment. *HR Focus*
         71(3):18-19 (March 1994).
      Kaplan, David A. Take down the girlie calendars. *Newsweek* 122(21):34 (November 22, 1993).
      Lee, Robert D., and Paul S. Greenlaw. The legal evolution of sexual harassment. *Public Administration Review*
         55(4):357-364 (July/August 1995).
      Leo, John. An empty ruling on harassment. [Editorial] *U.S. News and World Report* 115(21):20 (November 29,
         1993).
      Lissy, William E. Easier to prove sexual harassment. *Supervision* 55(7):20-21 (July 1994).
      Miller, William H. The quiet place on Capitol Hill. *Industry Week* 242(20):62 (October 18, 1993).
      Reynolds, Larry. Court rulings and proposed regs will guide harassment policies. *HR Focus* 71(4):1 (April
         1994).
      Rosen, Jeffrey. Reasonable women. *New Republic* 209(18):12-13 (November 1, 1993).
      Sachs, Andrea, Marc Hequet, Elaine Lafferty, and Joyce Leviton. "9-zip! I love it!": a dramatic decision
         produces new guidelines for judging sexual harassment. *Time* 142(22):44-45 (November 22, 1993).
      Seligman, Daniel. Growth situation. *Fortune* 128(15);195-196, 199 (December 13, 1993).
      Woolsey, Christine. Court struggles to define sexual harassment. *Business Insurance* 27(43):2, 80 (October 18,
         1993).
      ———. Employers review harassment policies. *Business Insurance* 27(47):1, 4 (November 15, 1993).

3847. Izumi Seimitsu Kogyo Kabushiki Kaisha v. U.S. Philips Corp.   November 30, 1993
      510 US 27   126 LEd2d 396   114 SCt 425
      Geisel, Jerry. PPO regulation upheld. *Business Insurance* 27(50):2, 51 (December 6, 1993).
      Miller, William H. The quiet place on Capitol Hill. *Industry Week* 242(20):62 (October 18, 1993).

3848. United States v. James Daniel Good Real Property   December 13, 1993
      510 US 43   126 LEd2d 490   114 SCt 492
         Almanac (1994):314
         Editorials (1993):1554-1555
         Guide (West): (1995):111-113
         Sup Ct Yearbook (1992-93):219-220; (1993-94):78-79
      Chemerinsky, Erwin. Supreme Court review: civil forfeiture: a diminishing power. *Trial* 30(4):66-68 (April
         1994).
      Rosenbloom, David H. Fuzzy law from the High Court. [Editorial] *Public Administration Review* 54(6):503-
         506 (November/December 1994).

3849. John Hancock Mutual Life Insurance Co. v. Harris Trust and Savings Bank · · · December 13, 1993
     510 US 86   126 LEd2d 524   114 SCt 517

     Sup Ct Review (1994):429-540
     Sup Ct Yearbook (1993-94):64

Roberts, Sally. ERISA liability defined: High Court says insurers are fiduciaries as annuity managers. *Business Insurance* 27(52):2, 41 (December 20, 1993).

Woolsey, Christine. Court struggles to define sexual harassment. *Business Insurance* 27(43):2, 80 (October 18, 1993).

3850. Ratzlaf v. United States   January 11, 1994
     510 US 135   126 LEd2d 615   114 SCt 655

     Guide (West): (1995):81-83
     Sup Ct Review (1994):429-540
     Sup Ct Yearbook (1993-94):76

Ignorance of the law as an excuse expanded by Supreme Court. *Journal of Taxation* 80(3):130 (March 1994).

Keneally, Kathryn. Congress loosens Supreme Court's interpretations of 'specific intent.' *Journal of Taxation* 82(2):110-115 (February 1995).

———. Supreme Court raises "specific intent" threshold for some criminal violations. *Journal of Taxation* 81(1):44-48 (July 1994).

Simon, Lindsey H. Supreme Court review: the Supreme Court's interpretation of the word "willful": ignorance of the law as an excuse to prosecutions for structuring currency transactions. *Journal of Criminal Law and Criminology* 85(4):1161-1188 (Spring 1995).

3851. Weiss v. United States   January 19, 1994
     510 US 163   127 LEd2d 1   114 SCt 752

     Sup Ct Yearbook (1992-93):219; (1993-94):94-95

3852. Thunder Basin Coal Co. v. Reich   January 19, 1994
     510 US 200   127 LEd2d 29   114 SCt 771

     Sup Ct Yearbook (1993-94):105-106

3853. Schiro v. Farley, Superintendent, Indiana State Prison   January 19, 1994
     510 US 222   127 LEd2d 47   114 SCt 783

     Sup Ct Yearbook (1992-93):220; (1993-94):73-74

Lane, James R. Supreme Court review: Fifth Amendment—the covert narrowing of double jeopardy precedent: the Supreme Court's real reason for hearing Schiro v. Farley. *Journal of Criminal Law and Criminology* 85(4):909-935 (Spring 1995).

3854. National Organization of Women (NOW) v. Scheidler   January 24, 1994
     510 US 249   127 LEd2d 99   114 SCt 798

     Almanac (1982):377-378; (1994):311
     Editorials (1994):108-113
     Guide (West): (1995):5-8
     Sup Ct Review (1994):129-168
     Sup Ct Yearbook (1992-93):223; (1993-94):26-31, 99-100, 113-118R

Blakey, G. Robert. The RICO racket. *National Review* 46(9):61-62, 76 (May 16, 1994).

Gaffney, Edward McGlynn, Jr. Anti-abortion racketeers? *Commonweal* 120(19):6-7 (November 5, 1993).

Glasser, Susan B. Activists weigh fallout from ruling against Operation Rescue. *Ms.* 4(6):93 (May/June 1994).

Kennedy, John W. Open season on pro-lifers? *Christianity Today* 38(3):52 (March 7, 1994).

Randolph, Jennifer G. Supreme Court review: RICO—the rejection of an economic motive requirement. *Journal of Criminal Law and Criminology* 85(4):1189-1222 (Spring 1995).

RICO cuts both ways. [Editorial] *Nation* 258(6):181 (February 14, 1994).

Van Biema, David, Julie Johnson, Elizabeth Taylor, and Sarah Tippit. Your activist, my mobster: a ruling by the High Court enables foes to use a voracious racketeering law against pro-life leaders. *Time* 143(6):32-33 (February 7, 1994).

Vitiello, Michael. Has the Supreme Court really turned RICO upside down? An examination of NOW v. Scheidler. *Journal of Criminal Law and Criminology* 85(4):1223-1257 (Spring 1995).

3855. Albright v. Oliver   January 24, 1994
    510 US 266   127 LEd2d 114   114 SCt 807
    Sup Ct Yearbook (1992-93):225; (1993-94):100

Dripps, Donald A. Supreme Court review: the 'near miss' doctrine: wide of the mark. *Trial* 30(5):78-80 (May 1994).

Wunsch, Eric J. Supreme Court review: Fourth Amendment and Fourteenth Amendment—malicious prosecution and (section) 1983: is there a constitutional violation remediable under section 1983? *Journal of Criminal Law and Criminology* 85(4):878-908 (Spring 1995).

3856. ABF Freight Systems, Inc. v. National Labor Relations Board (NLRB)   January 24, 1994
    510 US 317   127 LEd2d 152   114 SCt 835
    Sup Ct Yearbook (1992-93):225; (1993-94):106

Miller, William H. The quiet place on Capitol Hill. *Industry Week* 242(20):62 (October 18, 1993).

Stark, Sheldon J. The after-acquired evidence doctrine: an insidious defense. *Trial* 31(3):26-33 (March 1995).

3857. Department of Revenue of Oregon v. ACF Industries, Inc.   January 24, 1994
    510 US 332   127 LEd2d 165   114 SCt 843
    Sup Ct Yearbook (1993-94):111-112

3858. Northwest Airlines, Inc. v. County of Kent, Michigan   January 24, 1994
    510 US 355   127 LEd2d 183   114 SCt 855
    Sup Ct Review (1994):429-540
    Sup Ct Yearbook (1992-93):218-219; (1993-94):61

Kent upheld. *Aviation Week and Space Technology* 140(5):19 (January 31, 1994).

Phillips, Edward H. High Court confronts "reasonable fee" issue. *Aviation Week and Space Technology* 139(23):28-30 (December 6, 1993).

Proctor, Paul. Excessive fee Court date. *Aviation Week and Space Technology* 138(25):15 (June 21, 1993).

Supreme Court to hear airport fees case. *Aviation Week and Space Technology* 139(18):35 (November 1, 1993).

3859. Caspari, Superintendent, Missouri Eastern Correctional Center v. Bohlen   February 23, 1994
    510 US 383   127 LEd2d 236   114 SCt 948
    Sup Ct Yearbook (1993-94):79-80

3860. Hagen v. Utah   February 23, 1994
    510 US 399   127 LEd2d 252   114 SCt 958
    Sup Ct Review (1994):429-540
    Sup Ct Yearbook (1993-94):95

3861. American Dredging Co. v. Miller   February 23, 1994
    510 US 443   127 LEd2d 285   114 SCt 981
    Sup Ct Review (1994):429-540
    Sup Ct Yearbook (1993-94):64-65

3862. Federal Deposit Insurance Corporation (FDIC) v. Meyer   February 23, 1994
    510 US 471   127 LEd2d 308   114 SCt 996
    Sup Ct Yearbook (1993-94):101

3863. United States Department of Defense v. Federal Labor Relations Authority (FLRA)   February 23, 1994
    510 US 487   127 LEd2d 325   114 SCt 1006
    Sup Ct Review (1994):429-540
    Sup Ct Yearbook (1992-93):222-223; (1993-94):93

3864. Elder v. Holloway   February 23, 1994
    510 US 510   127 LEd2d 344   114 SCt 1019
      Sup Ct Yearbook (1993-94):100-101

3865. Fogerty v. Fantasy, Inc.   March 1, 1994
    510 US 517   127 LEd2d 455   114 SCt 1023
      Sup Ct Review (1994):429-540
      Sup Ct Yearbook (1993-94):63

3866. Liteky v. United States   March 7, 1994
    510 US 540   127 LEd2d 474   114 SCt 1147
      Sup Ct Review (1994):429-540
      Sup Ct Yearbook (1993-94):70

Citera, Toni-Ann. Supreme Court review: a look at the extrajudicial source doctrine under 28 U.S.C. §455. *Journal of Criminal Law and Criminology* 85(4):1114-1135 (Spring 1995).

3867. Campbell, aka Skyywalker v. Acuff-Rose Music, Inc.   March 7, 1994
    510 US 569   127 LEd2d 500   114 SCt 1164
      Almanac (1994):312
      Editorials (1994):304-307
      Guide (West): (1995):75-77
      Sup Ct Yearbook (1992-93):215-218; (1993-94):62-63

Buchsbaum, Herbert. The law in your life: rap and the law. *Scholastic Update* 126(2):12-14 (September 17, 1993).

Van Biema, David, Greg Aunapu, Patrick E. Cole, and Kristen Lippert-Martin. Parodies regained. *Time* 143(12):46 (March 21, 1994).

3868. Victor v. Nebraska   March 22, 1994
      Coupled with Sandoval v. California
    511 US 1   127 LEd2d 583   114 SCt 1239
      Guide (West): (1995):93-95
      Sup Ct Yearbook (1993-94):82

Dripps, Donald A. Supreme Court review: reasonable doubt: uncertainty about 'moral certainty' continues. *Trial* 30(7):83-86 (July 1994).

Kenney, Shelagh. Supreme Court review: Fifth Amendment—upholding the constitutional merit of misleading reasonable doubt jury instructions. *Journal of Criminal Law and Criminology* 85(4):989-1027 (Spring 1995).

3869. United States v. Granderson   March 22, 1994
    511 US 39   127 LEd2d 611   114 SCt 1259
      Guide (West): (1995):326-328
      Sup Ct Review (1994):429-540
      Sup Ct Yearbook (1993-94):85

3870. Powell v. Nevada   March 30, 1994
    511 US 79   128 LEd2d 1   114 SCt 1280
      Guide (West): (1995):95-96
      Sup Ct Yearbook (1993-94):71-71

3871. Oregon Waste Systems, Inc. v. Department of Environmental Quality of the State of Oregon   April 4, 1994
      Coupled with Columbia Resource Co. v. Department of Environmental Quality of the State of Oregon
    511 US 93   128 LEd2d 13   114 SCt 1345
      Almanac (1994):313
      Guide (West): (1995):55-56
      Sup Ct Review (1995):217-276
      Sup Ct Yearbook (1993-94):23, 90

High Court strikes down out-of-state waste fees. *American City and County* 109(7):16 (June 1994).

3872. J.E.B. v. Alabama ex rel. T. B.   April 19, 1994
       511 US 127   128 LEd2d 89   114 SCt 1419
          Almanac (1994):312
          Editorials (1994):486-491
          Guide (West): (1995):237-239, 541-564R
          Sup Ct Yearbook (1992-93):219; (1993-94):36-39, 70-71, 131-142R
      Chemerinsky, Erwin. Supreme Court review: the end of gender-based peremptory challenges. *Trial* 30(8):69, 72-73 (August 1994).
      ———. Gender-based juries? *Trial* 31(8):34-37 (August 1995).
      Deverman, Beth A. Supreme Court review: Fourteenth Amendment—equal protection: the Supreme Court's prohibition of gender-based peremptory challenges. *Journal of Criminal Law and Criminology* 85(4):1028-1061 (Spring 1995).
      High Court rules prospective jurors can't be excluded based on their gender. *Jet* 86(1):39 (May 9, 1994).
      Rosen, Jeff. Oversexed. *New Republic* 210(20):12, 14 (May 16, 1994).
      Too peremptory by half. *Economist* 331(7860):27 (April 23-29, 1994).

3873. Central Bank of Denver, N.A. v. First Interstate Bank of Denver, N.A.   April 19, 1994
       511 US 164   128 LEd2d 119   114 SCt 1439
          Guide (West): (1995):156-157
          Sup Ct Review (1994):429-540
          Sup Ct Yearbook (1992-93):219; (1993-94):22, 44-46, 66-67, 119-131R
      Hanson, Randall K., and Joanne W. Rockness. Gaining a new balance in the courts: some of the liability burden has disappeared, but a heavy weight remains. *Journal of Accountancy* 178(2):40-44 (August 1994).
      Miller, William H. The quiet place on Capitol Hill. *Industry Week* 242(20):62 (October 18, 1993).

3874. McDermott, Inc. v. AmClyde and River Don Casting Ltd.   April 20, 1994
       511 US 202   128 LEd2d 148   114 SCt 1461
          Sup Ct Yearbook (1993-94):65-66
      Pagnani, Frederick J., Jr. Recent Court rulings aid professional liability. *Best's Review* (Property/Casualty Insurance Edition) 96(1):52-55 (May 1995).

3875. Boca Grande Club, Inc. v. Florida Power and Light Co., Inc.   April 20, 1994
       511 US 222   128 LEd2d 165   114 SCt 1472
          Sup Ct Yearbook (1993-94):65

3876. United States v. Irvine   April 20, 1994
       511 US 224   128 LEd2d 168   114 SCt 1473
          Sup Ct Yearbook (1993-94):68
      High Court says 1979 disclaimer of pre-'32 trust interest triggers gift tax. *Practical Accountant* 27(2):12 (June 1994)
      McCue, Howard M., III. Supreme Court to hear Irvine case—may reconsider Jewett. *Trusts and Estates* 132(12):22-24 (December 1993).

3877. Landgraf v. USI Film Products et al.   April 26, 1994
       511 US 244   128 LEd2d 229   114 SCt 1483
          Almanac (1994):314
          Guide (West): (1995):134-136
          Sup Ct Review (1994):429-540
          Sup Ct Yearbook (1992-93):223-224; (1993-94):102-103, 104
      Miller, William H. The quiet place on Capitol Hill. *Industry Week* 242(20):62 (October 18, 1993).
      Murphy, Betty Southard, Wayne E. Barlow, and D. Diane Hatch. 1991 Civil Rights Act not retroactive. *Personnel Journal* 73(7):24 (July 1994).

Woolsey, Christine. Civil rights law not meant to be retroactive: Court. *Business Insurance* 28(18):2, 61 (May 2, 1994).

3878. Rivers v. Roadway Express, Inc.   April 26, 1994
511 US 298   128 LEd2d 274   114 SCt 1510
     Guide (West): (1995):136-138
     Sup Ct Review (1994):429-540
     Sup Ct Yearbook (1992-93):224; (1993-94):102-103
Murphy, Betty Southard, Wayne E. Barlow, and D. Diane Hatch. 1991 Civil Rights Act not retroactive. *Personnel Journal* 73(7):24 (July 1994).
Woolsey, Christine. Civil rights law not meant to be retroactive: Court. *Business Insurance* 28(18):2, 61 (May 2, 1994).

3879. Stansbury v. California   April 26, 1994
511 US 318   128 LEd2d 293   114 SCt 1526
     Guide (West): (1995):91-93
     Sup Ct Yearbook (1993-94):81

3880. City of Chicago v. Environmental Defense Fund (EDF)   May 2, 1994
511 US 328   128 LEd2d 302   114 SCt 1108
     Almanac (1994):313
     Guide (West): (1995):140-142
     Sup Ct Review (1994):429-540
     Sup Ct Yearbook (1992-93):221-222; (1993-94):22-23, 88-89
Bradford, Hazel, and Debra K. Rubin. High Court deems plant ash toxic. *ENR* 232(19):8-9 (May 9, 1994).
Miller, William H. The quiet place on Capitol Hill. *Industry Week* 242(20):62 (October 18, 1993).
Perlman, Ellen. A costly ruling on hazardous waste. *Governing* 7(10):12 (July 1994).
Solid waste management: Washington, D.C. *American City and County* 109(2):14 (February 1994).

3881. United States v. Alvarez-Sanchez   May 2, 1994
511 US 350   128 LEd2d 319   114 SCt 1599
     Sup Ct Yearbook (1993-94):81-82

3882. Beecham v. United States   May 16, 1994
511 US 368   128 LEd2d 383   114 SCt 1669
     Sup Ct Yearbook (1993-94):83

3883. Kokkonen v. Guardian Life Insurance Co. of America   May 16, 1994
511 US 375   128 LEd2d 391   114 SCt 1673
     Sup Ct Yearbook (1993-94):71

3884. C & A Carbone, Inc. v. Town of Clarkstown, New York   May 16, 1994
511 US 383   128 LEd2d 399   114 SCt 1677
     Almanac (1994):313
     Guide (West): (1995):56-58
     Sup Ct Review (1995):217-276
     Sup Ct Yearbook (1992-93):222; (1993-94):23, 89-90
Diederich, Michael D., Jr. Can municipalities manage their own solid waste? *Environment* 37(4):3, 45 (May 1995).
Miller, William H. The quiet place on Capitol Hill. *Industry Week* 242(20):62 (October 18, 1993).
Phalon, Richard. Bargains in garbage. *Forbes* 154(4):104 (August 15, 1994).
Supreme Court rulings affect waste industry. *American City and County* 109(8):14 (July 1994).
Terrazas, Michael. Going with the flow of flow control. *American City and County* 110(11):60-64, 68, 72, 75 (October 1995).
Ward, Janet. Court ruling hurts locals. [Editorial] *American City and County* 109(8):4 (July 1994).

3885. Security Services, Inc. v. Kmart Corp.   May 16, 1994
     511 US 431   128 LEd2d 433   114 SCt 1702
      Sup Ct Yearbook (1993-94):91-92

3886. Dalton, Secretary of the Navy v. Specter   May 23, 1994
     511 US 462   128 LEd2d 497   114 SCt 1719
      Almanac (1994):435-436
      Editorials (1993):290-295; (1994):614-617
      Guide (West): (1995):374-375
      Sup Ct Yearbook (1993-94):93-94
     Supreme Court challenge. *Aviation Week and Space Technology* 140(10):19 (March 7, 1994).

3887. Custis v. United States   May 23, 1994
     511 US 485   128 LEd2d 517   114 SCt 1732
      Sup Ct Review (1994):429-540
      Sup Ct Yearbook (1993-94):83-84

3888. Posters 'N' Things, Ltd. v. United States   May 23, 1994
     511 US 513   128 LEd2d 539   114 SCt 1747
      Sup Ct Yearbook (1993-94):75-76

3889. BFP v. Resolution Trust Corp.   May 23, 1994
     511 US 531   128 LEd2d 556   114 SCt 1757
      Sup Ct Review (1994):429-540
      Sup Ct Yearbook (1993-94):62

3890. National Labor Relations Board (NLRB) v. Health Care & Retirement Corp.   May 23, 1994
     511 US 571   128 LEd2d 586   114 SCt 1778
      Sup Ct Review (1994):429-540
      Sup Ct Yearbook (1993-94):25, 105
     Cimini, Michael H., and Charles J. Muhl. Developments in industrial relations: Supreme Court rules on nurses. *Monthly Labor Review* 117(8):62 (August 1994).
     DiCesare, Constance B. The law and work: update and stay tuned. *Monthly Labor Review* 118(8):79 (July 1995).
     Gostin, Lawrence O. Law and medicine. *JAMA: The Journal of the American Medical Association* 273(21): 1688-1689 (June 7, 1995).
     Yarborough, Mary Helen. LPNs as supervisors: far-reaching impact? *HR Focus* 71(8):3 (August 1994).

3891. Staples v. United States   May 23, 1994
     511 US 600   128 LEd2d 608   114 SCt 1793
      Sup Ct Review (1994):429-540
      Sup Ct Yearbook (1993-94):76-77
     Lefevour, Martin T. Supreme Court review: 26 U.S.C. § 5861(d) requires mens rea as to the physical characteristics of the weapon. *Journal of Criminal Law and Criminology* 85(4):1136-1160 (Spring 1995).

3892. Associated Industries of Missouri v. Lohman, Director of Revenue of Missouri   May 23, 1994
     511 US 641   128 LEd2d 639   114 SCt 1815
      Sup Ct Yearbook (1993-94):110

3893. Morgan Stanley and Co., Inc. v. Pacific Mutual Life Insurance Co.   May 23, 1994
     511 US 658   128 LEd2d 654   114 SCt 1827
      Sup Ct Yearbook (1993-94):67

3894. Waters v. Churchill   May 31, 1994
     511 US 661   128 LEd2d 686   114 SCt 1878

Sup Ct Yearbook (1993-94):97-98

Rosenbloom, David H. Fuzzy law from the High Court. [Editorial] *Public Administration Review* 54(6):503-506 (November/December 1994).

3895. PUD No. 1. of Jefferson County & City of Tacoma v. Washington Department of Ecology   May 31, 1994
Jefferson County PUD v. Ecology Department of Washington
511 US 700   128 LEd2d 716   114 SCt 1900
   Sup Ct Review (1994):429-540
   Sup Ct Yearbook (1993-94):90-91
Behnke, Jom, and Harold Dondis. The Clean Water Act and federally licensed utilities. *Public Utilities Fortnightly* 132(20):42-46 (November 1, 1994).

3896. Nichols v. United States   June 6, 1994
511 US 738   128 LEd2d 745   114 SCt 1921
   Sup Ct Yearbook (1993-94):84-85

3897. Department of Revenue of Montana v. Kurth Ranch June 6, 1994
511 US 767   128 LEd2d 767   114 SCt 1937
   Guide (West): (1995):109-111
   Sup Ct Yearbook (1993-94):23, 77
Hildy, John. Supreme Court review: Fifth Amendment—double jeopardy and the dangerous drug tax. *Journal of Criminal Law and Criminology* 85(4):936-961 (Spring 1995).

3898. Key Tronics Corp. v. United States   June 6, 1994
511 US 809   128 LEd2d 797   114 SCt 1960
   Sup Ct Yearbook (1993-94):89
Begley, Ronald. Cost recovery ruling gets mixed response. *Chemical Week* 154(23):12 (June 15, 1994).
Court rules legal expenses not recoverable in superfund. *Chemical Marketing Reporter* 245(25):18 (June 20, 1994).
Lenckus, Dave. Legal costs unrecoverable from other PRPs: High Court. *Business Insurance* 28(24):2, 20 (June 13, 1994).

3899. Farmer v. Brennan, Warden   June 6, 1994
511 US 825   128 LEd2d 811   114 SCt 1970
   Sup Ct Yearbook (1993-94):82-83

3900. Digital Equipment Corp. v. Desktop Direct, Inc.   June 6, 1994
511 US 863   128 LEd2d 842   114 SCt 1992
   Sup Ct Yearbook (1993-94):71

3901. Romano v. Oklahoma   June 13, 1994
512 US 1   129 LEd2d 1   114 SCt 2004
   Guide (West): (1995):43-45
   Sup Ct Yearbook (1993-94):73

3902. United States v. Carlton   June 13, 1994
512 US 26   129 LEd2d 22   114 SCt 2018
   Guide (West): (1995):116-118
   Sup Ct Yearbook (1993-94):67-68
Huffaker, John B. Retroactive change for stock sales to ESOPs upheld. *Journal of Taxation* 81(2):119 (August 1994).
Moore, Stephen, and Michael Markson. Tax unfairness. *National Review* 46(32):28 (April 18, 1994).
Supreme Court upholds retroactive amendment of estate tax statute. *Taxes* 72(7):397 (July 1994).
Willens, Robert. Does Carlton end the retroactivity debate? *Journal of Accountancy* 178(4):27-28 (October 1994).

3903. City of Ladue v. Gilleo   June 13, 1994
       512 US 43   129 LEd2d 36   114 SCt 2038
           Almanac (1994):313-314
           Editorials (1994):744-747
           Guide (West): (1995):172-174
           Sup Ct Yearbook (1993-94):23, 97
       Boedecker, Karl A., and Fred W. Morgan. The evolution of First Amendment protection for commercial
           speech. *Journal of Marketing* 59(1):38-47 (January 1995).
       Hernandez, Debra Gersh. Banning select signs in windows of private homes is unconstitutional. *Editor and*
           Publisher 127(29):18-19 (July 16, 1994).
       Newman, Judith B. A sign of the times. *People Weekly* 41(10):115, 117 (March 21, 1994).

3904. Department of Taxation and Finanace of New York v. Milhelm, Attea and Brothers, Inc.   June 13, 1994
       512 US 61   129 LEd2d 52   114 SCt 2028
           Guide (West): (1995):290-291
           Sup Ct Yearbook (1993-94):112

3905. O'Melveny & Myers v. Federal Deposit Insurance Co. (FDIC)   June 13, 1994
       512 US 79   129 LEd2d 67   114 SCt 2048
           Sup Ct Yearbook (1993-94):69
       Clolery, Paul. Fraud detection central to Supreme Court case. *Practical Accountant* 27(2):6-7 (February 1994).
       Zolkos, Rodd. Supreme Court ruling may ease liability risk for advisors to S&L's. *Business Insurance* 28(25):3,
           15 (June 20, 1994).

3906. Howlett v. Birkdale, Shipping Co., S.A.   June 13, 1994
       512 US 92   129 LEd2d 78   114 SCt 2057
           Sup Ct Yearbook (1993-94):65

3907. Livadas v. Bradshaw, California Labor Commissioner   June 13, 1994
       512 US 107   129 LEd2d 93   114 SCt 2068
           Sup Ct Yearbook (1993-94):107-108

3908. Ibanez v. Florida, Department of Business and Professional Regulation, Board of Accountancy June 13, 1994
       512 US 136   129 LEd2d 118   114 SCt 2084
           Guide (West): (1995):167-169
           Sup Ct Yearbook (1993-94):97
       Baliga, Wayne. Nonpracticing CPA can advertise CPA designation, U.S. Supreme Court says. *Journal of*
           Accountancy 179(3):26 (March 1995).
       Boedecker, Karl A., and Fred W. Morgan. The evolution of First Amendment protection for commercial
           speech. *Journal of Marketing* 59(1):38-47 (January 1995).
       Clolery, Paul. High Court rules CPAs can tout their credentials. *Practical Accountant* 27(8):9 (August 1994).
       Turman, Lloyd A. The press corps can write: but when will they learn to read? *Vital Speeches* 61(3):75-76
           (November 15, 1994).

3909. Simmons v. South Carolina   June 18, 1994
       512 US 154   129 LEd2d 133   114 SCt 2187
           Guide (West): (1995):45-46
           Sup Ct Yearbook (1993-94):74-75

3910. West Lynn Creamery, Inc. v. Healy   June 17, 1994
       512 US 186   129 LEd2d 157   114 SCt 2205
           Guide (West): (1995):58-60
           Sup Ct Review (1995):217-276
           Sup Ct Yearbook (1993-94):23, 109-110

3911. MCI Telecommunications Corp. v. American Telephone & Telegraph Co.   June 17, 1994
      Coupled with United States v. AT&T, Co.
  512 US 218   129 LEd2d 182   114 SCt 2223
     Sup Ct Review (1994):429-540
     Sup Ct Yearbook (1993-94):91
    Safire, William. Scalia v. Merriam-Webster. *New York Times Magazine* (section 6, part 1):30-32 (November 20, 1994).

3912. Hawaiian Airlines, Inc. v. Norris   June 20, 1994
      Coupled with Finazzo v. Norris
  512 US 246   129 LEd2d 203   114 SCt 2239
     Sup Ct Review (1994):429-540
     Sup Ct Yearbook (1993-94):107

3913. Director, Office of Workers' Compensation Programs, Department of Labor   June 20, 1994
     v. Greenwich Collieries, Inc.
  512 US 267   129 LEd2d 221   114 SCt 2251
     Sup Ct Review (1994):429-540
     Sup Ct Yearbook (1993-94):108

3914. Barclays Bank PLC v. Franchise Tax Board of California   June 20, 1994
      Coupled with Colgate-Palmolive Co. v. Franchise Tax Board of California
  512 US 298   129 LEd2d 244   114 SCt 2268
     Guide (West): (1995):384-385
     Sup Ct Yearbook (1993-94):110-111
    McArthur, J. William, Jr., and Kendall L. Houghton. In Barclays, U.S. Supreme Court finds for California, which was banking on it. *Journal of Taxation* 81(3):176-179 (September 1994).
    Smart move. *Economist* 328(7829):86 (September 18-24, 1993).
    Unhappy returns for Barclays. *Economist* 331(7869):79 (June 25-July 1, 1994).

3915. Reed v. Farley, Superintendent, Indiana State Prison June 20, 1994
  512 US 339   129 LEd2d 277   114 SCt 2291
     Sup Ct Yearbook (1993-94):85-86

3916. Dolan v. City of Tigard   June 24, 1994
  512 US 374   129 LEd2d 304   114 SCt 2309
     Almanac (1994):310-311
     Guide (West): (1995):118-119
     Sup Ct Yearbook (1993-94):39-41, 108-109, 154-168R
    Carpenter, Betsy. This land is my land: environmentalism is colliding with the rights of property owners. *U.S. News and World Report* 116(10):65-69 (March 14, 1994).
    Cohen, Jonathan E. A constitutional safety valve: the variance in zoning and land-use based environmental controls. *Boston College Environmental Affairs Law Review* 22(2):307-364 (Winter 1995).
    High Court limits cities' rights. *American City and County* 109(10):26-27 (September 1994).
    Platt, Rutherford H. Law: parsing Dolan. *Environment* 36(8):4-5, 43 (October 1994).
    Rosenbloom, David H. Fuzzy law from the High Court. [Editorial] *Public Administration Review* 54(6):503-506 (November/December 1994).
    Spencer, Leslie. Legalized extortion. *Forbes* 153(4):98 (February 14, 1994).
    Walters, Jonathan. Tightening the screws on 'takings.' *Governing* 7(11):18-20 (August 1994).

3917. Honda Motor Co. Ltd. v. Oberg   June 24, 1994
  512 US 415   129 LEd2d 336   114 SCt 2331
     Almanac (1994):314
     Guide (West): (1995):100-102
     Sup Ct Yearbook (1993-94):23, 42-43, 112, 143-153R

Chemerinsky, Erwin. Supreme Court review: punitive damages and the Constitution. *Trial* 30(10):90-92 (October 1994).

Wojcik, Joanne. High Court affirms limits on punitive awards. *Business Insurance* 28(27):3, 10 (July 4, 1994).

3918. Davis v. United States   June 24, 1994
  512 US 452   129 LEd2d 362   114 SCt 2350
   Godless 122-123
   Guide (West): (1995):97-98
   Sup Ct Yearbook (1993-94):80-81

Dripps, Donald A. Supreme Court review: 'Maybe I should talk to a lawyer': ambiguous invocations of Miranda. *Trial* 30(9):90-92 (September 1994).

Levenberg, Thomas O. Supreme Court review: Fifth Amendment—responding to ambiguous requests for counsel during custodial interrogations. *Journal of Criminal Law and Criminology* 85(4):962-988 (Spring 1995).

3919. Heck v. Humphrey   June 24, 1994
  512 US 477   129 LEd2d 383   114 SCt 2364
   Sup Ct Review (1994):429-540
   Sup Ct Yearbook (1993-94):101-102

3920. Thomas Jefferson University, dba Thomas Jefferson University Hospital   June 24, 1994
  v. Shalala, Secretary of Health and Human Services
  512 US 504   129 LEd2d 405   114 SCt 2381
   Sup Ct Review (1994):429-540
   Sup Ct Yearbook (1993-94):92

Gostin, Lawrence O. Law and medicine. *JAMA: The Journal of the American Medical Association* 273(21): 1688-1689 (June 7, 1995).

Jaschik, Scott. Supreme Court rejects millions in Medicare claims sought by universities with teaching hospitals. *Chronicle of Higher Education* 40(44):A34 (July 6, 1994).

3921. Consolidated Rail Corp. (CONRAIL) v. Gottshall   June 24, 1994
  512 US 532   129 LEd2d 427   114 SCt 2396
   Sup Ct Review (1994):429-540
   Sup Ct Yearbook (1993-94):106-107

George, James A., and Michelle M. O'Daniels. Recoverable damages in admiralty and maritime cases: muddied waters after Miles v. Apex Marine. *Trial* 31(5):58-65 (May 1995).

Woolsey, Christine. Court struggles to define sexual harassment. *Business Insurance* 27(43):2, 80 (October 18, 1993).

3922. Shannon v. United States   June 24, 1994
  512 US 573   129 LEd2d 459   114 SCt 2419
   Sup Ct Review (1994):429-540
   Sup Ct Yearbook (1993-94):80

Ellias, Randi. Supreme Court review: should courts instruct juries as to the consequences to a defendant of a "not guilty by reason of insanity" verdict? *Journal of Criminal Law and Criminology* 85(4):1062-1083 (Spring 1995).

3923. Williamson v. United States   June 27, 1994
  512 US 594   129 LEd2d 476   114 SCt 2431
   Sup Ct Review (1994):429-540
   Sup Ct Yearbook (1993-94):78

Dripps, Donald A. Supreme Court review: reining in the against-interest exception. *Trial* 30(11):100-101 (November 1994).

Duck, Emily F. Supreme Court review: the Williamson standard for the exception to the rule against hearsay for statements against penal interest. *Journal of Criminal Law and Criminology* 85(4):1084-1113 (Spring 1995).

3924. Turner Broadcasting System, Inc. v. Federal Communication Commission (FCC)   June 27, 1994
512 US 622   129 LEd2d 497   114 SCt 2445

Almanac (1994):312-313
Guide (West): (1995):71-73
Sup Ct Review (1994):57-128
Sup Ct Yearbook (1993-94):52-55, 95-96, 193-219R

Hernandez, Debra Gersh. Cable operators and the First Amendment: U.S. Supreme Court says they have the same rights and protections as other media. *Editor and Publisher* 127(29):14-15 (July 16, 1994).

Huber, Peter W. Must-carry and the Bill of Rights. *Forbes* 154(5):94 (August 29, 1994).

Press, Aric. Tacking toward moderation. *Newsweek* 124(2):58 (July 11, 1994).

3925. Board of Education of Kiryas Joel Village School District v. Grumet   June 27, 1994
        Coupled with Board of Education of Monroe-Woodbury Central School District v. Grumet
        Coupled with Attorney General of New York v. Grumet
512 US 687   129 LEd2d 546   114 SCt 2481

Almanac (1994):313
Editorials (1994):816-823
Guide (West): (1995):161-164, 467-502R
Sup Ct Yearbook (1993-94):23, 49-52, 96, 168-193R

Bork, Robert H. What to do about the First Amendment. *Commentary* 99(2):23-29 (February 1995).

Carter, Stephen L. Let us pray. *New Yorker* 70(40):60-74 (December 5, 1994).

Church-state separation case to be heard. *Christian Century* 111(1):8-9 (January 5-12, 1994).

Cooke, Ronald J. The religious schools controversy. *America* 172(5):17-19 (February 18, 1995).

Court rules against religious school district. *Christian Century* 111(21):678-679 (July 13-20, 1994).

Drinan, Robert F. The Constitution and handicapped Hasidim children. *America* 170(7):8-11 (February 26, 1994).

Gest, Ted. The Supreme Court: a reluctant referee. *U.S. News and World Report* 117(12):84 (September 26, 1994).

Grumet, Louis. Breaching the wall. *American School Board Journal* 181(5):26-28 (May 1994).

Kaplan, David A. A question of separation. *Newsweek* 122(24):72 (December 13, 1993).

Kiryas Joel: victory from defeat. [Editorial] *America* 171(2):3 (July 16-23, 1994).

Loconte, Joe. Will Court reshape church-state test? *Christianity Today* 38(6):50 (May 16, 1994).

Ostling, Richard N., and Jeff Hooten. Is there a place for God in school? *Time* 143(15):60-61 (April 11, 1994).

Press, Aric. Tacking toward moderation. *Newsweek* 124(2):58 (July 11, 1994).

Rabkin, Jeremy. The curious case of Kiryas Joel. *Commentary* 98(5):58-61 (November 1994).

Rapps, Dennis. The case for Kiryas Joel. *American School Board Journal* 181(5):28 (May 1994).

Religionists divided over church-state case. *Christian Century* 111(11):346-347 (April 6, 1994).

Roberts, Steven V. Reaching out a hand through a wall of fear. *U.S. News and World Report* 115(23):10-11 (December 13, 1993).

Rosen, Jeff. Village people. *New Republic* 210(15):11-12, 14 (April 11, 1994).

Scrap the 'Lemon test,' say Southern Baptists. *Christian Century* 111(7):219-220 (March 2, 1994).

Sullivan, Winnifred Fallers. The USCC & the rebbe. *Commonweal* 121(10):6-7 (May 20, 1994).

3926. Madsen v. Women's Health Center, Inc.   June 30, 1994
512 US 753   129 LEd2d 593   114 SCt 2516

Almanac (1994):311, 355
Editorials (1994):824-827
Guide (West): (1995):2-5, 503-540R
Sup Ct Review (1994):129-168
Sup Ct Yearbook (1993-94):26-31, 98-99, 266-291R

Buckley, William F. What are they arguing about? *National Review* 46(10):70-71 (May 30, 1994).

Chemerinsky, Erwin. Looking ahead to the new term. *Trial* 30(12):81-83 (December 1994).

Gostin, Lawrence O. Law and medicine. *JAMA: The Journal of the American Medical Association* 273(21): 1688-1689 (June 7, 1995).

Kennedy, John W. Buffer-zone case tests free speech. *Christianity Today* 38(7):48 (June 20, 1994).

Press, Aric. Tacking toward moderation. *Newsweek* 124(2):58 (July 11, 1994).

Van Biema, David, Ann Blackman, Andrea Sachs, and Sarah Tippit. Keep your distance: in a blow to pro-lifers, the High Court lets stand an exclusion zone against antiabortion protesters. *Time* 144(2):25 (July 11, 1994).

Van Biema, David, Julie Johnson, Elizabeth Taylor, and Sarah Tippit. Your activist, my mobster: a ruling by the High Court enables foes to use a voracious racketeering law against pro-life leaders. *Time* 143(6):32-33 (February 7, 1994).

3927. International Union, United Mine Workers v. Bagwell   June 30, 1994
       United Mine Workers v. Bagwell
       512 US 821   129 LEd2d 642   114 SCt 2552
           Guide (West): (1995):99-100
           Sup Ct Yearbook (1992-93):225; (1993-94):68-69
       Miller, William H. The quiet place on Capitol Hill. *Industry Week* 242(20):62 (October 18, 1993).

3928. McFarland v. Scott, Director, Texas Department of Criminal Justice, Institutional Division   June 30, 1994
       512 US 849   129 LEd2d 666   114 SCt 2568
           Guide (West): (1995):39-41
           Sup Ct Yearbook (1993-94):46-49, 72-73, 256-266R
       Kaplan, David A. Catch-22 at the High Court. *Newsweek* 123(15):68 (April 11, 1994).

3929. Holder, Individually and in his Official Capacity   June 30, 1994
           as County Commissioner for Blekley County, Georgia v. Hall
       512 US 874   129 LEd2d 687   114 SCt 2581
           Almanac (1994):312
           Guide (West): (1995):393-395
           Sup Ct Review (1994):429-540
           Sup Ct Yearbook (1992-93):221; (1993-94):34-36, 87-88, 232-256R
       Bolick, Clint. Bad fences. *National Review* 47(6):51-53 (April 3, 1995).
       Davis, Olethia. Tenuous interpretation: Sections 2 and 5 of the Voting Rights Act. *National Civic Review* 84(4):310-322 (Fall/Winter 1995).
       Leo, John. Rejecting electoral 'homelands.' [Editorial] *U.S. News and World Report* 117(8):19 (August 22, 1994).
       McCoy, Frank. Racial politics and the High Court. *Black Enterprise* 24(3):25 (November 1993).
       Van Biema, David, Wendy Cole, and Michael Riley. Snakes or ladders?: a controversial Supreme Court decision on racial redistricting uncovers a can of worms. *Time* 142(2):30-31 (July 12, 1993).

3930. Tuilaepa v. California   June 30, 1994
           Coupled with Proctor v. California
       512 US 967   129 LEd2d 750   114 SCt 2630
           Guide (West): (1995):46-48
           Sup Ct Yearbook (1993-94):75

3931. Johnson, Speaker of the Florida House of Representatives v. DeGrandy   June 30, 1994
           Coupled with DeGrandy v. Johnson
           Coupled with United States v. Florida
       512 US 997   129 LEd2d 775   114 SCt 2647
           Almanac (1994):312
           Guide (West): (1995):395-397
           Sup Ct Yearbook (1992-93):220-221; (1993-94):31-33, 86-87, 219-231R

Davis, Olethia. Tenuous interpretation: Sections 2 and 5 of the Voting Rights Act. *National Civic Review* 84(4): 310-322 (Fall/Winter 1995).

Ehrenhalt, Alan. The Court that forgot about politics. *Governing* 8(3):7-8 (December 1994).

McCoy, Frank. Racial politics and the High Court. *Black Enterprise* 24(3):25 (November 1993).

Weber, Ronald E. Redistricting and the courts: judicial activism in the 1990s. *American Politics Quarterly* 23(2):204-228 (April 1995).

3932. United States v. Shabani   November 1, 1994
    513 US 10   130 LEd2d 225   115 SCt 382
        Guide (West): (1995):108-109
        Sup Ct Yearbook (1994-95):81

3933. U.S. Bancorp Mortgage Co. v. Bonner Mall Partnership   November 8, 1994
    513 US 18   130 LEd2d 233   115 SCt 386
        Sup Ct Yearbook (1993-94):299-300; (1994-95):76

    Ceniceros, Roberto. Decision will keep rulings on the books. *Business Insurance* 28(46):1, 4 (November 14, 1994).
    ———. High Court ruling may have wide impact. *Business Insurance* 28(48):1, 16 (November 28, 1994).
    Fisch, Jill E. Supreme Court review: post-settlement vacatur: a case of disappearing decisions. *Trial* 31(2):86-88 (February 1995).
    Yang, Catherine. Rulings for sale?: the High Court weights "precedent snuffing." *Business Week* (3394):56 (October 17, 1994).

3934. Hess v. Port Authority Trans-Hudson Corp.   November 14, 1994
    513 US 30   130 LEd2d 245   115 SCt 394
        Sup Ct Yearbook (1994-95):114-115

3935. United States v. X-Citement Video, Inc.   November 29, 1994
    513 US 64   130 LEd2d 372   115 SCt 464
        Guide (West): (1994):352-355; (1995):286-288
        Sup Ct Review (1995):71-98
        Sup Ct Yearbook (1993-94):302; (1994-95):81-82
    Caplan, Lincoln. Uneasy days in Court. *Newsweek* 124(15):62-64 (October 10, 1994).

3936. Federal Elections Commission v. National Rifle Association Political Victory Fund   December 6, 1993
    513 US 88   130 LEd2d 439   115 SCt 537
        Almanac (1994):36
        Sup Ct Yearbook (1993-94):302-303; (1994-95):92

3937. Reich v. Collins, Revenue Commission of Georgia   December 6, 1994
    513 US 106   130 LEd2d 454   115 SCt 547
        Sup Ct Yearbook (1993-94):307; (1994-95):117

3938. Brown, Secretary of Veterans Affairs v. Gardner   December 12, 1994
    513 US 115   130 LEd2d 462   115 SCt 552
        Almanac (1995):8-18
        Sup Ct Yearbook (1993-94):303; (1994-95):101

3939. Nebraska Department of Revenue v. Loewenstein   December 12, 1994
    513 US 123   130 LEd2d 470   115 SCt 557
        Sup Ct Yearbook (1994-95):116

3940. Interstate Commerce Commission (ICC) v. Transcon Lines   January 10, 1995
    513 US 138   130 LE2d 562   115 SCt 689
        Sup Ct Yearbook (1994-95):98

3941. Tome v. United States   January 10, 1995
    513 US 150   130 LEd2d 574   115 SCt 696
      Sup Ct Review (1995):277-321
      Sup Ct Yearbook (1994-95):83
    Burns, Robert P. Supreme Court review: foreword: bright lines and hard edges: anatomy of a criminal evidence
      decision. *Journal of Criminal Law and Criminology* 85(4):843-877 (Spring 1995).

3942. Asgrow Seed Co. v. Winterboer dba DeeBees   January 18, 1995
    513 US 179   130 LEd2d 682   115 SCt 788
      Sup Ct Yearbook (1993-94):298-299; (1994-95):70

3943. United States v. Mezzanatto   January 18, 1995
    513 US 196   130 LEd2d 697   115 SCt 797
      Sup Ct Yearbook (1994-95):83-84

3944. American Airlines, Inc. v. Wolens   January 18, 1995
    513 US 219   130 LEd2d 715   115 SCt 817
      Sup Ct Yearbook (1993-94):297; (1994-95):67
    McTague, Jim. Big decisions: some important business cases are on the Supreme Court docket. *Barron's*
      74(40):23 (October 3, 1994).
    Miller, William H. Order in the court. *Industry Week* 243(1):56 (October 3, 1994).

3945. NationsBank of North Carolina, N.A. v. Variable Annuity Life Insurance Co. (VALIC)   January 18, 1995
      Coupled with Ludwig, Comptroller of Currency v. Variable Annuity Life Insurance Co. (VALIC)
    513 US 251   130 LEd2d 740   115 SCt 810
      Sup Ct Yearbook (1993-94):298; (1994-95):67-68
    Hofmann, Mark A. Punitive damages appeal to be heard by High Court. *Business Insurance* 29(15):10 (January
      30, 1995).
    McLeod, Douglas. High Court takes bank annuity case. *Business Insurance* 28(24):21 (June 13, 1994).
    McTague, Jim. Big decisions: some important business cases are on the Supreme Court docket. *Barron's*
      74(40):23 (October 3, 1994).
    1993 litigation scorecard. *Best's Review* (Life/Health Insurance Edition) 94(10):32 (February 1994).

3946. Allied-Bruce Terminix Cos., Inc. v. Dobson   January 18, 1995
    513 US 265   130 LEd2d 753   115 SCt 834
      Sup Ct Yearbook (1993-94):300; (1994-95):74
    McTague, Jim. Big decisions: some important business cases are on the Supreme Court docket. *Barron's*
      74(40):23 (October 3, 1994).

3947. Schlup v. Delo, Superintendent, Potosi Correctional Center   January 23, 1995
    513 US 298   130 LEd2d 808   115 SCt 851
      Almanac (1995):6-41
      Sup Ct Yearbook (1993-94):301; (1994-95):86-87
    Chemerinsky, Erwin. Supreme Court review: innocence and habeas corpus. *Trial* 31(4):79-81 (April 1995).

3948. McKennon v. Nashville Banner Publishing Co.   January 23, 1995
    513 US 352   130 LEd2d 852   115 SCt 879
      Sup Ct Yearbook (1993-94):306; (1994-95):110
    Brady, Robert L. After-acquired evidence will not bar discrimination suits. *HR Focus* 72(5):18 (May 1995).
    DiCesare, Constance B. The law at work: the after-acquired evidence rule. *Monthly Labor Review* 118(5):62
      (May 1995).
    Hofmann, Mark A. Court bars popular defense from employment bias suits. *Business Insurance* 29(5):2, 10
      (January 30, 1995).
    Lissy, William E. After-acquired evidence of employee's wrongdoing. *Supervision* 56(7):12-13 (July 1995).

McTague, Jim. Big decisions: some important business cases are on the Supreme Court docket. *Barron's* 74(40):23 (October 3, 1994).

Miller, William H. Order in the Court. *Industry Week* 243(1):56 (October 3, 1994).

Stark, Sheldon J. The after-acquired evidence doctrine: an insidious defense. *Trial* 31(3):26-33 (March 1995).

3949. Duncan, Warden v. Henry   January 23, 1995
513 US 364   130 LEd2d 865   115 SCt 887
Sup Ct Yearbook (1994-95):84

3950. Lebron v. National Railroad Passenger Corp.   February 21, 1995
Lebron v. Amtrack
513 US 374   130 LEd2d 902   115 SCt 951
Sup Ct Yearbook (1993-94):304; (1994-95):99-100
Chemerinsky, Erwin. Supreme Court review: state action. *Trial* 31(9):82-84 (September 1995).

3951. Milwaukee Brewery Workers' Pension Plan v. Jos. Schlitz Brewing Co.   February 21, 1995
513 US 414   130 LEd2d 932   115 SCt 981
Sup Ct Yearbook (1994-95):112-113
Miller, William H. Order in the Court. *Industry Week* 243(1):56 (October 3, 1994).

3952. O'Neal v. McAninch, Warden   February 21, 1995
513 US 432   130 LEd2d 947   115 SCt 992
Sup Ct Yearbook (1993-94):301-302; (1994-95):86

3953. United States v. National Treasury Employees Union   February 22, 1995
513 US 454   130 LEd2d 964   115 SCt 1003
Sup Ct Yearbook (1993-94):303-304; (1994-95):24, 105-106
Hernandez, Debra Gersh. Federal workers can receive pay for outside writing. *Editor and Publisher* 128(15):16-17 (April 15, 1995).

3954. Harris v. Alabama   February 22, 1995
513 US 504   130 LEd2d 1004   115 SCt 1031
Sup Ct Yearbook (1993-94):301; (1994-95):77-78

3955. Jerome B. Grubart, Inc. v. Great Lakes Dredge & Dock Co.   February 22, 1995
513 US 527   130 LEd2d 1024   115 SCt 1043
Sup Ct Yearbook (1993-94):298; (1994-95):68-69
Krizan, William G. Admiralty court gets flood cases. *ENR* 234(9):10 (March 6, 1995).

3956. Anderson, Director, California Department of Social Services v. Green   February 22, 1995
513 US 557   130 LEd2d 1050   115 SCt 1059
Sup Ct Yearbook (1994-95):97
Chemerinsky, Erwin. Looking ahead to the new term. *Trial* 30(12):81-83 (December 1994).
Gest, Ted. Courts: the next arena. *U.S. News and World Report* 118(2):36-37 (January 16, 1995).

3957. Gustanfson v. Alloyd Co., Inc. aka Alloyd Holdings, Inc.   February 28, 1995
513 US 561   131 LEd2d 1   115 SCt 1061
Sup Ct Review (1995):99-124
Sup Ct Yearbook (1993-94):297-298; (1994-95):70-71

3958. Arizona v. Evans   March 1, 1995
514 US 1   131 LEd2d 34   115 SCt 1185
Sup Ct Yearbook (1994-95):90-91

3959. Swint v. Chambers County Commission   March 1, 1995
    514 US 35   131 LEd2d 60   115 SCt 1203
    Sup Ct Yearbook (1993-94):306-307; (1994-95):73

3960. Mastrobuono v. Shearson Lehman Hutton   March 6, 1995
    514 US 52   131 LEd2d 76   115 SCt 1212
    Sup Ct Yearbook (1994-95):75
    Huth, William E., and Keith Highet. International decisions. *American Journal of International Law* 89(3):601-604 (July 1995).
    Karp, Richard. A blow to brokers: High Court rules investors can get punitive damages. *Barron's* 75(11):12-13 (March 13, 1995).
    Pettit, Dave. Brokers on edge: Supreme Court to review rights of customers. *Barron's* 74(42):13 (October 17, 1994).
    Spiro, Leah Nathans. Abusive brokers beware. *Business Week* (3416):110 (March 20, 1995).

3961. Curtiss-Wright Corp. v. Schoonejongen   March 6, 1995
    514 US 73   131 LEd2d 94   115 SCt 1223
    Sup Ct Yearbook (1994-95):112
    DiCesare, Constance B. Retirement health benefits. *Monthly Labor Review* 118(7):78 (July 1995).
    Geisel, Jerry. Drop in health care costs tops benefit news of '95. *Business Insurance* 29(53):26 (December 25, 1995).
    ————. ERISA case now before High Court could erode pre-emption. *Business Insurance* 28(41):3, 26 (October 10, 1994).
    High Court takes benefit case. *Business Insurance* 28(40):2 (October 3, 1994).
    Lenckus, Dave. Court considers plan amendment. *Business Insurance* 29(4):1, 20 (January 23, 1995).
    ————. Court protects plan amendments. *Business Insurance* 29(53):27 (December 25, 1995).
    ————. High Court shifts focus of benefit cutback suits. *Business Insurance* 29(11):1, 10 (March 13, 1995).
    ————. Plan language warrants attention: threat of retiree litigation a major concern for employers. *Business Insurance* 28(53):35 (December 26, 1994).

3962. Shalala, Secretary of Health and Human Services v. Guernsey Memorial Hospital   March 6, 1995
    514 US 87   131 LEd2d 106   115 SCt 1232
    Sup Ct Yearbook (1994-95):98-99

3963. Goeke, Superintendent, Renz Correctional Center v. Branch   March 20, 1995
    514 US 115   131 LEd2d 152   115 SCt 1275
    Sup Ct Yearbook (1994-95):85

3964. Director, Office of Workers' Compensation Programs, Department of Labor   March 21, 1995
    v. Newport News Shipbuilding & Dry Dock Co.
    514 US 122   131 LEd2d 160   115 SCt 1278
    Sup Ct Yearbook (1994-95):113-114

3965. Anderson, Director, California Department of Social Services v. Edwards   March 22, 1995
    514 US 143   131 LEd2d 178   115 SCt 1291
    Sup Ct Yearbook (1994-95):96-97

3966. Qualitex Co. v. Jacobson Products Co., Inc.   March 28, 1995
    514 US 159   131 LEd2d 248   115 SCt 1300
    Sup Ct Yearbook (1994-95):73
    Kelly, David M. Rainbow of ideas to trademark color. *Advertising Age* 66(17):20-22 (April 24, 1995).
    Sachs, Andrea. High Court's ruling may color ad plans. *Advertising Age* 66(15):30 (April 10, 1995).

3967. Oklahoma Tax Commission v. Jefferson Lines, Inc. April 3, 1995
    514 US 175   131 LEd2d 261   115 SCt 1331
    Sup Ct Yearbook (1994-95):116-117

Dell'Isola, Mark, and Sara Ann Hull. State sales tax on interstate transportation service valid. *CPA Journal* 65(7):62-64 (August 1995).

3968. Plaut v. Spendthrift Farm, Inc.   April 18, 1995
514 US 211   131 LEd2d 328   115 SCt 1447
Sup Ct Yearbook (1993-94):298; (1994-95):24, 71

3969. Shalala, Secretary of Health and Human Services v. Whitecotton   April 18, 1995
514 US 268   131 LEd2d 374   115 SCt 1477
Sup Ct Yearbook (1994-95):99

3970. Freightliner Corp. v. Myrick   April 18, 1995
514 US 280   131 LEd2d 385   115 SCt 1483
Sup Ct Yearbook (1994-95):97

Coben, Larry E. Where does Myrick lead us? No preemption of defective restraint system claims. *Trial* 31(9):36-39 (September 1995).

3971. Heintz v. Jenkins   April 18, 1995
514 US 291   131 LEd2d 395   115 SCt 1489
Sup Ct Yearbook (1994-95):75

3972. Celotex Corp. v. Edwards   April 19, 1995
514 US 300   131 LEd2d 403   115 SCt 1494
Sup Ct Yearbook (1994-95):68

3973. McIntyre v. Ohio Elections Commission   April 19, 1995
514 US 334   131 LEd2d 426   115 SCt 1511
Sup Ct Yearbook (1993-94):302; (1994-95):24, 57-60, 104-105, 119-127R

3974. Stone v. Immigration and Naturalization Service (INS)   April 19, 1995
514 US 386   131 LEd2d 465   115 SCt 1537
Sup Ct Yearbook (1994-95):106

3975. Kyles v. Whitley, Warden   April 19, 1995
514 US 419   131 LEd2d 490   115 SCt 1555
Sup Ct Yearbook (1993-94):301; (1994-95):85-86

3976. Rubin, Secretary of the Treasury v. Coors Brewing Co.   April 19, 1995
514 US 476   131 LEd2d 532   115 SCt 1585
Sup Ct Yearbook (1993-94):304; (1994-95):24, 103-104

Bovard, James. Beer bust: censorship of commercial speech blocks the pursuit of happiness. [Editorial] *Barron's* 74(47):66 (November 21, 1994).

Colford, Steven W. Two ad cases will gauge new justice. *Advertising Age* 65(43):40 (October 10, 1994).

McTague, Jim. Big decisions: some important business cases are on the Supreme Court docket. *Barron's* 74(40):23 (October 3, 1994).

Miller, William H. Order in the Court. *Industry Week* 243(1):56 (October 3, 1994).

Seligman, Daniel, and Alicia Hills Moore. The winding road to the First Amendment. *Fortune* 132(1):211-212 (July 10, 1995).

3977. California Department of Corrections v. Morales   April 25, 1995
514 US 499   131 LEd2d 588   115 SCt 1597
Sup Ct Yearbook (1994-95):89

3978. United States v. Williams   April 25, 1995
514 US 527   131 LEd2d 608   115 SCt 1611

Sup Ct Yearbook (1994-95):72

Cuonzo, George P. High Court extends standing to sue to third parties. *Taxes* 73(11):618-621 (November 1995).

Kafka, Gerald A., and Rita A. Cavanagh. Supreme Court expands refund jurisdiction to include some third-party payors. *Journal of Taxation* 83(3):139-144 (September 1995).

Supreme Court uphold third party's standing to bring claim for tax refund. *Taxes* 73(5):226 (May 1995).

Wagenbrenner, Anne. Supreme Court nixes IRS attempt to limit refund suits to 'taxpayers.' *Journal of Accountancy* 180(1):36-37 (July 1995).

3979. United States v. Lopez   April 26, 1995
    514 US 549   131 LEd2d 262   115 SCt 1624
        Almanac (1995):6-40-6-41, D-15-16R
        Sup Ct Review (1995):125-215
        Sup Ct Yearbook (1993-94):300-301; (1994-95):24, 43-46, 79-80, 128-142R

American survey: the passing of William Brennan. *Economist* 336(7922):28 (July 8-14, 1995).

Caplan, Lincoln. Uneasy days in Court. *Newsweek* 124(15):62-64 (October 10, 1994).

Chemerinsky, Erwin. Looking ahead to the new term. *Trial* 30(12):81-83 (December 1994).

———. Supreme Court review: changing course: Lopez limits congressional powers. *Trial* 31(6):86-89 (June 1995).

———. Supreme Court review: race and the Supreme Court. *Trial* 31(10):86-88 (October 1995).

Clinton seeks to save school gun ban. *American School Board Journal* 182(6):15 (June 1995).

Dripps, Donald A. Supreme Court review: don't make a federal case out of it. *Trial* 31(1):90-92 (January 1995).

Fedarko, Kevin, Nina Burleigh, J. F. O. McAllister, and Andrea Sachs. A gun ban is shot down: a historic Supreme Court decision opens the door to redefining the power of the federal government. *Time* 145(19):85 (May 8, 1995).

Gest, Ted. After 58 years, the Court says no. *U.S. News and World Report* 118(18):15 (May 8, 1995).

Graglia, Lino A. Case studies. *National Review* 47(12):32-33 (June 26, 1995).

Kaplan, David A. This Court's not on TV. *Newsweek* 126(15):64 (October 9, 1995).

Lacayo, Richard, and Andrea Sachs. The soul of a new majority: in most of the Supreme Court's important rulings this year, combination was five right, four left. *Time* 146(2):46-48 (July 10, 1995).

Press, Aric, and Bruce Shenitz. The limits of commerce. *Newsweek* 125(19):72 (May 8, 1995).

Rosen, Jeff. Fed up. *New Republic* 212(21):13-14 (May 22, 1995).

Schwartz, Herman. Judgment days. [Editorial] *Nation* 261(13):452-454 (October 23, 1995).

Sowell, Thomas. Is the Constitution superfluous? [Editorial] *Forbes* 155(12):61 (June 5, 1995).

Supreme Court: attack and retreat. *Economist* 335(7913):29 (May 6-12, 1995).

Will, George F. Rethinking 1937. [Editorial] *Newsweek* 125(20):70 (May 15, 1995).

3980. New York State Conference of Blue Cross & Blue Shield Plans v. Travelers Insurance Co.   April 26, 1995
        Coupled with George E. Pataki v. Travelers Insurance Co.
        Coupled with Hospital Association of New York State v. Travelers Insurance Co.
    514 US 645   131 LEd2d 695   115 SCt 1671
        Sup Ct Yearbook (1994-95):98

Geisel, Jerry. Drop in health care costs tops benefit news of '95. *Business Insurance* 29(53):26 (December 25, 1995).

———. Health care law and disorder: courts divided on states' funding statutes. *Business Insurance* 28(48):1, 21 (November 28, 1994).

———. State surcharges meet resistance. *Business Insurance* 29(4):1, 20 (January 23, 1995).

Hofmann, Mark A. States win key ERISA victory. *Business Insurance* 29(18):1, 50 (May 1, 1995).

———. Narrowing ERISA pre-emption sparks fears. *Business Insurance* 29(53):28 (December 25, 1995).

Lemov, Penelope. High Court lowers a barrier to state health care reform. *Governing* 8(10):59 (July 1995).

McMenamin, Brigid. One-size-fits-all medicine. *Forbes* 155(9):60-61 (April 24, 1995).

Schachner, Michael, and Christine Woolsey. Ruling narrows ERISA pre-emption shield. *Business Insurance* 29(20):1, 20 (May 15, 1995).

Voelker, Rebecca. ERISA ruling creates options for state reforms. *JAMA: The Journal of the American Medical Association* 274(14):1106-1107 (October 11, 1995).

Woolsey, Christine. Plan protests provider law: suit claims 'any willing provider' law pre-empted by ERISA. *Business Insurance* 29(29):1, 103 (July 17, 1995).

3981. United States v. Robertson   May 1, 1995
     514 US 669   131 LEd2d 714   115 SCt 1732
     Sup Ct Yearbook (1994-95):43-46, 80-81
Supreme Court: attack and retreat. *Economist* 335(7913):29 (May 6-12, 1995).

3982. Kansas v. Colorado   May 15, 1995
     514 US 673   131 LEd2d 759   115 SCt 1733
     Sup Ct Yearbook (1994-95):117-118

3983. Hubbard v. United States   May 15, 1995
     514 US 695   131 LEd2d 779   115 SCt 1754
     Almanac (1995):6-41
     Sup Ct Yearbook (1994-95):78-79

3984. City of Edmonds, Washington v. Oxford House   May 15, 1995
     514 US 725   131 LEd2d 801   115 SCt 1776
     Sup Ct Yearbook (1994-95):108-109
Group homes triumph in Supreme Court. *Planning* 61(7):27-28 (July 1995).
Lauber, Daniel. Group think. *Planning* 61(10):11-13 (October 1995).

3985. Reynoldsville Casket Co. v. Hyde   May 15, 1995
     514 US 749   131 LEd2d 820   115 SCt 1745
     Sup Ct Yearbook (1994-95):76-77

3986. Purkett, Superintendent, Farmington Corrections Center v. Elem   May 15, 1995
     514 US 765   131 LEd2d 834   115 SCt 1769
     Sup Ct Yearbook (1994-95):88
Dripps, Donald A. Supreme Court review: 'I didn't like the way he looked.' *Trial* 31(7):94-96 (July 1995).

3987. U.S. Term Limits, Inc. v. Thornton   May 22, 1995
     Coupled with Bryant, Attorney General of Arkansas v. Bobbie E. Hill
     514 US 779   131 LEd2d 881   115 SCt 1842
     Almanac (1994):314-315; (1995):6-38-6-39, D-17-D-18R
     Editorials (1995):588-597
     Sup Ct Yearbook (1993-94):292-297; (1994-95):24, 40-43, 94-95, 142-162R
Bryant, Winston. Is it constitutional for states to limit congressional terms by restricting ballot access? *Congressional Digest* 74(4):104, 106 (April 1995).
Caplan, Lincoln. Uneasy days in Court. *Newsweek* 124(15):62-64 (October 10, 1994).
Chemerinsky, Erwin. Looking ahead to the new term. *Trial* 30(12):81-83 (December 1994).
Chua-Eoan, Howard G., Laurence I. Barrett, Wendy Cole, Andrea Sachs, and Richard Woodbury. A coming to terms: voters love to restrict incumbents, but the Supreme Court may squash the idea. *Time* 144(23):41-42 (December 5, 1994).
Gest, Ted. Term limits: detour ahead. *U.S. News and World Report* 118(22):11 (June 5, 1995).
Graglia, Lino A. Case studies. *National Review* 47(12):32-33 (June 26, 1995).
Robben, Elizabeth J. Is it constitutional for states to limit congressional terms by restricting ballot access? *Congressional Digest* 74(4):105, 107 (April 1995).
Rosen, Jeffrey. Coming to terms. *New Republic* 211(24);18, 20 (December 12, 1994).
———. Terminated. *New Republic* 212(24);12, 14 (June 12, 1995).
Silverstein, Kenneth. Term limits proposals gathering steam. *American City and County* 109(10):16 (September 1994).

Sowell, Thomas. Hypocrisy. [Editorial] *Forbes* 156(6):80 (September 11, 1995).

Term limits: back from the dead? *Economist* 335(7916):26-27 (May 27-June 2, 1995).

3988. Wilson v. Arkansas   May 22, 1995
      514 US 927   131 LEd2d 976   115 SCt 1914
        Sup Ct Yearbook (1994-95):91

Dripps, Donald A. Supreme Court review: will the real Fourth Amendment please stand up? *Trial* 31(11):80-82 (November 1995).

3989. First Options of Chicago, Inc. v. Kaplan   May 22, 1995
      514 US 938   131 LEd2d 985   115 SCt 1920
        Sup Ct Yearbook (1994-95):74

3990. Nebraska v. Wyoming   May 30, 1995
      515 US 1   132 LEd2d 1   115 SCt 1933
        Sup Ct Yearbook (1994-95):118

3991. North Star Steel Co. v. Thomas   May 30, 1995
           Coupled with Crown Cork & Seal Co., Inc. v. United Steelworkers
      515 US 29   132 LEd2d 27   115 SCt 1927
        Sup Ct Yearbook (1994-95):111-112

DiCesare, Constance B. The law at work: deadline for WARN suits. *Monthly Labor Review* 118(10):48 (October 1995).

3992. Garlotte v. Fordice, Governor of Mississippi   May 30, 1995
      515 US 39   132 LEd2d 36   115 SCt 1948
        Sup Ct Yearbook (1994-95):84-85

3993. Reno, Attorney General v. Koray   June 5, 1995
      515 US 50   132 LEd2d 46   115 SCt 2021
        Sup Ct Yearbook (1994-95):91-92

3994. Missouri v. Jenkins   June 12, 1995
      515 US 70   132 Led2d 63   115 Sct 2038
        Editorials (1995):716-719
        Sup Ct Yearbook (1993-94):293; (1994-95):36-40, 110-111, 183-202R

Caplan, Lincoln. Uneasy days in Court. *Newsweek* 124(15):62-64 (October 10, 1994).

Chemerinsky, Erwin. Supreme Court review: race and the Supreme Court. *Trial* 31(10):86-88 (October 1995).

Demagnetised. *Economist* 335(7919):29 (June 17-23, 1995).

High Court rules on integration and hiring. *American School Board Journal* 182(8):13-14 (August 1995).

Jaschik, Scott. Justice Thomas stresses the role of predominantly black colleges. *Chronicle of Higher Education* 41(41):A22 (June 23, 1995).

Schwartz, Herman. Judgment days. [Editorial] *Nation* 261(13):452-454 (October 23, 1995).

Sendor, Benjamin. Kansas City and the limits of desegregation. *American School Board Journal* 182(9):18-20 (September 1995).

Silverstein, Ken. Equal opportunity on trial. *Scholastic Update* (Teachers' Edition) 127(6):22-24 (November 18, 1994).

White, Jack E. Uncle Tom justice. [Editorial] *Time* 145(26):36 (June 26, 1995).

Will, George F. From Topeka to Kansas City. [Editorial] *Newsweek* 125(26):66 (June 26, 1995).

3995. Ryder v. United States   June 12, 1995
      515 US 177   132 LEd2d 136   115 SCt 2031
        Sup Ct Yearbook (1994-95):100

3996. City of Milwaukee v. Cement Division, National Gypsum Co. June 12, 1995
    515 US 189   132 LEd2d 148   115 SCt 2091
      Sup Ct Yearbook (1994-95):69

3997. Adarand Constructors, Inc. v. Pena, Secretary of Transportation June 12, 1995
    515 US 200   132 LEd2d 158   115 SCt 2097
      Almanac (1995):6-24-25, 6-38-39,D-20R
      Editorials (1995):664-673
      Sup Ct Review (1995):1-43
      Sup Ct Yearbook (1993-94):293; (1994-95):2, 5, 27-32, 106-107, 162-182R

Adarand influences cases. *ENR* 235(7):11 (August 14, 1995).

Affirmative action: death by judges? *Economist* 335(7919):28 (June 17-23, 1995).

Affirmative action under fire. *Scholastic Update* 128(2):3 (September 15, 1995).

Amar, Akhil Reed, and Neal Katyal. School colors. *New Republic* 213(3-4):24-25 (July 17-24, 1995).

Asst. Atty. Gen. Deval Patrick says administration ready for affirmative action battle. *Jet* 88(8):4 (July 3, 1995).

Barlow, Wayne E., D. Diane Hatch, and Betty Southard Murphy. Recent legal decisions affect you. *Personnel Journal* 74(8):92 (August 1995).

Caplan, Lincoln. Uneasy days in Court. *Newsweek* 124(15):62-64 (October 10, 1994).

The challenge to affirmative action. *HR Focus* 72(8):19 (August 1995).

Chemerinsky, Erwin. Looking ahead to the new term. *Trial* 30(12):81-83 (December 1994).

———. Supreme Court review: race and the Supreme Court. *Trial* 31(10):86-88 (October 1995).

Cimini, Michael H., and Charles J. Muhl. Supreme Court rules on affirmative action. *Monthly Labor Review* 118(9):48 (September 1995).

Court decreases opportunity for minority firms. *Planning* 61(8):20-22 (August 1995).

Courting trouble. *National Review* 47(13):16-18 (July 10, 1995).

Crock, Stan, and Michele Galen. 'A thunderous impact' on equal opportunity. *Business Week* (3430):37 (June 26, 1995).

The end of affirmative action. *New Republic* 213(1):7 (July 3, 1995).

Excerpts from opinions on affirmative action. *Chronicle of Higher Education* 41(41):A22R (June 23, 1995).

Gest, Ted. Thomas's bias cases: will the justice influence his colleagues in upcoming disputes over race? *U.S. News and World Report* 117(18):63-64 (November 7, 1994).

Gest, Ted, Steven V. Roberts, Kenneth T. Walsh, Jim Impoco, and Karen Mitchell. Back to the politicians: a Supreme Court ruling will fuel the fight over affirmative action. *U.S. News and World Report* 118(25):38-39 (June 26, 1995).

Jaschik, Scott. Blow to affirmative action. *Chronicle of Higher Education* 41(41):A21-A23 (June 23, 1995).

Klein, Joe. The end of affirmative action. *Newsweek* 125(7):36-37 (February 13, 1995).

Korman, Richard, and Tom Ichniowski. Feds face narrower options. *ENR* 234(24):8-9 (June 19, 1995).

———. Is Randy Pech the next Croson? *ENR* 234(3):10 (January 23, 1995).

———. U.S. agencies stick to pre-Adarand plans. *ENR* 234(25):10-11 (June 26, 1995).

Lacayo, Richard, and Andrea Sachs. The soul of a new majority: in most of the Supreme Court's important rulings this year, combination was five right, four left. *Time* 146(2):46-48 (July 10, 1995).

Lowery, Mark. Down but not out. *Black Enterprise* 26(2):15 (September 1995).

McCoy, Frank. Will the High Court end federal set-asides? *Black Enterprise* 25(5):24 (December 1994).

Minority set-asides: change ahead. *Nation's Business* 83(10):24 (October 1995).

Puddington, Arch. Will affirmative action survive? *Commentary* 100(4):22-26 (October 1995).

Rosen, Jeff. Dancing days. *New Republic* 212(7):18-19 (February 13, 1995).

Schwartz, Herman. Judgment days. [Editorial] *Nation* 261(13):452-454 (October 23, 1995).

Seligman, Daniel, and Patty de Llosa. The scrutinizers. *Fortune* 132(2):170 (July 24, 1995).

Silverstein, Ken. Equal opportunity on trial. *Scholastic Update* (Teachers' Edition) 127(6):22-24 (November 18, 1994).

What's ahead for affirmative action? *Jet* 88(9):6 (July 10, 1995).

White, Jack E. Uncle Tom justice. [Editorial] *Time* 145(26):36 (June 26, 1995).

3998. Wilton v. Seven Falls Co. June 12, 1995
    515 US 277   132 LEd2d 214   115 SCt 2137

Sup Ct Yearbook (1994-95):75-76

3999. Metropolitan Stevedore Co. v. Rambo   June 12, 1995
         515 US 291   132 LEd2d 226   115 SCt 2144
         Sup Ct Yearbook (1994-95):114
     DiCesare, Constance B. The law at work: erratum. *Monthly Labor Review* 118(7):79 (July 1995).
     ———. The law at work: workers' compensation. *Monthly Labor Review* 118(5):63 (May 1995).

4000. Johnson v. Jones   June 12, 1995
         515 US 304   132 LEd2d 238   115 SCt 2151
         Sup Ct Yearbook (1994-95):107-108

4001. Kimberlin v. Quinlan   June 12, 1995
         515 US 321   132 LEd2d 252   115 SCt 2552
         Sup Ct Yearbook (1994-95):108

4002. Commissioner of Internal Revenue v. Schleier   June 14, 1995
         515 US 323   132 LEd2d 294   115 SCt 2159
         Sup Ct Yearbook (1994-95):72
     Barlow, Wayne E., D. Diane Hatch, and Betty Southard Murphy. Recent legal decisions affect you. *Personnel Journal* 74(8):92 (August 1995).
     DiCesare, Constance B. The law at work: backpay, damages can be taxed. *Monthly Labor Review* 118(10):48 (October 1995).
     Elwood, Robert M. Supreme Court's ruling on taxation of discrimination damages provides little resolution. *Journal of Taxation* 83(3):148-152 (September 1995).
     High Court holds ADEA damages fully taxable. *Practical Accountant* 28(8):14 (August 1995).
     Himelstein, Linda, Ira Sager, and Keith H. Hammonds. The $20,000 sweepstakes for folks who got the ax. *Business Week* (3418):55 (April 3, 1995).
     IRS goes after ADEA awards in light of Schleier decision. *Taxes* 73(11):629 (November 1995).
     Luscombe, Mark A. Taxation of discrimination awards. *Taxes* 73(11):587-594 (November 1995).
     No exclusion for ADEA damages—not received on account of personal injury, court says. *Journal of Taxation* 83(2):66 (August 1995).
     No exclusion for ADEA settlement proceeds. *Taxes* 73(7):338 (July 1995).

4003. Chandris, Inc. v. Latsis   June 14, 1995
         515 US 347   132 LEd2d 314   115 SCt 2172
         Sup Ct Yearbook (1994-95):113

4004. Witte v. United States   June 14, 1995
         515 US 389   132 LEd2d 351   115 SCt 2199
         Sup Ct Yearbook (1994-95):82-83

4005. Gutierrez de Martinez v. Lamagno   June 14, 1995
         515 US 417   132 LEd2d 375   115 SCt 2227
         Sup Ct Yearbook (1994-95):95-96

4006. Oklahoma Tax Commission v. Chickasaw Nation   June 14, 1995
         515 US 450   132 LEd2d 400   115 SCt 2214
         Sup Ct Yearbook (1994-95):116

4007. Sandin, Unit Team Manager, Halawa Correctional Facility v. Conner   June 19, 1995
         515 US 472   132 LEd2d 418   115 SCt 2293
         Sup Ct Yearbook (1994-95):89-90
     Chemerinsky, Erwin. Supreme Court review: race and the Supreme Court. *Trial* 31(10):86-88 (October 1995).

4008. United States v. Gaudin
    515 US 506   132 LEd2d 444
    Sup Ct Yearbook (1994-95):87-88

        June 19, 1995
        115 SCt 2310

4009. Vimar Seguros y Reaseguros, S.A. v. M/V Sky Reefer
    515 US 528   132 LEd2d 462
    Sup Ct Yearbook (1994-95):69-70

        June 19, 1995
        115 SCt 2322

4010. Hurley v. Irish-American Gay, Lesbian and Bisexual Group of Boston
    515 US 557   132 LEd2d 487
    Sup Ct Yearbook (1994-95):104
    Free speech: the scornin' o' the pink. *Economist* 335(7920):26 (June 24-30, 1995).
    Wackerman, Daniel T. Mind's eye. [Editorial] *America* 173(2):5 (July 15-22, 1995).

        June 19, 1995
        115 SCt 2338

4011. National Private Truck Council, Inc. v. Oklahoma Tax Commission
    515 US 582   132 LEd2d 509
    Sup Ct Yearbook (1994-95):115

        June 19, 1995
        115 SCt 2351

4012. United States v. Aguilar
    515 US 593   132 LEd2d 520
    Sup Ct Yearbook (1994-95):79

        June 21, 1995
        115 SCt 2357

4013. Florida Bar Association v. Went For It, Inc.
    515 US 618   132 LEd2d 541
    Sup Ct Yearbook (1994-95):102-103
    Colford, Steven W. Two ad cases will gauge new justice. *Advertising Age* 65(43):40 (October 10, 1994).

        June 21, 1995
        115 SCt 2371

4014. Vernonia School District, 47J v. Wayne Acton
    515 US 646   132 LEd2d 564
    Editorials (1995):720-727
    Sup Ct Yearbook (1994-95):47-50, 109-110, 202-214R
    Adams, Kathleen, and Nick Catoggio. The Supreme Court: a principal's best friend *Time* 146(2):14 (July 10, 1995).
    Chemerinsky, Erwin. Supreme Court review: race and the Supreme Court. *Trial* 31(10):86-88 (October 1995).
    Courtside: drug test passes court test. *Phi Delta Kappan* 77(2):187-188 (October 1995).
    Dripps, Donald A. Supreme Court review: will the real Fourth Amendment please stand up? *Trial* 31(11):80-82 (November 1995).
    High Court upholds random drug tests for athletes. *Jet* 88(10):46 (July 17, 1995).
    Mahon, J. Patrick. Vernonia v. Acton: should schools conduct random drug tests of student athletes? *NASSP Bulletin* 79(573):52-55 (October 1995).
    McCallum, Jack, and Christian Stone. Courting controversy. *Sport Illustrated* 83(2):11 (July 10, 1995).
    Sendor, Benjamin. Will the real conservative please stand up? *American School Board Journal* 182(10):22, 44 (October 1995).

        June 26, 1995
        115 SCt 2386

4015. Babbitt, Secretary of the Interior
    v. Sweet Home Chapter of Communities for a Great Oregon
    515 US 687   132 LEd2d 597
    Almanac (1995):5-14
    Editorials (1995):804-807
    Sup Ct Yearbook (1994-95):60-63, 95, 260-271R
    Endangered species issues still live on. *ENR* 235(2):16 (July 10, 1995).
    Endangered species: nature, nurture and property rights. *Economist* 336(7922):24-25 (July 8-14, 1995).
    Lacayo, Richard, and Andrea Sachs. The soul of a new majority: in most of the Supreme Court's important rulings this year, combination was five right, four left. *Time* 146(2):46-48 (July 10, 1995).
    Protecting animal and human habitats. *Science News* 148(3):43 (July 15, 1995).

        June 29, 1995

        115 SCt 2407

Salvesen, David. Endangered species get Supreme Court reprieve. *Planning* 61(8):20 (August 1995).

Stone, Richard. Court upholds need to protect habitat. *Science* 269(5220):23 (July 7, 1995).

4016. United States v. Hayes   June 29, 1995
        Coupled with Louisiana v. Hayes
    515 US 737   132 LEd2d 635   115 SCt 2431
      Almanac (1995):6, 39-40
      Sup Ct Review (1995):45-70
      Sup Ct Yearbook (1994-95):32-36, 93-94

Chemerinsky, Erwin. Supreme Court review: race and the Supreme Court. *Trial* 31(10):86-88 (October 1995).

High Court rules against redistricting in Georgia. *Jet* 88(10):4 (July 17, 1995).

Silverstein, Ken. Equal opportunity on trial. *Scholastic Update* (Teachers' Edition) 127(6):22-24 (November 18, 1994).

4017. Capital Square Review and Advisory Board v. Pinette   June 29, 1995
    515 US 753   132 LEd2d 650   115 SCt 2440
      Sup Ct Review (1995):323-391
      Sup Ct Yearbook (1994-95):53-57, 101-102, 248-260R

Chemerinsky, Erwin. Supreme Court review: free speech or religious freedom: revisiting the establishment clause. *Trial* 31(12):16-19 (December 1995).

———. Supreme Court review: race and the Supreme Court. *Trial* 31(10):86-88 (October 1995).

Doerr, Edd. Church and state: wobbly wall. *Humanist* 55(5):36-37 (September/October 1995).

The sign on the cross. [Editorial] *America* 173(2):3 (July 15-22, 1995).

4018. Rosenberger v. Rector and Visitors of the University of Virginia   June 29, 1995
    515 US 819   132 LEd2d 700   115 SCt 2510
      Guide (West): (1995):159-161
      Sup Ct Review (1995):323-391
      Sup Ct Yearbook (1994-95):50-53, 102, 215-232R

American survey: the passing of William Brennan. *Economist* 336(7922):28 (July 8-14, 1995).

Chemerinsky, Erwin. Supreme Court review: free speech or religious freedom: revisiting the establishment clause. *Trial* 31(12):16-19 (December 1995).

———. Supreme Court review: race and the Supreme Court. *Trial* 31(10):86-88 (October 1995).

Doerr, Edd. Church and state: wobbly wall. *Humanist* 55(5):36-37 (September/October 1995).

Drinan, Robert F. University funding for religious activities. *America* 172(1):16-18 (January 14-21, 1995).

Ferranti, Jennifer. High Court mandates equal treatment for religion. *Christianity Today* 39(9):62 (August 14, 1995).

———. Time to strip the lemon Pledge? *Christianity Today* 39(1):47, 49 (January 9, 1995).

Gaffney, Edward McGlynn, Jr. At Jefferson's university. *Commonweal* 122(8):6-7 (April 21, 1995).

Gest, Ted. A long-anticipated right turn. *U.S. News and World Report* 119(2):9 (July 10, 1995).

Hernandez, Debra Gersh. Supreme Court orders funding of religion-oriented student publication. *Editor and Publisher* 128(27):18-19, 39 (July 15, 1995).

Jaschik, Scott. Court decision forces changes at U. of Virginia. *Chronicle of Higher Education* 42(2):A44-A45 (September 8, 1995).

———. High Court appears divided on university aid to religious groups. *Chronicle of Higher Education* 41(26):A27 (March 10, 1995).

———. High Court bars U. of Virginia from denying funds to religious newspaper. *Chronicle of Higher Education* 41(43):A24-A25 (July 7, 1995).

———. Religious-activities ruling may force colleges to alter rules. *Chronicle of Higher Education* 41(44):A22-A23 (July 14, 1995).

Lacayo, Richard, and Andrea Sachs. The soul of a new majority: in most of the Supreme Court's important rulings this year, combination was five right, four left. *Time* 146(2):46-48 (July 10, 1995).

McFarland, Steve. A tenuous victory for religious freedom. [Editorial] *Christianity Today* 39(9):18-19 (August 14, 1995).

O'Connor, Sandra Day. Excerpts from Justice O'Connor's concurring opinion in decision on religious activities. *Chronicle of Higher Education* 41(44):A23 (July 14, 1995).

Public funds for religious speech. [Editorial] *America* 173(5):3 (August 26-September 2, 1995).

Religious speech, public money. *Christian Century* 112(9):286-287 (March 15, 1995).

Schwartz, Herman. Judgment days. [Editorial] *Nation* 261(13):452-454 (October 23, 1995).

Student fees refunded at Va. *Editor and Publisher* 128(51):15 (December 23, 1995).

The sign on the cross. [Editorial] *America* 173(2):3 (July 15-22, 1995).

Souter, David H. Justice Souter's dissent on funds for religious activities. *Chronicle of Higher Education* 41(43):A29-A33R (July 7, 1995).

Text of Court's ruling on funds for religious activities. *Chronicle of Higher Education* 41(43):A26-A29R (July 7, 1995).

Two principles collide on a Virginia campus. [Editorial] *America* 172(12):3 (April 8, 1995).

White, Lawrence. The profound consequences of the 'Rosenberger' ruling. [Editorial] *Chronicle of Higher Education* 41(44):B1-B3 (July 14, 1995).

4019. Miller v. Johnson   June 29, 1995
      Coupled with Abrams v. Johnson
      Coupled with United States v. Johnson
    515 US 900   132 LEd2d 762   115 SCt 2475
     Almanac (1995):6-39-6-40, D-23R
     Editorials (1995):794-803
     Sup Ct Review (1995):45-70
     Sup Ct Yearbook (1994-95):24, 32-36, 93, 232-248R

American survey: the passing of William Brennan. *Economist* 336(7922):28 (July 8-14, 1995).

Can black Congressional members survive Supreme Court blow? *Jet* 88(11):8 (July 24, 1995).

Chemerinsky, Erwin. Supreme Court review: race and the Supreme Court. *Trial* 31(10):86-88 (October 1995).

Davis, Olethia. Tenuous interpretation: Sections 2 and 5 of the Voting Rights Act. *National Civic Review* 84(4):310-322 (Fall/Winter 1995).

Engstrom, Richard L. Shaw, Miller and the districting thicket. *National Civic Review* 84(4):323-336 (Fall/Winter 1995).

Fineman, Howard. Shifting racial lines. *Newsweek* 126(2):38-39 (July 10, 1995).

Gest, Ted. A long-anticipated right turn. *U.S. News and World Report* 119(2):9 (July 10, 1995).

———. Thrilling tales from yesteryear. *U.S. News and World Report* 119(13):74 (October 2, 1995).

Higginbotham, A. Leon, Jr. 50 years of civil rights. *Ebony* 51(1):148-154 (November 1995).

Lacayo, Richard, and Andrea Sachs. The soul of a new majority: in most of the Supreme Court's important rulings this year, combination was five right, four left. *Time* 146(2):46-48 (July 10, 1995).

McCoy, Frank. Under Supreme attack. *Black Enterprise* 26(3):24 (October 1995).

Schwartz, Herman. Judgment days. [Editorial] *Nation* 261(13):452-454 (October 23, 1995).

Will, George F. The Voting Rights Act at 30. [Editorial] *Newsweek* 126(2):64 (July 10, 1995).

Zimmerman, Joseph F. Election systems and representative democracy: reflections on the Voting Rights Act of 1965. *National Civic Review* 84(4):287-309 (Fall/Winter 1995).

4020. Citzens Bank of Maryland v. Strumpf   October 31, 1995
    516 US 16   133 LEd2d 258   116 SCt 286
     Sup Ct Yearbook (1994-95):280-281

Cocheo, Steve, and Michael Crotty. Come first Monday in October, banking has a date in court. *ABA Banking Journal* 87(10):7 (October 1995).

4021. National Labor Relations Board (NLRB) v. Town & Country Electric, Inc.   November 11, 1995
    516 US 85   133 LEd2d 371   116 SCt 450
     Sup Ct Yearbook (1994-95):287

Krizan, William G. Large mountain of salt is piling up at NLRB. *ENR* 235(21):8 (November 20, 1995).

4022. Thompson v. Keohane   November 29, 1995
    516 US 99   133 LEd2d 383   116 SCt 457

Sup Ct Yearbook (1994-95):282-283

4023. Bailey v. United States   December 6, 1996
      Coupled with Robinson v. United States
      516 US 137   133 LEd2d 472   116 SCt 501
        Sup Ct Yearbook (1994-95):282

4024. Zicherman v. Korean Air Lines   January 16, 1996
      516 US 217   133 LEd2d 596   116 SCt 629
        Sup Ct Yearbook (1994-95):289-290
      Hofmann, Mark A. Fiduciary liability in review: High Court to rule on ERISA plan participants' ability to sue.
        Business Insurance 29(41):71 (October 9, 1995).

4025. Bank One, Chicago, N.A. v. Midwest Bank and Trust Co.   January 17, 1996
      516 US 264   133 LEd2d 635   116 SCt 637
      Cocheo, Steve, and Michael Crotty. Come first Monday in October, banking has a date in court. *ABA Banking
        Journal* 87(10):7 (October 1995).

4026. Libretti v. United States   November 7, 1995
      516 US 271   133 LEd2d 271   116 SCt 356
        Sup Ct Yearbook (1994-95):281-282

4027. D. Grant Peacock v. Jack L. Thomas   February 21, 1996
      516 US 349   133 LEd2d 817   116 SCt 862
      Gest, Ted. Thrilling tales from yesteryear. *U.S. News and World Report* 119(13):74 (October 2, 1995).
      Hofmann, Mark A. Fiduciary liability in review: High Court to rule on ERISA plan participants' ability to sue.
        Business Insurance 29(41):71 (October 9, 1995).

4028. Matsushita Electric Industrial Co. v. Epstein   February 27, 1996
      516 US 367   134 LEd2d 6   116 SCt 873
        Sup Ct Yearbook (1994-95):280

4029. Hercules, Inc. v. United States   March 4, 1996
      516 US 417   134 LEd2d 47   116 SCt 981
        Sup Ct Yearbook (1994-95):285-286
      Hofmann, Mark A. Fiduciary liability in review: High Court to rule on ERISA plan participants' ability to sue.
        Business Insurance 29(41):71 (October 9, 1995).

4030. Bennis v. State of Michigan   March 4, 1996
      516 US 442   134 LEd2d 068   116 SCt 994
        Sup Ct Yearbook (1994-95):281
      Cocheo, Steve, and Michael Crotty. Come first Monday in October, banking has a date in court. *ABA Banking
        Journal* 87(10):7 (October 1995).

4031. Varity Corp. v. Howe   March 19, 1996
      516 US 489   134 LEd2d 130   116 SCt 1065
        Sup Ct Yearbook (1994-95):287-288
      Hofmann, Mark A. Defining moment for fiduciary duty: employers await ERISA ruling. *Business Insurance*
        29(45):1, 60 (November 6, 1995).
        ———. Don't twist case into bad law. [Editorial] *Business Insurance* 29(45):8 (November 6, 1995).
        ———. Fiduciary liability in review: High Court to rule on ERISA plan participants' ability to sue. *Business
        Insurance* 29(41):71 (October 9, 1995).

4032. Wisconsin v. City of New York   March 20, 1996
      Coupled with Oklahoma v. City of New York

Coupled with Department of Commerce v. City of New York
517 US 1   134 LEd2d 167   116 SCt 1091
  Sup Ct Yearbook (1994-95):273

4033. Barnett Bank of Marion County, North America v. Nelson   March 26, 1996
      517 US 25   134 LEd2d 237   116 SCt 1103
        Almanac (1995):2-78, 2-84
      Friedman, Amy S. Agents file response to Barnett's certiorari bid. *National Underwriter* (Life and
        Health/Financial Services Edition) 99(31):4 (July 31, 1995).
      Hofmann, Mark A. Fiduciary liability in review: High Court to rule on ERISA plan participants' ability to sue.
        Business Insurance 29(41):71 (October 9, 1995).

4034. Seminole Tribe v. Florida   March 27, 1996
      517 US 44   134 LEd2d 252   116 SCt 1114
        Sup Ct Yearbook (1994-95):288

4035. Morse v. Republican Party of Virginia   March 27, 1996
      517 US 186   134 LEd2d 347   116 SCt 1186
        Sup Ct Yearbook (1994-95):285

4036. O'Connor v. Consolidated Coin Caterers Corp.   April 1, 1996
      517 US 308   134 LEd2d 433   116 SCt 1307
      Hofmann, Mark A. High Court to consider age bias. *Business Insurance* 29(47):2, 32 (November 20, 1995).

4037. Lonchar v. Thomas   April 1, 1996
      517 US 314   134 LEd2d 440   116 SCt 1293
        Sup Ct Yearbook (1994-95):283

4038. United States v. Armstrong   May 13, 1996
      517 US 456   134 LEd2d 687   116 SCt 1480
        Editorials (1995):1368-1371

4039. 44 Liquormart, Inc. v. Rhode Island   May 13, 1996
      517 US 484 134   LEd2d 711   116 SCt 1495
        Sup Ct Yearbook (1994-95):287
      Court should curb ad bans. *Advertising Age* 66(47):9 (November 20, 1995).
      Winfield, Richard N., and Mark R. Anderson. Liquor ad case may expand speech rights. *Editor and Publisher*
        128(46):5 (November 18, 1995).

4040. BMW of North America v. Ira Gore Jr.   May 20, 1996
      517 US 559   134 LEd2d 809   116 SCt 1589
        Sup Ct Yearbook (1994-95):288-289
      Another chance to get it right. [Editorial] *Business Insurance* 29(43):8 (October 23, 1995).
      Gest, Ted. Thrilling tales from yesteryear. *U.S. News and World Report* 119(13):74 (October 2, 1995).
      Hager, Mark M., and Ned Miltenberg. Punitive damages and the free market: a law and economics perspective.
        Trial 31(9):28-35 (September 1995).
      Hofmann, Mark A. Court gives mixed signals. *Business Insurance* 29(42):1, 4 (October 16, 1995).
      ————. Punitive damages appeal to be heard by High Court. *Business Insurance* 29(15):10 (January 30, 1995).
      ————. Punitive damages back before Court. *Business Insurance* 29(41):1, 70-71 (October 9, 1995).

4041. Romer v. Evans   May 20, 1996
      517 US 620   134 LEd2d 855   116 SCt 1620
        Sup Ct Yearbook (1994-95):272-280
      Dripps, Donald A. Supreme Court review: gay rights at the crossroads. *Trial* 31(5):80-81 (May 1995).

Hetter, Katia. Gay rights issues bust out all over. *U.S. News and World Report* 119(13):71-74 (October 2, 1995).

Leo, John. No more rights turns. [Editorial] *U.S. News and World Report* 119(16):34 (October 23, 1995).

Rosen, Jeff. Disoriented. *New Republic* 213(7):24-26 (October 23, 1995).

4042. United States v. International Business Machines Corp. (IBM)   June 10, 1996
517 US 843   135 LEd2d 124   116 SCt 1793
Hofmann, Mark A. Premium tax questioned: export clause ruling may have import for business. *Business Insurance* 29(51):3, 12 (December 18, 1995).

4043. Shaw v. Hunt   June 13, 1996
      Coupled with Pope v. Hunt
517 US 899   135 LEd2d 207   116 SCt 1894
   Almanac (1995):12-4
   Sup Ct Yearbook (1994-95):284

4044. Bush v. Vera   June 13, 1996
      Coupled with Lawson v. Vera
      Coupled with United States v. Vera
517 US 952   135 LEd2d 248   116 SCt 1941
   Almanac (1995):12-3-12-4
   Sup Ct Yearbook (1994-95):284-285
McCoy, Frank. Under Supreme attack. *Black Enterprise* 26(3):24 (October 1995).

4045. Brown v. Pro Football, Inc. dba Washington Redskins   June 20, 1996
518 US 231   135 LEd2d 521   116 SCt 2116
McCallum, Jack, and Kostya Kennedy. A Supreme test. *Sport Illustrated* 83(27):15-16 (December 25, 1995-January 1, 1996).

4046. Lewis v. Casey   June 24, 1996
518 US 343   135 LEd2d 606   116 SCt 2174
   Sup Ct Yearbook (1994-95):283

4047. United States v. Virginia   June 26, 1996
518 US 515   135 LEd2d 735   116 SCt 2264
Jaschik, Scott. U.S. seeks reversal to let VMI stay all male. *Chronicle of Higher Education* 41(39):A27 (June 9, 1995).

Leo, John. Return of the ERA. [Editorial] *U.S. News and World Report* 119(24):28 (December 18, 1995).

Rosen, Jeffrey. Boys and girls. *New Republic* 210(7):14, 16 (February 14, 1994).

Seligman, Daniel. Women on the rat line. *Fortune* 127(9):104 (May 3, 1993).

WORDS AND PHRASES INDEX

This is an index to the words and phrases argued in the United States Supreme Court. After each word is an entry number not a page number.

abstention doctrine, 1190, 1224, 1337, 1481
acquiring, 1681
act of state doctrine, 1181
activity, 1107
actual controversy, 1537
actual legitimate cost, 780
actual malice, 1296, 1319, 1431, 1732
agency records, 2068
agent, 1088
aid and comfort, 808
alarm limit, 1928
anti-busing law, 1447
arguing, 1069
attorney general, 1639
the average person, 1584

bad faith, 2102
bail out provision, 2089
barge, 785
Bernstein exception, 1505
bill of attainder, 1230
blackmail, 1408
block booking, 870
blue ribbon juries, 853
broker-dealer distinction, 1717
Bruton rule, 1488
business insurance, 1352, 1961
business league, 1970
business or personal expenses, 1250
business or property, 2008

cannon shot doctrine, 89
carnal knowledge, 1656
Carroll doctrine, 521
case and/or controversy, 811, 849, 1338
checker, 1858
chilling effect, 1428, 1510, 1522
civil action, 2053
clear and convincing, 1987
clear and present danger, 446, 448, 451, 456, 667,
    885, 895, 903, 914, 926
clear proof, 1251
close judicial scrutiny, 1978
Colgate doctrine, 450

collateral estoppel, 1401
commerce, 651, 737
common benefit, 1571
company town, 819
compulsory process, 1293
conduct unbecoming an officer and a gentleman,
    1652
contemporary community standards, 1841
contracting out, 1207
control test, 1815
convenience and needs defense, 1666
county unit system, 1146
criminal prosecution, 1743
criminal syndicalism, 554, 555, 657

days, 573
debt adjusting, 1149
delinquency, 1284
dependent, 1569
directly affects, 742
doctrine of selective exclusiveness, 146
doctrine of vested rights, 24
double-bunking, 1992
drug courier profile, 2099
dual school system, 1396
due process, 917
due process of law, 890
dwelling, 1042

economic or geographic market, 1261
economic power, 1817
employee committee, 1059
employees, 717, 790
employer, 1411
endangered species, 1923
enterprise concept, 1340
establishment clause, 1167
ex post facto law, 24
exhaustion of military remedies, 1743
extortion, 1553

facial overbreadth, 1598
failing company, 1356
fair and equitable, 715

fair return, 574
fair value, 780
fair value dicta, 329
fairness doctrine, 1374
family, 1631
Feres doctrine, 899
fighting words, 1456
final judgment, 1137
flat fee registration tax, 1898
foreign state, 1907
forum non conveniens, 844
free exercise clause, 1167, 1170
free-transfer plan, 1331
free will, 1585
freedom-of-choice plan, 1329, 1330
freeport doctrine, 154

gag order, 1258, 1791
general welfare, 507
gift, 805
girlie picture magazine, 1317
golden fleece award, 2024
good cause transfer, 1164
good faith, 2102
gross income, 707
guarantee clause, 143

habeas corpus, 1802
Hair (the musical), 1686
heat of passion, 1701
History of the United States Decision-Making
    Process on Vietnam Policy, 1532
hit-and-run statute, 1453
hot oil produced, 627

I know it when I see it, 1196
implied-reservation-of-water-doctrine, 1944
in custody, 1359
inappropriate, 2411
income, 1886
incompetency, 1035
incorporation doctrine, 595
Indian country, 818, 1676, 1684
industry-wide, 1970
influencing, 581
injury to business or property, 1484
inpact of actuality, 1381
interpretation test, 1217
interrogation, 2093
interstate compacts, 85
irrebuttable presumptions, 1617

jostling, 1415
judicial integrity, 1801

Ker-Frisbie doctrine, 254, 921
knowingly violating regulation, 1454

labor organization, 1059
legal clinics, 1872
legitimate legislative sphere, 1695
lemon test, 1468
lessee, 1559
loan shark, 1450
lobbying activities, 939
lookout, 147

managerial employees, 1634
manipulative, 1746
manipulative practices, 1173
maritime employment, 2038
medically indicated, 1793
meeting competition, 1937
member of crew, 706, 785
militant, 1005
Miranda warnings, 1260, 1359, 1430, 2016, 2093
moral character, 1005, 1100
moral turpitude, 1004
mother's insurance benefits, 2028
motor vehicle, 587

necessity, 1023
neighborhood school zoning, 1445
neutral principles of law, 2033
nolle prosequi, 1276
nonforfeitable, 2096
non-Indian community, 1676
no-strike clause, 1409
noxious products doctrine, 348, 444

obesity cure, 594
objectionable, 2411
obscene, 1247
obscenity, 1245
open field doctrine, 516
ordinary, 702
organize, 1012
original package doctrine, 103, 396, 174, 183
original package test, 1723
otherwise qualified, 2011

panic peddling activities, 1452
parade or procession, 732
pass on theory, 1851
passing on defense, 1344
pecuniary loss, 1917
Pentagon papers, 1532
person, 842, 1051, 1091, 1244, 1321, 1464, 1532,
    1772, 1880, 1897
personal stake, 2076

petty offenses, 1415
physical penetration and trespass test, 1443
piracy, 71, 1579
plain view, 1466
point sources, 1820
police power, 1126
political or religious activities, 1480
political question doctrine, 143, 1122
political subdivision, 1946
press, 1257
the prevailing usage at law, 923
private attorney general theory, 1694
private speech, 1954
privilege of doing business, 1824
probable cause, 892, 1138
Procunier test, 1637
production of goods for commerce, 725
property, 1507, 2111
public aspects, 1308
public figure, 1662
public interest, 1574
public official, 1240
Puerto Ricans, 1262

reasonable-doubt standard, 1400
reasonable grounds, 1044
red flag law, 589
release time programs, 865, 927
religion, 1855
religious beliefs, 1412
required records doctrine, 1308, 1309, 1310
right of privacy, 1269
right to remain silent, 1200
right to sue, 2110
river system, 1438
Roth-Sindermann doctrine, 1530, 1531
rule of reason, 320, 1490, 1903

sacrilegious, 929
sale, 1702
scab, 1660
scalping securities, 1173
search and seizure, 1306
section of country geographic market, 1169, 1666
securities, 1441
seizure, 1546, 1803
self-organization, 581
separate but equal doctrine, 312, 688, 954, 1160
service-connected offenses, 1689
service-oriented crimes, 1689
sexual promiscuity, 1318
Sherbert doctrine, 1170
short selling, 1995
Shreveport doctrine, 421
silver platter doctrine, 1082

similar relief, 1150
snail darter, 1923
special public interest, 1599
speech and conduct, 1456
speech and nonspeech, 1326
spike mike, 1094
state action doctrine, 198, 1195, 1505, 1672, 2065
state replevin statues, 1507
state statutes, 1566
states, 1493
statute, what is a, 1114
steering, 1979
Stencel doctrine, 899
subterfuge, 1879
subversive, 1303
subversive organization, 1303
summary disposition, 923
Sunday blue laws, 1101, 1102, 1104
suspect class, 1561

taking, 2037, 2111
target of search, 1947
terminal laborer, 1858
third-party technique, 1090
ticket scalpers, 545
tippees, 2070
tomatoes, 292
treasury warrant, 152
trust busting, 401
trustee, 615

under color, 1091
under color of a statute, 1909
under color of state law, 1967
unfair methods of competition, 1483
unrelated person, 1596

valuable mineral deposits, 2104
viability determination, 1953
vertical price-fixing, 398
Vietnam war, 1307
void contract, 1386
voluntary and intelligent, 1405

wages, 1886
war claims for damages, 148
Watergate tapes, 1874
well-pleaded complaint, 1932
what is a statute, 1114
white ghetto, 1539
white person, 622
wildcat strike, 2043
wilful, 760
wilfully, 620
will not handle agreement, 1280

Watergate tapes, 1667
wrongful force, 1553

yellow dog contracts, 375, 376, 422

POPULAR LAW NAME INDEX

This indexes the cases that argued a law like the Federal Employers' Liability Act (FELA). Each entry number (not page number) is arranged by full law name and acronym name, e.g. FELA (Federal Employers' Liability Act).

AAA (Agricultural Adjustment Act), 643, 644, 758, 1115

ADEA (Age Discrimination in Employment Act), 1879, 1994, 2275, 2476, 2766, 2868, 2870, 3370, 3390, 3562, 3593, 3607, 3781, 3948, 4002, 4036

AECA (Arms Control Export Act), 2565

AFDC (Aid to Families with Dependent Children), 1402, 2136, 2141, 2385, 2793, 3129, 3203, 3956

AFDC-UF (Aid to Families with Dependent Children, Unemployment Fathers Program), 2022

AHTA (Anti-Head Tax Act), 3858

APA (Administrative Procedure Act), 907, 922, 1367, 1394, 1492, 1550, 1580, 1691, 1698, 1757, 1919, 2044, 2164, 2184, 3827, 3886, 3913

Acts of Confiscation, 15, 20

Adamson Eight-Hour Act of 1916, 437

Administrative Procedure Act (APA), 907, 922, 1367, 1394, 1492, 1550, 1580, 1691, 1698, 1757, 1919, 2044, 2164, 2184, 3827, 3886, 3913

Admiralty Jurisdiction Act, 1383

Adolescent Family Life Act, 3281

Adoption Assistance and Child Welfare Act of 1980, 3667

Age Discrimination in Employment Act of 1967 (ADEA), 1879, 1994, 2275, 2476, 2766, 2868, 2870, 3370, 3390, 3562, 3593, 3607, 3781, 3948, 4002, 4036

Agricultural Adjustment Act (AAA), 1152

Agricultural Adjustment Act of 1933 (AAA), 643, 644

Agricultural Adjustment Act of 1938 (AAA), 758

Agricultural Marketing Agreement Act, 2700

Agricultural Marketing Agreement Act of 1937, 695, 742, 759

Aid to Families with Dependent Children (AFDC), 1402, 2385, 2793, 3129, 3203, 3956. *See also* Social Security, AFDC.

Aid to Families with Dependent Children, Unemployment Fathers Program (AFDC-UF), 2022. *See also* Social Security, AFDC-UF.

Airline Deregulation Act, 3944

Airline Deregulation Act of 1978, 3112, 3695

Airport and Airway Development Act of 1970, 2601

Airport and Airway Development Act of 1982, 3094

Airport and Airway Revenue Act of 1970, 1898

Airport Development Acceleration Act of 1973, 2601

Alaska National Interest Lands Conservation Act of 1980, 3108

Alien Immigration Act of 1903, 386

Alien Land Law of 1913, 493

Alien Property Custodian Act of 1943, 1278

Alien Registration Act of 1940, 724, 922, 1012

Anti-Crime Law of 1984, 3300

Anti-Drug Abuse Act of 1986, 3530

Anti-Drug Abuse Act of 1988, 3869, 3928

Anti-Head Tax Act (AHTA) of 1973, 3858

Anti-Injunction Act, 1766, 2157

Antinarcotic Act, 530

Anti-Slavery Act of 1866, 3353

Armed Career Criminal Act of 1984, 3887

Arms Export Control Act (AECA), 2565

Articles of War of 1929, 821

Ashburton Treaty of 1842, 253

Atomic Energy Act, 2612

Atomic Energy Act of 1946, 948

Atomic Energy Act of 1954, 2505

BLA (Base Labor Agreement), 2347

Bail Reform Act of 1964, 3464

Bail Reform Act of 1984, 3148

Balanced Budget and Emergency Deficit Control Act of 1985, 3058

Bank Holding Company Act, 2182

Bank Holding Company Act of 1956, 2862, 2929

Bank Holding Company Act of 1987, 3421

Bank Merger Act of 1960, 1169

Bank Merger Act of 1966, 1666

Bank of the United States Act of 1791, 74

Bank of the United States Act of 1816, 74

Bank Security Act of 1970, 1752, 2521

Bank Service Corporation Act of 1962, 1394

Banking Act of 1933, 2734

Bankruptcy Act, 625, 696, 699, 701, 715, 750, 1239, 1265, 1332

Bankruptcy Act of 1898, 2330

Bankruptcy Act of 1978, 2416

Bankruptcy Act of 1984, 3889

Bankruptcy Code, 3368, 3662

Bankruptcy Code of 1978, 3311
Bankruptcy Reform Act of 1978, 2446, 2538, 2637
Base Labor Agreement (BLA) of 1968, 2347
Bituminous Coal Conservation Act of 1935, 651
Black Lung Benefits Act, 3913
Black Lung Benefits Act of 1972, 3430
Black Lung Reform Act of 1977, 3293
Boulder Canyon Project Act, 1162, 1176, 2121
Briand-Kellogg Peace Pact, 626
Buck Act, 1226
Buy Indian Act, 2100

CERCLA (Comprehensive Environmental Response
    Compensation and Liability Act), 2700, 2951,
    3349, 3898
COGSA (Carriage of Goods by Sea Act), 4009
CZMA (Coastal Zone Management Act), 2614
Cable Communications Policy Act, 3807
Cable Television Consumer Protection and
    Competition Act of 1992, 3924
Capper-Volstead Act, 1920
Carriage of Goods by Sea Act of 1936 (COGSA),
    4009
Census Act, 2324
Central Intelligence Agency Act, 1657
Central Intelligence Information Act, 2760
Cheyenne River Act, 3822
Child Abuse Act of 1984, 3000
Child Labor Tax Act of 1919, 484, 485
Chinese Exclusion Acts, 330
Chinese Exclusion Act of 1888, 263
Chinese Laundry Laws, 248
Civil Aeronautics Act, 862
Civil Rights Act, 692, 1163, 1224, 1907, 3050
Civil Rights Act of 1866, 869, 872, 1253, 1343,
    1349, 2242, 2731, 3140, 3141
Civil Rights Act of 1870, 1253
Civil Rights Act of 1871, 912, 1279, 1510, 1633,
    1725, 1748, 1967, 2010, 2102, 2226, 2494, 2501,
    2593, 2676, 2735, 2780, 2834, 2855, 2889, 3079
Civil Rights Act of 1875, 198, 231
Civil Rights Act of 1883, 368
Civil Rights Act of 1957, 1067
Civil Rights Act of 1964, 1208, 1209, 1252, 1264,
    1314, 1425, 1435, 1444, 1446, 1570, 1615, 1619,
    1678, 1712, 1739, 1748, 1781, 1787, 1788, 1806,
    1842, 1843, 1846, 1855, 1870, 1871, 1878, 1883,
    1904, 1936, 1940, 1945, 1973, 2004, 2010, 2027,
    2056, 2094, 2110, 2135, 2151, 2165, 2179, 2183,
    2189, 2194, 2209, 2242, 2326, 2349, 2357, 2365,
    2386, 2387, 2398, 2420, 2493, 2528, 2543, 2558,
    2586, 2599, 2688, 2711, 2804, 3017, 3045, 3049,
    3059, 3065, 3111, 3170, 3195, 3287, 3332, 3342,
    3346, 3348, 3353, 3366, 3391, 3424, 3433, 3515,
    3544, 3546, 3690, 3728, 3837, 3948

Civil Rights Act of 1964, Bennett Amendment, 2245
Civil Rights Act of 1968, 1349, 1424, 1539
Civil Rights Act of 1981, 3830
Civil Rights Act of 1983, 3919
Civil Rights Act of 1984, 2638
Civil Rights Act of 1991, 3846, 3877, 3878
Civil Rights Attorney's Fee Awards Act of 1976,
    2106, 2107, 2136, 2141, 2154, 2329, 2514, 2652,
    2676, 2758, 2833, 2889, 2894, 2966, 3035, 3062
Civil Rights of Institutionalized Persons Act of 1980,
    2400
Civil Service Reform Act of 1978, 2606, 2812, 2882,
    3436
Civil Service Retirement Act, 2063
Civil War Amendments, Jim Crow Laws, 231
Clayton Act, 716, 842, 945, 1007, 1077, 1169, 1261,
    1484, 1555, 1627, 1666, 1681, 1699, 1813, 1851,
    1880, 1959, 2008, 2227, 2232, 2235, 2253, 2399,
    2465, 2482, 2487, 2535, 3066, 3188, 3447
Clayton Act of 1914, 467, 487, 581, 728, 806, 807
Clayton Act of 1950, 1130
Clean Air Act, 1494, 2588, 2609, 2983, 3051, 3206,
    3484
Clean Air Act 1970 Amendment, 1780
Clear Air Act of 1977, 2721
Clean Water Act, 1493, 2791, 3083, 3131, 3215,
    3654, 3679, 3725, 3733, 3895
Clean Water Act of 1975, 2916
Coal Mine Health and Safety Act of 1969, 1612,
    3293
Coastal Zone Management Act of 1972 (CZMA),
    2614
Commerce Clause, 88, 2742, 3532, 3645, 3884
Commodity Exchange Act, 2360, 2583
Common Law, 14
Communications Act, 3369. See also Federal
    Communications Act.
Communications Act of 1934, 674, 700, 932, 1976,
    2201, 2281, 2988. See also Federal
    Communications Act of 1934.
Communist Control Act, 1107
Communist Control Act of 1954, 983
Comprehensive Drug Abuse Prevention and Control
    Act of 1970, 2193, 2854
Comprehensive Drug Abuse Prevention and Control
    Act of 1981, 3762
Comprehensive Employment and Training Act, 2984
Comprehensive Environmental Response,
    Compensation and Liability Act of 1980
    (CERCLA), 2700, 2951, 3349, 3898
Comprehensive Environmental Response,
    Compensation and Liability Act of 1986, 3898
Comstock Act of 1873, 209, 2570
Condemnation Act of 1888, 836
Confiscation Act of 1861, 180

Conformity Act of 1934, 723
Consumer Credit Protection Act, 1450
Consumer Product Safety Act, 2112
Control Shares Acquisitions Act, 3119
Convention on Service Abroad of Judicial and
    Extrajudicial Documents in Civil and Commercial
    Matters of 1969, 3263
Copyright Act, 3445
Copyright Act of 1976, 2768, 3345
Criminal Appeals Act, 1448, 1474
Criminal Justice Act of 1964, 2042
Crimes Act of 1790, 99
Crude Oil Windfall Profit Tax Act of 1980, 2533
Curtis Act of 1898, 751

DOHSA (Death on the High Seas Act), 1373, 1413,
    1541, 1616, 1917, 3023
Davis-Bacon Act, 2206
Death on the High Seas Act of 1920 (DOHSA), 1373,
    1413, 1541, 1616, 1917, 3023
Debt Collection Act of 1982, 3778
Declaratory Judgment Act, 1053. *See also* Federal
    Declaratory Judgment Act of 1934.
Defense Base Closure and Realignment Act of 1990,
    3886
Defense Bases Act, 1027
Defense Production Act of 1950, 930
Deficit Reduction Act of 1984, 2793, 3203
Department of Transportation Act of 1966, 1434
Desert Land Act, 976
Developmentally Disabled Assistance and Bill of
    Rights Act of 1975, 2207
Displaced Persons Act of 1948, 2176
District of Columbia Court Reform and Criminal
    Procedure Act of 1970, 1566
Douglas Amendment, 2862
Drug Conspiracy Statute of 1970, 3932
Dryer Act, 1613
Due Process Clause, 3042, 3093

EAHCA (Education for All Handicapped Children
    Act), 2419, 2755, 2758, 2839, 3221
ERISA (Employee Retirement Income Security Act),
    2096, 2225, 2568, 2571, 2852, 2878, 2893, 3117,
    3118, 3153, 3307, 3329, 3344, 3398, 3488, 3517,
    3665, 3707, 3742, 3781, 3799, 3804, 3849, 3961,
    3980, 4027, 4031
ESA (Endangered Species Act), 1923, 3700, 4015
Eagle Protection Act, 2037, 3004
Economic Stabilization Act of 1970, 1697
Education for All Handicapped Children Act, 2755,
    2839
Education for All Handicapped Children Act of 1975
    (EAHCA), 2419, 2758, 3221

Educational Amendments of 1972, 1641, 1993, 2366,
    2436, 2638, 3652
Eight Hour Law of 1892, 882
Elementary and Secondary Education Act of 1965,
    1338, 2529, 2808
Elementary and Secondary Education Act of 1978,
    2807
Embargo Act of 1807, 52, 62
Emergency Bank Act of 1933, 632
Emergency Deficiency Appropriation Act of 1943,
    828
Emergency Price Control Act of 1942, 782, 784, 831,
    843, 876
Emergency School Aid of 1972, 1577, 1641, 2040
Employee Retirement Income Security Act (ERISA),
    2096, 2568, 2571, 3117, 3118, 3153, 3344, 3781,
    3804, 4027
Employee Retirement Income Security Act of 1974
    (ERISA), 2225, 2852, 2878, 2893, 3307, 3329,
    3398, 3488, 3513, 3517, 3665, 3707, 3742, 3799,
    3849, 3961, 3980
Employee Retirement Income Security Act of 1994
    (ERISA), 4031
Employers" Liability Act of 1906, 373
Employers" Liability Act of 1908, 435
Endangered Species Act of 1973 (ESA), 1923, 3700,
    4015
Endangered Species Act of 1994 (ESA), 4015
Energy Policy and Conservation Act of 1975, 1766
Energy Reorganization Act of 1974, 3468
Enforcement Act, 219
Enforcement Acts of 1870, 197, 198
Equal Access Act, 2956
Equal Access Act of 1984, 3473
Equal Access to Justice Act, 3471, 3592, 3631, 3831
Equal Employment Opportunity Act of 1972, 1649,
    1712
Equal Pay Act, 1904, 2245
Equal Pay Act of 1963, 1645, 2209
Equal Protection Clause, 1174, 2197, 2832, 3872
Equal Rights Act, 2005
Erdman Act of 1898, 375
Espionage Act of 1917, 446, 448, 449, 451, 456, 458,
    948
Ethics in Government Act of 1978, 3282, 3953
Ex Post Facto Clause, 3977
Excise Technical Changes Act of 1958, 1237
Executive Salary Cost-of-Living Adjustment Act,
    2163
Expediting Act, 1555

FACA (Federal Advisory Committee Act), 3358
FCA (False Claim Act), 2582, 3336
FECA (Federal Elections Campaign Act), 1727,
    2276, 2291, 2336, 2453

FECA (Federal Employees' Compensation Act), 2474, 2692

FELA (Federal Employers' Liability Act), 2131, 2229, 3254, 3383, 3921, 3934

FHA (Fair Housing Act), 1809, 1979, 2325, 3984

FICA (Federal Insurance Contributions Act), 2248

FIFRA (Federal Insecticide, Fungicide and Rodenticide Act), 2727, 2904, 3611, 3839

FLSA (Fair Labor Standards Act), 725, 726, 754, 798, 810, 877, 1340, 1771, 2091, 2205, 2245, 2784, 2836, 2965, 3183

FOIA (Freedom of Information Act), 1547, 1710, 1983, 2067, 2068, 2075, 2112, 2324, 2368, 2370, 2531, 2647, 2760, 2829, 3244, 3322, 3389, 3633, 3800, 3863

FSLMRS (Federal Service Labor-Management Relations Statute), 3461

FTCA (Federal Torts Claim Act), 886, 899, 938, 979, 1849, 2086, 2474, 2478, 2719, 2890, 3144, 3258, 3279, 3339, 3543, 3548, 3640, 3766, 3796, 4005

FUTA (Federal Unemployment Tax Act), 2237, 2248, 3084

Fair Debt Collection Practices Act, 3971

Fair Housing Act (FHA), 3984

Fair Housing Act of 1968 (FHA), 1809, 1979, 2325

Fair Labor Standards Act (FLSA), 877, 2091, 2205, 2245, 2784, 2836, 2965, 3183

Fair Labor Standards Act of 1938 (FLSA), 725, 726, 754, 798, 810

Fair Labor Standards Act of 1961 (FLSA), 1340

Fair Labor Standards Act of 1974 (FLSA), 1771

Fairness Doctrine, 1574

False Claim Act (FCA), 2582, 3336

Family Farmer Bankruptcy Act of 1986, 3231

Federal Advisory Committee Act of 1972 (FACA), 3358

Federal Agricultural Fair Practices Act, 2705

Federal-Aid Highway Act of 1968, 1434

Federal Alcohol Administration Act (1935), 3976

Federal Alien Registration Act of 1940, 724

Federal Arbitration Act, 2468, 2621, 2794, 3172

Federal Arbitration Act of 1952, 950

Federal Aviation Act of 1958, 1710

Federal Aviation Act of 1978, 2547

Federal Bank Robbery Act, 2544

Federal Cigarette Labeling and Advertising Act of 1965, 3723

Federal Civil Forfeiture Statute of 1981, 3840

Federal Communications Act, 750, 1017, 1374. *See also* Communications Act.

Federal Communications Act of 1934, 1574. *See also* Communications Act of 1934.

Federal Corp Insurance Act of 1945, 854

Federal Corrupt Practices Act, 1516

Federal Declaratory Judgment Act of 1934, 648. *See also* Declaratory Judgment Act

Federal Elections Campaign Act of 1971 (FECA), 1727, 2291, 2336, 2453

Federal Elections Campaign Act of 1979 (FECA), 2276

Federal Election Campaign Fund Act Amendment of 1971, 2802

Federal Employees' Compensation Act (FECA), 2474, 2692

Federal Employees' Liability Reform and Tort Compensation Act, 3543

Federal Employers' Liability Act (FELA), 1184, 1413, 1616, 2051, 3109, 3200, 3510, 3635

Federal Employers' Liability Act of 1907 (FELA), 3934

Federal Employers' Liability Act of 1908 (FELA), 3254, 3921

Federal Employers' Liability Act of 1982 (FELA), 3383

Federal Employers' Liability and Compensation Act, 2131, 2229

Federal Export Clause, 4042

Federal Firearms Act of 1938, 772

Federal Food, Drug, and Cosmetic Act, 1390, 2814. *See also* Food, Drug and Cosmetic Act.

Federal Food, Drug and Cosmetic Act of 1938, 777, 858

Federal Habeas Corpus Statute of 1977, 3782

Federal Insecticide, Fungicide, and Rodenticide Act (FIFRA), 2904, 3839

Federal Insecticide, Fungicide, and Rodenticide Act of 1972 (FIFRA), 3611

Federal Insecticide, Fungicide, and Rodenticide Act of 1978 (FIFR), 2727

Federal Insurance Contributions Act (FICA), 2248

Federal Interpleader Act, 2383

Federal Judiciary Act of 1789, 134, 681

Federal Kidnapping Act, 921, 1316, 1405

Federal Labor Standards Act, 3791

Federal Labor Standards Act of 1938, 3390

Federal Land and Management Act of 1976, 2825

Federal Land Policy and Management Act, 2565

Federal Liquor Enforcement Act of 1936, 892

Federal Magistrates Act, 2130, 3620

Federal Maritime Lien Act, 3586

Federal Mine Safety and Health Act of 1977, 2263

Federal Motor Carrier Act of 1935, 717

Federal Narcotics Act, 1071

Federal Obscenity Statute, 1246

Federal Old-Age Survivors and Disability Insurance Benefits Program, 1822

Federal Payment in Lieu of Taxes Act, 2773

Federal Power Act, 1478, 2323, 2512, 2682, 3514

Federal Power Act of 1920, 722

Federal Power Act of 1935, 1176
Federal Property and Administrative Services Act, 2100
Federal Property and Administrative Services Act of 1949, 2306
Federal Railroad Safety Act of 1970, 3783
Federal Rules of Criminal Procedure, 2786, 3943
Federal Rules of Evidence, 3943
Federal Service Labor-Management Relations Statute (FSLMRS), 3461
Federal Smith Act, 983, 995
Federal Tobacco Inspection Act of 1935, 689
Federal Torts Claim Act (FTCA), 899, 938, 979, 1849, 2086, 2474, 2478, 2719, 2890, 3144, 3258, 3279, 3339, 3543, 3548, 3640, 3766, 3796, 4005
Federal Tort Claims Act of 1948, 886
Federal Trade Commission Act, 1039, 1169, 1483, 1681
Federal Trade Commission Act of 1914, 594, 601, 602
Federal Trade Commission Act of 1931, 639
Federal Unemployment Tax Act (FUTA), 2237, 2248
Federal Unemployment Tax Act of 1977, 3084
Federal Water Pollution Control Act, 2145, 2271, 2358
Federal Water Pollution Control Act Amendments of 1972, 1820, 2069, 2217
Federal Water Pollution Control Act Amendments of 1977, 2158
Federal Water Power Act of 1920, 722
Federal Wire Tapping Act, 932
Federal Youth Correction Act of 1950 (YCA), 2297, 2490
Feres Doctrine, 2890, 3144
Filled Milk Act of 1923, 683
Financial Institutions Supervisory Act of 1966, 3625
Fisherman's Protection Act of 1967, 3043
Flag Protection Act of 1989, 3475
Flood Control Act, 3053
Food and Agriculture Act of 1965, 1395
Food and Drugs Act of 1906, 607
Food, Drug and Cosmetic Act, 1700. *See also* Federal Food, Drug and Cosmetic Act.
Food, Drug and Cosmetic Act of 1958, 3839
Food Stamp Act, 3038
Food Stamp Act of 1964, 1595, 1596
Food Stamp Act of 1971, 1595
Foraker Act of 1900, 344
Force Act of 1870, 197, 198
Force Act of 1871, 229
Foreign Agents Registration Act of 1938, 3134
Foreign Commerce Clause, 3396
Foreign Corrupt Practices Act, 3400
Foreign Sovereign Immunities Act of 1976, 2517, 3301, 3701, 3771

Fort Laramie Treaty of 1851, 2200
Fort Laramie Treaty of 1868, 2149, 2200
Fourteenth Amendment. *See* Equal Protection Clause.
Frazier-Lemke (Farm Mortgage) Act of 1934, 638
Frazier-Lemke (Farm Mortgage) Act of 1935, 659
Freedom of Information Act (FOIA), 1547, 1710, 1983, 2067, 2068, 2075, 2112, 2324, 2368, 2370, 2531, 2647, 2760, 2829, 3244, 3322, 3389, 3633, 3863
Freedom of Information Act of 1966 (FOIA), 3800
Friendship, Commerce and Navigation Treaty, 2387
Fugitive Slave Act of 1793, 136
Fugitive Slave Act of 1850, 155
Futures Trading Act of 1921, 486

Gas Policy Act of 1978, 2236
General Allotment Act, 1753, 2081, 2575
General Crimes Act, 1894
Glass-Steagall Act, 2182, 2734
Glass-Steagall Act of 1933, 2736
Glass-Steagall Banking Act of 1933, 1441
Gramm-Rudman-Hollings Anti-Deficit Act of 1985, 3058
Great Sioux Reservation Treaty of 1868, 1830
Gun Control Act of 1968, 1498, 2471
Gun-Free School Zones Act 1990, 3979

Habeas Corpus Act of 1863, 162
Hague Service Convention, 3263
Handicapped Education Act of 1975, 3354
Harbor Workers' Compensation Act, 3913
Harrison Antinarcotic Act of 1914, 481
Harrison Narcotics Act of 1914, 447
Harrison Narcotic Act of 1919, 597
Hart-Scott-Rodino Antitrust Improvements Act of 1976, 2487
Hatch Act of 1939, 1597
Hatch Act of 1940, 840, 841
Hepburn Act of 1906, 388
Higher Education Act of 1965, 2754
Higher Education Facilities Act of 1963, 1469
Hobbs Act, 981, 1553, 2074, 2810, 3573
Hobbs Act of 1984, 3691
Housing Act of 1937, 3237
Housing Act of 1949, 2478
Housing Act of 1954, 1042
Housing and Rent Act of 1947, 864
Hyde Amendment of 1976, 2147, 2148

IDEA (Individuals with Disabilities Education Act), 3845
IDRA (Insanity Defense Reform Act), 3922
IEEPA (International Emergency Economic Powers Act), 2288, 2737

Immigration and Nationality Act, 1081, 2565, 2610, 3636

Immigration and Nationality Act of 1952, 1029, 1085, 1123, 1141, 1228, 1534, 2176, 2279, 2432, 2444, 3211

Immigration and Nationality Act of 1992, 3641

Immigration Reform and Control Act of 1986, 3534

Immunity Act of 1954, 982

Import-Export Clause, 2450

Independent Offices Appropriation Act of 1952, 1625, 1626

Indian Appropriation Act of 1885, 249

Indian Civil Rights Act of 1968, 1889, 1907

Indian Claims Commission Act, 2081, 2149, 2787

Indian Commerce Clause, 2439, 4034

Indian Financing Act of 1974, 2439

Indian Gaming Regulatory Act, 4034

Indian General Allotment Act of 1883, 3797

Indian General Allotment Act of 1887, 3638

Indian Land Consolidation Act of 1983, 3145

Indian Major Crimes Act of 1885, 3761

Indian Mineral Leasing Act of 1938, 2853

Indian Reorganization Act of 1934, 1649, 2830

Indian Self-Determination and Education Assistance Act, 2439

Individuals with Disabilities Education Act (IDEA), 3845

Insanity Defense Reform Act of 1984 (IDRA), 3922

Internal Revenue Code, 933, 2522

Internal Revenue Code of 1934, 1111

Internal Revenue Code of 1939, 967, 978, 988, 1006, 1022, 1023, 1140, 1153

Internal Revenue Code of 1954, 1076, 1140, 1203, 1250, 1463, 1679, 1757, 1834, 1886, 1925, 1955, 1970, 2060, 2186, 2228, 2309, 2322, 3388, 3454, 3756

Internal Security Act, 1107

Internal Security Act of 1950, 959, 983, 994, 1018, 1235, 1695

International Emergency Economic Powers Act of 1977 (IEEPA), 2288, 2737

Interstate Agreement on Detainers, 2174, 2908

Interstate Commerce Act, 898, 1086, 1550, 1580, 2192, 2359, 3359

Interstate Commerce Act of 1887, 322, 324

Interstate Commerce Act of 1940, 806, 812

Interstate Land Sales Full Disclosure Act, 1769

Interstate River Compact, 3599

Investment Advisers Act of 1940, 1173, 1990, 2036, 2184, 2863

Investment Company Act of 1940, 1389, 1717, 2184, 3565

Investment Company and Investment Advisers Acts, 1990

Japanese American Exclusion Act 1942, 800, 801

Jencks Act, 1107, 1313, 1709

Jim Crow Laws, 231

Jones Act, 944, 1027, 1045, 1184, 1411, 1413, 1616, 1818, 2430, 3200, 3510, 3528, 3628, 3861

Jones Act of 1920, 4003

Jones Act of 1929, 585

Judicial Code, 739

Judiciary Act, 119, 140, 145

Judiciary Act of 1789, 44, 49, 66, 82, 85, 116, 134, 141, 155, 159

Judiciary Act of 1801, 36

Judiciary Acts of 1802, 35, 36

Juvenile Delinquency Act, 3664

Keating-Owen Child Labor Law of 1916, 444

Keating-Owen Child Labor Tax of 1919, 485

Ku Klux Klan Act of 1871, 198, 229, 3749

LHWCA (Longshoremen's and Harbor Workers' Compensation Act), 598, 706, 785, 826, 1027, 1383, 1413, 1858, 2038, 2131, 2166, 2211, 2338, 2456, 2519, 2523, 2551, 2725, 2800, 3383, 3628, 3722, 3744, 3906, 3999, 4003

LMRDA (Labor-Management Reporting and Disclosure Act), 1230, 1280, 1571, 1698, 1811, 2363, 2384, 2710, 2745, 3299, 3385, 3398, 3533, 3629, 3398

Labor Management Act, 1078

Labor Management Relations Act, 1050, 1063, 1214, 1275, 1409, 1612, 1646, 1734, 2208, 2220, 2234, 2280, 2335, 2355, 2374, 2407, 2831, 3449

Labor Management Relations Act of 1947, 895, 930, 1119, 1121, 1251, 2043, 2264, 3425, 3519, 3629, 3819. *See also* Taft-Hartley Act of 1947.

Labor-Management Reporting and Disclosure Act (LMRDA), 1571, 2363, 2710

Labor-Management Reporting and Disclosure Act of 1959 (LMRDA), 1230, 1280, 1698, 1811, 2384, 2745, 3299, 3385, 3398, 3533, 3629, 3398

Landrum-Griffin Amendments, 1280

Lanham Act, 2378, 2769

Lantham Act Trademark Act of 1946, 936

Legal Tender Act of 1862, 177, 182

Legislative Branch Appropriation Act of 1977, 1979, 2163

Limited Liability Act, 3499

Lloyd-La Follette Act, 1632

Local Government Antitrust Act of 1984, 2820

Longshoremen's and Harbor Workers' Compensation Act (LHWCA), 706, 1027, 1383, 1413, 1858, 2338, 2519, 2523, 2551, 2725, 2800, 3383, 3628, 3722, 3744, 3999, 4003

Longshoremen's and Harbor Workers' Compensation Act of 1927 (LHWCA), 598, 785, 826

Longshoremen's and Harbor Workers' Compensation Act of 1972 (LHWCA), 2038, 2131, 2166, 2211, 2456, 3906

Low-Level Radioactive Waste Policy Amendments Act of 1985, 3714

MSAWPA (Migrant and Seasonal Agricultural Workers Protection Act), 3428

Magnuson Fishery Conservation and Management Act, 3043

Major Crimes Act, 1831, 1894

Mandamus and Venue Act of 1962, 2053

Management Labor Relations Act of 1947, 895

Mann Act, 1041, 2518

Mann White-Slave Traffic Act of 1910, 412, 434

Marijuana Tax Act, 1368

Marine Protection, Research and Sanctuaries Act of 1972, 2271

McCarran Act of 1945, 832

McCarran Amendment, 1740, 3789

McCarran-Ferguson Act, 1352, 2233, 2816, 3702, 3817

McCarran-Ferguson Act of 1945, 1039, 1939, 1961, 2417, 3843

Medical Assistance (Medicaid) Program, 1860, 1861. *See also* Social Security Act, Medicaid program

Menominee Termination Act of 1954, 1328

Merchant Marine Act of 1920, 535

Merchant Marine Act of 1936, 2055

Mexican Cession Act of 1854, 740

Migrant and Seasonal Agricultural Workers Protection Act of 1983 (MSAWPA), 3428

Migratory Bird Act of 1918, 459

Migratory Bird Conservation Act, 2479

Migratory Bird Hunting Stamp Act, 2479

Migratory Bird Treaty Act, 2037

Migratory Bird Treaty of 1916, 459

Military Reconstruction Act, 165, 169

Military Selective Service Act, 1847, 2273, 2806

Military Selective Service Act of 1967, 1436

Militia Act of 1795, 100

Millers-Tydings Act of 1937, 913

Mineral Lands Leasing Act of 1970, 2287

Mineral Leasing Act of 1920, 2104, 2215

Missouri Compromise of 1820, 154

Money Laundering Act of 1986, 3850

Montgomery Amendment of 1986, 3477

Montreal Agreement, 3330

Motor Carrier Act of 1980, 2701, 3493, 3769

Multiemployer Pension Plan Amendment Act, 3146

Multiemployer Pension Plan Amendments Act of 1980, 2716, 2944, 3820, 3951

Multiple-Use Sustained Yield Act of 1960, 1944

Multistate Tax Compact, 1885

Municipal Bankruptcy Act of 1934, 652

NEPA (National Environmental Policy Act), 1580, 1769, 1786, 1900, 2009, 2044, 2294, 2497, 2534

NFA (National Firearms Act), 660, 691, 1310, 1440, 3698, 3891

NGPA (Natural Gas Policy Act), 2461, 2537, 2579, 2931, 3522

NHPRDA (National Health Care Planning and Resources Development Act), 2252

NIRA (National Industrial Recovery Act), 627, 637, 711

NLRA (National Labor Relations Act), 662, 663, 664, 665, 666, 684, 687, 783, 986, 1059, 1065, 1154, 1183, 1207, 1220, 1275, 1294, 1297, 1377, 1497, 1520, 1573, 1660, 1671, 1678, 1682, 1699, 1733, 1776, 1815, 1910, 1964, 1971, 1991, 2019, 2059, 2124, 2127, 2266, 2296, 2304, 2312, 2355, 2371, 2457, 2491, 2492 2507, 2527, 2536, 2546, 2573, 2584, 2637, 2745, 2852, 2960, 3116, 3139, 3152, 3153, 3217, 3385, 3432, 3559, 3648, 3767, 4021

NSA (National Security Act), 2829, 3260

Narcotics Control Act of 1956, 1044, 1138

Narcotic Drugs Import and Export Act, 1001

National Bank Act, 1394, 3945, 4033

National Bituminous Coal Wage Agreement of 1945, 842

National Blood Policy, 2851

National Childhood Vaccine Injury Act, 3969

National Environmental Policy Act (NEPA), 1900, 2044, 2497, 2534

National Environmental Policy Act of 1969 (NEPA), 1580, 1769, 1786, 2009, 2294

National Environmental Policy Act of 1982 (NEPA), 3334

National Firearms Act (NFA), 1310, 1440, 3698, 3891

National Firearms Act of 1934 (NFA), 660, 691

National Firearms Registration and Transfer Record, 3891

National Gas Act, 2236, 2286. *See also* Natural Gas Act.

National Health Care Planning and Resources Development Act (NHPRDA), 2252

National Housing Act, 835, 1042, 1463

National Industrial Recovery Act (NIRA), 711

National Industrial Recovery Act of 1933 (NIRA), 627, 637

National Labor Relations Act (NLRA), 684, 783, 986, 1059, 1065, 1154, 1183, 1207, 1220, 1275, 1294, 1297, 1377, 1497, 1520, 1573, 1660, 1671, 1678, 1682, 1699, 1733, 1776, 1815, 1910, 1964, 1971, 1991, 2019, 2059, 2124, 2127, 2266, 2296, 2304, 2312, 2355, 2371, 2457, 2491, 2492, 2507, 2527, 2536, 2546, 2573, 2584, 2637, 2745, 2852,

2960, 3116, 3139, 3152, 3153, 3217, 3385, 3432,
  3559, 3648, 3767, 4021
National Labor Relations Act (NLRA) of 1935, 662,
  663, 664, 665, 666, 684, 687
National Minimum Drinking Age Act, 3190
National Motor Vehicle Theft Act of 1919, 587
National Parks Act of 1913, 709
National Pollution Discharge Elimination System,
  2069, 3215
National Prohibition Act of 1919, 521, 527, 546, 548,
  556, 558, 560, 567, 584, 585, 601, 602, 609, 610,
  612, 623
National Security Act of 1947 (NSA), 2829, 3260
National Sinking Fund Amendment of 1878, 214
National Stolen Property Act, 2340, 2896
National Traffic and Motor Vehicle Safety Act of
  1966, 2569, 3970
National Trails System Act Amendments of 1983,
  3406
National Transportation Act, 3190
Nationality Act of 1940, 931, 1024, 1025, 1026,
  1141, 1286, 2608
Natural Gas Act, 1320, 1724, 3234. *See also* National
  Gas Act.
Natural Gas Act of 1938, 745, 780
Natural Gas Policy Act of 1978 (NGPA), 2461, 2537,
  2579, 2931, 3522
Naturalization Act of 1906, 572, 591, 592
Neutrality Act of 1816, 1004
Newspaper Preservation Act of 1970, 3382
Newspaper Publicity Act of 1912, 414
Noise Control Act of 1972, 1568, 1642
Nonprofit Institutions Act, 1742
Norris-LaGuardia Act, 842, 1251, 1409, 1612, 2235,
  2266, 2407, 3132, 3359
Norris-La Guardia Act of 1932, 728

OCCA (Organized Crime Control Act), 1474, 1501,
  1638, 2160, 2602, 3097
OCSLA (Outer Continental Shelf Lands Act), 1373,
  1473, 2284, 2295, 2800, 3290
OSHA (Occupational Safety and Health Act), 1829,
  1911, 2062, 2152, 2153, 2260, 3542, 3712
Occupational Safety and Health Act (OSHA), 2152,
  3712
Occupational Safety and Health Act of 1970
  (OSHA), 1829, 1911, 2062, 2153, 2260, 3542
Omnibus Adjustment Act of 1926, 2121
Omnibus Budget Reconciliation Act of 1981, 2971
Omnibus Crime Control and Safe Streets Act, 1514,
  1620, 2877
Omnibus Crime Control and Safe Street Act of 1968,
  1475, 1523, 1639, 1640, 1812, 1908, 1982, 2001
Ordinance of 1787, 470
Organic Administration Act of 1897, 1944

Organized Crime Control Act of 1970 (OCCA),
  1474, 1501, 1638, 2160, 2602, 3097
Outer Continental Shelf Lands Act (OCSLA), 1373,
  1473, 2284, 2800, 3290
Outer Continental Shelf Lands Act of 1978
  (OCSLA), 2295

PURPA (Public Utility Regulatory Policies Act),
  2376, 2513
PWSA (Ports and Waterways Safety Act), 1888
Pacific Northwest Electric Power Planning and
  Conservation Act of 1980, 2702
Packers and Stockyards Act of 1921, 483
Packwood Amendment, 3043
Panama Canal Treaty, 3063
Paperwork Reduction Act of 1980, 3407
Passport Act of 1926, 1228, 2279
Patent Act, 1928
Pelly Amendment, 3043
Plant Variety Protection Act, 3942
Pole Attachment Act, 3099
Portal to Portal Act, 2205
Ports and Waterways Safety Act of 1972 (PWSA),
  1888
Postal Revenue and Federal Salary Act of 1967, 1404
Postal Service and Federal Employees Salary Act of
  1962, 1229
Power Plant and Industrial Fuel Use Act of 1978,
  2287
Pregnancy Discrimination Act, 2558, 2571
Pregnancy Discrimination Act of 1978, 3072, 3544
Presidential Recordings and Materials Preservation
  Act, 1874
Price-Anderson Act, 1932, 2612
Private Express Statutes, 3536
Privacy Act, 3863
Privacy Act of 1974, 2760
Privileges and Immunities Clause, 131, 2823
Protection of Children Against Sexual Exploitation
  Act of 1977, 3935
Public Broadcasting Act of 1967, 2742
Public Buildings Act of 1926, 836
Public Health Service Act, 2851
Public Health Service Act of 1970, 3570
Public Utility Holding Company Act of 1935, 763,
  851
Public Utility Regulatory Policies Act of 1978
  (PURPA), 2376, 2513
Public Vessels Act, 2474
Public Works Employment Act of 1977, 2151
Pueblo Lands Act of 1924, 2864
Pure Food and Drug Act of 1906, 396

Quiet Title Act, 3006
Quiet Title Act of 1972, 2508

RCRA (Resource Conservation and Recovery Act), 2791, 3381, 3679, 3880

RFRA (Religious Freedom Restoration Act), 3435

RICO (Racketeer Influenced and Corrupt Organizations Act), 2074, 2602, 2262, 2902, 2905, 3162, 3188, 3305, 3362, 3363, 3372, 3400, 3402, 3663, 3765, 3838, 3854

RLA (Railway Labor Act), 581, 661, 799, 990, 1113, 1998, 2266, 2342, 2672, 3109, 3359, 3912

Racial Bias Statute of 1866, 3170

Racketeer Influenced and Corrupt Organizations (RICO), 2262, 3162, 3188, 3305, 3362, 3363, 3663, 3765

Racketeer Influenced and Corrupt Organizations Act of 1970 (RICO), 2074, 2602, 2902, 2905, 3372, 3400, 3402, 3838, 3854

Rail Passenger Service Act of 1970, 2801

Railroad Retirement Act of 1934, 636

Railroad Retirement Act of 1974, 1957, 2162

Railroad Revitalization and Regulatory Reform Act of 1976, 3133

Railway Labor Act (RLA), 799, 990, 1113, 1998, 2266, 2342, 2672, 3109, 3359, 3912

Railway Labor Act of 1926, 581

Railway Labor Act of 1934, 661

Real Property Acquisition Policies Act, 2603

Reclamation Act of 1902, 1032, 1943

Reconstruction Civil Rights Act of 1871, 3749

Reduce Taxation Act of 1894, 301

Refugees Act of 1980, 2703, 3106, 3636, 3828

Regulate Commerce Act of 1887, 279

Rehabilitation Act of 1973, 2011, 2219, 2464, 2640, 2755, 2758, 2775, 2897, 3000, 3036, 3100, 3241

Religious Freedom Restoration Act (RFRA), 3435

Removal Act of 1875, 250

Rent Control, 3227

Resource Conservation and Recovery Act of 1976 (RCRA), 3381, 3679

Resource Conservation and Recovery Act (RCRA) of 1980, 2791

Resource Conservation and Recovery Act of 1984 (RCRA), 3880

Retail Competition Enforcement Act of 1987, 3245

Revenue Act of 1918, 576

Revenue Act of 1924, 579, 615, 618

Revenue Act of 1926, 583, 618

Revenue Act of 1928, 628, 679, 739

Revenue Act of 1932, 721, 727, 805

Revenue Act of 1934, 720

Revenue Act of 1936, 760

Revenue Act of 1938, 846

Rivers and Harbors Act of 1890, 332

Rivers and Harbors Appropriations Act of 1899, 2216

Robinson-Patman Act, 945, 1339, 1742, 1922, 1937, 1959, 2227, 2473, 2482, 2865, 3485, 3829

Robinson-Patman Act of 1936, 807, 1077

Rock Island Transition and Employee Assistance Act of 1980, 2330

Rosebud Indian Reservation 1889, 1830

Rules of Decision Act, 1289

Rural Electrification Act, 2512

SSI (Supplemental Social Income for the Aged, Blind and Disabled), 2320, 2402

Safety-appliance Act of 1893, 405

Second War Powers Act of 1942, 802

Secondary Education Act of 1965, 2900

Securities Act of 1933, 650, 950, 1702, 1746, 1995, 2105, 2173, 2459, 2587, 2850, 3338, 3957

Securities Act of 1934, 2070, 2459, 3162, 3233

Securities Exchange Act, 1157

Securities Exchange Act of 1933, 2850, 2866

Securities Exchange Act of 1934, 1352, 1386, 1702, 1746, 1951, 1956, 2013, 2105, 2334, 2459, 2587, 2794, 2850, 2858, 3162, 3213, 3408, 3594, 3623, 3806, 3873, 4028

Security Treaty, 1016

Sedition Act of 1798, 1179

Selective Service Act, 1266

Selective Service Act of 1917, 443

Selective Training and Service Act of 1940, 779, 822

Seneca Indians Treaty of 1797, 432

Sentencing Reform Act of 1984, 3300

Sequoia National Park Act of 1926, 1492

Serviceman's Group Life Insurance Act of 1965, 2292

Sheppard-Towner Maternity Act of 1921, 507

Sherman Act, 1356, 1817, 1864, 1872, 1897, 1903, 1937, 1939, 1977, 2045, 2065, 2232, 2235, 2252, 2253, 2311, 2367, 2394, 2434, 2733, 2820, 2879, 2906, 3401, 3576, 3843

Sherman Antitrust Act, 1717, 3793

Sherman Antitrust Act of 1890, 299, 320, 333, 355, 361, 376, 387, 398, 401, 413, 450, 467, 487, 488, 492, 503, 526, 549, 552, 604, 711, 716, 728, 759, 792, 806, 813, 814, 852, 870, 900, 913, 945, 949, 962, 963, 991, 1000, 1021, 1068, 1090, 1136, 1157, 1302, 1312, 1339, 1348, 1361, 1490, 1703, 2103, 2718, 2865

Sioux Treaty of 1868, 380

Slave Trade Act of 1818, 104

Slave Trade Clause, 95

Smith Act, 1057, 1058, 1093

Smith Act of 1940, 914, 1012, 1107

Snyder Act, 1622

Social Security Act, 1081, 1402, 1502, 1728, 1790, 1826, 1860, 1861, 1877, 1948, 2022, 2028, 2134,

2188, 2231, 2319, 2320, 2385, 2414, 2515, 2987, 3276
Social Security Act of 1935, 669, 670, 671, 1366, 1687, 1822
Social Security Act of 1972, 2272
Social Security Act of 1977, 2643
Social Security Amendment Act of 1983, 3016
Social Security Act, Aid to Families with Dependent Children (AFDC), 2136, 2141 *See also* Aid to Families with Dependent Children (AFDC).
Social Security Act, Medicaid Program, 2147, 2148 *See also* Medical Assistance (Medicaid) Program.
Social Security Act, Medicare Program, 2353, 2354
Social Security Act, Supplemental Security Income, 2402 *See also* Supplemental Social Income for the Aged, Blind and Disabled (SSI).
Soil Conservation and Domestic Allotment Act, 1395
Soldiers' and Sailors' Civil Relief Act of 1940, 3777
Solid Waste Disposal Act, 3725
Solomon Amendment, 2754
Speedy Trial Act, 2922, 2986
Speedy Trial Act of 1974, 3274
Staggers Rail Act of 1980, 2330, 2712, 3081
Stock-Raising Homestead Act of 1916, 2532
Submerged Lands Act, 1840, 2391
Subversive Activities Control Act of 1950, 987, 995, 1201, 1305
Subversive Activities Control Act of 1954, 1106, 1235
Summary Suspension Act of 1950, 994
Sunshine Act, 2673
Superfund, 2951, 3349
Supplemental Social Income for the Aged, Blind and Disabled (SSI), 2320 *See also* Social Security Act, Supplemental Security Income.
Supremacy Clause, 3308
Surface Mining Control and Reclamation Act of 1977, 2249, 2250
Surface Transportation Assistance Act of 1982, 3127
Surplus Property Act of 1944, 980

Taft-Hartley Act, 907, 1063, 1268, 2264, 2507, 3819. *See also* Labor Management Relations Act.
Taft-Hartley Act of 1947, 1634, 2264, 2892, 3242, 3890. *See also* Labor Management Relations Act of 1947.
Taft-Hartley Amendment, 1377
Taking Clause, 2944
Tariff Act of 1883, 292
Tariff Act of 1890, 282 *See also* Wilson Tariff Act of 1890.
Tariff Act of 1922, 562, 571, 613
Tariff Act of 1930, 613
Tax Equity and Fiscal Responsibility Act of 1982, 2633

Tax Injunction Act, 2199, 2293, 2396
Tax Injunction Act of 1982, 3396
Tax Reform Act of 1986, 3902
Tax Reform Bill of 1984, 2631
Tenure of Office Act of 1867, 536
Tonkin Bay Resolution of 1964, 1307
Trade Act of 1974, 1766
Trade Expansion Act of 1962, 1766
Trade Secrets Act, 1983
Trademark Act of 1946, 2378, 3729
Traders with Indians Statutes, 2143
Trading with the Enemy Act, 531, 1031, 1278
Transportation Act of 1920, 478, 492, 513
Treason Clause, 808
Treaty of 1783, 115
Treaty of 1794, 818
Treaty of 1819, 148
Treaty of 1852, 2542
Treaty of 1853, 264
Treaty of 1854, 2035
Treaty of 1855, 2035
Treaty of 1856, 751
Treaty of 1858, 3004
Treaty of 1859, 364, 746
Treaty of 1866, 751
Treaty of 1867, 1684
Treaty of 1868, 1043
Treaty of 1924, 613
Treaty of Paris of 1803, 111
Treaty of Peace of 1794, 115
Treaty with Great Britain of 1925, 548
Truth in Lending Act, 2054, 2246, 2247, 2445
Tucker Act, 343, 2081, 2288, 2375, 2575, 2916, 3406

Uniform Code of Military Justice, 992, 993, 1009, 1652, 1670, 1689, 1743, 3199
Uniform Criminal Extradition Act, 2174
Uniform Relocation Act of 1970, 2603
Uniformed Services Former Spouses' Protection Act, 3340
United States Housing Act of 1937, 1449
United States Warehouse Act of 1916, 847
Universal Military Training and Service Act, 966, 1412, 1470
Universal Military Training and Service Act of 1948, 1218, 1326
Urban Mass Transportation Act of 1964, 2380

Veterans' Benefits Act, 3144
Veterans' Emergency Housing Act of 1946, 1042
Veterans' Preference Act of 1950, 994
Veterans' Reemployment Rights Act, 3636
Victim and Witness Protection Act of 1982, 3452
Victims of Crime Act of 1984, 3451
Vietnam Era, Veterans' Assistance Act, 2114

Vietnam Era Veterans' Readjustment Assistance Act of 1974, 2261
Volstead Act of 1919, 463
Voting Rights Act, 2627, 2655, 3588, 3757, 3763, 3931
Voting Rights Act of 1965, 1244, 1262, 1355, 1360, 1423, 1567, 1590, 1711, 1736, 1745, 1821, 1946, 2087, 2089, 2244, 2390, 2451, 2472, 2792, 3082, 3604, 3605, 3647, 3841, 3929, 4019, 4035
Voting Rights Act Amendments of 1970, 1421
Voting Rights Act of 1981, 3841
Voting Rights Act of 1982, 3040

WARN (Worker Adjustment and Retraining Notification Act), 3991
Wagner-Peyser Act, 2432
War Claims Act of 1948, 1034
War Labor Disputes Act of 1943, 842
War Risk Insurance Act, 770

War-time Prohibition Act of 1918, 454
Warsaw Convention, 2799, 3330
Water Quality Improvement Act of 1970, 1565
Webb-Kenyon Act of 1913, 433
Westfall Act, 4005
Wetlands Act of 1961, 2479
Wheeler-Lea Amendment of 1938, 1483
White Slave Traffic Act of 1910, 412, 434
Wild Free-roaming Horses and Burros Act, 1765
Wildlife Refuge Revenue Sharing Act, 2215
Williams Act, 2404, 2858
Williams Act of 1968, 3119
Wilson Tariff Act of 1890, 552. *See also* Tariff Act of 1890.
Worker Adjustment and Retraining Notification Act (WARN), 3991

YCA (Federal Youth Correction Act), 2297, 2490

CASE SUBJECT INDEX

This index links each entry number of a case to a topic or subject.

Abortion, 1448, 1548, 1549, 1968, 3005, 3268, 3281, 3378, 3788
    advertising, 1705
    blockades, 3749
    consent of parent(s) or spouse, 1792, 1794, 2034, 2196, 2548, 2549, 3501, 3502, 3732;
      notification of, 3218
    counseling, 3570
    demonstrations, 3278, 3854, 3926
    doctors' views, 2977
    homeless, 1861, 1862, 2148
    lifesaving measures for fetus, 1953
    Medicaid, 1793, 1860, 1861, 2147, 2148
    performed in licensed medical facilities, 2550
    public hospitals, 1862
    second physician present, 2549
    wait period, 3732
Academic. *See* education, academic.
Access to government records, 2067, 2068, 2171, 2324, 2760; classified, 1547, 2294
Access to information, 2647, 2673, 3331. *See also* freedom of information.
Admiralty law. *See* maritime law.
Admission to the Union,
    Louisiana, 140
    Oklahoma, 404
Adoption, 1730, 1986, 2577, 3844
Adult bookstores/theaters, 1774, 2241, 2873, 2876, 2937, 3057, 3305
Advertising, 646, 749, 880, 1039, 1179, 1591, 1705, 1872, 2285, 2570, 2970, 3046, 3835, 4039
    alcohol, 2715, 4039
    birth control, 2570
    direct mailing, 3257
    discount airfares, 3695
    editorial advertising time, 1574, 2281
    eyeglasses, 968, 1171
    legal services, 1872, 2317, 2849, 3257, 3908, 4013
    magazines, 3773
    milk marketing, 2700
    political, 1661, 1905, 3950
    prescription drugs, 1756
    utility bill inserts, 2125, 2126, 2936

Aerial surveillance, 2982, 2983. *See also* search and seizure; wiretapping and surveillance.
    helicopter, 3302
Affirmative action, 2243, 2711, 2985, 3048, 3049, 3050, 3096, 3111, 3303, 3346, 3997. *See also* race discrimination; racial quotas.
    employment preferences, 1649
    federal, 3503
    set asides, 2151, 3821
    voluntary plan, 2027
Age discrimination, 2275, 2766, 2868, 2870, 3370, 3390, 3561, 3562, 3593, 3607, 3781, 3948, 4002, 4036
    mandatory retirement, 1783, 1879
    state, 1994, 2476
Agency regulations. *See* regulations; states, regulations.
Agriculture, 854, 2700, 3101
    cooperatives, 695, 1920, 2705
    disaster relief, 3011
    farm labor, 2006, 2432
    farms, 638, 659, 701, 857, 3231
    livestock, 242, 483; grazing, 399, 400, 406, 1944
    production, 643, 644, 758
    protection against disease or infection, 561
    state regulation, 759, 871, 1393
    tenant farmers, 1395
Aiding and abetting, 2108, 2438
Air pollution, 370, 426
    air quality standards, 1780, 2721
      business penalized, 3484
      state, 1073
    vehicle emissions, 1494, 3051, 3206
Airlines or airplanes or airports. *See* aviation.
Alcohol/liquor, 497, 540, 1392, 1537, 2065, 2434
    advertisements, 2715; price, 4039
    alcoholism, 3241
    chronic alcoholic, 1345
    beer, 1077, 1261, 1555, 2103, 2482
    contents labeling, 3976
    drinking age, 1808
    drunk driving, 999, 1263, 1784, 2466, 2681, 2706, 2743, 3316, 3456, 3664, 3842
    drunkenness, 11, 2466, 3187
    illegal distilling business, 1216

illegal transporting, 521, 560, 585, 623, 892, 1227
licenses (to sell), 2589, 2771
moonshine, 516, 523, 524, 1237
prohibition, 210, 257, 258, 433, 454, 463, 527,
    546, 548, 556, 558, 584, 601, 602, 609, 610,
    612
race discrimination, 1510
regulations, 141, 260, 270, 276, 641, 2448, 2998
sales, 1676, 2269, 2448, 3075, 3453; illegal, 284
students' possession, 1683
taxes. *See* corporate taxes, alcoholic beverages.
Aliens, 2661, 2695, 2703, 2723, 2759. *See also*
  immigration.
    asylum, 3106, 3151
    Australians, 816
    Belgians, 1534
    Bulgarians, 1081
    Canadian, 591, 592
    Chinese, 263
    Dutch, 1600
    Filipino, 3266
    French, 264
    G-4 visa status, 2415
    Greek, 922
    Haitians, 2888, 3633, 3828
    Hungarian, 572
    Irish, 3641
    Italians, 922
    Japanese, 280, 349, 493, 494, 509, 510, 511, 512,
        517, 525, 622, 857, 872
    Mexican, 959, 1464, 1719, 1803, 2843
    Puerto Ricans, 2432
    resident, 872, 1853, 2444
    Rumanians, 941
    Russian, 922
    Thai, 2610
    Ukrainian, 2176
    undocumented, 2389
Amendments to the Constitution. *See* Constitution,
  amendments.
Animal rights, 294, 3564. *See also* agriculture,
  livestock; endangered species; hunting; wildlife.
Antitrust, 355, 376, 997, 1007, 1494, 2312, 2487,
  2654, 2677, 2718, 2820, 2821, 2865, 2879, 2946,
  2959, 2992, 3066, 3119, 3245
    acquiring stock, 1681
    alcohol, 2065, 2434, 3075. *See also* antitrust,
      beer.
    anticompetitive activity, 991, 1261, 1356, 1703,
      3550, 3576
    beer, 1077, 1261, 1555, 2103, 2482. *See also*
      antitrust, alcohol.
    boycott, 1939
    by an association, 1903, 1920, 2367, 2465, 2798
    candy, 807, 945

city ordinance, 2311
cooperatives, 2865
electricity, 1897
entertainment, 503, 870, 962, 1053, 2235
foreign countries, 1136
gasoline, 360, 711, 1922
hospital, 2252
influencing legislation, 1090
insurance, 1961, 2252, 2399, 2417, 3843
meat dealers, 361, 604
mergers, 1130, 1169, 1261, 1386, 1555, 1813,
    3382, 3447, 3541
monopoly 237, 299, 320, 361, 387, 398, 401, 450,
    465, 467, 538, 549, 991, 1157, 1627, 1681,
    1717, 3752, 3793
newspapers, 814, 1356, 3382
nonprofit exemption, 1742
overcharging, 3496
price discrimination, 807, 945, 1077, 1742, 1937,
    1959, 2227, 2473, 2482, 3485
price fixing, 333, 492, 538, 624, 644, 711, 870,
    913, 1302, 1348, 1356, 1490, 1703, 1937, 1977,
    2103, 2253, 2394, 2644, 2990, 3245, 3328,
    3401, 3450, 3702
price war, 655, 3829
real estate, 2045
regulated industries, 1804
resale prices, 398, 450, 655, 900, 913, 945, 1068,
    1312, 2473
restraint of trade, 467, 526, 549, 552, 792, 806,
    813, 852, 855, 1136, 1490, 1681, 1804, 1864,
    1872, 2235, 2399
shipping rates, 1243
shoes, 1130
sports, 487, 949, 963, 1000, 1302, 1513, 2733,
    4045
taxicabs, 852
threefold damage, 387, 488, 716, 900, 1000,
    1136, 1243, 1312, 1339, 1344, 1484, 1813,
    1851, 1880, 2008, 2227, 2232, 2482
trading stamps, 1483
transporting, 413
tying agreements, 1021, 1361, 1699, 1817, 3697
unfair method of competition, 445, 594
Appeals, 1480, 1536, 1706, 1892, 2183, 2214, 2390,
  3959
    abstention, 1794
    aggravating factors, 3506
    briefs filed, 3637
    by a fugitive, 3768, 3963
    capital punishment, 948, 2564, 3033, 3443
    change in law, 1233
    direct appeal, 2651
    disclosure of evidence, 1274
    disqualification of counsel, 2628, 2871

errors, 645, 698, 2352, 2445

failure to obtain evidence, 1211

federal evidentiary hearings, 3681

filing, 937, 2917, 3524

harmless error, 835, 1099, 1273, 2620, 3052; by
    attorney, 1211, 2518. *See also* attorney, error.

interlocutory order, 2183

intervention, 389

lack of controversy, 2313

lack of evidence, 1194, 2029

moot point, 484, 960, 1974, 2076, 2219, 2330,
    2331, 2339, 2467, 2516, 3933

on set aside verdict, 1818

parallel litigation, 2468

prosecutorial vindictiveness, 2421

remanded, 1965, 2014, 2015, 2231, 2296, 2431,
    2467

substitute for appeal, 1802

validity of state law, 554, 555, 569, 2392

Appearance. *See* personal appearance.

Application for Stay, 1426, 1535, 1819, 1854, 2238,
    2468, 2785, 3615, 3734, 3788, 3844

Arbitration, 950, 1078, 1079, 1080, 1121, 1275,
    1612, 1619, 1823, 2234, 2468, 2528, 3338, 3562,
    3946, 3960, 3989

Armed Forces, 1027, 2883, 3144, 3199. *See also*
    military; national guard; veterans; war.

injuries, 3205

Arrest, 530, 892, 1279, 1359, 1716, 2078, 2267,
    2406, 2485

    bail denied, 2331

    Congress member, 26, 31, 1532

    drugs, 2828, 3842

    hearing, 3563, 3870

    incident to, 1608, 1609

    of children, 32, 2016

    pre-arrest silence, 2116

    probable cause, 1014, 1138, 1337, 2003

    in public place, 1773

    right to remain silent, 1707, 2337, 2925, 3782;
        denied, 3273

    under false identification, 2025

    without warrant, 521, 1044, 1165, 1726, 2003,
        2020, 2083

Arson. *See* fire.

Associations, 906, 1114, 1137, 1903, 2306, 3267. *See
    also* freedom of association.

    affiliated with radical organization, 816, 935,
        1066, 1081, 1100, 1107, 1347

    agreements, 3331

    boycotting, 2441

    campaign financing, 2276, 2300, 2453

    discipline, 1913, 1914

    dues, 3019

    as homeless, 3746

membership, 1036, 1066, 1087, 1148, 1235, 1254

political, 943, 2447, 3268

private clubs, 1510

regulations or standards, 2341, 2367

right to meet, 916

speech, 1526, 3465

subversive, 914, 916, 920, 959, 987, 1005, 1018,
    1029, 1030, 1035, 1057, 1058, 1093, 1100,
    1106, 1107, 1148, 1201, 1224, 1230, 1235,
    1272, 1303, 1305, 1427

Asylum, 3106, 3151, 3641, 3646, 3828

Attorneys, 164, 173, 190, 296, 923, 2518, 2877,
    3469, 3471, 3622. *See also* right to counsel.

    advertising, 1872, 2317, 2849, 3257, 3908, 4013

    bad faith conduct, 3590

    client privilege, 1751

    conduct, 2590, 3656; in proceedings, 2397

    debt collecting, 3971

    depositions, 2531

    error, 2772, 3750. *See also* appeals, harmless
        error, by attorney.

    fees, 42, 1314, 1571, 1577, 1641, 2106, 2107,
        2110, 2136, 2154, 2329, 2374, 2588, 2833,
        2889, 2894, 2966, 3035, 3045, 3051, 3062,
        3181, 3206, 3362, 3363, 3366, 3401, 3430,
        3741, 3865; assessing state, 1930; contingent
        fee, 3440; court fees, 21, 1694, 2133, 2652,
        3532; enhanced, 3725; expert witness fees,
        3540; filing deadline, 3831; formula, 2514;
        prevailing defendant or party, 1883, 2141,
        2514; self-representation, 3552

    frivolous lawsuits, 3387, 3479

    immunity, 3583

    independent counsel, 3282

    ineffective, 2912, 3029

    law school, 688, 856, 896, 1635, 2484

    legal assistance, 1353

    legal materials, 1836, 4046

    malpractice, 172, 186, 2042

    prosecuting attorney, 1731, 2318, 2786, 3830

    public defender, 2301, 2724

    representation, 3333

    solicitation of clients, 1913, 1914

    state bar, 811, 1004, 1005, 1100, 1114, 1600,
        1703, 2484, 2796, 3177; denied admission,
        1151, 1427; dues usage, 3465

    suspension, 2881

Automobiles, 880, 1227, 2781, 2923, 4040. *See also*
    air pollution, vehicle emissions; product liability,
    automobiles; search and seizure, automobiles;
    search and seizure, recreational vehicles.

    airbags, 2569

    contract, 2054, 2246

    design, 3263

    driver license, 2874

drunk driving, 999, 1263, 1784, 2466, 2681,
   2706, 2743, 3316, 3456, 3664
gasoline, 360, 711, 1922
hit and run, 1453
junk dealers, 1770
license plate, 1833
loans, 2054
manufacturing, 2906
odometer tampering, 3320
sobriety checkpoints, 3481
stolen, 522
title altering, 3516
traffic violation, 2940
used for stealing, 1096
Aviation, 1120, 2799. *See also* aerial surveillance.
   air cargo liability limits, 2662
   airlines, 862, 2298, 3036; advertising, 3695;
      deregulation, 3112; frequent flyer program,
      3944; liability, 3330; pilots, 3539; taxes, 2601,
      3094
   airplanes, 1710; accidents, 1541, 3339, 4024;
      crash, 2298, 2647; sales, 2547; stolen, 587
   airports, 1568, 3175, 3339, 3727, 3731, 3858;
      authority, 3600; parking lots, 2769
   fuel taxes, 3014
Awards from trials, 242, 1080, 2051, 2278, 2284,
   3026, 3055, 3205, 3214, 3384, 3434, 3471, 3513,
   3592, 3917
   valuation, 3254

Bail, 2331, 3148, 3149, 3464
Bankruptcy, 39, 48, 72, 101, 563, 608, 652, 1265,
   2774, 2838, 2934, 3885, 3905, 3940, 3983
   chapter 7 (liquidation), 3591, 3596
   chapter 11 (corporate reorganization), 696, 715,
      1332, 3368, 3596, 3972; corporate, 699, 2538,
      3457, 3632, 3650
   chapter 13 (reorganization), 2538, 3591, 4020
   court jurisdiction, 2416, 3662
   creditor, 3222, 3231, 3368
   debt payment, 3525
   federal-tax payments, 3467
   filing deadlines, 3680, 3772
   filing fees, 1544, 1557
   foreclosure sale, 701, 3889, 3933
   jury trial, 1239
   labor contract, 2637
   liens, 625, 1076, 2446, 2538, 3222, 3311, 3574,
      3575, 3644
   liquidation. *See* bankruptcy, chapter 7
   mortgage, 638, 659, 3231, 3808, 3815
   reorganization. *See* bankruptcy, chapter 13
   restitution obligations, 3069, 3458
   retirement plans, 3488, 3707
   transfer of funds, 3669

   uniformity requirement, 2330
Banks and banking, 73, 74, 91, 92, 151, 153, 654,
   1394, 2334, 2734, 2929, 2935, 3548, 3905. *See also*
   money; property, mortgage; regional banking.
   bankrupt, 563, 3905
   branches, 3078
   checking: account, 2422; hold, 4020; sufficient
      funds, 1265, 4025
   credit, 2887
   depositor, 1679; insurance, 393, 2991
   due-on-sale, 2418
   Federal Reserve Bank, 3625
   fraud, 300, 2422, 2544
   holding companies, 1487, 2109, 2182, 2736,
      3232, 3421
   incorporated, 117
   insurance sales, 1487, 2535, 3814, 3945, 4033
   interest, 2073
   international, 1278, 1505, 2554, 3271, 3462, 3701
   investment advisory service, 2109, 2182
   joint accounts, 2885
   loans, 2054, 2246, 2445, 2905, 4020
   mergers, 1169, 1666, 2767
   notes, 116, 128, 3408
   records, 1752, 3271
   securities sales, 1441, 2736, 3078
   taxes, 176, 704, 1463, 2460, 2594, 3556, 3557
   unincorporated, 106
Bargaining agreement. *See* labor; unions.
Benefits, 636, 669, 1554, 1904, 1935, 2063, 2162,
   2225, 2312, 2568, 2571, 2599, 2852, 2893, 2944,
   2987, 3016, 3118, 3225, 3344, 3398, 3614, 3665,
   3678, 3781. *See also* taxes in general, benefits.
   after termination, 3517
   disability, 770, 1629, 2515, 2812, 3276, 3340,
      3480. *See also* workers' compensation.
   discrimination, 1687, 1788, 1806, 1822, 1826,
      2022, 2088, 2558, 2599, 2643
   employers' obligations, 1956, 2523, 3799, 3820,
      3951
   health, 2335, 2558, 2878, 3742, 3961, 4031
   insurance. *See* insurance.
   investments as, 3781
   maternity leave. *See* pregnancy rights, maternity
      leave.
   mental health. *See* mental health, benefits.
   military, 16, 1569, 1847, 2277, 2292, 2898
   multiemployer benefit fund, 2280, 2667, 3146,
      3819
   pension mismanagement, 3804
   plans, 2716, 3117, 3665
   retirement. *See* retirement, benefits.
   Social Security. *See* Social Security.
   vacation, 3329
   veterans. *See* veterans, benefits.

unemployment. *See* unemployment,
  compensation.
  welfare. *See* welfare, benefits.
Bill of Rights. *See* Constitution, Bill of Rights;
  freedom of assembly; freedom of association;
  freedom of expression; freedom of information;
  freedom of press; freedom of religion; freedom of
  speech; right to counsel; right to petition; right to
  privacy.
Birth control, 762, 1109, 1231, 1489, 2570
  sales to minors, 1850
Block mergers, 3066
Bonds, 4, 192, 240, 582, 720, 3240
  mass transit, 1837
  railroads, 158, 631
  state, 230, 256
Boundary dispute, 181, 290, 1830, 2255, 2256, 2270,
  2302, 2657, 3500, 3579, 3739. *See also* freedom of
  religion, church property disputes.
  federal-state, 3677
  interstate, 2783, 2790
  oceanfront, 2391
  water, 2489
Boycotts, 477, 1939, 2127, 2441, 2573, 3242
Breathalyzer test, 2706
Bribery, 1158, 2308, 3372, 3400, 3411, 3691
  elections, 352, 1051, 2348
  federal grants, 2636
  influencing member of Congress, 1529
Broadcasting. *See* communications, broadcasting;
  television.
Business. *See* corporate taxes; corporations;
  employees; franchise; licensing, business; retail
  trade.

Cable television. *See* television, cable.
Campaign, *See* elections, campaign.
Candidates, *See* elections, candidates.
Capital punishment, 71, 93, 213, 948, 1528, 1795,
  1796, 1797, 1819, 1876, 2438, 2578, 2604, 2607,
  2744, 2779, 2867, 2930, 2980, 3022, 3033, 3128,
  3511, 3688, 3706, 3751, 3947
  abusive, 3719
  aggravating circumstances, 2098, 2361, 2564,
    3506, 3527, 3699, 3775
  by electricity, 273, 277, 838
  by legal injection, 2785, 2814
  children, 3285, 3375
  commutation of death sentence, 2597
  court error, 3737
  crimes impact, 3618
  death by legal injection, 2785, 2814
  death penalty, 2595, 2622, 3497
  death sentence, prior record, 2596
  exclusion for good behavior, 2973

extraneous circumstances, 887
factors (death), 2605
failure to execute, 838
indifferent to human life, 3122
insane, 3030
intentional murder, 3853
Judge's verdict, 3954; trial judge, 3504
jury, 1316, 1333, 1451, 1941, 2137, 2976, 2981,
  3143, 3341, 3418, 3930; instructions, 867,
  1410, 2564, 3086, 3420, 3422, 3431, 3497,
  3512, 3612, 3753, 3901, 3909
lesser offense, 1419, 2128, 2369
life sentence, 3185
mandatory, 1798, 1799, 1848, 2869, 3415, 3909
maximum punishment, 3566
mentally disabled, 3374
mitigating circumstances, 1941, 1942, 2314,
  3130, 3208, 3527, 3833
presentence report, 1827
right to counsel, 3367
robbery, 2930
stop execution, 2595, 2600, 2604, 2607, 2785,
  3928, 4037
testimony, 2000
third party appeal, 3443
victims impact, 3173, 3347
Casinos, 2745, 2999. *See also* gambling.
Censorship, 595, 998, 1013, 1064, 1110, 1133, 1196,
  1246, 1429, 1558, 1585, 1637, 1655, 1665, 2190,
  2230, 3219. *See also* child pornography;
  pornography.
  books, 1245
  bookstore, 1512, 3057
  by zoning, 1774
  community standards, 1656, 1841, 1852
  movies, 929, 1062, 1089, 1215, 1318, 1656, 1708,
    2072, 2129
  obscenity. *See* obscenity; post office, obscene
    matter.
  and pornography, 1015, 1364, 1584. *See also*
    freedom of speech, pornography.
  publications, 1139, 1247, 1283, 1317, 1404, 1527,
    1737, 3228
  sado-masochistic materials, 1852
  theater production, 1686
Charities, 2520, 2522, 3454. *See also* fund raising;
  nonprofits.
Child abuse, 2314, 2331, 3288, 3292, 3309, 3405,
  3870
  hearsay statements, 3507, 3642, 3941
  jurisdiction, 3705
  records, 3091
  testify, 3508
  trial, 3627
Child custody. *See* children, custody.

Child labor, 415, 444, 484, 485, 658, 781, 2091
Child Pornography, 1125, 2437, 3361, 3442, 3675, 3935. *See also* pornography.
Child support, 1556, 1882, 2350, 2530, 2957, 2971, 3142
   majority age, 1690
   Social Security insurance disregarded, 3482
Children, 330, 1318, 3965. *See also* abortion, consent of parent(s); illegitimate children; teenage pregnancy.
   abandonment, 2254
   arrest or confession, 32, 2016
   court jurisdiction, 1248, 1284, 1400
   criminal record, 1624, 1825, 2023, 2490
   custody, 1491, 2224, 2671, 3844; termination, 2240, 2345, 2428
   deport, 3770
   food stamps, 1595
   foster, 3667
   inheritance, 338, 1439
   institutionally commit, 2014, 2015
   parental notification, 3218
   preventive detention, 2698
   restricting access to objectionable materials, 3326
   right to jury trial, 1467
   sales of objectionable literature to, 1139, 1317
   sentenced as an adult, 2297, 3664
   Social Security benefits, 1790, 1877, 2028, 3404
   tried as an adult, 1696, 2297, 2314
   witness. *See* witness, children as.
Christmas Cribs/Crèche, 2642, 2824, 3379
Church and state, 2836, 2874, 2884, 2933, 2955, 3003. *See also* freedom of religion.
   church-operated hospital, 334
   evolution, 3176
   federal aid, 2900
   nativity scene, 2642, 2824, 3379. *See also* church and state, religious display.
   prayer, 1132, 1167, 1168, 1187, 2592, 2860, 3216, 3724
   private schools, 528, 578, 839, 1468, 1563, 1594, 1603, 1604, 2581, 3037, 3823; aid to, 1693, 1868, 2058; state aid, 2899; teachers, 1971; textbook loans, 1342, 1593
   private universities, 1469, 1602, 1768, 2522
   property, 271, 934, 1476, 2033
   public schools, 2956, 3473, 3811, 3925; Bible reading, 919, 1167, 1187; flag salute, 718, 773; prayer, 1132, 1167, 1168, 1187, 3724; religious instruction, 865, 927, 1346; Ten Commandments posted, 2156
   public universities, 2299, 4018
   records, 3268
   religious display, 2156, 4017. *See also* Christmas Cribs/Crèche; church and state, nativity scene.

   ritual sacrifices, 3818
   sacramental drug use, 3435
   solicitation regulation, 712, 767
   taxes, 1038, 1338, 1403, 2237, 2319, 2396, 2522, 2581, 3399
Cities, 580, 652, 719, 1897, 2954, 3105, 3314. *See also* local taxes.
   annexation, 371, 1711, 2089
   authority, 3248
   bonds, 3240
   as corporations, 151, 453
   desegregation of public areas, 1160, 1388
   elections, 3319
   employees, 1599, 2475, 2503, 3229, 3655, 3894. *See also* public employees, city.
   immunity, 2084, 3550
   liability, 1918, 2780, 2855, 3764
   ordinance, 211, 239, 248, 321, 360, 425, 428, 453, 537, 680, 744, 756, 765, 767, 768, 786, 905, 915, 940, 1126, 1524, 1525, 1661, 1708, 1754, 1845, 2020, 2057, 2285, 2300, 2311, 3171, 3227, 3278, 3326; adult theaters, 1774, 2241, 2937; airport, 1568; grandfather clause, 1782; health, 2548; permit, 901, 902, 942, 2321, 2332; residency, 2626; streets, 697, 874, 879, 880, 902; used to discrimination, 441, 694; zoning, 2241, 2937, 3550
   police, 127, 211, 416, 1762, 1782, 2576
   privately owned, 819
   property, 3773
   public displays, 2642
   public improvements, 383
   public transportation, 574
   regulations, 905, 3265
   taxes, 80, 371
   use of public facilities, 1686
Citizenship, 115, 145, 193, 330, 1758, 2305, 2368
   by race, 216, 622
   dual, 931, 1026
   expatriation, 1024, 1026
   foreign voting, 1024, 1286
   in territories, 65, 281
   loss, 1025, 1141
   naturalization, 12, 493, 494, 532, 1085, 2608; revoked, 776, 1286; unwillingness to bear arms, 572, 591, 592, 825
   of Japanese Americans, 774, 775, 800, 801
   of Native Americans, 238, 247
   of Slaves, 154
   outside country, 37, 1123
   revoked, 2176
   serving in foreign military, 1026
Civil Procedure, 2324, 3615
   filing documents, 937, 3637
   rule 11 (attorneys' signatures), 3479, 3537, 3656

rule 23 (Class Action), 469, 719, 1238, 1314, 1433, 1556, 1610, 1614, 1629, 1637, 1668, 1677, 1725, 1806, 2073, 2076, 2094, 2543, 2557, 2619, 3366, 3390, 3534, 4028; communication ban, 2242; parties, 1713, 1749, 1757, 1843, 2242, 2386, 2414
  rule 34 (privilege matter), 938, 1031
  rule 35 (physical or mental examination), 723, 1205
  rule 37 (failure to produce documents), 1031, 2133, 2373
  rule 52 (erroneous), 2965
  rule 56 (Summary Judgment), 814, 3027
  rule 57 (Judgments, declaratory). *See* judgments, declaratory.
  rule 65 (Injunctions). *See* injunctions.
Civil Rights, 231, 1252, 1253, 1458, 1909, 2010, 2135, 2155, 2210, 2494, 2623, 3096, 3128 *See also* criminal offenses; race discrimination; sex discrimination.
  private discrimination, 1777
  protests, 1117, 1194, 1197, 1198, 1242, 1264, 1301
  violations, 3350
Civil War. *See* War, Civil.
Class Action Suit. *See* civil procedure; rule 23 (Class Action).
Collective bargaining. *See* labor, collective bargaining; unions, collective bargaining.
Colleges and universities, 3855. *See also* school desegregation/segregation, universities.
  bargaining, 2629
  disabled denied, 2011
  discrimination, 688, 856, 896, 897, 1635, 1936, 1993, 2436
  dormitories, 3377
  faculty, 2059; contract renewal, 1530
  federal funding, 2638
  financial aid. *See* financial aid.
  law school, 688, 856, 896, 1635, 2484
  medical school, 1887, 1936
  newspaper, 1558
  private universities, 1469, 1602, 1768, 2522
  public universities, 626, 2299, 4018
  resident status, 1578, 2415
  sports, 2733, 3294
  tenure. *See* employment discrimination, tenure.
  unions, 3584
Commercial speech, 2994, 3046, 3201, 3257, 3377, 3976, 4039. *See also* freedom of speech.
  advertising. *See* advertising.
  billboards, 2285, 3550
  editorial advertising time, 1574, 2281
  flyers, 3773
  letterhead, 3469

  licensing, 2332, 3393
  political action committees, 3071, 3429
  real estate signs, 1838
  solicitation to obtain clients, 1913, 1914, 3787, 4013
  tradename, 1958
  utility bill inserts, 2125, 2126
Communications. *See also* television.
  broadcasting, 1171, 1374, 1574, 1919, 2281, 2464; radio, 1601
  indecent, 3369
  license, 946, 989, 1374, 1574, 1919, 2201, 2464, 3503
Community property, 583, 795, 1631, 2197, 2277, 3340
Confession, 327, 764, 996, 1138, 1185, 1341, 1430, 1488, 1515, 1865, 2634, 3417, 3881, 4022. *See also* self-incrimination, confession.
  admissibility, 1647, 1814
  by codefendant, 2841, 2996, 3123, 3124
  coerced, 647, 791, 859, 937, 1147, 1270, 1406, 2841, 3002, 3547; by drugs, 1143, 1199
  guilty plea. *See* guilty plea.
  of children, 32
  orally, 3085
  under hypnosis, 3583
  voluntariness, 705, 793, 1060, 1095, 1159, 1199, 1407, 1750, 2093, 2140, 2406, 2915, 3002
  without counsel, 2961, 3371
Confidentiality, 1751, 3613
Conflict with federal laws (pre-empted), 2705, 2712, 2745, 2851, 2852, 3054, 3517, 3767, 3907
Confrontation, 2996, 3123. *See also* witness, right to confront.
Congress, 283, 290, 1286. *See also* congressional investigations; Constitution.
  delegation of powers, 399, 400, 562, 1766
  immunity from suits, 1285, 1695
  implied powers, 74
  laws or legislation, 395, 842, 1874, 1879, 2100, 2112, 2130, 2166, 2188, 2259, 2476, 2535, 3359. *See also* conflict with federal laws (pre-empted); constitutionality, 35, 1067, 1244, 2022, 3112; construction, 2135, 2136, 2262, 2336, 2499; date effective, 282, 573, 623, 1883; intent, 3306
  legislative power, 359, 598, 651, 689, 784, 1771, 2153, 3058, 3190, 3569, 3600, 3979; over courts, 93, 571, 643; separation of powers, 3671
  veto, 2565, 3112
  war powers, 471, 472, 637
Congress Members. *See also* reapportionment and redistricting.
  armed forces reserves, 1658
  arrested, 26, 31, 1532

bail, 26
censured, 1376
discipline, 1529
immunity from suits, 1285, 1695
impeachment, 222
speech or debate clause, 1529, 1532, 2004, 2024
Congressional Investigations. *See also* Congress.
    authority, 1010, 1058, 1695
    liability, 912
    mode of hearing, 1166
    quorum, 891
    witnesses, 222, 543, 570, 593, 971, 972;
        contempt, 939, 1010, 1058, 1093, 1166;
        perjury, 891
Conspiracy, 446, 448, 451, 458, 622, 741, 835, 916,
    995, 1012, 1428, 1937, 2155, 2193, 2593, 2718,
    2724, 3250
    interference with civil rights, 1252, 1253, 1458,
        2010, 2494
    national secrets, 948
    to cause riot, 2053
Constitution, 362, 639, 1657, 1865, 2061, 2351,
    2565, 3282. *See also* Congress, laws or legislation;
    freedom of assembly; freedom of association;
    freedom of expression; freedom of information;
    freedom of press; freedom of religion; freedom of
    speech; right to counsel; right to petition; right to
    privacy.
        Amendments, 216, 217, 223, 231, 337, 385, 463,
            479, 480, 673, 839, 3341; ratification, 23, 460,
            461, 474
        Bill of Rights, 124, 189, 196, 197, 198, 208,
            1137, 1167, 1168
        guarantee of liberty, 505
        historical patterns, 2592
        oath to support, 1040
Contempt of court, 369, 520, 738, 829, 866, 904, 923,
    1131, 1259, 1501, 3394, 3927
    congressional witness, 939, 1010, 1058, 1093,
        1129, 1166, 1192
    failure to comply with order, 723, 842, 1301,
        2496
    jury hearing, 1664
Contraceptives. *See* birth control.
Contracts, 51, 56, 69, 81, 137, 317, 363, 511, 621,
    633, 2036, 2316, 2801, 3009, 3303, 3412, 3767
    arbitration, 2468
    breach or breaking contract, 965, 2286, 2691,
        3524, 3743
    conflict of interest, 1088
    employment, 1207, 1530, 1531, 2430, 2507, 2668
    government, 1032, 1088, 3279
    illegal promises, 2312
    labor, 394, 1935, 2528, 2637, 3167, 3172; fraud,
        788

lending, 2246, 2445
obligation, 1837
purchase, 2054
refusal of delivery, 888
tickets, 3558
union, 3225
Contractors, 703, 2344, 2486, 2499, 2725, 2732
Copyright, 870, 2847, 2896, 3345, 3793
    infringement, 3537
    music, 1579, 1977, 2768, 3445, 3865, 3867
    performance, 1875
    photographs, 236
    short story, 3445
    Supreme Court Reporter, 126
    telephone book, 3549
    video recorders, 2617
    video rentals, 3793
Corporate taxes, 485, 619, 643, 644, 1111, 2309,
    3236, 3388. *See also* banks and banking, taxes;
    licensing, taxes; state taxes, multinational
    corporations; taxes in general.
        alcoholic beverages, 168, 641, 1542, 3466, 3609
        capital assets, 3232
        customer list, 3779
        excise, 357, 641, 1223, 2113, 4042
        foreign subsidiaries, 2233, 3711
        highway-use, 3472
        home office, 3745
        international. *See* international business, taxes.
        interstate, 2077, 2115, 3529
        inventory, 1723, 1955, 3067
        mining, 502, 2186, 2287
        motor carrier, 1023, 1824, 2142, 3532
        out-of-state business, 464, 908, 1188, 1223, 3692,
            3708
        property, 3094
        S corporations, 3754
        sole ownership, 771
        subsidiaries, 883, 1970, 2423, 2424
        takeover expenses, 3653
        unitary, 3290
        valorem property tax. *See* corporate taxes,
            inventory.
        valuation, 713
Corporations, 46, 175, 285, 1188, 1905, 2310. *See
    also* banks and banking; corporate taxes;
    employees; franchise; international business;
    interstate business; retail trade; securities.
        arbitration, 3989
        bankruptcy, 696, 699, 715, 1332, 2538, 3457,
            3596, 3632, 3650, 3972
        business records, 1644, 3270
        charters, 75, 117, 129, 131, 189, 210, 211
        government entities as, 151, 316, 453, 648, 820,
            3950

holding companies, 1487, 2109, 2182, 3421
hostile takeovers, 2858, 3119
illegal, 2262
import-export, 4042
incorporated, 117
liability, 3088, 3115, 3249, 3723, 3843, 3970,
    4029; of directors, 1706, 1990, 4027
licensing. *See* licensing, business.
mail-order, 3692
management, 1634
mergers, 3321
minority-owned, 2151, 3997
multinational, 48, 103, 387, 2387, 3388, 3914.
    See also international business.
nonprofit. *See* nonprofits.
officers and directors, 1390, 1706, 1990, 3233
partnerships. *See* partnerships.
price fixing, 545
reorganization. *See* corporations, bankruptcy.
securities registration, 650
stockholders, 153, 180, 648, 651, 699, 1867,
    2619; race discrimination, 512
stocks, 274, 355, 457, 513, 2070
subsidiaries, 2935
takeover, 2404
trade secrets, 1638
unincorporated, 106
County, 3351, 3959
    ordinance, 2851
Court fees, 21, 1694, 2133, 2652, 3532
Court jurisdiction, 97, 118, 171, 191, 289, 378, 395,
    769, 821, 987, 1372, 1635, 2170, 2484, 2585, 2670
    across state lines, 2646
    appeals, 52, 681, 1667, 2134
    bankruptcy court, 2416, 3662
    children's court, 1248, 1284, 1400
    circuit court, 57, 60, 195, 225, 235, 240, 351, 739
    claims court, 827, 1134, 2063, 2081, 2354, 3802
    concurrent state courts, 2284
    customs court, 571
    district court, 53, 503, 1338, 1772, 3104, 3170,
        3545, 3802
    diversity, 815, 844, 1289, 1926, 3380, 3705
    diversity of citizenship, 469, 1493, 2217, 3412
    federal court, 36, 43, 49, 654, 997, 1251, 1566,
        1762, 1831, 1932, 2076, 2132, 2263, 2264,
        2380, 2568, 2810, 2812, 2814, 2871, 2911,
        2913, 2917, 2935, 3015, 3088, 3093, 3115,
        3155, 3174, 3191, 3200
    federal common law, 2217, 2232, 2856
    federal or state courts, 107, 108, 155, 239, 248,
        508, 983, 1119, 1376, 1475, 1740, 1990, 2159,
        2224, 2621, 2624, 2844, 3060, 3402, 3433,
        3534, 3716, 3905
    federal question, 2856

filing requirements, 2326, 3558
juvenile court. *See* court jurisdiction, children's
    court.
maritime court. *See* maritime law, court
    jurisdiction.
military court, 159, 1652, 1689, 2375
minimum contact, 1867, 2047, 2048, 2373
multistate courts, 2284, 3423
over Native Americans, 121, 1043, 1424, 2635,
    2691
political question, 1122, 1785, 3451
regulatory, 708, 763, 841, 1622, 1698, 1724,
    1728, 1829, 1919, 2044, 2158, 2164, 2184,
    2353, 2529, 2534, 2614, 3625, 3827
size of jury verdict, 1818
state court, 54, 57, 67, 77, 296, 382, 653, 1631,
    2333, 2645, 2887, 3944, 3946
sue in United States court, 1880, 2298, 2517
Supreme Court. *See* Supreme Court, jurisdiction.
tax court assignments, 3619
territorial court, 232, 249, 818, 1618, 1684, 2142
tribal court, 1730, 1894, 2856, 3089, 3860; over
    nonmember, 225, 1889, 3463
Court-Martial, 757, 977, 1016, 1670, 1689, 1743,
    3199, 3918, 3995
    non-service connected crimes, 1372
    of civilians, 992, 993, 1009
    of wartime desertion, 1025
Court order, 60, 119, 289, 617, 766, 997, 3104
    state action, 730
Court procedure, 13, 269, 3974
    burden of proof, 1857, 2644
    co-defendant, 741, 1185, 1222, 1323, 1455, 1488,
        1899, 1999, 2952
    criminal intent, 481, 2012, 2470
    discriminatory, 1614
    due process, 152, 234, 383, 890, 917, 1020, 1557,
        1738, 1850, 1856, 1992, 2002, 2047, 2239,
        2328, 2412, 2698, 2706, 2730, 2803, 2845,
        2848, 2872, 2908, 2923, 2969, 3032, 3038,
        3098, 3166; states' jurisdiction, 3460
    equity, 608
    extradition, 156, 921
    federal courts, 3735, 3983; abstention, 2397
    filing requirements, 2326
    guilt by association, 1216
    guilt by presence, 1237
    hearings, 1665, 1997, 2328, 2353, 2444, 2496,
        3413, 3563, 3567
    judicial disqualification, 3866
    legislative intent, 607, 2061; reasonableness, 683
    limitation to file, 2536
    mootness, 2643
    notification to parties, 3515
    pleading, 3015

records, 1008; confidential, 3735
remedies, 1563, 2420
separate offenses, 597, 1096
settlements, 3883, 3900
served summons, 2364
transcript, 3813 ; fees, 985, 1761
two-tier court system, 1508
want of jurisdiction, 2230, 2362
writ of error, 170, 273
Credit Cards. See money, credit cards.
Crime Boss, 3148
Criminal Law, 2896, 3098, 3183
Criminal offenses:
    against victims on basis of race, religion, ethnic
        origin or other status, 198, 229, 235, 809, 926,
        1253, 1375, 1458, 3720, 3816
    assessment to aid victims, 3451
    committed by or against Native Americans, 232,
        249, 310, 1043, 1831, 1894, 2635, 3761, 3860
    criminal intent, 481, 2012, 2470
    dangerous special offenders, 2160; leave state,
        2254
    elements, 2842
    felon possession of gun, 2471, 2815, 3882
    felon registration, 1020
    habitual, 340, 410, 755, 1118, 1271, 1304
Criminal records, 1624, 1825, 2023, 2490, 3091,
    3322
Criminals. See freedom of press, criminal story;
    prison inmates.
Cruel and unusual punishment. See capital
    punishment.
Cult (Santeria), 3818
Customs, 571, 2923, 3230
    duties, 183, 292, 342, 343, 344, 562, 2450
    United States Customs Service, 3318

Damage claims/suits, 252, 629, 980, 1344, 1458,
    1891, 2374, 2375, 2478, 2494, 2575, 2662, 2663,
    2668, 2724, 2735, 2780, 2794, 2834, 2835, 2855,
    2919, 2927, 2928, 2954, 3140, 3141, 3178, 3220,
    3354, 3738, 3813, 3955. See also suits.
    against a city, 3105
    against federal agencies, 761, 1465, 2454, 3862,
        3969
    against federal officials, 2053, 2086, 2408, 2409,
        2431, 2545
    against a state, 3349, 3354
    against the United States, 2650, 2719
    awards, 3026, 3214; tax, 2051, 2284
    fees, 3364
    jury trial, 3424
    loss of society, 1616, 2092
    loss of wages, 2551
    mental anguish, 1616

pension mismanagement, 3804
property, 2650
punitive, 967, 1080, 1998, 2086, 2278, 2612,
    2969, 3601, 3640, 3877, 3917, 3919, 3960,
    4040; evil intent, 2501; excessive fines, 3373,
    3538, 4040; jury guidelines, 3836
wrongful death, 2362, 2670
Death Penalty. See capital punishment.
Debts, 15, 29, 386, 2412, 3586, 3778, 3971
    business, 1153
    federal, 3073
    imprisonment, 102
    lien, 6, 1909, 2446. See also Property, lien
    payments, 20, 1450
    promissory note, 27
    state, 59, 230, 1149
Defamation. See Libel
Desegregation of: See also school desegregation/
    segregation.
    housing, 1748, 3394
    prison, 2463
    public areas, 1160, 1388
Disability benefits, 770, 1629, 2515, 2810, 3276,
    3480, 3913. See also veterans, disability benefits;
    workers' compensation.
    insurance, 645, 1648, 3117, 3293
Disabled Rights, 2640, 2755, 2758, 3221, 3354,
    3823, 3845, 3925, 3984
    deaf, 2011, 2119, 2219, 2419, 2464
    discrimination against disabled, 2775, 2839,
        3000, 3036
    employment, 3100
    mentally retarded, 2901, 3286, 3374
Discount retailers. See retail trade.
Discovery. See trial, discovery.
Discrimination. See affirmative action; age
    discrimination; benefits, discrimination; colleges
    and universities, discrimination; civil rights;
    criminal offenses; disabled rights, discrimination;
    education, discrimination; employment
    discrimination; housing, discrimination; juries,
    discrimination; licensing, used to discriminate;
    military, discrimination; property, discrimination;
    race discrimination; reverse discrimination; school
    desegregation/segregation; sex bias; sex
    discrimination.
District of Columbia, 40, 42, 869, 958, 3235
    criminal courts, 1566
    rent control, 471
    taxes, 80
Disturbing the peace, 712, 885, 903, 1142, 1212,
    1213, 1347, 1418, 1456. See also picketing.
    demonstration, 1117, 1156, 1194, 1197, 1242,
        3235, 3854, 3926
    disorderly conduct, 1069, 1508

riots, 1633, 2053

Divorce, 341, 960, 1732
    alimony, 1963
    court fees, 1433
    decree, 2292
    property settlement, 1128, 1957, 2526, 3340
    residency, 347, 367, 1673
    survivor benefits, 2987

Double jeopardy, 497, 980, 1019, 1379, 1381, 1401, 1540, 1643, 1894, 2628, 2632, 2664, 2694, 2707, 2740, 2818, 2854, 2945, 3397, 3456, 3668, 3842, 3897
    consecutive sentences, 2085
    conviction reversed, 1921, 2221, 2381
    criminal and civil sanction, 679, 3336
    cumulative sentences, 2458
    death hearings, 2980
    failure to execute, 838
    hung jury, 90
    like charges, 4004
    mistrial, 2372
    prosecution from two difference states, 2914
    retry case, 1696, 2181, 2979, 3182, 3291
    review of sentence, 2160
    second offense punishment, 305, 2193, 2458, 2914
    sentencing procedure, 3859
    state and federal prosecutions, 1048, 1049, 2214

Draft. *See* military, draft.

Driving under the Influence (DUI), 3316. *See also* automobiles, drunk driving.

Drugs, 917, 1135, 1443, 1545, 1756, 1767, 1856, 2101, 2193, 2541, 2658, 2764, 2809, 2828, 3101, 3274, 3726, 3842, 3860, 4038
    banned, 3435
    ceremonial usage, 3435
    forcibly administered, 2392, 3685
    found in search and seizure, 860, 951, 1071, 1138, 1165, 1193, 1277, 1337, 1465, 1536, 1773, 1863, 1975, 2039, 2099, 2140, 2150, 2213, 2309, 2477, 2539, 2553, 2555, 2556, 2591, 2809, 2150, 3560, 3606, 3794
    generic, 2378, 2483
    illegal substances, 3569, 3668, 3897
    labeling, 3060. *See also* drugs, warning labels.
    manufacturing, 2952
    marijuana fields, 2659
    pharmaceutical products, 2473, 3060
    possession, 1001, 1044, 1387
    prescription identity, 1816
    refusal to employ users, 1973
    selling, 447, 481, 597, 1028, 1311, 1387, 1417, 1430, 1689, 2952, 3189, 3582, 3621; drug related materials, 2332, 3888
    sentencing and drugs. *See* sentencing, drugs.
    smuggling, 2559, 2854, 2968, 3932
    testing, 2483, 3317, 3318, 3356; random, 4014
    therapy, 2392
    trafficking, 3280, 3325, 3848, 3923, 3981, 4023, 4026
    transporting, 1368
    used to get a confession, 1143, 1199
    warning labels, 858. *See also* drugs, labeling.

Drunk drivers. *See* automobiles, drunk driving.

Drunkenness, 11, 2466, 3187; chronic alcoholic, 1345

Due process. *See* court procedure, due process.

Education, 380, 2557. *See also* church and state; colleges and universities; school desegregation/segregation; students; teachers.
    academic decisions, 2921
    academic freedom, 1058, 1272, 1530, 1531, 2921
    academic standards, 2921
    continuing education, 1960
    discrimination, 1615, 1777, 1870, 1945, 2040, 2366, 3048, 3365, 4047
    employees, 2623
    federal construction grants, 1469
    financial aid, *See* financial aid.
    financing, 1561, 2040, 2529
    foreign languages taught, 505, 506, 544, 1615
    libraries, book banning, 2411
    mandatory attendance, 1496; public school, 528
    private schools, 2581, 2752; public funding, 1693, 1868, 2058, 2410, 2899; textbook loans, 1342, 1593
    public schools, 2510, 3811; Bible reading, 919, 1167, 1187; flag salute, 718, 773; prayer, 1132, 1167, 1187, 3724; religious instruction, 865, 927, 1346; Ten Commandments posted, 2156
    regulations, 3176
    residency requirements, 2510
    school board, 1378, 1807, 2443
    school bus, 3277
    school discipline, 1832
    school district, 1075, 1561, 3439
    students. *See* students.
    suspension hearing, 1677
    tax for schoolbooks, 578
    teachers. *See* teachers.
    teaching evolution, 1346
    undocumented aliens, 2389

Elections, 910, 1262, 1423, 1486, 2379, 2802, 3071. *See also* reapportionment and redistricting; voting rights.
    access to ballot, 3069, 3070, 3639
    access to media, 1257, 2281
    bribery, 352, 1051, 2348

campaign financing, 841, 1516, 1706, 1727, 2276, 2291, 2315, 2336, 2453, 3429, 3573, 3936

campaign literature, 1741, 3533, 3689, 3973

campaign participation, 1597, 1598

campaign posters, 2683

candidates, 1902, 2348, 2413, 2498, 3696; designate race, 1174; endorsement, 3310; exclusion from ballots, 1360; malice, 3364

city and county, 3319

county, 1461

independents, 3070

judges, 219, 3588, 3604, 3605

local, 1084, 1378, 1946, 2087, 2089, 2390, 2433, 2472, 3647

minority party, 3069

political contributions and expenditures, 2447, 2453. See also PACS.

political party conventions, 1535, 2185, 4035

presidential, 286; elector, 925; filing, 2498

primaries, 547, 603, 635, 736, 787, 943, 1146, 2185, 3070, 3696

procedures, 2627

registering: discrimination, 672, 1067, 1217; to vote, 1459

state, 1267, 1355, 1460, 1630, 3588, 3602

water districts, 1559, 1560, 2218

write-in, 3696

Electricity. See utilities, electricity.

Embezzlement, 918, 3308

Eminent domain, 142, 195, 419, 496, 498, 714, 827, 836, 961, 1126, 1933, 2041, 2117, 2161, 2249, 2250, 2426, 2603, 2684, 2696, 2712, 2761 compensation, 319, 802, 889, 2202

Emotional Distress Law, 3228

Employee benefits. See benefits.

Employees, 2296, 3167, 3172, 3356, 3665. See also attorneys; benefits; contracts, labor; federal government, employees; freedom of religion, working on Saturday; freedom of religion, working on Sunday; freedom of speech, employees; hours and wages; labor; personal appearance; post office, employees; pregnancy rights; public employees; railroads, employees; teachers; workplace safety. absenteeism, 3423

confrontation with, 1682

discharge, 2454, 2546, 2735, 2803, 3197, 3907

dislocated, 3112

dismissal, 489, 662, 1734, 1762, 1764, 1781, 2208, 2289, 2328, 2410, 2546, 3912; retaliatory, 907, 984, 2491, 2527, 2989, 3468

disciplinary action, 3229

grievances, 1078, 2234, 3598

harassment, 3109, 3353

investigated, 3114

involuntary servitude, 3286

job requirements, 3342

layoffs, 1220, 2266, 2365, 2516, 2962, 3025, 3054, 3315, 3991

leave of absence, 1878, 3084

lockout, 1002, 1220, 1776

military service, 1847, 3636

refusal to rehire, 1570, 2584

reinstated, 907, 3856

replacing, 2584

subcontracted, 1207, 2507

termination, 1034, 1055, 1632, 2545, 3118, 3656

testing, 1435, 1712, 1759, 1964, 1974, 2398. See also drugs, testing.

Employment Agency, 440, 566, 735

Employment discrimination, 1294, 2062, 2289, 2387, 2400, 2492, 2543, 2599, 2656, 2722, 2731, 2804, 2966, 3037, 3065, 3948

burden of proof of, 2189, 3837

disabled, 2640, 3100

drug users, 1973

employee testing, 1435, 1712, 1759, 1974, 2398, 3287

employment preferences, 1649

filing deadlines, 2165

files, 2179

hiring practices, 1739, 1927, 2425, 3492

intimidation not to work, 368

job bias, 3065, 3084

leave of absence, 1878, 3084

overseas, 3546

physical requirements, 1871, 1904

pre-school age children, 1425

prima facie case, 1940, 1945, 2189, 2349, 2398, 2493

race, 368, 799, 1435, 1570, 1619, 1712, 1759, 1781, 1870, 1940, 2027, 2056, 2110, 2194, 2357, 2365, 2386, 2398, 2493, 2586, 3424

religion, 2884, 3037, 3065, 3095, 3195, 3324

residency requirements, 2626

retroactive, 2420, 3877, 3878

salary, 2209

seniority, 799, 1154, 1739, 1842, 1843, 1846, 1855, 1878, 2056, 2326, 2349, 2357, 2711, 2985, 3315, 3348; credit, 1847

sex, 878, 1425, 1569, 1591, 1846, 1871, 2004, 2005, 2010, 2094, 2189, 2326, 3433

sexual orientation, 3260

speech, 1335, 1954, 2503, 2545, 2629, 3894, 3953

tenure, 664, 665, 1530, 1531, 3391

Endangered Species, 294, 459, 1923, 2037, 3004, 3700, 4015. See also animal rights; hunting; wildlife.

Energy, 2682, 2702

rates, 3012

sales, 3275

Entertainment, performer's act, 1875

Entrapment, 612, 1028, 1158, 1440, 3675

Environment, 2588, 2721, 2774, 2791, 2951, 3107, 3110, 3349. *See also* air pollution; endangered species; hunting; landfill; mining; noise pollution; nuclear power; oil; public land; roads; sewage; solid waste; suits, environmental; superfund; timber; utilities; water; wildlife.

    impact statements, 3334

Environmental hazards, 2075. *See also* hazardous waste, radioactive waste; sewage; solid waste; suits, environmental; water, pollution.

    air pollution, 2609

    asbestos, 3027

    impact statements, 1769, 1786, 2009, 2294, 2497, 2534

    state implementation plan to correct, 1780

Evidence, 468, 540, 560, 793, 808, 904, 1158, 1194, 1211, 1274, 1947, 2029, 2381, 2406, 2487, 2704, 2756, 2757, 2811, 3103, 3615, 3683, 3975, 4008. *See also* informant; wiretapping and surveillance.

    attorney-client privilege, 2171

    battered child, 3627

    burden of proof, 2644, 2837

    by co-defendant, 1185, 1222, 1323, 1455, 1488, 1999

    by searchlight, 556

    declaration of co-conspirator, 996, 1420

    destroyed, 3292

    discovery of evidence, 3032, 3174

    evaluated, 2168

    exclusionary rule, 1082, 1110, 1227, 1714, 1716, 1801, 1892, 2078, 2130, 2132, 2704, 2756, 2757, 2771, 3395

    favorable to accused, 2907

    federal rules, 3718

    fingerprints, 2813

    hearsay, 1323, 1417, 1420, 1551, 1621, 2000, 2138, 3923, 3941

    illegally obtained, 416, 516, 567, 700, 952, 999, 1082, 1110, 1172, 1313, 1611, 3395

    impeachment of witness, 1688

    insufficient, 3291

    intent, 449

    lack of, 2979

    multiple-object conspiracy, 3626

    new, 1731, 3751, 3947

    perjured, 630

    predisposed, 3675

    preponderance, 3525, 3717

    presumption, 1387, 1499

    prior conviction, 1775

    relevancy, 1870

    scientific, 3839

    standard of proof, 1987, 2177, 2345, 2459, 2580, 3525

    statistics, 1973

    suppress, 1639, 1640, 1908, 2130, 2539, 3029, 3280

    telephone conversation, 3189; intercepted on phone extension, 1017

    testimonial, 315, 1268, 1341, 3486

    third-party conduct, 2617

    to discredit testimony, 951

    two witness rule, 845

    used in another trial, 3397

    wrongfully seized, 1801, 1802

Evolution controversy, 3176

Ex post facto laws, 3169

Extradition, 156, 921, 3168, 3191

    of prison inmates, 2174

Facilities usage, 1686, 3243

    overnight, 2739

Fair trial, 499, 1105, 1232, 1258, 1324, 1551, 1704, 2178, 2620, 2653, 2665, 2686, 2728, 2729, 2786, 2789, 2837, 2841, 2907, 2958, 3002, 3039, 3622, 3676. *See also* trial.

Father's rights. *See* illegitimate children, paternity suits.

Federal courts. *See* court jurisdiction.

Federal government, 1547. *See also* damage claims/ suits, against United States; freedom of speech, against government; government agencies; suits, against federal government.

    as employer, 3461

    attorney general, 849, 911, 2487

    debts, 3073

    defraud, 491, 980, 2674, 2732, 2984, 3983

    employees, 617, 690, 1727, 1758, 2052, 2732, 3561, 4005; disability benefits, 3480; excluded from job because of military or jury service, 828, 1115; hiring favoritism, 3492; honoraria, 3953; payoff, 2308, 3411; political activities, 840, 841, 911, 994, 1597, 1660; termination, 1034, 1055, 1632, 2545; unions, 1660, 2606, 2975, 3436, 3863

    false claims by, 3336

    fee imposition, 3789

    food stamps. *See* welfare, food stamps.

    funding, 2900, 3036, 3570

    grants, 2207, 2529

    immunity, 17, 227, 938, 1629, 1938, 1967, 2588, 3053, 3650, 3679; taxes, 797

    in the public interest, 561, 831

    liability, 979, 2474, 3131, 3258, 4029

    loans, 3011

    loyalty oaths, 911, 974, 1115

paperwork, 2519
    private contractor, 2499
    separation of powers, 47
    surplus property, 2306
    treasury, 214, 632, 633
    working overseas, 882
Federal payment, 2773, 2787, 2807, 2808
Federal regulations. *See* food regulation; regulations.
Federal Reserve Bank, 3625
Federal-State relations, 2807, 2820, 2897, 3240
Felon. *See* criminal law; criminal offenses, felon
    possession of gun; criminal offenses, felon
    registration; criminal records.
Filings, 937, 2778, 2917, 3015, 3524, 3637
    deadlines, 2165, 2772, 3381, 3680, 3772, 3831
    fees, 1544, 1557
    requirements, 2326
Financial aid, 1853, 2415, 2754, 2829, 2933
Fire, 160, 418, 551, 792, 1291, 1332, 1915, 2602,
    2857, 2979; firefighters, 3346
Firearms. *See* guns.
Fishing. *See* hunting, fish. *See also* Native
    Americans, hunting and fishing rights.
Flag desecration, 1628, 1663
Flag burning, 1365, 3357, 3475
Food. *See also* food regulation.
    candy, 807, 945
    fruit, 586
    Milk, 2700
Food regulation, 3013
    adulteration, 396, 777, 1700
    Avocados, 1152
    beef, 272
    Cantaloupe, 1393
    imported, 354
    kosher, 519
    labeling, 607, 777, 858, 3060
    Milk, 683, 695, 742, 905, 1729, 2175
    Oleo margarine, 259, 298; offense, 358; tax, 357
    packaging/containers, 1393, 1859, 2175
    poultry dealers, 637
    Raisins, 759
    Shrimp, 568
    Tomatoes, 292
    Wheat, 758
Food Stamps, 3003, 3038, 3238. *See also* welfare,
    food stamps.
    fraud, 2842
Forfeiture, 1540, 2602, 2631, 3838
    assets, 3362, 3363
    automobile, 1227, 2923, 4030
    drugs law, 3740, 3762, 3840, 3848, 4026
    money, 2521
    personal papers, 245
    property, 1442

    ship outfitted for war, 318
Foster children, 3667
Franchise, 600, 1864, 2844
Freedom of assembly, 198, 916, 1036, 1142, 1212,
    1213, 1264, 1347, 1375
Freedom of association, 554, 569, 657, 694, 803,
    1216, 2749, 2802, 3069, 3070, 3639. *See also*
    associations.
    political, 1630, 1785, 2080, 2185, 3310
    restricted, 3326
Freedom of expression, 1456, 2230. *See also*
    censorship; child pornography; disturbing the
    peace; freedom of speech; obscenity; pornography.
    city ordinance, 1733, 1774, 2241
    nude dancing, 1537, 2241, 2269, 3610
    vulgar words, 1601
Freedom of information, 938, 1710, 2067, 2068,
    2075, 2112, 2673, 2760, 2829, 3800
    attorneys work product exemption, 2531
    Census, 2324
    classified, 1547, 2294, 3331
    open meetings, 3358; federal investigation, 2647
    police, 3389; records, 2370
    privacy, 1983, 2368, 3633, 3863
Freedom of press, 595, 1232, 1875, 1906, 1916,
    2488, 2685, 2750, 2847, 2967, 3265, 3322, 3335,
    3360 *See also* censorship; freedom of speech.
    advertising, 646
    book publishing, 2052, 3608
    confidentiality, 1533, 3613
    conflict of interest, 665
    contempt, 848
    criminal story, 1653, 1654, 1791, 1931, 3630
    defamation, 1662, 1732, 1981, 2026, 2646, 2967
    editorials, 738, 829, 1257, 1659, 3490
    elections, 1257
    flyers, 680, 926, 1452, 1511
    identity of charge child, 1825, 2023
    judicial proceedings coverage, 738
    libel and slander, 9, 359, 1269, 1685, 2645, 2646,
        2675; private figure, 2967; public figure, 1408,
        1662, 1732, 1981, 2024, 3024, 3228; public
        official, 1179, 1431, 1432
    malice, 1669
    postal regulation, 209
    press conference, 3622
    reporting, 829, 3427
    restraint, 1471, 1791, 3244
    trial coverage, 2152, 2403; pretrial coverage,
        2030, 2618, 3039
    university newspaper, 1558
Freedom of religion, 140, 712, 789, 865, 901, 927,
    1038, 1346, 1437, 1485, 1693, 1868, 1902, 2058,
    2204, 3095, 3176, 3195, 3239. *See also* church and
    state; freedom of press; freedom of speech.

Bible reading in school, 919, 1167, 1168, 1187
charitable contributions, 2356
church property dispute, 63, 150, 187, 934, 1351, 1476, 2033
conscientious objectors. *See* military, conscientious objectors.
distribution of literature, 680, 765, 767, 768, 819
flag salute, 718, 773
mandatory school attendance, 1496
prayer, 3216; atgraduation, 3724; moment of silence, 2860; at school, 1132, 1187
public forum, 2265
public worship, 902, 940, 942, 2299
religious display, 2156, 2642, 4017
religious publications, 756, 781, 786, 1202, 3304, 4018
religious test oath, 1108
Social Security number, 3003
societies, 934, 2956; meeting room, 3473, 3811
textbook loans, 1342, 1593
veto liquor licenses, 2448
working on Saturday, 1170, 1855
working on Sunday, 1101, 1102, 1103, 1104, 2884
Freedom of speech, 657, 884, 1064, 1093, 1229, 1264, 1534, 1558, 1606, 1632, 1663, 2072, 2125, 2126, 2683, 2726, 2739, 2742, 2802, 2806, 2817, 2849, 2863, 2936, 3057, 3071, 3816. *See also* censorship; commercial speech; freedom of expression; freedom of press; freedom of religion.
abusive language, 1660
against government, 667, 903, 914, 920
against military, 446, 448, 449, 451, 456, 458, 466, 1511, 1522, 1652, 1742, 2049; in Vietnam, 1266, 1326, 1354, 1456, 1532
against police, 3170
airports, 3175, 3727, 3731
anarchy, 529, 554, 589, 920
associations, 1526, 3465
before school board, 1807
boycotting, 2441, 3242
broadcasting, 1374
campaign literature, 1741, 3973
candidate for public office, 2348, 3310
canvassing, 915, 1754, 2057, 2265; door-to-door canvassing, 697
clear and present danger, 1807
disturbing the peace, 885, 903, 1212, 1213, 1347, 1456, 3235
draft card burning, 1326
editorials, 1659
employees, 1335, 1530, 1531, 1954, 2503, 2545, 2629, 3197, 3894, 3953
fighting words, 744, 1213, 1375, 1456, 3720
flag burning, 1365, 3357, 3475

flyers, 1854, 2313
handing out flyers, 697, 749, 765, 1452, 1511, 1521, 2504
libel and slander, 926, 1061, 1204, 1457, 1660, 2886, 3490, 3608; of a public figure, 1296, 2026; of a public official, 1240
loitering, 710
loudspeakers, 874, 879, 928
movies, 929, 1062, 1089, 1196, 1656, 1686, 1708, 3134
obscenity, 1215, 1245, 1246, 1584, 1585
offensive language, 744, 1456, 1601, 3228
on public grounds, 321, 2504
parades, 732, 4010; asking for police protection, 3713
parks, 901, 940, 942
petitions, 2049
picketing, 1212, 1213, 1524, 1525, 1733, 2123, 2441
political advertisement, 1661, 3950
political protest, 3475
political speech, 1408, 1598, 1727, 1874, 1905, 2503, 3134, 3602, 3689, 3903
pornography, 1015, 1112, 1139, 1247, 1364, 1457, 1584, 1708, 3442, 3838
press conference, 1131
propaganda, 3134
public forum, 2274, 2883, 2910
reporting, 829, 3427
sign, 1838, 3903
solicitation of contributions, 2057, 3505, 3727, 3731
speakers, 3211
stores or shopping centers, 1521, 2111
students, 2411, 3056
symbolic, 589, 1354, 1833, 3357
taxes, 1037, 1038
teacher, 1807, 1810, 1954, 2410, 2469
time and place restriction, 2265
unions, 895, 2384, 2469
Fund raising, 2726, 3284. *See also* charities; nonprofits.

Gambling, 382, 952, 1022, 1094, 1191, 1308, 1309, 1350, 1442, 1546, 1801, 2686, 3046, 3090, 3097, 4034. *See also* casinos.
Gas leases, 2853, 2887, 3108
Gerrymandering. *See* reappointment and redistricting, gerrymandering.
Government agencies, 322, 388, 478, 648, 650, 689, 717, 790, 862, 976, 1883, 2192, 2304, 2457, 2569, 3282, 3542, 3564, 3936, 3964. *See also* federal government; regulations.
administrative interpretation of law, 2009, 2201, 2248, 2279, 2291, 2310, 2562, 2846

administrative proceedings, 708, 763, 784, 841,
   995, 1106, 1622, 1698, 1724, 1728, 1919, 2044,
   2158, 2164, 2184, 2260, 2353, 2529, 2534,
   2810, 2812, 2814, 3217, 3625, 3827; injunction
   against, 1428, 1512, 2157; right to jury trial at,
   1829
claim payments, 307
conflict, 3514
disclosure, 1710, 2179
discontinued programs, 3801
expenditures, 1657
fees, 1625, 1626
investigations, 876, 1203, 1679, 1750, 1925,
   2060, 2171, 2647; confidential, 3800
judicial interpretation, 2614
open meetings, 3358
records, 2067, 2068, 2179, 2760
summons, 2238
Government contracts, 1032, 1088, 3279
Government corporations, 316, 648, 820, 3950
Grand juries, 212, 234, 337, 593, 1131, 1643, 3120,
   3427. *See also* juries.
   errors, 3272
   evidence, 1611, 2487, 3626, 3683; refusal to
      disclose location, 904
   indictment, 2826, 3272
   investigative powers, 1533
   judge as grand jury, 866
   lied (perjury), 2932
   materials, 2582, 2583
   procedures, 2938
   service because of race, 218, 331, 634, 752, 1564,
      2741, 2924. *See also* juries, service because of
      race.
   subpoena, 3526
   testimony, 711, 2060
   witness, 7, 366, 904, 1532, 1546, 1969; immunity
      of, 279, 969, 1501, 2066, 2455; refusal to
      testify, 1501, 1523, 1611, 3718
Gray market, 3230. *See also* retail trade.
Guilty plea, 1370, 1405, 1406, 1407, 1419, 1564,
   1643, 2339, 2541, 2912, 3834
   refusing, 2395
   voluntariness, 2462
Guns, 496, 660, 1475, 1498, 2098, 2632, 2714, 2926,
   2940, 2974, 3018, 3034, 3979, 4023. *See also*
   criminal offenses, felon possession of gun.
   carrying, 691, 1440, 1506, 2001, 2097, 2471,
      2958, 2980, 3882
   illegal possession, 295, 772, 1310, 1509, 2002,
      2490, 2815, 3660, 3891
   police shooting, 2819
   using, 2097

Habeas Corpus, 45, 162, 171, 219, 353, 499, 630,
   753, 757, 937, 1074, 1143, 1150, 1999, 2029, 2095,
   2177, 2428, 3121, 3312, 3419, 3422, 3506, 3554,
   3615, 3617, 3681, 3688, 3717, 3784, 3928, 3949,
   3963, 3975, 3992, 4022
   cause and prejudice, 3719
   conclusiveness of findings, 2605
   constitutional claims, 1865, 2351
   conviction invalid, 3919
   credibility of witness, 2462
   exhausted rule, 2333, 2351, 2924
   facts, 3681
   friend of court, 4037
   guilty plea, 1643, 2339
   limited scope, 1515
   new evidence, 1731, 3751, 3947
   new rule, 3661, 3753, 3809, 3859
   post conviction proceeding, 1358
   prosecuting attorney, 1731, 2318
   question not raised state court, 1147
   retroactive, 3497
   substitute for appeal, 1802
   trial-related errors, 3782, 3952
Handicapped. *See* disabled rights.
Hate crimes. *See* criminal offenses, against victims
   on basis of race, religion, ethnic origin or other
   status.
Hazardous waste, 2612, 3104, 3693. *See also*
   radioactive waste.
   cleanup costs, 2774, 2934, 3898
   incinerators, 3880
   licensing, 3712
   shipping, 1454
   storage, 2534
Health, 1063. *See also* insurance, health; medicine;
   workplace safety.
   asbestos, 3027
   benefits, *See* benefits, health.
   black lung, 3293, 3430, 3614, 3913
   environmental impact statement, 1769, 1900
   hearing aids, 2008
   inspections, 1052
   nursing homes, 2414
   occupational safety, 1047, 2062, 2153, 2260
   vaccinations, 362, 3258, 3969
Higher education. *See* colleges and universities.
Highway. *See* roads, highway.
Historical preservation, landmark, 1933
Homeless, 737, 753, 1042, 1482, 1549, 2511, 2525,
   3746. *See also* loitering.
   abortion, 1861, 1862, 2147, 2148
   deportation, 349
   divorce court fees, 1433
   Medicaid, 2147, 2148, 2188, 2320
   medical care, 1623, 1757

right to counsel, 1144, 1145, 1281, 1506, 1651,
     1966, 2042, 2090, 2240, 3367, 3928
right to free court transcript, 985, 1761
Hours and wages, 328, 363, 377, 423, 437, 508, 651,
   754, 1645, 2245, 2308, 2616, 3183. *See also*
   employees; labor; public employees.
   employment contract, 2430
   federal standards, 1697, 1771
   involuntary servitude, 394
   leave of absence, 1878, 2261, 3084
   maximum hours, 1340
   overtime, 439, 798, 882, 2205, 2965
   payment by coupons, 345
   salaries, 2163
   severance pay, 1214, 3153, 3411
   travel time, 810
   vacation pay, 3329
   wages, 2692, 2836; back pay, 2209, 3856;
      garnishment of, 2692, 2709, 2720; loss of,
      2551; minimum, 501, 653, 658, 725, 726, 1340,
      2784; rate determination of, 2206
   work week. *See* freedom of religion, working on
      Saturday; freedom of religion, working on
      Sunday.
Housing, 961, 2478. *See also* community property.
   desegregation, 1748, 3394
   discrimination, 1288, 1343, 1349, 1539, 1748; by
      race, 1809, 1979, 2325, 3289
   low income, 1449, 1748, 2044, 3790
   public housing tenants, 3079
   renting, 1042, 1288, 1539
   zoning, 441, 1713, 1809, 1845, 3984
Hunting. *See also* animal rights; endangered species;
   Native Americans, hunting and fishing rights;
   wildlife.
   Eagles, 3004
   Elk, 1912
   Fish, 649, 872, 1605, 1840
   Game birds, 308
   license fees, 1912
   skins and fur, 514
   Whales, 3043
Hustler (Periodical), 3228
Hypnosis, 3184, 3583

Illegitimate children, 1322, 1495, 3007. *See also*
   children.
   blood test, 2239
   inheritance, 1439, 1835, 1950
   paternity suits, 1491, 1985, 1986, 2350, 2530,
      2577, 3202, 3352
   rights, 1321
   Social Security benefits, 1790, 2028
   support, 1556, 2350, 2530
   survivor's benefits, 2063

Immigration, 3471. *See also* aliens.
   admission, 280; denied because of security, 941
   amnesty, 3825; denied, 3534
   asylum, 3106, 3151, 3641, 3646, 3828
   checkpoints, 1803
   deportation, 349, 816, 922, 959, 1018, 1070,
      1081, 2440, 2565, 2843, 3631, 3633, 3641,
      3974; of children, 3770; left country, 2610
   employment, 263, 293, 386, 1893, 1978, 2305; of
      illegal aliens, 1599, 3634
   entry and re-entry, 941
   false statements, 3246
   financial aid. *See* Financial aid
   illegal entry, 2922
   naturalization, 532, 3266; denied, 2608; false
      answers, 1085, 2176; revoked, 3246
   refugees, 3106
   registration, 724
   resident aliens, 872, 1853; reentry, 2444
Immunity, 3, 17, 227, 279, 575, 690, 703, 797, 938,
   969, 1184, 1279, 1285, 1629, 1633, 1695, 1731,
   1788, 1810, 1888, 1896, 1907, 1938, 1965, 1967,
   2046, 2066, 2074, 2084, 2102, 2106, 2136, 2155,
   2268, 2275, 2278, 2344, 2375, 2408, 2409, 2431,
   2455, 2480, 2486, 2554, 2588, 2624, 2676, 2677,
   2735, 2784, 2823, 2877, 2897, 2950, 3053, 3204,
   3220, 3350, 3365, 3448, 3453, 3583, 3650, 3679,
   3686, 3743, 3766, 3813, 3830, 3864, 3934, 4000,
   4029
Impeachment, 222, 639, 1034, 1688, 2762, 2763,
   3747
Importing-exporting. *See* corporations, importing-
   exporting; food regulation, imported; international
   business, importing-exporting; interstate business,
   importing-exporting; state taxes, imported
   merchandise.
Income taxes, 301, 303, 430, 464, 1487, 2248, 2971.
   See also corporation taxes; local taxes; Native
   Americans, taxes; state taxes; taxes in general.
   back pay awards, 3690, 4002
   bankruptcy trustee, 3651
   business expense, 619, 727, 739, 778, 924, 1046,
      2481, 3126
   Canadians, 3313
   charities, 2520, 2522, 3454
   commissions, 721
   deductions, 575, 620, 702, 727, 1022, 1250, 1901,
      2481
   depletion allowance, 2228, 3756
   dividends, 640
   dues, 1111, 3019
   evading, 679, 760, 933, 988, 1006
   exemption, 685, 1970, 2522, 3063; denied, 3268,
      3343
   false return, 1006, 2516

foreclosure, 221
futures, 486, 978
gains, 771, 846, 978, 3321
gift, 720, 1128, 2388
gross income, 967
joint filings, 576
loan, 2509
lobbying expenses, 739, 1046, 2520
losses, 1153
lunch expenses reimbursement, 1886
medical expenses, 3126
not filing, 3521
overpayment, 579, 583, 615
partnership, 599, 1140, 1554, 3603
property sales, 2509
receivership, 605
royalties, 2611
separate filings, 583, 795
social clubs, 3494
stocks, 457, 590, 628, 640, 702, 1128, 1398, 2481
tax returns, 2615
tax shelter, 3055
trust, 618, 707, 2322
unconstitutionality, 1657, 1658
utilities, 3392
withholding, 3080
Independent-Law Counsel, 3282
Indians. *See* Native Americans.
Indictment, 2826; of codefendant, 2918
Indigents. *See* homeless.
Informant, 761, 974, 1044, 1268, 1311, 1350, 1443, 1509, 2539, 2553
    prison, 2118, 3031, 3547, 3554
    privilege identity, 1001, 1277
Inheritance, 338, 1439, 1835, 1950, 2631
    tax, 539, 582, 3237
Injunction, 440, 483, 888, 1418, 1582, 1787, 1923, 1968, 2075, 2219, 2568, 2710, 3150, 3564, 3734
    against federal proceedings, 1428, 1512, 2157
    against police, 2502
    against state officials, 1725
    against state proceedings, 1224, 1512, 2157, 2293
    enforcement, 519, 782, 2358
    in labor disputes, 678, 728, 729, 842, 930, 1063, 1409, 2407, 2960, 3927
    national health and safety, 1063
    parade, 1854
    petroleum production, 611, 1766
    protection of business operations, 1325
    remedy, 2199
    restraining order, 604, 1471, 1691
    taxes, 2633; state, 2396
    temporary, 1452
    unfair competition, 445
    violation, 403

Insanity, 326, 873, 893, 1099, 1127, 1256, 1857, 2580, 3684, 3685, 3922. *See also* mental health.
    defense, 2789, 2925, 3030, 3068
Insider Trading, 2070, 2587, 2866, 3213
Insurance, 130, 175, 317, 393, 676, 743, 832, 1039, 1352, 2127, 2167, 2399, 2852, 3883
    agent, 721, 854, 1065, 3665
    annuity, 3849
    beneficiary, 2292
    benefits, 1687
    claim, 2048, 2932, 2969
    corporate liability, 3843
    court awards, 3513
    disability. *See* Disability benefits, insurance
    fire, 418, 792, 2602
    fraud, 3538
    health, 2252, 2417, 3742
    life policy, 618, 731
    liquidate, 3817
    medical malpractice, 1939
    payments, 3355
    rehabilitation proceedings, 2343
    self-insurance, 3126
    sold by undertakers, 881
    sold through banks, 1487, 2535, 3814, 3945, 4040
    taxes, 1834, 2233, 2816
    underwriting, 1961
    unemployment, 3084, 3095, 3324
International business, 354, 541, 817, 861, 1278, 1505, 2055, 2327, 2554, 2670, 2906, 2931, 2959, 3271, 3462, 3701, 3847. *See also* corporations, multinational.
    confiscation, 1755
    importing-exporting, 342, 343, 344, 965, 1181, 1723
    investments, 3093
    seized assets, 1031
    taxes, 908, 1723, 1988, 2574, 3014
International Law, 1505, 3263
    Argentina, 130, 3701
    asylum, 3106, 3151
    extradition, 253, 254, 3704
    foreign courts, 304
    foreign government sovereignty, 1181, 1755, 2517, 2554, 3771
    foreign offenses, 992, 993, 1009, 1016
    high sea, 733
    immunity, 3, 2554
    maritime law. *See* maritime law.
    neutrality, 38
    power to regulate citizens abroad, 936
    property seizure, 531, 668, 1031
    sue in United States court, 1880, 2298, 2517
    treaty, 50, 111, 255, 263, 264, 459, 510, 512, 517, 743, 877, 1009, 1016, 1988, 2061, 2347, 2387,

3063, 3313; violation, 254, 548, 613, 3704, 3759. *See also* Native Americans, treaties.

Warsaw Convention, 3555, 4024

International Relations, 656

    Agreements, 3043, 3174

    British property claims after revolution, 15, 20

    claims against foreign government, 2288

    conflicts concerning the sea, 86, 89, 336, 614, 733

    foreign attachment testimony, 10

    foreign minister, 3, 99

    foreign officials, bribery, 3400

    military: bases outside United States, 1027; expedition, 313, 318

    visa, 1534, 3211

Internment, 800, 801, 3155. *See also* Japanese Americans; war.

Interrogation, 791, 1014, 1060, 1200, 1260, 1430, 1647, 1722, 2093, 2797, 3136, 3474, 3547, 3597, 3879

    by IRS agents, 1750

    custodial, 1814, 2016, 2223, 3518

    of corporation, 1390

    request for counsel, 2641, 2788, 2961, 3262, 3417, 3419, 3518, 3784, 3879, 4022; waived, 3913. *See also* right to counsel, during interrogation.

    secret, 1185

    videotaped, 3486

Interstate boundaries. *See* boundary disputes, interstate.

Interstate business, 131, 149, 188, 206, 272, 299, 308, 348, 518, 722, 837, 1729, 1924, 1929, 1967, 2077, 2115, 2175, 2404, 3192, 3529, 3694, 3935, 3967, 3981, 3985

    and intrastate, 421

    arbitration, 3946

    carriers, 178, 224, 297, 322, 407, 409, 411, 413, 421, 513, 666, 677, 806, 875, 1054, 1884, 2203, 2359, 3493, 3769; discrimination, 1086

    city regulations, 905

    ethanol, 3253

    federal regulation, 144, 322, 324, 388, 405, 407, 637, 683, 847, 1208, 1209, 1984, 2442

    importing-exporting, 270, 568, 1770, 3020

    obstructing, 302

    rates, 2988

    regulation power, 792, 1152, 2249, 2250, 2323, 3885

    state proprietary action, 2122

    telephone and telegraph, 207, 3296

    transporting, 412, 433, 737, 1393, 1454, 1824

    stolen goods, 2340

Interstate disputes, 2566

Japanese Americans, 774, 775, 800, 801

Job discrimination. *See* employment discrimination.

Judgments, 401, 411, 1867, 2253, 2365, 2798, 3027, 3524, 3933

    binding effect, 1737

    collateral, 2343; estoppel, 1951, 2159, 2541, 2608, 2609

    debts owed, 3778

    declaratory, 565, 974, 1053, 1209, 1429, 1548, 1549, 1673, 1809, 2183, 2568

    economic regulation, 1782

    final judgment awards, 3592

    interest, 3996

    libel summary, 3024

    modification, 1096, 2329

    notification, 3589

    payments, 3434

    pending, 3998

    relitigate, 2572

Judges, 269, 2676, 3504, 3954

    appointed, 3995

    as jury, 866

    assignment, 1134

    bias, 546, 829, 2969

    elections, 219, 3588, 3604, 3605

    immunity, 1896, 2155

    impeachment, 3747

    lay, 1784

    magistrates, 2130, 3567, 3620

    military, 3851, 3995

    misconduct, 1906

    obstruction of justice, 4012

    salaries, 2163

    state, 3607

    trial, 4008

Judicial procedure. *See* court procedure.

Juries, 2779, 3785, 4008. *See also* capital punishment, jury; grand juries.

    alternate jurors, 3785

    demeanor, 3187

    discrimination, 1952, 2978, 3074

    evidence evaluation, 2168

    hung jury, 90

    impartial, 1105, 1258, 1545, 1735, 2212, 2318, 3198, 3581

    instructions, 300, 620, 698, 1216, 1700, 1895, 2012, 2050, 2051, 2191, 2351, 2352, 2597, 2837, 3052, 3196, 3255, 3612, 3809, 3836; on harmless error, 2470, 3580; on lesser offense, 988, 2369; on mitigating circumstances, 3420, 3431; on presumption of innocence, 1996; on reasonable doubt, 3512, 3805, 3868. *See also* capital punishment, jury, instructions.

    opposition to capital punishment, 1941, 2137, 2981, 3143

peremptory challenges, 246, 452, 456; because
    bilingual, 3578; because of death penalty views,
    1333, 2137, 3269; because of race, 1219, 3074,
    3312, 3551, 3587, 3676, 3986; because of sex,
    3872. *See also* juries, voir dire examination.
petty offenses, 358
proof of prejudice, 2178
selection, 853, 1334, 1545, 1735, 3403, 3587,
    3620; based on race, 588, 937, 953, 975, 1219,
    2212, 3074, 3531, 3710; tax records, 937. *See
    also* juries, voir dire examination.
service: because of race, 216, 217, 218, 223, 331,
    634, 1219. *See also* grand juries, service
    because of race.; because of sex, 1116
size, 1416, 1890, 1980, 2120, 2618
special, 853
summons for, 8
verdict, 3187, 4008. *See also* trial, verdict.
voir dire examination, 588, 1735, 1841, 2212,
    2618, 2620, 3706
Jurisdiction. *See* court jurisdiction.
Juveniles. *See* children.

Kidnapping, 254, 1316, 1405, 2518, 2914

Labor, 2342, 2947. *See also* child labor; employees;
    hours and wages; unions.
    arbitration, 1078, 1079, 1080, 1121, 1612, 1619,
        1823, 2234, 2528, 2667, 2962, 3562
    bargaining, 2782, 3154; impasse, 1220, 2304;
        process, 708, 1059, 3432; time, 2606. *See also*
        labor, duty to bargain.
    boycotting, 477, 2127, 2573
    coercing union organization, 581, 662, 663, 664,
        666, 1377
    collective bargaining, 661, 687, 790, 1079, 1121,
        1207, 1275, 1409, 1971, 2027, 2606, 2649,
        2831, 3256, 3519, 3541, 3559, 3598, 3791,
        3890, 4045; agreement, 783, 1119, 1214, 1646,
        1699, 1823, 2043, 2124, 2220, 2528, 2882,
        2891, 3152, 3767, 3907; employee exclusion,
        2296; remedies, 2380; successorship clause,
        1646; termination, 2637
    confrontation with employee, 1682
    continuing education requirement, 1960
    duty to bargain, 1065, 1497, 1671, 2266
    extortion, 981
    government interference, 687, 930, 3386
    hiring hall, 1910, 2371, 2425, 3385
    hiring immigrants, 263, 293, 386, 1599, 1893,
        1978, 2305, 3634
    hiring restrictions, 2475
    injunction on labor dispute. *See* injunction, in
        labor dispute.

interference to organize, 986, 1294, 1377, 2019,
    2527
jury trial, 3425
labor disputes. *See* labor disputes.
managerial exclusion, 2059, 2491, 2782
military service, 1847, 3636
negotiations, 3386; with union, 1807, 3436, 3461
no strike rule, 1612, 2492
picketing, 477, 678, 710, 729, 747, 748, 884,
    1050, 1325, 1524, 1733, 1910, 2127
references, 3571
remedies, 3425, 3856
strike, 684, 1002, 1154, 1294, 2043, 3401; hiring
    during, 2584
subcontracting employees, 1207, 2507
supervisors, 3890
unfair labor practices, 684, 708, 1220, 1739,
    1776, 1998, 2019, 2280, 2507, 2527, 3217
Labor Contracts. *See* contracts, labor.
Labor Disputes, 488, 526, 678, 728, 729, 842, 930,
    1002, 1063, 1121, 1251, 1297, 1409, 1553, 1764,
    1972, 2043, 2407, 2492, 2960, 3132, 3214
Land, 64, 66, 83, 857. *See also* community property;
    Native Americans, land; public land.
    claims, 120, 122, 135, 139, 278, 2660, 3113
    eminent domain, 142, 496, 498, 714, 824, 827,
        836, 961, 1126, 2037, 2041, 2161, 2864;
        compensation for, 319, 802, 889, 2202, 3145
    oceanfront, 2391
    off-shore, 849, 2295
    outer continental shelf, 3108
    right of way, 275, 1120, 2479
    title, 50, 61, 97, 2508, 3113, 3224
    wetland, 2479, 2916
    zoning, 537, 1631, 1713
Land-Use Planning, 3164, 3209
Landfill, 3693, 3694
    filing lawsuit deadlines against, 3381
Law enforcement. *See* police.
Laws (Statutes). *See* Congress, laws or legislation;
    states, laws.
Liability 350, 373, 381, 420, 535, 826, 979, 1045,
    1918, 2046, 2084, 2229, 2408, 2474, 2662, 2780,
    2855, 2920, 3015, 3109, 3131, 3220, 3233, 3249,
    3258, 3314, 3330, 3360, 3499, 3543, 3764, 3843,
    3899, 3906, 4009, 4025, 4027, 4029. *See also*
    product liability.
Libel, 9, 359, 926, 1061, 1179, 1204, 1240, 1269,
    1408, 1431, 1432, 1457, 1660, 1662, 1685, 1732,
    1981, 2024, 2026, 2646, 2675, 2875, 2886, 2967,
    3024, 3228, 3364, 3490, 3608
Licensing, 942, 1912, 2332, 2550
    broadcasting, 946, 989, 1374, 1574, 1919, 2201,
        2464, 3503

business, 248, 541, 566, 600, 735, 1215, 1840, 2321

    hazardous waste, 3712

    medicine, 261; suspension, 1691

    pawnbrokers, 517

    professional, 2796

    prostitution, 3393

    religious publications, 786

    taxes, 194, 646, 660, 767, 871, 1066, 1753

    used to discriminate, 732, 756, 872

Lien. *See* bankruptcy, lien; debts, lien; taxes in general, lien.

Liquor. *See* alcohol/liquor.

Loans. *See* banks and banking, loans.

Lobbying, 939, 1090, 1113, 2520

    expenses, 739, 1046

Local taxes, 192. *See also* cities, taxes; income taxes; state taxes; taxes in general.

    excise, 3638

    property, 429, 3439, 3638, 3777

    school district, 1075, 1561, 3439

Loitering, 710, 1069, 2511, 2697

Lotteries, 220, 348, 3835

Low income housing. *See* housing, low income; housing, public housing tenants.

Loyalty Oaths, 163, 164

    federal, 911, 974, 1115

    state, 910, 935, 1035, 1037, 1038, 1254, 1272, 1303

Mail. *See* post office.

Maritime law, 38, 98, 255, 318, 3874, 3875. *See also* international relations, conflicts concerning the sea; workers' compensation, maritime workers; shipping; water.

    court jurisdiction, 70, 86, 147, 160, 491, 598, 614, 766, 944, 1045, 1473, 1541, 3861, 3955

    dry dock, 559

    prize, 34, 84, 95, 336, 2435

    shipbuilding, 2055

    ship collision, 147, 372, 381, 2405, 3996; foreign government immunity, 804

    ship salvage, 133

    ship seizure, 89, 613, 2553

    ship owners, 1411; debts, 3586; liability, 350, 381, 420, 535, 826, 1045, 1047, 2229, 3008, 3499, 3906, 4009

    wrongful death, 191, 199, 252, 476, 1373, 1413, 1616, 1917, 3023, 3510

Marriage and relationships, 1882, 2674, 3156

    adultery or premarital relations, 1489

    co-habitation, 1631; interracial, 1206, 3295

    community property, 583, 795, 1631, 2197, 2277, 3340

    divorce. *See* divorce.

    interracial, 1292; sexual relations, 228, 1206

    polygamy, 212, 265, 271

    spouses' income, 2272

    tax returns, 576, 583, 596, 599

Maternity leave. *See* pregnancy rights, maternity leave.

Martial Law, 162

    Hawaii, 823

    Rhode Island, 143

    Texas, 611

Medicaid/Medicare, 1793, 1860, 1861, 2134, 2147, 2148, 2188, 2231, 2272, 2320, 2353, 2354, 2402, 3483, 3812, 3920, 3962, 3980

    care facilities, 2846

Medicine. *See also* drugs; health; workplace safety.

    blood plasma, 2851

    care to homeless, 1623, 1757

    dentist, 2992

    disconnect life support, 3498

    disease, 3100

    doctors, 261, 1691, 2977, 3250, 3543; malpractice, 1939; professional review, 3250

    hearing aids, 2008

    hospitals, 334, 3640

    license, 261, 1691

    medical devices, 3489

    medical school, 1887, 1936

    physical exam, 3356

    treatment, 899, 1805, 2576, 3938

    vaccines, 362, 3258, 3969

Mental health. 2188, 3034, 3068. *See also* disabled rights, mentally retarded; hypnosis; insanity.

    benefits, 2852, 2893

    distress, 3555

    drug therapy, 2392, 3413

    federal grants, 2207

    forced antipsychotic drug, 3685

    health plan, 2399

    institutionally committed, 1241, 1504, 2580; children, 2014, 2015; confinement, 1715, 2393; involuntary, 1127, 1987, 2079, 3832; voluntary, 3410

    prison inmate, 2079; drug therapy, 3413; evaluation, 3252

    psychiatric testimony, 2222, 2595

    sterilization, 550

Mergers. *See* antitrust, mergers; banks and banking, mergers; block mergers; corporations, mergers.

Military, 313, 318, 877, 2049, 2358, 3279 *See also* armed forces; freedom of speech, against military; national guard; veterans; war.

    base access, 1115, 1741

    base closure, 3886

    bases outside the country, 1027

    benefits, 16, 1569, 1847, 2292, 2898

compulsory training, 626
conscientious objectors, 591, 626, 779, 811, 825, 966, 1218, 1412, 1436, 1470
court jurisdiction, 159, 1652, 1689, 2375
court-martial. *See* court martial.
doctors' liability, 3543
discrimination, 2540
draft, 100, 443, 446, 448, 449, 822, 966, 1326, 1437, 2273; evasion, 1123, 1141; registration, 2754, 2806; resistors to the 2754, 2806
duty, 443, 572, 1025, 3777
honorably discharged, 2346
judges, 3851, 3995
medical treatment, 899, 3938
officer promotion, 1674
reserves, 2261
schools, 4047
secrets, 938
servicemen injuries, 2890
servicemen off duty, 886
serving in foreign military, 1026
state, 76, 243
surveillance of civilians, 1522
tax refunds, 3937
taxes on benefits, 3678
trespassing, 2883
weapons, 2294
Mineral rights. *See* oil, leases; gas leases; mining, mineral rights income.
Mining, 285, 424, 488, 498, 502, 526, 651, 1627, 1786, 2104, 2186, 2215, 2270, 2287, 3509, 3614
claims, 2307, 2825
gravel, 2532
lease, 2295, 2611, 2614
mineral rights income, 2382
permits, 3110
safety, 417, 3449, 3852; hours, 328; and strike, 1612
strip, 2249, 2250
Money, 4, 116, 2521, 2734. *See also* banks and banking; Federal Reserve Bank; treasury.
check fraud, 2422. *See also* banks and banking, checking.
counterfeit, 3881
credit card, 2073; billing errors, 2247; fraud, 1613; stolen, 1726
gold certificates, 632, 633
legal tender, 177, 182, 233, 631
reporting requirements, 3850
scrip, 345
Motor transportation industry, 3127 *See also* railroads, carriers; shipping.
carriers, 1023, 1054, 1824, 1884, 2142, 2203, 2359, 3493, 3532, 3769

Movies. *See* censorship, movies; copyright; freedom of speech, movies.
Municipal employees. *See* public employees, city.
Murder, 2098, 2945. *See also* capital punishment; criminal law; criminal offenses.
elements, 1701, 3259
malicious, 3052
premeditation, 2029
self-defense, 3098
sentencing, 1949
Music copyrights. *See* copyright, music.

National forests. *See* public land, national forests.
National Guard, 1161, 3477. *See also* armed forces; military; states, military; war.
civilian employment, 3636
riot control, 1633
National parks. *See* public land, national parks.
National security, 948, 982, 994, 1055, 1305, 1514, 2279
Central Intelligence agents' book publication, 2052
classified nuclear weapons, 2294
espionage, 1070
Native Americans, 2100, 2795, 2853, 2856, 2995, 3004, 3006, 3009, 3239, 3384, 3616, 3801
alcohol/liquor license, 2589
ceremonial drug use, 3435
Cherokee Nation, 310, 395
citizenship, 238, 247
court jurisdiction, 121, 1043, 1424, 2635, 2691, 2856
crimes. *See* criminal offenses, committed by or against Native Americans.
employment preferences, 1649
gambling, 3097, 4034. *See also* gambling.
hunting and fishing rights, 311, 364, 432, 746, 1327, 1328, 1605, 1680, 2035, 2200, 2542, 2909, 3004, 3006, 3108
land, 56, 87, 346, 374, 500, 740, 818, 964, 1618, 1676, 1684, 1763, 1830, 2081, 2149, 2200, 2572, 2589, 2635, 2864, 2995, 3113, 3145, 3376, 3822, 3860; payment for, 2787
liquor license, 2589
schools, 380
self-regulation, 2542
Seminole Nation, 751
statute jurisdiction, 2439
taxes, 1226, 1562, 1753, 1763, 2142, 2143, 2439, 3535, 3638, 3797, 4006; oil and gas, 2316, 2830
territories, 118, 121, 2149; court jurisdiction, 232, 249, 818, 1618, 1684, 2142

treaties, 118, 121, 346, 751, 1328, 1562, 1680, 1684, 1830, 2035, 2149, 2200, 2995, 3004, 3376

tribal courts, 1730, 1894, 3089; over non-members, 225, 1889, 3463

tribal membership, 1907

water rights, 374, 1162, 1438, 1740, 2200, 2489, 2572, 2585, 3009

welfare benefits, 1622

Natural Gas, 745, 780, 1724, 2236, 2931. *See also* utilities.

piping, 402

price control, 2461

rates, 2286, 2579

transporting, 402, 3234

Negligence, 224, 392, 979, 2478

awards, 242

fire, 160, 1332

liability, 373

maintenance of airport, 3339

personal injury, 2284

Newspapers, 814, 1356, 3382. *See also* college and universities, newspaper; freedom of press.

Noise pollution, 1120, 1568, 1642, 3600

Nonprofits, 1036, 1742, 2970, 3268, 3284, 3716. *See also* charities; fund raising.

charters, 3716

disbarred, 1036

Nuclear power, 1900, 2505, 2534, 2810, 3297, 3455, 3468

accidents, 1932, 2497

power plant, 3275

Nuisance: book store as, 3057

Obscenity, 1112, 1215, 1245, 1246, 1584, 1585, 1601, 2007, 2873, 2876, 2972, 3135, 3305

Oil, 627, 1565, 2145, 2533, 2830, 3998

gasoline, 360, 711, 1922

leases, 570, 2853, 3108, 3264

petroleum products, 611, 1766

royalties, 3264

PACS, 3071, 3429. *See also* elections, political contributions and expenditures.

Pardon, 123, 520, 1670, 2258, 3166

Parole and Probation, 2076, 2747, 2848, 3166, 3977

hearing, 1997

ineligibility, 3909

liability, 2046

rescinded, 2290

violation, 2908

Partnerships, 2688, 3236, 3412

Patents, 408, 538, 855, 863, 1177, 1178, 1638, 1962, 2195, 2617, 3308, 3795, 3847, 3942

chemical process, 2144

fruit, 586

human-made micro-organisms, 2119

infringement, 2524

mathematical formula, 1928, 2187

medical-device substitutes, 3489

oil shale, 2104

Paternity suits. *See* illegitimate children, paternity suits.

Pensions and benefits. *See* benefits; disability benefits; retirement, benefits; unemployment, compensation; welfare, benefits.

Personal appearance, 1747. *See also* employees.

beard, 1545

obesity, 3545

Picketing, 477, 678, 710, 729, 747, 748, 884, 1050, 1212, 1213, 1325, 1524, 1525, 1910, 2127, 2123, 2441, 3278. *See also* disturbing the peace.

on private property, 1733

Piracy, 18, 71, 78, 79. *See also* maritime law, prize.

Plea bargaining, 1881, 1949, 2395, 2708, 2912, 3105, 3182, 3943, 4026. *See also* sentencing.

misunderstood terms, 2339

Police, 127, 211, 416, 1762, 1782, 2305, 2576, 3171, 3855

assaulted by, 2780

chokeholds, 2502

collective bargaining, 3791

hair grooming, 1747

immunity, 2950, 3204

mandatory retirement, 1783

misconduct, 1725

mislead on charges filed, 2953

officer killing mandatory death sentence, 1848

records, 2370, 3389

sheriff, 3959

shootings, 2819

testimony, 2958; perjured, 2480

violence, 2502

Political Action Committee. *See* PACS.

Pornography, 1015, 1112, 1139, 1247, 1364, 1457, 1584, 1708, 3369, 3838. *See also* child pornography.

Post Office, 836, 1015, 2765, 3505

employees, 3536

fraud, 431, 778, 789, 796, 1075, 1613, 2826, 2932, 3196, 3213, 3320

international mailing, 3536

mail delivery, 302, 1229, 1637, 1665, 2570

mail-order, 3692

obscene matter, 1133, 1246, 1404, 1655, 1841

postmaster, 307

rates, 356, 414, 2562

regulations, 209, 1229

stolen credit cards, 1726

unstamped mail, 2274

Pre-Empted, 2705, 2712, 2745, 2851, 2852, 3054,
    3517, 3767, 3907
Pregnancy rights, 1648, 1721, 1806, 2558. *See also*
    teenage pregnancy.
        fetal protection, 3544
        maternity leave, 1617, 1878, 1918, 2326, 2571,
            3037, 3072
President,
        communication privilege, 1667
        constitutional question, 2061
        electors, 286, 925
        elections, 286, 2498
        executive order, 627, 930, 2288.
        immunity from damage liability, 2408
        papers, 1874
        powers, 100, 165, 269, 282, 424, 536, 562, 668,
            862, 930, 1766, 1874, 2737, 3058, 3076, 3477
        proclamation authority, 656
        removal from office, 639, 1034
        veto power, 573, 3076
Press conference and releases, 1061, 1131, 3622
        false claims, 3830
Price fixing. *See* antitrust, price fixing.
Prison Inmates, 2086, 2748, 2845, 3165. *See also*
    pardon.
        access to courts, 1353
        access to legal materials, 1836, 4046
        beatings, 809, 2501. *See also* prison inmates, use
            of excessive force.
        credit for time served, 1379, 2180, 3666, 3993
        disciplinary action, 2154, 2872, 2919
        drug therapy, 3413
        escape, 2050
        frivolous suits, 3682
        grievance, 3657
        hearings, 1665, 3413
        hurt, 2927, 2928, 2949
        informant, 2118, 3031, 3547, 3554. *See also*
            informant.
        labor union, 1866
        legal assistance, 1353
        mail censorship, 1637, 1665
        marriage, 3156
        media, 1931; interviews, 1653, 1654, 4001
        medical care, 1805
        reading materials, 3335
        refused religious publications, 1202
        religious liberty, 1485
        segregated, 2463
        transfer, 1778, 1779, 2079, 2174, 2259, 2506
        transporting, 2911
·   treatment, 4007
        use of excessive force, 3567, 3649. *See also*
            prison inmates, beatings.
        visitors, 3337

Prisons and Jails, 1637, 1778, 1930, 2251, 2506
        abuse, 3682
        bad conditions, 3601; hearings on, 3567
        bail hearings, 3563
        confinement, 2463; solitary confinement, 277,
            2154
        consent decrees, 3643
        disciplinary proceedings, 1749, 2845
        liability, 3899
        loss of property, 2226
        preventive detention for children, 2698
        regulation, 1654
        riots, 2949
        searches of cells, 2746
        smoking exposure, 3824
Privacy, 1983, 2368, 2659, 3212, 3244, 3633, 3863.
    See also right to privacy.
Privileges and immunities. *See* immunity.
Probate, 1472
Probation. *See* parole and probation.
Product liability, 2112, 3008, 3279
        automobiles, 2047, 3263
        safety, 2904
        warranty, 3423
Property, 13, 94, 208, 241, 441, 490, 1343, 2226,
    2306, 2650, 2825, 3351
        abandoned, 184
        airspace rights, 1120
        assessment, 3298
        claims, 2435
        community property. *See* community property.
        damage, 703
        destruction, 561
        discrimination, 509, 510, 511, 525, 533, 1349
        disputes, 63, 150, 187, 934, 1351, 1476, 2033
        donation, 2388
        eminent domain, 195, 419, 1933, 2041, 2117,
            2202, 2249, 2250, 2426; cash interest, 2161.
            See also land, eminent domain.
        eviction, 3738
        farms, 638, 659, 701, 857
        foreclosure, 28, 701, 2526, 3889
        government owned, 1765, 3505
        inherited by noncitizens, 264, 525
        lease: race discrimination, 509, 510, 511, 525
        lien, 125, 2426, 3574, 3589. *See also* bankruptcy,
            lien; debts, lien; taxes in general, lien.
        minerals, 3998
        mortgage, 137, 621, 638, 659, 2418, 2509, 2561,
            3808, 3815
        public use, 185, 580, 3916
        restrictive or racial covenants, 868, 869, 947
        sales, 3006
        seized, 1442, 1507, 2923, 3762
        settlements. *See* divorce, property settlement.

shopping centers, 2111

survey, 278

takings, 124, 138, 185, 314, 319, 365, 419, 580, 824, 827, 889, 1126, 1933, 2307, 2426, 3028, 3099, 3406, 3733

taxes, 301, 303, 429, 846, 1636, 1763, 2199, 2594, 3298, 3439, 3638, 3709, 3777, 3857. *See also* taxes in general, property.

title, 115, 122, 565, 605, 2508, 3161

tribunal awards, 3384

zoning, 564, 1631, 2117, 2202, 2210

Prostitution, 412, 434, 2697, 4030

restrict by license, 3393

Public employees. *See also* employees; federal government, employees.

city, 1599, 2475, 2503, 3229, 3655, 3894

county, 2080

discharge, 2803

hiring favoritism, 1762

police. *See* police.

state, 685, 935, 984, 1108, 1340, 1598, 1697, 1839, 1893, 1969, 1989, 2005, 2629, 3571, 3624

taxes on benefits, 3678

Public land, 114, 321, 438, 500, 836, 901, 940, 942, 2504, 2683, 2822, 3044, 3773. *See also* land; property, government owned.

fire, 551

horses, 1765

interstate highways, 1434

livestock grazing, 399, 400, 406, 1944

mining, 424, 2215, 2532, 3110, 3509

national forests, 1944, 3239

national parks, 306, 323, 406, 709, 1492, 2739

oil lease, 570

power plants, 976

state, 3161

trespassing, 391

utilities right-of-way, 709

wildlife refuges, 2215

Public officials, 2301, 2724. *See also* Congress; federal government; government agencies.

bribery, 3691

defamation by, 1738, 1981, 2024

defamation of, 1179, 1204, 1240, 1319, 1431, 1432, 1457

immunity, 1938, 2064, 2074, 2102, 2268, 2409, 2431, 2735, 2877, 3220, 4000; President of the United States, 2408

liability, 1918, 2084, 3220

oath to support Constitution, 1040

press release, 1061

religious activities, 1108

suits, 227, 888, 1633, 2053

Public property. *See* public land.

Public sector employees. *See* public employees.

Public television. *See* television, public/non-commercial.

Public transportation, 928, 2380

buses, 830, 1279

cities, 574

school buses, 3277

subway, 574

Punishment, 14, 44, 340, 390, 403, 410, 452, 1345, 1370, 1749, 2303, 2463. *See also* capital punishment; sentencing.

assessment to aid victims, 3451

drug addict, 1135

failure to pay fines, 2190, 2525

harm, 2438

harsher than recommended, 3566

mandatory life sentence, 1949, 2071

maximum, 2001, 3566

misdemeanor, 2090

pretrial detention, 1992

second offense punishment, 305, 2193, 2458

solitary confinement, 277, 1479, 1930, 2154

Punitive damages. *See* damage claims/suits, punitive.

Race bias, 216, 217, 218, 223, 331, 634, 752, 1219, 1564, 3059, 3178, 3342

Race discrimination, 1252, 2398, 2433, 3140, 3141, 4038. *See also* affirmative action; employment discrimination, race; school desegregation/segregation.

by boat, 861

by bus, 830, 1279

by railroads, 266, 312, 730, 734, 898

employment preferences, 1649

in a cemetery, 970

in a restaurant, 1086, 1098, 1117, 1155, 1156, 1194, 1195, 1197, 1198, 1209, 1314

in benefits, 2599

in education, 335, 557, 954, 958, 973, 1186, 1615, 870, 1873, 2040, 2522; higher, 688, 856, 896, 897, 1635, 1936; private school, 1777

in hotels/motels, 1208

in housing, 533, 1349, 1809, 1979, 2325, 3289

in leasing property, 509, 510, 511, 525

in military, 2540

in prison, 2463

in private clubs, 1510

in public parks and other recreational areas, 1160, 1388

in public swimming pools, 1462

in union bargaining, 1678

on juries, 2741, 3676

property restrictions, 868, 869, 947

stockholders, 512

Racial quotas, 2985, 3096

Racial harassment, 3353
Racketeering, 1553, 2262, 2905, 3188, 3305, 3372,
3718, 3765, 3838, 3854, 3981
    prior conviction on, 2902, 3402
Radioactive waste, 3679, 3714. *See also* hazardous
waste.
Railroads, 214, 224, 266, 287, 312, 320, 419, 436,
730, 812, 1021, 1090, 2801, 3163, 3934
    abandonment, 2192, 2712
    Amtrak, 3670, 3950
    carriers, 534, 734, 898, 1184
    crossings, 319, 3783
    employees, 437, 661, 799, 990, 2330, 3109, 3132,
        3703, 3921; negligence, 373, 392
    flat cars, 3081
    land grant, 500, 740
    liability, 535, 681, 3254, 3635
    livestock, 242
    rates, 201, 202, 203, 204, 205, 244, 251, 268, 297,
        322, 329, 378, 388, 421, 492, 513, 1550, 1580,
        2449; discrimination, 806; intrastate, 478
    right-of-way, 275, 389
    safety, 405
    state-owned, 2342
    taxes, 250, 713, 3133
Rape, 1274, 1334, 1372, 1538, 1876, 1934, 2085,
2198, 2403, 3029, 3047, 3295, 3360, 3568;
    victim's name released, 1685
Rates, 356, 414, 1243, 2286, 2562, 2579, 2821, 2988,
3012. *See also* railroads, rates; regulations, rates;
utilities, rates.
    excessive, 3372
    setting, 2206, 3297
Real Estate sale, 41, 134, 2045
    developer, 3827
    discrimination, 1343, 1979, 2325
    restrictive covenant, 533, 947
    unfair trade practice, 1769
Reapportionment and redistricting, 833, 1234, 1255,
1821, 2244, 3082, 3672, 3757, 3763, 3931
    at-large election, 1736, 1745
    board of supervisors, 1461
    Census count, 3730, 4032
    City council, 1745, 2451
    congressional districts, 2560
    county commissioners, 1315
    college board of trustees, 1391
    disapportionate in population size, 1175, 1362,
        1363, 2563
    gerrymandering, 1084, 2560, 3041, 3841, 4016,
        4019, 4043, 4044; minority legislative districts,
        3040
    population disparity, 2563

    state legislature, 1122, 1189, 1190, 1210, 1459,
        1460, 1552, 1567, 1581, 1582, 1583, 1844,
        3041
Refugees, 3106
Regional banking, 2862
Registration of stock, 2850. *See also* corporations,
stocks; securities.
Regulations, 447, 486, 691, 840, 1697, 1970, 1983,
2376, 2542, 2689, 2929, 3081, 3164, 3209, 3670,
3970 *See also* cities, regulations; food regulation;
securities, regulations; states, regulations; trucking
regulations.
    accounting, 409, 3962
    agency, 3127, 3248
    alcohol, 141, 260, 270, 276, 641, 2448, 2589,
        2715, 2998
    coal industry, 651, 1786
    commercial sponges industry, 733
    deregulate, 3112
    drug testing, 2483
    economic, 1782
    enforcement of decisions, 3542
    environmental, 2983
    funding, 3570
    housing, 3790
    hydraulic projects, 1033, 3455
    insecticides and pesticides, 2727, 2904, 3611
    interstate business, 144, 322, 388, 405, 407, 637,
        683, 792, 847, 1152, 1208, 1209, 1984, 2249,
        2250, 2323, 2442
    judicial power to review, 851, 907, 1320, 1394,
        1395, 1434, 1478, 1786, 2164, 2320, 2449,
        2513, 2588, 2606, 3801
    livestock, 483
    mail, 209, 1229
    Medicaid/Medicare, 2134, 2231, 2272, 2320,
        2354, 3483, 3812, 3920, 3962, 3980; payments,
        2353
    mining, 1786, 3614
    national guard to duty, 3477
    natural gas, 2931
    oil industry, 627, 2533
    paperwork, 2135, 3407
    price, 742, 1760
    prisons and jails, 1654
    public land, 399, 400, 1434
    rates, 324, 745, 780, 1550, 1625, 1626, 2449,
        2513, 2579, 2990, 3099, 3493, 3514, 3522,
        3885, 3940
    rulemaking, 989, 1580, 1634, 1746, 1900, 1919,
        2201, 2513, 2515, 2534, 2569
Social Security, 1502, 1687, 1948, 2319, 2385,
    2515, 2678, 2687, 2690, 2793, 2993, 3001,
    3016, 3021, 3159; eligibility, 1081, 1728, 1877,
    3487, 3831

summons, 2648
telephone/telegraph, 207, 946, 3911
textile industry, 726, 2260
violation, 2359
welfare payments, 3409, 3956, 3965
Relations. *See also* international relations.
with Belgium, 255
with Britain, 253, 548, 613; territory, 877
with Cuba, 313, 318, 1505, 2737
with France, 30, 55, 304
with Iran, 2288
with Japan, 1016, 2387
with Peru, 254
with Philippines, 2347
with Soviet Union, 668, 743, 2407
with Spain, 148
with Taiwan, 2061
with Venezuela, 325
Religious harassment, 3065. *See also* employment
discrimination, religion.
Remedies, 1563, 1964, 2232, 2380, 2420, 2924,
3425, 3856
private, 1993, 2209, 2216
reject settlement offer, 2194
state, 1994, 2400
timely claim, 1846
Rent and renters, 1042, 1288, 1539, 2857
control, 471, 472, 831, 864, 2946, 3227, 3674
eviction, 1481
notification, 2364
Reservation. *See* Native Americans, land.
Residency requirements, 347, 367, 1673, 2510, 2626,
2796, 3010, 3177
Restitution, 3452, 3458
Retail Trade, 2111, 3230. *See also* gray markets;
sales.
discount, 3245
wholesale, 3075
Retirement, 3849
benefits, 1957, 2096, 2162, 2225, 2277, 2599,
2812, 3307, 3323, 3329; suing for, 2643
early retirement plans, 3344
mandatory, 636, 1783, 1879
plans, 3707; bankrupt, 3488
Reverse discrimination, 3346
Right to assemble. *See* freedom of assembly.
Right to counsel, 606, 686, 1125, 1200, 1304, 1503,
1589, 1722, 2301, 2500, 2567, 2628, 2679, 2680,
2693, 2704, 2778, 2789, 2918, 3031, 3333, 3750,
3928. *See also* attorneys.
assigned, 606, 753; not notified, 3252
assistance, 1414, 1899, 2095, 3138, 3208
bail hearing, 3597
cannot pay for, 3362, 3363, 3367
children, 1248

confession, 3417
conflict of interest, 3251
court-martial, 1743
defendants' representative too, 3251
denied, 1159, 2953, 3518
disqualifying, 2170, 2190
during interrogation, 1828, 2961, 3262. *See also*
interrogation, request for counsel.
homeless, 1144, 1145, 1281, 1506, 1651, 1966,
2042, 2090, 2240, 3928
incriminating statements, 1828
lied, 2942
multiple representations, 2095
perjured, 2942
retroactive, 1477, 2644
self represented, 2625
waived, 1256, 1718, 2223, 3834, 3918
without counsel's knowledge, 2169
Right to Petition, 2049, 2875, 2898
Right to Privacy, 890, 1052, 1231, 1306, 1489, 1548,
1738, 1816, 2123, 3042, 3360. *See also* privacy.
birth control, 1850
disconnect life-support, 3498
invasion, 1669, 1685, 1751
newsworthy person, 1269
telephone numbers, 2017
Right to Remain Silent. *See* arrest, right to remain
silent.
Rights of Handicapped. *See* disabled rights.
Riots. *See* conspiracy, to cause riot; disturbing the
peace, riots; prisons and jails, riots.
Roads, 534, 749, 3239
built through national parks, 1434
closure, 2210
construction, 2100
highway use tax, 3472
injunction against parades, 1301, 1854
regulation, 677, 697, 874, 879, 880, 902, 1054
right to travel, 1458
turnpikes, 316
Robbery, 2544, 2765, 2930, 2943; armed, 2958, 2980

Sales. *See also* retail trade.
airplanes, 2547
objectionable literature to children, 1139, 1317
of rail line, 3359
property, 3006
School. *See* education, school.
School desegregation/segregation, 557, 954, 955,
956, 957, 958, 973, 1163, 1517, 1577, 1587, 1873,
2031, 3673, 3994
attorney's fees, 1641
boundary change, 1384
busing, 1444, 1447, 1668, 2427, 2429, 3523
closing public schools, 1186

faculty allocations, 1236, 1238, 1369, 1445
high school, 335, 1787
local plans, 1040, 1329, 1330, 1331, 1382, 1385, 2427
private schools, 1593
remedies, 1444, 1445, 1447, 1518, 1869
school board duty, 2032
school transfer, 1164
taxes to correct, 3439
unitary system, 1396, 1446
universities, 384, 897, 3728
School Land Grant funds, 3044
Search and seizure, 245, 452, 516, 540, 558, 609, 834, 890, 932, 1082, 1110, 1233, 1295, 1358, 1802, 2003, 2591, 2630, 2658, 2659, 2661, 2753, 2756, 2757, 2811, 2819, 2840, 3317, 3318. *See also* aerial surveillance.
   and arrest, 1165, 1180, 1182, 1380, 1466, 1608, 1609, 1650, 2020, 2083, 3958
   anonymous tip, 3476
   at friends, 3441
   automobiles, 521, 585, 892, 1172, 1180, 1227, 1414, 1466, 1509, 1575, 1588, 1592, 1650, 1720, 1800, 1803, 1947, 1975, 2018, 2172, 2598, 2781, 2940, 3077, 3437, 3476; closed containers, 2282, 2283, 2377, 3572, 3585
   backpack, 3077
   bank records, 1752, 2132
   barn, 3101
   beeper, 2477, 2751
   beyond 12-mile sea limit, 556
   boat. *See* search and seizure, ship.
   body cavity, 1992
   border searches, 1588, 1714, 1719, 1720, 1803, 2172, 2903
   burglar's tools, 1337
   bus passengers, 3606
   by government agents, 2099, 2150
   by government agency, 1070, 1422, 1911, 2263, 3103
   by inspector, 1052, 1642, 1915; building inspector, 1290; fire marshal, 1291, 2612; health inspector, 1083; mining inspector, 2263
   by officer, 524, 527, 560, 1263
   by private person, 475
   by school officials, 2777, 3478
   co-conspirators, 3794
   consent, 1334, 1498, 1575, 1726; third party, 1466, 1621, 3495
   corporate paperwork, 366, 455, 584, 601
   covert entry, 1982
   detain for, 2021, 2267, 2485, 2511, 2598, 2903, 3325
   drugs, 860, 951, 1071, 1138, 1165, 1193, 1277, 1337, 1465, 1536, 1773, 1863, 1975, 2039,

2099, 2140, 2150, 2213, 2309, 2477, 2539, 2553, 2555, 2556, 2559, 2591, 2809, 2827, 2903, 2950, 3560, 3606, 3794
   felon, 3210
   fire investigation, 1915. *See also* search and seizure, by inspector, fire marshal.
   forcible, 1392
   garbage, 3194, 3247
   highway checkpoints, 1720, 1975, 3481
   home, 2401
   hotel room, 1070, 1182, 1268
   in company lobby, 2616
   in foreign country, 3414
   in hot pursuit, 1287, 1773
   investigatory stops, 2770
   jail, 1129; cell, 2746
   junkyard, 3179
   knock and announce, 3988
   luggage, 1863, 2018, 2485, 2556, 2559, 2827
   newspaper, 1916
   obscene publications, 1112, 2007, 2873
   other items found, 1364, 1789
   pat down, 2039
   physical evidence, 1546, 1576
   plain view, 1466, 1975, 2083, 2309, 2495, 3470
   possession/ownership of seized goods, 2139, 2140
   probable cause, 1350, 1789, 1915, 2139, 2267, 2377, 2539, 2950; unreasonable, 3102
   property, 1031, 1442, 1507, 3762
   protective sweep, 3416
   random, 1975, 3606
   recreational vehicles, 2940
   requiring identification, 2021
   search for weapons, 1336
   ship, 89, 613, 2553, 2968
   sobriety checkpoints. *See* search and seizure, highway checkpoints.
   stop and frisk, 1336, 1337, 1509, 2809, 3810
   trash, 3194, 3247
   using beeper, 2477, 2751
   warrant, 1863, 1916, 1934, 2950, 2972, 3280; computer error, 3958; not named, 2213; open-ended, 2007; second warrant, 610
   warrantless, 416, 468, 530, 585, 602, 860, 1091, 1392, 1465, 1498, 1575, 1576, 1592, 1911, 2017, 2018, 2039, 2129, 2263, 2377, 2401, 2556, 2681, 2813, 3077, 3102, 3114, 3204, 3438, 3441
   wrong address, 523, 3092
Secrecy, 2582, 2583, 3358
Securities, 815, 2173, 2717, 2736, 2805, 2850, 2858, 3078, 3234, 3893, 3939, 3960, 4028
   Accountants' misstatements, 2013
   arbitration, 950, 3338

Broker, 3061, 3261; commission, 3172
certificate of deposit, 2334
commodities, 2360, 3061
derivative action, 3565
disciplinary proceedings, 2184
employee benefit plan, 1956
false registration statement, 2459
forged, 2340
fraud, 288, 1173, 1702, 1746, 1995, 2036, 2070,
    2105, 2360, 2459, 3055, 3162, 3213, 3603,
    3663, 3806, 3873, 3968
insider information or trading, 2070, 2587, 2866,
    3213
investment advisor, 2109, 2182, 2619; illegal
    transactions, 1173
investment funds, 1441
merger, 3594
misrepresentation, 950, 1386
mutual fund sales, 1717
proxy statements, 1352, 1386, 1951, 3623
regulation, 2863
reorganization, 763, 851
scienter requirement, 2105, 2587
stock exchange, 1157
stock value, 1389, 1702, 3957
stockholders, 2794, 3186, 3233
unclaimed, 3776
Sedition, 914, 982, 987, 1005, 1008, 1057, 1106,
    1107, 1201, 1235, 1305, 1526
    states, 983, 1011, 1012, 1272, 1303
Self-incrimination, 291, 309, 385, 468, 794, 850, 906,
    917, 969, 1106, 1200, 1235, 1308, 1309, 1310,
    1359, 1405, 1416, 1442, 2118, 2634, 2714, 2743,
    2797, 2953, 3033, 3087, 3136, 3207, 3271
    automobile accident, 1453
    blood test, 999, 1263, 2466
    business records, 876, 1543, 1789, 2496, 2639,
        3270
    by reporting violation, 2145
    by silence, 1225, 1273, 1895, 2191
    by talking, 3085
    child custody, 1284, 3405
    confession, 1260, 1270, 3068, 3438
    handwriting, 1299
    invoking privilege, 971, 972, 984, 1191, 1192,
        1225, 1390, 2191
    law presumption of guilt, 1368
    police lineup, 1298, 1299
    private papers, 475
    protection, 982
    registration and possession of guns, 1440
    state immunity laws, 1969
    to psychologist, 3047
    undercover agent, 3474
    waving rights, 3597

    witness. *See* witness, self-incrimination.
Seniority Systems, 1154, 1739, 1842, 1843, 1846,
    1847, 1855, 1878, 2056, 2326, 2349, 2357, 2711,
    2985, 3315, 3348
Sentencing, 353, 2221, 2525, 2747, 3198, 3300,
    3506, 3512, 3566, 3618, 3699, 3853. *See also* plea
    bargaining; punishment.
    by jury, 1572, 3255, 3418
    children, 2297, 3664
    commutation or clemency, 2258
    concurrent terms, 3147, 3992
    consecutive sentences, 2085, 3992
    credit for time served, 1379, 3993
    cumulative sentences, 2458
    drugs, 2082, 2303, 3530, 3582, 3621, 3687, 3803,
        3869, 4004
    gang membership, 3658
    guidelines, 3792; misapplied, 3577, 3595, 3660
    guns, 2001, 3018, 3803, 3882, 3887
    harder, 3816, 3954
    improper sentencing, 3530
    mandatory life, 1949, 2071, 3527, 3621
    misdemeanor, 2090
    multiple counts, 3798
    multiple felonies, 3459
    murder. *See* Murder
    psychiatric evaluation before, 3252
    reduced, 3687
    reforms improper sentencing, 3491
    repeat offender, 1477, 3736, 3896
    review, 2160
    right to speak at sentencing, 1092
    second offense punishment, 305, 2193, 2458;
        longer than first, 2941
    vacate or void, 1150
    witness perjury, 3760
Separation of powers, 47, 3058, 3282
Severance pay. *See* hours and wages, severance pay.
Sewage, 339, 473, 616, 2217, 3654
Sex bias, 3072, 3137
Sex discrimination, 193, 377, 423, 501, 653, 658,
    1116, 1878, 1986, 2198, 2688, 2749, 2804, 2835,
    3017, 3267, 3332
    in alimony, 1963
    in benefits, 1687, 1788, 1806, 1822, 1826, 1904,
        2022, 2088, 2558, 2599
    in child support, 1690
    in community property, 2197
    in education, 1945, 1993, 2366, 2436, 2638, 4047
    in employment, 878, 1425, 1569, 1591, 1846,
        1871, 2004, 2005, 2010, 2094, 2189, 2326,
        3433
    in estate administration, 1472
    in federally funded programs, 2366
    in law, 190, 296

in liquor sales, 1808
in military, 1674, 2273
in Social Security benefits, 1826, 2651
in taxes, 1636
in voting, 672
in wages, 1645, 2245
on juries, 1675, 1952
Sexual harassment, 3017, 3846
in schools, 3652
Sexual orientation discrimination, 3260, 4010, 4041
Shipping, 409, 1086, 1393, 1454, 1459, 2340, 2359,
3183, 3193, 3234, 3301, 3493, 3769
by boat, 37, 62, 78, 1888, 2124, 2211, 3301
by bus, 666, 875
by railroad, 224, 297, 322, 407, 411, 413, 421,
433, 513, 806, 3081
by truck, 677, 1054, 1824, 1884, 2203, 2990,
3081, 3885
people, 412, 737
rates, 2821
Slavery, 5, 95, 107, 109, 132, 434
escape, 145
evidence, 58
fugitives, 136, 155
servitude, 394
slave trade, 104, 133
Smoking/tobacco, 1753, 3824, 3904
price, 68
regulation, 689
taxes, 2113
Smuggling, 1540, 2340, 2559, 2854, 2968, 3932
Social Security, 670, 671, 1081, 1502, 1569, 1687,
1728, 1822, 1826, 1948, 2136, 2188, 2319, 2385,
2515, 2651, 2643, 2678, 2687, 2690, 2793, 2987,
2993, 3001, 3003, 3016, 3021, 3159, 3482, 3487,
3831
children's benefits, 1790, 1877, 2028, 3404
Social Science Data Use, 3042
Solid waste, 1929, 3694, 3871, 3884
Sodomy, 3042
Sports, 949, 4045
college, 2733, 3294
compete, 3734
State and local government, 2946, 3016. *See also*
local government taxes; states; state taxes.
State powers. *See* states, authority.
State taxes, 462, 837, 2257, 2293, 2396, 2713, 2738,
3897. *See also* corporate taxes; income taxes; local
taxes; Native Americans, taxes; taxes in general.
agreement between states, 1885
aid to church-related colleges, 1602, 2581
aircraft, 1898
airlines, 2601
animal skins and fur, 514
bank deposits, 704

benefits, 669, 3678, 3826
business, 174, 183, 188, 194, 502, 646, 1023,
1188, 1226, 1924, 2077, 2142, 3193, 3296,
3327, 3396, 3692, 3715, 3759, 3857, 3892,
4011
cable television services, 3553
capital gains, 3708
coal, 495, 2287
custom duties, 2450
estate, 2383
exceptions from taxes, 1037, 1562, 3160
federal securities, 113, 3939
gasoline, 553, 2115, 2236
immunity to pay, 690, 797; federal contractor,
2344, 2486
imported merchandise, 168, 174, 183
income, 642, 3323
inheritance, 539, 582
interstate goods, 3192
mortgage, 2561
multinational corporations, 676, 832, 875, 908,
1282, 1542, 1723, 2233, 2423, 2424, 2574,
3914
Native Americans, 1753, 1763, 2113, 2439, 3797,
4006
overpayment, 596
property tax, 429, 1636, 1763, 1988, 2199, 2594,
3857; assessment, 3709
railroad property, 250, 3133
refunds, 3937
sales, 2143, 2344, 2488, 2859, 3014, 3253, 3399,
3553, 3786, 3967; at tribal store, 2113, 3535,
3904
separate filings, 596
windfall, 3327
States, 339, 2385, 2571, 3776, 4034. *See also*
injunction, against state proceedings; state taxes.
amendment, 2180, 4041; ratification, 693
attorney general, 2877; proceedings, 1011, 1057
authority, 12, 17, 29, 82, 110, 220, 237, 295, 459,
466, 529, 724, 759, 843, 849, 983, 1152, 1623,
1771, 2131, 2174, 2175, 2323, 2376, 2476,
2512, 2537, 2576, 2612, 2621, 2712, 2784,
2960
bonds, 2633
business, 251, 655, 695, 742, 2122; regulation,
103, 110, 127, 175, 194, 200, 206, 244, 270,
272, 312, 317, 329, 393, 402, 407, 418, 508,
515, 545, 568, 624, 649, 677, 733, 812, 847,
968, 1542, 1672, 1729, 1756, 1770, 1859, 1884,
1958, 2109, 2203, 3910
capital city, 404
compact, 714, 909, 2552
debts, 59, 230, 1149
elections. *See* elections, state.

employees, 685, 935, 984, 1108, 1340, 1598, 1697, 1839, 1893, 1969, 1989, 2005, 2629, 3571, 3624; bargaining agreement, 3152; overtime, 3791

immunity, 1629, 1965, 2046, 2624, 3448, 3453, 3743, 3934

land claims and disputes, 85, 112, 122, 3161

laws, 397, 476, 673, 1101, 1102, 1272, 1448, 1565, 1628, 1701, 1852, 1922, 1929, 2006, 2203, 2505, 3153, 3166, 3378

lawsuits, 256, 267, 1184, 1633, 1672, 1673, 1888, 1965, 2136, 2452, 3059. *See also* suits, against state.

legislative chaplains, 2592

legislative investigations, 1148; witness, contempt, 1129, 1192

legislators, 1266, 3216

legislature: immunity, 2106; speech or debate clause, 2074; unicameral, 2592; vetoes, 2592

liability claims, 3723

military, 76, 243

officials, 1725, 2724; immunity, 2046, 2735, 3350; liability, 1091, 3624; office, 2413

police power, 259, 1816

property, 2435

referendum, 1449

regulations, 141, 146, 200, 201, 202, 203, 204, 205, 268, 433, 649, 759, 830, 871, 1039, 1054, 1171, 1352, 1393, 1605, 1691, 1804, 1888, 2418, 2461, 2512, 2589, 2947, 2988, 3020, 3119, 3980. *See also* cities, regulations; regulations.

residency requirements, 1623, 1673, 1927, 2382

selection of governor, 1267

water rights, 314, 379, 682, 1032, 1162, 1438, 1944, 2121, 2216, 2442, 2452, 2489, 2552, 2585, 3599, 3780, 3789, 3982, 3990

zoning, 2448

Statutes. *See* Congress, laws or legislation; states, laws.

Statutes of Limitations, 96, 2327, 2834, 2957, 3116, 3178, 3188, 3264, 3985
    securities, 3603
    taxes, 1203

Sterilization, 550, 755, 1896

Stockholders or stocks. *See* corporations, stockholders; securities.

Streets. *See* roads.

Strike. *See* boycotting; labor, strike; unions, striking.

Students, 1526, 2299, 2411, 3855. *See also* education.
    academic dismissal, 1887
    death, 3741
    disabled, 2419, 3354
    discipline, 1832

expulsion, 3221

extracurricular clubs/societies, 2956, 3473

financial aid. *See* financial aid.

newspaper, 3219

obscenity, 3056

paddling, 1832

rights, 2777

suspension, 1677, 1683, 1891, 2443

wearing of armbands in protest, 1354

Suits, 22, 53, 65, 436, 888, 1394, 2013, 2053, 2147, 2306, 2802, 3682. *See also* damage/claims suits.
    against federal government, 479, 828, 1492, 1658, 1849, 2216, 2474, 2540; fraudulent, 761; spending, 1338
    against state, 256, 267, 1672, 1673, 3059, 3616
    back wages, 2206, 2209
    between states, 2452
    broker, 3261
    environmental, 1492, 2271, 3725
    immunity, 3830; compensation, 575; court reporter, 3813; federal government, 17, 227, 938, 1629, 1967, 2275, 3766, 3864, 4029; federal government agencies, 1938; federal government contractor, 703; local government, 2084, 2278; membership, 1907; military, 2375; police, 1279, 2102, 4000; private individuals, 3686; prosecution, 1731; school boards, 1810; states, 1184, 1633, 1788, 1888, 1965, 2136; waiver, 2624
    international, 1880, 2298, 2517
    private individuals, 2360, 3083
    prosecution, 3855
    school board, 1683
    settlements, 3874, 3875
    wrongful death, 1373, 1633, 1917, 1926, 2051, 2086, 2474, 3023

Sunday work laws, 2884, 3324. *See also* freedom of religion, working on Sunday.

Superfund, 2951, 3349

Supreme Court, 2504, 2555
    complaint by state, 1161
    denied to hear, 3844
    dismissed, 2630, 3688, 3847
    divided court, 1083, 1538, 2195, 2268, 2315, 2341, 2817, 2818, 2822, 2823, 2824, 2827, 2828, 2874, 2920, 3146, 3211, 3893
    foreign relations, 1181
    hypothetical issues, 2313
    judicial review, 16, 35, 425, 429, 507, 693, 970, 2243, 2361
    jurisdiction, 25, 66, 159, 482, 667, 764, 806, 975, 1494, 2148, 2224, 2236, 2450, 2512, 2598, 2651, 3067; lack, 2362
    justices, appointment, 675
    remanded, 3511, 4001

reporter, 126
reversed decision, 2728
special master, 2256, 2257, 2302, 2452, 2552
supplemental decree, 2255, 2270

Taxes in general, 447, 578, 660, 1038, 2648, 2666, 2669, 2880, 2999, 3240. *See also* banks and banking, taxes; corporate taxes; income taxes; local taxes; Native Americans, taxes; state taxes.
    accounting methods, 1140, 1543, 1901, 1955
    bankrupt taxpayer, 3467
    bookkeeping, 3157
    crude oil, 2533
    customs duties, 183, 292, 342, 343, 344, 562
    delinquent taxpayer, 2885, 3774, 3978
    direct, 19, 176, 221
    estate, 539, 731, 1289, 2997, 3902
    exemption, 685, 1970, 2880, 3019; for nonprofits, 2970; for private schools, 2752; for religious organizations, 1403, 1476, 1480; tax free, 2767
    food, 357
    gift, 805, 2322, 2631, 2997, 3426, 3876
    guns, 3698
    information fraud, 1203
    inheritance, 3237
    judge, 179
    late filing, 2772
    lien, 2885
    life insurance, 1834, 2233, 2816
    loan, 2631
    magazines, 3125
    natural resources, 2316
    of awards, 2051, 2284
    of states' activities, 820
    on losses, 3090
    on unlawful activity, 1308, 1309
    property, 301, 303, 846, 2526. *See also* property, taxes.
    records, 2648, 3212
    refund, 2773
    religious objection, 2319
    retroactive, 1003, 3902
    severance, 2830
    Social Security, 670, 671, 2319
    state bonds, 2633
    stocks, 2805, 3186
    summons, 1925, 2776, 3313
    tolls, 188
    user fee, 1898
Teachers, 920, 984, 1035, 1335, 1617, 1764, 1839, 1946, 1960, 1971, 1978, 2040, 2948, 2985
    certification, 3342
    contractual renewal, 1531, 2668
    fitness, 1087
    speech, 1807, 1810, 1954, 2410, 2469

    suspension, 3026
Teenage pregnancy, 3281
Telephone or telegraph, 207, 504, 946, 1017, 2603, 2864, 3189, 3372, 3911
    book, 3549
    dial-a-porn, 3369
    telephone numbers, 2017
    taxes, 3296
    telephone wires, 567, 674, 1306
Television, 2075. *See also* communications, broadcasting.
    cable, 1625, 1976, 2311, 2426, 2994, 3099, 3248, 3807, 3924
    public, noncommercial, 2742
    sports, 2733
Term limits, 3987
Territories, 121, 1684, 2149. *See also* citizenship, in territories; court jurisdiction, territorial court; District of Columbia.
    Florida, 108
    Georgia, 118
    Guam, 3444
    Hawaii, 544, 823, 867
    Louisiana, 111
    Nebraska, 281
    Philippine Islands, 359, 390
    Puerto Rico, 342, 343, 344, 482, 2379; standing to sue, 2432
    Utah, 212, 213, 265, 271
Testimony. *See* witness, testimony.
Timber, 391, 964, 2081, 2575, 3239, 3671
Torts, 420, 559, 886, 979, 1383, 1541, 2478, 2890, 3054, 3144, 3543, 3548, 3766, 3796, 3874, 3905, 4005
    hospitals, 3640
    servicemen, 899, 1849
    state, 3152, 3220
Toxic waste. *See* hazardous waste.
Trade Secret, 2727
Trademarks or Tradenames, 215, 594, 936, 1124, 1958, 2769, 3201, 3230, 3729, 3900, 3966
    copying, 1177, 1178
    infringement, 2378, 3150
    using for product identity sales, 655
Transportation and transporting. *See* interstate business, carriers; public transportation; roads, shipping.
Travel, 1948
    international, 1029, 1030, 1228; denied, 2737
    interstate, 1252
    passport issued, 1029, 1030, 1201, 1228; outside United States, 1123; revoked, 2279
    tickets, 3558
    visa, 1534, 3211

Treason, 1, 2, 45, 808, 845, 931, 948; malicious
   words, 11
Treasury, 214, 632, 633
Treaty. *See* international law, treaty; Native
   Americans, treaties.
Trespass, 391, 1197, 1198, 1264, 1276, 1325
Trial, 105, 262, 866, 995, 1744, 2050, 2597, 3627
      accused: absence, 3748; disruptive and removed,
         1399; drugged during, 3685
      bail hearing, 3563
      bond hearing, 3464
      change of venue, 1105, 1258
      children tried as an adult, 1696, 2297, 2314
      discovery, 3223; investigator's report, 1709
      errors, 3782, 3952
      fair trial. *See* fair trial.
      false testimony, 1731, 2480
      in another state, 3758, 3915
      incompetent to stand, 1072, 1504, 3721
      joint, 3755
      jury, 196, 315, 337, 482, 577, 770, 992, 1053,
         1124, 1259, 1324, 1389, 1415, 1467, 1500,
         1664, 1829, 1951, 2086, 2137, 2275, 3131,
         3424, 3629, 3927; evidence evaluation, 2168;
         size, 1586, 1980, 2120
      media coverage, 1232, 1258, 1704, 1791, 2030,
         2152, 2178, 2403
      mistrial, 2372
      motion for a new trial, 629, 975
      prosecutor's disclosure, 1775
      retry case, 2747
      right to a speedy trial, 1276, 1474, 1519, 2346,
         2521, 2922, 2926, 2986, 3274, 3726, 3915
      right to fair. *See* fair trial.
      second trial, 1696, 2181, 2941
      self-representation, 1718
      verdict, 1499, 1500, 1921, 2128, 2381, 2764. *See
         also* juries, verdict.
Trucking regulation, 2701. *See also* interstate
   business, carriers; shipping.
Trust Fund, 226, 247, 2523, 2667
      notification, 894
      taxes, 618, 707, 2322

Unemployment: compensation, 1170, 1721, 1728,
   1972, 2114, 2204, 2237, 2248, 3025, 3054;
   insurance, 3084, 3095, 3324
Unfair competition, 445, 465
Unions, 661, 662, 1866, 1971, 2124, 2209, 2264,
   2266, 2469, 2491, 2891, 2975, 3217, 3243, 3584,
   3629, 3819, 3863. *See also* injunction, in labor
   disputes.
      affiliated with another union, 2943
      agency shop. *See* unions, union shop.
      back-to-work agreement, 3539
      bargaining, 3154
      bargaining unit, 1634, 2304
      boycotting, 376, 403, 467, 813, 2355, 2573, 3242;
         at secondary business, 1183, 1280, 3132
      bylaws or Constitution violations, 3629
      collective bargaining, 2606, 2962, 3139, 3767.
         See also labor, collective bargaining.
      contracts, 3225
      discipline of members, 3139
      dues' fees, 2672, 2948, 3283, 3584
      election, 1367, 1698, 1811, 2006, 2710, 3533
      employee committee, 1059
      expelled, 1571
      extortion, 981
      fair representation, 1275, 1998, 2536, 3116;
         denied, 2335, 2425, 2454, 3425
      fining a member, 1297, 1573, 2892
      grievance procedures, 1214, 1678, 1734, 1964,
         1989, 2205, 2208, 2454, 2536, 3519;
         arbitration, 1275, 2234
      labor violence, 1251
      membership, 375, 422, 555, 664, 665, 666, 884,
         1154, 2363, 2384, 2465, 2989; forced, 2457
      negligence, 3449
      negotiations, 1807, 3436, 3461
      nonmembers, 2593, 2943, 2948; fees, 3283
      nonunion labor, 549, 747, 990, 1325, 1699, 2235
      officers, 3299
      officials, 794, 1230, 1319, 2363, 2492;
         embezzlement, 3398
      organizing, 442, 581, 783, 803, 986, 1377, 1520,
         3648, 4021
      pensions, 3819
      picketing, 1910, 2123, 2355, 2371, 3132; on
         private property, 1733
      political activities, 1113, 1516
      political strike, 2355, 2407
      representatives, 799, 1682, 2371, 2465, 2507,
         2745
      right to bargain, 442, 1991, 2649
      secondary activity, 1815, 2127, 2573
      strikebreakers, 1573, 3432
      striking, 488, 526, 663, 728, 1002, 1121, 1297,
         1409, 1553, 1764, 1972, 2043, 2492, 3054;
         economic, 3315; political strike, 895; wildcat,
         2220
      union shop, 990, 1113, 1839, 2948, 3584
      use of abusive language, 1660
      work stoppages, 1776, 2407
Universities. *See* colleges and universities.
Utilities, 687, 851. *See also* gas leases; oil; telephone
   or telegraph.
      bill inserts, 2125, 2126, 2936
      cable television. *See* television, cable.
      coal usage, 2287, 3514, 3645

electricity, 438, 542, 648, 1176, 1478, 1626,
    1672, 1760, 1804, 1897, 2218, 2512, 2513
ethanol, 3253
hydroelectric energy, 2323, 2963
ice, 600
natural gas, 1320, 1626, 1724, 2286, 2537, 3234.
    See also natural gas.
power plants, 976
rates, 504, 542, 574, 745, 780, 1176, 1320, 2963,
    2988, 3012, 3522
regulation, 2376
right-of-way, 709, 2603

Vaccines, 362, 3258, 3969
Vested Rights, 24
Veterans, 1037, 2114, 2261, 3142, 3241, 3266, 3640
    benefits, 2898
    disability benefits, 3142, 3340
    preferential employment, 2005
    retirement pay, 2277
    tax exemptions, 2880
Vietnam War. *See* War, Vietnam.
Vindictiveness, 2730
Voting Rights, 265, 1067, 1189, 1355, 1391, 1423,
    1560, 2087, 2218, 2627, 2655, 2792, 2832, 3040,
    3041. *See also* elections; reapportionment and
    redistricting.
    age, 1421
    at-large system, 2433
    criminals, 2832
    gerrymandering. *See* reapportionment and
        redistricting, gerrymandering.
    literacy test, 427, 1056, 1244, 1421, 1590
    local elections, 2390
    outside country, 1024, 1286
    political party affiliation, 1630
    polling tax, 672, 1249, 4035
    procedural change, 2472
    property taxes, 1692
    Puerto Ricans, 1262, 2379
    race restrictions, 197, 235, 331, 351, 352, 427,
        547, 603, 635, 692, 736, 787, 943, 1146, 1217,
        1360, 1711, 2089, 2244, 2451, 2472, 3082
    residency requirement, 1486
    state, 1567; county commissioner, 3929
    women, 193, 480

Wages. *See* hours and wages.
War:
    Civil, 165; blockades, 157, 161, 166, 167;
        confiscation, 173, 180, 182; Native American
        claims, 751; reconstruction, 169, 173, 184
    claims for damages, 325
    claims for property, 15, 20, 531, 802, 1031, 1278
    damage, 3301

price controls during wartime, 782, 784, 831, 843,
    864
prohibition of arms sales, 656
trial for war crimes, 821, 977
Revolutionary, 15, 20
Vietnam, 1307, 1426; classified information,
    1471, 1532; opposition to war, 1266, 1326,
    1354, 1436, 1532; protest, 1418, 1456, 1521,
    1606, 1658
World War I: prohibition, 454; resistance to, 451,
    456, 458, 466
World War II, 757; curfew, 774, 775; exclusion
    and relocation, 800, 801; gasoline ration
    coupons, 834; leasing buildings, 802, 824, 889
Warrant. *See* search and seizure, warrant.
Water, 1033, 1888, 2216. *See also* maritime law.
    coastline, 2939
    dam building, 470, 722, 1923, 1943
    districts, 1559, 1560, 2218
    flood control, 3053
    Great Lakes, 518, 1493, 2217
    irrigation, 314, 1032, 2121
    land underneath, 287, 2391, 2508
    offshore, 849, 2295
    outer continental shelf, 2614, 3108
    pollution, 339, 616, 909, 1493, 1820, 2069, 2158,
        2217, 2271, 2358, 2791, 3131, 3654, 3895;
        cross state lines, 3083; enforcement of no,
        3215; mineral, 397; oil spill, 1565, 2145
    public access, 2041
    reclamation project, 1943
    reservoirs, 3053
    rights, 314, 374, 379, 682, 1032, 1162, 1438,
        1740, 1944, 2121, 2200, 2216, 2442, 2452,
        2489, 2552, 2572, 2585, 2699, 3009, 3158,
        3599, 3780, 3789, 3982, 3990
    rivers, 88, 110, 146, 147, 149, 178, 332, 365; boat
        collision on, 2405
    tide, 3224
    wetlands, 2916
    wharf construction, 617
Weights and Measures, 515
Welfare, 507, 1557, 3003, 3064, 3129, 3203, 3309
    aid to families with dependent children, 1366,
        1402, 1422, 1502, 2022, 2385, 2913, 2971,
        3956, 3965
    aliens, 1464
    benefits, 1622, 2793; computation, 1502
    food stamps, 1595, 1596, 2861. *See also* food
        stamps.
    Medicaid, 2402
    payments, 3409, 3956, 3965
    residency requirement, 1366, 1464, 1948
    termination procedure, 1397

Wildlife, 2215, 2479, 3020. *See also* agriculture, livestock; animal rights; endangered species; hunting.
    protection, 1765, 1984, 2037.
Wills, 138, 338, 1835
Wiretapping and surveillance, 700, 1158, 1522, 1546, 1982, 2686, 2877, 4012. *See also* aerial surveillance; evidence.
    authorization, 1639, 1640
    eavesdropping, 1295, 1357, 1514
    identification of person, 1812
    interception of communication, 1523, 1620, 1908
    radio transmitter, 932, 1443
    recording conversations, 750, 952, 1094, 1129
    sealed, 3446
    telephone numbers, 2017
    telephone wires, 567, 674, 1306
    validity of order, 1812
Witness, 33, 1106, 3223
    alibi, 1416
    business records, 1789, 2496, 2639. *See also* self-incrimination, business records.
    children as, 3180, 3288, 3507, 3508
    congressional witnesses, 222, 543, 570, 593, 971, 972
    credibility, 1274, 1707, 2462
    cross-examine, 1551, 1624, 1767, 2101, 2116, 2337, 2964, 3226, 3295
    deportation, 2440
    expert witness fees, 3170, 3540
    failure to testify, 698
    grand juries, 7, 366, 904, 1532, 1546, 1969; immunity, 279, 969, 1501, 2066, 2455; refusal to testify, 1501, 1523, 1611, 3718
    handwriting, 2060
    identification of accused, 1298, 1300, 1313, 1503, 1538, 1856, 1892, 2078, 3226
    immunity, 2480
    intimidation, 2494
    leading questions, 1099
    news reporters' privilege, 1533, 1916
    on own behalf, 291, 1097, 1341, 1451
    probation officer, 2634
    psychiatric testimony, 2222, 2595
    reimbursement fees, 3520
    right to confront, 1151, 1221, 1222, 1277, 1311, 1323, 1371, 1417, 1455, 1551, 2138, 2952, 2964, 2996, 3123, 3507, 3642; children, 3180; via closed-circuit television, 3508

right to present, 1293
right to silence, 1722, 1750, 1767, 1895, 2337, 2466, 3207
self-incrimination, 1451, 1501, 1644, 1647, 1709, 1749, 1751, 1895, 2066, 2082, 2222, 2223, 2455, 3207
sequestration, 1744
spouse as, 1041, 2064
subpoena, 794, 3520
tampering with, 3105
testimony, 293, 315, 1221, 1667, 1688, 1744, 2064, 2918, 2942, 2952, 3207, 3508, 3856, 3949, 3975; third party testimony, 1709; under hypnosis, 3184. *See also* witness, psychiatric testimony.
truthfulness, 1607, 2101, 2942
Workers' Compensation, 435, 817, 1184, 1473, 1495, 1648, 2088, 2146, 2523, 2725, 2800, 3118, 3200, 3380, 3428
    after retiring, 2225, 3744
    black lung, 3293, 3430, 3614, 3913
    claim, 2338, 3256
    disability status, 2166
    maritime workers, 199, 598, 706, 785, 826, 1027, 1413, 2092, 2211, 2229, 2430, 2456, 2519, 2551, 3383, 3528, 3628, 3722, 3744, 3964, 3999, 4003; foreign seaman, 1045, 1411; on land, 2038, 2131; on pier, 1383, 1858
    railroad workers, 2283
    retroactive, 3659
Workplace Safety, 1047, 2062, 2153, 2260, 3127, 3544, 3655. *See also* mining, safety.
    accidents, 1932, 2497, 3200
    transporting employees, 3428
Wrongful death. *See* damage claims/suits, wrongful death; maritime law, wrongful death; suits, wrongful death.

Yarmulkes, 2955

Zoning, 441, 537, 564, 1631, 1713, 1809, 1845, 2117, 2202, 2210, 2241, 2895, 2901, 2937, 3107, 3984
    billboards, 3550
    Native American, 3376
    permit and impact fees, 3209

CASE NAMES AND POPULAR CASE NAMES INDEX

Each entry (not page number) leads to the case by any parties involved, including coupled cases. Note government agencies are not under their abbreviations but the full agency name, e.g. INS is filed under Immigration and Naturalization Service (INS). Use of city names is a problem so look under both the official city name and under City of, e.g. Los Angeles and City of Los Angeles. Any popular case names are given in quotation marks "Alabama and Mississippi Boundary Case."

44 Liquormart, Inc. v. Rhode Island, 4039

47th Street Photo, Inc. v. Coalition to Preserve the Integrity of American Trademarks, 3230

50 Acres of Land; United States v., 2761

92 Buena Vista Ave.; United States v., 3762

324 Liquor Corp. v. Duffy, 3075

356 Bales of Cotton; American Insurance Co. v., 108

$8,850 in United States Currency; United States v., 2521

A & P Tea Co. v. Cottrell, 1729

A.B. Dick Co.; Henry v., 408

ABF Freight Systems, Inc. v. National Labor Relations Board (NLRB), 3856

ACF Industries, Inc.; Department of Revenue v., 3857

ALA Schechter Poultry Corp. v. United States, 637

ANR Pipeline Co.; Schneidewind v., 3234

ARAMCO; Equal Employment Opportunity Commission (EEOC) v., 3546

ARC America Corp.; California v., 3328

ARM; United States Catholic Conference v., 3268

ASARCO Inc. v. Idaho State Tax Commission, 2423

AT&T, Co.; MCI Telecommunications v., 3911

———; Lorance v., 3348

———; United States v., 3911

AT&T Technologies, Inc. v. Communication Workers of America, 2962

Aaron v. Securities Exchange Commission (SEC), 2105

———; Cooper v., 1040

Abate v. Mundt, 1461

Abbate v. United States, 1049

Abbott; Thornburgh v., 3335

Abbott & Associates, Inc.; Illinois v., 2487

Abbott Laboratories v. Portland Retail Druggist Association, 1742

———; Jefferson County Pharmaceutical Association, Inc. v., 2473

Abe v. Richardson, 1255

Abel v. United States, 1070

———; United States v., 2763

Abend; Stewart v., 3445

Aberdeen and Rockfish Railroad Co. v. Students Challenging Regulatory Agency Procedures (SCRAP), 1580

Abernathy v. Sullivan, 1179

Ableman v. Booth, 155

Abney; Evans v., 1388

Abood v. Detroit Board of Education, 1839

Abortion Rights Mobilization, Inc.; United States Catholic Conference v., 3268

Abourezk; Regan v., 3211

Abrahamson; Brecht v., 3782

Abram; Breithaupt v., 999

Abrams v. Martin, 2698

——— v. United States, 451

Abrams, Jr. v. Johnson, 4019

Abramson; Federal Bureau of Investigation (FBI) v., 2370

Acevedo; California v., 3585

Achilli v. United States, 1006

Ackerman; Ferri v., 2042

Ackley; Chicago, Milwaukee and St. Paul Railroad Co. v., 203

Action Automotive, Inc.; National Labor Relations Board (NLRB) v., 2782

Acton; Vernonia School District v., 4014

Actors Equity Association; H.A. Artists & Associates Inc. v., 2235

Acuff-Rose Music; Campbell v., 3867

Adair v. United States, 375

Adams; Cuyler v., 2174

———; Mennonite Board of Missions v., 2561

——— v. Tanner, 440

———; Terry v., 943

——— v. Texas, 2137

——— v. United States, 769

——— v. Williams, 1509

Adams Fruit Co. v. Ramsford Barrett, 3428

Adamson v. California, 850

———; Ricketts v., 3182

Adarand Constructors, Inc. v. Pena, Secretary of Transportation, 3997

Adderley v. Florida, 1264

Addington v. Texas, 1987

Addyston Pipe and Steel Co. v. United States, 333

Adkins v. Children's Hospital of the District of Columbia, 501

——— v. Lyons, 501

Adler v. Board of Education of the City of New York, 920

Administrator, Federal Aviation Administration (FAA) v. Robertson, 1710

Administrator; Opp Cotton Mills v., 726

Administrator of General Services; Nixon v., 1874

Advanced Lightweight; Laborers Health and Welfare v., 3225

Aeschliman; Consumer Power Co. v., 1900

Aetna Casualty & Surety Co.; Rodrigue v., 1373

———; Weber v., 1495

Aetna Life Insurance Co. v. Lavoie, 2969

Afroyim v. Rusk, Secretary of State, 1286

Agee; Haig v., 2279

Agency Holding Corp. v. Malley-Duff and Associates, Inc., 3188

Agins v. City of Tiburon, 2117

Agnello v. United States, 530

Agricultural Board; Michigan Canners & Freezers v., 2705

Aguilar v. Felton, 2900

——— v. Texas, 1193

———; United States v., 4012

Aguillard; Edwards v., 3176

Agurs; United States v., 1775

Ahlers; Norwest Bank of Worthington v., 3231

Aiello; Geduldig v., 1648

Aikens; United States Postal Service, Board of Governors v., 2493

Air Courier Conference of America v. American Postal Workers Union, AFL-CIO, 3536

Air France v. Saks, 2799

Air Line Pilots Association, International v. O'Neill, 3539

——— v. Thurston, 2766

Air Pollution Variance Board of Colorado v. Western Alfalfa Corp., 1642

Air Reduction Sales Co. v. Commissioner of Internal Revenue, 833

Ake v. Oklahoma, 2789

Akin v. United States, 1740

Akron Center for Reproductive Health, Inc.; Akron v., 2548

———; Ohio v., 3502

Al-Khazraji; Saint Francis College v., 3140

Alabama; Bailey v., 394

———; Baldwin v., 2869

———; Beck v., 2128

———; Boykin v., 1370

———; Douglas v., 1222

———; Harris v., 3954

———; Heath v., 2914

———; J.E.B. v., 3872

———; Marsh v., 819

———; McKinney v., 1737

———; Mills v., 1257

———; NAACP v., 1036

———; Norris v., 634

———; Pace v., 228

———; Patterson v., 606

———; Powell v., 606

———; Swain v., 1219

———; Taylor v., 2406

———; Thornhill v., 710

——— v. United States, 1161

———; Weems v., 606

——— v. White, 3476

Alabama Midland Railway Co.; ICC v., 324

Alabama Power Co. v. Davis, 1847

"Alabama and Mississippi Boundary Case," 2790

"Alabama Power Case," 1847

Aladdin's Castle, Inc.; Mesquite v., 2321

Alaska; Davis v., 1624

———; Kenai Peninsula Borough v., 2215

———; United States v., 3677

———; Watt v., 2215

Alaska Airlines, Inc. v. Brock, 3112

Albemarle Paper Co. v. Moody, 1712

Albernaz v. United States, 2193

Albers; Whitley v., 2949

Albertini; United States v., 2883

Alberts v. California, 1015

Albertson v. Subversive Activities Control Board (SACB), 1235

Albonico; Madera Irrigation District v., 1032

Albrecht v. Herald Co., 1312

Albright v. Oliver, 3855

Alcan Aluminium, Ltd.; Franchise Tax Board v., 3396

Alderman v. United States, 1357

Aldinger v. Howard, 1772

Aldridge v. United States, 588

Alessi v. Raybestos-Manhattan, Inc., 2225

Alexander v. Gardner-Denver Co., 1619

——— v. Holmes County Board of Education, 1382

——— v. United States, 3838

Alexander, Governor of Tennessee v. Choate, 2775

Alexandria; Breard v., 915

Alexandria Scrap Corp.; Hughes v., 1770

Alexandria Women's Health Clinic; Bray v., 3749

Alford; North Carolina v., 1419

———; United States v., 551

Alfred Dunhill of London, Inc. v. Republic of Cuba, 1755

Alfred H. Mayer Co.; Jones v., 1343

Alfred L. Snapp & Son, Inc. v. Puerto Rico, 2432

Algonquin, SNG, Inc.; Federal Energy Administration v., 1766

Allain; Papasan v., 3044

Allard; Andrus v., 2037

Allegheny County; Griggs v., 1120

Allegheny Pittsburgh Coal Co. v. County Commissioner of Webster County, West Virginia, 3298

Allen; Board of Education of Central School District No. 1 v., 1342

———; Board of Pardons v., 3166

———; Brown v., 937

———; County Court of Ulster County v., 2002

———; Daniels v., 937

——— v. Illinois, 3047

———; Illinois v., 1399

———; James v., 6

——— v. McCurry, 2159

———; Mueller v., 2581

———; Pulliam v., 2676

———; Speller v., 937

——— v. State Board of Elections, 1355

——— v. United States, 315

——— v. Wright, 2752

Allen Bradley Co. v. Local Union No. 3, International Brotherhood of Electrical Workers, 813

Allen Park Public Schools v. Bradley, 1668

Allgeyer v. Louisiana, 317

Alliance Resources Corp.; TXO Production Corp. v., 3836

Allied-Bruce Terminix Cos., Inc. v. Dobson, 3946

Allied International, Inc.; International Longshoremen's Assoc. v., 2355

Allied-Signal, Inc. v. Director, Division of Taxation, 3708

Allied Structural Steel Co. v. Spannaus, 1935

Alling; Sherlock v., 199

Allis-Chalmers Corp. v. Lueck, 2831

Allis-Chalmers Manufacturing Co.; National Labor Relations Board (NLRB) v., 1297

Alloyd Co., Inc.; Gustanfson v., 3957

Allred v. United States, 870

Allstate Insurance Co. v. Hague, 2167

Allwright; Smith v., 787

Almeida-Sanchez v. United States, 1588

Aloha Airlines, Inc. v. Director of Taxation of Hawaii, 2601

Alpine Ridge Group; Cisneros v., 3790

Alton; Alton v., 960

——— v. Alton, 960

Alton Railroad Co.; Railroad Retirement Board (RRB) v., 636

Aluminum Co. of America v. Central Lincoln Peoples' Utility District, 2702

Alvarez-Machain; United States v., 3704

Alvarez-Sanchez; United States v., 3881

Alvez; American Export Lines, Inc. v., 2092

Alyeska Pipeline Service Co. v. Wilderness Society, 1694

Amalgamated Food Employees Union, Local 590 v. Logan Valley Plaza Inc., 1325

Amax Coal Co.; National Labor Relations Board (NLRB) v., 2280

Amazon Petroleum Co. v. Ryan, 627

Ambach v. Norwick, 1978

Ambler Realty Co.; Village of Euclid v., 537

AmClyde; McDermott v., 3874

Amerada Hess Corp. v. Division, Director of Taxation, New Jersey Department of Treasury, 3327

Amerada Hess Shipping Corp.; Argentina Republic v., 3301

American Academy of Orthopaedic Surgeons; Marrese v., 2798

American Airlines, Inc. v. Wolens, 3944

American Automobile Assocation (AAA) v. United States, 1111

American Banana Co. v. United Fruit Co., 387

American Bank & Trust Co. v. Dallas County, 2594

American Bar Endowment; United States v., 3019

American Brands, Inc.; Carson v., 2183

American Broadcasting Co. v. Democratic National Committee, 1574

——— v. Federal Communications Commission (FCC), 2281

——— v. WNCN Listerners Guild, 2201

American Cetacean Society; Baldridge v., 3043

———; Japan Whaling Association v., 3043

American Civil Liberties Union; Chabad v., 3379

——— v. Federal Communication Commission (FCC), 1976

American Civil Liberties Union, Greater Pittsburgh Chapter; Allegheny, County of v., 3379

———; City of Pittsburgh v., 3379

American College of Obstetricians & Gynecologists; Thornburgh v., 3005

American College of Physicians; United States v., 2970

American Communications Association v. Douds, 895

American Construction Co. v. Jacksonville, Tampa and Key West Railway Co., 289

——— v. Pennsylvania Company for Insurance on Lives and Granting Annuities, 289

American Dredging Co. v. Miller, 3861

American Electric Power Service Corp.; American
    Paper Institute, Inc. v., 2513
———; Federal Energy Regulatory Commission
    (FERC) v., 2513
American Electric Power System v. Sierra Club
    Federal, 1786
American Export Lines, Inc. v. Alvez, 2092
American Express Co. v. Koerner, 2247
———; James Clark Distilling Co. v., 433
American Foreign Service Association v. Garfinkel,
    3331
American Fruit Growers, Inc. v. Brogdex Co., 586
American Guarantee and Liability Insurance Co.;
    Glona v., 1322
American Hospital and Life Insurance Co.; Federal
    Trade Commission (FTC) v., 1039
American Hospital Association; Bowen v., 3000
——— v. National Labor Relations Board (NLRB),
    3559
American Iron and Steel Institute v. Natural
    Resources Defense Council (NRDC), 2721
American Insurance Co. and the Ocean Insurance Co.
    v. 356 Bales of Cotton, Canter, Claimant, 108
American Manufacturing Co.; United Steelworkers
    of America v., 1078
American Medical Association (AMA) v. Federal
    Trade Commission (FTC), 2341
American Mini Theatres, Inc.; Young v., 1774
American National Red Cross v. S.G., 3716
American Natonal Bank & Trust Co. of Chicago v.
    Haroco, Inc., 2905
American Newspaper Publishers Assn. v. National
    Citizens, 1919
American Oil Co. (AMOCO) v. Neill, 1223
American Paper Institute, Inc. v. American Electric
    Power ServiceCorp., 2513
American Petroleum Institute; Industrial Union
    Department v., 2153
———; Marshall v., 2153
American Postal Workers Union, AFL-CIO; Air
    Courier Conference of America v., 3536
American Press Co.; Grosjean v., 646
American Savings Bank; Nobelman v., 3808
American Shipbuilding co. v. National Labor
    Relations Board (NLRB), 1220
American Society of Composers, Authors and
    Publishers v. Columbia Broadcasting System,
    Inc. (CBS), 1977
American Society of Mechanical Engineers, Inc. v.
    Hydrolevel Corp., 2367
American Steamboat Co. v. Chase, 191
American Stores Co.; California v., 3447
American Textile Manufacturers Institute, Inc. v.
    Donovan, 2260
American Theatres Association v. United States, 870

American Tobacco Co. v. Patterson, 2349
American Train Dispatchers Association; Norfolk &
    Western Railway Co. v., 3541
American Trucking Association; Interstate
    Commerce Commission (ICC) v., 2701
——— v. Scheiner, 3193
——— v. Smith, Director, Arkansas Highway and
    Transportation Department, 3472
———; United States v., 717
American Warehousemen's Association v. Brooks,
    1909
American Waterways Operators, Inc.; Askew v.,
    1565
American Wholesale Grocers Association v. Swift
    and Co., 604
Americans for Change; Federal Elections
    Commission v., 2315
Americans United for Separation of Church and
    State, Inc.; Valley Forge Christian College v.,
    2306
Amerind v. Mancari, 1649
Ames; Champion v., 348
———; Smyth v., 329
"Amish School Case," 1496
Amoco Production Co. v. Village of Gambell,
    Alaska, 3108
Amoco Production Co. and Marathon Oil Co. v.
    Jicarilla Apache Indian Tribe, 2316
Amos; Corp. of Presiding Bishop of the Church of
    Jesus Christ of Latter-Day Saints v., 3195
———; Hadnott v., 1360
———; United States v., 3195
Amtrack; Lebron v., 3950
Anchor Motor Freight, Inc.; Hines v., 1734
Anders v. California, 1281
——— v. Floyd, 1968
Anderson; Boyce v., 109
——— v. Celebrezze, Secretary of State of Ohio,
    2498
——— v. City of Bessemer City, North Carolina,
    2804
——— v. Committee for Public Education and
    Religious Liberty, 1594, 1603
——— v. Creighton, 3204
———; Jenkins v., 2116
——— v. Liberty Lobby, Inc., 3024
——— v. Martin, 1174
Anderson, Director, California Department of Social
    Services v. Green, 3956
——— v. Edwards, 3965
Anderson Brothers Ford and Ford Motor Credit v.
    Valencia, 2246
Andreas; Illinois v., 2591
Andres v. United States, 867
Andresen v. Maryland, 1789

Andrews v. Andrews, 347
———; Andrews v., 347
Andrus v. Allard, 2037
——— v. Glover Construction Co., 2100
——— v. Shell Oil Co., 2104
——— v. Sierra Club, 2009
Anheuser-Busch, Inc.; Federal Trade Commission
    (FTC) v., 1077
Aniskoff; Conroy v., 3777
Ankenbrandt, as Next Friend and Mother of L.R. v.
    Richards, 3705
Ansonia Board of Education v. Philbrook, 3065
The Antelope, 95
Antelope; United States v., 1831
Antoine v. Byers & Anderson, Inc., 3813
——— v. Washington, 1680
Apex Hosiery Co. v. Leader, 716
Apex Marine Corp.; Miles v., 3510
Apfelbaum; United States v., 2066
Apodaca v. Oregon, 1500
Appalachian Electric Power Co.; United States v.,
    722
"Appalachian I," 722
Appollon, 89
Aptheker v. Secretary of State, 1201
Arabian American Oil Co.; Equal Employment
    Opportunity Commission (EEOC) v., 3546
Arabian American Oil Co. and Aramco Services Co.;
    Bourseslan v., 3546
Arave, Warden v. Creech, 3775
Arcadia, Ohio v. Ohio Power Co., 3514
Arcambel v. Wiseman, 21
Arcara v. Cloud Books, 3057
Ardestani v. Immigration and Naturalization Service
    (INS), 3631
Argentina Republic v. Amerada Hess Shipping Corp.,
    3301
Argersinger v. Hamlin, Sheriff, 1506
Arizona v. California, 1162, 2489
———; California v., 2256
———; Edwards v., 2223
——— v. Evans, 3958
——— v. Fulminante, 3547
——— v. Hicks, 3102
———; Jobin v., 756
——— v. Manypenny, 2214
——— v. Maricopa County Medical Society, 2394
——— v. Mauro, 3136
———; Miranda v., 1260
———; Poland v., 2980
——— v. Roberson, 3262
——— v. Rumsey, 2694
——— v. San Carlos Apache Tribe of Arizona, 2585
———; Schad v., 3612
———; Tison v., 3122

Arizona; United States v., 1421
———; Walton v., 3504
———; Westbrook v., 1256
——— v. Youngblood, 3292
Arizona ex rel. Sullivan; Southern Pacific Co. v., 812
Arizona Electric Power Cooperative v. Mid-
    Louisiana Gas Co., 2579
Arizona Governing Committee for Tax Deferred
    Annuity and Deferred Compensation Plans v.
    Norris, 2599
Arizona State Bar; Baird v., 1427
Arizona State Tax Commission; Central Machinery
    Co. v., 2143
———; McClanahan v., 1562
———; Warren Trading Post Co. v., 1226
Arkansas; Epperson v., 1346
———; Gent v., 1283
———; Holloway v., 1899
——— v. Oklahoma, 3654
———; Rock v., 3184
——— v. Sanders, 2018
———; Tennessee v., 2302
———; Whitmore v., 3443
———; Wilson v., 3988
Arkansas Best Corp. v. Commissioner, 3232
Arkansas-Best Freight System; Barrentine v., 2205
Arkansas Electric Cooperative Corp. v. Arkansas
    Public Service Commission, 2512
Arkansas Louisiana Gas Co. v. Hall, 2286
Arkansas Public Service Commission; Arkansas
    Electric Cooperative Corp. v., 2512
Arkansas State Highway Employees, Local 315;
    Smith v., 1989
Arkansas Valley Land and Cattle Co. v. Mann, 262
Arkansas Writers' Project, Inc. v. Charles O.
    Ragland, 3125
Arkoma Associates; Carden v., 3412
Arline; School Board of Nassau County v., 3100
"Arlington Case," 227
Armco Inc. v. Hardesty, Tax Commissioner of West
    Virginia, 2713
Armstrong; United States v., 4038
Army and Air Force Exchange Service v. Sheehan,
    2375
Arn; Thomas v., 2917
Arnett, Director v. Kennedy, 1632
Arnold, Schwinn and Co.; United States v., 1302
Aronson v. Quick Point Pencil Co., 1962
Arsenal Building Corp. v. Walling, 754
Arthur Young & Co.; United States v., 2648
Artist M.; Suter v., 3667
Arver v. United States, 443
Asahi Metal Industry Co. v. Superior Court of
    California, 3093
Asakura v. City of Seattle, 517

Asgrow Seed Co. v. Winterboer dba DeeBees, 3942
Ash; Cort v., 1706
———; United States v., 1589
Ashcraft v. Tennessee, 791
Ashcroft; Gregory v., 3607
———; Planned Parenthood of Kansas City v., 2549
Ashe v. Swenson, 1401
Ashland Oil, Inc. v. Governor of Maryland, 1922
Ashton v. Cameron County Water Improvement
    District, No. One, 652
Ashwander v. Tennessee Valley Authority (TVA),
    648
Askew v. Amerian Waterways Operators, Inc., 1565
Aspen Highlands Skiing Corp.; Aspen Skiing Co. v.,
    2879
Aspen Skiing Co. v. Aspen Highlands Skiing Corp.,
    2879
Asphalt Products Co. v. Commissioner of Internal
    Revenue, 3157
———; Commissioner v., 3157
Associated Builders; Building Trades Council v.,
    3767
Associated Builders and Contractors of
    Massachusetts/Rhode Island, Inc.;
    Massachusetts Water Resources Authority v.,
    3767
Associated Dry Goods Corp.; Equal Employment
    Opportunity Commission (EEOC) v., 2179
Associated Enterprises v. Toltec Watershed
    Improvement District, 1560
Associated General Contractors of California, Inc. v.
    California State Council of Carpenters, 2465
Associated Industries of Missouri v. Lohman,
    Director of Revenue of Missouri, 3892
Associated Press (AP); International News Service
    v., 445
——— v. National Labor Relation Board (NLRB),
    665
——— v. United States, 814
———; United States v., 814
——— v. Walker, 1296
Association of Data Processing Service
    Organizations, Inc. v. Camp, 1394
Astoria Federal Savings and Loan Association v.
    Solimino, 3593
Astroline Communications Co. Limited Partnership
    v. Shurberg Broadcasting of Hartford, Inc.,
    3503
Atascadero State Hospital v. Scanlon, 2897
Atchison, Topeka and Santa Fe Railroad Co. v. Buell,
    3109
———; National Railroad Passenger Corp. v., 2801
Atherton v. Atherton, 341
———; Atherton v., 341
Atherton Mills v. Johnston, 484

Atkins v. Rivera, 3021
Atkins, Commissioner of the Massachusetts
    Department of Public Welfare v. Parker, 2861
Atkinson; United States v., 645
Atlantic Richfield Co.; Ray v., 1888
——— v. USA Petroleum Co., 3450
Atlantic Transport Co. of West Virginia v. Imbrovek,
    420
Atlas Roofing Co., Inc. v. Occupational Safety and
    Health Review Commission, 1829
Atonio; Wards Cove Packing Co. v., 3342
Attleboro; Public Utilities Commission v., 542
Attorney General of Massachusetts; A Book named
    "John Cleland's Memoirs of a Woman of
    Pleasure" v., 1245
Attorney General of New York v. Grument, 3925
——— v. Soto-Lopez, 3010
Attorney General of Texas; League of United Latin
    American Citizens v., 3605
Attorney Registration and Disciplinary Commission;
    Peel v., 3469
Attrill; Huntington v., 288
August; Delta Air Lines, Inc. v., 2194
Austin v. Kentucky, 1283
———; Low v., 183
———; National Association of Letter Carriers v.,
    1660
——— v. United States, 3840
Austin, Michigan Secretary of State v. Michigan
    State Chamber of Commerce, 3429
Automated Medical Laboratories; Hillsborough
    County v., 2851
Automatic Canteen Co. of America v. Federal Trade
    Commission (FTC), 945
Automobile Club of Michigan v. Commissioner of
    Internal Revenue, 1003
Autry v. Estelle, Director, Texas Department of
    Corrections, 2600
Avagliano; Sumitomo Shoji America, Inc. v., 2387
Avery; Johnson v., 1353
——— v. Midland County, Texas, 1315
"Avocado Pear Case," 1152
Ayers, Ex parte, 256
——— v. Fordice, Governor of Mississippi, 3728
———; In re, 256
Aznavorian; Califano v., 1948

B.E. Tilley; Mead Corp. v., 3344
B.F. Keith Vaudeville Exchange; Hart v., 503
BFP v. Resolution Trust Corp., 3889
B.J.F.; Florida Star v., 3360
BMW of North America v. Ira Gore Jr., 4040
BT Investment Managers, Inc.; Lewis v., 2109
Babbitt v. United Farm Workers National Union,
    2006

Babbitt, Secretary of the Interior v. Sweet Home Chapter of Communities for a Great Oregon, 4015

Babcock & Wilcox Co.; National Labor Relations Board (NLRB) v., 986

"Baby Doe Case," 3000

"Baby Jane Doe Case," 3000

Bacchus Imports, LTD. v. Dias, Director of Taxation of Hawaii, 2738

Bachowski; Dunlop v., 1698

Bacon; Blum v., 2385

Badaracco v. Commissioner of Internal Revenue, 2615

Badders v. United States, 431

Baer; Rosenblatt v., 1240

———— v. United States, 446

Baggett; McConnell v., 1189

————; Vann v., 1189

Baggot; United States v., 2583

Bagley; United States v., 2907

Bagwell; International Union, United Mine Workers v., 3927

Bailey v. Alabama, 394

———— v. Drexel Furniture Co., 485

———— v. United States, 4023

————; United States v., 2050

Bair; Moorman Manufacturing Co. v., 1924

Baird v. Arizona State Bar, 1427

————; Bellotti v., 1794, 2034

————; Eisenstadt v., 1489

————; Hunerwadel v., 1794, 2034

———— v. State Bar of Arizona, 1427

"Baird I," 1794

"Baird II," 2034

Bakelite Corp.; Ex Parte, 571

Baker v. Carr, 1122

———— v. General Motors Corp., 3054

———— v. McCollan, 2025

————; South Carolina v., 3240

Bakery and Pastry Drivers & Helpers Local 802 of the International Brotherhood of Teamsters v. Wohl, 748

Bakke; Regents of University of California v., 1936

Balaam; Santa Barbara County Water Agency v., 1032

Baldasar v. Illinois, 2090

Baldridge v. American Cetacean Socity, 3043

Baldrige; McNichols v., 2324

Baldrige, Secretary of Commerce v. Shapiro, 2324

Baldwin v. Alabama, 2869

———— v. Fish and Game Commission of Montana, 1912

———— v. Montana Fish and Game Commission, 1912

———— v. Missouri, 582

Baldwin v. New York, 1415

Balint; United States v., 481

Balkcom; Solesbee v., 893

Ball; Grand Rapids School District v., 2899

———— v. James, 2218

———— v. United States, 2815

Ballard; Schlesinger v., 1674

————; United States v., 789

Ballew v. Georgia, 1890

Ballin; United States v., 283

Baltimore; Barron v., 124

Baltimore; Johnson v., 2868

Baltimore and Ohio Railroad Co.; Norman v., 631

Baltimore City Department of Social Services v. Bouknight, 3405

Baltimore Gas and Electric Co. v. Natural Resources Defense Council, Inc. (NRDC), 2534

Balzac v. Porto Rico, 482

Banco Nacional de Cuba v. Sabbatino, 1181

————; First National City Bank v., 1505

Banco Para El Comercio Exterior De Cuba; First National City Bank v., 2554

Bandemer; Davis v., 3041

"Bank Cases," 74, 91

Bank One, Chicago, N.A. v. Midwest Bank and Trust Co., 4025

Bank of Augusta v. Earle, 131

Bank of Columbia v. Okely, 73

Bank of Commonwealth of Kentucky; Briscoe v., 128

Bank of Marin v. England, 1265

Bank of North America; Turner v., 27

Bank of Nova Scotia v. United States, 3272

Bank of Texas v. Childs, 2594

Bank of the United States v. Deveaux, 46

———— v. Halstead, 94

————; Osborn v., 91

———— v. Planters' Bank of Georgia, 92

———— v. Primrose, 131

BankAmerica Corp. v. United States, 2535

Bankers Life & Casualty Co. v. Crenshaw, 3249

Bankers Trust Co.; United States v., 631

Bantam Books, Inc. v. Sullivan, 1139

Banton; Tyson and Brother-United Theatre Ticket Offices, Inc. v., 545

Baptist Hospital, Inc.; National Labor Relations Board (NLRB) v., 2019

Bar of Examiners; Schware v., 1004

Barasch; Duquesne Light Co. v., 3297

Barber; Minnesota v., 272

Barbier v. Connolly, 239

Barbour; Barton v., 224

Barclay v. Florida, 2596

Barclays Bank PLC v. Franchise Tax Board of California, 3914

Barefoot v. Estelle, Director, Texas Department of Corrections, 2595

Barenblatt v. United States, 1058

Bark Springbok, The, 166

Barker v. Kansas, 3678

—— v. Wingo, Warden, 1519

Barlow v. Collins, 1395

Barlow's, Inc.; Marshall v., 1911

Barnes; Burke v., 3076

——; Jones v., 2590

Barnes, Prosecuting Attorney of St. Joseph County, Indiana v. Glen Theatre, Inc., 3610

Barnett Bank of Marion County, North America v. Nelson, 4033

Barnette; West Virginia Board of Education v., 773

Barnette; West Virginia State Board of Education v., 773

Barney's Lessee; Hawkins v., 120

Barnhill v. Johnson, Trustee, 3669

Barnwell; South Carolina v., 677

Barr v. City of Columbia, 1194

—— v. Matteo, 1061

Barreme; Little v., 38

Barrentine v. Arkansas-Best Freight System, Inc., 2205

Barresi; McDaniel v., 1446

Barrett; Adams Fruit Co. v., 3428

——; Connecticut v., 3085

Barron v. Mayor and City Council of Baltimore, 124

Barrows v. Jackson, 947

Barry; Boos v., 3235

——; Smith v., 3637

——; St. Paul Fire and Marine Insurance Co. v., 1939

Bartels v. Iowa, 506

Bartkus v. Illinois, 1948

Bartlett; Solem v., 2635

Barton v. Barbour, 224

Bartow County Tax Assessors; First National Bank v., 2805

Bas v. Tingy, 30

Basic, Inc. v. Levinson, 3233

Bass v. Federal Power Commission (FPC), 1320

——; United States v., 1475

Bassett; South Chicago Coal & Dock Co. v., 706

Basye; United States v., 1554

Batchelder; United States v., 2001

Bateman Eichler, Hill Richards, Inc. v. Berner, 2866

Bates v. Little Rock, 1066

—— v. State Bar of Arizona, 1872

Bath Iron Works Corp. v. Director, Office of Workers' Compensation Programs, 3744

Batson v. Kentucky, 2978

Battin; Colgrove v., 1586

Baxstrom v. Herold, 1241

Baxter v. Palmigiano, 1749

Bayside Fish Flour Co. v. Gentry, 649

Bazemore v. Friday, 3048

Beach Communications, Inc.; Federal Communications Commission (FCC) v., 3807

Beacon Brass Co.; United States v., 933

Beacon Theatres, Inc. v. Westover, 1053

Beal, Secretary, Department of Public Welfare of Pennsylvania v. Doe, 1860

Bearden v. Georgia, 2525

Beason; Davis v., 265

Beatty v. Kurtz, 114

Beauchamp; Sturges and Burns Manufacturing Co. v., 415

Beauharnais v. Illinois, 926

Beaver River Power Co. v. United States, 438

Beazer; New York City Transit Authority v., 1973

Bechtel Power Corp. v. Pennsylvania, 2425

Beck v. Alabama, 2128

——; Communications Workers of America v., 3283

Becker; New York State on Kennedy v., 432

——; New York State ex rel. Kennedy v., 432

—— v. United States, 2238

Beckwith v. United States, 1750

——; Webb's Fabulous Pharmacies, Inc. v., 2161

Bedford Cut Stone Co. v. Journeymen Stone Cutters' Association of North America, 549

Beecham v. United States, 3882

Beecher v. Boston Chapter, NAACP, 2516

"Beef Trust Case," 361

Beer v. United States, 1745

Begier, Trustee v. Internal Revenue Service (IRS), 3467

Beilan v. Board of Public Education, 1035

Belden; Esteben v., 189

Belknap, Inc. v. Hale, 2584

Bell; Buck v., 550

——; Grove City College v., 2638

—— v. Maryland, 1197

——; North Haven Board of Education v., 2366

—— v. Ohio, 1942

—— v. Texas, 1271

—— v. United States, 2544

—— v. Wolfish, 1992

Bell, Secretary of Education v. New Jersey and Pennsylvania, 2529

Bell Aerospace Co.; National Labor Relations Board (NLRB) v., 1634

Bellanca; New York State Liquor Authority v., 2269

Belle Terre v. Boraas, 1631

Bellis v. United States, 1644

Bellotti; First National Bank v., 1905

——; First National Bank of Boston v., 1905

Bellotti, Attorney General of Massachusetts v. Baird, 1794, 2034
Bellwood; Gladstone, Realtors v., 1979
Belmont; United States v., 668
Belton; Gebhart v., 954, 957, 973
——; New York v., 2283
Beltran v. Myers, Director, California State Department of Health, 2231
Bender v. Williamsport Area School District, 2956
"Bendectin Case," 3839
Benjamin; Prudential Insurance Co. v., 832
Bennett, Secretary of Education v. Kentucky Department of Education, 2808
—— v. New Jersey, 2807
Bennett Mining Co. v. Lord, 502
Bennis v. State of Michigan, 4030
Benson; Crowell v., 598
——; Curtin v., 406
Benton v. Maryland, 1381
"Benzene Case," 2153
Berea College v. Kentucky, 384
Berger v. New York, 1295
Bergeron; Blanchard v., 3306
Bergna v. Stanford Daily, 1916
Berkeley; Fisher v., 2946
Berkeley, California; Citizens Against Rent Control/Coalition for Fair Housing v., 2300
Berkemer, Sheriff of Franklin County, Ohio v. McCarty, 2743
Berkovitz v. United States, 3258
Berman v. Parker, 961
Bermuda; The, 161
Bernal v. Fainter, Secretary of State of Texas, 2695
Bernalillo County Assessor; Hooper v., 2880
Bernard; Gulf Oil Co. v., 2242
Berner; Bateman Eichler, Hill Richards, Inc. v., 2866
Bernhard; Ross v., 1389
Berra v. United States, 988
Berry v. City of Dallas, 3393
Bertine; Colorado v., 3077
Bessemer City; Anderson v., 2804
Bethel School District No. 403 v. Fraser, 3056
BethEnergy Mines, Inc.; Pauley v., 3614
Beto; Cruz v., 1485
——; Reed v., 1271
Betts v. Brady, Warden, 753
——; Public Employees Retirement System v., 3370
Betty-Louise Felton; Chancellor of the Board of Education of the City of New York v., 2900
——; Secretary, United States Department of Education v., 2900
Bevans; United States v., 70
Bi-Metallic Investment Co. v. State Board of Equalization of Colorado, 429

Bibb v. Navajo Freight Lines, Inc., 1054
Bicron Corp.; Kewanee Oil Co. v., 1638
Biddle; Green v., 85
Bidwell; De Lima v., 342
——; Downes v., 344
Bigelow v. Virginia, 1705
Biggers; Neil v., 1538
Biggins; Hazen Paper Co. v., 3781
Bildisco and Bildisco; National Labor Relations Board (NLRB) v., 2637
Bill Johnson's Restaurants, Inc. v. National Labor Relations Board (NLRB), 2527
Billings; Providence Bank v., 117
Birkdale, Shipping Co., S.A.; Howlett v., 3906
Birmingham; Walker v., 1301
Bisceglia; United States v., 1679
Bishop; Maxwell v., 1410
—— v. Wood, 1762
Biswell; United States v., 1498
Bitzer; Fitzpatrick v., 1788
—— v. Matthews, 1788
Bivens v. Six Unknown Named Agents of Federal Bureau of Narcotics, 1465
Biwabic Mining Co. v. Lord, 502
Black; Stringer v., 3661
Black, Director, Missouri Department of Corrections and Human Resources v. Romano, 2848
Black Bird Creek Marsh Co.; Wilson v., 110
"Black Monday Case," 637
Blacker; McPherson v., 286
Blackfeet Tribe; Montana v., 2853
Blackledge, Warden v. Perry, 1643
Bladel; Michigan v., 2961
Blair; Ray v., 925
Blaisdell; Home Building and Loan Assocation v., 621
Blake; Loughborough v., 80
——; Winona and St. Peter Railroad Co. v., 204
Blakely v. United States, 161
Blanchard v. Bergeron, 3306
Bland; United States v., 592
Blanton v. North Las Vegas, 3316
Blatchford, Commissioner, Department of Community and Regional Affairs of Alaska v. Native Village of Noatak, 3616
Blau v. United States, 904
Bliss Dairy, Inc.; United States v., 2481
Block v. Hirsh, 471
——; Parker v., 2861
Block, Secretary of Agriculture v. Community Nutrition Institution, 2700
—— v. Neal, 2478
—— v. North Dakota ex rel. Board of University and School Lands, 2508

Block, Sheriff of the County of Los Angeles v.
    Rutherford, 2748
Blockburger v. United States, 597
Blue Chip Stamps v. Manor Drug Stores, 1702
Blue Cross of Kansas City; National Gerimedical
    Hospital and Gerontology Center v., 2252
Blue Shield of Virginia v. McCready, 2399
Blum v. Bacon, 2385
Blum, Commissioner, New York State Department of
    Social Services v. Stenson, 2652
——— v. Yaretsky, 2414
Blumstein; Dunn v., 1486
Blundo; International Terminal Operating Co., Inc.
    v., 1858
Blystone v. Pennsylvania, 3415
Board of Airport Commissioners of the City of Los
    Angeles v. Jews for Jesus, Inc., 3175
Board of Commissioners; Monroe v., 1331
Board of Commissioners of Jackson; Monroe v.,
    1331
Board of Curators of the University of Missouri v.
    Horowitz, 1887
———; Papish v., 1558
Board of Directors of Rotary International v. Rotary
    Club of Duarte, 3137
Board of Education; Adler v., 920
———; Brown v., 954, 973
———; Doremus v., 919
———; Pickering v., 1335
Board of Education, Community Unit School District
    187, Cahokia, Illinois; McNeese v., 1163
Board of Education of Central School District No. 1
    v. Allen, 1342
Board of Education of Ewing Township; Everson v.,
    839
Board of Education of Kiryas Joel Village School
    District v. Grumet, 3925
Board of Education of Knoxville; Goss v., 1164
Board of Education of Los Angeles; Crawford v.,
    2429
Board of Education of Memphis City Schools;
    Northcross v., 1577
Board of Education of Monroe-Woodbury Central
    School District v. Grumet, 3925
Board of Education of Oklahoma City v. National
    Gay Task Force, 2817
Board of Education of Oklahoma City Public
    Schools; Dowell v., 1384
Board of Education of Oklahoma City Public
    Schools, Independent School District No. 89,
    Okalahoma County, Oklahoma v. Dowell, 3523
Board of Education of Paris Union School District
    No. 95 v. Vail, 2668
Board of Education of Rogers, Arkansas v.
    McCluskey, 2443

Board of Education of School District No. 71,
    Champaign County; McCollum, Illinois ex rel.
    v., 865
Board of Education of the City School District of
    New York v. Harris, 2040
Board of Education of the Gould School District;
    Raney v., 1330
Board of Education of the Hendrick Hudson Central
    School District v. Rowley, 2419
Board of Education of the Memphis, Tennessee, City
    Schools; Northcross v., 1396
Board of Education of the Westside Community
    Schools (Dist. 66) v. Mergens, 3473
Board of Education, Island Trees Union Free School
    District No. 26 v. Pico, 2411
Board of Equalization; Jimmy Swaggart Ministries
    v., 3399
———; Western Air Lines v., 3094
Board of Estimate v. Morris, 3319
Board of Governors; Securities Industry Assn. v.,
    2734, 2736
Board of Governors of Federal Reserve System v.
    Dimension Financial Corp., 2929
——— v. Investment Co. Institute, 2182
——— v. MCorp Financial, Inc., 3625
———; Northeast Bancorp v., 2862
Board of License Commissioners of the Town of
    Tiverton v. Pastore, Liquor Control
    Administrator of Rhode Island, 2771
Board of Pardons v. Allen, 3166
Board of Public Education; Beilan v., 1035
Board of Public Works of Maryland; Roemer v.,
    1768
Board of Regents; Keyishian v., 1272
———; Slochower v., 984
Board of Regents of State Colleges v. Roth, 1530
Board of Regents of Florida; Patsy v., 2400
Board of Regents of University of Oklahoma; NCAA
    v., 2733
———; Sipuel v., 856
Board of School Commissioners of Mobile County;
    Davis v., 1445
Board of Supervisors of Elections; Gerende v., 910
Board of Trustees of Keene State College v.
    Sweeney, 1945
Board of Trustees of the State University of New
    York (SUNY) v. Fox, 3377
Board of Trustees of the Village of Scarsdale v.
    McCreary, 2824
Board of Wardens of Port; Cooley v., 146
Bob Jones University v. United States, 2522
Bob-Lo Excursion Co. v. Michigan, 861
Bobbie E. Hill; Bryant, Attorney General of Arkansas
    v., 3987

Boca Grande Club, Inc. v. Florida Power and Light
    Co., Inc., 3875
Boddie v. Connecticut, 1433
Bodine; Christian Feigenspan, Co. v., 463
Boeing Co., Inc. v. United States, 3411
Bohemian Distributing Co. v. Norman Williams Co.,
    2434
Bohlen; Caspari v., 3859
Bohning v. Ohio, 506
Bolden; Mobile v., 2087
Boles; Califano v., 2028
———; Crabtree v., 1118
———; Oyler v., 1118
Bolger v. Youngs Drug Products Corp., 2570
Bolling v. Sharpe, 958, 973
Bollinger; Commissioner of Internal Revenue v.,
    3236
Bollman and Swartwout, Ex Parte, 45
Bolton; Doe v., 1549
——— v. Martin, 8
Bond v. Floyd, 1266
Bonito Boats, Inc. v. Thunder Craft Boats, Inc., 3308
Bonjorno v. Kaiser Aluminum and Chemical Corp.,
    3434
———; Kaiser Aluminum and Chemical Corp. v.,
    3434
Bonner Mall Partnership; U.S. Bancorp Mortgage
    Co. v., 3933
A Book named "John Cleland's Memoirs of a
    Woman of Pleasure" v. Attorney General of
    Massachusetts, 1245
Boos v. Barry, 3235
Booster Lodge No. 405 v. National Labor Relations
    Board (NLRB), 1573
Booth; Ableman v., 155
——— v. Maryland, 3173
———; United States v., 155
Boraas; Belle Terre v., 1631
Bordenkircher v. Hayes, 1881
Bordon; Luther v., 143
Boren; Craig v., 1808
Bose Corp. v. Consumers Union of United States,
    Inc., 2675
Bostick; Florida v., 3606
Boston and Maine Corp.; Interstate Commerce
    Commission (ICC) v., 3670
———; National Railroad Passenger Corp. v., 3670
———; Norris v., 144
Boston Beer Co. v. Massachusetts, 210
Boston Chapter, NAACP; Beecher v., 2516
———; Boston Firefighters Union, Local 718 v.,
    2516
Boston Firefighters Union, Local 718 v. Boston
    Chapter, NAACP, 2516

Boston Police Patrolmen's Association v. Castro,
    2516
Bouie v. Columbia, 1198
Bouknight; Baltimore v., 3405
———; Maurice M. v., 3405
Boulder, Colorado; Community Communications
    Company, Inc. v., 2311
Bounds v. Smith, 1836
"La Bourgogne," 381
Bourjaily v. United States, 3189
Bourland; South Dakota v., 3822
Bourseslan v. Arabian American Oil Co. and Aramco
    Services Co., 3546
Bove v. New York, 853
Bowden v. Fort Smith, 756
Bowen v. City of New York, 2993
Bowen v. Gilliard, 3203
——— v. Michigan Academy of Family Physicians,
    3001
——— v. Owens, 2987
——— v. Public Agencies Opposed to Social
    Security Entrapment, 3016
——— v. Roy, 3003
——— v. United States Postal Service (USPS), 2454
Bowen v. Yuckert, 3159
Bowen, Secretary of Health and Human Services v.
    American Hospital Association, 3000
———; Chan Kendrick v., 3281
———; Kendrick v., 3281
Bowerbank; Hodgson v., 49
———; Hodgson and Thompson v., 49
Bowers; Corliss v., 579
——— v. Hardwick, 3042
Bowles; Hecht Co. v., 782
Bowman v. Chicago and Northwestern Railway Co.,
    258
———; James v., 352
———; United States v., 491
Bowman Transportation Co.; Franks v., 1739
Bowsher v. Synar, 3058
Bowsher, Comptroller General of the United States v.
    Merck & Co., Inc., 2499
Boyce v. Anderson, 109
Boyd v. Nebraska ex. rel. Thayer, 281
——— v. United States, 245, 282
Boyde v. California, 3418
Boykin v. Alabama, 1370
Boyle; United States v., 2772
——— v. United Technologies Corp., 3279
Boynton; Dempsey v., 463
——— v. Virginia, 1086
Boys Markets, Inc. v. Retail Clerk Union, Local 770,
    1409
Bracker; White Mountain Apache Tribe v., 2142

Bradfield v. Roberts, Treasurer of the United States, 334
Bradley; Allen Park Public Schools v., 1668
———; Diamond v., 2195
———; Fallbrook Irrigation District v., 314
——— v. Fisher, 186
———; Grosse Point Public School System v., 1668
———; Milliken v., 1668, 1869
——— v. School Board of City of Richmond, 1641
——— v. School Board of Richmond, 1236
Bradshaw; Livadas v., 3907
———; Oregon v., 2567
Bradwell v. Illinois, 190
Brady; Betts v., 753
———; Complete Auto Transit, Inc. v., 1824
——— v. United States, 1405
Brailsford; Georgia v., 15
Bram v. United States, 327
Branch; Goeke v., 3963
——— v. Texas, 1528
Brandenburg v. Ohio, 1375
Brandhove; Tenney v., 912
Brandon v. Holt, Director of Police for the City of Memphis, 2780
Branstad; Puerto Rico v., 3191
Branti v. Finkel, 2080
Branzburg v. Hayes, 1533
Braswell v. United States, 3270
Brathwaite; Manson v., 1856
Braunfeld v. Brown, 1103
Braunskill; Hilton v., 3149
Braxton v. United States, 3577
Bray v. Alexandria Women's Health Clinic, 3749
Bread Political Action Committee v. Federal Election Commission (FEC), 2336
Breard v. Alexandria, Louisiana, 915
Brecht v. Abrahamson, Superintendent, Dodge Correctional Institution, 3782
Breckenridge; Griffin v., 1458
Breed v. Jones, 1696
Breedlove v. Suttles, as Tax Collector, 672
Breininger v. Sheet Metal Workers International Association, Local Union No. 6, 3385
Breithaupt v. Abram, 999
Brendale v. Confederate Tribes & Bands of Yakima Indian Nation, 3376
Brennan; Corning Glass Works v., 1645
———; Farmer v., 3899
Bresler; Greenbelt Cooperative Publishing Association v., 1408
Brewer; Northbrook National Insurance Co. v., 3380
——— v. Williams, 1828
Brewster; United States v., 1529
Bridges v. California, 738

——— v. Wixon, District Director, Immigration and Naturalization Service, 816
Briggs v. Elliot, 954, 955, 973
———; Malley v., 2950
———; Stafford v., 2053
Brigham; Randall v., 172
Brignoni-Ponce; United States v., 1719
Brinegar v. United States, 892
Brinkman; Dayton Board of Education v., 1873, 2032
Briscoe v. LaHue, 2480
——— v. Louisiana, 1117
——— v. President and Directors of the Bank of Commonwealth of Kentucky, 128
Broadcast Music, Inc. v. Columbia Broadcasting System, Inc. (CBS), 1977
Broadrick v. Oklahoma, 1598
Broadwell v. United States, 358
Brock; Alaska Airlines, Inc. v., 3112
———; Citicorp Industrial Credit Inc. v., 3183
Brock; International Union, United Automobile, Aerospace and Agricultural Implement Workers of America v., 3025
——— v. Pierce County, 2984
——— v. Roadway Express, Inc., 3127
Brockbank dba Brockbank Apparel Co.; United States v., 824
Brockett v. Spokane Arcades, Inc., 2876
Brogdex Co.; American Fruit Growers v., 586
Bronson v. Kinzie, 137
———; McCarthy v., 3567
Brooke Group Ltd. v. Brown and Williamson Tobacco Corp., 3829
Brooks; American Warehousemen's Association v., 1909
———; Flagg Brothers, Inc. v., 1909
———; Lefkowitz v., 1909
——— v. Southern Pacific Co., 373
——— v. United States, 522, 886
Brotherhood; Missouri-Kansas-Texas Railroad Co. v., 3163
Brotherhood of Locomotive Engineers; Interstate Commerce Commission (ICC) v., 3163
Brotherhood of Maintenance of Way Employees; Burlington Northern Railroad Co. v., 3132
Brotherhood of Railway and Steamship Clerks; Texas and New Orleans Railroad Co. v., 581
Brotherhood of Railway Carmen; CSX Transportation, Inc. v.; 3541
Brown v. Allen, 937
——— v. Board of Education of Topeka, Kansas, 954, 973
———; Braufeld v., 1103
———; California v., 3086
———; Carey v., 2123
———; Chrysler Corp. v., 1983

————; Frommhagen v., 1630

———— v. Glines, 2049

———— v. Hartlage, 2348

———— v. Illinois, 1716

———— v. Louisiana, 1242, 2120

————; International Organization of Masters, Mates & Pilots v. Brown; Masters, Mates & Pilots v., 3533

————; Kingsley Books, Inc. v., 1013

———— v. Maryland, 103

———— v. Mississippi, 647

————; O'Brien v., 1535

————; Parker v., 759

————; Pickett v., 2530

———— v. Pro Football, Inc. dba Washington Redskins, 4045

————; Reading Co., 1332

———— v. Slaughter, 132

———— v. Socialist Workers '74 Campaign Committee (Ohio), 2447

————; Storer v., 1630

———— v. Texas, 2021

————; Texas v., 2495

———— v. Thomson, Secretary of State of Wyoming, 2563

———— v. United States, 62, 395, 3074

————; United States v., 1230

———— v. Walker, 309

"Brown I," 954

"Brown II," 973

Brown, Director, Department of Law and Public Safety, Division of Gaming Enforcement, State of New Jersey v. Hotel & Restaurant Employees & Bartenders International Union, Local 54, 2745

Brown, Secretary of Veterans Affairs v. Gardner, 3938

Brown and Williamson Tobacco; Brooke Group Ltd. v., 3829

Brown-Forman Distillers Corp. v. New York State Liquor Authority, 2998

Brown Shoe Co. v. United States, 1130

Brownell; Perez v., 1024

Browning; Nashville, C & St. L. Ry. v., 713

————; Nashville, Chattanooga and St. Louis Railway v., 713

Browning-Ferris Industries, Inc. v. Kelco Disposal Inc., 3373

Bruce; Burnet, Commissioner of Internal Revenue v., 590

Bruce Church, Inc.; Pike v., 1393

Bruch; Firestone Tire and Rubber Co. v., 3307

Bruno v. United States, 698

Brunswick Associates Limited Partnership; Pioneer Investment Services Co. v., 3772

Brunswick Corp. v. Pueblo Bowl-O-Mat, Inc., 1813

Brush; McElvaine v., 277

Brushaber v. Union Pacific Railroad Co., 430

Bruton v. United States, 1323

Bryan; Burns Banking Co. v., 515

———— v. Itasca County, Minnesota, 1763

Bryant; California Brewers Assocation v., 2056

———— v. Yellen, 2121

———— v. Zimmerman, 569

Bryant, Attorney General of Arkansas v. Bobbie E. Hill, 3987

Buchanan v. Kentucky, 3198

———— v. Warley, 441

Buck v. Bell, 550

Buckley; Corrigan v., 533

———— v. Fitzsimmons, 3830

———— v. Valeo , 1727

Buck's Stove and Range Co.; Gompers v., 403

Buczynski v. General Motors, Corp., 2225

Buell; Atchison, Topeka and Santa Fe Railroad Co. v., 3109

Bufferd v. Commissioner of Internal Revenue Service, 3754

Buffington, Collector of Internal Revenue v. Day, 179

Buie; Maryland v., 3416

Building and Construction Trades of the Metropolitan District v. Associated Builders and Contractors of Massachusetts/Rhode Island, Inc., 3767

Building Trades Council v. Associated Builders, 3767

Bull; Calder v., 24

Bullington v. Missouri, 2221

Bullock; Cabana v., 2930

————; Texas Monthly v., 3304

Bulova Watch Co.; Steele v., 936

Bumper v. North Carolina, 1334

Bunting v. Oregon, 439

Bunton v. Patterson, 1355

Burbank v. Lockheed Air Terminal, Inc., 1568

Burbine; Moran v., 2953

Burch v. Louisiana, 1980

————; Zinermon v., 3410

Burdeau v. McDowell, 475

Burdick v. Takushi, Director of Elections of Hawaii, 3696

Burdine; Texas Dept. of Community Affairs v., 2189

Bureau of Alcohol, Tobacco and Firearms v. Federal Labor Relations Authority, 2606

Bureau of Revenue of New Mexico; Ramah Navajo School Board, Inc. v., 2439

Burford; Ex Parte, 44

Burger, Ex Parte, 757

———— v. Kemp, 3208

Burger; New York v., 3179
Burger King Corp. v. Rudzewicz, 2844
Burget; Patrick v., 3250
Burgett v. Texas, 1304
Burke v. Barnes, 3076
———; United States v., 3690
Burks v. Lasker, 1990
——— v. United States, 1921
Burleson; Journal of Commerce and Commercial
    Bulletin v., 414
Burlington Northern, Inc.; Schreiber v., 2858
——— v. United States, 2449
Burlington Northern Railroad Co. v. Brotherhood of
    Maintenance of Way Employees, 3132
——— v. Ford, 3703
——— v. Oklahoma Tax Commission, 3133
——— v. Woods, 3088
Burnet v. Leininger, 599
———; North American Oil Consolidated v., 605
Burnet, Commissioner of Internal Revenue v. Bruce,
    590
——— v. Logan, 590
——— v. Wells, 618
Burnett v. Grattan, 2731
Burnham v. Superior Court of California, 3460
Burns; Elrod v., 1785
———; In re, 1467
——— v. Reed, 3583
Burns v. Richardson, 1255
——— v. United States, 3595
Burns International Security Services, Inc.; National
    Labor Relations Board (NLRB) v., 1497
Burrow-Giles Lithographic Co. v. Sarony, 236
Burson, Attorney General and Reporter for
    Tennessee v. Freeman, 3689
Burton v. Clyne, 483
——— v. Wilmington Parking Authority, 1098
Bush v. Lucas, 2545
——— v. Vera, 4044
Busic v. United States, 2097
Business Electronics Corp. v. Sharp Electronics
    Corp., 3245
Business Executives' Move for Vietnam Peace;
    Federal Communications Commission (FCC)
    v., 1574
———; Post-Newsweek Stations, Capital Area, Inc.
    v., 1574
Business Guides, Inc. v. Chromatic Communications
    Enterprises, Inc., 3537
Bustamonte; Schneckloth v., 1575
Butchers' Benevolent Association v. Crescent City
    Live-stock Landing and Slaughter-House Co.,
    189

Butchers' Union Slaughterhouse and Live stock
    Landing Co. v. Crescent City Livestock
    Landing and Slaughter-house Co., 237
Butchers' Union Slaughterhouse v. Crescent City
    Slaughterhouse, 237
Butenko v. United States, 1357
Butler v. McKellar, 3419
——— v. Michigan, 998
———; United States v., 643
Butterworth v. Smith, 3427
Buttfield v. Stranahan, 354
Button; NAACP v., 1137
———; National Association for the Advancement
    of Colored People (NAACP) v., 1137
Butts; Curtis Publishing Co. v., 1296
——— v. Harrison, 1249
Butz v. Economou, 1938
Buxton v. Ullman, 1109
Byars v. United States, 540
Byers; California v., 1453
Byers & Anderson, Inc.; Antoine v., 3813
Bynum; Martinez v., 2510
Byrd; Dean Witter Reynolds Inc. v., 2794

C & A Carbone, Inc. v. Town of Clarkstown, New
    York, 3884
C & P Telephone Company of Virignia; Norfolk
    Redevelopment and Housing Authority v., 2603
C. & S. Airlines v. Waterman Corp., 862
C.B. & Q. R. R. Co. v. Iowa, 201
CIO; Hague v., 694
CSX Transportation, Inc. v. Brotherhood of Railway
    Carmen, 3541
——— v. Easterwood, 3783
CTS Corp. v. Dynamics Corp. of America, 3119
Caban v. Mohammed, 1986
Cabana v. Bullock, 2930
Cabazon Band of Mission Indians; California v.,
    3097
Cabell v. Chavez-Salido, 2305
Cabot Carbon; National Labor Relations Board
    (NLRB) v., 1059
Cady v. Dombrowski, 1592
Cafeteria and Restaurant Workers Union, Local 473,
    AFL-CIO v. McElroy, 1115
Cage v. Louisiana, 3512
Calandra; United States v., 1611
Calder v. Bull, 24
——— v. Jones, 2646
Caldor, Inc.; Estate of Thornton v., 2884
Caldwell v. Mississippi, 2867
———; United States v., 1533
Califano v. Aznavorian, 1948
——— v. Boles, 2028
——— v. Jobst, 1877

——— v. Westcott, 2022
Califano, Secretary of Health, Education and Welfare
    v. Goldfarb, 1822
——— v. Webster, 1826
California v. ARC America Corp., 3328
——— v. Acevedo, 3585
———; Adamson v., 850
———; Alberts v., 1015
——— v. American Stores Co., 3447
———; Anders v., 1281
———; Arizona v., 1162, 2489
——— v. Arizona and the United States, 2256
———; Boyde v., 3418
———; Bridges v., 738
——— v. Brown, 3086
——— v. Byers, 1453
——— v. Cabazon Band of Mission Indians, 3097
——— v. Carney, 2840
——— v. Central Pacific Railroad Co., 250
———; Chapman v., 1273
———; Chimel v., 1380
——— v. Ciraolo, 2982
———; Cockrill v., 525
———; Cohen v., 1456
———; Douglas v., 1145
———; Edwards v., 737
———; Faretta v., 1718
——— v. Federal Energy Regulatory Commission
    (FERC), 3455
———; Gilbert v., 1299
———; Goldstein v., 1579
——— v. Grace Brethren Church, 2396
——— v. Green, 1417
——— v. Greenwood, 3247
———; Griffin v., 1225
———; Harrington v., 1371
———; Hartford Fire Insurance Co. v., 3843
——— v. Hodari D., 3560
———; Horton v., 3470
———; Hurtado v., 234
———; Irvine v., 952
———; Ker v., 1165
——— v. Krivda, 1536
———; Lambert v., 1020
——— v. LaRue, 1537
———; Martinez v., 2046
———; McGautha v., 1451
———; Medina v., 3721
———; Merrett Underwriting Agency Management
    Ltd. v., 3843
———; Miller v., 1584
———; Morrison v., 622
———; Oyama v., 857
———; Proctor v., 3930
——— v. Ramos, 2597

California; Robbins v., 2282
———; Robinson v., 1135
———; Rochin v., 917
——— v. Rooney, 3194
———; Sandoval v., 3868
———; Schmerber v., 1263
——— v. Secretary of the Interior, 2614
———; Secretary of the Interior v., 2614
——— v. Sierra Club, 2216
——— v. Skelly Oil Co., 1320
———; Smith v., 1064
——— v. Southern Pacific Railroad Co., 250
———; Stansbury v., 3879
——— v. Stewart, 1260
———; Stoner v., 1182
———; Stromberg v., 589
———; Summa Corp. v., 2660
——— v. Superior Court of California, 3168
——— v. Trombetta, 2706
———; Tuilaepa v., 3930
——— v. United States, 1943
———; United States v., 849, 3786
——— v. Usery, 1771
———; Western Oil and Gas Association v., 2614
———; Whitney v., 554
——— v. Yellen, 2121
———; Young v., 697
California Board of Equalization; Western and
    Southern Life Insurance Co. v., 2233
California Brewers Assocation v. Bryant, 2056
California Coastal Commission v. Granite Rock Co.,
    3110
———; Nollan v., 3209
California Department of Corrections; Minnick v.,
    2243
——— v. Morales, 3977
California Federal Savings and Loan Association v.
    Mark Guerra, Director of Fair Employment and
    Housing, 3072
California Medical Association v. Federal Election
    Commission (FEC), 2276
California Men's Advisory Council; Rowland v.,
    3746
California Men's Colony; Rowland v., 3746
California Public Service Commission v. Federal
    Communications Commission (FCC), 2988
California Retail Liquor Dealers Assocation v.
    Midcal Aluminum, Inc., 2065
California ex rel State Lands Commission v. United
    States, 2391
California State Council of Carpenters; Associated
    General Contractors of California, Inc. v., 2465
Calvert Distillers Corp.; Schwegmann Brothers v.,
    913

Camara v. Municipal Court of the City and County of San Francisco, 1290

Camden; United Building and Construction Trades Council v., 2626

Camenisch; University of Texas v., 2219

Cameron County Water Improvement District; Ashton v., 652

Camfield v. United States, 323

Caminetti v. United States, 434

Cammarano v. United States, 1046

Camp; Association of Data Processing Service Organizations, Inc. v., 1394

———; Investment Company Institute (ICI) v., 1441

Campbell; Heckler v., 2515

———; Reed v., 3007

——— v. United States, 1268

Campbell, aka Skyywalker v. Acuff-Rose Music, Inc., 3867

Canada; Missouri ex rel. Gaines v., 688

Cannon; Davidson v., 2928

——— v. University of Chicago, 1993

Canter; American Insurance Co. v., 108

Cantor dba Selden Drugs Co. v. Detroit Edison Co., 1804

Cantrell v. Forest City Publishing Co., 1669

Cantwell v. Connecticut, 712

Capital Cities Cable, Inc. v. Crisp, Director, Oklahoma Alcoholic Beverage Control Board, 2715

Capital Gains Research Bureau, Inc.; Securities Exchange Commission (SEC) v., 1173

"Capital Punishment Cases of 1972," 1528

"Capital Punishment Cases of 1976," 1795, 1796, 1797, 1798, 1799

Capital Square Review and Advisory Board v. Pinette, 4017

Caplin and Drysdale, Chartered v. United States, 3363

Caputo; Northeast Marine Terminal Co. v., 1858

Carbon Fuel Co. v. United Mine Workers, 2043

Carchman, Mercer County Prosecutor v. Nash, 2908

Carden v. Arkoma Associates, 3412

Cardinal Chemical Co. v. Morton International, Inc., 3795

Cardoza-Fonseca; Immigration and Naturalization Service (INS) v., 3106

Cardwell, Warden v. Lewis, 1650

Carey v. Brown, 2123

———; New York Gaslight Club, Inc. v., 2110

——— v. Piphus, 1891

——— v. Population Services International, 1850

———; United Jewish Organization v., 1821

Cargill, Inc. v. Monfort of Colorado, Inc., 3066

Carl W. Stotts; Memphis Fire Department v., 2711

Carlisle; Respublica v., 1

Carlson v. Green, 2086

Carlton; United States v., 3902

Carmack; United States v., 836

Carmen v. Idaho, 2467

Carmichael v. Gulf States Paper Corp., 669

——— v. Southern Coal and Coke Co., 669

Carnation Co. v. Pacific Westbound Conference, 1243

Carney; California v., 2840

Carnival Cruise Lines, Inc. v. Shute, 3558

Carnley v. Cochran, 1125

Carolene Products Co.; United States v., 683

Carolina Environment Study Group; Duke Power Co. v., 1932

———; United States Nuclear Regulatory Commission v., 1932

Carpenter v. United States, 3213

Carpenters; Sears, Roebuck and Co. v., 1910

Carpenters and Joiners Union of America, Local No. 213 v. Ritter's Cafe, 747

Carr; Baker v., 1122

——— v. Montgomery County Board of Education, 1369

——— v. Young, 1087

Carrier; Murray v., 3032

Carroll v. President and Commissioners of Princess Anne County, Maryland, 1347

——— v. United States, 521

Carson v. American Brands, Inc., t/a American Tobacco Co., 2183

Carter v. Carter Coal Co., 651

———; Florence County School District No. 4 v., 3845

———; Goldwater v., 2061

———; Helvering v., 651

——— v. Kentucky, 2191

——— v. United States, 3280

——— v. West Feliciana Parish School Board, 1385

Carter Coal Co.; Carter v., 651

Cartier, Inc.; K Mart Corp. v., 3230

Casal; Florida v., 2555

Case v. Los Angeles Lumber Products Co., 696

Casey; Lewis v., 4046

———; Planned Parenthood of Southeastern Pennsylvania v., 3732

———; West Virginia University Hospital, Inc. v., 3540

Caspari, Superintendent, Missouri Eastern Correctional Center v. Bohlen, 3859

Cassius Clay v. United States, 1470

Castillo; Lyng v., 3038

Castleberry; Oklahoma v., 2827

Castro; Boston Police Patrolmen's Association v., 2516

Catalano, Inc. v. Target Sales, Inc., 2103

Catalina Foothills School District; Zobrest v., 3823

Catawba Indian Tribe; South Carolina v., 2995

Caterpillar, Inc. v. Williams, 3167

Cathedral Academy v. Committee for Public Education and Religious Liberty, 1594

Catholic Action of Hawaii-Peace Education Project; Weinberger v., 2294

Catholic Bishop of Chicago; National Labor Relations Board (NLRB) v., 1971

Catholic Social Services, Inc.; Reno v., 3825

Catrett; Celotex Corp. v., 3027

Cauble; Supreme Tribe of Ben-Hur v., 469

Causby; United States v., 827

Ceccolini; United States v., 1892

Celebrezze; Anderson v., 2498

Celotex Corp. v. Catrett, 3027

—— v. Edwards, 3972

Cement Division, National Gypsum Co.; Milwaukee v., 3996

Centennial Savings Bank FSB; United States v., 3557

Center Moriches Union Free School District; Lamb's Chapel v., 3811

Central Bank of Denver, N.A. v. First Interstate Bank of Denver, N.A., 3873

Central Bank of Nigeria; Verlinden B.V. v., 2517

Central Baptist Church; Diffenderfer v., 1476

Central Greyhound Lines v. Mealey, 875

Central Gulf Lines, Inc.; Exxon Corp. v., 3586

Central Hanover Bank and Trust Co.; Mullane v., 894

Central Hardware Co. v. National Labor Relations Board (NLRB), 1520

Central Hudson Gas and Electric Corp. v. Public Service Commission of New York, 2126

Central Illinois Public Service Co. v. United States, 1886

Central Intelligence Agency (CIA) v. Sims, 2829

——; Sims v., 2829

Central Lincoln Util. Dist.; Aluminum Co. v., 2702

Central Machinery Co. v. Arizona State Tax Commission, 2143

Central Pacific Railroad Co.; California v., 250

Central Railroad Co.; New York v., 181

Central States, Southeast & Southwest Areas Pension Fund v. Central Transport, Inc., 2878

Central Transport, Inc.; Central States Pension Fund v., 2878

Certain Named and Unnamed Undocumented Alien Children; Texas v., 2389

Chabad v. American Civil Liberties Union, 3379

Chadha; Immigration and Naturalization Service (INS) v., 2565

——; United States House of Representatives v., 2565

——; United States Senate v., 2565

Chadwick; United States v., 1863

Chae Chan Ping v. United States, 263

Chaffin v. Stynchcombe, 1572

Chakrabarty; Diamond v., 2119

Chamberlin v. Dade County Board of Public Instruction, 1187

Chambers v. Florida, 705

—— v. Maroney, Superintendent, 1414

——; Marsh v., 2592

—— v. Mississippi, 1551

—— v. NASCO, Inc., 3590

——; United States v., 623

Chambers County Commission; Swint v., 3959

Champion v. Ames, 348

Champion International Corp. v. International Woodworkers of America, 3170

Chan Kendrick v. Otis R. Bowen, Secretary of Health and Human Services, 3281

——; United Families of America v., 3281

Chandler; Corbett v., 949

—— v. Florida, 2178

——; Kowalaski v., 949

Chancellor of the Board of Education of the City of New York v. Betty-Louise Felton., 2900

Chandris, Inc. v. Latsis, 4003

Chaney; Heckler v., 2814

Channel Two Television, Co. v. National Citizens, 1919

Chaplinsky v. New Hampshire, 744

Chapman v. California, 1273

——; Respublica v., 2

——; Rhodes v., 2251

—— v. United States, 3582

Chappell v. Wallace, 2540

Chardon v. Fernandez, 2289

—— v. Fumero Soto, 2557

Charles; Diamond v., 2977

Charles D. Bonanno Linen Service, Inc. v. National Labor Relations Board (NLRB), 2304

Charles Dowd Box Co. v. Courtney, 1119

Charles River Bridge v. Warren Bridge, 129

Charles Wolff Packing Co. v. Court of Industrial Relations Wolff Packing Co. v. Court of Industrial Relations, 508

Charleston; Weston v., 113

Charlotte-Mecklenburg Board of Education; Swann v., 1444

The Charming Betsy, 37

The Charming Betsy; Murry v., 37

Chase; Steamboat Co. v., 191

Chastain; Ferry v., 563

Chauffeurs, Teamsters and Helpers, Local No. 391 v. Terry, 3425

Chauffeurs, Local No. 391 v. Terry, 3425

Chaunt v. United States, 1085

Chavez; United States v., 1640

Chavez-Salido; Cabell v., 2305
Chavis; Whitcomb v., 1460
Cheek; Prudential Insurance Co. v., 489
——— v. United States, 3521
Cheff v. Schnackenberg, 1259
Chema v. United States, 3394
Chemical Construction, Corp.; Kremer v., 2365
Chemical Manufacturers Association v. Natural
    Resources Defense Council (NRDC), 2791
Chemical Waste Management, Inc. v. Hunt, 3693
"Chenery I," 763
"Chenery II," 851
Chenery Corp.; Securities Exchange Commission
    (SEC) v., 763, 851
"Cherokee Indian Cases," 118, 121
Cherokee Nation v. Georgia, 118
Cherokee Nation of Oklahoma; United States v.,
    3113
"Cherokee Trust Funds," 247
Cherry v. Committee for Public Education and
    Religious Liberty, 1603
Chesapeake and Ohio Railway Co. v. Schwalb, 3383
Chesapeake & Potomac Telephone Company of
    Virgina; Norfolk Redevelopment and Housing
    Authority v., 2603
Chesapeake Bay Foundation, Inc.; Gwaltney of
    Smithfield, Ltd. v., 3215
Chesny; Marek v., 2889
Chesterfield County School Board; Cohen v., 1617
Chevron Oil Co. v. Huson, 1473
Chevron U.S.A. Inc. v. Natural Resources Defense
    Council, Inc. (NRDC), 2721
Chiarella v. United States, 2070
Chicago; Chicago, Burlington and Quincy Railroad
    v., 319
——— v. Illinois Central Railroad Co., 287
———; Termininiello v., 885
———; Times Film Corp. v., 1089
Chicago & N.W. Tr. Co.; Hayfield Northern R. Co.
    v., 2712
Chicago and Northwestern Railway Co.; Bowman v.,
    258
———; Keogh v., 492
———; Peik v., 202
Chicago and North Western Transportation Co. v.
    Kalo Brick & Tile Co., 2192
Chicago and Southern Airlines v. Waterman
    Steamship Corp., 862
Chicago Auditorium Association; Willing v., 565
Chicago, Burlington and Quincy Railroad Co. v.
    Chicago, 319
——— v. Cutts, 201
——— v. Iowa, 201
———; Railroad Commission of Wisconsin v., 478

Chicago, Milwaukee and St. Paul Railroad Co. v.
    Ackley, 203
——— v. Minnesota, 268
Chicago Teachers Union, Local No. 1 v. Hudson,
    2948
Chickasaw Nation; Oklahoma Tax Commission v.,
    4006
"Child Labor Tax Case," 485
Children's Hospital; Adkins v., 501
Childs; Bank of Texas v., 2594
———; Wynnewood Bank & Trust v., 2594
Chilicky; Schweiker v., 3276
Chimel v. California, 1380
"Chinese Exclusion Case," 263
Chisholm v. Georgia, 17
Chisom v. Roemer, Governor of Louisiana, 3604
Choate; Alexander v., 2775
Chrestenson; Valentine v., 749
Chrisman; Washington v., 2309
Christian Echoes National Ministry; United States v.,
    1480
Christian Feigenspan, Co. v. Bodine, 463
Christiansburg Garment Co. v. Equal Employment
    Opportunity Commission (EEOC), 1883
"Christmas-Tree Case," 3379
Christoffel v. United States, 891
Chromatic Communications Enterprises, Inc.;
    Business Guides, Inc. v., 3537
Chrysler Corp. v. Brown, 1983
Chrysler Motors Corp.; J. Truett Payne Company Inc.
    v., 2227
Church of Scientology of California v. Internal
    Revenue Service (IRS), 3212
Church of the Lukumi Babalu Aye, Inc. v. City of
    Hialeah, 3818
Churchill; Waters v., 3894
——— v. United States, 3735
Cincinnati; Pembaur v., 2954
——— v. Reakirt, 580
——— v. Richards, 580
——— v. Vester, 580
Cincinnati, New Orleans & Texas Pacific Railway;
    Interstate Commerce Commission (ICC) v., 322
"Cincinnati Newsrack Case," 3773
Cipollone v. Liggett Group, Inc., 3723
Ciraolo; California v., 2982
Cisneros; Darby v., 3827
Cisneros, Secretary of Housing and Urban
    Developmment v. Alpine Ridge Group, 3790
Citibank, N.A. v. Wells Fargo Asia Ltd., 3462
Citicorp Industrial Credit Inc. v. Brock, 3183
Citizen Band Potawatomi Indian Tribe; Oklahoma
    Tax Commission v., 3535
Citizens Against Rent Control/Coalition for Fair
    Housing v. City of Berkeley, California, 2300

Citizens Bank of Maryland v. Strumpf, 4020

Citizens for Abatement of Aircraft Noise, Inc.; Washington Airports Authority v., 3600

Citizens for a Better Environment; Schaumburg v., 2057

Citizens Publishing Co. v. United States, 1356

Citizens' Savings and Loan Association of Cleveland v. Topeka Loan Association v. Topeka, 192

Citizens to Preserve Overton Park, Inc. v. Volpe, Secretary, Department of Transportation, 1434

City and County of San Francisco v. Skelly Oil Co., 1320

City Disposal Systems, Inc.; National Labor Relations Board (NLRB) v., 2649

City of Akron v. Akron Center for Reproductive Health, Inc., 2548

City of Burlington v. Dague, 3725

City of Cambridge; Nectow v., 564

City of Canton v. Harris, 3314

City of Chicago v. Environmental Defense Fund (EDF), 3880

——— v. Great Lakes Dredge & Dock Co., 3955

City of Cincinnati v. Discovery Network, Inc., 3773

City of Cleburne, Texas v. Cleburne Living Center, Inc., 2901

City of Columbia v. Omni Outdoor Advertising, Inc., 3550

City of Dallas; Berry v., 3393

———; M.J.R., Inc. v., 3393

——— v. Stanglin, 3326

City of East Cleveland; Moore v., 1845

City of Edmonds, Washington v. Oxford House, 3984

City of Harrisonville v. W.S. Dickey Clay Manufacturing Co., 616

City of Hialeah; Church of the Lukumi Babalu Aye, Inc., 3818

City of Houston v. Hill, 3171

City of Ladue v. Gilleo, 3903

City of Lakewood v. Plain Dealer Publication Co., 3265

City of Lockhart v. United States, 2472

City of Los Angeles v. Los Angeles Gas and Electric Corp., 453

——— v. Lyons, 2502

——— v. Skelly Oil Co., 1320

City of Madison, Joint School District No. 8 v. Wisconsin Employment Relations Commission, 1807

City of Memphis v. Greene, 2210

City of Mesquite v. Aladdin's Castle, Inc., 2321

City of Milwaukee v. Cement Division, National Gypsum Co., 3996

——— v. Illinois and Michigan, 2217

City of Mobile, Alabama v. Bolden, 2087

City of New York; Department of Commerce v., 4032

———v. Federal Communications Commission (FCC), 3248

——— v. National Sea Clammers Association, 2271

———; O'Neill v., 2934

———; Oklahoma v., 4032

———; Wisconsin v., 4032

City of Newport v. Fact Concerts, Inc., 2278

City of Oklahoma City v. Tuttle, 2855

City of Pittsburgh v. American Civil Liberties Union of Greater Pittsburgh Chapter., 3379

City of Pleasant Grove v. United States, 3082

City of Port Arthur, Texas v. United States, 2451

City of Renton v. Playtime Theatres, Inc., 2937

City of Revere v. Massachusetts General Hospital, 2576

City of Richmond v. J.A. Croson Co., 3303

——— v. United States, 1711

City of Riverside v. Rivera, 3035

City of Rome v. United States, 2089

City of St. Louis v. Praprotnik, 3229

City of San Diego v. Skelly Oil Co., 1320

City of Tacoma v. Taxpayers of Tacoma, 1033

City of Tiburon; Agins v., 2117

City of Virginia Beach v. Howell, 1552

City of West Branch, Michigan; McDonald v., 2663

Civil Aeronautics Board v. Waterman Steamship Corp., 862

Civil Service Commission; Guardians Association v., 2586

"Civil Rights Cases," 231

Claiborne Hardware, Co.; National Association for Advancement of Colored People (NAACP) v., 2441

Clara Watson v. Fort Worth Bank and Trust, 3287

Clark Distilling Co. v. Western Maryland Railway Co., 433

Clark; Commissioner v., 3321

———; Field and Co. v., 282

———; Honda v., 1278

———; R.C. Tway Coal Co. v., 651

——— v. Roemer, Governor of Louisiana, 3588

———; Rose v., 3052

———; Town of Pawlet v., 64

———; United States v., 2063, 2308

Clark, Secretary of the Interior v. Community for Creative Non-Violence, 2739

Clarke v. Clarke, 338

———; Clarke v., 338

——— v. Haberle Crystal Springs Brewing Co., 575

——— v. Securities Industry Association, 3078

Class; New York v., 2940

Classic; United States v., 736

Clauson; Zorach v., 927

Clayton; Gilfillan v., 2234

———— v. International Union, United Automobile, Aerospace and Agricultural Implement Workers of America, 2234

Clayton Brokerage Co. of St. Louis, Inc. v. Leist, 2360

Cleary; Goesaert v., 878

Cleavinger v. Saxner, 2919

Cleburne Living Center, Inc.; Cleburne v., 2901

Clements, Governor of Texas v. Fashing, 2413

Clemons v. Mississippi, 3431

Clemtree Garner; Memphis Police Department v., 2819

Cleveland; Executive Jet Aviation, Inc. v., 1541

———— v. Hope Natural Gas Co., 780

————; International Association of Fire Fighters v., 3050

———— v. Loudermill, 2803

Cleveland Board of Education v. La Fleur, 1617

Cleveland-Cliffs Iron Co. v. Lord, 502

Clifford; Helvering v., 707

————; Michigan v., 2613

Clinchfield Coal Co. v. Director, Office of Workers' Compensation Programs, United States Department of Labor, 3614

Cloud Books; Arcara v., 3057

Clover Leaf Creamery Co.; Minnesota v., 2175

Cloyd W. Miller Co.; Woods v., 864

Clutchette; Enomoto v., 1749

Clyne; Burton v., 483

Coalition to Preserve the Integrity of American Trademarks; 47th Street Photo, Inc. v., 3230

————; United States v., 3230

Coastal Corp.; Willy v., 3656

Cobb; Shaare Tefila Congregation v., 3141

Cochran; Carnley v., 1125

———— v. Louisiana Board of Education, 578

Cockrill v. California, 525

Codispoti v. Pennsylvania, 1664

Coffin v. United States, 300

Coffy v. Republic Steel Corp., 2114

Cogdell; United States v., 2050

Cohen v. California, 1456

———— v. Chesterfield County School Board, 1617

———— v. Cowles Media Inc., dba Minneapolis Star & Tribune Co., 3613

————; Flast v., 1338

Cohens v. Virginia, 82

Cohn; Cox Broadcasting Corp. v., 1685

————; G.D. Searle & Co. v., 2327

Coker v. Georgia, 1876

Colautti v. Franklin, 1953

Colburn; Delaware River Joint Toll Bridge Commission v., 714

Colby v. Driver, 2053

Cole v. Georgia, 2686

————; Hall v., 1571

————; Wyatt v., 3686

———— v. Young, 994

Colegrove v. Green, 833

Coleman; Havens Realty Corp. v., 2325

———— v. McGrath, 922

———— v. Miller, 693

———— v. Thompson, 3615, 3688

Colgate v. Harvey, Tax Commissioner of Vermont, 642

————; United States v., 450

Colgate-Palmolive Co. v. Franchise Tax Board of California, 3914

Colgrove v. Battin, 1586

Collector v. Day, 179

Collet v. Collet, 12

————; Collet v., 12

Collins; Barlow v., 1395

———— v. City of Harker Heights, Texas, 3655

————; Frisbie v., 921

————; Graham v., 3753

———— v. Hardyman, 916

————; Herrera v., 3751

————; Reich v., 3937

————; Thomas v., 803

Collins, Director, Texas Department of Criminal Justice v. Youngblood, 3491

Colonial American Life Insurance Co. v. Commissioner, 3355

Colonnade Catering Corp. v. United States, 1392

Colorado v. Bertine, 3077

————; Bi-Metallic Investment Co. v., 429

———— v. Connelly, 3068

————; Kansas v., 3982

———— v. New Mexico, 2452, 2699

———— v. Nunez, 2630

————; Patterson v., 369

———— v. Spring, 3087

————; Wolf v., 890

Colorado River Water Conservation District v. United States, 1740

Colten v. Kentucky, 1508

Colton v. Southern California Edison Co., 1176

Columbia; Barr v., 1194

————; Bouie v., 1198

———— v. Omni Outdoor Advertising, Inc., 3550

Columbia Broadcasting System, Inc. (CBS); American Society of Composers, Authors and Publishers v., 1977

————; Broadcast Music, Inc. v., 1977

———— v. Democratic National Committee, 1574

———— v. Federal Communications Commission (FCC), 2281

Columbia Pictures Corp. v. United States, 870

Columbia Pictures Industries, Inc.; Professional Real Estate Investors, Inc. v., 3793

Columbia Resource Co. v. Department of Environmental Quality of the State of Oregon, 3871

Columbus Board of Education v. Penick, 2031

Comegys; Holmes v., 10

Commercial Metals Co.; Southern Pacific Transportation, Co. v., 2359

Commissioner; Arkansas Best Corp. v., 3232

———— v. Asphalt Products Co., 3157

————; Automobile Club of Michigan v., 1003

————; Badaracco v., 2615

———— v. Bollinger, 3236

————; Colonial American Life Insurance Co. v., 3355

————; Corn Products Refining Co. v., 978

————; Cottage Savings Association v., 3556

————; Crane v., 846

————; Dickman v., 2631

————; F. Strauss and Son, Inc. v., 1046

————; Freytag v., 3619

————; Graham v., 3343

———— v. Groetzinger, 3090

————; INDOPCO, Inc. v., 3653

————; Lilly v., 924

————; Moline Properties v., 771

————; National Carbide Corp. v., 883

————; Paulsen v., 2767

————; Portland Golf Club v., 3494

————; Tank Truck Rentals, Inc. v., 1023

————; Textile Mills Securities Corp. v., 739

————; Thor Power Tool Co. v., 1955

Commissioner of Internal Revenue; Air Reduction Sales Co. v., 833

————; Asphalt Products Co. v., 3157

————_; Bufferd v., 3754

———— v. Clark, 3321

———— v. Engle et ux., 2611

———— v. Estate of Bosch, 1289

———— v. Fink, 3186

———— v. First Security Bank of Utah, N.A., 1487

———— v. Harmon, 795

———— v. Heininger, 778

————; Hernandez v., 3343

————; Higgins v., 727

————; Hillsboro National Bank v., 2481

———— v. Indianapolis Power & Light Co., 3392

———— v. Keystone Consolidated Industries, Inc., 3799

———— v. Lincoln Savings and Loan Association, 1463

———— v. Portland Cement Company of Utah, 2186

————; Pure Carbonic, Inc. v., 883

———— v. Schleier, 4002

Commissioner of Internal Revenue; Schlude v., 1140

———— v. Soliman, 3745

———— v. Sullivan, 1022

———— v. Tellier, 1250

———— v. Tufts, 2509

————; United Missouri Bank of Kansas v., 2388

———— v. Wemyss, 805

————; Whipple v., 1153

Commissioner, Immigration and Naturalization Service (INS) v. Jean, 3471

Commissioner of Taxes; Mobil Oil Corp. v., 2077

Commissioners and Mental Health/Mental Retardation Administrator for Bucks County v. Halderman, 2297

Committee for Public Education and Religious Liberty (PEARL); Anderson v., 1594, 1603

————; Cathedral Academy v., 1594

————; Cherry v., 1603

———— ; Levitt v., 1594

————; Levitt and Nyquist v., 1594

———— v. Nyquist, Commissioner of Education of the State of New York, 1603

———— v. Regan, 2058

Committee of Character and Fitness; Willner v., 1151

Committee on Legal Ethics of the West Virginia State Bar v. Triplett, 3430

Commodity Futures Trading Commission v. Schor, 3061

———— v. Weintraub, 2838

Common Cause v. Schmitt, 2315

Commonwealth of Edison Co. v. Natural Resources Defense Council, Inc. (NRDC), 2534

———— v. Montana, 2287

Commonwealth of Pennsylvania v. Dillon, 32

Communications Workers of America; AT&T Technologies, Inc. v., 2962

———— v. Beck, 3283

Communist Party of United States v. Subversive Activities Control Board, 987, 1106

Community Communications Co., Inc. v. City of Boulder, Colorado, 2311

Community for Creative Non-Violence; Clark v., 2739

Community Health Services; Heckler v., 2687

Community Nutrition Institute; Block v., 2700

————; Young v., 3013

Community Television of Southern California v. Gottfried, 2464

Community for Non-Violence v. Reid, 3345

Compagnie Generale Transatlantique; Kermarec v., 1047

Compagnie des Bauxites de Guinee; Insurance Corporation of Ireland Ltd. v., 2373

Compass Shipping Co. Ltd.; Rodriguez v., 2229

Compco Corp. v. Day-Brite Lightening, Inc., 1178

Complete Auto Transit, Inc. v. Brady, 1824
—— v. Reis, 2220
Conboy; Pillsbury Co. v., 2455
Concerned Neighbors in Action; Stringfellow v.,
    3104
Concrete Pipe and Products of California, Inc. v.
    Construction Laborers Pension Trust for
    Southern California, 3820
Condon; Nixon v., 603
Confederate Tribes and Bands of Yakima; Brendale
    v., 3376
Confederated Salish & Kootenai Tribes; Moe v.,
    1753
Confederated Tribes and Bands of the Yakima Indian
    Nation; County Yakima v., 3376, 3638
——; Wilkinson v., 3376
Confederated Tribes of the Colville Indian
    Reservation v. Washington, 2113
——; Washington v., 2113
Connaughton; Harte-Hanks Communications, Inc. v.,
    3364
Connecticut v. Barrett, 3085
——; Boddie v., 1433
——; Cantwell v., 712
—— v. Doehr, 3589
——; Fahy v., 1172
——; Geer v., 308
——; Griswold v., 1231
—— v. Johnson, 2470
——; Palko v., 673
—— v. Teal, 2398
"Connecticut Anti-Contraception Case," 1231
Connecticut Board of Pardons v. Dumschat, 2258
Connecticut Department of Income Maintenance v.
    Heckler, Secretary of Health and Human
    Services, 2846
Connecticut General Life Insurance Co. v. Johnson,
    676
Connecticut National Bank v. Germain, Trustee for
    the Estate of O'Sullivan's Fuel Oil Co., Inc.,
    3662
Connelie; Foley v., 1893
Connell; Vermilya-Brown Co. v., 877
Connell Construction Co. v. Plumbers and
    Steamfitters Local Union No. 100, 1699
Connelly; Colorado v., 3068
Conner; Sandin v., 4007
Connick, District Attorney v. Myers, 2503
Connolly; Barbier v., 239
—— v. Pension Benefit Guaranty Corp. , 2944
Connor v. Finch, 1844
——; Finch v., 1844
Conrad; Southeastern Promotions, Ltd. v., 1686
"Conrail Case," 2640
Conroy v. Aniskoff, 3777

Consolidated Coal Co.; Costle v., 2158
—— v. Director, Office of Workers'
    Compensation Programs, United States
    Department of Labor, 3614
Consolidated Coin Caterers Corp.; O'Connor v.,
    4036
Consolidated Edison Co. of New York v. National
    Labor Relations Board (NLRB), 687
—— v. Public Service Commission of New York,
    2125
Consolidated Freightways Corp.; Kassel v., 2203
Consolidated Rail Corp. (CONRAIL) v. Darrone,
    Administratrix of the Estate of LeStrange, 2640
—— v. Gottshall, 3921
—— v. Railway Labor Executives' Association,
    3356
——; West v., 3116
Constantin; Sterling v., 611
——; United States v., 641
Construction Laborers Pension Trust; Concrete Pipe
    and Products v., 3820
Construction Laborers Vacation Trust; Franchise Tax
    Board v., 2568
Consumer Alert v. State Farm, 2569
Consumer Life Insurance Co.; United States v., 1834
Consumer Power Co. v. Aeschliman, 1900
Consumer Product Safety Commission v. GTE
    Sylvania, Inc., 2112
Consumers Union of the United States, Inc.; Bose
    Corp. v., 2675
——; GTE Sylvania, Inc. v., 2075
——; Supreme Court of Virginia v., 2106
——; Virginia Supreme Court v., 2106
Container Corp. of America v. California Franchise
    Tax Board, 2574
——; United States v., 1348
"Contempt Pardon Case," 520
Continental Bank Corp.; Lewis v., 3421
Continental Oil Co. v. Federal Power Commission
    (FPC), 1320
—— v. Governor of Maryland, 1922
Continental Ore Co. v. Union Carbide and Carbon
    Co., 1136
Continental Trust Co.; Hyde v., 301
Continental TV, Inc. v. GTE Sylvania, Inc., 1864
Contractors Association of Eastern Pennsylvania v.
    Pennsylvania, 2425
Conway Corp.; Federal Power Commission (FPC),
    1760
Cook v. United States, 613
Cook County; Soldal v., 3738
Cook County Officers Electoral Board v. Reed, 3639
Cooley v. Board of Wardens of Port of Philadelphia,
    146
Coolidge v. New Hampshire, 1466

————; United States v., 67
Cooper v. Aaron, 1040
———— v. Federal Reserve Bank of Richmond, 2722
————; Kovacs v., 879
———— v. Pate, 1202
————; Reiter v., 3769
———— v. Telfair, 29
Coors Brewing Co.; Rubin v., 3976
Coosaw Mining Co. v. South Carolina, 285
Cooter & Gell v. Hartmarx Corp., 3479
Coplin v. United States, 3063
Coppage v. Kansas, 422
Copperweld Corp. v. Independence Tube Corp., 2718
Corbett v. Chandler, 949
Corbin; Grady v., 3456
Corbitt v. New Jersey, 1949
Corliss v. Bowers, Collector of Internal Revenue, 579
Corn Products Refining Co. v. Commissioner of
    Internal Revenue (IRS), 978
———— v. Federal Trade Commission (FTC), 807
Cornelius, Acting Director, Office of Personnel
    Management v. NAACP Legal Defense and
    Educational Fund, Inc., 2910
———— v. Nutt, 2882
Corning Glass Works v. Brennan, Secretary of Labor,
    1645
————; Brennan, Secretary of Labor v., 1645
Coronado Coal Co. v. United Mine Workers of
    America, 526
————; United Mine Workers v., 488
Corp. of the Presiding Bishop of the Church of Jesus
    Christ of Latter-Day Saints v. Amos, 3195
Corporation of New Orleans v. Winter, 65
Corrigan v. Buckley, 533
————; Truax v., 477
Costle v. Consolidated Coal Co., 2158
Cort v. Ash, 1706
————; Rusk v., 1123, 1141
Cortese; Parham v., 1507
Cortez; United States v., 2172
Cory v. Western Oil & Gas Assn., 2822
Cory, Controller of the State of California v. White,
    Attorney General of Texas, 2383
Costle v. Pacific Legal Foundation, 2069
Cottage Savings Assocation v. Commissioner of
    Internal Revenue, 3556
Cotton v. Scotland Neck City Board of Education,
    1518
"Cotton Dust Case," 2260
Cottrell; A & P Tea Co. v., 1729
————; Great Atlantic and Pacific Tea Co. v., 1729
Couch v. United States, 1543
Council of the City of Emporia; Wright v., 1517
Councilman; Schlesinger v., 1689
Counselman v. Hitchcock, 279

County Board of Education Richmond, Georgia;
    Cummings v., 335
County Commissioner of Webster County; Allegheny
    Pittsburgh Coal Co. v., 3298
County Commission of Webster County, West
    Virginia; East Kentucky Energy Corp. v., 3298
County Court of Ulster County, New York v. Allen,
    2002
County of Allegheny v. American Civil Liberties
    Union of Greater Pittsburgh Chapter, 3379
County of Allegany, New York v. United States,
    3714
County of Cortland, New York v. United States, 3714
County of Harris, Texas; Xerox Corp. v., 2450
County of Imperial, California v. Munoz, 2157
County of Kent; Northwest Airlines v., 3858
County of Los Angeles v. Davis, 1974
————; First English Evangelical Lutheran Church
    v., 3164
————; Japan Line, Ltd. v., 1988
————; Valley Unitarian-Universalist Church, Inc.
    v., 1038
County of Oneida; Oneida Indian Nation of New
    York v., 1618
County of Oneida, New York v. Oneida Indian
    Nation of New York State, 2795
County of Riverside, California v. McLaughlin, 3563
County of Washington, Oregon v. Gunther, 2245
County of Yakima v. Confederated Tribes and Bands
    of the Yakima Indian Nation, 3376, 3638
County School Board of Prince Edward County;
    Davis v., 954, 956, 973
————; Griffin v., 1186
County School Board; Green v., 1329
Court of Industrial Relations; Wolff Packing Co. v.,
    508
Courtney; Charles Dowd Box Co. v., 1119
Coutu; Universities Research Association v., 2206
Covert; Reid v., 993, 1009
Covington and Lexington Turnpike Road Co. v.
    Sandford, 316
Cowles Media Co.; Cohen v., 3613
Cox v. Louisiana, 1212, 1213
———— v. New Hampshire, 732
————; Quirin v., 757
"Cox I," 1212
"Cox II," 1213
Cox Broadcasting Corp. v. Cohn , 1685
Coxe v. Huston, 26
———— v. M'Clenachan, 26
Coy v. Iowa, 3288
Coyle v. Smith, 404
Coyne; Fort Halifax Packing Co. v., 3153
Crabtree v. Boles, 1118
Craig v. Boren, 1808

Craig v. Harney, Sheriff, 848
———; Maryland v., 3508
——— v. Missouri, 116
Cramer v. United States, 500, 808
Crampton v. Ohio, 1451
Crane v. Commissioner of Internal Revenue, 846
———; Ex Parte , 119
——— v. Kentucky, 3002
Cravalho v. Richardson, 1255
Crawford v. Board of Education of the City of Los
        Angeles, 2429
Crawford Fitting Co. v. J.T. Gibbons, Inc., 3170
"Crèche I," 2642
"Crèche II," 2834
Creech; Arave v., 3775
Creighton; Anderson v., 3204
Crenshaw; Bankers Life and Casualty Co. v., 3249
Crescent City Livestock Landing and Slaughter
        House Co.; Butchers' Benevolent Association
        v., 189
Crescent City Slaughterhouse; Butchers' Union
        Slaughterhouse v., 237
Crest Street Community Council; North Carolina
        Department of Transportation v., 3062
Crews; United States v., 2078
Crisp; Capital Cities Cable, Inc. v., 2715
Criswell; Western Air Lines, Inc. v., 2870
Cronic; United States v., 2679
Crosby v. United States, 3748
Crouter v. Lemon, 1604
Crow Dog; Ex Parte, 232
Crow Tribe; National Farmers Union Insurance Cos.
        v., 2856
Crowell v. Benson, 598
Crowley; Furniture Moving Drivers v., 2710
Crown, Cork & Seal Co., Inc. v. Parker, 2543
——— v. United Steelworkers, 3991
Crown Kosher Super Market; Gallagher v., 1104
Crown Life Insurance v. Malley-Duff Associates,
        Inc., 3188
Crowninshield; Sturges v., 72
Cruikshank; United States v., 198
Cruz v. Beto, Corrections Director, 1485
——— v. New York, 3123
Cruzan v. Director, Missouri Department of Health,
        3498
——— v. Harmon, Director, Missouri Department of
        Health, 3498
Cumming v. County Board of Education Richmond,
        Georgia, 335
Cummings; Gaffney v., 1581
——— v. Missouri, 163
Cunningham v. Neagle, 269
Cupp v. Murphy, 1576
Cupp, Superintendent v. Naughten, 1607

Curlett; Murray v., 1167, 1168
Curran; Merrill Lynch Pierce Fenner & Smith, Inc.
        v., 2360
Currie v. United States, 157
Currin v. Wallace, Secretary of Agriculture, 689
Curtin v. Benson, 406
Curtin Matheson Scientific, Inc.; National Labor
        Relations Board (NLRB) v., 3432
Curtis Publishing Co. v. Butts, 1296
Curtiss; Strawbridge v., 43
Curtiss-Wright Export Corp.; United States v., 656
Curtiss-Wright Corp. v. Schoonejongen, 3961
Custis v. United States, 3887
Cuyler v. Adams, 2174
——— v. Sullivan, 2095

D. Grant Peacock v. Jack L. Thomas, 4027
Dade County Bd. of Public Instruction; Chamberlin
        v., 1187
Dagenhart; Hammer v., 444
Daggett; Karcher v., 2560
Dague; Burlington v., 3725
Dahl; Pinter v., 3261
Daily Income Fund, Inc. v. Fox, 2619
Daily Mail Publishing Co.; Smith v., 2023
Dairy Queen, Inc. v. Wood, 1124
Dairymen's League Cooperative Association v. Rock
        Royal Co-operative, Inc., 695
Dalby; Pirate v., 5
Dalia v. United States, 1982
Dallas; FW/PBS, Inc. v., 3393
———; FW/PBS, Inc. dba Paris Adult Bookstores II
        v., 3393
———; Interstate Circuit, Inc. v., 1318
———; United Artists Corp. v., 1318
Dallas County; American Bank and Trust Co. v.,
        2594
Dallas Independent School District; Jett v., 3365
Dalm; United States v., 3426
Dalton, Secretary of the Navy v. Specter, 3886
Damarest v. Manspeaker, 3520
Dames & Moore v. Regan, Secretary of Treasury,
        2288
Damron; Ocala Star-Banner Co. v., 1432
"Danbury Hatters Case," 376
Dandridge v. Williams, 1402
Danforth; Planned Parenthood of Central Missouri v.,
        1792
Daniel v. Family Security Life Insurance Co., 881
———; International Brotherhood of Teamsters, etc.
        v., 1956
Daniels v. Allen, 937
——— v. Williams, 2927
Dann; United States v., 2787

Danziger, Acting Chairman, Casino Control Commission of New Jersey v. Hotel & Restaurant Employees & Bartenders International Union, Local 54, 2745

Darby v. Cisneros, Secretary of Housing and Urban Development, 3827

———; United States v., 725

Darden; Nationwide Mutual Insurance Co. v., 3665

——— v. Wainwright, Secretary, Florida Department of Corrections, 3022

Darkow v. United States, 456

Darlington, Inc.; Federal Housing Administration (FHA) v., 1042

Darrone; Consolidated Rail Corp. (CONRAIL) v., 2640

"Dartmouth College Case," 75

Daubert v. Merrell Dow Pharmaceuticals, Inc., 3839

D'Auchy; Wiscart v., 22

Daugherty; McGrain v., 543

Davenport; Pennsylvania Department of Public Welfare v., 3458

Davida Johnson; Lucious Abrams, Jr. v., 4019

——— v. United States, 4019

Davidowitz; Hines v., 724

Davidson v. Cannon, 2928

——— v. City of New Orleans, 208

Davis; Alabama Power Co. v., 1847

——— v. Alaska, 1624

——— v. Bandemer, 3041

——— v. Beason, 265

——— v. Board of School Commissioners of Mobile County, 1445

———; County of Los Angeles v., 1974

——— v. County of School Board of Prince Edward County, 954, 956, 973

———; Helvering v., 671

———; Hutto v., 2303

———; International Longshoremen's Association v., 2989

——— v. Massachusetts, 321

——— v. Passman, 2004

———; Parker v., 182

———; Paul v., 1738

——— v. Scherer, 2735

———; Smith v., 797

———; Southeastern Community College v., 2011

———; Steward Machine Co. v., 670

——— v. United States, 834, 1128, 3454, 3918

———; United States v., 1128, 1398

———; Washington v., 1759

Dawson v. Delaware, 3658

Dawson Chemical Co. v. Rohm and Haas Co., 2144

Day; Collector v., 179

———; Buffington, Collector of Internal Revenue v., 179

Day; Heckler v., 2690

———; Manual Enterprise, Inc. v., 1133

Day-Brite Lightening, Inc.; Compco, Inc. v., 1178

"Dayton I," 1873

"Dayton II," 2032

Dayton v. Dulles, Secretary of State, 1030

Dayton Board of Education v. Brinkman, 1873, 2032

Dayton Christian Schools, Inc. v. Ohio Civil Rights Commission, 3037

Dayton-Goose Creek Railway Co. v. United States, 513

"Deadly Force Case," 2819

Deal v. United States, 3798

Dean Milk Co. v. City of Madison, Wisconsin, 905

Dean Witter Reynolds Inc. v. Byrd, 2794

DeBenedictis; Keystone Bituminous Coal Association v., 3107

DeBoer; DeBoer v., 3844

——— v. Schmidt, 3844

DeBoer, aka Baby Girl Clausen v. DeBoer, 3844

Debs; In re , 302

——— v. United States, 449

DeCoteau v. District County Court for the Tenth Judicial District, 1684

Dedeaux; Pilot Life Insurance Co. v., 3117

Deering; Duplex Printing Press v., 467

Defenders of Wildlife; Lujan v., 3700

DeFillippo; Michigan v., 2020

DeFunis v. Odegaard, 1635

DeGeofroy v. Riggs, 264

DeGrandy v. Johnson, 3931

———; Johnson v., 3931

DeJonge v. Oregon, 657

de la Cuesta; Fidelity Federal Savings and Loan Assoc. v., 2418

Delaware; Dawson v., 3658

———; Franks v., 1934

———; Neal v., 223

——— v. New York, 3776

——— v. Prouse, 1975

——— v. Van Arsdall, 2964

Delaware River Joint Toll Bridge Commission v. Colburn, 714

Delaware State College v. Ricks, 2165

"Delaware Valley I," 3051

"Delaware Valley II," 3206

Delaware Valley Citizens' Council; Pennsylvania v., 3051

Delaware Valley Citizens' Council for Clean Air; Pennsylvania v., 3206

DelCostello v. International Brotherhood of Teamsters, 2536

Deleet Merchandising Corp. v. United States, 2615

Delgado; Immigration and Naturalization Service (INS) v., 2661

Delia; United States v., 772
De Lima v. Bidwell, 342
Delli Paoli v. United States, 996
Dellmuth v. Muth, 3354
Delo; Schlup v., 3947
De Longchamps; Respublica v., 3
De Los Santos; Scindia Steam Navigation Co. Ltd v., 2211
Delta Air Lines, Inc. v. August, 2194
———; Shaw v., 2571
Demisay; Local 144 Nursing Home Pension Fund v., 3819
Democratic National Committee; American Broadcasting Co. v., 1574
———; Columbia Broadcasting System, Inc. v., 1574
Democratic Party of the United States v. National Conservative Political Action Committee, 2802
——— v. Wisconsin ex. rel. LaFollette, 2185
Democratic Senatorial Campaign Committee; Federal Election Commission (FEC) v., 2291
Democratic Senatorial Campaign Committee ; National Republican Senatorial Committee v., 2291
Dempsey v. Boynton, 463
———; Moore v., 499
Den, Murray's Lessee v. Hoboken Land and Improvement Co., 152
Dennis v. Higgins, Director, Nebraska Department of Motor Vehicles, 3532
——— v. Sparks, 2155
Dennison; Kentucky v., 156
Denno; Jackson v., 1199
———; Stovall v., 1300
Dent v. West Virginia, 261
Denton, Director of Corrections of California v. Hernandez, 3682
Denver; Londoner v., 383
Denver School District No. 1; Keyes v., 1587
Department of Commerce v. City of New York, 4032
——— v. Montana, 3672
Department of Conservation; LaCoste v., 514
Department of Defense; Perpich v., 3477
Department of Employment Security; Turner v., 1721
Department of Environmental Quality; Oregon Waste Systems v., 3871
Department of Environmental Quality of the State of Oregon; Columbia Resource Co. v., 3871
Department of Game; Puyallup Tribe v., 1327
Department of Game of Washington; Kautz v., 1327
——— v. Puyallup Tribe, 1605
———; Puyallup Tribe v., 1605
Department of Revenue; Exxon Corp. v., 2115
———; National Bellas Hess, Inc. v., 1282
———; Norton Co. v., 908

Department of Revenue of Montana v. Kurth Ranch, 3897
Department of Revenue of Oregon v. ACF Industries, Inc., 3857
Department of Social Services; Lassiter v., 2240
———; Monell v., 1918
Department of Taxation and Finanace of New York v. Milhelm, Attea and Brothers, Inc., 3904
Department of Transportation v. State Farm, 2569
Department of Treasury v. Galioto, 3034
———; Stevens v., 3561
Department of Treasury, Internal Revenue Service v. Federal Labor Relations Authority (FLRA), 3436
DePasquale; Gannett Co., Inc. v., 2030
Deposit Guaranty National Bank v. Roper, 2073
Deputy v. du Pont, 702
Dern; United States ex rel. Greathouse v., 617
———; Greathouse v., 617
Des Moines Independent Community School District; Tinker v., 1354
Desktop Direct, Inc.; Digital Equipment Corp. v., 3900
DeShaney v. Winnebago County Department of Social Services, 3309
——— v. United States, 914
Deshawn Green; Anderson, Director, California Department of Social Services v., 3956
Deslions v. LaCompagnie General Transatlantique, 381
Detroit; Huron Portland Cement Co. v., 1073
Detroit Board of Education; Abood v., 1839
Detroit Edison; Cantor v., 1804
——— v. National Labor Relations Board (NLRB), 1964
Detroit Local Joint Executive Board; Howard Johnson Co. v., 1646
Deveaux; Bank of the United States v., 46
Devex Corp.; General Motors Corp. v., 2524
Dewey; Donovan v., 2263
Dewsnup v. Timm, 3644
Diamond v. Charles, 2977
Diamond, Commissioner of Patents and Trademarks v. Bradley, 2195
——— v. Chakrabarty, 2119
——— v. Diehr, 2187
Dias; Bacchus Imports, LTD. v. , 2738
DiCenso; Earley v., 1468
———; Robinson v., 1468
Dickerson; Minnesota v., 3810
Dickerson, Director, Bureau of Alcohol, Tobacco and Firearms v. New Banner Institute, Inc., 2471
Dickinson Public Schools; Kadrmas v., 3277
Dickman v. Commissioner of Internal Revenue, 2631
Diedrich v. Commissioner of Internal Revenue, 2388

Diehr; Diamond v., 2187
Diffenderfer v. Central Baptist Church of Miami, Florida, 1476
DiFrancesco; United States v., 2160
Diggs v. United States, 434
Digital Equipment Corp. v. Desktop Direct, Inc., 3900
Dillon; Commonwealth v., 32
——— v. Gloss, 474
Dimension Financial Corp.; Board of Governors of Federal Reserve System, 2929
Dimick v. Schiedt, 629
Dion; United States v., 3004
Dionisio; United States v., 1546
Director, Division of Taxation; Allied-Signal, Inc. v., 3708
Director, Missouri Department of Health; Cruzan v., 3498
Director, Office of Workers' Compensation Programs, Department of Labor; Bath Iron Works Corp. v., 3744
——; Clinchfield Coal Co. v., 3614
——; Consolidation Coal Co. v., 3614
——— v. Greenwich Collieries, Inc., 3913
——— v. Maher Terminals, 3913
Director, Office of Workers' Compensation Programs, Department of Labor; Morrison-Knudsen Construction Co. v., 2523
——— v. Newport News Shipbuilding & Dry Dock Co., 3964
——— v. Perini North River Associates, 2456
——; Potomac Electric Power Co. v., 2166
——; U.S. Industries/Federal Sheet Metal, Inc. v., 2338
Director, Division of Taxation, New Jersey Department of Treasury; Texaco, Inc. and Tenneco Oil Co. v., 3327
Director of Taxation of Hawaii; Aloha Airlines, Inc. v., 2601
——; Hawaiian Airlines, Inc. v., 2601
Dirks v. Securities and Exchange Commission (SEC), 2587
DiSanto v. Pennsylvania, 541
Discovery Network; Cincinnati v., 3773
District County Court; DeCoteau v., 1684
District Court; Fisher v., 1730
——; Kennerly v., 1424
——; Oklahoma Publishing Co. v., 1825
District Court for Eagle County; United States v., 1438
District of Columbia Court of Appeals v. Feldman, 2484
District of Columbia v. Greater Washington Board of Trade, 3742

Division, Director of Taxation; Amerada Hess Corp. v., 3327
Dix; West River Bridge Co. v., 142
Dixson v. United States, 2636
——; United States v., 3842
"Dixon-Yates Case," 1088
Dobbins v. Los Angeles, 360
Dobson; Allied-Bruce Terminix Co. v., 3946
Dock McKoy, Jr. v. North Carolina, 3420
Dodd; United States v., 828
Dodge v. Woolsey, 153
Dodson; Polk Country v., 2301
Doe; Beal v., 1860
——— v. Bolton, Attorney General, 1549
——; Heller v., 3832
——; Honing v., 3221
——; Plyler v., 2389
——; Poelker v., 1862
——— v. Ullman, 1109
——— v. United States, 3271
——; United States v., 2639
——; Webster v., 3260
"Doe II," 3271
Doehr; Connecticut v., 3589
Doggett v. United States, 3726
Doherty; Immigration and Naturalization Service (INS) v., 3641
Dolan v. City of Tigard, 3916
Dole; South Dakota v., 3190
——— v. United Steelworkers of America, 3407
Dollar Park and Fly, Inc.; Park 'N Fly, Inc. v., 2769
Dombrowski; Cady v., 1592
——— v. Eastland, 1285
——— v. Pfister, 1224
Domestic and Foreign Commerce Corp.; Larson v., 888
Donaldson; O'Connor v., 1715
Donnelly; Lynch v., 2642
——; Parma Board of Education v., 2803
——; Yellow Freight System, Inc. v., 3433
Donohue; Lathrop v., 1114
Donovan; American Textile Manufacturers Institute v., 2260
——— v. Dewey, 2263
——; National Cotton Council of America v., 2260
——— v. Penn Shipping Co., Inc., 1818
——— v. San Antonio Metropolitan Transit Authority, 2784
——; United States v., 1812
Donovan, Secretary of Labor v. Lone Steer, Inc., 2616
Dooley v. United States, 343
Doremus v. Board of Education of Borough of Hawthorne, 919

Doremus; United States v., 447
Dorr v. United States, 359
Dorrance; Van Horne's Lessee v., 13
Dorsey; Fortson v., 1210
Dothard v. Rawlinson, 1871
Dotterweich; United States v., 777
Douds; American Communications Association v., 895
Dougall; Sugarman v., 1599
Douglas T. Smith v. Ishmael Jaffree, 2860
Dougherty County, Georgia, Board of Education v. White, 1946
Douglas v. Alabama, 1222
——— v. California, 1145
Douglas, Commissioner, Virginia Marine Resources Commission v. Seacoast Products, Inc., 1840
Douglass; Huidekoper's Lessee v., 41
Dow; Maxwell v., 337
Dow Chemical Co. v. United States, 2983
Dowd; Irvin v., 1105
Dowell v. Board of Education of Oklahoma City Public Schools, 1384
———; Board of Education of Oklahoma City Public Schools v., 3523
Dowling v. United States, 2896, 3397
Downes v. Bidwell, 344
Doyle; Mt. Healthy City School District v., 1810
——— v. Ohio, 1767
Dr. Miles Medical Co. v. John D. Park and Sons Co., 398
Draper v. United States, 1044
"Dred Scott Case," 154
Drexel Furniture Co.; Bailey v., 485
Drug Enforcement Administration (DEA); Shapiro v., 2760
Druggists Mutual Insurance Co.; Wengler v., 2088
Driver; Colby v., 2053
Dryer v. Sims, 909
Dryfoos v. Edwards, 454
Dubuque; Gelpcke v., 158
Duckworth v. Eagan, 3371
Duffy; 324 Liquor Corp. v., 3075
———; Phyle v., 873
Dugger; Hitchcock v., 3130
———; Parker v., 3527
Duke Power Co. v. Carolina Environment Study Group, Inc., 1932
———; Griggs v., 1435
Dukes; New Orleans v., 1782
Dulles; Dayton v., 1030
———; Kent v., 1029
Dulles; Nishikawa v., 1026
———; Trop v., 1025
Dumbra v. United States, 527
Dumschat; Connecticut Board of Pardons v., 2258

Dun & Bradstreet, Inc. v. Greenmoss Builders, Inc., 2886
Dunaway v. New York, 2003
Duncan v. Kahanamoku, 823
——— v. Louisiana, 1324
Duncan, Warden v. Henry, 3949
Dunlop v. Bachowski, 1698
Dunn; United States v., 3101
Dunn, Governor v. Blumstein, 1486
Dunnigan; United States v., 3760
Duplex Printing Press v. Deering, 467
du Pont; Deputy v., 702
DuPont; Shanks v., 115
Duquesne Light Co. v. Barasch, 3297
Duren v. Missouri, 1952
Durham County; R.J. Reynolds Tobacco Co. v., 3067
Durham Lumber Co.; United States v., 1076
Duris; Pallas Shipping Agency, Ltd. v., 2519
Duro v. Reina, Chief of Police, 3463
Durousseau v. United States, 52
Duryee; Mills v., 59
Dusky v. United States, 1072
Dutton, Warden v. Evans, 1420
Dyer County Board of Education; Webb v., 2833
Dynamics Corp. of America; CTS Corp. v., 3119
Dyson, Chief of Police of Dallas v. Stein, 1429

E.C. Knight Co.; United States v., 299
EDF; Chicago v., 3880
E.G. Shinner and Co.; Lauf v., 678
E.I. du Pont; United States v., 991, 1007
E.I. DuPont de Nemours Co. v. Train, Administrator, Environmental Protection Agency (EPA), 1820
Eagan; Duckworth v., 3371
Eagerton; Exchange Oil and Gas Corp. v., 2537
———; Exxon Corp. v., 2537
Earl; Lucas v., 576
Earle; Bank of Augusta v., 131
———; New Orleans and Carrollton Railroad Co. v., 131
Earley v. DiCenso, 1468
East Carroll Parish School Board v. Marshall, 1736
East Cleveland; Moore v., 1845
East Kentucky Energy Corp. v. County Commission of Webster County, West Virginia, 3298
East River Steamship Corp. v. Transamerica Delaval Inc., 3008
East Texas Motor Freight System, Inc. v. Rodriguez, 1843
Eastern Airlines, Inc. v. Floyd, 3555
——— v. Mahfoud, 2920
Eastern Band of Cherokee Indians v. United States, 247
Eastern Kentucky Welfare Rights Organization; Simon v., 1757

Eastern Railroad Presidents Conference v. Noerr Motor Freight, Inc., 1090

Eastland v. United States Servicemen's Fund, 1695

Easterwood; CSX Transportation, Inc. v., 3783

Eastland; Dombrowski v., 1285

Eastman Kodak Co. v. Image Technical Services, Inc., 3697

Eau Claire; Hallie v., 2820

Eckerhart; Hensley v., 2514

Economou; Butz v., 1938

Economy Light and Power Co. v. United States, 470

Eddings v. Oklahoma, 2314

Edelman, Director of Illinois Department of Public Aid v. Jordan, 1629

Edenfield v. Fane, 3787

Edgar v. MITE Corp., 2404

Edge Broadcasting Co.; United States v., 3835

Edmondson Oil Company, Inc.; Lugar v., 2412

Edmonson v. Leesville Concrete Co., 3587

Edward J. DeBartolo Corp. v. Florida Gulf Coast Building and Construction Trades Council, 3242

——— v. National Labor Relations Board (NLRB), 2573

Edwards v. Aguillard, 3176

———; Anderson v., 3965

——— v. Arizona, 2223

——— v. California, 737

———; Celotex Corp. v., 3972

———; Dryfoos v., 454

———; Heckler v., 2651

——— v. South Carolina, 1142

Egan; United States v., 1523

Ehrler; Kay v., 3552

Eichman; United States v., 3475

Eight Thousand Eight Hundred and Fifty Dollars in United States Currency; United States v., 2521

Eisenstadt, Sheriff v. Baird, 1489

Eisner v. Macomber, 457

Ekiu v. United States, 280

Elder v. Holloway, 3864

Eldridge; Mathews v., 1728

Electric Auto-Lite Co.; Mills v., 1386

Elem; Purkett v., 3986

Elfbrandt v. Russell, 1254

Eli Lilly and Co. v. Medtronic, Inc., 3489

Elias-Zacarias; Immigration and Naturalization Service (INS) v., 3646

Elisa Chan v. Korean Air Lines, Ltd. (KAL), 3330

Elk v. Wilkins, 238

Elkins v. United States, 1082

———; Whitehill v., 1303

Elliott; Briggs v., 954, 955, 973

——— v. Wiltz, 230

———; University of Tennessee v., 3059

Ellis v. Brotherhood of Railway, Airline & Streamship Clerks, Freight Handlers, Express & Station Employees, 2672

———; Parker v., 1074

Ellzey; Hepburn v., 40

Elmendorf v. Taylor, 96

Elrod v. Burns, 1785

Elstad; Oregon v., 2797

Ely v. Klahr, 1459

Emison; Growe v., 3757

Empire Storage and Ice Co.; Giboney v., 884

Employers Insurance; Musick, Peeler & Garrett v., 3806

"Employers' Liability Case," 373

Employment Division, Department of Human Resources of Oregon v. Alfred L. Smith, 3435

Emporium Capwell Co. v. Western Addition Community Organization, 1678

Emspak v. United States, 972

Endo; Ex Parte, 801

Energy Action Educational Foundation; Watt v., 2295

Energy Reserves Group, Inc. v. Kansas Power and Light Co., 2461

Energy Resources Co., Inc.; United States v., 3457

Engel v. Vitale, 1132

England; Bank of Marin v., 1265

Engle; Commissioner v., 2611

———; Koehler v., 2653

——— v. Isaac, 2351

English v. General Electric Co., 3468

Enmons; United States v., 1553

Enmund v. Florida, 2438

Enomoto v. Clutchette, 1749

Enterprise Association of Pipefitters Local 638; National Labor Relations Board (NLRB) v., 1815

Enterprise Association of Steam, etc; National Labor Relations Board (NLRB) v., 1815

Enterprise Wheel and Car Corp.; United Steelworkers of America v., 1080

Environmental Defense Fund; Chicago v., 3880

Environmental Protection Agency (EPA) v. Mink, 1547

——— v. National Crushed Stone Association, 2158

——— v. Natural Resource Defense Council (NRDC), 2721, 2791

——— v. National Sea Clammers Assocation, 2271

——— v. Oklahoma, 3654

———; Union Electric Co. v., 1780

Environmental Tectonics Corp.; W.S. Kirkpatrick and Co. v., 3400

Epperson v. Arkansas, 1346

Epstein; Matsushita Electric Industrial Co. v., 4028

Equal Employment Opportunity Commission
       (EEOC) v. Arabian American Oil Co.
       (ARAMCO), 3546
—— v. Associated Dry Goods Corp., 2179
——; Ford Motor Co. v., 2420
——; Christiansburg Garment Co. v., 1883
—— v. Federal Labor Relations Authority, 2975
——; General Telephone Co. v., 2094
—— v. Mayor and City Council of Baltimore,
       2868
——; Newport News Shipbuilding and Dry Dock
       Co. v., 2558
——; Sheet Metal Workers' International
       Association v., 3049
—— v. Shell Oil Co., 2656
——; University of Pennsylvania v., 3391
—— v. Wyoming, 2476
Equitable Trust Co. of New York; Hicks v., 531
——; United States v., 531
Erickson; Hunter v., 1349
Erickson, Warden v. Feather, 1684
Erie Railroad Co. v. Tompkins, 681
Erie Resistor Corp.; National Labor Relations Board
       (NLRB) v., 1154
Erika, Inc.; United States v., 2354
Ernst and Ernst v. Hochfelder, 1746
Ernst and Young; Reves v., 3408, 3765
Erwin; Westfall v., 3220
Erznoznik v. City of Jacksonville, 1708
Escambia County, Florida v. McMillan, 2655
Escobedo v. Illinois, 1200
Escondido; Yee v., 3674
Escondido Mutual Water Co. v. La Jolla Rincon, San
       Pasqual, Pauma and Pala Band of Mission
       Indians, 2682
Espinoza; O'Dell v., 2362
Estate of Bosch; Commissioner v., 1289
Estate of Cowart v. Nicklos Drilling Co., 3722
Estate of Shabazz; O'Lone v., 3165
Estate of Donald E. Thornton v. Caldor, Inc., 2884
Esteben v. Louisiana ex rel. Belden, 189
Estelle; Autry v., 2600
——; Barefoot v., 2595
—— v. Gamble, 1805
——; Rummel v., 2071
Estelle, Corrections Director v. Smith, 2222
Estelle, Warden v. McGuire, 3627
Estep v. United States, 822
Estes v. Texas, 1232
Etowah County Commission; Presley v., 3647
Eu v. San Francisco County Democratic Central
       Committee, 3310
Eubank; Helvering v., 721
Euge; United States v., 2060
Evans v. Abney, 1388

——; Arizona v., 3958
——; Dutton v., 1420
——; Hopper v., 2369
—— v. Jeff D., 2966
——; Oscar Mayer and Co. v., 1994
——; Romer v., 4041
—— v. United States, 3691
——; United Air Lines, Inc. v., 1846
Everson v. Board of Education of Ewing Township,
       839
Evatt; Yates v., 3580
Everhart; Sullivan v., 3409
Evitts, Superintendent, Blackburn Correctional
       Complex v. Lucey, 2778
Ewing; Regents of University of Michigan v., 2921
Ex Parte Ayers, 256
—— Bakelite Corp., 571
—— Bollman, 45
—— Bollman and Swartwout, 45
—— Burger, 757
—— Burford, 44
—— Crane, 119
—— Garland, 164
—— Grossman, 520
—— Haupt, 757
—— Heinek, 757
—— Jackson, 209
—— Kan-gi-Shun-ca (Otherwise known as Crow
       Dog), 232
—— Kemmler, 273
—— Kerling, 757
—— Levitt, 675
—— Lockwood, 296
—— McCabe, 256
—— McCardle, 171
—— Milligan, 162
—— Mitsuye Endo, 801
—— Neubauer, 757
—— Quirin, 757
—— Republic of Peru, 766
—— Scott, 256
—— Siebold, 219
—— Swartwout, 45
—— Thiel, 757
—— Vallandigham, 159
—— Virginia, 217
—— Virginia and Coles, 218
—— Yarbrough, 235
—— Young, 378
Exchange Oil and Gas Corp. v. Eagerton, 2537
Executive Jet Aviation, Inc. v. Cleveland, 1541
"Expatriation Cases," 1024, 1025
Exxon Corporation v. Central Gulf Lines, Inc., 3586
—— v. Eagerton, Commissioner of Revenue of
       Alabama, 2537

———— v. Governor of Maryland, 1922

———— v. Hunt, 2951

———— v. Wisconsin Department of Revenue, 2115

FMC Corp. v. Holliday, 3513

F.S. Royster Guano Co. v. Virginia, 464

F. Strauss and Son, Inc. v. Commissioner of Internal Revenue, 1046

F.W. Woolworth Co. v. Taxation and Revenue Department of the State of New Mexico, 2424

F.W./PBS, Inc. dba Paris Adult Bookstores II v. City of Dallas, 3393

Fabe; United States Department of Treasury v., 3817

Fact Concerts, Inc.; Newport v., 2278

Fahy v. Connecticut, 1172

Fainter; Bernal v., 2695

Fair Assessment in Real Estate Association, Inc. v. McNary, 2293

Fairchild v. Hughes, 479

Fairfax-Brewster School, Inc. v. Gonzales, 1777

Fairfax's Devisee v. Hunter's Lessee, 61

Fairley v. Patterson, 1355

Falbo v. United States, 779

Falcon; General Telephone Co. of Southwest v., 2386

Fall River Dyeing and Finishing Corp. v. National Labor Relations Board (NLRB), 3154

Fallbrook Irrigation District v. Bradley, 314

Falls City Industries, Inc. v. Vanco Beverage, Inc., 2482

Falstaff Brewing Corp.; United States v., 1555

Falwell; Hustler Magazine, Inc. v., 3228

Family Security Life Insurance Co.; Daniel v., 881

Fane; Edenfield v., 3787

"Fanny Hill Case," 1245

Fano; Meachum v., 1778

Fantasy, Inc.; Fogerty v., 3865

Fare v. Michael C., 2016

Faretta v. California, 1718

Fargo Women's Health Organization v. Schafer, 3788

Farley; Reed v., 3915

————; Schiro v., 3853

Farmar v. United States, 2611

Farmer v. Brennan, Warden, 3899

Farmer's Loan and Trust Co.; Reagan v., 297

————; Pollock v., 301, 303

————; Stone v., 244

Farrar and Smith, Co-Administrators of Estate of Joseph D. Farrar v. Hobby, 3741

Farrey v. Sanderfoot, 3574

Farrington v. Tokushige, 544

Fashing; Clements v., 2413

Fauntleroy v. Lum, 382

Fay v. New York, 853

Fay, Warden v. Noia, 1147

Feather; Erickson, Warden v., 1684

Federal Baseball Club of Baltimore, Inc. v. National League of Professional Baseball Clubs, 487

Federal Bureau of Investigation (FBI) v. Abramson, 2370

Federal Communications Commission (FCC); American Broadcasting, Co., Inc. v., 2281

————; American Civil Liberties Union v., 1976

———— v. Beach Communications, Inc., 3807

———— v. Business Executives' Move for Vietnam Peace, 1574

————; CBS, Inc. v., 2281

————; California Public Service Commission v., 2988

————; City of New York v., 3248

———— v. Florida Power Corp., 3099

————; Florida Public Service Commission v., 2988

———— v. Gottfried, 2464

———— v. ITT World Communications, Inc., 2673

———— v. League of Women Voters of California, 2742

————; Louisiana Public Service Commission v., 2988

————; Metro Broadcasting, Inc. v., 3503

———— v. Midwest Video Corp., 1976

————; National Association of Broadcasters v., 1919

————; National Broadcasting Co., Inc. v., 2281

———— v. National Citizens Committee for Broadcasting (NCCB), 1919

————; Public Utilities Commission of Ohio v., 2988

———— v. RCA Communications,Inc., 946

———— v. Pacifica Foundation, 1601

————; Red Lion Broadcasting Co. v., 1374

————; Sable Communications v., 3369

————; Turner Broadcasting System, Inc. v., 3924

———— v. WNCN Listeners Guild, 2201

Federal Crop Insurance Corp. v. Merrill, 854

Federal Deposit Insurance Corporation (FDIC) v. Philadelphia Gear Corp., 2991

———— v. Meyer, 3862

————; O'Melveny & Myers v., 3905

Federal Elections Commission (FEC) v. Americans for Change, 2315

————; Bread Political Action Committee v., 2336

————; California Medical Association v., 2276

———— v. Democratic Senatorial Campaign Committee, 2291

———— v. Massachusetts Citizens for Life, Inc., 3071

———— v. National Conservative Political Action Committee, 2802

———— v. National Rifle Association (NRA) Political Victory Fund, 3936

———— v. National Right to Work Committee, 2453

Federal Energy Administration v. Algonquin SNG, Inc., 1766

Federal Energy Regulatory Commission (FERC) v. American Electric Power Service Corp., 2513

———; California v., 3455

——— v. Mid-Louisiana Gas Co., 2579

——— v. Mississippi, 2376

——— v. United Distribution Co., 3522

Federal Housing Administration (FHA) v. Darlington, Inc., 1042

Federal Labor Relations Authority (FLRA); Bureau of Alcohol, Tobacco and Firearms v., 2606

———; Department of Defense v., 3863

———; Department of Treasury v., 3436

———; Equal Employment Opportunity Commission (EEOC) v., 2975

———; Fort Stewart Schools v., 3461

———; United States Department of Defense v., 3863

Federal Power Commission (FPC); Bass v., 1320

———; Continental Oil Co. v., 1320

——— v. Conway Corp., 1760

——— v. Florida Power and Light Co., 1478

——— v. Hope Natural Gas Co., 780

———; Hunt Oil Co. v., 1320

———; Mobil Oil Corp. v., 1320

——— v. Natural Gas Pipeline Co., 745

———; Natural Gas Pipeline Co. v., 745

——— v. New England Power Co., 1626

———; New Mexico v., 1320

——— v. Oregon, 976

——— v. Skelly Oil Co., 1320

——— v. Southern California Edison Co.,1176

———; Standard Oil Co. of Texas v., 1320

———; Sun Oil Co. v., 1320

———; Superior Oil Co. v., 1320

——— v. Transcontinental Gas Pipe Line Corp., 1724

Federal Reserve Bank of Richmond; Cooper v., 2722

Federal Trade Commission (FTC); AMA v., 2341

——— v. American Hospital and Life Insurance Co., 1039

———; American Medical Association v., 2341

——— v. Anheuser-Busch, Inc., 1077

———; Automatic Canteen Co. of America v., 945

———; Corn Products Refining Co. v., 807

——— v. Gratz, 465

———; Great Atlantic & Pacific Tea, Co. v., 1959

——— v. Grolier, Inc., 2531

——— v. Indiana Federation of Dentists, 2992

——— v. National Casualty Co., 1039

——— v. Raladam Co., 594

——— v. Sperry & Hutchinson Co., 1483

——— v. Standard Oil Co. of California, 2164

——— v. Superior Court Trial Lawyers Association, 3401

———; Superior Court Trail Lawyers Association v., 3401

——— v. Ticor Title Insurance Co., 3702

Federal Water and Gas Corp.; Securities and Exchange Commission (SEC) v., 851

Federated Department Stores, Inc. v. Moitie, 2253

Fedorenko v. United States, 2176

Feeney; Massachusetts v., 2005

———; Personnel Administrator of Massachusetts v., 2005

———; Port Authority Trans-Hudson Corp. v. , 3448

Feenstra; Kirchberg v., 2197

Feiner v. New York, 903

Feist Publications, Inc. v. Rural Telephone Services Co., Inc., 3549

Feldman; District of Columbia Court of Appeals v., 2484

———; Marcus Brown Holding Co. v., 472

Felix; United States v., 3668

Felton; Aguilar v., 2900

Fenno; Veazie Bank v., 176

Felton; Chancellor of the Board of Education of the City of New York v., 2900

———; Miller v., 2915

———; Secretary, United States Department of Education v., 2900

Ferber; New York v., 2437

Ferens v. John Deere Co., 3423

Feres v. United States, 899

Ferguson v. Georgia, 1097

———; Plessy v., 312

——— v. Skrupa, 1149

Fernandez; Chardon v., 2289

Ferreira; United States v., 148

Ferri v. Ackerman, 2042

Ferris Faculty Assocation; Lehnert v., 3584

Ferry v. Chastain, 563

——— v. James, 563

——— v. Lloyd, 563

——— v. Ramsey, 563

——— v. Ramsey Petroleum Co., 563

Fetters v. United States ex rel. Cunningham, 593

Feuerstein; Kalb v., 701

Fex v. Michigan, 3758

Fibreboard Paper Products Corp. v. National Labor Relations Board (NLRB), 1207

Fidelity Federal Savings & Loan Association v. De La Cuesta, 2418

Field and Co. v. Clark, 282

Filardo; Foley Bros. v., 882

Filburn; Wickard v., 758

Financial Institution Employees, Local 1182; National Labor Relations Board (NLRB) v., 2943

———; Seattle-First National Bank v., 2943

Finazzo v. Norris, 3912

Finch v. Connor, 1844

———; Connor v., 1844

———; United States v., 1844

Fink; Commissioner of Internal Revenue v., 3186

Finkel; Branti v., 2080

Finkelstein; Sullivan v., 3487

Finley; Pennsylvania v., 3138

——— v. United States, 3339

Finnegan v. Leu, 2363

Finney; Hutto v., 1930

Firestone; Time, Inc. v., 1732

Firefighters Local Union No. 1784 v. Stotts, 2711

Firestone Tire and Rubber Co. v. Richard Bruch, 3307

——— v. Risjord, 2170

First Alabama Bank; Parsons Steel, Inc. v., 2935

First English Evangelical Lutheran Church of Glendale v. County of Los Angeles, 3164

First Interstate Bank; Central Bank v., 3873

First National Bank; Gully v., 654

First National Bank of Atlanta v. Bartow County Board of Tax Assessors, 2805

First National Bank of Boston v. Bellotti, 1905

First National City Bank v. Banco Nacional de Cuba, 1505

——— v. Banco Para El Comercio Exterior De Cuba, 2554

First National Maintenance Corp. v. National Labor Relations Board (NLRB), 2266

First Options of Chicago, Inc. v. Kaplan, 3989

First Security Bank of Utah; Commissioner v., 1487

First Unitarian Church v. County of Los Angeles, 1038

FirsTier Mortgage Co., aka Realbanc, Inc. v. Investors Mortgage Insurance Co., 3524

Fish and Game Commission; Baldwin v., 1912

———; Takahashi v., 872

———; Torao Takahashi v., 872

Fisher; Bradley v., 186

——— v. City of Berkeley, 2946

——— v. District Court of the Sixteenth Judicial District of Montana, 1730

——— v. United States, 1751

———; United States v., 39

———; Yamataya v., 349

Fiske v. Kansas, 555

Fitzgerald; Harlow v., 2409

———; Nixon v., 2408

Fitzhugh; Propeller Genessee Chief v., 147

Fitzpatrick v. Bitzer, Chairman, State Employees' Retirement Commission, 1788

Fitzsimmons; Buckley v., 3830

Fixa v. Heilberg, 1229

"Flag-Burning Case," 3475

"Flag Desecration Case," 1365

"Flag Salute Cases," 718, 773

Flagg Brothers, Inc. v. Brooks, 1909

Flanagan v. United States, 2628

Flast v. Cohen, Secretary of Health, Education, and Welfare, 1338

Fleming; Howard v., 353

Flemming, Secretary of Health, Education and Welfare v. Nestor, 1081

Fletcher v. Peck, 51

——— v. Rhode Island, 141

——— v. Weir, 2337

Flint; Robins Dry Dock and Repair Co. v., 559

Flint Ridge Development Co. v. Scenic Rivers Association of Oklahoma, 1769

Flipside, Hoffman Estates, Inc.; Hoffman Estates v., 2332

Flood v. Kuhn, 1513

Flook; Parker v., 1928

Florence County School District Four v. Carter by and Through Carter, 3845

Flores; Reno v., 3770

———; United States v., 614

Florida; Adderley v., 1264

———; Barclay v., 2596

——— v. Bostick, 3606

——— v. Casal, 2555

———; Chambers v., 705

———; Chandler v., 2178

———; Enmund v., 2438

———; Gardner v., 1827

———; Gustafson v., 1609

———; Hayes v., 2813

———; Hildwin v., 3341

———; Hoyt v., 1116

———; Ibanez v., 3908

——— v. Jimeno, 3572

———; McLaughlin v., 1206

——— v. Mellon, 539

———; Miller v., 3169

———; Murphy v., 1704

———; Pennekamp v., 829

———; Proffitt v., 1796

——— v. Riley, 3302

———; Robinson v., 1195

——— v. Royer, 2485

———; Schneble v., 1488

———; Seminole Tribe v., 4034

———; Skiriotes v., 733

———; Sochor v., 3699

Florida; Spaziano v., 2744

———; Tibbs v., 2381

———; United States v., 3931

——— v. Wells, 3437

———; Williams v., 1416

Florida Bar Association v. Went For It, Inc., 4013

Florida Department of Business and Professional Regulation; Ibanez v., 3908

Florida Department of Revenue; Wardair Canada, Inc. v., 3014

Florida Department of State v. Treasure Salvors, Inc., 2435

Florida Division of Alcoholic Beverages and Tobacco; McKesson Corp. v., 3466

Florida East Coast Railway Co.; United States v., 1550

Florida Gulf Coast Building and Construction Trades Council; Edward J. DeBartolo Corp. v., 3242

Florida Legislative Investigation Committee; Gibson v., 1148

Florida Lime and Avocado Growers, Inc. v. Paul, 1152

Florida Power and Light Co., Inc.; Boca Grande Club, Inc. v., 3875

———; Federal Power Commission (FPC) v., 1478

——— v. Lorion, DBA Center for Nuclear Responsibility, 2810

Florida Power Corp.; Federal Communications Commission (FCC) v., 3099

Florida Public Services Commission v. Federal Communications Commission (FCC), 2988

Florida Star v. B.J.F., 3360

"Florida Telegraph Case," 207

Flower v. United States, 1511

Flowers; United Steelworkers of America v., 2536

Floyd; Anders v., 1968

———; Bond v., 1266

———; Eastern Airlines, Inc. v., 3555

Flynn; Holbrook v., 2958

Flynt v. Ohio, 2230

Fogerty v. Fantasy, Inc., 3865

Foley v. Connelie, 1893

Foley Bros., Inc. v. Filardo, 882

Follett v. Town of McCormick, South Carolina, 786

Fontenot; Rickert Rice Mills v., 644

Food Store Employees Union, Local No. 347, Amalgamated Meat Cutters and Butchers Workermen of North America v. Gissel Packing Co., 1377

"Footnote Four," 683

Ford; Burlington Northern Railroad Co. v., 3703

——— v. Georgia, 3531

———; P.C. Pfeiffer Co. v., 2038

——— v. United States, 548

——— v. Wainwright, Secretary, Florida Department of Corrections, 3030

"Ford Memoirs," 2847

Ford Motor Co. v. Equal Employment Opportunity Commmission (EEOC), 2420

——— v. National Labor Relations Board (NLRB), 1991

Ford Motor Credit Co. v. Milhollin, 2054

——— v. Millhollin, 2054

Fordice; Garlotte v., 3992

———; United States v., 3728

Fordice, Governor of Mississippi; Ayers v., 3728

Foremost Insurance Co. v. Richardson, 2405

Forest City Publishing Co.; Cantrell v., 1669

Forklift Systems, Inc.; Harris v., 3846

Forsham v. Harris, 2068

Forsyth; Mitchell v., 2877

Forsyth County, Georgia v. Nationalist Movement, 3713

Fort Gratiot Landfill v. Michigan Department of Natural Resources, 3694

Fort Gratiot Sanitary Landfill, Inc. v. Michigan Department of Natural Resources, 3694

Fort Halifax Packing Co. Inc. v. Coyne, 3153

Fort Smith; Bowden v., 756

Fort Stewart Schools v. Federal Labor Relations Authority (FLRA), 3461

Fort Wayne Books, Inc. v. Indiana, 3305

Fort Worth Bank and Trust; Watson v., 3287

"Fortner I," 1361

"Fortner II," 1817

Fortner Enterprises, Inc. v. United States Steel Corp., 1361

———; United States Steel Corp. v., 1817

Fortson v. Dorsey, 1210

——— v. Morris, 1267

Fortune; Schiavone v., 3015

Forty-Fourth General Assembly of Colorado; Lucas v., 1190

Foster; Mitchum v., 1512

———; Port Authority Trans-Hudson Corp. v., 3448

Foster and Elam v. Neilson, 111

Foster-Fountain Packing Co. v. Haydel, 568

Foucha v. Louisiana, 3684

Foust; International Brotherhood of Electrical Workers v., 1998

Fowler v. Lindsey, 25

——— v. Miller, 25

——— v. Rhode Island, 940

Fox; Board of Trustees v., 3377

———; Daily Income Fund, Inc. v., 2619

———; State University of New York, Board of Trustees v., 3377

Frady; United States v., 2352

Franchise Tax Board v. Alcan Aluminium, Ltd., 3396

———; Barclays Bank PLC v., 3914

———; Container Corp. of America v., 2574

Franchise Tax Board of California; Colgate-Palmolive Co. v., 3914

——— v. Construction Laborers Vacation Trust For Southern California, 2568

——— v. United States Postal Service, 2709

Francis, Warden v. Franklin, 2837

Frank v. Maryland, 1052

Frank Lyon Co. v. United States, 1901

Franklin; Colautti v., 1953

———; Francis v., 2837

——— v. Gwinnett County Public Schools, 3652

Franklin, Secretary of Commerce v. Massachusetts, 3730

Franklin Mint Corp.; Trans World Airlines, Inc. v., 2662

Franks v. Bowman Transportation Co., 1739

Franks v. Delaware, 1934

Fraser; Bethel School District v., 3056

Fraser, Trenholm and Co. v. United States, 161

Frazee v. Illinois Department of Employment Security, 3324

Frazier v. Heebe, 3177

Frazier; Green v., 462

Fred Irey, Jr., Inc. v. Occupational Safety and Health Review Commission, 1829

Freed; United States v., 1440

Freedman v. Maryland, 1215

Freeland and Krontz; Taylor v., 3680

Freeman; Burson v., 3689

——— v. Hewit, 837

——— v. Pitts, 3673

Freightliner Corp. v. Myrick, 3970

Fretwell; Lockhart v., 3750

Freytag v. Commissioner of Internal Revenue, 3619

Frick v. Webb, 512

Friday; Bazemore v., 3048

———; United States v., 3048

Friedman v. Rogers, 1958

———; Rogers v., 1958

Friedman-Harry Marks Clothing Co.; National Labor Relations Board (NLRB) v., 664

Frisbie v. Collins, 921

Frisby v. Schultz, 3278

Fritz; United States Railroad Retirement Board v., 2162

Frohwerk v. United States, 448

Frommhagen v. Brown, 1630

Frontiero v. Richardson, 1569

Frost DBA Frost and Frost Trucking Co. v. Railroad Commission of California, 534

Frothingham v. Mellon, 507

Fruehauf Trailer Co.; National Labor Relations Board (NLRB) v., 663

Fruit and Vegetable Packers and Warehousemen, Local 760; National Labor Relations Board (NLRB) v., 1183

Fry v. United States, 1697

Fuentes v. Shevin, Attorney General, 1507

Fugate v. New Mexico, 2818

"Fugitive Slave Cases," 136, 155

Fullilove v. Klutznick, 2151

Fulminante; Arizona v., 3547

Fulton; United States v., 2963

Fumero Soto; Chardon v., 2557

Funk Brothers Seed Co. v. Kalo Inoculant Co., 863

Furman v. Georgia, 1528

Furnco Construction Corp. v. Waters, 1940

G. D. Searle & Co. v. Cohn, 2327

GTE Sprint Communications Group v. Sweet, 3296

GTE Sylvania, Inc.; Consumer Product Safety Commission v., 2112

——— v. Consumers Union of the United States, Inc., 2075

———; Continental TV, Inc. v., 1864

Gade, Director, Illinois Environmental Protection Agency v. National Solid Wastes Management Association, 3712

Gaffney v. Cummings, 1581

Gagne; Maher v., 2141

Gainey; United States v., 1216

Galigher Co.; United States v., 824

Galioto; United States Department of Treasury, Bureau of Alcohol, Tobacco and Firearms v., 3034

Gallagher v. Crown Kosher Super Market of Massachusetts, 1104

Galloway v. United States, 770

Galvan v. Press, Immigration and Naturalization Service, 959

Gambell; Amoco Production Co. v., 3108

Gambino v. United States, 560

Gamble; Estelle v., 1805

Gannett Co., Inc. v. DePasquale, 2030

Garcia v. San Antonio Metropolitan Transit Authority, 2784

———; Western Fuel Co. v., 476

———; Wilson v., 2834

Garcia et al. v. United States, 2765

Garden State Bar Assoc.; Middlesex County Ethics Committee v., 2397

Gardner; Brown v., 3938

——— v. Florida, 1827

Gardner-Denver Co.; Alexander v., 1619

Garfinkel; American Foreign Service Association v., 3331

Garland, Ex Parte, 164

Garlotte v. Fordice, Governor of Mississippi, 3992

Garmon; San Diego Building Trades v., 1050

Garner; Grogan v., 3525

——— v. Louisiana, 1117

———; Memphis Bank and Trust Co. v., 2460

———; Memphis Police Department v., 2819

———; Tennessee v., 2819

Garnett; Leser v., 480

——— v. United States, 2854

Garrison v. Louisiana, 1204

———; Maryland v., 3092

Garrity v. New Jersey, 1270

Gates; Illinois v., 2539

Gateway Coal Co. v. United Mine Workers of
America, 1612

Gathers; South Carolina v., 3347

Gaubert; United States v., 3548

Gaudet; Sea-Land Service, Inc. v., 1616

Gaudin; United States v., 4008

Gault; In re, 1284

Gautreaux; Hills v., 1748

Geary; Renne, San Francisco City Attorney v., 3602

Gebhart v. Belton, 954, 957, 973

Geders v. United States, 1744

Geduldig v. Aiello, 1648

Geer v. Connecticut, 308

Gelbard v. United States, 1523

Gelpcke v. City of Dubuque, 158

General Building Contractors Association, Inc. v.
Pennsylvania, 2425

General Dynamics Corp.; United States v., 1627,
3126

General Electric Co. v. Gilbert, 1806

———; English v., 3468

———; United States v., 538

General Motors Corp.; Baker v., 3054

———; Buczynski v., 2225

——— v. Devex Corp., 2524

——— v. Romein, 3659

——— v. United States, 3484

———; United States v., 802

——— v. Washington, 1188

———; Washington v., 1494

General Telephone Co. of the Northwest, Inc. v.
Equal Employment Opportunity Commission
(EEOC), 2094

General Telephone Co. of the Southwest v. Falcon,
2386

General Utilities and Operating Co. v. Helvering,
Commissioner of Internal Revenue, 640

Generix Drug Corp.; United States v., 2483

Gent v. Arkansas, 1283

Gentile v. State Bar of Nevada, 3622

Gentry; Bayside Fish Flour Co. v., 649

George C. Wallace, Governor of Alabama v. Jaffree,
2860

George E. Pataki v. Travelers Insurance Co., 3980

Georgia; Ballew v., 1890

———; Bearden v., 2525

——— v. Brailsford, 15

———; Cherokee Nation v., 118

———; Chisholm v., 17

———; Coker v., 1876

———; Cole v., 2686

———; Ferguson v., 1097

———; Ford v., 3531

———; Furman v., 1528

———; Godfrey v., 2098

———; Green v., 2000

———; Gregg v., 1795

———; Jackson v., 1528

———; James B. Beam Distilling Co. v., 3609

———; Jenkins v., 1656

——— v. McCollum, 3710

———; Nobles v., 326

——— v. Pennsylvania Railroad Co., 806

———; Reid v., 2150

——— v. South Carolina, 3500

———; Stanley v., 1364

——— v. Stanton, 169

——— v. Tennessee Copper Co., 370, 426

——— v. United States, 1567

———; Waller v., 2686

———; Williams v., 975

———; Wood v., 1131, 2190

———; Worcester v., 121

Geraghty; United States Parole Committee v., 2076

Gerende v. Board of Supervisors of Elections of
Baltimore City, 910

Gerald D.; Michael H. v., 3352

Gerhardt; Helvering v., 685

Germain, Connecticut National Bank v., 3662

German Alliance Insurance Co. v. Lewis, 418

Gertz v. Robert Welch, Inc., 1662

Gettysburg Electric Railway Co.; United States v.,
306

Giarratano; Murray v., 3367

Gibbons v. Ogden, 88

———; Railway Labor Executives Assoc. v., 2330

Gibbs; United Mine Workers v., 1251

Giboney v. Empire Storage and Ice Co., 884

Gibson v. Florida Legislative Investigation
Committee, 1148

Gideon v. Wainwright, 1144

Gilbert v. California, 1299

———; General Electric Co. v., 1806

———; Gulf Oil Corp. v., 844

——— v. Minnesota, 466

Gilbertson; Lampf, Pleva, Lipkind, Prupis &
Petigrow v., 3603

Giles v. Harris, 351

Giles v. Maryland, 1274
Gilfillan v. Clayton, 2234
Gilleo; Ladue v., 3903
Gillette v. United States, 1436
Gilley; Siegert v., 3571
Gilliam v. School Board City of Hopewell, 1236
Gilliard; Bowen v., 3203
Gillock; United States v., 2074
Gilmer v. Interstate/Johnson Lane Corp., 3562
Gilmore; Old Dominion Steamship Co. v., 372
———— v. Taylor, 3809
———— v. Utah, 1819
Gingles; Thornburgh v., 3040
Ginsberg v. New York, 1317
Ginzburg v. United States, 1246
Giordana; United States v., 1639
Girard; Wilson v., 1016
Girard's Executors; Vidal v., 138
Girouard v. United States, 825
Gissel Packing Co.; Food Store Employees Union,
    Local No. 347, Amalgamated Meat Cutters and
    Butchers Workermen of North America v.,
    1377
————; National Labor Relations Board (NLRB) v.,
    1377
Gitlow v. New York, 529
Givhan v. Western Line Consolidated School
    District, 1954
Gizoni; Southwest Marine, Inc. v., 3628
Gladstone, Realtors v. Village of Bellwood, 1979
Glasgow, Inc. v. Pennsylvania, 2425
Glass v. the Sloop Betsey, 18
Glasser v. United States, 741
Glen Theatre, Inc; Barnes v., 3610
Glenn; R.C. Tway Coal Co. v., 651
Glenshaw Glass Co.; Commissioner v., 967
Glidden Co. v. Zdanok, 1134
Glines; Brown v., 2049
Globe Newspaper Co. v. Superior Court for the
    County of Norfolk, 2403
Glona v. American Guarantee and Liability Insurance
    Co. , 1322
Gloss; Dillion v., 474
Glover; Tower v., 2724
Glover Construction Co.; Andrus v., 2100
Go-Bart Importing Co. v. United States, 584
Gobitis; Minersville School District v., 718
Godfrey v. Georgia, 2098
Godinez, Warden v. Moran, 3834
Goeke, Superintendent, Renz Correctional Center v.
    Branch, 3963
Goesaert v. Cleary, 878
Goguen; Smith v., 1628
"Gold Clause Cases," 631, 632, 633
Goldberg v. Kelly, 1397

Goldberg; Rostker v., 2273
———— v. Sweet, Director of Illinois Department of
    Revenue, 3296
Goldblatt v. Town of Hempstead, New York, 1126
"Golden State I," 2960
"Golden State II," 3386
Golden State Transit Corp. v. City of Los Angeles,
    3386
———— v. Los Angeles, 2960
Goldfarb; Califano v., 1822
———— v. Virginia State Bar, 1703
Goldman v. United States, 750
Goldsboro Christian School v. United States, 2522
Goldstein v. California, 1579
Goldwater v. Carter, 2061
Gollust v. Mendell, 3594
Gomez v. Toledo, 2102
Gomillion v. Lightfoot, 1084
Gompers v. Buck's Stove and Range Co., 403
Gong Lum v. Rice, 557
Gonzales; Fairfax-Brewster School, Inc. v., 1777
Good Samaritan Hospital v. Shalala, Secretary of
    Health and Human Services, 3812
Goode; Norfolk and Western Railway Co. v., 3383
————; Rizzo v., 1725
————; Wainwright v., 2605
Gooding; United States v., 104
Goodman v. Lukens Steel Co., 3178
————; United Steelworkers of America v., 3178
Goodrich Transit; Interstate Commerce Commission
    (ICC) v., 409
Goodwin; United States v., 2395
Goodyear Tire & Rubber Co.; United States v., 3388
Gordon; Trimble v., 1835
Gore; BMW of North America v., 4040
Goss v. Board of Education of Knoxville, Tennessee,
    1164
———— v. Lopez, 1677
Gottfried; Community Television of Southern
    California v., 2464
————; Federal Communications Commission
    (FCC) v., 2464
Gottshall; Consolidated Rail Corp. (CONRAIL) v.,
    3921
Gould, Inc.; Wisconsin Department of Industry v.,
    2947
Gouled v. United States, 468
Gouveia; United States v., 2693
Government of India; Pfizer, Inc. v., 1880
Governor of Georgia v. Saundry African Slaves, 107
Governor of Maryland; Ashland Oil, Inc. v., 1922
————; Continental Oil Co. v., 1922
————; Exxon Corp. v., 1922
————; Gulf Oil Corp. v., 1922
————; Shell Oil Co. v., 1922

Gozlon-Peretz v. United States, 3530
Grace; United States v., 2504
Grace Brethren Church; California v., 2396
———— v. United States, 2396
————; United States v., 2396
Grady v. Corbin, 3456
Graham v. Collins, Director, Texas Department of
    Criminal Justice, Institutional Division, 3753
———— v. Commissioner of Internal Revenue, 3343
————; Kentucky v., 2894
————; Stone v., 2156
————; Strader v., 145
————; Weaver v., 2180
———— v. West Virginia, 410
Graham, Commissioner v. Richardson, 1464
Grahl v. United States, 443
Granberry v. Greer, 3121
Granderson; United States v., 3869
"Grandfather Clause Case," 427
Granfinanciera, S.A. v. Paul C. Nordberg, 3368
"Granger Cases," 200, 201, 202, 203, 204, 205
Granite Rock Co.; California Coastal Commission v.,
    3110
"Grant Parish Case," 198
Grattan; Burnett v., 2731
Gratz; FTC v., 465
Grau v. United States, 609
Graubard v. United States, 443
Gravel v. United States, 1532
Graves v. New York ex rel. O'Keefe, 690
Gray; Herb's Welding, Inc. v., 2800
———— v. Mississippi, 3143
———— v. Sanders, 1146
————v. United States, 3196
Gray-Cannon Lumber Co.; United States v., 824
"Gray Market" Case, 3230
Gray Panthers; Schweiker v., 2272
Grayned v. City of Rockford, 1525
Great American Savings and Loan Association v.
    Novotny, 2010
Great Atlantic and Pacific Tea Co. v. Cottrell, 1729
———— v. Federal Trade Commission (FTC), 1959
Great Dane Trailers, Inc.; National Labor Relations
    Board (NLRB) v., 1294
Great Lakes Dredge & Dock Co.; City of Chicago v.,
    3955
————; Jerome B. Grubart v., 3955
Greater Washington Board of Trade; District of
    Columbia v., 3742
Green; Anderson v., 3956
———— v. Biddle, 85
————; California v., 1417
————; Carlson v., 2086
————; Colegrove v., 833

———— v. County School Board of New Kent
    County, Virginia, 1329
———— v. Frazier, 462
———— v. Georgia, 2000
———— v. Mansour, Director, Michigan Department
    of Social Services, 2913
————; McDonnell Douglas Corp. v., 1570
———— v. United States, 567, 1019, 1092
————; United States v., 981
Green Bay Co.; Pumpelly v., 185
Green Bay and Mississippi Canal Co.; Pumpelly v.,
    185
"Green Monday" Case, 2736
Greenbelt Cooperative Publishing Association v.
    Bresler, 1408
Greenburgh Civic Assns.; U. S. Postal Service v.,
    2274
Greene v. Lindsey, 2364
————; Memphis v., 2210
Greenfield; Wainwright v., 2925
Greenholtz v. Inmates of the Nebraska Penal and
    Correctional Complex, 1997
Greenhow; Pleasants v., 240
Greenman; Juilliard v., 233
Greenmoss Builders; Dun & Bradstreet, Inc. v., 2886
Greenough; Trustees v., 226
Greenville; Peterson v., 1155
Greenwich Collieries; Director, Office of Workers'
    Compensation Programs v., 3913
————; California v., 3247
————; McDonough Power Equipment Inc. v., 2620
Greer v. Benjamin Spock, 1741
————; Granberry v., 3121
———— v. Miller, 3207
Gregg v. Georgia, 1795
Gregory v. Ashcroft , 3607
———— v. Helvering, Commissioner of Internal
    Revenue, 628
————; Kentucky Distilleries & Warehouse Co. v.,
    463
Gregory Lee Johnson; Texas v., 3357
Grendel's Den, Inc.; Larkin v., 2448
Griffin v. Breckenridge, 1458
———— v. California, 1225
———— v. County School Board of Prince Edward
    County, 1186
———— v. Illinois, 985
————; Lovell v., 680
———— v. Oceanic Contractors, Inc., 2430
———— v. United States, 3626
———— v. Wisconsin, 3210
Griffith v. Kentucky , 3074
Griffiths; In re, 1600
Griggs v. County of Allegheny, 1120
———— v. Duke Power Co., 1435

——— v. Provident Consumer Discount Co., 2445

———; United States v., 899

Grimes v. Raymond Concrete Pile Co., 1027

Grimaud; United States v., 399

Grimsdell DBA Grocer Printing Co.; United States v., 824

Griswold v. Connecticut, 1231

———; Hepburn v., 177

Groetzinger; Commissioner v., 3090

Grogan v. Garner, 3525

Grolier, Inc.; Federal Trade Commission (FTC) v., 2531

Grosjean v. American Press Co., 646

Grosse Pointe Public School System v. Bradley, 1668

Grossman; Ex Parte, 520

Grosso v. United States, 1309

Group Life and Health Insurance Co. aka Blue Shield of Texas v. Royal Drug Co., dba Royal Pharmacy of Castle Hills, 1961

Grove City College v. Bell, Secretary of Education, 2638

Groves v. Ring Screw Workers, Ferndale Division, 3519

——— v. Slaughter, 132

Grovey v. Townsend, 635

Growe, Secretary of State of Minnesota v. Emison, 3757

Grumet; Attorney General of New York v., 3925

———; Board of Education v., 3925

———; Board of Education of Kiryas Joel Village School District v., 3925

———; Board of Education of Monroe-Woodbury Central School District v., 3925

Guaranty Trust Co. of New York v. York, 815

Guardian Life Insurance Co. of America; Kokkonen v., 3883

Guardians Association v. Civil Service Commission of the City of New York, 2586

Guernsey Memorial Hospital; Shalala v., 3962

Guerra; California Federal Savings and Loan Association v., 3072

Guest; United States v., 1252

"Guffey Coal Case," 651

Guidry v. Sheet Metal Workers National Pension Fund, 3398

Guinn v. United States, 427

Guinn and Beal v. United States, 427

Gulf Offshore Co. v. Mobil Oil Corp., 2284

Gulf Oil Co. v. Bernard, 2242

——— v. Gilbert, 844

——— v. Governor of Maryland, 1922

Gulf States Paper Corp.; Carmichael v., 669

Gully v. First National Bank in Meridian, 654

Gunn v. University Committee to End the War in Vietnam, 1418

Gunther; County of Washington v., 2245

Gus. Leisy and Co. v. Hardin, 270

Gustafson v. Florida, 1609

Gustanfson v. Alloyd Co., Inc. aka Alloyd Holdings, Inc., 3957

Gutierrez de Martinez v. Lamagno, 4005

Guy W. Capps, Inc.; United States v., 965

Guyot; Hilton v., 304

Gwaltney of Smithfield, Ltd. v. Chesapeake Bay Foundation, Inc., 3215

Gwinnett County Public Schools; Franklin v., 3652

Gyer's Lessee v. Irwin, 31

H.A. Artists & Associates, Inc. v. Actors' Equity Association, 2235

H.J. Inc. v. Northwestern Bell Telephone Co., 3372

H.L. v. Matheson, Governor of Utah, 2196

"Habeas Corpus Case," 219

Haberle Crystal Springs Brewing Co.; Clarke v., 575

Habluetzel; Mills v., 2350

Hackney; Jefferson v., 1502

Hadacheck v. Sebastian , 428

Haddock v. Haddock, 367

———; Haddock v., 367

Hadley v. Junior College District of Metropolitan Kansas City, Missouri, 1391

Hadnott v. Amos, 1360

Hafer v. Melo, 3624

Hagan; Pollard's Lessee v., 139

Hagen v. Utah, 3860

Haggerty; United States v., 3475

Hague; Allstate Insurance Co. v., 2167

——— v. Committee for Industrial Organization (CIO), 694

Hahn; Nordlinger v., 3709

Haig, Secretary of State v. Agee, 2279

Haigh v. United States, 161

Haile; Mason v., 102

Haines v. Kerner, 1479

Haitian Centers Council; Sale v., 3828

Haitian Refugee Center, Inc.; McNary v., 3534

Halderman; Commissioners and Mental Health/Mental Retardation Administrator for Bucks County v., 2297

———; Mayor of City of Philadelphia v., 2297

———; Pennhurst Parents-Staff Association v., 2297

———; Pennhurst State School and Hospital v., 2624, 2207

Hale; Belknap, Inc. v., 2584

———; United States v., 1707

Hale and Henkel, 366

Halifax Local No. 425 v. Moody, 1712

Hall; Arkansas Louisiana Gas Co. v., 2286

——— v. Cole, 1571

——— v. De Cuir, 206

Hall; Helicopteros Nacionales de Colombia v., 2670
———; Holder v., 3929
———; Hope Natural Gas Co. v., 553
Hallstrom v. Tillamook County, 3381
Halper; United States v., 3336
Halperin; Kissinger v., 2268
Halstead; Bank of the United States v., 94
Ham v. South Carolina, 1545
"The Hamilton," 372
Hamilton v. Kentucky Distilleries and Warehouse
      Co., 454
——— v. Regents of the University of California,
      626
Hamilton Bank; Williamson Planning Commission
      v., 2895
Hamlin; Argersinger v., 1506
Hamling v. United States, 1655
Hammer v. Dagenhart, 444
Hampton; Hanrahan v., 2107
———; Johnson v., 2107
——— v. Mow Sun Wong, 1758
Hampton County Election Commission; NAACP v.,
      2792
Handley v. Stutz, 274
Hanover Shoe, Inc. v. United Shoe Machinery Corp.,
      1344
———; United Shoe Machinery Corp. v., 1344
Hanrahan v. Hampton, 2107
Hans v. Louisiana, 267
Hansberry v. Lee, 719
Hanson; Railway Employees' Department v., 990
Happersett; Minor v., 193
Harbison; Knoxville Iron Co. v., 345
Hardesty; Armco, Inc. v., 2713
Hardin; Leisy v., 270
Hardison; International Association of Machinists
      and Aerospace Workers v., 1855
———; Trans World Airlines, Inc., 1855
Hardwick; Bowers v., 3042
Hardy; Holden v., 328
Hardyman; Collins v., 916
Haring, Lieutenant, Arlington County Police
      Department v. Prosise, 2541
Harisiades v. Shaughnessy, 922
Harker Heights; Collins v., 3655
Harlow v. Fitzgerald, 2409
Harmelin v. Michigan, 3621
Harmon; Commissioner v., 795
Harney; Craig v., 848
Haroco, Inc.; American National Bank & Trust Co.
      v., 2905
Harper v. Virginia Department of Taxation, 3826
——— v. Virginia State Board of Elections, 1249
———; Washington v., 3413

Harper & Row, Publishers, Inc., v. Nation
      Enterprises, 2847
Harrah Independent School District v. Martin, 1960
Harrington v. California, 1371
Harris v. Alabama, 3954
———; Board of Education v., 2040
———; City of Canton v., 3314
——— v. Forklift Systems, Inc., 3846
———; Forsham v., 2068
———; Giles v., 351
——— v. James, 563
——— v. Lloyd, 563
——— v. McRae, 2147
——— v. New York, 1430
———; New York v., 3438
———; Pulley v., 2622
——— v. Ramsey, 563
——— v. Ramsey Petroleum Co., 563
———; United States v., 229
———; Younger v., 1428
Harris Trust and Savings Bank; John Hancock
      Mutual Life Insurance Co. v., 3849
Harrisburg; The, 252
Harrison; Butts v., 1249
———; Norwood v., 1593
——— v. Sterry, 48
——— v. United States, 1341
Harry N. Walters, Administrator of Veterans' Affairs
      v. National Association of Radiation Survivors,
      2898
Hart v. B.F. Keith Vaudeville Exchange, 503
Harte-Hanks Communications, Inc. v. Connaughton,
      3364
Hartford Fire Insurance Co. v. California, 3843
Hartigan v. Zbaraz, 3218
Hathorn v. Lovorn, 2390
Hartlage; Brown v., 2348
Hartmarx Corp.; Cooter & Gell v., 3479
Hartzell Propeller, Inc. v. Reyno, 2298
Harvey; Colgate v., 642
———; Michigan v., 3417
Hasbrouck; Texaco, Inc. v., 3485
Haskell; Noble State Bank v., 393
Haslip; Pacific Mutual Life Insurance Co. v., 3538
Hass; Oregon v., 1688
Hasting; United States v., 2518
Haupt, Ex Parte, 757
——— v. United States, 845
Havens; United States v., 2101
Havens Realty Corp. v. Coleman, 2325
Haverty; International Stevedoring Co. v., 535
Hawaii v. Standard Oil Co. of California, 1484
Hawaii Housing Authority v. Midkiff, 2696
Hawaiian Airlines, Inc. v. Director of Taxation of
      Hawaii, 2601

——— v. Norris, 3912
"Hawke No. 1," 460
"Hawke No. 2," 461
Hawke v. Smith, 460, 461
Hawkins v. Barney's Lessee, 120
——— v. United States, 1041
Hayburn's Case, 16
Haydel; Foster Fountain Packing Co. v., 568
Hayden; Warden v., 1287
Hayes; Bordenkirsher v., 1881
———; Branzburg v., 1533
——— v. Florida, 2813
———; Louisiana v., 4016
———; United States v., 4016
Hayfield Northern Railroad Co., Inc. v. Chicago &
    North Western Transporation Co., 2712
Haymes, Montanye v., 1779
Haynes v. United States, 1310
——— v. Washington, 1159
Hays v. United States, 434
Hazelwood School District v. Kuhlmeier, 3219
——— v. United States, 1870
Hazen Paper Co. v. Biggins, 3781
Head v. New Mexico Board of Examiners in
    Optometry, 1171
Healy v. James, 1526
Heart of Atlanta Motel, Inc. v. United States, 1208
Health Care & Retirement Corp.; National Labor
    Relations Board (NLRB) v., 3890
Healy; West Lynn Creamery v., 3910
Hearst Publications, Inc.; National Labor Relations
    Board (NLRB) v., 790
Heath v. Alabama, 2914
Hechler; International Brotherhood of Electrical
    Workers v., 3152
Hecht Co. v. Bowles, 782
Heck v. Humphrey, 3919
Heckler; Connecticut Department of Income
    Maintenance v., 2846
Heckler, Secretary of Health and Human Services v.
    Campbell, 2515
——— v. Chaney, 2814
——— v. Community Health Services of Crawford
    County, Inc., 2687
——— v. Day, 2690
——— v. Edwards, 2651
——— v. Mathews, 2643
——— v. Ringer, 2678
——— v. Turner, 2793
Hedden; Nix v., 292
Heebe; Frazier v., 3177
Heffron v. International Society for Krishna
    Consciousness, Inc.(ISKCON), 2265
Heilberg; Fixa v., 1229
Heinek, Ex Parte, 757

Heinek v. Preisler, 1362
Heinhold Commodities, Inc. v. Leist, 2360
Heininger; Commissioner v., 778
Heintz v. Jenkins, 3971
Heisler v. Thomas Colliery Co., 495
"Heisler Trilogy," 553
Heitner; Shaffer v., 1867
Helicopteros Nacionales de Colombia, S.A. v. Hall,
    2670
Hellenic Lines, Ltd. v. Rhoditis, 1411
Heller, Secretary, Kentucky Cabinet for Human
    Resources v. Doe, 3832
Helling v. McKinney, 3824
Helm; Solem v., 2578
Helms; Hewitt v., 2463, 3181
———; Jones v., 2254
Helvering v. Carter, 651
———; General Utilities and Operating Co. v., 640
———; Gregory v., 628
——— v. Horst, 720
——— v. Le Gierse, 731
———; Welch v., 619
——— v. Wilson, 685
Helvering, Commissioner of Internal Revenue v.
    Clifford, 707
——— v. Davis, 671
——— v. Eubank, 721
——— v. Gerhardt, 685
——— v. Mitchell, 679
Hemme; United States v., 2997
Henderson; Tollett v., 1564
——— v. United States, 898, 2986
Hendricks County Rural Electric Membership Corp.
    v. National Labor Relations Board (NLRB),
    2296
Hendricks County Rural Electric Membership Corp.;
    National Labor Relations Board v., 2296
Henkel; Hale v., 366
Henry v. A.B. Dick Co., 408
———; Duncan v., 3949
———; Middendorf v., 1743
——— v. Mississippi, 1211
———; United States v., 2118
Hensley v. Eckerhart, 2514
———; United States v., 2770
Hepburn v. Griswold, 177
———; Mima Queen v., 58
Hepburn and Dundas v. Ellzey, 40
Hepner v. United States, 386
Hepps; Philadelphia Newspapers, Inc. v., 2967
Herald Co.; Albrecht v., 1312
Herb's Welding, Inc. v. Gray, 2800
Herbert v. Lando, 1981
———; Northern Pacific Railroad Co. v., 246
Hercules, Inc. v. United States, 4029

Herion; Paulussen v., 2957
Herman and MacLean v. Huddleston, 2459
Hernandez v. Commissioner of Internal Revenue,
    3343
———; Denton v., 3682
——— v. New York, 3578
——— v. Texas, 953
———; Underhill v., 325
Herndon v. Lowry, 667
———; Nixon v., 547
Herold; Baxstrom v., 1241
Herrera v. Collins, Director, Texas Department of
    Criminal Justice, Institutional Division, 3751
Herweg v. Ray, Governor of Iowa, 2320
Hess v. Indiana, 1606
——— v. Port Authority Trans-Hudson Corp., 3934
———; United States ex rel. Marcus v., 761
Hester v. United States, 516
Heublein, Inc. v. South Carolina Tax Commission,
    1542
Hewit; Freeman v., 837
Hewitt v. Helms, 2463, 3181
Hewitt Associates; Mertens v., 3804
"Hialeah Case," 3818
Hicklin v. Orbeck, 1927
Hicks; Arizona v., 3102
——— v. Equitable Trust Co. of New York, 531
——— v. Merchantile Trust Co., 531
———; St. Mary's Honor Center v., 3837
Higginbotham; Mobil Oil Corp. v., 1917
Higgins v. Commissioner of Internal Revenue, 727
———; Dennis v., 3532
Higginson; Moosman v., 28
———; Smyth v., 329
Hildwin v. Florida, 3341
"The Hill Case," 1269
Hill; Bryant, Attorney General of Arkansas v., 3987
———; Houston v., 3171
——— v. Lockhart, Director, Arkansas Department
    of Correction, 2912
——— v. Stone, 1692
———; Superintendent v., 2872
———; Tennessee Valley Authority (TVA) v., 1923
——— v. Texas, 752
———; Time, Inc. v., 1269
———; United States v., 3756
——— v. Wallace, 486
Hill Military Academy; Pierce v., 528
Hillery; Procunier v., 1653
———; Vasquez v., 2924
Hills v. Gautreaux, 1748
Hills v. Scenic Rivers Association of Oklahoma,
    1769
Hillsboro National Bank v. Commissioner of Internal
    Revenue, 2481

Hillsborough County, Florida v. Automated Medical
    Laboratories, Inc., 2851
Hilton v. Guyot, 304
——— v. Braunskill, 3149
——— v. South Carolina Public Railways
    Commission, 3635
Hinderlider v. La Plata River and Cherry Creek Ditch
    Co., 682
Hines v. Anchor Motor Freight, Inc., 1734
——— v. Davidowitz, 724
Hinkle; Yamashita v., 494
Hinton v. United States, 2636
Hirsh; Block v., 471
Hipolite Egg Co. v. United States, 396
Hirabayashi v. United States, 774
Hishon v. King and Spalding, 2688
Hisquierdo v. Hisquierdo, 1957
———; Hisquierdo v., 1957
Hitchcock; Counselman v., 279
——— v. Dugger, 3130
———; Wolf v., 346
Hitchman Coal and Coke Co. v. Mitchell, 442
Hoagland; Wurts v., 241
Hobby; Farrar v., 3741
———; Peters v., 974
——— v. United States, 2741
Hoboken Land and Improvement Co.; Murray's
    Lessee v., 152
Hochfelder; Ernst and Ernst v., 1746
Hocking Valley Railway Co.; Swift and Co. v., 436
Hodari D.; Califonria v., 3560
"Hodel I," 2250
"Hodel II," 2249
Hodel v. Irving, 3145
——— v. Village of Gambell, 3108
——— v. Virginia Surface Mining and Reclamation
    Association, Inc., 2249
Hodel, Acting Secretary of the Interior v. Indiana,
    2250
Hodge; Hurd v., 869
———; Urciolo v., 869
Hodges v. United States, 368
Hodgson v. Minnesota, 3501
———; Minnesota v., 3501
Hodgson and Thompson v. Bowerbank, 49
Hoeper v. Tax Commission of Wisconsin, 596
Hoffa v. United States, 1268
Hoffman; Mexico v., 804
Hoffmann-La Roche, Inc. v. Sperling, 3390
Hogan; Malloy v., 1191
———; Mississippi University of Women v., 2436
———; Schweiker v., 2402
Hohri; United States v., 3155
Hoke v. United States, 412
Holbrook v. Flynn, 2958

Holden v. Hardy, 328

Holder; Schlagenhauf v., 1205

Holder, Individually and in his Official Capacity as
County Commissioner for Blekley County,
Georgia v. Hall, 3929

"Holding Company Case," 689

Holland v. Illinois, 3403

———; Missouri v., 459

Holliday; FMC Corp. v., 3513

Hollingsworth v. Virginia, 23

Holloway v. Arkansas, 1899

———; Elder v., 3864

Hollywood Motor Car Company, Inc.; United States
v., 2421

Holmes v. Comegys, 10

——— v. Securities Investor Protection Corp., 3663

Holmes County Board of Education; Alexander v.,
1382

Holohan; Mooney v., 630

Holt; Brandon v., 2780

Holywell Corp. v. Smith, 3651

Home Building and Loan Assocation v. Blaisdell,
621

Home State Bank; Johnson v., 3591

Honda v. Clark, Attorney General, 1278

Honda Motor Co. Ltd. v. Oberg, 3917

Honing v. Doe, 3221

Hooper v. Bernalillo County Assessor, 2880

Hooven & Allison Co.; Limbach, Tax Commissioner
of Ohio v., 2666

Hoover v. Ronwin, 2677

Hope Natural Gas Co.; Cleveland v., 780

———; Federal Power Commission (FPC) v., 780

——— v. Hall, 553

Hopkins; Le v., 248

———; Price Waterhouse v., 3332

———; Wo Le v., 248

———; Yick Wo v., 248

Hopper v. Evans, 2369

Horowitz; Board of Curators v., 1887

Horst; Helvering v., 720

Horton v. California, 3470

Hortonville Education Association; Hortonville Joint
School District No. 1 v., 1764

Hortonville Joint School District No. 1 v. Hortonville
Education Association, 1764

Hospital Association of New York State v. Travelers
Insurance Co., 3980

Hoston v. Louisiana, 1117

"Hot Oil Case," 627

Hotel & Restaurant Employees & Bartenders
International Union, Local 54; Danziger, Acting
Chairman, Casino Control Commission of New
Jersey v., 2745

Hotel Employees; Brown v., 2745

Houchins v. KQED, Inc., 1931

Hough v. The Western Transportation Co., 160

Houghton v. Payne, 356

Household Manufacturing, Inc.; Lytle v., 3424

Houston v. Moore, 76

Houston, East and West Texas Railway Co. v. United
States , 421

Houston Lawyers' Association v. Texas, 3605

Howard; Aldinger v., 1772

——— v. Fleming, 353

——— v. Illinois Central Railroad Co., 373

——— v. North Carolina, 353

"Howard Hughes Estates Case," 2383

Howard Johnson Co., Inc. v. Detroit Local Joint
Executive Board, Hotel and Restuarant
Employees and Bartenders International Union,
AFL-CIO, 1646

Howe v. Smith, Attorney General, 2259

———; Varity Corp. v., 4031

Howell; City of Virginia Beach v., 1552

———; Mahan v., 1552

Howes Leather Co.; La Buy v., 997

Howlett v. Birkdale, Shipping Co., S.A., 3906

——— v. Rose, as Superintendent of Schools for
Pinellas County, Florida, 3478

Hoyt v. Florida, 1116

Hubbard v. United States, 3983

Huddleston; Herman and MacLean v., 2459

———; Itel Containers International Corp. v., 3759

Hudgens v. National Labor Relations Board (NLRB),
1733

Hudson; Chicago Teachers Union v., 2948

——— v. Louisiana, 2181

——— v. Palmer, 2746

Hudson and Goodwin; United States v., 54

Hudson County Water Co. v. McCarter, 379

Hughes v. Alexandria Scrap Corp., 1770

———; Fairchild v., 479

———; Parham v., 1985

——— v. Oklahoma, 1984

——— v. Rowe, 2154

Hughes Properties; United States v., 2999

Hughey v. United States, 3452

Huidekoper's Lessee v. Douglass, 41

Hull Memorial Presbyterian Church; Presbyterian
Church, 1351

Humes; Missouri Pacific Railroad v., 242

Humphrey; Heck v., 3919

Humphrey's Executor (Rathbun) v. United States,
639

Hunerwadel v. Baird, 1794, 2034

Hunt; Chemical Waste Management, 3693

———; Exxon Corp. v., 2951

———; Local Loan Co. v., 625

——— v. McNair, Governor, 1602

Hunt; Murphy v., 2331
———; Pope v., 4043
———; Shaw v., 4043
——— v. Washington State Apple Advertising
    Commission, 1859
Hunt Oil Co. v. Federal Power Commission (FPC),
    1320
Hunter v. Erickson, 1349
———; Missouri v., 2458
——— v. Pittsburgh, 371
——— v. Underwood, 2832
Hunter's Lessee; Fairfax's Devisee v., 61
———; Martin v., 66
Huntington v. Attrill, 288
——— v. Huntington Branch, NAACP, 3289
Huntington Branch, NAACP; Huntington v., 3289
Hurd v. Hodge, 869
Hurley v. Irish-American Gay, Lesbian and Bisexual
    Group of Boston, 4010
Huron Portland Cement Co. v. Detroit, Michigan,
    1073
Hurst v. Hurst, 33
———; Hurst v., 33
"Hurst's Case," 33
Hurtado v. California, 234
Huson; Chevron Oil Co. v., 1473
Hustler Magazine, Inc. and Larry C. Flynt v. Jerry
    Falwell, 3228
Hustler Magazine, Inc.; Keeton v., 2645
Huston; Coxe v., 26
Husty v. United States, 585
Hutcheson; United States v., 728
Hutchinson v. Proxmire, 2024
Hutto v. Davis, 2303
——— v. Finney, 1930
Hyde v. Continental Trust Co., 301
——— v. Continental Trust Co. of New York, 303
———; Jefferson Parish Hospital District No. 2 v.,
    2654
———; Reynoldsville Casket Co. v., 3985
Hyde Park; Northwestern Fertilizer Co. v., 211
Hydrolevel Corp.; American Society of Mechanical
    Engineers, Inc. v., 2367
Hygrade Provision Co., Inc. v. Sherman, 519
Hylton v. United States, 19
———; Ware v., 20
Hynes v. Mayor and Council of the Borough of
    Oradell, 1754
——— v. Oradell, 1754

IAAF; Reynolds v., 3734
IBM; United States v., 4042
INDOPCO, Inc. v. Commissioner Internal Revenue
    Service, 3653
ITT Continental Baking Co.; United States v., 1681

ITT World Communications, Inc.; Federal
    Communications Commission (FCC) v., 2673
Ibanez v. Florida, Department of Business and
    Professional Regulation, Board of Accountancy,
    3908
Icicle Seafoods, Inc. v. Worthington, 2965
Idaho; Carmen v., 2467
———; Lankford v., 3566
——— v. Laura Lee Wright, 3507
———; National Organization of Women v., 2467
———; United States v., 1421, 3789
Idaho ex rel. Evans, Governor of Idaho v. Oregon
    and Washington, 2566
Idaho State Tax Commission; ASARCO, Inc. v.,
    2423
Illinois v. Abbott & Associates, Inc., 2487
——— v. Allen, 1399
Illinois; Allen v., 3047
——— v. Andreas, 2591
———; Baldasar v., 2090
———; Bartkus v., 1948
———; Beauharnais v., 926
———; Bradwell v., 190
———; Brown v., 1716
——— v. City of Milwaukee, Wisconsin, 1493
———; Escobedo v., 1200
——— v. Gates, 2539
———; Griffin v., 985
———; Holland v., 3403
———; Illinois Brick Co. v., 1851
———; Illinois Central Railroad v., 287
———; James v., 3395
——— v. Kentucky, 3579
———; Ker v., 254
———; Kirby v., 1503
——— v. Krull, 3103
——— v. Lafayette, 2556
———; Lee v., 2996
———; McCray v., 1277
———; Milwaukee v., 2217
———; Missouri v., 339
———; Morgan v., 3706
———; Munn v., 200
———; Patterson v., 3273
——— v. Perkins, 3474
———; Pope v., 3135
———; Presser v., 243
———; Rakas v., 1947
——— v. Rodriguez, 3495
———; Scott v., 1966
———; Smith v., 1311
———; Stanley v., 1491
———; Taylor v., 3223
———; Wabash, St. Louis and Pacific Railway v.,
    251

———; Ward v., 1852
———; White v., 3642
———; Witherspoon v., 1333
———; Ybarra v., 2039
Illinois Brick Co. v. Illinois, 1851
Illinois Broadcasting Co., Inc. v. National Citizens, 1919
Illinois Central Railroad Co.; Chicago v., 287
———; Howard v., 373
——— v. Illinois, 287
———; Interstate Commerce Commission (ICC) v., 388
Illinois Commerce Commission v. Sante Fe Elevator Corp., 847
Illinois Department of Revenue; Rockford Life Insurance Co. v., 3160
Illinois Deptartment of Employment Security; Frazee v., 3324
Illinois ex rel. McCollum v. Board of Education of School District No. 71, Champaign County, 865
Image Technical Services, Inc.; Eastman Kodak Co. v., 3697
Imbler v. Pachtman, 1731
Imbrovek; Atlantic Transport Co. of West Virginia v., 420
Immigration and Naturalization Service (INS); Ardestani v., 3631
——— v. Cardoza-Fonseca, 3106
——— v. Chadha, 2565
——— v. Delgado, 2661
——— v. Doherty, 3641
——— v. Elias-Zacarias, 3646
——— v. Lopez-Mendoza, 2759
——— v. Manzano, 3266
——— v. National Center for Immigrants' Rights, Inc., 3634
——— v. Pangilinan, 3266
——— v. Phinpathya, 2610
——— v. Rios-Pineda, 2843
——— v. Stevic, 2703
———; Stone v., 3974
Imperial Irrigation District v. Yellen, 2121
Imrex Co.; Sedima, S.P.R.L. v., 2902
In re R.M.J., 2317
In re Burrus, 1467
In re Debs, 302
In re Gault, 1284
In re Griffiths, 1600
In re Hurst, 33
In re Neagle, 269
In re Oliver, 866
In re Pappas, 1533
In re Permian Basin Area Rate Cases, 1320
In re Primus, 1913
In re Rahrer, 276

In re Sarah, 86
In re Snyder, 2881
In re Summers, 811
In re The Santissima Trinidad, 84
In re the Three Friends, 318
In re Wildenhus, 255
In re Winship, 1400
In re Yamashita, 821
Inadi; United States v., 2952
"Income Tax Cases," 301, 303
Inda; United States v., 399
Independence; Owen v., 2084
Independence Tube Corp.; Copperweld Corp. v., 2718
Independent Federation of Flight Attendants v., TWA, Inc., 2326
———; Trans World Airlines, Inc. (TWA) v., 3315
——— v. Zipes, 3366
Independent Insurance Agents of America, Inc.; Ludwig v., 3814
———; United States Bank v., 3814
India; Pfizer, Inc. v., 1880
Indian Towing Co. v. United States, 979
Indiana; Ft. Wayne Books, Inc. v., 3305
———; Hess v., 1606
———; Hodel v., 2250
———; Jackson v., 1504
———; Ramirez v., 2828
———; Sappenfield v., 3305
Indiana Federation of Dentists; Federal Trade Commission (FTC) v., 2992
Indianapolis Power & Light Co.; Commissioner of Internal Revenue v., 3392
Industrial Union Department, AFL-CIO v. American Petroleum Institute, 2153
Ingersoll-Rand Co. v. McClendon, 3517
Ingraham v. Wright, 1832
Inmates of the Nebraska Penal and Correction Complex; Greenholtz v., 1997
Inmates of the Suffolk County Jail; Rapone, Commissioner of Corrections of Massachusetts v., 3643
———; Rufo v., 3643
Innis; Rhode Island v., 2093
Insilco Broadcasting Corporation v. WNCN Listeners Guild, 2201
Institutionalized Juveniles; Secretary of Public Welfare v., 2015
"Insular Cases," 342, 344
Insurance Agents International Union; National Labor Relations Board (NLRB) v., 1065
"Insurance Antitrust Case," 3843
Insurance Corp. of Ireland, Ltd. v. Compagnie des Bauxites de Guinee, 2373
Internal Revenue; Corn Products Refining Co. v., 978

Internal Revenue; Diedrich v., 2388
———; Jewett v., 2322
Internal Revenue Commissioner v. Glenshaw Glass
    Co., 967
Internal Revenue Service; Begier v., 3467
———; Church of Scientology v., 3212
International Association of Machinists v. Street,
    1113
International Association of Machinists and
    Aerospace Workers v. Hardison, 1855
International Boxing Club; United States v., 963
International Brotherhood of Electrical Workers
    (IBEW) v. Foust, 1998
——— v. Hechler, 3152
——— v. National Labor Relations Board, 687
International Brotherhood of Electrical Workers,
    Local 71; Wooddell v., 3629
International Brotherhood of Electrical Workers,
    Local 340; NLRB v., 3139
International Brotherhood of Teamsters; DelCostello
    v., 2536
——— v. United States, 1842
International Brotherhood of Teamsters, Chauffeurs,
    Warehousemen and Helpers of America v.
    Daniel, 1956
International Longshoremen's Association, AFL-CIO
    v. Allied International, Inc., 2355
——— v. Davis, 2989
———; Jacksonville Bulk Terminals, Inc. v., 2407
———; National Labor Relations Board (NLRB) v.,
    2124
International Minerals and Chemical Corp.; United
    States v., 1454
International News Service v. Associated Press, 445
International Organization of Masters, Mates & Pilots
    v. Brown Masters, Mates & Pilots v. Brown,
    3533
International Paper Co. v. Ouellette, 3083
———; Zahn v., 1610
International Parts Corp.; Perma Life Mufflers, Inc.
    v., 1339
International Primate Protection League v.
    Administrators of Tulane Educational Fund,
    3564
International Salt Co., Inc. v. United States, 855
International Shoe Co. v. Washington, 817
International Soceity for Krishna Consciousness
    (ISKCON); Heffron v., 2265
———; Lee v., 3731
International Society for Krishna Consciousness, Inc.
    (ISKCON) and Brian Rumbaugh v. Lee, 3727
International Stevedoring Co. v. Haverty, 535
International Terminal Operating Co., Inc. v. Blundo,
    1858
———; Romero v., 1045

International Union, Automobile, UAW; Lyng v.,
    3238
International Union, United Automobile, Aerospace
    and Agricultural Implement Workers of
    America v. Brock, 3025
——— v. Johnson Controls Inc., 3544
International Union, United Mine Workers v.
    Bagwell, 3927
International Woodworkers of America; Champion
    International Corp. v., 3170
International Workers Order, Inc. v. McGrath, 911
Interstate Circuit, Inc. v. Dallas, 1318
Interstate Commerce Commission (ICC) v. Alabama
    Midland Railway Co., 324
——— v. American Trucking Associations, Inc.,
    2701
——— v. Boston and Maine Corp., 3670
——— v. Brotherhood of Locomotive Engineers,
    3163
——— v. Cincinnati, New Orleans and Texas Pacific
    Railway Co., 322
——— v. Goodrich Transit Co., 409
——— v. Illinois Central Railroad Co., 388
———; Preseault v., 3406
——— v. Texas, 3081
——— v. Transcon Lines, 3940
Interstate Iron Co. v. Lord, 502
Interstate/Johnson Lane Corp.; Gilmer v., 3562
Investment Company Institute (ICI) v. Camp, 1441
———; Federal Reserve v., 2182
Investors Mortgage Insurance Co.; FirsTier Mortgage
    Co. v., 3524
Inwood Laboratories, Inc. v. Ives Laboratories, Inc.,
    2378
Iowa; Bartels v., 506
———; Chicago, Burlington and Quincy Railroad v.,
    201
———; Coy v., 3288
———; Sosna v., 1673
Iowa Department of Revenue; Shell Oil Co. v., 3290
Iowa Department of Revenue and Finance; Kraft
    General Foods, Inc. v., 3711
Iowa Mutual Insurance Co. v. LaPlante, 3089
Irish-American Gay, Lesbian & Bisexual Group;
    Hurley v., 4010
Irvin v. Dowd, 1105
Irvine v. California, 952
———; United States v., 3876
Irving; Hodel v., 3145
Irving Independent School District v. Tatro, 2755
Irving Trust Co.; Schoenthal v., 608
Irvis; Moose Lodge #107 v., 1510
Irwin v. Department of Veterans Affairs, 3515
———; Geyer's Lessee v., 31
Isaac; Engle v., 2351

Ishmael Jaffree; Douglas T. Smith v., 2860
"Island Trees Case," 2411
Itasca County; Bryan v., 1763
Itel Containers International Corp. v. Huddleston,
     Commissioner of Revenue of Tennessee, 3759
Ivanhoe Irrigation District v. McCracken, 1032
Ivanov v. United States, 1357
Ives Laboratories, Inc.; Inwood Laboratories, Inc. v.,
     2378
Izumi Seimitsu Kogyo Kabushiki Kaisha v. U.S.
     Philips Corp., 3847

J. Truett Payne Co., Inc. v. Chrysler Motors Corp.,
     2227
J. Weingarten, Inc.; National Labor Relations Board
     (NLRB) v., 1682
J.A. Croson Co.; Richmond v., 3303
J.E.B. v. Alabama ex rel. T. B. , 3872
J.I. Case Co. v. National Labor Relations Board
     (NLRB), 783
J.R.; Parham v., 2014
J.T. Gibbons, Inc.; Crawford Fitting Co. v., 3170
J. W. Hampton, Jr. and Co. v. United States, 562
Jackman v. Rosenbaum Co., 490
Jackson; Barrows v., 947
——— v. Denno, Warden, 1199
———; Ex Parte, 209
——— v. Georgia, 1528
——— v. Indiana, 1504
——— v. Kelly, 119
——— v. Metropolitan Edison Co., 1672
———; Michigan v., 2961
———; United States v., 1316
——— v. Virginia, 2029
Jackson Board of Education; Wygant v., 2985
Jackson Municipal Separate School District;
     Singleton v., 1385
Jackson Transit Authority v. Local Division 1285,
     Amalgamated Transit Union, AFL-CIO-CLC,
     2380
Jackson Vinegar Co.; Yazoo and Mississippi Valley
     Railroad v., 411
Jacksonville; Erznoznik v., 1708
———; Northeastern Flordia Chapter of the
     Associated General Contractors v., 3821
———; Papachristou v., 1482
Jacksonville Bulk Terminals, Inc. v. International
     Longshoremen's Association, 2407
Jacksonville Railway; American Construction Co. v.,
     289
Jacobellis v. Ohio, 1196
Jacobsen; United States v., 2658
Jacobson v. Massachusetts, 362
——— v. United States, 3675
Jacobson Products Co.; Qualitex Co. v., 3966

Jaffree; Smith v., 2860
———; Wallace v., 2860
Jago v. Van Curen, 2290
Jakobson; United States v., 1218
James v. Allen, 6
———; Ball v., 2218
——— v. Bowman, 352
———; Ferry v., 563
———; Harris v., 563
———; Healy v., 1526
——— v. Illinois, 3395
——— v. Kentucky, 2665
———; United States v., 3053
——— v. Valtierra, 1449
———; Wyman v., 1422
James B. Beam Distilling Co. v. Georgia, 3609
James Clark Distilling Co. v. American Express Co.,
     433
——— v. Western Maryland Railway Co., 433
James Daniel Good Real Property; United States v.,
     3848
James M. Brooks v. United States, 886
Jamison v. Texas, 765
Janis; United States v., 1801
Japan Line, Ltd. v. County of Los Angeles, 1988
Japan Whaling Association v. American Cetacean
     Society, 3043
"Japanese American Concentration Camp Case," 800
"Japanese American Curfew Case," 774
"Japanese American Internment Cases," 774, 800,
801
"Japanese Immigrant Case," 349
Jay Burns Baking Co. v. Bryan, 515
"Jaybird Party Case," 943
Jean; Commissioner, Immigration and Naturalization
     Service (INS) v., 3471
——— v. Nelson, Commissioner, Immigration and
     Naturalization Service, 2888
Jeff D.; Evans v., 2966
Jeffers; Lewis v., 3506
Jefferson v. Hackney, Commissioner, 1502
——— v. United States, 899
Jefferson County Pharmaceutical Association, Inc. v.
     Abbott Laboratories, 2473
Jefferson County PUD v. Ecology Department of
     Washington, 3895
Jefferson Lines, Inc.; Oklahoma Tax Commission v.,
     3967
Jefferson Parish Hospital District No. 2 v. Hyde,
     2654
Jencks v. United States, 1008
Jenkins v. Anderson, Warden, 2116
——— v. Georgia, 1656
———; Heintz v., 3971
———; Missouri v., 3439, 3994

Jensen, Director, Department of Motor Vehicles of
    Nebraska v. Quaring, 2874
Jerome B. Grubart, Inc. v. Great Lakes Dredge &
    Dock Co., 3955
Jerrico, Inc.; Marshall v., 2091
Jerry T. O'Brien, Inc.; Securities Exchange
    Commission (SEC) v., 2717
Jersey Shore State Bank v. United States, 3080
Jett v. Dallas Independent School District, 3365
Jewel Ridge Coal Corp. v. Local No. 6167, United
    Mine Workers, 810
Jewett v. Commissioner of Internal Revenue, 2322
Jews for Jesus, Inc.; Board of Airport Commissioners
    v., 3175
Jicarilla Apache Indian Tribe; Amoco Production Co.
    and Marathon Oil Co. v., 2316
———; Merrion v., 2316
"Jim Crow Laws," 312
Jim McNeff, Inc. v. Todd, 2507
Jimeno; Florida v., 3572
Jimmy Swaggart Ministries v. Board of Equalization
    of California, 3399
Jobin v. Arizona, 756
Jobst; Califano v., 1877
Joe Mario Trevino v. Texas, 3676
John D. Park and Sons Co.; Dr. Miles Medical Co. v.,
    398
John Deere Co.; Ferens v., 3423
John Doe; United States v., 3120
John Doe Agency and John Doe Government Agency
    v. John Doe Corporation, 3389
John Doe Corporation; John Doe Agency, 3389
John E. Mallard v. United States District Court for
    Southern District of Iowa, 3333
John Hancock Mutual Life Insurance Co. v. Harris
    Trust and Savings Bank, 3849
Johns; United States v., 2781
Johnson; Abrams, Jr. v., 4019
——— v. Avery, Commissioner of Corrections, 1353
———; DeGrandy v., 3931
———; Barnhill v., 3669
———; Connecticut General Life Insurance Co. v.,
    676
———; Connecticut v., 2470
——— v. Hampton, 2107
——— v. Home State Bank, 3591
——— v. Jones, 4000
———; Kelley v., 1747
——— v. Louisiana, 1499
———; Mabry v., 2708
——— v. Mayor and City Council of Baltimore,
    2868
———; Miller v., 4019
——— v. Mississippi, 3259
———; Mississippi v., 165

———; Nicirema Operating Co. v., 1383
———; Ohio v., 2707
——— v. Texas, 3833
———; Texas v., 3357
——— v. Transportation Agency, Santa Clara
    County, 3111
———; Traynor v., 1383
——— v. United States, 860
———; United States v., 215, 2401, 3144, 4019
———; Washington Metropolitan Transit Authority
    v., 2725
——— v. Zerbst, 686
Johnson, Speaker of the Florida House of
    Representatives v. DeGrandy, 3931
Johnson & Graham's Lessee v. William M'Intosh, 87
Johnson Controls, Inc.; Auto United Union Workers
    v., 3544
———; International Union, United Auto Workers
    v., 3544
Johnston; Atherton Mills v., 484
Joint Anti-Fascist Refugee Committee v. McGrath,
    911
Joint Meeting of Essex and Union Counties v.
    National Sea Clammers Association, 2271
Jones v. Alfred H. Mayer Co., 1343
———; Breed v., 1696
———; Calder v., 2646
———; Johnson v., 4000
———; Local 926, International Union of Operating
    Engineers v., 2491
——— v. North Carolina Prisoners' Labor Union,
    Inc., 1866
——— v. Opelika, 756
——— v. Securities and Exchange Commission
    (SEC), 650
——— v. United States, 1071, 2580
———; Vitek v., 2079
———; Watson v., 187
——— v. Wolf, 2033
Jones, Superintendent, Great Meadow Correctional
    Facility v. Barnes, 2590
Jones, Warden v. Helms, 2254
Jones & Laughlin Steel Corp.; NRLB v., 662
——— v. Pfeifer, 2551
Jordan; Edelman v., 1629
———; Quern v., 1965
Joseph Burstyn, Inc. v. Wilson, 929
Joseph E. Seagrams and Sons; Kiefer-Stewart Co. v.,
    900
Joseph H. Munson Co., Inc.; Secretary of State v.,
    2726
Jos. Schlitz Brewing Co.; Milwaukee Brewery
    Workers' Pension Plan v., 3951
Joseph Triner Corp.; McNeil v., 655

Journal of Commerce and Commercial Bulletin v. Burleson, 414

Journeymen Stone Cutters Association of North America; Bedford Cut Stone Co. v., 549

Joy v. St. Louis, 275

Juilliard v. Greenman, 233

Jumel; Louisiana v., 230

Junior College District; Hadley v., 1391

Jurek v. Texas, 1797

Justices of Boston Municipal Court v. Lydon, 2664

K Mart Corp. v. Cartier, Inc., 3230

———; Security Services, Inc. v., 3885

KQED, Inc.; Houchins v., 1931

Kadrmas v. Dickinson Public Schools, 3277

Kagama alias Pactah Billy; United States v., 249

Kahanamoku; Duncan v., 823

Kahn v. Shevin, 1636

———; United States v., 1620

Kaiser Aetna v. United States, 2041

Kaiser Aluminum and Chemical Corp. v. Bonjorno, 3434

———; Bonjorno v., 3434

——— v. Weber, 2027

Kaiser Steel Corp. v. Mullins, 2312

Kalb v. Feuerstein, 701

——— v. Luce, 701

Kalo Brick & Tile Co.; Chicago & N.W. Tr. Co. v., 2192

Kalo Inoculant Co.; Funk Bros. Co. v., 863

Kamen v. Kemper Financial Services, Inc., 3565

Kan-gi-Shun-ca (Otherwise known as Crow Dog), Ex Parte, 232

Kann v. United States, 796

Kansas; Barker v., 3678

——— v. Colorado, 3982

———; Coppage v., 422

———; Fiske v., 555

———; Mugler v., 257

——— v. Utilicorp United Inc., 3496

Kansas ex rel. Tufts v. Ziebold, 257

Kansas Natural Gas Co.; West v., 402

Kansas Power and Light Co.; Energy Reserves Group, Inc., 2461

Kaplan; First Options v., 3989

Karcher v. May, 3216

Karcher, Speaker, New Jersey Assembly v. Daggett, 2560

Karlen; Strycker's Bay Neighborhood Council, Inc. v., 2044

Karo; United States v., 2751

Kasmir; United States v., 1751

Kassel v. Consolidated Freightways Corp. of Delaware, 2203

Kastigar v. United States, 1501

Katchen v. Landy, 1239

Katt; Testa v., 843

Katz v. United States, 1306

Katzenbach v. McClung, 1209

——— v. Morgan, 1262

———; South Carolina v., 1244

Kaufman v. Lee, 227

——— v. United States, 1358

Kautz v. Department of Game of Washington, 1327

Kawakita v. United States, 931

Kay v. Ehrler, 3552

Keane v. National Democratic Party, 1535

Keating; Southland Corp. v., 2621

Kedroff v. Saint Nicholas Cathedral of Russian Orthodox Church in North America, 934

Keefe; Organization for a Better Austin v., 1452

Keene; Meese v., 3134

Keene Corp. v. United States, 3802

Keeney, Superintendent, Oregon State Penitentiary v. Tamayo-Reyes, 3681

Keeper of the Common Jail; Mali and Wildenhus v., 255

Keeton v. Hustler Magazine, Inc., 2645

Keith Exchange; Hart v., 503

Keith J. Hudson v. Jack McMillian, 3649

Kelco Disposal Inc.; Browning-Ferris Industries, Inc. v., 3373

Keller v. State Bar of California, 3465

Kelley; Goldberg v., 1397

——— v. Johnson, 1747

——— v. Maryland, 901

Kelly; Jackson v., 119

——— v. Robinson, 3064

Kemmler, Ex Parte, 273

Kemp; Burger v., 3208

———; McCleskey v., 3128

Kemper Financial Services, Inc.; Kamen v., 3565

Kenai Peninsula Borough v. Alaska, 2215

Kendrick; Bowen v., 3281

———; United Families of America v., 3281

Kennedy; Arnett v., 1632

——— v. Mendoza-Martinez, 1141

———; Oregon v., 2372

Kennerly v. District Court of Ninth Judicial District of Montana, 1424

Kent v. Dulles, Secretary of State, 1029

——— v. United States, 1248

Kentucky; Austin v., 1283

———; Batson v., 2978

———; Berea College v., 384

———; Buchanan v., 3198

———; Carter v., 2191

———; Colten v., 1508

———; Crane v., 3002

——— v. Dennison, 156

Kentucky; Griffith v., 3074
———; Illinois v., 3579
———; James v. , 2665
———; Madden v., 704
———; Olden v., 3295
———; Rawlings v., 2140
———; Stanford v., 3375
——— v. Stincer, 3180
——— v. Whorton, 1996
Kentucky Bar Association; Shapero v., 3257
Kentucky, dba Bureau of State Police v. Graham,
    2894
Kentucky Department of Corrections v. Thompson,
    3337
Kentucky Department of Education; Bennett v., 2808
Kentucky Distilleries & Warehouse Co. v. Gregory,
    463
———; Hamilton v., 454
Keogh v. Chicago and Northwestern Railway, 492
Keohane; Thompson v., 4022
Ker v. California, 1165
——— v. Illinois, 254
Kerling, Ex Parte, 757
Kermarec v. Compagnie Generale Transatlantique,
    1047
Kern County Water Agency v. Sierra Club, 2216
Kerner; Haines v., 1479
Kerr-McGee Corp. v. Navajo Tribe of Indians, 2830
———; Silkwood v., 2612
Kewanee Oil Co. v. Bicron Corp., 1638
Key Tronics Corp. v. United States, 3798
Keyes v. Denver School District No. 1, 1587
"Keyes Case," 1587
Keyishian v. Board of Regents of the University of
    the State of New York, 1272
Keystone Bituminous Coal Association v.
    DeBenedictis, 3107
Keystone Consolidated Industries; Commissioner v.,
    3799
Kidd v. Pearson, 260
Kiefer-Stewart Co. v. Joseph E. Segrams and Sons,
    Inc., 900
Kilbourn v. Thompson, 222
Kilpatrick v. United States, 3272
Kimball Laundry Co. v. United States, 889
Kimberlin v. Quinlan, 4001
Kimmelman v. Morrison, 3029
King v. St. Vincent's Hospital, 3636
——— v. United States, 1268
King and Spalding; Hishon v., 2688
Kingsley Books, Inc. v. Brown, 1013
Kingsley International Pictures Corp. v. Regents of
    University of State of New York, 1062
Kinsella v. Krueger, 992, 1009
Kinzie; Bronson v., 137

Kirby v. Illinois, 1503
Kirby Forest Industries, Inc. v. United States, 2684
Kirchberg v. Feenstra, 2197
Kirkpatrick v. Preisler, 1362
Kirschbaum v. Walling, 754
Kissinger v. Halperin, 2268
——— v. Reporters Committee for Freedom of the
    Press, 2067
Klahr; Ely v., 1459
Klamath Tribe; Oregon Fish & Wildlife Dept. v.,
    2909
Klayminc v. United States, 3150
Klein; United States v., 184
Kleindienst v. Mandel, 1534
Kleppe v. New Mexico, 1765
Kleppe, Secretary of the Interior v. Sierra Club, 1786
Klevenhagen; Moreau v., 3791
Kline; Vlandis v., 1578
Klintock; United States v., 78
Klopfer v. North Carolina, 1276
Klutznick; Fullilove v., 2151
Kneip; Rosebud Sioux Tribe v., 1830
Knight; Minnesota Community College Faculty
    Association v., 2629
———; Minnesota State Board for Community
    Colleges v., 2629
——— v. United States Land Assocation, 278
Knoll; Springfield Township School District v., 2835
Knoop; Piqua Branch Bank v., 151
———; Piqua Branch of the State Bank of Ohio v.,
    151
Knotts; United States v., 2477
Knox v. Lee, 182
Knoxville Iron Co. v. Harbison, 345
Koerner; American Express Co. v., 2247
Koehler, Warden v. Engle, 2653
Kohl v. United States, 195
Kohn; Rendell-Baker v., 2410
Kois v. Wisconsin, 1527
Kokinda; United States v., 3505
Kokkonen v. Guardian Life Insurance Co. of
    America, 3883
Kolender v. Lawson, 2511
Koller; Richardson-Merrell, Inc. v., 2871
Konigsberg v. State Bar of California, 1005, 1100
"Konigsberg I," 1005
"Konigsberg II," 1100
Koray; Reno v., 3993
Kordel; United States v., 1390
Korean Air Lines (KAL); Chan v., 3330
——— v. Zicherman, 4024
———; Zicherman v., 4024
Korematsu v. United States, 800
Kosak v. United States, 2650
Kotteakos v. United States, 835

Kovacs v. Cooper, 879
———; Ohio v., 2774
Kowalaski v. Chandler, 949
Kozminski; United States v., 3286
Kraemer; Shelley v., 868
Kraft General Foods, Inc. v. Iowa Department of Revenue and Finance, 3711
Kramer; Santosky v., 2345
——— v. Union Free School District, No. 15, 1378
——— v. United States, 443
Kras; United States v., 1544
Krause, Administrator v. Rhodes, 1633
Kremer v. Chemical Construction Corp., 2365
Kretske v. United States, 741
Kreuger; Kinsella v., 1009
Krivda; California v., 1536
Kroger; Owen Equipment and Erection Co. v., 1926
Krueger; Kinsella v., 992
Krull; Illinois v., 3103
"Ku Klux Klan Act," 2593
"The Ku-Klux Case," 235
Kuhlmann v. Wilson, 3031
Kuhlmeier; Hazelwood School District v., 3219
Kuhn; Flood v., 1513
Kungys v. United States, 3246
Kunz v. New York, 902
Kurth Ranch; Department of Revenue v., 3897
Kurtz; Beatty v., 114
Kurtzman; Lemon v., 1468, 1563
Kush v. Rutledge, 2494
Kyles v. Whitley, Warden, 3975

LTV Corp.; Pension Benefit Guaranty Corp. v., 3488
La Buy v. Howes Leather Co., 997
LaCompagnie General Transatlantique; Deslions v., 381
LaCoste v. Department of Conservation of Louisiana, 514
LaFayette v. Louisiana Power and Light Co., 1897
La Fleur; Cleveland Board of Education v., 1617
LaFollette; Democratic Party of the United States v., 2185
LaHue; Briscoe v., 2480
La Jolla Band of Mission Indians; Escondido Mutual Water Co. v., 2682
LaPlante; Iowa Mutual Insurance Co. v., 3089
La Plata River Cherry Creek Ditch Co.; Hinderlider v., 682
LaRocca v. United States, 2097
LaRue; California v., 1537
LaSalle National Bank; Rosewell v., 2199
———; United States v., 1925
Labine v. Vincent, 1439
Labor and Industrial Relations Commission; Wimberly v., 3084

Laborers Health & Welfare Trust Fund for Northern California v. Advanced Lightweight Concrete Co., 3225
"Lady Chatterley's Lover," 1062
Lafayette; Illinois v., 2556
Laidlaw v. Organ, 68
Laird; Massachusetts v., 1426
———; Stuart v., 36
Laird, Secretary of Defense v. Tatum, 1522
Lake Country Estates, Inc. v. Tahoe Regional Planning Agency, 1967
Lakeside v. Oregon, 1895
Lalli v. Lalli, 1950
———; Lalli v., 1950
Lamagno; Gutierrez de Martinez v., 4005
Lamb's Chapel and John Steigerwald v. Center Moriches Union Free School District, 3811
Lambert v. California, 1020
Lamborn v. Pennsylvania, 767
Lamont v. Postmaster General of United States, 1229
Lamont, dba Basic Pamphlets v. Postmaster General, 1229
Lampf, Pleva, Lipkind, Prupis & Petigrow v. Gilbertson, 3603
Landano; United States Department of Justice v., 3800
Landgraf v. USI Film Products et al., 3877
Landmark Communications, Inc. v. Virginia, 1906
Lando; Herbert v., 1981
Landon, District Director of the Immigration and Naturalization Service v. Plasencia, 2444
Landreth; Landreth Timber Co. v., 2850
Landreth Timber Co. v. Landreth, 2850
Landy; Katchen v., 1239
Lane; Teague v., 3312
——— v. United States, 2932
———; United States v., 2932
——— v. Williams, 2339
——— v. Wilson, 692
Lankford v. Idaho, 3566
Lanza v. New York, 1129
———; United States v., 497
Larkin v. Grendel's Den, Inc., 2448
———; Withrow v., 1691
Larry Witters v. Washington Department of Services for the Blind, 2933
Larsen; Lauritzen v., 944
———; Negre v., 1436, 1437
Larson v. Domestic and Foreign Commerce Corp., 888
——— v. Valente, 2356
Lasker; Burks v., 1990
Lassiter v. Department of Social Services of Durham County, North Carolina, 2240

Lassiter v. Northampton County Board of Election, 1056
Late Corporations of the Church of Jesus Christ of Latter-Day Saints v. United States, 271
Lathrop v. Donohue, 1114
Latsis; Chandris, Inc. v., 4003
Lau v. Nichols, 1615
Lauf v. E.G. Shinner and Co., 678
Lauritzen v. Larsen, 944
Lavoie; Aetna v., 2969
Lawlor; Loewe v., 376
Lawrence v. Paul, 202
Lawrence County v. Lead-Deadwood School District No. 40-1, 2773
Lawrence H. Crandon v. United States, 3411
Lawson; Kolender v., 2511
——— v. Vera, 4044
Lawton v. Steele, 294
Le v. Hopkins, 248
Le Gierse; Helvering v., 731
Lead-Deadwood School District; Lawrence County v., 2773
Leader; Apex Hosiery Co. v., 716
League of United Latin American Citizens v. Attorney General of Texas, 3605
League of Women Voters of California; Federal Communications Commission (FCC) v., 2742
Leary v. United States, 1368
Leatherman v. Tarrant County Narcotics Intelligence and Coordination Unit, 3764
Leathers, Commissioner or Revenues of Arkansas v. Medlock, 3553
———; Medlock v., 3553
Lebron v. Amtrack, 3950
——— v. National Railroad Passenger Corp., 3950
Lechmere, Inc. v. National Labor Relations Board (NLRB), 3648
Lee; Hansberry v., 719
——— v. Illinois, 2996
——— v. International Society for Krishna Consciousness, Inc. (ISKCON), 3731
———; International Society for Krishna Consciousness, Inc. (ISKCON) v., 3727
———; Kaufman v., 227
———; Knox v., 182
——— v. Mississippi, 859
———; United States v., 227, 556, 2319
———; Williams v., 1043
———; Winston v., 2811
——— v. Weisman, 3724
Lee Optical of Oklahoma, Inc.; Williamson v., 968
Lees v. United States, 293
Leesville Concrete Co.; Edmonson v., 3587
Lefkowitz v. Brooks, 1909
———; United States v., 601

"Legal Tender Cases," 233
"Legal Tender Acts Case," 177
Leger; Sailor v., 1464
Legrant; Washington v., 1366
Lehman v. City of Shaker Heights, 1661
——— v. Lycoming County Children's Service Agency, 2428
Lehman, Secretary of the Navy v. Nakshian, 2275
Lehnert v. Ferris Faculty Assocation, 3584
Lehr v. Robertson, 2577
Leininger; Burnet v., 599
Leist; Clayton Brokerage Co. of St. Louis, Inc. v., 2360
———; Heinhold Commodities, Inc. v., 2360
———; New York Mercantile Exchange v., 2360
Lemke v. United States, 456
"Lemon I," 1468
"Lemon II," 1563
Lemon; Crouter v., 1604
——— v. Kurtzman, 1468, 1563
——— v. Kurtzman, Superintendent of Public Instruction of the Commonwealth of Pennsylvania, 1468, 1563
———; Sloan v., 1604
Leon; United States v., 2756
Leser v. Garnett, 480
Lessee of Livingston v. Moore, 125
Lessee of Waddell; Martin v., 135
Leu; Finnegan v., 2363
Leupp; Quick Bear v., 380
Levinson; Basic, Inc. v., 3233
Levitt, Ex Parte, 675
———; Tafflin v., 3402
Levitt and Nyquist v. Committee for Public Education and Religious Liberty (PERL), 1594
Levy v. Louisiana Through the Charity Hospital of Louisiana, 1321
____; Parker v., 1652
Lewis v. BT Investment Managers, Inc., 2109
———; Cardwell v., 1650
——— v. Casey, 4046
———; German Alliance Insurance Co. v., 418
———; Richmond v., 3737
———; Transamerica Mortgage Advisors, Inc. (TAMA) v., 2036
——— v. United States, 842
———; United States v., 842
Lewis, Comptroller of the State of Florida v. Continental Bank Corp., 3421
Lewis, Director, Arizona Department of Corrections v. Jimmie Wayne Jeffers, 3506
Lewis and Fox Co. v. Sherman, 519
Lewis Publishing Co. v. Morgan, 414
Liberty Lobby; Anderson v., 3024
Library of Congress v. Shaw, 3045

Libretti v. United States, 4026

"License Cases," 141

Liebmann; New State Ice Co. v., 600

Liepelt; Norfolk and Western Railway Co. v., 2051

Liggett Group, Inc.; Cipollone v., 3723

Light v. United States, 400

Lightfoot; Gomillion v., 1084

Lilly v. Commissioner of Internal Revenue Service, 924

Limbach; New Energy Co. v., 3253

Limbach, Tax Commissioner of Ohio v. Hooven & Allison Co., 2666

Lincoln, Acting Director, Indian Health Service v. Vigil, 3801

Lincoln Savings and Loan Association; Commissioner of Internal Revenue v., 1463

Linda R.S. v. Richard D., 1556

Lindahl v. Office of Personnel Management (OPM), 2812

Linden Lumber Division, Summer & Co. v. National Labor Relations Board (NLRB), 1671

Lindsey; Fowler v., 25

——; Greene v., 2364

—— v. Normet, 1481

Lindsley v. Natural Carbonic Gas Co., 397

"Lineup Cases," 1298, 1299, 1300

Lingle v. Norge Division of Magic Chef, Inc., 3256

Linkletter v. Walkers, 1233

Linmark Associates, Inc. v. Township of Willingboro, 1838

Liparota v. United States, 2842

Liteky v. United States, 3866

Little v. Barreme, 38

—— v. Streater, 2239

Little Rock; Daisy Bates v., 1066

——; Reinman v., 425

"Little Rock Desegregation Crisis," 1040

Littleton; O'Shea v., 1614

Litton; Pepper v., 699

Litton Financial Printing Division v. National Labor Relations Board (NLRB), 3598

Livadas v. Bradshaw, California Labor Commissioner, 3907

Lloyd; Ferry v., 563

——; Harris v., 563

Lloyd Corp. v. Tanner, 1521

Lo-Ji Sales, Inc. v. New York, 2007

Local 28 of Sheet Metal Workers' International Association v. Equal Employment Opportunity Commission (EEOC), 3049

Local 93, International Association of Firefighters, etc. v. Cleveland, 3050

Local 112, United Brotherhood of Carpenters and Joiners of America; Summit Valley Industries, Inc. v., 2374

Local 144 Nursing Home Pension Fund v. Demisay, 3819

Local 174, Teamsters Chauffeurs, Warehousemen and Helpers of America v. Lucas Flour Co., 1121

Local 408, International Brotherhood of Teamsters v. National Labor Relations Board, 2637

Local 926, International Union of Operating Engineers, AFL-CIO v. Jones, 2491

Local 3489, United Steelworkers of America, AFL-CIO v. Usery, Secretary of Labor, 1811

Local Division 1285 Amalgamted Transit Union; Jackson Transit Authority v., 2380

Local Loan Co. v. Hunt, 625

Local No. 82, Furniture & Piano Moving, Furniture Store Drivers, Helpers, Warehousemen & Packers v. Crowley, 2710

Local No. 358, Bakery Workers; Nolde Brothers, Inc., 1823

Local No. 6167, United Mine Workers; Jewel Ridge Coal Corp. v., 810

Local Union 759, International Union of the United Rubber, Cork, Linoleum and Plastic Workers of America; W.R. Grace and Co. v., 2528

Local Union No. 3; Allen-Bradley Co. v., 813

——, International Brotherhood of Electrical Workers; Allen-Bradley Co. v., 813

Lochner v. New York, 363

Locke; United States v., 2825

Lockett v. Ohio, 1941

Lockhart; Hill v., 2912

—— v. McCree, 2981

—— v. Nelson, 3291

Lockhart, Director, Arkansas Department of Corrections v. Fretwell, 3750

Lockheed Air Terminal; Burbank v., 1568

Lockheed Aircraft Corp. v. United States, 2474

Lockwood; Ex Parte, 296

Lodge; Rogers v., 2433

Lodge 76, International Association of Machinists and Aerospace Workers v. Wisconsin Employment Relations Commission, 1776

Loew's Inc. v. United States, 870

Loewe v. Lawlor, 376

Loewenstein; Nebraska Department of Revenue v., 3939

Loftsgaarden; Randall v., 3055

Logan; Burnet v., 590

—— v. Zimmerman Brush Co., 2328

Logan Valley Plaza Inc.; Amalgamated Food Employees v., 1325

Lohman; Associated Industries v., 3892

The Lola, 336

Lombard v. Louisiana, 1156

Lomenzo; WMCA v., 1234

Lonberger; Marshall v., 2462
Lonchar v. Thomas, 4037
Londoner v. Denver, 383
Lone Steer, Inc.; Donovan v., 2616
Lone Wolf v. Hitchcock, 346
Long; Michigan v., 2598
Long Island Railroad Co.; Transportation Union v., 2342
Longo v. United States, 3394
Longshoremen; National Labor Relations Board (NLRB) v., 2891
Lopez; Goss v., 1677
——— v. United States, 1158
———; United States v., 3979
Lopez-Mendoza; Immigration and Naturalization Service (INS) v., 2759
Lorain Journal Co.; Milkovich v., 3490
Lorance v. AT&T Technologies, Inc., 3348
Lord; Bennett Mining Co. v., 502
———; Biwabic Mining Co. v., 502
———; Cleveland-Cliffs Iron Co. v., 502
———; Interstate Iron Co. v., 502
———; Mesaba-Cliffs Iron Mining Co. v., 502
———; Oliver Iron Mining Co. v., 502
———; Republic Iron and Steel Co. v., 502
"Lord's Day Statute," 1104
Lorenzetti; United States v., 2692
Loretto v. Teleprompter Manhattan CATV Corp., 2426
Lorion; Florida Power & Light Co. v., 2810
Lorion, dba Center for Nuclear Responsibility; United States Nuclear Regulatory Commission v., 2810
Los Angeles; Dobbins v., 360
———; Golden State Transit Corp. v., 2960, 3386
——— v. Los Angeles Gas and Electric Corp., 453
——— v. Preferred Communications, Inc., 2994
Los Angeles, Department of Water and Power v. Manhart, 1904
Los Angeles County; First Unitarian Church v., 1038
Los Angeles Gas and Electric Corp.; Los Angeles, 453
Los Angeles Lumber Products Co.; Case v., 696
"Lottery Case," 348
Loud Hawk; United States v., 2926
Loudermill; Cleveland Board of Education v., 2803
Loughborough v. Blake, 80
Louisiana; Allgeyer v., 317
———; Briscoe v., 1117
———; Brown v., 1242, 2120
———; Burch v., 1980
———; Cage v., 3512
———; Cox v., 1212, 1213
———; Duncan v., 1324
———; Foucha v., 3684

———; Garner v., 1117
———; Garrison v., 1204
———; Hans v., 267
——— v. Hayes, 4016
———; Hoston v., 1117
———; Hudson v., 2181
———; Johnson v., 1499
——— v. Jumel, 230
———; Levy v., 1321
———; Lombard v., 1156
———; Maryland v., 2236, 2257
——— v. Mississippi, 2657
———; Mississippi v., 3739
———; Perry v., 3511
———; Roberts v., 1799, 1848
———; Shea v., 2788
———; Sullivan v., 3805
———; Taylor v., 1675
——— v. United States, 1217
———; United States v., 2270, 2790
"Louisiana Bond Case," 230
"Louisiana Boundary Case," 2270
"Louisiana Common Carrier Case," 206
"Louisiana's Creationism Case," 3176
Louisana ex rel. Belden; Esteben v., 189
Louisiana ex rel. Francis v. Resweber, 838
Louisiana Board of Education; Cochran v., 578
Louisiana Power and Light Co.; LaFayette v., 1897
Louisiana Public Service Commission v. Federal Communications Commission (FCC), 2988
Louisville; Thompson v., 1069
Louisville and Nashville Railroad; Steele v., 799
Louisville Joint Stock Land Bank v. Radford, 638
Louisville, New Orleans and Texas Railway Co. v. Mississippi, 266
Lovell v. City of Griffin, 680
Lovett; United States v., 828
Loving v. Virginia, 1292
Lovorn; Hathorn v., 2390
Low v. Austin, 183
Lowe v. Securities and Exchange Commission (SEC), 2863
Lowry; Herndon v., 667
Lucas; Bush v., 2545
——— v. Earl, 576
——— v. Forty-Fourth General Assembly of the State of Colorado, 1190
———; Mathews v., 1790
———; Michigan v., 3568
——— v. South Carolina Coastal Council, 3733
"Lucas Decision," 3733
Lucas Flour Co.; Teamsters v., 1121
Luce; Kalb v., 701
——— v. United States, 2762
Lucey; Evitts v., 2778

Lucious Abrams, Jr. v. Davida Johnson, 4019
Ludwig v. Independent Insurance Agents of America, Inc., 3814
Ludwig, Comptroller of Currency v. Variable Annuity Life Insurance co. (VALIC), 3945
Lueck; Allis-Chalmers Corp. v., 2831
Lugar v. Edmondson Oil Co., 2412
Lujan, Secretary of the Interior v. Defenders of Wildlife, 3700
——— v. National Wildlife Federation, 3509
Lukens Steel Co.; Goodman v., 3178
Lukhard v. Reed, 3129
Lum; Fauntleroy v., 382
Lundy; Rose v., 2333
Lurk v. United States, 1134
Luther v. Borden, 143
Lybrand; McCain v., 2627
Lycoming County Children's Services Agency; Lehman v., 2428
Lydon; Justices of Boston Municipal Court v., 2664
Lynaugh; Penry v., 3374
Lynch v. Overholser, 1127
Lynch, Mayor of Pawtucket v. Donnelly, 2642
Lyng v. Castillo, 3038
Lyng v. International Union, Automobile, Aerospace and Agricultural Implement Workers of America, UAW, 3238
——— v. Northwest Indian Cemetery Protective Association, 3239
——— v. Payne, 3011
Lynn; Sheet Metal Workers International Association v., 3299
Lyons; Adkins v., 501
———; Los Angeles v., 2502
——— v. Oklahoma, 793
Lytle v. Household Manufacturing, Inc., Schwitzer Turbo-chargers, 3424

M'Clung v. Silliman, 83
M'Cormick v. Sullivant, 97
M'Faddon; Schooner Exchange v., 55
M'Kim v. Voorhies, 57
M.J.R., Inc. v. City of Dallas, 3393
MCI Telecommunications Corp. v. American Telephone & Telegraph Co., 3911
MCorp Financial, Inc.; Board of Governors of the Federal Reserve System v., 3625
M/V Sky Reefer; Vimar Seguros y Reaseguros v., 4009
Mabry, Commissioner, Arkansas Department of Correction v. Johnson, 2708
MacCollom; United States v., 1761
MacDonald; United States v., 2346
MacDonald, Sommer and Frates v. County of Yolo, 3028

Macintosh; United States v., 591
Mack v. Russell County Commission, 3647
Mackay Radio and Telegraph Co.; National Labor Relations Board (NLRB) v., 684
——— v. RCA Communications, Inc., 946
Macomber; Eisner v., 457
Macon; Maryland v., 2873
Madden v. Kentucky, 704
Maddox; Republic Steel Corp. v., 1214
Madera Irrigation District v. Albonico, 1032
——— v. Steiner, 1032
Madigan; McCarthy v., 3657
Madison; Dean Milk Co. v., 905
———; Marbury v., 35
Madrazo; Governor of Georgia v., 107
Madsen v. Women's Health Center, Inc., 3926
Maggio, Warden v. Williams, 2604
Mahan v. Howell, 1552
Maher v. Gagne, 2141
Maher, Commissioner of Social Services of Connecticut v. Roe, 1861
Maher Terminals; Director, Office of Workers' Compensation Programs, Department of Labor v., 3913
Mahfoud; Eastern Air Lines, Inc. v., 2920
Mahon; Pennsylvania Coal Co. v., 498
Maine v. Moulton, 2918
——— v. Taylor, 3020
——— v. Thiboutot, 2136
——— v. Thornton, 2659
———; United States v., 2255, 2783, 2939
Maislin Industries, U.S., Inc. v. Primary Steel, Inc., 3493
Mali and Wildenhus v. Keeper of the Common Jail, 255
Malley v. Briggs, 2950
Malley-Duff and Associates, Inc.; Agency Holding Corp. v., 3188
———; Crown Life Insurance v., 3188
Malloy v. Hogan, Sheriff, 1191
Mallory v. United States, 1014
Maltezos v. Pennsylvania, 767
Mancari; Amerind v., 1649
———; Morton v., 1649
Mandel; Kleindienst v., 1534
Manhart; Los Angeles, Department of Water and Power v., 1904
Manigualt v. Springs, 365
Manitowoc Products Co.; Sawyer v., 463
Mann; Arkansas Valley Land and Cattle Co. v., 262
Manor Drug Stores; Blue Chip Stamps v., 1702
Mansell v. Mansell, 3340
———; Mansell v., 3340
Manson v. Brathwaite, 1856
Mansour; Green v., 2913

Manspeaker; Damarest v., 3520

Manual Enterprise, Inc. v. Day, Postmaster General, 1133

Manypenny; Arizona v., 2214

Manzano; Immigration and Naturalization Service (INS) v., 3266

Mapp v. Ohio, 1110

Marathon Pipe Line Co.; Northern Pipeline Construction, Co. v., 2416

———; United States v., 2416

Marbury v. Madison, 35

Marchant; United States v., 105

Marchetti v. United States, 1308

Marcus v. Search Warrant of Property at 104 East Tenth Street, Kansas City, Missouri, 1112

Marcus Brown Holding Co., Inc. v. Feldman, 472

Marek v. Chesny, Individually, and as Administrator of the Estate of Chesny, 2889

Marianna Flora, 98

Maricopa County; Memorial Hospital v., 1623

Maricopa County Medical Society; Arizona v., 2394

Marine Bancorporation; United States v., 1666

Marine Bank v. Weaver, 2334

Marion; United States v., 1474

Maroney; Chambers v., 1414

Marrese v. American Academy of Orthopaedic Surgeons, 2798

Marron v. United States, 558

Marsh v. Alabama, 819

———; Richardson v., 3124

Marsh, Nebraska State Treasurer v. Chambers, 2592

Marshall v. American Petroleum Institute, 2153

———; East Carroll Parish School Board v., 1736

——— v. Jerrico, Inc., 2091

———; Whirlpool Corp. v., 2062

Marshall, Secretary of Labor v. Barlow's, Inc., 1911

Marshall, Superintendent, Southern Ohio Correctional Facility v. Lonberger, 2462

Martin; Abrams v., 2698

———; Anderson v., 1174

———; Bolton v., 8

——— v. City of Struthers, Ohio, 768

———; Harrah Independent School District v., 1960

——— v. Hunter's Lessee, 66

——— v. New York v., 818

——— v. Lessee of Waddell, 135

——— v. Mott, 100

——— v. Ohio, 3098

———; Schall v., 2698

——— v. Wilks, 3346

Martin, Secretary of Labor v. Occupational Safety and Health Review Commission, 3542

Martin Marietta Corp.; Phillips v., 1425

Martinez v. California, 2046

———; Procunier v., 1637

———; Santa Clara Pueblo v., 1907

Martinez, as Next Friend of Morales v. Bynum, 2510

Martinez-Fuerte; United States v., 1803

Marvel Entertainment Group; Pavelic and LeFlore v., 3387

Maryland; Andresen v., 1789

———; Bell v., 1197

———; Benton v., 1381

———; Booth v., 3173

———; Brown v., 103

——— v. Buie, 3416

——— v. Craig, 3608

———; Frank v., 1052

———; Freedman v., 1215

——— v. Garrison, 3092

———; Giles v., 1274

———; Kelley v., 901

——— v. Louisiana, 2236, 2257

——— v. Macon, 2873

———; McCulloch v., 74

———; McGowan v., 1101

———; Mills v., 3255

———; Niemotko v., 901

——— v. Sandra Ann Craig, 3508

———; Smith v., 2017

——— v. Wirtz, Secretary of Labor, 1340

Mascitti v. McGrath, 922

Mason v. Haile, 102

Massachusetts; A Book named "John Cleland's Memoirs of a Woman of Pleasure" v., 1245

———; Boston Beer Co. v., 210

———; Davis v., 321

———; Franklin v., 3730

——— v. New Hampshire, 2323

———; Jacobson v., 362

——— v. Laird, 1426

———; McDonald v., 340

——— v. Mellon, 507

———; Metropolitan Life Insurance Co. v., 2852

——— v. Morash, 3329

———; Nichols v., 697

——— v. Oakes, 3361

———; Pervear v., 168

———; Plumley v., 298

———; Prince v., 781

——— v. Sheppard, 2757

———; Thurlow v., 141

——— v. United States, 1898

Massachusetts Board of Retirement v. Murgia, 1783

"Massachusetts Boundary Case," 2255

Massachusetts Citizens for Life, Inc.; Federal Elections Commission (FEC) v., 3071

Massachusetts Council of Construction Employers, Inc.; White v., 2475

Massachusetts Department of Education; Burlington School Commission v., 2839

Massachusetts General Hospital; City of Revere v., 2576

Massachusetts Mutual Life Insurance Co. v. Russell, 2893

Massachusetts Water Resources Authority v. Associated Builders and Contractors of Massachusetts/Rhode Island, Inc., 3767

Massiah v. United States, 1185

Masson v. New Yorker Magazine, 3608

———— v. The New Yorker, 3608

Mastrobuono v. Shearson Lehman Hutton, 3960

Mata; Sumner v., 2177

Matheson; H.L. v., 2196

Matthews; Bitzer v., 1788

———— v. Eldridge, 1728

————; Heckler v., 2643

———— v. Lucas, 1790

————; Morris v., 2945

————; Perkins v., 1423

Mathewson; Satterlee v., 112

Mathiason; Oregon v., 1814

Matlock; United States v., 1621

Matsushita Electric Industrial Co. v. Epstein, 4028

———— v. Zenith Radio Corp., 2959

Matteo; Barr v., 1061

Mattox v. United States, 3063

Mauclet; Nyquist v., 1853

Maurice M. v. Bouknight, 3405

Mauro; Arizona v., 3136

Maxwell v. Bishop, Superintendent, 1410

———— v. Dow, 337

————; Sheppard v., 1258

May; Karcher v., 3216

Mayes; Talton v., 310

Maynard; Wooley v., 1833

Mayor, Aldermen and Commonalty of the City of New York v. Miln, 127

Mayor and City Council of Baltimore; Equal Employment Opportunity Commission (EEOC) v., 2868

————; Johnson v., 2868

Mayor and Council of the Borough of Oradell; Hynes v., 1754

Mayor of City of Philadelphia v. Halderman, 2297

Mayor of Washington, D.C. v. Davis, 1759

"Maximum Rate Case," 322

Maze; United States v., 1613

Mazurie; United States v., 1676

McAninch; O'Neal v., 3952

McBoyle v. United States, 587

McBratney; United States v., 225

McBride; Ribnik v., 566

McCabe, Ex Parte, 256

McCain v. Lybrand, 2627

McCardle, Ex Parte, 171

McCarter; Hudson County Co. v., 379

McCarthy v. Bronson, 3567

———— v. Madigan, 3657

McCarty; Berkemer v., 2743

———— v. McCarty, 2277

————; McCarty v., 2277

McClanahan v. Arizona State Tax Commission, 1562

McClenachan; Coxe v., 26

McClendon; Ingersoll-Rand Co. v., 3517

McCleskey v. Kemp, Superintendent, Georgia Diagnostic and Classification Center, 3128

———— v. Zant, Superintendent, Georgia Diagnostic and Classification Center, 3554

McClung; Katzenbach v., 1209

———— v. Silliman, 83

McClure; Schweiker v., 2353

McCluskey; Board of Education of Rogers Arkansas v., 2443

McCollan; Baker v., 2025

McCollum v. Board of Education, 865

————; Georgia v., 3710

McConnell v. Baggett, 1189

McCormack; Powell v., 1376

McCormick; Follett v., 786

———— v. Sullivant, 97

———— v. United States, 3573

McCracken; Ivanhoe Irrigation District v., 1032

McCrary; Runyon v., 1777

———— v. Runyon et ux. d/b/a Bobbe's School, 1777

McCrary; Southern Independent School Assocation v., 1777

McCray v Illinois, 1277

———— v. United States, 357

McCready; Blue Shield of Virginia v., 2399

McCreary; Board of Trustees of the Village of Scarsdale v., 2824

McCree; Lockhart v., 2981

McCulloch v. Maryland, 74

McCullough; Texas v., 2941

McCurry; Allen v., 2159

McDaniel v. Barresi, 1446

———— v. Paty, 1902

———— v. Sanchez, 2244

McDermott; United States by and through Internal Revenue Service v., 3774

McDermott, Inc. v. AmClyde and River Don Casting Ltd., 3874

McDermott International, Inc. v. Wilander, 3528

McDonald v. City of West Branch, Michigan, 2663

———— v. Massachusetts, 340

———— v. Santa Fe Trail Transportation Co., 1781

———— v. Smith, 2875

McDonnell; Wolff v., 1665

McDonnell Douglas Corp. v. Green, 1570
McDonough Power Equipment, Inc. v. Greenwood,
    2620
McDowell; Burdeau v., 475
McElroy; Cafeteria and Restaurant Workers Union
    v., 1115
———; Cafeteria Workers Union v., 1115
——— v. United States, 2340
McElvaine v. Brush, 277
McFaddon; Schooner Exchange v., 55
McFarland v. Scott, Director, Texas Department of
    Criminal Justice, Institutional Division, 3928
McGautha v. California, 1451
McGhee v. Sipes, 868
McGinley; Two Guys from Harrison-Allentown v.,
    1102
McGowan v. Maryland, 1101
McGrain v. Daugherty, 543
McGrath; Coleman v., 922
———; International Workers Order, Inc. v., 911
———; Joint Anti-Fascist Refugee Committee v.,
    911
———; Mascitti v., 922
———; National Council of American-Soviet
    Friendship, Inc.v., 911
McGuire; Estelle v., 3627
McInnis v. United States, 567
McIntire v. Wood, 60
McIntosh; Johnson v., 87
McIntyre v. Ohio Elections Commission, 3973
McKaskle, Acting Director, Texas Department of
    Corrections v. Wiggins, 2625
McKeiver v. Pennsylvania, 1467
McKellar; Butler v., 3419
McKelvie; Nebraska District of Evangelical Lutheran
    Synod v., 506
McKennon v. Nashville Banner Publishing Co., 3948
McKesson Corp. v. Division of Alcoholic Beverages
    and Tobacco, 3466
——— v. Florida Division of Alcoholic Beverages
    and Tobacco, 3466
McKim v. Voorhies, 57
McKinney v. Alabama, 1737
———; Helling v., 3824
McLain v. Real Estate Board of New Orleans, Inc.,
    2045
McLaughlin; County of Riverside, California v.,
    3563
——— v. Florida, 1206
———; Riverside v., 3563
——— v. United States, 2974
McLaurin v. Oklahoma State Regents for Higher
    Education, 897
McLean Credit Union; Patterson v., 3353
McMahon; Shearson/American Express, Inc. v., 3162

McMann v. Richardson, 1406
———; United Air Lines, Inc. v., 1879
McMillan; Escambia County, Florida v., 2655
——— v. Pennsylvania, 3018
McMillian; Hudson v., 3649
McNabb v. United States, 764
McNair; Hunt v., 1602
McNally v. United States, 3196
McNamara; Mora v., 1307
McNary; Fair Assessment in Real Estate Association,
    Inc. v., 2293
McNary, Commissioner of Immigration and
    Naturalization v. Haitian Refugee Center, Inc.,
    3534
McNeese v. Board of Education, Community Unit
    School District 187, Cahokia, Illinois, 1163
McNeil v. Joseph Triner Corp., 655
——— v. United States, 3796
——— v. Wisconsin, 3597
McNichols v. Baldrige, 2324
McPherson v. Blacker, 286
———; Rankin v., 3197
McQuillan; Spectrum Sports v., 3752
McRae; Harris v., 2147
Meachum v. Fano, 1778
Mead Corp. v. B.E. Tilley, 3344
Meadowmoor Dairies, Inc.; Milk Wagon Drivers
    Union v., 729
———; Milk Wagon Drivers Union of Chicago,
    Local 753 v., 729
Mealey; Central Greyhound Lines v., 875
Mechanik; United States v., 2938
Medina v. California, 3721
Medlock; Leathers v., 3553
——— v. Leathers, Commissioner of Revenues of
    Arkansas, 3553
Medtronic, Inc.; Eli Lilly and Co. v., 3489
Meek v. Pittenger, 1693
Meese v. Keene, 3134
Melkonyan v. Sullivan, Secretary of Health and
    Human Services, 3592
Mellon; Florida v., 539
———; Frothingham v., 507
———; Massachusetts v., 507
Melo; Hafer v., 3624
Members of the City Council of the City of Los
    Angeles v. Taxpayers for Vincent, 2683
Memoirs v. Massachusetts v., 1245
Memorial Hospital v. Maricopa County, 1623
Memphis; Watson v., 1160
Memphis and Charleston Railroad Co.; Robinson v.,
    231
Memphis Bank & Trust Co. v. Garner, 2460
Memphis Community School District v. Stachura,
    3026

Memphis Fire Department v. Carl W. Stotts, 2711
Memphis Police Department v. Cleamtree Garner, 2819
Mendell; Gollust v., 3594
Mendenhall; United States v., 2099
Mendoza; United States v., 2608
Mendoza-Lopez; United States v., 3151
Mendoza-Martinez; Kennedy v., 1141
Mennonite Board of Missions v. Adams, 2561
Menominee Tribe of Indians v. United States, 1328
"Mental Health Case," 1241
Merchantile Trust Co.; Hicks v., 531
———; United States v., 531
———; White v., 531
Merck & Co.; Bowsher v., 2499
Mercury Construction Corp.; Moses H. Cone Memorial Hospital v., 2468
Mergens; Board of Education v., 3473
———; Westside Community Schools v., 3473
Meritor Savings Bank, FSB v. Mechelle Vinson, 3017
Merrell Dow Pharmaceuticals; Daubert v., 3839
——— v. Thompson, 3060
Merrett Underwriting Agency Management Ltd. v. California, 3843
Merrill; Federal Crop Insurance Corp. v., 854
Merrill Lynch, Pierce, Fenner and Smith, Inc. v. Curran, 2360
Merrion, dba Merrion & Bayless v. Jicarilla Apache Tribe, 2316
Mertens v. Hewitt Associates, 3804
Mesaba-Cliffs Iron Mining Co. v. Lord, 502
Mesaroch v. United States, 995
Mescalero Apache Tribe; New Mexico v., 2542
Metcalf & Eddy, Inc.; Puerto Rico Aqueduct and Sewer Authority v., 3743
Methow Valley Citizens Council; Robertson v., 3334
Metro Broadcasting, Inc. v. Federal Communications Commission (FCC), 3503
Metromedia, Inc. v. City of San Diego, 2285
———; Rosenbloom v., 1457
Metropolitan Cooperative Milk Producers Bargaining Agency v. Rock Royal Co-operative, Inc., 695
Metropolitan Edison Co.; Jackson v., 1672
——— v. National Labor Relations Board (NLRB), 2492
——— v. People Against Nuclear Energy (PANE), 2497
Metropolitan Housing Development Corp.; Arlington Heights v., 1809
Metropolitan Life Insurance Co. v. Massachusetts, 2852
——— v. Taylor, 3118
——— Trafficante v., 1539
——— v. Ward, 2816

Metropolitan Stevedore Co. v. Rambo, 3999
Metropolitan Washington Airports Authority v. Citizens for Abatement of Aircraft Noise, Inc., 3600
Meyer; Federal Deposit Insurance Corporation (FDIC) v., 3862
——— v. Nebraska, 505
Mezei; Shaughnessy v. United States ex rel., 941
Mezzanatto; United States v., 3943
Miami Herald Publishing Co. v. Tornillo, 1659
Michael C.; Fare v., 2016
Michael H. v. Gerald D., 3352
Michael M. v. Superior Court of Sonoma County, 2198
Michelin Tire Corp. v. Wages, Tax Commissioner, 1723
Michigan; Bennis v., 4030
——— v. Bladel, 2961
———; Bob-Lo Excursion Co. v., 861
———; Butler v., 998
——— v. Clifford, 2613
——— v. DeFillippo, 2020
———; Fex v., 3758
———; Harmelin v., 3621
——— v. Harvey, 3417
——— v. Jackson, 2961
——— v. Long, 2598
——— v. Lucas, 3568
——— v. Mid-Louisiana Gas Co., 2579
——— v. Mosley, 1722
——— v. Summers, 2267
——— v. Tucker, 1647
——— v. Tyler, 1915
Michigan Academy of Family Physicians; Bowen v., 3001
Michigan Canners & Freezers Association, Inc. v. Agricultural Marketing and Bargaining Board, 2705
Michigan Chamber of Commerce; Austin v., 3429
Michigan Citizens for an Independent Press v. Thornburgh, 3382
Michigan Department of Natural Resources; Fort Gratiot Sanitary Landfill, Inc. v., 3694
Michigan Department of State Police v. Rick Sitz, 3481
———; Will v., 3350
Michigan Department of Treasury; Davis v., 3323
———; Trinova Corp. v., 3529
Midcal Aluminum, Inc.; California Retail Liquor Dealers Association v., 2065
Middendorf v. Henry, 1743
Middlesex County Ethics Committee v. Garden State Bar Association, 2397
Middlesex County Sewerage Authority v. National Sea Clammers Association, 2271

Midkiff; Hawaii Housing Authority v., 2696

Midland County; Avery v., 1315

Midlantic National Bank v. New Jersey Department of Environmental Protection, 2934

Mid-Louisiana Gas Co.; Arizona Electric Power Cooperative v., 2579

———; Federal Energy Regulatory Commission v., 2579

———; Michigan v., 2579

———; Public Service Commission v., 2579

Midwest Bank and Trust Co.; Bank One, Chicago, N.A. v., 4025

Midwest Oil Co.; United States v., 424

Midwest Video Corp.; Federal Communications Commission (FCC) v., 1976

———; National Black Media Coalition v., 1976

Migra v. Warren City School District Board of Education, 2623

Milanovich v. United States, 1096

Miles v. Apex Marine Corp., 3510

Milhelm, Attea and Brothers; Department of Taxation v., 3904

Milhollin; Ford Motor Credit Co. v., 2054

Milk Wagon Drivers Union of Chicago, Local 753 v. Meadowmoor Dairies, Inc., 729

Milkovich v. Lorain Journal Co., 3490

Miller; American Dredging Co. v., 3861

——— v. California, 1584

———; Coleman v., 693

——— v. Fenton, Superintendent, Rahway State Prison, 2915

——— v. Florida, 3169

———; Fowler v., 25

———; Greer v., 3207

——— v. Johnson, 4019

——— v. Schoene, 561

——— v. Texas, 295

——— v. United States, 157, 180

———; United States v., 691, 1752, 2826

——— v. Wilson, 423

——— v. Zbaraz, 2148

Milligan; Ex Parte, 162

"Milliken I," 1668

"Milliken II," 1869

Milliken, Governor of Michigan v. Bradley, 1668, 1869

Mills v. Alabama, 1257

——— v. Duryee, 59

——— v. Electric Auto-Lite Co., 1386

——— v. Habluetzel, 2350

——— v. Maryland, 3255

——— v. Rogers, 2392

Mills Music, Inc. v. Snyder, 2768

Millsap; Quinn v., 3351

Miln; New York v., 127

Milton v. Wainwright, Corrections Director, 1515

Milwaukee; Illinois v., 1493

———; Snyder v., 697

Milwaukee Brewery Workers' Pension Plan v. Jos. Schlitz Brewing Co., 3951

Mima Queen v. Hepburn, 58

Minersville School District v. Gobitis, 718

Mink; EPA v., 1547

Minneapolis Star & Tribune Co. v. Minnesota Commissioner of Revenue, 2488

Minnesota v. Barber, 272

———; Chicago, Milwaukee and St. Paul Railroad Co. v., 268

——— v. Clover Leaf Creamery Co., 2175

——— v. Dickerson, 3810

———; Gilbert v., 466

——— v. Hodgson, 3501

———; Hodgson v., 3501

——— v. Murphy, 2634

——— v. Olson, 3441

———; Near v., 595

———; Shevlin-Carpenter Co. v., 391

"Minnesota Abortion Case," 3501

Minnesota Commissioner of Revenue; Minneapolis Star and Tribune Co. v., 2488

Minnesota Community College Faculty Association v. Knight, 2629

"Minnesota Mortgage Moratorium Case," 621

Minnesota Public Interest Research Group; Selective Service System v., 2754

"Minnesota Rate Cases," 268

Minnesota State Board for Community Colleges v. Knight, 2629

Minnich; Rivera v., 3202

Minnick v. California Department of Corrections, 2243

——— v. Mississippi, 3518

Minor v. Happersett, 193

"Minstrels Case," 145

"Miracle Case," 929

Miranda v. Arizona, 1260

Misco, Inc.; United Paperworkers International Union v., 3214

Mishkin v. New York, 1247

Mississippi; Brown v., 647

———; Caldwell v., 2867

———; Chambers v., 1551

———; Clemons v., 3431

———; Federal Energy Regulatory Commission (FERC) v., 2376

———; Gray v., 3143

———; Henry v., 1211

——— v. Johnson, 165

———; Johnson v., 3259

———; Lee v., 859

——— v. Louisiana, 3739

———; Louisiana v., 2657

———; Louisville, New Orleans and Texas Railway
     Co. v., 266

———; Minnick v., 3518

———; Mississippi Power and Light Co. v., 3275

———; Papasan v., 3044

———; Phillips Petroleum Co. v., 3224

——— v. Stanton, 169

———; Stone v., 220

———; Williams v., 331

Mississippi Power and Light Co. v. Mississippi, 3275

Mississippi University for Women v. Hogan, 2436

Mississippi Valley Generating Co.; United States v.,
     1088

Missouri; Baldwin v., 582

———; Bullington v., 2221

———; Craig v., 116

———; Cummings v., 163

———; Duren v., 1952

——— v. Holland, 459

——— v. Hunter, 2458

——— v. Illinois, 339

——— v. Jenkins, 3439, 3994

——— v. Moore, 305

———; Welton v., 194

———; Wilkins v., 3375

Missouri ex rel. Gaines v. Canada, 688

Missouri ex rel. Southwestern Bell Telephone Co. v.
     Public Service Commission of Missouri, 504

Missouri-Kansas-Texas Railroad Co. v. Brotherhood,
     3163

———v. Texas, 3081

Missouri Pacific Railroad v. Humes, 242

Mistretta v. United States, 3300

Mitchell v. Forsyth, 2877

———; Helvering v., 679

———; Hitchman Coal and Coke Co. v., 442

———; Oregon v., 1421

———; State v., 3816

———; Texas v., 1421

Mitchell; United Parcel Service, Inc. v., 2208

———; United Public Workers v., 840

——— v. United States, 734

———; United States v., 2081, 2575

———; Venegas v., 3440

———; Wisconsin v., 3816

"Mitchell II," 2575

Mitchum dba Book Mart v. Foster, 1512

Mite Corp.; Edgar v., 2404

Mitsubishi Motors Corp. v. Soler Chrysler-Plymouth,
     Inc., 2906

Mitsuye Endo; Ex Parte, 801

Mobil Oil Corp. v. Commissioner of Taxes of
     Vermont, 2077

Mobil Oil Corp. v. Federal Power Commission
     (FPC), 1320

———; Gulf Offshore Co. v., 2284

——— v. Higginbotham, 1917

Mobil Oil Exploration & Producing Southeast, Inc. v.
     United Distribution Co., 3522

Mobile, Jackson and Kansas City Railroad Co. v.
     Turnipseed, 392

Moe v. Confederated Salish & Kootenai Tribes of
     Flathead Reservation, 1753

Moffitt; Ross v., 1651

Mohammed; Caban v., 1986

Mohasco Corp. v. Silver, 2135

Moitie; Federated Department Stores, Inc. v., 2253

Moline Properties, Inc. v. Commissioner of Internal
     Revenue, 771

Molzof, Personal Representative of the Estate of
     Molzof v. United States, 3640

Monell v. Department of Social Services of the City
     of New York, 1918

Monessen Southwestern Railway Co. v. Morgan,
     3254

Monfort of Colorado, Inc.; Cargill, Inc. v., 3066

"Monkey Law Case," 1346

Monroe v. Board of Commissioners of Jackson,
     Tennessee, 1331

——— v. Pape, 1091

——— v. Standard Oil Co., 2261

Monsanto; United States v., 3362

Monsanto Co.; Ruckelshaus v., 2727

——— v. Spray-Rite Service Corp., 2644

Montalvo-Murillo; United States v., 3464

Montana v. Blackfeet Tribe of Indians, 2853

———; Commonwealth Edison Co. v., 2287

———; Department of Commerce v., 3672

——— v. North Cheyenne Tribe, 2585

———; Sandstrom v., 2012

——— v. United States, 2200

———; United States Department of Commerce v.,
     3672

Montana Fish and Game Commission; Baldwin v.,
     1912

Montanye, Former Superintendent v. Haymes, 1779

Montgomery County Board of Education; Carr v.,
     1369

———; United States v., 1369

Montoya de Hernandez; United States v., 2903

Moody; Albemarle Paper Co. v., 1712

———; Halifax Local No. 425 v., 1712

Mooney v. Holohan, Warden, 630

Moore v. City of East Cleveland, Ohio, 1845

——— v. Dempsey, 499

———; Houston v., 76

———; Livingston v., 125

———; Missouri v., 305

Moore; St. Louis Brewing Association v., 463
Moorman Manufacturing Co. v. Bair, 1924
Moose Lodge, No. 107 v. Irvis, 1510
Mora v. McNamara, 1307
Moragne v. States Marine Lines, Inc., 1413
Morales; California Department of Corrections v., 3977
Morales, Attorney General of Texas v. Trans World Airlines, Inc., 3695
Moran v. Burbine, 2953
———; Godinez v., 3834
Morash; Massachusetts v., 3329
More; United States v., 42
Moreau v. Klevenhagen, Sheriff of Harris County, Texas, 3791
Morehead v. New York ex rel. Tipaldo, 653
Moreno; Toll v., 2415
———; United States Department of Agriculture (USDA) v., 1596
Morgan v. Illinois, 3706
———; Katzenbach v., 1262
———; Lewis Publishing Co. v., 414
———; Monessen Southwestern Railway Co. v., 3254
———; Morgan's Heirs v., 69
———; New York City Board of Elections v., 1262
——— v. Virginia, 830
Morgan Stanley and Co., Inc. v. Pacific Mutual Life Insurance Co., 3893
Morgan's Heirs v. Morgan, 69
Morissette v. United States, 918
Morris; Board of Estimate v., 3319
———; Fortson v., 1267
——— v. Mathews, 2945
———; New York City Board of Estimate v., 3319
———; Ponterio v., 3319
———; Wharton v., 4
Morris, Warden v. Slappy, 2500
Morrison v. California, 622
———; Kimmelman v., 3029
——— v. Olson, 3282
———; United States v., 2169
Morrison-Knudsen Construction Co. v. Director, Office of Workers' Compensation Programs, United States Department of Labor, 2523
Morse v. Republican Party of Virginia, 4035
Mortier; Wisconsin Public Intervenor v., 3611
Morton; Sierra Club v., 1492
———; United States v., 2720
Morton, Secretary of the Interior v. Mancari, 1649
——— v. Ruiz, 1622
Morton International, Inc.; Cardinal Chemical Co. v., 3795
Moses H. Cone Memorial Hospital v. Mercury Construction Corp., 2468

Moskal v. United States, 3516
Mosley; Michigan v., 1722
———; Police Department of Chicago v., 1524
Mossman v. Higginson, 28
Motor Vehicle Manufacturers Association of the United States, Inc. v. State Farm Mutual Automobile Insurance Co., 2569
Mott; Martin v., 100
Mottaz; United States v., 3006
Moulton; Maine v., 2918
Mount Ephraim; Schad v., 2241
Mountain States Telephone and Telegraph Co. v. Pueblo of Santa Ana, 2864
Mow Sun Wong; Hampton v., 1758
Mowder v. Pennsylvania, 767
Mt. Healthy City School District Board of Education v. Doyle, 1810
Mu'Min v. Virginia, 3581
Mueller v. Allen, 2581
Mugler v. Kansas, 257
Muhammad Ali v. United States, 1470
Mulcahy; Same v., 685
Mulkey; Reitman v., 1288
Mullane v. Central Hanover Bank and Trust Co., 894
Mullaney v. Wilbur, 1701
Muller v. Oregon, 377
Mullins; Kaiser Steel Corp. v., 2312
Multistate Tax Commission; United States Steel Corp. v., 1885
Mundt; Abate v., 1461
Municipal Court of San Francisco; Camara v., 1290
Municipality No. 1 of the City of New Orleans; Permoli v., 140
Muniz; Pennsylvania v., 3486
Munn v. Illinois, 200
Munoz; County of Imperial, California v., 2157
Munoz-Flores; United States v., 3451
Munro v. Socialist Workers Party, 3069
Munson; Secretary of State v., 2726
Murdock v. Pennsylvania, 767
———; United States v., 620
Murgia; Massachusetts Board of Retirement v., 1783
Murphy; Cupp v., 1576
——— v. Florida, 1704
——— v. Hunt, 2331
———; Minnesota v., 2634
——— v. Waterfront Commission of New York Harbor, 1192
Murray v. Carrier, 3032
——— v. Curlett, 1167, 1168
——— v. Giarratano, 3367
———; Smith v., 3033
———; Turner v., 2976
——— v. United States, 3280

———; United States Department of Agriculture v., 1595

Murry v. Schooner The Charming Betsy, 37

Musick, Peeler & Garrett v. Employers Insurance of Wausau, 3806

Muskrat v. United States, 395

Muth; Dellmuth v., 3354

Myers; Beltran v., 2231

———; Connick v., 2503

——— v. United States, 536

Myrick; Freightliner Corp. v., 3970

NAACP v. Alabama ex rel. Patterson, 1036

——— v. Button, 1137

——— v. Claiborne Hardware Co., 2441

——— v. Hampton County Election Commission, 2792

——— v. New York, 1590

NAACP Legal Defense & Educational Fund; Cornelius v., 2910

NASD; United States v., 1717

NASCO, Inc.; Chambers v., 3590

NFL; Radovich v., 1000

NRDC; American Iron and Steel Institute v., 2721

———; Baltimore Gas and Electric Co. v., 2534

———; Chemical Manufacturers Assn. v., 2791

———; Chevron U.S.A. Inc. v., 2721

———; Commonwealth of Edison Co. v., 2534

———; Environmental Protection Agency (EPA) v., 2721, 2791

———; United States Nuclear Regulatory Commission v., 2534

———; Vermont Yankee Nuclear Power Corp. v., 1900

Nachman Corp. v. Pension Benefit Guaranty Corp. , 2096

Nacirema Operating Co. v. Johnson, 1383

Naftalin; United States v., 1995

Nakshian; Lehman v., 2275

Nantahala Power & Light Co. v. Thornburg, 3012

Nardone v. United States, 674, 700

Nash; Carchman v., 2908

Nashville Banner Publishing Co.; McKennon v., 3948

Nashville Gas Co. v. Satty, 1878

Nashville, Chattanooga and St. Louis Railway v. Browning, 713

Nation Enterprises; Harper & Row v., 2847

National Association for the Advancement of Colored People (NAACP) v. Alabama ex rel. Patterson, 1036

——— v. Button, 1137

——— v. Claiborne Hardware Co., 2441

——— v. Hampton County Election Commission, 2792

——— v. New York, 1590

National Association for the Advancement of Colored People (NAACP), Legal Defense & Educational Fund; Cornelius v., 2910

National Association of Broadcasters v. Federal Communications Commission (FCC), 1919

——— v. WNCN Listeners Guild, 2201

National Association of Greeting Card Publishers v. United States Postal Service, 2562

National Association of Letter Carriers; United States Civil Service Commission, v., 1597

National Association of Radiation Survivors; Walters v., 2898

National Association of Securities Dealers, Inc. (NASD) v. Securities Exchange Commission (SEC), 1441

———; United States v., 1717

National Bank of Commerce; United States v., 2885

National Bellas Hess, Inc. v. Department of Revenue of Illinois, 1282

National Black Media Coalition v. Midwest Video Corp., 1976

National Black Police Association; Velde v., 2431

National Broadcasting Co., Inc. v. Federal Communications Commission (FCC), 2281

National Broiler Marketing Association v. United States, 1920

National Cable Television Association v. United States, 1625

National Carbide Corp. v. Commissioner of Internal Revenue, 883

National Casualty Co.; Federal Trade Commission (FTC) v., 1039

National Center for Immigrants' Rights, Inc.; Immigration and Naturalization Service (INS) v., 3634

National Citizens Committee for Broadcasting; American Newspaper Publishers Assn. v., 1919

———; Channel Two Television, Co. v., 1919

———; Illinois Broadcasting Co., Inc. v., 1919

———; Federal Communications Commission (FCC) v., 1919

———; Post Co. v., 1919

National Collegiate Athletic Association (NCAA) v. Board of Regents of the University of Oklahoma, 2733

——— v. Tarkanian, 3294

National Conservative Political Action Committee; Democratic Party of the United States v., 2802

National Conservative Political Action Committee; Federal Elections Commission (FEC) v., 2802

National Cotton Council of America v. Donovan, 2260

National Council of American-Soviet Friendship, Inc.v. McGrath, 911

National Crushed Stone Association; Environmental
    Protection Agency (EPA) v., 2158
National Democratic Party; Keane v., 1535
National Farmers Union Insurance Cos. v. Crow
    Tribe of Indians, 2856
National Federation of Blind, Inc.; Riley v., 3284
National Football League (NFL); Radovich v., 1000
National Gay Task Force; Board of Education v.,
    2817
National Gerimedical Hospital and Gerontology
    Center v. Blue Cross of Kansas City, 2252
National Labor Relations Board (NLRB); ABF
    Freight Systems, Inc. v., 3856
——— v. Action Automotive, Inc., 2782
——— v. Allis-Chalmers Manufacturing Co., 1297
——— v. Amax Coal Co., 2280
———; American Hospital Association v., 3559
———; American Shipbuilding Co. v., 1220
———; Associated Press Co. v., 665
——— v. Babcock and Wilcox Co., 986
——— v. Baptist Hospital, Inc., 2019
——— v. Bell Aerospace Co., Division of Textron,
    Inc., 1634
——— v. Bildisco and Bildisco, 2637
———; Bill Johnson's Restaurants, Inc. v., 2527
——— v. Burns International Security Services, Inc.,
    1497
——— v. Cabot Carbon Co., 1059
——— v. Catholic Bishop of Chicago, 1971
———; Central Hardware Co. v., 1520
National Labor Relations Board; Charles D. Bonanno
    Linen Service Inc. v., 2304
——— v. City Disposal Systems,Inc., 2649
———; Consolidated Edison Co. v., 687
——— v. Curtin Matheson Scientific, Inc., 3432
———; Detroit Edison, Co. v., 1964
———; Edward J. DeBartolo Corp. v., 2573
——— v. Enterprise Association of Steam, Hot
    Water, Hydraulic Sprinkler, Pneumatic Tube,
    Ice Machine and General Pipefitters of New
    York and Vicinity, Local Union No. 638, 1815
——— v. Erie Resistor Corp., 1154
———; Fall River Dyeing and Finishing Corp. v.,
    3154
———; Fibreboard Paper Products Corp. v., 1207
——— v. Financial Institution Employees, Local
    1182, 2943
———; First National Maintenance Corp. v., 2266
———; Ford Motor Co. v., 1991
——— v. Friedman-Harry Marks Clothing Co., Inc.,
    664
——— v. Fruehauf Trailer Co., 663
——— v. Fruit and Vegetable Packers and
    Warehousemen, Local 760, 1183
——— v. Gissel Packing Co.,1377

——— v. Great Dane Trailers, Inc., 1294
——— v. Health Care & Retirement Corp., 3890
——— v. Hearst Publications, Inc., 790
——— v. Hendricks County Rural Electric
    Membership Corp., 2296
———; Hendricks County Rural Electric
    Membership Corp. v., 2296
———; Hudgens v., 1733
——— v. Insurance Agents International Union,
    1065
———; International Brotherhood of Electrical
    Workers v., 687
——— v. International Brotherhood of Electrical
    Workers, Local 340, 3139
——— v. International Longshoremen's Association,
    AFL-CIO, 2124, 2891
———; J.I. Case Co. v., 783
——— v. J. Weingarten, Inc., 1682
——— v. Jones and Laughlin SteelCo., 662
———; Lechmere v., 3648
———; Linden Lumber Div. Summer & Co. v.,
    1671
———; Litton Financial Printing Divison v., 3598
———; Local 408, International Brotherhood of
    Teamsters v., 2637
——— v. Mackay Radio and Telegraph Co., 684
———; Metropolitan Edison Co. v., 2492
———; National Licorice Co. v., 708
———; National Woodwork Manufacturer's Assn
    v., 1280
———; Oregon-Columbia Chapter, Associated
    General Contractors of America v., 2371
———; Pacific Northwest Chapter of the Associated
    Builders and Contractors Inc. v., 2371
———; Pattern Makers v., 2892
———; Ranco, Inc. v., 986
——— v. Retail Store Employees Union, Local
    1001, 2127
——— v. Seamprufe, Inc., 986
———; Shepard v., 2457
———; Sinclair Co. v., 1377
——— v. Stockholders Publishing Co., 790
———; Sure-Tan, Inc. v. , 2723
——— v. Times-Mirror Co., 790
——— v. Town & Country Electric, Inc., 4021
——— v. Transportation Management Corp., 2546
——— v. Truck Drivers Local Union, No. 449, 1002
——— v. Truck Drivers Union, Local 413, 1671
——— v. United Food & Commercial Workers
    Union, Local 23, 3217
———; United Mine Workers of American v., 2280
———; United Steelworkers of America v., 895
———; Universal Camera Corp. v., 907
———; Washington, Virginia and Maryland Coach
    Co. v., 666

———; Woelke & Romero Framing Inc. v., 2371

——— v. Wyman-Gordon Co., 1367

——— v. Yeshiva University, 2059

National Labor Review Board v. Western Addition Community Organization, 1678

National League; Federal Baseball Club of Baltimore, Inc. v., 487

National League of Cities v. Usery, 1771

National Licorice Co. v. National Labor Relations Board, 708

National Muffler Dealers Association, Inc. v. United States, 1970

National Organization of Women (NOW) v. Idaho, 2467

——— v. Scheidler, 3854

National Private Truck Council, Inc. v. Oklahoma Tax Commission,4011

"National Prohibition Cases," 463

National Railroad Passenger Corp. v. Atchison, Topeka & Santa Fe Railway Co., 2801

——— v. Boston and Maine Corp., 3670

———; Lebron, 3950

National Republican Senatorial Committee v. Democratic Senatorial Campaign Committee, 2291

National Rifle Association Political Victory Fund; Federal Elections Commission (FEC) v., 3936

National Right to Work Committee; Federal Elections Commission (FEC) v., 2453

National Sea Clammers Association; City of New York v., 2271

———; Environmental Protection Agency (EPA) v., 2271

———; Joint Meeting of Essex and Union Counties v., 2271

———; Middlesex County Sewerage Authority v., 2271

National Securities, Inc.; Securities Exchange Commission (SEC) v., 1352

National Socialist Party of America v. Village of Skokie, 1854

National Society of Professional Engineers v. United States, 1903

National Solid Wastes Management Association; Gade v., 3712

National Treasury Employees Union; United States v., 3953

——— v. William Von Raab, 3318

National Wholesale Grocers Association v. Swift and Co., 604

National Wildlife Federation; Lujan v., 3509

National Woodwork Manufacturers Association v. National Labor Relations Board, 1280

Nationalist Movement; Forsyth County v., 3713

NationsBank of North Carolina, N.A. v. Variable Annuity Life Insurance Co. (VALIC), 3945

Nationwide Mutual Insurance Co. v. Darden, 3665

"Native American Citizenship Case," 238

Natural Carbonic Gas Co.; Lindsley v., 397

Natural Gas Pipeline Co.; Federal Power Commission (FPC) v., 745

Natural Resource Defense Council (NRDC); American Iron and Steel Institute v., 2721

———; Baltimore Gas and Electric Co. v., 2534

———; Chemical Manufacturers Assn. v., 2791

———; Chevron U.S.A. Inc. v., 2721

———; Commonwealth of Edison Co. v., 2534

———; Environmental Protection Agency v., 2721, 2791

———; United States Nuclear Regulatory Commission v., 2534

———; Vermont Yankee Nuclear Power Corp. v., 1900

Naughton; Cupp v., 1607

Navajo Freight Lines, Inc.; Bibb v., 1054

Navajo Tribe; Kerr-McGee Corp. v., 2830

"Nazi Saboteurs Cases," 757

Neagle; Cunningham v., 269

Neagle; In re, 269

Neal; Block v., 2478

——— v. Delaware, 223

Near v. Minnesota ex rel. Olsen, 595

Nebbia v. New York, 624

Nebraska; Boyd v., 281

———; Meyer v., 505

———; Olsen v., 735

———; Victor v., 3868

——— v. Wyoming, 3780, 3990

Nebraska ex rel. Douglas; Sporhase v., 2442

Nebraska Department of Revenue v. Loewenstein, 3939

Nebraska District of Evangelical Lutheran Synod v. McKelvie, 506

Nebraska Press Association v. Stuart, 1791

Nectow v. City of Cambridge, 564

Negonsott v. Samuels, Warden, 3761

Negre v. Larsen, 1436, 1437

Neil, Warden v. Biggers, 1538

Neill; American Oil Co. v., 1223

Neilson; Foster v., 111

Nelson; Barnett Bank v., 4033

———; Jean v., 2888

———; Lockhart v., 3291

———; Pennsylvania v., 983

———; Saudi Arabia v., 3771

Nelson, Warden v. O'Neil, 1455

Nestor; Flemming v., 1081

Neubauer, Ex Parte, 757

Neuberger v. United States, 532

Nevada; Powell v., 3870
——; Riggins v., 3685
—— v. United States, 2572
Neville; South Dakota v., 2466
New; Wilson v., 437
New Banner Institute, Inc.; Dickerson v., 2471
New Energy Co. of Indiana v. Limbach, 3253
New England Power Co.; Federal Power Commission
    (FPC) v., 1626
—— v. New Hampshire, 2323
New Hampshire; Chaplinsky v., 744
——; Coolidge v., 1466
——; Cox v., 732
——; Massachusetts v., 2323
——; New England Power Co. v., 2323
——; Pierce v., 141
——; Poulos v., 942
——; Roberts v., 2323
——; Sweezy v., 1011
New Hampshire Department of Employment
    Security; White v., 2329
New Jersey; Bell v., 2529
——; Bennett v., 2807
——; Corbitt v., 1949
——; Garrity v., 1270
——; New York v., 473
—— v. Palmer, 463
——; Philadelphia v., 1929
—— v. Portash, 1969
——; Schneider v., 697
—— v. T.L.O., 2777
——; Twining v., 385
New Jersey; United States Trust Co. of New York v.,
    1837
—— v. Wilson, 56
New Jersey Department of Environmental Protection;
    Midlantic Protection v., 2934
——; O'Neill v., 2934
New Mexico; Colorado v., 2452, 2699
—— v. Federal Power Commission (FPC), 1320
——; Fugate v., 2818
——; Kleppe v., 1765
—— v. Mescalero Apache Tribe, 2542
——; Oklahoma v., 3599
——; Texas v., 2552, 3158
——; United States v., 1944, 2344
New Mexico Board of Examiners of Optometry;
    Head v., 1171
New Orleans; Davidson v., 208
—— v. Dukes, dba Louisiana Concessions, 1782
—— v. Winter, 65
New Orleans and Carrollton Railroad Co. v. Earle,
    131
New State Ice Co. v. Liebmann, 600
New York; Baldwin v., 1415

—— v. Belton, 2283
——; Berger v., 1295
—— v. Bernard Harris, 3438
——; Bove v., 853
——; Bowen v., 2993
—— v. Burger, 3179
—— v. Central Railroad Co., 181
—— v. Class, 2940
——; Cruz v., 3123
——; Delaware v., 3776
——; Dunaway v., 2003
——; Fay v., 853
——; Feiner v., 903
—— v. Ferber, 2437
——; Ginsberg v., 1317
——; Gitlow v., 529
——; Graves v., 690
——; Harris v., 1430
——; Hernandez v., 3578
——; Kunz v., 902
——; Lanza v., 1129
——; Lo-Ji Sales, Inc. v., 2007
——; Lochner v., 363
—— v. Miln, 127
——; Mishkin v., 1247
——; National Association for the Advancement
    of Colored People (NAACP) v., 1590
——; Nebbia v., 624
—— v. New Jersey, 473
——; New York State Club Association v., 3267
—— v. Oneida Indian Nation of New York, 2795
—— v. P.J. Video, Inc., 2972
——; Patterson v., 1857
New York; Payton v., 2083
——; Peters v., 1337
—— v. Quarles, 2714
——; Railway Express Agency v., 880
——; Redrup v., 1283
——; Regan v., 969
——; Riddick v., 2083
——; Saia v., 874
——; Sibron v., 1337
——; Spano v., 1060
——; Street v., 1365
—— v. United States, 820, 3714
—— v. Uplinger, 2697
——; Vignera v., 1260
——; Williams v., 887
"New York II," 3714
New York ex rel. Bryant v. Zimmerman, 569
New York ex rel. O'Keefe; Graves v., 690
New York ex rel. Ray v. Martin, 818
New York ex rel. Tipaldo; Morehead v., 653
New York Central Railroad Co. v. White, 435
New York City Board of Elections v. Morgan, 1262

New York City Board of Estimate v. Morris, 3319
New York City; Penn Central Transportation v., 1933
New York City Transit Authority v. Beazer, 1973
New York Gaslight Club, Inc. v. Carey, 2110
New York Mercantile Exchange v. Leist, 2360
"New York Mineral Waters Case," 820
New York State ex rel. Kennedy v. Becker, 432
New York State Club Association v. New York, 3267
New York State Conference of Blue Cross & Blue
    Shield Plans v. Travelers Insurance Co., 3980
New York State Crime Victims Board; Simon &
    Schuster v., 3630
New York State Department of Labor; New York
    Telephone Co. v., 1972
New York State Liquor Authority v. Bellanca, DBA
    The Main Event, 2269
———; Brown-Forman Distillers Corp. v., 2998
New York State on Relation of Kennedy v. Becker,
    432
New York Stock Exchange; Silver v., 1157
New York Yankees; Toolson v., 949
New York Telephone Co. v. New York Department
    of Labor, 1972
New York Times Co. v. Sullivan, 1179
——— v. United States, 1471
New Yorker Magazine; Masson v., 3608
Newark Morning Ledger Co. v. United States, 3779
Newman v. Piggie Park Enterprises, Inc., 1314
Newport News Shipbuilding and Dry Dock Co.;
    Director, Office of Workers' Compensation
    Programs v., 3964
——— v. Equal Employment Opportunity
    Commission (EEOC), 2558
Ngiraingas v. Sanchez, 3444
Niagara Frontier Tariff Bureau, Inc.; Square D Co. v.,
    2990
Nichols; Lau v., 1615
——— v. Massachusetts, 697
——— v. United States, 3896
———; United States v., 231
Nicklos Drilling Co.; Cowart v., 3722
Niemotko v. Maryland, 901
Nishikawa v. Dulles, Secretary of State, 1026
Nix v. Hedden, 292
——— v. Whiteside, 2942
Nix, Warden of the Iowa State Penitentiary v.
    Williams, 2704
Nixon v. Administrator of General Services, 1874
——— v. Condon, 603
——— v. Fitzgerald, 2408
——— v. Herndon, 547
——— v. United States, 1667, 3747
———; United States v., 1667
"Nixon I," 547
"Nixon II," 603

"Nixon Tape Case," 1667
Noatak; Blatchford v., 3616
Nobelman v. American Savings Bank, 3808
Noble State Bank v. Haskell, 393
Nobles v. Georgia, 326
———; United States v., 1709
Noerr Motor Freight, Inc.; Eastern Railroad
    Presidents Conference v., 1090
Noia; Fay v., 1147
Nolde Brothers, Inc. v. Local No. 358, Bakery &
    Confectionary Workers Union, AFL-CIO, 1823
Nollan v. California Coastal Commission, 3209
Nordberg; Granfinanciera v., 3368
Nordic Village, Inc.; United States v., 3650
Nordlinger v. Hahn, 3709
Norfolk and Western Railway Co. v. American Train
    Dispatchers Association, 3541
——— v. Goode, 3383
——— v. Liepelt, 2051
Norfolk Redevelopment and Housing Authority v.
    Chesapeake & Potomac Telephone Co. of
    Virginia, 2603
Norge Division of Magic Chef, Inc.; Lingle v., 3256
Norman v. Baltimore and Ohio Railroad Co., 631
——— v. Reed, 3639
Norman Williams Co.; Bohemian Distributing Co. v.,
    2434
———; Rice v., 2434
———; Wine and Spirits Wholesalers of California
    v., 2434
Normet; Lindsey v., 1481
Norris v. Alabama, 634
———; Arizona Governing Committee for Tax
    Deferred Annuity and Deferred Compensation
    Plans v., 2599
——— v. Boston, 144
———; Finazzo v., 3912
———; Hawaiian Airlines, Inc. v., 3912
North v. Russell, 1784
North American Oil Consolidated v. Burnet,
    Commissioner of Internal Revenue, 605
North Carolina v. Alford, 1419
———; Bumper v., 1334
———; Howard v., 353
———; Klopfer v., 1276
———; McKoy v., 3420
———; Parker v., 1407
——— v. Pearce, 1379
———; Woodson v., 1798
North Carolina Department of Transportation v. Crest
    Street Community Council, Inc., 3062
North Carolina Life and Accident and Health
    Insurance Guaranty Association; Underwriters
    National Assurance Co. v., 2343

North Carolina Prisoners' Labor Union, Inc.; Jones
  v., 1866
North Carolina State Board of Education v. Swann,
  1447
North Cheyenne Tribe; Montana v., 2585
North Dakota; Block v., 2508
———; Quill Corp. v., 3692
——— v. United States, 2479, 3453
North Haven Board of Education v. Bell, Secretary of
  Education, 2366
North Las Vegas; Blanton v., 3316
North Star Steel Co. v. Thomas, 3991
Northampton County Board of Election; Lassiter v.,
  1056
Northbrook National Insurance Co. v. Brewer, 3380
Northcross v. Board of Education of the Memphis
  City Schools, 1396, 1577
——— v. Memphis Board of Education, 1577
Northeast Bancorp, Inc. v. Board of Governors of the
  Federal Reserve System, 2862
Northeast Marine Terminal Co., Inc. v. Caputo, 1858
Northeastern Florida Chapter of the Associated
  General Contractors of America v. City of
  Jacksonville, Florida, 3821
Northern Pacific Railroad Co. v. Herbert, 246
——— v. United States, 1021
Northern Pipeline Construction Co. v. Marathon Pipe
  Line Co., 2416
Northern Securities Co. v. United States, 355
Northwest Airlines, Inc. v. County of Kent,
  Michigan, 3858
——— v. Transport Workers Union of America,
  AFL-CIO, 2209
Northwest Indian Cemetery Protective Association;
  Lyng v., 3239
Northwest Wholesale Stationers, Inc. v. Pacific
  Stationery & Printing Co., 2865
Northwestern Bell Telephone Co.; H.J. Inc. v., 3372
Northwestern Fertilizer Co. v. Hyde Park, 211
Norton v. Warner, Co., 785
Norton Co. v. Department of Revenue of Illinois, 908
Nortz v. United States, 632
Norwest Bank of Worthington v. Ahlers, 3231
Norwick; Ambach v., 1978
Norwood v. Harrison, 1593
Norwood's Lessee; Owings v., 50
Novotny; Great American Savings and Loan
  Association v., 2010
Noyes v. Rock Royal Co-operative, Inc., 695
Nunez; Colorado v., 2630
Nunn v. United States, 438
Nunnemaker; Ylst v., 3617
Nutt; Cornelius, Acting Director, Office of Personnel
  Management v., 2882

Nyquist v. Committee for Public Education and
  Religious Liberty, 1603
———; Committee for Public Education &
  Religious Liberty v., 1603
———; Committee for Public Education v., 1603
——— v. Mauclet, 1853

OPM; Lindahl v., 2812
Oakes; Massachusetts v., 3361
O'Bannon v. Town Court Nursing Center, 2134
Oberg; Honda Motor Co. v., 3917
O'Brien v. Brown, 1535
———; United States v., 1326
———; Webb v., 511
Ocala Star-Banner Co. v. Damron, 1432
O'Callahan v. Parker, Warden, 1372
Occupational Safety and Health Review
  Commission; Atlas Roofing Co., Inc. v., 1829
———; Fred Irey, Jr., Inc. v., 1829
———; Martin v., 3542
Oceanic Contractors, Inc.; Griffin v., 2430
O'Connor v. Consolidated Coin Caterers Corp., 4036
——— v. Donaldson, 1715
——— v. Ortega, 3114
——— v. United States, 3063
Odegaard; DeFunis v., 1635
O'Dell v. Espinoza, 2362
Office of Disciplinary Counsel; Zauderer v., 2849
Office of Personnel Management v. Richmond, 3480
Offshore Logistics, Inc. v. Tallentire, 3023
Ogden; Gibbons v., 88
——— v. Saunders, 101
Ohio v. Akron Center for Reproductive Health, 3502
———; Bell v., 1942
Ohio; Bohning v., 506
———; Brandenburg v., 1375
———; Crampton v., 1451
———; Doyle v., 1767
———; Flynt v., 2230
———; Jacobellis v., 1196
——— v. Johnson, 2707
——— v. Kovacs, DBA B & W Enterprises, 2774
———; Lockett v., 1941
———; Mapp v., 1110
———; Martin v., 3098
———; Osborne v., 3442
———; Pohl v., 506
———; Powers v., 3551
——— v. Roberts, 2138
———; Terry v., 1336
———; Tumey v., 546
———; United States Department of Energy v., 3679
———; Wood v., 1767
Ohio ex rel. Eaton v. Price, 1083

Ohio Civil Rights Commission v. Dayton Christian Schools, Inc., 3037

Ohio Elections Commission; McIntyre v., 3973

Ohio Power Co.; Arcadia v., 3514

Ohio State Bar Association; Ohralik v., 1914

Ohralik v. Ohio State Bar Association, 1914

Ojeda Rios; United States v., 3446

Okanogan Indians v. United States, 573

Okely; Bank of Columbia v., 73

Oklahoma; Ake v., 2789

———; Arkansas v., 3654

———; Broadrick v., 1598

——— v. Castleberry, 2827

——— v. City of New York, 4032

———; Eddings v., 2314

———; Environmental Protection Agency (EPA) v., 3654

———; Hughes v., 1984

———; Lyons v., 793

——— v. New Mexico, 3599

———; Romano v., 3901

———; Ross v., 3269

———; Skinner v., 755

———; Thompson v., 3285

——— v. United States Civil Service Commission, 841

———; Wyoming v., 3645

Oklahoma ex rel. Williamson; Skinner v., 755

Oklahoma Publishing Co. v. District Court in and for Oklahoma County, Oklahoma, 1825

Oklahoma State Regents; McLaurin v., 897

Oklahoma Tax Commission; Burlington Northern Railroad v., 3133

——— v. Chickasaw Nation, 4006

——— v. Citizen Band Potawatomi Indian Tribe of Oklahoma, 3535

——— v. Jefferson Lines, Inc., 3967

———; National Private Truck Council, Inc. v., 4011

——— v. Sac and Fox Nation, 3797

Olano; United States v., 3785

Old Dearborn Distributing Co. v. Seagram Distillers Corp., 655

Old Dominion Branch, No. 496, National Association of Letter Carriers, AFL-CIO v. Austin, 1660

Old Dominion Steamship Co. v. Gilmore, 372

Olden v. Kentucky, 3295

Olim v. Wakinekona, 2506

Oliphant v. Suquamish Indian Tribe, 1889

Oliver; Albright v., 3855

Oliver; In re, 866

——— v. United States, 2659

Oliver Iron Mining Co. v. Lord, 502

Olmstead v. United States, 567

O'Lone v. Estate of Shabazz, 3165

Olsen v. Nebraska ex rel. Western Reference and Bond Association, Inc., 735

Olson; Minnesota v., 3441

———; Morrison v., 3282

O'Melveny & Myers v. Federal Deposit Insurance Co. (FDIC), 3905

Omni Outdoor Advertising, Inc.; Columbia v., 3550

On Lee v. United States, 932

One 1958 Plymouth Sedan v. Pennsylvania, 1227

One Assortment of 89 Firearms; United States v., 2632

One Lot Emerald Cut Stones and One Ring v. United States, 1540

Oneida Indian Nation; County of Oneida v., 2795

Oneida Indian Nation of New York v. County of Oneida, 1618

———; New York v., 2795

O'Neal v. McAninch, Warden, 3952

O'Neil; Nelson v., 1455

——— v. Vermont, 284

O'Neill; Air Line Pilots Association (ALPA) v., 3539

——— v. City of New York, 2934

——— v. New Jersey Department of Environmental Protection, 2934

——— v. Synar, 3058

Opelika; Jones v., 756

"Operation Sunshine," 4031

Opp Cotton Mills v. Administrator of Wage and Hour Division of Department of Labor, 726

Opperman; South Dakota v., 1800

Oradell; Hynes v., 1754

Orbeck; Hicklin v., 1927

Oregon; Apodaca v., 1500

——— v. Bradshaw, 2567

———; Bunting v., 439

———; DeJonge v., 657

——— v. Elstad, 2797

———; Federal Power Commission v., 976

——— v. Hass, 1688

———; Idaho ex rel. v., 2566

——— v. Kennedy, 2372

———; Lakeside v., 1895

——— v. Mathiason, 1814

——— v. Mitchell, 1421

———; Muller v., 377

"Oregon Case," 528

Oregon-Columbia Chapter, Associated General Contractors of America v. National Labor Relations Board (NLRB), 2371

Oregon Department of Fish and Wildlife v. Klamath Indian Tribe, 2909

Oregon-Washington Carpenters Employers Pension Trust Fund v. R.A. Gray & Co., 2716

Oregon Waste Systems, Inc. v. Department of Environmental Quality of the State of Oregon, 3871
Organ; Laidlaw v., 68
Organization for a Better Austin v. Keefe, 1452
Oritz; United States v., 1720
Orozco v. Texas, 1359
Orr v. Orr, 1963
———; Orr v., 1963
Ortega; O'Connor v., 3114
———; United States v., 99
Ortega-Rodriguez v. United States, 3768
Ortwein v. Schwab, 1557
Osborn v. President, Directors and Co. of the Bank of United States, 91
Osborne v. Ohio, 3442
Oscar Mayer and Co. v. Evans, 1994
Osceola; The, 350
O'Shea v. Littleton, 1614
Oswald; Respublica v., 9
Otis R. Bowen, Secretary of Health and Human Services v. Chan Kendrick, 3281
Ouellette; International Paper Co. v., 3083
Overholser; Lynch v., 1127
Owen v. City of Independence, Missouri, 2084
——— v. Owen, 3575
———; Owen v., 3575
Owen Equipment and Erection Co. v. Kroger, 1926
Owens; Bowen v., 2987
———; United States v., 3226
Owings v. Norwood's Lessee, 50
——— v. Speed, 81
Oyama v. California, 857
Oyler v. Boles, Warden, 1118
Oxford House; Edmonds v., 3984
Ozawa v. United States, 493

P.C. Pfeiffer Co., Inc. v. Ford, 2038
P.J. Video, Inc.; New York v., 2972
PUD No. 1 of Jefferson County & City of Tacoma v. Washington Department of Ecology, 3895
Pabst Brewing Co.; United States v., 1261
Pace v. Alabama, 228
Pachtman; Imbler v., 1731
Pacific and Arctic Railway; United States v., 413
Pacific Legal Foundation; Costle v., 2069
Pacific Gas and Electric Co. v. Public Utilities Commission, 2936
——— v. Skelly Oil Co., 1320
——— v. State Energy Resources Conservation and Development Commission, 2505
Pacific Mutual Insurance Co. v. Haslip, 3538
Pacific Mutual Life Insurance Co.; Morgan Stanley and Co., Inc. v., 3893

Pacific Northwest Chapter of the Associated Builders and Contractors Inc. v. National Labor Relations Board (NLRB), 2371
Pacific Stationery; Northwest Stationers v., 2865
Pacific Westbound Conference; Carnation Co. v., 1243
Pacifica Foundation; Federal Communications Commission (FCC) v., 1601
Padilla; United States v., 3794
Page, Excecutor of Miller v. United States, 180
Painter; Sweatt v., 896
Palko v. Connecticut, 673
Pallas Shipping Agency, Ltd. v. Duris, 2519
Palmer; Hudson v., 2746
———; New Jersey v., 463
———; Rhode Island v., 463
——— v. Thompson, Mayor, 1462
———; United States v., 71
Palmigiano; Baxter v., 1749
Palmore v. Sidoti, 2671
——— v. United States, 1566
Panama Refining Co. v. Ryan, 627
Pangilinan; Immigration and Naturalization Service (INS) v., 3266
Papachristou v. City of Jacksonville, 1482
Papasan v. Allain, Governor of Mississippi, 3044
Pape; Monroe v., 1091
———; Time, Inc. v., 1431
Papish v. Board of Curators of the University of Missouri, 1558
Pappas; In re, 1533
Paquete Habana; The, 336
Paradise; United States v., 3096
Paralyzed Veterans of America; Department of Transportation v., 3036
Paramount Pictures, Inc.; United States v., 870
A Parcel of Land; United States v., 3762
Parden v. Terminal Railway of Alabama State Docks Department, 1184
Parham v. Cortese, 1507
——— v. Hughes, 1985
——— v. J.R., a minor, 2014
———; Woodruff v., 174
Paris Adult Theatre I v. Slaton, 1585
Park; United States v., 1700
Park 'N Fly, Inc. v. Dollar Park and Fly, Inc., 2769
Parke, Davis and Co.; United States v., 1068
Parke, Warden v. Raley, 3736
Parker; Atkins v., 2861
———; Berman v., 961
——— v. Block, 2861
———; Crown, Cork & Seal Co., Inc. v., 2543
——— v. Davis, 182
——— v. Dugger, Secretary, Florida Department of Corrections, 3527

———— v. Ellis, 1074

———— v. North Carolina, 1407

————; O'Callahan v., 1372

———— v. Randolph, 1999

Parker, Acting Commissioner of Patents and Trademarks v. Flook, 1928

Parker, Director of Agriculture v. Brown, 759

Parker, Warden v. Levy, 1652

Parklane Hosiery Co., Inc. v. Shore, 1951

Parks; Saffle v., 3422

———— v. United States, 1268

Parma Board of Education v. Donnelly, 2803

Parr v. United States, 1075

Parratt v. Taylor, 2226

Parrish; West Coast Hotel Co. v., 658

Parsons Steel, Inc. v. First Alabama Bank, 2935

Pasadena City Board of Education v. Spangler, 1787

"Passenger Cases," 144

Passman; Davis v., 2004

Pastore; Tiverton Board of License Commissioners v., 2771

Pataki v. Travelers Insurance Co., 3980

Pate; Cooper v., 1202

Patrick v. Burget, 3250

Patsy v. Board of Regents of the State of Florida, 2400

Pattern Makers' League of North America, AFL-CIO v. National Labor Relations Board (NLRB), 2892

Patterson v. Alabama, 606

————; American Tobacco Co. v., 2349

————; Bunton v., 1355

———— v. Colorado ex rel. Attorney General of Colorado, 369

————; Fairley v., 1355

———— v. Illinois, 3273

———— v. McLean Credit Union, 3353

———— v. New York, 1857

Patterson, Trustee v. Shumate, 3707

Patton v. United States, 577

———— v. Yount, 2728

Paty; McDaniel v., 1902

Paul v. Davis, 1738

————; Florida Lime and Avocado Growers, Inc. v., 1152

————; Lawrence v., 202

————; Rodgers v., 1238

———— v. Virginia, 175

Paul S. Davis v. Michigan Department of Treasury, 3323

Paula A. Hobbie v. Unemployment Appeals Commission of Florida and Lawton & Co., 3095

Pauley, Survivor of Pauley v. BethEnergy Mines, Inc., 3614

Paulsen et ux. v. Commissioner of Internal Revenue, 2767

Paulussen v. Herion, 2957

Pavelic and LeFlore v. Marvel Entertainment Group, Division of Cadence Industries Corp., 3387

Pawlet v. Clark, 64

"Pawtucket, R.I. Crèche Case," 2642

Payne; Houghton v., 356

————; Lyng v., 3011

———— v. Tennessee, 3618

Payner; United States v., 2132

Payton v. New York, 2083

Pearce; North Carolina v., 1379

Pearson; Kidd v., 260

Peck; Fletcher v., 51

Peel v. Attorney Registration and Disciplinary Commission of Illinois, 3469

Peik v. Chicago and Northwestern Railway Co., 202

Pell v. Procunier, Director, California Department of Corrections, 1653

Peltier; United States v., 1714

Pembaur v. City of Cincinnati, 2954

Pena; Adarand Constructors v., 3997

Penick; Columbus Board of Education v., 2031

Penn Central Transporation Co. v. New York City, 1933

Penn Security Life Insurance Co.; United States v., 1834

Penn Shipping Co.; Donovan v., 1818

Pennekamp v. Florida, 829

Pennell v. City of San Jose, 3227

Pennhurst Parents-Staff Assocation v. Halderman, 2207

Pennhurst State School and Hospital v. Halderman, 2207, 2624

————; Pennsylvania Association for Retarded Citizens v., 2297

Pennsylvania; Bechtel Power Corp. v., 2425

————; Blystone v., 3415

————; Codispoti v., 1664

————; Contractors Association of Eastern Pennsylvania v., 2425

———— v. Delaware Valley Citizens' Council for Clean Air, 3051, 3206

————; DiSanto v., 541

———— v. Finley, 3138

————; General Building Contractors Association, Inc. v., 2425

————; Glasgow, Inc. v., 2425

————; Lamborn v., 767

————; McKeiver v., 1467

————; McMillan v., 3018

————; Maltezos v., 767

————; Mowder v., 767

———— v. Muniz, 3486

Pennsylvania; Murdock v., 767
——— v. Nelson, 983
———; One 1958 Plymouth Sedan v., 1227
———; Perisich v., 767
———; Philadelphia and Reading Railroad Co. v.,
    188
———; Plymouth Coal v., 417
———; Powell v., 259
———; Prigg v., 136
——— v. Ritchie, 3091
———; Seders v., 767
———; Smalis v., 2979
———; Sun Ship, Inc. v., 2131
———; Twitchell v., 170
———; Tzanes v., 767
——— v. Union Gas Co., 3349
———; United Engineers and Constructors v., 2425
——— v. Wheeling and Belmont Bridge Co., 149
Pennsylvania Association for Retarded Citizens v.
    Pennhurst State School and Hospital, 2297
Pennsylvania Bureau of Correction v. United States
    Marshals Service, 2911
Pennsylvania Coal Co. v. Mahon, 498
Pennsylvania Company for Insurance on Lives and
    Granting Annuities; American Construction Co.
    v., 289
Pennsylvania Department of Public Welfare v.
    Davenport, 3458
Pennsylvania Railroad Co.; Georgia v., 806
Pennzoil Co. v. Texaco, Inc., 3115
Penry v. Lynaugh, 3374
Pensacola Telegraph Co. v. Western Union
    Telegraph Co., 207
Pension Benefit Guaranty Corp.; Connolly v., 2944
    ——— v. LTV Corp., 3488
———; Nachman Corp. v., 2096
——— v. R.A. Gray & Co., 2716
———; Woodward Sand Co., Inc. v., 2944
——— v. Yahn & McDonnnell, Inc., 3146
"Pentagon Papers," 1532
"Pentagon Papers Case," 1471
People Against Nuclear Energy (PANE);
    Metropolitan Edison Co. v., 2497
———; United States Nuclear Regulatory
    Commission v., 2497
Pepper v. Litton, 699
Percheman; United States v., 122
Peretz v. United States, 3620
Perez v. Brownell, 1024
——— v. United States, 1450
———; United States v., 90
Perfetto; Rowoldt v., 1018
Perini North Rivers Associates; Director, Office of
    Workers' Compensation Programs, United
    States Department of Labor v., 2456

Perisich v. Pennsylvania, 767
Perkins; Illinois v., 3474
——— v. Matthews, Mayor, 1423
Perma Life Mufflers, Inc. v. International Parts
    Corp., 1339
"Permian Basin Area Rate Cases," 1320
Permoli v. Municipality No. 1 of the City of New
    Orleans, 140
Perpich v. Department of Defense, 3477
Perry; Blackledge v., 1643
——— v. Louisiana, 3511
——— v. Sindermann, 1531
——— v. Thomas, 3172
——— v. United States, 633
Perry Education Association v. Perry Local
    Educators' Association, 2469
Perry Local Educators' Assocation; Perry Education
    Association v., 2469
Personnel Administrator of Massachusetts v. Feeney,
    2005
Peru; Ex Parte, 766
Pervear v. Commonwealth of Massachusetts, 168
Peter v. United States, 1218
Peterhoff; The, 167
Peters v. Hobby, 974
——— v. New York, 1337
———; United States v., 47
———; Wheaton v., 126
Peterson v. City of Greenville, 1155
Petty Motors Co.; United States v., 824
Pfeifer; Jones and Laughlin Steel Corp. v., 2551
Pfister; Dombrowski v., 1224
Pfizer, Inc. v. Government of India, 1880
——— v. India, 1880
Philadelphia v. New Jersey, 1929
Philadelphia Gear Corp.; Federal Deposit Insurance
    Corporation (FDIC) v., 2991
Philadelphia National Bank; United States v., 1169
Philadelphia Newspapers, Inc. v. Hepps, 2967
Philadelphia and Reading Railroad Co. v.
    Pennsylvania, 188
Philbrook; Ansonia Board of Education v., 3065
Philko Aviation, Inc. v. Shacket et ux., 2547
Phillips v. Martin Marietta Corp., 1425
———; Smith v., 2318
Phillips Petroleum Co. v. Mississippi, 3224
——— v. Shutts, 2887
Phinpathya; Immigration and Naturalization Service
    v., 2610
Phyle v. Duffy, Warden, 873
Pickering v. Board of Education of Township High
    School District 205, Will County, Illinois, 1335
Pickett v. Brown, 2530
Pico; Board of Education Island Trees Union Free
    School District No. 26 v., 2411

Pierce v. Hill Military Academy , 528
——— v. New Hampshire, 141
——— v. Society of Sisters of Holy Names of Jesus
    and Mary, 528
——— v. United States, 458
Pierce County; Brock v., 2984
Pierson v. Ray, 1279
Piggie Park Enterprises, Inc.; Newman v., 1314
Pike v. Bruce Church, Inc., 1393
Pillsbury Co. v. Conboy, 2455
Pilot Life Insurance Co. v. Everate W. Dedeaux,
    3117
Pinette; Capital Square Review and Advisory Board
    v., 4017
Pinhas; Summit Health, Ltd. v., 3576
Pink; United States v., 743
Pinter v. Dahl, 3261
Pioneer Investment Services Co. v. Brunswick
    Associates Limited Partnership, 3772
Pipefitters Local Union, No. 562 v. United States,
    1516
Piper; Roadway Express, Inc. v., 2133
———; Supreme Court of New Hampshire v., 2796
Piper Aircraft Co. v. Reyno, 2298
Piphus; Carey v., 1891
Piqua Branch of the State Bank of Ohio v. Knoop,
    151
Pirate alias Belt v. Dalby, 5
Pireno; Union Labor Life Insurance, Co. v., 2417
Pitot; Sere v., 53
Pittenger; Meek v., 1693
Pitts; Freeman v., 3673
Pittsburgh; Hunter v., 371
Pittsburgh & Lake Erie Railroad Co. v. Railway
    Labor Executives' Association, 3359
Pittsburgh Commission on Human Relations;
    Pittsburgh Press Co. v., 1591
Pittsburgh Press Co. v. Pittsburgh Commission on
    Human Relations, 1591
Pittston Coal Group v. Sebben, 3293
Place; United States v., 2559
Plain Dealer Publications Co.; Lakewood v., 3265
Planned Parenthood Association of Kansas City,
    Missouri, Inc. v. Ashcroft, Attorney General of
    Missouri, 2549
Planned Parenthood of Central Missouri v. Danforth,
    Attorney General of Missouri, 1792
Planned Parenthood of Southeastern Pennsylvania v.
    Casey, Governor of Pennsylvania, 3732
Planters' Bank of Georgia; Bank of the United States
    v., 92
Plasencia; Landon v., 2444
Plaut v. Spendthrift Farm, Inc., 3968
Playtime Theatres, Inc.; Renton v., 2937
Pleasants v. Greenhow, 240

Plessy v. Ferguson, 312
Plumbers and Pipefitters, AFL-CIO; Local No. 334
    v., 2264
Plumbers and Steamfitters, Local Union 100; Connell
    Construction Co. v., 1699
Plumley v. Massachusetts, 298
Plyler, Superintendent v. Doe, 2389
Plymouth; The, 160
Plymouth Coal Co. v. Pennsylvania, 417
"Pocket Veto Case," 573
Poe v. Ullman, State Attorney, 1109
Poe, Collector of Internal Revenue v. Seaborn, 583
Poelker v. Doe, 1862
Pohl v. Ohio, 506
Pointer v. Texas, 1221
Poland v. Arizona, 2980
Police Department of Chicago v. Mosley, 1524
Polk County v. Dodson, 2301
Pollak; Public Utilities Commission of District of
    Columbia v., 928
Pollard, Lessee v. Hagan, 139
Pollock v. Farmers' Loan and Trust Co., 301, 303
——— v. Williams, Sheriff, 788
Pond v. Walden, 2307
Ponte, Superintendent, Massachusetts Correctional
    Institution v. Real, 2845
Ponterio v. Morris, 3319
Pope v. Hunt, 4043
——— v. Illinois, 3135
Popular Democratic Party; Rivera-Rodriguez v., 2379
Population Services International; Carey v., 1850
Port Authority Trans-Hudson Corp. v. Feeney, 3448
———; Hess v., 3934
——— v. Foster, 3448
"Port Gibson, MS case," 2441
Portash; New Jersey v., 1969
Porter v. Warner Holding Co., 831
Porterfield v. Webb, 510
Portland Cement Co. of Utah; Commissioner of
    Internal Revenue v., 2186
Portland Golf Club v. Commissioner of Internal
    Revenue, 3494
Portland Retail Druggist Association; Abbott
    Laboratories v., 1742
Porto Rico; Balzac v., 482
Portsmouth Harbor Land and Hotel Co. v. United
    States, 496
Porvenzano; United States Department of Justice v.,
    2760
Posadas de Puerto Rico Associates, dba Condado
    Holiday Inn v. Tourism Co. of Puerto Rico,
    3046
Post Co. v. National Citizens, 1919
Posters 'N' Things, Ltd. v. United States, 3888

Post-Newsweek Stations, Capital Area, Inc. v.
    Business Executives' Move for Vietnam Peace,
    1574
Postmaster General; Lamont v., 1229
Potomac Electric Power Co. v. Director Office of
    Workers Compensation Programs, United States
    Department of Labor, 2166
Poulos v. New Hampshire, 942
Powell v. Alabama, 606
——— v. McCormack, 1376
——— v. Nevada, 3870
——— v. Pennsylvania, 259
———; Stone v., 1802
——— v. Texas, 1345
———; United States v., 1203, 2764
Powers v. Ohio, 3551
Praprotnik; City of St. Louis v., 3229
Pratt v. Westcott, 2022
Prebyterian Church in United States v. Mary
    Elizabeth Blue Hull Memorial Presbyterian
    Church, 1351
Preciat v. United States, 157
Preferred Communications, Inc.; Los Angeles v.,
    2994
Preisler; Heinkel v., 1362
———; Kirkpatrick v., 1362
Preseault v. Interstate Commerce Commission (ICC),
    3406
President and Commissioners of Princess Anne;
    Carroll v., 1347
Presley v. Etowah County Commission, 3647
Press; Galvan v., 959
Press-Enterprise Co. v. Superior Court of California,
    Riverside County, 2618
——— v. Superior Court of California for the
    County of Riverside, 3039
Presser v. Illinois, 243
Preston v. United States, 1180
Price; Eaton v., 1083
———; Ohio ex rel. Eaton v., 1083
———; United States v., 1253
Price Waterhouse v. Ann Hopkins, 3332
Prichard; Weinberg v., 1552
Prigg v. Pennsylvania, 136
Primary Steel, Inc.; Maislin Industries v., 3493
Primrose; Bank of United States v., 131
Primus; In re, 1913
Prince v. Massachusetts, 781
——— v. San Francisco, 1037
Princeton University v. Schmid, 2313
"Prize Cases," 157
Pro Football, Inc.; Brown v., 4045
Proctor v. California, 3930
Procunier v. Hillery, 1653
———; Pell v., 1653

———; Skillern v., 2785
Procunier, Director, California Department of
    Corrections v. Martinez, 1637
Professional Real Estate Investors, Inc. v. Columbia
    Pictures Industries, Inc., 3793
Proffitt v. Florida, 1796
Propeller Genessee Chief v. Fitzhugh, 147
Prosise; Haring v., 2541
Prosser's Moving and Storage Co. v. Robbins, 2667
Prouse; Delaware v., 1975
Providence Bank v. Billings and Pittman, 117
"Providence Hospital Case," 334
Providence Journal Co.; United States v., 3244
Provident Consumer Discount Co.; Griggs v., 2445
Proxmire; Hutchinson v., 2024
Prudential Insurance Co. v. Benjamin, 832
——— v. Cheek, 489
Pruneyard Shopping Center v. Robins, 2111
Ptasynski; United States v., 2533
Public Agencies Opposed to Social Security
    Entrapment; Bowen v., 3016
Public Citizen v. United States Department of Justice,
    3358
Public Employees Retirement System of Ohio v.
    Betts, 3370
Public Employment Relations Board; Regents of the
    University of California v., 3243
Public Service Commission; Central Hudson Gas and
    Electric Corp. v., 2126
Public Service Commission of Missouri; Missouri ex
    rel. Southwestern Bell Telephone Co. v., 504
Public Service Commission of the State of New York
    v. Mid-Louisiana Gas Co., 2579
Public Utilities; Consolidated Edison Co. v., 2125
Public Utilities Commission; Pacific Gas and Electric
    Co. v., 2936
Public Utilities Commission of District of Columbia
    v. Pollak, 928
Public Utilities Commission of Ohio v. Federal
    Communications Commission, 2988
Public Utilities Commission of Rhode Island v.
    Attleboro Steam and Electric Co., 542
Pueblo Bowl-O-Mat, Inc.; Brunswick Corp. v., 1813
Puerto Rico v. Branstad, 3191
Puerto Rico ex rel. Barez; Alfred L. Snapp & Son
    Inc. v., 2432
Puerto Rico Aqueduct and Sewer Authority v.
    Metcalf & Eddy, Inc., 3743
Puget Sound Gillnetters Association v. United States
    District Court for the Western District of
    Washington, 2035
Pulley, Warden v. Harris, 2622
Pulliam, Magistrate for the County of Culpeper,
    Virginia v. Allen, 2676
Pullman Co.; Railroad Commission of Texas v., 730

Pullman-Standard v. Swint, 2357
Pumpelly v. Green Bay Co., 185
———— v. Green Bay and Mississippi Canal Co., 185
Pure Carbonic, Inc. v. Commissioner of Internal
    Revenue, 883
Purkett, Superintendent, Farmington Corrections
    Center v. Elem, 3986
"Puyallup I," 1327
"Puyallup II," 1605
Puyallup Tribe; Department of Game v., 1605
———— v. Department of Game of Washington,
    1327, 1605
Pyramid Lake Paiute Tribe of Indians v. Truckee-
    Carson Irrigation District, 2572

Qualitex Co. v. Jacobson Products Co., Inc., 3966
Quaring; Jensen v., 2874
Quarles; New York v., 2714
————; Toth v., 977
Queen v. Hepburn, 58
Quern v. Jordan, 1965
Quick Bear v. Leupp, 380
Quick Point Pencil Co.; Aronson v., 1962
Quill Corp. v. North Dakota, 3692
Quilter; Voinovich v., 3763
Quinlan; Kimberlin v., 4001
Quinn v. Millsap, 3351
———— v. United States, 971
————; United States v., 2968
Quirin v. Cox, 757
————; Ex Parte, 757

R. Enterprises, Inc.; United States v., 3526
R.A. Gray & Co.; Oregon-Washington Carpenters
    Employers Pension Trust Fund v., 2716
————; Pension Benefit Guaranty Corp. v., 2716
R.A.V. v. City of St. Paul, Minnesota, 3720
RCA Communications, Inc.; FCC v., 946
————; Mackay Radio and Telegraph Co. v., 946
R.C. Tway Coal Co. v. Clark, 651
———— v. Glenn, 651
R.J. Reynolds Tobacco Co. v. Durham County, North
    Carolina, 3067
R.L.C.; United States v., 3664
R.M.J.; In re, 2317
Race Horse; Ward v., 311
Radcliff Materials Inc.; Texas Industries, Inc. v.,
    2232
Raddatz; United States v., 2130
Radford; Louisville Joint Stock Land Bank v., 638
Radio, Television News Directors Association;
    United States v., 1374
Radloff; Toibb v., 3596
Radovich v. National Football League (NFL), 1000
Ragland; Arkansas Writers' Project, Inc. v., 3125

Rahrer; In re, 276
————; Wilkerson v., 276
Railway Clerks; Ellis v., 2672
"Railroad Commission Cases," 244
Railroad Commission; Frost & Frost Trucking Co. v.,
    534
Railroad Commission of Texas v. Pullman Co., 730
Railroad Commission of Wisconsin v. Chicago,
    Burlington and Quincy Railroad Co., 478
Railroad Retirement Board (RRB) v. Alton Railroad
    Co., 636
Railway Employees' Department, American
    Federation of Labor v. Hanson, 990
Railway Express Agency v. New York, 880
Railway Labor Executives' Association;
    Consolidated Rail Corp. (CONRAIL) v., 3356
————; Conrail v., 3356
———— v. Gibbons, 2330
————; Pittsburgh & Lake Erie Railroad Co. v.,
    3359
————; Skinner v., 3317
Raines; United States v., 1067
Rakas v. Illinois, 1947
Rake v. Wade, Trustee, 3815
Raladam Co.; Federal Trade Commission (FTC) v.,
    594
Raley; Parke v., 3736
Ralston, Warden v. Robinson, 2297
Ramah Navajo School Board, Inc. v. Bureau of
    Revenue of New Mexico, 2439
Rambo; Metropolitan Stevedore Co. v., 3999
Ramirez v. Indiana, 2828
Ramos; California v., 2597
Ramsey; Ferry v., 563
————; Harris v., 563
Ramsey Petroleum Co.; Harris v., 563
Ranco, Inc. v. National Labor Relations Board
    (NLRB), 986
Randall v. Brigham, 172
———— v. Loftsgaarden, 3055
————; Speiser v., 1037
Randolph; Parker v., 1999
Raney v. Board of Education of the Gould School
    District, 1330
Rankin v. McPherson, 3197
Rapone, Commissioner of Corrections of
    Massachusetts v. Inmates of the Suffolk County
    Jail, 3643
Rathbun v. United States, 1017
Ratzlaf v. United States, 3850
Rauscher; United States v., 253
Rawlings v. Kentucky, 2140
Rawlinson; Dothard v., 1871
Rawson; United Steelworkers v., 3449
Ray v. Blair, 925

Ray; Herweg v., 2320
———; Pierson v., 1279
——— v. United States, 3147
———; United States Department of State v., 3633
Ray, Governor of Washington v. Atlantic Richfield
    Co., 1888
Raybestos-Manhattan, Inc.; Alessi v., 2225
Raymond Concrete Pile Co.; Grimes v., 1027
Raymond Motor Transporation, Inc. v. Rice, 1884
Readers' Digest Association; Wolston v., 2026
Reading Co. v. Brown, 1332
Reagan v. Farmers' Loan and Trust Co., 297
Reakirt; Cincinnati v., 580
Real; Ponte v., 2845
Real Estate Board of New Orleans; McLain v., 2045
Rector and Visitors of the University of Virginia;
    Rosenberger v., 4018
Red Lion Broadcasting Co. v. Federal
    Communications Commission (FCC), 1374
Redhail; Zablocki v., 1882
Redington; Touche Ross and Co., 2013
Redrup v. New York, 1283
Reed v. Beto, 1271
———; Burns v., 3583
——— v. Campbell, 3007
———; Cook County Officers Electoral Board v.,
    3639
——— v. Farley, Superintendent, Indiana State
    Prison, 3915
———; Lukhard v., 3129
———; Norman v., 3639
——— v. Reed, 1472
———; Reed v., 1472
——— v. Ross, 2729
———; Schick v., 1670
Reese; United States v., 197
Reeves, Inc. v. Stake, 2122
Regan; Committee for Public Education and
    Religious Liberty v., 2058
———; Dames & Moore v., 2288
——— v. New York, 969
———; South Carolina v., 2633
Regan, Secretary of the Treasury v. Taxation with
    Representation of Washington, 2520
——— v. Time, Inc., 2750
Regan v. Wald, 2737
Regenbogen v. United States, 835
Regents of University of New York; Kingsley
    International Pictures Corp. v., 1062
Regents of the University of California v. Bakke,
    1936
———; Hamilton v., 626
——— v. Public Employment Relations Board ,
    3243

Regents of the University of Michigan v. Ewing,
    2921
Regester; White v., 1582
"Regional Banking Compact Case," 2862
Rehner; Rice v., 2589
Reich v. Collins, Revenue Commission of Georgia,
    3937
———; Thunder Basin Coal Co. v., 3852
Reid; Community for Non-Violence v., 3345
——— v. Covert, 993, 1009
——— v. Georgia, 2150
———; Southern Railway Co. v., 407
Reina; Duro v., 3463
Reinecke, formerly Collector of Internal Revenue v.
    Smith, 615
Reinman v. Little Rock, 425
Reis; Complete Auto Transit, Inc. v., 2220
Reiter v. Cooper, 3769
——— v. Sonotone Corp., 2008
Reitman v. Mulkey, 1288
Rendell-Baker v. Kohn, 2410
Renne, San Francisco City Attorney v. Geary, 3602
Reno; Shaw v., 3841
Reno, Attorney General v. Catholic Social Services,
    Inc., 3825
——— v. Flores, 3770
——— v. Koray, 3993
Reporters Committee for Freedom of Press;
    Kissinger v., 2067
———; United States Department of Justice v., 3322
Reproductive Health Services; Webster v., 3378
Republic National Bank of Miami v. United States,
    3740
Republic of Argentina v. Weltover, Inc., 3701
Republic of Cuba; Alfred Dunhill v., 1755
Republic of Mexico v. Hoffman, 804
Republic of Peru; Ex Parte, 766
Republic Iron and Steel Co. v. Lord, 502
Republic Steel Corp.; Coffy v., 2114
——— v. Maddox, 1214
Republican Party; Morse v., 4035
Republican Party of Connecticut; Tashjian v., 3070
Republican Party of Illinois; Rutan v., 3492
Republican Party of the State of Connecticut;
    Tashjian v., 3070
Reservists Committee to Stop the War; Schlesinger
    v., 1658
Resolution Trust Corp.; BFP v., 3889
Respublica v. Carlisle, 1
——— v. Chapman, 2
——— v. De Longchamps, 3
——— v. Oswald, 9
——— v. Shaffer, 7
——— v. Weidel, 11
Resweber; ex rel. Francis v., 838

———; Louisiana ex rel. Francis v., 838
Retail Clerk Union; Boys Market, Inc. v., 1409
Retail Store Employees Union; National Labor
        Relation Board (NLRB) v., 2127
Reves v. Ernst & Young, 3408, 3765
Review Board of the Indiana Employment Security
        Division; Thomas v., 2204
Rex Trailer Co., Inc. v. United States, 980
Reyno; Hartzell Propeller, Inc. v., 2298
———; Piper Aircraft Co. v., 2298
Reynolds v. International Amateur Athletic
        Federation (IAAF), 3734
——— v. Smith, 1366
——— v. United States, 212
———; United States v., 938
Reynolds, et al. v. Sims, 1189
Reynoldsville Casket Co. v. Hyde, 3985
Rhinehart; Seattle Times Co., DBA The Seattle
        Times v., 2685
Rhode Island; 44 Liquormart, Inc., 4039
———; Fletcher v., 141
———; Forty-four Liquormart, 4039
———; Fowler v., 940
——— v. Innis, 2093
——— v. Palmer, 463
———; Scheuer v., 1633
"Rhode Island and New York Boundary Case," 2783
"Rhode Island School-Prayer Case," 3724
Rhodes; Krause, Administrator v., 1633
Rhodes, Governor of Ohio v. Chapman, 2251
Rhoditis; Hellenic Lines, Ltd. v., 1411
Ribnik v. McBride, 566
Rice; Gong Lum v., 557
———; Raymond Motor Transporation, Inc. v., 1884
——— v. Santa Fe Elevator Corp., 847
———; Simpson v., 1379
——— v. Sioux City Memorial Park Cemetery, 970
———; Wolff, Warden v., 1802
Rice, Director, Department of Alcoholic Beverage
        Control of California v. Norman Williams Co.,
        2434
——— v. Rehner, 2589
Richard D.; Linda R.S. v., 1556
Richards; Ankenbrandt v., 3705
———; Cincinnati v., 580
——— v. Washington Terminal Co., 419
Richardson; Abe v., 1255
———; Burns v., 1255
———; Cravalho v., 1255
———; Foremost Insurance Co. v., 2405
———; Frontiero v., 1569
———; Graham v., 1464
——— v. Marsh, 3124
———; McMann v., 1406
———; Tilton v., 1469

Richardson v. United States, 2740
———; United States v., 1657
Richardson-Merrell, Inc. v. Koller, an infant, by and
        through Koller et ux., her natural guardians,
        2871
Richmond; Bradley v., 1641
——— v. Lewis, Director, Arizona Department of
        Corrections, 3737
———; Office of Personnel Management v., 3480
———; Rogers v., 1095
——— v. United States, 1012
Richmond County Board of Education; Cumming v.,
        335
Richmond Newspapers, Inc. v. Virginia, 2152
Rickert Rice Mills v. Fontenot, 644
Ricketts v. Adamson, 3182
Ricks; Delaware State College v., 2165
Riddick v. New York, 2083
Ridgway v. Ridgway, 2292
———; Ridgway v., 2292
Riggs; DeGeofroy v., 264
———; Geofroy v., 264
Riggins v. Nevada, 3685
"Right to Die Case," 3498
Riley; Florida v., 3302
——— v. National Federation of the Blind of North
        Carolina, Inc., 3284
Ring Screw Workers; Groves v., 3519
Ringer; Heckler v., 2678
Rio Grande Dam and Irrigation Co.; United States v.,
        332
Rios-Pineda; Immigration and Naturalization Service
        (INS) v., 2843
Risjord; Firestone Tire and Rubber Co. v., 2170
Ristaino v. Ross, 1735
Ritchie; Pennsylvania v., 3091
Ritter's Cafe; Carpenters and Joiners Union v., 747
Rivera; Atkins v., 3021
Rivera; City of Riverside v., 3035
——— v. Minnich, 3202
Rivera-Rodriguez v. Popular Democratic Party, 2379
Rivers v. Roadway Express, Inc., 3878
Riverside Bayview Homes, Inc.; United States v.,
        2916
Rives; Virginia v., 217
Rizzo v. Goode, 1725
Roadway Express, Inc.; Brock v., 3127
——— v. Piper, 2133
——— Rivers v., 3878
Roanoke Redevelopment and Housing Authority;
        Wright v., 3079
Robbins v. California, 2282
———; Prosser's Moving and Storage Co. v, 2667
———; Schneider Moving & Storage Co. v., 2667
Robel; United States v., 1305

Roberson; Arizona v., 3262
Robert Welch, Inc.; Gertz v., 1662
Roberts; Bradfield v., 334
——— v. New Hampshire, 2323
——— v. Louisiana, 1799, 1848
———; Ohio v., 2138
———; Thigpen v., 2730
——— v. United States, 2082
Roberts, Acting Commissioner, Minnesota
    Department of Human Rights v. United States
    Jaycees, 2749
Robertson; Administrator, Federal Aviation
    Administration (FAA) v., 1710
———; Lehr v., 2577
——— v. Methow Valley Citizens Council, 3334
——— v. Seattle Audubon Society, 3671
———; United States v., 3981
Robins; Pruneyard Shopping Center v., 2111
Robins Dry Dock and Repair Co. v. Flint, 559
Robinson v. California, 1135
——— v. DiCenso, 1468
——— v. Florida, 1195
———; Kelly v., 3064
——— v. Memphis and Charleston Railroad Co.,
    231
———; Ralston v., 2297
———; Smith v., 2758
———; United Mine Workers of America Health
    and Retirement Funds v., 2335
——— v. United States, 4023
———; United States v., 1608
Rochin v. California, 917
Rock v. Arkansas, 3184
Rock Royal Co-operative, Inc.; Dairymen's League
    Cooperative Association v., 695
———; Metropolitan Cooperative Milk Producers
    Bargaining Agency v., 695
———; Noyes v., 695
———; United States v., 695
Rockefeller; Wells v., 1363
Rockford; Grayned v., 1525
Rockford Life Insurance Co. v. Illinois Department
    of Revenue, 3160
Rodgers v. Paul, 1238
———; United States v., 2526, 2674
Rodrigue v. Aetna Casualty and Surety Co., 1373
Rodriguez v. Compass Shipping Co., Ltd., 2229
———; East Texas Motor Freight System, Inc. v.,
    1843
———; Illinois v., 3495
Rodriguez; San Antonio Independent School District
    v., 1561
———; Southern Conference of Teamsters v., 1843
———; Teamsters Local Union 657 v., 1843

Rodriguez de Quijas v. Shearson/American Express,
    Inc., 3338
Roe; Maher v., 1861
——— v. Wade, 1548
———; Whalen v., 1816
Roemer v. Board of Public Works of Maryland, 1768
———; Chisom v., 3604
———; Clark v., 3588
Roemer, Governor of Louisiana; United States v.,
    3604
Rogers v. Friedman, 1958
———; Friedman v., 1958
——— v. Lodge, 2433
———; Mills v., 2392
——— v. Richmond, Warden, 1095
———; Societe Internationale Pour Participations
    Industrielles v., 1031
———; Texas Optometric Association v., 1958
——— v. United States, 906
Rohm and Haas Co.; Dawson Chemical Co. v., 2144
Rojas-Contreras; United States v., 2922
Romano; Black v., 2848
——— v. Oklahoma, 3901
———; United States v., 1237
Romein; General Motors Corp. v., 3659
Romeo; Youngberg v., 2393
Romer v. Evans, 4041
Romero v. International Terminal Operating Co.,
    1045
Romero-Barcelo; Weinberger v., 2358
Ron Pair Enterprises; United States v., 3311
Ronald Reagan v. Abourezk, 3211
Ronwin; Hoover v., 2677
Rooney; California v., 3194
Roper; Deposit Guaranty National Bank v., 2073
Rosales-Lopez v. United States, 2212
Rose v. Clark, 3052
———; Howlett v., 3478
——— v. Rose, 3142
———; Rose v., 3142
Rose, Warden v. Lundy, 2333
Rosebud Sioux Tribe v. Kneip, 1830
Rosenbaum Co.; Jackman v., 490
Rosenberg v. United States, 948
Rosenberger v. Rector and Visitors of the University
    of Virginia, 4018
Rosenblatt v. Baer, 1240
Rosenbloom v. Metromedia, Inc., 1457
Rosewell v. LaSalle National Bank, Trustee, 2199
Ross v. Bernhard, 1389
——— v. Moffitt, 1651
——— v. Oklahoma, 3269
———; Reed v., 2729
———; Ristaino v., 1735
———; United States v., 2377

Rossi; Weinberger v., 2347

Rostker, Director of Selective Service v. Goldberg, 2273

Rotary Club of Duarte; Board of Directors of Rotary International v., 3137

Roth; Board of Regents v., 1530

——— v. United States, 741, 1015

Rottenberg v. United States, 784

Roviaro v. United States, 1001

Rowan Companies, Inc. v. United States, 2248

Rowan dba American Book Service v. United States Post Office, 1404

Rowe; Hughes v., 2154

Rowland v. California Men's Advisory Council, 3746

——— v. California Men's Colony, 3746

Rowland, Former Director, California Department of Corrections v. California Men's Colony, Unit II Men's Advisory Council, 3746

Rowley; Board of Education v., 2419

Rowoldt v. Perfetto, Immigration and Naturalization Service, 1018

Roy; Bowen v., 3003

Royal Drug Co.; Group Life and Health Insurance Co. v., 1961

Royer; Florida v., 2485

Rubin v. United States, 2173

Rubin, Secretary of the Treasury v. Coors Brewing Co., 3976

Ruby; Sisson v., 3499

Ruckelshaus, Administrator, Environmental Protection Agency (EPA) v. Monsanto Co., 2727

——— v. Sierra Club, 2588

Rudzewicz; Burger King Corp. v., 2844

Rufo, Sheriff of Suffolk County v. Inmates of the Suffolk County Jail, 3643

Ruiz; Morton v., 1622

Rumely; United States v., 939

Rumery; Newton v., 3105

Rummel v. Estelle, 2071

Rumsey; Arizona v. , 2694

Runyon et ux., dba Bobbe's School v. McCrary, 1777

———; McCrary v., 1777

Rural Telephone Services Co., Inc.; Feist Publications, Inc. v., 3549

Rusk; Afroyim v., 1286

——— v. Cort, 1141

——— v. Savchuk, 2048

———; Zemel v., 1228

Rusk, Secretary of State v. Cort, 1123

Russell; Elfbrandt v., 1254

———; Massachusetts Mutual Life Insurance Co. v., 2893

———; North v., 1784

Russell; Salve Regina College v., 3545

——— v. United States, 2857

Russell County Commission; Mack v., 3647

Russello v. United States, 2602

Rust v. Sullivan, Secretary of Health and Human Services, 3570

Rutan v. Republication Party of Illinois, 3492

Rutherford; Block v., 2748

Rutledge; Kush v., 2494

Ryan; Amazon Petroleum Co. v., 627

———; Panama Refining Co. v., 627

———; United States v., 231

Ryder v. United States, 3995

Rylander; United States v., 2496

S. Simcha Goldman v. Weinberger, 2955

SCRAP; Aberdeen and Rockfish Railroad Co. v., 1580

———; United States v., 1580

S.G.; American National Red Cross v., 3716

Sabbatino; Banco Nacional de Cuba v., 1181

Sable Communications of California, Inc. v. Federal Communications Commission (FCC), 3369

Sac and Fox Nation; Oklahoma Tax Commission v., 3797

Sacher, et al. v. United States, 923

Sadlowski; United Steelworkers of America v., 2384

Saffle v. Parks, 3422

Safley; Turner v., 3156

Saia v. New York, 874

Sailor v. Leger, 1464

Sain; Townsend v., 1143

Saint Francis College v. Al-Khazraji, AKA Allan, 3140

Saint Nicholas Cathedral; Kedroff v., 934

Saks; Air France v., 2799

Sale, Acting Commissioner, Immigration and Naturalization Service v. Haitian Centers Council, Inc., 3828

Salerno; United States v., 3148, 3718

Saline Bank; United States v., 106

Salve Regina College v. Russell, 3545

Salvucci; United States v., 2139

Salyer Land Co. v. Tulare Lake Basin Water Storage District, 1559

Same v. Mulcahy, 685

Samuel L. Skinner v. Railway Labor Executives' Association, 3317

Samuels; Negonsott v., 3761

San Antonio Independent School District v. Rodriguez, 1561

San Antonio Metropolitan Transit Authority; Donovan v., 2784

———; Garcia v., 2784

San Carlos Apache Tribe; Arizonia v., 2585

San Diego; Metromedia, Inc. v., 2285
———; San Diego Gas & Electric Co. v., 2202
San Diego Building Trades Council v. Garmon, 1050
San Diego Gas and Electric Co. v. City of San Diego, 2202
San Francisco; Prince v., 1037
———; United States v., 709
San Francisco Arts and Athletics, Inc. (SFAA) v. United States Olympic Committee (USOC), 3201
San Francisco County Democratic Central Committee; Eu v., 3310
San Jose; Pennell v., 3227
Sanchez; McDaniel v., 2244
———; Ngiraingas v., 3444
Sandberg; Virginia Bankshares, Inc. v., 3623
Sanderfoot; Farrey v., 3574
Sanders; Arkansas v., 2018
———; Gray v., 1146
———; Wesberry v., 1175
——— v. United States, 1150, 2129
Sandford; Covington and Lexington Turnpike Road Co. v., 316
———; Dred Scott v., 154
Sandin, Unit Team Manager, Halawa Correctional Facility v. Conner, 4007
Sandoval v. California, 3868
Sandra Ann Craig; Maryland v., 3508
Sandstrom v. Montana, 2012
Sanitary District of Chicago v. United States, 518
Santa Ana; Mountain States Telephone and Telegraph Co. v., 2864
Santa Barbara County Water Agency v. Balaam, 1032
Santa Clara County v. Southern Railway Co., 250
Santa Clara Pueblo v. Martinez, 1907
Santa Fe Elevator Corp.; Illinois Commerce Commission v., 847
——— Rice v., 847
Santa Fe Pacific Railroad; United States v., 740
———; United States ex rel. Hualpai Indians v., 740
Santa Fe Trail Transporation Co.; McDonald v., 1781
Santana; United States v., 1773
Santosky v. Kramer, 2345
Santissima Trinidad; In re, 84
Sappenfield v. Indiana, 3305
Sarah; In re, 86
Sarony; Burrow-Giles Lithographic Co. v., 236
Satterlee v. Mathewson, 112
Satterwhite v. Texas, 3252
Satty; Nashville Gas Co. v., 1878
Satz v. Sherman, 519
Saudi Arabia v. Nelson, 3771
Saunders; Ogden v., 101
Sauvinet; Walker v., 196

Savchuk; Rush v., 2048
Sawyer v. Manitowoc Products Co., 463
——— v. Smith, Interim Warden, 3497
——— v. Whitley, Warden, 3719
———; Youngstown Sheet and Tube Co. v., 930
Saxbe, Attorney General v. Washington Post Co., 1654
Saxner; Cleavinger v., 2919
Scales v. United States, 1107
Scanlon; Atascadero State Hospital v., 2897
"Scarsdale Crèche Case," 2834
Scenic Rivers Association; Flint Ridge Development v., 1769
Scenic Rivers Association of Oklahoma; Hills v., 1769
Schad v. Arizona, 3612
——— v. Borough of Mount Ephraim, 2241
Schaefer; Shalala v., 3831
Schaeffer v. United States, 456
Schafer; Fargo Women's Health Organization v., 3788
Schall, Commissioner of New York City Department of Juvenile Justice v. Martin, 2698
Scheidler; National Organization of Women (NOW) v., 3854
Scheiner; American Trucking Association v., 3193
Schempp; Abington School District v., 1167
Schenck v. United States, 446
Scherer; Davis v., 2735
Scheuer, Administratix v. Rhodes, 1633
Schiavone v. Fortune, AKA Time, Inc., 3015
Schick v. Reed, Chairman, United States Board of Parole, 1670
——— v. United States, 358
Schiedt; Dimick v., 629
Schiro v. Farley, Superintendent, Indiana State Prison, 3853
Schlagenhauf v. Holder, 1205
Schleier; Commissioner v., 4002
Schlesinger v. Councilman, 1689
Schlesinger, Secretary of Defense v. Ballard, 1674
——— v. Reservists Committee to Stop the War, 1658
Schlude v. Commissioner of Internal Revenue, 1140
Schlunk; Volkswagenwerk Aktiengesellschaft v., 3263
Schlup v. Delo, Superintendent, Potosi Correctional Center, 3947
Schmerber v. California, 1263
Schmid; Princeton University v., 2313
Schmidt; DeBoer v., 3844
Schmitt; Common Cause v., 2315
Schmuck v. United States, 3320
Schnackenberg; Cheff v., 1259
Schneble v. Florida, 1488

Schneckloth v. Bustamonte, 1575
Schneider v. State of New Jersey (Town of
    Irvington), 697
Schneider Moving & Storage Co. v. Robbins, 2667
Schneiderman v. United States, 776, 1012
Schneidewind v. ANR Pipeline Co., 3234
Schoene; Miller v., 561
Schoenthal v. Irving Trust Co., 608
School Board City of Hopewell; Gilliam v., 1236
School Board of Nassau County, Florida and Craig
    Marsh, Superintendent of Schools of Nassau
    County, Florida v. Arline, 3100
School Board of Richmond; Bradley v., 1236
School Committee of the Town of Burlington,
    Massachusetts v. Department of Education of
    Massachusetts, 2839
"School Desegregation Cases," 954, 955, 956, 957,
    1329, 1330, 1331, 1444, 1445, 1446, 1447
School District of Abington Township v. Schempp,
    1167
School District of the City of Grand Rapids v. Ball,
    2899
"School Prayer Case," 1132
Schoonejongen; Curtiss-Wrigth Corp. v., 3961
Schooner Amistad; United States v., 133
Schooner Exchange v. M'Faddon, 55
Schooner Peggy; United States v., 34
Schor; Commodity Futures Trading Commission v.,
    3061
Schreiber v. Burlington Northern, Inc., 2858
Schultz; Frisby v., 3278
Schwab; Ortwein v., 1557
Schwalb; Chesapeake and Ohio Railway Co. v., 3383
Schware v. Board of Bar of Examiners of New
    Mexico, 1004
Schwegmann Brothers v. Calvert Distillers Corp.,
    913
——— v. Seagram Distillers Corp., 913
Schweiker v. Chilicky, 3276
Schweiker, Secretary of Health and Human Services
    v. Gray Panthers, 2272
——— v. Hogan, 2402
——— v. McClure, 2353
——— v. Wilson, 2188
Schwimmer; United States v., 572
Scindia Steam Navigation Co., LTD. v. De Los
    Santos, 2211
Scotland Neck City Board of Education; Cotton v.,
    1518
———; United States v., 1518
Scott, Ex Parte, 256
——— v. Illinois, 1966
———; McFarland v., 3928
——— v. Sandford, 154
——— v. United States, 1908

Scott; United Brotherhood of Carpenters and Joiners
    v., 2593
"Scottsboro Boys Cases," 606, 634
"Scottsboro Cases," 606, 634
Screws v. United States, 809
Scripps-Howard Broadcasting Co.; Zacchini v., 1875
Sea-Land Services, Inc. v. Gaudet, 1616
Seaborn; Poe v., 583
Seacoast Products, Inc.; Douglas v., 1840
Seagram Distillers Corp.; Old Dearborn Distributing
    Co. v., 655
———; Schwegmann Brothers v., 913
Seampruf, Inc.; National Labor Relations Board
    (NLRB) v., 986
Search Warrant; Marcus v., 1112
Sears, Roebuck and Co. v. San Diego County District
    Council of Carpenters, 1910
——— v. Stiffel Co., 1177
Seas Shipping Co. v. Sieracki, 826
Seaton; Vitarelli v., 1055
Seatrain Shipbuilding Corp. v. Shell Oil Co., 2055
Seattle; Asakura v., 517
———; See v., 1291
Seattle Audubon Society; Robertson v., 3671
Seattle-First National Bank v. Financial Institution
    Employees, Local 1182, 2943
Seattle School District No. 1; Washington v., 2427
Seattle Times Co., dba The Seattle Times v.
    Rhinehart, 2685
Sebastian; Hadacheck v., 428
Sebben; Pittston Coal Group v., 3293
"Second Legal Tender Act Cases," 182
Second National Bank of New Haven v. United
    States, 1289
Secretary of Labor; Tony & Susan Alamo Foundation
    v., 2836
Secretary of Public Welfare of Pennsylvania v.
    Institutionalized Juveniles, 2015
Secretary of State; Aptheker v., 1201
Secretary of State of Maryland v. Joseph H. Munson
    Co., Inc., 2726
Secretary of the Interior v. California, 2614
———; California v., 2614
Secretary of the Treasury; Sorenson v., 2971
Secretary, United States Department of Education v.
    Betty-Louise Felton, 2900
Securities Corporation General; United States v., 531
———; White v., 531
Securities Exchange Commission (SEC); Aaron v.,
    2105
——— v. Capital Gains Research Bureau, Inc., 1173
——— v. Chenery Corp., 763, 851
———; Dirks v., 2587
——— v. Federal Water and Gas Corp., 851
——— v. Jerry T. O'Brien, Inc., 2717

Securities Exchange Committion; Jones v., 650
———; Lowe v., 2863
———; National Association of Securities Dealers,
    Inc. (NASD) v., 1441
——— v. National Securities, Inc., 1352
———; Steadman v., 2184
——— v. United States Realty and Improvement
    Co., 715
Securities Industry Association v. Board of
    Governors of the Federal Reserve System, 2734,
    2736
———; Clarke v., 3078
———; Security Pacific National Bank v., 3078
Securities Investor Protection Corp.; Holmes v., 3663
Security Industrial Bank; United States v., 2446
Security Pacific National Bank v. Securities Industry
    Association, 3078
Security Services, Inc. v. Kmart Corp., 3885
Seders v. Pennsylvania, 767
Sedima, S.P.R.L. v. Imrex Co., Inc., 2902
See v. City of Seattle, 1291
Seeger; United States v., 1218
Segura v. United States, 2753
Seiter; Wilson v., 3601
Seldin; Warth v., 1713
"Selective Draft Law Cases," 443
Selective Service System v. Minnesota Public
    Interest Research Group, 2754
Sells Engineering, Inc.; United States v., 2582
Seminole Nation v. United States, 751
Seminole Tribe v. Florida, 4034
Senate v. Synar, 3058
"Separate but Equal Case," 312
Sere and Laralde v. Pitot, 53
Seven Falls Co.; Wilton v., 3998
Sgro v. United States, 610
Shaare Tefila Congregation v. Cobb, 3141
Shabani; United States v., 3932
Shacket; Philko Aviation, Inc. v., 2547
Shaffer v. Heitner, 1867
———; Respublica v., 7
———; v. Valtierra, 1449
Shaker Heights; Lehman v., 1661
Shalala; Good Samaritan Hospital, Inc. v., 3812
———; Thomas Jefferson University v., 3920
Shalala, Secretary of Health and Human Services v.
    Guernsey Memorial Hospital, 3962
——— v. Schaefer, 3831
——— v. Whitecotton, 3969
Shanks v. DuPont, 115
Shannon v. United States, 3922
Shapero v. Kentucky Bar Association, 3257
Shapiro; Baldrige v., 2324
——— v. Drug Enforcement Administration, 2760
——— v. Thompson, 1366

——— v. United States, 876
"Shared Time Case," 2899
Sharp Electronics Corp.; Business Electronics Corp.
    v., 3245
Sharpe; Bolling v., 958, 973
———; United States v., 2809
Shaughnessy; Harisiades v., 922
——— v. United States ex rel. Mezei, 941
Shaw v. Hunt, 4043
———; Library of Congress v., 3045
——— v. Reno, Attorney General, 3841
Shaw, Acting Commissioner, New York State
    Division of Human Rights v. Delta Air Lines,
    Inc., 2571
Shea v. Louisiana, 2788
Shearer; United States v., 2890
Shearson/American Express, Inc. v. McMahon, 3162
———; Rodriguez v., 3338
Shearson Lehman Hutton; Mastrobuono v., 3960
Sheehan; Army and Air Force Exchange Service v.,
    2375
Sheet Metal Workers; Breininger v., 3385
Sheet Metal Workers International Association v.
    Lynn, 3299
Sheet Metal Workers National Pension Fund; Guidry
    v., 3398
Shell Oil Co.; Andrus v., 2104
———; Equal Employment Opportunity
    Commission v., 2656
——— v. Governor of Maryland, 1922
——— v. Iowa Department of Revenue, 3290
———; Seatrain Shipbuilding Corp. v., 2055
Shelley v. Kraemer, 868
Shelton v. Tucker, 1087
Shepard v. National Labor Relations Board (NLRB),
    2457
Sheppard; Massachusetts v., 2757
——— v. Maxwell, Warden, 1258
Sherbert v. Verner, 1170
Sherlock v. Alling, 199
Sherman; Hygrade Provision Co. v., 519
———; Lewis and Fox Co. v., 519
———; Satz v., 519
——— v. United States, 1028
Shevin; Fuentes v., 1507
———; Kahn v., 1636
Shevlin-Carpenter Co. v. Minnesota, 391
Shirey; United States v., 1051
Shore; Parklane Hosiery Co., Inc. v., 1951
Short; Texaco, Inc. v., 2307
Shreveport Grain and Elevator Co.; United States v.,
    607
"Shreveport Rate Case," 421
Shubert; United States v., 962
Shulman v. United States, 750

Shuman; Sumner v., 3185
Shumate; Patterson v., 3707
Shurberg Broadcasting of Hartford, Inc.; Astroline Communications Co. Limited Partnership v., 3503
Shute; Carnival Cruise Lines, Inc. v., 3558
Shutts; Phillips Petroleum Co. v., 2887
Sibbach v. Wilson and Co., 723
Sibron v. New York, 1337
Sicurella v. United States, 966
Sidoti; Palmore v., 2671
"Sick Chicken Case," 637
Siebold; Ex Parte, 219
Siegert v. Gilley, 3571
Sieracki; Seas Shipping Co. v., 826
Sierra Club; Andrus v., 2009
———; California v., 2216
———; Kern County Water Agency v., 2216
———; Kleppe v., 1786
——— v. Morton, 1492
———; Ruckelshaus v., 2588
Sierra Club Federal; American Electric Power System v., 1786
Sifuentes v. United States, 1803
Silkwood, Administrator of the Estate of Silkwood v. Kerr-McGee Corp., 2612
Silliman; M'Clung v., 83
Silver; Mohasco Corp. v., 2135
——— v. New York Stock Exchange, 1157
"Silver Springs Monkeys Case," 3564
Silverman v. United States, 1094
Silverthorne Lumber Co. v. United States, 455
"Simants Case," 1791
Simmons v. South Carolina, 3909
——— v. United States, 1313
Simon v. Eastern Kentucky Welfare Rights Organization, 1757
Simon & Schuster, Inc. v. Members of New York State Crime Victims Board, 3630
Simopoulos v. State of Virginia, 2550
Simpson v. Rice, 1379
Sims v. Central Intelligence Agency (CIA), 2829
———; Dryer, State ex rel. v., 909
———; Reynolds v., 1189
———; West Virginia v., 909
———; State v., 909
Sinclair v. United States, 570
Sinclair Co. v. National Labor Relations Board (NLRB), 1377
Sindermann; Perry v., 1531
Singleton v. Jackson Municipal Separate School District, 1385
———; United States v., 231
——— v. Wulff, 1793
"Sinking Fund Case," 214

Sioux City Memorial Park Cemetery; Rice v., 970
Sioux Nation of Indians; United States v., 2149
Sipes; McGhee v., 868
———; Vaca v., 1275
Sipuel v. Board of Regents of the University of Oklahoma, 856
Sisal Sales Corp.; United States v., 552
Sisson v. Ruby, 3499
Sitz; Michigan State Police v., 3481
Six Unknown Named Agents of the Federal Bureau of Narcotics; Bivens v., 1465
Skelly Oil Co.; California v., 1320
———; City and County of San Francisco v., 1320
———; City of Los Angeles v., 1320
———; City of San Diego v., 1320
———; Federal Power Commission (FPC) v., 1320
———; Pacific Gas & Electric Co. v., 1320
Skidmore v. Swift and Co., 798
Skillern v. Procunier, Director, Texas Department of Corrections, 2785
Skinner v. Oklahoma ex rel. Williamson, 755
Skipper v. South Carolina, 2973
Skiriotes v. Florida, 733
Skokie; National Socialist Party v., 1854
Skrupa; Ferguson v., 1149
Slappy; Morris v., 2500
Slaton; Paris Adult Theatre I v., 1585
Slaughter; Brown v., 132
———; Groves v., 132
"Slaughterhouse Case," 189
"Slave Ship Case," 95
Sloan v. Lemon, 1604
Slochower v. Board of Higher Education of City of New York, 984
Sloop Betsey; Glass v., 18
Smalis v. Pennsylvania, 2979
Smith v. Allwright, 787
———; American Trucking Association v., 3472
——— v. Arkansas State Highway Employees, Local 315, 1989
——— v. Barry, 3637
———; Bounds v., 1836
———; Butterworth v., 3427
——— v. California, 1064
———; Coyle v., 404
——— v. Daily Mail Publishing Co., 2023
——— v. Davis, 797
———; Employment Division, Department of Human Resources of Oregon v., 3435
———; Estelle v., 2222
———; Hawke v., 460, 461
———; Holywell Corp. v., 3651
———; Howe v., 2259
——— v. Illinois, 1311
——— v. Jaffree, 2860

Smith v. Maryland, 2017
———; McDonald v., 2875
——— v. Murray, 3033
——— v. Phillips, 2318
———; Reinecke v., 615
———; Reynolds v., 1366
——— v. Robinson, Rhode Island Associate
    Commissioner of Education, 2758
———; Sawyer v., 3497
———; Smyth v., 329
——— v. Swormstedt, 150
——— v. Turner, 144
——— v. United States, 822, 3766, 3803
———; United States v., 79, 3543, 3651
——— v. Wade, 2501
Smith, Sheriff v. Goguen, 1628
Smith, dba Intrigue v. United States, 1841
Smyth v. Ames, 329
——— v. Higginson, 329
——— v. Smith, 329
Snepp v. United States, 2052
Snyder; In re, 2881
———; Mills Music, Inc. v., 2768
——— v. Milwaukee, 697
Sochor v. Florida, 3699
"Social Security Act Cases," 670, 671
Socialist Workers '74 Campaign Committee; Brown
    v., 2447
Socialist Workers Party; Munro v., 3069
Societe Internationale Pour Participations
    Industrielles v. Rogers, 1031
Societe Nationale Industrielle Aerospatiale v. United
    States District Court for Southern District of
    Iowa, 3174
Society for Krishna Consciousness v. Lee,
    Superintendent of Port Authority Police, 3727
Society of Sisters; Pierce v., 528
Socony-Vacuum Oil Co.; United States v., 711
Sokolow; United States v., 3325
Soldal v. Cook County, Illinois, 3738
Soler Chrysler-Plymouth; Mitsubishi Motors v., 2906
Solem, Warden, South Dakota State Penitentiary v.
    Helm, 2578
——— v. Bartlett, 2635
——— v. Stumes, 2641
Solesbee v. Balkcom, 893
Soliman; Commissioner v., 3745
Solimino; Astoria Federal Savings and Loan
    Association v., 3593
Solorio v. United States, 3199
"Son of Sam Law Case," 3630
Sonoma County Superior Court; Michael M. v., 2198
Sonotone Corp.; Kathleen R. Reiter v., 2008
"Sony Betamax Case," 2617

Sony Corp. of America v. Universal City Studios,
    Inc., 2617
Sonzinsky v. United States, 660
Sorenson v. Secretary of the Treasury, 2971
Sorrells v. United States, 612
Sosna v. Iowa, 1673
Soto; Chardon v., 2557
Soto-Lopez; Attorney General of New York v., 3010
South Carolina v. Baker, 3240
——— v. Catawba Indian Tribe, 2995
———; Coosaw Mining Co. v., 285
———; Edwards v., 1142
——— v. Gathers, 3347
———; Georgia v., 3500
———; Ham v., 1545
——— v. Katzenbach, 1244
——— v. Regan, Secretary of the Treasury, 2633
———; Simmons v., 3909
———; Skipper v., 2973
South Carolina Coastal Council; Lucas v., 3733
South Carolina Public Railways Commission; Hilton
    v., 3635
South Carolina State Highway Department v.
    Barnwell Brothers, Inc., 677
South Carolina Tax Commission; Heublein v., 1542
———; Spencer v., 2823
South-Central Timber Development, Inc. v.
    Wunnicke, Commissioner, Department of
    Natural Resources of Alaska, 2689
South Chicago Coal and Dock Co. v. Bassett, 706
South Dakota v. Bourland, 3822
——— v. Dole, 3190
——— v. Neville, 2466
——— v. Opperman, 1800
———; St. Martin Evangelical Lutheran Church v.,
    2237
Southeastern Community College v. Davis, 2011
Southeastern Promotions, Ltd. v. Conrad, 1686
South-Eastern Underwriters Association; United
    States v., 792
Southard; Wayman v., 93
Southern California Edison Co.; Colton v., 1176
———; Federal Power Commission (FPC) v., 1176
Southern Conference of Teamsters v. Rodriguez,
    1843
Southern Coal and Coke Co.; Carmichael v., 669
Southern Independent School Association v.
    McCrary, 1777
Southern Motor Carriers Rate Conference, Inc. v.
    United States, 2821
Southern Pacific Co. v. Arizona ex rel. Sullivan, 812
———; Brooks v., 373
Southern Pacific Railroad Co.; California v., 250
Southern Pacific Transportation Co. v. Commercial
    Metals Co., 2359

Southern Railway Co. v. Reid, 407
———; Santa Clara County v., 250
——— v. United States, 405
Southland Corp. v. Keating, 2621
Southwest Marine, Inc. v. Gizoni, 3628
Sowders, Warden; Summitt v., 2168
———; Watkins v., 2168
Spalding v. Vilas, 307
Spallone v. United States, 3394
Spangler; Pasadena City Board of Education v., 1787
Spannaus; Allied Structural Steel Co. v., 1935
Spano v. New York, 1060
Sparkman; Stump v., 1896
Sparks; Dennis v., 2155
Spaziano v. Florida, 2744
Specter; Dalton v., 3886
Spectrum Sports v. McQuillan, dba Sorboturf
    Enterprises, 3752
Speed; Owings v., 81
Speiser v. Randall, 1037
Speller v. Allen, 937
Spence v. Washington, 1663
Spencer v. Texas, 1271
Spencer et ux. v. South Carolina Tax Commission,
    2823
Spendthrift Farm, Inc.; Plaut v., 3968
Sperling; Hoffman-La Roche, Inc. v., 3390
Sperry & Hutchinson Co.; Federal Trade
    Commission (FTC) v., 1483
Sperry Corp.; United States v., 3384
Spies v. United States, 760
Spinelli v. United States, 1350
Spock; Greer v., 1741
Spokane Arcades, Inc.; Brockett v., 2876
Sporhase v. Nebraska ex rel. Douglas, Attorney
    General, 2442
Spray-Rite Service Corp.; Monsanto Co. v., 2644
Spring; Colorado v., 3087
Springbok; The, 166
Springer v. United States, 221
Springfield Township School District v. Knoll, 2835
Springs; Maniguault v., 365
Square D Co. v. Niagara Frontier Tariff Bureau, Inc.,
    2990
St. Amant v. Thompson, 1319
St. Francis College v. Al-Khazraji, aka Allan, 3140
St. Louis; Joy v., 275
St. Louis Brewing Association v. Moore, 463
St. Louis, Kansas City and Colorado Railroad Co. v.
    Wabash Railroad Co., 389
St. Martin Evangelical Lutheran Church and
    Northwestern Lutheran Academy v. South
    Dakota, 2237
St. Mary's Honor Center v. Hicks, 3837

St. Nicholas Cathedral of Russian Orthodox Church
    of North America; Kedroff v., 934
St. Paul; R.A.V. v., 3720
St. Paul Fire and Marine Insurance Co. v. Barry,
    1939
St. Vincent's Hospital; King v., 3636
Stachura; Memphis Community School District v.,
    3026
Stafford v. Briggs, 2053
——— v. Wallace, 483
Stake; Reeves, Inc. v., 2122
Standard Oil Co.; Hawaii v., 1484
———; Monroe v., 2261
Standard Oil Co. of California; Federal Trade
    Commission (FTC) v., 2164
Standard Oil Co. of New Jersey v. United States, 401
Standard Oil Co. of Texas v. Federal Power
    Commission (FPC), 1320
Standefer v. United States, 2108
Stanford v. Kentucky, 3375
Stanford Daily; Bergna v., 1916
———; Zurcher v., 1916
Stanglin; Dallas v., 3326
Stanley v. Georgia, 1364
——— v. Illinois, 1491
———; United States v., 231, 3205
"Stanley Case," 3205
Stansbury v. California, 3879
Stanton; Georgia v., 169
———; Mississippi v., 169
——— v. Stanton, 1690
———; Stanton v., 1690
Staples v. United States, 3891
State Bar of Arizona; Baird v., 1427
———; Bates v., 1872
State Bar of California; Keller v., 3465
———; Konigsberg v., 1005, 1100
State Bar of Nevada; Gentile v., 3622
State Board of Elections; Allen v., 1355
State Energy Resources Conservation and
    Development Commission; Pacific Gas and
    Electric Co. v., 2505
State Farm; Consumer Alert v., 2569
———; Department of Transportation v., 2569
State Farm Mutual Automobile Insurance Co.; Motor
    Vehicle Manufacturers Association v., 2569
"State Freight Tax Case," 188
State Oil and Gas Board of Mississippi;
    Transcontinental Gas Pipe Line Corp. v., 2931
State of Wisconsin v. Yoder, 1496
States Marine Lines, Inc.; Moragne v., 1413
Stauffer Chemical Co.; United States v., 2609
Steadman v. Securities and Exchange Commission
    (SEC), 2184
Steagald v. United States, 2213

Steamboat Co. v. Chase, 191
"Steamboat Monopoly Cases," 88, 146
Steamer Daniel Ball v. United States, 178
Steamer Harrisburg v. Rickards, 252
The Steamer Peterhoff, 167
"Steel I," 523
"Steel II," 524
"Steel Seizure Case," 930
Steele v. Bulova Watch Co., 936
———; Lawton v., 294
——— v. Louisville and Nashville Railroad, 799
——— v. United States, No. 1, 523
——— v. United States, No. 2, 524
"Steelworkers Trilogy Cases," 1078, 1079, 1080
Steer; White v., 823
Steffens; United States v., 215
Stein; Dyson v., 1429
Steiner; Madera Irrigation District v., 1032
Stencel Aero Engineering Corp. v. United States,
     1849
Stenson; Blum v., 2652
Stephens; Zant v., 2361, 2564
Sterling v. Constantin, 611
Sternbach v. United States, 282
Sterry; Harrison v., 48
Stevens v. Department of Treasury, 3561
Stevic; Immigration and Naturalization Service (INS)
     v., 2703
Steward Machine Co. v. Davis, 670
Stewart v. Abend, Authors Research Co., 3445
———; California v., 1260
——— v. United States, 1099
Stiffel Co.; Sears, Roebuck and Co. v., 1177
Stincer; Kentucky v., 3180
Stinson v. United States, 3792
Stockholders Publishing Co.; National Labor
     Relations Board (NLRB) v. 790
Stone v. Farmers' Loan and Trust Co., 244
——— v. Graham, 2156
———; Hill v., 1692
——— v. Immigration and Naturalization Service
     (INS), 3974
——— v. Mississippi, 220
——— v. Wisconsin, 205
Stone, Warden v. Powell, 1802
Stoner v. California, 1182
"Stop and Frisk Cases," 1336, 1337
Storer v. Brown, 1630
Storer Broadcasting Co.; United States v., 989
Stotts; Firefighters Local Union No. 1784 v., 2711
———; Memphis Fire Department v., 2711
Stovall v. Denno, 1300
Strader v. Graham, 145
Stranahan; Buttfield v., 354
Strauder v. West Virginia, 216

Strawbridge v. Curtiss, 43
Streater; Little v., 2239
Street; International Association of Machinists v.,
     1113
———; Tennessee v., 2841
——— v. New York, 1365
Strickland; Wood v., 1683
Strickland, Superintendent, Florida State Prison v.
     Washington, 2680
Stringer v. Black, Commissioner, Mississippi
     Department of Corrections, 3661
Stringfellow v. Concerned Neighbors in Action, 3104
Stromberg v. California, 589
Stroop; Sullivan v., 3482
Stroud v. United States, 452
Strumpf; Citizens Bank v., 4020
Struthers; Martin v., 768
Strycker's Bay Neighborhood Council, Inc. v.
     Karlen, 2044
Stuart v. Laird, 36
———; Nebraska Press Association v., 1791
———; United States v., 3313
Students Challenging Regulatory Agency Procedures
     (SCRAP); Aberdeen and Rockfish Railroad Co.
     v., 1580
———; United States v., 1580
Stumes; Solem v., 2641
Stump v. Sparkman, 1896
Sturges v. Crowninshield, 72
Sturges and Burn Manufacturing Co. v. Beauchamp,
     415
Stutz; Handley v., 274
Stynchcombe; Chaffin v., 1572
Subversive Activities Control Board; Albertson v.,
     1235
———; Communist Party v., 987, 1106
Suffolk Insurance Co.; Williams v., 130
"Sugar Trust Case," 299
Sugarman v. Dougall, 1599
Sullivan; Abernathy v., 1179
———; Bantam Books, Inc. v., 1139
———; Commissioner v., 1022
———; Cuyler v., 2095
——— v. Louisiana, 3805
———; Melkonyan v., 3592
———; New York Times Co. v., 1179
———; Rust v., 3570
———; United States v., 858
——— v. Wainwright, 2607
Sullivan, Secretary of Health and Human Services v.
     Everhart, 3409
——— v. Finkelstein, 3487
——— v. Stroop, 3482
——— v. Zebley, 3404
Sullivant; McCormick v., 97

Sumitomo Shoji America, Inc. v. Avagliano, 2387
Summa Corp. v. California ex rel. State Lands Commission, 2660
Summers; In re, 811
———; Michigan v., 2267
Summit Health, Ltd. v. Pinhas, 3576
Summit Valley Industries, Inc. v. Local 112, United Brotherhood of Carpenters and Joiners of America, 2374
Summitt v. Sowders, Warden, 2168
Sumner v. Mata, 2177
——— v. Shuman, 3185
Sun v. United States, 1138
Sun Oil Co. v. Federal Power Commission (FPC), 1320
——— v. Wortman, 3264
Sun Ship, Inc. v. Pennsylvania, 2131
"Sunday Closing Law Cases," 1101, 1102, 1103, 1104
Sundry African Slaves v. Madrazo, 107
"Superfund Law" Case, 2951
Superintendent, Massachusetts Correctional Institution at Walpole v. Hill, 2872
Superior Court; Burnham v., 3460
Superior Court of California; Asahi Metal Industry Co. v., 3093
———; California v., 3168
———; Times-Mirror Co. v., 738
Superior Court of California, Riverside County; Press-Enterprise Co. v., 2618
Superior Court of California for the County of Riverside; Press-Enterprise Co. v., 3039
Superior Court for Norfolk; Globe Newspaper Co. v., 2403
Superior Court Trail Lawyers Association v. Federal Trade Commission (FTC), 3401
Superior Oil Co. v. Federal Power Commision (FPC), 1320
Supreme Court of New Hampshire v. Piper, 2796
Supreme Court of Virginia v. Consumers Union of the United States, 2106
Supreme Tribe of Ben-Hur v. Cauble, 469
Suquamish Indian Tribe; Oliphant v., 1889
Sure-Tan, Inc. v. National Labor Relations Board (NLRB), 2723
Suter v. Artist M., 3667
Suttles; Breedlove v., 672
Swain v. Alabama, 1219
Swan; Wilco v., 950
Swank; United States v., 2228
Swann v. Charlotte-Mecklenburg Board of Education, 1444
———; Charlotte-Mecklenburg Board of Education v., 1444

Swann; North Carolina State Board of Education v. , 1447
Swartwout; Ex Parte, 45
Sweeney; Board of Trustees v., 1945
Sweatt v. Painter, 896
Sweet; GTE Sprint Communications Group v., 3296
———; Goldberg v., 3296
Sweet Home; Babbitt v., 4015
Sweezy v. New Hampshire by Wyman, 1011
Swenson; Ashe v., 1401
Swift v. Tyson, 134
Swift and Co.; American Wholesale Grocers Association v., 604
——— v. Hocking Valley Railway Co., 436
———; National Wholesale Grocers Association v., 604
———; Skidmore v., 798
——— v. United States, 361
———; United States v., 604
Swint v. Chambers County Commission, 3959
———; Pullman-Standard v., 2357
———; United Steelworkers of America v., 2357
Swormstedt; Smith v., 150
Sykes; Wainwright v., 1865
Synar; Bowsher v., 3058
———; O'Neill v., 3058
———; Senate v., 3058
System Federation, No. 40; Virginian Railway Co. v., 661

T.I.M.E.-D.C., Inc. v. United States, 1842
T.L.O.; New Jersey v., 2777
TWA, Inc.; Independent Federation of Flight Attendants v., 2326
TXO Production Corp. v. Alliance Resources Corp., 3836
Taco Cabana, Inc.; Two Pesos, Inc. v., 3729
Tafflin v. Levitt, 3402
Tahoe Regional Planning Agency; Lake Country Estates, Inc. v., 1967
Takahashi v. Fish and Game Commission, 872
Takushi; Burdick v., 3696
Tallentire; Offshore Logistics, Inc. v., 3023
Talton v. Mayes, 310
Tamayo-Reyes; Keeney v., 3681
Tank Truck Rentals, Inc. v. Commissioner of Internal Revenue, 1023
Tanner; Adams v., 440
———; Lloyd Corp. v., 1521
——— v. United States, 3187
Target Sales, Inc.; Catalino, Inc. v., 2103
Tarkanian; National Collegiate Athletic Association (NCAA) v., 3294
Tarrant County Narcotics Unit; Leatherman v., 3764
Tashjian v. Republican Party of Connecticut, 3070

Tatro; Irving Independent School District v., 2755
Tatum; Laird v., 1522
Tax Commission; Hoeper v., 596
———; Walz v., 1403
Taxation and Revenue Department of New Mexico;
        F.W. Woolworth, Co. v., 2424
Taxation with Representation; Regan v., 2520
Taxpayers for Vincent; City Council v., 2683
———; Members of the City Council v., 2683
Taxpayers of Tacoma; Tacoma v., 1033
Taylor v. Alabama, 2406
———; Elmendorf v., 96
——— v. Freeland & Krontz, 3680
———; Gilmore v., 3809
——— v. Illinois, 3223
——— v. Louisiana, 1675
———; Maine v., 3020
———; Metropolitan Life Insurance Co. v., 3118
———; Parratt v., 2226
———; Terrett v., 63
——— v. United States, 602, 3459
———; United States v., 3274
Teague v. Lane, 3312
Teal; Connecticut v., 2398
Teamsters Local Union 657 v. Rodriguez, 1843
Tee-Hit-Ton Indians v. United States, 964
Teleprompter Manhattan CATV Corp.; Loretto v.,
        2426
Telfair; Cooper v., 29
Tellier; Commissioner of Internal Revenue v., 1250
Tennessee v. Arkansas, 2302
———; Ashcraft v., 791
——— v. Garner, 2819
———; Payne v., 3618
——— v. Street, 2841
———; Virginia v., 290
Tennessee Copper Co.; Georgia v., 370, 426
Tennessee Valley Authority; Ashwander v., 648
——— v. Hill, 1923
Tenney v. Brandhove, 912
Terance v. Thompson, 509
Terminal Railway of Alabama State Docks
        Department; Parden v., 1184
Terminiello v. Chicago, 885
Terrett v. Taylor, 63
Terry v. Adams, 943
———; Chauffeurs, Local No. 391 v., 3425
——— v. Ohio, 1336
"Test Oath Cases," 163, 164
Testa v. Katt, 843
Texaco, Inc. v. Hasbrouck, 3485
———; Pennzoil Co. v., 3115
——— v. Short, 2307

Texaco, Inc. and Tenneco Oil Co. v. Director,
        Division of Taxation, New Jersey Department
        of Treasury, 3327
Texas; Adams v., 2137
———; Addington v., 1987
———; Aguilar v., 1193
———; Bell v., 1271
———; Branch v., 1528
——— v. Brown, 2495
———; Brown v., 2021
———; Burgett v., 1304
——— v. Certain Named and Unnamed
        Undocumented Alien Children, 2389
———; Estes v., 1232
——— v. Gregory Lee Johnson, 3357
———; Hernandez v., 953
———; Hill v., 752
———; Houston Lawyers' Association v., 3605
———; ICC v., 3081
———; Jamison v., 765
——— v. Johnson, 3357
———; Johnson v., 3833
———; Jurek v., 1797
——— v. McCullough, 2941
———; Miller v., 295
———; Missouri-Kansas-Texas Railroad Co. v.,
        3081
——— v. Mitchell, 1421
——— v. New Mexico, 2552, 3158
———; Orozco v., 1359
———; Pointer v., 1221
———; Powell v., 1345
———; Satterwhite v., 3252
———; Spencer v., 1271
———; Trevino v., 3676
———; United States v., 3778
———; Washington v., 1293
——— v. White, 173
Texas and New Orleans Railroad Co. v. Brotherhood
        of Railway and Steamship Clerks, 581
Texas and Pacific Railway Co. v. United States, 421
Texas Department of Community Affairs v. Burdine,
        2189
Texas Department of Highways and Public
        Transportation; Welch v., 3200
Texas Industries, Inc. v. Radcliff Materials, Inc.,
        2232
Texas Monthly v. Bullock, 3304
Texas Optometric Association, Inc. v. Rogers, 1958
"Texas Primary Cases," 943, 547, 603
"Texas White Primary Case," 547
Textile Mills Securities Corp. v. Commissioner of
        Internal Revenue , 739
Textile Workers; National Labor Relations Board
        (NLRB) v., 1573

The New Yorker; Masson v., 3608

Thiboutot; Maine v., 2136

Thiel, Ex Parte, 757

Thigpen, Commissioner, Mississippi Department of Corrections v. Roberts, 2730

Thomas v. Arn, 2917

———— v. Collins, 803

————; Lonchar v., 4037

————; North Star Steel Co. v., 3991

————; Peacock v., 4027

————; Perry v., 3172

———— v. Review Board of the Indiana Employment Security Division, 2204

———— v. Washington Gas Light Co., 2146

Thomas, Administrator, United States Environmental Protection Agency (EPA) v. Union Carbide Agricultural Products Co., 2904

Thomas Colliery Co.; Heisler v., 495

Thomas Jefferson University, DBA Thomas Jefferson University Hospital v. Shalala, Secretary of Health and Human Services, 3920

Thompson v. City of Louisville, 1069

————; Coleman v., 3615, 3688

————; Kentucky Department of Corrections v., 3337

———— v. Keohane, 4022

————; Kilbourn v., 222

————; Merrell Dow Pharmaceuticals, Inc. v., 3060

———— v. Oklahoma, 3285

————; Palmer v., 1462

————; Shapiro v., 1366

————; St. Amant v., 1319

————; Terance v., 509

Thompson/Center Arms Co.; United States v., 3698

Thomson; Brown v., 2563

Thor Power Tool Co. v. Commissioner, Internal Revenue Service, 1955

Thornburg; Nantahala Power & Light Co. v., 3012

Thornburgh v. Abbott, 3335

———— v. Gingles, 3040

————; Michigan Citizens for an Independent Press v., 3382

Thornburgh, Governor of Pennsylvania v. American College of Obstetricians & Gynecologists, 3005

Thornhill v. Alabama, 710

Thornton; Maine v., 2659

————; U.S. Term Limits, Inc. v., 3987

Three Affiliated Tribes of the Fort Berthold Reservation v. Wold Engineering, P.C., 2691, 3009

Three Friends; In re the, 318

Thunder Basin Coal Co. v. Reich, 3852

Thunder Craft Boats, Inc.; Bonito Boats, Inc. v., 3308

Thurlow v. Massachusetts, 141

Thurston; Air Line Pilots Association International v., 2766

————; TWA v., 2766

Tibbs v. Florida, 2381

Ticor Title Insurance Co.; Federal Trade Commission (FTC) v., 3702

Tiffany Fine Arts, Inc. v. United States, 2776

Tigard; Dolan v., 3916

Tileston v. Ullman, 762

Tillamook County; Hallstrom v., 3381

Tilton v. Richardson, Secretary of Department of Health, Education and Welfare, 1469

Timbers of Inwood Forest Associates, Ltd; United Savings Association v., 3222

Time, Inc. v. Firestone, 1732

———— v. Hill, 1269

———— v. Pape, 1431

————; Regan v., 2750

Times Film Corp. v. Chicago, 1089

Times-Mirror Co.; National Labor Relations Board (NLRB) v., 790

Times-Mirror Co. v. Superior Court of California, 738

Timm; Dewsnup v., 3644

Tingy; Bas v., 30

Tinker v. Des Moines Independent Community School District, 1354

Tipaldo; Morehead v., 653

Tison v. Arizona, 3122

Todd; Jim McNeff, Inc. v., 2507

Toibb v. Radloff, 3596

Tokushige; Farrington v., 544

Toledo; Gomez v., 2102

Toll, President, University of Maryland v. Moreno, 2415

Tollett v. Henderson, 1564

Toltec Watershed Improvement District; Associated Enterprises v., 1560

Tome v. United States, 3941

Tompkins; Erie Railroad v., 681

Tony and Susan Alamo Foundation v. Secretary of Labor, 2836

Toolson v. New York Yankees, 949

Toomer v. Witsell, 871

Topco Associates, Inc.; United States v., 1490

Topeka; Loan Association v., 192

Torcaso v. Watkins, 1108

Tornillo; Miami Herald Publishing Co. v., 1659

Tot v. United States, 772

Touby v. United States, 3569

Touche Ross and Co. v. Redington, 2013

Tourism Co. of Puerto Rico; Posadas de Puerto Rico Associates v., 3046

Town & Country Electric, Inc.; National Labor Relations Board (NLRB) v., 4021

Town Court Nursing Center; O'Bannon v., 2134

Town of Clarkstown; C & A Carbone v., 3884

Town of Hallie v. City of Eau Claire, 2820

Town of Hempstead; Goldblatt v., 1126

Town of Huntington, New York v. Huntington Branch, NACCP, 3289

Town of Newton v. Rumery, 3105

Town of Pawlet v. Clark, 64

Tower, Public Defender of Douglas County, Oregon v. Glover, 2724

Towns of Battleboro and Dummerston; West Bridge Co. v., 142

Townsend; Grovey v., 635

———— v. Sain, Sheriff, 1143

Township of Willingboro; Linmark Associates, Inc. v., 1838

"Trade-mark Case," 215

Trafficante v. Metropolitan Life Insurance Co., 1539

"Trail of Tears Cases," 118, 121

Train; E.I. du Pont de Nemours v., 1820

Trammel v. United States, 2064

Trans World Airlines, Inc. (TWA) v. Franklin Mint Corp., 2662

———— v. Hardison, 1855

———— v. Independent Federation of Flight Attendants (IFFA), 3315

———— v. Morales v., 3695

———— v. Thurston, 2766

————; Zipes v., 2326

Trans-Missouri Freight Association; United States v., 320

Transamerica Delaval; East River Steamship Corp. v., 3008

Transamerica Mortgage Advisors, Inc. (TAMA) v. Lewis, 2036

Transcon Lines; Interstate Commerce Commission (ICC) v., 3940

Transcontinental Gas Pipe Line Corp.; Federal Power Commission (FPC) v., 1724

———— v. State Oil and Gas Board of Mississippi, 2931

Transport Workers Union; Northwest Airlines, Inc. v., 2209

Transportation Agency, Santa Clara County; Johnson v., 3111

Transportation Management Corp.; National Labor Relations Board (NLRB) v., 2546

Travelers Insurance Co.; George E. Pataki v., 3980

————; Hospital Association of New York State v., 3980

————; New York State Conference of Blue Cross & Blue Shield Plans v., 3980

————; Pataki v., 3980

Traynor v. Johnson, 1383

———— v. Turnage, 3241

Treasure Salvors, Inc.; Florida Department of State v., 2435

Tribune Co. v. United States, 814

Trimble v. Gordon, 1835

Trinova Corp. v. Michigan Department of Treasury, 3529

Triplett; Committee on Legal Ethics of the West Virginia State Bar v., 3430

————; United States Department of Labor v., 3430

Trombetta; California v., 2706

Trop v. Dulles, Secretary of State, 1025

Truax v. Corrigan, 477

Truck Drivers Union, Local 413; National Labor Relations Board (NLRB) v., 1671

Truck Drivers Local Union, No. 449; National Labor Relations Board (NLRB) v., 1002

Truckee-Carson Irrigation District; Pyramid Lake Paiute Tribe of Indians v., 2572

———— v. United States, 2572

"Trucking Industry Rate Case," 3769

Trustees v. Greenough, 226

Trustees of Dartmouth College v. Woodward, 75

Tucker; Michigan v., 1647

————; Shelton v., 1087

————; United States v., 1477

Tufts; Commissioner of Internal Revenue v., 2509

———— v. Ziebold, 257

Tuilaepa v. California, 3930

Tulane Educational Fund; Primate Protection League v., 3564

Tulare Lake Basin Water Storage; Salyer Land Co. v., 1559

Tulee v. Washington, 746

Tull v. United States, 3131

Tully; Westinghouse Electric Corp. v., 2669

Tumey v. Ohio, 546

Turkette; United States v., 2262

Turnage; Traynor v., 3241

Turner v. Department of Employment Security and Board of Review of the Industrial Commission of Utah, 1721

————; Heckler v., 2793

———— v. Murray, 2976

———— v. President, Directors and Company of the Bank of North America, 27

———— v. Safley, 3156

————; Smith v., 144

———— v. United States, 1387

Turner Broadcasting System, Inc. v. Federal Communication Commission (FCC), 3924

Turnipseed; Mobile, Jackson and Kansas City Railroad v., 392

Tuten v. United States, 2490

Tuttle; Oklahoma City v., 2855

Tutun v. United States, 532

Twining v. New Jersey, 385
Twitchell v. Commonwealth of Pennsylvania, 170
Two Guys from Harrison-Allentown, Inc. v. McGinley, 1102
Two Pesos, Inc. v. Taco Cabana, Inc., 3729
Tyler; Michigan v., 1915
Tyler Pipe Industries v. Washington State Department of Revenue, 3192
Tyson; Swift v., 134
Tyson and Brother-United Theatre Ticket Officers, Inc. v. Banton, 545
Tzanes v. Pennsylvania, 767

U.S. Bancorp Mortgage Co. v. Bonner Mall Partnership, 3933
U.S. District Court for Southern District; Mallard v., 3333
U.S. Industries/Federal Sheet Metal, Inc. v. Director, Office of Workers' Compensation Programs, United States Department of Labor, 2338
U.S. Jaycees; Roberts v., 2749
U.S. Marshals; Pennsylvania Bureau of Correction v., 2911
U.S. Philips Corp.; Izumi Seitmitsu Kogyo Kaisha v., 3847
U.S. Realty and Import Co.; Securities Exchange Commission (SEC) v., 715
U.S.; Southern Motor Carriers Rate Conference v., 2821
U.S. Term Limits, Inc. v. Thornton, 3987
USA Petroleum Co.; Atlantic Richfield Co. v., 3450
USI Film Products; Landgraf, 3877
USOC; SFAA v., 3201
The Ucayali, 766
Ullman; Buxton v., 1109
———; Doe v., 1109
———; Poe v., 1109
———; Tileston v., 762
Ullmann v. United States, 982
Underhill v. Hernandez, 325
Underwood; Hunter v., 2832
Underwriters National Assurance Co. v. North Carolina Life and Accident and Health Insurance Guaranty Association, 2343
Unemployment Appeals Comm.; Hobbie v., 3095
Union Bank v. Wolas, 3632
Union Carbide Agriculture Products Co.; Thomas v., 2904
Union Carbide and Carbon Co.; Continental Ore Co. v., 1136
Union Electric Co. v. Environmental Protection Agency (EPA), 1780
Union Free School District; Kramer v., 1378
Union Gas Co.; Pennsylvania v., 3349
Union Labor Life Insurance Co. v. Pireno, 2417

Union Pacific Railroad Co.; Brushaber v., 430
——— v. United States, 214
United Air Lines, Inc. v. Evans, 1846
——— v. McMann, 1879
United Artists Corp. v. United States, 870
——— v. Dallas, 1318
United Association of Journeymen & Apprentices of the Plumbing and Pipefitting Industry of the United States and Canada, AFL-CIO v. Local 334, United Association of Journeymen & Apprentices of the Plumbing and Pipefitting Industry of the United States and Canada, 2264
United Auto Workers; Clayton v., 2234
United Brotherhood of Carpenters & Joiners of America, Local 610, AFL-CIO v. Scott, 2593
United Building & Construction Trades Council of Camden County and Vicinity v. Mayor and Council of the City of Camden, 2626
United Distribution Co.; Federal Energy Regulatory Commission v., 3522
———; Mobil Oil Exploration & Producing Southeast, Inc. v., 3522
United Engineers and Constructors v. Pennsylvania, 2425
United Families of America v. Chan Kendrick., 3281
United Farm Workers National Union; Babbitt v., 2006
United Food Workers; National Labor Relations Board (NLRB) v., 3217
United Fruit Co.; American Banana Co. v., 387
United Jewish Organization of Williamsburgh, Inc. (UJO) v. Carey, 1821
United Mine Workers v. Bagwell, 3927
———; Carbon Fuel Co. v., 2043
——— v. Coronado Coal Co., 488
———; Coronado Coal Co. v., 526
———; Gateway Coal Co. v., 1612
——— v. Gibbs, 1251
——— v. National Labor Relations Board, 2280
——— v. United States, 842
———; United States v., 842
United Mine Workers of America Health & Retirement Funds v. Robinson, 2335
United Missouri Bank of Kansas v. Commissioner of Internal Revenue, 2388
United Paperworkers International Union v. Misco, Inc., 3214
United Parcel Service, Inc. v. Mitchell, 2208
——— v. United States Postal Service, 2562
United Public Workers of America v. Mitchell, 840
United Railways and Electric Co. of Baltimore v. West, 574
United Retail and Wholesale Employees Teamsters Union, Local No. 115 Pension Plan v. Yahn & McDonnell, Inc., 3146

United Savings Association of Texas v. Timbers of
   Inwood Forest Associates, Ltd., 3222
United Shoe Machinery Corp. v. Hanover Shoe, Inc.,
   1344
———; Hanover Shoe, Inc. v., 1344
United States v. 50 Acres of Land, 2761
——— v. 92 Buena Vista Avenue, Rumson, New
   Jersey, 3762
——— v. $8,850 in United States Currency, 2521
———; AAA v., 1111
——— v. AT&T, Co., 3911
———; Abbate v., 1049
——— v. Abel, 2763
———; Abel v., 1070
———; Abrams v., 451
———; Achilli v., 1006
———; Adair v., 375
———; Adams v., 769
———; Addyston Pipe and Steel Co. v., 333
———; Agnello v., 530
——— v. Aguilar, 4012
——— v. Agurs, 1775
———; Akin v., 1740
———; Alabama v., 1161
——— v. Alaska, 3677
———; Albernaz v., 2193
——— v. Albertini, 2883
———; Alderman v., 1357
———; Aldridge v., 588
———; Alexander v., 3838
——— v. Alford, 551
———; Allen v., 315
———; Allred v., 870
———; Almeida-Sanchez v., 1588
——— v. Alvarez-Machain, 3704
——— v. Alvarez-Sanchez, 3881
——— v. American Bar Endowment, 3019
——— v. American College of Physicians, 2970
———; American Theatres Association v., 870
——— v. American Trucking Association, Inc., 717
——— v. Amos, 3195
———; Andres v., 867
——— v. Antelope, 1831
——— v. Apfelbaum, 2066
——— v. Appalachian Electric Power Co., 722
——— v. Arizona, 1421
——— v. Armstrong, 4038
——— v. Arnold, Schwinn and Co., 1302
——— v. Arthur Young & Co., 2648
———; Arver v., 443
——— v. Ash, 1589
——— v. Associated Press, 814
———; Associated Press (AP) v., 814
——— v. Atkinson, 645
———; Austin v., 3840

———; Badders v., 431
———; Baer v., 446
——— v. Baggot, 2583
——— v. Bagley, 2907
——— v. Bailey, 2050
———; Bailey v., 4023
——— v. Balint, 481
———; Ball v., 2815
——— v. Ballard, 789
——— v. Ballin, 283
———; Bank of Nova Scotia v., 3272
———; BankAmerica Corp. v., 2535
——— v. Bankers Trust Co., 631
———; Barenblatt v., 1058
——— v. Bass, 1475
——— v. Basye, 1554
——— v. Batchelder, 2001
——— v. Beacon Brass Co., 933
———; Beaver River Power Co. v., 438
———; Becker v., 2238
———; Beckwith v., 1750
———; Beecham v., 3882
———; Beer v., 1745
———; Bell v., 2544
———; Bellis v., 1644
——— v. Belmont, 668
———; Berkovitz v., 3258
———; Berra v., 988
——— v. Bevans, 70
——— v. Bisceglia, 1679
——— v. Biswell, 1498
———; Blakely v., 161
——— v. Bland, 592
———; Blau v., 904
——— v. Bliss Dairy, Inc., 2481
———; Blockburger v., 597
———; Bob Jones University v., 2522
———; Boeing Co., Inc. v., 3411
——— v. Booth, 155
———; Bourjaily v., 3189
——— v. Bowman, 491
———; Boyd v., 245, 282
——— v. Boyle, Executor of the Estate of Boyle,
   2772
———; Brady v., 1405
———; Bram v., 327
———; Braswell v., 3270
———; Braxton v., 3577
——— v. Brewster, 1529
——— v. Brignoni-Ponce, 1719
———; Brinegar v., 892
———; Broadwell v., 358
——— v. Brockbank dba Brockbank Apparel Co.,
   824
———; Brooks v., 522

———; Brooks v., 886
——— v. Brown, 1230
———; Brown v., 62, 395, 3074
———; Brown Shoe Co. v., 1130
———; Bruno v., 698
———; Bruton v., 1323
——— v. Burke, 3690
———; Burks v., 1921
———; Burlington Northern Inc. v., 2449
———; Burns v., 3595
———; Busic v., 2097
———; Butenko v., 1357
——— v. Butler, 643
———; Byars v., 540
——— v. Calandra, 1611
——— v. Caldwell, 1533
——— v. California, 849, 3786
———; California v., 1943
———; California ex rel. California Lands
     Commission v., 2391
———; Camfield v., 323
———; Caminetti v., 434
———; Cammarano v., 1046
———: Campbell v., 1268
———; Caplin and Drysdale v., 3363
——— v. Carlisle, 1
——— v. Carlton, 3902
——— v. Carmack, 836
——— v. Carolene Products Co., 683
———; Carpenter v., 3213
———; Carroll v., 521
———; Carter v., 3280
——— v. Causby, 827
——— v. Ceccolini, 1892
——— v. Centennial Savings Bank FSB (Resolution
     Trust Corporation, Receiver), 3557
———; Central Illinois Public Services v., 1886
——— v. Chadwick , 1863
———; Chae Chan Ping v., 263
——— v. Chambers, 623
——— v. Chapman, 2
———; Chapman v., 3582
———; Chaunt v., 1085
——— v. Chavez, 1640
———; Cheek v., 3521
———; Chema v., 3394
——— v. Cherokee Nation of Oklahoma, 3113
———; Chiarella v., 2070
——— v. Christian Echoes National Ministry, Inc.,
     1480
———; Christoffel v., 891
———; Church of Jesus Christ of Latter Day Saints
     v., 271
———; Church of Scientology of California v., 3735
———; Citizens Publishing Co. v., 1356

United States v. City and County of San Francisco,
     709
——— v. City of Fulton, 2963
———; City of Lockhart v., 2472
———; City of Port Arthur v., 2451
———; City of Richmond v., 1711
——— v. Clark, 2063, 2308
——— v. Classic, 736
——— v. Coalition to Preserve the Integrity of
     American Trademarks, 3230
———; Coffin v., 300
——— v. Cogdell, 2050
——— v. Colgate and Co., 450
———; Colonnade Catering Corp. v., 1392
———; Colorado River Water Conservation District
     v., 1740
———; Columbia Pictures Corp. v., 870
——— v. Constantine, 641
——— v. Consumer Life Insurance Co., 1834
——— v. Container Corp. of America, 1348
———; Cook v., 613
——— v. Coolidge, 67
———; Coplin v., 3063
——— v. Cortez, 2172
———; Couch v., 1543
———; County of Allegany, New York v., 3714
———; County of Cortland, New York v., 3714
———; Cramer v., 500, 808
——— v. Crews, 2078
——— v. Cronic, 2679
———; Crosby v., 3748
——— v. Cruikshank, 198
———; Currie v., 157
——— v. Curtiss-Wright Export Corp. et al., 656
———; Custis v., 3887
———; Dalia v., 1982
——— v. Dalm, 3426
——— v. Dann, 2787
——— v. Darby, 725
———; Darkow v., 456
——— v. Davida Johnson , 4019
——— v. Davis, 1128, 1398
———; Davis v., 834, 1128, 3454, 3918
———; Dayton-Goose Creek Railway Co. v., 513
——— v. De Longchamps, 3
———; Deal v., 3798
———; Debs v., 449
———; Deleet Merchandising Corp. v., 2615
——— v. Delia, 772
———; Delli Paoli v., 996
———; Dennis v., 914
——— v. DiFrancesco, 2160
———; Diggs v., 434
——— v. Dion, 3004
——— v. Dionisio, 1546

United States v. District Court in and for County of
  Eagle, 1438
——— v. Dixon and Foster, 3842
———; Dixson v., 2636
——— v. Dodd, 828
——— v. Doe, 2639
———; Doe v., 3271
———; Doggett v., 3726
——— v. Donovan, 1812
———; Dooley v., 343
——— v. Doremus, 447
———; Dorr v., 359
——— v. Dotterweich, 777
———; Dow Chemical Co. v., 2983
———; Dowling v., 2896, 3397
———; Draper v., 1044
———; Dumbra v., 527
——— v. Dunn, 3101
——— v. Dunningan, 3760
——— v. Durham Lumber Co., 1076
———; Durousseau v., 52
———; Dusky v., 1072
——— v. E.C. Knight Co., 299
——— v. E.I. du Pont de Nemours and Co., 991,
  1007
———; Eastern Band of Cherokee Indians v., 247
———; Economy Light and Power Co. v., 470
——— v. Edge Broadcasting Co., 3835
——— v. Egan, 1523
——— v. Eichman, 3475
——— v. Eight Thousand Eight Hundred and Fifty
  Dollars ($8,850) in United States Currency,
  2521
———; Ekiu v., 280
———; Elkins v., 1082
———; Emspak v., 972
——— v. Energy Resources Co., Inc., 3457
——— v. Enmons, 1553
——— v. Equitable Trust Co. of New York, 531
——— v. Erika, Inc., 2354
———; Estep v., 822
——— v. Euge, 2060
———; Evans v., 3691
———; Falbo v., 779
——— v. Falstaff Brewing Corp., 1555
———; Farmar v., 2611
———; Fedorenko v., 2176
——— v. Felix, 3668
———; Feres v., 899
——— v. Ferreira, 148
———; Fetters v., 593
——— v. Finch, 1844
———; Finley v., 3339
———; Fisher v., 1751
——— v. Fisher, Assignees of Blight, 39

———; Flanagan v., 2628
——— v. Flores, 614
——— v. Florida, 3931
——— v. Florida East Coast Railway Co., 1550
———; Flower v., 1511
———; Ford v., 548
——— v. Fordice, Governor of Mississippi, 3728
——— v. Frady, 2352
———; Frank Lyon Co. v., 1901
———; Fraser, Trenholm and Co. v., 161
——— v. Freed, 1440
——— v. Friday, 3048
———; Frohwerk v., 448
———; Fry v., 1697
——— v. Gainey, 1216
——— v. Galigher Co., 824
———; Galloway v., 770
———; Gambino v., 560
———; Garcia v., 2765
———; Garrett v., 2854
——— v. Gaubert, 3548
——— v. Gaudin, 4008
———; Geders v., 1744
———; Gelbard v., 1523
——— v. General Dynamics Corp., 1627, 3126
——— v. General Electric Co., 538
——— v. General Motors Co., 802
———; General Motors Corp. v., 3484
——— v. Generix Drug Corp., 2483
———; Georgia v., 1567
——— v. Gettysburg Electric Railway Co., 306
——— v. Gillock, 2074
———; Gillette v., 1436
———; Ginzburg v., 1246
——— v. Giordana, 1639
———; Girouard v., 825
———; Glasser v., 741
———; Go-Bart Importing Co. v., 584
———; Goldman v., 750
———; Goldsboro Christian School v., 2522
——— v. Gooding, 104
——— v. Goodwin, 2395
——— v. Goodyear Tire & Rubber Co., 3388
———; Gouled v., 468
——— v. Gouveia, 2693
———; Gozlon-Peretz v., 3530
——— v. Grace, 2504
——— v. Grace Brethren Church, 2396
———; Grace Brethren Church v., 2396
———; Grahl v., 443
——— v. Granderson, 3869
———; Grau v., 609
———; Graubard v., 443
———; Gravel v., 1532
———; Gray v., 3196

——— v. Gray-Cannon Lumber Co., 824
——— v. Green, 981
———; Green v., 567 , 1019, 1092
———; Griffin v., 3626
———; Griggs v., 899
——— v. Grimaud, 399
——— v. Grimsdell dba Grocer Printing Co., 824
———; Grosso v., 1309
——— v. Guest, 1252
———; Guinn v., 427
———; Guinn and Beal v., 427
——— v. Guy W. Capps, Inc., 965
——— v. Haggerty, 3475
———; Haigh v., 161
——— v. Hale, 1707
——— v. Halper, 3336
———; Hamling v., 1655
———; Hampton and Co. v., 562
——— v. Harris, 229
———; Harrison v., 1341
——— v. Hasting, 2518
———; Haupt v., 845
——— v. Havens, 2101
———; Hawkins v., 1041
——— v. Hayes, 4016
———; Haynes v., 1310
———; Hays v., 434
———; Hazelwood School District v., 1870
———; Heart of Atlanta Motel, Inc. v., 1208
——— v. Hemme, 2997
———; Henderson v., 898, 2986
——— v. Henry, 2118
——— v. Hensley, 2770
———; Hepner v., 386
———; Hercules, Inc. v., 4029
———; Hester v., 516
——— v. Hill, 3756
———; Hinton v., 2636
———; Hipolite Egg Co. v., 396
———; Hirabayashi v., 774
———; Hobby v., 2741
———; Hodges v., 368
———; Hoffa v., 1268
——— v. Hohri, 3155
———; Hoke v., 412
——— v. Hollywood Motor Car Co., Inc., 2421
———; Houston, East and West Texas Railway Co. v., 421
———; Hubbard v., 3983
——— v. Hudson and Goodwin, 54
——— v. Hughes Properties, 2999
———; Hughey v., 3452
———; Humphrey's Executor v., 639
———; Husty v., 585
——— v. Hutcheson, 728

United States; Hylton v., 19
——— v. ITT Continental Baking Co., 1681
——— v. Idaho, 1421
——— v. Idaho ex rel. Director, Idaho Department of Water Resources, 3789
——— v. Inadi, 2952
——— v. Inda, 399
———; Indian Towing Co. v., 979
——— v. International Boxing Club of New York, 963
———; International Brotherhood of Teamsters v., 1842
——— v. International Business Machines Corp. (IBM), 4042
——— v. International Minerals and Chemical Corp., 1454
———; International Salt Co. v., 855
——— v. Irvine, 3876
———; Ivanov v., 1357
——— v. Jackson, 1316
——— v. Jacobsen, 2658
———; Jacobson v., 3675
——— v. Jakobson, 1218
——— v. James, 3053
——— v. James Daniel Good Real Property, 3848
———; James M. Brooks v., 886
——— v. Janis, 1801
———; Jefferson v., 899
———; Jencks v., 1008
———; Jersey Shore State Bank v., 3080
——— v. John Doe, 3120
——— v. Johns, 2781
——— v. Johnson, 215, 2401, 3144, 4019
———; Johnson v., 860
———; Jones v., 1071, 2580
——— v. Judge Peters, 47
——— v. Kagama alias Pactah Billy, 249
——— v. Kahn, 1620
———; Kaiser Aetna v., 2041
———; Kann v., 796
——— v. Karo, 2751
——— v. Kasmir, 1751
———; Kastigar v., 1501
———; Katz v., 1306
———; Kaufman v., 1358
———; Kawakita v., 931
———; Keene Corp. v., 3802
———; Kent v., 1248
———; Key Tronics Corp. v., 3798
———; Kilpatrick v., 3272
———; Kimball Laundry Co. v., 889
———; King v., 1268
———; Kirby Forest Industries, Inc. v. , 2684
———; Klayminc v., 3150
——— v. Klein, 184

United States v. Klintock, 78
——— v. Knotts, 2477
———; Kohl v., 195
——— v. Kordel, 1390
———; Korematsu v., 800
———; Kosak v., 2650
———; Kotteakos v., 835
——— v. Kozminski, 3286
———; Kramer v., 443
——— v. Kras, 1544
———; Kretske v., 741
———; Kungys v., 3246
——— v. Lane, 2932
———; Lane v., 2932
——— v. Lanza, 497
———; LaRocca v., 2097
——— v. LaSalle National Bank, 1925
———; Lawrence H. Crandon v., 3411
———; Leary v., 1368
——— v. Lee, 227, 556, 2319
———; Lees v., 293
——— v. Lefkowitz, 601
———; Lemke v., 456
——— v. Leon, 2756
——— v. Lewis, 842
———; Lewis v., 842
———; Libretti v., 4026
———; Light v., 400
———; Liparota v., 2842
———; Liteky v., 3866
——— v. Locke, 2825
———; Lockheed Aircraft Corp. v., 2474
———; Loew's Inc. v, 870
———; Longo v., 3394
——— v. Lopez, 3979
———; Lopez v., 1158
——— v. Lorenzetti, 2692
——— v. Loud Hawk, 2926
——— v. Louisiana, 2270, 2790
———; Louisiana v., 1217
——— v. Lovett, 828
———; Luce v., 2762
———; Lurk v., 1134
——— v. MacCollom, 1761
——— v. MacDonald, 2346
——— v. Macintosh, 591
——— v. Maine, 2255, 2939
——— v. Maine et al., 2783
———; Mallory v., 1014
——— v. Marathon Pipe Line Co., 2416
——— v. Marchant & Colson, 105
———; Marchetti v., 1308
——— v. Marine Bancorporation, Inc., 1666
——— v. Marion, 1474
———; Marron v., 558
——— v. Marsha B. Kokinda, 3505
——— v. Martinez-Fuerte, 1803
———; Massachusetts v., 1898
———; Massiah v., 1185
——— v. Matlock, 1621
———; Mattox v., 3063
——— v. Maze, 1613
——— v. Mazurie, 1676
———; McBoyle v., 587
——— v. McBratney , 225
———; McCormick v., 3573
———; McCray v., 357
———; McElroy v., 2340
———; McInnis v., 567
———; McLaughlin v., 2974
———; McNabb v., 764
———; McNally v., 3196
———; McNeil v., 3796
——— v. Mechanik, 2938
——— v. Mendenhall, 2099
——— v. Mendoza, 2608
——— v. Mendoza-Lopez, 3151
———; Menominee Tribe of Indians v., 1328
——— v. Mercantile Trust Co., 531
———; Mesaroch v., 995
——— v. Mezzanatto, 3943
——— v. Midwest Oil Co., 424
———; Milanovich v., 1096
——— v. Miller, 691, 1752, 2826
———; Miller v., 157, 180
——— v. Mississippi Valley Generating Co., 1088
———; Mistretta v., 3300
——— v. Mitchell, 2081, 2575
———; Mitchell v., 734
———; Molzof v., 3640
——— v. Monsanto, 3362
——— v. Montalvo-Murillo, 3464
———; Montana v., 2200
——— v. Montgomery County Board of Education, 1369
——— v. Montoya de Hernandez, 2903
——— v. More, 42
———; Morissette v., 918
——— v. Morrison, 2169
——— v. Morton, 2720
———; Moskal v., 3516
——— v. Mottaz, 3006
———; Muhammad Ali v., 1470
——— v. Munoz-Flores, 3451
——— v. Murdock, 620
———; Murray v., 3280
———; Muskrat v., 395
———; Myers v., 536
——— v. Naftalin, 1995
———; Nardone v., 674, 700

——— v. National Association of Securities Dealers, Inc. (NASD), 1717

——— v. National Bark of Commerce, 2885

———; National Broiler Marketing Association v., 1920

———; National Cable Television Association v., 1625

———; National Muffler Dealers Association v., 1970

———; National Society of Professional Engineers v., 1903

——— v. National Treasury Employees Union, 3953

———; Neuberger v., 532

———; Nevada v., 2572

——— v. New Mexico, 1944, 2344

———; New York v., 820, 3714

———; New York Times Co. v., 1471

———; Newark Morning Ledger Co. v., 3779

——— v. Nichols, 231

———; Nichols v., 3896

——— v. Nixon, 1667

———; Nixon v., 1667, 3747

——— v. Nobles, 1709

——— v. Nordic Village, Inc., 3650

———; North Dakota v., 2479, 3453

———; Northern Pacific Railway Co. v., 1021

———; Northern Securities Co. v., 355

———; Nortz v., 632

———; Nunn v., 438

——— v. O'Brien, 1326

———; O'Connor v., 3063

——— v. Ojeda Rios, 3446

———; Okanogan Indians v., 573

——— v. Olano, 3785

———; Oliver v., 2659

———; Olmstead v., 567

———; On Lee v., 932

——— v. One Assortment of 89 Firearms, 2632

———; One Lot Emerald Cut Stones and One Ring v., 1540

——— v. Ortega, 99

———; Ortega-Rodriguez v., 3768

——— v. Ortiz, 1720

——— v. Oswald, 9

——— v. Owens, 3226

———; Ozawa v., 493

——— v. Pabst Brewing Co., 1261

——— v. Pacific and Arctic Railway and Navigation Co., 413

——— v. Padilla, 3794

——— v. Palmer, 71

———; Palmore v., 1566

——— v. Paradise, 3096

——— v. Paramount Pictures, Inc., 870

——— v. A Parcel of Land, 3762

United States v. Park, 1700

——— v. Parke, Davis and Co., 1068

———; Parks v., 1268

———; Parr v., 1075

———; Patton v., 577

——— v. Payner, 2132

——— v. Peltier, 1714

——— v. Penn Security Life Insurance Co., 1834

——— v. Percheman, 122

———; Peretz v., 3620

——— v. Perez, 90

———; Perez v., 1450

———; Perry v., 633

———; Peter v., 1218

——— v. Petty Motors Co., 824

——— v. Philadelphia National Bank, 1169

———; Pierce v., 458

———; Pipefitters Local Union, No. 562 v., 1516

——— v. Pink, 743

——— v. Place, 2559

———; Pleasant Grove v., 3082

———; Portsmouth Harbor Land and Hotel Co. v., 496

———; Posters 'N' Things, Ltd. v., 3888

——— v. Powell, 1203, 2764

———; Preciat v., 157

———; Preston v., 1180

——— v. Price, 1253

——— v. Providence Journal Co., 3244

——— v. Ptasynski, 2533

——— v. Quinn, 2968

———; Quinn v., 971

——— v. R. Enterprises, Inc., 3526

——— v. R.L.C., 3664

——— v. Raddatz, 2130

——— v. Radio, Television News Directors Association, 1374

——— v. Raines, 1067

———; Rathbun v., 1017

———; Ratzlaf v., 3850

——— v. Rauscher, 253

———; Ray v., 3147

——— v. Reese, 197

———; Regenbogen v., 835

——— v. Rene Martin Verdugo-Urquidez, 3414

———; Republic National Bank of Miami v., 3740

———; Rex Trailer Co., Inc. v., 980

——— v. Reynolds, 938

———; Reynolds v., 212

——— v. Richardson, 1657

———; Richardson v., 2740

———; Richmond v., 1012

——— v. Rio Grande Dam and Irrigation Co., 332

——— v. Riverside Bayview Homes, Inc., 2916

——— v. Robel, 1305

United States; Roberts v., 2082
——— v. Robertson, 3981
——— v. Robinson, 1608
———; Robinson v., 4023
——— v. Rock Royal Co-operative Inc., 695
——— v. Rodgers, 2526, 2674
——— v. Roemer, Governor of Louisiana, 3604
———; Rogers v., 906
——— v. Rojas-Contreras, 2922
——— v. Romano, 1237
———; Rome v., 2089
——— v. Ron Pair Enterprises, 3311
———; Rosales-Lopez v., 2212
———; Rosenberg v., 948
——— v. Ross, 2377
———; Roth v., 741, 1015
———; Rottenberg v., 784
———; Roviaro v., 1001
———; Rowan Cos. v., 2248
———; Rubin v., 2173
——— v. Rumely, 939
———; Russell v., 2857
———; Russello v., 2602
——— v. Ryan, 231
———; Ryder v., 3995
——— v. Rylander, 2496
——— v. S.A. Empresa De Viacao Aerea Rio
    Grandense (VARIG Airlines), 2719
——— v. SCRAP, 1580
———; Sacher v., 923
——— v. Salerno, 3148, 3718
——— v. Saline Bank of Virginia, 106
——— v. Salvucci, 2139
———; Sanders v., 1150, 2129
——— v. Santa Fe Pacific Railroad, 740
——— v. Santana, 1773
———; Sanitary District of Chicago v., 518
———; Scales v., 1107
———; Schaeffer v., 456
———; Schechter Poultry Corp. v., 637
———; Schenck v., 446
———; Schick v., 358
———; Schmuck v., 3320
———; Schneiderman v., 776, 1012
——— v. Schooner Amistad, 133
——— v. Schooner Peggy, 34
——— v. Schwimmer, 572
——— v. Scotland Neck City Board of Education,
    1518
———; Scott v., 1908
———; Screws v., 809
———; Second National Bank of New Haven v.,
    1289
——— v. Securities Corporation General, 531
——— v. Security Industrial Bank, 2446

——— v. Seeger, 1218
———; Segura v., 2753
——— v. Sells Engineering, Inc., 2582
———; Seminole Nation v., 751
———; Sgro v., 610
——— v. Shabani, 3932
——— v. Shaffer, 7
———; Shannon v., 3922
———; Shapiro v., 876
——— v. Sharpe, 2809
———; Shaughnessy v., 941
——— v. Shearer, Individually and as
    Administratrix for the Estate of Shearer, 2890
———; Sherman v., 1028
——— v. Shirey, 1051
——— v. Shreveport Grain and Elevator Co., 607
——— v. Shubert, 962
———; Shulman v., 750
———; Sicruella v., 966
———; Sifuentes v., 1803
———; Silverman v., 1094
———; Silverthorne Lumber Co. v., 455
———; Simmons v., 1313
———; Sinclair v., 570
——— v. Singleton, 231
——— v. Sioux Nation of Indians, 2149
——— v. Sisal Sales Corp., 552
——— v. Smith, 79, 3543, 3651
———; Smith v., 822, 1841, 3766, 3803
———; Snepp v., 2052
——— v. Socony-Vacuum Oil Co., 711
——— v. Sokolow, 3325
———; Solorio v., 3199
———; Sonzinsky v., 660
———; Sorrells v., 612
——— v. South-Eastern Underwriters Association,
    792
———; Southern Railway Co. v., 405
———; Spallone v., 3394
——— v. Sperry Corp., 3384
———; Spies v., 760
———; Spinelli v., 1350
———; Springer v., 221
———; Standard Oil v., 401
———; Standefer v., 2108
——— v. Stanley, 231, 3205
———; Staples v., 3891
——— v. Stauffer Chemical Co., 2609
———; Steagald v., 2213
———; Steamer Daniel Ball v., 178
———; Steele v., 523, 524
——— v. Steffens, 215
———; Stencel Aero Engineering Corp. v., 1849
———; Sternbach v., 282
———; Stewart v., 1099

———; Stinson v., 3792
——— v. Storer Broadcasting Co., 989
———; Stroud v., 452
——— v. Stuart, 3313
——— v. Students Challenging Regulatory Agency
    Procedures (SCRAP), 1580
——— v. Sullivan, 858
——— v. Swank, 2228
——— v. Swift and Co., 604
———; Swift and Co. v., 361
———; T.I.M.E.-D.C., Inc. v., 1842
———; Tanner v., 3187
——— v. Taylor, 3274
———; Taylor v., 602, 3459
———; Tee-Hit-Ton Indians v., 964
——— v. Texas, 3778
———; Texas and Pacific Railway Co. v., 421
——— v. The Three Friends, 318
——— v. Thompson/Center Arms Co., 3698
———; Tiffany Fine Arts, Inc. v., 2776
———; Tome v., 3941
——— v. Topco Associates, Inc., 1490
———; Tot v., 772
———; Touby v., 3569
———; Trammel v., 2064
——— v. Trans-Missouri Freight Association, 320
———; Tribune Co. v., 814
———; Truckee-Carson Irrigation District, 2572
——— v. Tucker, 1477
———; Tull v., 3131
——— v. Turkette, 2262
———; Turner v., 1387
———; Tuten v., 2490
———; Tutun v., 532
———; Ullmann v., 982
———; Union Pacific Railroad Co. v., 214
———; United Artists Corp. v., 870
——— v. United Mine Workers of America, 842
———; United Mine Workers of America v., 842
——— v. United States Coin and Currency, 1442
——— v. United States District Court for the Eastern
    District of Michigan, 1514
——— v. United States Gypsum Co., 1937
———; United Steelworkers of America v., 1063
———; Upjohn Co. v., 2171
———; Utah Division of State Lands v., 3161
———; Utah Power and Light Co. v., 438
———; Universal Pictures Co. v., 870
——— v. Valenzuela-Bernal, 2440
——— v. Vera, 4044
——— v. Villamonte-Marquez, 2553
——— v. Virginia, 4047
———; Vogel v., 456
——— v. Vogel Fertilizer Co., 2310
——— v. Von Neumann, 2923

United States v. Vuitch, 1448
——— v. Wade, 1298
———; Wade v., 3687
———; Walder v., 951
———; Walter v., 2129
———; Wangerin v., 443
——— v. Ward dba L.O. Ward Oil and Gas
    Operations, 2145
———; Washington v., 2035, 2113, 2486
——— v. Washington Post Co., 1471
———; Wasman v., 2747
———; Watkins v., 1010
——— v. Watson, 828, 1726
———; Wayte v., 2806
——— v. Weber, 2027
——— v. Weber Aircraft Corp., 2647
———; Weeks v., 416
———; Weems v., 390
———; Weiss v., 3851
——— v. Wells Fargo Bank, 3237
———; Welsh v., 1412
———; Werner v., 456
———; West Virginia v., 3073
———; Westover v., 1260
———; Whalen v., 2085
———; Wheat v., 3251
——— v. Wheeler, 1894
——— v. White, 794, 1443
——— v. White Star Line, 409
——— v. Whiting Pools, Inc., 2538
———; Wiborg v., 313
———; Wiener v., 1034
——— v. Wiggs dba Chicago Flexible Shaft Co.,
    824
———; Wilkinson v., 1093
——— v. Will, 2163
——— v. Williams, 3683, 3978
———; Williams v., 2422, 3660
———; Williamson v., 3923
——— v. Wilson, 123, 3666
———; Wilson v., 291
——— v. Wiltberger, 77
———; Wiltberger v., 77
——— v. Winans, 364
———; Winters v., 374
———; Witte v., 4004
——— v. Wittemann, 215
——— v. Wong Kim Ark, 330
———; Wong Sun v., 1138
——— v. Worrall, 14
——— v. Wrightwood Dairy Co., 742
——— v. X-Citement Video, Inc., 3935
———; Yakus v., 784
———; Yasui v., 775
———; Yates v., 1012

United States; Yellin v., 1166
———— v. Yellow Cab Co., 852
———— v. Yermian, 2732
———— v. Young, 2786
————; Young v., 3150
————; Zafiro v., 3755
———— v. Zbaraz, 2148
United States by and through Internal Revenue
    Service (IRS) v. McDermott, 3774
United States ex rel. Greathouse v. Dern, 617
United States ex rel. Hualpai Indians v. Santa Fe
    Pacific Railroad, 740
United States ex rel. Marcus v. Hess, 761
United States ex rel. Toth v. Quarles, 977
United States Catholic Conference v. Abortion Rights
    Mobilization, Inc. (ARM), 3268
United States Civil Service Commission v. National
    Association of Letter Carriers, AFL-CIO, 1597
————; Oklahoma v., 841
United States Coin and Currency; United States v.,
    1442
United States Department of Agriculture (USDA) v.
    Murray, 1595
———— v. Moreno, 1596
United States Department of Commerce v. Montana,
    3672
United States Department of Defense v. Federal
    Labor Relations Authority (FLRA), 3863
United States Department of Energy v. Ohio, 3679
United States Department of Justice (USDOJ) v.
    Landano, 3800
————v. Provenzano, 2760
————; Public Citizen v., 3358
———— v. Reporters Committee for Freedom of the
    Press, 3322
————; Washington Legal Foundation v., 3358
United States Department of Labor v. Triplett, 3430
United States Department of State v. Ray, 3633
———— v. Washington Post Co., 2368
United States Department of Transportation v.
    Paralyzed Veterans of America, 3036
United States Department of Treasury v. Fabe,
    Superintendent of Insurance of Ohio , 3817
United States District Court; Societe Nationale v.,
    3174
United States District Court for Eastern District;
    United States v., 1514
United States District Court for the Western District
    of Washington; Puget Sound Gillnetters
    Association v., 2035
United States Gypsum Co.; United States v., 1937
United States House of Representatives v. Chadha,
    2565
United States Jaycees; Roberts v., 2749
United States Land Association; Knight v., 278

United States National Bank of Oregon v.
    Independent Insurance Agents of America, Inc.,
    3814
United States Nuclear Regulatory Commission v.
    Carolina Environment Study Group, Inc., 1932
———— v. Lorion, dba Center for Nuclear
    Responsibility, 2810
———— v. People Against Nuclear Energy (PANE),
    2497
———— v. Natural Resources Defense Council, Inc.
    (NRDC), 2534
United States Olympic Committee (USOC); San
    Francisco Arts and Athletics (SFAA) v., 3201
United States Parole Commission v. Geraghty, 2076
United States Post Office; Bowen v., 2454
———— v. Council of Greenburgh Civic Associations,
    2274
————; Franchise Tax Board of California v., 2709
————; National Association of Greeting Card
    Publishers v., 2562
————; Rowan v., 1404
————; United Parcel Service of America v., 2562
United States Postal Service, Board of Governors v.
    Aikens, 2493
United States Railroad Retirement Board v. Fritz,
    2162
United States Senate v. Chadha, 2565
United States Servicemen's Fund; Eastland v., 1695
United States Steel Corp. v. Fortner Enterprises, Inc.,
    1817
————; Fortner Enterprises, Inc. v., 1361
———— v. Multistate Tax Commission, 1885
United States Trust Co. of New York v. New Jersey,
    1837
United Steelworkers; Crown Cork & Seal Co. v.,
    3991
United Steelworkers of America v. American
    Manufacturing Co., 1078
————; Dole v., 3407
———— v. Enterprise Wheel and Car Corp., 1080
———— v. Flowers, 2536
———— v. Goodman, 3178
———— v. National Labor Relations Board (NLRB),
    895
———— v. Rawson, 3449
———— v. Sadlowski, 2384
———— v. Swint, 2357
———— v. United States, 1063
————; Usery v., 1811
———— v. Warrior and Gulf Navigation Co., 1079
———— v. Weber, 2027
United Technologies Corp.; Boyle v., 3279
United Transportation Union v. Long Island Railroad
    Co., 2342
Universal Amusement Co.; Vance v., 2072

Universal Camera Corp. v. National Labor Relations Board (NLRB), 907

Universal City Studios, Inc.; Sony Corp. of America v., 2617

Universal Pictures Co. v. United States, 870

Universities Research Association, Inc. v. Coutu, 2206

University Committee to End War; Gunn v., 1418

University of Chicago; Cannon v., 1993

"University of Missouri at Kansas City Case," 2299

University of Pennsylvania v. Equal Employment Opportunity Commission (EEOC), 3391

University of Tennesse v. Elliott, 3059

University of Texas v. Camenisch, 2219

Updegraff; Wieman v., 935

Uphaus v. Wyman, 1057

Upjohn Co. v. United States, 2171

Uplinger; New York v., 2697

Urciolo v. Hodge, 869

Usery; California v., 1771

———; Local 3489, United Steelworkers of America v., 1811

———; National League of Cities v., 1771

———; United Steelworkers of America Local 3489 v., 1811

Utah; Gilmore v., 1819

———; Hagen v., 3860

———; Wilkerson v., 213

Utah Division of State Lands v. United States, 3161

Utah Power and Light Co. v. United States, 438

Utilicorp United Inc.; Kansas v., 3496

Vaca v. Sipes, 1275

Vail; Board of Education of Paris Union School District No. 95 v., 2668

Valco; Buckley v., 1727

Valencia; Anderson Bros. Ford v., 2246

Valente; Larson v., 2356

Valentine v. Chrestensen, 749

Valenzuela-Bernal; United States v., 2440

Vallandigham; Ex Parte, 159

Valley Forge Christian College v. Americans United for Separation of Church and State, Inc., 2306

Valley Unitarian-Universalist Church, Inc. v. County of Los Angeles, 1038

Valtierra; James v., 1449

———; Shaffer v., 1449

Van Arsdall; Delaware v., 2964

Van Curen; Jago v., 2290

Van Horne's Lessee v. Dorrance, 13

Vance v. Universal Amusement Co., 2072

Vanco Beverage, Inc.; Falls City Industries, Inc. v., 2482

"Vanguard Cases," 3050

Vann v. Baggett, 1189

Variable Annuity Life Insurance Co. (VALIC); Ludwig, Comptroller of Currency v., 3945

———; NationsBank v., 3945

Varig Airlines; United States v., 2719

Varity Corp. v. Howe, 4031

Vasquez v. Hillery, 2924

Veazie Bank v. Fenno, 176

Velde v. National Black Police Association, Inc., 2431

Venegas v. Mitchell, 3440

Vera; Bush v., 4044

———; Lawson v., 4044

———; United States v., 4044

Verdugo-Urquidez; United States v., 3414

Verlinden B. V. v. Central Bank of Nigeria, 2517

Vermilya-Brown Co., Inc. v. Connell, 877

Vermont; O'Neil v., 284

———; Williams v., 2859

Vermont Yankee Nuclear Power Corp. v. Natural Resources Defense Council (NRDC), 1900

Verner; Sherbert v., 1170

Vernonia School District, 47J v. Wayne Acton, 4014

———; Acton, 4014

Vester; Cincinnati v., 580

Veterans Administration; Irwin v., 3515

Victor v. Nebraska, 3868

Vidal v. Girard's Executors, 138

Vidal v. Mayor, Aldermen and Citizens of Philadelphia, Executors of Girard, 138

Vigil; Lincoln v., 3801

Vignera v. New York, 1260

Vilas; Spalding v., 307

Village of Arlington Heights v. Metropolitan Housing Development Corp., 1809

Village of Belle Terre v. Boraas, 1631

Village of Euclid v. Ambler Realty Co., 537

Village of Gambell; Hodel v., 3108

Village of Hoffman Estates v. Flipside, Hoffman Estates, Inc., 2332

Village of Schaumburg v. Citizens for Better Environment, 2057

Villamonte-Marquez; United States v., 2553

Vimar Seguros y Reaseguros, S.A. v. M/V Sky Reefer, 4009

Vincent; Labine v., 1439

———; Widmar v., 2299

Vinson; Meritor Savings Bank v., 3017

Vinton Branch of Mountain Trust Bank of Roanoke; Wright v., 659

Virginia; Bigelow v., 1705

———; Boynton v., 1086

———; Cohens v., 82

———; Ex Parte, 217

———; F.S. Royster Guano Co. v., 464

———; Hollingsworth v., 23

Virginia; Jackson v., 2029
———; Landmark Communications, Inc. v., 1906
———; Loving v., 1292
———; Morgan v., 830
———; Mu'Min v., 3581
———; Paul v., 175
———; Richmond Newspapers, Inc. v., 2152
——— v. Rives, 217
———; Simopoulos v., 2550
——— v. Tennessee, 290
———; United States v., 4047
Virginia and Coles; Ex Parte, 218
Virginia Bankshares, Inc. v. Sandberg, 3623
Virginia Citizens Consumer Council; Virginia State
    Board of Pharmacy v., 1756
"Virginia Coupon Cases," 240, 256
Virginia Department of Taxation; Harper v., 3826
Virginia Hospital Association; Wilder v., 3483
"Virginia Private School Case," 1777
Virginia State Bar; Goldfarb v., 1703
Virginia State Board of Elections; Harper v., 1249
Virginia State Board of Pharmacy v. Virginia
    Citizens Consumer Council, Inc., 1756
Virginia Surface Mining and Reclamation
    Association; Hodel v., 2249
Virginian Railway Co. v. System Federation, No. 40,
    Railway Employees Department of the
    American Federation of Labor, 661
Vitale; Engel v., 1132
Vitarelli v. Seaton, Secretary of the Interior, 1055
Vitek v. Jones, 2079
Vlandis v. Kline, 1578
Vogel v. United States, 456
Vogel Fertilizer Co.; United States v., 2310
Voinovich, Governor of Ohio v. Quilter, Speaker Pro
    Tempore of Ohio House of Representatives,
    3763
Volkswagenwerk Aktiengesellschaft v. Schlunk,
    3263
Volpe; Citizens to Preserve Overton Park, Inc. v.,
    1434
Von Neumann; United States v., 2923
Von Raab; National Treasury Employees Union v.,
    3318
Voorhies, M'Kim v., 57
———; McKim v., 57
Vuitch; United States v., 1448

W.A. Ross Construction Co.; Yearsley v., 703
W.R. Grace and Co. v. Local Union 759,
    International Union of the United Rubber, Cork,
    Linoleum & Plastic Workers of America, 2528
W.S. Dickey Clay Manufacturing Co.; City of
    Harrisonville v., 616

W.S. Kirkpatrick and Co. v. Environmental Tectonics
    Corp., International, 3400
WMCA, Inc. v. Lomenzo, Secretary of State of New
    York, 1234
WNCN Listeners Guild; American Broadcasting
    Companies, Inc. v., 2201
———; Federal Communications Commission
    (FCC) v., 2201
———; Insilco Broadcasting Corporation v., 2201
———; National Association of Broadcasters v.,
    2201
Wabash Railroad; St. Louis, Kansas City and
    Colorado Railroad v., 389
Wabash, St. Louis and Pacific Railway v. Illinois,
    251
Waddell; Martin v., 135
Wade; Rake v., 3815
———; Roe v., 1548
———; Smith v., 2501
——— v. United States, 3687
———; United States v., 1298
Wages, Tax Commissioner; Michelin Tire Corp. v.,
    1723
"Wagner Act Cases," 662, 663, 664, 665
Wainwright; Darden v., 3022
———; Ford v., 3030
———; Gideon v., 1144
——— v. Goode, 2605
——— v. Greenfield, 2925
———; Milton v., 1515
———; Sullivan v., 2607
——— v. Sykes, 1865
Wainwright, Secretary, Florida Department of
    Corrections v. Witt, 2779
Wakinekona; Olim v., 2506
Wald; Regan v., 2737
Walden; Pond v., 2307
Walder v. United States, 951
Walker; Associated Press v., 1296
——— v. Birmingham, 1301
———; Brown v., 309
——— v. Sauvinet, 196
Walkers; Linkletter v., 1233
Wallace; Chappell v., 2540
———; Currin v., 689
———; Hill v., 486
———; Stafford v., 483
Wallace, Governor of Alabama v. Jaffree, 2860
Waller v. Georgia, 2686
Walling; Arsenal Building Corp. v., 754
———; Kirschbaum v., 754
Walter v. United States, 2129
———; Wolman v., 1868

Walters, Administrator of Veterans' Affairs v. National Association of Radiation Survivors, 2898

Walton v. Arizona, 3504

Walz v. Tax Commission of New York City, 1403

Wandell's Lessee; Martin v., 135

Wangerin v. United States, 443

Ward v. Illinois, 1852

———; Metropolitan Life Insurance Co. v., 2816

——— v. Race Horse, 311

———; United States v., 2145

Ward's Cove Packing Co. v. Atonio, 3342

Wardair Canada, Inc. v. Florida Department of Revenue, 3014

Warden, Maryland Penitentiary v. Hayden, 1287

Ware v. Hylton, 20

Warley; Buchanan v., 441

Warner, Co.; Norton v., 785

Warner Holding Co.; Porter v., 831

Warren Bridge; Charles River Bridge v., 129

Warren City School District Board of Education; Migra v., 2623

Warren McCleskey v. Kemp, Superintendent, Georgia Diagnostic and Classification Center, 3128

Warren Trading Post Co. v. Arizona State Tax Commission, 1226

Warrior and Gulf Navigation Co.; United Steelworkers of America v., 1079

Warth v. Seldin, 1713

Washington; Antoine v., 1680

——— v. Chrisman, 2309

Washington v. Confederated Tribes of the Colville Indian Reservation, 2113

———; Confederated Tribes of the Colville Indian Reservation v., 2113

——— v. Davis, 1759

——— v. General Motors Corp., 1494

———; General Motors Corp. v., 1188

———; Haynes v., 1159

———; International Shoe Co. v., 817

——— v. Legrant, 1366

——— v. Seattle School District No. 1, 2427

———; Spence v., 1663

———; Strickland v., 2680

——— v. Texas, 1293

———; Tulee v., 746

——— v. United States, 2035, 2113, 2486

——— v. Walter Harper, 3413

——— v. Washington State Commercial Passenger Fishing Vessel Association, 2035

Washington Department of Ecology; PUD No. 1 of Jefferson County v., 3895

Washington Dept. of Services for the Blind; Witters v., 2933

Washington Gas Light Co.; Thomas v., 2146

Washington Legal Foundation v. United States Department of Justice (USDOJ), 3358

Washington Metropolitan Area Transit Authority v. Johnson, 2725

Washington Post Co.; Saxbe v., 1654

———; United States v., 1471

———; United States Department of State v., 2368

Washington State Apple Advertising Commission; Hunt v., 1859

Washington State Commercial Passenger Fishing Vessel Assn.; Washington v., 2035

Washington State Department of Revenue; Tyler Pipe Industries v., 3192

Washington Terminal Co.; Richards v., 419

Washington, Virginia and Maryland Coach Co. v. National Labor Relations Board (NLRB), 666

Wasman v. United States, 2747

Waterfront Commission; Murphy v., 1192

Waterman Steamship Corp.; C&S Airlines v., 862

———; Chicago and Southern Airlines v., 862

———; Civil Aeronautics Board v., 862

Waters v. Churchill, 3894

———; Furnco Construction Corp. v., 1940

Watkins v. Sowders, Warden, 2168

———; Torcaso v., 1108

——— v. United States, 1010

Watson v. City of Memphis, 1160

——— v. Jones, 187

———; United States v., 828, 1726

Watt v. Alaska, 2215

Watt, Secretary of the Interior v. Energy Action Educational Foundation, 2295

——— v. Western Nuclear, Inc., 2532

Wayman v. Southard, 93

Wayte v. United States, 2806

Weaver v. Graham, 2180

———; Marine Bank v., 2334

Webb v. County Board of Education of Dyer County, Tennessee, 2833

———; Frick v., 512

———; Porterfield v., 510

——— v. O'Brien, 511

——— v. Webb, 2224

———; Webb v., 2224

Webb's Fabulous Pharmacies, Inc. v. Beckwith, 2161

Weber v. Aetna Casualty and Surety Co., 1495

———; Kaiser Aluminum and Chemical Corp. v., 2027

———; United States v., 2027

———; United Steelworkers of America v., 2027

Weber Aircraft Corp.; United States v., 2647

Webster; Califano v., 1826

——— v. Doe, 3260

Webster, Attorney General of Missouri v.
    Reproductive Health Services, 3378
Weeks v. United States, 416
Weems v. Alabama, 606
——— v. United States, 390
Weidle; Respublica v., 11
Weinberg v. Prichard, 1552
Weinberger; Goldman v., 2955
——— v. Wiesenfeld, 1687
Weinberger, Secretary of Defense v. Catholic Action
    of Hawaii/Peace Education Project, 2294
——— v. Romero-Barcelo, 2358
——— v. Rossi, 2347
Weingarten, Inc.; National Labor Relations Board
    (NLRB), 1682
Weintraub; Commodity Futures Trading Commission
    v., 2838
Weir; Fletcher v., 2337
Weiser; White v., 1583
Weisman; Lee v., 3724
Weiss v. United States, 3851
Welch v. Helvering, Commissioner of Internal
    Revenue, 619
——— v. Texas Department of Highways and Public
    Transportation, 3200
Wells; Burnet v., 618
———; Florida v., 3437
——— v. Rockefeller, 1363
Wells Fargo Asia Ltd.; Citibank, N.A. v., 3462
Wells Fargo Bank; United States v., 3237
Welsh v. United States, 1412
——— v. Wisconsin, 2681
Welton v. Missouri, 194
Weltover, Inc.; Republic of Argentina v., 3701
Wemyss; Commissioner of Internal Revenue v., 805
Wengler v. Druggists Mutual Insurance Co., 2088
Went For It, Inc.; Florida Bar v., 4013
Werner v. United States, 456
Wesberry v. Sanders, 1175
West v. Conrail, 3116
——— v. Consolidated Rail Corp. (CONRAIL),
    3116
——— v. Kansas Natural Gas Co., 402
———; United Railways and Electric Co. of
    Baltimore v., 574
———; Wright v., 3717
West Bridge Co. v. Towns of Battleboro and
    Dummerston, 142
West Coast Hotel Co. v. Parrish, 658
West Feliciana Parish School Board; Carter v., 1385
West Lynn Creamery, Inc. v. Healy, 3910
West River Bridge Co. v. Dix, 142
West Virginia; Dent v., 261
———; Graham v., 410
———; Strauder v., 216

——— v. United States, 3073
West Virginia ex rel. Dyer v. Sims, 909
West Virginia State Board of Education v. Barnette,
    773
West Virginia University Hospital, Inc. v. Casey,
    3540
Westbrook v. Arizona, 1256
Westcott; Califano v., 2022
———; Pratt v., 2022
Western Addition Community Organization;
    Emporium Capwell Co. v., 1678
———; National Labor Review Board (NLRB) v.,
    1678
Western Air Lines v. Board of Equalization, 3094
——— v. Criswell, 2870
Western Alfalfa Corp.; Air Pollution Variance Board
    of Colorado v., 1642
Western and Southern Life Insurance Co. v. State
    Board of Equalization of California, 2233
Western Fuel Co. v. Garcia, 476
Western Line Consolidated School District; Givhan
    v., 1954
Western Maryland Railway Co.; Clark Distilling Co.
    v., 433
———; James Clark Distilling Co. , 433
Western Nuclear, Inc.; Watt v., 2532
Western Oil and Gas Association v. California, 2614
———; Cory v., 2822
Western Reference and Bond Association, Inc.;
    Olsen v. Nebraska ex rel., 735
Western Transportation Co.; Hough v., 160
Western Union Telegraph Co.; Pensacola Telegraph
    Co. v., 207
Westfall v. Erwin, 3220
Westinghouse Electric Corp. v. Tully, 2669
Weston v. City of Charleston, 113
Westover; Beacon Theatres, Inc. v., 1053
——— v. United States, 1260
Whalen v. United States, 2085
Whalen, Commissioner of Health of New York v.
    Roe, 1816
Wharton v. Morris, 4
Wheat v. United States, 3251
Wheaton v. Peters, 126
Wheeler; United States v., 1894
Wheeling and Belmont Bridge Co.; Pennsylvania v.,
    149
Whipple v. Commissioner of Internal Revenue, 1153
Whirlpool Corp. v. Marshall, 2062
Whitcomb, Governor of Indiana v. Chavis, 1460
White; Alabama v., 3476
———; Cory v., 2383
———; Dougherty County, Georgia Board of
    Education v., 1946
——— v. Illinois, 3642

———— v. Massachusetts Council of Construction Employers, Inc., 2475

———— v. Mechanics Securities Corp., 531

———— v. New Hampshire Department of Employment Security, 2329

————; New York Central Railroad Co. v., 435

———— v. Regester, 1582

———— v. Securities Corporation General, 531

———— v. Steer, 823

————; Texas v., 173

————; United States v., 794, 1443

———— v. Weiser, 1583

White Mountain Apache Tribe v. Bracker, 2142

"White Primary Case," 943

White Star Line; United States v., 409

Whitecotton; Shalala v., 3969

Whitehill v. Elkins, President, University of Maryland, 1303

Whiteside; Nix v., 2942

Whitley v. Albers, 2949

————; Kyles v., 3975

————; Sawyer v., 3719

———— v. Williams, 1355

Whiting Pools, Inc.; United States v., 2538

Whitmore v. Arkansas, 3443

Whitney v. California, 554

Whorton; Kentucky v., 1996

Wiborg v. United States, 313

Wickard, Secretary of Agriculture v. Filburn, 758

Widmar v. Vincent, 2299

Wieman v. Updegraff, 935

Wiener v. United States, 1034

Wiesenfeld; Weinberger v., 1687

Wiggins; McKaskle v., 2625

Wiggs dba Chicago Flexible Shaft Co.; United States v., 824

Wilander; McDermott International, Inc. v., 3528

Wilbur; Mullaney v., 1701

Wilco v. Swan, 950

Wildenhus; In re, 255

"Wildenhus Case," 255

Wilder v. Virginia Hospital Association, 3483

Wilderness Society; Alyeska Pipeline Service Co. v., 1694

Wilkerson v. Rahrer, 276

———— v. Utah, 213

Wilkins; Elk v., 238

———— v. Missouri, 3375

Wilkinson v. Confederated Tribes and Bands of Yakima Indian Nation, 3376

———— v. United States, 1093

Wilks; Martin v., 3346

Will v. Michigan Department of State Police, 3350

————; United States v., 2163

William A. Frazee v. Illinois Department of Employment Security, 3324

William L. Webster, Attorney General of Missouri v. Reproductive Health Services, 3378

William Wrigley Jr.; Wisconsin Department of Revenue v., 3715

Williams; Adams v., 1509

————; Brewer v., 1828

————; Caterpillar, Inc. v., 3167

————; Dandridge v., 1402

————; Daniels v., 2927

———— v. Florida, 1416

———— v. Georgia, 975

————; Lane v., 2339

———— v. Lee, 1043

————; Maggio v., 2604

———— v. Mississippi, 331

———— v. New York, 887

————; Nix v., 2704

————; Pollock v., 788

———— v. Suffolk Insurance Co., 130

———— v. United States, 2422, 3660

————; United States v., 3683, 3978

———— v. Vermont, 2859

————; Whitley v., 1355

————; Withrow v., 3784

———— v. Zbaraz, 2148

————; Zobel v., 2382

"Williams I," 1828

"Williams II," 2704

Williamson v. Lee Optical of Oklahoma Inc., 968

———— v. United States, 3923

Williamson County Regional Planning Commission v. Hamilton Bank of Johnson City, 2895

Williamsport Area School District; Bender v., 2956

Willing v. Chicago Auditorium Association, 565

Wilmington Parking Authority; Burton v., 1098

Willner v. Committee on Character and Fitness, 1151

Willy v. Coastal Corp., 3656

Wilson v. Arkansas, 3988

———— v. Black Bird Creek Marsh Co., 110

———— v. Garcia, 2834

———— v. Girard, 1016

————; Helvering v., 685

————; Joseph Burstyn, Inc. v., 929

————; Kuhlmann v., 3031

————; Lane v., 692

————; Miller v., 423

———— v. New, 437

————; New Jersey v., 56

————; Schweiker v., 2188

———— v. Seiter, 3601

———— v. United States, 291

————; United States v., 123, 3666

Wilson and Co.; Sibbach v., 723

Wilton v. Seven Falls Co., 3998
Wiltz; Elliott v., 230
Wimberly v. Labor and Industrial Relations
    Commission of Missouri, 3084
Winans; United States v., 364
Wine and Spirits Wholesalers of California v.
    Norman Williams Co., 2434
Wingo; Barker v., 1519
Winnebago County Department of Social Services;
    DeShaney v., 3309
Winona and St. Peter Railroad Co. v. Blake, 204
Winship; In re, 1400
Winston, Sheriff v. Lee, 2811
Winter; Corporation of New Orleans v., 65
Winterboer DBA DeeBees; Asgrow Seed Co. v.,
    3942
Winters v. United States, 374
Wirtz; Maryland v., 1340
Wiscart v. D'Auchy, 22
Wisconsin v. City of New York, 4032
———; Griffin v., 3210
———; Kois v., 1527
———; McNeil v., 3597
——— v. Mitchell, 3816
———; Stone v., 205
———; Welsh v., 2681
——— v. Yoder, 1496
Wisconsin ex rel. LaFollette; Democratic Party of the
    United States v., 2185
Wisconsin Department of Industry, Labor and
    Human Relations v. Gould, Inc., 2947
Wisconsin Department of Revenue v. William
    Wrigley Jr., 3715
Wisconsin Employment Relations Commission;
    Madison Joint School District v., 1807
———; International Association of Machinists v.,
    1776
Wisconsin Public Intervenor and Town of Casey v.
    Mortier Wisconsin Forestry/Right-of-Way/Turf
    Coalition, 3611
"Wiseguy Case," 3630
Wiseman; Arcambel v., 21
Witherspoon v. Illinois, 1333
Withrow v. Larkin, 1691
——— v. Williams, 3784
Witsell; Toomer v., 871
Witt; Wainwright v., 2779
Witte v. United States, 4004
Wittemann; United States v., 215
Wixon; Bridges v., 816
Wo Le v. Hopkins, 248
Woelke & Romero Framing, Inc. v. National Labor
    Relations Board (NLRB), 2371
Wohl; Bakery & Pastry Drivers & Helpers Local 802
    v., 748

Wolas; Union Bank v., 3632
Wold Engineering; Three Affiliated Tribes v., 2691
———; Three Affiliated Tribes of Fort Berthold
    Reservation v., 3009
Wolens; American Airlines, Inc. v., 3944
Wolf v. Colorado, 890
———; Jones v., 2033
Wolff v. McDonnell, 1665
Wolff, Warden v. Rice, 1802
Wolfish; Bell v., 1992
Wolman v. Walter, 1868
Wolston v. Reader's Digest Association, 2026
Women's Health Center; Madsen v., 3926
Wong Kim Ark; United States v., 330
Wong Sun v. United States, 1138
Wood; Bishop v., 1762
———; Dairy Queen, Inc. v., 1124
——— v. Georgia, 1131, 2190
——— v. Ohio, 1767
———; McIntire v., 60
——— v. Strickland, 1683
Wooddell v. International Brotherhood of Electrical
    Workers, Local 71, 3629
Woodruff v. Parham, 174
Woods; Burlington Northern Railroad Co. v., 3088
——— v. Cloyd W. Miller Co., 864
Woodson v. North Carolina, 1798
———; World-Wide Volkswagen Corp. v., 2047
Woodward; Trustees of Dartmouth College v., 75
Woodward Sand Co., Inc. v. Pension Benefit
    Guaranty Corp., 2944
Wooley v. Maynard, 1833
Woolsey; Dodge v., 153
Worcester v. Georgia, 121
World-Wide Volkswagen Corp. v. Woodson, 2047
Worrall; United States v., 14
Worthington; Icicle Seafoods, Inc. v., 2965
Wortman; Sun Oil Co. v., 3264
Wright; Allen v., 2752
——— v. City of Roanoke Redevelopment and
    Housing Authority, 3079
——— v. Council of the City of Emporia, 1517
———; Idaho v., 3507
———; Ingraham v., 1832
——— v. Vinton Branch of the Mountain Trust Bank
    of Roanoke, Virginia, 659
Wright, Warden v. West, 3717
Wrightwood Dairy Co.; United States v., 742
Wulff; Singleton v., 1793
Wunnicke; South-Central Timber Dev. v., 2689
Wurts v. Hoagland, 241
Wyatt v. Cole, 3686
Wygant v. Jackson Board of Education, 2985
Wyman v. James, 1422
———; Uphaus v., 1057

Wyman-Gordon Co.; NLRB v., 1367
Wynnewood Bank & Trust v. Childs, 2594
Wyoming; EEOC v., 2476
———; Nebraska v., 3780
———; Nebraska v., 3990
——— v. Oklahoma, 3645

X-Citement Video, Inc.; United States v., 3935
Xerox Corp. v. County of Harris, Texas, 2450

Yahn & McDonnell; Pension Benefit Guaranty Corp.
    v., 3146
———; United Retail and Wholesale Employees
    Teamsters Union, Local No. 115 Pension Plan
    v., 3146
Yakus v. United States, 784
Yamashita v. Hinkle, 494
——— v. Styer, 821
———; In re, 821
Yamataya v. Fisher, 349
Yarbrough; Ex parte, 235
Yaretsky; Blum v., 2414
Yasui v. United States, 775
Yates v. Evatt, Commissioner, South Carolina
    Department of Corrections, 3580
——— v. United States, 1012
Yazoo and Mississippi Valley Railroad Co. v.
    Jackson Vinegar Co.,411
Ybarra v. Illinois, 2039
Yearsley v. W.A. Ross Construction Co., 703
Yee v. City of Escondido, California, 3674
Yellen; Bryant v., 2121
———; California v., 2121
———; Imperial Irrigation District v., 2121
Yellin v. United States, 1166
Yellow Cab Co.; United States v., 852
Yellow Freight System, Inc. v. Donnelly, 3433
Yermian; United States v., 2732
Yeshiva University; National Labor Relations Board
    v., 2059
———; Yeshiva University Faculty Association v.,
    2059
Yeshiva University Faculty Association v. Yeshiva
    University, 2059
Yick Wo v. Hopkins, 248
Ylst, Warden v. Nunnemaker, 3617
Yoder; Wisconsin v., 1496
Yolo County; MacDonald, Sommer and Frates v.,
    3028
York; Guaranty Trust Co. v., 815
Young v. California, 697
———; Carr v., 1087

Young; Cole v., 994
——— v. Community Nutrition Institute, 3013
———; Ex Parte, 378
———; United States v., 2786
——— v. United States ex rel. Vuitton et Fils S.A.,
    3150
Young, Mayor of Detroit v. American Mini Theatres,
    Inc., 1774
Youngblood; Arizona v., 3292
———; Collins v., 3491
Youngberg v. Romeo, 2393
Younger v. Harris, 1428
Youngs Drug Products Corp.; Bolger v., 2570
Youngstown Sheet and Tube Co. v. Sawyer, 930
Yount; Patton v., 2728
Yuckert; Bowen v., 3159

Zablocki v. Redhail, 1882
Zacchini v. Scripps-Howard Broadcasting Co., 1875
Zafiro v. United States, 3755
Zahn v. International Paper Co., 1610
Zant, Superintendent; McCleskey v., 3554
Zant, Warden v. Stephens, 2361, 2564
Zauderer v. Office of Disciplinary Counsel of the
    Supreme Court of Ohio, 2849
Zbaraz; Hartigan v., 3218
———; Miller v., 2148
———; United States v., 2148
———; Williams v., 2148
Zdanok; Glidden Co. v., 1134
Zebley; Sullivan v., 3404
Zemel v. Rusk, Secretary of State, 1228
Zenith Radio Corp.; Matsushita Electric Industrial
    Co. v., 2959
Zerbst; Johnson v., 686
Zicherman v. Korean Air Lines, 4024
Zicherman; Korean Air Lines v., 4024
Ziebold; Kansas ex rel. Tufts v., 257
———; Tufts v., 257
Zimmerman Brush Co.; Logan v., 2328
———; New York ex rel. Bryant v., 569
———; Bryant v., 569
Zinermon v. Burch, 3410
Zipes; Independent Federation of Flight Attendants
    v., 3366
——— v. Trans World Airlines, Inc. (TWA), 2326
Zobel v. Williams, Commissioner of Revenue, and
    Alaska, 2382
Zobrest v. Catalina Foothills School District, 3823
Zorach v. Clauson, 927
Zurcher v. Stanford Daily, 1916

ABOUT THE AUTHOR

Kelly Janousek holds a B.A. in Social Science from Western Michigan University, M.L.I.S. from University of Pittsburgh and a Paralegal Certificate from Mississippi University for Women. Currently a librarian at California State University, Long Beach she collects and instructs in legal information, political science, government information, and public policy and administration. She is also active in the Association of College and Research Libraries, Law and Political Science Section, and past-chair of Reference and Users Services Association, Business and Reference Services Section.